Invitation to Psychology

FOURTH EDITION

Carole Wade • Carol Tavris

Dominican University of California

PEARSON
Prentice
Hall

Upper Saddle River, NJ 07458

Library of Congress Cataloging-in-Publication Data

Wade, Carole.
 Invitation to psychology / Carole Wade, Carol Tavris. —4th ed.
  p.   cm.
 Includes bibliographical references and index.
 ISBN 0-13-175063-1
 1. Psychology—Textbooks.   I. Tavris, Carol.   II. Title.
 BF121.W265 2008
 150—dc22   2006102412

Editorial Director: Leah Jewell
Executive Editor: Jessica Mosher
Editorial Assistant: Jessica Kupetz
Editor in Chief, Development: Rochelle Diogenes
Assessment Editor: Kerri Scott
Media Editor: Bryan Hyland
Director of Marketing: Brandy Dawson
Senior Marketing Manager: Jeanette Moyer
Marketing Assistant: Laura Kennedy
Assistant Managing: Maureen Richardson
Production Liaison: Maureen Richardson/Nicole Girrbach
Manufacturing Manager: Nick Sklitsis
Manufacturing Buyer: Sherry Lewis

Interior Design: Kathy Mrozek
Cover Design: Kathy Mrozek
Cover Illustration/Photo: Jess Kugler/Index Stock
   Imagery, Inc.
Director, Image Resource Center: Melinda Patelli
Manager, Rights & Permissions: Zina Arabia
Interior Image Specialist: Beth Brenzel
Cover Image Specialist: Karen Sanatar
Image Permission Coordinator: Joanne Dippel
Photo Researcher: Barbara Salz
Composition/Full-Service Project Management:
   Prepare, Inc.
Printer/Binder: Courier Companies, Inc.

Credits and acknowledgments borrowed from other sources and reproduced, with permission, in this textbook appear on appropriate page within text (or on pages C-1–C-4).

Pearson Education, Ltd.
Pearson Education Australia PTY, Limited
Pearson Education Singapore, Pte., Ltd.
Pearson Education North Asia Ltd.
Pearson Education, Canada, Ltd.
Pearson Educaciòn de Mexico, S.A. de C.V.
Pearson Education–Japan
Pearson Education Malaysia, Pte., Ltd.
Pearson Education, Upper Saddle River, NJ

10 9 8 7 6 5 4 3 2 1

ISBN-13:   978-0-13-175063-0
ISBN-10:   0-13-175063-1

contents at a glance

PART *One*   Your Self

At the heart of psychology lies a question: What is a person? This section shows how psychologists from five schools of thought address this question. What traits define personality, and where do they come from? What milestones occur on the way to becoming a person?

PART *Two*   Your Body

We cannot understand our psychological selves without understanding our physical selves. These chapters describe how brain activity, neurons, and hormones affect your psychological functioning, and how you are able to sense and perceive the world around you.

PART *Three*   Your Mind

"I think, therefore I am," said the philosopher René Descartes. This section discusses the impressive ways in which human beings think—and why they so often fail to think and reason well—and explores the puzzles and paradoxes of memory.

PART *Four*   Your Environment

Even unsociable hermits are influenced by their surroundings and by other people. In these chapters you will learn how physical and social environments—from the immediate situation to the larger cultural context—affect your actions and attitudes.

PART *Five*   Your Mental Health

At some point, many of us struggle with psychological problems, which range from everyday difficulties to incapacitating conditions. This part describes the major mental and emotional disorders and evaluates the therapies that have been designed to treat them.

PART *Six*   Your Life

A satisfying life depends on having healthy emotions, coping well with stress, and knowing how to reach your goals. In these closing chapters, we see how the influences discussed in the previous units—personality, body, mind, and environment—affect your emotions, well-being, and four of life's fundamental motives: love, sex, eating, and work.

contents

to the instructor

Psychology textbooks have always had a little problem with length. William James's two-volume classic, *Principles of Psychology* (1890), took him 12 long years to write and weighed in at a hefty 1,393 pages. (And today's students think *they* have it hard!) Just two years after it was published, James followed it with *Psychology, Briefer Course*, which was much shorter, under 500 pages. But James was not happy with his briefer book; in a letter to his publishers, he complained that he had left out "all bibliography and experimental details, all metaphysical subtleties and digressions, all quotations, all humor and pathos, all interest in short. . . ." (quoted in Weiten & Wight, 1992).

The great James was probably too hard on himself; he was entirely incapable of writing anything dull or uninteresting. Nevertheless, we kept his words in mind as we were working on our own "briefer" introduction to psychology. From the outset, we were guided by a philosophy that we hoped would help us avoid some of the pitfalls of the genre:

1. A brief book should have not only fewer chapters than a longer book but also its own meaningful organization.
2. Students at all levels need critical-thinking tools for evaluating psychological issues intelligently.
3. Brief or long, a textbook needs to use examples, analogies, lively writing, and a strong narrative sense to pull students into the material and make it relevant to their lives.
4. Students remember more if they learn actively.
5. Research on culture, gender, and biology should be mainstreamed throughout the book wherever it is relevant.

In the rest of this preface, we describe how we have tried to incorporate our philosophy into this book, and changes made in this edition.

1. Brevity and Organization

We know that instructors often feel hard-pressed to cover all the material of a 17- or 18-chapter introductory text in a semester or quarter. The 14 chapters in this book cover the major topics in introductory psychology but are organized differently than in our 17-chapter edition. We wanted to do two things: engage students quickly and provide a logical scaffolding for the diverse topics in psychology. The first chapter, which introduces students to the field and to the fundamentals of critical and scientific thinking, is followed by six sections, each consisting of two chapters (in one case, three). The title of each section invites the reader to consider how the discipline of psychology can illuminate aspects of his or her own life and provides the reader with a personal frame of reference for assimilating the information:

- **PART ONE: YOUR SELF** examines major theories of personality (Chapter 2) and development (Chapter 3). These are high-interest topics for students and will draw them into the course right away. Moreover, starting off with these chapters allows us to avoid redundancy in coverage of the major schools of psychology—biological, learning, cognitive, sociocultural, and psychodynamic. Instead of introducing these perspectives in the first chapter and then having to explain them again in a much later personality chapter, we cover them once, in this section.

- **PART TWO: YOUR BODY** explores the many ways in which the brain, neurons, and hormones affect psychological functioning (Chapter 4), body rhythms and states of consciousness (Chapter 5), and the neurological and psychological underpinnings of sensation and perception (Chapter 6).

- **PART THREE: YOUR MIND** discusses the impressive ways in which human beings think and reason—and why they so often fail to think and reason well (Chapter 7)—and explores the puzzles and paradoxes of memory (Chapter 8).

- **PART FOUR: YOUR ENVIRONMENT** covers basic principles of learning (Chapter 9) and the impact of social and cultural contexts on behavior (Chapter 10). Combining learning and social psychology in the same part is a break from convention, but we think it makes good sense, for these two fields share an emphasis on external influences on behavior.

- **PART FIVE: YOUR MENTAL HEALTH** reviews the major mental and emotional disorders (Chapter 11) and evaluates the therapies designed to treat them (Chapter 12).

- **PART SIX: YOUR LIFE** shows how mind, body, and environment influence emotions, stress, and health (Chapter 13) and the fundamental motives that drive people: eating and appetite, love and sex, and work and achievement (Chapter 14).

Naturally, we could not include every topic that might be found in a longer book, but we have retained those that are truly essential in an introductory course. In most cases, you will find these topics in the chapters where you expect them to be, but there are a few exceptions. For example, eating disorders are not discussed in the chapter on psychological disorders; instead, we discuss them in the context of psychological, genetic, and cultural factors in eating, overweight, and dieting (Chapter 14). If at first you do not see a topic that interests you, we urge you to look for it in the table of contents or the index.

2. Critical and Scientific Thinking

Since we introduced critical thinking in the first edition of our longer book, in the 1980s, we have been gratified to see its place in the study of psychology grow. Without critical-thinking skills, learning ends at the classroom door.

In this book, too, our goal is to get students to reflect on what they learn, resist leaping to conclusions on the basis of personal experience alone (so tempting in psychological matters), apply rigorous standards of evidence, and listen to competing views. As in our longer book, we introduce eight basic guidelines to critical and scientific thinking in the first chapter and then teach and model these guidelines throughout the book.

We use a critical-thinking icon, a light bulb, together with a tab like the one shown here to draw the reader's at-

tention to some (but not all) of the critical-thinking discussions in the text. The light bulb and tab are meant to say to students, "Listen up! As you read about this topic, you will need to be especially careful about assumptions, evidence, and conclusions." The critical-thinking light bulb also appears in many of the Quick Quizzes to alert students to items that give them practice in critical thinking.

True critical thinking, we have always maintained, cannot be reduced to a set of rhetorical questions or to a formula for analyzing studies. Because it is a process of evaluating claims and ideas, it must be woven into a book's narrative. We try to model critical thinking for students in our evaluations not only of popular but unsupported ideas in the popular culture but also in our evaluations of unsupported academic or clinical beliefs: for example, that projective tests like the Rorschach are reliable and valid ways of assessing pathology, emotional disorders, or the likelihood of child sexual abuse (they aren't), and that posttraumatic interventions such as Critical Incident Stress Debriefing reliably help survivors of disasters avoid developing PTSD (they don't). Likewise, we try to convey the importance of critical thinking and empirical evidence in our coverage of psychological issues that have evoked emotional debate, such as children's eyewitness testimony, multiple personality disorder, recovered memories, parental versus peer influence on children, the role of biology in addiction, definitions of racism and sexism, and many others.

3. Liveliness and Relevance

Virginia Woolf once said that fiction is not dropped like a pebble upon the ground but, like a spider's web, is attached to life at all four corners. The same principle applies to good textbook writing. Authors of texts at all levels have a unique opportunity to combine scholarly rigor and authority with warmth and compassion in conveying what psychologists know (and still seek to know) about the predicaments and puzzles of life.

Right from the outset, we want students to see that psychology can deepen our understanding of those predicaments and puzzles. Its lessons apply to the world and to us all as individuals. Each chapter, therefore, begins with a feature called **Psychology in the News** that presents a real news item: for example, a 66-year-old Romanian woman giving birth; the emotionally divisive case of Terri Schiavo; a rape victim whose mistaken eyewitness testimony sent an innocent man to prison for years; a Supreme Court decision about a religious group's ritual use of a hallucinogenic tea; a child who died during a session of "rebirthing" therapy in Colorado; and a college student who claimed to have been addicted to games on the Internet.

We use these stories to raise issues that will be addressed in the chapter. Then, at the end of the chapter, we revisit the opening story to show how concepts and findings that the reader has been studying illuminate the issues raised. We think this device helps promote critical thinking and also helps students appreciate that psychology is indeed "attached to life at all four corners."

At the end of each chapter, another feature, **Taking Psychology with You**, draws on research reported in the chapter to tackle practical topics, such as living with chronic pain (Chapter 6), eliminating bad habits (Chapter 9), getting along with people of other cultures (Chapter 10), and evaluating self-help programs and books (Chapter 12).

4. Active Learning

One of the soundest findings about learning is that you can't just sit there like a sack of potatoes while it happens. You have to be actively involved, whether practicing the new skill or encoding new material. Our textbook includes several pedagogical features that encourage students to become actively involved in what they are reading.

What's Ahead introduces each major section within a chapter with a set of brief questions. These are not merely rhetorical but are intended to be provocative or intriguing enough to arouse students' curiosity: In a competition, why is the third-place winner often happier than the second-place winner? How can merely sitting in a doctor's office make you feel sick? What is the "Big Lie," and why does it work so well?

Quick Quizzes throughout each chapter encourage active learning by inviting students to check their progress while they are reading and to go back and review if necessary. The quizzes do more than test for memorization of definitions; they let students know whether they comprehend what they have read. Mindful of the common tendency to skip quizzes or to peek at the answers, we have used various formats and have included entertaining examples in order to motivate students to test themselves.

As mentioned earlier, many of the quizzes also include critical-thinking questions, identified by the light bulb symbol, that require more than recognition or recall. For example: What kinds of questions should a critical thinker ask about a new drug for depression? If a woman's job performance is declining, what else besides low achievement might be the reason? Why should consumers be cautious about accepting the success of a therapy, self-help program, or drug on the basis of some individual's enthusiastic testimonial?

Get Involved exercises provide an entertaining approach to active learning. Some consist of quick demonstrations (e.g., swing a flashlight in a dark closet to see how briefly images remain in sensory memory); some are simple mini-studies (e.g., violate a social norm and see what happens); and some help students relate course material to their own lives (e.g., if you drink, list the motives you have for doing so). Instructors may want to assign some of these exercises to the entire class and then discuss the results and what they mean.

Other pedagogical features include **graphic illustrations** of complex concepts; a **running glossary** that defines boldfaced technical terms on the pages where they occur for handy reference and study; a **cumulative glossary** at the back of the book; a list of **key terms** at the end of each chapter with page numbers so that students can find the sections where the terms are covered; **chapter outlines**; and **chapter summaries** in paragraph form to help students review major concepts.

5. Mainstreaming Culture, Gender, and Biology

Of course, all introductory textbooks are divided into chapters that cover particular topics or subfields, such as the brain, emotion, developmental psychology, and social psychology. Increasingly, however, some areas of investigation can no longer be squeezed into a single chapter, because they are relevant to topics throughout the course. This is especially true of findings from the bookends of human behavior, culture and biology, as well as research on gender, that little subject of immense interest!

Where possible, therefore, we have tried to integrate research in these areas wherever it applies rather than relegating studies on gender, culture, or biology to an intellectual ghetto of separate chapters or boxed features.

For example, we cover many gender differences in this book—in sexual attitudes and motives, sexual coercion, body satisfaction, depression, antisocial personality disorder, children's play preferences, and ways of expressing love, intimacy, and emotion, to mention just a few. (You will find many other topics in the index.) We do not equate "gender" with "women," either. We have been particularly attentive to research on the psychology of men, for example by considering the underdiagnosis of male depression and the rise of eating disorders and distorted body images in young men. In many cases, we have tried to go beyond mere description of differences by examining competing explanations for them: biological and evolutionary influences, social roles, gender socialization, gender schemas, and the power of current situations and experiences to shape people's choices and lives.

GENDER

For examples of how we treat gender issues, see our discussions of:

- Sex differences in the brain (pp. 141–142)
- Gender and emotion (pp. 446–447)
- Gender and heroism (p. 348)
- Transgender identity (pp. 93–95)
- Evolutionary theories of sexual behavior (pp. 476–478)
- Weight and eating disorders in women and men (pp. 487–489)

Nor do we focus exclusively on gender differences. Many differences, though reliable, are trivial in terms of real-life importance. And gender similarities, though they are often overlooked, are every bit as important and interesting as the eternal search for differences. We therefore include findings on similarities, too—for example, that men and women do not, overall, differ in mood swings in the course of an average month (Chapter 5), in obedience to authority (Chapter 10), or even, in spite of average differences in brain lateralization, in their actual performance on many cognitive tasks.

In recent years, and certainly in the aftermath of 9/11, most psychologists have come to appreciate the profound influence of culture on all aspects of life, from nonverbal behavior to the deepest attitudes about how the world should be. Thus we raise empirical findings about culture and ethnicity, as topics warrant, throughout the book: for example, in our discussions of addiction, mental disorders, social norms, emotional expression, group differences in IQ scores and academic achievement, motivational conflicts, personality, psychotherapy, rules about time, attitudes toward weight and the ideal body, and the effectiveness of medication. (Again, we refer you to the index for a complete listing of topics.) In addition, Chapter 2 highlights cultural factors in personality and Chapter 10 contains extended discussions of ethnocentrism, prejudice, and cross-cultural relations. We try to apply critical thinking to our coverage of culture, teaching students to avoid the twin temptations of ethnocentrism and stereotyping.

CULTURE

For examples of how we treat culture, see our discussions of:
- Cultural influences on personality (pp. 61–65)
- Ethnic identity and acculturation (pp. 350–351)
- Ethnocentrism (p. 352)
- Addiction rates and drug abuse (pp. 389–390)
- Attitudes toward achievement (p. 252)

Anyone who is awake and conscious knows that we are in the midst of a biomedical revolution that is transforming science and psychology. Findings from the Human Genome Project, studies of behavioral genetics, astonishing discoveries about the brain, technologies such as PET scans and fMRI, the proliferation of medications for psychological disorders—all have had a profound influence on our understanding of human behavior and on interventions to help people with chronic problems. This work, too, can no longer be confined to a single chapter; accordingly, we report new findings from the biological front wherever they are relevant throughout the book, in our discussions of the brain, memory, emotion, stress, child development, aging, mental illness, personality, and many other topics. But just as we do with culture and gender, we apply principles of critical thinking to this domain of research, too. We caution students about the dangers of reducing complex behaviors solely to biology, overgeneralizing from limited data, failing to consider other explanations, and oversimplifying solutions (e.g., as promises of miracle drugs often do).

BIOLOGY

For examples of how we cover biological research, see our discussions of:
- Genetics and personality (pp. 53–57)
- Stem cells and the production of new neurons (pp. 121–122)
- Schizophrenia (pp. 395–397)
- Sexual desire and behavior (pp. 474–476)
- Weight and body shape (pp. 485–486)

What's New in This Edition?

In this fourth edition of *Invitation to Psychology*, we have retained the text's basic approach, organization, and pedagogy. We have made no changes just for the sake of making changes. Many of the book's features have been tested by time and student reaction; students and instructors like them.

One important new feature in every chapter is a section called **Close-up on Research**, in which we take a provocative research question and show how investigators have set about answering it, from start to finish. Because an essential aspect of the scientific enterprise is critical thinking, we have woven our eight critical-thinking guidelines into this feature and have highlighted them in boldface. We show students how the process works from the first questions a psychological scientist asks ("What might be a better predictor of male violence than testosterone?" "Why is human touch emotionally and even physically beneficial?" "Do posttraumatic interventions help or hurt?") to defining terms (how exactly can we measure the development of conscience in children?) to considering other explanations for the findings. Each of these features also contains a graph or table of the results so that students can get practice in reading these important presentations of data.

CLOSE-UP ON RESEARCH

For examples of this feature, see:
- Hugs and Health (pp. 460–461)
- How to Kill Intrinsic Motivation (pp. 319–320)
- The Plastic Brain (pp. 123–124)
- How Not to Interview Children (pp. 271–272)
- Does Crisis Debriefing Help? (pp. 422–423)

Further, this edition features **Concept Maps**, visual summaries at the end of each chapter that organize the material and show relationships between topics at a glance. Instructors and students will find this way of summarizing material to be a useful study aid.

This edition also contains some new chapter-opening stories, and throughout the book we have added the latest research on cutting-edge issues and controversies, from findings on stem cells and neuronal growth throughout life to research on reasons for the obesity epidemic worldwide. A list of all deletions, additions, and modifications in the fourth edition is available to adopters of the third edition, so that no one will have to guess why we made particular changes. We hope this support will make the transition from the previous edition to this one as painless as possible. You can obtain this information from your Prentice Hall representative or by writing to: Marketing Manager, Psychology; Prentice Hall Publishers; One Lake Street; Upper Saddle River, New Jersey 07458.

Instructor and Student Supplements to Accompany *Invitation to Psychology*, Fourth Edition

Prentice Hall has made every effort to provide superb supplements that will save you preparation time and enhance the classroom experience. For access to all instructor supplements for *Invitation to Psychology*, Fourth Edition, go to *http://prenhall.com/irc* and follow the directions to register (or log in if you already have a user name and password).

Once you have registered and your status as an instructor is verified, you will be e-mailed a login name and password. Click on the "online catalogue" link, then on "psychology," then on "introductory psychology," and finally Wade/Tavris *Invitation to Psychology*, 4e. Under the description of each supplement is a link that allows you to download and save the supplement to your desktop.

Hard copies of the supplements can be requested through your Prentice Hall sales representative. If you do not know your sales representative, go to *http://prenhall.com/replocator/* and follow the directions. For technical support for any of your Prentice Hall products, you and your students can contact *http://247.prenhall.com/* or call customer technical support at 1-800-677-6337.

Supplements for Instructors

Test Item File (978-0-13-232973-6) This excellent test bank, developed by Rose Suggett (Southeast Community College) and Doug Radke, contains over 3,000 multiple-choice, true/false, and essay questions, each referenced to the relevant page in the textbook. A *Total Assessment Guide* chapter overview makes creating tests easier by providing a grid that organizes all test items by text section and question type/level of difficulty. All multiple-choice questions are categorized as factual, conceptual, or applied. A developmental editor has carefully reviewed every question to ensure the highest-quality items and consistency with text content.

Prentice Hall's TestGen (978-0-13-232972-9) Available on one dual-platform CD-ROM, this computerized test generator program provides instructors "best in class" features in a user-friendly program. Create tests using the TestGen Wizard and easily select questions with drag-and-drop or point-and-click functionality. Add or modify test questions using the built-in Question Editor. TestGen also offers algorithmic functionality, which allows for the creation of unlimited versions of a single test. The Quiz Master feature allows for online test delivery. TestGen comes complete with an instructor gradebook and full technical support. It is available online through the Instructor's Resources Center or on the Instructor's Resource CD-ROM.

NEW **Prentice Hall's Testing Platform** *MyTest* This new alternative to TestGen is a powerful assessment-generation program that helps instructors easily create and print quizzes, tests, and exams, as well as homework or practice handouts. You can create questions, evaluations, or assignments online, which gives you flexibility and the ability to manage your course work at any time, anywhere you are.

NEW **PowerPoint Presentation and Classroom Response Questions** A completely redesigned PowerPoint presentation, created by Brian Malley (University of Michigan) for *Invitation to Psychology*, Fourth Edition, incorporates the text art and outlines the key points for each text chapter. Classroom Response Questions ("clicker" questions), also created for the fourth edition, are designed to promote animated class discussion. Available on the Instructor's CD-ROM or online at *http://prenhall.com/irc*.

Classroom Response Systems Pearson Education offers the benefits of partnerships with two of the leading classroom-response systems on the market. Customers using a Classroom Response System with their text are entitled to student and department savings, and Prentice Hall will be happy to help you set one up or expand your current system. For more information about Classroom Response Systems, visit *http://www.prenhall.com/crs*

Instructor's Resource Manual (978-0-13-232972-9) The Instructor's Resource Manual offers an abundant collection of resources prepared by Alan Swinkles (St. Edwards University). For each chapter, you'll find activities, exercises, assignments, handouts, and demonstrations for in-class use, as well as guidelines on integrating many media resources into your classroom and syllabus. The material for each chapter is organized according to a convenient Chapter Lecture Outline to save you preparation time.

Instructor's CD-ROM (978-0-13-157320-8) The Instructor's Resource CD-ROM brings all of the Fourth Edition instructor resources together: the PowerPoint presentations, the electronic files for the Instructor's Resource Manual materials, and the Test Item File to help you customize your lecture notes.

Instructor's Resource Binder (978-0-13-239311-9) This binder includes an extensive collection of teaching resources for new and experienced instructors alike. Organized by chapter, it includes the Instructor's Resource Manual, the Test Item file, Prentice Hall's Introductory Psychology transparencies, the Instructor's Resource CD-ROM, and the TestGen computerized testing software.

Color Transparencies (978-0-13-192699-8) A set of full-color transparencies is available at the Instructor's Resource Center online at *http://prenhall.com/irc* or on CD-ROM, as well as in acetate format. Lecture notes to accompany the transparencies for use in the classroom are also available online.

College Teaching Tips **(978-0-13-614317-8)** Fred W. Whitford (Montana State University) has drawn on his own teaching experiences over the last 25 years to help new instructors or graduate teaching assistants manage the myriad tasks required to teach an introductory course effectively and solve the array of problems a new instructor can expect. The guide has been completely revised and updated from the former *Teaching Psychology: A Guide for the New Instructor*, Fourth Edition.

Movies as Illustrations for Introductory Psychology **(978-0-13-145510-8)** Steven R. Rouse (Pepperdine University) has assembled 45 different movie scenes, several for each textbook chapter, that can be used to spark discussion and clarify concepts covered in class. This collection includes summaries of the scenes, notes that link the movie scenes to topics in introductory psychology, and discussion questions that engage the class in conversation about the scene.

Media and Online Resources for Instructors and Students

NEW **VangoNotes** Allow students to download chapter reviews, tests, and study aids and listen to them on any MP3 player, whenever they want, wherever they are. VangoNotes are easy to use; just download and go. They are efficient; they can be used in the car, at the gym, walking to class, or wherever else the student wishes. For more information or to download, go to *www.VangoNotes.com*.

 NEW MyPsychLab for *Invitation to Psychology, 4/E* Continual feedback is important for successful student progress. New to this edition, *MyPsychLab* allows instructors to assess student progress and adapt course material to meet the specific needs of the class, and it enables students to assess their progress by taking online self-assessment tests. The tests have a large base of questions that are different from those in the test bank and other supplements. Different kinds of questions are used for pretests and posttests, including multiple-choice, text match, ranking, fill in the blank, and drag and drop.

After taking the pretest, students get a customized study plan that includes a variety of tools to help them master the material. The tools include e-book exercises, simulations, and activities. Students can use these to study key content areas and then take posttests, as often as they want, to see how they are doing. Items selected for pretests and posttests are randomized, so if students opt to take the posttest again, they have exposure to additional questions for the same content area. By allowing students to assess their own progress, *MyPsychLab* helps students become more "classroom-ready" as well.

For instructors, *MyPsychLab* records the pretest, study plan, and posttest results in the form of individual student grades as well as an aggregate report of class progress. The instructor can then adapt course material to suit the needs of individual students or the class as a whole. *MyPsychLab* saves instructors time by charting student progress and by including course materials such as extra lecture notes, PPT slides, and activities right at hand. Instructors can then select whatever specific materials they need to help students with particular areas of difficulty.

Students access *MyPsychLab* through an access code packaged with their text; they can also buy it online at *www.mypsychlab.com*. Your Prentice Hall representative can provide you with an instructor's code and more information.

 LIVE!PSYCH Media Library The *Live!Psych* media library is a series of experiments, simulations, and activities to offer students an interactive way to master the major concepts presented in introductory psychology and to reinforce the scientific nature of the discipline. Designed to get students to interact with the material and to appeal to different learning styles, these media activities were created in consultation with psychology instructors and carefully reviewed by a board of experts to ensure accuracy and pedagogical effectiveness. *Live!Psych* experiments were principally designed by Linda Lockwood (Metro State College), the content author, and members of the *Live!Psych* review board. The *Live!Psych* media library is available through *MyPsychLab* or on a CD-ROM (0-13-194774-5). See *http://www.prenhall.com/livepsych*.

 Research Navigator™ helps students find, cite, and conduct research with three exclusive databases: EBSCO's ContentSelect Academic Journal Database, *The New York Times* Search by Subject Archive, and Best of the Web Link Library. Available through *MyPsychLab* or packaged with the text. See *http://www.researchnavigator.com*.

Video Classics in Psychology CD-ROM (0-13-189154-5) This CD-ROM offers original footage of some of the best-known classic experiments in psychology, including Milgram's obedience study, Watson's Little Albert, Bandura's Bobo doll, Pavlov's dog, Harlow's monkey, and others. Students can also see interviews with renowned contributors to the field like B. F. Skinner, Carl Rogers, Erik Erickson, and Carl Jung. Each video is preceded by background information on the importance of the experiment or researcher to the field and is followed by questions that connect the video to concepts presented in the text.

 SafariX WebBook Students can buy an online subscription to *Invitation to Psychology*, Fourth Edition, at a 50 percent savings. With the SafariX WebBook, students can search the text, make notes online, print out reading assignments that incorporate lecture notes, and bookmark important passages. See *www.safarix.com*.

Companion Web site Visit the Prentice Hall Introductory Psychology Web site for many resources, including links to useful sites in the major areas of psychology and links to current real-world issues. The Web site is available to all. Go to *http://www.prenhall.com/wade*.

Video Resources for Instructors

Prentice Hall has an extensive video and media library and video packages available to qualified adopters of *Invitation to Psychology*, Fourth Edition. Ask your Prentice Hall sales representative for details on these and other media packages.

Introductory Psychology Teaching Films Boxed Set (0-13-192687-X) This multi-DVD set, organized by chapter topics, contains 100 short video clips. The clips, from 5 to 15 minutes long, come from popular video sources for psychology classroom use, such as ABC News, the *Films for the Humanities* series, and PBS.

Prentice Hall Lecture Launcher Video for Introductory Psychology (0-13048640-X) This video consists of short clips from the *Films for the Humanities and Sciences* library, edited to provide brief and compelling video content for launching and enhancing your lectures.

***Films for the Humanities and Sciences* Video Library** Qualified adopters can select videos on various topics in psychology from the extensive library of *Films for the Humanities and Sciences*. See *http://www.films.com*.

Supplementary Texts

Contact your Prentice Hall representative to package any of these supplementary texts with *Invitation to Psychology*, Fourth Edition. A package ISBN is required for your bookstore order.

Student Study Guide for *Invitation to Psychology*, Fourth Edition (978-0-13-232474-8) The Fourth Edition study guide contains material to help reinforce students' understanding of the concepts covered in the text. Each chapter provides an overview to introduce students to the chapter, learning objective exercises to test students' understanding of the main themes, and a multiple-choice pretest and posttests for gauging students' progress.

***Current Directions in Introductory Psychology: Readings from the American Psychological Society* (978-0-13-152367-8)** This reader includes 20 articles from the APS journal *Current Directions in Psychological Science*. These timely, cutting-edge articles, chosen with the undergraduate audience in mind, allow students to read about current, exciting research in psychology in the words of the scientists themselves.

***Readings in Pseudoscience and the Paranormal* (978-0-13-152367-8)** This new, topically organized text, by Timothy J. Lawson (College of Mount St. Joseph), presents the differences between science and pseudoscience in a fun, interesting way. Lawson uses original sources to illustrate some of the pseudoscientific claims that students are exposed to through the media, the Internet, and pop psychology books.

***TIME* Special Edition: Psychology (978-0-13-152367-8)** These 15 lively *TIME* magazine articles about current issues and debates in psychology are perfect for discussion groups, in-class debates, or research assignments.

***Forty Studies That Changed Psychology*, Fifth Edition (978-0-13-114729-4)** Roger Hock (Mendocino College) presents the seminal research studies that have shaped modern psychology, including an overview of the environment that gave rise to each study, its experimental design, its findings, and its impact on current thinking in the discipline.

***The Psychology Student Writer's Manual*, Second Edition (978-0-13-041382-6)** If you require your students to write papers, this invaluable manual, by Jill M. Scott (University of Central Oklahoma), Russell Koch (University of Central Oklahoma), Gregory M. Scott (University of Central Oklahoma), and Stephen M. Garrison (University of Central Oklahoma), is for you. It will show your students how to prepare research reports, write term papers, and improve their overall writing ability. The authors cover fundamental aspects of writing, from structure and grammar to content and citations.

***The Psychology Major: Careers and Strategies for Success*, Third Edition (978-0-13-198751-7)** Eric Landrum (Idaho State University) and Stephen Davis (Texas Wesleyan University) offer valuable information on career options available to psychology majors, tips for improving their academic performance, and a guide to the APA style of research reporting.

***How to Think Like a Psychologist: Critical Thinking in Psychology*, Second Edition (978-0-13-015046-2)** Donald McBurney (University of Pittsburgh) uses a question-and-answer format to explore some of the most common questions students ask about psychology.

Acknowledgments

Like any other cooperative effort, writing a book requires a support team. We are indebted to the following reviewers for their many insightful and substantive suggestions during the development of this and previous editions of *Invitation to Psychology* and for their work on supplements. (Please note that the affiliations of some individuals may have changed since they reviewed our book.)

Paul Ackerman, Wichita State University
Nelson Adams, Winston-Salem State University
Lloyd Anderson, Bismarck State College
Susan A. Anderson, University of South Alabama
Kevin J. Apple, James Madison University
Eva Glahn Atkinson, Brescia University
Ronald Baenninger, Temple University
Judith Barker, Cuyahoga Community College
Linda M. Bastone, SUNY-Purchase College
Jim Beers, John Jay College of Criminal Justice
Dan Bellack, Trident Technical College
Kathleen Bey, Palm Beach Community College
Martin Bink, Western Kentucky University
Lynn Brandsma, Chestnut Hill College
John Bouseman, Hillsborough Community College
Michael A. Britt, Marist College
Kimberly Brown, Ball State University
Robert Bruel, Kean College
Dan Brunsworth, Kishwaukee College
Cheryl Busbee, CUNY BMCC
Sharon K. Calhoun, Indiana University–Kokomo
David N. Carpente, Southwest Texas State University
Sally Carr, Lakeland Community College
Loren Cheney, Community College of Rhode Island
Richard Coelho, Lansing Community College
Norman Culbertson, Yakima Valley College
Mark Cummins, Dason College
William Curtis, Camden County College
Gregory Cutler, Bay de Noc Community College

Betty Davenport, Campbell University
Nat DeAnda, Los Medanos College
Virginia Diehl, Western Illinois University
Lynn Dodson, Seattle Central Community College
Evelyn Doody, Community College of Southern Nevada
Kimberly Duff, Cerritos College
Laurel End, Mt. Mary College
William Fabricius, Arizona State University
Bryan Fantie, American University
Vivian Ferry, Community College of Rhode Island
Andrew Geoghegan, Longview Community College
Richard Girard, New Hampshire Community Technical College
Randy Gold, Cuesta College
Peter Graham, Pensacola Junior College
David Grilly, Cleveland State University
Bea Gattuso Grosh, Millersville University
Jack Harnett, Virginia Commonwealth University
Roger Harnish, Rochester Institute of Technology
James E. Hart, Edison Community College
Peter C. Hill, Grove City College
Susan Horton, Mesa Community College
Charles Huffman, James Madison University
Gene Indenbaum, SUNY-Farmingdale
Linda A. Jackson, Michigan State University
Sherri Jackson, Jacksonville University
Craig Johnson, Towson State University
Jim Jokerst, Aims Community College
Patricia Kemerer, Ivy Tech Community College
Steve Kilianski, Rutgers University
David Klein, Stark State College of Technology
Katherine Kocel, Jackson State University
Anne Kollath, Allan Hancock College
James H. Korn, Saint Louis University
Andrea Lassiter, Minnesota State University
Patsy Lawson, Volunteer State Community College
Gary Levy, University of Wyoming
John F. Lindsay, Jr., Georgia College and State University
Laura Madson, New Mexico State University
Peter Maneno, Normandale Community College
Donna B. Mantooth, Georgia Highlands College
Lyla Maynard, Des Moines Area Community College
Phil McClung, West Virginia University at Parkersburg
Cynthia McCormick, Armstrong Atlantic State University
Judith McLaughlin, Montana State University, Billings
Holly McQuillan, Porterville Community College
Elizabeth Meadows, Central Michigan University
Rafael Mendez, Bronx Community College
Judi Misale, Truman State University
Karen Mottarella, University of Central Florida
Diana P. Nagel, Northwest Arkansas Community College
Benjamin Newberry, Kent State University
J. Ken Nishita, California State University, Monterey Bay
Peggy Norwood, Metro State College of Denver
Orlando Olivares, Bridgewater State College
Kristine R. Palmer, Richland Community College
David Perkins, College of St. Elizabeth
Wade Pickren, Southeastern Oklahoma State University
Michelle Pilati, Rio Hondo College
Paula M. Popovich, Ohio University
Amy Posey, Benedictine College
Jack Powell, University of Hartford
Judith Pratt, Longview Community College
Shirley Pritchett, Northeast Texas Community College
Jeffery A. Ratliff-Crain, University of Minnesota, Morris
Steven Richman, Nassau Community College
Mark P. Rittman, Cuyahoga Community College
Denis Sabat, Mary Washington College
Claire St. Peter Pipkin, West Virginia University
Moises Salinas, Central Connecticut State University
Lee Schrock, Kankakee Community College
Suzanne Schultz, Umpqua Community College
Charles Slem, Cal Poly-San Luis Obispo
Angela Simon, El Camino College
Christina S. Sinisi, Charleston Southern University
Holly Straub, University of South Dakota
Rose Suggett, Southeast Community College, Lincoln
Ed Valsi, Oakland Community College
Lynda Vannice, Umpqua Community College
Matthew Westra, Longview Community College
Fred Whitford, Montana State University
Edmond Zuromski, Community College of Rhode Island

We are also grateful to our superb editorial and production teams at Prentice Hall. "Cooperation in pursuit of mutual goals" is known to build alliances, and over the years we have forged a strong and affectionate alliance with this remarkable group. Our deepest thanks to our former Executive Editor Jennifer Gilliland and our current one, Jessica Mosher, who supervised the revision from start to finish, offering wonderful suggestions and keeping the project on track; to Nicole Girrbach, who coordinated all of the complex details of production with exceptional efficiency and patience; and to Assistant Managing Editor Maureen Richardson, who always somehow puts together all the myriad elements of a book while responding thoughtfully to her authors' concerns (i.e., doing almost everything we want). Once again we thank Barbara Salz for her persistence in tracking down new photographs from sometimes recalcitrant sources.

As always, our greatest thanks go to Howard Williams and Ronan O'Casey, who for so many years and editions have bolstered us with their love, humor, good cheer, and good coffee, even when we are suffering from Deadline Dysphoria Disorder.

We hope that you will enjoy reading and using *Invitation to Psychology,* and that your students will find it a true invitation to the field we love. We welcome your reactions, experiences using it, and suggestions for improvements or for teaching from it.

Carole Wade
Carol Tavris

to the student

If you are reading this introduction, you are starting your introductory psychology course on the right foot. It always helps to get a general picture of what you are about to read before charging forward.

Our goal in this book is to guide you to think critically and imaginatively about psychological issues, and to help you apply what you learn to your own life and the world around you. We ourselves have never gotten over our initial excitement about psychology, and we have done everything we can think of to make the field as absorbing for you as it is for us. However, what you bring to this book is as important as what we have written—we can pitch ideas at you, but you have to step up to the plate to connect with them. This text will remain only a collection of pages with ink on them unless you choose to read actively. The more involved you are in your own learning, the more successful the book and your course will be, and the more enjoyable, too.

Getting Involved

To encourage you to read and study actively, we have included some special features:

- Every chapter opens with **Psychology in the News**, an actual story from the media related to issues that will be discussed in the chapter. Do not skip these stories! We return to them at the end of the chapter, where we show you how findings from psychology might help you understand each story in particular and others like it that you will encounter. How do you feel about a 66-year-old woman who gives birth to a baby— or an 80-year-old man who fathers one? Why would a rich man who could easily attract consenting sexual partners nonetheless commit rape? What motivated Lance Armstrong to recover from cancer and go on to win the Tour de France bicycle race seven times?

- Each chapter contains several **Get Involved** exercises, entertaining little experiments or explorations you can do that demonstrate what you are reading about. In Chapter 2, for instance, you get to assess your own basic personality traits, and in Chapter 12, you can find out how your own thoughts affect your moods. Some Get Involved exercises take only a minute; others are ministudies that you can do by observing or interviewing others.

- In Chapter 1, we will introduce you to the basic guidelines of **critical and scientific thinking**, the principles we hope will help you distinguish unsupported claims or "psychobabble" from good, scientific reasoning. The iden-

tifying icon for critical thinking is a light bulb. Throughout the book, some (but not all) of our critical-thinking discussions are signaled in the text by a small tab that includes the light bulb and the topic being critically examined, like the one shown here. We will be telling you about many lively and passionate debates in psychology: debates about sex and gender differences, the meaning of dreams, psychotherapy, recovered memories, "multiple personality disorder," and many other topics. We hope our coverage of these debates will increase your involvement with the ongoing discoveries of psychology.

Thinking Critically About . . .

- Every chapter also contains a **Close-up on Research** section, in which we take a closer look at how psychological scientists do what they do—the ways they think critically and use established methods to investigate interesting problems. We hope that by reading these you will gain a deeper appreciation of what goes into all those studies you hear about in the news—and what makes the good ones good.

- Every chapter contains several **Quick Quizzes** that test your understanding, retention, and ability to apply what you have read to examples. Do not let the word "quiz" give you a sinking feeling. These quizzes are for your practical use and even, we hope, for your enjoyment. Some contain a critical-thinking item, denoted by the light bulb symbol. The answers we give for these items are only suggestions; feel free to come up with different ones. These questions ask you to reflect on what you have read and to apply the critical-thinking guidelines described in Chapter 1. But if you take the time to respond thoughtfully to them, we think you will become more engaged with the material, learn more, and become a more sophisticated user of psychology.

- At the end of each chapter, a feature called **Taking Psychology with You** will suggest ways you can apply what you have learned to everyday concerns (such as how to boost your motivation or improve your memory) as well as to serious problems, such as how to live with chronic pain or help a friend who seems suicidal.

How to Study

In our years of teaching, we have found that certain study strategies can vastly improve learning, and so we offer the following suggestions. Reading Chapter 8, on memory, and Chapter 9, on learning, will also be helpful.

- Before starting a chapter, browse through it, looking at the pictures and reading the headings to get an idea of what is in store. Do not read the text as you might read a novel, taking in large chunks at a sitting. To get the most from your studying, we recommend that you read only a part of each chapter at a time.

- Instead of simply reading silently, nodding along saying "hmmmmm" to yourself, try to restate what you have read in your own words at the end of each major section. Some people find it helpful to write down main points. Do not count on getting by with just one reading of a chapter. Most people need to go through the material at least twice and then review the main points several times before an exam.

- When you have finished a chapter, read the **Summary** and also the **Concept Map** for the chapter, which provides a visual summary of the material and shows how the topics are related. Using the list of **Key Terms**, try to define and discuss each term to see how well you understand and remember it. If you need to review a term, a page number is given to tell you where it is first mentioned in the chapter.

- Important new terms in this textbook are printed in **boldface** and are defined in the margin of the page on which they appear or on the facing page. The **marginal glossary** permits you to find these terms and concepts easily, and it will help you when you study for exams. A complete glossary also appears at the end of the book.

- If you are assigned a term project or a report, you may need to track down some references or do further reading. Throughout the book, discussions of studies and theories include citations in parentheses that look like this: (Aardvark & Zebra, 2006). A citation tells you who the authors of a book or paper are and when their work was published. You can then look up the full reference in the **References** at the end of the book, where you will also find a *Name Index* and a *Subject Index*. The Name Index lists the name of every author cited and the pages where each person's work is discussed. If you remember the name of a psychologist but not where he or she was mentioned, look up the name in the index. The Subject Index lists all the major topics mentioned in the book. If you want to review material on, say, depression, you can look up "depression" in the Subject Index and find each place it is mentioned.

You might also want to make use of a number of study tools that accompany this text; check them out online at *www.myPearsonstore.com*.

- The **Student Study Guide**, available at your bookstore or online at *www.mypearsonstore.com*, is an excellent learning resource. It contains review materials, exercises, and practice tests to help you understand and apply the concepts in the book. Each chapter provides an overview, learning objective exercises to check your understanding of the main themes, and pretests and posttests for gauging your progress.

- **VangoNotes** contain quick reviews, exercises, practice tests, and key concepts that you can download onto any MP3 player, to use whenever you want to want to study or to review material just before an exam. Go to *http://www.VangoNotes.com*.

- *MyPsychLab* is an online resource that helps you see exactly how you are doing in your course—what you understand well and where you need more work. Based on how you do on a pretest, you are provided with your own customized study plan with simulations and activities that help you master the material you are reading. You can continue to quiz yourself by taking the posttest as many times as you want. Go to *http://www.mypsychlab.com*.

- For additional information about psychology and its links to research and news events, as well as yet another way to take online quizzes that provide immediate feedback, go to the **Companion Web site** at *http://www.prenhall.com/wade*.

We have done our utmost to convey our own enthusiasm about psychology. But it is your efforts as much as ours that will determine whether you find psychology to be exciting or boring, and whether the field will make a difference in your own life. This book is our way of inviting you into the world of psychology. Our warmest welcome!

Carole Wade
Carol Tavris

about the authors

Carole Wade earned her Ph.D. in cognitive psychology at Stanford University. She began her academic career at the University of New Mexico, where she taught courses in psycholinguistics and developed the first course at the university on the psychology of gender. She was professor of psychology for ten years at San Diego Mesa College, then taught at College of Marin and Dominican University of California. In addition to this text, she and Carol Tavris have written *Psychology*; *Psychology in Perspective*; and *The Longest War: Sex differences in perspective*. Dr. Wade has a long-standing interest in making psychology accessible to students and the general public. For many years she has focused her efforts on the teaching and promotion of critical-thinking skills, diversity issues, and the enhancement of undergraduate education in psychology. She chaired the APA Board of Educational Affairs's Task Force on Diversity Issues at the Precollege and Undergraduate Levels of Education in Psychology, as well as the APA's Public Information Committee; has been a G. Stanley Hall lecturer at the APA convention; and served on the steering committee for the National Institute on the Teaching of Psychology. Dr. Wade is a Fellow of the American Psychological Association and a charter member of the Association for Psychological Science. When she isn't busy with her professional activities, she can be found riding the trails of northern California on her Morgan horse, McGregor, or one of his Arabian stablemates, Condé or Ricochet.

Carol Tavris earned her Ph.D. in the interdisciplinary program in social psychology at the University of Michigan, and as a writer and lecturer she has sought to educate the public about the importance of critical and scientific thinking in psychology. In addition to this text, she and Carole Wade have written *Psychology*; *Psychology in Perspective*; and *The Longest War: Sex differences in perspective*. Dr. Tavris is also coauthor, with Elliot Aronson, of *Mistakes Were Made (But Not by Me): Why we justify foolish beliefs, bad decisions, and hurtful acts*; and author of *The Mismeasure of Woman* and *Anger: The misunderstood emotion*. She has written on psychological topics for a wide variety of magazines, journals, edited books, and newspapers. Many of her book reviews and opinion essays for *The Los Angeles Times*, *The New York Times Book Review*, *Scientific American*, and other publications have been collected in *Psychobabble and Biobunk: Using psychology to think critically about issues in the news*. Dr. Tavris lectures widely on, among other topics, pseudoscience in psychology and psychiatry, anger, and the science and politics of research on gender. She has taught in the psychology department at UCLA and at the Human Relations Center of the New School for Social Research in New York. She is a Fellow of the American Psychological Association and a charter Fellow of the Association for Psychological Science; a member of the board of the Council for Scientific Clinical Psychology and Psychiatry; and a member of the editorial board of the APS journal *Psychological Science in the Public Interest*. When she is not writing or lecturing, she can be found walking the trails of the Hollywood Hills with her border collie, Sophie.

psychology in the news

"Cheeseburger Bill" Wins in House

WASHINGTON, DC, OCTOBER 19, 2005. In what is being called a "weighty victory" for fast-food chains, the House of Representatives today approved the "cheeseburger" bill, officially known as the Personal Responsibility in Food Consumption Act. The new law prohibits overweight people from suing fast-food manufacturers and chains for making them fat. The bill now goes to the Senate, where it faces an uncertain future.

Zaniness on Parade in Pasadena

PASADENA, CA, NOVEMBER 19, 2005. The 29th annual Doo Dah Parade, a joyful celebration of wacky weirdness, will take place tomorrow in Pasadena. The event encourages marchers to shed their inhibitions and dress outrageously. Last week, a new Doo Dah Queen was chosen in a public tryout open to people of "all genders, ages, sizes, shapes, beliefs, and persuasions."

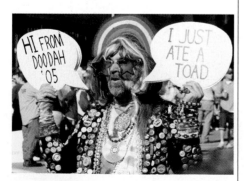

Nearly anything goes at Pasadena's annual Doo Dah Parade.

This year, for the first time, the parade will be headed up by the BBQ Hibachi Marching Grill Team.

New Orleans Evacuated

NEW ORLEANS, LA, AUGUST 31, 2005. Reeling from the devastation caused by Hurricane Katrina, residents of the Gulf Coast are continuing to stream out of the area. Even before the hurricane made landfall in Louisiana two days ago, over 1.2 million people were under orders to leave. By yesterday, levees in New Orleans had failed and 80 percent of the city was under water. Many of those who remain are without food, water, or toilets, and a sense of desperation is mounting. Experts predict a high incidence of post-traumatic stress disorder.

James Nielsen/ZUMA Press

With most of the city under water, refugees are fleeing New Orleans, some with no more than the clothes on their backs.

Canada Legalizes Gay Marriage

TORONTO, ONT., CANADA, JULY 20, 2005. Following the lead of Belgium, the Netherlands, and Spain, Canada today became the fourth nation to legalize gay marriage. Conservative and religious opponents reacted with anger and vowed to get the law reversed. In the United States, too, gay marriage remains a divisive and inflammatory issue. Only one state, Massachussets, recognizes gay marriage; Vermont and Connecticut, like several European countries, permit civil unions for gay men and lesbians, but not marriage.

Pakistani Woman Honored

NEW YORK, NY, NOVEMBER 3, 2005. At a gala event at Lincoln Center last night, *Glamour* Magazine honored Mukhtaran Bibi, a Pakistani woman who became an international symbol of resistance to injustice after being gang-raped in 2002 on orders by a neighboring tribal council. The rape was in retaliation for an alleged affair between Mukhtaran's brother and a woman from the neighboring tribe. Although tradition demanded that she kill herself, Mukhtaran instead pressed charges against her attackers, who were convicted, released after an appeal, and then re-imprisoned. She has become an advocate for the health and security of women, using government compensation and donated funds to build two schools and a police station in her village. At the *Glamour* banquet, Brooke Shields introduced the devout Muslim as a person who "showed the world the real meaning of the word honor."

What Is Psychology?

If you are in the habit of reading the news, you may have come across the five stories shown here. Newspapers, magazines, and news shows are full of tales of heroism and courage, murder and mayhem, personal accomplishment and emotional controversies. But why, you may be wondering, are we starting this book with these stories? What on earth do they have to do with psychology?

The answer is: Everything.

People usually associate psychology with mental and emotional disorders, personal problems, and psychotherapy. But psychologists take as their subject the entire spectrum of beautiful and brutish things that human beings do—the kinds of things you read and hear about every day. Psychologists reading these particular stories would want to know why obesity has become epidemic in North America: Is it because of people's lack of willpower, or do the large portions and fatty foods served by restaurants have something to do with it? They would be curious to know why some people,

psychology The discipline concerned with behavior and mental processes and how they are affected by an organism's physical state, mental state, and external environment; often represented by Ψ, the Greek letter psi (usually pronounced "sy").

empirical Relying on or derived from observation, experimentation, or measurement.

like the jovial marchers in the Doo Dah Parade, are extroverts, whereas others find comfort in quiet conformity: Is it because of genes, biology, or upbringing? They would wonder why people become straight, gay, or bisexual—and why so many straight people fear or detest homosexuality. They would want to know what enables some individuals, like Mukhtaran Bibi, to stand up for their rights and the rights of others, even at great personal risk, whereas others stay silent. They would ask why people respond in such vastly different ways to a disaster, some resorting to lawlessness, some putting their own lives in jeopardy to save others. They would have other questions about Hurricane Katrina, too: Were criticisms of the government's rescue efforts just a matter of 20/20 hindsight, or had officials been "in denial" about the seriousness of the storm? How prevalent is psychological trauma after such a catastrophe, and what kind of "crisis counseling"—if any—might be able to help those survivors who suffer from it?

If you want to know what psychology is about, then, the news is a pretty good place to start. Indeed, in this book we will be discussing all the issues raised by these stories and many others in the news. But psychology is not just about behavior that is newsworthy. Psychologists are also interested in how ordinary human beings—and other animals, too—learn, remember, solve problems, perceive, feel, and get along (or fail to get along) with others. They are, therefore, as likely to study commonplace experiences—rearing children, gossiping, remembering a shopping list, daydreaming, making love, and making a living—as exceptional ones.

If you have ever wondered what makes people tick, or if you want to gain some insight into your own behavior, then you are in the right course. We invite you now to step into the world of psychology, the discipline that dares to explore the most complex topic on earth: you.

GET INVOLVED

Read All About It

To get an idea of just how broad a discipline psychology is, take any newspaper and circle the headlines of stories about which psychology might be able to offer insights. Don't skip the sports, business, and "people" sections! How many headlines did you mark?

WHAT'S *Ahead*

- What's the difference between psychology and plain old common sense?
- How old is the science of psychology?
- Was Sigmund Freud the official founder of scientific psychology?
- What are the major perspectives in psychology?

The Science of Psychology

Psychology can be defined as *the discipline concerned with behavior and mental processes and how they are affected by an organism's physical state, mental state, and external environment*. This definition, however, is a little like defining a car as a vehicle for transporting people from one place to another without explaining how a car differs from a train or a bus, how a Ford differs from a Ferrari, or how a catalytic converter works. To get a clear picture of what psychology is, you are going to need to know more about its methods, its findings, and its ways of interpreting information.

Psychology, Pseudoscience, and Common Sense

Let's begin by considering what psychology is *not*. First, the psychology that you are about to study bears little relation to the popular psychology ("pop psych") often found in self-help books or on talk shows. In recent years, the public's appetite for psychological information has created a huge market for "psychobabble": pseudoscience and quackery covered by a veneer of psychological language. Pseudoscience (*pseudo* means "false") promises quick fixes to life's problems, such as "reliving" the supposed trauma of birth to resolve your current unhappiness, or "reprogramming" your brain to make it more creative. Serious psychology is more complex, more informative, and, we think, far more helpful than psychobabble because it is based on rigorous research and **empirical** evidence—evidence gathered by careful observation, experimentation, and measurement.

Second, serious psychology differs radically from such nonscientific competitors as graphology (handwriting analysis), fortune-telling, numerology, and the most popular, astrology. Like psychologists, promoters of these competing systems try to explain people's problems and predict their behavior. If you are having romantic problems, for example, an astrologer may advise you to choose an Aries instead of an Aquarius as your next love, and a "past-lives channeler" may say it's because you were jilted in a former life. Belief in these unscientific approaches is widespread, even in scientifically advanced countries; between one-third and one-half of Americans and Canadians believe in astrology, and 27 percent of Americans have sought out a fortune-teller or psychic for advice (De Robertis & Delaney, 2000; National Science Board, 2000). Yet whenever the predictions of psychics, astrologers, and the like are put to the test, they turn out to be so vague as to be meaningless ("Spirituality will increase next year") or just plain wrong (Park, 2000; Radford, 2005; Shermer, 1997). What should have been the fatal blow to astrological and psychic claims occurred on September 11, 2001, when the World Trade Center was destroyed. Not one psychic or astrologer had predicted that devastating event.

Third, psychology is not just a fancy name for common sense. Psychological research often produces findings that directly contradict prevailing beliefs, and throughout this book you will be discovering many of them. For example, are unhappy memories "repressed" and then accurately recalled years later, as if they had been recorded on videotape? Are most abused children destined to become abusive parents themselves? Do policies of abstinence from alcohol reduce rates of alcoholism? If you play Beethoven tapes to your infant, will your baby become smarter? At the start

of an introductory psychology course, many students hold beliefs such as these—beliefs that have been promoted in popular books and TV shows, or that are based on "commonsense" notions in the culture. Empirical evidence, however, has shown that these and many other widely held ideas about human behavior are, in fact, wrong.

CLOSE-UP on Research

Mistaken Beliefs About Human Behavior

One purpose of an introductory course like the one you are taking is to correct such misconceptions—by teaching you how psychologists study them and showing you how their research might confirm or dispel ideas that many of us take for granted. How many students come into their first psych course with a bunch of mistaken ideas in their heads—and can a semester of learning really dislodge those ideas?

To answer these questions, Annette Kujawski Taylor and Patricia Kowalski (2004) gave 90 introductory students a "Psychological Information" questionnaire on the first day of class. The test consisted of 36 true/false items—for example, "Under hypnosis you can perform feats that are otherwise impossible," "Too much sugar causes hyperactivity in children," "At any point in time, we use only 10 percent of our brains," and "Listening to Mozart will enhance your thinking and creativity." The students also rated their confidence in each of their responses on a scale of 1 (not at all confident) to 10 (very confident). All of the items were on topics that the course was scheduled to cover, and all of them were false. As a group, the students failed the test miserably: Their accuracy was only 38.5 percent, which is actually worse than chance, and they had more confidence in their wrong answers than their correct ones. Moreover, students with high grade-point averages did no better than those with low ones. So much for common sense!

During the last week of class, the same students took another test, one that included all of the earlier items plus 12 new true items that were randomly mixed in but not scored. This time, we're happy to say, the students' overall accuracy was

I see you being less gullible in the future.

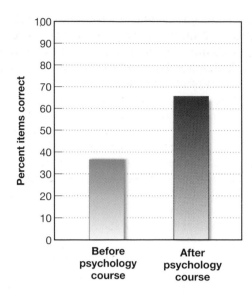

much better: 66.3 percent (see the above figure). The researchers attributed this change (which was larger than in similar studies done previously by other researchers) in part to the fact that instruction had explicitly focused on the scientific evidence refuting such beliefs. (As you will be seeing, we take the same approach in this book.) Yet even at the end of the course, more than a third of the students' responses were wrong, meaning that there was still plenty of room for improvement. The researchers then dug deeper into the evidence by analyzing the students' confidence ratings. They found that by the end of the semester, the students had gained confidence in their correct beliefs and lost confidence in their still incorrect beliefs, suggesting that they were beginning to be unsure about their misconceptions and perhaps were on the way to giving them up. If so, they were learning one of the most important lessons in science: that uncertainty about untested assumptions and beliefs can be a good thing.

Throughout this book and your introductory course, you, too, will repeatedly learn that "popular opinion" and "common sense" are not always reliable guides to human behavior. The kind of research you will be learning about won't always provide the answers you might have wished for, and sometimes it will be unable to provide final answers; our goal, however, is to show you why the scientific investigation of even our most

phrenology The now discredited theory that different brain areas account for specific character and personality traits, which can be "read" from bumps on the skull.

cherished beliefs can lead to answers that are far more sensible than "common sense." On the other hand, psychological findings do not have to be surprising or counterintuitive to be important. Like scientists in other fields, psychological scientists strive not only to discover new phenomena and correct mistaken ideas but also to deepen our understanding of an already familiar world—by identifying the varieties of love, the origins of violence, or the reasons that a great song can lift our hearts.

The Birth of Modern Psychology

Most of the great thinkers of history, from Aristotle to Zoroaster, raised questions that today would be called psychological. They wanted to know how people take in information through their senses, use information to solve problems, and become motivated to act in brave or villainous ways. They wondered about the elusive nature of emotion, and whether it controls us or is something we can control. Like today's psychologists, they wanted to *describe*, *predict*, *understand*, and *modify* behavior in order to add to human knowledge and increase human happiness. But unlike modern psychologists, scholars of the past did not rely heavily on empirical evidence. Often their observations were based simply on anecdotes or descriptions of individual cases.

This does not mean that the forerunners of modern psychology were always wrong. On the contrary, they often had insights and made observations that were verified by later work. Hippocrates (c. 460 B.C.–c. 377 B.C.), the Greek physician known as the founder of modern medicine, observed patients with head injuries and inferred that the brain must be the ultimate source of "our pleasures, joys, laughter, and jests as well as our sorrows, pains, griefs, and tears." And so it is. In the first century A.D., the Stoic philosophers observed that people do not become angry or sad or anxious because of actual events but because of their explanations of those events. And so they do.

But without empirical methods, the forerunners of psychology also committed terrible blunders. A good example comes from the early 1800s, when the theory of **phrenology** (Greek for "study of the mind") became wildly popular in Europe and America. Inspired by the writings and lectures of Austrian physician Joseph Gall (1758–1828), phrenologists argued that different

Bumpy logic? Phrenology, a nineteenth-century pseudoscientific fad, linked bumps on the skull with character traits. On this phrenology "map," notice the tiny space allocated to self-esteem and the large one devoted to cautiousness!

brain areas accounted for specific character and personality traits, such as "stinginess" and "religiosity," and that such traits could be "read" from bumps on the skull. Thieves, for example, supposedly had large bumps above the ears. When phrenologists examined people who had "stealing bumps" but were not thieves, they explained away this counterevidence by saying that other bumps represented positive traits that must be holding the person's thieving impulses in check. In the United States, parents, teachers, and employers flocked to phrenologists for advice (Benjamin, 1998). But phrenology was a classic pseudoscience—sheer nonsense.

At about the time that phrenology was peaking in popularity, several pioneering men and women in Europe and America were starting to study psychological issues using scientific methods. In 1879, the first psychological laboratory was officially established in Leipzig, Germany, by Wilhelm Wundt (VIL-helm Voont). Wundt (1832–1920), who was trained in medicine and philosophy, promoted a method called *trained introspection*, in which volunteers were taught to carefully observe, analyze, and describe their own sensations, mental images, and emotional reactions. Wundt's introspectors might take as long as 20 minutes to report their inner experiences during a 1.5-second experiment. The goal was to break behavior down into its most basic elements, much as a chemist might analyze water into hydrogen plus oxygen. Most psychologists eventually rejected trained introspection as too subjective, but Wundt still is usually credited for formally initiating the movement to make psychology a science. Many early psychologists in North America were trained in Wundt's laboratory.

Another early approach to scientific psychology, called **functionalism**, emphasized the function or purpose of behavior, as opposed to its analysis and description. One of functionalism's leaders was William James (1842–1910), an American philosopher, physician, and psychologist. Attempting to grasp the nature of the mind through introspection, wrote James (1890/1950), is "like seizing a spinning top to catch its motion, or trying to turn up the gas quickly enough to see how the darkness looks." Inspired in part by the evolutionary theories of British naturalist Charles Darwin (1809–1882), James and other functionalists instead asked how various actions help a person or animal adapt to the environment. This emphasis on the causes and consequences of behavior was to set the course of psychological science.

Psychology also has roots in Vienna, Austria, where it first developed as a method of psychotherapy. While researchers were at work in their laboratories, struggling to establish psychology as a science, Sigmund Freud (1856–1939), an obscure neurologist, was in his office listening to his patients' reports of depression, nervousness, and obsessive habits. Freud became convinced that their symptoms had mental, not bodily, causes. His patients' distress was due, he concluded, to conflicts and emotional traumas that had originated in early childhood and were too threatening to be remembered consciously, such as forbidden sexual feelings for a parent. Freud's ideas eventually evolved into a broad theory of personality, and both his theory and his methods of treating people with emotional problems became known as **psychoanalysis**.

From its early beginnings in philosophy, natural science, and medicine, psychology eventually grew into a complex discipline encompassing many

functionalism An early psychological approach that emphasized the function or purpose of behavior and consciousness.

psychoanalysis A theory of personality and a method of psychotherapy, originally formulated by Sigmund Freud, that emphasizes unconscious motives and conflicts.

different specialties, perspectives, and methods. (In other chapters, you will be learning more about the history of psychology and the people who played a prominent role in its development.) Today the field is like a large, sprawling family. The members of this family have common great-grandparents, and many of the cousins have formed alliances, but some are quarreling and a few are barely speaking to one another.

Psychology's Present

The various approaches to psychology eventually evolved into five major theoretical perspectives, which now predominate in the field. These approaches reflect different questions that psychologists ask about human behavior, different assumptions about how the mind works, and, most important, different ways of explaining why people do what they do.

1 The **biological perspective** focuses on how bodily events affect behavior, feelings, and thoughts. Electrical impulses shoot along the intricate pathways of the nervous system. Hormones course through the bloodstream, telling internal organs to slow down or speed up. Chemical substances flow across the tiny gaps that separate one microscopic brain cell from another. Biological psychologists study how these physical events interact with events in the external environment to produce perceptions, memories, and behavior. They also investigate the contribution of genes and other biological factors to the development of abilities and personality traits. A popular biological specialty, **evolutionary psychology**, follows in the tradition of functionalism by focusing on how genetically influenced behavior that was functional or adaptive during our evolutionary past may be reflected in many of our present behaviors, mental processes, and traits. The biological perspective has had a profound impact on nearly all areas of psychology and we therefore feature biological findings throughout this book.

2 The **learning perspective** is concerned with how the environment and experience affect a person's (or a nonhuman animal's) actions. Within this perspective, *behaviorists* focus on the environmental rewards and punishers that maintain or discourage specific behaviors. Behaviorists do not invoke the mind

What makes us who we are? Psychologists approach the puzzles of human behavior from five major perspectives: biological, learning, cognitive, sociocultural, and psychodynamic.

to explain behavior; they prefer to stick to what they can observe and measure directly: acts and events taking place in the environment. For example, do you have trouble sticking to a schedule? A behaviorist would analyze the environmental distractions that could help account for this common problem. *Social-cognitive learning theorists*, on the other hand, combine elements of behaviorism with research on thoughts, values, and intentions. They believe that people learn not only by adapting their behavior to the environment but also by imitating others and by thinking about the events happening around them. As we will see in other chapters, the learning perspective has many practical applications.

3 The **cognitive perspective** emphasizes what goes on in people's heads—how peo-

biological perspective
A psychological approach that emphasizes bodily events and changes associated with actions, feelings, and thoughts.

evolutionary psychology
A field of psychology emphasizing evolutionary mechanisms that may help explain human commonalities in cognition, development, emotion, social practices, and other areas of behavior.

learning perspective A psychological approach that emphasizes how the environment and experience affect a person's or animal's actions; it includes behaviorism and social-cognitive learning theories.

cognitive perspective
A psychological approach that emphasizes mental processes in perception, memory, language, problem solving, and other areas of behavior.

ple reason, remember, understand language, solve problems, explain experiences, acquire moral standards, and form beliefs. (The word *cognitive* comes from the Latin for "to know.") Using clever methods, cognitive psychologists infer mental processes from observable behavior. One of the most important contributions of this perspective has been to show how people's thoughts and explanations of events affect their actions, feelings, and choices. All of us are constantly seeking to make sense of the world and of our own physical and mental states. Our ideas may not always be realistic or sensible, but they continually influence our behavior. The cognitive approach is one of the strongest forces in psychology, and it has inspired an explosion of research on the intricate workings of the mind.

4 The **sociocultural perspective** focuses on social and cultural forces outside the individual, forces that shape every aspect of behavior, from how we kiss to what and where we eat. Most of us underestimate the impact of other people, the social context, and cultural rules on nearly everything we do: how we perceive the world, express joy or grief, manage our households, and treat our friends and enemies. We are like fish that are unaware they live in water, so obvious is water in their lives. Sociocultural psychologists study the water— the social and cultural environments that people "swim" in every day.

5 The **psychodynamic perspective** deals with unconscious dynamics within the individual, such as inner forces, conflicts, or instinctual energy. It has its origins in Freud's theory of psychoanalysis, but many other psychodynamic theories now exist. Psychodynamic psychologists try to dig below the surface of a person's behavior to get to the roots of personality; they think of themselves as archeologists of the mind. As we will see in Chapter 2, psychodynamic psychology is the thumb on the hand of psychology—connected to the other fingers, but also set apart from them because it differs radically from the others in its language, methods, and standards of acceptable evidence. Many psychological scientists believe that psychodynamic approaches belong in philosophy or literature rather than in academic psychology. But psychotherapists and laypeople are often

attracted to the psychodynamic perspective's emphasis on such grand psychological issues as the power of sexuality and the universal fear of death.

We will be encountering the major findings and methods of these five approaches in the rest of this book. The differences among these schools of thought are very real; a psychoanalyst's explanation of your personality will not be the same as a cognitive psychologist's, and neither account will be the same as that of a biological, learning, or sociocultural psychologist. However, not all psychologists feel they must swear allegiance to one approach or another. Many draw on what they take to be the best features of diverse schools of thought.

In addition, many psychologists have been affected by psychological movements and intellectual trends that do not fit neatly into any of the major perspectives. One such movement, **humanist psychology**, which gained force in the 1960s, emphasizes free will, personal growth, resilience, and the achievement of human potential and self-fulfillment. Humanists argue that psychology should focus on what really matters to most people—their uniquely human hopes and aspirations. Although many researchers regard humanism as a philosophy of life rather than a systematic or scientific approach to psychology, this movement has had considerable influence both inside and outside the field. A contemporary research specialty known as *positive psychology* follows in the footsteps of humanism by focusing on the qualities that enable people to be happy, optimistic, and resilient in times of stress (Gable & Haidt, 2005; Seligman & Csikszentmihalyi, 2000). And humanism has had a direct influence on psychotherapy and the human potential and self-help movements.

Despite the diversity of psychological approaches, however, most psychological scientists agree on certain basic guidelines about what is and what is not acceptable in their discipline. Nearly all reject supernatural explanations of events—evil spirits, psychic forces, miracles, and so forth. Most believe in the importance of gathering empirical evidence and not relying on hunches or personal belief. This insistence on rigorous standards of proof is what sets psychology apart from nonscientific explanations of human experience.

sociocultural perspective A psychological approach that emphasizes social and cultural influences on behavior.

psychodynamic perspective A psychological approach that emphasizes unconscious dynamics within the individual, such as inner forces, conflicts, or the movement of instinctual energy.

humanist psychology A psychological approach that emphasizes free will, personal growth, resilience, and the achievement of human potential.

QUICK quiz

Here is your first Quick Quiz. Try it; you won't be graded!

A. See whether psychology's past is still present in your memory.

1. *True or false?* Psychology's forerunners relied heavily on empirical evidence.

2. Credit for founding modern scientific psychology usually goes to _____.

3. Early psychologists who emphasized how behavior helps an organism adapt to its environment were known as _____.

B. To find out whether you understand the five major perspectives in psychology, match each possible explanation of anxiety on the left with a perspective on the right.

1. Anxious people often think about the future in distorted ways.

2. Anxiety is due to forbidden, unconscious desires.

3. Anxiety symptoms often bring hidden rewards, such as being excused from exams.

4. Excessive anxiety can be caused by a chemical imbalance.

5. A national emphasis on competition and success promotes anxiety about failure.

     a. learning
     b. psychodynamic
     c. sociocultural
     d. biological
     e. cognitive

Answers:

A. 1. false   2. Wilhelm Wundt   3. functionalists   B. 1. e   2. b   3. a   4. d   5. c

WHAT'S *Ahead*

- If someone is a psychologist, why can't you assume that the person is a therapist?

- If you decided to call yourself a psychotherapist, would you be breaking the law?

- What's the difference between a clinical psychologist and a psychiatrist?

What Psychologists Do

basic psychology The study of psychological issues in order to seek knowledge for its own sake rather than for its practical application.

applied psychology The study of psychological issues that have direct practical significance; also, the application of psychological findings.

Now you know the main viewpoints that guide psychologists in their work. But what do psychologists actually do with their time between breakfast and dinner?

The professional activities of psychologists generally fall into three broad categories: (1) teaching and doing research in colleges and universities; (2) providing health or mental-health services, often referred to as *psychological practice*; and (3) conducting research or applying its findings in nonacademic settings such as business, sports, government, law, and the military (see Table 1.1). Some psychologists move flexibly across these areas. A re-

searcher might also provide counseling services in a mental-health setting, such as a clinic or a hospital; a university professor might teach, do research, and serve as a consultant in legal cases.

Psychological Research

Most psychologists who do research have doctoral degrees (Ph.D.s or Ed.D.s, doctorates in education). Some, seeking knowledge for its own sake, work in **basic psychology**; others, concerned with the practical uses of knowledge, work in **applied psychology**. A psychologist doing basic research might ask, "How does peer pressure influence people's attitudes and behavior?" An applied psychologist might ask, "How can knowledge about peer pressure be used to reduce binge drinking in colleges?"

Psychologists doing basic and applied research have made important scientific contributions in areas as diverse as health, education, child development, testing, conflict resolution, marketing, industrial design, worker productivity, and urban planning. Their findings are the focus of this book and of your course. Yet scientific research is the aspect of the discipline least recognized and understood by the public (Benjamin, 2003). We hope that by the time you finish this book, you will have

TABLE 1.1
What Is a Psychologist?

Not all psychologists do clinical work. Many do research, teach, work in business, or consult. The professional activities of psychologists with doctorates fall into three general categories.

Academic/Research Psychologists	Clinical Psychologists	Psychologists in Industry, Law, or Other Settings
Specialize in areas of pure or applied research, such as:	*Do psychotherapy and sometimes research; may work in any of these settings:*	*Do research or serve as consultants to institutions on, for example:*
Human development	Private practice	Sports
Psychometrics (testing)	Mental-health clinics	Consumer issues
Health	General hospitals	Advertising
Education	Mental hospitals	Organizational problems
Industrial/organizational psychology	Research laboratories	Environmental issues
Physiological psychology	Colleges and universities	Public policy
Sensation and perception		Opinion polls
Design and use of technology		Military training
		Animal behavior
		Legal issues

a greater understanding of what research psychologists do and of their contributions to human knowledge and welfare.

Psychological Practice

Psychological practitioners, whose goal is to understand and improve people's physical and mental health, work in mental hospitals, general hospitals, clinics, schools, counseling centers, the criminal justice system, and private practice. Since the late 1970s, the proportion of psychologists who are practitioners has steadily increased; practitioners now account for over two-thirds of new psychology doctorates and members of the American Psychological Association (APA), psychology's largest professional organization.

Some practitioners are *counseling psychologists*, who generally help people deal with problems of everyday life, such as test anxiety, family conflicts, or low job motivation. Others are *school psychologists*, who work with parents, teachers, and stu-

dents to enhance students' performance and resolve emotional difficulties. The majority, however, are *clinical psychologists*, who diagnose, treat, and study mental or emotional problems. Clinical psychologists are trained to do psychotherapy with severely disturbed people, as well as with those who are simply troubled or unhappy and want to learn to handle their problems better.

In almost all states, a license to practice clinical psychology requires a doctorate. Most clinical psychologists have a Ph.D., some have an Ed.D., and a smaller but growing number have a Psy.D. (doctorate in psychology, pronounced "sy-dee"). Clinical psychologists typically do four or five years of graduate work in psychology, plus at least a year's internship under the direction of a practicing psychologist. Clinical programs leading to a Ph.D. or Ed.D. are usually designed to prepare a person both as a scientist and as a practitioner; they require completion of a *dissertation*, a major scholarly project (usually involving research) that contributes to knowledge in the field. Programs leading to a

Psychological researchers and practitioners work in all sorts of settings, from classrooms to courtrooms. Here Linda Bartoshuk (top) uses technology to study how the anatomy of the tongue influences the way we experience different tastes. A clinical psychologist (center) helps a couple in therapy. And Louis Herman (bottom) studies a dolphin's ability to understand an artificial language comprised of hand signals; in response to the gestural sequence "person" and "over," the dolphin will leap over the person in the pool.

Psy.D. focus on professional practice and do not usually require a dissertation, although they typically require the student to complete a major study, theoretical paper, or literature review. Psy.D. programs now enroll about a quarter of all doctoral candidates in psychology (Norcross, Kohout, & Wicherski, 2005).

People often confuse *clinical psychologist* with three other terms: *psychotherapist*, *psychoanalyst*, and *psychiatrist*. But these terms mean different things. A psychotherapist is simply someone who does any kind of psychotherapy. The term is not legally regulated; in fact, in most states, anyone can say that he or she is a "therapist" of one sort or another without having any training at all. A psychoanalyst is a person who practices one particular form of therapy, psychoanalysis. To call yourself a psychoanalyst, you must have an advanced degree, get specialized training at a psychoanalytic institute, and undergo extensive psychoanalysis yourself. A psychiatrist is a medical doctor (M.D.) who has done a three-year residency in psychiatry under the supervision of more experienced physicians to learn to diagnose and treat mental disorders. Like some clinical psychologists, some psychiatrists do research on mental problems, such as depression or schizophrenia, instead of working with patients.

Psychiatrists and clinical psychologists do similar work, but psychiatrists, because of their medical training, are more likely to focus on possible biological causes of mental disorders and often treat these problems with medication. They can write prescriptions and, at present, most clinical psychologists cannot. (In the United States, New Mexico and Louisiana have given prescription privileges to psychologists who receive special training, and other states are also considering doing so.) Psychiatrists, however, are often untrained in current psychological theories and methods and unfamiliar with current research in psychology (Luhrmann, 2000).

Other mental-health professionals include licensed clinical social workers (LCSWs); marriage, family, and child counselors (MFCCs); and counselors with specific specialties. These professionals ordinarily treat general problems in adjustment and family conflicts rather than serious mental disturbance, although their work may bring them into contact with people who have serious problems—violent delinquents, people with drug addictions, sex offenders, and individuals involved in domestic violence or child abuse. Licensing requirements vary from state to state but usually include a mas-

TABLE 1.2
Types of Psychotherapists

Just as not all psychologists are psychotherapists, not all psychotherapists are clinical psychologists. Here are the major terms used to refer to mental-health professionals:

Psychotherapist	A person who does psychotherapy; may have anything from no degree to an advanced professional degree; the term is unregulated.
Clinical psychologist	Diagnoses, treats, and/or studies mental and emotional problems, both mild and severe; has a Ph.D., an Ed.D., or a Psy.D.
Psychoanalyst	Practices psychoanalysis; has specific training in this approach after an advanced degree (usually, but not always, an M.D. or a Ph.D.); may treat any kind of emotional disorder or pathology.
Psychiatrist	Does work similar to that of a clinical psychologist but is likely to take a more biological approach; has a medical degree (M.D.) with a specialty in psychiatry.
Licensed clinical social worker (LCSW); marriage, family, and child counselor (MFCC)	Typically treats common individual and family problems but may also deal with more serious problems such as addiction or abuse. Licensing requirements vary but generally has at least an M.A. in psychology or social work.

ter's degree in psychology or social work and one or two years of supervised experience. (For a summary of the types of psychotherapists and the training they receive, see Table 1.2.)

Many research psychologists, and some practitioners, are worried about an increase in the number of counselors and psychotherapists who are unschooled in research methods and the empirical findings of psychology and who use unvalidated therapy techniques (Beutler, 2000; Lilienfeld, Lynn, & Lohr, 2003; Peterson, 2003). In 1987, such concerns contributed to the formation of a national organization devoted to the needs and interests of psychology as a science, the American Psychological Society (APS) (recently renamed the Association for Psychological Science). Many practitioners, on the other hand, argue that psychotherapy is an art and that research findings are largely irrelevant to the work they do with clients. In Chapter 12, we will return to the important issue of the widening gap in training and attitudes between scientists and many therapists.

Psychology in the Community

During the second half of the twentieth century, psychology expanded rapidly in terms of scholars, publications, and specialties. The American Psychological Association now has 54 divisions. Some represent major fields such as developmental psychology or physiological psychology. Others represent specific research or professional interests, such as the psychology of women, the psychology of men, ethnic minority issues, sports, the arts, environmental concerns, gay and lesbian issues, peace, psychology and the law, and health.

As psychology has grown, psychologists have found ways to contribute to their communities in about as many fields as you can think of. They consult with companies to improve worker satisfaction and productivity. They establish programs to improve race relations and reduce ethnic tensions. They advise commissions on how pollution and noise affect mental health. They do rehabilitation training for people who are physically or mentally disabled. They educate judges and juries about eyewitness testimony. They assist the police in emergencies involving hostages or disturbed persons. They conduct public-opinion surveys. They run suicide-prevention hot lines. They advise zoos on the care and training of animals. They help coaches improve the athletic performances of their teams. And on and on. Is it any wonder that people are often a little fuzzy about what a psychologist is?

QUICK quiz

Can you match the specialties on the left with their defining credentials and approaches on the right?

1. psychotherapist
2. psychiatrist
3. clinical psychologist
4. research psychologist
5. psychoanalyst

   a. Trained in a therapeutic approach started by Freud.

   b. Has a Ph.D., Psy.D., or Ed.D. and does research on, or psychotherapy for, mental-health problems.

   c. May have any credential, or none.

   d. Has an advanced degree (usually a Ph.D.) and does applied or basic research.

   e. Has an M.D.; tends to take a medical approach to emotional problems.

Answers:

1.c 2.e 3.b 4.d 5.a

WHAT'S *Ahead*

- Can a person be too open-minded?

- What guidelines can help you evaluate psychological claims?

- What's the secret of a good scientific definition?

- Why is a psychological theory unscientific if it explains anything that could conceivably happen?

- What's wrong with drawing conclusions about behavior from a collection of anecdotes?

Critical and Scientific Thinking in Psychology

One of the greatest benefits of studying psychology is that you learn not only how the brain works in general but also how to use yours in particular—by thinking critically. **Critical thinking** is the ability and willingness to assess claims and make objective judgments on the basis of well-supported reasons and evidence rather than emotion or anecdote. Critical thinkers are able to look for flaws in arguments and to resist claims that have no support. They realize that criticizing an argument is not the same as criticizing the person making it, and they are willing to engage in vigorous debate about the validity of an idea. Critical thinking, however, is not merely negative thinking. It includes the ability to be creative and constructive—the ability to come up with alternative explanations for events, think of implications of research findings, and apply new knowledge to social and personal problems.

Most people know that you have to exercise the body to keep it in shape, but they may not realize that clear thinking also requires effort and practice. All around us we can see examples of flabby thinking. Sometimes people justify their mental laziness by proudly telling you they are open-minded. But not all opinions are created equal. It's good to be open-minded, many scientists have observed, but not so open that your brains fall out!

Critical thinking is not only indispensable in ordinary life; it is also fundamental to all science, including psychological science. By exercising critical thinking, you will be able to distinguish serious psychology from the psychobabble that clutters the airwaves and bookstores. (In the study of introductory students' misconceptions described earlier, students who did well on a critical-thinking test showed the greatest improvement on the misconceptions test.) Critical thinking requires logical skills, but other skills and dispositions are also important (Anderson, 2005; Halpern, 2002; Levy, 1997; Paul, 1984; Ruggiero, 1997). Here are eight essential critical-thinking guidelines that we will be emphasizing throughout this book.

Ask Questions; Be Willing to Wonder What is the one kind of question that most exasperates parents of young children? "Why is the

critical thinking The ability and willingness to assess claims and make objective judgments on the basis of well-supported reasons and evidence rather than emotion or anecdote.

sky blue, Mommy?" "Why doesn't the plane fall?" "Why don't pigs have wings?" Unfortunately, as children grow up, they tend to stop asking "why" questions like these. (Why do you think this is?)

"The trigger mechanism for creative thinking is the disposition to be curious, to wonder, to inquire," observed Vincent Ruggiero (1988). "Asking 'What's wrong here?' and/or 'Why is this the way it is, and how did it come to be that way?' leads to the identification of problems and challenges." We hope that you will not approach psychology as received wisdom but will ask many questions about the theories and findings we present in this book. Be on the lookout, too, for questions about human behavior that have not yet been asked—the way a psychological scientist would. When the editors of the prestigious journal *Science* recently identified 125 important puzzles that scientists hope to solve over the next decades, several of those puzzles were psychological in nature (Kennedy & Norman, 2005).

"I still don't have all the answers, but I'm beginning to ask the right questions."

Define Your Terms Once you have raised a general question, the next step is to frame it in clear and concrete terms. Vague or poorly defined terms in a question can lead to misleading or incomplete answers. For example, have you ever wondered whether animals can use language? The answer depends on how you define language. If you mean "a system of communication," then birds do it, bees do it, and even worms do it. But if you mean "a system of communication that combines sounds or gestures into an infinite number of structured utterances that convey meaning" (which is how linguists define it), then as far as anyone can tell, only people use language, though some animals are able to acquire some aspects of language in special settings (see Chapter 7).

For scientists, defining terms means being precise about just what it is that they're studying. Researchers often start out with a **hypothesis**, a statement that attempts to describe or explain a given behavior. Initially, this hypothesis may be stated quite generally, as in, say, "Misery loves company." But before any research can be done, the hypothesis must be made more precise. For example, "Misery loves company" might be rephrased as "People who are anxious about a threatening situation tend to seek out others facing the same threat."

A hypothesis, in turn, leads to explicit predictions about what will happen in a particular situation. In a prediction, terms such as *anxiety* or *threatening situation* are given **operational definitions**, which specify how the phenomena in question are to be observed and measured. "Anxiety" might be defined operationally as a score on an anxiety questionnaire; "threatening situation" might be defined as the threat of an electric shock. The prediction might be, "If you raise people's anxiety scores by telling them they are going to receive electric shocks, and then you give them the choice of waiting alone or with others in the same situation, they will be more likely to choose to wait with others than they would be if they were not anxious." The prediction can then be tested, using systematic methods.

Examine the Evidence Have you ever heard someone in the heat of argument exclaim, "I just know it's true, no matter what you say" or "That's my opinion; nothing's going to change it"? Have you ever made such statements yourself? Accepting a conclusion without evidence, or expecting others to do so, is a sure sign of lazy thinking. A critical thinker asks, "What evidence supports or refutes this argument and its opposition? How reliable is the evidence?" If checking the reliability of the evidence directly is not practical, the person considers whether it came from a reliable source (Lipps, 2004). Reliable authorities exercise critical thinking themselves, have education or experience that establishes their expertise, share their evidence openly, and are trusted by other experts.

In scientific research, an idea may initially generate excitement because it is plausible, imaginative, or appealing, but as we have seen, eventually it must be backed by empirical evidence if it is to be taken seriously. A collection of anecdotes or an appeal to authority will not do. Here's an example

hypothesis A statement that attempts to predict or to account for a set of phenomena; scientific hypotheses specify relationships among events or variables and are empirically tested.

operational definition A precise definition of a term in a hypothesis, which specifies the operations for observing and measuring the process or phenomenon being defined.

When demonstrating "levitation" and other supposedly magical phenomena, illusionists such as André Kole exploit people's tendency to trust the evidence of their own eyes even when such evidence is misleading. Critical thinkers ask about the nature and reliability of the evidence for a phenomenon.

involving childhood autism, a serious mental disorder. Autistic children often live in a silent world of their own, cut off from normal social interaction. They may rock back and forth for hours, and sometimes they do self-destructive things, such as poking pencils in their ears. At one time, many clinicians thought that autism was caused by rejecting, cold "refrigerator mothers." Their belief was influenced by the writings of the eminent psychoanalyst Bruno Bettelheim, who drew his conclusions from just a few case studies of autistic children whose mothers had psychological problems. When proper studies were finally done, using objective testing procedures and a larger, more representative group of autistic children and their parents, scientists learned that parents of autistic children are as psychologically healthy as any other parents. Today we know that autism stems from a neurological problem rather than from any psychological problems of the mothers and that certain genes probably increase susceptibility to the disorder (Ingram et al., 2000). But because so many people uncriti-

principle of falsifiability The principle that a scientific theory must make predictions that are specific enough to expose the theory to the possibility of disconfirmation.

cally accepted Bettelheim's claims, thousands of women blamed themselves for their children's disorder and suffered needless guilt and remorse.

Analyze Assumptions and Biases

Assumptions are beliefs that are taken for granted, and *biases* are assumptions that keep us from considering the evidence fairly or that cause us to ignore the evidence entirely. Critical thinkers try to identify and evaluate the unspoken assumptions on which claims and arguments may rest—in the books they read, the political speeches they hear, and the advertisements that bombard them every day. In science, as in other fields, a questioning attitude toward assumptions is what drives progress. Some of the greatest scientific advances have been made by those who dared to doubt what everyone else assumed to be true: that the sun revolves around the earth, that illness can be cured by applying leeches to the skin, that madness is a sign of demonic possession.

Critical thinkers are willing to analyze and test not only other people's assumptions but also their own (which is much harder). Researchers put their own assumptions to the test by stating a hypothesis in such a way that it can be *refuted*, or disproved by counterevidence. This principle, known as the **principle of falsifiability**, does not mean that the hypothesis *will* be disproved, only that it *could be* if contrary evidence were to be discovered.

Another way of saying this is that a scientist must risk disconfirmation by predicting not only what will happen but also what will *not* happen if the hypothesis is correct. In the "misery loves company" study, the hypothesis would be supported if most anxious people sought each other out, but disconfirmed if most anxious people went off alone to sulk and worry, or if anxiety had no effect on their behavior (see Figure 1.1). A willingness to risk disconfirmation forces the scientist to take negative evidence seriously and to abandon mistaken assumptions. Any researcher who refuses to do this is not a true scientist.

Many violations of the principle of falsifiability occur in everyday life. For example, when police officers believe a suspect is guilty, they may take even the person's protestations of innocence as evidence of guilt ("He's just covering up"). Of course, many guilty people claim they are innocent, but so do innocent people. Interviewers in such situations must therefore be open to evidence that disconfirms their beliefs. Similarly, many people who firmly believe in alien abductions violate the principle of falsifiability when they are faced with evidence

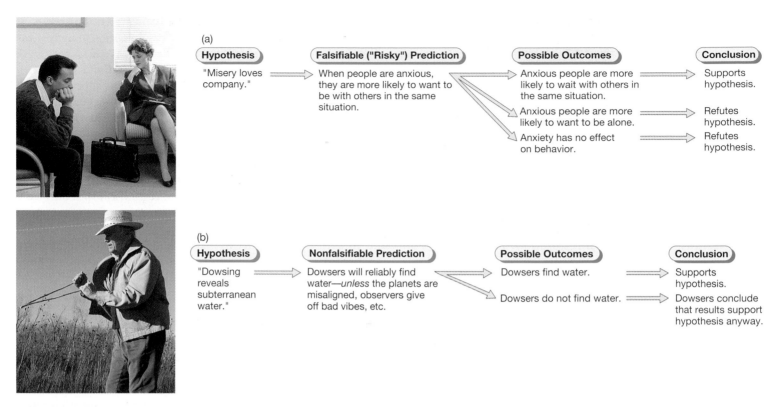

FIGURE 1.1

The Principle of Falsifiability

The scientific method requires researchers to expose their ideas to the possibility of counterevidence, as in row (a). In contrast, people claiming psychic powers, such as dowsers (who say they can find underground water with a "dowsing rod" that bends when water is present), typically interpret all possible outcomes as support for their assertions, as in row (b). Their claims are therefore untestable.

that "alien spaceships" are merely natural phenomena or weather balloons. True believers will insist that the government must be covering up the truth, or that aliens must have clever, sneaky ways of disguising their spacecraft. By simply explaining away all counterevidence, they avoid ever putting their beliefs to the test.

Avoid Emotional Reasoning

Emotion has a place in critical thinking and in science, too. Passionate commitment to a view motivates people to think boldly, to defend unpopular ideas, and to seek evidence for creative new theories. But emotional conviction alone cannot settle arguments.

All of us are apt to feel threatened and get defensive whenever our most treasured beliefs are challenged. We value these beliefs highly, in part because they offer explanations for phenomena that might otherwise seem puzzling or frightening and because they simplify a complicated world (Preston & Epley, 2005). You probably already hold strong beliefs about child rearing, drugs, the causes of crime, racism, the origins of intelligence, gender

differences, homosexuality, and many other issues of concern to psychologists. As you read this book, you may find yourself quarreling with findings that you dislike. Disagreement is fine; it means that you are reading actively and are engaged with the material. All we ask is that you think about why you are disagreeing. Is it because the evidence is unpersuasive or because the results make you feel anxious or annoyed?

Don't Oversimplify

A critical thinker looks beyond the obvious, resists easy generalizations, and rejects either–or thinking. For example, is it better to feel you have control over what happens to you, or to accept with tranquility whatever life serves up? Either answer oversimplifies. As we will see in Chapter 13, control has many important benefits, but sometimes it's best to "go with the flow."

One common form of oversimplification is *argument by anecdote*—generalizing from a personal experience or a few examples to everyone: One crime committed by a paroled ex-convict means that parole should be abolished; one friend who hates his or her school means that everybody who goes there hates it. Anecdotes are often the source of stereotyping as well: One dishonest welfare mother means they are all dishonest; one encounter with an unconventional Californian means they are all flaky. Critical and scientific thinkers want more evidence than one or two stories before drawing such sweeping conclusions.

Consider Other Interpretations

A critical thinker creatively formulates hypotheses that offer reasonable explanations of the topic at hand. In science, the goal is to arrive at a **theory**, an organized system of assumptions and principles that purports to explain certain phenomena and how they are related. A scientific theory is not just someone's personal opinion, as in "It's only a theory" or "I have a theory about why he told that lie." It is true that some scientific theories are tentative, pending more research, but some, like the theories of gravity and evolution, are accepted by virtually all scientists. Theories that come to be accepted by the scientific community make as few assumptions as possible and account for many empirical findings.

Before settling on an explanation of some behavior, however, critical thinkers are careful not to shut out alternative possibilities. They generate as many interpretations of the evidence as they can before choosing the most likely one. For example, suppose a news magazine reports that people who are chronically depressed are more likely than nondepressed people to develop cancer. Before concluding that depression causes cancer, you would need to consider some other possibilities. Perhaps depressed people are more likely to smoke and to drink excessively, and it is these unhealthful habits that increase their cancer risk. Or perhaps, in studies of depression and cancer, early, undetected cancers were responsible for the patients' feelings of depression.

Tolerate Uncertainty

Ultimately, learning to think critically teaches us one of the hardest lessons of life: how to live with uncertainty. Sometimes there is little or no evidence available to examine. Sometimes the evidence permits only tentative conclusions. Sometimes the evidence seems strong enough to permit strong conclusions . . . until, exasperatingly, new evidence throws our beliefs into disarray. Critical thinkers are willing to accept this state of uncertainty. They are not afraid to say, "I don't know" or "I'm not sure."

In science, tolerating uncertainty means that researchers must avoid drawing firm conclusions until other researchers have repeated, or *replicated*, their studies and verified their findings. Secrecy is a big "no-no" in science; you must be willing to tell others where you got your ideas and how you tested them so that others can challenge the findings if they think the findings are wrong. Replication is an essential part of the scientific process because sometimes what seems to be a fabulous phenomenon turns out to be only a fluke.

The need to accept a certain amount of uncertainty does not mean that we must abandon all assumptions, beliefs, and convictions. That would be impossible, in any case: We all need values and principles to guide our actions. As Vincent Ruggiero (1988) wrote, "It is not the embracing of an idea that causes problems—it is the refusal to relax that embrace when good sense dictates doing so."

As you read this book, keep in mind the eight guidelines we have described. Practice in critical thinking really can help students bulk up their "thinking muscles" and understand psychological concepts better. That is why we have given you many opportunities to apply these guidelines to psychological theories and to the personal and social

Many questions currently have no firm answers. For example, several explanations of sexual orientation have been offered, but no one theory can account for the many variations of both homosexuality and heterosexuality, as we will see in Chapter 14.

theory An organized system of assumptions and principles that purports to explain a specified set of phenomena and their interrelationships.

issues that affect us all. Starting with the next chapter, the "Close-up on Research" feature will high-

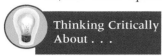
Thinking Critically About . . .

light some of the guidelines that you should keep in mind when reading about a particular study. From time to time, a blue tab with a light bulb symbol, like the one shown here, will highlight a discussion in which one or more of our critical-thinking guidelines are especially relevant. In Quick Quizzes, the light bulb will indicate questions that give you prac-

tice in applying the guidelines yourself. Keep in mind, however, that critical thinking is important throughout the book, not only where the light bulb appears.

Critical thinking is a tool to guide us on a life-long quest for understanding—a tool that we must keep sharpening. And it is as much an attitude as it is a set of skills. True critical thinking, in the words of philosopher Richard W. Paul (1984), is "fair-mindedness brought into the heart of everyday life."

QUICK *quiz*

Can you say how the guidelines to critical thinking were violated in each of the following cases?

1. For years, writer Norman Cousins told how he had cured himself of a rare, life-threatening disease through a combination of humor and vitamins. In a best-selling book, he recommended the same approach to others.

2. Benjamin Rush, an eighteenth-century physician, believed that yellow fever should be treated by bloodletting. Many of his patients died, but Rush did not lose faith in his approach; he attributed each recovery to his treatment and each death to the severity of the disease (Stanovich, 1996).

3. In recent years, several newsmagazines have run stories claiming that U.S. schoolchildren have too much homework. They have cited numerous examples of kids who are stressed out because they are overworked.

Answers:

1. Cousins oversimplified, arguing by anecdote instead of examining evidence from controlled studies that included people who were not helped by humor and vitamins, and he may have been reasoning emotionally because of his own dramatic recovery.   2. Rush failed to analyze and test his assumptions; he violated the principle of falsifiability, interpreting a patient's survival as support for his hypothesis and explaining away each death by saying that the person had been too ill for the treatment to work. Thus, there was no possible counterevidence that could refute the theory (which, by the way, was dead wrong—the "treatment" was actually as dangerous as the disease).   3. These claims rely on anecdotal "evidence." And, by the way, they are false. Empirical studies find that time spent daily on homework increased from an average of 16 minutes in 1981 to slightly more than 19 minutes in 1997 and has not changed much since; half of all 3- to 12-year-olds say they do no homework at all (Brown Center on Education Policy, 2003). Students who are overburdened by homework are the exception, not the rule.

WHAT'S *Ahead*

- From what group are participants in psychological studies most often drawn—and why does it matter?

- When are psychological case studies informative, and when are they useless?

- Why do psychologists often observe people in laboratories instead of simply watching them in everyday situations?

- What's the test of a good test?

- Why should you be skeptical about psychological tests that appear in magazines and newspapers and on the Internet?

- What's the difference between a psychological survey and a poll of listeners on talk radio?

Descriptive Studies: Establishing the Facts

Psychologists gather evidence to support their hypotheses by using different methods, depending on the kinds of questions they want to answer. These methods are not mutually exclusive, however. Just as a police detective may rely on DNA samples, fingerprints, and interviews of suspects to figure out "who done it," psychological sleuths often draw on different techniques at different stages of an ongoing investigation.

No matter what technique is used, one major challenge facing any researcher is to select the participants ("subjects") for the study. Ideally, the researcher would prefer to get a **representative sample**, a group of participants that accurately represents the larger population that the researcher is interested in. Suppose you wanted to learn about drug use among college sophomores. Questioning or observing every sophomore in the country would obviously not be practical; instead, you would need to recruit a sample. You could use special selection procedures to ensure that this sample contained the same proportion of women, men, blacks, whites, poor people, rich people, Catholics, Jews, and so on as in the general population of college sophomores. Even then, a sample drawn just from your own school or town might not produce results applicable to the entire country or even your state.

Most people do not realize that a sample's size is less critical than its representativeness. A small but representative sample may yield extremely accurate results, whereas a study that fails to use proper sampling methods may yield questionable results, no matter how large the sample. In practice, psychologists and others who study human behavior must often settle for a sample of people who happen to be available, and more often than not, this means college students. Psychologist Peter Killeen notes, with tongue only partly in cheek, that students are "cheaper than white rats, and they're more similar to the population to which we hope to generalize. And they seldom bite" (quoted in Jaffe, 2005). But because college students differ in many ways from nonstudents, conclusions based on college students do not always generalize to the population at large, and they should be accepted with caution until the research is replicated with nonstudents (R. Peterson, 2001).

We turn now to the specific methods used most commonly in psychological research. As you read about these methods, you may want to list their advantages and disadvantages in order to remember them better, and then check your list against the one in Table 1.3 on page 30. We will begin with **descriptive methods**, which allow researchers to describe and predict behavior but not necessarily to choose one explanation over competing ones.

Case Studies

A **case study** (or *case history*) is a detailed description of a particular individual, based on careful observation or on formal psychological testing. It may include information about a person's childhood, dreams, fantasies, experiences, relationships, and hopes—anything that will provide insight into the person's behavior. Case studies are most common-

ly used by clinicians, but sometimes academic researchers use them as well, especially when they are just beginning to study a topic or when practical or ethical considerations prevent them from gathering information in other ways.

For example, suppose you want to know whether the first few years of life are critical for acquiring a first language. Can children who have missed out on hearing speech (or, in the case of deaf children, seeing signs) "catch up" later? Obviously, psychologists cannot answer this question by isolating children and seeing what happens! So instead they have studied unusual cases of language deprivation.

One such case involved a 13-year-old girl who had been cruelly locked up in a small room since infancy. Her mother, a battered wife, barely cared for her, and no one in the family spoke a word to her. If she made the slightest sound, her severely disturbed father beat her with a large piece of wood. When she was finally rescued, Genie, as researchers called her, did not know how to chew or to stand erect, and her only sounds were high-pitched whimpers. Eventually, she began to use words and understand short sentences, but even after many years, her grammar and pronunciation remained abnormal. She never learned to use pronouns correctly, ask questions, produce proper negative sentences, or use the little word endings that communicate things like tense and possession (Curtiss, 1977, 1982;

This picture, drawn by Genie, a young girl who endured years of isolation and mistreatment, shows one of her favorite pastimes: listening to researcher Susan Curtiss playing the piano. Genie's drawings were used along with other case material to study her mental and social development.

representative sample A group of individuals, selected from a population for study, which matches that population on important characteristics such as age and sex.

descriptive methods Methods that yield descriptions of behavior but not necessarily causal explanations.

case study A detailed description of a particular individual being studied or treated.

observational study
A study in which the researcher carefully and systematically observes and records behavior without interfering with the behavior; it may involve either naturalistic or laboratory observation.

GET INVOLVED

A Study of Personal Space

Try a little naturalistic observation of your own. Go to a public place where people seat themselves, such as a movie theater or a cafeteria with large tables. You might recruit some friends to help you; you can divide the area into sections and assign each observer one section to observe. As individuals and groups sit down, note how many seats they leave between themselves and the next person. On the average, how far do people tend to sit from strangers? Once you have your results, see how many possible explanations you can come up with.

Rymer, 1993). This sad case, along with similar ones, suggests that a critical period exists for language development, with the likelihood of mastering a first language declining steadily after early childhood and falling off drastically at puberty (Pinker, 1994).

Case studies illustrate psychological principles in a way that abstract generalizations and cold statistics never can, and they produce a more detailed picture of an individual than other methods do. In biological research, cases of patients with brain damage have yielded important clues to how the brain is organized (see Chapter 4). But in most instances, case studies have serious drawbacks. Information is often missing or is hard to interpret (for example, no one knows whether Genie was born with mental deficits). The observer may have biases that cause him or her to notice some facts and overlook others. The person who is the focus of the study may report selective or inaccurate memories. And that person may be unrepresentative of the group that the researcher is interested in; therefore, this method has only limited usefulness for deriving general principles of behavior. For all these reasons, case studies are usually only sources, rather than tests, of hypotheses. You should be extremely cautious about pop-psych books and TV programs that present only testimonials and vivid case histories as evidence.

Observational Studies

In **observational studies**, the researcher observes, measures, and records behavior while taking care to avoid intruding on the people (or animals) being observed. The primary purpose of *naturalistic observation* is to find out how people or other animals act in their normal social environments. Psychologists use naturalistic observation wherever people happen to be—at home, on playgrounds or streets, in schoolrooms, or in offices. Often, however, researchers prefer making their observations in a laboratory setting. In *laboratory observation*, they have more control. They can use sophisticated equipment, determine how many people will be observed at once, maintain a clear line of vision, and so forth.

Suppose that you wanted to know how infants of different ages respond when left with a stranger. The most efficient approach might be to have parents and their infants come to your laboratory, observe them playing together for a while through a one-way window, then have a stranger enter the room and, a few minutes later, have the parent leave. You could record signs of distress, interactions with the stranger, and other behavior, checking your observations against those of others to ensure accuracy. If you did this, you would find that very young infants carry on cheerfully with whatever they are doing when the parent leaves. However, by the age of about 8 months, children will often burst into tears or show other signs of what child psychologists call "separation anxiety" (see Chapter 3).

The man on the left is slumbering for science. By sleeping in the laboratory instead of in the natural environment of their own homes, volunteers can provide researchers with valuable information about brain and muscle activity during sleep.

One shortcoming of laboratory observation is that the presence of researchers and special equipment may cause participants to behave differently than they would in their usual surroundings. Further, observational studies, like other descriptive studies, are more useful for describing behavior than for explaining it. If we observe infants protesting whenever a parent leaves the room, we cannot be sure why they are protesting. Is it because they have become attached to their parents and want them nearby, or have they learned from experience that crying brings an adult with a cookie and a cuddle? Observational studies alone cannot answer such questions.

Tests

Psychological tests, sometimes called *assessment instruments*, are procedures for measuring and evaluating personality traits, emotional states, aptitudes, interests, abilities, and values. Typically, tests require people to answer a series of written or oral questions. The answers may then be totaled to yield a single numerical score, or a set of scores. *Objective tests*, also called *inventories*, measure beliefs, feelings, or behaviors of which an individual is aware; *projective tests* are designed to tap unconscious feelings or motives (see Chapter 11).

At one time or another, you no doubt have taken a personality test, an achievement test, or a vocational-aptitude test. Hundreds of psychological tests are used in industry, education, the military, and the helping professions. Some are given to individuals, others to large groups. These measures help clarify differences among individuals, as well as differences in the reactions of the same person on different occasions or at different stages of life. Tests may be used to promote self-understanding, to evaluate treatments and programs, or, in scientific research, to draw generalizations about human behavior. Well-constructed psychological tests are a great improvement over simple self-evaluation because many people have a distorted view of their own abilities and traits. For example, in the workplace, employees tend to overestimate their skills and CEOs are overconfident in their judgments. Both in school and on the job, people are often blissfully unaware of their own lack of competence (Dunning, Heath, & Suls, 2004).

One test of a good test is whether it is **standardized**—that is, whether uniform procedures exist for giving and scoring the test. It would hardly be fair to give some people detailed instructions and plenty of time and others only vague in-

Many people attach a lot of importance to their test scores!

structions and limited time. Those who administer the test must know exactly how to explain the tasks involved, how much time to allow, and what materials to use. Scoring is usually done by referring to **norms**, or established standards of performance. The usual procedure for developing norms is to give the test to a large group of people who resemble those for whom the test is intended. Norms determine which scores can be considered high, low, or average.

Test construction presents many challenges. For one thing, the test must be **reliable**—that is, it must produce the same results from one time and place to the next. A vocational-interest test is not reliable if it tells Tom that he would make a wonderful engineer but a poor journalist, but then gives different results when Tom retakes the test a week later. Nor is it reliable if alternate forms of the test, intended to be comparable, yield different results.

To be useful, a test must also be **valid**—that is, it must measure what it is designed to measure. A creativity test is not valid if what it actually measures is verbal sophistication. The validity of a test is often measured by its ability to predict independent measures, or *criteria*, of the trait in question. The criterion for a scholastic aptitude test might be college grades; the criterion for a test of shyness might be behavior in social situations. Among psychologists, controversy exists about the validity of even some widely used tests, such as IQ tests and the Scholastic Assessment Test (SAT).

Criticisms and reevaluations of psychological tests keep psychological assessment honest

psychological tests Procedures used to measure and evaluate personality traits, emotional states, aptitudes, interests, abilities, and values.

standardize In test construction, to develop uniform procedures for giving and scoring a test.

norms In test construction, established standards of performance.

reliability In test construction, the consistency of test scores from one time and place to another.

validity The ability of a test to measure what it was designed to measure.

and scientifically rigorous. In contrast, the pop-psych tests frequently found in magazines and newspapers and on the Internet usually have not been evaluated for either validity or reliability. These questionnaires often have inviting headlines such as "What Breed of Dog Are You Most Like?" or "The Seven Types of Lover," but they are merely lists of questions that someone thought sounded good.

Surveys

Psychological tests usually generate information about people indirectly. In contrast, **surveys** are questionnaires and interviews that gather information by asking people *directly* about their experiences, attitudes, or opinions. Most of us are familiar with national opinion surveys, such as the Gallup and Roper polls. Surveys have been done on many topics, from Internet use to sexual preferences.

Surveys produce bushels of data, but they are not easy to do well. Sampling problems are often an issue. For example, when a radio talk-show host surveys listeners about a political issue, the results

Thinking Critically About Opinion Polls and Surveys

are not likely to generalize to the population as a whole, even if thousands of people respond. Why? As a group, people who listen to talk radio are likely to hold different opinions than those who prefer, say, a classical music station.

The Internet sometimes provides researchers with huge samples that are more diverse than traditional ones in terms of gender, socioeconomic status, and geographic region, and are thus more representative of the general population (Gosling et al., 2004). However, all surveys and polls, even those on the Internet, are vulnerable to the problem of **volunteer bias**: Those who feel strongly enough to volunteer their opinions may differ from those who stay silent. When you read about a survey (or any other kind of study), always ask who participated. A biased, nonrepresentative sample does not necessarily mean that a survey is worthless or uninteresting, but it does mean that the results may not hold true for other groups.

Yet another problem with surveys is that people sometimes lie, especially when the survey is about a touchy topic ("What? Me do that disgusting/dishonest/fattening thing? Never!"). The likelihood of lying is reduced when respondents are guaranteed anonymity. Computer technolo-

gy can help in this regard because people are more likely to feel anonymous when they "talk" to a computer than when they fill out a paper-and-pencil questionnaire (Turner et al., 1998). Also, there are ways to check for lying—for example, by asking a question several times with different wording. But not all surveys use these techniques, and even when people are trying to be truthful, they may misinterpret the survey questions or misremember the past.

When you hear about the results of a survey or opinion poll, you also need to consider which questions were (and were not) asked and how the questions were phrased. The questions a researcher asks may reflect his or her assumptions about the topic or may be designed to further a particular agenda (Ericksen & Steffen, 1999). Many years ago, famed sex researcher Alfred Kinsey made it his practice always to ask, "*How many times have you* (masturbated, had nonmarital sex, etc.)?" rather than "*Have you ever* (masturbated, had nonmarital sex, etc.)?" The first type of question elicits more truthful responses than the second because it decreases the respondent's potential self-consciousness about having done the act in question. The second way of phrasing the question would have permitted embarrassed respondents to reply with a simple but dishonest "No."

As you can see, although surveys can be extremely informative, they must be conducted and interpreted carefully.

surveys Questionnaires and interviews that ask people directly about their experiences, attitudes, or opinions.

volunteer bias A shortcoming of findings derived from a sample of volunteers instead of a representative sample; the volunteers may differ from those who did not volunteer.

"Are you (a) contented, (b) happy, (c) very happy, (d) wildly happy, (e) deliriously happy?"

QUICK quiz

Be careful how you interpret these questions.

A. Which descriptive method would be most appropriate for studying each of the following topics? (All of them, by the way, have been investigated by psychologists.)

1. Ways in which the games of boys differ from those of girls
2. Changes in attitudes toward nuclear disarmament after a TV movie about nuclear holocaust
3. The math skills of children in the United States versus Japan
4. Physiological changes that occur when people watch violent movies
5. The development of a male infant who was reared as a female after his penis was accidentally burned off during a routine surgery

    a. case study
    b. naturalistic observation
    c. laboratory observation
    d. survey
    e. test

B. Professor Flummox gives her new test of aptitude for studying psychology to her psychology students at the start of the year. At the end, of the year, she finds that those who did well on the test averaged only a C in the course. The test lacks _____.

Answers:

A. 1.b 2.d 3.e 4.c 5.a   B. validity

WHAT'S *Ahead*

- If two things are "negatively" correlated, such as grades and TV watching, what is the relationship between them?

- If attention problems in children and time spent watching TV are "positively" correlated, does that mean TV causes attention problems?

Correlational Studies: Looking for Relationships

In descriptive research, psychologists often want to know whether two or more phenomena are related and, if so, how strongly. For example, are students' grade-point averages related to the number of hours they spend watching television? To find out, a psychologist would do a **correlational study**.

Measuring Correlations

The word **correlation** is often used as a synonym for "relationship." Technically, however, a correlation is a numerical measure of the *strength* of the relationship between two things. The "things" may

be events, scores, or anything else that can be recorded and tallied. In psychological studies, such things are called **variables** because they can vary in quantifiable ways. Height, weight, age, income, IQ scores, number of items recalled on a memory test, number of smiles in a given time period— anything that can be measured, rated, or scored can serve as a variable.

A **positive correlation** means that high values of one variable are associated with high values of the other, and that low values of one variable are associated with low values of the other:

Variable 1   Variable 2

Positive Correlation

Height and weight are positively correlated, for example; so are IQ scores and school grades. Rarely is a correlation perfect, however. Some tall people weigh less than some short ones; some people with average IQs are superstars in the classroom, and some with high IQs get poor grades. Figure 1.2(a) shows a positive correlation between men's educational level and their annual income.

correlational study A descriptive study that looks for a consistent relationship between two phenomena.

correlation A measure of how strongly two variables are related to each other.

variables Characteristics of behavior or experience that can be measured or described by a numeric scale; variables are manipulated and assessed in scientific studies.

FIGURE 1.2
Correlations
Graph (a) shows a positive correlation: In general, income rises with education. Graph (b) shows a negative correlation: In general, the higher people's incomes are, the fewer dental problems they have. Graph (c) shows a zero correlation between height and aggressiveness.

A **negative correlation** means that high values of one variable are associated with low values of the other:

Figure 1.2(b) shows a negative correlation between average income and the incidence of dental disease for groups of 100 families; in general, as you can see, the higher the income, the fewer the dental problems. In the automobile business, the older the car, the lower the price, except for antiques and models favored by collectors. As for human beings, in general, the older adults are, the fewer miles they can run, the fewer crimes they are likely to commit, and the fewer hairs they have on their heads. And remember our question about hours spent watching TV and grade-point averages? They're negatively correlated: Spending lots of hours in front of the television is associated with lower grades, possibly because TV watching cuts into study time (Potter, 1987; Ridley-Johnson, Cooper, & Chance, 1983). (That may be why the more hours children spend in front of the television, the less likely they are later on to get through college, even after controlling for IQ, behavioral problems, and socioeconomic status [Hancox, Milne, & Poulton, 2005]). See whether you can think of other variables that are negatively correlated. Remember that a negative correlation means a relationship exists; the more of one thing, the less of another. If there is no relationship between two variables, as in Figure 1.2(c), we say that they are *uncorrelated*. For example, shoe size and IQ scores are uncorrelated.

The statistic used to express a correlation is called the **coefficient of correlation**. This number conveys both the size of the correlation and its direction. A perfect positive correlation has a coefficient of +1.00, and a perfect negative correlation has a coefficient of −1.00. Suppose you weighed ten people and listed them in order, from lightest to heaviest, then measured their heights and listed them in order, from shortest to tallest. If the names on the two lists were in exactly the same order, the correlation between weight and height would be +1.00. If the correlation between two variables is +.80, it means that the two are strongly related. If the correlation is −.80, the relationship is just as strong, but it is negative. When there is no association between two variables, the coefficient is zero or close to zero.

Cautions About Correlations

Correlational studies are common in psychology and are often reported in the news. But beware: Correlations can be misleading. The important thing to remember is that *a correlation does not necessarily establish causation*. It is easy to assume that if A predicts B, then A must be causing B—that is,

positive correlation An association between increases in one variable and increases in another or between decreases in one and in the other.

negative correlation An association between increases in one variable and decreases in another.

coefficient of correlation A measure of correlation that ranges in value from −1.00 to +1.00.

making B happen—but that is not necessarily so. For example, a study recently discovered a positive correlation between the number of hours that children watch television between ages 1 and 3 and their risk of having attention problems by age 7 (Christakis et al., 2004). The news media jumped on this finding and implied that watching TV *causes* later attention problems. Now, that might be true, but it is also possible that attention problems cause TV watching: Perhaps children who have attention problems early on are more attracted to television than calmer children are. Or perhaps the harried parents of distractable children are more likely than other parents to rely on TV as a babysitter. It's also possible that neither variable causes the other directly: Perhaps parents who allow their young kids to watch a lot of TV have attention problems themselves, and, therefore, they create a home environment that fosters hyperactivity and inattentiveness. Likewise, a negative correlation between TV watching and grades might exist because heavy TV watchers have less time to study, but it is also possible that they have some personality trait that attracts them to TV and makes them dislike studying, or that they use TV as an escape when their grades are low, or that TV is especially appealing to people who are not academically inclined . . . you get the idea.

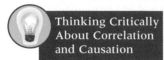 **Thinking Critically About Correlation and Causation**

The moral of the story: When two variables are associated, one variable may or may not be causing the other.

QUICK quiz

Are you clear about correlations?

A. Identify each of the following as a positive or negative correlation:

1. The higher a male monkey's level of the hormone testosterone, the more aggressive he is likely to be.

2. The older people are, the less frequently they tend to have sexual intercourse.

3. The hotter the weather, the more crimes against persons (such as muggings) tend to occur.

B. Now see whether you can generate two or three possible explanations for each of the preceding findings.

Answers:

A. 1. positive 2. negative 3. positive B. 1. The hormone may cause aggressiveness, or acting aggressively may stimulate hormone production. 2. Older people may have less interest in sex than younger people, have less energy or more physical ailments, or simply have trouble finding partners. 3. Hot temperatures may make people edgy and cause them to commit crimes; potential victims may be more plentiful in warm weather because more people go outside; criminals may find it more comfortable to be out committing their crimes in warm weather than in cold. (Our explanations for these correlations are not the only ones possible.)

WHAT'S *Ahead*

- Why do psychologists rely so heavily on experiments?

- What, exactly, do control groups control *for*?

- In a double-blind experiment, who is "blind" and what aren't they supposed to "see"?

The Experiment: Hunting for Causes

Researchers gain plenty of information from descriptive studies, but when they want to actually track down the causes of behavior, they rely heavily on the experimental method. An **experiment** allows the researcher to *control*, or manipulate, the situation being studied. Instead of being a passive recorder of what is going on, the researcher actively does something that he or she believes will affect people's behavior and then observes what happens. These procedures allow the experimenter to draw conclusions about cause and effect—about what causes what.

All psychological studies must conform to certain ethical guidelines, but such guidelines are especially important in experimental research because of this element of manipulation. In nearly all colleges and universities, a review committee must approve all studies and be sure they conform to federal regulations. In addition, the American

experiment A controlled test of a hypothesis in which the researcher manipulates one variable to discover its effect on another.

Psychological Association (APA) has a code of ethics, stating that subjects in a study must voluntarily consent to participate and must know enough about the study to make an intelligent decision, a doctrine known as **informed consent**. Researchers must protect participants from physical and mental harm, and if any risk exists, must warn them and give them an opportunity to withdraw at any time.

The APA's code also covers the humane treatment of research animals, which are used in only a small minority of psychological studies but are crucial to progress in some fields, especially biological psychology and behavioral research. Because of heated debates over animal rights and welfare, the APA's guidelines for using animals have been made more comprehensive in recent years. In addition, federal regulations governing the housing and care of animals have been strengthened and are constantly being reevaluated. Every experiment involving vertebrates must now be reviewed by a committee that includes representatives from the research institution and the community.

Experimental Variables

Imagine that you are a psychologist and you come across reports that cigarette smoking improves reaction time on simple tasks. You have a hunch that nicotine may have the opposite effect, however, when the task is as complex and demanding as driving a car. Therefore, you decide to do an experiment to test your hypothesis. In a laboratory, you ask smokers to "drive" using a computerized driving simulator equipped with a stick shift and a gas pedal. The object, you tell them, is to maximize the distance covered by driving as fast as possible on a winding road while avoiding collisions with other cars. At your request, some of the participants smoke a cigarette immediately before climbing into the driver's seat. Others do not. You are interested in comparing how many collisions the two groups have. The basic design of this experiment is illustrated in Figure 1.3, which you may want to refer back to as you read the next few pages.

The aspect of an experimental situation manipulated or varied by the researcher is known as

informed consent The doctrine that human research subjects must participate voluntarily and must know enough about a study to make an intelligent decision about whether to participate.

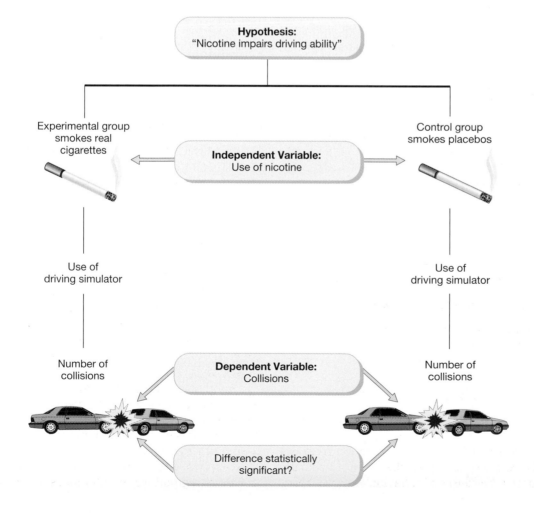

FIGURE 1.3
Do Smoking and Driving Mix?
The text describes this experimental design to test the hypothesis that nicotine in cigarettes impairs driving skills.

the **independent variable**. The reaction of the subjects—the behavior that the researcher tries to predict—is the **dependent variable**. Every experiment has at least one independent and one dependent variable. In our example, the independent variable is nicotine use: one cigarette versus none. The dependent variable is the number of collisions.

Ideally, everything in the experimental situation except the independent variable is held constant—that is, kept the same for all participants. You would not have some people use a stick shift and others an automatic, unless shift type were an independent variable. Similarly, you would not have some people go through the experiment alone and others perform in front of an audience. Holding everything but the independent variable constant ensures that whatever happens is due to the researcher's manipulation and nothing else. It allows you to rule out other interpretations.

Understandably, students often have trouble keeping independent and dependent variables straight. You might think of it this way: The dependent variable—the outcome of the study—*depends* on the independent variable. When psychologists set up an experiment, they think, "If I do X, the people in my study will do Y." The "X" represents the independent variable; the "Y" represents the dependent variable:

Experimenter manipulates	Subjects' behavior *depends* on what experimenter does
↓	↓
Independent Variable → affects →	**Dependent Variable**

Most variables may be either independent or dependent, depending on what the experimenter wishes to find out. If you want to know whether eating chocolate makes people nervous, then the amount of chocolate eaten is the independent variable. If you want to know whether feeling nervous makes people eat chocolate, then the amount of chocolate eaten is the dependent variable.

Experimental and Control Conditions

Experiments usually require both an experimental condition and a comparison, or **control condition**. People in the control condition are treated exactly like those in the experimental condition, except that they are not exposed to the same treatment, or manipulation of the independent variable. Without a control condition, you cannot be sure that the behavior you are interested in would not have occurred anyway, even without your manipulation. In some studies, the same subjects can be used in both the control and the experimental conditions; they are said to serve as their own controls. In other studies, people are assigned to either an *experimental group* or a *control group*.

In our nicotine experiment, the participants who smoke before driving make up the experimental group, and those who do not smoke make up the control group. We want these two groups to be roughly the same in terms of average driving skill. It would not do to start out with a bunch of reckless roadrunners in the experimental group and a bunch of tired tortoises in the control group. We probably also want the two groups to be similar in average intelligence, education, smoking history, and other characteristics, so that none of these variables will affect our results. One way to accomplish this is to use **random assignment** of people to one group or another—for example, by randomly assigning them numbers and putting those with even numbers in one group and those with odd numbers in another group. If we have enough participants in our study, individual characteristics that could possibly affect the results are likely to be roughly balanced in the two groups, so we can safely ignore them.

We now have two groups. We also have a problem. In order to smoke, people in the experimental group must light up and inhale. These acts might set off certain expectations—of feeling relaxed, getting nervous, feeling confident, or whatever. These expectations, in turn, might affect driving performance. It would be better to have the control group do everything the experimental group does except use nicotine. Therefore, let's change our experimental design a bit. Instead of having participants in the control group refrain from smoking, we will give them a **placebo**, a fake treatment.

Placebos, which are critical when testing new drugs, often take the form of pills or injections containing no active ingredients. (For example, to see what placebos revealed in a study of Viagra

independent variable
A variable that an experimenter manipulates.

dependent variable A variable that an experimenter predicts will be affected by manipulations of the independent variable.

control condition In an experiment, a comparison condition in which subjects are not exposed to the same treatment as are those in the experimental condition.

random assignment A procedure for assigning people to experimental and control groups in which each individual has the same probability as any other of being assigned to a given group.

placebo An inactive substance or fake treatment used as a control in an experiment.

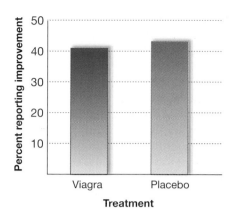

FIGURE 1.4

Does Viagra Work for Women?

Placebos are essential to determine whether people taking a new drug improve because of the drug or because of their expectations about it. In one study, 41 percent of women taking Viagra said their sex lives had improved. It sounds impressive, but 43 percent taking a placebo pill also said their sex lives had improved (Basson et al., 2002).

for women's sexual problems, see Figure 1.4.) In our nicotine study, we will use phony cigarettes that taste and smell like the real thing but contain no active ingredients. Our control subjects will not know their cigarettes are fakes and will have no way of distinguishing them from real ones. Now if they have substantially fewer collisions than the experimental group, we will feel safe in concluding that nicotine increases the probability of an auto accident.

Control groups, by the way, are also crucial in many nonexperimental studies. For example, in recent years, some psychotherapists have published books arguing that teenage girls develop special problems with self-esteem, confidence, and body image. But unless they have also tested or surveyed a comparable group of teenage boys, there is no way of knowing whether these problems are unique to girls or typical of all adolescents—or none of them. (For the answer, see Chapter 3.)

Experimenter Effects

Because expectations can influence the results of a study, participants should not know whether they are in an experimental or a control group. When this is so (as it usually is), the experiment is said to be a **single-blind study**. But participants are not the only ones who bring expectations to the laboratory; so do researchers. And researchers' expectations and hopes for a particular result may cause them to inadvertently influence the participants' responses through facial expressions, posture, tone of voice, or some other cue. Such **experimenter effects** can be powerful; even an experimenter's friendly smile can affect people's responses in a study (Rosenthal, 1994).

One solution to the problem of experimenter effects is to do a **double-blind study**. In such a study, the person running the experiment, the one having actual contact with the participants, also does not know who is in which group until the data have been gathered. Double-blind procedures are standard in drug research. Different doses of a drug are coded in some way, and the person administering the drug is kept in the dark about the code's meaning until after the experiment. To run our nicotine study in a double-blind fashion, we would keep the person dispensing the cigarettes from knowing which ones were real and which were placebos.

Advantages and Limitations of Experiments

Because experiments allow conclusions about cause and effect, and because they permit researchers to distinguish real effects from placebo effects, they have long been the method of choice in psychology.

However, like all methods, the experiment has its limitations. Just as in other kinds of studies, the participants are not always representative of the larger population. As we noted earlier, most volunteers in academic experiments are college students, who differ in many ways from people who are not in school. Moreover, in an experiment, the researcher determines which questions are asked and which behaviors are recorded, and the participants try to do as they are told. In their desire to cooperate, advance scientific knowledge, or present themselves in a positive light, they may act in ways that they ordinarily would not (Kihlstrom, 1995).

Thus, research psychologists confront a dilemma: The more control they exercise over the situation, the more unlike real life it may be. For this reason, many psychologists have

single-blind study An experiment in which subjects do not know whether they are in an experimental or a control group.

experimenter effects Unintended changes in subjects' behavior due to cues inadvertently given by the experimenter.

double-blind study An experiment in which neither the participants nor the individuals running the study know which participants are in the control group and which are in the experimental group until after the results are tallied.

Carefully conducted field research can provide important information about behavior in "real life." For example, psychologists have studied how people in crowded places, like this outdoor café, modify their gaze and body position to preserve a sense of privacy.

field research
Descriptive or experimental research conducted in a natural setting outside the laboratory.

called for more **field research**, the careful study of behavior in natural contexts such as schools and the workplace, using both descriptive and experimental methods. For example, a psychologist interested in ways of reducing prejudice might study that problem not just in the laboratory but also in offices and schools.

Every research method has both strengths and weaknesses. Did you make a list of each method's advantages and disadvantages, as we suggested earlier? If so, compare it now with the one in Table 1.3.

TABLE 1.3
Research Methods in Psychology: Their Advantages and Disadvantages

Method	Advantages	Disadvantages
Case study	Good source of hypotheses. Provides in-depth information on individuals. Unusual cases can shed light on situations or problems that are unethical or impractical to study in other ways.	Vital information may be missing, making the case hard to interpret. The person's memories may be selective or inaccurate. The individual may not be representative or typical.
Naturalistic observation	Allows description of behavior as it occurs in the natural environment. Often useful in first stages of a research program.	Allows researcher little or no control of the situation. Observations may be biased. Does not allow firm conclusions about cause and effect.
Laboratory observation	Allows more control than naturalistic observation. Allows use of sophisticated equipment.	Allows researcher only limited control of the situation. Observations may be biased. Does not allow firm conclusions about cause and effect. Behavior may differ from behavior in the natural environment.
Test	Yields information on personality traits, emotional states, aptitudes, and abilities.	Difficult to construct tests that are reliable and valid.
Survey	Provides a large amount of information on large numbers of people.	If sample is nonrepresentative or biased, it may be impossible to generalize from the results. Responses may be inaccurate or untrue.
Correlational study	Shows whether two or more variables are related. Allows general predictions.	Does not permit identification of cause and effect.
Experiment	Allows researcher to control the situation. Permits researcher to identify cause and effect and to distinguish placebo effects from treatment effects.	Situation is artificial, and results may not generalize well to the real world. Sometimes difficult to avoid experimenter effects.

QUICK quiz

There are many advantages and no disadvantages of taking this quiz.

A. Name the independent and dependent variables in studies designed to answer the following questions:

   1. Whether sleeping after learning a poem improves memory for the poem

   2. Whether the presence of other people affects a person's willingness to help someone in distress

   3. Whether people get agitated from listening to heavy-metal music

B. On a talk show, Dr. Blitznik announces a fabulous new program: Chocolate Immersion Therapy (C.I.T.). "People who spend one day a week doing nothing but eating chocolate are soon cured of eating disorders, depression, drug abuse, and poor study habits," claims Dr. Blitznik. What should you find out about C.I.T. before signing up?

Answers:

A. 1. Opportunity to sleep after learning is the independent variable; memory for the poem is the dependent variable. 2. The presence of other people is the independent variable; willingness to help others is the dependent variable. 3. Exposure to heavy-metal music is the independent variable; agitation is the dependent variable. B. Some questions to ask: Is there research showing that people who go through C.I.T. did better than those in a control group who did not have the therapy or who had a different therapy—say, Broccoli Immersion Therapy? If so, how many people were studied? How were they selected, and how were they assigned to the therapy and no-therapy groups? Did the person running the experiment know who was getting C.I.T. and who was not? How long did the "cures" last? Has the research been replicated?

WHAT'S *Ahead*

- In psychological studies, why are averages sometimes misleading?

- How can psychologists tell whether a finding is impressive or trivial?

- Why are some findings statistically significant but unimportant in practical terms?

Evaluating the Findings

If you are a psychologist who has just done an observational study, a survey, or an experiment, your work has only just begun. Once you have some results in hand, you must do three things with them: (1) describe them, (2) assess how reliable and meaningful they are, and (3) figure out how to explain them.

Why Psychologists Use Statistics

Let's say that 30 people in the nicotine experiment smoked real cigarettes and 30 smoked placebos. We have recorded the number of collisions for each person on the driving simulator. Now we have 60 numbers. What can we do with them?

The first step is to summarize the data. The world does not want to hear how many collisions each person had. It wants to know what happened in the nicotine group as a whole, compared with what happened in the control group. To provide this information, we need numbers that sum up our data. Such numbers, known as **descriptive statistics**, are often depicted in graphs and charts.

A good way to summarize the data is to compute group averages. The most commonly used type of average is the **arithmetic mean**. (For two other types, see the Appendix.) The mean is calculated by adding up all the individual scores and dividing the result by the number of scores. We can compute a mean for the nicotine group by adding up the 30 collision scores and dividing the sum by 30. Then we can do the same for the control group. Now our 60 numbers have been boiled down to 2. For the sake of our example, let's assume that the nicotine group had an average of 10 collisions, whereas the control group's average was only 7.

We must be careful, however, about how we interpret these averages. It is possible that no one in our nicotine group actually had 10 collisions. Perhaps half the people in the group were motoring maniacs and had 15 collisions, whereas the others were more cautious and had only 5. Perhaps almost all the subjects had 9, 10, or 11 collisions. Perhaps the number of accidents ranged from 0 to 15. The mean does not tell us about such variability in the subjects' responses. For that, we need other descriptive

descriptive statistics
Statistics that organize and summarize research data.

arithmetic mean An average that is calculated by adding up a set of quantities and dividing the sum by the total number of quantities in the set.

Averages can be misleading if you don't know the extent to which events deviated from the statistical mean and how they were distributed.

standard deviation A commonly used measure of variability that indicates the average difference between scores in a distribution and their mean.

inferential statistics Statistical procedures that allow researchers to draw inferences about how statistically meaningful a study's results are.

significance tests Statistical tests that assess how likely it is that a study's results occurred merely by chance.

statistics. For example, the **standard deviation** tells us how clustered or spread out the individual scores are around the mean; the more spread out they are, the less "typical" the mean is. (For details, see the Appendix.) Unfortunately, when research is reported in newspapers or on the nightly news, you usually hear only about the mean.

At this point in our nicotine study, we have one group with an average of 10 collisions and another with an average of 7. Should we break out the champagne? Try to get on TV? Call our mothers? Better hold off. Perhaps if one group had an average of 15 collisions and the other an average of 1, we could get excited. But rarely does a psychological study hit you between the eyes with a sensationally clear result. In most cases, there is some possibility that the difference between the two groups was due simply to chance. Perhaps the people in the nicotine group just happened to be a little more accident-prone, and their behavior had nothing to do with the nicotine.

To find out how impressive the data are, psychologists use **inferential statistics**. These statistics do not merely describe or summarize the data; they permit a researcher to draw inferences (conclusions based on evidence) about how meaningful the findings are. Like descriptive statistics, inferential statistics involve the application of mathematical formulas to the data (again, see the Appendix for details). Historically, the most commonly used inferential statistics have been **significance tests**, which tell researchers how likely a result was to have occurred by chance. In our nicotine study, a significance test will tell us how likely it is that the difference between the nicotine group and the placebo group occurred by chance. It is not possible to rule out chance entirely, but if the likelihood that a result occurred by chance is extremely low, we say that the result is *statistically significant*. This means that the probability that the difference is "real" is overwhelming—not certain, mind you, but overwhelming.

By convention, psychologists consider a result to be significant if it would be expected to occur by chance 5 or fewer times in 100 repetitions of the study. Another way of saying this is that the result is significant at the .05 ("point oh five") level. If the difference could be expected to occur by chance in 6 out of 100 studies, we would have to say that the results failed to support the hypothesis—that the difference we obtained might well have occurred merely by chance—although we might still want to do further research to be sure. You can see that psychologists refuse to be impressed by just any old result.

By the way, a nicotine study similar to our hypothetical example was actually done (Spilich, June, & Renner, 1992). Smokers who lit up before driving got a little farther on the simulated road, but they also had significantly more collisions on average (10.7) than did temporarily abstaining smokers (5.2) or nonsmokers (3.1). After hearing about this research, the head of Federal Express banned smoking on the job among all of the company's drivers.

QUICK quiz

Check your understanding of the descriptive–inferential distinction by mentally placing a check in the appropriate column for each phrase:

	Descriptive Statistics	Inferential Statistics
1. Summarize the data	_____	_____
2. Give likelihood of data occurring by chance	_____	_____
3. Include the mean	_____	_____
4. Give a measure of statistical significance	_____	_____
5. Tell you whether to call your mother about your results	_____	_____

Answers:

1. descriptive 2. inferential 3. descriptive 4. inferential 5. inferential

From the Laboratory to the Real World

The last step in any study is to figure out what the findings mean. Trying to understand behavior from uninterpreted findings is like trying to become fluent in Swedish by reading a Swedish–English dictionary. Just as you need the grammar of Swedish to tell you how the words fit together, the psychologist needs hypotheses and theories to explain how the facts that emerge from research fit together.

Choosing the Best Explanation

Sometimes it is hard to choose between competing explanations. Does nicotine disrupt driving by impairing coordination, by increasing a driver's vulnerability to distraction, by interfering with the processing of information, by distorting the perception of danger—or by some combination of these factors? In interpreting any study, we must not go too far beyond the facts. Several explanations may fit those facts equally well, which means that more research will be needed to determine the best one.

Sometimes the best interpretation of a finding does not emerge until a hypothesis has been tested in different ways. If the findings of studies using different methods converge, there is greater reason to be confident about them. On the other hand, if they conflict, researchers will know they must modify their hypotheses or do more research.

Here's an example. When psychologists compare the mental-test scores of young people and old people, they usually find that younger people consistently outscore older ones. This type of research, in which groups are compared at a given time, is called **cross-sectional**:

Cross-Sectional Study

Different groups compared at one time:

Group A (20-year-olds)
Group B (50-year-olds)   compared
Group C (80-year-olds)

But **longitudinal studies** can also be used to investigate mental abilities across the life span. In a longitudinal study, the same people are followed over a period of time and are reassessed at regular intervals:

Longitudinal Study

Same group compared at different times:

Group A at age 20 → Group A at age 50 → Group A at age 80

In contrast to cross-sectional studies, longitudinal studies find that as people age, they sometimes continue to perform as well as they ever did on certain mental tests. A *general* decline in ability may not occur until people reach their 70s or 80s (Salthouse, 2004; Schaie, 1993). Why do results from the two types of studies conflict? Probably because cross-sectional studies measure generational differences; younger generations tend to outperform older ones because they are better educated or are more familiar with the tests used. Without longitudinal studies, we might falsely conclude that all types of mental ability inevitably decline sharply with advancing age.

Judging the Result's Importance

Sometimes psychologists agree on the reliability and meaning of a finding but not on its ultimate relevance for theory or practice. Statistical significance alone does not provide the answer (Killeen, 2005). A result may be statistically significant at the "point oh-five level" yet be small and of little consequence in everyday life because the independent variable does not explain most of the variation in people's behavior. On the other hand, a result may not quite reach statistical significance yet be worth following up on (Falk & Greenbaum, 1995; Hunter, 1997). Because of these problems, many psychologists now prefer other statistical procedures that reveal how powerful the independent variable really is—how much of the variation in the data the variable accounts for.

One popular statistical technique, called **meta-analysis**, combines and analyzes data from many studies, instead of assessing each study's results separately. Meta-analysis tells the researcher how much of the variation in scores across all the studies examined can be explained by a particular variable. For example, a meta-analysis of nearly 50 years of research found that gender accounts for a good deal of the variance in performance on certain spatial–visual tasks, with males doing better on the average (Voyer, Voyer, & Bryden, 1995). In contrast, other meta-analyses have shown that gender accounts for only 1 to 5 percent of the variance on tests of verbal ability, math ability, and aggressiveness (Hyde, 2005). Although gender differences on these tests are reliable, they are small, and scores for males and females greatly overlap.

Techniques such as meta-analysis are useful because rarely does one study prove anything, in psychology or any other field. That is why you should be suspicious of headlines that announce a sudden major scientific breakthrough based on a single study. Such breakthroughs do occur, but they are rare.

Thinking Critically About "Significant" Research Findings

cross-sectional study A study in which individuals of different ages are compared at a given time.

longitudinal study A study in which individuals are followed and periodically reassessed over a period of time.

meta-analysis A procedure for combining and analyzing data from many studies; it determines how much of the variance in scores across all studies can be explained by a particular variable.

Psychological Topics

Psychologists use scientific methods to study many puzzles of human behavior. Why does human touch reduce anxiety and feel so comforting? Why do people strive to become champion athletes in spite of physical disabilities? What causes people to become anorexic, and even starve themselves to death? And what could motivate terrorists to kill themselves and thousands of innocent people?

psychology in **the news**
REVISITED

Now that you have finished the first chapter of this book, you are ready to explore more deeply what psychologists have learned about human behavior.

At the start of each of the remaining chapters, we will present a real story from the news, one that raises some intriguing psychological questions. Then, at the end of the chapter, we will revisit the story to show how the material you have learned can help answer those questions. If you are ready to share the excitement of studying human behavior; if you love mysteries and want to know not only who did it but also why they did it; if you are willing to reconsider what you think you think . . . then you are ready to read on.

➤TAKING ➤PSYCHOLOGY ➤WITH ➤YOU

What Psychology Can Do for You—and What It Can't

If you intend to become a psychologist or a mental-health professional, you have an obvious reason for taking a course in psychology. But psychology can contribute to your life in many ways, whether you plan to work in the field or not. Here are a few things psychology can do for you:

● **Make you a more informed person.** One purpose of education is to acquaint people with their cultural heritage and with human achievements in literature, the arts, and science. Because psychology plays a large role in contemporary society, being a well-informed person requires knowing something about psychological methods and findings.

● **Satisfy your curiosity about human nature.** When the Greek philosopher Socrates admonished his students, "Know thyself," he was only telling them to do what most people want to do anyway. Psychology—along with the other social sciences, literature, history, and philosophy—can contribute to a better understanding of yourself and others.

● **Help you increase control over your life.** Psychology cannot solve all your problems, but it does offer helpful techniques for handling your emotions, improving your memory, and eliminating unwanted habits. It can also foster an attitude of objectivity that is useful for analyzing your behavior and your relationships.

● **Help you on the job.** A bachelor's degree in psychology is useful for getting a job in a helping profession, for example as a welfare caseworker or a rehabilitation counselor. Anyone who works as a nurse, doctor, member of the clergy, police officer, or teacher can also put psychology to work on the job. So can waiters, flight attendants, bank tellers, salespeople, receptionists, and others whose jobs involve customer service. Finally, psychology can be useful to those whose jobs require them to predict people's behavior—for example, labor negotiators, politicians, advertising copywriters, managers, product designers, buyers, market researchers, magicians. . . .

● **Give you insights into political and social issues.** Crime, drug abuse, discrimination, and war are not only social issues but also psychological ones. Psychological knowledge alone cannot solve the complex political, social, and ethical problems that plague every society, but it can help citizens make informed judgments about them. For example, if you know how social and cultural practices affect rates of illegal drug use and abuse, this knowledge may affect your views about drug policies.

We are optimistic about psychology's role in the world, but we want to caution you that sometimes people expect things from psy-

chology that it can't deliver. Psychology can not tell you the meaning of life. A philosophy about the purpose of life requires not only knowledge but also reflection and a willingness to learn from life's experiences. Nor does psychological understanding relieve people of responsibility for their actions. Knowing that your short temper is a result, in part, of your unhappy childhood does not give you a green light to yell at your family or mistreat your own kids. Most important, as we have repeatedly emphasized, psychology will not provide you with simple answers to complex questions. Instead, it offers findings from many perspectives, which the critical thinker will try to evaluate and integrate.

Yet despite the complexity of behavior and the lack of simple answers to human problems, psychologists have made enormous progress in unraveling the secrets of the human brain, mind, and heart. At the

end of each chapter, starting with the next one, the "Taking Psychology with You" feature will suggest ways to apply psychological findings to your own life—at school, on the job, or in your relationships.

Bent Offerings, *St. Petersburg Times*

SUMMARY

The Science of Psychology

• *Psychology* is the discipline concerned with behavior and mental processes and how they are affected by an organism's external and internal environment. Psychology's methods and reliance on *empirical evidence* distinguish it from pseudoscience and "psychobabble."

• Psychological findings sometimes confirm, but often contradict, "common sense." As we saw in the "Close-Up on Research" feature, an introductory psychology course can correct many misconceptions about human behavior. But a result does not have to be surprising or counterintuitive to be scientifically important.

• Psychology's forerunners made some valid observations and had some useful insights, but without rigorous empirical methods, they also made serious errors in the description and explanation of behavior, as in the case of *phrenology*.

• The official founder of scientific psychology was Wilhelm Wundt, who established the first psychological laboratory in 1879, in Leipzig, Germany. Wundt emphasized the analysis of experience into basic elements through *trained introspection*. A competing approach, *functionalism*, which was inspired in part by the evolutionary theories of Charles Darwin, emphasized the functions of behavior. One of

its leading proponents was William James. Psychology as a method of psychotherapy was born in Vienna, with the work of Sigmund Freud and the establishment of *psychoanalysis*.

• Five points of view predominate today in psychology. The *biological perspective* emphasizes bodily events associated with actions, thoughts, and feelings, and also genetic contributions to behavior. Within this perspective, a popular specialty, *evolutionary psychology*, emphasizes the purposes and functions of behavior, as functionalism did. The *learning perspective* emphasizes how the environment and a person's history affect behavior; within this perspective, *behaviorists* reject mentalistic explanations and *social-cognitive learning theorists* combine elements of behaviorism with the study of thoughts, values, and intentions. The *cognitive perspective* emphasizes mental processes in perception, problem solving, belief formation, and other human activities. The *sociocultural perspective* explores how social contexts and cultural rules affect an individual's beliefs and behavior. And the *psychodynamic perspective*, which originated with Freud's theory of psychoanalysis, emphasizes unconscious motives, conflicts, and desires; it differs greatly from the other approaches in its methods and standards of evidence.

• Each approach has made important contributions to psychology, but many, if not most, psychologists draw on more than one school of thought. And many have been influenced by movements that do not fall neatly into one of the five perspectives we have discussed. For example, a contemporary research specialty called *positive psychology* follows in the footsteps of *humanist psychology* by focusing on the positive aspects of human behavior.

What Psychologists Do

• Psychologists do research and teach in colleges and universities, provide mental-health services (*psychological practice*), and conduct research and apply findings in a wide variety of nonacademic settings. *Applied psychology* is concerned with the practical uses of psychological knowledge. *Basic psychology* is concerned with knowledge for its own sake.

• *Psychotherapist* is an unregulated term for anyone who does therapy, including persons who have no credentials or training at all. Licensed therapists differ according to their training and approach. *Clinical psychologists* have a Ph.D., an Ed.D., or a Psy.D.; *psychiatrists* have an M.D.; *psychoanalysts* are trained in psychoanalytic institutes; and licensed clinical social workers, counselors with various specialties, and marriage, family, and child counselors may have a variety of postgraduate degrees. Many psychologists are concerned about an increase in poorly trained psychotherapists who lack credentials or a firm understanding of research methods and findings.

Critical and Scientific Thinking in Psychology

• One benefit of studying psychology is the development of *critical-thinking* skills and attitudes. The critical thinker asks questions, defines terms clearly, examines the evidence, analyzes assumptions and biases, avoids emotional reasoning, avoids oversimplification, considers alternative interpretations, and tolerates uncertainty. These activities not only are useful in ordinary life but also are the basis of the scientific method. For example, scientists are required to state hypotheses and predictions precisely and formulate operational definitions ("define your terms"); to gather empirical evidence; to comply with the *principle of falsifiability* ("analyze assumptions"); to be cautious in settling on a theory ("consider other interpretations"); and to resist drawing firm conclusions until results are replicated ("tolerate uncertainty").

Descriptive Studies: Establishing the Facts

• Psychological scientists try whenever possible to use samples that are representative of the larger population they wish to describe. In practice, however, they must often rely on college students as subjects, and although in many cases the consequences are probably minimal, in other cases the conclusions should be generalized with caution.

• *Descriptive methods* allow psychologists to describe and predict behavior but not necessarily to choose one explanation over others. Such methods include case studies, observational studies, psychological tests, and surveys, as well as correlational methods.

• *Case studies* are detailed descriptions of individuals. They are often used by clinicians, and they can be valuable in exploring new research topics and addressing questions that would otherwise be difficult to study. But because information is often missing or hard to interpret, and because the person under study may not be representative of people in general, case studies are typically sources rather than tests of hypotheses.

• In *observational studies*, the researcher systematically observes and records behavior without interfering in any way with the behavior. *Naturalistic observation* is used to find out how people behave in their natural environments. *Laboratory observation* allows more control and the use of special equipment; behavior in the laboratory, however, may differ in certain ways from behavior in natural contexts.

• *Psychological tests* are used to measure and evaluate personality traits, emotional states, aptitudes, interests, abilities, and values. A good test is one that has been *standardized*, is scored using established *norms*, and is both *reliable* and *valid*. Critics have questioned the reliability and validity of even some widely used tests.

• *Surveys* are questionnaires or interviews that ask people directly about their experiences, attitudes, and opinions. They are difficult to do well; sampling problems are often an issue, and the results can be affected by a *volunteer bias*. Findings can also be affected by biased questions and by the fact that respondents sometimes lie, misremember their experiences, or misinterpret the questions.

Correlational Studies: Looking for Relationships

• In descriptive research, studies that look for relationships between phenomena are known as *correlational*. A *correlation* is a measure of the strength of a positive or negative relationship between two variables and is expressed by the *coefficient of correlation*. A correlation does not necessarily demonstrate a causal relationship between the variables.

The Experiment: Hunting for Causes

• *Experiments* allow researchers to control the situation being studied, manipulate an *independent variable*, and assess the effects of the manipulation on a *dependent variable*. Because of the element of manipulation, ethical guidelines are especially important in experimental research. These guidelines govern studies with human beings, who must give *informed consent* before participating, and also with animals, which must be treated humanely.

• Experimental studies usually require a comparison or *control condition* and often involve *random assignment* of subjects to experimental and control groups. In some studies, people in the control group receive a *placebo*. *Single-blind* and *double-blind* procedures can be used to prevent the expectations of the subjects or the experimenter from affecting the results. Because experiments allow conclusions about cause and effect, they have long been the method of choice in psychology. However, like laboratory observations, experiments create a special situation that may call forth behavior not typical in other environments. Many psychologists, therefore, have called for more *field research*.

Evaluating the Findings

• Psychologists use *descriptive statistics*, such as the *arithmetic mean* and *standard deviation*, to summarize data. They use *inferential statistics* to find out how impressive the data are. *Significance tests* tell the researcher how likely it is that the results of a study occurred merely by chance. The results are said to be *statistically significant* if this likelihood is very low.

• Choosing among competing interpretations of a finding can be difficult, and care must be taken to avoid going beyond the facts. Sometimes the best interpretation does not emerge until a hypothesis has been tested in more than one way—for example, by using both *cross-sectional* and *longitudinal methods*.

• Statistical significance does not always imply real-world importance because the amount of variation in the data accounted for by a particular variable may be small. Conversely, a result that does not quite reach significance may be potentially useful. Therefore, many psychologists are now turning to other statistical measures. The technique of *meta-analysis*, for example, reveals how much of the variation in scores across many different studies can be explained by a particular variable.

KEY TERMS

Use this list to check your understanding of terms and people in this chapter. If you have trouble with a term, you can find it on the page listed.

The Science of Psychology

Psychology is the discipline concerned with behavior and mental processes and how they are affected by an organism's external and internal environment. Unlike pseudoscientific approaches to behavior, it relies on empirical data.

The Birth of Modern Psychology

- Wilhelm Wundt founded the first psychology laboratory in Leipzig, Germany, in 1879 and emphasized the analysis of experience through trained introspection.
- American William James emphasized the adaptive nature of behavior, an approach known as **functionalism.**
- Sigmund Freud developed **psychoanalysis,** an early form of psychotherapy, in Vienna, Austria.

Today's Five Major Psychological Perspectives

- The **biological perspective** focuses on how bodily events interact with the external environment to affect behavior, feelings, and thoughts.
- The **learning perspective** emphasizes the environment's effect on behavior.
- The **cognitive perspective** emphasizes mental processes in reasoning, memory, perception, language, problem solving, and beliefs.
- The **sociocultural perspective** focuses on the influence of social and cultural forces on behavior.
- The **psychodynamic perspective** looks at unconscious dynamics, such as inner forces, conflicts, and instinctual energy.

What Psychologists Do

- Conduct research in **basic psychology,** to gain knowledge for its own sake; and **applied psychology,** to find practical uses for knowledge.
- Teach.
- Provide mental health services (psychological practice).

- Psychotherapist is an unregulated term.
- Clinical psychologists have Ph.D., Ed.D., or Psy.D. degrees.
- Psychiatrists have M.D. degrees.
- Psychoanalysts have completed training in psychoanalytic institutes.

Critical and Scientific Thinking in Psychology

- Asking questions
- Defining terms
- Examining evidence
- Analyzing assumptions, beliefs taken for granted, and biases, beliefs that prevent us from considering the evidence fairly.
  — **Principle of falsifiability,** the statement of a hypothesis in such a way that it can be disproved by counterevidence
- Avoiding emotional reasoning

- Avoiding oversimplification
- Considering alternative interpretations
  — Scientific goal is a **theory,** or an organized system of assumptions and principles to explain a set of phenomena and their interrelationships
- Tolerating uncertainty; in science, avoiding firm conclusions until others have **replicated,** or repeated the studies with the same results

Principle of falsifiablility

(a)

Hypothesis	Falsifiable ("Risky") Prediction	Possible Outcomes	Conclusion
"Misery loves company."	When people are anxious, they are more likely to want to be with others in the same situation.	Anxious people are more likely to wait with others in the same situation.	Supports hypothesis.
		Anxious people are more likely to want to be alone.	Refutes hypothesis.
		Anxiety has no effect on behavior.	Refutes hypothesis.

(b)

Hypothesis	Nonfalsifiable Prediction	Possible Outcomes	Conclusion
"Dowsing reveals subterranean water."	Dowsers will reliably find water—*unless* the planets are misaligned, observers give off bad vibes, etc.	Dowsers find water.	Supports hypothesis.
		Dowsers do not find water.	Dowsers conclude that results support hypothesis anyway.

Research Methods in Psychology

Descriptive Studies: Establishing the Facts

- **Representative sample:** group of participants accurately represents the larger population that the researcher is interested in.
- **Case study:** a detailed description of a particular individual, based on observation or formal psychological testing.
- **Observational study:** careful observation, measurement, and recording of behavior without intruding on the subjects.
- **Psychological tests:** assessment instruments that measure and evaluate personality traits, emotional states, aptitudes, interest, abilities, and values.
- **Surveys:** questionnaires or interviews that ask people directly about their experiences, attitudes, or opinions.

Correlational Studies: Looking for Relationships

A **positive** or **negative correlation** is a measure of the strength of a relationship between two variables but does not demonstrate causation.

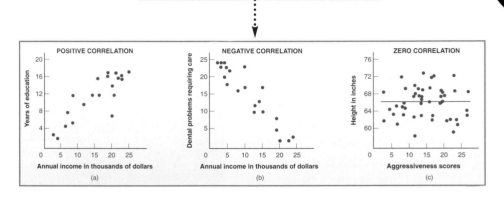

The Experiment: Hunting for Causes

- **Experiments** allow researchers to control the situation lable to measure the effects on a **dependent variable**.

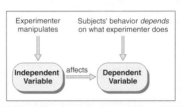

- Experiments usually require a **control condition** in which subjects are not exposed to the experimental condition.
- Participation in an experimental or control group is determined by **random assignment.**
- Drug experiments typically include the use of a **placebo,** an inactive substance used as a control.

Experimenter Effects

The expectations of participants can influence a study's results. Solution:
- **Single-blind study:** an experiment in which subjects do not know whether they are in an experimental or a control group.

A researcher's expectations can also unintentionally influence the study's outcome. Solution:
- **Double-blind study:** an experiment in which neither the participants nor the individuals running the study know which participants are in the control group and which are in the experimental group until after the results are tallied.

Evaluating the Findings

- **Descriptive statistics** (including the **arithmetic mean** and **standard deviation**) organize and summarize data.
- **Inferential statitstics** help to determine how meaningful the findings are.
- **Significance tests** measure the probability that the study's findings could have occurred by chance.
- Interpretation of findings may need to await studies using different methods. E.g., **cross-sectional** studies compare subjects of different ages; **longitudinal** methods follow subjects over many years.

- **Meta-analysis** combines and analyzes data from many studies to determine how much of the variance across all studies can be explained by a particular variable.

"American Taliban" Sentenced to 20 Years

ALEXANDRIA, VA, OCTOBER 4, 2002. John Walker Lindh, the "American Taliban," was sentenced today to a term of 20 years in prison without possibility of parole in exchange for pleading guilty to two counts of "supplying services to the Taliban." Known to the Taliban as Abdul Hamid, Lindh attended militant training camps in Afghanistan and later joined the Taliban's fight against the Northern Alliance, allies of the Americans.

His lawyers and family say that Lindh was a lonely, somewhat lost young man on a spiritual quest who

John Walker Lindh at home at age 12 and as a student in a religious school in Pakistan.

got in over his head when he went to the Middle East. In his 21 years, Lindh had already taken on many names and identities. In Internet chat rooms, he posed as a black rapper ("doodoo" and "John Doe") and also as Dr. J, Hine E. Craque, and Mr. Mujahid.

In his midteens, in his hometown of San Anselmo, California, he became a Muslim and began wearing white robes, calling himself Suleyman al-Lindh. After studying at the Islamic Center of San Francisco, he told his parents he wanted to go to the Middle East and become a serious scholar of Islam. He traveled to Yemen, where he became convinced that a proper Mus-

lim should train for a military jihad (holy war) to create a pure Islamic state. Eventually he made his way to Pakistan and then Afghanistan, where he fell in with the Taliban.

During the U.S. war in Afghanistan following the attacks of September 11, 2001, Lindh was caught in a shootout between a group of fellow Taliban prisoners and the Northern Alliance. The Americans captured him, put him in isolation, and interrogated him harshly for information. Public sentiment against Lindh was strong and vehement in the emotional aftermath of 9/11, and most Americans regarded his actions as treasonous.

While in prison awaiting trial, Lindh has remained a faithful Muslim, praying toward Mecca five times a day and studying the Koran in Arabic.

loyal

Lindh, as he appeared when captured with Taliban fighters in Afganistan.

Theories of Personality

Who is John Walker Lindh: a shy boy on a spiritual quest or a traitor to his country? Was he born with a disposition toward rebelliousness, or did something happen in his life that caused him to end up in Afghanistan? Is his personality characterized by the sweet, loving, and spiritual qualities that his family sees, or by anger, defiance, and violence? Who is the real John Walker Lindh? *Is* there a real one?

In this chapter, we will see how psychologists address such questions. In psychology, **personality** refers to a distinctive pattern of behavior, mannerisms, thoughts, and emotions that characterizes an individual over time. This pattern consists of many distinctive **traits**, habitual ways of behaving, thinking, and feeling: shy, outgoing, hostile, gloomy, confident, ambitious, and so on. The schools of psychology described in Chapter 1 differ in their view of the origins and stability of those traits.

personality A distinctive and relatively stable pattern of behavior, thoughts, motives, and emotions that characterizes an individual.

trait A characteristic of an individual, describing a habitual way of behaving, thinking, or feeling.

psychoanalysis A theory of personality and a method of psychotherapy developed by Sigmund Freud; it emphasizes unconscious motives and conflicts.

psychodynamic theories Theories that explain behavior and personality in terms of unconscious dynamics within the individual.

For much of the twentieth century, Freudian psychoanalytic theory was the dominant approach to explaining personality differences. Its sweeping view held that a person's conflicts, guilts, defenses, and ways of dealing with others could be traced to unconscious dynamics originating in early childhood. By the end of the twentieth century, however, biological research was offering an entirely different view of personality: that about half of the variation in human personality traits is due to genetic variations and has nothing to do with unconscious motives or how your parents treated you.

In this chapter, we will begin with the oldest theory of personality, the psychodynamic one, so that you will have a sense of how influential it was, why it still appeals to many, and why many of its ideas have become outdated. Next we will consider evidence for the newest approach, the genetic view. Few scientists think any more that babies are tiny lumps of clay, shaped entirely by their experiences, or that parents alone determine whether their infant becomes an adventurer, a sourpuss, a rap star, . . . or John Walker Lindh. On the other hand, if only half of the human variation in personality traits is due to genetics, what is responsible for the other half?

To answer that question, we will then examine some of the leading approaches to personality that are neither psychodynamic nor biological: the environmental view, which emphasizes the role of social learning, situations, parents, and peers; the cultural view, which emphasizes cultural influences on traits and behavior; and the humanist view, which emphasizes self-determination and free will.

When we are done, we will return to the puzzle of John Walker Lindh. As you read, ask yourself: Is personality set in childhood, or can adult experiences shape and even transform our traits? Which aspects of our personalities seem to be inborn and which are learned? Which has more influence on our behavior: our personality or the situation we are in?

WHAT'S *Ahead*

- In Freud's theory of personality, why are the id and the superego always at war?
- When people say you're being "defensive," what defenses might they be thinking of?
- How do psychologists regard Freud today—as a genius or a fraud?
- What would Carl Jung have had to say about Harry Potter's arch-enemy, Lord Valdemort?
- What are the "objects" in the object-relations approach to personality?

Psychodynamic Theories of Personality

A man apologizes for "displacing" his frustrations at work onto his family. A woman suspects that she is "repressing" a childhood trauma. An alcoholic reveals that he is no longer "in denial" about his drinking. A teacher informs a divorcing couple that their 8-year-old child is "regressing" to immature behavior. All of this language—about displacing, repressing, denying, and regressing—can be traced to the first psychodynamic theory of personality, Sigmund Freud's theory of **psychoanalysis**.

Freud's theory is called **psychodynamic** because it emphasizes the movement of psychological energy within the person in the form of attachments, conflicts, and motivations. Today's psychodynamic theories differ from Freudian theory and from one another, but they all share an emphasis on unconscious processes going on within the mind. They also share an assumption that adult personality and ongoing problems are formed primarily by experiences in early childhood. These experiences produce unconscious thoughts and feelings, which later form characteristic habits, conflicts, and often self-defeating behavior.

No one disputes the profound influence that Sigmund Freud had on the twentieth century, but there is enormous dispute about the lasting value of his work. Freud saw himself as one of the great geniuses of history, and many people agree with that assessment. But many contemporary scientists think he was a flat-out fraud whose ideas have not stood the test of time—a "dinosaur in the history of ideas" (Medawar, 1982). In this section, we will introduce you to Freud's ideas and then to two modern psychodynamic approaches. We will also try to show you why attitudes toward Freud today range from reverence to contempt, and why he evokes such controversy.

Freud and Psychoanalysis

To enter the world of Sigmund Freud is to enter a realm of unconscious motives, guilty secrets, unspeakable yearnings, and conflicts between desire and duty. These unseen forces, Freud be-

Sigmund Freud (1856–1939).

2 The **ego**, the second system to emerge, is a referee between the needs of instinct and the demands of society. It bows to the realities of life, putting a rein on the id's desire for sex and aggression until a suitable, socially appropriate outlet for it can be found. The ego, said Freud, is both conscious and unconscious, and it represents "reason and good sense."

3 The **superego**, the last system of personality to develop, represents morality and parental authority; it includes the conscience, the inner voice that says you did something wrong. The superego, which is partly conscious but largely unconscious, judges the activities of the id, handing out good feelings of pride and satisfaction when you do something well and handing out miserable feelings of guilt and shame when you break the rules.

"VERY WELL I'LL INTRODUCE YOU. EGO MEET ID. NOW GET BACK TO WORK."

lieved, have far more power over our personalities than our conscious intentions do. The unconscious reveals itself, said Freud, in art, dreams, jokes, apparent accidents, and slips of the tongue (which came to be called "Freudian slips"). The British member of Parliament who referred to the "honourable member from Hell" when he meant to say "from Hull," said Freud (1920/1960), was revealing his actual, unconscious appraisal of his colleague.

The Structure of Personality

In Freud's theory, personality consists of three major systems: the id, the ego, and the superego. Any action we take or problem we have results from the interaction and degree of balance among these systems (Freud, 1905, 1920/1960, 1923/1962).

1 The **id**, which is present at birth, is the reservoir of unconscious psychological energies and the motives to avoid pain and obtain pleasure. The id contains two competing instincts: the life, or sexual, instinct (fueled by psychic energy called the **libido**) and the death, or aggressive, instinct. As energy builds up in the id, tension results. The id may discharge this tension in the form of reflex actions, physical symptoms, or uncensored mental images and unbidden thoughts.

According to Freud, the healthy personality must keep all three systems in balance. Someone who is too controlled by the id is governed by impulse and selfish desires. Someone who is too controlled by the superego is rigid, moralistic, and bossy. Someone who has a weak ego is unable to balance personal needs and wishes with social duties and realistic limitations.

If a person feels anxious or threatened when the wishes of the id conflict with social rules, the ego has weapons at its command to relieve the tension. These unconscious strategies, called **defense mechanisms**, deny or distort reality, but they also protect us from conflict and anxiety. They become unhealthy only when they cause self-defeating behavior and emotional problems. Here are some of the primary defenses identified by Freud and later analysts (A. Freud, 1967; Vaillant, 1992):

1 *Repression* occurs when a threatening idea, memory, or emotion is blocked from consciousness. A woman who had a frightening childhood experience that she cannot remember, for example, is said to be repressing her memory of it. Freud used the term to mean both *unconscious* expulsion of disturbing material from awareness and *conscious* suppression of such material, but modern analysts tend to think of repression only as an unconscious defense mechanism (McNally, 2003).

id In psychoanalysis, the part of personality containing inherited psychic energy, particularly sexual and aggressive instincts.

libido (li-BEE-do) In psychoanalysis, the psychic energy that fuels the life or sexual instincts of the id.

ego In psychoanalysis, the part of personality that represents reason, good sense, and rational self-control.

superego In psychoanalysis, the part of personality that represents conscience, morality, and social standards.

defense mechanisms Methods used by the ego to prevent unconscious anxiety or threatening thoughts from entering consciousness.

*"I'm sorry, I'm not speaking to anyone tonight.
My defense mechanisms seem to be out of order."*

2 *Projection* occurs when a person's own unacceptable or threatening feelings are repressed and then attributed to someone else. A person who is embarrassed about having sexual feelings toward members of a different ethnic group, for example, may project this discomfort onto them, saying, "Those people are dirty-minded and oversexed."

3 *Displacement* occurs when people direct their emotions toward things, animals, or other people that are not the real object of their feelings. A boy who is forbidden to express anger toward his father, for example, may "take it out" on his toys or his younger sister. When displacement serves a higher cultural or socially useful purpose, as in the creation of art or inventions, it is called *sublimation*. Freud argued that society has a duty to help people sublimate their unacceptable impulses for the sake of civilization. Sexual passion may be sublimated into the creation of art or literature; aggressive impulses may be sublimated into competitive sports.

4 *Reaction formation* occurs when a feeling that produces unconscious anxiety is transformed into its opposite in consciousness. A woman who is afraid to admit to herself that she fears her husband may instead cling to the belief that she loves him deeply. A person who is aroused by erotic images may angrily assert that pornography is disgusting. How does such a transformed emotion differ from a true emotion? In reaction formation the professed feeling is excessive, and the person is extravagant and compulsive about demonstrating it, as when a woman says of an abusive husband: "Of course I love him! I *never* have any bad thoughts about him! He's perfect!"

5 *Regression* occurs when a person reverts to a previous phase of psychological development. An 8-year-old boy who is anxious about his parents' divorce may regress to earlier habits of thumb sucking or clinging. Adults may regress to immature behavior when they are under pressure—for example, by having temper tantrums when they don't get their way.

6 *Denial* occurs when people refuse to admit that something unpleasant is happening, such as mistreatment by a partner; that they have a problem, such as drinking too much; or that they are feeling a forbidden emotion, such as anger. Denial protects a person's self-image and preserves the illusion of invulnerability: "It can't happen to me."

The Development of Personality

Freud argued that personality develops in a series of *psychosexual stages*, in which sexual energy takes different forms as the child matures. Each new stage produces a certain amount of frustration, conflict, and anxiety. If these are not resolved properly, normal development may be interrupted, and the child may remain *fixated*, or stuck, at the current stage.

For example, said Freud, some people remain fixated at the *oral stage*, which occurs during the first year of life, when babies experience the world through their mouths. As adults, they will seek oral gratification in smoking, overeating, nail biting, or chewing on pencils; some may become clinging and dependent, like a nursing child. Others remain fixated at the *anal stage*, at ages 2 to 3, when toilet training and control of bodily wastes are the key issues. They may become "anal retentive," holding everything in, obsessive about neatness and cleanliness. Or they may become just the opposite, "anal expulsive"—messy and disorganized.

For Freud, however, the most crucial stage for the formation of personality was the *phallic (Oedipal) stage*, which lasts roughly from age 3 to age 5 or 6. During this stage, said Freud, the child unconsciously wishes to possess the parent of the other sex and to get rid of the parent of the same sex. Children often announce proudly, "I'm going to marry Daddy (or Mommy) when I grow up," and they reject the same-sex "rival." Freud (1924a, 1924b) labeled this phenomenon the **Oedipus complex**, after the Greek legend of King Oedipus, who unwittingly killed his father and married his mother.

Boys and girls, Freud believed, go through the Oedipal stage differently. Boys are discovering the pleasure and pride of having a penis, so when they see a naked girl for the first time, they are horrified. Their unconscious exclaims (in effect), "Her penis has been cut off! Who could have done such a thing to her? Why, it must have been her powerful father. And if he could do it to her, my father could do it to me!" This realization, said Freud, causes the boy to repress his desire for his mother and identify with his father. He accepts his father's authority and the father's standards of conscience and morality; the superego has emerged.

Freud admitted that he did not quite know what to make of girls, who, lacking the penis, could not go through the same steps. He speculated that a girl, upon discovering male anatomy, would panic that she had only a puny clitoris instead of a stately penis. She would conclude that she already had lost her penis. As a result, Freud said, girls do not have the powerful motivating fear that boys do to give up their Oedipal feelings and develop a strong superego; they have only a lingering sense of "penis envy."

Freud believed that when the Oedipus complex is resolved, at about age 5 or 6, the child's personality is fundamentally formed. Unconscious conflicts with parents, unresolved fixations and guilts, and attitudes toward the same and the other sex will continue to replay themselves throughout life. The child settles into a supposedly nonsexual *latency stage*, in preparation for the *genital stage*, which begins at puberty and leads to adult sexuality.

In Freud's view, then, your adult personality is shaped by how you progressed through the early psychosexual stages, which defense mechanisms you developed to reduce anxiety, and whether your ego is strong enough to balance the conflict between the id (what you would like to do) and the superego (your conscience).

As you might imagine, Freud's ideas were not exactly received with yawns. Sexual feelings in 5-year-olds! Repressed longings in respectable adults! Unconscious meanings in dreams! Penis envy! This was strong stuff in the early years of the twentieth century, and before long psychoanalysis had captured the public imagination in Europe and America. But it also produced a sharp rift with the emerging schools of empirical psychology.

This rift continues to divide scholars today. Many believe that the overall framework of his theory is timeless and brilliant, even if some specific ideas have proved faulty (Westen, 1998). Others think that psychoanalytic theory is nonsense, with little empirical support, and that Freud was not the brilliant theoretician, impartial scientist, or even successful clinician that he claimed to be. On the contrary, they note, Freud often bullied his patients into accepting his explanations of their symptoms, and he ignored all evidence disconfirming his ideas (McNally, 2003; Powell & Boer, 1995; Sulloway, 1992; Webster, 1995). In one famous case, he pressured an 18-year-old patient, "Dora" (Ida Bauer), to accept the unwanted sexual advances of one of her father's friends, attributing her "hysterical" refusal to her own supposedly repressed sexual desires. Dora angrily left treatment after three months (Lakoff & Coyne, 1993).

On the positive side, Freud welcomed women into the profession of psychoanalysis, wrote eloquently about the devastating results to women of society's suppression of their sexuality, and argued, ahead of his time, that homosexuality was neither a sin nor a perversion but a "variation of the sexual function" and "nothing to be ashamed of" (Freud, 1961). Freud was thus a mixture of intellectual vision and blindness, sensitivity and arrogance. His provocative ideas left a powerful legacy to psychology—one that others began to tinker with immediately.

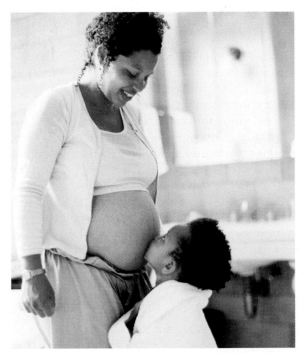

Freud believed that during the Oedipal stage, little boys fantasize about marrying their mothers and regard their fathers as rivals.

Oedipus complex In psychoanalysis, a conflict occurring in the phallic (Oedipal) stage, in which a child desires the parent of the other sex and views the same-sex parent as a rival.

QUICK quiz

Have Freudian concepts registered in your unconscious? Which Freudian concepts do the following events suggest?

1. A 4-year-old girl wants to snuggle on Daddy's lap but refuses to kiss her mother.
2. A celibate priest writes poetry about sexual passion.
3. A man who is angry at his boss shouts at his kids for making noise.
4. A woman whose father was cruel to her when she was little insists over and over that she loves him dearly.
5. A racist justifies segregation by saying that black men are only interested in sex with white women.
6. A 9-year-old boy who moves to a new city starts having tantrums.

Answers:

1. Oedipus complex   2. sublimation   3. displacement   4. reaction formation   5. projection   6. regression

Other Psychodynamic Approaches

Some of Freud's followers stayed in the psychoanalytic tradition and modified Freud's theories from within. Women, as you might imagine, were not too pleased about "penis envy." Clara Thompson (1943/1973) and Karen Horney [HORN-eye] (1926/1973) argued that it was insulting philosophy and bad science to claim that half the human race is dissatisfied with its anatomy. When women feel inferior to men, they said, we should look for explanations in the disadvantages that women live with and their second-class status. In fact, Horney added, if anyone has an envy problem, it is men. Men have "womb envy": They envy women's ability to bear children.

Others broke away from Freud, or were actively rejected by him, and went off to start their own schools. Today, there are many psychodynamic approaches, but two are especially popular: those of Carl Jung and of the object-relations theorists.

Jungian Theory Carl Jung (1875–1961) was originally one of Freud's closest friends and a member of his inner circle, but the friendship ended with a furious quarrel about the nature of the unconscious. In addition to the individual's own unconscious, said Jung (1967), all human beings share a vast **collective unconscious**, containing universal memories, symbols, images, and themes, which he called **archetypes**.

An archetype can be an image, such as the "magic circle," called a *mandala* in Eastern religions, which Jung thought symbolizes the unity of life and "the totality of the self." Or it can be a figure found in fairy tales, legends, and popular stories, such as the Hero, the nurturing Earth Mother, the Powerful Father, or the Wicked Witch. It can even be an aspect of the self. For example, the *shadow* archetype reflects the prehistoric fear of wild animals and represents the bestial, evil side of human nature. Scholars have found that some basic archetypes, such as the Hero and the Earth Mother, do appear in the stories and images of virtually every society (Campbell, 1949/1968; Neher, 1996). Jungians would consider Darth Vader, Dracula, the Dark Lord Sauron, and Harry Potter's tormentor Valdemort as expressions of the shadow archetype.

Two of the most important archetypes, in Jung's view, are those of maleness and femaleness. Jung (like Freud) recognized that "masculine" and "feminine" qualities exist in both sexes. The *anima* represents the feminine archetype in men; the *animus* represents the masculine archetype in women. Problems can arise, however, if a person tries to repress his or her internal, opposite archetype—that is, if a man denies his softer feminine side or if a woman denies her masculine side.

Although Jung shared with Freud a fascination with the darker aspects of the personality, he (along with other dissenters from Freudian orthodoxy) had confidence in the positive, forward-moving strengths of the ego. He believed that people are motivated not only by past conflicts, but also by their future goals

---

collective unconscious In Jungian theory, the universal memories and experiences of humankind, represented in the symbols, stories, and images (archetypes) that occur across all cultures.

archetypes [AR-ki-types] Universal, symbolic images that appear in myths, art, stories, and dreams; to Jungians, they reflect the collective unconscious.

In The Wizard of Oz, *the Wicked Witch of the West is a beloved example of the archetype of evil.*

and their desire to fulfill themselves. Jung was also among the first to identify extroversion/introversion as a basic dimension of personality. Nonetheless, many of Jung's ideas were more suited to mysticism and philosophy than to empirical psychology, which may be why so many Jungian ideas became popular with New Age movements.

Jung had a psychotic breakdown after his split with Freud. And he revealed his own dark side when he supported the Nazis, writing vicious attacks on Jews and claiming that their collective unconscious differed from that of gentiles. (So much for its universality.) But he continued to treat patients and attract many worshipful followers by virtue of his charisma (Hayman, 2001). Like Freud, therefore, Jung left a troubling personal legacy along with theories that appealed to legions of believers.

The Object-Relations School

Freud essentially regarded the baby as if it were an independent, greedy little organism ruled by its own instinctive desires; other people were relevant only insofar as they gratified the infant's drives or blocked them. But by the 1950s, increased awareness of the importance of human attachments led to the emergence of the **object-relations school**, developed in Great Britain by Melanie Klein, D. W. Winnicott, and others.

To object-relations theorists, the central problem in life is to find a balance between the need for independence and the need for others. This balance requires constant adjustment to separations and losses: small ones that occur during quarrels, moderate ones such as leaving home for the first time, and major ones such as divorce or death. The way we react to these separations, according to object-relations analysts, is largely determined by our experiences in the first year or two of life.

The reason for the clunky word "object" in object relations, instead of the warmer word "human" or "parent," is that the infant's attachment is not only to a real person (usually the mother) but also to the infant's evolving perception of her. The child creates a *mental representation* of the mother—someone who is kind or fierce, protective or rejecting. The child's representations of important adults, whether realistic or distorted, unconsciously affect personality throughout life, influencing how the person relates to others: with trust or suspicion, acceptance or criticism (Goldstein, 2002; Westen, 1998).

The object-relations school also departs from Freudian theory regarding the nature of male and female development (Sagan, 1988; Winnicott, 1957/1990). In the object-relations view, children of both sexes identify first with the mother. Girls, who are the same sex as the mother, do not need to separate from her; the mother treats a daughter as an extension of herself. But boys, to develop a

object-relations school A psychodynamic approach that emphasizes the importance of the infant's first two years of life and the baby's formative relationships, especially with the mother.

According to object-relations theory, a baby constructs unconscious representations of his or her parents, which will influence the child's relations with others throughout life.

masculine identity, must break away from the mother; the mother encourages a son to be independent and separate. Thus men, in this view, develop more rigid boundaries between themselves and other people than women do.

Evaluating Psychodynamic Theories

Although modern psychodynamic theorists differ in many ways, they share a general belief that to understand personality we must explore its unconscious dynamics and origins. Many psychologists in other fields, however, regard most psychodynamic ideas as literary metaphors rather than as scientific explanations (Cioffi, 1998; Crews, 1998). Critics argue that psychodynamic theories are guilty of three scientific failings:

Thinking Critically About Psychodynamic Ideas

1 *Violating the principle of falsifiability.* As we saw in Chapter 1, a theory that is impossible to disconfirm in principle is not scientific. Many psychodynamic concepts about unconscious motivations are, in fact, impossible to confirm or disconfirm. Followers often accept an idea because it seems intuitively right or their experience seems to support it. Anyone who doubts the idea or offers disconfirming evidence is then accused of being "defensive" or "in denial." This way of dismissing criticism is neither scientific nor fair!

Some psychodynamic ideas can be tested empirically. For example, Freud thought that playing or observing aggressive sports would channel aggressive energy into a socially accepted form, and thus reduce it. But decades of empirical research find just the opposite: Aggressive sports often increase the hostility and aggression of participants and observers, such as these soccer fans.

2 *Drawing universal principles from the experiences of a few atypical patients.* Freud and most of his followers generalized from a few individuals, often patients in therapy, to all human beings. Of course, the problem of overgeneralizing from small samples occurs in other areas of psychology too, and sometimes valid insights about human behavior can be obtained from case studies. The problem occurs when the observer fails to confirm these observations by studying other samples and incorrectly infers that what applies to some individuals applies to all. For example, some psychodynamically oriented therapists, accepting Freud's notion of a childhood latency stage, have assumed that if a child masturbates or takes part in sex play, the child has probably been sexually molested. But masturbation and sexual curiosity are by no means typical only of abused children; these are normal and common behaviors among children in the general population (Friedrich et al., 1998; Lamb, 2002).

3 *Basing theories of personality development on retrospective accounts and the fallible memories of patients.* Most psychodynamic theorists have not observed random samples of children at different ages, as modern child psychologists do, to construct their theories of development. Instead they have worked backward, creating theories based on themes in adults' recollections of childhood. The analysis of memories can be an illuminating way to achieve insights about our lives; in fact, it is the only way we can think about our own lives! But, as we will see in Chapter 8, memory is often inaccurate, influenced as much by what is going on in our lives now as by what happened in the past. If you are currently not getting along with your mother, you may remember all the times when she was hard on you and forget the counterexamples of her kindness.

Retrospective analysis has another problem: It creates an *illusion of causality* between events. People often assume that if A came before B, then A must have caused B. For example, if your mother spent three months in the hospital when you were 5 years old and today you feel anxious and insecure in college, an object-relations analyst would probably draw a connection between the two facts. But a lot of other things could be causing your anxiety and insecurity, such as being away from home for the first time at a large and impersonal college.

In recent years, some psychologists have been testing psychodynamic ideas empirically. They have identified nonconscious processes in thought, memory, and behavior; and they have found evidence for many of the major defense mechanisms, such as reaction formation, projection, denial, and displacement (Baumeister, Dale, & Sommer, 1998; Cramer, 2000; Marcus-Newhall et al., 2000). More generally, research confirms the psychodynamic idea that we are often unaware of the motives behind our own puzzling or self-defeating actions. However, the modern, empirical study of personality has taken quite a different turn from the all-embracing observations and intuitions of Freud and his descendants.

QUICK quiz

Are you feeling defensive about answering this quiz?

1. An 8-year-old boy is behaving aggressively, hitting classmates and disobeying his teacher. Which of the following explanations of his behavior might come from a Freudian, Jungian, or object-relations analyst?

   a. The boy is expressing his shadow archetype.

   b. The boy is expressing the aggressive energy of the id and has not developed enough ego control.

   c. The boy has had unusual difficulty separating from his mother and is compensating by behaving aggressively.

2. In the 1950s and 1960s, many psychoanalysts, observing unhappy gay men who had sought therapy, concluded that homosexuality was a mental illness. What violation of the scientific method were they committing?

Answers:

1. a. Jung b. Freud c. object-relations analyst   2. The analysts were drawing inappropriate conclusions from atypical patients in therapy, failing to test these conclusions with gay men who were not in therapy or with heterosexuals. When such research was done, using appropriate control groups, it turned out that gay men were not more mentally disturbed or depressed than heterosexuals (Hooker, 1957).

WHAT'S *Ahead*

- How reliable are those tests that tell you what "personality type" you are?

- How can psychologists tell which personality traits are more central or important than others?

- Which five dimensions of personality seem to describe people the world over?

The Modern Study of Personality

People love to fit themselves and their friends into "types." They have been doing it forever. Early Greek philosophers thought our personalities fell into four fundamental categories depending on mixes of body fluids. For example, if you were an angry, irritable sort of person, you supposedly had an excess of choler, and even now the word *choleric* describes a hothead. And if you were slow-moving and unemotional, you supposedly had an excess of phlegm, making you a "phlegmatic" type.

Popular Personality Tests That particular theory is long gone, but other unscientific tests of personality types still exist, aimed at predicting how people will do at work, whether they will get along with others, or whether they will succeed as leaders. One such test, the Myers-Briggs Type Indicator, is hugely popular in business, at motivational seminars, and with matchmaking services; at least 2.5 million Americans a year take it (Gladwell, 2004). The test assigns people to one of 16 different types, depending on how the individual combines various tendencies, such as being introverted or extroverted or being someone who relies on logic or intuition. Unfortunately, the Myers-Briggs is not much more reliable than measuring body fluids; one study found that fewer than half of the respondents scored as the same type a mere five weeks later. And there is little evidence to support the test's key premise that knowledge of a person's type reliably predicts behavior on the job or in relationships (Barbuto, 1997; Paul, 2004; Pittenger, 1993).

> **Thinking Critically About Personality Tests**

The four basic personality types

objective tests (inventories) Standardized questionnaires requiring written responses; they typically include scales on which people are asked to rate themselves.

factor analysis A statistical method for analyzing the intercorrelations among various measures or test scores; clusters of measures or scores that are highly correlated are assumed to measure the same underlying trait or ability (factor).

In addition, the personality-assessment industry has developed more than 2,500 personality tests to measure specific traits and tendencies that business and government would love to be able to identify: for example, the tendency to steal, take drugs, or be disloyal on the job (Ehrenreich, 2001). But it is important to think critically about these tests, because many of them are nearly useless from a scientific point of view. (In "Taking Psychology with You," we discuss handwriting analysis, another popular but unreliable effort to measure personality.)

However, there are also many measures of personality traits that are scientifically valid and useful in research. **Objective tests (inventories)** are standardized questionnaires that require written responses, typically to multiple-choice or true-false items. They provide information about literally hundreds of different aspects of personality, including needs, values, interests, self-esteem, emotional problems, and typical ways of responding to situations. For example, the Minnesota Multiphasic Personality Inventory (MMPI) is used to assess personality disorders (see Chapter 11). And the Multidimensional Personality Questionnaire (MPQ) is often used to identify key di-

mensions of personality and the traits that make up each one (Krueger, 2000).

Using well-constructed inventories, psychologists have identified hundreds of traits, ranging from sensation seeking (the enjoyment of risk) to "erotophobia" (the fear of sex). Are some of these traits more important or central than others? Do some of them overlap or cluster together?

Clustering Traits For Gordon Allport, one of the most influential psychologists in the empirical study of personality, the answer to both questions was yes. Allport (1937, 1961) recognized that not all traits have equal weight and significance in people's lives. Most of us, he said, have 5 to 10 *central traits* that reflect a characteristic way of behaving, dealing with others, and reacting to new situations. For instance, some people see the world as a hostile, dangerous place, whereas others see it as a place for fun and frolic. *Secondary traits*, in contrast, are more changeable aspects of personality, such as music preferences, habits, casual opinions, and the like.

Raymond B. Cattell advanced the study of this issue by applying a statistical method called **factor analysis**. Performing a factor analysis is like adding water to flour: It causes the material to clump up into little balls. When applied to traits, this procedure identifies clusters of correlated items that seem to be measuring some common underlying factor. For example, the traits of assertiveness, willingness to tell jokes in large groups, and taking pleasure in meeting new people might share the common factor of extroversion.

Using questionnaires, life descriptions, and observations of thousands of people, Cattell (1965, 1973) measured dozens of personality traits, including humor, intelligence, creativity, dominance, and emotional disorders. Out of these he identified 16 factors, later noting that only six of them had been repeatedly confirmed.

Today, hundreds of factor-analytic studies support the existence of a cluster of central personality traits. Although researchers are still debating exactly how many traits belong to this inner core—some say three, others say as many as nine—most personality researchers agree on the centrality of five "robust factors," known informally as the *Big Five* (Jang et al., 1998; McCrae et al., 2005, 2006; Paunonen, 2003):

1 *Extroversion versus introversion* describes the extent to which people are outgoing or shy. It includes such traits as being talkative or silent, sociable or reclusive, adventurous or cautious, eager to be in the limelight or inclined to stay in the shadows.

2 *Neuroticism (negative emotionality) versus emotional stability* describes the extent to which a person suffers from such traits as anxiety, an inability to control impulses, and a tendency to feel negative emotions such as anger, guilt, contempt, and resentment. Neurotic individuals are worriers, complainers, and defeatists, even when they have no major problems. They are always ready to see the sour side of life and none of its sweetness.

3 *Agreeableness versus antagonism* describes the extent to which people are good-natured or irritable, cooperative or abrasive, secure or suspicious and jealous. It reflects the tendency to have friendly relationships or hostile ones.

4 *Conscientiousness versus impulsiveness* describes the degree to which people are responsible or undependable, persevering or quick to give up, steadfast or fickle, tidy or careless, self-disciplined or impulsive.

5 *Openness to experience versus resistance to new experience* describes the extent to which people are curious, imaginative, questioning, and creative or conforming, unimaginative, predictable, and uncomfortable with novelty.

The Big Five have emerged as distinct, central personality dimensions in most places around the

Where do you think this man would score on extroversion?

world, including Britain, Canada, the Czech Republic, China, Ethiopia, Turkey, the Netherlands, Japan, Spain, the Philippines, Hawaii, Germany, Portugal, Israel, South Korea, Russia, and Australia (Digman & Shmelyov, 1996; Katigbak et al., 2002; McCrae et al., 2005; Somer & Goldberg, 1999). One monumental research venture gathered data from thousands of people across 50 cultures. In this massive project as in many smaller ones, the five personality factors emerge whether you ask people for self-reports or

---

GET INVOLVED

Rate Your Traits

For each of the ten items that follow, write a number from 1 to 7 indicating the extent to which you see that trait as being characteristic of you, where 1 = "I *disagree* strongly that this trait describes me" to 7 = "I *agree* strongly that this trait describes me." Use the midpoint, 4, if you neither agree nor disagree that the trait describes you. (This self-test was designed by Samuel D. Gosling.)

1. _____ Extroverted, enthusiastic
2. _____ Critical, quarrelsome
3. _____ Dependable, self-disciplined
4. _____ Anxious, easily upset
5. _____ Open to new experiences, complex
6. _____ Reserved, quiet
7. _____ Sympathetic, warm
8. _____ Disorganized, careless
9. _____ Calm, emotionally stable
10. _____ Conventional, uncreative

To score yourself on The Big Five traits, use this key:

Extroversion:	High on question 1, low on question 6
Neuroticism:	High on question 4, low on question 9
Agreeableness:	High on question 7, low on question 2
Conscientiousness:	High on question 3, low on question 8
Openness:	High on question 5, low on question 10

Now ask a friend or relative to rate you on each of the 10 items. How closely does that rating match your own? If there is a discrepancy, what might be the reason for it?

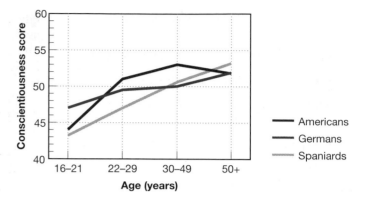

FIGURE 2.1

Consistency and Change in Personality

Although the Big Five traits are fairly stable, changes do occur over the life span. As you can see here, neuroticism (negative emotionality) is highest among young adults and then declines, whereas conscientiousness is lowest among young adults and then steadily increases. These changes may reflect common experiences that occur as young people grow up and leave home or as a common process of maturation (Costa et al., 1999).

have people assessed by friends or independent observers (McCrae et al., 2005; Terracciano & McCrae, 2006; Watson, Hubbard, & Wiese, 2000).

Moreover, the Big Five are remarkably stable over a lifetime, especially once a person hits 30. There is some good news, however, for crabby neurotics, especially young ones. A survey of thousands of people in 10 countries, and a separate meta-analysis of 92 longitudinal studies, found that although young people, ages 16 to 21, are the most neurotic (emotionally negative) and the least agreeable and conscientious, people tend to become more agreeable and conscientious and less negative between ages 30 and 40 (Costa et al., 1999; Roberts, Walton, & Viechtbauer, 2006) (see Figure 2.1). In later adulthood older people also tend to become less extroverted and less open to new experiences. Because these changes have

been found in many different countries, they may reflect the universality of adult experiences—such as work and family responsibilities—or common maturational changes over the life span.

The Big Five do not provide a complete picture of personality, of course. Clinical psychologists note that important traits involved in mental disorders are missing, such as psychopathy (impulsivity and lack of remorse), self-absorption, and obsessionality (Westen & Shedler, 1999). Personality researchers note that other important traits are missing, such as religiosity, dishonesty, humorousness, and conventionality (Abrahamson, Baker, & Caspi, 2002; Paunonen & Ashton, 2001). But the Big Five do seem to lie at the core of personality variations among healthy individuals. Where do these traits, and others, come from?

QUICK quiz

Show that you have the trait of conscientiousness by taking this quiz.

1. What is the advantage of inventories over tests of personality "types"?
2. Raymond Cattell advanced the study of personality by (a) developing case-study analysis, (b) using factor analysis, (c) devising the Myers-Briggs Type Indicator.
3. Which of the following are *not* among the Big Five personality factors? (a) introversion, (b) agreeableness, (c) psychoticism, (d) openness to experience, (e) intelligence, (f) neuroticism, (g) conscientiousness
4. Which one of the Big Five typically decreases by age 30? (a) agreeableness, (b) extroversion, (c) openness to experience, (d) neuroticism

Answers:

1. They have better reliability and validity.   2. b   3. c, e   4. d

WHAT'S *Ahead*

- Do puppies have personalities? What about octopuses?

- Is it possible to be born irritable or easygoing?

- To what extent are personality differences among people influenced by their genetic differences?

- Are people who have highly heritable personality traits stuck with them forever?

Genetic Influences on Personality

A mother we know was describing her two children: "My daughter has always been difficult, intense, and testy," she said, "but my son is the opposite, placid and good-natured. They came out of the womb that way." Was this mother right? Is it possible to be born touchy or good-natured? Or was she treating her two babies differently?

For centuries, efforts to understand why people differ from one another have swung from biological answers ("it's in their nature; they are born that way") to learning and environmental ones ("it's all a matter of nurture—how they are raised and the experiences they have"). The *nature–nurture* debate has been one of the longest-running either–or arguments in philosophy and psychology.

"THERE'S ANOTHER HEREDITARY DISEASE THAT RUNS IN THE ROYAL FAMILY. YOUR GRANDFATHER WAS A STUBBORN FOOL, YOUR FATHER WAS A STUBBORN FOOL, AND YOU ARE A STUBBORN FOOL."

Edward L. Thorndike (1903), one of the leading psychologists of the early 1900s, staked out the nature position by claiming that "in the actual race of life . . . the chief determining factor is heredity." But in stirring words that became famous, his contemporary, behaviorist John B. Watson (1925), insisted that experience could write virtually any message on the blank slate of human nature:

> Give me a dozen healthy infants, well-formed, and my own specified world to bring them up in and I'll guarantee to take any one at random and train him to become any type of specialist I might select—doctor, lawyer, artist, merchant-chief and yes, even beggar-man and thief, regardless of his talents, penchants, tendencies, abilities, vocations, and race of his ancestors.

Today, almost all psychologists who study personality regard biology and experience as interacting influences, each shaping the other over time. "The nature–nurture debate is over," said one researcher (Turkheimer, 2000). "The bottom line is that everything is heritable . . . [but the findings] do not show that genes are more fundamental than environments." In this section and the next, we will see what this means, by examining the interlaced influences of nature and nurture on personality.

How can heredity affect personality? **Genes**, the basic units of heredity, are made up of elements of *DNA* (deoxyribonucleic acid). These elements form chemical codes for the synthesis of proteins; proteins, in turn, affect virtually every aspect of the body, from its structure to the chemicals that keep it running. Genes can affect the behaviors we call "personality" through their effects on an infant's developing brain and nervous system.

Researchers currently measure genetic contributions to personality in three ways: by studying personality traits in other species, by studying the temperaments of human infants and children, and by doing heritability studies of twins and adopted individuals. These methods only permit us to *infer* the existence of relevant genes—just as, if you find your toddler covered in chocolate, it's pretty safe to infer that candy is somewhere close by. Scientists hope that the actual genes underlying temperaments and key traits will one day be discovered, and dozens of possible associations between specific genes and personality traits have already been reported (Fox et al., 2005b; Plomin et al., 2001). You will be hearing lots more about genetic discoveries in the coming years, so it is important to understand what they mean—and don't mean.

genes The functional units of heredity; they are composed of DNA and specify the structure of proteins.

temperaments
Physiological dispositions to respond to the environment in certain ways; they are present in infancy and are assumed to be innate.

Puppies and Personalities

A psychologist who was interviewed in the *Los Angeles Times* described Susie, one of his clients, as irritable, grumpy, and manipulative. Hardly a comment to make headlines, except that Susie is a bear (Gosling & John, 1999).

In recent years, scientists have been drawing on research in physiology, genetics, ecology, and ethology (the study of animals in their natural habitats) to investigate the nature of personality in our fellow animals, in order to better understand the evolutionary and biological underpinnings of human personality traits (Jones & Gosling, 2005). These investigators argue that just as it has been evolutionarily adaptive for human beings to vary in their ways of responding to the world and those around them, so it has been for animals. For example, it would be beneficial for a species if some, but not all, of its members were bold or impulsive enough to risk life and limb to confront a stranger or experiment with a new food and other members were more cautious.

When we think of an individual who has a personality, we usually think of a human being. But bears, dogs, pigs, hyenas, goats, cats, and, of course, our fellow primates also have distinctive, characteristic ways of behaving that make them different from their fellows (Gosling, 2001). So, surprisingly, does the humble, squishy octopus! When researchers dropped a crab into a tank of octopuses, some of them would aggressively grab that dinner right away; others seemed more passive and waited for the crab to swim near them; and some waited and attacked the crab when no one was watching (Mather & Anderson, 1993). Apparently,

you don't have to be a person to have a personality. You don't even have to be a primate.

In another imaginative set of studies, Samuel D. Gosling and his colleagues (2003) recruited dog owners and their dogs in a local park. All the owners provided personality assessments of their dogs and filled out the same personality inventory for themselves. The owners then designated another person who knew them and their dogs and who could judge the personalities of both. In a second study, the owners brought their dogs to an enclosed section of the park where three independent observers rated the dogs, so the researchers could compare the owners' judgments of their dogs' personalities with the observers' ratings. And in a third study, the investigators took photos of the dogs at play in order to examine the effects of breed and appearance on the animals' personalities. The dog owners, their friends, and the neutral observers all agreed quite strongly in their ratings of the dogs' personalities along four of the Big Five traits: extroversion, agreeableness, emotional reactivity (neuroticism), and openness to experience. (Conscientiousness requires considerable cognitive ability and so far has turned up only in humans and chimpanzees.)

To date, Gosling and his colleagues have found evidence of most of the Big Five traits in 64 different species. So when you hear your dog-crazy friend say, "Barkley is such a shy and nervous little pup, whereas Barker is outgoing and sociable," she is probably right.

Heredity and Temperament

Let's turn now to human personalities. Even in the first weeks after birth, human babies differ in activity level, mood, responsiveness, heart rate, and attention span (Belsky, Hsieh, & Crnic, 1996; Fox et al., 2005a). Some are irritable and cranky; others are placid and sweet-natured. Some will cuddle up in an adult's arms and snuggle; others squirm and fidget, as if they cannot stand being held. Some smile easily; others fuss and cry.

These differences appear even when you control for possible prenatal influences, such as the mother's nutrition, drug use, or problems with the pregnancy. The reason is that babies are born with genetically determined **temperaments**, dispositions to respond to the environment in certain ways. Temperaments include *reactivity* (how excitable, arousable, or responsive a baby is), *soothability* (how easy it is to calm an upset baby), and positive and negative emotionality. Temperaments are quite stable over time and may later form the basis of spe-

Group portraits of dogs, as of people, often reveal different personalities. Usually, someone is showing off, someone is grumpy, and someone isn't paying attention at all.

Extreme shyness and fear of new situations tend to be biologically based, stable aspects of temperament—both in human beings and in monkeys. On the right, a timid infant rhesus monkey cowers behind a friend in the presence of an outgoing stranger.

cific personality traits (Else-Quest et al., 2006; Rothbart, Ahadi, & Evans, 2000).

For example, highly reactive infants, even at 4 months of age, are excitable, nervous, and fearful; they overreact to any little thing, even a colorful picture placed in front of them. As toddlers, they tend to be wary and fearful of new things—toys that make noise, odd-looking robots—even when their moms arc right there with them. At 5 years, many of these children are still timid and uncomfortable in new situations. At 7 years, many still have symptoms of anxiety. They are afraid of being kidnapped, they need to sleep with the light on, and they are afraid of sleeping in an unfamiliar house—even if they have never experienced any sort of trauma.

In contrast, nonreactive infants take things easy. They lie there without fussing; they rarely cry; they babble happily. As toddlers, they are outgoing and curious about new toys and events. They continue to be easygoing and extroverted throughout childhood (Fox et al., 2005a; Kagan, 1997). Children at these two extremes differ physiologically, too (Rothbart, Ahadi, & Evans, 2000). During mildly stressful tasks, reactive children are more likely than nonreactive children to have increased heart rates, heightened brain activity, and high levels of stress hormones.

You can see, then, how biologically based temperaments might form the basis of the later personality traits we call "diligence," "assertiveness," "shyness," or "negative emotionality."

Heredity and Traits

A third way to study genetic contributions to personality is to estimate the **heritability** of specific traits within groups of children or adults. This method is favored by **behavioral geneticists**, sci-entists concerned with the genetic bases of behavior and personality traits. Within any group, individuals will vary in shyness, cheerfulness, impulsiveness, or any other quality. Heritability gives us a statistical estimate of the *proportion of the total variation in a trait that is attributable to genetic variation within a group.* Because the heritability of a trait is expressed as a proportion (such as .60 or 60/100), the maximum value it can have is 1.0 (which would mean that 100 percent of the variation in the trait was due to genetic variation).

We know that heritability is a tough concept to understand at first, so here's an example. Suppose that your entire psychology class takes a test of shyness, and you compute an average shyness score for the group. Some students will have scores close to the average, whereas others will have scores that are much higher or lower than the average. Heritability gives you an estimate of the extent to which your class's variation in shyness is due to genetic differences among the students who took the test. Note, however, that this estimate applies only to the group as a whole. It does not tell you anything about the impact of genetics on any *particular* individual's shyness or extroversion. You might be shy primarily because of your genes, but your friend might be shy with new people because of an embarrassing experience she had in a school play at the age of 8.

One obvious example of a highly heritable trait is height: Within a group of equally well-nourished individuals, most of the variation among them will be accounted for by their genetic differences. In contrast, table manners have low heritability because most variation among individuals is accounted for by differences in upbringing. Even highly heritable traits, however, can be modified by the environment. For example, although height

heritability A statistical estimate of the proportion of the total variance in some trait that is attributable to genetic differences among individuals within a group.

behavioral genetics An interdisciplinary field of study concerned with the genetic bases of individual differences in behavior and personality.

is highly heritable, malnourished children may not grow up to be as tall as they would have if given sufficient food. Conversely, if children eat an extremely nutritious diet, they may grow up to be taller than anyone thought they could.

Computing Heritability Scientists have no way to estimate the heritability of a trait or behavior directly, so they must infer it by studying people whose degree of genetic similarity is known. You might think that the simplest approach would be to compare blood relatives within families; everyone knows of families that are famous for some talent or personality trait. But the fact that a trait runs in a family doesn't tell us much, because close relatives usually share environments as well as genes. If Carlo's parents and siblings all love lasagna, that doesn't mean a taste for lasagna is heritable! The same applies if everyone in Carlo's family is shy, moody, or loves music.

A better approach is to study adopted children (e.g., Loehlin, Horn, & Willerman, 1996; Plomin & DeFries, 1985). Such children share half of their genes with each birth parent, but they grow up in a different environment, apart from their birth parents. On the other hand, they share an environment with their adoptive parents and siblings, but not their genes. Researchers can compare correlations between the children's traits and those of their

Identical twins Gerald Levey (left) and Mark Newman were separated at birth and raised in different cities. When they were reunited at age 31, they discovered some astounding similarities. Both were volunteer firefighters, wore mustaches, and were unmarried. Both liked to hunt, watch old John Wayne movies, and eat Chinese food. They drank the same brand of beer, held the can with the little finger curled around it, and crushed the can when it was empty. The challenge is to figure out which of these traits and behaviors are influenced strongly by heredity, which result from environmental factors such as social class and upbringing, and which are due merely to chance.

biological and adoptive relatives and can then use the results to estimate heritability.

Another approach is to compare identical twins with fraternal twins. *Identical twins* develop when a fertilized egg divides into two parts that then become separate embryos. Because the twins come from the same fertilized egg, they share all their genes, barring genetic mutations. (Identical twins may differ slightly at birth, however, because of differences in the blood supply to the two fetuses, or other chance factors.) In contrast, *fraternal twins* develop when a woman's ovaries release two eggs instead of one, and each egg is fertilized by a different sperm. Fraternal twins are wombmates, but they are no more alike genetically than any other two siblings (they share, on average, only half their genes), and they may be of different sexes.

Behavioral geneticists can estimate the heritability of a trait by comparing groups of same-sex fraternal twins with groups of identical twins. The assumption is that if identical twins are more alike than fraternal twins, then the increased similarity must be due to genetic influences. Perhaps, however, people do not treat identical and fraternal twins the same way. To avoid this problem, investigators have studied identical twins who were separated early in life and were reared apart. (Until relatively recently, adoption policies and attitudes toward births out of wedlock permitted such separations to occur.) In theory, separated identical twins share all their genes but not their environments. Any similarities between them should therefore be primarily genetic and should permit a direct estimate of heritability.

How Heritable Are Personality Traits? Findings from adoption and twin studies have provided compelling support for a genetic contribution to personality. Identical twins reared apart will often have unnerving similarities in gestures, mannerisms, and moods; indeed, their personalities often seem as similar as their physical features. If one twin tends to be optimistic, glum, or excitable, the other will probably be that way too (Braungert et al., 1992; Plomin et al., 2001).

Behavioral-genetic studies have produced remarkably consistent results on the heritability of traits. Whether the trait in question is one of the Big Five or one of many others from aggressiveness to overall happiness, heritability is typically around .50 (Bouchard, 1997a; Jang et al., 1998; Loehlin, 1992; Lykken & Tellegen, 1996; Waller et al., 1990). This means that within a group of people, about 50 percent of the variation in such traits is attributable to genetic differences among the individuals in the group. These findings have been replicated in many countries.

Some researchers have even reported high heritability for such specific activities as getting divorced (McGue & Lykken, 1992) and watching a lot of television in childhood (Plomin et al., 1990). How on earth can divorce and TV watching be heritable? Our prehistoric ancestors didn't get married, let alone divorced, and they certainly didn't watch TV! Perhaps, though, certain traits or temperaments that *are* heritable could predispose a person to do these things.

Evaluating Genetic Theories

We think you will agree that these behavioral-genetic findings are pretty amazing. Psychologists hope that one intelligent use of such findings will be to help people become more accepting of themselves and their children. Although we can all learn to make improvements and modifications to our personalities, most of us probably will never be able to *transform* our personalities because of our genetic dispositions and temperaments (Efran, Greene, & Gordon, 1998).

On the other hand, it is also important not to oversimplify, by claiming that "genes are everything," and overlook the role of the environment and experience in modifying traits. A genetic *predisposition* does not necessarily imply genetic *inevitability*. A person might have a gene that, for example, predisposes him or her to depression, but without certain environmental stresses or circumstances, the person will probably never become depressed (see Chapter 11). When people oversimplify, they mistakenly assume that personality problems that have a genetic component are

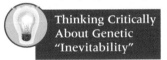
Thinking Critically About Genetic "Inevitability"

Separated at birth, the Mallifert twins meet accidentally.

permanent—say, that someone is "born to be bad" or to be a miserable grump forever. That belief can affect their behavior and actually make matters worse. Oversimplification can also lead people to incorrectly assume that if a problem, such as depression or shyness, has a genetic contribution, it will respond only to medication so there is no point trying other interventions; we discuss what is wrong with this assumption in Chapter 12.

As Robert Plomin (1989), a leading behavioral geneticist, observed, "The wave of acceptance of genetic influence on behavior is growing into a tidal wave that threatens to engulf the second message of this research: These same data provide the best available evidence for the importance of environmental influences." Let us now see what some of those influences might be.

QUICK quiz

We hope you have a few quiz-taking genes.

1. What three broad lines of research support the hypothesis that personality differences are due in part to genetic differences?

2. In behavioral-genetic studies, the heritability of personality traits, including the Big Five, is typically about (a) .50, (b) .90, (c) .10 to .20, (d) zero.

3. A newspaper headline announces: "Couch Potatoes Born, Not Made: Kids' TV Habits May Be Hereditary." Why is this headline misleading? What other explanations of the finding are possible? What aspects of TV watching *could* have a hereditary component?

Answers:

1. Research on animal personalities, human temperaments, and the heritability of traits   2. a   3. The headline implies that there is a "TV-watching gene," but there obviously isn't any such gene. The writer is failing to consider other explanations. For example, perhaps some temperaments dispose people to be sedentary or passive, and this disposition leads to a tendency to watch a lot of television.

social-cognitive learning theory A major contemporary learning view of personality, which holds that personality traits result from a person's learning history and his or her expectations, beliefs, perceptions of events, and other cognitions.

WHAT'S *Ahead*

- If personality traits are stable, why don't people always behave consistently across situations?

- How would a social-cognitive theorist explain why Madonna is so different as a performer and as a mom?

- How much can parents shape their children's personalities?

- How do your peers influence your personality?

Environmental Influences on Personality

The environment may account for half of the variation in personality, but what *is* the environment, exactly? In this section, we will consider the relative influence of three aspects of the environment: the particular situations you find yourself in, how your parents treat you, and who your peers are.

Situations and Social Learning

The very definition of a trait is that it is consistent across situations. But people often behave one way at home and a different way with their friends. The reason for people's inconsistency, according to behaviorists in the learning tradition, is that different behaviors are rewarded, punished, or ignored in different contexts. (In Chapter 9, we will examine in greater depth the important principles of behavioral theory.) For example, you are likely to be more extroverted in an audience of screaming, cheering *American Idol* fans than at home with relatives who would regard such noisy displays with alarm and condemnation. Because of such variations in our behavior across situations, strict behaviorists think it does not even make sense to talk about personality. In their view, people don't have traits; they simply show certain behavior patterns in some situations and not others.

A major contemporary learning view, **social-cognitive learning theory**, accounts for similarities in traits across situations and also for the inconsistencies that often occur. It holds that personality traits result, in part, from your learning history and your resulting expectations and beliefs. A child who studies hard and gets good grades, attention from teachers, admiration from friends, and praise from parents will come to expect that hard work in other situations will also pay off. That child will become, in terms of personality traits, "ambitious" and "industrious." A child who studies hard and gets poor grades, is ignored by teachers and parents, and is rejected by friends for being a grind will come to expect that working hard isn't worth it. That child will become (in the view of others) "unambitious" or "lazy."

Social-cognitive learning theory also emphasizes the continual interaction between your particular qualities and the situation you are in (Fleeson, 2004). Your temperament, habits, and beliefs influence how you respond to others, whom you hang out with, and the situations you seek (Bandura, 2001; Cervone & Shoda, 1999; Mischel

Who is the "real" Madonna—doting mother or flamboyant performer? According to social-cognitive learning theory, our genetic dispositions and personality traits cause us to choose some situations over others, but situations then influence which aspects of our personalities we express.

ZUMA Press

& Shoda, 1995). In turn, the situation influences your behavior and beliefs, rewarding some behaviors and extinguishing others. This process is called **reciprocal (mutual) determinism**.

The two-way process of reciprocal determinism (as opposed, say, to the one-way determinism of "genes determine everything" or "everything is learned") helps answer a question asked by everyone who has a sibling: What makes children who grow up in the same family so different, apart from their genes? The answer seems to be: experiences that affect each child differently, chance events that cannot be predicted, situations that children find themselves in, and peer groups that the children belong to (Harris, 2006; Plomin, Asbury, & Dunn, 2001; Rutter et al., 2001). Behavioral geneticists refer to these unique and chance experiences that are not shared with other family members as the **nonshared environment**: for example, being in Mrs. Miller's class in the fourth grade (which might inspire you to become a scientist), winning the lead in the school play (which might push you toward an acting career), or being bullied at school (which might have caused you to see yourself as weak and powerless). All these experiences work reciprocally with your own interpretation of them, your temperament, and your perceptions (did Mrs. Miller's class excite or bore you?).

Keeping the concept of reciprocal determinism in mind, let us take a look at two of the most powerful environmental influences in people's lives: their parents and their friends.

Parental Influence— and Its Limits

In April 1999, Dylan Klebold and Eric Harris, teenagers enraged at the popularity of school jocks and resentful about their own inadequacies, killed 12 classmates and a teacher at Columbine High School in Littleton, Colorado, in a coldly premeditated plan. Then they committed suicide. In the ensuing atmosphere of panic and blame, many people tried to find reasons for the boys' rampage. They blamed the boys' genes, the media, violent video games, the availability of guns, and, above all, their parents. The parents should have known, people said. They should have done something to prevent the tragedy. Or they did something very wrong in raising their sons; maybe they were neglectful or abusive.

These claims reflect an entrenched Western belief that parental child-rearing practices are the strongest influence, maybe even the *sole* influence, on children's personality development. For many decades, few psychologists thought to question this assumption, and many still accept it. Yet the belief that personality is primarily determined by how parents treat their children has begun to crumble under the weight of three lines of evidence (Harris, 1998, 2006):

1 *The shared environment of the home has little if any influence on personality.* In behavioral-genetic research, the "shared environment" includes the family you grew up with and the experiences and background you shared with your siblings and parents. If these had as powerful an influence as commonly assumed, then studies should find a strong correlation between the personality traits of adopted children and those of their adoptive parents. In fact, the correlation is weak to nonexistent, indicating that the influence of child-rearing practices and family life is nil compared to the influence of genetics (Cohen, 1999, Plomin, Asbury, & Dunn, 2001). As we just saw, it is only the nonshared environment that has a strong impact.

2 *Few parents have a single child-rearing style that is consistent over time and that they use with all their children.* Developmental psychologists have tried for many years to identify the effects of specific child-rearing practices on children's personality traits. The problem is that parents are inconsistent from day to day and over the years. Their child-rearing practices vary, depending on their own stresses, moods, and marital satisfaction (Harris, 1998; Holden & Miller, 1999). As one child we know said to her exasperated mother, "Why are you so mean to me today, Mommy? I'm this naughty every day." Moreover, parents tend to adjust their methods of child rearing according to the temperament of the child; they are often more lenient with easygoing children and more punitive with difficult ones.

3 *Even when parents try to be consistent in the way they treat their children, there may be little relation between what they do and how the children turn out.* Some children of troubled and abusive parents are resilient and do not suffer lasting emotional damage, as we will see in Chapter 3; some children of the kindest and most nurturing parents succumb to drugs, mental illness, or gangs. By all accounts, the parents of Dylan Klebold were loving and involved with their son (Garbarino & Bedard, 2001).

reciprocal determinism In social-cognitive theories, the two-way interaction between aspects of the environment and aspects of the individual in the shaping of personality traits.

nonshared environment Unique aspects of a person's environment and experience that are not shared with family members.

Of course, parents do influence their children in lots of ways. They contribute to their children's religious beliefs, intellectual and occupational interests, feelings of self-esteem or inadequacy, adherence to traditional or modern notions of masculinity and femininity, helpfulness to others, skills, and values (Beer, Arnold, & Loehlin, 1998; Krueger, Hicks, & McGue, 2001; McCrae et al., 2000). Above all, what parents do profoundly affects the quality of their relationship with their children—whether their children feel loved, secure, and valued or humiliated, frightened, and worthless (Harris, 1998).

Parents also have some influence even on traits in their children that are highly heritable. In one longitudinal study that followed children from age 3 to age 21, kids who were impulsive, uncontrollable, and aggressive at age 3 were far more likely than calmer children to grow up to be impulsive, unreliable, and antisocial, and more likely to commit crimes (Caspi, 2000). Early temperament was a strong and consistent predictor of these later personality traits. But not *every* child came out the same way. What protected some of those at risk, and helped them move in a healthier direction, was having parents who made sure they stayed in school, supervised them closely, and gave them consistent discipline. Another longitudinal study found that among children born with a genetic predisposition to extreme shyness and fearfulness, only those who had the gene *and* whose mothers had little social support (which increases stress) were still very shy at age 7 (Fox et al., 2005b). Perhaps the socially isolated mothers were extremely protective of their children, not exposing them to other people, and thus they were inadvertently rewarding their children's shyness rather than helping them modify it.

Nevertheless, it is clear that the parent–child relationship is not a one-way street in which parents determine everything about their kids. Because of reciprocal determinism, the relationship runs in both directions, with parents and children continually influencing one another. And yet, once children leave

Have you ever been in this situation, as the excluded student or the one doing the excluding? Being rejected by peers is one of the most painful experiences that adolescents report having.

home, starting in preschool, parental influence on children's behavior *outside* the home begins to wane. The "nonshared environment"—peers, chance events, and circumstances—takes over.

The Power of Peers

Should the parents of Dylan Klebold and Eric Harris have known how angry and resentful their sons felt in their private souls, angry enough to inflict a bloody revenge on their classmates? When two psychologists surveyed 275 freshmen at Cornell University, they found that most of them had "secret lives" and private selves that they never revealed to their parents (Garbarino & Bedard, 2001). Most reported committing crimes, drinking, doing drugs, and having sex without their parents' knowing anything about it. The researchers concluded that Dylan Klebold was just an extreme case of a common adolescent phenomenon: showing your parents only one facet of your personality and an entirely different one to your peers.

Children, like adults, live in two environments: their homes and their world outside the home. At home children learn how their parents want them to behave and what they can get away with; as soon as they leave home, however, they conform to the dress, habits, language, and rules of their peers. Children who were law-abiding in the fifth grade may start breaking the law in high school, if that is what it takes—or what they think it takes—to win the respect of their peers (Harris, 1998).

Adolescent culture often consists of many different peer groups, organized by interests (jocks,

GET INVOLVED

Situation and Self

Are you "a different person" when you are alone, with your parents, hanging out with friends, in class, or at a party? If so, in what ways? Do you have a "secret self" that you do not show to your family? Consider the Big Five factors (or any other personality traits that are important to you) as you answer these questions.

nerds, musicians, artists), ethnicity, or status and popularity. Unfortunately, children and teenagers who are temperamentally fearful and shy, have few or no friends, or are physically unattractive or weak are more likely than other kids to be bullied, victimized, and rejected by their peers (Hodges & Perry, 1999).

It has been difficult to tease apart the effects of parents and peers because parents usually try to arrange things so that their children's environments duplicate their own values and customs. To see which has the stronger influence on personality and behavior, therefore, we must look at situations in which these environments clash. For example, when parents value academic achievement and their child's peers do not, who wins? The answer, typically, is peers.

In a study of 15,000 students at nine different American high schools, researchers sought reasons for the average difference in school performance of Asian-Americans, African-Americans, Latinos, and whites (Steinberg, Dornbusch, & Brown, 1992). Asian-American students, who had the highest grades on the average, reported having the highest

level of peer support for academic achievement. They studied together in groups, cheered one another on, and praised one another's success. But many African-American students regarded academic success as a sign of selling out to the white establishment. High-achieving black students often said they had few black friends for this reason; they felt they had to choose between doing well in school and being popular with their peers (Ogbu, 2003). This dilemma affects students of *any* ethnicity or gender whose peer group thinks that academic success is only for nerds and sellouts (Arroyo & Zigler, 1995).

Peers, like parents, shape the expression of personality traits, causing us to emphasize some attributes or abilities and downplay others. Of course, as the theory of reciprocal determinism would predict, our temperaments and dispositions also cause us to select particular peer groups (if they are available) instead of others, and our temperaments also influence how we behave within the group. But once we are among peers, most of us go along with them, molding facets of our personalities to the pressures of the group.

QUICK quiz

We want to nurture your appreciation of quizzes because it's in our nature to give them to you.

1. What three lines of evidence have disputed the belief that parents are the major influence on their children's personalities?

2. Which contributes most to the variation among siblings in their personality traits: (a) the family environment that all of them share, (b) the way their parents treat them, or (c) the unique experiences they have that are not shared with their families?

Answers:

1. The shared family environment has little if any influence on personality; few parents have a consistent child-rearing style; and even when parents try to be consistent in the way they treat their children, there may be little relation between what they do and how the children turn out.   2. c

WHAT'S *Ahead*

• How does your culture influence your personality—and even whether you think you have a stable "self"?

• Why are punctuality and aggressiveness more than just individual personality traits?

• Why are men in the South and West more likely to get angry at personal insults than other American men are?

Cultural Influences on Personality

If you get an invitation to come to a party at 7 P.M., what time are you actually likely to get there? If someone gives you the finger or calls you a rude name, are you more likely to become furious or laugh it off?

It might seem that conscientiousness about time and quickness to anger are personality traits that result from genetic dispositions or experience. But culture has a profound effect on these reactions and many others. A **culture** is a program of shared rules that govern the behavior of members of a community or society, and a set of values and beliefs shared by most members of that community and passed from one generation to another (Lonner, 1995). In this section, we will consider some of the contributions of the cultural approach to understanding personality.

Culture, Values, and Traits

It is not always easy to see how cultural rules affect your own personality, but here's a demonstration. Take as much time as you like to answer this question: "Who are you?" "I am _____."

culture A program of shared rules that govern the behavior of members of a community or society and a set of values, beliefs, and attitudes shared by most members of that community.

individualist cultures
Cultures in which the self is regarded as autonomous, and individual goals and wishes are prized above duty and relations with others.

collectivist cultures
Cultures in which the self is regarded as embedded in relationships, and harmony with one's group is prized above individual goals and wishes.

Your response to "Who are you?" will be influenced by your cultural background, particularly whether your culture emphasizes individualism or community (Hofstede & Bond, 1988; Markus & Kitayama, 1991; Triandis, 1996). In **individualist cultures**, the independence of the individual often takes precedence over the needs of the group, and the self is often defined as a collection of personality traits ("I am outgoing, agreeable, and ambitious") or in occupational terms ("I am a psychologist"). In **collectivist cultures**, group harmony often takes precedence over the wishes of the individual, and the self is defined in the context of relationships and the community ("I am the son of a farmer, descended from three generations of storytellers on my mother's side and five generations of farmers on my father's side . . . ").

As Table 2.1 shows, individualist and collectivist ways of defining the self influence many aspects of life, including which personality traits we value, how we express emotions, and how much we value having relationships or maintaining freedom (Campbell et al., 1996; Kashima et al., 1995). Individualist and collectivist outlooks even affect how stable we perceive our personalities to be across situations. In a revealing study comparing Japanese and Americans, the Americans reported that their sense of self changes only 5 to 10 percent in different situations, whereas the Japanese said that 90 to 99 percent of their sense of self changes (de Rivera, 1989). For the group-oriented Japanese, it

Individualistic Americans exercise by running, walking, bicycling, and skating, all in different directions and wearing different clothes. Collectivist Japanese employees at their hiring ceremony exercise in identical fashion.

TABLE 2.1
Some Average Differences Between Individualist and Collectivist Cultures

Members of Individualist Cultures	Members of Collectivist Cultures
Define the self as autonomous, independent of groups.	Define the self as an interdependent part of groups.
Give priority to individual, personal goals.	Give priority to the needs and goals of the group.
Value independence, leadership, achievement, self-fulfillment.	Value group harmony, duty, obligation, security.
Give more weight to an individual's attitudes and preferences than to group norms as explanations of behavior.	Give more weight to group norms than to individual attitudes as explanations of behavior.
Attend to the benefits and costs of relationships; if costs exceed advantages, a person is likely to drop a relationship.	Attend to the needs of group members; if a relationship is beneficial to the group but costly to the individual, the individual is likely to stay in the relationship.

Source: Triandis, 1996.

is important to enact *tachiba*, to perform your social roles correctly so that there will be harmony with others. Americans, in contrast, tend to value "being true to yourself" and having a "core identity."

Culture and Traits When people fail to understand the influence of culture on behavior, they often attribute another person's mysterious or annoying actions to individual personality traits when they are really due to cultural norms.

Consider the apparently simple matter of *conversational distance*: how close people usually stand to one another when they are speaking (Hall, 1959, 1976). Arabs like to stand close enough to feel your breath, touch your arm, and see the pupils of your eyes—a distance that makes most white Americans, Canadians, and northern Europeans uneasy, unless they are talking intimately with a lover. The English and the Swedes stand farthest apart when they converse; southern Europeans stand closer, and Latin Americans and Arabs stand the closest (Keating, 1994; Sommer, 1969). One of our students from the Middle East told us he always thought his Anglo classmates were cold and aloof, even prejudiced against him, because they kept moving away from him in conversation. They, in turn, thought he had a "pushy" personality. They were all simply trying to reestablish the conversational distance that made them comfortable.

Or consider tardiness. Individuals differ in whether they try to be "on time" or are always late, but cultural norms affect how individuals regard time in the first place. In northern Europe, Canada, and the United States, time is organized into linear segments in which people do one thing "at a time" (Hall, 1983; Hall & Hall, 1990). The day is divided into appointments, schedules, and routines, and because time is a precious commodity, people don't like to "waste" time or "spend" too much time on any one activity (hence, the popularity of multitasking). In such cultures, therefore, it is considered the height of rudeness (or high status) to keep someone waiting. But in Mexico, southern Europe, the Middle East, South America, and Africa, time is organized along parallel lines. People do many things at once, and the needs of friends and family supersede mere appointments. Latinos and Middle Easterners think nothing of waiting for hours or days to see someone. The idea of having to be somewhere "on time," as if time were more important than a person, is unthinkable.

In culturally diverse North America, the two time systems keep bumping into each other. An Anglo judge in Miami got into hot water when he observed that "Cubans always show up two hours late for weddings"—late in his culture's terms, that is. The judge was accurate in his observation; the problem was his implication that something was wrong with Cubans for being "late." And "late" compared to what, by the way? The Cubans were perfectly on time for Cubans.

Culture and Testosterone

A good example of how culture gets into personality comes from the study of culture and male aggression. Richard Nisbett (1993) **analyzed the common assumption** that male violence is an inevitable result of testosterone. He **asked an interesting question**: Given that men everywhere have testosterone, why do rates of male aggressiveness vary enormously across cultures and throughout history?

By examining the evidence from historical records, Nisbett (1993) found that the American South, along with some western regions of the country originally settled by Southerners, have much higher rates of white homicide and other violence than the rest of the country has—but only particular kinds of violence: The use of fists or guns to protect a man's sense of honor, protect his property, or respond to perceived insults. Nisbett **considered various explanations**, such as poverty or racial tensions. But when he controlled for regional differences in poverty and the percentage of African-Americans in the population, by county, "southernness" remained an independent predictor of homicide. Nisbett also ruled out a history of slavery as an explanation: Regions of the South that had the highest concentrations of slaves in the past have the lowest white homicide rates today.

Nisbett hypothesized that the higher rates of violence in the South must derive from economic causes—that the higher rates occur in cultures that were originally based on herding, in contrast to cultures based on agriculture. People who depend economically on agriculture tend to develop and promote cooperative strategies for survival. But people who depend on their herds are extremely vulnerable; their livelihoods can be lost in an instant by the theft of their animals. To reduce the likelihood of theft, Nisbett theorized, herders learn to be hyperalert to

Arabs tend to stand much closer to one another than Westerners do. This "personality difference" is due to different cultural norms for conversational distance.

Many people assume that men can't help being violent because of their testosterone. But on average, men in agricultural economies are far more cooperative and nonviolent than men in herding economies. Amish farmers have always had very low rates of violence, whereas in the Old West, the cattle-herding cowboy culture was a violent one. (Fortunately, the shootout here is just a reenactment.)

any possibly threatening act and respond to it immediately with force. This would explain why cattle rustling and horse thievery were capital crimes in the Old West, and why Mediterranean and Middle Eastern herding cultures even today place a high value on male aggressiveness. When Nisbett **examined the evidence** for this hypothesis, looking at agricultural practices within the South, he found that homicide rates were indeed more than twice as high in the hills and dry plains areas (where herding occurs) as in farming regions.

The emphasis on aggressiveness and vigilance in herding communities, in turn, fosters a *culture of honor*, in which even apparently small disputes and trivial insults (trivial to people from other cultures, that is) put a man's reputation for toughness on the line, requiring him to respond with violence to restore his status (Cohen, 1998). Although the herding economy has become much less important in the South and West, the legacy of its culture of honor remains.

These regions have rates of honor-related homicides (such as murder to avenge a perceived insult to one's family) that are *five times higher* than in other regions of the country. Cultures of honor also have higher rates of domestic violence. Both sexes in such cultures believe it is appropriate for a man to physically assault a woman if he believes she is threatening his honor and reputation—say, by being unfaithful or by leaving him (Vandello & Cohen, 2003).

Next, Nisbett and his colleagues actually brought northern and southern male students into their lab to measure how these students would respond psychologically and physiologically to being insulted (Cohen et al., 1996). The physiological measures were levels of cortisol, a hormone associated with high levels of stress, and testosterone, which is associated with dominance and aggression. Participants were 173 white male undergraduates, who were told that the experiment would assess their performance on various tasks, and that the experimenter would be taking saliva samples to measure their blood sugar levels throughout the procedure. After the young men gave their baseline saliva sample, they had to walk down the hall to another room. As they did, a confederate of the experimenter—who seemed to be another student participant—bumped into them and called them an insulting name (a seven-letter word beginning with "a," if you want to know). In the final phase of the experiment, as the young men were filling out a questionnaire, the experimenter took a "post-bump" saliva sample from each of them. Northerners responded calmly to the insult; if anything, they thought it was funny. But many Southerners were immediately inflamed, and, as you can see in the figures on the left, their levels of cortisol and testosterone shot up.

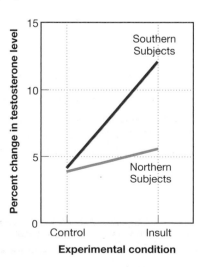

Nisbett and his colleagues have **considered other explanations** for variations in male aggressiveness across cultures. Their work identified only one particular contributing factor: being raised in a culture of honor. Another factor has to do with the dangers a culture faces. In cultures in which competition for resources is fierce and survival is difficult, men are "toughened up" and pushed to take risks, even with their lives (Gilmore, 1990). In contrast, in cultures in which resources are abundant and there are no serious hazards or enemies to worry about—such as the Ifaluk, the Tahitians, and the people of Sudest Island near New Guinea— men do not feel they have to prove themselves and they are not raised to be tough and aggressive (Lepowsky, 1994; Levy, 1984). When a society becomes more peaceful, so do its men.

Evaluating Cultural Approaches

A woman we know, originally from England, married a Lebanese man. They were happy together but had the usual number of marital misunderstandings and squabbles. After a few years, they visited his hometown in Lebanon, where she had never been before. "I was stunned," she told us. "All the things I thought he did because of his *personality* turned out to be because he's *Lebanese*! Everyone there was just like him!"

Our friend's reaction illustrates both the contributions and the limitations of cultural studies of personality. She was right in recognizing that some of her husband's behavior was attributable to his culture; for example, his Lebanese notions of time were very different from her English notions. But

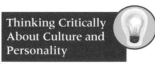

Thinking Critically About Culture and Personality

she was wrong to infer that the Lebanese are all like him: Individuals are affected by their culture, but they vary within it.

Cultural psychologists face the problem of how to describe cultural influences on personality without stereotyping (Church & Lonner, 1998). As one student of ours put it, "How come when we students speak of 'the' Japanese or 'the' blacks or 'the' whites or 'the' Latinos, it's called stereotyping, and when you do it, it's called 'cross-cultural psychology'?" This question shows excellent critical thinking! The study of culture does not rest on the assumption that all members of a culture behave the same way or have the same personality traits. As we have seen in this chapter, people vary according to their temperaments, beliefs, and learning histories, and this variation occurs within every culture.

Moreover, regional variations occur in every society. America may be an individualist culture overall, but the deep South, with its history of strong regional identity, is more collectivist than the rugged, independent West (Vandello & Cohen, 1999). The Chinese and the Japanese both value group harmony, but the Chinese are more likely to promote individual achievement, whereas the Japanese are more likely to strive for group consensus (Dien, 1999).

Finally, in spite of their differences, cultures have many human concerns and needs in common—for love, attachment, family, work, and religious or communal tradition. Nonetheless, cultural rules are what, *on average*, make Swedes different from Bedouins and Cambodians different from Italians. The traits that we value, our sense of self versus community, and our notions of the right way to behave—all key aspects of personality—begin with the culture in which we are raised.

QUICK quiz

At the moment, you live in a culture that values the importance of quizzes.

1. Cultures whose members regard the "self" as a collection of stable personality traits are (individualist/collectivist).
2. A Mexican visitor to England wonders why everyone he meets seems to stand too far away from him in conversation. When he moves closer, they move away. Mexico and England have different rules of _____.
3. Why, according to one theory, do men in the American South and West respond more aggressively to perceived insults than other American men do?

Answers:

1. individualist   2. conversational distance   3. These men come from regions in which economies based on herding gave rise to "cultures of honor," requiring males to be vigilant and aggressive toward potential threats.

You are never too old for self-actualization. Hulda Crooks, shown here at age 91 climbing Mt. Fuji, took up mountain climbing at 54. "It's been a great inspiration for me," she said. "When I come down from the mountain I feel like I can battle in the valley again." She died at the age of 101.

humanist psychology
A psychological approach that emphasizes personal growth, resilience, and the achievement of human potential.

unconditional positive regard To Carl Rogers, love or support given to another person with no conditions attached.

existentialism A philosophical approach that emphasizes the inevitable dilemmas and challenges of human existence.

WHAT'S *Ahead*

- How does the humanist vision of personality differ from psychodynamic and genetic views?

- In the humanist view, what's wrong with saying to a child, "I love you because you've been good"?

The Inner Experience

A final way to look at personality starts with the person's own point of view. Psychologists who take a *humanist* approach to personality emphasize our uniquely human capacity to determine our own actions and futures. Biology may hand us temperamental dispositions that limit us, the environment may deal us some tough experiences, our parents may treat us as we would not have wished, but we have the free will to transcend these forces.

Humanist Approaches

Humanist psychology was launched as a movement in the early 1960s. The movement's chief leaders—Abraham Maslow (1908–1970), Carl Rogers (1902–1987), and Rollo May (1909–1994)—argued that it was time to replace psychoanalysis and behaviorism with a "third force" in psychology, one that would draw a fuller picture of human potential and personality.

Abraham Maslow The trouble with psychology, said Maslow (1970, 1971), was that it had ignored many of the positive aspects of life, such as joy, laughter, love, happiness, and *peak experiences*, rare moments of rapture caused by the attainment of excellence or the experience of beauty. The traits that Maslow thought most important to personality were not the Big Five, but rather were the qualities of the *self-actualized person*—the person who strives for a life that is meaningful, challenging, and satisfying.

For Maslow, personality development could be viewed as a gradual progression toward self-actualization. Most psychologists, he argued, had a lopsided view of human nature, a result of their emphasis on studying emotional problems and negative traits such as neuroticism or insecurity. As Maslow (1971) wrote, "When you select out for careful study very fine and healthy people, strong people, creative people . . . then you get a very different view of mankind. You are asking how tall can people grow, what can a human being become?"

Carl Rogers Rogers, like Freud, derived many of his ideas from observing his clients in therapy. As a clinician, Rogers (1951, 1961) was interested not only in why some people cannot function well but also in what he called the fully functioning individual. How you behave depends on your subjective reality, Rogers said, not on the external reality around you. Fully functioning people experience *congruence*, or harmony, between the image they project to others and their true feelings and wishes. They are trusting, warm, and open rather than defensive or intolerant. Their beliefs about themselves are realistic.

To become fully functioning people, Rogers maintained, we all need **unconditional positive regard**, love and support for the people we are, without strings (conditions) attached. This doesn't mean that Winifred should be allowed to kick her brother when she is angry with him or that Wilbur may throw his dinner out the window because he doesn't like pot roast. In these cases, a parent can correct the child's behavior without withdrawing love from the child. The child can learn that the behavior, not the child, is what is bad. "House rules are 'no violence,' children," is a very different message from "You are horrible children for behaving so badly."

Unfortunately, Rogers observed, many children are raised with *conditional* positive regard: "I will love you if you behave well, and I won't love you if you behave badly." Adults often treat each other this way, too. People treated with conditional regard begin to suppress or deny feelings or actions that they believe are unacceptable to those they love. The result, said Rogers, is incongruence, a sense of being out of touch with your feelings, of not being true to your "real self," which in turn produces low self-regard, defensiveness, and unhappiness. A person experiencing incongruence scores high on neuroticism, becoming bitter and negative.

Rollo May May shared with the humanists a belief in free will. But he also emphasized some of the inherently difficult and tragic aspects of the human condition, including loneliness, anxiety, and alienation. In books such as *Love and Will* and *The Meaning of Anxiety*, May brought to American psychology elements of the European philosophy of **existentialism**. This doctrine emphasizes the inevitable challenges of human existence, such as the search for the meaning of life, the need to confront death, and living with the burden of responsibility for our actions.

Free will, however, carries a price in anxiety and despair, which is why so many people try to escape from freedom into narrow certainties and blame others for their misfortunes. For May, our personalities reflect the ways we cope with the struggles to find meaning in existence, to use our freedom wisely, and to face suffering and death bravely. May popularized the humanist idea that we can choose to make the best of ourselves by drawing on inner resources such as love and courage, but he added that we can never escape the harsh realities of life and loss.

Evaluating Humanist Approaches

As with psychodynamic theories, the major criticism of humanist psychology is that many of its assumptions are untestable. Freud looked at humanity and saw destructive drives, selfishness, and lust. Maslow and Rogers looked at humanity and saw cooperation, selflessness, and love. May looked at humanity and saw fear of freedom, loneliness, and the struggle for meaning. These differences, say critics, may tell us more about the observers than about the observed.

Many humanist concepts, although intuitively appealing, are hard to define operationally (see Chapter 1). How can we know whether a person is self-fulfilled or self-actualized? How can we tell whether a woman's decision to quit her job and become a professional rodeo rider represents an "escape from freedom" or a freely made choice? And what exactly is unconditional positive regard? If it is defined as unquestioned support of a child's efforts at mastering a new skill, or as assurance that the child is loved in spite of his or her mistakes, then it is clearly a good idea. But in the popular culture, unconditional positive regard has often been interpreted as an unwillingness ever to say "no" to a

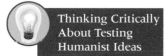
Thinking Critically About Testing Humanist Ideas

IF YOU WERE AN ICEBERG...

THE PART EVERYONE GETS TO SEE

ALL THE GREAT ASPECTS OF YOUR PERSONALITY

S. Harris

child, or to offer constructive criticism and set limits, which children need.

Despite such concerns, humanist psychologists have added balance to the study of personality. Influenced in part by the humanists, psychologists in the contemporary field of "positive psychology" are studying many positive human traits, such as courage, helpfulness to others, the motivation to excel, and self-confidence. Stress researchers have discovered the benefits of humor and hope. Developmental psychologists are studying ways to foster children's empathy and creativity.

Finally, the humanist and existential argument that we have the power to choose our own destinies, even when fate delivers us into tragedy, has fostered a new appreciation of human resilience in the face of adversity.

QUICK quiz

Exercise free will, as a humanist would advise you to, by choosing to take this quiz.

1. According to Carl Rogers, a man who loves his wife only when she is looking her best is giving her positive regard that is (a) conditional or (b) unconditional.

2. The humanist who described the importance of having peak experiences was (a) Abraham Maslow, (b) Rollo May, (c) Carl Rogers.

3. A humanist and a Freudian psychoanalyst are arguing about human nature. What underlying assumptions about psychology and human potential are they likely to bring to their discussion? How can they resolve their differences without either–or thinking?

Answers:

1. a   2. a   3. The Freudian assumes that human nature is basically selfish and destructive; the humanist assumes that it is basically loving and life-affirming. They can resolve this either–or debate by recognizing that human beings have both capacities, and that the situation and culture often determine which capacity is expressed at a given time.

psychology in the news REVISITED

How are the dimensions of personality woven together in the case of John Walker Lindh, whose apparent change of personality was described in the news item at the start of this chapter? After going to prison, Lindh changed his first name again, to Hamza, after the uncle of Mohammed. His devotion to Islam has not wavered. In 2006, Lindh's parents, who had kept their silence since their son's conviction, began traveling the country to tell their son's story and urge President George Bush to grant him clemency. Their son did not have a "personality change," they maintain, nor did he do anything treasonous; he was a victim of the times and of America's anger toward Muslims in the aftermath of 9/11. Their son has, they say, *always* been idealistic and spiritual.

A psychodynamic theorist would look for unconscious motives in Lindh's embrace of a radically different culture. Was his anger at the American way of life a displacement of anger toward his parents (who had divorced) or toward other authority figures? Was his attraction to a rigidly all-male environment a reflection of repressed homosexual feelings or an unconscious hostility toward women?

Psychologists taking a biological view of personality would emphasize the possible genetic contributions to Lindh's personality traits, such as his introversion. They would point out that young people in their late teens, the period of Lindh's restless travels to the Middle East, are the most neurotic (emotionally negative), the least agreeable and conscientious, and the most open to new experience. Other traits characterizing this young man probably remained stable over the years, merely taking different form as he grew older.

Psychologists who take a learning or environmental perspective would examine situational influences on personality. When people are in a situation in which militant or aggressive behavior is rewarded—with attention, excitement, comradeship, and a sense of power over what they view as a corrupt system—they may become political revolutionaries or religious warriors. For John Walker Lindh, by all accounts a young man who felt isolated, lonely, and alienated from his peers in America, finding a group of welcoming, like-minded men in the Middle East must have felt exhilarating. A social-cognitive learning theorist would also emphasize the process of reciprocal determinism. Just as the situation rewarded and encouraged certain traits and attitudes in Lindh, his own traits and attitudes would have attracted him to that situation to begin with. And just as the parents of Dylan Klebold and Eric Harris had no clue about the hidden, angry facet of their sons' personalities, so too it was not unusual for the parents of John Walker Lindh to have had no clue about their son's growing estrangement from them.

Cultural psychologists might observe that although Lindh tried hard to shuck his identity as an American, much of his behavior and attitudes in fact reflect deeply ingrained American values and cultural norms. The most fundamental of these is individualism: Lindh (and his parents) took for granted his right to seek spiritual fulfillment in any way he chose, even when such a quest took him away from his family and meant placing his own goals and wishes above those of his parents.

Finally, in the humanist view, all of us are free to write and rewrite our life narratives, and to choose the beliefs and values that guide our lives. From this perspective, Hamza Walker Lindh's commitment to Islam is something he freely chose for himself, a decision as authentic and deeply felt as those his agemates might make about choosing a career, a religion different from their parents', or a political philosophy. But humanists would also remind us that the private man, the one who lives inside Lindh's skin, could be quite different from his public persona.

Ultimately, we can only guess at who the "real" Hamza (John) Walker Lindh is or what his motives were. Nonetheless, all of us can use the insights of the theorists in this chapter to better understand ourselves and the people we love. Each of us is a mix of genetic influences, learned habits, the pressure of peers, new experiences, cultural norms, unconscious fears and conflicts, and our own private visions of possibility. This mix gives each of us the stamp of our personality, the qualities that make us feel uniquely . . . us.

➤TAKING ➤PSYCHOLOGY ➤WITH ➤YOU

How to Avoid the "Barnum Effect"

How well does the following paragraph describe you?

> Some of your aspirations tend to be pretty unrealistic. At times you are extroverted, affable, sociable, while at other times you are introverted, wary, and reserved. You pride yourself on being an independent thinker and do not accept others' opinions without satisfactory proof. You prefer a certain amount of change and variety, and you become dissatisfied when hemmed in by restrictions and limitations. At times you have serious doubts as to whether you have made the right decision or done the right thing.

When people believe that this description was written just for them, as the result of a personalized horoscope or handwriting analysis, they all say the same thing: "It describes me *exactly*!" Everyone thinks this description is accurate because it is vague enough to apply to almost everyone and it is flattering (don't we all consider ourselves to be "independent thinkers"?).

This is why many psychologists worry about the "Barnum effect" (Snyder & Shenkel, 1975). P. T. Barnum was the great circus showman who said, "There's a sucker born every minute." He knew that the formula for success was to "have a little something for everybody"—and that is just what unscientific personality profiles, horoscopes, and handwriting analysis (graphology) have in common. They have "a little something for everyone" and therefore are nonfalsifiable.

For example, graphologists claim that they can identify your personality traits from the form and distribution of your handwritten letters (Beyerstein, 1996). Wide spacing between words means you feel isolated and lonely. If your lines drift upward, you are an "uplifting" optimist, and if your lines droop downward, you are a pessimist who feels you are being "dragged down." If you make large capital *I*'s, you have a large ego.

Yet whenever graphology has been tested empirically, it has failed. A meta-analysis of 200 published studies found no validity or reliability to graphology in predicting work performance, aptitudes, or personality. No school of graphology fared better than any other, and no graphologist was able to perform better than untrained amateurs making guesses from the same materials (Dean, 1992; Klimoski, 1992).

If handwriting analysis were just an amusing game, no one would worry about it, but graphologists have been hired by companies to predict a person's leadership ability, attention to detail, willingness to be a good team player, honesty, and even criminal tendencies (Beyerstein, 1996). How would you feel if you were turned down for a job because some graphologist branded you a potential thief because you have "desire-for-possession hooks" on your *S*'s?

If you do not want to be taken in by graphology or the many other "personality" assessments that rely on the Barnum effect, research offers this advice:

● **Beware of all-purpose descriptions that could apply to anyone.** Sometimes you doubt your decisions; who among us has not? Sometimes you feel outgoing and sometimes shy; who does not? Do you "have sexual secrets that you are afraid of confessing"? Just about everybody does.

● **Beware of your own selective perceptions.** Most of us are so impressed when an astrologer, psychic, or graphologist gets something right that we overlook all the descriptions that are plain wrong.

● **Resist flattery.** It is easy to reject a profile that describes you as selfish or stupid. Watch out for the ones that tell you how wonderful and smart you are, what a great leader you will be, or how modest you are about your abilities.

If you keep your critical faculties with you, you won't end up paying hard cash for soft answers or taking a job you despise because it fits your "personality type." In other words, you'll have proved Barnum wrong.

SUMMARY

• *Personality* refers to an individual's distinctive and relatively stable pattern of behavior, motives, thoughts, and emotions. Personality is made up of many different *traits*, characteristics that describe a person across situations.

Psychodynamic Theories of Personality

• Sigmund Freud was the founder of *psychoanalysis*, which was the first *psychodynamic* theory. Modern psychodynamic theories share an emphasis on unconscious processes and a belief in the formative role of childhood experiences and early, unconscious conflicts.

• According to Freud, the personality consists of the *id* (the source of sexual energy, which he called the *libido*, and the aggressive instinct); the *ego* (the source of reason); and the *superego* (the source of conscience). *Defense mechanisms* protect the ego from unconscious anxiety. They include, among others, repression, projection, displacement (one form of which is sublimation), reaction formation, regression, and denial.

• Freud believed that personality develops in a series of *psychosexual stages*, with the *phallic (Oedipal) stage* most crucial. During this stage, Freud believed, the *Oedipus complex* occurs, in which the child desires the parent of the other sex and feels rivalry with the same-sex parent. When the Oedipus complex is resolved, the child identifies with the same-sex parent, but females retain a lingering sense of inferiority and "penis envy"—a notion later contested by female psychoanalysts like Clara Thompson and Karen Horney.

• Carl Jung believed that people share a *collective unconscious* that contains universal memories and images, or *archetypes*. Personality, in this view, includes many archetypes, such as the *shadow* (evil) and the *anima* and *animus*.

• The *object-relations school* emphasizes the importance of the first two years of life rather than the Oedipal phase; the infant's relationships to important figures, especially the mother, rather than sexual needs and drives; and the problem in male development of breaking away from the mother.

• Psychodynamic approaches have been criticized for violating the principle of falsifiability; for overgeneralizing from atypical patients to everyone; and for basing theories on the unreliable memories and retrospective accounts of patients, which can create an *illusion of causality*. However, some psychodynamic ideas have received empirical support, including the existence of nonconscious processes and defenses.

The Modern Study of Personality

• Most popular tests that divide personality into "types" are not valid or reliable. In research, psychologists typically rely on *objective tests (inventories)*, such as the Minnesota Multiphasic Personality Inventory or the Multidimensional Personality Questionnaire, to identify and study personality traits and disorders.

• Gordon Allport argued that people have a few *central traits* that are key to their personalities and a greater number of *secondary traits* that are less fundamental. Raymond Cattell used *factor analysis* to identify clusters of traits that he considered the basic components of personality.

• There is strong evidence for the *Big Five* dimensions of personality: extroversion versus introversion, neuroticism (negative emotionality) versus emotional stability, agreeableness versus antagonism, conscientiousness versus impulsiveness, and openness to experience versus resistance to new experience. Although these dimensions are quite stable over time and across circumstances, some of them do change over the life span, reflecting maturational development or common adult responsibilities.

Genetic Influences on Personality

• The nature–nurture debate is one of the oldest controversies in philosophy and psychology, but it is pretty much over. Today most psychologists recognize that *genes*, the basic units of heredity, account for about half of the variation in human traits, but the environment and experience account for the other half.

• One line of evidence for the biological origins of personality differences comes from studies of many other species, including octopuses, pigs, hyenas, bears, horses, dogs, and primates. Such studies reveal variation in many of the same characteristic traits that humans have.

• Individual differences in *temperaments*—ways of reacting to the environment—appear to be inborn, emerging early in life and influencing subsequent personality development. Temperamental differences in extremely reactive and nonreactive children may be due to physiological variations in their responses to change and novelty.

• *Behavioral-genetic* data from twin and adoption studies suggest that the *heritability* of many adult personality traits is around .50. Genetic influences create dispositions and set limits on the expression of specific traits. But even traits that are highly heritable can be modified throughout life by circumstances and learning.

Environmental Influences on Personality

• People often behave inconsistently in different circumstances because behaviors that are rewarded in one situation may be punished or ignored in another. According to *social-cognitive learning theorists*, personality results from the interaction of aspects of the environment and aspects of the individual in a pattern of *reciprocal determinism*.

• Behavioral geneticists have found that an important influence on personality is the *nonshared environment*, the unique experiences that each child in a family has.

• Three lines of evidence challenge the popular assumption that parents have the greatest impact on their children's personalities and behavior: (1) Behavioral-genetic studies find that shared family environment has little if any influence on personality; (2) few parents have a consistent child-rearing style over time and with all their children; and (3) even when parents try to be consistent, there may be little relation between what they do and how the children turn out. However, parents can modify their children's temperaments, prevent children at risk of delinquency and crime from choosing a path of antisocial behavior, modify the extent of a child's shyness, influence many of their children's values and attitudes, and teach them to be kind and helpful. And, of course, parents profoundly affect the quality of their relationship with their children.

• One major environmental influence on personality is peer groups, which can be more powerful than parents. Most children and teenagers behave differently with their parents than with their peers.

Cultural Influences on Personality

• Many qualities that Western psychologists treat as individual personality traits are heavily influenced by *culture*. People from *individualist cultures* define themselves in different terms than those from *collectivist cultures*, and they perceive their "selves" as more stable across situations. People vary in their notions of appropriate *conversational distance* and in their attitudes toward time and being "on time."

• As described in the "Close-up on Research," male violence is not simply a result of male testosterone but also is influenced by the economic requirements of the culture a man grows up in: Herding economies foster male aggressiveness more than agricultural economies do. Men in *cultures of honor*, including certain regions of the American South and West, are more likely to become angry when they feel insulted and to behave aggressively to restore their sense of honor than are men from other cultures. When they are insulted, their levels of cortisol and testosterone rise quickly, whereas men from other cultures generally do not show this reaction.

• Cultural theories of personality face the problem of describing broad cultural differences and their influences on personality without promoting stereotypes or overlooking universal human needs.

The Inner Experience

• *Humanist psychologists* focus on a person's subjective sense of self and the free will to change. They emphasize human potential and the strengths of human nature, as in Abraham Maslow's concepts of *peak experiences* and *self-actualization*. Carl Rogers stressed the importance of *unconditional positive regard* in creating a "fully functioning" person. Rollo May brought *existentialism* into psychology, emphasizing some of the inherent challenges of human existence that result from having free will, such as the search for meaning in life.

• Critics observe that many ideas from humanist psychology are subjective and difficult to measure, but the field has fostered research on many positive aspects of personality, such as optimism, hope, and resilience under adversity.

Psychology in the News, Revisited

• Genetic influences, life experiences and learned habits, the pressure of specific situations, cultural norms, unconscious fears and conflicts, and our private sense of the "inner self" all combine in complex ways to create our distinctive personalities.

KEY TERMS

personality   42

trait   42

Sigmund Freud   42

psychoanalysis   42

psychodynamic theories   42

id   43

libido   43

ego   43

superego   43

defense mechanisms   43

repression   43

projection   44

displacement and sublimation   44

reaction formation   44

regression   44

denial   44

psychosexual stages (oral, anal, phallic, latency, genital)   44–45

Oedipus complex   45

Clara Thompson   46

Karen Horney   46

Carl Jung   46

collective unconscious   46

archetypes   46

shadow   46

anima, animus   46

object-relations school   47

mental representations   47

illusion of causality   48

objective tests (inventories)   50

Gordon Allport   50

central traits   50

secondary traits   50

Raymond B. Cattell   50

factor analysis   50

the "Big Five" personality traits   50

genes   53

temperament   54

heritability   55

behavioral geneticists   55

identical and fraternal twins   56

social-cognitive learning theory   58

reciprocal determinism   59

nonshared environment   59

culture   61

individualist versus collectivist cultures   62

conversational distance   63

culture of honor   64

humanist psychology   66

Abraham Maslow   66

peak experiences   66

self-actualization   66

Carl Rogers   66

congruence   66

unconditional positive regard   66

Rollo May   66

existentialism   66

- **Personality:** a distinctive pattern of behavior, mannerisms, thoughts, and emotions that characterizes an individual over time.
- **Traits:** habitual ways of behaving, thinking, and feeling.

Psychodynamic Theories of Personality

Psychodynamic theories emphasize unconscious processes, the role of childhood experiences, and unconscious conflicts.

Freud

To Freud, personality consists of three systems, which ideally should be in balance.
- **Id**
- **Ego**
- **Superego**

Defense mechanisms, such as repression, denial, and projection, serve to protect the ego from conflict, but they can distort reality and case self-defeating behavior.

Psychosexual stages of personality development:
- Oral
- Anal
- Phallic (Oedipal)
- Latency
- Genital

Jung

Jung believed that all people share a **collective unconscious**, consisting of universal memories and **archetypes**—universal symbols, stories, or human characters representing good, evil, and other mythic qualities.

Object-Relations School

The **object relations school** emphasizes the importance of the first two years of life and formative relationships, especially with the mother.

Evaluating Psychodynamic Theories

These theories:
- Violate the principle of falsifiability
- Draw universal principles from the experiences of a few atypical patients
- Are based on retrospective accounts and fallible memories of patients

Measuring Personality Traits

Personality Tests

- Many popular personality tests, especially those designed to identify "types," lack reliability and validity.
- **Objective tests** (inventories) are standardized questionnaires about needs, values, interests, emotional problems, typical ways of responding to situations, and personality traits.

Clustering Traits

- Gordon Allport believed that people have a few central, defining traits and other secondary traits that are more changeable.
- Raymond B. Cattell used **factor analysis** to identify the core clusters of personality traits.
- Factor-analytic studies today support the existence of basic personality dimensions, known informally as the Big Five:
  — Extroversion versus introversion
  — Neuroticism versus emotional stability
  — Agreeableness versus antagonism
  — Conscientiousness versus impulsiveness
  — Openness to experience versus resistance to new experience

The Big Five dimensions have been documented around the world, emerging whether people are asked for self-reports or are assessed by others. They are remarkably stable over a lifetime, although neuroticism tends to decrease and conscientiousness to increase in young adulthood.

The Modern Study of Personality

Genetic Infuences

Animal Personalities

Some researchers study the biological basis of personality by identifying traits in other species. They have found evidence for some of the Big Five in species as varied as octopuses, bears, and dogs.

Temperament

Babies are born differing in certain key **temperaments**, such as reactivity and soothability, which may form the basis of later personality traits.

Heredity and Traits

- Some researchers investigate genetic contributions to personality by doing **heritability** studies of twins and adopted individuals.
- **Behavioral-genetic** data from these studies show that the heritability of most traits is about 50%.

Evaluating Genetic Theories

- A genetic predisposition does not imply genetic inevitability.
- Today, almost all psychologists who study personality regard biology and experience as interacting influences.

Environmental Infuences

Social-cognitive learning theory:
- Holds that personality traits result in part from a person's learning history and resulting expectations and beliefs.
- Emphasizes **reciprocal determinism**, the two-way interaction between a person's qualities and the specific demands of the situation.
- The most influential experiences that shape personality are those in the **nonshared environment**, unique and chance events not shared with parents and siblings.

The Power of Parents

- Few parents have a single child-rearing style that is consistent over time and that they use with all their children.
- Even when parent try to be consistent, there may be little relation between what they do and how the children turn out.
- Parents do influence their children's interests, self-esteem, religious views and other values, and can modify their children's genetic predispositions.

The Power of Peers

Peer groups' influence can be more powerful than parents' influence on a child's personality development.

Cultural Infuences

A **culture** is a program of shared rules or values that govern the behavior of members of a community or society.
- In **individualist cultures**, the independence of the individual often takes precedence over the needs of the group.
- In **collectivist cultures**, group harmony often takes precedence over the wishes of the individual.

Culture and Traits

- When people fail to understand the influence of culture on behavior, they may misattribute a person's behavior to personality. For example, cultures differ in rules for conversational distance and notions of time.

- Male aggressiveness is often less a matter of testosterone or personality than of cultural norms, determined turn by a culture's economy and notions of male honor.

Evaluating Cultural Approaches

- Cultural psychologists face the problem of how to describe cultural influences on personality without stereotyping.
- Individuals are affected by their culture, but they vary within it.

The Inner Experience

Humanist psychology emphasizes a person's subjective sense of self.
- Abraham Maslow introduced the concepts of **peak experiences** and **self-actualization**.
- Carl Rogers stressed the importance of **unconditional positive regard**.
- Rollo May's inclusion of **existentialism** emphasized some of the inherent human challenges that result from free will.

Many humanist assumptions are untestable and hard to define operationally, but humanist ideas about positive human traits, such as courage and resilience, have added balance to the study of personality.

Age Record Broken as 66-Year-Old Woman Gives Birth

BUCHAREST, ROMANIA, JANUARY 16, 2005. A 66-year-old unmarried professor of literature today became the world's oldest woman ever to have given birth. Adriana Iliescu became pregnant through in vitro fertilization using sperm and egg from anonymous donors. The baby, Eliza Maria, weighs only a little over 3 pounds, and her twin sister was stillborn. The mother told the news media that she was "more than happy" with her baby and felt she had been given a "new lease on life." Members of her family are long-lived, she said, so she is not worried about dying before her child reaches maturity.

The news of the baby's birth spurred considerable debate in Romania and around the world about the ethics of women past the age of fertility using artificial insemination to become pregnant. One church official in Bucharest said it was "shocking." Some fertility experts and ethicists have misgivings about facilitating the pregnancies of older women, although they admit it is hard to draw the line between "acceptable" and "too old." Dr. Mark Sauer, who pioneered the use of donor eggs in older women, has said of older women having children, "I lose my comfort level after 55 because I have to believe that there are quality-of-life issues involved in raising a child at that age." An old woman dealing with a teenager, he added, "may have some problems."

Other rare cases of women who have conceived late in life have made headlines around the world. In 2003, a 65-year-old Indian woman, a schoolteacher, gave birth to a boy. It was the first child for Satyabhama Mahapatra and her husband, who had been married for 50 years. Mahapatra had been impregnated with an egg from her 26-year-old niece, which had been fertilized by her husband. And in Los Angeles in 1997, a 63-year-old woman, Arceli Keh, gave birth to a daughter, also with sperm donated by her husband.

Across the globe, countries are wrestling with the complicated biological, ethical, and legal issues that late in vitro pregnancies create. In many European nations, legislation prohibits in vitro procedures after age 50. But opponents of such restrictions point out that no country prohibits older men from conceiving children, so why should there be limits on women, if they are healthy enough to maintain a full-term pregnancy?

Adriana Iliescu, age 66, after giving birth to Eliza Maria.

Development Over the Life Span

How do *you* react to the idea of a 66-year-old woman having a baby? Would it make any difference if the mother were "only" 55 years old, or 50? What if she were older than 66? Do you feel the same about older fathers as you do about older mothers? A few months after the birth of Eliza Maria and all of the attendant publicity that followed, the news quietly noted the death of James Doohan, who had played Scotty in the original *Star Trek* series and movies. Doohan had become a father for the fourth time in 2000, at the age of 80, when his second wife, Wende (then 43), gave birth to their daughter. But the birth of the Doohan's baby had not made headlines, in spite of the father's age. Doohan died five years later of pneumonia and Alzheimer's disease. Was it loving and natural, or selfish and unethical, for James Doohan to father a child when he was 80? Is there a right time to become a parent? For that matter, is there a right time to do anything in life—go to school, get married, retire . . . die?

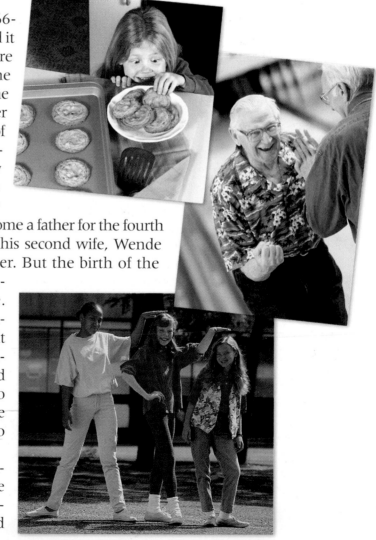

During the first half of the twentieth century, the answer would have been a resounding "yes." Going to college, starting a family, choosing a job, and

socialization The process by which children learn the behaviors, attitudes, and expectations required of them by their society or culture.

advancing up the ladder to retirement were all events that tended to happen in sequence. But because of demographic changes, an unpredictable economy, a high divorce rate, advances in reproductive technology, and many other forces, millions of people today do things out of order, if they do them at all. Going to college, having children, changing careers, or starting new families may occur in almost any decade of adulthood.

Psychologists are probably no better equipped than anyone else to address the many ethical issues raised by these changes, such as whether a woman should forgo pregnancy if she can't realistically expect to be around until her child grows up. But *developmental psychologists*, who study universal aspects of life-span development as well as cultural and individual variations, can help us think critically about the question of "natural" life stages.

Developmental psychologists focus on physiological and cognitive changes across the life span and on **socialization**, the process by which children learn the attitudes and behaviors expected of them by society. In this chapter, we will explore some of their major findings, starting at the very beginning of human development, with the period from conception to birth, and continuing through adulthood into old age. At the end of the chapter, we will tell you how Adriana Iliescu and her daughter are doing. As you read, ask yourself what it means, in psychological terms, to be young, middle-aged, or old, and why so many people feel uneasy about the prospect of postmenopausal motherhood.

Developmental psychologists study people across the life span. They would have a living laboratory with this six-generation family, which includes Sara Knauss, age 118 (center); her daughter, age 95 (right), her grandson, age 73 (center), her great-granddaughter, age 49 (standing with her dad), her great-great granddaughter, age 27 (on floor), and her great-great-great grandson, age 3.

WHAT'S *Ahead*

- How can a pregnant woman reduce the risk of damage to the embryo or fetus?
- Given a choice, what do newborns prefer to look at?
- How does culture affect how a baby physically matures?
- Why is cuddling so important for infants (not to mention adults)?
- If you have a 1-year-old, why shouldn't you worry if your baby cries when left with a new baby-sitter?

From Conception Through the First Year

A baby's development, before and after birth, is a marvel of *maturation*, the unfolding of genetically influenced behavior and physical characteristics. In only 9 months of a mother's pregnancy, a cell grows from a dot this big (.) to a squalling bundle of energy that

looks just like Aunt Sarah. In another 15 months, that bundle of energy grows into a babbling toddler who is curious about everything. No other time in human development brings so many changes, so fast.

Prenatal Development

Prenatal development is divided into three stages: the germinal, the embryonic, and the fetal. The *germinal stage* begins at fertilization, when the male sperm unites with the female ovum (egg); the fertilized single-celled egg is called a *zygote*. The zygote soon begins to divide, and in 10 to 14 days it has become a cluster of cells that attaches itself to the wall of the uterus. The outer portion of this cluster will form part of the placenta and umbilical cord, and the inner portion becomes the embryo. The placenta, connected to the embryo by the umbilical cord, serves as the growing embryo's link for food from the mother. It allows nutrients to enter and wastes to exit, and it screens out some, but not all, harmful substances.

Once implantation is complete, about two weeks after fertilization, the *embryonic stage* begins, lasting until the eighth week after conception, at which point the embryo is only $1\frac{1}{2}$ inches long. From the fourth to the eighth weeks, the hormone testosterone is secreted by rudimentary testes in embryos that are genetically male; without this hormone, the embryo will develop to be anatomically female. After 8 weeks, the *fetal stage* begins. The organism, now called a *fetus*, further develops the organs and systems that existed in rudimentary form in the embryonic stage. Although it used to be thought that the last trimester was the most important time for growth of the nervous system, we now know that important events in neural development occur throughout gestation (Nelson, Thomas, & de Haan, 2006).

Many parents hope to have an influence on their offspring even before their babies are born.

Although the womb is a fairly sturdy protector of the growing embryo or fetus, some harmful influences can cross the placental barrier (O'Rahilly & Müller, 2001). These influences include the following:

1 *German measles* (rubella), especially early in the pregnancy, can affect the fetus's eyes, ears, and heart. The most common consequence is deafness. Rubella is preventable if the mother has been vaccinated, which can be done up to three months before pregnancy.

2 *X-rays or other radiation and toxic chemicals such as lead or mercury* can cause fetal abnormalities and deformities. Exposure to lead, found in old paint, and mercury, found in contaminated fish, is also associated with attention problems and lower IQ scores (Newland & Rasmussen, 2003).

3 *Sexually transmitted diseases* can cause mental retardation, blindness, and other physical disorders. Genital herpes affects the fetus only if the mother has an outbreak at the time of delivery, which exposes the newborn to the virus as the baby passes through the birth canal. (This risk can be avoided by having a cesarean section.) HIV, the virus that causes AIDS, can also be transmitted to the fetus, especially if the mother has developed AIDS and has not been treated.

4 *Cigarette smoking* during pregnancy increases the likelihood of miscarriage, premature birth, abnormal fetal heartbeat, and an underweight baby. The negative effects may last long after birth, showing up in increased rates of infant sickness, sudden infant death syndrome (SIDS), asthma, and, in later childhood, hyperactivity, learning difficulties, and even antisocial behavior (Button, Thapar, & McGuffin, 2005).

5 *Regular consumption of alcohol* can kill neurons throughout the fetus's developing brain and impair the child's later mental abilities, attention span, and academic achievement (Ikonomidou et al., 2000; Streissguth, 2001). Having more than two drinks a day significantly increases the risk of *fetal alcohol syndrome (FAS)*, which is associated with low birth weight, a smaller brain, facial deformities, lack of coordination, and mental retardation. FAS is the leading cause of nonhereditary mental retardation, but it is simply the extreme end of a spectrum of alcohol-related birth defects that range from mild to severe (Sampson et al., 2000). Because alcohol can affect many different aspects of fetal brain development, most specialists recommend that a pregnant woman abstain from drinking alcohol.

6 *Drugs other than alcohol* can be harmful to the fetus, whether they are illicit ones such as morphine, cocaine, and heroin, or commonly used legal substances such as antibiotics, antihistamines, tranquilizers, acne medication, and diet pills. Cocaine can cause subtle impairments in children's cognitive and language abilities and larger ones in the ability to manage impulses and frustrations (Lester, LaGasse, & Seifer, 1998; Stanwood & Levitt, 2001).

The lesson is clear. A pregnant woman does well to stop smoking and drinking alcohol, and to take no other drugs of any kind unless they are medically necessary—and then to accept the fact that her child will never be properly grateful for all that sacrifice!

The Infant's World

Newborn babies could never survive on their own, but they are far from being passive and inert. As a result of evolution, many abilities, tendencies, and characteristics are universal in human beings and are present at birth or develop very early, given certain experiences.

TABLE 3.1
Reflexes of the Newborn Baby

Reflex	Description
Rooting	An infant touched on the cheek or corner of the mouth will turn toward the touch and search for something to suck on.
Sucking	An infant will suck on anything suckable, such as a nipple or finger.
Swallowing	An infant can swallow, though this reflex is not yet well coordinated with breathing.
Moro or "startle"	In response to a loud noise or a physical shock, an infant will throw its arms outward and arch its back.
Babinski	In response to a touch on the bottom of the foot, the infant will splay its toes outward and then curl them in. (In adults, the toes just curl in.)
Grasp	In response to a touch on the palm of the hand, an infant will grasp.
Stepping	If held so that the feet just touch the ground, an infant will show "walking" movements, alternating the feet in steps.

The sucking and grasping reflexes at work.

contact comfort In primates, the innate pleasure derived from close physical contact; it is the basis of an infant's first attachment.

Newborns begin life with several *motor reflexes,* automatic behaviors that are necessary for survival (see Table 3.1). They will grasp tightly a finger pressed on their palms. They will turn their heads toward a touch on the cheek or corner of the mouth and search for something to suck on, a handy rooting reflex that allows them to find the breast or bottle. Many of these reflexes eventually disappear, but others—such as the knee-jerk, eye-blink, and sneeze reflexes—remain.

Babies are also equipped with a set of inborn perceptual abilities. They can see, hear, touch, smell, and taste (bananas and sugar water are in; rotten eggs are out). A newborn's visual focus range is only about 8 inches, the average distance between the baby and the face of the person holding the baby, but visual ability develops rapidly. Newborns can distinguish contrasts, shadows, and edges. They can discriminate their mother or other primary caregiver on the basis of smell, sight, or sound almost immediately. Within a couple of months, they show evidence of depth perception (see Chapter 6).

Despite commonalities, however, many aspects of infants' maturation depend on cultural customs that govern how their parents hold, touch, feed, and talk to them (Rogoff, 2003). For example, in most of North America, babies are expected to sleep for eight uninterrupted hours by the age of 4 or 5 months. This milestone is considered a sign of neurological maturity, although many babies wail when the parent puts them in the crib at night and leaves the room. But among Mayan Indians, rural Italians, African villagers, Indian Rajput villagers, and urban Japanese, this nightly clash of wills rarely occurs because the infant sleeps with the mother for the first year or two of life, waking and nursing about every four hours. These differences in babies' sleep arrangements reflect cultural and parental values. Mothers in close-knit agricultural communities believe it is important to sleep with the baby in order to forge a close bond; many white North American parents believe it is important to foster the child's independence as soon as possible (Keller et al., 2005; Morelli et al., 1992).

Attachment

Emotional attachment is a universal capacity of all primates and is important for health and survival all through life. By becoming attached to a caregiver, children gain a secure base from which they can explore the environment and a haven of safety to return to when they are afraid (Bowlby, 1982).

Contact Comfort Attachment begins with physical touching and cuddling between infant and parent. Margaret and Harry Harlow first demonstrated the importance of touching, or **contact comfort**, by raising infant rhesus monkeys with two kinds of artificial mothers (Harlow, 1958; Harlow & Harlow, 1966). The first was a forbidding construction of wires and warming lights with a milk bottle connected to it. The second was constructed of wire and covered in foam rubber and cuddly terry cloth (see Figure 3.1). At the time, many psychologists thought that babies become attached to their mothers simply because mothers provide food (Blum, 2002). But the Harlows' baby monkeys ran to the terry-cloth "mother" when they were frightened or startled, and cuddling up to it calmed them down. Human children, too, often seek contact comfort when they are in an unfamiliar situation, are scared by a nightmare, or fall and hurt themselves.

Separation and Security

Once babies are emotionally attached to the mother or other caregiver, separation can be a wrenching experience. Between 6 and 8 months of age, babies become wary or fearful of strangers. They wail if they are put in an unfamiliar setting or are left with an unfamiliar person. And they show **separation anxiety** if the primary caregiver temporarily leaves them. This reaction usually continues until the middle of the second year, but many children show signs of distress at parental separation until they are about 3 years old (Hrdy, 1999). All children go through this phase, although cultural child-rearing practices influence how strongly the anxiety is felt and how long it lasts. In cultures where babies are raised with lots of adults and other children, separation anxiety is not as intense or as long-lasting as it can be in societies like Japan, where babies form attachments primarily or exclusively with the mother (Rothbaum et al., 2000).

To determine the nature of the attachment between mothers and babies, Mary Ainsworth (1973, 1979) devised an experimental method called the *Strange Situation*. A mother brings her baby into an unfamiliar room containing lots of toys. After a while a stranger comes in and attempts to play with the child. The mother leaves the baby with the stranger. She then returns and plays with her child, and the stranger leaves. Finally, the mother leaves the baby alone for three minutes and then returns. In each case, observers carefully note how the baby behaves with the mother, with the stranger, and when the baby is alone.

Ainsworth divided children into three categories on the basis of their reactions to the Strange Situation. Some babies are *securely attached*: They cry or protest if the mother leaves the room; they welcome her back and then play happily again; they are clearly more attached to the mother than to the stranger. Other babies are *insecurely attached*, and this insecurity can take two forms. The child may be *avoidant*, not caring if the mother leaves the room, making little effort to seek contact with her on her return, and treating the stranger about the same as the mother. Or the child may be *anxious or ambivalent*, resisting contact with the mother at reunion but protesting loudly if she leaves. Anxious or

separation anxiety The distress that most children develop, at about 6 to 8 months of age, when their primary caregivers temporarily leave them with others.

FIGURE 3.1
The Comfort of Contact
Infants need cuddling as much as they need food. In Margaret and Harry Harlow's studies, infant rhesus monkeys were reared with a cuddly terry-cloth "mother" and with a bare wire "mother" that provided milk (left). The infants would cling to the terry mother when they were not being fed, and when they were frightened (as the infant on the right was by a toy spider put in his enclosure), it was the terry mother they ran to.

STYLES OF ATTACHMENT

ambivalent babies may cry to be picked up and then demand to be put down, or they may behave as if they are angry with the mother and resist her efforts to comfort them. Insecure attachment is associated with later emotional and behavioral problems in children, such as aggressiveness, poor social relationships, and acting out (Gauthier, 2003; Mickelson, Kessler, & Shaver, 1997; NICHD Early Child Care Research Network, 2006).

What Causes Insecure Attachment?

Ainsworth believed that insecure attachment results primarily from the way mothers treat their babies during the first year. Mothers who are sensitive and responsive to their babies' needs, she said, create securely attached infants; mothers who are uncomfortable with or insensitive to their babies create insecurely attached infants. To many, the implication was that babies needed exactly the right kind of mothering from the very start in order to become securely attached, and that putting a child in day care would retard this important development—notions that caused insecurity among many mothers!

Ainsworth's measure of attachment, however, did not take the baby's experience into account. Babies who become attached to many adults, because they live in large extended families or have spent a lot of time with adults in day care, may seem to be avoidant in the Strange Situation because they don't panic when their mothers leave. But perhaps they have simply learned to be comfortable with strangers. Moreover, although there is a modest correlation between a mother's sensitivity and a child's secure attachment, this doesn't tell us which causes what, or whether something else causes both sensitivity and attachment (De Wolff & van IJzendoorn, 1997). Programs designed to help new mothers become less anxious and more attuned to their babies do help some moms become more sensitive, but these programs only modestly affect the child's degree of secure attachment (Bakermans-Kranenburg, van IJzendoorn, & Juffer, 2003).

The emphasis on maternal sensitivity also overlooks the fact that most children form a secure attachment to their mothers in spite of wide variations in child-rearing practices (Mercer, 2006). For example, German babies are frequently left on their own for a few hours at a stretch by mothers who believe that even babies should become self-reliant. And among the Efe of Africa, babies spend about half their time away from their mothers in the care of older children and other adults

"Please, Jason. Don't you want to grow up to be an autonomous person?"

(Tronick, Morelli, & Ivey, 1992). Yet German and Efe children are not insecure, and they develop as normally as children who spend more time with their mothers.

Likewise, time spent in day care has no effect on the security of a child's attachment. In a major longitudinal study of more than 1,000 children, researchers compared infants who were in child care 30 hours or more a week, from age 3 months to age 15 months, with children who spent less than 10 hours a week in child care. The two groups did not differ on any measure of attachment, and children in high-quality day care—where the caregivers were well trained and child–staff ratios were small—did better on measures of social, language, and cognitive development than children at home (NICHD Early Child Care Research Network, 2002).

What factors, then, do promote insecure attachment?

• *Abandonment and deprivation in the first two years of life.* For example, Romanian babies raised in orphanages for their first two years are less likely than babies adopted earlier to become securely attached to their eventual adoptive parents, although most ultimately do fine (Rutter et al., 2004).

• *Parenting that is abusive, neglectful, or erratic because the parent is chronically irresponsible or depressed.* In one longitudinal study, children whose mothers had suffered from postpartum depression, leading the women to be either too intrusive with their infants or too remote and insensitive, were more likely to be insecurely attached at 18 months (Tomlinson, Cooper, & Murray, 2005).

- *The child's own genetically influenced temperament.* Babies who are fearful and prone to crying from birth are more likely to show insecure behavior in the Strange Situation (Belsky et al., 1996; Seifer et al., 1996).

- *Changing, stressful circumstances in the child's family.* Infants and young children may temporarily shift from secure to insecure attachment, becoming clingy and fearful of being left alone, if their families are undergoing a period of stress, as during parental divorce or a parent's chronic illness (Belsky et al., 1996; Mercer, 2006).

The bottom line, however, is that infants are biologically disposed to become attached to their caregivers, and normal, healthy attachment will occur within a wide range of cultural, family, and individual variations in child-rearing customs.

QUICK quiz

Are you feeling secure, anxious, or avoidant about quizzes?

1. Name as many potentially harmful influences on fetal development as you can.
2. Melanie is playing happily on a jungle gym at her child-care center when she falls off and scrapes her knee. She runs to her caregiver for a consoling cuddle. Melanie is seeking _____.
3. A baby left in the Strange Situation does not protest when his mother leaves the room, and he seems to ignore her when she returns. What style of attachment is this behavior said to reflect?
4. In item 3, what else besides the child's style of attachment could be causing the child's reaction?

Answers:

1. German measles early in pregnancy; exposure to radiation, lead, or toxic chemicals; sexually transmitted diseases; the mother's use of cigarettes, alcohol, or other drugs   2. contact comfort   3. insecure (avoidant)   4. the child's own temperament and the child's familiarity with being temporarily left alone

WHAT'S *Ahead*

- Why do so many parents speak baby talk?
- Is language an innate ability or an acquired one?
- What important accomplishment are infants revealing when they learn to play peekaboo?
- Why will most 5-year-olds choose a tall, narrow glass of lemonade over a short, fat glass containing the same amount?

Cognitive Development

A friend of ours told us about a charming exchange he had with his 2-year-old grandson. "You're very old," the little boy said. "Yes, I am," said his grandfather. "I'm very new," said the child. Two years old, and already this little boy's mind is working away, making observations, trying to understand the differences he observes, and using language (creatively!) to describe them. The development of language and thought from infancy throughout childhood is a marvel to anyone who knows a child—or was one.

Language

Try to read this sentence aloud:

Kamaunawezakusomamamanenohayawe-wenimtuwamaanasana.*

Can you tell where one word begins and another ends? Unless you know Swahili, the syllables of this sentence will sound like gibberish.

Well, to a baby learning its native tongue, every sentence must, at first, be gibberish. How, then, does an infant pick out discrete syllables and words from the jumble of sounds in its environment, much less figure out what those words mean? And how is it that in only a few short years, children not only understand thousands of words but can also produce and understand an endless number of new word combinations?

From Cooing to Communicating

The process of acquiring language begins in the first months, with crying and cooing. Even at this early stage, babies are highly responsive to the

---

Kama unaweza kusoma maneno haya, wewe ni mtu wa maana sana means, in Swahili, "If you can read these words, you are a remarkable person."

telegraphic speech A child's first word combinations, which omit (as a telegram did) unnecessary words.

pitch, intensity, and sound of language, and they react to the emotions and rhythms in voices. When most adults speak to babies, their pitch is higher and more varied than usual, and their intonation is exaggerated. Adult use of baby talk, which researchers call *parentese*, has been documented all over the world, from Sweden to Australia to Japan. Parentese helps babies learn the melody and rhythm of their native language (Fernald & Mazzie, 1991).

In what has to have been one of the most adorable research projects ever, three investigators compared the way mothers spoke to their babies and to pets, which also tend to evoke baby talk. They found that mothers exaggerate vowel sounds for their babies but not for Puffy the poodle or Cuddles the cat, suggesting that parentese is, indeed, a way of teaching language to infants (Burnham, Kitamura, & Vollmer-Conna, 2002).

By 4 to 6 months of age, babies can often recognize their own names and other words that are regularly spoken with emotion, such as "Mommy" and "Daddy." They also know many of the key consonant and vowel sounds of their native language and can distinguish such sounds from those of other languages (Kuhl et al., 1992). Over time, exposure to the baby's native language reduces the child's ability to perceive speech sounds in other languages. Thus, Japanese infants can hear the difference between the English sounds *la* and *ra*, but older Japanese children and Japanese adults cannot. Because this contrast does not exist in their language, they become insensitive to it.

Between 6 months and 1 year, infants become increasingly familiar with the sound structure of their native language. They are able to distinguish words from the flow of speech. They will listen longer to nonsense words that violate their expectations of what words should sound like and even to sentences that violate their expectations of how sentences should be structured (Jusczyk, 2002; Jusczyk, Houston, & Newsome, 1999). They start to babble, making many ba-ba and goo-goo sounds, endlessly repeating sounds and syllables. Then, at about a year of age, though the timing varies considerably, children start to name things. They already have some mental concepts for familiar people and objects, and their first words represent these concepts ("mama," "doggie," "car").

Also at the end of the first year, babies develop a repertoire of symbolic gestures, another important tool of communication. They gesture to refer to objects (e.g., sniffing to indicate "flower"), to request things (e.g., smacking the lips for "food"),

to describe objects (e.g., raising the arms for "big"), and to reply to questions (e.g., opening the palms or shrugging the shoulders for "I don't know"). They clap in response to pictures of things they like, from Teletubbies to baseball games. Children whose parents encourage them to use gestures acquire larger vocabularies, have better comprehension, are better listeners, and are less frustrated in their efforts to communicate than babies who are not encouraged to use gestures (Goodwyn & Acredolo, 1998). When babies begin to speak, they continue to gesture along with their words (just as adults gesture when talking), suggesting that gestures are not a substitute for language but are deeply related to its development (Mayberry & Nicoladis, 2000).

Between the ages of 18 months and 2 years, toddlers begin to produce words in two- or three-word combinations ("Mama here," "go 'way bug," "my toy"). The child's first combinations of words have a common quality: They are **telegraphic**. When people had to pay for every word in a telegram, they quickly learned to drop unnecessary articles (*a*, *an*, or *the*) and auxiliary verbs (such as *is* or *are*), but they still conveyed the message. Similarly, the two-word sentences of toddlers omit articles, auxiliary verbs, other parts of speech, and word endings, but

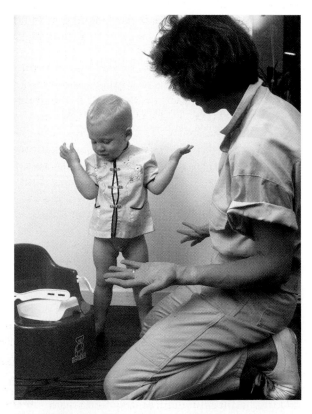

Conversational gestures emerge early!

they are still remarkably accurate in conveying meanings. Children use two-word sentences to locate things ("here toy"), make demands ("more milk"), negate actions ("no want," "all-gone milk"), describe events ("Bambi go," "hit ball"), describe objects ("pretty dress"), show possession ("Mama dress"), and ask questions ("Where Daddy?"). Pretty good for a little kid, don't you think?

At about this age, children develop another impressive talent: the rapid acquisition of new words. By the age of 6, the average child has a vocabulary of between 8,000 and 14,000 words, meaning that children acquire up to 8 new words a day between the ages of 1 and 6. They absorb new words as they hear them. They form a quick impression of a word's likely meaning by using their knowledge of grammatical contexts, and from the social context in which they hear the words used (Golinkoff & Hirsh-Pasek, 2006; Rice, 1990). The process of absorbing and understanding thousands of new words continues up through adolescence.

How on earth do children do all this?

The Innate Capacity for Language

At one time, most psychologists assumed that children acquired language by imitating adults and paying attention when adults corrected their mistakes. Then along came linguist Noam Chomsky (1957, 1980), who argued that language was far too complex to be learned bit by bit, as one might learn a list of world capitals.

Language, he noted, is not just any old communication system. It is a system that enables us to combine elements that are themselves meaningless into utterances that convey meaning, and to reject utterances that are not acceptable in our native tongue. It permits us to express and comprehend an infinite number of novel utterances, created on the spot. This ability is essential, because except for a few fixed phrases ("How are you?" "Get a life"), most of the utterances we produce or hear over a lifetime are new.

The task facing children, said Chomsky, is far more complicated than merely figuring out which sounds form words. They must also take the *surface structure* of a sentence—the way the sentence is actually spoken or signed—and apply grammatical rules (*syntax*) in order to infer an underlying *deep structure* that contains meaning. For example, although "Mary kissed John" and "John was kissed by Mary" have different surface structures, any 5-year-old knows that the two sentences have essentially the same deep structure, in which Mary is the actor and John gets the kiss.

Because no one actually teaches us grammar when we are toddlers, said Chomsky, the human brain must contain a **language acquisition device**, an innate mental module that allows young children to develop language if they are exposed to an adequate sampling of conversation. Just as a bird is designed to fly, human beings are designed to use language. Children's brains are sensitive to the core features common to all languages, such as nouns and verbs, subjects and objects, and negatives. These common features occur even in languages as seemingly different as Mohawk and English, or Okinawan and Bulgarian (Baker, 2001; Cinque, 1999).

Over the years, linguists and *psycholinguists* (researchers who study the psychology of language) have gathered many types of evidence to support the Chomskyan position:

1 *Children in different cultures go through similar stages of linguistic development.* For example, they will often form their first negatives simply by adding *no* or *not* at the beginning or end of a sentence ("No get dirty"). At a later stage, they will use double negatives ("He don't want no milk"; "Nobody don't like me"), even when their language does not allow such constructions (Klima & Bellugi, 1966; McNeill, 1966).

2 *Children combine words in ways that adults never would.* They reduce a parent's sentences ("Let's go to the store!") to their own two-word versions ("Go store!") and make many charming errors that an adult would not ("The alligator goed kerplunk," "Daddy taked me," "Hey, Horton heared a Who") (Ervin-Tripp, 1964; Marcus et al., 1992). Such errors, which psycholinguists call *overregularizations*, are not random; they show that the child has grasped a grammatical rule (add the *t* or *d* sound to make a verb past tense, as in *walked* and *hugged*) and is merely overgeneralizing it (*taked*, *goed*).

language acquisition device According to many psycholinguists, an innate mental module that allows young children to develop language if they are exposed to an adequate sampling of conversation.

Even when parents try to correct their children's syntax, it usually doesn't work.

3 *Adults do not consistently correct their children's syntax, yet children learn to speak or sign correctly anyway.* Learning explanations of language acquisition assume that children are rewarded for saying the right words and punished for making errors. But parents do not stop to correct every error in their children's speech, so long as they can understand what the child is trying to say (Brown, Cazden, & Bellugi, 1969). Indeed, parents often *reward* children for incorrect statements! The 2-year-old who says "Want milk!" is likely to get it; most parents would not wait for a more grammatical (or polite) request.

4 *Children who are not exposed to adult language may invent a language of their own.* Deaf children who have never learned a standard language, either signed or spoken, have made up their *own* sign languages, and across cultures these languages show similarities in sentence structure. For example, children in America and Taiwan have produced similar languages, as have children in Spain and Turkey (Goldin-Meadow, 2003). A group of deaf children in Nicaragua created a home-grown but grammatically complex sign language that is unrelated to Spanish (Senghas & Coppola, 2001).

5 *Infants as young as 7 months can derive simple linguistic rules from a string of sounds.* If babies are repeatedly exposed to artificial "sentences" with an ABA pattern, such as "Ga ti ga" or "Li na li," until they get bored, they will then prefer new sentences with an ABB pattern (such as "Wo fe fe") over new sentences with an ABA pattern (such as "Wo fe wo"). (They indicate this preference by looking longer at a flashing light

These deaf Nicaraguan children have invented their own grammatically complex sign language.

associated with the novel pattern than one associated with the familiar pattern.) Conversely, when the original sentences have an ABB structure, babies will prefer novel ones with an ABA structure. To many researchers, these responses suggest that babies can discriminate the different types of structures (Marcus et al., 1999). Astonishingly, this ability emerges even before they can understand or produce any words.

Chomsky's ideas revolutionized thinking about language and human nature. Many psycholinguists today believe that an innate facility for language evolved in human beings because it was extraordinarily beneficial (Pinker, 1994, 1999). In particular, it permitted our prehistoric ancestors to convey precise information about time, space, and events (as in "Honey, are you going on the mammoth hunt today?") and allowed them to negotiate alliances that were necessary for survival ("If you share your nuts and berries with us, we'll share our mammoth with you"). Language may also have developed because it provides the human equivalent of the mutual grooming that other primates rely on to forge social bonds (Dunbar, 2004). Just as other primates will clean, stroke, and groom each other for hours as a sign of affection and connection, human friends will sit for hours and chat over coffee.

The Influence of Learning on Language Despite the evidence for Chomsky's view that language is innate, some theorists argue that instead of inferring grammatical rules, children learn the probability that any given word or syllable will follow another, something infants as young as 8 months are able to do (Saffran, Aslin, & Newport, 1996; Seidenberg, MacDonald, & Saffran, 2002). In this view, infants are more like statisticians than grammarians.

Even theorists who emphasize an inborn grammatical capacity acknowledge that in any behavior as complex as language, nurture must also play a role. Although most children have the capacity to acquire language from mere exposure to it, parents do help things along. They may not go around correcting their children's speech all day, but they do recast and expand their children's clumsy or ungrammatical sentences ("Monkey climbing!" "Yes, the monkey is climbing the tree") (Bohannon & Stanowicz, 1988). Children, in turn, often imitate those recasts and expansions, suggesting that they are learning from them (Bohannon & Symons, 1988).

Language, therefore, depends on both biological readiness and social experience. Abused children who are not exposed to language during their early years (such as Genie, whom we mentioned in Chapter 1), rarely speak normally or catch up grammatically. Such sad evidence suggests a *critical period* in language development during the first few years of life or possibly the first decade. During these years, children need exposure to language and opportunities to practice their emerging linguistic skills in conversation with others.

QUICK quiz

Please use your human capacity for language to answer these questions.

1. "More cake!" and "Mommy come" are examples of _____ speech.

2. The central distinction between human language and other communication systems is that language (a) allows for the generation of an infinite number of new utterances, (b) is spoken, (c) is learned only after explicit training, (d) expresses meaning directly through surface structures.

3. What did Chomsky mean by a "language acquisition device"?

4. What five findings support the existence of an innate language acquisition device?

Answers:

1. telegraphic 2. a 3. an innate mental module that permits young children to develop language if they are exposed to it 4. Children everywhere go through similar stages of linguistic development; children combine words in ways that adults would not; adults do not consistently correct their children's syntax; groups of children not exposed to adult language may make up their own; and infants who are only a few months old appear to distinguish different sentence structures.

Thinking

Children do not think the way adults do. At age 2, they may call all large animals by one name (say, "horsie") and all small animals by another (say, "bug"). At 4, they may protest that a sibling has more fruit juice when it is only the shapes of the glasses that differ, not the amount of juice.

In the 1920s, Swiss biologist *Jean Piaget* [Zhan Pee-ah-ZHAY] (1896–1980) proposed a theory of cognitive development to explain these childish mistakes. Piaget's keen observations of children and his brilliant ideas caused a revolution in thinking about how thinking develops. Piaget's great insight was that children's errors are as interesting as their correct responses. Children will say things that seem cute or wildly illogical to adults. But the strategies that children use to think and solve problems, said Piaget, are not random or meaningless. They reflect a predictable interaction between the child's maturational stage and the child's experience in the world.

Piaget's Theory of Cognitive Stages

According to Piaget (1929/1960, 1984), as children develop, they must make constant mental adaptations to new observations and experiences. Sometimes they *assimilate* new information into their existing mental categories; for example, a German shepherd and a terrier both fit the category *dogs*. At other times, however, children must change their mental categories to *accommodate* their new experiences; for example, a cat does not belong to the category *dogs* and a new category is required, one for *cats*. Both processes are constantly interacting, Piaget said, as children go through four stages of cognitive development:

1 *The sensorimotor stage (birth to age 2).* In this stage, the infant learns through concrete actions: looking, touching, hearing, putting things in the mouth, sucking, grasping. "Thinking" consists of coordinating sensory information with bodily movements. Gradually these movements become more purposeful, as the child explores the environment and learns that specific movements will produce

This baby is not intentionally trying to drive his parents crazy. Like a good little scientist, he is trying to figure out cause and effect. Will the dish break? Will there be a noise? Will mom come with more food?

object permanence
The understanding, which develops throughout the first year, that an object continues to exist even when you cannot see it or touch it.

egocentric thinking
Seeing the world from only your own point of view; the inability to take another person's perspective.

conservation The understanding that the physical properties of objects—such as the number of items in a cluster or the amount of liquid in a glass—can remain the same even when their form or appearance changes.

specific results. Swatting a cloth away will reveal a hidden toy; letting go of a fuzzy toy duck will cause it to drop out of reach; banging on the table with a spoon will produce dinner (or Mom, taking the spoon away).

A major accomplishment at this stage, said Piaget, is **object permanence**, the understanding that something continues to exist even if you cannot see it or touch it. In the first few months, he observed, infants seem to follow the motto "out of sight, out of mind." They will look intently at a little toy, but if you hide it behind a piece of paper they will not look behind the paper or make an effort to get the toy. By about 6 months of age, however, infants begin to grasp the idea that the toy exists whether or not they can see it. If a baby of this age drops a toy from her playpen, she will look for it; she also will look under a cloth for a toy that is partially hidden. By 1 year of age, most babies have developed an awareness of the permanence of some objects; even if a toy is covered by a cloth, it must be under there. This is when they love to play peekaboo.

Object permanence, said Piaget, represents the beginning of the child's capacity to use mental imagery and symbols. The child becomes able to hold a concept in mind, to learn that the word *fly* represents an annoying, buzzing creature, and that *Daddy* represents a friendly, playful one.

2 *The preoperational stage (ages 2 to 7).* During this stage, the use of symbols and language accelerates. A 2-year-old is able to pretend, for instance, that a large box is a house, table, or train. But Piaget described this stage largely in terms of what the child cannot do. For example, children lack the cognitive abilities necessary for understanding abstract principles and *mental operations*. An operation is a train of thought that can be run backward or forward. Multiplying 2 times 6 to get 12 is an operation; so is the reverse operation, dividing 12 by 6 to get 2. Thus a preoperational child knows that Jessie is his sister, but he may not get the reverse operation, the idea that he is Jessie's brother. Piaget also believed (mistakenly, as we will see) that preoperational children cannot take another person's point of view because their thinking is **egocentric**: They see the world only from their own frame of reference and cannot imagine that others see things differently.

Further, said Piaget, preoperational children cannot grasp the concept of **conservation**, the notion that physical properties do not change when their forms or appearances change. Children at this age are unable to understand that an amount of liquid or a number of pennies remains the same even if you pour the liquid from one glass to another of a different size or if you stack the pennies (see Figure 3.2). If you pour liquid from a short, fat glass into a tall,

FIGURE 3.2
Piaget's Principle of Conservation
In a typical test for conservation of number (left), the number of blocks is the same in two sets, but those in one set are then spread out and the child must say whether one set has more blocks than another. Preoperational children think that the set that takes up more space has more blocks. In a test for conservation of quantity (right), the child is shown two short glasses with equal amounts of liquid. Then the contents of one glass are poured into a tall, narrower glass, and the child is asked whether one container now has more. Most preoperational children do not understand that pouring liquid from a short glass into a taller one leaves the amount of liquid unchanged. They judge only by the height of liquid in the glass.

narrow glass, preoperational children will say there is more liquid in the second glass. They attend to the appearance of the liquid (its height in the glass) to judge its quantity, so they are misled.

3 *The concrete operations stage (ages 7 to 12).* By this stage, children have developed significantly and have overcome some of their earlier limitations. They are able to take other people's perspectives and they make fewer logical errors. However, Piaget observed, these newfound abilities are usually tied to information that is concrete, that is, to actual experiences that have happened or concepts that have a tangible meaning to them. So children at this stage still make errors of reasoning when they are asked to think about abstract ideas ("patriotism" or "future education") or things that are not physically at hand. During these years, nonetheless, children's cognitive abilities expand rapidly. They come to understand the principles of conservation, reversibility, and cause and effect. They learn mental operations, such as addition, subtraction, multiplication, and division.

4 *The formal operations stage (age 12 through adulthood).* In this last stage, teenagers become capable of abstract reasoning. They understand that ideas can be compared and classified, just as objects can. They are able to reason about situations they have not experienced firsthand, and they can think about future possibilities. They are able to search systematically for answers to problems. They are able to draw logical conclusions from premises common to their culture and experience.

Table 3.2 summarizes Piaget's stages of cognitive development.

Current Views of Cognitive Development Piaget was a brilliant observer of children, and his major point has been well supported: New reasoning abilities depend on the emergence of previous ones. You cannot learn algebra before you can count, and you cannot learn philosophy before you understand logic. Since Piaget's original work, however, research has built on, expanded, and in some areas revised his ideas:

1 *Cognitive abilities develop in continuous, overlapping waves rather than discrete steps or stages.* If you observe children at different ages, as Piaget did, it will seem that they reason differently. But if you study the everyday learning of children at any given age, you will find that a child may use several different strategies to solve a problem, some more complex or accurate than others (Siegler, 2006). Learning occurs gradually, with retreats to former ways of thinking as well as advances to new ones. Children's reasoning ability also depends on the circumstances—who is asking them questions, the specific words used, the materials used, and what they are reasoning about—and not just on the stage they are in. In short, cognitive development is *continuous*; new abilities do not simply pop up when a child is a certain age (Courage & Howe, 2002).

2 *Preschoolers are not as egocentric as Piaget thought.* Most 3- and 4-year-olds *can* take another person's perspective (Flavell, 1999). When 4-year-olds play with 2-year-olds, for example,

TABLE 3.2
Summary of Piaget's Stages of Cognitive Development

Stage	Major Accomplishments
Sensorimotor (ages 0–2)	Object permanence Beginning of capacity to use mental images and symbols
Preoperational (ages 2–7)	Accelerated use of symbols and language
Concrete operations (ages 7–12)	Understanding of conservation Understanding of reversibility Understanding of cause and effect
Formal operations (age 12–adulthood)	Abstract reasoning Ability to compare and classify ideas

theory of mind The human ability to think about the way one's own mind and the minds of others work, and how cognitions and feelings affect behavior.

they modify and simplify their speech so the younger children will understand (Shatz & Gelman, 1973). One preschooler we know showed her teacher a picture she had drawn of a cat and an unidentifiable blob. "The cat is lovely," said the teacher, "but what is this thing here?" "That has nothing to do with you," said the child. "That's what the *cat* is looking at."

By about ages 3 to 4, children also begin to understand that you cannot predict what a person will do just by observing a situation or knowing the facts. You also have to know what the person is feeling and thinking; the person might even be lying. They start asking why other people behave as they do ("Why is Johnny so mean?"). In short, they are developing a **theory of mind**, a system of beliefs about how their own and other people's minds work and how people are affected by their beliefs and emotions. They start using verbs like *think* and *know,* and by age 4 they understand that what another person thinks might not match their own beliefs (Flavell, 1999; Lillard, 1998; Wellman, Cross, & Watson, 2001). To cognitive psychologists, the ability to understand that people can have false beliefs is a major milestone, because it means the child is beginning to question how we know things. The ability to think this way is a foundation for later higher-order, scientific thinking.

3 *Children understand far more than Piaget gave them credit for—and some adults understand far less.* Taking advantage of the fact that infants look longer at novel or surprising stimuli than at familiar ones, psychologists have designed delightfully imaginative methods of testing what babies know. These methods reveal that babies may be born with mental modules or core knowledge systems for numbers, the spatial relations of objects, some basic categories, and other features of the physical world (Quinn, 2002; Spelke, 2000). For example, at only 4 months of age, babies will look longer at a ball if it seems to roll through a solid barrier, leap between two platforms, or hang in midair than they do when the ball obeys the laws of physics. This suggests that the unusual event is surprising to them (see Figure 3.3). And infants as young as $2\frac{1}{2}$ to $3\frac{1}{2}$ months are aware that objects continue to exist even when masked by other objects, a form of object permanence that Piaget never imagined possible in babies so young (Baillargeon, 1999).

Conversely, not all adolescents and adults develop the ability for formal reasoning and reflective judgment. Some never develop the capacity

Possible event

Impossible event

FIGURE 3.3
Testing Infants' Knowledge
In this clever procedure, a baby watches as a box is pushed from left to right along a striped platform. The box is pushed until it reaches the end of the platform (a possible event) or until only a bit of it rests on the platform (an impossible event). Babies look longer at the impossible event, suggesting that it surprises them. Somehow they know that an object needs physical support and can't just float on air (Baillargeon, 1994).

for formal operations, and others think concretely unless a specific problem requires abstract thought.

4 *Cognitive development is spurred by the growing speed and efficiency of information processing.* Children reason just as Piaget said they do, with the tasks he gave them, but subsequent cognitive research has discovered why their thinking changes. As children mature, their working memory expands, they become better able to inhibit irrelevant and distracting thoughts and focus on a problem, and their general speed of processing increases. All of these changes help them reason more logically and efficiently (Luna et al., 2004).

5 *Cognitive development depends on the child's education and culture.* The Russian psychologist Lev Vygotsky (1896–1934), born in the same year as Piaget, differed from Piaget in emphasizing the sociocultural influences on children's cognitive development. Vygotsky was right. Culture—the world of tools, language, rituals, beliefs, games, and social institutions—profoundly shapes and structures children's cognitive development, fostering some abilities and neglecting others (Tomasello, 2000). For example, traditional nomadic hunting peoples, such as the Inuit of Canada and the Aborigines of Australia, do not quantify things and do not need to (Dasen, 1994; Gordon, 2004). The Aborigines have number words only up to five; after that, all quantities are described as "many." In such cultures, the conservation of quantity develops late, if at all. But nomadic hunters excel in spatial abilities, because spatial orientation is crucial for finding water holes and successful hunting routes. In contrast, children who live in settled agricultural communities, such as the Baoulé of the Ivory Coast, develop rapidly in the ability to quantify and much more slowly in spatial reasoning.

As you see, our understanding of children's cognitive maturation has undergone significant modification since Piaget's time. Nonetheless, Piaget left an enduring legacy: the insight that children are not passive vessels into which education and experience are poured. Children actively interpret their worlds, using their developing abilities to assimilate new information and figure things out.

Experience and culture influence cognitive development. Children who work with clay, wood, and other materials, such as this young potter in India, tend to understand the concept of conservation sooner than children who have not had this hands-on practice.

QUICK quiz

Please actively interpret this quiz.

1. Understanding that two rows of six pennies are equal in number, even if one row is spread out and the other is stacked up, is an example of _____.

2. Understanding that a toy exists even after Mom puts it in her purse is an example of _____, which develops during the _____ stage.

3. A 5-year-old who tells his dad that "Sally said she saw a bunny but she was lying" has developed a _____.

4. List five findings that have expanded or modified aspects of Piaget's theory.

Answers:

1. conservation   2. object permanence, sensorimotor   3. theory of mind   4. The changes from one stage to another occur in continuous, overlapping waves rather than distinct stages. Children are less egocentric than Piaget thought. Children know more and know it earlier than he believed, whereas some adults understand less. Children's cognitive development is spurred by the growing expansion of working memory and speed of information processing. And cognitive development is affected by cultural practices and experiences.

WHAT'S *Ahead*

- Are children born to be selfish little savages or do they have a "moral sense"?
- What is wrong with "because I say so" as a way of getting children to behave?
- Why are some children able to resist a forbidden treat whereas others gobble it up as soon as adults are out of sight?

Learning to Be Good

How do children learn to tell right from wrong, resist the temptation to behave selfishly, and obey the rules of social conduct? In the 1960s, Lawrence Kohlberg (1964), inspired by Piaget's work, argued that children's ability to understand right from wrong evolved along with the rest of their cognitive abilities, progressing through three levels. In studies of how children reason about moral dilemmas, he found that very young children obey rules because they fear being punished if they disobey, and later because they think it is in their best interest to obey. At about age 10, their moral judgments shift to ones based on conformity and loyalty to others, and then to an understanding of the rule of law. In adulthood, a few individuals go on to develop a moral standard based on universal human rights. For example, Martin Luther King, Jr., fought against laws supporting segregation; Mohandas

How do children learn to resist temptation?

Gandhi advocated nonviolent solutions to injustice in India; and Susan B. Anthony fought for women's right to vote.

Kohlberg was right that moral reasoning ability increases during the school years. Unfortunately, so do cheating, lying, cruelty, and the cognitive ability to rationalize these actions. As Thomas Lickona (1983) wryly summarized, "We can reach high levels of moral reasoning, and still behave like scoundrels." Accordingly, developmental psychologists today place greater emphasis on how children learn to regulate their own emotions and behavior. Most children learn to inhibit their wishes to beat up their younger siblings, steal a classmate's toy, or scream at the top of their lungs if they don't get their way. The child's emerging ability to understand right from wrong, and to behave accordingly, depends on the emergence of conscience and moral emotions such as shame, guilt, and empathy (Kochanska et al., 2005).

Even very young children are capable of feeling empathy for others and taking another person's point of view. They do not obey rules only because they are afraid of what will happen to them if they disobey, but also because they understand right from wrong. By age 5, they know the difference between doing the right thing and obeying orders; for example, they know it is wrong to hurt someone even if a teacher tells them to (Turiel, 2002). Therefore, many psychologists conclude that the capacity for understanding right from wrong, like that for language, is inborn. As Jerome Kagan (1984) wrote, "Without this fundamental human capacity, which nineteenth-century observers called a *moral sense,* the child could not be socialized."

The moral sense and a desire to behave well with others can be nurtured or extinguished, however, by experiences in a child's life. For example, when you did something wrong as a child, did the adults in your family spank you, shout at you, threaten you, or explain the error of your ways? One of the most common methods used by parents to enforce moral standards and good behavior is **power assertion**, which includes threats, physical punishment, depriving the child of privileges, and generally taking advantage of being bigger, stronger, and more powerful. Of course, a parent may have no alternative other than "Do it because I say so!" if the child is too young to understand a rule or impishly keeps trying to break it. But when power assertion consists of sheer parental bullying and frequent physical punishment, it is associated with greater aggressiveness in children, reduced empathy, and poorer moral reasoning (Gershoff, 2002; Hoffman, 1994; Lopez, Bonenberger, & Schneider, 2001). When parents are verbally abusive, insulting and ridiculing the child ("You are so stupid, I wish you had never been born"), the results are especially devastating (Moore & Pepler, 2006).

This does not mean that power assertion has the same effects on all children, in all environments, and in all cultures (Collins et al., 2000). For one thing, cultures tend to differ in their preferred methods of discipline; Chinese and African-American families are often sterner than middle-class white families, but the children generally regard their parents' discipline as evidence of concern, not abusiveness. Thus, the context in which the discipline occurs makes an enormous difference. Is the parent–child relationship fundamentally loving and trusting or one full of hostility and fighting?

Consider spanking. "My parents spanked me and I am fine," some people say, and they may well be right. The occasional, moderate use of spanking has no long-term detrimental outcomes for most middle-class children (Baumrind, Larzelere, & Cowan, 2002). The reason is that it typically occurs in an otherwise loving context as a quick action of

power assertion A method of child rearing in which the parent uses punishment and authority to correct the child's misbehavior.

Power Assertion
The parent uses physical force, threats, insults, or other kinds of power to get the child to obey.

Examples: *"Do it because I say so"; "Stop that right now"; hitting*

Result: *The child obeys, but only when the parent is present; the child often feels resentful.*

last resort when a child is misbehaving. Physical punishment backfires, however, when it is used inappropriately or harshly, causing the child to become angry and resentful. Many parents resort to spanking whenever they don't know what else to do. If the family atmosphere is one of anger, quarreling, and constant efforts to subdue the children, the use of physical punishment can easily spiral out of control (Gershoff, 2002). Moreover, harsh but ineffective discipline methods are then often transmitted to the next generation: Aggressive parents teach their children that the way to raise children is by behaving aggressively (Capaldi et al., 2003).

Thinking Critically About Spanking

A strategy that is more successful than spanking and other forms of power assertion is **induction**, in which the parent appeals to the child's own abilities, empathy, helpful nature, affection for others, and sense of responsibility. A parent using induction might explain to a misbehaving child that the child's actions could harm or upset another person ("You made Doug cry; it's not nice to bite"; "You must never poke anyone's eyes because that could hurt them seriously"). Or the parent might appeal to the child's own helpful inclinations ("I know you're a person who likes to be good to others"), which is far more effective than citing external reasons to be good ("You'd better be nice or you won't get dessert"). Children whose parents use induction and emphasize the importance of empathy tend to feel guilty if they hurt others. They are more likely to internalize standards of right and wrong

and be considerate of others (Berkowitz & Grych, 2000; Eisenberg et al., 2002; Hoffman, 1994).

Induction is not the same as being overly *permissive*—letting children do anything they want—or being uninvolved or unconcerned. Parents who use induction tend to be *authoritative* and democratic rather than arbitrarily *authoritarian* or permissive. That is, they give emotional support to the child and listen to the child's concerns and wishes, but they also require good behavior; they set high but reasonable expectations and teach their children how to meet them (Baumrind, 1989, 1991; Berkowitz & Grych, 2000). They have high demands for maturity and self-control in their children, but they also express a lot of sensitivity and warmth and they are highly involved with their children's lives. Their children have greater skills in *self-regulation*, the ability to control and modify their impulses, thoughts, and feelings, than do children of parents who rely on power assertion.

CLOSE-UP on Research

Self-Control and Conscience

As we have just seen, parenting styles are linked with whether and how children learn to behave themselves. Yet some psychologists have **questioned the assumption** that styles of discipline are the primary ingredient in determining a child's moral behavior. They have wondered whether something might intervene between how the parent treats the child and the child's willingness to listen. As we saw in discussing maternal sensitivity and the child's attachment style, one possibility is the child's own temperament.

To explore the links between parental discipline, the child's self-regulation, and the emergence of conscience, Grazyna Kochanska and Amy Knaack (2003) conducted a longitudinal study of 106 children. They **asked three questions**: At what age does self-regulation emerge? Is it related to the later internalization of moral standards? Is it related to how a mother disciplines her child? The researchers studied young children at ages 22, 33, and 45 months, measuring the children's self-regulatory abilities and observing the mothers' methods of discipline as they interacted with their

Induction

The parent appeals to the child's good nature, empathy, love for the parent, and sense of responsibility to others, and offers explanations of rules.

Examples: *"You're too grown up to behave like that"; "Fighting hurts your little brother."*

Result: *The child tends to internalize reasons for good behavior.*

induction A method of child rearing in which the parent appeals to the child's own resources, abilities, sense of responsibility, and feelings for others in correcting misbehavior.

children. When the children were 56 and 73 months, the researchers measured the development of conscience and a "moral self."

The researchers **defined their terms**. They defined self-regulation as "effortful control," the child's ability to suppress his or her initial wish to do something in favor of doing something else that is not as much fun. But how would you measure this ability in a little kid? Kochanska and Knaack designed a series of tests, all cleverly disguised as games. Some of the games required the child to whisper instead of shout, walk instead of run, ignore the dominant image in a picture and find a more subtle one, and delay gratification by not reaching immediately for an M&M under a cup or resisting the urge to open a bag to get a toy inside.

The researchers also measured the mothers' use of induction or power assertion in several ways. One was to observe what the mothers did when they were asked to get their child to clean up the play area or to prevent the child from playing with some appealing, easily accessible toys. Did the mother explain the reasons for her request to the child (induction) or did she issue strict orders (power assertion)? After interacting with her child, the mother left the room, and the child was free to obey or disobey, as the researchers observed what the child did in her absence.

When the children were 56 months old, the researchers assessed their moral development. They had the children play a game in which the experimenter held two large puppets that took opposite positions on nine moral actions. For example, one puppet would say, "When I'm by myself, I usually don't do things Mom says not to do" and the other would say, "Sometimes, when I'm by myself, I do things Mom says not to do." The children had to say which puppet they were more like. The nine moral actions included being willing to apologize, feeling empathy, being concerned about others' wrongdoing, feeling guilty after doing something naughty or wrong, and being concerned about their parents' feelings. The researchers also measured the children's actual behavior—for example, whether they cheated on the rules in playing a ball-tossing game. Then the researchers devised a composite conscience score for each child. Finally, when the children were 73 months old, their mothers rated them on the frequency of antisocial problems such as being irritable and quick to fly off the handle, destroying their own or others' belongings, or fighting with other children.

The researchers, therefore, **amassed considerable evidence** to examine. First, as you can see in the first row of the table on the right, the correlations between effortful self-control, measured at 22, 33, and 45 months of age, and the children's later conscience score at 56 months were positive, very high, and statistically significant (except for the very youngest children). Second, the correlations between effortful control and later antisocial problems were negative and also statistically significant, meaning that children who were most able to regulate their impulses early in life were least likely to get in trouble later by fighting or destroying things.

Third, you can see that the child's ability to delay gratification and regulate feelings was also negatively associated with the mother's use of power assertion, meaning that mothers who ordered their children to "behave" tended to have children who were impulsive and aggressive.

| | Child Effortful Control | | | |
	22 Months	33 Months	45 Months	Overall
Conscience score at 56 months	.21	.59	.64	.58
Aggression problems at 73 months	−.28	−.33	−.32	−.37
Mother's use of power assertion	−.33	−.49	−.52	−.54

The researchers **considered another interpretation** of that last correlational finding: Perhaps some mothers relied on power assertion *because* their children were impulsive and aggressive and did not behave. Indeed, in this study, children who were defiant and rebellious were more likely to provoke power assertion by their mothers. Moreover, the children's ability or inability to control their actions was consistent over time and across all tasks, suggesting that it was due to a personality trait.

Other longitudinal studies have replicated the stability of self-regulation (Raffaelli, Crockett, & Shen, 2005). However, the mother's use of power assertion independently continued to predict the child's effortful control and conscience score. This pattern of findings teaches us to **avoid oversimplification**, for example, by concluding that "it's all in what the mother does" or that "it's all in the child's personality." Mothers and children, it seems, raise each other.

QUICK quiz

••

Exercise self-regulation by taking this quiz.

1. What is a major limitation of cognitive theories of moral reasoning in understanding how children develop a conscience?

2. Which method of disciplining an aggressive child is most likely to teach empathy? (a) induction, (b) authoritarian firmness, (c) power assertion, (d) spanking

3. What early ability predicts the development of conscience later on?

Answers:

1. Moral behavior is not necessarily related to the ability to reason morally.   2. a   3. self-regulation, the ability to control one's immediate impulses and wishes.

WHAT'S *Ahead*

- Why do some people fail to identify themselves as either male or female?

- How would a biologically oriented psychologist explain why most little boys and girls are "sexist" in their choice of toys?

- What happens to children's notions about gender once they are able to distinguish males from females?

- How do teachers unintentionally reinforce aggressiveness in boys?

- If a little girl "knows" that girls can't be doctors, does this mean she will never go to medical school?

Gender Development

No parent ever excitedly calls a relative to exclaim, "It's a baby! It's a $7\frac{1}{2}$-pound, black-haired baby!" The baby's sex is the first thing everyone notices and announces. How soon do children themselves notice that boys and girls are different sexes and understand which sex they themselves are? How do children learn the rules of masculinity and femininity, the things that boys do that are different from what girls do? Why, as one friend of ours observed, do most preschool children act like the "gender police," insisting, say, that boys can't be nurses and girls can't be doctors? And why do some children come to feel they don't belong to the sex everyone else thinks they do?

Gender Identity

Let's start by clarifying some terms. **Gender identity** refers to a child's sense of being male or female, of belonging to one sex and not the other.

Gender typing is the process of socializing children into their gender roles and, thus, reflects society's ideas about which abilities, interests, traits, and behaviors are appropriately masculine or feminine. A person can have a strong gender identity and not be gender typed: A man may be confident in his maleness and not feel threatened by doing "unmasculine" things such as needlepointing a pillow; a woman may be confident in her femaleness and not feel threatened by doing "unfeminine" things such as serving in combat.

In the past, psychologists tried to distinguish the terms *sex* and *gender*, reserving "sex" for the physiological or anatomical attributes of males and females and "gender" for differences that are learned. Thus they might speak of a sex difference in the frequency of baldness but a gender difference in fondness for romance novels. Today, these two terms are often used interchangeably because, as we have noted repeatedly in this book, nature and nurture are inextricably linked. It is not easy to separate physiological and anatomical traits from psychological ones (Golombok & Fivush, 1994; Roughgarden, 2004).

The complexity of sex and gender development is especially apparent in the cases of people who do not fit the familiar categories of male and female. Every year, thousands of babies are born with **intersex conditions**, formerly known as hermaphroditism. In these conditions, which occur in about one of every 2,000 births, chromosomal or hormonal anomalies cause the child to be born with ambiguous genitals, or genitals that conflict with the infant's chromosomes. A child who is genetically female, for example, might be born with an enlarged clitoris that looks like a penis. A child who is genetically male might be born with androgen insensitivity, a condition that causes the external genitals to appear to be female (Roughgarden, 2004; Zucker, 1999).

gender identity The fundamental sense of being male or female; it is independent of whether the person conforms to the social and cultural rules of gender.

gender typing The process by which children learn the abilities, interests, personality traits, and behaviors associated with being masculine or feminine in their culture.

intersex conditions (intersexuality) Conditions, occurring in about one of every 2,000 births, in which chromosomal or hormonal anomalies cause a child to be born with ambiguous genitals, or genitals that conflict with the infant's chromosomes.

As adults, many intersexed individuals call themselves *transgender,* a term describing a broad category of people who do not fit comfortably into the usual categories of male and female, masculine and feminine. Some are comfortable living with the physical and psychological attributes of both sexes, considering themselves to be "gender queer" and even refusing to be referred to as he or she. But many feel uncomfortable in their sex of rearing and wish to be considered a member of the other sex; their gender identity is at odds with their anatomical sex or appearance. They are *transsexual,* feeling that they are male in a female body or vice versa; they often try to make a full transition to the other sex through surgery or hormones or by simply taking on the dress and attributes of the sex they wish to be. Intersexed people and transsexuals have been found in virtually all cultures throughout history (Denny, 1998; Roughgarden, 2004).

Influences on Gender Development

To understand the typical course of gender development, as well as the variations, developmental psychologists study the interacting influences of biology, cognition, and learning on gender identity and gender typing.

Biological Influences Starting in the preschool years, boys and girls congregate primarily with other children of their sex, and most prefer the toys and games of their own sex (Maccoby, 1998). They will play together if required to, but given their druthers, they usually choose to play with same-sex friends. The kind of play that young boys and girls enjoy also differs, on average. Little boys, like young males in all primate species, are more likely than females to go in for physical roughhousing, risk taking, and aggressive displays. These sex differences occur all over the world, almost regardless of how adults treat children—for example, whether they encourage boys and girls to play together or separate them (Lytton & Romney, 1991; Maccoby, 1998, 2002). Similarly, many parents lament that although they try to give their children the same toys, it makes no difference; their sons want trucks and guns and their daughters want dolls.

Biological researchers believe that these play and toy preferences have a basis in prenatal hormones, particularly the presence or absence of prenatal androgens (masculinizing hormones). Girls who were exposed to prenatal androgens in the womb are later more likely than nonexposed girls to prefer "boys' toys" such as cars and fire engines, and they are also more physically aggressive than other girls (Berenbaum & Bailey, 2003). Most androgenized girls, however, develop a female gender identity and do not see themselves as male in any way.

What, then, does create gender identity? In the past, most psychologists thought it was almost entirely learned, a result of the child's socialization and learning. Today, many think it is hardwired. One way of answering the question is to study children whose sex of rearing was discrepant with their anatomical or genetic sex as a result of accidents at birth or having been born with ambiguous genitals. What sex do they identify with? When Kenneth Zucker (1999) reviewed the hundreds of cases

Throughout history and across cultures, there have been transgender people. Some women have lived as men, as did the eighteenth-century pirates Ann Bonny and Mary Read (left). Some men have lived as women, as did We-Wha, a Zuni Indian man, shown in a photo taken about 1885. Today many transgender individuals are outspoken about their sexual and gender identities. Luke Woodward (right), who was born and raised female, has come out as a male and is active in a campus movement to make life better for fellow transgender students.

Ann Bonny *and* Mary Read *convicted of Piracy Nov.ʳ 28ᵗʰ 1720 at a Court of Vice Admiralty held at* Sᵗ Jago de la Vega *in ẏ Island of Jamaica.*

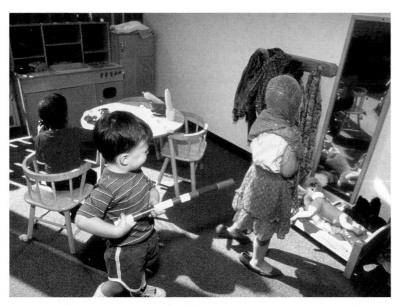

Look familiar? In a scene typical of many nursery schools and homes, the boy builds a gun out of anything he can, and the girl dresses up in any pretty thing she can find. Psychologists (and parents) debate whether such gender typing is biologically based or a result of the emergence of gender schemas.

of such children, he found that the answer is enormously complex, depending on the interactions of genes, prenatal hormones, anatomical structures, and experiences in life.

For example, consider the results of a longitudinal follow-up study of 16 genetic males who had a rare condition that caused them to be born without a penis. The babies were otherwise normal males, with testicles and appropriate androgen levels. Fourteen of these babies had been socially and surgically assigned to the female sex, according to the custom when they were born. But the parents of two of the boys did not consent to the procedure and raised their sons as male. Those two developed a male gender identity. All 16 have interests and attitudes that are considered typical of males. But of the 14 who were surgically reassigned as females, eight have declared themselves male, five are living as females, and one has an unclear gender identity (Reiner & Gearheart, 2004).

Because of the many factors involved in gender identity, a fierce battle is currently raging among physicians, sex researchers, and intersexed people

Thinking Critically About Gender Identity themselves about the best approach to take with intersexed babies (Zucker, 1999). Should physicians intervene surgically or hormonally, or do nothing and eventually let the child decide what sex he or she wishes to be? For the present, we will all have

to live with uncertainty about what the best course of action is, until we know better how nature and nurture interact to produce a gender identity as male, female, or trans.

Cognitive Influences Cognitive psychologists explain the mystery of children's gender segregation and toy and play preferences by studying the children's changing cognitive abilities. Even before babies can speak, they recognize that there are two genders. By the age of 9 months, most babies can discriminate male from female faces (Fagot & Leinbach, 1993), and they can match female faces with female voices (Poulin-Dubois et al., 1994). By the age of 2 to 3, toddlers can label themselves as boys or girls, but it is not until the age of 4 or 5 that most children develop a stable gender identity, a sense of themselves as being male or female regardless of what they wear or how they behave. Only then do they understand that what boys and girls do does not necessarily indicate what sex they are: A girl remains a girl even if she can climb a tree, and a boy remains a boy even if he has long hair.

Cognitive processes are involved in the behavioral differences between boys and girls that emerge during the preschool years. Once children can label themselves and others consistently as being a boy or a girl, they change their behavior to conform to the category they belong to. They begin to prefer same-sex playmates and sex-traditional toys without being explicitly taught to do so (Martin, Ruble, & Szkrybalo, 2002). They become more gender typed in their toy play, games, aggressiveness, and verbal skills than children who still cannot consistently label males and females. Most notably, girls stop behaving aggressively (Fagot, 1993). It is as if they go along behaving like boys until they know they are girls. At that moment, but not until that moment, they seem to decide: "Girls don't do this; I'm a girl; I'd better not either."

It's great fun to watch 3- to 5-year-old children struggle to figure out what makes boys and girls different: "The ones with eyelashes are girls; boys don't have eyelashes," said one 4-year-old to her aunt in explaining her drawing. After dinner at an Italian restaurant, a 4-year-old told his parents that

gender schema A cognitive schema (mental network) of knowledge, beliefs, metaphors, and expectations about what it means to be male or female.

he'd got the answer: "Men eat pizza and women don't" (Bjorkland, 2000). By the age of 5, children consolidate their knowledge, with all of its mistakes and misconceptions, into a **gender schema**, a mental network of beliefs and expectations about what it means to be male or female and about what each sex is supposed to wear, do, feel, and think (Bem, 1993; Martin & Ruble, 2004). Gender schemas even include metaphors. For example, after age 4, children of both sexes will usually say that rough, spiky, black, or mechanical things are male and that soft, pink, fuzzy, or flowery things are female; that black bears are male and pink poodles are female (Leinbach, Hort, & Fagot, 1997). Gender schemas are most rigid between ages 5 and 7; at this age, it's really hard to dislodge a child's notion of what boys and girls can do (Martin, Ruble, & Szkrybalo, 2002). A little girl at this stage will tell you stoutly that "girls can't be doctors" even if her own mother is a doctor.

One puzzle of gender development is that virtually all over the world, boys' gender schemas are more rigid than girls' are. That is, boys express stronger preferences for masculine toys and activities than girls do for feminine ones, and boys are harsher on themselves and other boys who fail to behave in gender-typed ways (Bussey & Bandura, 1992; Maccoby, 1998). One reason may be that most societies value masculine occupations and traits more than feminine ones, and males have higher status. So when boys behave like (or play with) girls, they lose status, and when girls behave like boys, they gain status (Serbin, Powlishta, & Gulko, 1993).

Many people retain inflexible gender schemas throughout their lives, feeling uncomfortable or

angry with men or women who break out of traditional roles—let alone with transgendered individuals who don't fit either category or want to change the one they grew up with. However, with increasing experience and cognitive sophistication, older children often become more flexible in their gender schemas, especially if they have friends of the other sex and if their families and cultures encourage such flexibility (Martin & Ruble, 2004). Children begin to modify their gender schemas, understanding, say, that women can be engineers and men can be cooks.

Cultures and religions, too, differ in their schemas for the roles of women and men. In all industrialized nations, for example, it is taken for granted that women and men alike should be educated; indeed, laws mandate a minimum education for both sexes. But in Afghanistan, even after the overthrow of the Taliban and its prohibition on female education, many girls who attend school still receive death threats. Gender schemas can be very powerful, and events that challenge their legitimacy can be enormously threatening. How flexible are your own gender schemas?

Learning Influences A third influence on gender development is the environment, which is full of subtle and not-so-subtle messages about what girls and boys are supposed to do. Behavioral and social-cognitive learning theorists study how the process of gender socialization instills these messages in children (Bussey & Bandura, 1999). Although many adults say they treat boys and girls equally or that "my little girl was just naturally feminine but my boy was born to be a boxer," research disputes their claims.

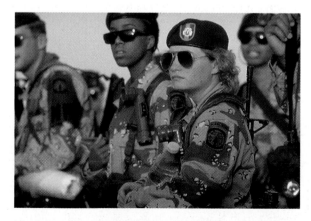

Not long ago, the idea of women serving in the military and men teaching preschoolers would have offended or at least startled many people. Today, as a result of changing economic conditions, gender schemas have become less rigid in Western countries, and these images have lost their power to shock.

Can You Imagine Being the Other Sex?

If you woke up tomorrow and found that you had been transformed into a member of the other sex, how would your life change, if at all? Would anything be different about your attitudes, behavior, habits, experiences, choices, preferences, and feelings? Write down your first reactions and then ask a few of your male and female friends the same question. If possible, ask young children, too. Do their answers differ depending on their sex? If so, how? What does this exercise reveal about gender socialization and schemas?

Gender socialization begins at the moment of birth. Parents tend to portray their newborn girls as more feminine and delicate than boys, and boys as stronger and more athletic than girls, although it is hard to know how athletic a newborn boy could be and all newborns are pretty delicate (Karraker, Vogel, & Lake, 1995). Many parents are careful to dress their baby in outfits they consider to be the correct color and pattern for his or her sex. Clothes don't matter to the infant, of course, but they are signals to adults about how to treat the child. Adults often respond to the same baby differently, depending on whether the child is dressed as a boy or a girl (Stern & Karraker, 1989).

Adults respond to boys and girls differently even when the children are behaving in exactly the same way. In one observational study, 12- to 16-month-old boys and girls were equally assertive (as measured by the frequency of their efforts to get an adult's attention) and verbal (as measured by their attempts to communicate with others). But teachers responded far more often to assertive boys than to shy ones and to verbal girls than to non-verbal ones. Subtly, the teachers were reinforcing gender-typed behavior. When the researchers observed the same children a year later, a gender difference was now apparent, with boys behaving more assertively and girls talking more to teachers (Fagot et al., 1985). Social-learning theorists believe that the teachers' reinforcements created this gender difference, although it is also possible that the teachers were merely anticipating changes that would have occurred anyway because of genetic influences.

Parents, teachers, and other adults convey their beliefs and expectations about gender even when they are entirely unaware that they are doing so. For example, when parents believe that boys are naturally better at math or sports and that girls are naturally better at English, they unwittingly communicate those beliefs by how they respond to a child's success or failure. They may tell a son who did well in math, "You're a natural math whiz, Johnny!" But if a daughter gets good grades, they may say, "Wow, you really worked hard in math, Joanie, and it shows!" The implication is that girls have to try hard but boys have a natural gift. Messages like these are not lost on children. Both sexes tend to lose interest in activities that are supposedly not natural for them, even when they all start out with equal abilities (Dweck, 2006; Frome & Eccles, 1998).

In today's fast-moving world, society's messages to men and women keep shifting. As a result, gender

cathy®   **by Cathy Guisewite**

development has become a lifelong process, in which gender schemas, attitudes, and behavior evolve as people have new experiences and as society itself changes. Five-year-old children may behave like sexist piglets while they are trying to figure out what it means to be male or female. Their behavior is shaped by a combination of hormones, genetics, gender schemas, parental and social lessons, religious and cultural customs, and experiences. But their gender-typed behavior as 5-year-olds often has little to do with how they will behave at 25 or 45. Children can grow up in an extremely gender-typed family and yet, as adults, find themselves in careers or relationships they would never have imagined for themselves. If 5-year-olds are the gender police, many adults end up breaking the law.

QUICK quiz

Quiz-taking is appropriate behavior for all sexes and genders.

1. Three-year-old Paulo thinks that if he changed from wearing pants to wearing dresses he could become a girl. He still lacks a stable _____.

2. *True or false:* All intersexed people are transsexual.

3. A biological psychologist would say that a 3-year-old boy's love of going "vroom, vroom" with his truck collection is probably a result of _____.

4. Which statement about gender schemas is *false*? (a) They are present in early form by 1 year of age; (b) they are permanent conceptualizations of what it means to be masculine or feminine; (c) they eventually expand to include many meanings and associations to being male and female; (d) they probably reflect the status of women and men in society.

5. Herb hopes his 4-year-old daughter will become a doctor like him, but she refuses to play with the toy stethoscope he bought her and insists that she will be a princess when she grows up. What conclusions can Herb draw about his daughter's future career?

Answers:

1. gender identity 2. false 3. biological factors such as prenatal hormones, specifically androgens 4. b 5. Not many. His daughter's rigid gender-typed behavior is typical when children are acquiring gender schemas, but it does not predict much of anything about her adult interests or occupation.

WHAT'S *Ahead*

- What are the advantages and disadvantages of going through puberty earlier than most of your classmates?

- Should teenage criminals be considered "not guilty by reason of adolescence"?

- During adolescence, are extreme turmoil and unhappiness the exception or the rule?

Adolescence

Adolescence refers to the period of development between **puberty**, the age at which a person becomes capable of sexual reproduction, and adulthood. In some cultures, the time span between puberty and adulthood is only a few months; a sexually mature boy or girl is expected to marry and assume adult tasks. In modern Western societies, however, teenagers are not considered emotionally mature enough to assume the rights, responsibilities, and roles of adulthood.

The Physiology of Adolescence

Until puberty, boys and girls produce roughly the same levels of male hormones (androgens) and female hormones (estrogens). At puberty, the brain's pituitary gland begins to stimulate hormone production in the adrenal and reproductive glands. From puberty on, boys have a higher level of androgens than girls do, and girls have a higher level of estrogens than boys do.

In boys, the reproductive glands are the testes (testicles), which produce sperm; in girls, the reproductive glands are the ovaries, which release eggs. During puberty, these sex organs mature and the individual becomes capable of reproduction. In girls, the development of breasts and **menarche**, the onset of menstruation, are signs of sexual maturity. In boys, the signs are the onset of nocturnal emissions and the growth of the testes, scrotum, and penis. Hormones are also responsible for the emergence of *secondary sex characteristics*, such as a

puberty The age at which a person becomes capable of sexual reproduction.

menarche [men-ARR-kee] The onset of menstruation.

deepened voice and facial and chest hair in boys and pubic hair in both sexes.

The onset of puberty depends on both genetic and environmental factors. Menarche, for example, depends on a female's having a critical level of body fat, which is necessary to sustain a pregnancy. Body fat triggers the hormonal changes associated with puberty (Chehab et al., 1997). An increase in body fat among children in developed countries may help explain why the average age of puberty declined in Europe and North America until the mid-twentieth century. The average age of menarche now occurs at about 12 years and 8 months in white girls and a few months earlier in black girls.

Early and Late Puberty Individuals vary enormously in the onset and length of puberty. If you entered puberty before most of your classmates, or if you matured much later than they did, you know that your experience of adolescence was different from that of the average teenager (whoever that is). Going through puberty out of sync with one's peers can produce feelings of alienation and depression and body-image distortions that can lead to eating disorders (Ricciardelli & McCabe, 2004).

Early-maturing boys generally have a more positive view of their bodies than late-maturing boys do, and their relatively greater size and strength give them a boost in sports and the prestige that being a good athlete brings young men. But they are also more likely to smoke, drink alcohol, use other drugs, and break the law than later-maturing boys (Cota-Robles, Neiss, & Rowe, 2002; Duncan et al., 1985).

Some early-maturing girls have the prestige of being socially popular, but, partly because others in their peer group regard them as being sexually precocious, they are also more likely to fight with their parents, drop out of school, have a negative body image, and be angry or depressed. Early menarche itself does not cause these problems; rather, it tends to accentuate existing behavioral problems and family conflicts. Girls who go through puberty relatively late, in contrast, have a more difficult time at first, but by the end of adolescence many are happier with their appearance and are more popular than their early-maturing classmates (Caspi & Moffitt, 1991; Stattin & Magnusson, 1990).

Brain Development When people think of physical changes in adolescence, they usually think of body maturation and the effects of hormones on mood and sexuality. But the brain

To their embarrassment, children typically reach puberty at different times. These girls are all the same age, but they differ considerably in physical maturity.

undergoes significant developmental changes, too. New connections among brain cells are added and others are pruned away (see Chapter 4). One researcher compares what happens to the brain during adolescence with remodeling a house—the basic structure is still there, but it's updated and streamlined. Changes occur primarily in the prefrontal cortex, which is responsible for impulse control and planning, and the limbic system, which is involved in emotional processing (Spear, 2000; Walker, 2002). In Chapter 11 we will see that errors in the "remodeling" process during adolescence may be involved in the onset of schizophrenia and other disorders in vulnerable individuals.

In 2005, the Supreme Court banned the death penalty for juveniles as cruel and unusual punishment, partly on the basis of research showing that adolescents often get into trouble because of the neurological immaturity of their brains. Some researchers have concluded from this evidence that many teenagers who commit crimes should be considered "less guilty by reason of adolescence." Do you agree?

The Psychology of Adolescence

The media love sensational stories about teenagers who are angry, live in emotional turmoil and anguish, feel lonely, hate their parents, and lack self-esteem. How realistic is this portrait of adolescence? Not very. The rate of violent crimes committed by

Thinking Critically About "Adolescent Turmoil"

FIGURE 3.4
Gender (Non)differences in Self-Esteem

Popular books claim that girls and women have much lower self-esteem than boys and men, starting in adolescence. But studies of nearly 150,000 American adolescents find that the difference is very small (Kling et al., 1999).

adolescents has actually been plummeting steadily since 1993. As for self-worth, two meta-analyses of studies of nearly 150,000 young people found no sudden adolescent drop in self-esteem for either sex. As you can see in Figure 3.4, although males on average had slightly higher self-esteem than females, the difference was very small (Kling et al., 1999).

Similarly, studies of representative samples of adolescents find that only a small minority are seriously troubled, angry, or unhappy. Most teenagers have supportive families, a sense of purpose and self-confidence, good friends, and the skill to cope with their problems. Extreme turmoil and unhappiness are the exception, not the rule. Adolescent rebellion is more a matter of generational attitudes and cultural norms than of anything inherent in adolescent development. The baby-boom generation protested the authority of their parents and even created the term "generation gap," but most of the teenage and college-age children of baby boomers feel close to their parents, whom they typically see as allies rather than adversaries (Howe & Strauss, 2003).

Nevertheless, three kinds of problems are more common during adolescence than during childhood or adulthood: conflict with parents, mood swings and depression, and higher rates of reckless, rule-breaking, and risky behavior (Spear, 2000). In Western societies, these problems are the downside of growing up. Although quarrels with parents can be painful, they tend to signify a change from one-sided parental authority to a more reciprocal adult relationship. Rule-breaking often occurs because teenagers are developing their own standards and values, often by trying on the styles, actions, and attitudes of their

"So I blame you for everything—whose fault is that?"

peers, in contrast to those of their parents. Peers become especially important because they represent the values and style of the generation that teenagers identify with, the generation that they will share experiences with as adults (Bukowski, 2001; Harris, 1998; Hartup, 1999). As adults, many people report that rejection by peers during adolescence was more devastating than punitive treatment by parents.

Adolescents who are lonely, depressed, worried, or angry tend to express these concerns in ways characteristic of their sex. Boys are more likely than girls to externalize their emotional problems in acts of aggression and other antisocial behavior. Girls, in contrast, are more likely than boys to internalize their feelings and problems, for example by becoming withdrawn or developing eating disorders (Zahn-Waxler, 1996).

QUICK quiz

If you are not in the midst of adolescent turmoil, try these questions.

1. The onset of menstruation is called _____.
2. What is the difference between *puberty* and *adolescence*?
3. Extreme turmoil and rebellion in adolescence are (a) nearly universal, (b) the exception rather than the rule, (c) rare.
4. *True or false:* Teenage boys have much higher self-esteem than teenage girls do.

Answers:

1. menarche   2. *Puberty* refers to the physiological process of sexual maturation; *adolescence* is a social category marking the years between puberty and adulthood.   3. b   4. false

WHAT'S *Ahead*

- What feelings are common during emerging adulthood, the years from 18 to 25?

- Does menopause make most women depressed and irrational?

- Do men go through a male version of menopause?

- Which mental abilities decline in old age and which do not?

Adulthood

According to ancient Greek legend, the Sphinx was a monster—half lion, half woman—who terrorized passersby on the road to Thebes. The Sphinx would ask each traveler a question and then murder those who failed to answer correctly. (The Sphinx was a pretty tough grader.) The question was this: What animal walks on four feet in the morning, two feet at noon, and three feet in the evening? Only one traveler, Oedipus, knew the solution to the riddle. The animal, he said, is Man, who crawls on all fours as a baby, walks upright as an adult, and limps in old age with the aid of a staff.

The Sphinx was the first life-span theorist. Since then, many philosophers, writers, and scientists have speculated on the course of adult development. Are the changes of adulthood predictable, like those of childhood? What are the major psychological issues of adult life? Is mental and physical deterioration in old age inevitable?

Stages and Ages

One of the first modern theorists to propose a life-span approach to psychological development was psychoanalyst Erik H. Erikson (1902–1994). Just as children progress through stages, he said, so do adults. Erikson (1950/1963, 1982) wrote that all individuals go through eight stages in their lives. Each stage is characterized by a "crisis," a particular challenge, which ideally should be resolved before the individual moves on.

1 *Trust versus mistrust* is the challenge that occurs during the baby's first year, when the baby depends on others to provide food, comfort, cuddling, and warmth. If these needs are not met, the child may never develop the essential trust of others necessary to get along in the world.

2 *Autonomy (independence) versus shame and doubt* is the challenge that occurs when the child is a toddler. The young child is learning to be independent and must do so without feeling too ashamed or uncertain about his or her actions.

3 *Initiative versus guilt* is the challenge that occurs as the preschooler develops. The child is acquiring new physical and mental skills, setting goals, and enjoying newfound talents but must also learn to control impulses. The danger lies in developing too strong a sense of guilt over his or her wishes and fantasies.

4 *Competence versus inferiority* is the challenge for school-age children, who are learning to make things, use tools, and acquire the skills for adult life. Children who fail these lessons of mastery and competence may come out of this stage feeling inadequate and inferior.

5 *Identity versus role confusion* is the great challenge of adolescence, when teenagers must decide who they are, what they are going to do, and what they hope to make of their lives. The term *identity crisis* describes what Erikson considered to be the primary conflict of this stage. Those who resolve it will come out of this stage with a strong identity, ready to plan for the future. Those who do not will sink into confusion, unable to make decisions.

6 *Intimacy versus isolation* is the challenge of young adulthood. Once you have decided who you are, said Erikson, you must share yourself with another and learn to make commitments. No matter how successful you are in work, you are not complete until you are capable of intimacy.

7 *Generativity versus stagnation* is the challenge of the middle years. Now that you know who you are and have an intimate relationship, will you sink into complacency and selfishness, or will you experience "generativity"—creativity and renewal? Parenthood is the most common means for the successful resolution of this stage, but people can be productive, creative, and nurturant in other ways, in their work or their relationships with the younger generation.

8 *Ego integrity versus despair* is the final challenge of old age. As they age, people strive to reach the ultimate goals—wisdom, spiritual tranquility, an acceptance of their lives. Just as the healthy child will not fear life, said Erikson, the healthy adult will not fear death.

Erikson recognized that cultural and economic factors affect people's progression through these stages. Some societies, for example, make

According to Erik Erikson, children must master the crisis of competence and older adults must resolve the challenge of generativity. This child and her grandmother are certainly helping each other with their life tasks! But are the needs for competence and generativity important at only one stage of life?

the passages relatively easy. If you know you are going to be a farmer like your parents and you have no alternative, then moving from adolescence into young adulthood is not a terribly painful step (unless you hate farming). If you have many choices, however, as adolescents in urban societies often do, the transition can become prolonged. Some people put off making choices and never resolve their "identity crisis." Similarly, cultures that place a high premium on independence and individualism will make it difficult for many of their members to resolve Erikson's sixth crisis, that of intimacy versus isolation.

Erikson's work reminds us that development is never finished; it is an ongoing process. His work was important because he placed adult development in the context of family and society, and he specified many of the essential concerns of adulthood: trust, competence, identity, generativity, and the ability to enjoy life and accept death.

Because Erikson discussed these themes in terms of their relative importance at different ages, many readers of his work assumed that the psychological concerns he identified occur at only one crucial time of life. Erikson was well aware that they can occur out of order, although that was not his emphasis. Later researchers, working at a time when people's lives had become less traditional and predictable, discovered just how out of order they can be. Although in Western societies adolescence is often a time of confusion about identity and aspirations, an identity crisis is not limited to the teen years. A man who has worked in one job all his life, and then is laid off and must find an entirely new career, may have an identity crisis too. Likewise, competence is not mastered once and for all in childhood. People learn new skills

and lose old ones throughout their lives, and their sense of competence rises and falls accordingly. Moreover, people who are highly generative, in terms of being committed to helping their communities or the next generation, tend to do volunteer work or choose occupations that allow them to contribute to society throughout their lives (Mansfield & McAdams, 1996).

Stage theories, therefore, are not an adequate way of understanding how adults grow and change, or remain the same, across the life span. As one wise psychologist observed many years ago, "there is not one process of aging, but many; there is not one life course followed, but multiple courses. . . . The variety is as rich as the historic conditions people have faced and the current circumstances they experience" (Pearlin, 1982).

The Transitions of Life

Of course, certain events do tend to occur at particular times in life: going to school, learning to drive a car, having a baby, retiring from work. In all societies, people rely on a *social clock* to determine whether they are on time for these transitions or off time. The social clock consists of norms governing what most other people of the same age and historical generation are expected to do (Moen & Wethington, 1999; Neugarten, 1979).

Cultures have different social clocks. In some, young men and women are supposed to marry and start having children right after puberty, and work responsibilities come later. In others, a man may not marry until he has shown that he can support a family, which might not be until his 30s. But in all cultures, doing the right thing at the right time, compared to your friends, is reassuring. When nearly everyone your age goes through the same experience or enters a new role at the same time, adjusting to these transitions is relatively easy. Conversely, if you aren't doing these things and hardly anyone you know is doing them either, you will not feel out of step.

In modern societies today, social clocks are not telling time the way they once did. Most people will face unanticipated transitions—events that happen without warning, such as being fired from a job because of downsizing. And many people have to deal with nontransitions—events that they *expect* to happen that do not: for example, not getting married at the age they expected, not getting promoted, not being able to afford to retire, or not being able to have children (Schlossberg & Robinson, 1996). With this in mind, let's consider some of the major transitions of life.

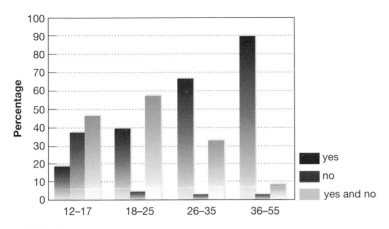

FIGURE 3.5
Are You an Adult Yet?
When people are asked, "Do you feel that you have reached adulthood?" the percentage that answers "yes" steadily increases over time. But as you can see, people between the ages of 18 and 25, emerging adults, are most likely to say "yes and no" (Arnett, 2000).

Emerging Adulthood In industrialized nations, major demographic changes have postponed the timing of career decisions, marriage or cohabitation, and parenthood until a person's late 20s on the average. Many young people between the ages of 18 and 25 (would that include anyone you know?) are in college and at least partly dependent financially on their parents. This phenomenon has created a phase of life that some call *emerging adulthood* (Arnett, 2000). When emerging adults are asked whether they feel they have reached adulthood, the majority answer: in some ways yes, in some ways no. (See Figure 3.5.)

In certain respects, emerging adults have moved beyond adolescence into maturity, becoming more emotionally controlled, more confident, and less angry and alienated (Roberts, Caspi, & Moffitt, 2001). But

they are also the group most likely to live unstable lives, feel unrooted, and take risks. Emerging adults move more often than people in other demographic groups do—back to their parents' homes and then out again, from one city to another, from living with roommates to living on their own. And their rates of risky behavior (such as binge drinking, having unprotected sex, and driving at high speeds or while drunk) are higher than those of any other age group, including adolescents.

Of course, not all young people in this age group are alike. Some groups within the larger society, such as Mormons, promote early marriage and parenthood. And young people who are poor, who have dropped out of school, who had a child at 16, or who have few opportunities for good jobs will not have the leisure to explore many options. But the overall shift in all industrialized nations toward a global economy, increased education, and delayed career and family decisions suggests that emerging adulthood is likely to grow in importance as a distinct phase of prolonged exploration and freedom.

The Middle Years For most women and men, the midlife years between 35 and 65 are the prime of life (MacArthur Foundation, 1999; Mroczek & Sprio, 2005). These years are typically a time of the greatest psychological well-being, good health, productivity, and community involvement. When crises occur, it is for reasons related not to aging but to specific life-changing events, such as illness or the loss of a job or spouse (Wethington, 2000).

But doesn't menopause make most midlife women depressed, irritable, and irrational?

Doonesbury

BY GARRY TRUDEAU

"You're As Old As You Feel"

Ask five people, about a decade apart in age, and one of whom is at least 70, how old they are and how old they feel. (You may include yourself.) What is the gap, if any, between their chronological age and their psychological age? Is the gap larger among the older individuals? If so, ask why they perceive an age gap between their actual years and how old they feel.

Menopause, which usually occurs between ages 45 and 55, is the cessation of menstruation after the ovaries stop producing estrogen and progesterone. Menopause does produce physical symptoms in many women, notably hot flashes, as the vascular system adjusts to the decrease in estrogen. But only about 10 percent of all women have unusually severe physical symptoms.

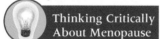 Thinking Critically About Menopause

The negative view of menopause as a syndrome that causes depression and other negative emotional reactions is based on women who have had an early menopause following a hysterectomy (removal of the uterus) or who have had a lifetime history of depression. But these women are not typical. According to many surveys of thousands of healthy, randomly chosen women in the general population, most women view menopause with relief (that they no longer have to worry about pregnancy or menstrual periods) or with no particular feelings at all. The vast majority have only a few physical symptoms (which can be annoying and bothersome but are temporary) and most do not become depressed; only 3 percent even report regret at having reached menopause (McKinlay, McKinlay, & Brambilla, 1987). In one recent study of 1,000 postmenopausal women, fewer than half reported physical symptoms and only 5 percent of those complained of mood symptoms (Ness, Aronow, & Beck, 2006).

Although women lose their fertility after menopause and men theoretically remain fertile throughout their lives, men have a biological clock too. Testosterone diminishes, although it never drops as sharply in men as estrogen does in women. The sperm count may gradually drop, and the sperm that remain are more susceptible to genetic mutations that can increase the risk of certain diseases in children conceived by older fathers (Wyrobek et al., 2006). For example, fathers over 50 have three times the risk of conceiving a child who develops schizophrenia as fathers under age 25 (Malaspina, 2001), and older fathers increase the probability that their child will be autistic (Reichenberg et al., 2006).

The physical changes of midlife do not by themselves predict how people will feel about aging or how they will respond to it (Schaie & Willis, 2002). How a culture views aging, as something natural and inevitable or a process to be fought and slowed down, is far more important to how people adjust.

Old Age

When does old age start? Not long ago you would have been considered old in your 60s. Today, the fastest-growing segment of the population in North America consists of people over the age of 85. There were 4 million Americans age 85 or older in 2000, and the Census Bureau projects that there may be as many as 31 million by 2050. Close to 1 million of them will be over the age of 100. How will these people do? *Gerontologists*, researchers who study aging and the old, have been providing some answers.

Various aspects of intelligence, memory, and other forms of mental functioning decline significantly with age. Older adults score lower on tests of reasoning, spatial ability, and complex problem solving than do younger adults. The ability to produce and spell familiar words declines, a change that often causes great frustration and annoyance (Burke & Shafto, 2004). It takes older people longer to remember names and retrieve dates and other information; in fact, the speed of cognitive processing in general slows down significantly. However, older people vary considerably, with some declining mentally and others remaining sharp (Salthouse, 2006).

Fortunately, not all cognitive abilities worsen with age. **Fluid intelligence** is the capacity for deductive reasoning and the ability to use new information to solve problems. It reflects an inherited predisposition, and it parallels other biological capacities in its growth and later decline (Bosworth & Schaie, 1999; Li et al., 2004). **Crystallized intelligence** consists of the knowledge and skills that are built up over a lifetime, the kind of intelligence that gives us the ability to do arithmetic, define words, or

menopause The cessation of menstruation and of the production of ova; it is usually a gradual process lasting up to several years.

fluid intelligence The capacity for deductive reasoning and the ability to use new information to solve problems; it is relatively independent of education and tends to decline in old age.

crystallized intelligence Cognitive skills and specific knowledge of information acquired over a lifetime; it is heavily dependent on education and tends to remain stable over the lifetime.

take political positions. It depends heavily on education and experience, and it tends to remain stable or even improve over the life span (see Figure 3.6). This is why physicians, lawyers, teachers, farmers, musicians, insurance agents, politicians, psychologists, and people in many other occupations can continue working well into old age.

Thinking Critically About "Inevitable" Declines in Old Age

Psychologists have made great strides in separating conditions once thought to be an inevitable part of old age from those that are preventable or treatable:

- Apparent senility in the elderly is often caused by malnutrition, prescription medications, harmful combinations of medications, and even over-the-counter drugs (such as sleeping pills and antihistamines), all of which can be hazardous to old people.

- Depression, passivity, and memory problems may result from the loss of meaningful activity, intellectual stimulation, goals to pursue, and control over events (Hess, 2005; Langer, 1983; Schaie & Zuo, 2001).

- Weakness, frailty, and even some diseases associated with old age are often caused by being inactive and sedentary (Booth & Neufer, 2005).

Many of the physical and mental losses of old age are genetically based, but many have to do with be-

The two images of old age: More and more old people are living healthy, active, mentally stimulating lives. But with increasing longevity, others are falling victim to degenerative diseases such as Alzheimer's.

havioral and psychological factors. A crucial protective factor is aerobic exercise and strength training, which maintain physical strength and flexibility, boost the brain's blood supply, promote the development of new cells, and can even suppress genetic predispositions for various infirmities (Booth & Neufer, 2005). The result is greatly improved cognitive functioning in

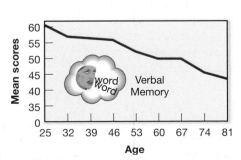

FIGURE 3.6
Changes in Mental Functioning over Time
As these graphs show, some intellectual abilities tend to dwindle with age, but numerical and verbal abilities remain relatively steady over the years.

skills such as planning, concentration, and scheduling (Colcombe & Kramer, 2004). Mental stimulation also seems to promote the growth of neural connections in the brain, even well into old age (Hultsch et al., 1999; Kleim et al., 1998). Even short-term training programs in memory, solving problems, and concentration for people between 65 and 94 produce significant cognitive gains. These improvements counteract the cognitive decline that would normally have occurred without the training (Ball et al., 2002).

Perhaps the best news is that as people get older, most become better able to regulate their negative feelings and emphasize the positive. The frequency of intense negative emotions is highest among people aged 18 to 34, then drops sharply to age 65. After 65, it levels off, rising only slightly among old people facing crises of illness and bereavement

(Charles & Carstensen, 2004; Charles, Reynolds, & Gatz, 2001). Apparently, many people do grow wiser, or at least more tranquil, with age.

Some researchers who study aging are therefore optimistic. In their view, people who have challenging occupations and interests, who remain active mentally and physically, and who adapt flexibly to change are likely to maintain their cognitive abilities. "Use it or lose it," they say. Other researchers, however, are less optimistic (Salthouse, 2006). "When you've lost it, you can't use it," they reply. They are worried about the growing numbers of people living into their 90s and 100s, when rates of cognitive impairment and dementia rise dramatically. The challenge for society is to make sure that the many people who will be living beyond 90 can keep using their brains instead of losing them.

QUICK quiz

You are never too old (or young) to answer this quiz.

1. The key psychological issue during adolescence, said Erikson, is a(n) _____ crisis.

2. What new phase of life development has been created because of demographic changes, and what years does it include?

3. Most women react to menopause by (a) feeling depressed, (b) regretting the loss of femininity, (c) going a little crazy, (d) feeling relieved or neutral.

4. Which of these statements about the decline of mental abilities in old age is *true*? (a) It can rarely be lessened with training programs; (b) crystallized intelligence inevitably declines sharply; (c) it is sometimes a result of medication or disease rather than aging; (d) it begins to accelerate once people reach age 65.

5. Suddenly, your 80-year-old grandmother has become confused and delusional. Before concluding that old age has made her senile, what other explanations should you rule out?

Answers:

1. identity 2. emerging adulthood, ages 18 to 25 3. d 4. c 5. You should rule out the possibility that she is taking medications, including nonprescription drugs.

WHAT'S *Ahead*

- Do terrible childhood experiences inevitably affect a person forever?
- What makes most children resilient in the face of adversity?

The Wellsprings of Resilience

Most people take it for granted that the path from childhood to adolescence to adulthood is a fairly straight one. We think of the lasting attitudes, habits, and values our parents taught us. We continue to have deep attachments to our families, even when we are fighting with them. And many people carry with them the scars of emotional wounds they suffered as children. Children who have been beaten, neglected, or constantly subjected to verbal or physical abuse by their parents are more likely than other children to have emotional problems, become delinquent and violent, commit crimes, drop out of school, develop mental disorders such as depression, and develop chronic stress-related illnesses (Emery & Laumann-Billings, 1998; Margolin & Gordis, 2004; Repetti, Taylor, & Seeman, 2002).

And yet, when research psychologists began to question the entrenched assumption that early trauma always has long-lasting effects and considered the evidence for alternative views, they got quite a different picture. Most children, they found, are remarkably resilient, eventually overcoming even the devastating effects of war, having abusive or alcoholic parents, or being sexually molested (Cohen, 1999; Kaufman & Zigler, 1987; McNally, 2003; Rathbun, DiVirgilio, & Waldfogel, 1958; Rind, Tromovitch, & Bauserman, 1998; West & Prinz, 1987). One researcher, whose team studied hundreds of vulnerable children from birth to age 32, was surprised by their results: "As we watched these children grow from babyhood to adulthood," she wrote, "we could not help but respect the self-righting tendencies within them that produced normal development under all but the most persistently adverse circumstances" (Werner, 1989).

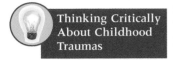

Thinking Critically About Childhood Traumas

Many of the children who outgrow early deprivation and trauma have easygoing temperaments or personality traits, such as self-efficacy and self-control, that help them roll with even severe punches. They have a secure attachment style, which helps them work through traumatic events in a way that heals their wounds and restores hope and emotional balance (Mikulincer, Shaver, & Horesh, 2006). If children lack these secure attachments with their own parents, they may be rescued by love and attention from their siblings, extended family, peers, or other caring adults. And some have experiences outside the family—in schools, places of worship, or other organizations—that give them a sense of competence, moral support, solace, religious faith, and self-esteem (Cowen et al., 1990; Garmezy, 1991; Masten, 2001).

Perhaps the most powerful reason for the resilience of so many children, and for the changes that adults make throughout life, is that we are all constantly interpreting our experiences. We can decide to repeat the mistakes our parents made or break free of them. We can decide to remain set in our ways or to strike out in new directions at age 20, 50, or 70. We can think about our setbacks and victories, our problems and our accomplishments, and decide for ourselves whether we want to remain prisoners of childhood . . . or to be liberated by the possibilities of adulthood.

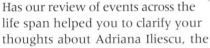

psychology in the news REVISITED

Has our review of events across the life span helped you to clarify your thoughts about Adriana Iliescu, the woman who gave birth at age 66? On the child's first birthday, her mother gave her a party and told the press, "I can't describe how I feel when I hug her, when I kiss her. It's a special kind of feeling. And [raising her] is not as tough as I had expected." But Eliza Maria was only a year old at the time. When she is an energetic 6-year-old and her mother is 72, will her mother be able to handle that? How will it be for Eliza Maria, at 16, to have a mother who is 82? What if her mother becomes ill? Iliescu is unmarried and says she does not have much of an extended family or many friends. She admits she has no plans for the child if she should become ill and unable to care for her.

The concept of the social clock can help us understand why so many people feel queasy about a woman getting pregnant so late in life: She is obviously off time! Yet, as we have also seen, the whole concept of natural stages is out of date. Increasingly, age is what we make of it; reaching a certain age has few if any inevitable consequences. Iliescu may seem unusual, but in fact millions of older people, required by unforeseen circumstances to rear their grandchildren, have risen to the challenge.

But some ethicists and social critics are concerned about the medical, social, and psychological costs of pregnancy and raising a child so late in life. They point out that for every successful pregnancy among older women, there are thousands of failures. They worry that stories about women like Iliescu raise women's expectations to unreasonable heights and create false hopes that technology can easily overcome any biological limitations. In fact, the older a woman is, the greater her chance of developing medical problems in pregnancy, such as gestational diabetes and high blood pressure. Moreover, we have seen that age brings a decline in some cognitive and physical abilities. So it seems legitimate to worry about whether elderly parents,

Adriana Iliescu with Eliza Maria on the baby's first birthday.

of either sex, will have the mental resources and energy to guide their children through the many hurdles of childhood and adolescence.

Adriana Iliescu's decision to have a baby at her age is extremely rare. Fewer than 300 American women over age 50 give birth each year. The birthrate for women in their 40s, however, is much higher (Roan, 2002). Having a child in one's 40s used to seem as weird and unnatural as Iliescu's decision to have a baby at 66, but now that it is more common, with celebrities having babies in their late 40s, it doesn't seem as off time as it once did. Will giving birth after 50 come to be seen the same way?

In the next decades, as the world changes in countless unpredictable ways, the territory of adulthood will continue to expand, providing new frontiers as well as fewer signposts and road maps to guide us. Increasingly, age will be what we make of it.

►TAKING ►PSYCHOLOGY ►WITH ►YOU

Bringing Up Baby

Every year or so another best-selling book arrives to tell parents they've been doing it all wrong. Years ago the public was warned that the most crucial thing was bonding: The mother had to bond with her baby right away, right after birth, or dire things would happen to the baby's development. Then it turned out that although immediate bonding is certainly nice, adopted babies will bond to parents just fine even if they have been adopted several days, months, or years after birth (Eyer, 1992).

Throughout the twentieth century and still today, countless books have advised parents to treat their children in very specific, if contradictory, ways: Pick them up, don't pick them up; respond when they cry, don't respond when they cry; let them sleep with you, never let them sleep with you; be highly sensitive to their every need so they will securely attach to you, don't overreact to their every mood or complaint or you will spoil them (Hulbert, 2003).

No need to panic. As we have seen in this chapter, babies and young children thrive under a wide variety of child-rearing methods. They bring their own temperaments to the matter, too: Most respond readily to induction; others require stricter discipline. And as children grow up, they are subject to the influences of their peers and generation and to particular experiences that shape their interests and aspirations.

Well, then, how should you treat your children? Should you be strict or lenient, powerful or permissive? Should you require your child to stop having tantrums, to clean up his or her room, to be polite? Should you say, "Oh, nothing I do will matter, anyway?" or "Children need to express themselves in any way they please?" Even granted the limitations of what parents can do, child development research does suggest certain overall guidelines to help parents teach children to be confident, considerate, and helpful:

● **Set high expectations that are appropriate to the child's age and temperament, and teach the child how to meet them.** Some parents make few demands on their children, either unintentionally or because they believe a parent should not impose standards. Others make many demands, such as requiring children to be polite, help with chores, control their anger, be thoughtful of others, and do well in school. The children of parents who make few demands tend to be aggressive, impulsive, and immature. The children of parents who have high expectations tend to be helpful and above average in competence and self-confidence (Damon, 1995). But the demands must be appropriate for the child's age. You can't expect 2-year-olds to dress themselves, and before you can expect children to get up on time, they have to know how to use an alarm clock.

● **Explain, explain, explain.** Induction—telling a child why you have applied a rule—teaches a child to be responsible. Punitive methods ("Do it or I'll spank you") may result in compliance, but the child will tend to disobey as soon as you are out of sight. Explanations also teach children how to reason and understand; they reward curiosity and open-mindedness. While setting standards for your children, you can also allow them to express disagreements and feelings. This does not mean you have to argue with a 4-year-old about the merits of table manners or permit antisocial and destructive behavior. Once you have explained a rule, you need to enforce it consistently.

● **Encourage empathy.** Call the child's attention to the effects of his or her actions on others, appeal to the child's sense of fair play and desire to be good, and teach the child to take another person's point of view. As we saw, even very young children are capable of empathy. Vague orders, such as "Don't fight," are less effective than showing the child how fighting disrupts and hurts others. For boys especially, aggression and empathy are strongly and negatively related: the higher the one, the lower the other (Eisenberg et al., 2002).

● **Notice, approve of, and reward good behavior.** Many parents punish the behavior they dislike, a form of attention that often is rewarding to the child. It is much more effective to praise the behavior you do want, which teaches the child how to behave.

Even with the best skills and intentions, you cannot control everything that happens to your child or your child's basic temperamental dispositions. "The idea that we can make our children turn out any way we want is an illusion. Give it up," advises Judith Harris (1998). But, she adds, parents do have the power to make their children's lives miserable or secure. And they deeply affect the quality of the relationship they will have with their child throughout life: one filled with conflict and resentment, or one that is close and loving.

SUMMARY

From Conception Through the First Year

• *Developmental psychologists* study people's growth and change over the life span. They study *socialization*, the process by which children learn the rules and behavior society expects of them, and *maturation*, the unfolding of genetically influenced behavior and characteristics.

• Prenatal development consists of the *germinal*, *embryonic*, and *fetal* stages. Harmful influences that can adversely affect the fetus's development include German measles, toxic chemicals (such as lead and mercury), some sexually transmitted diseases, cigarettes, alcohol (which can cause *fetal alcohol syndrome* and cognitive deficits), illegal drugs, and even over-the-counter medications.

• Babies are born with *motor reflexes* and a number of perceptual abilities. But many aspects of infants' maturation depend on cultural customs that govern how their parents hold, touch, feed, and talk to them.

• Babies' innate need for *contact comfort* gives rise to emotional attachment to their caregivers, and by the age of 6 to 8 months, infants begin to feel *separation anxiety*. Studies of the *Strange Situation* have distinguished *secure* from *insecure* attachment; insecurity can take one of two forms, *avoidant* or *anxious–ambivalent* attachment.

• Styles of attachment are relatively unaffected by the normal range of child-rearing practices and also by whether or not babies spend time in day care. Insecure attachment is promoted by parents' rejection, mistreatment, or abandonment of their infants; by a mother's postpartum depression, which can affect her ability to care for the baby; by the child's own fearful, insecure temperament; or by stressful family situations.

Cognitive Development

• Infants are responsive to the pitch, intensity, and sound of language, which may be why adults in many cultures speak to babies in *parentese*, using higher-pitched words and exaggerated intonation. At 4 to 6 months of age, babies begin to recognize the sounds of their own language. They go through a babbling phase from age 6 months to 1 year, and at about 1 year, they start saying single words and using symbolic gestures. At age 2, children speak in two- or three-word *telegraphic* sentences that convey a variety of messages.

• Language allows us to express and comprehend an infinite number of novel utterances. Noam Chomsky argued that the ability to take the *surface structure* of any utterance and apply rules of *syntax* to infer its underlying *deep structure* must depend on an innate faculty for language, a *language acquisition device*. Many findings support this view: Children from different cultures go through similar stages of language development; children's language is full of *overregularizations* that reflect grammatical rules; adults do not consistently correct their children's syntax; children who have never been exposed to adult language often invent their own; and infants who are only a few months old appear to distinguish different sentence structures.

• Nonetheless, parental practices, such as repeating correct sentences verbatim and recasting incorrect ones, aid in language acquisition. Cases of children deprived of exposure to language suggest that a *critical period* exists for acquiring a first language.

• Jean Piaget argued that cognitive development depends on an interaction between maturation and a child's experiences in the world. Children's thinking changes and adapts through *assimilation* and *accommodation*. Piaget proposed four stages of cognitive development: *sensorimotor* (birth to age 2), during which the child learns *object permanence*; *preoperational* (ages 2 to 7), during which language and symbolic thought develop, although the child is *egocentric* in reasoning; *concrete operations* (ages 7 to 12), during which the child comes to understand mental *operations*, *conservation*, reversibility, and cause and effect; and *formal operations* (age 12 to adulthood), during which abstract reasoning develops.

• Researchers have modified and expanded Piaget's work. The changes from one stage to another occur in continuous, overlapping waves rather than distinct stages. Child are less egocentric than Piaget thought. Children know more and know it earlier than he believed, whereas some adults understand less. Children's cognitive development is spurred by the growing expansion of working memory and speed of information processing. And cognitive development is affected by cultural practices and experiences.

Learning to Be Good

• Lawrence Kohlberg proposed that as children mature cognitively, they go through three levels of moral reasoning. But people can reason morally without behaving morally. Developmental psychologists study how children learn to internalize standards of right and wrong and behave accordingly. This ability depends on the emergence of conscience and the moral emotions of guilt, shame, and empathy, and on the ability of children to learn to regulate their impulses, wishes, and feelings.

• Parental methods of discipline have different consequences for a child's moral behavior. *Power assertion* is associated with children who are aggressive and fail to internalize moral standards. However, the effects of physical punishment, such as spanking, depend on the family context and on the severity and frequency of the punishment. *Induction* is associated with children who develop empathy and internalized moral standards and who can resist temptation. In general, *authoritative* parents, who use induction and set limits, have better results with their children than do *authoritarian* or permissive parents.

• As discussed in "Close-up on Research," the ability of very young children to regulate and control their impulses and feelings is associated with the subsequent internalization of moral standards and conscience. This ability is enhanced by mothers who use induction as a primary form of discipline. It also may reflect a relatively stable personality trait, because it tends to emerge very early in life and to be consistent over time and across situations.

Gender Development

• Gender development includes the emerging awareness of *gender identity*, the cognitive understanding that a person is biologically male or female regardless of what he or she does or wears, and *gender typing*, the process by which boys and girls learn what it means to be masculine or feminine.

• Some individuals are born with *intersex* physical conditions and may consider themselves to be *transgender*. Some live comfortably with the physical and psychological attributes of both sexes; others are *transsexual*, feeling that they are male in a female body or vice versa.

• Biological psychologists account for gender differences in behavior in terms of genes and prenatal hormones, observing that universally, young boys and girls prefer different toys and games and playing with other children of their own sex. Cognitive psychologists study how children develop *gender schemas* of "male" and "female" categories and qualities, which in turn shape their gender-typed behavior. Gender schemas tend to be inflexible at first. They become more flexible as the child cognitively matures and assimilates new information, if the child lives in a culture that promotes flexible gender schemas. Learning theorists study the direct and subtle reinforcers and social messages that foster gender typing.

• Gender development changes over the life span, depending on people's experiences with work and family life and on larger events in society.

Adolescence

• *Adolescence* begins with the physical changes of *puberty*. In girls, puberty is signaled by *menarche* and the development of breasts; in boys, it begins with the onset of nocturnal emissions and the development of the testes, scrotum, and penis. Boys and girls who enter puberty early tend to have a more difficult adjustment than do those who enter puberty later than average.

• The adolescent brain undergoes significant developmental changes, too. New connections among brain cells are added and others are pruned away, especially in the prefrontal cortex and the limbic system.

• Most adolescents do not go through extreme emotional turmoil, anger, or rebellion. However, conflict with parents, mood swings and depression, and reckless behavior do increase in adolescence. The peer group becomes especially important. Boys tend to externalize their emotional problems in acts of aggression and other antisocial behavior; girls tend to internalize their problems by becoming depressed or developing eating disorders.

Adulthood

• Erik Erikson proposed that life consists of eight stages, each with a unique psychological challenge, or crisis, that must be resolved, such as an *identity crisis* in adolescence. Erikson identified many of the essential concerns of adulthood and showed that development is a lifelong process. However, psychological issues or crises are not confined to particular chronological periods or stages.

• Adults often evaluate their development according to a *social clock* that determines whether they are on time or off time for a particular event. When most people in an age group go through the same event at about the same time, transitions are easier than when people feel "out of step."

• In industrialized nations, major demographic changes have postponed the timing of career decisions, marriage or commitment to a partner, and parenthood until a person's late 20s on the average. The result is a new life phase between the ages of 18 and 25, *emerging adulthood*. For many, this phase is qualitatively different from both adolescence and adulthood.

• The middle years are generally not a time of turmoil or crisis but the prime of most people's lives. In women, *menopause* begins in the late 40s or early 50s. Many women have temporary physical symptoms, but most do not regret the end of fertility or become depressed and irritable. In middle-aged men, hormone production slows down but fertility continues, although mutations in sperm increase the risk of birth defects in offspring of older fathers.

• *Gerontologists* have revised our ideas about old age, now that people are living longer and healthier lives. The speed of cognitive processing slows down, and *fluid intelligence* parallels other biological

capacities in its eventual decline. *Crystallized intelligence*, in contrast, depends heavily on culture, education, and experience, and it tends to remain stable or even improve over the life span.

• Many supposedly inevitable results of aging, such as senility, depression, and physical frailty, are often avoidable. They may result from disease, medications, or poor nutrition, and also from a lack of stimulation, control of one's environment, and exercise. Exercise and mental stimulation promote the growth of synapses in the human brain, even well into old age, although some mental losses are inevitable.

The Wellsprings of Resilience

• Children who experience violence or neglect are at risk of having emotional and physical problems later in life. But the majority of children are resilient and are able to overcome early traumatic experiences. Psychologists now study not only the sad consequences of neglect, poverty, and violence but also the origins of resilience under adversity, which they find more common than was once believed.

KEY TERMS

Developmental psychologists study people's growth and change over the life span. They begin with socialization, the process by which children learn the attitudes and behaviors expected of them by their society.

Conception Through the First Year

Stages of Prenatal Development

- Germinal
- Embryonic
- Fetal

Prenatal Influences

- Some diseases, including German measles and sexually transmitted diseases
- Cigarettes, drugs, alcohol (which can cause fetal alcohol syndrome)
- Exposure to X-rays or toxic chemicals

The Infant's World

- Babies are born with motor reflexes, including:
  — rooting
  — sucking
  — grasping
  — Babinski
- Newborns also have some innate perceptual abilities.
- Cultural influences affect maturational milestones, such as an infant's sleeping through the night.

Attachment

Attachment begins with **contact comfort**, or touching and cuddling between infant and parent.

At about 8 months of age, babies develop separation anxiety if their primary caregiver temporarily leaves them.

Styles of attachment are unaffected by normal child-rearing practices and whether a child goes to daycare. Insecure attachment is promoted by extreme deprivation in infancy; abusive or erratic parenting; stressful family changes; and the child's own fearful temperament.

Babies may be securely or insecurely attached. Insecure babies may, in turn, be avoidant or anxious-ambivalent.

Cognitive Development

Language Development

- First months: crying and cooing
- 4 to 6 months: recognition of own names and other words and sounds of their language
- 6 months to 1 year: babbling phase
- Around 1 year: single words and symbolic gestures
- Around 2 years: 2-3 word **telegraphic** sentences

Noam Chomsky argued that the human brain contains a **language acquisition device** to enable young children to acquire language readily. Children learn to take the surface structure of a sentence and apply grammatical rules (syntax) to infer an underlying deep structure, which contains the sentence's meaning.

Findings supporting Chomsky's view:
1. Children in different cultures go through similar stages of linguistic development.
2. Children combine words in ways that adults never would.
3. Adults do not consistently correct their children's syntax, yet children learn language correctly.
4. Children who are not exposed to adult language may invent a language of their own.
5. Infants as young as 7 months can derive simple linguistic rules from a string of sounds.

Thinking

Jean Piaget argued that cognitive development depends on an interaction between maturation and a child's experience, and adapts through **assimilation** and **accommodation.**

Piaget's four stages of cognitive development:
1. Sensorimotor (birth to age 2): child learns **object permanence**
2. Preoperational (ages 2 to 7): development of language and symbolic thought
3. Concrete operations (ages 7 to 12): understanding of **conservation**, identity, and serial ordering
4. Formal operations (age 12 to adulthood): development of abstract reasoning

Findings challenge many of Piaget's views:
1. Cognitive abilities develop in continuous, overlapping waves, rather than in discrete stages.
2. Preschoolers are not as **egocentric** as Piaget thought.
3. Children understand far more than Piaget gave them credit for.
4. Cognitive development is spurred by the growing speed and efficiency of information processing.
5. Cognitive development depends on the child's education and culture.

Learning to be Good

Moral Behavior

Parental methods of discipline often have different consequences for children's moral behavior.
- **Power assertion** is associated with children who are aggressive and fail to internalize moral standards.
- **Induction** is associated with children who develop empathy and internalized moral standards and who can resist tempation.
- Authoritative parents, who use induction and set limits, tend to have better results with their children than do authoritarian or permissive parents.
- Young children's ability to regulate their impulses is associated with later internalized moral standards and conscience.

Gender Development

Gender identity: The cognitive understanding that a person is biologically male or female.
Gender typing: The process by which boys and girls learn what it means to be masculine or feminine.
Intersex conditions, in which children are born with ambiguous genitals, or genitals that conflict with their chromosomes; as adults, they may consider themselves **transgender**.

- **Biological psychologists** account for gender differences in behavior in terms of genes and prenatal hormones.
- **Cognitive psychologists** study how children develop gender schemas of "male" and "female" qualities, which shape their gender-typed behavior.
- **Learning theorists** study the direct and subtle reinforcers and social messages that foster gender typing.
- People's gender schemas, attitudes, and behavior evolve throughout their lives, with new experiences and societal changes.

Adolescence

Biological Changes

- Adolescence begins with the physical changes of **puberty**, including menarche in females and genital maturation in males.
- The brain goes through significant development as new connections among brain cells are added and others are pruned away.

Psychological Issues

- The stereotype of "adolescent turmoil"—rebellion and misery—is inaccurate for most teens. However, conflicts with parents, mood swings, and rule-breaking behavior do increase.
- The peer group becomes especially important.

The Transitions of LIfe

- Adults often evaluate their own development according to a **social clock**, comparing their own life events with others at the same stage.
- "Emerging adulthood" describes a life phase that occurs between 18 and 25, as many young people postpone career decisions, marriage, and parenthood.
- The middle years are the prime of most people's lives. **Menopause** begins in women during their late 40s or early 50s, while men experience a reduction of hormone production.

Adulthood

Erik Erikson's Stages

- Trust versus mistrust
- Autonomy (independence) versus shame and doubt
- Initiative versus guilt
- Competence versus inferiority
- Identity versus role confusion
- Intimacy versus isolation
- Generativity versus stagnation
- Ego integrity versus despair

Old Age

- Research in the field of **gerontology** shows that **fluid intelligence** parallels other biological capacities in its eventual decline, while **crystallized intelligence** tends to remain stable or even improve over the life span.
- Senility, depression, and physical frailty in old age are often the result of disease, medication, poor nutrition, and lack of stimulation and control of one's environment. Exercise and mental stimulation promote the growth of synapses in the human brain, even well into old age.

Schiavo's Parents Appeal to High Court

PINELLAS PARK, FL, MARCH 24, 2005. The ongoing struggle over the fate of severely brain-damaged Terri Schiavo, 41, headed to the Supreme Court Wednesday as her parents, Mary and Bob Schindler, made a last-ditch attempt to keep their daughter alive. For the past seven years, the Schindlers have waged a legal battle with their daughter's husband, Michael, who is her legal guardian and who says that Terri told him she would not want to be kept alive artificially. Her feeding tube was removed by court order last Friday.

According to court-appointed doctors, Schiavo has been in a "persistent vegetative state" for 15 years, ever since a potassium imbalance possibly brought on by an eating disorder caused her to

Terri Schiavo before her brain damage.

have a heart attack, which temporarily cut off oxygen to her brain. She can breathe on her own but cannot eat or drink. Unlike patients who are in a coma, people in a vegetative state are awake. They open their eyes, have some reflexes, and can even make noises and facial expressions. But they cannot think, feel emotions, or understand anything going on around them, and after a certain amount of time has passed, they have no chance of recovery. They are not technically brain dead, because the lower parts of the brain, which control functions such as breathing and heartbeat, are still functioning. But they have no conscious awareness of themselves or others. Schiavo's parents, however, insist that their daughter can respond to them with a smile, that she is in a "minimally conscious state" rather than a persistent vegetative state, and that she could get better with therapy.

The Schiavo case has had extraordinary political and legal ramifications. Schiavo has become a symbol for both the right-to-life movement and the right-to-die movement. On March 21, Congress called a special session and passed emergency legislation permitting the case to be heard in federal court, and President Bush interrupted a vacation to sign the bill, although polls showed that most Americans opposed the intervention. Yesterday, the U.S. Eleventh Circuit Court of Appeals in Atlanta rejected the Schindlers' request to have the feeding tub reinserted. The Florida Senate, on a 21–18 vote, also defeated an emergency measure designed to keep Schiavo alive. Meanwhile, Florida Governor Jeb Bush and the state's social services agency have petitioned the state court to allow them to take protective custody of Schiavo.

Schiavo in a videotape made by her parents many years after her brain damage.

CHAPTER

4

Neurons, Hormones, and the Brain

The tragic case of Terri Schiavo riveted the world in 2005. It raised not only ethical and legal questions but also some difficult medical and psychological ones. How can we know whether a person really is in a persistent vegetative state and has become incapable of all higher mental function? Why, in the video released by her family, did Terri appear to respond to her mother by turning her head and smiling? Could new technology provide a better understanding of her condition?

Millions of people suffer from disorders affecting the brain and nervous system, such as Lou Gehrig's disease, Alzheimer's, and Parkinson's. Some of these diseases harm the brain but leave the rest of the body alone. Others weaken or deform the body but leave the parts of the brain involved in thought and creativity alone. The brain's effects on our minds and bodies remind us that the 3-pound organ inside our skulls provides the bedrock for everything we

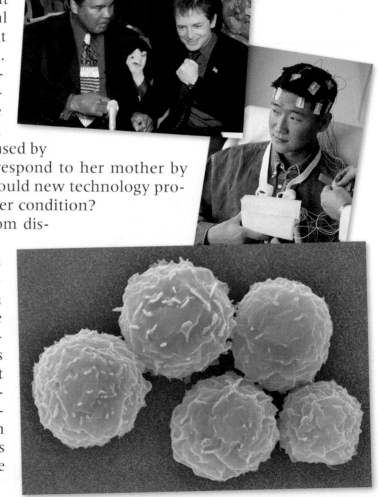

central nervous system (CNS) The portion of the nervous system consisting of the brain and spinal cord.

do and think. *Neuropsychologists*, along with neuroscientists from other disciplines, study the brain and the rest of the nervous system in hopes of gaining a better understanding of consciousness, perception, memory, emotion, stress, mental disorders, and even self-identity.

At this very moment, your own brain, assisted by other parts of your nervous system, is busily taking in these words. Whether you are excited, curious, or bored, your brain is registering some sort of emotional reaction. As you continue reading, your brain will (we hope) store away much of the information in this chapter. Later on, your brain may enable you to smell a flower, climb the stairs, greet a friend, solve a personal problem, or chuckle at a joke. But the brain's most startling accomplishment is its knowledge that it is doing all these things. This self-awareness makes brain research different from the study of anything else in the universe. Scientists must use the cells, biochemistry, and circuitry of their own brains to understand the cells, biochemistry, and circuitry of brains in general.

William Shakespeare called the brain "the soul's frail dwelling house." Actually, this miraculous organ is more like the main room in a house filled with many alcoves and passageways—the "house" being the nervous system as a whole. Before we can understand the windows, walls, and furniture of this house, we need to become acquainted with the overall floor plan. It's a pretty technical plan, which means that you will be learning many new terms, but you will need to know these terms in

The study of this mysterious 3-pound organ raises many challenging questions. Why can a small glitch in the brain's circuits be devastating to some people, whereas others can function with major damage? How do experiences in life alter our brains? And where in this collection of cells and circuits are the mind and our sense of self to be found?

order to understand how biological psychologists go about studying psychological topics.

As you read, keep the case of Terri Schiavo in mind. In this book, we cannot address the moral, political, and religious motives that triggered strong passions and angry public rhetoric over Terri's fate. But the information that you will learn in this chapter may help you think about what it means to be conscious and mentally aware and may help explain why there was so much controversy about Terri's mental state.

WHAT'S *Ahead*

- Why do you automatically pull your hand away from something hot "without thinking"?

- In an emergency, which part of your nervous system whirls into action?

The Nervous System: A Basic Blueprint

The function of a nervous system is to gather and process information, produce responses to stimuli, and coordinate the workings of different cells. Even the lowly jellyfish and the humble earthworm have the beginnings of such a system. In very simple organisms that do little more than move, eat, and eliminate wastes, the "system" may be no more than one or two nerve cells. In human beings, who do such complex things as dance, cook, and take psychology courses, the nervous system contains billions of cells. Scientists divide this intricate network into two main parts: the central nervous system and the peripheral (outlying) nervous system (see Figure 4.1).

The Central Nervous System

The **central nervous system (CNS)** receives, processes, interprets, and stores incoming sensory information—information about tastes, sounds, smells, color, pressure on the skin, the state of internal organs, and so forth. It also sends out messages destined for muscles, glands, and internal organs. The CNS is usually conceptualized as having two components: the brain, which we will con-

FIGURE 4.1

The Central and Peripheral Nervous Systems

The central nervous system includes the brain and the spinal cord. The peripheral nervous system consists of 43 pairs of nerves that transmit information to and from the central nervous system. Twelve pairs of cranial nerves in the head enter the brain directly; 31 pairs of spinal nerves enter the spinal cord at the spaces between the vertebrae.

sider in detail later, and the **spinal cord**. The spinal cord is actually an extension of the brain. It runs from the base of the brain down the center of the back, protected by a column of bones (the spinal column), and it acts as a bridge between the brain and the parts of the body below the neck.

The spinal cord produces some behaviors on its own without any help from the brain. These **spinal reflexes** are automatic, requiring no conscious effort. For example, if you accidentally touch a hot iron, you will immediately pull your hand away, even before your brain has had a chance to register what has happened. Nerve impulses bring a message to the spinal cord (hot!), and the spinal cord immediately sends out a command via other nerve impulses, telling muscles in your arm to contract and to pull your hand away from the iron. (Reflexes above the neck, such as sneezing and blinking, involve the lower part of the brain rather than the spinal cord.)

The neural circuits underlying many spinal reflexes are linked to other neural pathways that run up and down the spinal cord, to and from the brain. Because of these connections, reflexes can sometimes be influenced by thoughts and emotions. An example is erection in men, a spinal reflex that can be inhibited by anxiety or distracting thoughts and initiated by erotic thoughts. Some reflexes can be brought under conscious control. If you concentrate, you may be able to keep your knee from jerking when it is tapped, as it normally would. Similarly, most men can learn to voluntarily delay ejaculation, another spinal reflex. (Yes, they can.)

The Peripheral Nervous System

The **peripheral nervous system (PNS)** handles the central nervous system's input and output. It contains all portions of the nervous system outside the brain and spinal cord, right down to nerves in the tips of the fingers and toes. If your brain could not collect information about the world by means of a peripheral nervous system, it would be like a radio without a receiver. In the peripheral nervous system, *sensory nerves* carry messages from special receptors in the skin, muscles, and other internal and external sense organs to the spinal cord, which sends them along to the brain. These nerves put us in touch with both the outside world and the activities of our own bodies. *Motor nerves* carry orders from the central nervous system to muscles, glands, and internal organs. They enable us to move, and they cause glands to contract and to secrete substances, including chemical messengers called *hormones*.

Scientists further divide the peripheral nervous system into two parts: the somatic (bodily) nervous system and the autonomic (self-governing) nervous system. The **somatic nervous system**, sometimes called the *skeletal nervous system*, consists of nerves that are connected to sensory receptors and to the skeletal muscles that permit voluntary action. When you feel a bug on your arm, or when you turn off a light or write your name, your somatic system is active. The **autonomic nervous system** regulates the functioning of blood vessels,

spinal cord A collection of neurons and supportive tissue running from the base of the brain down the center of the back, protected by a column of bones (the spinal column).

spinal reflexes Automatic behaviors produced by the spinal cord without brain involvement.

peripheral nervous system (PNS) All portions of the nervous system outside the brain and spinal cord; it includes sensory and motor nerves.

somatic nervous system The subdivision of the peripheral nervous system that connects to sensory receptors and to skeletal muscles; sometimes called the *skeletal nervous system*.

autonomic nervous system The subdivision of the peripheral nervous system that regulates the internal organs and glands.

sympathetic nervous system The subdivision of the autonomic nervous system that mobilizes bodily resources and increases the output of energy during emotion and stress.

parasympathetic nervous system The subdivision of the autonomic nervous system that operates during relaxed states and that conserves energy.

glands, and internal (visceral) organs such as the bladder, stomach, and heart. When you see someone you have a crush on and your heart pounds, your hands get sweaty, and your cheeks feel hot, you can blame your autonomic nervous system.

The autonomic nervous system works more or less automatically, without your conscious control. Some people, however, have learned to heighten or suppress their autonomic responses intentionally, using a technique called *biofeedback* (Miller, 1978). Monitoring devices track the bodily process in question and produce a signal, such as a light or a tone, whenever the desired autonomic response occurs— for example, a change in blood pressure, blood flow, or heart rate. The method for producing the response may be prearranged or left up to the participant. Some clinicians are using biofeedback to treat high blood pressure, asthma, and migraine headaches. It is not clear, though, whether the autonomic responses are being controlled directly or by changing voluntary responses such as breathing, which in turn affects the autonomic nervous system.

The autonomic nervous system is itself divided into two parts: the **sympathetic nervous system** and the **parasympathetic nervous system**. These two parts work together, but in opposing ways, to adjust the body to changing circumstances (see Figure 4.2). The sympathetic system acts like the accelerator of a car, mobilizing the body for action and an output of energy. It makes you blush, sweat, and breathe more deeply, and it pushes up your heart rate and blood pressure. As we will see in Chapter 13, when you are in a situation that requires you to fight, flee, or cope, the sympathetic nervous system whirls into action. The parasympathetic system is more like a brake: It does not stop the body, of course, but it does tend to slow things down or keep them running smoothly. It enables the body to conserve and store energy. If you have to jump out of the way of a speeding motorcyclist, sympathetic nerves increase your heart rate. Afterward, parasympathetic nerves slow it down again and keep its rhythm regular.

Parasympathetic Division

Constricts pupils
Stimulates tear glands
Strongly stimulates salivation
Slows heartbeat
Constricts bronchial tubes in lungs
Activates digestion
Inhibits glucose release by liver

Sympathetic Division

Dilates pupils
Weakly stimulates salivation
Stimulates sweat glands
Accelerates heartbeat
Dilates bronchial tubes in lungs
Inhibits digestion
Increases epinephrine,
   norepinephrine secretion
   by adrenal glands
Relaxes bladder wall
Decreases urine volume
Stimulates glucose release by liver
Stimulates ejaculation in males

Contracts bladder wall
Stimulates genital erection (both
   sexes) and vaginal lubrication
   (females)

FIGURE 4.2
The Autonomic Nervous System
In general, the sympathetic division of the autonomic nervous system prepares the body to expend energy and the parasympathetic division restores and conserves energy. Sympathetic nerve fibers exit from areas of the spinal cord shown in red in this illustration; parasympathetic fibers exit from the base of the brain and from spinal cord areas shown in green.

QUICK quiz

Pause now to test your memory by mentally filling in the missing parts of the nervous system "house." Then see whether you can briefly describe what each part of the system does.

Answers:

1. central: processes, interprets, and stores information and issues orders to muscles, glands, and organs   2. peripheral: transmits information to and from the CNS   3. spinal cord: serves as a bridge between the brain and the peripheral nervous system, produces reflexes   4. somatic: controls the skeletal muscles   5. sympathetic: mobilizes the body for action, energy output   6. parasympathetic: conserves energy, maintains the body in a quiet state

WHAT'S *Ahead*

- Which cells are the nervous system's "communication specialists," and how do they "talk" to each other?

- Are you born with all the brain cells you'll ever have?

- How do learning and experience alter the brain's circuits?

- What happens when levels of brain chemicals called neurotransmitters are too low or too high?

- Which brain chemicals mimic the effects of morphine by dulling pain and promoting pleasure?

- Do men and women have different "sex hormones"?

Communication in the Nervous System

The blueprint we just described provides only a general idea of the nervous system's structure. Now let's turn to the details.

The nervous system is made up in part of **neurons**, or *nerve cells*. Neurons are the brain's communication specialists, transmitting information to, from, and within the central nervous system. They are held in place by **glia**. or *glial cells* (from the Greek for "glue"), which make up 90 percent of the brain's cells.

neuron A cell that conducts electrochemical signals; the basic unit of the nervous system; also called a *nerve cell*.

glia [GLY-uh or GLEE-uh] Cells that support, nurture, and insulate neurons, remove debris when neurons die, and modify neuronal functioning.

Spinal cord (motor neuron) Thalamus Cerebellum Cortex

The Structure of the Neuron

As you can see in Figure 4.4, a neuron has three main parts: *dendrites*, a *cell body*, and an *axon*. The **dendrites** look like the branches of a tree; indeed, the word *dendrite* means "little tree" in Greek. Dendrites act like antennas, receiving messages from as many as 10,000 other nerve cells and transmitting these messages toward the cell body. They also do some preliminary processing of those messages. The **cell body**, which is shaped roughly like a sphere or a pyramid, contains the biochemical machinery for keeping the neuron alive. As we will see later, it also determines whether the neuron should "fire"— transmit a message to other neurons—depending on inputs from other neurons. The **axon** (from the Greek for "axle") transmits messages away from the cell body to other neurons or to muscle or gland cells. Axons commonly divide at the end into branches called *axon terminals*. In adult human beings, axons vary from only 4 thousandths of an inch to a few feet in length. Dendrites and axons give each neuron a double role: As one researcher put it, a neuron is first a catcher, then a batter (Gazzaniga, 1988).

Many axons, especially the larger ones, are insulated by a surrounding layer of fatty material

For a long time, people thought that glial cells merely provided scaffolding for the more important and exciting neurons. We now know, however, that glial cells have many vital functions: They provide neurons with nutrients and insulate them, protect the brain from toxic agents, and remove cellular debris when neurons die. Glial cells also communicate chemically with each other and with neurons, and without them neurons probably could not function effectively. One type of glial cell appears to give neurons the go-ahead to start "talking" to each other (Ullian, Christopherson, & Barres, 2004). And over time, glia help determine which neural connections get stronger or weaker, suggesting that they play a vital role in learning and memory (Fields, 2004).

It's neurons, though, that are considered the building blocks of the nervous system, though in structure they are more like snowflakes than blocks, exquisitely delicate and differing from one another greatly in size and shape (see Figure 4.3). In the giraffe, a neuron that runs from the spinal cord down the animal's hind leg may be 9 feet long! In the human brain, neurons are microscopic. No one is sure how many neurons the human brain contains, but a typical estimate is 100 billion, about the same number as there are stars in our galaxy, and some estimates go much higher.

dendrites A neuron's branches that receive information from other neurons and transmit it toward the cell body.

cell body The part of the neuron that keeps it alive and determines whether it will fire.

axon A neuron's extending fiber that conducts impulses away from the cell body and transmits them to other neurons or to muscle or gland cells.

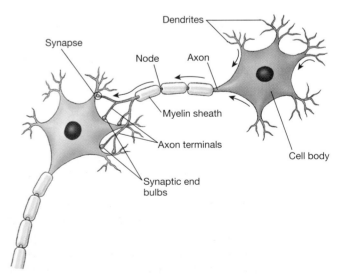

FIGURE 4.4
The Structure of a Neuron
Incoming neural impulses are received by the dendrites of a neuron and are transmitted to the cell body. Outgoing signals pass along the axon to terminal branches.

called the **myelin sheath**, which is made up of glial cells. Constrictions in this covering, called *nodes*, divide it into segments, which make it look a little like a string of link sausages (see Figure 4.4 again). One purpose of the myelin sheath is to prevent signals in adjacent cells from interfering with each other. Another, as we will see shortly, is to speed up the conduction of neural impulses. In individuals with multiple sclerosis, loss of myelin causes erratic nerve signals, leading to loss of sensation, weakness or paralysis, lack of coordination, or vision problems.

In the peripheral nervous system, the fibers of individual neurons (axons and sometimes dendrites) are collected together in bundles called **nerves**, rather like the lines in a telephone cable. The human body has 43 pairs of peripheral nerves; one nerve from each pair is on the left side of the body, and the other is on the right. Most of these nerves enter or leave the spinal cord, but the 12 pairs that are in the head, the *cranial nerves*, connect directly to the brain. In Chapter 6, we will discuss cranial nerves that are involved in the senses of smell, hearing, and vision.

Neurons in the News

Until recently, neuroscientists assumed that if neurons in the central nervous system were injured or damaged, they could never regenerate (grow back). But then the conventional wisdom got turned upside down. Animal studies showed that severed axons in the spinal cord *can* regrow when treated with certain nervous system chemicals (Schnell & Schwab, 1990). Researchers are now working to fine-tune this process and are exploring other approaches as well. Many are hopeful that regenerated axons will eventually enable people with spinal cord injuries to use their limbs again (Kraft, 2005).

Scientists have also had to rethink another entrenched assumption, which was accepted for most of the twentieth century despite some contradictory evidence: that mammals produce no new CNS cells after infancy. In the early 1990s, Canadian neuroscientists, working with mice, immersed immature cells from the animals' brains in a growth-promoting protein and showed that these cells could give birth to new neurons. Even more astonishingly, the new neurons then continued to divide and multiply (Reynolds & Weiss, 1992). One of the researchers, Samuel Weiss, said that this result "challenged everything I had read; everything I had learned when I was a student" (quoted in Barinaga, 1992).

Since then, scientists have discovered that the human brain and other body organs also contain such cells, which are now referred to as **stem cells.** These, too, give rise to new neurons when treated in the laboratory. Stem cells involved in learning and memory seem to divide and mature throughout adulthood—a discovery that holds tremendous promise for human well-being (Eriksson et al., 1998; Gage et al., 1998; Gould et al., 1998; Gould, Reeves, et al., 1999). We may even have some control over that process: In animal studies, physical exercise and mental activity promote the production and survival of these new cells (Gould, Beylin, et al., 1999; Kempermann, Brandon, & Gage, 1998; van Praag, Kempermann, & Gage, 1999). On the other hand, stress can inhibit the production of new cells, and nicotine can kill them (Berger, Gage, & Vijayaraghavan, 1998; Gould et al., 1998).

Stem-cell research is one of the hottest areas in biology and neuroscience and also one of the most hotly debated. In the United States, federal funding for stem-cell research has faced strong resistance by antiabortion activists. The reason: Scientists prefer working with cells from aborted fetuses and from embryos that are a few days old, which consist of just a few cells. (Fertility clinics store many such embryos because several "test tube" fertilizations are created for every patient who hopes to become pregnant; eventually, the extra embryos are destroyed.) Embryonic stem (ES) cells are especially useful because they can differentiate into any type of cell, from

In an area associated with learning and memory, new cells develop from immature stem cells, and physical and mental stimulation promotes their production and survival. These mice, which have toys to play with, tunnels to explore, wheels to run on, and other mice to share their cage with, will grow more cells than mice living alone in standard cages.

myelin sheath A fatty insulation that may surround the axon of a neuron.

nerve A bundle of nerve fibers (axons and sometimes dendrites) in the peripheral nervous system.

stem cells Immature cells that renew themselves and have the potential to develop into mature cells; given encouraging environments, stem cells from early embryos can develop into any cell type.

Tiny stem cells like these (magnified 1,200 times in this photo) have provoked both excitement and controversy.

neurons to kidney cells, whereas those from adults are far more limited and are also harder to keep alive.

Scientists are now working to develop methods for extracting ES cells while avoiding destruction of the embryo (Chung et al., 2005). Some scientists have also reported success in coaxing stem cells from adult organs, such as bone marrow and skin, to transform themselves into brain cells (e.g., Brazelton et al., 2000; Toma et al., 2001). A team in Germany, working with mice, recently reported success in turning cells that produce sperm into cells with many characteristics of ES cells (Guan et al., 2006). However, other attempts at finding alternatives to ES cells have been unsuccessful, and we still do not know whether adult stem cells can develop reliably into more than one kind of tissue in human beings.

In 2001, an executive order by President George W. Bush required American researchers who rely on federal funding (which is most of them) to get their cells from only a few, already established sources; new cell lines cannot be developed. Unfortunately, for technical reasons the existing cells can never be transplanted into human beings. Scientists and patient-advocacy groups, however, have been pressing for the ban to be lifted because transplanted stem cells may eventually help people recover from diseases of the brain (such as Alzheimer's) and from damage to the spinal cord and other parts of the body. Scientists have recently had some success in animals. For example, in one study, mice with recent spinal cord injuries regained much of their ability to walk normally after being injected with stem cells derived from human fetal brain tissue. Microscopic analysis showed that most of the cells had turned into either neurons or a particular type of glial cell (Cummings et al., 2005).

Each year brings more incredible findings about neurons, findings that only a short time ago would have seemed like science fiction. A long road lies ahead, and many daunting technical hurdles remain to be overcome before these findings yield practical benefits for human patients. Eventually, however, new treatments for medical and psychological disorders may be among the most stunning contributions of this line of basic biological research.

synapse The site where transmission of a nerve impulse from one nerve cell to another occurs; it includes the axon terminal, the synaptic cleft, and receptor sites in the membrane of the receiving cell.

How Neurons Communicate

Neurons do not directly touch each other, end to end. Instead, they are separated by a tiny space called the *synaptic cleft*, where the axon terminal of one neuron nearly touches a dendrite or the cell body of another. The entire site—the axon terminal, the cleft, and the covering membrane of the receiving dendrite or cell body—is called a **synapse**. Because a neuron's axon may have hundreds or even thousands of terminals, a single neuron may have synaptic connections with a great many others. As a result, the number of communication links in the nervous system runs into the trillions or perhaps even the quadrillions.

When we are born, most of these synapses have not yet formed, but during infancy, new synapses proliferate at a great rate (see Figure 4.5). Axons and dendrites continue to grow, and tiny projections on dendrites, called *spines*, increase in size and in number, producing more complex connections among the brain's nerve cells. Just as new learning and stimulating environments promote the production of new neurons, they also produce the greatest increases in synaptic complexity (Diamond, 1993; Greenough & Anderson, 1991; Greenough & Black, 1992; Rosenzweig, 1984). During childhood, unused synaptic connections are also "pruned away" as cells or their branches die and are not replaced, leaving behind a more efficient neural network. Such pruning may be as important as synaptic growth (Kolb, Gibb, & Robinson, 2003). But these changes—pruning and increases in synaptic density—are not confined to the early years; they continue all through life.

At birth   3 months   6 months   15 months

FIGURE 4.5
Getting Connected
Neurons in a newborn's brain are widely spaced, but they immediately begin to form new connections. These drawings show the marked increase in the number of connections from birth to age 15 months.

CLOSE-UP on Research

The Plastic Brain

The brain's remarkable **plasticity**, its flexibility in adapting to new experiences, may help explain why people with brain damage sometimes have amazing recoveries—why individuals who cannot recall simple words after a stroke may be speaking normally within a matter of months, and why patients who cannot move an arm after a head injury may regain full use of it after physical therapy. Their brains have rewired themselves to adapt to the damage (Liepert et al., 2000).

It has long been documented that some blind people are superior to sighted people at identifying things by touch and at tasks requiring an acute sense of hearing. One research team with an interest in brain plasticity **raised an intriguing question**: When people who have been blind from birth or early childhood try to determine where a sound is coming from, what happens in the part of the brain that in sighted people processes visual information? The researchers reasoned that brain regions normally devoted primarily to vision might "switch gears" in some blind individuals and begin to process input from other senses instead. To **gather evidence** for this hypothesis, they used brain-scan technology called positron-emission tomography (PET, to be described later in this chapter) to examine the brains of people who were localizing sounds heard through speakers. Some of the participants were sighted; others had been blind from early in life. When the participants heard sounds through both ears, activity in the occipital lobe, an area associated with vision, decreased in the sighted persons but not in the blind ones. When one ear was plugged, blind participants with superior skill at localizing sound showed activation in two areas of the occipital cortex; neither sighted people nor blind people without superior ability showed such activation. What's more, the degree of activation in these regions was correlated with the blind people's accuracy on the task, as you can see on the graph on this page (Gougoux et al., 2005). The brains of those with the best performance had apparently adapted to blindness by recruiting visual areas to take part in activities involving hearing—a dramatic example of plasticity.

Building on this research, the researchers **asked a different question**: What would hap-

The purple circles to the left of the vertical dotted line represent blind participants with low error rates in a sound-localization task; those to the right represent blind participants with high error rates. The graph shows that error rates for blind participants are correlated with changes in cerebral blood flow (CBF) in a particular visual area of the brain. The greater the changes (indicating more activity in this region), the greater a person's accuracy.

pen if sighted persons were blindfolded, so that they, too, were "blind"? In a series of studies, sighted people wore blindfolds for five days. Before they donned the blindfolds, brain scans showed that the visual areas in their brains were quiet during tasks requiring hearing or touch (for example, touching Braille letters). By day 5, however, these areas were lighting up during the tasks. Then, after the blindfolds were removed, the visual centers once again quieted down (Pascual-Leone et al., 2005).

The researchers have **considered different interpretations** of brain plasticity in blind individuals. One is that the brains of blind people have formed new connections in the visual centers to handle sound or touch. But in the blindfold studies, the changes in activity in the visual areas of sighted people's brains happened extremely quickly, probably too quickly for new connections to be established. The researchers therefore suggest that the visual areas of the brain possess the "computational machinery" necessary for processing nonvisual information, machinery that remains dormant until circumstances require its activation (Amedi et al., 2005). These explanations are not mutually exclusive: In sighted people, existing neural machinery may be able to take over new tasks in a pinch; in those who have been blind for most of their lives, new connections may have time to form, permitting more lasting structural changes in the brain's wiring.

plasticity The brain's ability to change and adapt in response to experience, for example, by reorganizing or growing new neural connections.

Whatever the explanation, this research teaches us that the brain is a dynamic organ: Its circuits are continually being modified in response to information, challenges, and changes in the environment. As scientists come to understand this process better, they may be able to apply their knowledge by designing improved rehabilitation programs for people with sensory impairments, developmental disabilities, and brain injuries.

FIGURE 4.6
Neurotransmitter Crossing a Synapse
Neurotransmitter molecules are released into the synaptic cleft between two neurons from vesicles (chambers) in the transmitting neuron's axon terminal. The molecules then bind to receptor sites on the receiving neuron. As a result, the electrical state of the receiving neuron changes and the neuron becomes either more likely to fire an impulse or less so, depending on the type of transmitter substance.

Neurons speak to one another, or in some cases to muscles or glands, in an electrical and chemical language. When a nerve cell is stimulated, a brief change in electrical voltage, called an **action potential**, occurs. (The details of this process are beyond the scope of this book.) The action potential produces an electrical current, or impulse. If an axon is unmyelinated, the action potential at each point in the axon gives rise to a new action potential at the next point; thus, the impulse travels down the axon somewhat as fire travels along the fuse of a firecracker. But in myelinated axons, the process is a little different. For certain reasons having to do with the physics of the process, conduction of a neural impulse beneath the sheath is impossible. Instead, the action potential "hops" from one node to the next. (More precisely, the action potential regenerates at each node.) This arrangement allows the impulse to travel faster than it could if the action potential had to be regenerated at every point along the axon. Nerve impulses travel more slowly in babies than in older children and adults because when babies are born, the myelin sheaths on their axons are not yet fully developed.

When a neural impulse reaches the axon terminal's buttonlike tip, it must get its message across the synaptic cleft to another cell. At this point, *synaptic vesicles*, tiny sacs in the tip of the axon terminal, open and release a few thousand molecules of a chemical substance called a **neurotransmitter**. Like sailors carrying a message from one island to another, these molecules then disperse across the synaptic cleft (see Figure 4.6).

When they reach the other side, the neurotransmitter molecules bind briefly with *receptor sites*, special molecules in the membrane of the receiving neuron's dendrites (or sometimes cell body), fitting these sites much as a key fits a lock. Changes occur in the receiving neuron's membrane, and the ultimate effect is either *excitatory* (a voltage shift in a positive direction) or *inhibitory* (a voltage shift in a negative direction), depending on which receptor sites have been activated. If the effect is excitatory, the probability that the receiving neuron will fire increases; if it is inhibitory, the probability decreases. Inhibition in the nervous system is extremely important. Without it, we could not sleep or coordinate our movements. Excitation of the nervous system would be overwhelming, producing convulsions.

What any given neuron does at any given moment depends on the net effect of all the messages being received from other neurons. Only when the cell's voltage reaches a certain threshold will it fire. Thousands of messages, both excitatory and inhibitory, may be coming into the cell. Essentially, the neuron must average them. The message that reaches a final destination depends on the rate at which individual neurons are firing, how many are firing, what types of neurons are firing, and where the neurons are located. It does not depend on how strongly the neurons are firing, however, because a neuron always either fires or it doesn't. Like the turning on of a light switch, the firing of a neuron is an *all-or-none* event.

Chemical Messengers in the Nervous System

The nervous system "house" would remain forever dark and lifeless without chemical couriers such as the neurotransmitters. Let's look more closely now at these substances and at two other types of chemical messengers: endorphins and hormones.

Neurotransmitters: Versatile Couriers

As we have seen, neurotransmitters make it possible for one neuron to excite or inhibit another. Neurotransmitters exist not only in the brain but also in the spinal cord, the peripheral nerves, and certain glands. Through their effects on specific nerve circuits, these substances can affect mood, memory, and well-being. The nature of the effect depends on the type of neurotransmitter, its location, and its level. Hundreds of substances are known or suspected to be neurotransmitters, and the number keeps growing. Here are a few of the better-understood neurotransmitters and some of their known or suspected effects:

- **Serotonin** affects neurons involved in sleep, appetite, sensory perception, temperature regulation, pain suppression, and mood.

- **Dopamine** affects neurons involved in voluntary movement, learning, memory, emotion, and, possibly, response to novelty.

- **Acetylcholine** affects neurons involved in muscle action, cognitive functioning, memory, and emotion.

- **Norepinephrine** affects neurons involved in increased heart rate and the slowing of intestinal activity during stress, and neurons involved in learning, memory, dreaming, waking from sleep, and emotion.

- **GABA (gamma-aminobutyric acid)** functions as the major inhibitory neurotransmitter in the brain.

- **Glutamate** functions as the major excitatory neurotransmitter in the brain; it is released by about 90 percent of the brain's neurons.

Harmful effects can occur when neurotransmitter levels are too high or too low. Low levels of serotonin have been associated with severe depression and other mental disorders. Abnormal GABA levels have been implicated in sleep and eating disorders and in convulsive disorders, including epilepsy. People with Alzheimer's disease lose brain cells responsible for producing acetylcholine, and this deficit helps account for their devastating memory problems. A loss of dopamine is responsible for the tremors and rigidity of Parkinson's disease. In multiple sclerosis, immune cells overproduce glutamate, which damages or kills the glial cells that normally make myelin.

We want to warn you, however, that pinning down the relationship between neurotransmitter abnormalities and behavioral abnormalities is extremely tricky. Each neurotransmitter plays multiple roles, and the functions of different substances often overlap. Further, it is always possible that something about a disorder leads to abnormal neurotransmitter levels instead of the other way around. Although drugs that boost or decrease levels of particular neurotransmitters are sometimes effective in treating disorders, this fact does not necessarily mean that abnormal neurotransmitter levels are *causing* the disorders. After all, aspirin can relieve a headache, but headaches are not caused by a lack of aspirin!

Many of us regularly ingest things that affect our own neurotransmitters. For example, most recreational drugs produce their effects by blocking or enhancing the actions of neurotransmitters. So do some herbal remedies. St. John's wort, which many people take for depression, prevents the cells that release serotonin from reabsorbing excess molecules that have remained in the synaptic cleft; as a result, serotonin levels rise. Many people do not realize that such remedies, because they affect the nervous system's biochemistry,

action potential A brief change in electrical voltage that occurs when a neuron is stimulated; it serves to produce an electrical impulse.

neurotransmitter A chemical substance that is released by a transmitting neuron at the synapse and that alters the activity of a receiving neuron.

Muhammad Ali and Michael J. Fox both have Parkinson's disease, which involves a loss of dopamine-producing cells. They have used their fame to draw public attention to the disorder.

endorphins [en-DOR-fins] Chemical substances in the nervous system that are similar in structure and action to opiates; they are involved in pain reduction, pleasure, and memory and are known technically as *endogenous opioid peptides.*

hormones Chemical substances, secreted by organs called glands, that affect the functioning of other organs.

endocrine glands Internal organs that produce hormones and release them into the bloodstream.

melatonin A hormone, secreted by the pineal gland, that is involved in the regulation of daily biological rhythms.

oxytocin A hormone, secreted by the pituitary gland, that stimulates uterine contractions during childbirth, facilitates the ejection of milk during nursing, and seems to promote, in both sexes, attachment and trust in relationships.

adrenal hormones Hormones that are produced by the adrenal glands and that are involved in emotion and stress.

can interact with other medications and can be harmful in high doses. Even ordinary foods can influence the availability of neurotransmitters in the brain, as we discuss in "Taking Psychology with You."

Endorphins: The Brain's Natural Opiates

Another intriguing group of chemical messengers is known collectively as *endogenous opioid peptides*, or more popularly as **endorphins**. Endorphins have effects similar to those of opiate drugs; that is, they reduce pain and promote pleasure. They are also thought to play a role in appetite, sexual activity, blood pressure, mood, learning, and memory. Some endorphins function as neurotransmitters, but most act primarily by altering the effects of neurotransmitters—for example, by limiting or prolonging those effects.

Endorphins were identified in the early 1970s. Candace Pert and Solomon Snyder (1973) were doing research on morphine, a pain-relieving and mood-elevating opiate derived from heroin, which is made from poppies. They found that morphine works by binding to receptor sites in the brain. This seemed odd. As Snyder later recalled, "We doubted that animals had evolved opiate receptors just to deal with certain properties of the poppy plant" (quoted in Radetsky, 1991). Pert and Snyder reasoned that if opiate receptors exist, then the body must produce its own internally generated, or *endogenous*, morphinelike substances, which they named "endorphins." Soon they and other researchers confirmed this hypothesis.

Endorphin levels seem to shoot up when an animal or a person is afraid or under stress. This is no accident; by making pain bearable in such situations, endorphins give a species an evolutionary advantage. When an organism is threatened, it needs to do something fast. Pain, however, can interfere with action: A mouse that pauses to lick a wounded paw may become a cat's dinner; a soldier who is overcome by an injury may never get off the

"PSST—ENDORPHINS. AND THEY'RE PERFECTLY LEGAL."

battlefield. But, of course, the body's built-in system of counteracting pain is only partly successful, especially when painful stimulation is prolonged.

In Chapter 14, we will see that a link also exists between endorphins and the pleasures of social contact. Research with animals suggests that in infancy, contact with the mother stimulates the flow of endorphins, which strengthens the infant's bond with her. Some researchers now think that this "endorphin rush" also occurs in the early stages of passionate love between adults, accounting for the feeling of euphoria that "falling" for someone creates (Diamond, 2004).

Hormones: Long-Distance Messengers

Hormones, which make up the third class of chemical messengers, are produced primarily in **endocrine glands**. They are released directly into the bloodstream, which carries them to organs and cells that may be far from their point of origin. Hormones have dozens of jobs, from promoting bodily growth to aiding digestion to regulating metabolism.

Neurotransmitters and hormones are not always chemically distinct; the two classifications are like clubs that admit some of the same members. A particular chemical, such as norepinephrine, may belong to more than one classification, depending on where it is located and what function it is performing. Nature has been efficient, giving some substances more than one task to perform.

The following hormones, among others, are of particular interest to psychologists:

1 **Melatonin**, which is secreted by the *pineal gland* deep within the brain, helps to regulate daily biological rhythms and promotes sleep, as we will discuss further in Chapter 5.

2 **Oxytocin**, which is secreted by another small gland within the brain, the *pituitary gland*, enhances uterine contractions during childbirth and facilitates the ejection of milk during nursing. Psychologists are interested in this hormone because recent research suggests that it also contributes to relationships in both sexes by promoting attachment and trust (see Chapter 14).

3 **Adrenal hormones**, which are produced by the *adrenal glands* (organs that are perched right above the kidneys), are involved in emotion and stress (see Chapter 13). These hormones also rise in response to nonemotional conditions, such as heat, cold, pain, injury, burns, and physical exercise, and in response to some drugs, such as caffeine and nicotine. The outer part of each adrenal gland produces *cortisol*, which increases blood-sugar levels and boosts energy. The inner part produces *epinephrine* (popularly known as adrenaline) and *norepinephrine*. When adrenal hormones are released in your body, activated by the sympathetic nervous system, they increase your arousal level and prepare you for action.

Adrenal hormones also enhance memory. If you give people a drug that prevents their adrenal glands from producing these hormones, they will remember less about emotional stories than a control group will (Cahill et al., 1994). Conversely, if you give epinephrine to animals right after learning, their memories will improve (McGaugh, 1990). The link between emotional arousal and memory makes evolutionary sense: Arousal tells the brain that an event or piece of information is important enough to encode and store for future use. Very high levels of adrenal hormones, however, sometimes impair memory for learned tasks; a moderate level may be optimal. To remember material for a test, therefore, you should probably aim for an arousal level somewhere between "hyper" and "laid back."

4 **Sex hormones**, which are secreted by tissue in the *gonads* (testes in men, ovaries in women) and also by the adrenal glands, include three main types, all occurring in both sexes but in differing amounts and proportions in males and females after the onset of puberty. *Androgens* (the most important of which is *testosterone*) are masculinizing hormones

produced mainly in the testes but also in the ovaries and the adrenal glands. Androgens set in motion the physical changes males experience at puberty—for example, a deepened voice and facial and chest hair—and cause pubic and underarm hair to develop in both sexes. Testosterone also influences sexual arousal in both sexes. *Estrogens* are feminizing hormones that bring on physical changes in females at puberty, such as breast development and the onset of menstruation, and that influence the course of the menstrual cycle. *Progesterone* contributes to the growth and maintenance of the uterine lining in preparation for a fertilized egg, among other functions. Estrogens and progesterone are produced mainly in the ovaries but are also produced in the testes and the adrenal glands.

Researchers are now studying the possible involvement of sex hormones in behavior not directly related to sex and reproduction. For example, some researchers believe that the body's natural estrogen may contribute to improved learning and memory by promoting the formation of synapses in certain areas of the brain (Maki & Resnick, 2000; Sherwin, 1998a; Wickelgren, 1997). But the most common belief about the nonsexual effects of sex hormones—that fluctuating levels of estrogen and progesterone make most women "emotional" before menstruation—has not been borne out by research, as we will see in Chapter 5.

sex hormones
Hormones that regulate the development and functioning of reproductive organs and that stimulate the development of male and female sexual characteristics; they include androgens, estrogens, and progesterone.

QUICK *quiz*

Get your glutamate going by taking this quiz.

A. Which word in parentheses better fits each of the following definitions?

1. Basic building blocks of the nervous system (*nerves, neurons*)
2. Cell parts that receive nerve impulses (*axons, dendrites*)
3. Site of communication between neurons (*synapse, myelin sheath*)
4. Opiatelike substance in the brain (*dopamine, endorphin*)
5. Chemicals that make it possible for neurons to communicate (*neurotransmitters, hormones*)
6. Hormone closely associated with emotional excitement (*epinephrine, estrogen*)

B. *True or false:* To remember the material in this chapter well, you should be as relaxed as possible while studying.

C. Imagine that you are depressed, and you hear about a medication for depression that affects the levels of several neurotransmitters thought to be involved in the disorder. Based on what you have learned, what questions would you want to ask before deciding whether to try the treatment?

Answers:

A. 1. neurons 2. dendrites 3. synapse 4. endorphin 5. neurotransmitters 6. epinephrine B. false (Can you say why?) C. You might want to ask, among other things, about side effects (each neurotransmitter has several functions, all of which might be affected by the treatment); about evidence that the treatment works; about whether there is any reason to believe that your own neurotransmitter levels are abnormal; and about whether there could be other reasons for your depression.

WHAT'S *Ahead*

- Why are patterns of electrical activity in the brain called "brain waves"?

- What scanning techniques reveal changes in brain activity while people listen to music or solve math problems?

- Is there a "gum-chewing center" in the brain?

Mapping the Brain

electroencephalogram (EEG) A recording of neural activity detected by electrodes.

transcranial magnetic stimulation (TMS) A method of stimulating brain cells, using a powerful magnetic field produced by a wire coil placed on a person's head; it can be used by researchers to temporarily inactivate neural circuits and is also being used therapeutically.

We come now to the main room of the nervous system "house": the brain. A disembodied brain stored in a formaldehyde-filled container is unexciting—a putty-colored, wrinkled glob of tissue that looks a little like an oversized walnut. It takes an act of imagination to envision this modest-looking organ writing *Hamlet*, discovering radium, or inventing the paper clip.

In a living person, of course, the brain is encased in a thick protective vault of bone. How, then, can scientists study it? One approach is to study patients who have had a part of the brain damaged or removed because of disease or injury. Another, the *lesion method*, involves damaging or removing sections of brain in animals and then observing the effects.

Electrical and Magnetic Detection

The brain can also be probed with devices called *electrodes*. Some electrodes are coin-shaped and are simply pasted or taped onto the scalp. They detect the electrical activity of millions of neurons in particular regions of the brain and are widely used in research and medical diagnosis. The electrodes are connected by wires to a machine that translates the electrical energy from the brain into wavy lines on a moving piece of paper or a screen. That is why electrical patterns in the brain are known as "brain waves." Different wave patterns are associated with sleep, relaxation, and mental concentration (see Chapter 5).

A brain-wave recording is called an **electroencephalogram (EEG)**. A standard EEG is useful but not very precise because it reflects the activities of many cells at once. "Listening" to the brain with an EEG machine is like standing outside a sports stadium: You know when something is happening, but you can't be sure what it is or who is doing it. Fortunately, computer technology can be combined with EEG technology to get a clearer picture of brain activity patterns associated with specific events and mental processes; the computer suppresses all the background "noise,"

leaving only the pattern of electrical responses to the event being studied.

For even more precise information, researchers use *needle electrodes*, very thin wires or hollow glass tubes that can be inserted into the brain, either directly in an exposed brain or through tiny holes in the skull. Only the skull and the membranes covering the brain need to be anesthetized; the brain itself, which processes all sensation and feeling, paradoxically feels nothing when touched. Therefore, a human patient or an animal can be awake and not feel pain during the procedure. Needle electrodes can be used both to record electrical activity from the brain and to stimulate the brain with weak electrical currents. Stimulating a given area often results in a specific sensation or movement. Microelectrodes are so fine that they can be inserted into single cells.

A more recently devised method of stimulating the brain, **transcranial magnetic stimulation (TMS)**, delivers a large current through a wire coil placed on a person's head. The current produces a magnetic field about 40,000 times greater than the earth's natural magnetic field (Travis, 2000). This procedure causes neurons under the coil to fire. It can be used to produce motor responses (say, a twitch in the thumb or a knee jerk) and can also be used by researchers to temporarily inactivate an area and observe the effects on behavior—functioning, in effect, as a "virtual" (and temporary) lesion method. The drawback is that when neurons fire, they cause many other neurons to become active too, so it is often hard to tell which neurons are critical for a particular task. Still, TMS has produced some important findings—for example, that a brain area involved in processing visual patterns is also active when a person merely imagines the stimulus (Kosslyn et al.,

Electrodes are used to produce an overall picture of electrical activity in different areas of the brain.

This microelectrode is being used to record the electrical impulses generated by a single cell in the brain of a monkey.

FIGURE 4.7
PET Scans of Metabolic Activity in the Brain
The PET scanner on the left will detect biochemical activity in specific brain areas. In the scans on the right, arrows and the color red indicate areas of highest activity and violet indicates areas of lowest activity as a person does different things.

1999). TMS has also been used to treat depression, as we will see in Chapter 12.

Scanning the Brain Since the mid-1970s, even more amazing doors to the brain have opened. The **PET scan (positron-emission tomography)** goes beyond anatomy to record biochemical changes in the brain as they are happening. One type of PET scan takes advantage of the fact that nerve cells convert glucose, the body's main fuel, into energy. A researcher can inject a patient with a glucoselike substance that contains a harmless radioactive element. This substance accumulates in brain areas that are particularly active and are consuming glucose rapidly. The substance emits radiation, which in turn is detected by a scanning device, and the result is a computer-processed picture of biochemical activity on a display screen, with different colors indicating different activity levels. Other kinds of PET scans measure blood flow or oxygen consumption, which also reflects brain activity.

PET scans, which were originally designed to diagnose abnormalities, have produced evidence that certain brain areas in people with emotional disorders are either unusually quiet or unusually active. But PET technology can also show which parts of the brain are active during ordinary activities and emotions. It lets researchers see which areas are busiest when a person hears a song, recalls a sad memory, works on a math problem, shifts attention from one task to another, or sees his or her sweetheart enter the room. The PET scans in Figure 4.7 show what an average healthy brain looks like when a person is doing different tasks.

Another technique, **MRI (magnetic resonance imaging)**, allows the exploration of "inner space" without injecting chemicals. Powerful magnetic fields and radio frequencies are used to produce vibrations in the nuclei of atoms making up body organs, and the vibrations are then picked up as signals by special receivers. A computer analyzes the signals, taking into account their strength and duration, and converts them into a high-contrast picture of the organ (see Figure 4.8). An ultrafast version of MRI, called *functional MRI*, can capture brain changes many times a second as a person performs a task, such as reading a sentence or solving a puzzle.

PET scan (positron-emission tomography) A method for analyzing biochemical activity in the brain, using injections of a glucoselike substance containing a radioactive element.

MRI (magnetic resonance imaging) A method for studying body and brain tissue, using magnetic fields and special radio receivers.

FIGURE 4.8
MRI of a Child's Brain
This MRI shows a child's brain—and the bottle he was drinking from while the image was obtained.

Still other scanning methods are becoming available with each passing year. Researchers are using brain scans to correlate activity in specific brain areas with everything from racial attitudes to moral reasoning to spiritual meditation. Researchers in an applied field called "neuromarketing" are even using them to study which parts of the brain are activated while people watch TV commercials or political ads. A word of caution, though: These images can convey oversimplified and sometimes misleading impressions. For example, by manipulating the color scales used in PET scans, researchers can make small contrasts look dramatic and larger ones look insignificant. An individual's brain can even be made to appear completely different depending on the colors used (Dumit, 2004).

Moreover, brain scans alone do not tell us precisely what is happening inside a person's head, either mentally or physiologically. They tell us *where* things happen but not *how* they happen—for example, how different brain circuits connect to produce behavior. Enthusiasm for new technology has produced a mountain of findings, but it has also resulted in some unwarranted conclusions about "brain centers" or "critical circuits" for this or that behavior. One scientist (cited in Wheeler, 1998) drew this analogy: A researcher scans the brains of gum-chewing volunteers, finds out which parts of their brains are active, and concludes that he or she has found the brain's "gum-chewing center"!

Descriptive studies using brain scans, then, are just a first step in understanding brain processes. Nonetheless, they are an exciting first step. We will be reporting many findings from PET scan and MRI research throughout this book. The brain can no longer hide from researchers behind the fortress of the skull. It is now possible to get a clear visual image of our most enigmatic organ without so much as lifting a scalpel.

localization of function Specialization of particular brain areas for particular functions.

brain stem The part of the brain at the top of the spinal cord, consisting of the medulla and the pons.

pons A structure in the brain stem involved in, among other things, sleeping, waking, and dreaming.

medulla [muh-DUL-uh] A structure in the brain stem responsible for certain automatic functions, such as breathing and heart rate.

WHAT'S *Ahead*

- Which brain part acts as a "traffic officer" for incoming sensations?

- Which brain part is the "gateway to memory"—and what cognitive catastrophe occurs when it is damaged?

- Why is it a good thing that the outer covering of the human brain is so wrinkled?

- How did a bizarre nineteenth-century accident illuminate the role of the frontal lobes?

A Tour Through the Brain

Most modern brain theories assume that different brain parts perform different (though overlapping) tasks. This concept, known as **localization of function**, goes back at least to Joseph Gall (1758–1828), the Austrian anatomist who thought that personality traits were reflected in the development of specific areas of the brain (see Chapter 1). Gall's theory of phrenology was completely wrongheaded (so to speak), but his general notion of specialization in the brain had merit.

To learn about what the various brain structures do, let's take an imaginary stroll through the brain. Pretend, now, that you have shrunk to a microscopic size and that you are wending your way through the "soul's frail dwelling house," starting at the lower part, just above the spine. Figure 4.9 shows the major structures we will encounter along the tour; you may want to refer to it as we proceed. Keep in mind, though, that in any activity—feeling an emotion, having a thought, performing a task—many different structures are involved. Our description, therefore, is a simplification.

The Brain Stem

We begin at the base of the skull with the **brain stem**, which looks like a stalk rising out of the spinal cord. Pathways to and from upper areas of the brain pass through its two main structures: the medulla and the pons. The **pons** is involved in (among other things) sleeping, waking, and dreaming. The **medulla** is responsible for bodily functions that do not have to be consciously willed, such as breathing and heart rate. Hanging has long been used as a method of execution

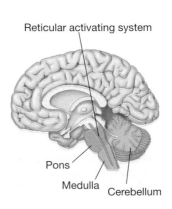

Reticular activating system

Pons

Medulla   Cerebellum

because when it breaks the neck, nervous pathways from the medulla are severed, stopping respiration.

Extending upward from the core of the brain stem is the **reticular activating system (RAS)**. This dense network of neurons, which extends above the brain stem into the center of the brain and has connections with higher areas, screens incoming information and arouses the higher centers when something happens that demands their attention. Without the RAS, we could not be alert or perhaps even conscious.

The Cerebellum

Standing atop the brain stem and looking toward the back part of the brain, we see a structure about the size of a small fist. It is the **cerebellum**, or "lesser brain," which contributes to a sense of balance and coordinates the muscles so that movement is smooth and precise. If your cerebellum were damaged, you would probably become exceedingly clumsy and uncoordinated. You might have trouble using a pencil, threading a needle, or even walking. In addition, this structure is involved in remembering certain simple skills and acquired reflexes (Daum & Schugens, 1996; Krupa, Thompson, & Thompson, 1993). Evidence has also accumulated that the cerebellum, which was once considered just a motor center, is not as "lesser" as its name implies: It appears to play a part in such complex cognitive tasks as analyzing sensory information, solving problems, and understanding words (Fiez, 1996; Gao et al., 1996; Müller, Courchesne, & Allen, 1998).

The Thalamus

Deep in the brain's interior, we can see the **thalamus**, the busy traffic officer of the brain. As sensory messages come into the brain, the thalamus directs them to higher centers. For example, the sight of a sunset sends signals that the

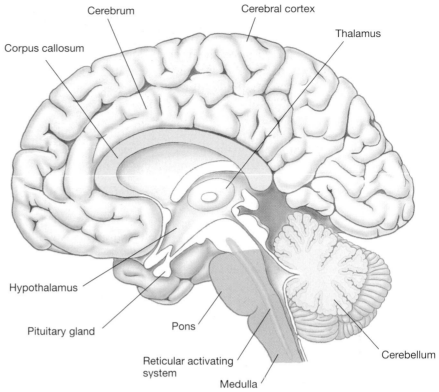

Cerebrum
Cerebral cortex
Thalamus
Corpus callosum
Hypothalamus
Pituitary gland
Pons
Reticular activating system
Medulla
Cerebellum

FIGURE 4.9
The Human Brain
This cross section depicts the brain as if it were split in half. The view is of the inside surface of the right half and shows the structures described in the text.

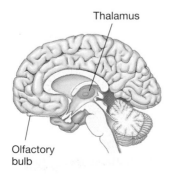

Thalamus
Olfactory bulb

thalamus directs to a vision area, and the sound of an oboe sends signals that the thalamus sends on to an auditory area. The only sense that completely bypasses the thalamus is the sense of smell, which has its own private switching station, the *olfactory bulb*. The olfactory bulb lies near areas involved in emotion. Perhaps that is why particular odors—the smell of fresh laundry, gardenias, a steak sizzling on the grill—often rekindle memories of important personal experiences.

The Hypothalamus and the Pituitary Gland

Beneath the thalamus sits a structure called the **hypothalamus** (*hypo* means "under"). It is involved in drives associated with the survival of both the individual and the species—hunger, thirst, emotion, sex, and reproduction. It regulates body temperature by triggering sweating or shivering, and it controls the complex operations of the autonomic nervous system. It also contains the biological clock that controls the body's daily rhythms (see Chapter 5).

reticular activating system (RAS) A dense network of neurons in the core of the brain stem; it arouses the cortex and screens incoming information.

cerebellum A brain structure that regulates movement and balance and that is involved in some cognitive tasks.

thalamus A brain structure that relays sensory messages to the cerebral cortex.

hypothalamus A brain structure involved in emotions and drives vital to survival; it regulates the autonomic nervous system.

Hanging down from the hypothalamus, connected to it by a short stalk, is a cherry-sized endocrine gland called the **pituitary gland**, which we mentioned earlier in our discussion of hormones. The pituitary is often called the body's "master gland" because the hormones it secretes affect many other endocrine glands. The master, however, is really only a supervisor. The true boss is the hypothalamus, which sends chemicals to the pituitary, telling it when to "talk" to the other endocrine glands. The pituitary, in turn, sends hormonal messages out to these glands.

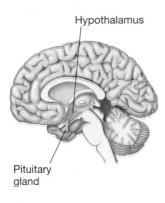

Hypothalamus

Pituitary gland

The hypothalamus, along with the two structures we will come to next, has often been considered part of a loosely interconnected set of structures called the **limbic system**, shown in Figure 4.10. (*Limbic* comes from the Latin for "border": These structures form a sort of border between the higher and lower parts of the brain.) Some anatomists also include parts of the thalamus in this system. Structures in this region are heavily involved in emotions that we share with other animals, such as rage and fear (MacLean, 1993). The usefulness of speaking of the limbic system as an integrated set of structures is now in dispute, because these structures also have other functions, and because parts of the brain outside of the limbic system are also involved in emotion. However, the term *limbic system* is still in wide use among researchers, so we thought you should know it.

The Amygdala

The **amygdala** (from the ancient Greek word for "almond") is responsible for evaluating sensory information, quickly determining its emotional importance, and contributing to the initial decision to approach or withdraw from a person or situation (see Chapter 13). For example, it instantly assesses danger or threat. The amygdala also plays an important role in mediating anxiety and depression; PET scans find that depressed and anxious patients show increased neural activity in

pituitary gland A small endocrine gland at the base of the brain that releases many hormones and regulates other endocrine glands.

limbic system A group of brain areas involved in emotional reactions and motivated behavior.

amygdala [uh-MIG-dul-uh] A brain structure involved in the arousal and regulation of emotion and the initial emotional response to sensory information.

hippocampus A brain structure involved in the storage of new information in memory.

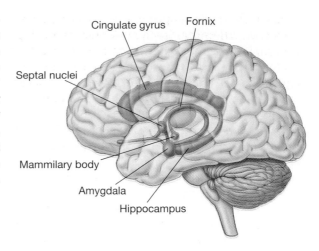

Cingulate gyrus   Fornix

Septal nuclei

Mammilary body

Amygdala

Hippocampus

FIGURE 4.10
The Limbic System
Structures of the limbic system play an important role in memory and emotion. The text describes two of these structures, the amygdala and the hippocampus. The hypothalamus is also often included as part of the limbic system.

this limbic structure (Davidson et al., 1999; Drevets, 2000).

The Hippocampus

Another important area traditionally classified as limbic is the **hippocampus**, which has a shape that must have reminded someone of a sea horse, for in Latin that is what its name means. This structure compares sensory information with what the brain has learned to expect about the world. When expectations are met, it tells the reticular activating system to cool it. There's no need for neural alarm bells to go off every time a car goes by, a bird chirps, or you feel your saliva trickling down the back of your throat!

The hippocampus has also been called the "gateway to memory." It enables us to form spatial memories so that we can accurately navigate through our environment (Maguire et al., 2000). Along with adjacent brain areas, it also enables us to form new memories about facts and events—the kinds of information you need to identify a flower, tell a story, or recall a vacation trip. This information is then stored in the cerebral cortex, which we will be discussing shortly. For example, when you recall meeting someone yesterday, various aspects of the memory—information about the person's greeting, tone of voice, appearance, and location—are probably stored in different locations in the cortex (Damasio et al., 1996; Squire, 1987). But without the hippocampus, the information would never get to these destinations. Moreover, the hippocampus may bind together the diverse aspects of a memory at the time it is formed, so that even though these aspects are stored in different places, the memory can be retrieved as one coherent entity (Squire & Zola-Morgan, 1991).

We know about the gateway function of the hippocampus in part from research on brain-damaged patients with severe memory problems. The case of one man, known to researchers as H. M., is probably the most intensely studied in the annals of medicine (Corkin, 1984; Corkin et al., 1997; Milner, 1970; Ogden & Corkin, 1991). In 1953, when H. M. was 27, surgeons removed most of his hippocampus, along with part of his amygdala. The operation was a last-ditch effort to relieve H. M.'s severe and life-threatening epilepsy. People with epilepsy, a neurological disorder that has many causes and takes many forms, often have seizures. Usually, the seizures are brief, mild, and controllable by drugs, but in H. M.'s case, they were unrelenting and uncontrollable.

The operation did achieve its goal: Afterward, the young man's seizures were milder and could be managed with medication. His memory, however, had been affected profoundly. Although H. M. continued to recall most events that had occurred before the operation, he could no longer remember new experiences for much longer than 15 minutes; they vanished like water down the drain. With sufficient practice, H. M. could acquire new physical or problem-solving skills, such as playing tennis or solving a puzzle, but he could not remember the training sessions in which he learned these skills. He would read the same magazine over and over without realizing it. He could not recall the day of the week, the year, or even his last meal. Most scientists attribute these deficits to an inability to form new memories for long-term storage.

Today, many years later, H. M., now elderly, will occasionally recall an unusually emotional event, such as the assassination of someone named Kennedy. He sometimes remembers that both his parents are dead, and he knows he has memory problems. But according to Suzanne Corkin, who studied H. M. extensively, these "islands of remembering" are the exceptions in a vast sea of forgetfulness. This good-natured man still does not know the scientists who have studied him for decades. He thinks he is much younger than he is, and he can no longer recognize a photograph of his own face; he is stuck in a time warp from the past.

Scientists are starting to understand just what happens in the hippocampus and in nearby structures during the formation of a long-term memory. For example, some synaptic pathways become more easily excitable and therefore more receptive to further impulses (Bliss & Collingridge, 1993). Release of the neurotransmitter glutamate may play a critical role in this process (Antonova et al., 2001). But these changes and others take time, which probably explains why memories remain vulnerable to disruption for a while after they are stored. Just as concrete takes time to set, memories require a period of *consolidation*, or stabilization, before they solidify.

The Cerebrum

At this point in our tour, the largest part of the brain still looms above us. It is the cauliflower-like **cerebrum**, where the higher forms of thinking take place. The complexity of the human brain's circuitry far exceeds that of any computer in existence, and much of its most complicated wiring is packed into this structure. Compared with many other creatures, we humans may be ungainly, feeble, and thin-skinned, but our well-developed cerebrum enables us to overcome these limitations and creatively control our environment (and, some would say, to mess it up).

The cerebrum is divided into two separate halves, or **cerebral hemispheres**, connected by a large band of fibers called the **corpus callosum**. In general, the right hemisphere is in charge of the left side of the body and the left hemisphere is in charge of the right side of the body. As we will see shortly, the two hemispheres also have somewhat different tasks and talents, a phenomenon known as **lateralization**.

The Cerebral Cortex Working our way right up through the top of the brain, we find that the cerebrum is covered by several thin layers of densely packed cells known collectively as the **cerebral cortex**. Cell bodies in the cortex, as in many other parts of the brain, produce a grayish tissue; hence the term *gray matter*. In other parts of the brain (and in the rest of the nervous system), long, myelin-covered axons prevail, providing the brain's *white matter*. Although the cortex is only about 3 millimeters (1/8 inch) thick, it contains almost three-fourths of all the cells in the human brain. The cortex has many crevasses and wrinkles, which enable it to contain its billions of neurons without requiring us to have the heads of giants—heads that would be too big to permit us to be born. In other

cerebrum [suh-REE-brum] The largest brain structure, consisting of the upper part of the brain; it is in charge of most sensory, motor, and cognitive processes. From the Latin for "brain."

cerebral hemispheres The two halves of the cerebrum.

corpus callosum [CORE-pus ca-LOW-suhm] The bundle of nerve fibers connecting the two cerebral hemispheres.

lateralization Specialization of the two cerebral hemispheres for particular operations.

cerebral cortex A collection of several thin layers of cells covering the cerebrum; it is largely responsible for higher mental functions. *Cortex* is Latin for "bark" or "rind."

occipital [ahk-SIP-uh-tuhl] lobes Lobes at the lower back part of the brain's cerebral cortex; they contain areas that receive visual information.

parietal [puh-RYE-uh-tuhl] lobes Lobes at the top of the brain's cerebral cortex; they contain areas that receive information on pressure, pain, touch, and temperature.

temporal lobes Lobes at the sides of the brain's cerebral cortex; they contain areas involved in hearing, memory, perception, emotion, and (in the left lobe, typically) language comprehension.

frontal lobes Lobes at the front of the brain's cerebral cortex; they contain areas involved in short-term memory, higher-order thinking, initiative, social judgment, and (in the left lobe, typically) speech production.

mammals, which have fewer neurons, the cortex is less crumpled; in rats, it is quite smooth.

Lobes of the Cortex
In each cerebral hemisphere, deep fissures divide the cortex into four distinct regions, or lobes (see Figure 4.11):

- The **occipital lobes** (from the Latin for "in back of the head") are at the lower back part of the brain. Among other things, they contain the *visual cortex*, where visual signals are processed. Damage to the visual cortex can cause impaired visual recognition or even blindness.

- The **parietal lobes** (from the Latin for "pertaining to walls") are at the top of the brain. They contain the *somatosensory cortex*, which receives information about pressure, pain, touch, and temperature from all over the body. The areas of the somatosensory cortex that receive signals from the hands and the face are disproportionately large because these body parts are particularly sensitive. Parts of the parietal lobes are also involved in attention and various mental operations.

- The **temporal lobes** (from the Latin for "pertaining to the temples") are at the sides of the brain, just above the ears, behind the temples. They are involved in memory, perception, and emotion, and they contain the *auditory cortex*, which processes sounds. An area of the left temporal lobe known as *Wernicke's area* is involved in language comprehension.

- The **frontal lobes**, as their name indicates, are located toward the front of the brain, just under the skull in the area of the forehead. They contain the *motor cortex*, which issues orders to the 600 muscles of the body that produce voluntary movement. In the left frontal lobe, a region known as *Broca's area* handles speech production. During short-term memory tasks, areas in the frontal lobes are especially active (Goldman-Rakic, 1996). The frontal lobes are also involved in emotion and in the ability to make plans, think creatively, and take initiative.

Because of their different functions, the lobes of the cerebral cortex tend to respond differently when stimulated. If a surgeon applied electrical current to your somatosensory cortex in the parietal lobes, you would probably feel a tingling in your skin or a sense of being gently touched. If your visual cortex in the occipital lobes were electrically stimulated, you might report a flash of light or swirls of color. But eerily, many areas of your cortex, when stimulated, would do nothing at all. These "silent" areas are sometimes called the *association cortex* because they are involved in higher mental processes.

Psychologists are especially interested in the most forward part of the frontal lobes, the *prefrontal cortex*. This area barely exists in mice and rats and takes up only 3.5 percent of the cerebral cortex in cats and about 7 percent in dogs, but it accounts for fully 29 percent of the cortex in human beings.

Scientists have long known that the frontal lobes, and the prefrontal cortex in particular, must have something to do with personality. The first clue appeared in 1848, when a bizarre accident drove an inch-thick, 3 1/2-foot-long iron rod clear through the head of a young railroad worker named Phineas Gage. As you can see in Figure 4.12, the rod (which is still on display at Harvard University, along with Gage's skull) entered beneath his left eye and exited through the top of his head, destroying much of his prefrontal cortex (H. Damasio et al., 1994). Miraculously, Gage survived this trauma and retained the ability to speak, think, and remember. But according to accounts of the accident, his friends complained that he was "no longer Gage." In a sort of Jekyll-and-Hyde transformation, he had changed from a mild-mannered, friendly, efficient worker into a foul-mouthed, ill-tempered, undependable lout who could not hold a steady job or stick to a plan. His employers had to let him go, and he was reduced to exhibiting himself as a circus attraction.

Today, there is some controversy about the exact details of this sad incident. For example, no one is

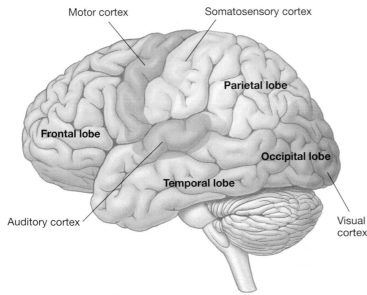

FIGURE 4.11
Lobes of the Cerebrum
Deep fissures divide the cortex of each cerebral hemisphere into four regions.

FIGURE 4.12
A Famous Skull
On the left is Phineas Gage's skull and a cast of his head. You can see where an iron rod penetrated his skull, altering his behavior and personality dramatically. The exact location of the brain damage remained controversial for almost a century and a half, until Hanna and Antonio Damasio and their colleagues (1994) used measurements of Gage's skull and MRIs of normal brains to plot possible trajectories of the rod. The reconstruction on the right shows that the damage occurred in an area of the prefrontal cortex associated with emotional processing and rational decision making.

really sure what Gage was like before his accident; his doctors may have exaggerated the extent of his personality transformation (Macmillan, 2000). But many other cases of brain injury, whether from stroke or trauma, support the conclusion that most scientists draw from the Gage case: that parts of the frontal lobes are involved in social judgment, rational decision making, and the ability to set goals and to make and carry through plans. Like Gage, people with damage in these areas sometimes mismanage their finances, lose their jobs, and abandon their friends. Interestingly, the mental deficits that characterize damage to these areas are often ac-

companied by a flattening out of emotion and feeling, which suggests that normal emotions are necessary for everyday reasoning and the ability to learn from mistakes (Damasio, 1994, 2003).

The frontal lobes also govern the ability to do a series of tasks in the proper sequence and to stop doing them at the proper time. The pioneering Soviet psychologist Alexander Luria (1980) studied many cases in which damage to the frontal lobes disrupted these abilities. One man observed by Luria kept trying to light a match after it was already lit. Another planed a piece of wood in the hospital carpentry shop until it was gone and then went on to plane the workbench!

QUICK quiz

It's time again to see how your own brain is working.

Match each description on the left with a term on the right.

1. Filters out irrelevant information.
2. Known as the "gateway to memory."
3. Controls the autonomic nervous system; involved in drives associated with survival.
4. Consists of two hemispheres.
5. Wrinkled outer covering of the brain.
6. Site of the motor cortex; associated with planning and taking initiative.

a. reticular activating system
b. cerebrum
c. hippocampus
d. cerebral cortex
e. frontal lobes
f. hypothalamus

Answers:

1.a 2.c 3.f 4.b 5.d 6.e

WHAT'S *Ahead*

- If the two cerebral hemispheres were out of touch, would they feel different emotions and think different thoughts?

- Why do researchers often refer to the left hemisphere as "dominant"?

- Should you sign up for a program that promises to perk up the right side of your brain?

The Two Hemispheres of the Brain

We have seen that the cerebrum is divided into two hemispheres that control opposite sides of the body. Although similar in structure, these hemispheres have somewhat separate talents, or areas of specialization.

Split Brains: A House Divided

In a normal brain, the two hemispheres communicate with each other across the corpus callosum, the bundle of fibers that connects them. Whatever happens in one side of the brain is instantly flashed to the other side. What would happen, though, if the two sides were cut off from each other?

In 1953, Ronald E. Myers and Roger W. Sperry took the first step toward answering this question by severing the corpus callosum in cats. Normally, each eye (in cats and in humans) transmits messages to both sides of the brain (see Figure 4.13). After this procedure, a cat's left eye sent information only to the left hemisphere and its right eye sent information only to the right hemisphere.

At first, the cats did not seem to be affected much by this drastic operation. But Myers and Sperry showed that something profound had happened. They trained the cats to perform tasks with one eye blindfolded. For example, a cat might have to push a panel with a square on it to get food but ignore a panel with a circle. Then the researchers switched the blindfold to the cat's other eye and tested the animal again. Now the cats behaved as if they had never learned the trick. Apparently, one side of the brain did not know what the other side was doing. It was as if the animals had two minds in one body. Later studies confirmed this result with other species, including monkeys (Sperry, 1964).

In all the animal studies, ordinary behavior, such as eating and walking, remained normal. Encouraged by this finding, a team of surgeons in the

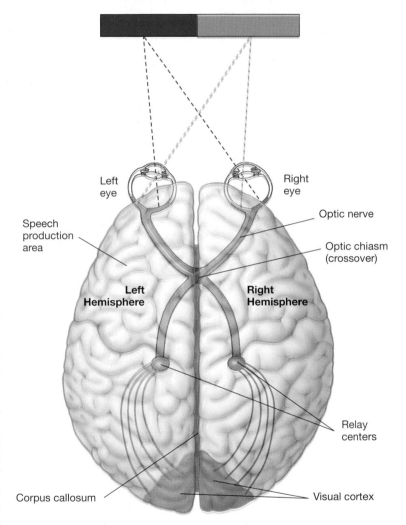

FIGURE 4.13
Visual Pathways

Each cerebral hemisphere receives information from the eyes about the opposite side of the visual field. Thus, if you stare directly at the corner of a room, everything to the left of the juncture is represented in your right hemisphere and vice versa. This is so because half the axons in each optic nerve cross over (at the optic chiasm) to the opposite side of the brain. Normally, each hemisphere immediately shares its information with the other one, but in split-brain patients, severing the corpus callosum prevents such communication.

early 1960s decided to try cutting the corpus callosum in patients suffering from debilitating, uncontrollable epilepsy. In severe forms of this disease, disorganized electrical activity spreads from an injured area to other parts of the brain. The surgeons reasoned that cutting the connection between the two halves of the brain might stop the spread of electrical activity from one side to the other. The surgery was done, of course, for the sake of the patients, who were desperate. But there was a bonus for scientists, who would be able to find out what each cerebral hemisphere can do when it is quite literally cut off from the other.

The results of this *split-brain surgery* generally proved successful. Seizures were reduced and sometimes disappeared completely. In their daily lives, split-brain patients did not seem much affected by the fact that the two sides of their brains were incommunicado. Their personalities and intelligence remained intact; they could walk, talk, and in general lead normal lives. Apparently, connections in the undivided deeper parts of the brain kept body movements and other functions normal. But in a series of ingenious studies, Sperry and his colleagues (and later other researchers) showed that perception and memory had been affected, just as they had been in earlier animal research. In 1981, Sperry won a Nobel Prize for his work.

It was already known that the two hemispheres are not mirror images of each other. In most people, language is largely handled by the left hemisphere; thus, a person who suffers brain damage

because of a stroke—a blockage in or rupture of a blood vessel in the brain—is much more likely to have language problems if the damage is in the left side than if it is in the right. Sperry and his colleagues wanted to know how splitting the brain would affect language and other abilities.

To understand this research, you must know how nerves connect the eyes to the brain. (The human patients, unlike Myers and Sperry's cats, did not have these nerves cut.) If you look straight ahead, everything in the left side of the scene before you—the visual field—goes to the right half of your brain, and everything in the right side of the scene goes to the left half of your brain. This is true for both eyes (refer back to Figure 4.13).

The procedure was to present information only to one or the other side of the patients' brains. In one early study (Levy, Trevarthen, & Sperry, 1972), the researchers took photographs of different faces, cut them in two, and pasted different halves together. The reconstructed photographs were then presented on slides. The person was told to stare at a dot on the middle of the screen, so that half the image fell to the left of this point and half to the right. Each image was flashed so quickly that the person had no time to move his or her eyes. When the patients were asked to say what they had seen, they named the person in the right part of the image (which would be the little boy in Figure 4.14). But when they were asked to point with their left hands to the face they had seen, they chose the person in the left side of the image (the mustached man in the figure). Further, they claimed

"Look at the center of the slide."

(a)

(b)   "Point to the person you saw."

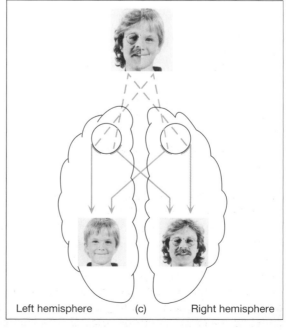

Left hemisphere   (c)   Right hemisphere

FIGURE 4.14

Divided View

When split-brain patients were shown composite photographs (a) and were then asked to pick out the face they had seen from a series of intact photographs (b), they said they had seen the face on the right side of the composite—yet they pointed with their left hands to the face that had been on the left. Because the two cerebral hemispheres could not communicate, the verbal left hemisphere was aware of only the right half of the picture, and the relatively mute right hemisphere was aware of only the left half.

they had noticed nothing unusual about the original photographs! Each side of the brain saw a different half-image and automatically filled in the missing part. Neither side knew what the other side had seen.

Why did the patients name one side of the picture but point to the other? Speech centers are in the left hemisphere. When the person responded with speech, it was the left side of the brain doing the talking. When the person pointed with the left hand, which is controlled by the right side of the brain, the right hemisphere was giving its version of what the person had seen.

In another study, the researchers presented slides of ordinary objects and then suddenly flashed a slide of a nude woman. Both sides of the brain were amused, but because only the left side has speech, the two sides responded differently. When the picture was flashed to one woman's left hemisphere, she laughed and identified it as a nude. When it was flashed to her right hemisphere, she said nothing but began to chuckle. Asked what she was laughing at, she said, "I don't know . . . nothing . . . oh—that funny machine." The right hemisphere could not describe what it had seen, but it reacted emotionally just the same (Gazzaniga, 1967).

The Two Hemispheres: Allies or Opposites?

The split-brain operation is still being performed, and split-brain patients continue to be studied. Research on left–right differences is also being done with people whose brains are intact (Springer & Deutsch, 1998). Electrodes and brain scans are used to measure activity in the left and right hemispheres while people perform different tasks. The results confirm that nearly all right-handed people and a majority of left-handers process language mainly in the left hemisphere. The left side is also more active during some logical, symbolic, and sequential tasks, such as solving math problems and understanding technical material.

Because of its cognitive talents, many researchers refer to left-hemisphere *dominance.* They believe that the left hemisphere usually exerts control over the right hemisphere. Split-brain researcher Michael Gazzaniga (1983) once argued that without help from the left side, the right side's mental skills would probably be "vastly inferior to the cognitive skills of a chimpanzee." He and others also believe that a mental "module" in the left hemisphere is constantly trying to explain actions and emotions generated by brain parts whose workings are nonverbal and outside of awareness. As one neuropsychologist put it, the left hemisphere is the brain's spin doctor (Broks, 2004).

Other researchers, including Sperry (1982), have rushed to the right hemisphere's defense. The right side, they point out, is no dummy. It is superior in problems requiring spatial–visual ability, the ability you use to read a map or follow a dress pattern, and it excels in facial recognition and the ability to read facial expressions. It is active during the creation and appreciation of art and music. It rec-

GET INVOLVED

TAP, TAP, TAP

Have a right-handed friend tap on a paper with a pencil held in the right hand for one minute. Then have the person do the same with the left hand, using a fresh sheet of paper. Finally, repeat the procedure, having the person talk while tapping. For most people, talking will decrease the rate of tapping—but more for the right hand than for the left, probably because both activities involve the same hemisphere (the left one), and there is competition between them. (Left-handed people vary more in terms of which hemisphere is dominant for language, so the results for them will be less predictable.)

ognizes nonverbal sounds, such as a dog's barking. The right hemisphere also has some language ability. Typically, it can read a word briefly flashed to it and can understand an experimenter's instructions. In a few split-brain patients, the right hemisphere's language ability has been quite well developed, showing that individual variation exists in brain lateralization.

Some researchers have also credited the right hemisphere with having a cognitive style that is

Thinking Critically About "Right Brain/Left Brain" Theories

intuitive and holistic (in which things are seen as wholes), in contrast to the left hemisphere's more ra-

tional and analytic mode. Over the years, this idea has been oversold by books and programs that promise to make people more creative by making them more "right-brained." But the right hemisphere is not always a hero: For example, it contains regions that process fear and sadness, emotions that often cause us to withdraw from others. Further, the differences between the two hemispheres are relative, not absolute—a matter of degree. In most real-life activities, the two sides cooperate naturally, with each making a valuable contribution. As Sperry (1982) himself once noted, "The left–right dichotomy . . . is an idea with which it is very easy to run wild."

QUICK quiz

Use as many parts of your brain as necessary to answer these questions.

1. Keeping in mind that both sides of the brain are involved in most activities, see whether you can identify which of the following is (are) more closely associated with the left hemisphere: (a) enjoying a musical recording, (b) wiggling the left big toe, (c) giving a speech in class, (d) balancing a checkbook, (e) recognizing a long-lost friend

2. Thousands of people have taken courses and bought tapes that promise to develop the "creativity" and "intuition" of their right hemispheres. What characteristics of human thought might explain the eagerness of some people to glorify "right-brainedness" and disparage "left-brainedness" (or vice versa)?

Answers:

1. c, d   2. One possible answer: Human beings like to make sense of the world, and one easy way to do that is to divide humanity into opposing categories. This kind of either-or thinking can lead to the conclusion that fixing up one brain hemisphere (e.g., making "left-brained," "right-brained") types more "right-brained") will make individuals happier and the world a better place. If only it were that simple!

WHAT'S *Ahead*

- Why do some brain researchers think that a unified "self" is only an illusion?

- Do men talk about sports and women about feelings because their brains are different?

Two Stubborn Issues in Brain Research

If you have mastered the definitions and descriptions in this chapter, you are prepared to read popular accounts of advances in neuropsychology. But many questions remain about how the brain works, and we will end this chapter with two of them.

Where Is the Self?

When we think about the remarkable blob of tissue in our heads that allows us to remember, to dream, and to think—the blob that can make our existence a hideous nightmare when it is damaged or diseased—we are led, inevitably, to a question that has been pondered for thousands of years: Where, exactly, is the self?

When you say, "I am feeling happy," your left hemisphere, your serotonin receptors, your endorphins, and all sorts of other brain parts and processes are active, but who, exactly, is the "I" doing the feeling? When you say, "My mind is playing tricks on me," who is the "me" watching your mind play those tricks, and who is it that's being tricked? When you say, "My brain isn't working too well today," where is the "you" observing "your" brain? Isn't the self observing itself a little like a finger pointing at its own tip?

"THEN IT'S AGREED—YOU CAN'T HAVE A MIND WITHOUT A BRAIN, BUT YOU CAN HAVE A BRAIN WITHOUT A MIND."

Most religions resolve the problem by teaching that an immortal self or soul exists entirely apart from the mortal brain. But modern brain scientists usually consider mind to be a matter of matter. They may have personal religious convictions about a soul or a spiritual response to the awesome complexity and interconnectedness of nature, but most assume that what we call "mind," "consciousness," or "self-awareness" can be explained in physical terms as a product of the cerebral cortex.

Our conscious sense of a unified self may even be an illusion. Neurologist Richard Restak (1983, 1994) has noted that many of our actions and choices occur without any direction by a conscious self. He concludes that "the brains of all creatures are probably organized along the lines of multiple centers and various levels." Cognitive scientist Daniel Dennett (1991) suggests that the brain or mind consists of independent brain parts that deal with different aspects of thought and perception, constantly conferring with each other and revising their "drafts" of reality. Likewise, Michael Gazzaniga (1985, 1998) has argued that the brain is organized as a loose confederation of independent modules, or mental systems, all working in parallel, with most of these modules operating outside of conscious awareness. As we saw, Gazzaniga believes that one verbal mod-

Thinking Critically About the Brain and the Self

ule, an "interpreter" (usually in the left hemisphere), is constantly explaining the actions, moods, and thoughts produced by the other modules. The result is the sense of a unified self (Gazzaniga, 1998; Roser & Gazzaniga, 2004).

Interestingly, the idea that the brain consists of modules and that the self is an illusion is consistent with the teachings of many Eastern spiritual traditions. Buddhism, for example, teaches that the self is not a unified thing but rather a collection of thoughts, perceptions, concepts, and feelings that shift and change from moment to moment. To Buddhists, the unity and the permanence of the self are a mirage. Such notions are contrary, of course, to what most people in the West, including psychologists, have always believed about their selves.

Over a century ago, William James (1890/1950) described the "self-as-knower," the inner sense we all have of being a distinct person who thinks, feels, and acts. But the age-old mind–brain puzzle continues to plague philosophers and scientists. Even in these days of modern technology, the neural circuits responsible for our sense of self remain hazy. One possibility is that an area in the prefrontal cortex, directly behind the eyes in the cleft between the two hemispheres, binds together perceptions and memories throughout the brain to produce a sense of oneself (Macrae, Kelley, & Heatherton, 2004).

But no one yet has a clear picture of how the inner life of the mind, our sense of subjective experience, is linked to the physical processes of the brain. Some brain-injured patients who, like H. M., are unable to store new memories about their experiences can nonetheless describe what kind of person they have been since the injury occurred— shy or outgoing, calm or worried, cautious or brave. Others, who have lost the ability to remember anything that happened to them *prior* to the injury, nonetheless retain the ability to describe what their personality traits were before the injury occurred (Klein et al., 2002). How are their brains able to know themselves? Equally mysterious, some patients with severe degeneration of the frontal lobes have unimpaired memories and language yet undergo a change in "self" comparable to Phineas Gage's transformation. One woman, a lifelong conservative, began to declare that "Republicans should be taken off the earth" (Miller et al., 2001).

Psychologists, neuroscientists, and cognitive scientists hope eventually to learn more about how our brains and nervous systems give rise to the self-as-knower. In the meantime, what do you think about the existence and location of your own "self" . . . and who, by the way, is doing the thinking?

Are There "His" and "Her" Brains?

A second stubborn issue for brain scientists concerns the existence of sex differences in the brain. On this issue, either–or thinking is a great temptation for many people. Because of the centuries of prejudice against women and a legacy of biased research on gender differences, some scientists and laypeople do not even want to consider the possibility that the brains of women and men might differ, on average, in some ways. Others go overboard in the opposite direction, convinced that most, if not all, differences between the sexes are in fact "all in the brain." To evaluate this issue intelligently, we need to ask two separate questions: *Do* the brains of males and females differ anatomically? And if so, what, if anything, do the differences have to do with men's and women's behavior, abilities, or ways of solving problems?

Let's consider the first question. Many anatomical and biochemical sex differences have been found in animal brains, especially in areas related to reproduction, such as the hypothalamus, but in other areas as well. Advances in technology have revealed some intriguing differences in human brains as well. For example, in a study of nine autopsied brains, researchers found that the women's brains had an average of 11 percent more cells in areas of the cortex associated with the processing of auditory information; in fact, all of the women had more of these cells than did any of the men (Witelson, Glazer, & Kigar, 1994). Brain scans show that parts of the frontal lobes and the limbic system are also larger in women, relative to the overall size of their brains, whereas parts of the parietal cortex and the amygdala are larger in men (Goldstein et al., 2001; Gur et al., 2002). Women also have more cortical folds in the frontal and parietal lobes (Luders et al., 2004).

Researchers are also using brain scans to search for average sex differences in brain activity while people work on particular tasks. In one study (Shaywitz et al., 1995), 19 men and 19 women were asked to say whether pairs of nonsense words rhymed, a task that required them to process and compare sounds. MRI scans showed that in both sexes an area at the front of the left hemisphere was activated. But in 11 of the women and none of the men, the corresponding area in the right hemisphere was also active. In another MRI study, ten men and ten women listened to a John Grisham thriller being read aloud. Men and women alike showed activity in the left temporal lobe, but women also showed some activity in the right temporal lobe, as you can

FIGURE 4.15

Gender and the Brain

When women and men listened to a John Grisham thriller read aloud, they showed activity in the left temporal lobe, but women also showed some activity in the right temporal lobe (Phillips et al., 2001). (Because of the orientation of these MRI images, the left hemisphere is seen on the right and vice versa.) Along with other evidence, these results suggest a sex difference in lateralization on tasks involving language.

see in Figure 4.15 (Phillips et al., 2001). These findings, along with many others, provide evidence for a sex difference in lateralization: For some types of tasks, especially those involving language, men seem to rely more heavily on one side of the brain whereas women tend to use both sides.

Thus, the answer to our first question is that yes, average sex differences in the brain do exist. But we are still left with our second question: *What do the differences mean for the behavior or personality traits of men and women in ordinary life?* Some popular writers have been quick to assume that brain differences explain, among other things, women's allegedly superior intuition, women's love of talking about feelings and men's love of talking about sports, women's greater verbal ability, men's edge in math ability, and why men won't ask for directions when they're lost. There are at least three problems with such conclusions:

1 *These supposed gender differences (in intuition, abilities, and so forth) are stereotypes.* In each case, the overlap between the sexes is greater than the difference between them. As we saw in Chapter 1, even when differences are statistically significant they are often quite small in practical terms (Hyde, 2000).

2 *A brain difference does not necessarily explain behavior or performance.* In the rhyme-judgment study, for example, both sexes did

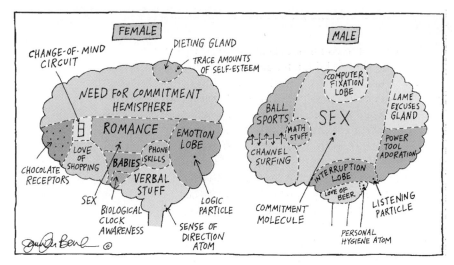

Cartoons like this one make most people laugh because men and women do differ, on average, in things like "love of shopping" and "power-tool adoration." But what does the research show about sex differences in the brain—and what they mean in real life?

way brains are organized and how they function. If you are a string musician, the area in your brain associated with music production is likely to be larger than that of nonmusicians (Jancke, Schlaug, & Steinmetz, 1997). If you are a cab driver, the area in your hippocampus responsible for visual representations of the environment is likely to be larger than average (Maguire et al., 2000). Analogously, males and females often have different experiences, which may be literally shaping their brains. That is why, in commenting on the study that had people listen to a John Grisham novel, one of the researchers noted: "We don't know if the difference is because of the way we're raised, or if it's hardwired in the brain" (quoted in Hotz, 2000).

equally well, despite the differences in their MRIs. The same has been true in other studies: Males and females may show different patterns of brain activity during a particular task, but they do not generally differ in their ability to do it. As for how brain differences might be related to more general mental abilities, or how men and women make judgments or behave socially, speculations are as plentiful as swallows in summer, but at present they remain just that—speculations.

3 *Sex differences in the brain could be the result rather than the cause of behavioral differences.* Experiences in life are constantly sculpting the circuitry of the brain, affecting the

In sum, the answer to our second question, whether physical differences are linked to behavior, is "It's uncertain." Animal studies have provided tantalizing clues, suggesting that sex differences in the brain influence reactions to acute or chronic stress, the likelihood of suffering depression, memory for emotional events, strategies for navigating around the environment, and other aspects of behavior (Cahill, 2005). But we simply do not yet know which, if any, of these findings are important for how human males and females manage their everyday lives—their work, their relationships, their families. It is important to keep an open mind about new findings on sex differences in the brain, but because the practical significance of these findings (if any) is not yet clear, it is also important not to oversimplify. The topic of sex differences in the brain is a sexy one, and research in this area can easily be exaggerated and misused.

QUICK quiz

Men and women alike have brains that can answer these questions.

1. Many brain researchers and cognitive scientists believe that the self is not a unified "thing" but is instead a collection of _____.

2. Name three reasons we should not assume that sex differences in the brain explain reported gender differences in behavior or cognition.

Answers:

1. independent modules or mental systems 2. Most of the reported gender differences are stereotypes and are small in practical terms; a biological difference does not necessarily have important behavioral implications; and brain differences could be the result rather than the cause of behavioral differences.

Now that you know more about the workings of the brain, let's return to the sad case of Terri Schiavo. The U.S. Supreme Court refused to intervene, as did Florida's appellate courts, and a few days after Schiavo's feeding tube was withdrawn the Schindlers ended their legal battle to keep her alive. She died shortly thereafter of dehydration, reportedly experiencing a painless and peaceful death.

Political and religious debates will continue over the rights of incapacitated people, the meaning of "death by natural causes," and when life should end if a person has left no written instructions. But the information in this chapter, and an increased understanding of the brain, can help us to separate what we might wish to be true about a patient's mental abilities from what really is true.

A few years before her death, a scan of Schiavo's brain had shown widespread destruction of brain cells in the cerebral cortex and their replacement by fluid. Yet her parents and many people who viewed the videotape the Schindlers made of her were convinced that she could recognize relatives, track objects with her eyes, and respond to questions. To a loving and desperately hopeful family, Terri's responses seemed to be evidence that she could recognize them and that her mind was functioning,

even if she could not speak. What they and many others did not realize is that activity in the brain stem can produce automatic, reflexive responses, including facial expressions and eye movements, without any awareness or thought on the patient's part and without any connection to events in the environment. The public never saw videos of Terri in her more common, clearly nonresponsive state.

Indeed, an autopsy performed after Schiavo's death confirmed that the injury to her brain had been massive and irreversible. Her visual cortex was no longer functioning, leaving her blind. Her brain, discolored and scarred, had shrunk to less than half the normal size; no amount of treatment could have repaired that kind of damage. The cause of her collapse so many years earlier remained uncertain; there was no evidence of an eating disorder, and also no evidence of abuse or strangulation, which the Schindlers had raised as a morbid possibility. But the consequences of her collapse were all too clear.

Of course, people will continue to differ about when, if ever, the time is right to discontinue the medical interventions that are keeping a person alive, even someone whose higher brain regions no longer function. But decisions in such difficult cases need to start with an understanding of the brain and its relationship to awareness of oneself and the environment. In the near future, brain-scan techniques such as functional MRI may reveal the degree of brain activity in severely brain-damaged patients when they are exposed to external stimuli, and may therefore help doctors distinguish with greater certainty between minimally conscious and persistent vegetative states (Schiff et al., 2005).

The study of our most miraculous organ, the brain, can also help us understand the abilities we all take for granted—the joys, memories, perceptions, sensations, emotions, thoughts, and dreams that having a healthy, functioning brain allows us to experience. But analyzing a human being in terms of physiology alone is like analyzing the Taj Mahal solely in terms of the materials that were used to build it. Even if we could monitor every cell and circuit of the brain, we would still need to understand the circumstances, thoughts, and cultural rules that affect whether we are gripped by hatred, consumed by grief, lifted by love, or transported by the transcendent moments of life.

TERRI'S BRAIN   HEALTHY BRAIN

The scan on the left, which was made in 2002 (three years before Terry Schiavo's death), using a method called computer-assisted tomography (CT), shows severe atrophy in her brain. The dark areas are massively enlarged ventricles filled with cerebral spinal fluid, which had by then replaced much of her cerebral cortex. On the right is a normal brain, showing typical small ventricles.

➤TAKING ➤PSYCHOLOGY ➤WITH ➤YOU

Food for Thought: Diet and Neurotransmitters

"Vitamin improves sex!" "Mineral boosts brain-power!" "Chocolate chases the blues!" Claims like these have long given nutritional theories of behavior a bad reputation. In the late 1960s, when Nobel laureate Linus Pauling proposed treating some mental disorders with massive doses of vitamins, few researchers listened. Mainstream medical authorities classified Pauling's vitamin therapy with such infamous cure-alls as snake oil and leeches.

Today, most mental-health professionals remain skeptical of nutritional cures for mental illness. But the underlying premise of nutritional treatments, that diet affects the brain and therefore behavior, is no longer considered a loony idea. Diet may indeed make a difference in cognitive function and in some types of disorders. In one double-blind study, researchers asked depressed patients to abstain from refined sugar and caffeine. Over a three-month period, these patients showed significantly more improvement in their symptoms than did another group of patients who instead refrained from eating red meat and from using artificial sweeteners (Christensen & Burrows, 1990).

Diet can also affect how well the brain functions. A week after a mild knock on the head, rats on a diet supplemented with omega-3 fish oil learned more quickly than control rats, and their brains had higher levels of a protein that encourages nerve cells to grow and form new connections (Wu, Ying, & Gómez-Pinilla, 2004). On the other hand, rats fed a high-fat, high-sugar diet—one comparable to diets popular in the Western world—learned more slowly than did rats on a standard diet and produced lower levels of proteins associated with learning and memory (Molteni et al.,

2002). In other research, older people took a daily supplement containing modest amounts of vitamins, minerals, and trace elements; at the end of a year, they showed improvements in short-term memory, problem-solving ability, abstract thinking, and attention, when compared to control subjects taking a placebo (Chandra, 2001). The B vitamin niacin in particular—a vitamin found in lean meats, legumes, milk, coffee, tea, and fortified cereals—may protect against Alzheimer's disease and mental decline in the elderly (Morris et al., 2004). The same may be true for the B vitamin folate, which is found in dark green, leafy vegetables, in some beans, and in fruits such as oranges and strawberries (Durga et al., 2006).

Some of the most exciting work on diet and behavior has looked at the role played by nutrients in the synthesis of neurotransmitters, the brain's chemical messengers. *Tryptophan*, an amino acid found in protein-rich foods (dairy products, meat, fish, and poultry), is a precursor (building block) of serotonin. *Tyrosine*, another amino acid found in proteins, is a precursor of norepinephrine, epinephrine, and dopamine. *Choline*, a component of the lecithin found in egg yolks, soy products, and liver, is a precursor of acetylcholine.

In the case of tryptophan, the path between the dinner plate and the brain is indirect. Tryptophan leads to the production of serotonin, which reduces alertness, promotes relaxation, and hastens sleep. Because tryptophan is found in protein, you might think that a high-protein meal would make you drowsy and that carbohydrates (sweets, bread, pasta, potatoes) would make you relatively alert. Actual-

ly, the opposite is true. High-protein foods contain several amino acids, not just tryptophan, and they all compete for a ride on carrier molecules headed for brain cells. Because tryptophan occurs in foods in small quantities, it doesn't stand much of a chance if all you eat is protein. It is in the position of a tiny child trying to push aside a crowd of adults for a seat on the subway.

Carbohydrates, however, stimulate the production of the hormone insulin, and insulin causes all the other amino acids to be drawn out of the bloodstream while having little effect on tryptophan. So carbohydrates increase the odds that tryptophan will make it to the brain. Paradoxically, then, a high-carbohydrate, no-protein meal is likely to make you relatively calm or lethargic and a high-protein one is likely to promote alertness, all else being equal (Spring, Chiodo, & Bowen, 1987). Research with people who tend to become frustrated, angry, or depressed in stressful situations suggests that high-carbohydrate food can actually reduce these responses and help such people cope (Markus et al., 2000).

Keep in mind, though, that many other factors influence mood and behavior, that the effects of nutrients are subtle, and that some of these effects depend on a person's age, the circumstances, and even the time of day. Further, nutrients interact with each other in complex ways. If you don't eat protein, you won't get enough tryptophan, but if you go without carbohydrates, the tryptophan found in protein will be useless.

In sum, if you're looking for brain food, you are most likely to find it not in a magic pill but in a well-balanced diet.

SUMMARY

• The brain is the bedrock of consciousness, perception, memory, and emotion.

The Nervous System: A Basic Blueprint

• The function of the nervous system is to gather and process information, produce responses to stimuli, and coordinate the workings of different cells. Scientists divide it into the *central nervous system (CNS)* and the *peripheral nervous system (PNS)*. The CNS includes the brain and *spinal cord* (which

produces *spinal reflexes* on its own); it receives, processes, interprets, and stores information and sends messages destined for muscles, glands, and organs. The PNS transmits information to and from the CNS by way of *sensory* and *motor nerves*.

• The peripheral nervous system consists of the *somatic nervous system*, which permits sensation and voluntary actions, and the *autonomic nervous system*, which regulates blood vessels, glands, and internal (visceral) organs. The autonomic system usually functions without conscious control but can be influenced through *biofeedback*.

• The autonomic nervous system is divided into the *sympathetic nervous system*, which mobilizes the body for action, and the *parasympathetic nervous system*, which conserves energy.

Communication in the Nervous System

• Neurons are the basic units of the nervous system. They are held in place by *glial cells*, which nourish, insulate and protect them, and enable them to function properly. Each neuron consists of *dendrites*, a *cell body*, and an *axon*. In the peripheral nervous system, axons (and sometimes dendrites) are collected together in bundles called *nerves*. Many axons are insulated by a *myelin sheath* that speeds up the conduction of neural impulses and prevents signals in adjacent cells from interfering with one another.

• Recent research has undermined two old assumptions: that neurons in the human central nervous system cannot be induced to regenerate and that no new neurons form after early infancy. In the laboratory, neurons in the CNS have been induced to regenerate. And scientists have learned that *stem cells* in brain areas associated with learning and memory give rise to new neurons and continue to divide and mature throughout adulthood. A stimulating environment seems to enhance this process.

• Communication between two neurons occurs at the *synapse*. Many synapses have not yet formed at birth. During development, axons and dendrites continue to grow as a result of both physical maturation and experience with the world, and throughout life, new learning results in new synaptic connections in the brain. Thus, the brain's circuits are not fixed and immutable but are continually changing in response to information, challenges, and changes in the environment, a phenomenon known as *plasticity*. As we saw in the "Close-up on Research," in some people who have been blind from an early age, brain regions usually devoted to vision are activated by sound and touch—a dramatic example of plasticity. Such people show superior performance in tasks involving these senses.

• When a wave of electrical voltage *(action potential)* reaches the end of a transmitting axon, *neurotransmitter* molecules are released into the *synaptic cleft*. When these molecules bind to *receptor sites* on the receiving neuron, that neuron becomes either more likely to fire or less so. The message that reaches a final destination depends on how frequently particular neurons are firing, how many are firing, what types are firing, and where they are located.

• Through their effects on neural circuits, neurotransmitters play a critical role in mood, memory, and psychological well-being. Abnormal levels of neurotransmitters have been implicated in several disorders, including depression, Alzheimer's disease, and Parkinson's disease.

• *Endorphins*, which act primarily by modifying the action of neurotransmitters, reduce pain and promote pleasure. Endorphin levels seem to shoot up when an animal or person is afraid or is under stress. Endorphins have also been linked to the pleasures of social contact.

• *Hormones*, produced mainly by the *endocrine glands*, affect and are affected by the nervous system. Psychologists are especially interested in *melatonin*, which promotes sleep and helps regulate bodily rhythms; oxytocin, which plays a role in attachment and trust; *adrenal hormones* such as *epinephrine* and *norepinephrine*, which are involved in emotions, memory, and stress; and the *sex hormones*, which are involved in the physical changes of puberty, the menstrual cycle *(estrogens* and *progesterone)*, and sexual arousal *(testosterone)*.

Mapping the Brain

• Researchers study the brain by observing patients with brain damage; by using the lesion method with animals; and by using such techniques as *electroencephalograms (EEGs)*, *transcranial magnetic stimulation (TMS)*, *positron-emission tomography (PET scans)*, and *magnetic resonance imaging (MRI)*.

• Brain scans reveal which parts of the brain are active during different tasks but do not tell us precisely what is happening, either physically or mentally, during the task. They do not reveal discrete "centers" for particular functions, and they must be interpreted cautiously.

A Tour Through the Brain

• All modern brain theories assume *localization of function*, although a particular area may have several functions, and many areas are likely to be involved in any particular activity.

• In the lower part of the brain, in the *brain stem*, the *medulla* controls automatic functions such as heartbeat and breathing, and the *pons* is involved in sleeping, waking, and dreaming. The *reticular activating system (RAS)* screens incoming information and is responsible for alertness. The *cerebellum* contributes to balance and muscle coordination and may also play a role in some higher mental operations.

• The *thalamus* directs sensory messages to appropriate higher centers. The *hypothalamus* is involved in emotion and in drives associated with survival. It also controls the operations of the autonomic nervous system and sends out chemicals that tell the pituitary gland when to "talk" to other endocrine glands. Along with other structures, such as the amygdala and the hippocampus, the hypothalamus has traditionally been considered part of the *limbic system*, which is involved in emotions that we share with other animals. However, the usefulness of speaking of the limbic system as an integrated set of structures is now in dispute.

• The *amygdala* is responsible for evaluating sensory information and quickly determining its emotional importance and for the initial decision to approach or withdraw from a person or situation. The *hippocampus* has been called the "gateway to memory" because it plays a critical role in the formation of long-term memories for facts and events.

• Much of the brain's circuitry is packed into the *cerebrum*, which is divided into two *cerebral hemispheres* and is covered by thin layers of cells known collectively as the *cerebral cortex*. The *occipital, parietal, temporal,* and *frontal lobes* of the cortex have specialized (but partially overlapping) functions. The *association cortex* appears to be responsible for higher mental processes. The frontal lobes, particularly areas in the *prefrontal cortex*, are involved in social judgment, the making and carrying out of plans, and decision making.

The Two Hemispheres of the Brain

• Studies of *split-brain* patients, who have had the *corpus callosum* cut, show that the two cerebral hemispheres have somewhat different talents, a phenomenon known as *lateralization*. In most people, language is processed mainly in the left hemisphere, which generally is specialized for logical, symbolic, and sequential tasks. The right hemisphere is associated with spatial–visual tasks, facial recognition, the creation and appreciation of art and music, and the processing of negative emotions. In most mental activities, however, the two hemispheres cooperate as partners, with each making a valuable contribution.

Two Stubborn Issues in Brain Research

• One of the oldest questions in the study of the brain is where the "self" resides. Many brain researchers and cognitive scientists believe that a unified self may be something of an illusion. Some argue that the brain operates as a collection of independent modules or mental systems, perhaps with one of them functioning as an "interpreter." An area in the prefrontal cortex may be critical for a unified sense of self. But much remains to be learned about the relationship between the brain and the mind.

• Brain scans and other techniques have revealed some differences in the brains of males and females in some anatomical structures, and in lateralization during tasks involving language (with females more likely to use both hemispheres). Controversy exists, however, about what these differences mean in real life. Speculation has often focused on behavioral or cognitive differences that are small and insignificant. Biological differences do not necessarily explain behavioral ones, and sex differences in experience could affect brain organization rather than the other way around.

Psychology in the News, Revisited

• Knowledge about the brain can help us think critically about decisions involving extraordinary measures to keep a person who is in a persistent vegetative state alive. In evaluating research on the role of the functioning brain in behavior, however, it is important to remember that findings on the brain are most illuminating when they are integrated with psychological and cultural ones.

KEY TERMS

central nervous system (CNS)   116

spinal cord   117

spinal reflexes   117

peripheral nervous system (PNS)   117

sensory nerves   117

motor nerves   117

somatic nervous system   117

autonomic nervous system   117

biofeedback   118

sympathetic nervous system   118

parasympathetic nervous system   118

neuron   119

glia   119

dendrites   120

cell body   120

axon   120

axon terminals   120

myelin sheath   121

nerve   121

stem cells   121

synaptic cleft   122

synapse   122

plasticity   123

action potential   124

synaptic vesicles   124

neurotransmitter   124

receptor sites   124

endorphins   126

hormones   126

endocrine glands   126

melatonin   126

oxytocin   126

adrenal hormones   126

cortisol   126

epinephrine and norepinephrine   127

sex hormones (androgens, estrogens, progesterone)   127

lesion method   128

electrode   128

electroencephalogram (EEG)   128

transcranial magnetic stimulation (TMS)   128

PET (positron-emission tomography) scan   129

MRI (magnetic resonance imaging)   129

localization of function   130

brain stem   130

pons   130

medulla   130

reticular activating system (RAS)   131

cerebellum   131

thalamus   131

olfactory bulb   131

hypothalamus   131

pituitary gland   132

limbic system   132

amygdala   132

hippocampus   132

consolidation   133

cerebrum   133

cerebral hemispheres   133

corpus callosum   133

lateralization   133

cerebral cortex   133

occipital lobes   134

visual cortex   134

parietal lobes   134

somatosensory cortex   134

temporal lobes   134

auditory cortex   134

Wernicke's area   134

frontal lobes   134

motor cortex   134

Broca's area   134

association cortex   134

prefrontal cortex   134

split-brain surgery   137

(hemispheric) dominance   138

Neuropsychologists study the brain and the rest of the nervous system to gain a better understanding of consciousness, perception, memory, emotion, stress, mental disorders, and self-identity.

The Nervous System: A Basic Blueprint

Nervous System

Central Nervous System (processes, interprets, stores information; issues orders to muscles, glands, organs)

Peripheral Nervous System (transmits information to and from the CNS)

Brain

Spinal Cord (bridge between brain and peripheral nerves)

Somatic Nervous System (controls skeletal muscles)

Autonomic Nervous System (regulates glands, blood vessels, internal organs)

Sympathetic Nervous System (mobilizes body for action, energy output)

Parasympathetic Nervous System (conserves energy, maintains quiet state)

Mapping the Brain

Methods for studying the brain:
- Observing patients with brain damage; lesion method
- **Electroencephalogram (EEG):** brain-wave recording
- **Transcranial magnetic stimulation (TMS):** used as a "virtual" lesion method
- **Positron-emission tomography (PET scan):** method for analyzing biochemical activity in the brain
- **Magnetic resonance imaging (MRI):** method for studying body and brain tissue, using magnetic fields and special radio receivers

Communication in the Nervous System

- **Neurons:** basic units of the nervous system, composed of **dendrites**, a **cell body**, and an **axon**
- **Glial cells:** hold neurons in place as well as nourish, insulate, and protect them
- **Nerves:** bundles of axons and some dendrites in the peripheral nervous system
- **Myelin sheath:** speeds up the conduction of neural impulses and prevents adjacent cells from interfering with one another
- **Stem cells:** seem to give rise to new neurons throughout adulthood

How Neurons Communicate

Communication between neurons occurs at **synapses**, most of which develop after birth:
1. **Action potential** (changes in electrical voltage) produces a neutral impulse.
2. **Neurotransmitter** molecules are released into the synaptic cleft and bind to receptor sites on the receiving neuron.
3. Receiving neuron becomes more likely to fire or less likely to fire.

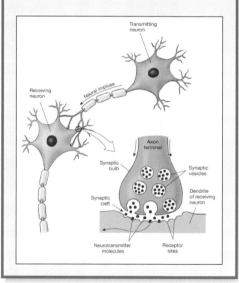

Chemical Messengers in the Nervous System

Neurotransmitters such as serotonin, dopamine, and acetylcholine play a critical role in mood, memory, and psychological well-being.
1. **Endorphins** modify the action of neurotransmitters to reduce pain and promote pleasure.
2. **Hormones** are chemical substances, secreted by glands that affect the functioning of other organs.
   - **Melatonin** promotes sleep.
   - **Oxytocin** plays a role in attachment and trust.
   - **Adrenal hormones,** such as epinephrine and norepinephrine, are involved in emotions, memory, and stress.
   - **Sex hormones** are involved in the physical changes of puberty; estrogen and progesterone are involved in the menstrual cycle and testosterone is involved in sexual arousal.

A Tour Through the Brain

All modern brain theories assume **localization of function**.

The **brain stem** is in the lower brain.
- The **medulla** controls automatic functions such as heartbeat and breathing.
- The **pons** is involved in sleeping, waking, and dreaming.
- The **reticular activating system (RAS)**, a dense network of neurons, screens incoming information and is responsible for alertness.

The **cerebellum** contributes to balance and muscle coordination.

- The **thalamus** directs sensory messages.
- The **hypothalamus** is involved in emotion and drives vital to survival and controls operations of the autonomic nervous system. It controls the **pituitary gland,** or master gland.
- **Limbic system:** group of brain areas involved in emotional reactions and motivated behavior.
- The **amygdala** evaluates sensory information and determines its emotional importance and helps to make the initial decision to approach or withdraw from a situation.
- The **hippocampus** plays a critical role in long-term memory for facts and events.
- The **cerebrum** contains much of the brain's circuitry; it is divided into two **cerebral hemispheres** and covered by thin layers of cells, or the **cerebral cortex.**

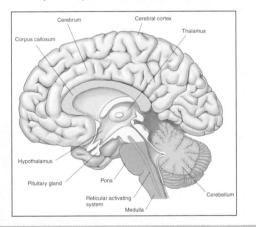

The Two Hemispheres of the Brain

Split Brains

- **Lateralization** is the specializing of each hemisphere.
- The left hemisphere is more active in processing language, logic, and symbolic–sequential tasks.
- The right hemisphere is associated with spatial-visual tasks, facial recognition, the creation and appreciation of art and music, and the processing of negative emotions.
- In most mental activities, the two sides cooperate.

Two Stubborn Issues in Brain Research

Where is the Self?

The issue of where the "self" resides in the brain is unanswered, with some researchers viewing the brain as a collection of independent modules or mental systems, perhaps with one functioning as "interpreter." An area of the prefrontal cortex may bind together perceptions and memories that produce a sense of self.

Are There "His" and "Her" Brains?

Brain scans reveal differences in lateralization in male and female brains during language tasks, but the real-life significance of these and other findings is still unknown.

Lobes of the Cerebral Cortex

- The **occipital lobes** contain the visual cortex.
- The **parietal lobes** contain the somatosensory cortex, which receives information about pressure, pain, touch, and temperature.
- The **temporal lobes** involve memory, perception, and emotion.
- The **frontal lobes** are involved in social judgment, the making and carrying out of plans, and decision making. Also contains the motor cortex, which controls voluntary movement, and Broca's area, which handles speech production.
- The association cortex appears to be responsible for higher mental process.

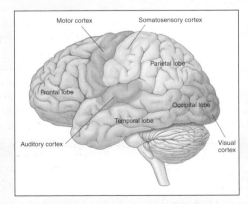

Supreme Court Says Okay To Hallucinogenic Tea

WASHINGTON, DC, FEBRUARY 21, 2006. In a unanimous decision, the nation's highest court today ruled that a small church in New Mexico may use a hallucinogenic tea from Brazil as part of a religious ritual.

The 140 members of the O Centro Espirita Beneficiente Uniao do Vegetal (UDV), which blends Christian beliefs and South American traditions, believe they can connect with God only by drinking the unpleasant-tasting hoasca tea twice a month at four-hour ceremonies. Because the tea contains an illegal Schedule 1 drug known as DMT, the government argued that its use violates a federal narcotics law and its importation violates a 1971 international treaty. When Chief Justice John Roberts asked if the government's position would be the same if the religion's followers used only one drop of the tea once a year, a government lawyer said yes.

But the justices were critical of the government's "zero tolerance" position. Several noted that peyote, derived from a cactus, is already allowed in Native American rituals. "Peyote seems to have been administered without the sky falling in," said Justice Stephen Breyer. Lawyers for the church also argued that use of the tea is comparable to the use of wine in the Christian sacrament of Communion.

Use of hoasca in the Amazon basin began before the conquest of South America by Europeans in the sixteenth century. Despite efforts by the Europeans to eradicate the practice, indigenous peoples continued to use the tea for both sacramental and medicinal purposes. Many South American groups today still believe that the drug frees the soul from its confinement in the body, allows visions and magical experiences, and leads to a sense of contact with the supernatural. The drug is also used in traditional folk healing.

The government contends that hoasca is unsafe, has a high potential for abuse, and could be used for nonreligious purposes. However, research conducted in Brazil has found that health problems among users have been minor and extremely rare, and that the drug has not caused any personality or cognitive problems. No nonreligious uses have been documented thus far in North America.

The Supreme Court ruling took note of a 1993 law, the Religious Freedom Restoration Act, which requires the government to allow religious practices unless it has a compelling reason not to do so. Because of their interest in freedom from government interference, several religious groups, including Mormons, Catholic bishops, Jews, Seventh-Day Adventists, Hindus, and Sikhs, filed briefs in favor of the New Mexico church.

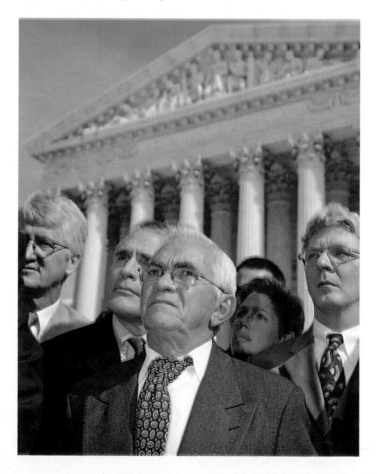

Members of the tiny U.S. branch of the Uniao do Vegetal church on the steps of the Supreme Court during hearings on their case.

Consciousness: Body Rhythms and Mental States

The drug in hoasca tea is just one of many used by people throughout the world to alter *consciousness*, the awareness of oneself and the environment. But consciousness also changes in predictable ways without any help from drugs. Each day, we all experience swings in mood, alertness, and efficiency. Each night, we all undergo a dramatic shift in consciousness when the ordinary rules of logic are suspended in the dream world of sleep. Performance and mood may be subject to much longer cycles as well, stretching over a month's time or even the seasons of the year. Why do these changes occur? And—religious motivations aside—why do some people deliberately try to alter their ordinary states of consciousness?

In this chapter we will see that the mental and physical aspects of consciousness are as intertwined as sunshine and shadow: Fluctuations in subjective experience are accompanied by predictable ups and downs in brain activity and hormone levels. We will begin with a discussion of the body's natural rhythms, which ebb

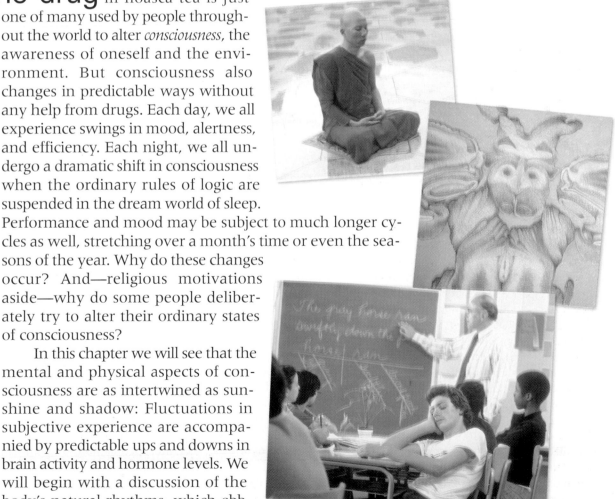

and flow over time. Next we will zero in on one particularly fascinating state of consciousness: dreaming. And then we will explore what psychologists have learned about two techniques used to alter consciousness deliberately: hypnosis and the use of recreational drugs. (We will discuss drug *abuse* and addiction in Chapter 11.)

This chapter will give you a better understanding of the human fascination with "altered states of consciousness" and why some people use drugs to achieve them. As you read, ask yourself: Are all drugs equally dangerous? Do religious motives justify making exceptions to drug laws? What if those New Mexico church members had been distilling vodka privately and using it in a religious ritual or growing grapevines to make a house wine for sale? Are our current drug policies realistic? We will return to these issues at the end of the chapter.

WHAT'S *Ahead*

- Why do you feel "out of sync" when you fly across time zones or change shifts at work?

- If you feel sad in the winter, do you have SAD?

- Does "PMS" cause most women to feel depressed or irritable before their periods?

Biological Rhythms: The Tides of Experience

biological rhythm A periodic, more or less regular fluctuation in a biological system; it may or may not have psychological implications.

endogenous Generated from within rather than by external cues.

circadian [sur-CAY-dee-un] rhythm A biological rhythm with a period (from peak to peak or trough to trough) of about 24 hours; from the Latin *circa*, "about," and *dies*, "a day."

At some point you may have come across an ad on the Internet for a "biorhythm chart" that supposedly foretells fluctuations in mood, alertness, and physical performance over your entire lifetime—solely on the basis of when you were born. Well, save your money: Biorhythm charts are pseudoscientific hogwash. It *is* true, however, that human beings experience dozens of periodic, fairly regular ups and downs in physiological functioning, which is what scientists mean when they speak of **biological rhythms**. A biological clock in our brains governs the waxing and waning of hormone levels, urine volume, blood pressure, and even the responsiveness of brain cells to stimulation. Many of these rhythms continue to occur even in the absence of external time cues; they are **endogenous**, or generated from within.

Many biological rhythms, called **circadian rhythms**, occur approximately every 24 hours. The best-known circadian rhythm is the sleep–wake cycle, but there are hundreds of others. For example, body temperature fluctuates about 1 degree centigrade each day, peaking, on average, in the late afternoon and hitting a low point, or trough, in the wee hours of the morning. Other rhythms occur less frequently than once a day—for example, the female menstrual cycle, which occurs every 28 days on average. Still others occur more frequently than once a day, many of them on about a 90-minute cycle. These include physiological changes during sleep and (unless social customs intervene) stomach contractions, hormone levels, susceptibility to visual illusions, verbal and spatial performance, brain-wave responses during cognitive tasks, alertness, and daydreaming (Escera, Cilveti, & Grau, 1992; Klein & Armitage, 1979; Kripke, 1974; Lavie, 1976).

Biological rhythms influence everything from the effectiveness of medicines taken at different times of the day to alertness and performance on the job. With a better understanding of these internal tempos, we may be able to design our days to take better advantage of our bodies' natural tempos. Let's look more closely at how these cycles operate.

Circadian Rhythms

Circadian rhythms exist in plants, animals, insects, and human beings. They reflect the evolutionary adaptation of organisms to the many changes associated with the rotation of the earth on its axis, such as changes in light, air pressure, and temperature.

In most societies, external time cues abound, and people's bodies become synchronized to them, following a strict 24-hour schedule. To identify endogenous circadian rhythms, therefore, scientists must isolate volunteers from sunlight, clocks, environmental sounds, and all other cues to time. Some hardy souls have spent weeks or even months alone in caves and salt mines, linked to the outside world only by a one-way phone line and a cable transmitting physiological measurements to the surface. Nowadays, however, volunteers usually live in specially designed rooms equipped with audio systems, comfortable furniture, and temperature controls.

When participants in these studies have been allowed to sleep, eat, and work whenever they wished, free of the tyranny of the timepiece, a few have lived a day that is much shorter or longer than 24 hours. If allowed to take daytime naps, however, most people soon settle into a day that averages about 24.3 hours (Moore, 1997). And when people are put on an artificial 28-hour "day," in an environment free of all time cues, their body temperature and certain hormone levels follow a

Stefania Follini (left) spent 4 months in a New Mexico cave (top), 30 feet underground, as part of an Italian study on biological rhythms. Her only companions were a computer and two friendly mice. In the absence of clocks, natural light, or changes in temperature, she tended to stay awake 20 to 25 hours and then sleep for 10. Because her days were longer than usual, when she emerged she thought she had been in the cave for only 2 months.

cycle that is very close to 24 hours—24.18 hours to be precise (Czeisler et al., 1999). These rhythms are remarkably similar from one person to the next.

The Body's Clock Circadian rhythms are controlled by a biological clock, or overall coordinator, located in a tiny teardrop-shaped cluster of cells in the hypothalamus called the **suprachiasmatic nucleus (SCN)**. Neural pathways from special receptors in the back of the eye transmit information to the SCN and allow it to respond to changes in light and dark. The SCN then sends out messages that cause the brain and body to adapt to these changes. Other clocks also exist, scattered around the body, and some may operate independently of the SCN, but for most circadian rhythms, the SCN is regarded as the master pacemaker.

The SCN regulates fluctuating levels of hormones and neurotransmitters, and they in turn provide feedback that affects the SCN's functioning. For example, during the dark hours, one hormone regulated by the SCN, **melatonin**, is secreted by the pineal gland, deep within the brain. The pineal gland responds to light and dark via complex connections that originate in the back of the eye. When you go to sleep in a darkened room, your melatonin level rises; when you wake up in the morning to a lightened room, it falls. Melatonin, in turn,

appears to help keep the biological clock in phase with the light–dark cycle (Haimov & Lavie, 1996; Lewy et al., 1992).

Melatonin treatments have been used to treat insomnia and synchronize disturbed sleep–wake cycles in blind people who lack light perception and whose melatonin production does not cycle normally (Sack & Lewy, 1997). But efforts to treat the insomnia of *sighted* people by giving them melatonin have had mixed results. Lots of people are taking over-the-counter melatonin supplements to help them sleep or to reduce jet lag, but it's unlikely that these supplements are very helpful. There are no federal standards to assure their quality, and no one has yet identified which dosages are effective (if any) or studied their long-term safety.

When the Clock Is Out of Sync
Under normal conditions, the rhythms governed by the SCN are synchronized, just as wristwatches can be synchronized. Their peaks may occur at different times, but they occur in phase with one

suprachiasmatic [soo-pruh-kie-az-MAT-ick] nucleus (SCN) An area of the brain containing a biological clock that governs circadian rhythms.

melatonin A hormone secreted by the pineal gland; it is involved in the regulation of circadian rhythms.

"IF WE EVER INTEND TO TAKE OVER THE WORLD,
ONE THING WE'LL <u>HAVE</u> TO DO IS SYNCHRONIZE OUR
BIOLOGICAL CLOCKS."

internal desynchronization A state in which biological rhythms are not in phase (synchronized) with one another.

another; thus if you know when one rhythm peaks, you can predict fairly well when another will do so. But when your normal routine changes, your circadian rhythms may be thrown out of phase with one another. Such **internal desynchronization** often occurs when people take airplane flights across several time zones. Sleep and wake patterns usually adjust quickly, but temperature and hormone cycles can take several days to return to normal. The resulting jet lag affects energy level, mental skills, and motor coordination.

Internal desynchronization also occurs when workers must adjust to a new shift. Efficiency drops, the person feels tired and irritable, accidents become more likely, and sleep disturbances and digestive disorders may occur. For police officers, emergency room personnel, airline pilots, truck drivers, and nu-

Travel can be exhausting, and jet lag makes it worse.

clear power plant operators, the consequences can be a matter of life and death. A National Commission on Sleep Disorders concluded that lack of alertness in night-shift equipment operators may have contributed, along with other factors, to the 1989 Exxon *Valdez* oil spill off the coast of Alaska and to disastrous accidents during the 1980s at two nuclear power plants, the Three Mile Island plant in the United States and the Chernobyl plant in Russia.

Night work itself is not necessarily a problem: With a schedule that always stays the same, even on weekends, people often adapt and do fine. However, many swing- and night-shift assignments are made on a rotating basis, so circadian rhythms never have a chance to resynchronize. Some scientists hope eventually to help rotating-shift workers resynchronize their rhythms by using melatonin or other techniques to "reset the clock" (Revell & Eastman, 2005), but so far these techniques are not ready for prime time. The best approach at present is to follow circadian principles by switching workers from one shift to another as infrequently as possible.

One reason that a simple cure for desynchronization has so far eluded scientists is that circadian rhythms are not perfectly regular and can be affected by illness, stress, fatigue, excitement, exercise, drugs, mealtimes, and ordinary daily experiences. Further, circadian rhythms differ greatly from individual to individual because of genetic differences (Hur, Bouchard, & Lykken, 1998). Some people are early birds, bouncing out of bed at the crack of dawn, whereas others are night owls who do their best work late at night and can't be pried out of bed until noon. (Schools are not designed to accommodate night owls.) You may be able to learn about your own personal pulses through careful self-observation, and you may want to try putting that information to use when planning your daily schedule.

Moods and Long-Term Rhythms

According to Ecclesiastes, "To every thing there is a season, and a time for every purpose under heaven." Modern science agrees. Seasonal cycles are common in nonhuman animals: Birds migrate south in the fall, bears hibernate in the winter, and marine animals become active or inactive, depending on bimonthly changes in the tides. In human beings, long-term cycles have been observed in everything from the threshold for tooth pain to conception rates. Folklore holds that our moods follow similar rhythms, particularly in response to seasonal changes and, in women, to menstrual changes. But do they?

GET INVOLVED

Measuring Your Alertness Cycles

For at least two days, except when you are sleeping, keep an hourly record of your mental alertness level, using this five-point scale: 1 = extremely drowsy or mentally lethargic; 2 = somewhat drowsy or mentally lethargic; 3 = moderately alert; 4 = alert and efficient; 5 = extremely alert and efficient.

Does your alertness level appear to follow a circadian rhythm, or does it rise and fall more frequently during the day? Are your cycles the same on weekends as during the week? Most important, how well does your schedule mesh with your natural fluctuations in alertness?

Does the Season Affect Moods?

Clinicians report that some people become depressed during particular seasons, typically winter, when periods of daylight are short—a pattern that has come to be known as **seasonal affective disorder (SAD)** (Rosenthal, 1998). During the winter months, SAD patients report feelings of sadness, lethargy, and drowsiness. To counteract the presumed effects of sunless days, some physicians and therapists have been treating SAD patients with phototherapy, having them sit in front of extremely bright fluorescent lights at specific times of the day, usually in the morning.

Evaluating the actual prevalence of SAD is difficult, however. Information comes mainly from clinical case reports rather than controlled studies, and, as we saw in Chapter 1, case studies have serious drawbacks. Many clinicians, extrapolating from patients who believe they suffer from SAD, think the disorder may affect as much as 20 percent of the population. But a national survey estimated the lifetime prevalence of major seasonal depression

These young Norwegian women are receiving light therapy for seasonal affective disorder (SAD). This type pf treatment is becoming increasingly popular and appears to be effective, but fewer people actually have SAD than is commonly thought, and its causes remain uncertain.

in the United States at only 0.4 percent, and the prevalence of major or minor seasonal depression at only 1 percent (Blazer, Kessler, & Swartz, 1998).

As for the effectiveness of light treatments, research on this question, too, has been flawed. A review of 173 light-treatment studies published between 1975 and 2003 found that only 20 had used an acceptable design and suitable controls (Golden et al., 2005). However, a meta-analysis of the data from those 20 studies did throw some light on the subject, so to speak. When people with SAD were exposed to either a brief period (e.g., 30 minutes) of bright light after waking or to light that slowly became brighter, simulating the dawn, their symptoms were in fact reduced. Light therapy even helped people with mild to moderate *non*-seasonal depression (see also Wirz-Justice et al., 2005).

> Thinking Critically
> About Seasonal
> Mood Changes

Some researchers have concluded that SAD patients must have some deficiency in the way they produce or respond to melatonin. For example, in one study, SAD patients produced melatonin for about half an hour longer at night in the winter than in the summer, whereas control subjects showed no such seasonal pattern (Wehr et al., 2001). However, why would light therapy also help some people with non-seasonal cases of depression? True cases of SAD may in fact have a biological basis, but the evidence to date remains inconclusive. When people get the winter blues, the reason could also be that they hate cold weather, are physically inactive, do not get outside much, or feel lonely during the winter holidays.

Does the Menstrual Cycle Affect Moods?

Controversy has also raged about another long-term rhythm, the monthly female menstrual cycle. During the first half of this cycle, an increase in the hormone estrogen causes the lining of the uterus to thicken in preparation for a possible pregnancy. At midcycle, the ovaries release a mature

seasonal affective disorder (SAD) A controversial disorder in which a person experiences depression during the winter and an improvement of mood in the spring.

egg, or ovum. Afterward, the ovarian sac that contained the egg begins to produce progesterone, which helps prepare the uterine lining to receive the egg. Then, if conception does not occur, estrogen and progesterone levels fall, the uterine lining sloughs off as the menstrual flow, and the cycle begins again.

The interesting question for psychologists is whether these physical changes are correlated

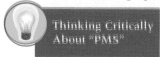
Thinking Critically About "PMS"

with emotional or intellectual changes, as folklore and tradition would have us believe. Most people seem to think so. In the 1970s, a vague cluster of physical and emotional symptoms associated with the days preceding menstruation—including fatigue, headache, irritability, and depression—came to be thought of as an illness and was given a label: "premenstrual syndrome" ("PMS"). Since then, several popular books and countless magazine articles have asserted that most women suffer from it. The medical literature, too, assumes a high incidence; when we scanned the abstracts of articles on "PMS" spanning three recent years, we found estimates ranging from 13 percent to "most women."

What does the evidence actually show? Many women do have *physical* symptoms associated with menstruation, including cramps, breast tenderness, and water retention, although women vary tremendously in this regard. And, of course, these physical symptoms can make some women feel grumpy or unhappy, just as pain can make men feel grumpy or unhappy. But *emotional* symptoms specifically associated with menstruation—notably, irritability and depression—are pretty rare, which is why we put "PMS" in quotation marks. Just as with SAD, more people claim to have symptoms than actually do. In reality, fewer than 5 percent of all women have such symptoms predictably over their cycles (Brooks-Gunn, 1986; Reid, 1991; Walker, 1994).

If true PMS is relatively uncommon, then why do so many women think they have it? One possibility is that they tend to notice feelings of depression or irritability when these moods happen to occur premenstrually but overlook times when such moods are *absent* premenstrually. Or they may label symptoms that occur before a period as "PMS" ("I am irritable and cranky; I must be getting my period") and attribute the same symptoms at other times of the month to a stressful day or a low grade on an English paper ("No wonder I'm irritable and cranky; I worked really hard on that paper and only got a C"). A woman's perceptions of her own emotional ups and downs can also be influenced by cultural attitudes and myths about menstruation. Some studies have encouraged biases in the reporting of premenstrual and menstrual symptoms by using questionnaires with gloomy, negative titles such as "Menstrual Distress Questionnaire."

To get around these problems, psychologists have polled women about their psychological and physical well-being without revealing the true purpose of the study (e.g., AuBuchon & Calhoun, 1985; Chrisler, 2000; Englander-Golden, Whitmore, & Dienstbier, 1978; Gallant, et al., 1991; Hardie, 1997; Parlee, 1982; Rapkin, Chang, & Reading, 1988; Slade, 1984; Vila & Beech, 1980; Walker, 1994). Using double-blind procedures, they have had women report symptoms for a single day and have then gone back to see what phase of the menstrual cycle the women were in; or they have had women keep daily records over on extended period of time. Some studies have included a control group that is usually excluded from research on hormones and moods: men!

CLOSE-UP on Research

Mood and "PMS"

Because so many people now take it for granted that most women have "PMS" and that it is a serious emotional problem for some, the two of us have sometimes been accused of bias for simply reporting the data disputing these assumptions. But stay with us as we describe more closely what the research has found.

In one typical study (McFarlane, Martin, & Williams, 1988), the researchers began by **asking**

"PMS" remedies line the shelves of drugstores, and most people assume that the syndrome is common—but is it?

the question, do women's moods differ from men's in a predictable way because of women's menstrual cycles? To find out, they examined changes in the pleasantness, arousal level, and stability of moods over time by having 15 women on birth-control pills, 12 normally cycling women, and 15 men rate their moods every day for 70 days. During this time, none of the participants knew that the study had anything to do with menstruation; they thought it was a straightforward study of mood and health. After the 70 days were up, the women then recalled their average moods for each week and phase of their menstrual cycle.

When the researchers **examined the evidence**, they found that in their daily reports, normally cycling women reported more pleasant moods than the other participants during the menstrual phase and the follicular phase (when an egg is forming). But there were no differences at all during the premenstrual phase. In fact, women's moods fluctuated less over the menstrual cycle than over days of the week! (Mondays, it seems, are tough for most people.) Moreover, women and men did not differ significantly in their emotional symptoms or the number of mood swings they reported at any time of the month, as you can see in the figure on this page. By comparing the women's daily reports with their retrospective reports, the researchers were also able to **question the cultural assumptions** about "PMS." The women *recalled* feeling more angry, irritable, and depressed in the premenstrual and menstrual phases than they had reported in their daily journals, showing that their retrospective reports had been influenced by their expectations and their belief that "PMS" is a reliable, recurring event.

All findings, of course, require replication before we can be confident of the result. In this case, other investigations have confirmed that most women do not have typical "PMS" symptoms even when they firmly believe that they do (Hardie, 1997; McFarlane & Williams, 1994). For example, although women have often reported that they cry premenstrually more than at other times, an interesting Dutch study that had women keep "crying and mood diaries" found no association between crying and phase of the menstrual cycle (van Tilburg & Becht, 2003). Even when women know that they are in a study of menstruation, most do not consistently report negative (or positive) psychological changes from one cycle to the next.

Like all good psychologists, researchers who do such studies are careful to **avoid oversimplification**. They do not conclude that "PMS" is

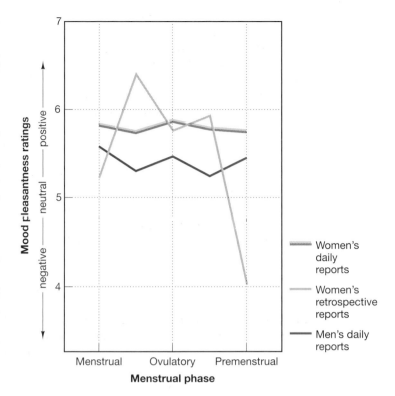

nonexistent. They do not deny that *some* women, in *some* months, have unpleasant moods before or during their periods. However, the accumulated research shows clearly that more women think they have "PMS" symptoms than actually do and that fewer women need to be treated for it than is commonly assumed.

The really important question, of course, is whether "PMS" affects women's ability to work, think, study, do brain surgery, or run a business. In the laboratory, some researchers have found that women tend be faster on tasks such as reciting words quickly or sorting objects manually before and after ovulation, when their estrogen is high (e.g., Saucier & Kimura, 1998). But empirical research has failed to establish any connection between phase of the menstrual cycle and real-world behavior in the vast majority of women. There is *no* relationship between phase of the menstrual cycle and work efficiency, problem solving, college exam scores, creativity, or any other behavior that matters in real life (Golub, 1992; Richardson, 1992). In a recent British study, female college students *said* that "PMS" interfered with their academic work, but the researchers could find no actual association between the number of symptoms reported by the students and their actual grades and test scores (Earl-Novell & Jessop, 2005). In the workplace, men and women report similar levels of stress, well-being, and ability to do the work required of them—and it doesn't matter whether the women are premenstrual, menstrual, postmenstrual, or nonmenstrual (Hardie, 1997).

These results are unknown to most people and have usually been ignored by doctors, therapists, and the media. During the 1970s, psychologists emphasized the psychological and cultural influences on women's experience of menstruation, but since the 1980s, premenstrual symptoms have come to be defined almost solely in medical and psychiatric terms (Parlee, 1994). In 1994, over the objections of many psychologists, the American Psychiatric Association included "premenstrual dysphoric disorder" (PMDD) in the *Diagnostic and Statistical Manual of Mental Disorders*, the official guide to psychiatric diagnosis. The label is supposed to describe a rare and incapacitating disorder, but its description includes the same hodgepodge of physical and emotional symptoms as "PMS" does. More recently, the antidepressant Prozac was repackaged and marketed as Sarafem, a medication supposedly just for PMDD.

As we have seen, for many people it isn't easy to avoid emotional reasoning when thinking about the menstrual cycle. Hormones do influence all of us, of course, as do many other internal processes. In a minority of cases, hormonal abnormalities or sudden hormonal changes can make women *and* men feel depressed, listless, irritable, or "not them-

"You've been charged with driving under the influence of testosterone."

For both sexes, the hormonal excuse rarely applies.

selves." Yet decades of research show that few women are likely to undergo personality shifts solely because of their hormones, and the same holds true for men. (In Chapter 13, we will see that testosterone doesn't "make" men violent.) In most instances, the body only provides the clay for people's symptoms and feelings; learning and culture mold that clay by teaching us which symptoms are important or worrisome and which are not. The impact of any bodily change depends on how we interpret it and how we respond to it.

QUICK quiz

There are no hormonal excuses for avoiding this quiz.

1. The functioning of the biological clock governing circadian rhythms is affected by the hormone _____.

2. Jet lag occurs because of _____.

3. For most women, the days before menstruation are reliably associated with (a) depression, (b) irritability, (c) elation, (d) creativity, (e) none of these, (f) a and b.

4. A researcher tells male subjects that testosterone usually peaks in the morning and that it probably causes hostility. She then asks them to fill out a "Hypertestosterone Syndrome Hostility Survey" in the morning and again at night. Based on your knowledge of menstrual-cycle findings, what do you think her study will reveal? How could she improve her study?

Answers:

1. melatonin   2. internal desynchronization   3. e   4. Because of the expectations that the men now have about testosterone, they may be biased to report more hostility in the morning. It would be better to keep them in the dark about the hypothesis and to measure their actual hormone levels at different points in the day, because individuals vary in their biological rhythms. Also, a control group of women could be added to see whether their hostility levels vary in the same way that men's do. Finally, the title on that questionnaire is pretty biased. A more neutral title, such as "Health and Mood Checklist," would be better.

WHAT'S *Ahead*

- How do brain waves change during the night?

- Why do we sleep?

- What happens when we go too long without enough sleep?

- Why might it be a good idea to take a daytime nap?

The Rhythms of Sleep

Perhaps the most perplexing of all our biological rhythms is the one governing sleep and wakefulness. Sleep, after all, puts us at risk: Muscles that are usually ready to respond to danger relax, and senses grow dull. As the late British psychologist Christopher Evans (1984) once noted, "The behavior patterns involved in sleep are glaringly, almost insanely, at odds with common sense." Then why is sleep such a profound necessity?

The Realms of Sleep

Let's start with some of the changes that occur in the brain during sleep. Until the early 1950s, little was known about the physiology of sleep. Then a breakthrough occurred in the laboratory of physiologist Nathaniel Kleitman, who at the time was the only person in the world who had spent his entire career studying sleep. Kleitman had given a graduate student, Eugene Aserinsky, the tedious task of finding out whether the slow, rolling eye movements that characterize the onset of sleep continue throughout the night. To both men's surprise, eye movements did occur, but they were rapid, not slow (Aserinsky & Kleitman, 1955). Using the electroencephalograph (EEG) to measure the brain's electrical activity (see Chapter 4), these researchers, along with another of Kleitman's students, William Dement, were able to correlate the rapid eye movements with changes in sleepers' brain-wave patterns (Dement, 1992). Adult volunteers were soon spending their nights sleeping in laboratories while scientists measured changes in their brain activity, muscle tension, breathing, and other physiological responses.

As a result of this research, today we know that during sleep, periods of **rapid eye movement (REM)** alternate with periods of fewer eye movements, or *non-REM (NREM) sleep*, in a cycle that recurs about every 90 minutes or so. The REM periods last from a few minutes to as long as an hour, averaging about 20 minutes in length. Whenever they begin, the pattern of electrical activity from the sleeper's brain changes to resemble that of alert wakefulness. Non-REM periods are themselves divided into shorter, distinct stages, each associated with a particular brain-wave pattern (see Figure 5.1).

When you first climb into bed, close your eyes, and relax, your brain emits bursts of *alpha waves*. On an EEG recording, alpha waves have a regular, slow rhythm and a high amplitude (height). Gradually, these waves slow down even further, and you drift off into slumber, passing through four stages:

- *Stage 1.* Your brain waves become small and irregular, and you feel yourself drifting on the edge of consciousness, in a state of light sleep. If awakened, you may recall fantasies or a few visual images.

- *Stage 2.* Your brain emits occasional short bursts of rapid, high-peaking waves called *sleep spindles*. Minor noises probably won't disturb you.

rapid eye movement (REM) sleep Sleep periods characterized by eye movement, loss of muscle tone, and dreaming.

FIGURE 5.1
Brain-Wave Patterns During Wakefulness and Sleep
Most types of brain waves are present throughout sleep, but different ones predominate at different stages.

- *Stage 3.* In addition to the waves characteristic of Stage 2, your brain occasionally emits *delta waves*, very slow waves with very high peaks. Your breathing and pulse have slowed down, your muscles are relaxed, and you are hard to rouse.

- *Stage 4.* Delta waves have now largely taken over, and you are in deep sleep. It will probably take vigorous shaking or a loud noise to awaken you. Oddly, though, if you talk or walk in your sleep, this is when you are likely to do so. The causes of sleepwalking, which occurs more often in children than adults, are still unknown, but they may involve unusual patterns of delta-wave activity (Bassetti et al., 2000).

This sequence of stages takes about 30 to 45 minutes. Then you move back up the ladder from Stage 4 to 3 to 2 to 1. At that point, about 70 to 90 minutes after the onset of sleep, something peculiar happens. Stage 1 does not turn into drowsy wakefulness, as one might expect. Instead, your brain begins to emit long bursts of very rapid, somewhat irregular waves. Your heart rate increases, your blood pressure rises, and your breathing gets faster and more irregular. Small twitches in your face and fingers may occur. In men, the penis becomes somewhat erect as vascular tissue relaxes and blood fills the genital area faster than it exits. In women, the clitoris enlarges and vaginal lubrication increases. At the same time, most skeletal muscles go limp, preventing your aroused brain from producing physical movement. You have entered the realm of REM.

Because the brain is extremely active while the body is entirely inactive, REM sleep has also been called "paradoxical sleep." It is during these periods that vivid dreams are most likely to occur. People report dreams when they are awakened from non-REM sleep, too; in one study, dream reports occurred 82 percent of the time when sleepers were awakened during REM sleep, but they also occurred 51 percent of the time when people were awakened during non-REM sleep (Foulkes, 1962). Non-REM dreams, however, tend to be shorter, less vivid, and more realistic than REM dreams, except in the hour or so before a person wakes up in the morning.

Occasionally, as the sleeper wakes up, a curious phenomenon occurs. The person emerges from REM sleep before the muscle paralysis characteristic of that stage has entirely disappeared, and becomes aware of an inability to move. About 30 percent of the general population has experienced at least one such episode, and about 5 percent have had a "waking dream" in this state. Their eyes are open, but what they "see" are dreamlike hallucinations, most often shadowy figures. They may even "see" a ghost or space alien sitting on their bed or hovering in a hallway, a scary image that they would regard as perfectly normal if it were part of a midnight nightmare. Instead of saying, "Ah! How interesting! I am having a waking dream!" some people interpret this experience literally and come to believe they have been visited by aliens or are being haunted by ghosts (Clancy, 2005; McNally, 2003).

REM and non-REM sleep continue to alternate throughout the night, with Stages 3 and 4 tending to become shorter or even to disappear and REM periods tending to get longer and closer together as the hours pass. This pattern may explain why you are likely to be dreaming when the alarm clock goes off in the morning. But the cycles are far from regular. An individual may bounce directly from Stage 4 back to Stage 2, or go from REM to Stage 2 and then back to REM. Also, the time between REM and non-REM is highly variable, differing from person to person and also within any given individual.

The reasons for REM sleep are still a matter of controversy. If you wake people up every time they lapse into REM sleep, nothing dramatic will happen. When finally allowed to sleep normally, however, they will spend a much longer time than usual in the REM phase, and it will be hard to rouse them. Electrical brain activity associated with REM may burst through into quiet sleep and even into wakefulness, as if the participants are making up for something they were deprived of. Some researchers have proposed that this "something" is connected with dreaming, but that idea has problems. For one thing, in rare cases, brain-damaged patients have lost the capacity to dream, yet they continue to show the normal sleep stages, including REM (Bischof & Bassetti, 2004). Moreover, although all mammals experience REM sleep—the only known exceptions are the bottlenose dolphin and the porpoise—it seems unlikely that rats and anteaters have the cognitive abilities required to construct dreams. Moles, which can hardly move their eyes at all,

Because cats sleep up to 80 percent of the time, it's easy to catch them in the various stages of slumber. A cat in non-REM sleep (left) remains upright, but during the REM phase (right), its muscles go limp and it flops onto its side.

nonetheless show EEG patterns associated with REM sleep. According to one well-known dream researcher, "no one, but no one, has been able to come up with a convincing explanation for REM sleep" (G. William Domhoff, personal communication).

Why We Sleep

Generally speaking, sleep appears to provide a time-out period, so that the body can eliminate waste products from muscles, repair cells, conserve or replenish energy stores, strengthen the immune system, and recover abilities lost during the day. When we do not get enough sleep, our bodies operate abnormally. For example, levels of hormones necessary for normal muscle development and proper immune-system functioning decline (Leproult, Van Reeth, et al., 1997).

Although most people can still get along reasonably well after a day or two of sleeplessness, sleep deprivation that lasts for four days or longer becomes uncomfortable and soon becomes unbearable. In animals, forced sleeplessness leads to infections and eventually death, and the same seems to be true for people. In one tragic case, a 51-year-old man abruptly began to lose sleep. After sinking deeper and deeper into an exhausted stupor, he developed a lung infection and died. An autopsy showed that he had lost almost all the large neurons in two areas of the thalamus that have been linked to sleep and hormonal circadian rhythms (Lugaresi et al., 1986).

The Mental Consequences of Sleeplessness Sleep is also necessary for normal mental functioning. Chronic sleep deprivation increases levels of the stress hormone cortisol, which may damage or impair brain cells that are necessary for learning and memory (Leproult et al., 1997). Also, new brain cells may either fail to develop or may mature abnormally (Guzman-Marin et al., 2005). Perhaps in part because of such damage, after the loss of even a single night's sleep, mental flexibility, attention, and creativity all suffer. After several days of staying awake, people may even begin to have hallucinations and delusions (Dement, 1978).

Of course, sleep deprivation rarely reaches that point, but people frequently suffer from milder sleep problems. According to the National Sleep Foundation, about 10 percent of adults are plagued by chronic insomnia—difficulty in falling or staying asleep. Insomnia can result from worry and anxiety, psychological problems, physical problems such as arthritis, and irregular or overly demanding work and study schedules. The result can be grogginess the next day.

Whatever your age, sometimes the urge to sleep is irresistible—especially because in fast-paced modern societies, may people do not get as much sleep as they need. Daytime drowsiness can interfere with reaction time, concentration, and the ability to learn.

sleep apnea A disorder in which breathing briefly stops during sleep, causing the person to choke and gasp.

narcolepsy A sleep disorder involving sudden and unpredictable daytime attacks of sleepiness or actual sleep.

(For advice on how to get a better night's sleep, see "Taking Psychology with You.")

Another cause of daytime sleepiness is **sleep apnea**, a disorder in which breathing periodically stops for a few moments, causing the person to choke and gasp. Sleep apnea has several causes, from blockage of air passages to failure of the brain to control respiration correctly, and over time it can cause high blood pressure and irregular heartbeat. In **narcolepsy**, another serious disorder, an individual is subject to irresistible and unpredictable daytime attacks of sleepiness or actual sleep, lasting from 5 to 30 minutes. When the person lapses into sleep, he or she is likely to fall immediately into the REM stage. A quarter of a million people in the United States suffer from this condition, many without knowing it. Narcolepsy seems to be caused by the degeneration of certain neurons in the hypothalamus, possibly due to an autoimmune malfunction or genetic abnormalities (Lin, Hungs, & Mignot, 2001; Mieda et al., 2004).

However, the most common cause of sleepiness is probably the most obvious one, staying up late and not allowing yourself to get enough sleep at night. Two-thirds of all Americans get fewer than the recommended seven or eight hours of sleep and American students get only about six hours a night, on average. Some people do fine on relatively few hours of sleep, but most need more than six hours for optimal performance and many adolescents need ten. When people don't get enough sleep, they are more likely to get into traffic and work accidents. The National Transportation Safety Board estimates that drowsiness is involved in 100,000 vehicle accidents a year, causing 1,500 road deaths and 71,000 injuries.

Don't doze off as we tell you this, but lack of sleep has also been linked to lower grades for everyone from very young kids to college students (Fallone et al., 2005; Wolfson & Carskadon, 1998). As sleep researcher James Maas (1998) has noted, many students drag themselves through the day "like walking zombies . . . moody, lethargic, and unprepared or unable to learn."

"Judith is someone who needs her sleep."

The Mental Benefits of Sleep Just as sleepiness can interfere with good mental functioning, a good night's sleep can promote it—and not just because you are well rested. Some researchers believe that sleep contributes to memory *consolidation*, a process by which the synaptic changes associated with recently stored memories become durable and stable, causing memory to become more reliable (Stickgold, 2005). Improvements in memory have been associated most closely with REM sleep and slow-wave sleep, and with memory for specific motor and perceptual skills. For example, when people or animals learn a perceptual task and are allowed to get normal REM sleep, their memory for the task is better the next day, even when they have been awakened during non-REM periods. But when they are deprived of REM sleep, their memories are impaired (Karni et al., 1994). And when people learn a computerized task—hitting keys when they see a dot in different places on a screen—some of the same brain areas that are active during the task are active later during REM sleep (Maquet et al., 2000).

If sleep enhances memory, perhaps it also enhances problem solving, which relies on information stored in memory. At least one study suggests that it does. German researchers gave volunteers a math test that required them to use two mathematical rules to generate one string of numbers from another and to deduce the final digit in the new sequence as quickly as possible. The volunteers were not told about a hidden shortcut that would enable them to calculate the final digit almost immediately. One group was trained in the evening and then got to snooze for eight hours before returning to the problem. Another group also got trained in the evening but then stayed awake for eight hours before coming back to the problem. A third group was trained in the morning and stayed awake all day, as they normally would, before taking the test. Those people who got the nighttime sleep were nearly three times likelier to discover the hidden shortcut as those in the other two groups (Wagner et al., 2004). On the basis of other research, the scientist who led this study attributed the insight-enhancing effects of sleep to the long-term storage of memories during deep (slow-wave) sleep, which occurs primarily during the first four hours of the night.

Remember this research the next time you are tempted to pull an all-nighter or shortchange yourself on your 40 winks. Even a quick nap can help your mental functioning (Mednick et al., 2002). Sleep is not a waste of time; it's an excellent use of it.

QUICK quiz

Wake up and take this quiz!

A. Match each term with the appropriate phrase.

1. REM periods
2. alpha
3. Stage 4 sleep
4. Stage 1 sleep

a. delta waves and talking in one's sleep
b. irregular brain waves and light sleep
c. relaxed but awake
d. active brain but inactive muscles

B. Sleep is necessary for normal (a) physical and mental functioning, (b) mental functioning but not physical functioning, (c) physical functioning but not mental functioning.

C. *True or false*: Only REM sleep has been associated with dreaming and memory consolidation.

Answers:

A.1.d 2.c 3.a 4.b B. a C. false

WHAT'S *Ahead*

- Why did Freud call dreams the "royal road to the unconscious"?

- How might your dreams be related to your current problems and concerns?

- How might dreams be related to ordinary daytime thoughts?

- Could dreams be caused by meaningless brain-stem signals?

Exploring the Dream World

For years, researchers believed that everyone dreams, and, indeed, most people who claim they never have dreams will in fact report them if they are awakened during REM sleep. However, as we noted earlier, there are rare cases of people who apparently do not dream at all. Most of these individuals have suffered some brain injury (Pagel, 2003).

In dreaming, the focus of attention is inward, though occasionally an external event, such as a wailing siren, can influence the dream's content. While a dream is in progress, it may be vivid or vague, terrifying or peaceful. It may also seem to make perfect sense—until you wake up and recall it as illogical, bizarre, and disjointed. Although most of us are unaware of our bodies or where we are while we are dreaming, some people report hav-

ing **lucid dreams**, in which they know they are dreaming and feel as though they are conscious (LaBerge & Levitan, 1995). A few even say that they can control the action in these dreams, much as a scriptwriter decides what will happen in a movie, although this ability is probably rare.

One issue that has bothered sleep researchers for years is whether the eye movements of REM sleep correspond to events and actions in a dream. Are the eyes tracking these images? Some researchers believe that in adult dreamers, eye movements do resemble those of waking life, when the eyes and head move in synchrony as the person moves about and shifts his or her gaze (J. H. Herman, 1992). But others think that eye movements are no more related to dream content than are inner-ear muscle contractions, which also occur during REM sleep.

Why do the images in dreams arise at all? Why doesn't the brain just rest, switching off all thoughts and images and launching us into a coma? Why, instead, do we spend our nights taking a chemistry exam, reliving an old love affair, flying through the air, or fleeing from monsters in the fantasy world of our dreams? We will consider four of the leading explanations and then evaluate them.

Dreams as Unconscious Wishes

One of the first psychological theorists to take dreams seriously was Sigmund Freud, the founder of psychoanalysis. After analyzing many of his patients' dreams and some of his own, Freud concluded that our nighttime fantasies provide insight

lucid dream A dream in which the dreamer is aware of dreaming.

into desires, motives, and conflicts of which we are unaware—a "royal road to the unconscious." In dreams, said Freud (1900/1953), we are able to express our unconscious wishes and desires, which are often sexual or violent in nature.

According to Freud, every dream is meaningful, no matter how absurd it may seem. But if a dream's message arouses anxiety, the rational part of the mind must disguise and distort it. Otherwise, the dream would intrude into consciousness and waken the dreamer. In dreams, therefore, one person may be represented by another—for example, a father by a brother—or even by several different characters. Similarly, thoughts and objects are translated into symbolic images. A penis may be disguised as a snake, umbrella, or dagger; a vagina as a tunnel or cave; and the human body as a house. Because reality is distorted in such ways, a dream resembles a psychosis, a severe mental disturbance; each night, we must become temporarily delusional so that our anxiety will be kept at bay and our sleep will not be disrupted.

To understand a dream, said Freud, we must distinguish its *manifest content*, the aspects of it that we consciously experience during sleep and may remember upon wakening, from its *latent* (hidden) *content*, the unconscious wishes and thoughts being expressed symbolically. Freud warned against the simpleminded translation of symbols, however—the kind of interpretation that often turns up in magazines and popular books promising to tell you exactly what your dreams mean. Each dream, said Freud, had to be analyzed in the context of the dreamer's waking life, as well as the person's associations to the dream's contents. Not everything in

a dream is symbolic. Sometimes, Freud cautioned, "A cigar is only a cigar."

Dreams as Efforts to Deal with Problems

Another explanation holds that dreams reflect the ongoing *conscious* preoccupations of waking life, such as concerns over relationships, work, sex, or health (Cartwright, 1977; Hall, 1953a, b). In this *problem-focused approach* to dreaming, the symbols and metaphors in a dream do not disguise its true meaning; they convey it. For example, psychologist Gayle Delaney told of a woman who dreamed she was swimming underwater. The woman's 8-year-old son was on her back, his head above the water. Her husband was supposed to take a picture of them, but for some reason he wasn't doing it, and she was starting to feel as if she were going to drown. To Delaney, the message was obvious: The woman was "drowning" under the responsibilities of child care, and her husband wasn't "getting the picture" (in Dolnick, 1990).

The problem-focused explanation of dreaming is supported by findings that dreams are more likely to contain material related to a person's current concerns than chance would predict (Domhoff, 1996). For example, among college students, who are often anxious about grades and tests, test-anxiety dreams are common: The dreamer is unprepared for or unable to finish an exam, or shows up for the wrong exam, or can't find the room where the exam is being given (Halliday, 1993; Van de Castle, 1994). (Sound familiar?) For their part, instructors often dream that they have forgotten their lecture notes at home, or that their notes contain only blank pages and they have nothing to say! Traumatic experiences can also affect people's dreams. In a cross-cultural study in which children kept dream diaries for a week, Palestinian children living in neighborhoods under threat of violence reported more themes of persecution and violence than did Finnish or Palestinian children living in peaceful environments (Punamaeki & Joustie, 1998).

Some psychologists believe that dreams not only reflect our waking concerns but also provide us with an opportunity to resolve them (Barrett, 2001; Cartwright, 1996). Rosalind Cartwright has been investigating this hypothesis for many years. Among people suffering from the grief of divorce, she finds, recovery is related to a particular pattern of dreaming: The first dream of the night often comes sooner than it ordinarily would, lasts longer, and is more emotional and storylike. Depressed

CAST OF DREAM

THE MONSTER . . . . . . YOUR FATHER
KIND WOMAN . . . . YOUR MOTHER
POLICEMAN . . . . YOUR ANALYST
FIRST STRANGER . . . . . YOUR BROTHER
SECOND STRANGER . . . YOUR SISTER
LITTLE BOY . . . . . YOU

These drawings from dream journals show that the images in dreams can be either abstract or literal and may reflect a person's concerns, problems, and interests. The two fanciful paintings represent the dreams of a person who worked all day long with brain tissue, which the drawings rather resemble. The desk (right) was sketched in 1939 by a scientist to illustrate his dream about a mechanical device for instantly retrieving quotations—a sort of early desktop computer!

people's dreams tend to get less negative and more positive as the night wears on, and this pattern, too, predicts recovery (Cartwright et al., 1998). Cartwright concludes that getting through a crisis or a rough period in life takes "time, good friends, good genes, good luck, and a good dream system."

Dreams as Thinking

Like the problem-focused approach, the *cognitive approach* to dreaming emphasizes current concerns, but it makes no claims about problem solving during sleep. In this view, dreaming is simply a modification of the cognitive activity that goes on when we are awake. In dreams, we construct reasonable simulations of the real world, drawing on the same kinds of memories, knowledge, metaphors, and assumptions about the world that we do when we are not sleeping (Antrobus, 1991, 2000; Domhoff, 2003; Foulkes, 1999). Thus the content of our dreams may include thoughts, concepts, and scenarios that may or may not be related to our daily problems. We are most likely to dream about our families, friends, studies, jobs, or recreational interests—topics that also occupy our waking thoughts.

In the cognitive view, the brain is doing the same kind of work during dreams as it does when we are awake, which is why parts of the cerebral cortex involved in perceptual and cognitive processing are highly activated during dreaming. The difference is that when we are asleep we are cut off from sensory input and feedback from the world and our bodily movements; the only input to the brain is its own

output. Our dreaming thoughts, therefore, tend to be more unfocused and diffuse than our waking ones—unless, of course, we're daydreaming!

This view predicts that if a person could be totally cut off from all external stimulation while awake, mental activity would be much like that during dreaming, with the same hallucinatory quality. In Chapter 6, we will see that this is, in fact, the case. The cognitive approach also predicts that as cognitive abilities and brain connections mature during childhood, dreams should change in nature, and they do. Toddlers may not dream at all in the sense that adults do. And although young children may experience visual images during sleep, their cognitive limitations keep them from creating true narratives until age 7 or 8 (Foulkes, 1999). Their dreams are infrequent and tend to be bland, static, and about everyday things ("I saw a dog; I was sitting"). But as they grow up, their dreams gradually become more and more intricate, dynamic, and storylike.

Dreams as Interpreted Brain Activity

A fourth approach to dreaming, the **activation–synthesis theory**, draws heavily on physiological research. According to this explanation, first proposed by J. Allan Hobson (1988, 1990), dreams are not "children of an idle brain," as Shakespeare called them. Rather, they are the result of neurons firing spontaneously in the lower part of the brain, in the pons, during REM sleep. These neurons control eye

activation–synthesis theory The theory that dreaming results from the cortical synthesis and interpretation of neural signals triggered by activity in the lower part of the brain.

ACTIVATION–SYNTHESIS THEORY OF DREAMS

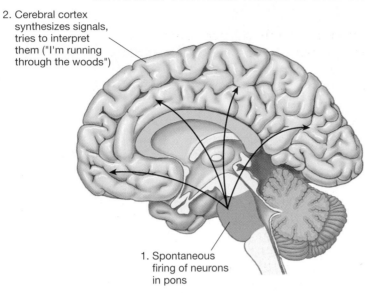

2. Cerebral cortex synthesizes signals, tries to interpret them ("I'm running through the woods")

1. Spontaneous firing of neurons in pons

movement, gaze, balance, and posture, and they send messages to sensory and motor areas of the cortex responsible during wakefulness for visual processing and voluntary action.

According to the activation–synthesis theory, the signals originating in the pons have no psychological meaning in themselves. But the cortex tries to make sense of them by *synthesizing*, or integrating, them with existing knowledge and memories to produce some sort of coherent interpretation. This is just what the cortex does when signals come from sense organs during ordinary wakefulness. The idea that one part of the brain interprets what has gone on in another—whether you are awake or asleep—is consistent with many modern theories of how the brain works (see Chapter 4).

When neurons fire in the part of the brain that handles balance, for instance, the cortex may generate a dream about falling. When signals occur that would ordinarily produce running, the cortex may manufacture a dream about being chased. Because the signals from the pons occur randomly, the cortex's interpretation—the dream—is likely to be incoherent and confusing. And because the cortical neurons that control the initial storage of new memories are turned off during sleep, we typically forget our dreams upon waking unless we write them down or immediately recount them to someone else.

Since Hobson's original formulation, he and his colleagues have added further details and modifications (Hobson, Pace-Schott, & Stickgold, 2000). The brain stem, they say, sets off responses in emotional and visual parts of the brain. At the same time, brain regions that handle logical thought and sensations

from the external world shut down. These changes would account for the fact that dreams tend to be emotionally charged, hallucinatory, and illogical.

Wishes, in this view, do not cause dreams; brain mechanisms do. Dream content, says Hobson (2002), may be "as much dross as gold, as much cognitive trash as treasure, and as much informational noise as a signal of something." That does not mean that dreams are meaningless. Hobson (1988) has argued that the brain "is so inexorably bent upon the quest for meaning that it attributes and even creates meaning when there is little or none to be found in the data it is asked to process." By studying these attributed meanings, you can learn about your unique perceptions, conflicts, and concerns—not by trying to dig below the surface of the dream, as Freud would, but by examining the surface itself. Or you can relax and enjoy the nightly entertainment that dreams provide.

Evaluating Dream Theories

How are we to evaluate these different attempts to explain dreaming? All four approaches account for some of the evidence, but each one also has its drawbacks.

Most psychologists today accept Freud's notion that dreams are more than incoherent ramblings of the mind—that they can have psychological meaning (Fisher & Greenberg, 1996). But most consider the traditional psychoanalytic interpretations of dreams to be far-fetched. No reliable rules exist for interpreting the supposedly latent content of dreams, and there is no objective way to know whether a particular interpretation is correct. Nor is there any convincing empirical support for most of Freud's claims. Freudian interpretations are common in popular books and newspaper columns and, of course, on the Internet, but they are only the writers' personal hunches.

Thinking Critically About Dream Theories

As for dreaming as a way of solving problems, it seems pretty clear that some dreams are related to current worries and concerns. But skeptics doubt that people can actually solve problems or resolve conflicts while sound asleep (Blagrove, 1996; Squier & Domhoff, 1998). Dreams, they say, merely give expression to our problems. The insights that people seem to gain into those problems could be occurring after they wake up and have a chance to think about what is troubling them.

The activation–synthesis theory has also come in for criticism (Domhoff, 2003). Not all dreams are as disjointed or as bizarre as the theory predicts; in fact,

Keep a Dream Diary

It can be fun to record your dreams. Keep a notebook or a tape recorder by your bedside. As soon as you wake up in the morning (or if you awaken during the night while dreaming), record everything you can about your dreams—even short fragments. After you have collected several dreams, see which theory or theories discussed in this chapter seem to best explain them. Do your dreams contain any recurring themes? Do they provide any clues to your current problems, activities, or concerns? (By the way, if you are curious about other people's dreams, you can find lots of them online at www.dreambank.net.)

many tell a coherent, if fanciful, story. Moreover, the activation–synthesis approach does not account well for dreaming that goes on outside of REM sleep. Some neuropsychologists emphasize different brain mechanisms involved in dreams, and many believe that dreams do reflect a person's goals and desires.

Finally, the cognitive approach to dreams is a fairly new one, so some of its specific claims remain to be tested against neurological and cognitive evidence. At present, however, it is a leading contender because it incorporates many elements of other theories and fits what we currently know about waking cognition and cognitive development.

Perhaps it will turn out that different kinds of dreams have different purposes and origins. We all know from experience that some of our dreams seem to be related to daily problems, some are vague and incoherent, and some are anxiety dreams that occur when we are worried or depressed. For the time being, we are going to have to live with uncertainty about what those fascinating stories and images in our sleeping brains really mean.

QUICK quiz

See if you can dream up an answer to this question.

In his dreams, Andy is an infant crawling through a dark tunnel looking for something he has lost. Which theory of dreams would be most receptive to each of the following explanations?

1. Andy recently found a valuable watch he had misplaced.
2. While Andy was sleeping, neurons in his pons that would ordinarily stimulate parts of the brain involved in leg-muscle movements were active.
3. Andy has repressed an early sexual attraction to his mother; the tunnel symbolizes her vagina.
4. Andy has broken up with his lover and is working through the emotional loss.

Answers:

1. the cognitive approach (the dreamer is thinking about a recent experience)   2. the activation–synthesis theory   3. psychoanalytic theory   4. the problem-focused approach

WHAT'S *Ahead*

- Can a hypnotist force you to do things against your will?
- Can hypnosis help you remember the past more accurately?
- What are the legitimate uses of hypnosis in psychology and medicine?
- Are hypnotized persons merely faking or playacting?

The Riddle of Hypnosis

For many years, stage hypnotists, "past-lives channelers," and some psychotherapists have been reporting that they can "age regress" hypnotized people to earlier years or even earlier centuries.

hypnosis A procedure in which the practitioner suggests changes in the sensations, perceptions, thoughts, feelings, or behavior of the subject.

Some therapists claim that hypnosis helps their patients accurately retrieve long-buried memories, and a few even claim that hypnosis has helped their patients recall alleged abductions by extraterrestrials. What are we to make of all this?

Hypnosis is a procedure in which a practitioner suggests changes in the sensations, perceptions, thoughts, feelings, or behavior of the subject (Kirsch & Lynn, 1995). The hypnotized person, in turn, tries to alter his or her cognitive processes in accordance with the hypnotist's suggestions (Nash & Nadon, 1997). Hypnotic suggestions typically involve performance of an action ("Your arm will slowly rise"), an inability to perform an act ("You will be unable to bend your arm"), or a distortion of normal perception or memory ("You will feel no pain," "You will forget being hypnotized until I give you a signal"). People usually report that their response to a suggestion feels involuntary, as if it happened without their willing it.

To induce hypnosis, the hypnotist typically suggests that the person being hypnotized feels relaxed, is getting sleepy, and feels the eyelids getting heavier and heavier. In a singsong or monotonous voice, the hypnotist assures the subject that he or she is

Is it hypnosis that enables the man stretched out between two chairs to hold the weight of the man standing on him, without flinching? This audience assumes so, but the only way to find out whether hypnosis produces unique abilities is to do research with control groups. It turns out that people can do the same thing even when they are not hypnotized.

sinking "deeper and deeper." Sometimes the hypnotist has the person concentrate on a color or a small object, or on certain bodily sensations. People who have been hypnotized report that the focus of attention turns outward, toward the hypnotist's voice. They sometimes compare the experience to being totally absorbed in a good movie or favorite piece of music. The hypnotized person almost always remains fully aware of what is going on and remembers the experience later unless explicitly instructed to forget it—and even then, the memory can be restored by a prearranged signal.

Because hypnosis has been used for everything from parlor tricks and stage shows to medical and psychological treatments, it is important to understand just what this procedure can and cannot achieve. We will begin with a look at the major findings on hypnosis; then we will consider two leading explanations of hypnotic effects.

The Nature of Hypnosis

Since the late 1960s, thousands of articles on hypnosis have appeared. Based on controlled laboratory and clinical research studies, most researchers agree on the following points (Kirsch & Lynn, 1995; Nash, 2001; Nash & Nadon, 1997):

1 *Hypnotic responsiveness depends more on the efforts and qualities of the person being hypnotized than on the skill of the hypnotist.* Some people are more responsive to hypnosis than others but why they are is unknown. Surprisingly, hypnotic susceptibility is unrelated to general personality traits such as gullibility, trust, submissiveness, or conformity (Nash & Nadon, 1997). And it is only weakly related to the ability to become easily absorbed in activities and the world of imagination, (Council, Kirsch, & Grant, 1996; Nash & Nadon, 1997).

2 *Hypnotized people cannot be forced to do things against their will.* Like drunkenness, hypnosis can be used to justify letting go of inhibitions ("I know this looks silly, but after all, I'm hypnotized"). Hypnotized individuals may even comply with a suggestion to do something that seems embarrassing or dangerous. But the individual is choosing to turn responsibility over to the hypnotist and to cooperate with the hypnotist's suggestions (Lynn, Rhue, & Weekes, 1990). There is no evidence that hypnotized people will do anything that actually goes against their morals or that constitutes a real threat to themselves or others (Laurence & Perry, 1988).

3 *Feats performed under hypnosis can be performed by motivated people without hypnosis.* Hypnotized subjects sometimes perform what seem like extraordinary mental or physical feats, but most research finds that hypnosis does not actually enable people to do things that would otherwise be impossible. With proper motivation, support, and encouragement, the same people could do the same things even without being hypnotized (Chaves, 1989; Spanos, Stenstrom, & Johnson, 1988).

4 *Hypnosis does not increase the accuracy of memory.* Many people assume that hypnosis can enhance the recall of forgotten experiences, but this is not true. In rare cases, hypnosis has been used successfully to jog the memories of crime victims, but usually the memories of hypnotized witnesses have been completely mistaken. Although hypnosis does sometimes boost the amount of information recalled, it also increases *errors*, perhaps because hypnotized people are more willing than others to guess, or because they mistake vividly imagined possibilities for actual memories (Dinges et al., 1992; Kihlstrom, 1994). The hypnotized person is often completely convinced that his or her memories are real, but they are not. Because pseudomemories and errors are so common in hypnotically induced recall, the American Psychological Association and the American Medical Association oppose the use of "hypnotically refreshed" testimony in courts of law.

"THE WITNESS HAS BARKED, MEOWED AND GIVEN US FIVE MINUTES OF BABY TALK. I'D SAY HYPNOSIS IS NOT THE ANSWER."

5 *Hypnosis does not produce a literal reexperiencing of long-ago events.* When clinical psychologist Michael Yapko (1994) surveyed 869 members of the American Association of Marriage and Family Therapists, he was alarmed to discover that more than half believed that "hypnosis can be used to recover memories from as far back as birth." This belief is just plain wrong. When people are regressed to an earlier age, their mental and moral performance remains adultlike (Nash, 1987). Their brain-wave patterns and reflexes do not become childish; they do not reason as children do or show child-sized IQs. They may use baby talk or report that they feel 4 years old again, but the reason is not that they are actually reliving the experience of being 4; they are just willing to play the role.

6 *Hypnotic suggestions have been used effectively for many medical and psychological purposes.* Although hypnosis is not of much use for finding out what happened in the past, it can be useful in the treatment of psychological and medical problems. Its greatest success is in pain management; some people experience dramatic relief of pain resulting from conditions as diverse as burns, cancer, and childbirth; others have learned to cope better emotionally with chronic pain. Hypnotic suggestions have also been used in the treatment of stress, anxiety, obesity, asthma, irritable bowel syndrom, chemotherapy-induced nausea, and even skin disorders (Nash & Barnier, 2007; Patterson & Jensen, 2003).

Theories of Hypnosis

Over the years, people have proposed many explanations of what hypnosis is and how it produces its effects. One early notion, that hypnosis is a "trance state," was eventually rejected by most researchers. Today, two competing theories predominate, with many scientists taking a position somewhere in the middle.

Dissociation Theories One leading approach was originally proposed by the late Ernest Hilgard (1977, 1986), who argued that hypnosis, like lucid dreaming and even simple distraction, involves **dissociation**, a split in consciousness in which one part of the mind operates independently of the rest of consciousness. In many hypnotized persons, said Hilgard, while most of the mind is subject to hypnotic suggestion, one part is a *hidden observer*, watching but not participating. Unless given special instructions, the hypnotized part remains unaware of the observer.

dissociation A split in consciousness in which one part of the mind operates independently of others.

A person whose arm is immersed in ice water ordinarily feels intense pain. But Ernest Hilgard, a pioneer in hypnosis research, found that when hypnotized people are told the pain will be minimal, they report little or no discomfort. Like the young woman shown here in one of Hilgard's studies, they seem unperturbed.

In his research, Hilgard attempted to question the hidden observer directly. In one procedure, hypnotized volunteers had to submerge an arm in ice water for several seconds, an experience that is normally excruciating. They were told that they would feel no pain, but that the nonsubmerged hand would be able to signal the level of any hidden pain by pressing a key. In this situation, many people said they felt little or no pain—yet at the same time, their free hand was busily pressing the key. After the session, these people continued to insist that they had been pain-free, unless the hypnotist asked the hidden observer to issue a separate report.

A related theory holds that during hypnosis, dissociation occurs between an "executive" system in the brain (probably in the frontal lobes) and other brain systems involved in thinking and acting (Woody & Bowers, 1994). The result is an altered state of consciousness similar to that found in patients with frontal lobe disorders. Because the dissociated systems are freed from control by the executive, they are more easily influenced by suggestions from the hypnotist. Like the activation–synthesis theory of dreaming, dissociation theories of hypnosis are consistent with modern brain theories, which hold that one part of the brain operates as a reporter and interpreter of activities carried out unconsciously by other brain parts (see Chapter 4).

DISSOCIATION THEORIES OF HYPNOSIS

Hypnotist induces hypnotic state

Split between hidden observer or executive control system and rest of mind

Person responds to suggestions ("I'm 4 years old")

The Sociocognitive Approach The second major approach to hypnosis, the *sociocognitive explanation*, holds that the effects of hypnosis result from an interaction between the social influence of the hypnotist (the "socio" part) and the abilities, beliefs, and expectations of the subject (the "cognitive" part) (Kirsch, 1997; Sarbin, 1991; Spanos, 1991). The hypnotized person is basically playing a role, one that has analogies in ordinary life, where we willingly submit to the suggestions of parents, teachers, doctors, therapists, and television commercials. In this view, even the "hidden observer" is simply a reaction to

the social demands of the situation and the suggestions of the hypnotist (Kirsch & Lynn, 1998).

The hypnotized person is not merely faking or playacting, however. A person who has been instructed to fool an observer by faking a hypnotic state will tend to overplay the role and will stop playing it as soon as the other person leaves the room. In contrast, hypnotized subjects continue to follow the hypnotic suggestions even when they think they are not being watched (Kirsch et al., 1989; Spanos et al., 1993). Like many social roles, the role of "hypnotized person" is so engrossing and involving that actions required by the role may occur without the person's conscious intent.

SOCIOCOGNITIVE THEORIES OF HYPNOSIS

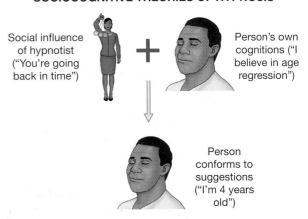

Social influence of hypnotist ("You're going back in time")

Person's own cognitions ("I believe in age regression")

Person conforms to suggestions ("I'm 4 years old")

Sociocognitive views explain why some people under hypnosis report spirit possession or "memories" of alien abductions (Clancy, 2005; Spanos, 1996). The individual goes to a therapist looking for an explanation of his or her nightmares, puzzling symptoms (such as waking up in the middle of the night in a cold sweat), or the waking dreams we described earlier. If the therapist already believes in alien abduction, he or she may hypnotize the person and then consciously or unconsciously shape the client's story by giving subtle or not-so-subtle hints about what the person should say.

The sociocognitive view can also explain apparent cases of past-life regression. In a fascinating program of research, Nicholas Spanos and his colleagues directed hypnotized Canadian university students to regress past their own births to previous lives. About a third of the students (who already believed in reincarnation) reported being able to do so. But when they were asked, while supposedly reliving a past life, to name the leader of their country, say whether the country was at peace or at war, or describe the money used in their community, the students could not do it. (One young man, who thought he was

Julius Caesar, said the year was 50 A.D. and he was emperor of Rome. But Caesar died in 44 B.C. and was never crowned emperor, and dating years as A.D. or B.C. did not begin until several centuries later.) Not knowing anything about the language, dates, customs, and events of their "previous life" did not

deter the students from constructing a story about it, however. They tried to fulfill the requirements of the role by weaving events, places, and persons from their present lives into their accounts and by picking up cues from the experimenter. The researchers concluded that the act of "remembering" another self involves the construction of a fantasy that accords with the rememberer's own beliefs and also the beliefs of others—in this case, those of the authoritative hypnotist (Spanos, Menary et al., 1991).

Psychologists who think hypnosis is a special state of consciousness involving dissociation and those who emphasize sociocognitive explanations agree on many issues. They agree, for example, that hypnosis does *not* cause memories to become sharper or allow early experiences to be "replayed" with perfect accuracy. Whatever hypnosis is, by studying it psychologists are learning much about human suggestibility, the power of imagination, and the way we perceive the present and remember the past.

QUICK quiz

We'd like to plant a suggestion in your mind—that you'd be wise to take this quiz.

A. *True or false:*

1. A hypnotized person is usually aware of what is going on and remembers the experience later.
2. Hypnosis gives us special powers that we do not ordinarily have.
3. Hypnosis reduces errors in memory.
4. Hypnotized people play no active part in controlling their behavior and thoughts.
5. According to Hilgard, hypnosis is a state of consciousness involving a "hidden observer."
6. Sociocognitive theorists view hypnosis as mere faking or conscious playacting.

B. Some people believe that hypnotic suggestions can bolster the immune system and help a person fight disease. However, support for this belief has so far been modest, and many studies have had methodological flaws (Miller & Cohen, 2001). One therapist dismissed these concerns by saying that a negative result just means that the hypnotist lacks skill or the right personality. As a critical thinker, can you spot what is wrong with his reasoning? (Think back to Chapter 1 and the way a scientific hypothesis must be stated.)

Answers:

A. 1. true 2. false 3. false 4. false 5. true 6. false   B. The therapist's argument violates the principle of falsifiability. If a result is positive, he counts it as evidence. But if a result is negative, he refuses to count it as counterevidence ("Maybe the hypnotist just wasn't good enough"). With this kind of reasoning, there is no way to tell whether the hypothesis is right or wrong.

WHAT'S *Ahead*

- In its physiological effects, is alcohol a "downer" or an "upper"?
- How do recreational drugs affect the brain?
- Why can a glass of wine make you feel tired at one time but sociable and pepped up at another?

Consciousness-Altering Drugs

In Jerusalem, hundreds of Hasidic men celebrate the completion of the reading of the holy Torah by dancing for hours in the streets; their goal is religious ecstasy. In South Dakota, several Lakota (Sioux) adults sit naked in the darkness and crushing heat of the sweat lodge; their goal is euphoria, the transcendence of pain, and possible connection with the Great Spirit of the Universe. In the Amazon jungle, a young man training to be a shaman, a religious leader, takes a whiff of hallucinogenic snuff made from the bark of the virola tree; his goal is to enter a trance and communicate with animals, spirits, and supernatural forces.

These three rituals, although seemingly quite different, are all aimed at release from the confines of ordinary consciousness. Cultures around the

All cultures have found ways to alter consciousness. The Maulavis of Turkey (left), the famous whirling dervishes, spin in an energetic but controlled manner in order to achieve religious rapture. People in many cultures meditate (center) as a way to quiet the mind and achieve spiritual enlightenment. And in some cultures, psychoactive drugs are used for religious or artistic inspiration, as in the case of the Huichol Indians of western Mexico (right), shown here harvesting hallucinogenic peyote mushrooms.

world have devised such practices, often as part of their religions. Because attempts to alter mood and consciousness appear to be universal, some writers believe they reflect a human need, one as basic as the need for food and water (Siegel, 1989).

William James (1902/1936), who was fascinated by alterations in consciousness, would have agreed. After inhaling nitrous oxide ("laughing gas"), he wrote, "Our normal waking consciousness, rational consciousness as we call it, is but one special type of consciousness, whilst all about it, parted from it by the filmiest of screens, there lie potential forms of consciousness entirely different." James hoped that psychologists would study these other forms of consciousness, but for half a century, few did. Then, during the 1960s, attitudes changed. During that decade of social upheaval, millions of people began to seek ways of deliberately producing *altered states of consciousness*, especially through the use of psychoactive drugs. Researchers became interested in the psychology, as well as the physiology, of such drugs. The filmy screen described by James finally began to lift.

Classifying Drugs

A **psychoactive drug** is a substance that alters perception, mood, thinking, memory, or behavior by changing the body's biochemistry. Around the world and throughout history, the most widely used drugs have been tobacco, alcohol, marijuana, mescaline, opium, cocaine, peyote—and, of course, tea and coffee. The reasons for taking such drugs vary: to alter consciousness, as part of a religious ritual, for recreation, to decrease physical pain or discomfort, or for psychological escape. But human beings are not the only species that likes to get high on occasion; so do many other animals. Baboons ingest tobacco, elephants love the alcohol in fermented fruit, and reindeer and rabbits seek out intoxicating mushrooms (Siegel, 1989).

In Western societies, a whole pharmacopeia of recreational drugs exists, and each year seems to see the introduction of new ones, both natural and synthetic. Most of these drugs can be classified as *stimulants, depressants, opiates,* or *psychedelics*, depending on their effects on the central nervous system and their impact on behavior and mood (see Table 5.1). Here we describe only their physiological and psychological effects; Chapter 11 covers addiction and Chapter 12 reviews drugs used in the treatment of mental and emotional disorders.

1 **Stimulants** *speed up activity in the central nervous system*. They include, among other drugs, nicotine, caffeine, cocaine, amphetamines ("uppers"), and methamphetamine ("meth"). In moderate amounts, stimulants produce feelings of excitement, confidence, and well-being or euphoria. In large amounts, they make a person anxious, jittery, and hyperalert. In very large doses, they may cause convulsions, heart failure, and death.

Amphetamines are synthetic drugs taken in pill form, injected, smoked, or inhaled. Methamphetamine is structurally similar to amphetamines and is used in the same ways; it comes in two forms, as a powder ("crank," "speed") or in a purer form, a crystalline solid ("glass," "ice"). Cocaine ("coke") is a natural drug derived from the coca plant. Rural

psychoactive drug A drug capable of influencing perception, mood, cognition, or behavior.

stimulants Drugs that speed up activity in the central nervous system.

TABLE 5.1
Some Psychoactive Drugs and Their Effects

Class of Drug	Type	Common Effects	Results of Abuse/Addiction
Amphetamines Methamphetamine	Stimulants	Wakefulness, alertness, raised metabolism, elevated mood	Nervousness, headaches, loss of appetite, high blood pressure, delusions, psychosis, heart damage, convulsions, death
Cocaine	Stimulant	Euphoria, excitation, boost of energy, suppressed appetite	Excitability, sleeplessness, sweating, paranoia, anxiety, panic, depression, heart damage, heart failure, injury to nose if sniffed
Tobacco (nicotine)	Stimulant	Varies from alertness to calmness, depending on mental set, setting, and prior arousal; decreases appetite for carbohydrates	*Nicotine:* heart disease, high blood pressure, impaired circulation, erectile problems in men, damage throughout the body due to lowering of a key enzyme *Tar:* lung cancer, emphysema, mouth and throat cancer, many other health risks
Caffeine	Stimulant	Wakefulness, alertness, shortened reaction time	Restlessness, insomnia, muscle tension, heartbeat irregularities, high blood pressure
Alcohol (1–2 drinks)	Depressant	Depends on setting and mental set; tends to act like a stimulant because it reduces inhibitions and anxiety	
Alcohol (several/many drinks)	Depressant	Slowed reaction time, tension, depression, reduced ability to store new memories or to retrieve old ones, poor coordination	Blackouts, cirrhosis of the liver, other organ damage, mental and neurological impairment, psychosis, possibly death
Tranquilizers (e.g., Valium); barbiturates (e.g., phenobarbital)	Depressant	Reduced anxiety and tension, sedation	Increased dosage needed for effects; impaired motor and sensory functions, impaired permanent storage of new information, withdrawal symptoms; possibly convulsions, coma, death (especially when taken with other drugs)
Opium, heroin, morphine	Opiate	Euphoria, relief of pain	Loss of appetite, nausea, constipation, withdrawal symptoms, convulsions, coma, possibly death
LSD, psilocybin, mescaline	Psychedelic	Exhilaration, visions and hallucinations, insightful experiences	Psychosis, paranoia, panic reactions
Marijuana	Mild psychedelic (classification controversial)	Relaxation, euphoria, increased appetite, reduced ability to store new memories, other effects depending on mental set and setting	Throat and lung irritation, possible lung damage if smoked heavily

depressants Drugs that slow down activity in the central nervous system.

opiates Drugs, derived from the opium poppy, that relieve pain and commonly produce euphoria.

psychedelic drugs Consciousness-altering drugs that produce hallucinations, change thought processes, or disrupt the normal perception of time and space.

workers in Bolivia and Peru chew coca leaf every day without apparent ill effects. In North America, the drug is usually inhaled, injected, or smoked in the highly refined form known as crack. These methods give the drug a more immediate, powerful, and dangerous effect than when coca leaf is chewed. Amphetamines, methamphetamine, and cocaine make users feel peppy but do not actually increase energy reserves. Fatigue, irritability, and depression may occur when the effects of these drugs wear off.

2 **Depressants** *slow down activity in the central nervous system*. They include alcohol, tranquilizers, barbiturates, and most of the common chemicals that some people inhale ("huffing"). Depressants usually make a person feel calm or drowsy, and they may reduce anxiety, guilt, tension, and inhibitions. In large amounts, they may produce insensitivity to pain and other sensations. Like stimulants, in very large doses they can cause irregular heartbeats, convulsions, and death.

People are often surprised to learn that alcohol is a central-nervous-system depressant. In small amounts, alcohol has some of the effects of a stimulant, because it suppresses activity in parts of the brain that normally inhibit impulsive behavior, such as loud laughter and clowning around. In the long run, however, it slows down nervous-system activity. Like barbiturates and opiates, alcohol can be used as an anesthetic; if you drink enough, you will eventually pass out. Over time, alcohol consumed in large quantities damages the liver, heart, and brain. Extremely large amounts can kill by inhibiting the nerve cells in the brain areas that control breathing and heartbeat. Every so often the news reports the death of a college student who had large amounts of alcohol "funneled" into him as part of an initiation or drinking competition. On the other hand, *moderate* social drinking—a drink or two of wine or liquor a day—is associated with a variety of health benefits, especially for adults over 40. These benefits include a reduced risk of heart attack and stroke, and antidiabetic effects (e.g., Davies et al., 2002; Mukamal et al., 2003; Reynolds et al., 2003).

3 **Opiates** *relieve pain*. They include opium, derived from the opium poppy; morphine, a derivative of opium; heroin, a derivative of morphine; and synthetic drugs such as methadone. All of these drugs mimic the action of endorphins, and most have a powerful effect on the emotions. When injected, they may produce a rush—a sudden feeling of euphoria. They may also decrease anxiety and motivation, although the effects vary.

4 **Psychedelic drugs** *disrupt normal thought processes, such as the perception of time and space*. Sometimes, psychedelics produce hallucinations, especially visual ones. Some psychedelics, such as lysergic acid diethylamide (LSD), are made in the laboratory. Others, such as mescaline (from the peyote cactus), *Salvia divinorum* (a plant native to Mexico), and psilocybin (from certain species of mushrooms), are natural substances. Emotional reactions to psychedelics vary from person to person and from one time to another for any individual. A "trip" may be mildly pleasant or unpleasant, a mystical revelation or a nightmare.

Some commonly used drugs fall outside these four classifications, combine elements of more than one category, or have uncertain effects. One is *marijuana* ("pot," "grass," "weed"), which is smoked or, less commonly, eaten in foods such as brownies, and is the most widely used illicit drug in North America and Europe. Some researchers classify it as a mild psychedelic, but others feel that its chemical makeup and its psychological effects place it outside the major classifications. The main active ingredient in marijuana is tetrahydrocannabinol (THC), derived from the hemp plant, *Cannabis sativa*. In some respects, THC appears to be a mild stimulant, increasing heart rate and making tastes, sounds, and colors seem more intense. But users often report reactions ranging from mild euphoria to relaxation or even sleepiness.

Although THC has not been shown to be carcinogenic, some researchers believe that very heavy smoking of the drug (which is high in tar) may increase the risk of lung damage (Barsky et al., 1998; Zhu et al., 2000). In moderate doses, marijuana can interfere with the transfer of information to long-term memory, a characteristic it shares with alcohol, and in large doses, it can cause hallucinations and a sense of unreality. Sometimes the drug impairs coordination, concentration, and reaction times, though it is not clear how long these effects last. On the other hand, some studies find that marijuana has medical benefits. It reduces the nausea and vomiting that often accompany chemotherapy treatment for cancer and AIDS; it reduces the physical tremors, loss of appetite, and other symptoms caused by multiple sclerosis; it helps reduce the frequency of seizures in some patients with epilepsy; and it alleviates the retinal swelling caused by glaucoma (Grinspoon & Bakalar, 1993; Zimmer & Morgan, 1997).

The Physiology of Drug Effects

Psychoactive drugs produce their psychological effects primarily by acting on brain neurotransmitters, the chemical substances that carry messages from one nerve cell to another. A drug may increase or decrease the release of neurotransmitters, prevent the reabsorption of excess neurotransmitter molecules by the cells that have released them, or block the effects of a neurotransmitter on a receiving nerve cell (see Chapter 4). Figure 5.2 shows how one drug, cocaine, increases the amount of norepinephrine and dopamine in the brain by blocking the reabsorption of these substances. Cocaine also seems to increase the transmission of serotonin (Rocha et al., 1998).

These biochemical changes affect cognitive and emotional functioning. For example, because of alcohol's effect on parts of the brain involved in judgment, drinkers often are unable to gauge their own competence. Just a couple of drinks can affect perception, response time, coordination, and balance, despite the drinker's own impression of unchanged

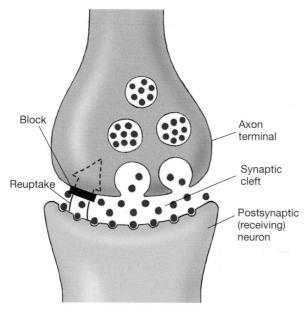

FIGURE 5.2
Cocaine's Effect on the Brain
Cocaine blocks the brain's reabsorption ("reuptake") of the neurotransmitters dopamine and norepinephrine, so levels of these substances rise. The result is overstimulation of certain brain circuits and a brief euphoric high. Then, when the drug wears off, a depletion of dopamine may cause the user to "crash" and become sleepy and depressed.

Block

Reuptake

Axon terminal

Synaptic cleft

Postsynaptic (receiving) neuron

or even improved performance. Liquor also affects memory, possibly by interfering with the work of serotonin. Information stored before a drinking session remains intact during the session but is retrieved more slowly (Haut et al., 1989). The ability to store new memories for later use also suffers after the consumption of only two or three drinks (Parker, Birnbaum, & Noble, 1976). Consuming small amounts does not seem to affect *sober* mental performance, but even occasional heavy drinking impairs later abstract thought. In other words, a Saturday-night binge is more dangerous than a daily drink.

As for other recreational drugs, there is little evidence that *light or moderate* use can damage the human brain enough to affect cognitive functioning, but nearly all researchers agree that heavy or frequent use is another matter (see Chapter 11). For example, one study found that heavy users of methamphetamine had damage to dopamine cells and performed more poorly than other people on tests of memory, attention, and movement, even though they had not used the drug for at least 11 months (Volkow et al., 2001).

Not all drugs are equally dangerous, however. Controversy exists especially about Ecstasy (MDMA), a synthetic drug that has properties of both a hallucinogen and a stimulant and that is said to increase empathy, insight, and energy. Ecstasy has provoked a great deal of hysteria; claims have been made, mostly on the basis of research with animals receiving huge doses, that the drug permanently damages serotonin cells, wipes out memory, and causes tremors like those of Parkinson's disease. But some of the best-known reports of these presumed dangers were based on research having major methodological problems; one influential report even had to be retracted in 2003 by the prestigious journal *Science* after irregularities and errors came to light. An impartial review of Ecstasy research concluded that there was no evidence that Ecstasy causes lasting damage "with the possible (but as yet unproven) exception of mild memory loss" (Kish, 2003). Heavy use may cause a reduction in serotonin levels, but this change has not been shown to be permanent, and it could be caused by other drugs that most heavy users take (Buchert et al., 2003).

The use of some psychoactive drugs, such as heroin and tranquilizers, can lead to **tolerance**: Over time, more and more of the drug is needed to get the same effect. When habitual heavy users stop taking a drug, they may suffer severe **withdrawal** symptoms, which, depending on the drug, may include nausea, abdominal cramps, sweating, muscle spasms, depression, and sleep problems.

tolerance Increased resistance to a drug's effects accompanying continued use.

withdrawal Physical and psychological symptoms that occur when someone addicted to a drug stops taking it.

The Psychology of Drug Effects

People often assume that the effects of a drug are automatic, the inevitable result of the drug's chem-

Thinking Critically About Drug Effects

istry ("I couldn't help what I said—the booze made me do it"). But reactions to a psychoactive drug involve

more than the drug's chemical properties. They also depend on a person's individual characteristics, experience with the drug, environmental setting, and mental set.

1 *Individual factors include body weight, metabolism, initial state of emotional arousal, personality characteristics, and physical tolerance for the drug.* For example, women generally get drunker than men on the same amount of alcohol because women are smaller, on average, and their bodies metabolize alcohol differently (Fuchs et al., 1995). Similarly, many Asians have a genetically determined adverse reaction to even small amounts of alcohol, which can cause severe headaches, facial flushing, and diarrhea (Cloninger, 1990). For individuals, a drug may have one effect after a tiring day and a different one after a rousing quarrel, or the effect may vary with the time of day because of the body's circadian rhythms. And some differences among individuals in their responses to a drug may be due to their personality traits. PET scans show that when people who are prone to anger and irritability wear nicotine patches, dramatic bursts of activity occur in the brain while they are working on competitive or aggressive tasks. These changes do not occur, however, in more relaxed and cheerful people or in control subjects wearing fake patches (Fallon et al., 2004).

2 *Experience with the drug refers to the number of times a person has taken it.* Trying a drug—a cigarette, an alcoholic drink, a stimulant—for the first time is often a neutral or unpleasant experience. But reactions typically change once a person has become familiar with the drug's effects.

3 *"Environmental setting" refers to the context in which a person takes the drug.* A person might have one glass of wine at home alone and feel sleepy but have three glasses of wine at a party and feel full of energy. Someone might feel happy and high drinking with good friends but fearful and nervous drinking with strangers. In one study of reactions to alcohol, most of the drinkers became

depressed, angry, confused, and unfriendly. Then it dawned on the researchers that anyone might become depressed, angry, confused, and unfriendly if asked to drink bourbon at 9:00 A.M. in a bleak hospital room, which was the setting for the experiment (Warren & Raynes, 1972).

4 *"Mental set" refers to expectations about the drug's effects and reasons for taking it.* Some people drink to become more sociable, friendly, or seductive; some drink to try to reduce feelings of anxiety or depression; and some drink in order to have an excuse for abusiveness or violence. Addicts use drugs to escape from the real world; people living with chronic pain use the same drugs in order to function in the real world (Portenoy, 1994). The motives for taking a drug greatly influence its effects.

Expectations can sometimes have a more powerful effect than the chemical properties of the drug itself. In several imaginative studies, researchers compared people who were drinking liquor (vodka and tonic) with those who *thought* they were drinking liquor but were actually getting only tonic and lime juice. (Vodka has a subtle taste, and most people could not tell the real and phony drinks apart.) The experimenters found a *"think–drink" effect*: Men behaved more belligerently when they thought they were drinking vodka than when they thought they were drinking plain tonic water, *regardless of the actual content of the drinks*. And both sexes reported feeling sexually aroused when they thought they were drinking vodka, whether they actually got vodka or not (Abrams & Wilson, 1983; Marlatt & Rohsenow, 1980).

Expectations and beliefs about drugs are, in turn, shaped by the culture in which you live. Many people start their day with a cup of coffee because it increases alertness, but when coffee was first introduced in Europe, people protested against it. Women said it suppressed their husbands' sexual performance and made men inconsiderate—and maybe it did! In the nineteenth century, Americans regarded marijuana as a mild sedative with no mind-altering properties. They did not expect it to give them a high, and it didn't; it merely put them to sleep (Weil, 1972/1986). Today, most people who smoke do it to get high, and that expectation has no doubt affected how people respond to the drug.

None of this means that alcohol and other drugs are merely placebos. Psychoactive drugs, as we have seen, do have physiological effects, many of them extremely potent. But an understanding of the psychological factors involved in drug use may help us think critically about the reactions individuals have to drugs and the use of drugs to excuse one's actions.

Cultural attitudes toward drugs vary with the times. Until recent decades, cigarette smoking was promoted as healthy and glamorous. And before it was banned in the United States in the 1920s, cocaine was widely touted as a cure for everything from toothaches to timidity. It was used in teas, tonics, throat lozenges, and even soft drinks (including, briefly, Coca-Cola, which derived its name from the coca plant).

QUICK quiz

There is no excuse for avoiding this quiz.

See whether you can name the following:

1. Three stimulants used illegally
2. Two drugs that interfere with the formation of new long-term memories
3. Three types of depressant drugs
4. A legal recreational drug that acts as a depressant on the central nervous system
5. Four factors that influence a person's psychological reactions to a drug

Answers:

1. cocaine, amphetamines, and methamphetamine   2. marijuana and alcohol   3. barbiturates, tranquilizers, and alcohol   4. alcohol   5. the person's physical condition, prior experience with the drug, mental set, and the environmental setting

As we have seen in this chapter, fluctuations and changes in consciousness, though interesting in themselves, also show us how expectations and explanations of our own mental and physical states affect what we do and how we feel. Research on SAD and "PMS," the purposes of sleep, the meaning of dreams, the nature of hypnosis, and the dangers and benefits of drugs have done much to dispel many popular but mistaken ideas about these topics. In this way, the scientific scrutiny of biological rhythms, dreaming, hypnotic suggestion, and drug-induced states has deepened our understanding of the intimate relationship between body and mind.

psychology in
the news
REVISITED

Let us return now to the interesting case of the church in New Mexico whose members use a hallucinogenic tea as part of a religious ritual. What is your reaction to this story?

Because the consequences of drug *abuse* are so devastating to individuals and to society, people often find it difficult to think critically about drug laws and policies; the debate becomes highly emotional. At one extreme, some people cannot accept evidence that their favorite drug—be it coffee, tobacco, alcohol, or marijuana—might have harmful effects. At the other extreme, some cannot accept evidence that their most hated drug— be it alcohol, morphine, marijuana, or the coca leaf—might not be dangerous in all forms or amounts and might even have some beneficial effects. Both sides often confuse potent drugs with others that have only subtle effects, and confuse light or moderate use with heavy or excessive use.

As we saw earlier, cultural attitudes toward a drug affect people's responses to it, and these attitudes vary with the times. Once a drug is declared illegal, many people assume it is deadly, even though some legal drugs are more dangerous than illegal ones. Addiction to prescription painkillers and sedatives used for recreational rather than medical purposes ("pharming") has risen dramatically in the past decade among teenagers and adults, yet these drugs are legal. Nicotine, which of course is legal, is as addictive as heroin and cocaine, which are illegal. Tobacco use contributes to more than 435,000 deaths in the United States every year, 24 times the number of deaths from all illegal forms of drug use combined (Fellows et al., 2002). Yet most people have a far more negative view of heroin and cocaine—and of hallucinogenic substances like peyote and hoasca tea—than of nicotine and prescription pain killers.

Emotions have run especially high in debates over marijuana. As we saw, heavy use of marijuana poses some physical risks. For most people, however, both the physical risks and the psychological ones are much lower than for other common drugs (Grant et al., 2003; Macleod et al., 2004). No deaths have ever been attributed to marijuana, and, as we also saw, the drug has some medical benefits. In recognition of these facts, Spain, Italy, Portugal, the Netherlands, and Belgium have decriminalized marijuana. But in the United States, where voters in 11 states (as of 2006) have approved the medical use of marijuana. Possession of any amount of pot remains illegal, and punishment for first offenses ranges from a few years in prison to life imprisonment without parole (Schlosser, 2003). Nearly half of all drug arrests nationwide are now for marijuana use. In many states, a person who has been convicted of marijuana possession cannot later get food stamps or welfare, which even convicted rapists and murderers are entitled to.

Some people are committed to the eradication of all currently illegal drugs, regardless of how they are used: for altering consciousness, coping with pain or illness, or participating in a religious ritual. Those at the other extreme think that all drugs should be decriminalized, no matter what their purpose. People in between those positions have tried to find a middle ground. Some would legalize marijuana for recreational and medicinal use, and perhaps also substances used in religious rituals, but would ban tobacco and most hard drugs. And some people feel that instead of punishing or incarcerating people who use drugs, society would be better off regulating where drugs are used (never at work or when driving, for example), providing treatment for addicts, and educating people about the benefits and hazards of particular drugs.

As you assess your own views about drugs, keep in mind what this chapter has reported about the universal human longing to experience altered states of consciousness. Human beings everywhere, throughout history, have sought ways to improve their moods and mental states when their biological rhythms temporarily ebb, and many have used them to seek spiritual enlightenment or seek connection with a divine power. Where, then, given this information, do you stand in the drug debate? Which psychoactive drugs, if any, should be prohibited? Can we create mental sets and environmental settings that promote safe recreational use of some drugs, minimize the likelihood of drug abuse, and permit the medicinal use of beneficial drugs? What do you think?

In debates over drug policy, emotional arguments and images (such as those in this poster from the 1930s) often take precedence over reasoning and research. Should any drugs be decriminalized, or permitted for treating medical problems or use in religious rituals? Why or why not?

➤TAKING ➤PSYCHOLOGY ➤WITH ➤YOU

How to Get a Good Night's Sleep

You hop into bed, turn out the lights, close your eyes, and wait for slumber. An hour later, you're still waiting. Finally you drop off, but at 3:00 A.M., to your chagrin, you're awake again. By the time the rooster crows, you have put in a hard day's night.

Insomnia affects most people at one time or another, and many people most of the time. No wonder that sleeping pills are a multimillion-dollar business. But many of these pills have side effects, such as making you feel a little foggy-headed the next day. Many hasten sleep only slightly and lose their effectiveness over time. Some can actually make matters worse; barbiturates, for example, greatly suppress REM sleep, a result that eventually causes wakefulness, and they also suppress Stages 3 and 4, the deeper stages of sleep. Although pills can be helpful on a temporary basis, they do not get at stress and anxiety that may be at the root of your insomnia, and once you stop taking the pills, your insomnia is likely to return. Sleep research suggests some alternatives:

• **Be sure you actually have a sleep problem.** Many people only *think* they sleep poorly. They overestimate how long it takes them to doze off and underestimate how much sleep they are getting. When they are observed in the laboratory, they usually fall asleep in less than 30 minutes and are awake only for very short periods during the night (Bonnet, 1990; Carskadon, Mitler, & Dement, 1974). The real test for diagnosing a sleep deficit is not how many hours you sleep—as we saw, people vary in how much they need—but how you feel during the day. Do you doze off without intending to? Do you feel drowsy in class or at meetings?

• **Get a correct diagnosis of the sleep problem.** Do you suffer from sleep apnea (see p. 154)? Do you have a physical disorder that is interfering with sleep? Do you live in a noisy place? (Try earplugs!) Are you fighting your personal biological rhythms by going to bed too early or too late? Do you go to bed early one night and late another? It's better to go to bed at about the same time every night and get up at the same time every morning.

• **Avoid excessive use of alcohol or other drugs.** Many drugs interfere with sleep. For instance, coffee, tea, cola, "energy drinks," and chocolate all contain caffeine, which is a stimulant; alcohol suppresses REM sleep; and some tranquilizers reduce Stage 4 sleep.

• **Use relaxation techniques.** For example, listening to soft music at bedtime, which slows down your heartbeat and breathing, can help older people sleep better and longer (Lai & Good, 2005), and it may help younger people as well.

• **Avoid lying awake for hours waiting for sleep.** Your frustration will cause arousal that will keep you awake. If you can't sleep, get up and do something else, preferably something dull and relaxing, in another room. When you feel drowsy, try sleeping again.

Finally, when insomnia is related to anxiety and worry, it makes sense to get to the source of your problems, and that may mean a brief round of cognitive-behavior therapy (CBT), which teaches you how to change the negative thoughts that are keeping you awake. A placebo-controlled study that compared the effectiveness of a leading sleep pill and a six-week course of CBT found that both approaches helped alleviate chronic insomnia, but CBT worked better both in the short run and the long run (Jacobs et al., 2004). Other research, too, finds that CBT helps people fall asleep sooner and stay asleep longer than pills do (Morin, 2004). (We discuss cognitive-behavior therapy in Chapter 13.)

Woody Allen once said, "The lamb and the lion shall lie down together, but the lamb will not be very sleepy." Like a lamb trying to sleep with a lion, you cannot expect to sleep well with stress hormones pouring through your bloodstream and worries crowding your mind. In an evolutionary sense, sleeplessness is an adaptive response to danger and threat. When your anxieties decrease, so may your sleepless nights.

SUMMARY

Biological Rhythms: The Tides of Experience

• *Consciousness* is the awareness of oneself and the environment. Changing states of consciousness are often associated with *biological rhythms*—periodic fluctuations in physiological functioning. These rhythms are typically synchronized to external cues, but many are also *endogenous*, generated from within. *Circadian* fluctuations occur about once a day; other rhythms occur less frequently or more frequently than that.

• When people live in isolation from all time cues, they tend to live a day that is slightly longer than 24 hours. Circadian rhythms are governed by a biological "clock" in the *suprachiasmatic nucleus (SCN)* of the hypothalamus. The SCN regulates and, in turn, is affected by the hormone *melatonin*, which is responsive to changes in light and dark and which increases during the dark hours. When a person's normal routine changes, the person may experience *internal desynchronization*, in which the usual circadian rhythms are thrown out of phase with one another. The result may be fatigue, mental inefficiency, and an increased risk of accidents.

• Folklore holds that moods follow a long-term biological rhythm. Some people do show a recurrence of depression every winter in a pattern that has been labeled *seasonal affective disorder* (SAD), but serious seasonal depression is rare. The causes of SAD are not yet clear but may involve an abnormality in the secretion of melatonin. Light treatments can be effective.

• Another long-term rhythm is the menstrual cycle, during which various hormones rise and fall. Well-controlled, double-blind studies on "PMS," such as the one described in "Close-up on Research," do not support claims that emotional symptoms are reliably and universally tied to the menstrual cycle. Overall, women and men do not differ in the emotional symptoms they report or in the number of mood swings they experience over the course of a month.

• Expectations and learning affect how both sexes interpret bodily and emotional changes. Few people of either sex are likely to undergo dramatic monthly mood swings or personality changes because of hormones.

The Rhythms of Sleep

• During sleep, periods of *rapid eye movement*, or *REM*, alternate with *non-REM sleep* in approximately a 90-minute rhythm. Non-REM sleep is divided into four stages on the basis of characteristic brain-wave patterns. During REM sleep, the brain is active, and there are other signs of arousal, yet most of the skeletal muscles are limp; vivid dreams are reported most often during REM sleep. Some people have had "waking dreams" when they emerge from REM sleep before the paralysis of that stage has subsided, and occasionally, people have interpreted the resulting hallucinations as real. The purposes of REM are still a matter of controversy.

• Sleep is necessary not only for bodily restoration but also for normal mental functioning. Many people get less than the optimal amount of sleep. Some suffer from insomnia, *sleep apnea*, or *narcolepsy*. Researchers are concerned about the growing number of sleep-deprived people in modern societies.

• Sleep may be necessary for the consolidation of memories. Improvements in memory due to sleep have been associated most closely with REM sleep and slow-wave sleep and with memory for specific skills. Sleep also seems to improve insight and problem solving.

Exploring the Dream World

• Dreams are often recalled as illogical and bizarre. Some people say they have *lucid dreams* in which they know they are dreaming. Researchers disagree about whether the eye movements of REM sleep are related to events and actions in dreams.

• The *psychoanalytic theory of dreams* holds that they allow us to gratify forbidden or unrealistic wishes and desires that have been forced into the unconscious part of the mind. In dreams, according to Freud, thoughts and objects are disguised as symbolic images.

• The *problem-solving approach to dreams* holds that they express current concerns. They may even help us solve current problems and work through emotional issues, especially during times of crisis. Findings on the dreams of divorced people support this view.

• The *cognitive approach to dreams* holds that they are simply a modification of the cognitive activity that goes on when we are awake. The difference is that during sleep we are cut off from sensory input from the world and our bodily movements, so our thoughts tend to be more diffused and unfocused. This explanation is supported by research on the content of dreams and changes in children's dreams as they mature cognitively.

• The *activation–synthesis theory of dreaming* holds that dreams occur when the cortex tries to make sense of, or interpret, spontaneous neural firing initiated in the pons. The resulting synthesis of these signals with existing knowledge and memories results in a dream. In this view, dreams do not disguise unconscious wishes, but they can reveal a person's perceptions, conflicts, and concerns.

• All of the current theories of dreams have some support, and all have weaknesses. Most psychologists today accept the notion that dreams are more than incoherent ramblings of the mind, but many psychologists quarrel with psychoanalytic interpretations. Some psychologists doubt that people can solve problems during sleep. The activation–synthesis theory does not seem to explain coherent, storylike dreams or non-REM dreams. The cognitive approach is now a leading contender, but some of its specific claims remain to be tested.

The Riddle of Hypnosis

• *Hypnosis* is a procedure in which the practitioner suggests changes in the sensations, perceptions, thoughts, feelings, or behavior of the subject, and the subject tries to comply. Although hypnosis has been used successfully for many medical and psychological purposes, it does not produce special abilities. Hypnosis can sometimes improve memory for facts about real events, but it also results in confusion between facts and vividly imagined possibilities. Therefore, "hypnotically refreshed" accounts are often full of errors and pseudomemories.

• A leading explanation of hypnosis and its effects is that hypnosis involves *dissociation*, a split in consciousness. In one version of this approach, the split is between a part of consciousness that is hypnotized and a *hidden observer* that watches but does not participate. In another version, the split is between an executive-control system in the brain and other brain systems responsible for thinking and acting. Dissociation theories are consistent with modern models of the brain.

• Another leading approach, the *sociocognitive explanation*, regards hypnosis as a product of normal social and cognitive processes. In this view, hypnosis is a form of role playing in which the hypnotized person uses active cognitive strategies, including imagination, to comply with the hypnotist's suggestions. The role is so engrossing that the person interprets it as real. Sociocognitive processes can account for the apparent age and past-life "regressions" of people under hypnosis and their reports of alien abductions: These individuals are simply playing a role based on fantasy, imagination, and suggestion.

Consciousness-Altering Drugs

• In all cultures, people have found ways to produce *altered states of consciousness*. For example, *psychoactive drugs* alter cognition and emotion by acting on neurotransmitters in the brain. Most psychoactive drugs are classified as *stimulants*, *depressants*, *opiates*, or *psychedelics*, depending on their central-nervous-system effects and their impact on behavior and mood. However, some common drugs, such as marijuana, fall outside these categories.

• When used frequently and in large amounts, some psychoactive drugs can damage neurons in the brain and impair learning and memory. Their use may lead to *tolerance*, in which increasing dosages are needed for the same effect, and *withdrawal* symptoms if a person tries to quit. But certain drugs, such as alcohol and marijuana, have been associated with some health benefits when used in moderation. And the effects of Ecstasy are controversial; much of the research has been flawed, and permanent negative effects so far are unproven.

• Reactions to a psychoactive drug are influenced not only by its chemical properties but also by the user's individual characteristics, prior experience with the drug, environmental setting, and *mental set*—the person's expectations and motives for taking the drug. Expectations can be even more powerful than the drug itself, as shown by the *"think–drink" effect*. Expectations and beliefs about drugs are in turn affected by a person's culture.

Psychology in the News, Revisited

• In the debate over drug policies, illustrated in this chapter's opening story, people often find it difficult to distinguish drug use from drug abuse and to separate issues of a drug's legality or illegality from the drug's potential dangers and benefits. But some are trying to find a middle ground in this debate.

KEY TERMS

Biological Rhythms: The Tides of Experience

Consciousness is the awareness of oneself and the environment.

Biological rhythms are periodic fluctuations in physiological functioning, synchronized to external cues or **endogenous** (generated from within).

Circadian Rhythms

Circadian rhythms occur about once a day.

Circadian rhythms are governed by a biological clock in the **suprachiasmatic nucleus (SCN)** in the hypothalamus.

SCN — Regulates → Neurotransmitters, hormones (e.g. melatonin) — Feedback → SCN

Melatonin, secreted by the pineal gland, helps keep the biological clock in phase with the light-dark cycle.

Internal desynchronization occurs when circadian rhythms are out of phase with one another.

Moods and Long-Term Rhythms

- In the treatment of **seasonal affective disorder** (SAD), a placebo effect may play a role, but light treatments are somewhat effective.
- Well-controlled double-blind studies of "PMS" do not support claims that emotional symptoms are tied to the menstrual cycle in most women, or that the menstrual cycle affects the ability to work or study.
- Expectations and learning affect interpretations of bodily and emotional changes.

The Rhythms of Sleep

Sleep is necessary not only for bodily restoration but for normal mental functioning.

Periods of **rapid eye movement** (REM) alternate with non-REM sleep in a 90-minute rhythm.
- The body is limp.
- The brain is active.
- Vivid dreams occur.

The reasons for REM sleep are still a matter of controversy.

Awake	Small, rapid
Stage 1	Small, irregular
Stage 2	Sleep spindles
Stage 3	Delta waves appear
Stage 4	Mostly delta
REM	Rapid, somewhat irregular

Mental Consequences of Sleeplessness

Sleep deprivation of even one night can result in reduced
- Mental flexibility
- Attention
- Creativity

Longer periods of sleep deprivation can result in
- Hallucinations
- Delusions

Sleep disorders include:
- **Sleep apnea**, in which breathing periodically stops for a few moments, causing the person to choke or gasp
- **Narcolepsy**, in which an individual is subject to irresistible and unpredictable daytime attacks of sleepiness or actual sleep, lasting from 5-30 minutes

Mental Benefits of Sleep

- Improved Memory
- Enhanced problem-solving ability

Exploring the Dream World

1. Freud concluded that our nighttime fantasies provide insight into desires, motives, and conflicts of which we are unaware.
2. The problem-focused explanation is that dreams reflect the ongoing conscious concerns of waking life and may help us resolve them.
3. The cognitive approach emphasizes current concerns, but makes no claims about problem solving during sleep.
4. The **activation-synthesis theory** holds that dreams occur when the cortex tries to make sense of spontaneous neural firing initiated in the pons during REM sleep.

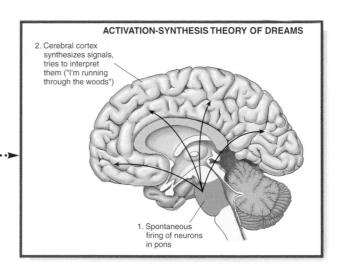

ACTIVATION-SYNTHESIS THEORY OF DREAMS

2. Cerebral cortex synthesizes signals, tries to interpret them ("I'm running through the woods")

1. Spontaneous firing of neurons in pons

The Riddle of Hypnosis

Hypnosis is a procedure in which the practitioner suggests changes in the sensations, perceptions, thoughts, feelings, or behavior of the subject.

- Hypnotic responsiveness depends more on the efforts and qualities of the person being hypnotized than on the skill of the hypnotist.
- Hypnotized people cannot be forced to do things against their will.
- Feats performed under hypnosis can be performed by motivated people without hypnosis.
- Hypnosis does not increase the accuracy of memory or produce a literal re-experiencing of long-ago events.
- Hypnotic suggestions have been used effectively for many medical and psychological purposes.

Theories of Hypnosis

1. The **dissociation** view is that hypnosis is a split in consciousness between a hypnotized part of the mind and a hidden observer or an executive control system.

DISSOCIATION THEORIES OF HYPNOSIS

Hypnotist induces hypnotic state

Split between hidden observer or executive control system and rest of mind

Person responds to suggestions ("I'm 4 years old")

2. The **sociocognitive** view regards the hypnotized person as using cognitive strategies, such as imagination, to comply with the hypnotist's suggestions.

SOCIOCOGNITIVE THEORIES OF HYPNOSIS

Social influence of hypnotist ("You're going back in time")

+

Person's own cognitions ("I believe in age regression")

Person conforms to suggestions ("I'm 4 years old")

Consciousness-Altering Drugs

Psychoactive drugs alter perception, mood, thinking, memory, or behavior by changing the body's biochemistry.

Drug classifications, based on their effects on the central nervous system, include:
- Stimulants
- Depressants
- Opiates
- Psychedelics

Marijuana may fall outside of these classifications.

The physiology of drug effects:
- The use of some psychoactive drugs can lead to tolerance: increased resistance to a drug's effects.
- When heavy users stop taking a drug, they may suffer severe **withdrawal symptoms**, which may include nausea, abdominal cramps, sweating, muscle spasms, depression, and sleep problems.

The psychology of drug effects:
- Effects may vary, depending on a person's physical condition (body weight, metabolism, etc.), experience with the drug, environmental setting, and mental set.

psychology in the news

UFO Sighting Over St. Louis

ST. LOUIS, MO, JANUARY 28, 2000. It seems to be UFO season in St. Louis and in nearby areas of southern Illinois. Two weeks ago, an Illinois truck driver and a miniature-golf course operator independently contacted police to report seeing a large object in the sky. According to the truck driver, the object looked like a floating house and had blinking lights. A police dispatcher alerted an officer in the field, and within a short period of time he and several other officers had seen the object, which eventually passed through five townships. Some said it looked like a massive elongated triangle emitting an intense white light; others said it was a large black arrowhead-shaped craft.

Now Stacy McKenna, 28, a St. Louis college student and waitress, says that several days after that incident, she saw three unidentified flying objects hovering over the freeway during rush-hour traffic. According to McKenna, they were shaped like triangles with white lights at each point. "At first they were just two bouncing, glowing lights," she reports. "Then another one dropped out of the sky. It was so huge, I screamed because I thought I was going to hit it." McKenna says she didn't believe in UFOs before, but now she is "intrigued."

Another witness, high school English teacher Stephen Winnacott, reports that he, too, has begun to reevaluate his beliefs about UFOs. "Before this experience I was skeptical," Winnacott said. "But now that I have seen something unexplainable, I will put more credibility in other UFO reports."

Dozens of other area residents have also reported seeing alien spacecraft this month. They have plenty of company. Over the years, UFO sightings have occurred throughout the world, especially in North America. California leads in the number of reported sightings, with Washington State in second place. A private pilot helped coin the term "flying saucer" many decades ago after seeing nine shiny disks skipping through the area, and thousands of reports of saucers and other mysterious objects have come in since.

One of the earliest UFO accounts occurred in the late 1940s, when a rancher noticed some strange pieces of metal strewn about his property near Roswell, New Mexico. When the Air Force quickly blocked off and cleared the site, stories circulated that a spacecraft had crashed and that alien corpses had been recovered. Today, thousands of believers in UFOs still flock to the International UFO Museum and Research Center's headquarters in Roswell.

Are these alien spacecraft? Many people who viewed these odd objects in the skies above Santos, Brazil, were convinced they were seeing UFOs.

CHAPTER

6

Sensation and Perception

We have all heard stories about UFOs and "flying saucers." Some of us scoff at them; others take them seriously. Why are these accounts so common? Are UFO sightings reported only by people who are silly or gullible, or do smart, savvy people also see alien aircraft? If such sightings are illusions, then why are those who report them so confident that what they saw was real? And why is one report often followed by several others in the same location: because there really are a lot of UFOs in the area or because of the power of suggestion?

In this chapter, we will try to answer these questions by exploring how our sense organs take in information from the environment and how the brain uses this information to construct a model of the world—a model that is not always accurate. We will focus on two closely connected sets of processes that enable us to know what is happening both inside our bodies and in the world beyond our own skins. The first process, **sensation**, is the detection of physical energy emitted or

If you stare at the cube, the surface on the outside and front will suddenly be on the inside and back, or vice versa, because your brain can interpret the sensory image in two different ways. The other purple and white drawing can also be perceived in two ways. Do you see them?

sensation The detection of physical energy emitted or reflected by physical objects.

perception The process by which the brain organizes and interprets sensory information.

sense receptors Specialized cells that convert physical energy in the environment or the body to electrical energy that can be transmitted as nerve impulses to the brain.

doctrine of specific nerve energies The principle that different sensory modalities exist because signals received by the sense organs stimulate different nerve pathways leading to different areas of the brain.

reflected by physical objects. The cells that do the detecting are located in the *sense organs*—the eyes, ears, tongue, nose, skin, and internal body tissues. Sensory processes produce an immediate awareness of sound, color, form, and other building blocks of consciousness. But to make sense of the world conveyed to us through our senses, we also need **perception**, a set of mental operations that organizes sensory signals into meaningful patterns. Our sense of vision produces a two-dimensional image on the back of the eye, but we *perceive* the world in three dimensions. Our sense of hearing brings us the sound of a C, an E, and a G played simultaneously on the piano, but we *perceive* a C major chord.

Sensation and perception are the foundation of learning, thinking, and acting, and findings on these topics can often be put to practical use—for example, in the design of hearing aids and industrial robots and in the training of flight controllers, astronauts, and other people who must make crucial decisions based on what they sense and perceive. An understanding of sensation and perception can also help us think more critically about our own experiences. As you read this chapter, ask yourself why people sometimes perceive things that are not there and, conversely, why they sometimes miss things that *are* there—looking without seeing, listening without hearing.

WHAT'S *Ahead*

- What kind of "code" in the nervous system helps explain why a pinprick and a kiss feel different?

- Why does your dog hear a "silent" doggie whistle when you can't?

- What bias can influence whether you think you hear the phone ringing when you are in the shower?

- What happens when people are deprived of all external sensory stimulation?

- Why do we sometimes fail to see an object that we're looking straight at?

Our Sensational Senses

At some point, you probably learned that there are five senses, corresponding to five sense organs: vision (eyes), hearing (ears), taste (tongue), touch (skin), and smell (nose). Actually, there are more than five senses, though scientists disagree about

the exact number. The skin, which is the organ of touch or pressure, also senses heat, cold, and pain, not to mention itching and tickling. The ear, which is the organ of hearing, also contains receptors that account for a sense of balance. The skeletal muscles contain receptors responsible for a sense of bodily movement.

All of our senses evolved to help us survive. Even pain, which causes so much human misery, is an indispensable part of our evolutionary heritage, for it alerts us to illness and injury. But sensory experiences contribute immeasurably to our lives even when they are not helping us stay alive. They entertain us, amuse us, soothe us, inspire us. If we really pay attention to our senses, said poet William Wordsworth, we can "see into the life of things" and hear "the still, sad music of humanity."

The Riddle of Separate Sensations

Sensation begins with the **sense receptors**, cells located in the sense organs. When these receptors detect an appropriate stimulus—light, mechanical pressure, or chemical molecules—they convert the energy of the stimulus into electrical impulses that travel along nerves to the brain. Sense receptors are like military scouts who scan the terrain for signs of activity. These scouts cannot make many decisions on their own. They must transmit what they learn to field officers—sensory neurons in the peripheral nervous system (see Chapter 4). The field officers in turn must report to generals at a command center—the cells of the brain. The generals are responsible for analyzing the reports, combining information brought in by different scouts, and deciding what it all means.

The "field officers" in the sensory system—the sensory nerves—all use exactly the same form of communication, a neural impulse. It is as if they must all send their messages on a bongo drum and can only go "boom." How, then, are we able to experience so many different kinds of sensations? The answer is that the nervous system *encodes* the messages. One kind of code, which is *anatomical*, was first described in 1826 by the German physiologist Johannes Müller, in his **doctrine of specific nerve energies**. According to this doctrine, different sensory modalities (such as vision and hearing) exist because signals received by the sense organs stimulate different nerve pathways leading to different areas of the brain. Signals from the eye cause impulses to travel along the optic nerve to the visual cortex. Signals from the ear cause impulses to travel along the auditory nerve to the auditory cortex. Light and sound waves produce different sensations because of these anatomical differences.

The doctrine of specific nerve energies implies that what we know about the world ultimately reduces to what we know about the state of our own nervous system: We see with the brain, not the eyes, and hear with the brain, not the ears. It follows that if sound waves could stimulate nerves that end in the visual part of the brain, we would "see" sound. Indeed, scientists hope one day to enable blind people to "see" by teaching them to interpret impulses from other senses that are then routed to the visual areas of the brain. Canadian neuroscientist Maurice Ptito, for example, is studying the effectiveness of a device that translates images from a camera into a pattern of electronic pulses that is sent to electrodes on the tongue, which in turn sends information about the pattern to areas of the brain that process images (Ptito et al., 2005). Using this device, congenitally blind people have learned to make out shapes, and their visual areas, long quiet, have suddenly become active.

A different sort of crossover occurs in a rare condition called **synesthesia**, in which the stimulation of one sense also consistently evokes a sensation in another. A person with synesthesia may say that the color purple smells like a rose, the aroma of cinnamon feels like velvet, or the sound of a note on a clarinet tastes like cherries (Cytowic, 2002; Martino & Marks, 2001). It may be that synesthetes have unusually direct connections between different sensory areas of the brain, such as those that handle vision and hearing, or an unusual number of connections between these areas (Nunn et al., 2002).

Synesthesia, however, is the exception, not the rule; for most of us, the senses remain separate.

Anatomical encoding alone does not completely explain why this is so, nor does it explain variations of experience *within* a particular sense—the sight of pink versus red, the sound of a piccolo versus the sound of a tuba, or the feel of a pinprick versus the feel of a kiss. An additional kind of code is therefore necessary. This second kind of code has been called *functional*.

Functional codes rely on the fact that sensory receptors and neurons fire, or are inhibited from firing, only in the presence of specific sorts of stimuli. At any particular time, then, some cells in the nervous system are firing and some are not. Information about *which* cells are firing, *how many* cells are firing, the *rate* at which cells are firing, and the *patterning* of each cell's firing constitutes a functional code. You might think of such a code as the neurological equivalent of the Morse code but much more complicated. Functional encoding may occur all along a sensory route, starting in the sense organs and ending in the brain.

Measuring the Senses

Just how sensitive are our senses? The answer comes from the field of *psychophysics*, which is concerned with how the physical properties of stimuli are related to our psychological experience of them. Drawing on principles from both physics and psychology, psychophysicists have studied how the strength or intensity of a stimulus affects the strength of sensation in an observer.

Absolute Thresholds One way to find out how sensitive the senses are is to show people a series of signals that vary in intensity and ask them to say which signals they can detect. The smallest amount of energy that a person can detect reliably

synesthesia A rare condition in which stimulation of one sense also evokes a sensation in another.

Different species sense the world differently. The flower on the left was photographed under normal light. The one on the right, photographed under ultraviolet light, is what a butterfly might see because butterflies have ultraviolet receptors. The hundreds of tiny bright spots are nectar sources.

absolute threshold
The smallest quantity of physical energy that can be reliably detected by an observer.

difference threshold
The smallest difference in stimulation that can be reliably detected by an observer when two stimuli are compared; also called *just noticeable difference (jnd)*.

is known as the **absolute threshold**. The word *absolute* is a bit misleading, though, because people detect borderline signals on some occasions and miss them on others. Reliable detection is said to occur when a person can detect a signal 50 percent of the time.

If you were having your absolute threshold for brightness measured, you might be asked to sit in a dark room and look at a wall or screen. You would then be shown flashes of light, varying in brightness, one flash at a time. Your task would be to say whether you noticed a flash. Some flashes you would never see. Some you would always see. And sometimes you would miss seeing a flash, even though you had noticed one of equal brightness on other trials. Such errors seem to occur in part because of random firing of cells in the nervous system, which produces fluctuating background noise, something like the background noise in a radio transmission.

By studying absolute thresholds, psychologists have found that our senses are very sharp indeed. If you have normal sensory abilities, you can see a candle flame on a clear, dark night from 30 miles away. You can hear a ticking watch in a perfectly quiet room from 20 feet away. You can taste a teaspoon of sugar diluted in 2 gallons of water, smell a drop of perfume diffused through a three-room apartment, and feel the wing of a bee falling on your cheek from a height of 1 centimeter (Galanter, 1962).

Yet despite these impressive sensory skills, our senses are tuned in to only a narrow band of physical energies. For example, we are visually sensitive to only a tiny fraction of all electromagnetic energy; we do not see radio waves or microwaves (see Figure

6.1). Other species can pick up signals that we cannot. Dogs can detect high-frequency sound waves that are beyond our range, as you know if you have ever called your pooch with a "silent" doggie whistle. Bats and porpoises can hear sounds two octaves beyond our range, and bees can see ultraviolet light, which merely gives human beings a sunburn.

Difference Thresholds Psychologists also study sensory sensitivity by having people compare two stimuli and judge whether they are the same or different. For example, a person might be asked to compare the weight of two blocks, the brightness of two lights, or the saltiness of two liquids. The smallest difference in stimulation that a person can detect reliably (again, half of the time) is called the **difference threshold** or *just noticeable difference (jnd)*. When you compare two stimuli, A and B, the difference threshold will depend on the intensity or size of A. The larger or more intense A is, the greater the change must be before you can detect a difference. If you are comparing the weights of two pebbles, you might be able to detect a difference of only a fraction of an ounce, but you would not be able to detect such a subtle difference if you were comparing two massive boulders.

Signal-Detection Theory Despite their usefulness, the procedures we have described have a serious limitation. Measurements for any given individual may be affected by the person's general tendency, when uncertain, to respond, "Yes, I noticed a signal (or a difference)" or, "No, I didn't notice anything." Some people are habitual yea-sayers, willing

FIGURE 6.1
The Visible Spectrum of Electromagnetic Energy
Our visual system detects only a small fraction of the electromagnetic energy around us.

to gamble that the signal was really there. Others are habitual naysayers, cautious and conservative. In addition, alertness, motives, and expectations can influence how a person responds on any given occasion. If you are in the shower and you are expecting an important call, you may think you heard the telephone ring when it did not. In laboratory studies, when observers want to impress the experimenter, they may lean toward a positive response.

Fortunately, these problems of *response bias* are not insurmountable. According to **signal-detection theory**, an observer's response in a detection task can be divided into a *sensory process*, which depends on the intensity of the stimulus, and a *decision process*, which is influenced by the observer's response bias. Methods are available for separating these two components. For example, the researcher can include some trials in which no stimulus is present and others in which a weak stimulus is present. Under these conditions, four kinds of responses are possible: The person (1) detects a signal that was present (a "hit"), (2) says the signal was there when it was not (a "false alarm"), (3) fails to detect the signal when it was present (a "miss"), or (4) correctly says that the signal was absent when it was absent (a "correct rejection").

Yea-sayers will have more hits than naysayers, but they will also have more false alarms because they are too quick to say, "Yup, it was there." Naysayers will have more correct rejections than yea-sayers, but they will also have more misses because they are too quick to say, "Nope, nothing was there." This information can be fed into a mathematical formula that yields separate estimates of a person's response bias and sensory capacity. The individual's true sensitivity to a signal of any particular intensity can then be predicted.

The old method of measuring thresholds assumed that a person's ability to detect a stimulus depended solely on the stimulus. Signal-detection theory assumes that there is no single threshold, because at any given moment, a person's sensitivity to a stimulus depends on a decision that he or she actively makes. Signal-detection methods have many real-world applications, from screening applicants for jobs requiring keen hearing to training air-traffic controllers, whose decisions about the presence or absence of a blip on a radar screen may mean the difference between life and death.

Sensory Adaptation

Variety, they say, is the spice of life. It is also the essence of sensation, for our senses are designed to respond to change and contrast in the environment. When a stimulus is unchanging or repetitious, sensation often fades or disappears. Receptors or nerve

signal-detection theory A psychophysical theory that divides the detection of a sensory signal into a sensory process and a decision process.

Now You See It, Now You Don't

Sensation depends on change and contrast in the environment. Hold your hand over one eye and stare at the dot in the middle of the circle on the right. You should have no trouble maintaining an image of the circle. However, if you do the same with the circle on the left, the image will fade. The gradual change from light to dark does not provide enough contrast to keep your visual receptors firing at a steady rate. The circle reappears only if you close and reopen your eye or shift your gaze to the X.

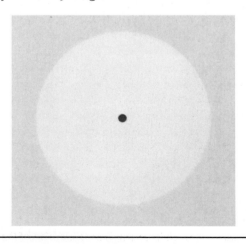

Is sensory deprivation pleasant or unpleasant? The answer isn't "either–or"; it depends on the circumstances and how you interpret your situation. Being isolated against your will can be terrifying, but many people have found an hour alone in a "flotation tank" to be calming and pleasant.

cells higher up in the sensory system get "tired" and fire less frequently. The resulting decline in sensory responsiveness is called **sensory adaptation**. Such adaptation is usually useful because it spares us from having to respond to unimportant information; for example, most of the time you have no need to feel your watch sitting on your wrist. Sometimes, however, adaptation can be hazardous, as when you no longer smell a gas leak that you noticed when you first entered the kitchen.

We never completely adapt to extremely intense stimuli—a terrible toothache, the odor of ammonia, the heat of the desert sun. And we rarely adapt completely to visual stimuli, whether they are weak or intense. Eye movements, voluntary and involuntary, cause the position of an object's image on the back of the eye to keep changing, so visual receptors located there do not have a chance to "fatigue." But in the laboratory, researchers can stabilize the image of a simple pattern, such as a line, at a particular point on the back of a person's eye. They use an ingenious device consisting of a tiny projector mounted on a contact lens. Although the eyeball moves, the image of the object stays focused on the same receptors. In minutes, the image begins to disappear.

What would happen if our senses adapted to *most* incoming stimuli? Would we sense nothing, or would the brain substitute its own images for the sensory experiences no longer available by way of the sense organs? In early studies of **sensory deprivation**, researchers studied this question by isolating male volunteers from all patterned sight and sound. Vision was restricted by a translucent visor, hearing by a U-shaped pillow and by background noise from an air conditioner and fan, and touch

sensory adaptation The reduction or disappearance of sensory responsiveness that occurs when stimulation is unchanging or repetitious.

sensory deprivation The absence of normal levels of sensory stimulation.

selective attention The focusing of attention on selected aspects of the environment and the blocking out of others.

by cotton gloves and cardboard cuffs. The volunteers took brief breaks to eat and use the bathroom, but otherwise they lay in bed, doing nothing. The results were dramatic. Within a few hours, many of the men felt edgy. Some were so disoriented that they quit the study the first day. Those who stayed longer became confused, restless, and grouchy. Many reported bizarre visions, such as a squadron of marching squirrels or a procession of marching eyeglasses. It was as though they were having the kind of "waking dreams" described in Chapter 5. Few people were willing to remain in the study for more than two or three days (Heron, 1957).

But the notion that sensory deprivation is unpleasant or even dangerous turned out to be an oversimplification (Suedfeld, 1975). Later research, using better methods, showed that hallucinations are less dramatic and less disorienting than had first been thought. Many people enjoy limited periods of deprivation, and some perceptual and intellectual abilities actually improve. Your response to sensory deprivation depends on your expectations and interpretations of what is happening. Reduced sensation can be scary if you are locked in a room for an indefinite period, but relaxing if you have retreated to that room voluntarily for a little time out—at, say, a luxury spa or a monastery.

Thinking Critically About Sensory Deprivation

Still, it is clear that the human brain requires a minimum amount of sensory stimulation in order to function normally. This need may help explain why people who live alone often keep the radio or television set running continuously and why prolonged solitary confinement is used as a form of punishment or even torture.

Sensing Without Perceiving

If too little stimulation can be bad for you, so can too much, because it can lead to fatigue and mental confusion. If you have ever felt exhausted, nervous, and headachy after a day crammed with hectic activities and deadlines, you know firsthand about sensory overload. When people find themselves in a state of overload, they often cope by blocking out unimportant sights and sounds and focusing only on those they find interesting or useful. Psychologists have called this the "cocktail party phenomenon" because at a cocktail party, a person typically focuses on just one conversation, ignoring other voices, the clink of ice cubes, and bursts of laughter across the room.

Even when overload is not a problem, our capacity for **selective attention**—the ability to focus on some parts of the environment and block out others—protects us from being overwhelmed by the countless sensory signals that are constantly impinging on our sense receptors. Competing sensory messages all enter the nervous system, however, and they get some processing, enabling us to pick up anything important, such as our own name spoken by someone several yards away.

That's the good news. The bad news is that selective attention, by its very nature, causes us to miss much that is going on around us; as a result, our conscious awareness of the environment is much less complete than most people think. We may even fail to consciously register objects that we are looking straight at, a phenomenon known as **inattentional blindness**: We look, but we do not see (Mack, 2003). When people are shown a video of a ball-passing game and are asked to count up the passes, they may even miss something as seemingly obvious as a man in a gorilla suit walking slowly through the ball court and thumping his chest (Simons & Chabris, 1999).

Selective attention, then, is a mixed blessing. It protects us from overload and allows us to focus on what's important, but it also deprives us of sensory information that we may need. That could be disastrous if you are so focused on listening to a voice on your cell phone while you are driving that you fail to see a pedestrian crossing the street in front of you.

In his films, famed director Alfred Hitchcock always appeared briefly in one scene, but few saw him even when they knew he'd be there—an instance of inattentional blindness.

QUICK quiz

If you are not on overload, try answering these questions.

1. Even on the clearest night, some stars cannot be seen by the naked eye because they are below the viewer's _____ threshold.

2. If you jump into a cold lake but moments later the water no longer seems so cold, sensory _____ has occurred.

3. If you are immobilized in a hospital bed, with no one to talk to and no TV or radio, and you feel edgy and disoriented, you may be suffering the effects of _____.

4. During a break from your job in a restaurant, you are so engrossed in a book that you fail to notice the clattering of dishes or orders being called out to the cook. This is an example of _____.

5. In real-life detection tasks, is it better to be a naysayer or a yea-sayer?

Answers:

1. absolute 2. adaptation 3. sensory deprivation 4. selective attention 5. Neither; it depends on the consequences of a "miss" or a "false alarm" and the probability of an event occurring. You might want to be a yea-sayer if you are just out the door, you think you hear the phone ringing, and you are expecting a call about a job interview. You might want to be a naysayer if you are just out the door, you think you hear the phone ringing, and you are on your way to a job interview and don't want to be late.

WHAT'S *Ahead*

- How does the eye differ from a camera?

- Why can we describe a color as bluish green but not as reddish green?

- If you were blind in one eye, why might you misjudge your distance from a painting on the wall but not the distance to buildings a block away?

- As a friend approaches, her image on your retina grows larger; why do you continue to see her as the same size?

- Why are perceptual illusions valuable to psychologists?

Vision

Vision is the most frequently studied of all the senses, and with good reason. More information about the external world comes to us through our eyes than through any other sense organ. Because we are most active in the daytime, we have been wired by evolution to take advantage of the sun's illumination. Animals that are active at night tend to rely more heavily on hearing.

What We See

The stimulus for vision is light; even cats, raccoons, and other creatures famous for their ability to get around in the dark need some light to see. Visible light comes from the sun and other stars and from light bulbs, and it is also reflected off objects. Light travels in the form of waves, and the *physical* characteristics of these waves affect three *psychological* aspects of our visual world: hue, brightness, and saturation.

1 Hue, the dimension of visual experience specified by color names, is related to the *wavelength* of light—that is, to the distance between

inattentional blindness Failure to consciously perceive something you are looking at because you are not attending to it.

hue The dimension of visual experience specified by color names and related to the wavelength of light.

brightness Lightness or luminance; the dimension of visual experience related to the amount (intensity) of light emitted from or reflected by an object.

saturation Vividness or purity of color; the dimension of visual experience related to the complexity of light waves.

retina Neural tissue lining the back of the eyeball's interior, which contains the receptors for vision.

rods Visual receptors that respond to dim light.

the crests of a light wave. Shorter waves tend to be seen as violet and blue, longer ones as orange and red. (We say "tend to" because other factors also affect color perception, as we will see later.) The sun produces white light, a mixture of all the visible wavelengths. Sometimes drops of moisture in the air act like a prism: They separate the sun's white light into the colors of the visible spectrum, and we are treated to a rainbow.

2 Brightness is the dimension of visual experience related to the amount, or *intensity*, of the light an object emits or reflects. Intensity corresponds to the amplitude (maximum height) of the wave. Generally speaking, the more light an object reflects, the brighter it appears. However, brightness is also affected by wavelength: Yellows appear brighter than reds and blues when physical intensities are actually equal.

3 Saturation (colorfulness) is the dimension of visual experience related to the *complexity* of light—that is, to how wide or narrow the range of wavelengths is. When light contains only a single wavelength, it is said to be pure, and the resulting color is said to be completely saturated. At the other extreme is white light, which lacks any color and is completely unsaturated. In nature, pure light is extremely rare. Usually, we sense a mixture of wavelengths, and we see colors that are duller and paler than completely saturated ones.

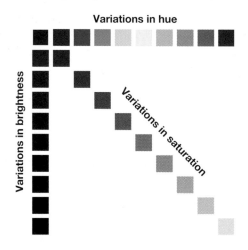

Variations in hue

Variations in brightness

Variations in saturation

An Eye on the World

Light enters the visual system through the eye, a wonderfully complex and delicate structure. As you read this section, examine Figure 6.2. Notice that the front part of the eye is covered by the transparent *cornea*. The cornea protects the eye and bends incoming light rays toward a *lens* located be-

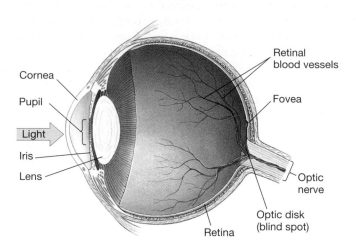

FIGURE 6.2
Major Structures of the Eye
Light passes through the pupil and lens and is focused on the retina at the back of the eye. The point of sharpest vision is at the fovea.

hind it. A camera lens focuses incoming light by moving closer to or farther from the shutter opening. However, the lens of the eye works by subtly changing its shape, becoming more or less curved to focus light from objects that are close by or far away. The amount of light that gets into the eye is controlled by muscles in the *iris*, the part of the eye that gives it color. The iris surrounds the round opening, or *pupil*, of the eye. When you enter a dim room, the pupil widens, or dilates, to let more light in. When you emerge into bright sunlight, the pupil contracts to allow less light in. You can see these changes by watching your eyes in a mirror as you change the lighting.

The visual receptors are located in the back of the eye, or **retina**. In a developing embryo, the retina forms from tissue that projects out from the brain, not from tissue destined to form other parts of the eye; thus, the retina is actually an extension of the brain. As Figure 6.3 shows, when the lens of the eye focuses light on the retina, the result is an upside-down image (which can actually be seen with an instrument used by eye specialists). Light from the top of the visual field stimulates light-sensitive receptor cells in the bottom part of the retina, and vice versa. The brain interprets this upside-down pattern of stimulation as something that is right side up.

About 120 to 125 million receptors in the retina are long and narrow and are called **rods**. Another 7 or 8 million receptors are cone shaped and are called, appropriately enough, **cones**. The center of the retina, or *fovea*, where vision is sharpest, contains only cones, clustered densely together. From the center to the periphery, the ratio of rods to cones increases, and the outer edges contain virtually no cones.

Rods are more sensitive to light than cones are. They enable us to see in dim light and at night. (Cats see well in dim light in part because they have a high proportion of rods.) Because rods occupy the outer edges of the retina, they also handle peripheral (side) vision. That is why you can sometimes see a star from the corner of your eye even though it is invisible to you when you gaze straight at it. But rods cannot distinguish different wavelengths of light so they are not sensitive to color, which is why it is often hard to distinguish colors clearly in dim light. The cones, on the other hand, are differentially sensitive to specific wavelengths of light and allow us to see colors. But they need much more light than rods do to respond, so they don't help us much when we are trying to find a seat in a darkened movie theater. (These differences are summarized in Table 6.1.)

We have all noticed that it takes some time for our eyes to adjust fully to dim illumination. This process of **dark adaptation** involves chemical changes in the rods and cones. The cones adapt quickly, within 10 minutes or so, but they never become very sensitive to the dim illumination. The rods adapt more slowly, taking 20 minutes or longer, but are ultimately much more sensitive. After the first phase of adaptation, you can see better but not well; after the second phase, your vision is as good as it will ever get.

Rods and cones are connected by synapses to *bipolar neurons*, which in turn communicate with

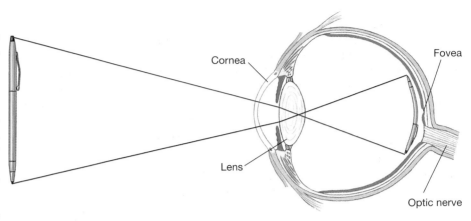

FIGURE 6.3
The Retinal Image
When we look at an object, the light pattern on the retina is upside down. René Descartes (1596–1650) was probably the first person to demonstrate this fact. He cut a piece from the back of an ox's eye and replaced the piece with paper. When he held the eye up to the light, he saw an upside-down image of the room on the paper.

neurons called **ganglion cells** (see Figure 6.4). The axons of the ganglion cells converge to form the *optic nerve*, which carries information out through the back of the eye and on to the brain. Where the optic nerve leaves the eye, at the *optic disk*, there are no rods or cones. The absence of receptors produces a blind spot in the field of vision. Normally, we are unaware of the blind spot because (1) the image projected on the spot is hitting a different, "nonblind" spot in the other eye; (2) our eyes move so fast that we can pick up the complete image; and (3) the brain fills in the gap. You can find your blind spot by following the instructions in the Get Involved exercise on the next page.

TABLE 6.1
Differences Between Rods and Cones

	Rods	Cones
How many?	120–125 million	7–8 million
Where most concentrated?	Periphery of retina	Center (fovea) of retina
How sensitive?	High sensitivity	Low sensitivity
Sensitive to color?	No	Yes

cones Visual receptors involved in color vision.

dark adaptation A process by which visual receptors become maximally sensitive to dim light.

ganglion cells Neurons in the retina of the eye, which gather information from receptor cells (by way of intermediate bipolar cells); their axons make up the optic nerve.

FIGURE 6.4
The Structures of the Retina
For clarity, all cells in this drawing are greatly exaggerated in size. In order to reach the receptors for vision (the rods and cones), light must pass through the ganglion and bipolar cells as well as the blood vessels that nourish them (not shown). Normally, we do not see the shadow cast by this network of cells and blood vessels because the shadow always falls on the same place on the retina, and such stabilized images are not sensed. But when an eye doctor shines a moving light into your eye, the treelike shadow of the blood vessels falls on different regions of the retina and you may see it—a rather eerie experience.

Find your blind spot

A blind spot exists where the optic nerve leaves the back of your eye. Find the blind spot in your left eye by closing your right eye and looking at the magician. Then slowly move the book toward and away from yourself. The rabbit should disappear when the book is between 9 and 12 inches from your eye.

Why the Visual System Is Not a Camera

Although the eye is often compared with a camera, the visual system, unlike a camera, is not a passive recorder of the external world. Instead of simply registering spots of light and dark, as in a photograph, neurons in the visual system build up a picture of the world by detecting its meaningful features.

Ganglion cells and neurons in the thalamus of the brain respond to simple features in the environment, such as spots of light and dark. But in mammals, special **feature-detector cells** in the visual cortex respond to more complex features. This fact was first demonstrated by David Hubel and Torsten Wiesel (1962, 1968), who painstakingly recorded impulses from individual cells in the brains of cats and monkeys. In 1981, they were awarded a Nobel Prize for their work. Hubel and Wiesel found that different neurons were sensitive to different patterns projected on a screen in front of an animal's eyes. Most cells responded maximally to moving or stationary lines that were oriented in a particular direction and located in a particular part of the visual field. One type of cell might fire most rapidly in response to a horizontal line in the lower right part of the visual field, another to a diagonal line at an angle in the upper left part of the visual field. In the real world, such features make up the boundaries and edges of objects.

Since this pioneering work was done, scientists have found that other cells in the visual system have more complex specialties, such as bull's-eyes and spirals (Gallant, Braun, & Van Essen, 1993). Some cells in the temporal lobe even appear to respond maximally to *faces* (Kanwisher, 2000; Ó Scalaidhe, Wilson, & Goldman-Rakic, 1997; Young & Yamane, 1992). Some scientists have concluded that evolution has equipped us with an innate *face module* in the brain. The existence of such a module could help explain why a person with brain damage may continue to recognize faces even after losing the ability to recognize other objects. In one case, a man could recognize a face made up entirely of vegetables, like the one in the painting on this page, but he could not recognize the vegetables (Moscovitch, Winocur, & Behrmann, 1997). Face modules could also help explain why infants show a strong preference for looking at faces.

A facility for deciphering faces makes evolutionary sense because it would have ensured our ancestors' ability to distinguish friend from foe or, in the case of infants, mothers from strangers. However, the existence of face modules remains controversial among neuroscientists. Some think that infants' apparent preference for faces is really a preference for curved lines, or eye contact, or patterns that have more elements in the upper part (e.g., two eyes) than in the lower part (e.g., just a mouth) (Turati, 2004). Moreover, some of the brain cells that supposedly make up the face module respond to other things, too, depending on a person's experiences and interests. In one fascinating study, cells in the presumed face module fired when car buffs examined pictures of classic cars but not when they looked at pictures of exotic birds, whereas the exact opposite was true for birdwatchers (Gauthier et al., 2000). Cars, of course, do not have faces!

Even if face and other specialized modules do exist, the brain cannot possibly contain a special area for every conceivable object. In general, the brain's job is to take fragmentary information about lines, angles, shapes, motion, brightness, texture, and patterns, and figure out that a chair is a chair, and that it is next to the dining room table. The perception of any given object probably depends

feature-detector cells Cells in the visual cortex that are sensitive to specific features of the environment.

Cases of brain damage support the idea that particular systems of brain cells are highly specialized. One man's injury left him unable to identify ordinary objects, which, he said, often looked like "blobs." Yet he had no trouble with faces, even when they were upside down or incomplete. When shown this painting, he could easily see the face, but he could not see the vegetables comprising it (Moscovitch, Winocur, & Behrmann, 1997).

trichromatic theory A theory of color perception that proposes three mechanisms in the visual system, each sensitive to a certain range of wavelengths; their interaction is assumed to produce all the different experiences of hue.

opponent-process theory A theory of color perception that assumes that the visual system treats pairs of colors as opposing or antagonistic.

on the activation of many cells in far-flung parts of the brain and on the overall pattern and rhythm of their activity (Bower, 1998).

How We See Colors

For 300 years, scientists have been trying to figure out why we see the world in living color. We now know that different processes explain different stages of color vision.

The Trichromatic Theory

The **trichromatic theory** (also known as the *Young-Helmholtz theory*) applies to the first level of processing, which occurs in the retina of the eye. The retina contains three basic types of cones. One type responds maximally to blue, another to green, and a third to red. The hundreds of colors we see result from the combined activity of these three types of cones.

Total color blindness is usually due to a genetic variation that causes cones of the retina to be absent or malfunctional. The visual world then consists of black, white, and shades of gray. Many species of animals are totally color-blind, but the condition is extremely rare in human beings. Most "color-blind" people are actually *color deficient.* Usually, the person is unable to distinguish red and green; the world is painted in shades of blue, yellow, brown, and gray. In rarer instances, a person may be blind to blue and yellow and may see only reds, greens, and grays. Color deficiency is found in about 8 percent of white men, 5 percent of Asian men, and 3 percent of black men and Native American men (Sekuler & Blake, 1994). Because of the way the condition is inherited, it is rare in women.

The Opponent-Process Theory

The **opponent-process theory** applies to the second stage of color processing, which occurs in ganglion cells in the retina and in neurons in the thalamus and visual cortex of the brain. These cells, known as *opponent-process cells,* either respond to short wavelengths but are inhibited from firing by long wavelengths, or vice versa (DeValois & DeValois, 1975). Some opponent-process cells respond in opposite fashion to red and green; that is, they fire in response to one and turn off in response to the other. Others respond in opposite fashion to blue and yellow. (A third system responds in opposite fashion to white and black and thus yields information about brightness.) The net result is a color code that is passed along to the higher visual centers. Because this code treats red and green, and also blue and yellow, as antagonistic, we can describe a color as bluish green or yellowish green but not as reddish green or yellowish blue.

Opponent-process cells that are *inhibited* by a particular color produce a burst of firing when the color is removed, just as they would if the opposing color were present. Similarly, cells that *fire* in response to a color stop firing when the color is removed, just as they would if the opposing color were present. These facts explain why we are susceptible to *negative afterimages* when we stare at a particular hue—why we see, for instance, red after staring at green (see the Get Involved exercise below). A sort of neural rebound effect occurs: The cells that switch on or off to signal the presence of "green" send the opposite signal ("red") when the green is removed and vice versa.

GET INVOLVED

A Change of Heart

Opponent-process cells that switch on or off in response to green send an opposite message—"red"—when the green is removed, producing a negative afterimage. Stare at the black dot in the middle of this heart for at least 20 seconds. Then shift your gaze to a white piece of paper or a white wall. Do you get a "change of heart"? You may see an image of a red or pinkish heart with a blue border.

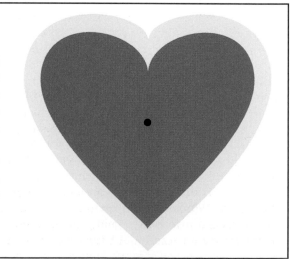

Constructing the Visual World

We do not see a retinal image; that image is merely grist for the mill of the mind, which actively interprets the image and constructs the world from the often fragmentary data of the senses. In the brain, sensory signals that give rise to vision, hearing, taste, smell, and touch are combined from moment to moment to produce a unified model of the world. This is the process of *perception.*

Form Perception To make sense of the world, we must know where one thing ends and another begins. In vision, we must separate the teacher from the lectern; in hearing, we must separate the piano solo from the orchestral accompaniment; in taste, we must separate the marshmallow from the hot chocolate. This process of dividing up the world occurs so rapidly and effortlessly that we take it completely for granted, until we must make out objects in a heavy fog or words in the rapid-fire conversation of someone speaking a foreign language.

The *Gestalt psychologists*, who belonged to a movement that began in Germany and was influential in the 1920s and 1930s, were among the first to study how people organize the world visually into meaningful units and patterns. In German, *Gestalt* means "form" or "configuration." The Gestalt psychologists' motto was "The whole is more than the sum of its parts." They observed that when we perceive something, properties emerge from the configuration as a whole that are not found in any particular component. When you watch a movie, for example, the motion you see is nowhere in the film, which consists of separate static frames projected at 24 frames per second.

One thing the Gestalt psychologists noted was that people always organize the visual field into *figure* and *ground*. The figure stands out from the rest of the environment (see Figure 6.5). Some things stand out as figure by virtue of their intensity or size; it is hard to ignore the blinding flash of a camera or a tidal wave approaching your piece of beach. The lower part of a scene tends to be seen as figure, the upper part as background (Vecera, Vogel, & Woodman, 2002). Unique objects also stand out, such as a banana in a bowl of oranges. Moving objects in an otherwise still environment, such as a shooting star, will usually be seen as figure. Indeed, it is hard to ignore a sudden change of any kind in the environment because our brains are geared to respond to change and contrast. However, selective

FIGURE 6.5
Figure and Ground
Which do you notice first in this drawing by M. C. Escher, the fish, geese, or salamanders? It will depend on whether you see the blue, red, or gold sections as figure or ground.

attention—the ability to concentrate on some stimuli and to filter out others—gives us some control over what we perceive as figure and ground, and sometimes it blinds us to things we would otherwise interpret as figure, as we saw earlier.

Other **Gestalt principles** describe strategies used by the visual system to group sensory building blocks into perceptual units (Kohler, 1929; Wertheimer, 1923/1958). The Gestalt psychologists believed that these strategies were present from birth or developed automatically early in infancy as a result of maturation. Modern research, however, suggests that at least some of them depend on experience (Quinn & Bhatt, 2005). Here are a few well-known Gestalt principles:

1 *Proximity.* Things that are near each other tend to be grouped together. Thus you perceive the dots on the left as two groups of dots, not as eight separate, unrelated ones. Similarly, you perceive the pattern on the right as vertical columns of dots, not as horizontal rows:

Gestalt principles
Principles that describe the brain's organization of sensory information into meaningful units and patterns.

2 *Closure.* The brain tends to fill in gaps in order to perceive complete forms. This is fortunate because we often need to decipher less-than-perfect images. The following figures are easily perceived as a triangle, a face, and the letter *e*, even though none of the figures is complete:

3 ***Similarity.*** Things that are alike in some way (for example, in color, shape, or size) tend to be perceived as belonging together. In the figure on the left, you see the circles as forming an *X*. In the one on the right, you see horizontal rows rather than vertical columns because the horizontally aligned stars are either all red or all outlined in red:

4 ***Continuity.*** Lines and patterns tend to be perceived as continuing in time or space. You perceive the figure on the left as a single line partially covered by an oval rather than as two separate lines touching an oval. In the figure on the right, you see two lines, one curved and one straight, instead of two curved and two straight lines, touching at one focal point:

Consumer products are sometimes designed with little thought for visual principles such as those formulated by the Gestalt psychologists, which is why it can be a major challenge to find the pause button on your DVD player's remote control or change from AM to FM on your car radio (Bjork, 2000; Norman, 1988). Good design requires, among other things, that crucial distinctions be visually obvious. For instance, knobs and switches with different functions should differ in color, texture, or shape, and they should stand out as

MONOCULAR CUES TO DEPTH

Most cues to depth do not depend on having two eyes. Some monocular (one-eyed) cues are shown here.

▼ LIGHT AND SHADOW
Both of these attributes give objects the appearance of three dimensions.

INTERPOSITION ▶
An object that partly blocks or obscures another one must be in front of the other one and is therefore seen as closer.

◀ MOTION PARALLAX
When an observer is moving, objects appear to move at different speeds and in different directions. The closer an object, the faster it seems to move; and close objects appear to move backward, whereas distant ones seem to move forward.

"figure." How would you use this information to re-design some of the products that you use?

Depth and Distance Perception

Ordinarily we need to know not only what something is but also where it is. Touch gives us this information directly, but vision does not, so we must infer an object's location by estimating its distance or depth.

To perform this remarkable feat, we rely in part on **binocular cues**—cues that require the use of two eyes. One such cue is **convergence**, the turning of the eyes inward, which occurs when they focus on a nearby object. The closer the object, the greater the convergence, as you know if you have ever tried to cross your eyes by looking at your own nose. As the angle of convergence changes, the corresponding muscular changes provide information to the brain about distance.

The two eyes also receive slightly different retinal images of the same object. You can prove this by holding a finger about 12 inches in front of your face and looking at it with only one eye at a time. Its position will appear to shift when you change eyes. Now hold up two fingers, one closer to your nose than the other. Notice that the amount of space between the two fingers appears to change when you switch eyes. The slight difference in lateral (sideways) separation between two objects as seen by the left eye and the right eye is called **retinal disparity**. Because retinal disparity increases as the distance between two objects increases, the brain can use it to infer depth and calculate distance.

Binocular cues help us estimate distances up to about 50 feet. For objects farther away, we use only **monocular cues**, cues that do not depend on using both eyes. One such cue is *interposition:* When an object is interposed between the viewer and a second object, partly blocking the view of the second object, the first object is perceived as being closer. Another monocular cue is *linear perspective:* When two lines known to be parallel appear to be coming together or converging, they imply the existence of depth. For example, if you are standing between railroad tracks, they appear to converge in the distance. These and other monocular cues are illustrated on these pages.

binocular cues Visual cues to depth or distance requiring two eyes.

convergence The turning inward of the eyes, which occurs when they focus on a nearby object.

retinal disparity The slight difference in lateral separation between two objects as seen by the left eye and the right eye.

monocular cues Visual cues to depth or distance that can be used by one eye alone.

RELATIVE SIZE ▶
The smaller an object's image on the retina, the farther away the object appears.

◀ RELATIVE CLARITY
Because of particles in the air—from dust, fog, or smog—distant objects tend to look hazier, duller, or less detailed.

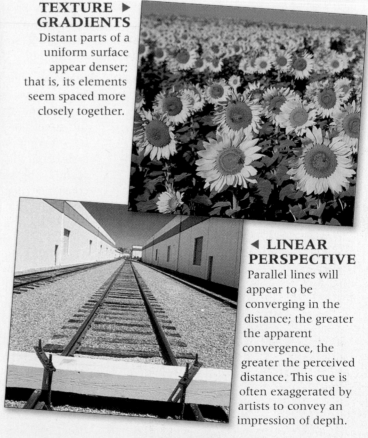

TEXTURE GRADIENTS ▶
Distant parts of a uniform surface appear denser; that is, its elements seem spaced more closely together.

◀ LINEAR PERSPECTIVE
Parallel lines will appear to be converging in the distance; the greater the apparent convergence, the greater the perceived distance. This cue is often exaggerated by artists to convey an impression of depth.

perceptual constancy
The accurate perception of objects as stable or unchanged despite changes in the sensory patterns they produce.

Visual Constancies: When Seeing Is Believing

Your perceptual world would be a confusing place without still another important perceptual skill. Lighting conditions, viewing angles, and the distances of stationary objects are all continually changing as we move about, yet we rarely confuse these changes with changes in the objects themselves. This ability to perceive objects as stable or unchanging even though the sensory patterns they produce are constantly shifting is called **perceptual constancy**. The best-studied constancies are visual, and they include the following:

1 *Shape constancy.* We continue to perceive objects as having a constant shape even though the shape of the retinal image produced by an object changes when our point of view changes. If you hold a pie plate directly in front of your face, its image on the retina will be round. When you set the plate on a table, its image becomes elliptical, yet you continue to identify the plate as round.

2 *Location constancy.* We perceive stationary objects as remaining in the same place even though the retinal image moves about as we move our eyes, heads, and bodies. As you drive along the highway, telephone poles and trees fly by—on your retina. But you know that these objects do not move on their own, and you also know that your body is moving, so you perceive the poles and trees as staying put.

3 *Size constancy.* We see an object as having a constant size even when its retinal image becomes smaller or larger. A friend approaching on the street does not seem to be growing; a car pulling away from the curb does not seem to be shrinking. Size constancy depends in part on familiarity with objects. You know that people and cars do not change size from moment to moment. It also depends on the apparent distance of an object. An object that is close produces a larger retinal image than the same object farther away, and the brain takes this into account. For example, when you move your hand toward your face, your brain registers the fact that the hand is getting closer, and you correctly perceive its unchanging size despite the growing size of its retinal image. There is, then, an intimate relationship between perceived size and perceived distance.

4 *Brightness constancy.* We see objects as having a relatively constant brightness even though the amount of light they reflect changes as the overall level of illumination changes. Snow remains white even on a cloudy day. We are not fooled because the brain registers the total illumination in the scene and we automatically take this information into account.

5 *Color constancy.* We see an object as maintaining its hue despite the fact that the wavelength of light reaching our eyes from the object may change as the illumination changes. For example, outdoor light is bluer than indoor light, and objects outdoors therefore reflect more blue light than those indoors. Conversely, indoor light from incandescent lamps is rich in long wavelengths and is therefore yellower. Yet an apple looks red whether you look at it in your kitchen or outside on the patio. Part of the explanation involves sensory adaptation, which we discussed earlier. Outdoors, we quickly adapt to short-wavelength (bluish) light, and indoors, we adapt to long-wavelength light. As a result, our visual responses are similar in the two situations. Also, when computing the color of a particular object, the brain takes into account *all* the wavelengths in the visual field immediately around the object. If an apple is bathed in bluish light, so, usually, is everything else around it. The increase in blue light reflected by the apple is canceled in the visual cortex by the increase in blue light reflected by the apple's surroundings, so the apple continues to look red.

Visual Illusions: When Seeing Is Misleading

Perceptual constancies allow us to make sense of the world. Occasionally, however, we can be fooled, and the result is a *perceptual illusion*. For psychologists, illusions are valuable because they are systematic errors that provide us with hints about the perceptual strategies of the mind.

Although illusions can occur in any sensory modality, visual illusions have been the best studied. Visual illusions sometimes occur when the strategies that normally lead to accurate perception are overextended to situations where they don't apply. Compare the lengths of the two vertical lines in Figure 6.6. If you are like most people, you perceive the line on the right as slightly longer than the one on the left. Yet they are exactly the same length. (Go ahead, measure them; everyone does.) This is the Müller-Lyer illusion, named after the German sociologist who first described it in 1889.

BIZARRO By DAN PIRARO

I HAVE NO SENSE OF DEPTH PERCEPTION. COULD YOU TELL ME — IS THAT SOMEONE STANDING WAY UP THERE ON THE CORNER, OR IS THERE A LITTLE MAN IN YOUR HAIR?

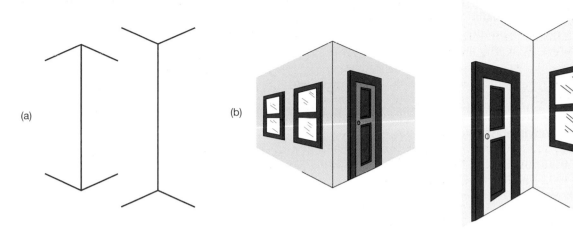

FIGURE 6.6
The Müller-Lyer Illusion
The two lines in (a) are exactly the same length. We are probably fooled into perceiving them as different because the brain interprets the one with the outward-facing branches as farther away, as if it were the far corner of a room, and the one with the inward-facing branches as closer, as if it were the near edge of a building (b).

One explanation for the Müller-Lyer illusion is that the branches on the lines serve as perspective cues that normally suggest depth (Gregory, 1963). The line on the left is like the near edge of a building; the one on the right is like the far corner of a room (see part b of the figure). Although the two lines produce retinal images of the same size, the one with the outward-facing branches suggests greater distance. We are fooled into perceiving it as longer because we automatically apply a rule about the relationship between size and distance that is normally useful: When two objects produce the

same size retinal image and one is farther away, the farther one is larger. The problem, in this case, is that there is no actual difference in the distance of the two lines, so the rule is inappropriate.

Some illusions are simply a matter of physics. Thus, a chopstick in a half-filled glass of water looks bent because water and air refract light differently. Other illusions occur due to misleading messages from the sense organs, as in sensory adaptation. Still others, like the Müller-Lyer illusion, seem to occur because the brain misinterprets sensory information. Figure 6.7 shows some other startling illusions.

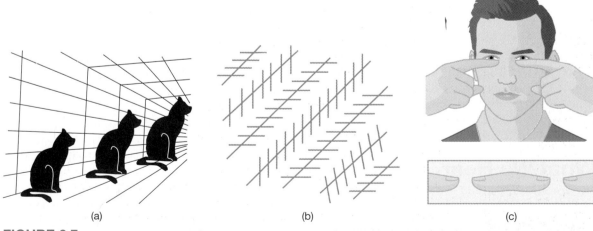

FIGURE 6.7
Fooling the Eye
Although perception is usually accurate, we can be fooled. In (a) the cats as drawn are exactly the same size; in (b) the diagonal lines are all parallel. To see the illusion depicted in (c), hold your index fingers 5 to 10 inches in front of your eyes as shown and then focus straight ahead. Do you see a floating "fingertip frankfurter"? Can you make it shrink or expand?

In everyday life, most illusions are harmless or entertaining. But sometimes illusions can contribute to industrial and automobile accidents. For example, because large objects often appear to move more slowly than small ones, drivers sometimes underestimate the speed of onrushing trains at railroad crossings and think they can beat the train, with tragic results.

QUICK quiz

This quiz is no illusion.

1. From an evolutionary point of view, people are most likely to have a mental module for recognition of (a) flowers, (b) bugs, (c) faces, (d) chocolate, (e) cars.

2. How can two Gestalt principles help explain why you can make out the Big Dipper on a starry night?

3. *True or false:* Binocular cues help us locate objects that are very far away.

4. Hold one hand about 12 inches from your face and the other one about 6 inches away. (a) Which hand will cast the smaller retinal image? (b) Why don't you perceive that hand as smaller?

Answers:

1. c 2. *Proximity* of certain stars encourages you to see them as clustered together to form a pattern; *closure* allows you to "fill in the gaps" and see the contours of a "dipper." 3. false 4. a. The hand that is 12 inches away will cast a smaller retinal image. b. Your brain takes the differences in distance into account in estimating size; also, you know how large your hands are. The result is size constancy.

WHAT'S *Ahead*

- Why does a note played on a flute sound different from the same note played on an oboe?

- If you habitually listen to loud music through headphones, what kind of hearing impairment are you risking?

- To locate the source of a sound, why does it sometimes help to turn or tilt your head?

Hearing

Like vision, the sense of hearing, or *audition*, provides a vital link with the world around us. Because social relationships rely so heavily on hearing, when people lose their hearing they sometimes come to feel socially isolated. That is why many hearing-impaired people feel strongly about teaching deaf children American Sign Language (ASL) or other gestural systems, which allow them to communicate with and forge close relationships with other signers.

What We Hear

The stimulus for sound is a wave of pressure created when an object vibrates (or, sometimes, when compressed air is released, as in a pipe organ). The vibration (or release of air) causes molecules in a transmitting substance to move together and apart. This movement produces variations in pressure that radiate in all directions. The transmitting substance is usually air, but sound waves can also travel through water and solids, as you know if you have ever put your ear to the wall to hear voices in the next room.

As with vision, *physical* characteristics of the stimulus—in this case, a sound wave—are related in a predictable way to *psychological* aspects of our experience:

1 **Loudness** is the dimension of auditory experience related to the *intensity* of a wave's pressure. Intensity corresponds to the amplitude, or maximum height, of the wave. The more energy contained in the wave, the higher it is at its peak. Perceived loudness is also affected by how high or low a sound is. If low and high sounds produce waves with equal amplitudes, the low sound may seem quieter.

Sound intensity is measured in units called *decibels* (dB). A decibel is one-tenth of a *bel*, a unit named for Alexander Graham Bell, the inventor of the telephone. The average absolute threshold of hearing in human beings is zero decibels. Decibels are not equally distant, as inches on a ruler are. A 60-decibel sound (such as that of a sewing machine) is not 50 percent louder than a 40-decibel sound (such as that of a whisper)—it is 100 times louder.

2 **Pitch** is the dimension of auditory experience related to the frequency of the sound wave and, to some extent, its intensity. *Frequency* refers to

loudness The dimension of auditory experience related to the intensity of a pressure wave.

pitch The dimension of auditory experience related to the frequency of a pressure wave; it is related to the height or depth of a tone.

how rapidly the air (or other medium) vibrates—that is, the number of times per second the wave cycles through a peak and a low point. One cycle per second is known as 1 *hertz* (Hz). The healthy ear of a young person normally detects frequencies in the range of 16 Hz (the lowest note on a pipe organ) to 20,000 Hz (the scraping of a grasshopper's legs).

3 **Timbre** is the distinguishing quality of a sound. It is the dimension of auditory experience related to the *complexity* of the sound wave—to the relative breadth of the range of frequencies that make up the wave. A pure tone consists of only one frequency, but in nature, pure tones are extremely rare. Usually what we hear is a complex wave consisting of several subwaves with different frequencies. A particular combination of frequencies results in a particular timbre. Timbre is what makes a note played on a flute, which produces relatively pure tones, sound entirely different from the same note played on an oboe, which produces very complex sounds.

When many sound-wave frequencies are present but are not in harmony, we hear noise. When all the frequencies of the sound spectrum occur, they produce a hissing sound called *white noise*. Just as white light includes all wavelengths of the visible light spectrum, so white noise includes all frequencies of the audible sound spectrum. People sometimes use white-noise machines to mask other sounds when they are trying to sleep.

An Ear on the World

As Figure 6.8 shows, the ear has an outer, a middle, and an inner section. The soft, funnel-shaped outer ear is well designed to collect sound waves, but hearing would still be quite good without it. The essential parts of the ear are hidden from view, inside the head.

A sound wave passes into the outer ear and through an inch-long canal to strike an oval-shaped membrane called the *eardrum.* The eardrum is so sensitive that it can respond to the movement of a

timbre The distinguishing quality of a sound; the dimension of auditory experience related to the complexity of the pressure wave.

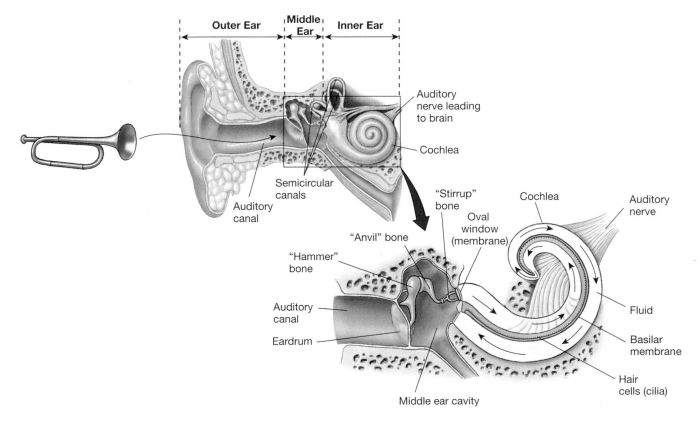

FIGURE 6.8
Major Structures of the Ear
Sound waves collected by the outer ear are channeled down the auditory canal, causing the eardrum to vibrate. These vibrations are then passed along to the tiny bones of the middle ear. Movement of these bones intensifies the force of the vibrations separating the middle and inner ear. The receptor cells for hearing (hair cells), located in the organ of Corti (not shown) within the snail-shaped cochlea, initiate nerve impulses that travel along the auditory nerve to the brain.

organ of Corti [CORE-tee] A structure in the cochlea containing hair cells that serve as the receptors for hearing.

cochlea [KOCK-lee-uh] A snail-shaped, fluid-filled organ in the inner ear, containing the organ of Corti, where the receptors for hearing are located.

single molecule! A sound wave causes it to vibrate with the same frequency and amplitude as the wave itself. This vibration is passed along to three tiny bones in the middle ear, the smallest bones in the human body. These bones, known informally as the "hammer," the "anvil," and the "stirrup," move one after the other, which has the effect of intensifying the force of the vibration. The innermost bone, the stirrup, pushes on a membrane that opens into the inner ear.

The actual organ of hearing, the **organ of Corti**, is a chamber inside the **cochlea**, a snail-shaped structure within the inner ear. This organ plays the same role in hearing that the retina plays in vision. It contains the all-important receptor cells, which in this case look like bristles and are called *hair cells*, or *cilia*. Brief exposure to extremely loud noises, like those from a gunshot or a jet airplane (140 dB), or sustained exposure to more moderate noises, like those from shop tools or truck traffic (90 dB), can injure these fragile cells. They flop over, like broken blades of grass, and if the damage reaches a critical point, hearing loss occurs. In modern societies, with their rock concerts, deafening bars, and millions of automobiles, snowmobiles, power saws, leaf blowers, jackhammers, and MP3 players (often played at full blast), such damage is common, even among teenagers and young adults. Scientists are now doing basic research on possible ways to grow new hair cells (Izumikawa et al., 2005; Sage et al., 2005), but these approaches have not yet led to therapies for hearing loss, and damage to these cells in human beings is currently irreversible.

The hair cells of the cochlea are embedded in the rubbery *basilar membrane*, which stretches across the interior of the cochlea. When pressure reaches the cochlea, it causes wavelike motions in fluid within the cochlea's interior. These waves of fluid push on the basilar membrane, causing it to move in

a wavelike fashion, too. Just above the hair cells is yet another membrane. As the hair cells rise and fall, their tips brush against it, and they bend. This causes the hair cells to initiate a signal that is passed along to the *auditory nerve*, which then carries the message to the brain. The particular pattern of hair-cell movement is affected by the manner in which the basilar membrane moves. This pattern determines which neurons fire and how rapidly they fire, and the resulting code in turn determines the sort of sound we hear. For example, we discriminate high-pitched sounds largely on the basis of where activity occurs along the basilar membrane; activity at different sites leads to different neural codes. We discriminate low-pitched sounds largely on the basis of the frequency of the basilar membrane's vibration; again, different frequencies lead to different neural codes.

Could anyone ever imagine such a complex and odd arrangement of bristles, fluids, and snail shells if it did not already exist?

Constructing the Auditory World

Just as we do not see a retinal image, so we do not hear a chorus of brushlike tufts bending and swaying in the dark recesses of the cochlea. Just as we do not see a jumbled collection of lines and colors, so we do not hear a chaotic collection of disconnected pitches and timbres. Instead, we use our perceptual powers to organize patterns of sound and to construct a meaningful auditory world.

For example, in class, your psychology instructor hopes you will perceive his or her voice as figure and the hum of a passing airplane, cheers from the athletic field, or distant sounds of a construction crew as ground. Whether these hopes are realized will depend, of course, on where you choose to direct your attention. Other Gestalt principles also seem to apply to hearing. The *proximity* of notes in a melody tells you which notes go together to form phrases; *continuity* helps you follow a melody on one violin when another violin is playing a different melody; *similarity* in timbre and pitch helps you pick out the soprano voices in a chorus and hear them as a unit; *closure* helps you understand a cell phone caller's words even when interference makes some of the individual sounds unintelligible.

Besides needing to organize sounds, we also need to know where they are coming from. We can estimate the *distance* of a sound's source by using loudness as a cue. For example, we know that a train sounds louder when it is 20 yards away than when it is a mile off. To locate the *direction* a sound

The sound level at a rock concert near the speakers is about 120 decibels and poses an immediate threat to a person's hearing.

is coming from, we depend in part on the fact that we have two ears. A sound arriving from the right reaches the right ear a fraction of a second sooner than it reaches the left ear, and vice versa. The sound may also provide a bit more energy to the right ear (depending on its frequency) because it has to get around the head to reach the left ear. It is hard to localize sounds that are coming from directly in back of you or from directly above your head because such sounds reach both ears at the same time. When you turn or cock your head, you are actively trying to overcome this problem. Many animals do not have to do this because the lucky creatures can move their ears independently of their heads.

papillae [pa-PILL-ee] Knoblike elevations on the tongue, containing the taste buds. (Singular: *papilla*.)

taste buds Nests of taste-receptor cells.

QUICK quiz

How well can you localize the answers to these questions?

1. Which psychological dimensions of hearing correspond to the intensity, frequency, and complexity of the sound wave?
2. Fred has a nasal voice and Ted has a gravelly voice. Which psychological dimension of hearing describes the difference?
3. An extremely loud or sustained noise can permanently damage the _____ of the ear.
4. During a lecture, a classmate draws your attention to a buzzing fluorescent light that you have not previously noticed. What will happen to your perception of figure and ground?

Answers:

1. loudness, pitch, timbre 2. timbre 3. hair cells (cilia) 4. The buzzing sound will become figure and the lecturer's voice will become ground, at least momentarily.

WHAT'S *Ahead*

- Why do saccharin and caffeine taste bitter to some people but not to others?
- Why do you have trouble tasting your food when you have a cold?
- Why is pain such a puzzle?

Other Senses

Psychologists have been particularly interested in vision and audition because of the importance of these senses to human survival. However, research on the other senses is growing dramatically, as awareness of how they contribute to our lives increases and new ways are found to study them.

Taste: Savory Sensations

Taste, or *gustation*, occurs because chemicals stimulate thousands of receptors in the mouth. These receptors are located primarily on the tongue, but some are also found in the throat, inside the cheeks, and on the roof of the mouth. If you look at your tongue in a mirror, you will notice many tiny bumps; they are called **papillae** (from the Latin for "pimples"), and they come in several forms. In all but one of these forms, the sides of each papil-

la are lined with **taste buds**, which up close look a little like segmented oranges (see Figure 6.9). Because of genetic differences, human tongues can have as few as 500 or as many as 10,000 taste buds (Miller & Reedy, 1990).

The taste buds are commonly referred to, mistakenly, as the receptors for taste. The actual receptor cells, however, are *inside* the buds, 15 to 50 to a bud. These cells send tiny fibers out through an opening in the bud; the receptor sites are on these fibers. The receptor cells are replaced by new cells about every ten

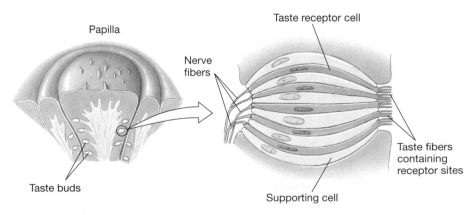

FIGURE 6.9
Taste Receptors
The illustration on the left shows taste buds lining the sides of a papilla on the tongue's surface. The illustration on the right shows an enlarged view of a single taste bud.

days. However, after age 40 or so, the total number of taste buds (and therefore receptors) declines.

Traditionally, researchers have considered four tastes to be basic: *salty, sour, bitter,* and *sweet,* each produced by a different type of chemical. Today, most researchers also include a fifth taste, *umami* (from the Japanese for "delicious"), which is the taste of monosodium glutamate (MSG); it is found in many protein-rich foods, including meat, shellfish, and seaweed. The basic tastes are part of our evolutionary heritage: Bitterness and sourness help us identify foods that are rancid or poisonous; sweetness helps us identify foods that are healthful or rich in calories; salt is necessary for all bodily functions; and umami may help us identify protein-rich foods.

The basic tastes can be perceived at any spot on the tongue that has receptors, and differences among the areas are small. Interestingly, the center of the tongue contains no taste buds, and so it cannot produce any sort of taste sensation. But, as in the case of the eye's blind spot, you will not usually notice the lack of sensation because the brain fills in the gap.

When you bite into an egg or a piece of bread or an orange, its unique flavor is composed of some combination of the four or five basic tastes, but the physiological details are still hazy. It has even been difficult to find the receptors for the basic tastes, although researchers have proposed candidates for the receptors that process bitter, sweet, and umami (Chaudhari, Landin, & Roper, 2000; Damak et al., 2003; Huang et al., 1999; Max et al., 2001; Montmayeur et al., 2001; Zhang et al., 2003).

Everyone knows that people live in somewhat different "taste worlds" (Bartoshuk, 1998). Some people love broccoli and others hate it. Some people can eat chili peppers that are burning hot, and others cannot tolerate the mildest jalapeño. One reason for these differences is genetic. In the United States, about 25 percent of people are *supertasters* who find saccharin, caffeine, broccoli, and many other substances to be unpleasantly bitter. (Women, especially Asian women, are overrepresented in this group.) "Tasters," in contrast, detect less bitterness, and "nontasters" detect none at all. Supertasters also perceive sweet tastes as sweeter and salty tastes as saltier than other people do, and they feel more burn from foods such as ginger, pepper, and hot chilies (Bartoshuk et al., 1998; Lucchina et al., 1998). Supertasters have more taste buds than other people, and certain papillae on their tongues are smaller, are more densely packed, and look different from those of nontasters (Reedy et al., 1993).

Other taste preferences are a matter of culture and learning. Many North Americans who enjoy raw oysters, raw smoked salmon, and raw herring are nevertheless put off by other forms of raw seafood that are popular in Japan, such as sea urchin and octopus. And within a given culture, some people will greedily gobble up a dish that makes others turn green. Some of these learned taste preferences probably begin in the womb or during breast-feeding. A baby whose mother drank carrot juice while pregnant or nursing is likely to be more enthusiastic about eating porridge mixed with carrot juice than porridge mixed with water, whereas babies without this exposure show no such preference (Mennella, Jagnow, & Beauchamp, 2001).

The attractiveness of a food can also be affected by its color, temperature, and texture. As Goldilocks found out, a bowl of cold porridge is not nearly as delicious as one that is properly heated. And any peanut butter fan will tell you that chunky and smooth peanut butters just don't taste the same. Even more important for taste is a food's odor. Subtle flavors such as chocolate and vanilla would have little taste if we could not smell them (see Figure 6.10). Smell's influence on flavor explains why you have trouble tasting your food when you have a stuffy nose. Most people who have chronic trouble detecting tastes have a problem with smell, not taste.

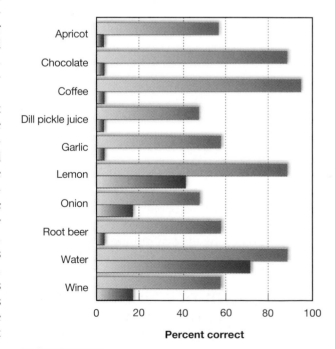

FIGURE 6.10
Taste Test
The orange bars show the percentages of people who could identify a substance dropped on the tongue when they were able to smell it. The blue bars show the percentage that could identify the substance when they were prevented from smelling it (Mozell et al., 1969).

Smell: The Sense of Scents

The great author and educator Helen Keller, who became blind and deaf as a toddler, once called smell "the fallen angel of the senses." Yet our sense of smell, or *olfaction*, although seemingly crude when compared to a bloodhound's, is actually quite good and is far more useful than most people realize.

The receptors for smell are specialized neurons embedded in a tiny patch of mucous membrane in the upper part of the nasal passage, just beneath the eyes (see Figure 6.11). Millions of receptors in each nasal cavity respond to chemical molecules in the air. When you inhale, you pull these molecules into the nasal cavity, but they can also enter from the mouth, wafting up the throat like smoke up a chimney. These molecules trigger responses in the receptors, and these responses combine to yield the yeasty smell of freshly baked bread or the spicy fragrance of a eucalyptus tree. Signals from the receptors are carried to the brain's olfactory bulb by the *olfactory nerve*, which is made up of the receptors' axons. From the *olfactory bulb*, they travel to a higher region of the brain.

Figuring out the neural code for smell has been a real challenge. Of the 10,000 or so smells we detect (rotten, burned, musky, fruity, spicy, flowery, resinous, putrid . . .), none seems to be more basic

Smell has not only evolutionary but also cultural significance. These pilgrims in Japan are purifying themselves with holy incense for good luck and health.

than any other. Moreover, as many as a thousand kinds of receptors exist, each kind responding to a part of an odor molecule's structure (Axel, 1995; Buck & Axel, 1991). (In 2004, Richard Axel and Linda Buck won a Nobel Prize for this discovery.) Distinct odors activate unique combinations of receptors, and signals from different types of receptors

FIGURE 6.11
Receptors for Smell
Airborne chemical molecules (vapors) enter the nose and circulate through the nasal cavity where the smell receptors are located. The receptors' axons make up the olfactory nerve, which carries signals to the brain. When you sniff, you draw more vapors into the nose and speed their circulation. Vapors can also reach the nasal cavity through the mouth by way of a passageway from the throat.

The Smell of Taste

Demonstrate for yourself that smell enhances the sense of taste. Take a bite of a slice of apple and chew on it, holding your nose as you do so, and then do the same with a slice of raw potato. You may find that you can't taste much difference! If you think you do taste a difference between the apple and the potato, maybe your expectations are influencing your response. Try the same thing again, but close your eyes and have someone else feed you the slices. Can you still tell them apart?

are combined in individual neurons in the brain. Some neurons seem to respond only to particular mixtures of odors rather than the individual odors in a mixture, which may explain why a mixture of clove and rose may be perceived as carnation rather than as two separate smells (Zou & Buck, 2006).

Although smell is less vital for human survival than for the survival of other animals, it is still important. We sniff out danger by smelling smoke, food spoilage, and gas leaks; thus, a deficit in the sense of smell is nothing to turn up your nose at. Such a loss can come about because of infection, disease, injury, or smoking. A person who has smoked two packs a day for ten years must abstain from cigarettes for ten more years before the sense of smell returns to normal (Frye, Schwartz, & Doty, 1990).

CLOSE-UP on Research

Nosy Behavior

Odors, of course, have psychological effects on us, which is why we buy perfumes and sniff flowers. Perhaps because olfactory centers in the brain are linked to areas that process memories and emotions, specific smells often evoke vivid, emotionally colored memories (Herz & Cupchik, 1995; Vroon, 1997). The smell of hot chocolate may trigger fond memories of cozy winter mornings from your childhood; the smell of rubbing alcohol may remind you of an unpleasant trip to the hospital. Odors can also influence people's everyday behavior, which is why shopping malls and hotels often install aroma diffusers in hopes of putting you in a good mood.

Many claims have been made for aroma's effects on behavior without much science to back up such claims. Now, however, some good science is starting to be done. For example, in three recent Dutch studies (Holland, Hendriks, & Aarts, 2005), researchers **asked an interesting question**: Can the citrus scent of an all-purpose cleaner (unobtrusively left in a hidden bucket) activate the mental concept *cleaning* and even affect people's "cleaning behavior"? In the first study, they presented strings of letters to participants and asked them to say whether each string formed a word. Half the strings were words and half were not. Participants exposed to the scent were quicker to identify cleaning-related words than control subjects were, as you can see in the figure below. They were also quicker at identifying cleaning-related words than other words. These results suggest that the scent made the concept *cleaning* more mentally accessible. In the second study, the researchers asked the participants to write down five activities they were planning to do during the rest of the day. Those exposed to the scent listed a cleaning activity more often than the other subjects did, again suggesting that the scent had activated the concept *cleaning*.

In the third study, the researchers first had participants fill out a questionnaire (one not related to

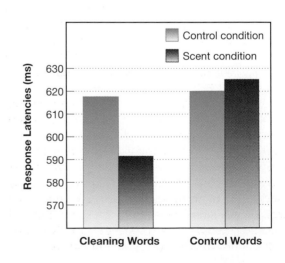

the study) and then moved them to another room where there was no scent and asked them to sit at a table and eat a crumbly biscuit. A hidden video camera recorded the participants' hand movements. People who had been previously exposed to the scent were much more likely than control subjects to wipe away the crumbs from the table! Apparently, activation of the concept *cleaning* made them more likely to clean up after themselves.

Can you think of an **alternative interpretation** of these results? One possibility is that the participants guessed the hypothesis. But the researchers had thought of that. After each study, they questioned the participants and found that none had been aware of the scent's influence. In fact, most were not even aware of having smelled the scent at all. "Together," write the researchers, "these observations provide compelling evidence that scent can have a nonconscious influence on thinking."

Senses of the Skin

The skin's usefulness is more than just skin deep. Besides protecting our innards, our 2 square yards of skin help us identify objects and establish intimacy with others. By providing a boundary between ourselves and everything else, the skin also gives us a sense of ourselves as distinct from the environment.

The basic skin senses include *touch* (or pressure), *warmth*, *cold*, and *pain*. Within these four types are variations such as itch, tickle, and painful burning. Although certain spots on the skin are especially sensitive to the four basic skin sensations, for many years scientists had difficulty finding distinct receptors for these sensations, except in the case of pressure. But then Swedish researchers found a new kind of nerve fiber that seems to be responsible for at least some types of itching (Schmelz et al., 1997). And scientists have also identified a possible cold receptor (McKemy, Neuhausser, & Julius, 2002; Peier et al., 2002).

Perhaps specialized fibers will also be discovered for other skin sensations. In the meantime, many aspects of touch continue to baffle science—for example, why gently touching adjacent pressure spots in rapid succession produces tickle; and why the simultaneous stimulation of warm and cold spots produces not a lukewarm sensation but the sensation of heat. Decoding the messages of the skin senses will eventually tell us how we are able to distinguish sandpaper from velvet and glue from grease.

The Mystery of Pain

Pain, which is not only a skin sense but also an internal sense, has come under special scrutiny. Pain differs from other senses in an important way: When the stimulus producing it is removed, the sensation may continue—sometimes for years. Chronic pain disrupts lives, puts stress on the body, and causes depression and despair. (For ways of coping with pain, see "Taking Psychology with You.")

The Gate-Control Theory of Pain

For many years, a leading explanation of pain has been the **gate-control theory**, which was first proposed by Canadian psychologist Ronald Melzack and British physiologist Patrick Wall (1965). According to this theory, pain impulses must get past a "gate" in the spinal cord. The gate is not an actual structure, but rather a pattern of neural activity that either blocks pain messages coming from the skin, muscles, and internal organs or lets those signals through. Normally, the gate is kept shut, either by impulses coming into the spinal cord from large fibers that respond to pressure and other kinds of stimulation or by signals coming down from the brain itself. But when body tissue is injured, the large fibers are damaged and smaller fibers open the gate, allowing pain messages to reach the brain unchecked.

If "gate" is open, then pain impulses reach the brain

"Gate" closed by incoming impulses from large fibers or from the brain; opened by impulses from smaller fibers

Because the gate-control theory emphasizes the role of the brain in controlling the gate, it correctly predicts that thoughts and feelings can influence our reactions to pain. When we dwell on our pain, focusing on it and talking about it constantly instead of acting in spite of it, we often intensify our experience of it (Sullivan, Tripp, & Santor, 1998). Conversely, when we are distracted from our pain, we may not feel it as we usually would, which is why we hear, from time to time, of athletes who are able to finish a performance despite sprained ankles or even broken bones. The gate-control theory also correctly predicts that mild pressure, or other kinds of stimulation, can interfere with severe or protracted pain by closing the spinal gate. When we vigorously rub a banged elbow or apply ice packs, heat, or stimulating ointments to injuries, we are applying this principle.

gate-control theory
The theory that the experience of pain depends in part on whether pain impulses get past a neurological "gate" in the spinal cord and thus reach the brain.

phantom pain The experience of pain in a missing limb or other body part.

kinesthesis [KIN-es-THEE-sis] The sense of body position and movement of body parts; also called *kinesthesia*.

Updating the Gate-Control Theory

The gate-control theory has been highly useful, but it does not fully explain the many instances of severe, chronic pain that occur without any sign of injury or disease whatsoever. In the strange phenomenon of **phantom pain**, for instance, a person continues to feel pain that seemingly comes from an amputated limb or from an organ that has been surgically removed. An amputee may feel the same aching, burning, or sharp pain from sores, calf cramps, throbbing toes, or even ingrown toenails that he or she endured before the surgery. Even when the spinal cord has been completely severed, amputees often continue to report phantom pain from areas below the break. There are no nerve impulses for the spinal cord gate to block or let through. So why is there pain?

These puzzles led Ronald Melzack (1992, 1993) to revise the gate-control theory. The brain, he says, not only responds to incoming signals from sensory nerves but also is capable of *generating* pain (and other sensations) entirely on its own. An extensive *matrix* (network) of neurons in the brain gives us a sense of our own bodies and body parts. When this matrix produces abnormal patterns of activity, the result is pain. Such abnormal patterns can occur not only because of input from peripheral nerves but also as a result of memories, emotions, expectations, or signals from various brain centers. In the case of phantom pain, the abnormal patterns may arise because of a lack of sensory stimulation or because of the person's efforts to move a nonexistent limb. Evidence that brain areas associated with a missing limb continue to function in its absence is consistent with this view (Davis et al., 1998).

Input from spinal cord
Signals from brain centers
Memories
Emotions
Expectations
Attention

Abnormal patterns of activity in a neural matrix

Pain

At present, however, no general theory completely explains phantom pain, or for that matter normal pain, which has turned out to be extremely complicated, both physiologically and psychologically. Different types of pain (from, say, a thorn, a bruise, or a hot iron) involve different chemical changes and different changes in nerve-cell activity at the site of injury or disease, as well as in the spinal cord and brain. These changes may suppress the pain or may amplify it by making neurons hyperexcitable. In addition, enormous variation exists among individuals: The same spinal condition that causes some people to live with agonizing back pain can be untroubling to others. One reason for this variation may be genetic differences in the production of pain-reducing endorphins (Zubieta et al., 2003). Another explanation has to do with differences in people's expectations. If you expect to feel pain, you may focus on it, producing a self-fulfilling prophecy, and if you expect *not* to feel pain, that expectation, too, can become self-fulfilling. Indeed, recent research with functional MRI shows that the stronger the pain a person expects to feel, the greater the activity in certain brain regions—and most of these regions are the same ones that respond to actual pain (Koyama et al., 2005).

Expectations about pain can be affected by placebos, your environment (for example, does it make you feel safe or apprehensive?), what your doctor tells you, psychological factors such as a focus on yourself, and cultural beliefs governing how appropriate it is to notice symptoms and express distress. These nonmedical influences on pain contribute to the rise and fall of pain epidemics, as in sudden, apparently mysterious outbreaks of back pain, whiplash, and repetitive-motion injuries (Gawande, 1998). The individuals who suffer during such epidemics are not faking it, and their pain is not "just in their heads." But it may be in their brains.

The Environment Within

We usually think of our senses as pipelines to the world around us, but two senses keep us informed about the movements of our own bodies. **Kinesthesis** tells us where our body parts are located and lets us know when they move. This information is provided by pain and pressure receptors located in the muscles, joints, and tendons (tissues that connect muscles to bones). Without kinesthesis, you could not touch your finger to your nose with your eyes shut. In fact, you would have trouble with any voluntary movement. Think of how hard walking is when your leg has fallen asleep or how clumsy chewing is when a dentist has numbed your jaw.

A school nurse and a teacher's aide examine Ashlyn Blocker's feet for injuries. Because of a rare condition, Ashlyn cannot feel pain from scrapes and scratches. Although pain causes much suffering, it is also useful because it alerts us to injuries and illness.

Equilibrium, or the sense of balance, gives us information about our bodies as a whole. Along with vision and touch, it lets us know whether we are standing upright or on our heads and tells us when we are falling or rotating. Equilibrium relies primarily on three **semicircular canals** in the inner ear (see Figure 6.8 on page 193). These thin tubes are filled with fluid that moves and presses on hairlike receptors whenever the head rotates. The receptors initiate messages that travel through a part of the auditory nerve not involved in hearing.

Normally, kinesthesis and equilibrium work together to give us a sense of our own physical reality, something we take utterly for granted but should not. Oliver Sacks (1985) told the heartbreaking story of Christina, a young British woman who suffered irreversible damage to her kinesthetic nerve fibers because of a mysterious inflammation. At first, Christina was as floppy as a rag doll; she could not sit up, walk, or stand. Then, slowly, she learned to do these things, relying on visual cues and sheer willpower. But her movements remained unnatural; she had to grasp a fork with painful force or she would drop it. More important, despite her remaining sensitivity to light touch on the skin, she could no longer experience herself as physically embodied: "It's like something's been scooped right out of me, right at the center. . . ."

With equilibrium, we come, as it were, to the end of our senses. Every second, millions of sensory signals reach the brain, which combines and integrates them to produce a model of reality from moment to moment. How does it know how to do this? Are our perceptual abilities inborn, or must we learn them? We turn next to this issue.

This break dancer obviously has exceptional kinesthetic talents and equilibrium.

QUICK quiz

See if you can make sense of the following quiz problems.

A. What explanation of each problem is most likely?

1. April always has trouble tasting foods, especially those with subtle flavors.

2. May has chronic shoulder pain, though the injury that initially caused it seems to have healed. [Hint: Think about the gate-control theory and its revision.]

3. June, a rock musician, does not hear as well as she used to.

B. After reading about the scent studies in the "Close-up on Research" feature, what further questions might you want to ask?

Answers:

A. 1. An impaired sense of smell, possibly due to disease, illness, or cigarette smoking. 2. Nerve fibers that normally close the pain "gate" may have been damaged, or a matrix of cells in the brain may be producing abnormal activity. 3. Hearing impairment has many causes, but in June's case, we might suspect that prolonged exposure to loud music has damaged the hair cells of her cochlea. B. Some questions to ask: Do other scents also affect behavior, and if so, which ones? (We do not want to oversimplify by assuming that similar results would occur for all scents.) Are pleasant and unpleasant scents equally likely to affect behavior? Would the effects be even stronger if the participants were aware of the scent? Most important, will other research replicate these initial findings?

WHAT'S *Ahead*

- Do babies see the world the way adults do?

- Why do blind children whose sight has been restored see better than adults in the same situation?

- What psychological motives could cause people to see the face of a religious figure on a cinnamon bun?

Perceptual Powers: Origins and Influences

What happens when babies first open their eyes? Do they see the same sights, hear the same sounds, smell the same smells, taste the same tastes as an adult does? Are their strategies for organizing the world wired into their brains from the beginning? Or is an infant's world, as William James once suggested, only a "blooming, buzzing confusion," waiting to be organized by experience and learning? The truth lies somewhere between these two extremes.

Inborn Abilities

In human beings, most basic sensory abilities and many perceptual skills are inborn or develop quite early. Infants can distinguish salty from sweet and can discriminate among odors. They can distinguish a human voice from other sounds. They will startle to a loud noise and turn their heads toward its source, showing that they perceive sound as being localized in space. Many visual skills, too, are present at birth

equilibrium The sense of balance.

semicircular canals Sense organs in the inner ear, which contribute to equilibrium by responding to rotation of the head.

or develop shortly afterward. Human infants can discriminate sizes and colors very early, possibly even right away. They can distinguish contrasts, shadows, and complex patterns after only a few weeks. And depth perception develops during the first few months.

Testing an infant's perception of depth requires considerable ingenuity. One clever procedure that was used for decades was to place infants on a device called a *visual cliff* (Gibson & Walk, 1960). The "cliff" is a pane of glass covering a shallow surface and a deep one (see Figure 6.12). Both surfaces are covered by a checkerboard pattern. The infant is placed on a board in the middle, and the child's mother tries to lure the baby across either the shallow or the deep side. Babies only 6 months of age will crawl across the shallow side but will refuse to crawl out over the cliff. Their hesitation shows that they have depth perception.

Of course, by 6 months of age, a baby has had quite a bit of experience with the world. But infants younger than 6 months can also be tested on the visual cliff, even though they cannot yet crawl. At only 2 months of age, babies show a drop in heart rate when placed on the deep side of the cliff but no change when they are placed on the shallow side. A slowed heart rate is usually a sign of increased attention. Thus, although these infants may not be frightened the way an older infant would be, it seems they can perceive the difference between the shallow and the deep sides of the cliff (Banks & Salapatek, 1984).

Critical Periods

Although many perceptual abilities are inborn, experience also plays a vital role. If an infant misses out on certain experiences during a crucial window of time—a *critical period*—perception will be impaired. Innate abilities will not survive because cells in the nervous system deteriorate, change, or fail to form appropriate neural pathways.

One way to study critical periods is to see what happens when the usual perceptual experiences of early life fail to take place. To do so, researchers often study animals whose sensory and perceptual systems are similar to our own. For example, like human beings, cats are born with the ability to detect horizontal and vertical lines and other spatial orientations; at birth, kittens' brains are equipped with the same kinds of feature-detector cells that adult cats have. But if they are deprived of normal visual experience, these cells deteriorate or change, and perception suffers (Crair, Gillespie, & Stryker, 1998; Hirsch & Spinelli, 1970).

In one famous study, kittens were exposed to either vertical or horizontal black and white stripes. Special collars kept them from seeing anything else, even their own bodies. After several months, the kittens exposed only to vertical stripes seemed blind to all horizontal contours; they bumped into horizontal obstacles, and they ran to play with a bar that an experimenter held vertically but not to a bar held horizontally. In contrast, those exposed

Glass over pattern

Shallow side

Glass surface

Deep side

Floor as seen through glass

FIGURE 6.12
A Cliff-Hanger
Infants as young as 6 months usually hesitate to crawl past the apparent edge of a visual cliff, which suggests that they are able to perceive depth.

only to horizontal stripes bumped into vertical obstacles and ran to play with horizontal bars but not vertical ones (Blakemore & Cooper, 1970).

Critical periods for sensory development also exist in human beings. When adults who have been blind from infancy have their vision restored, they may see, but often they do not see well. Their depth perception may be poor, causing them to trip constantly, and they cannot always make sense of what they see. To identify objects, they may have to touch or smell them. They may have trouble recognizing faces and emotional expressions. They may even lack size constancy and may need to remind themselves that people walking away from them are not shrinking in size (Fine et al., 2003). But if an infant's congenital blindness is corrected early, during a critical period during the first nine months or so, the prognosis is much better (though visual discriminations may never become entirely normal). In one study of infants who underwent corrective surgery when they were from 1 week to 9 months of age, improvement started to occur after as little as one hour of visual experience (Maurer et al., 1999).

Similar findings apply to hearing. When adults who were born deaf, or who lost their hearing before learning to speak, receive cochlear implants (devices that stimulate the auditory nerve and allow auditory signals to travel to the brain), they tend to find sounds confusing. In fact, they sometimes ask to have the implants removed. But cochlear implants are more successful in children and in adults who became deaf late in life (Rauschecker, 1999). The children presumably have not yet passed through the critical period for the processing of sounds, and the adults have already had years of auditory experience.

In sum, our perceptual powers are both wired in and dependent on experience. Because neurological connections in infants' brains and sensory systems are not completely formed, their senses are far less acute than an adult's. It takes time and experience for their sensory abilities to develop fully. But an infant's world is clearly not the blooming, buzzing confusion that William James took it to be.

Psychological and Cultural Influences on Perception

The fact that some perceptual processes appear to be innate does not mean that all people perceive the world in the same way. Because we care about what we see, hear, taste, smell, and feel, psychological factors can influence what we perceive and how we perceive it. Here are a few of these factors:

1 *Needs.* When we need something, have an interest in it, or want it, we are especially likely to perceive it. For example, hungry individuals are faster than others at seeing words related to hunger when the words are flashed briefly on a screen (Wispé & Drambarean, 1953).

2 *Beliefs.* What we hold to be true about the world can affect our interpretation of ambiguous sensory signals. When the World Trade Center was attacked, many people thought they saw the face of the devil (or some said Osama bin Laden) in the smoke billowing from the towers. In a Nashville coffee shop, a cinnamon bun was shellacked and enshrined because people thought they saw a likeness of the famous nun Mother Teresa in it. Images that remind people of a crucified Jesus have been reported on walls, dishes, pieces of toast, and plates of spaghetti, causing great excitement among those who believe that divine messages can be found on everyday objects—until other explanations emerge. In California, an image of Jesus on a garage door drew large crowds; it turned out to be caused by two streetlights that merged the shadows of a bush and a "For Sale" sign in the yard.

3 *Emotions.* Emotions can also influence our interpretation of sensory information. A small child afraid of the dark may see a ghost instead of a robe hanging on the door or a monster instead of a beloved doll. Pain, in particular, is affected by emotion. Soldiers who are seriously wounded often deny being in much pain, even though they are alert and are not in shock. Their relief at being alive may offset the anxiety and fear that contribute so much to pain (although distraction and the body's own pain-fighting mechanisms may also be involved). Conversely, negative emotions such as anger, fear, sadness, or depression can prolong and intensify a person's pain (Fernandez & Turk, 1992; Fields, 1991).

4 *Expectations.* Previous experiences often affect how we perceive the world (Lachman, 1996). The tendency to perceive what you expect is

We often see what we expect or need to see. After the attacks of 9/11, some people looked at this famous image of smoke billowing from the World Trade Center and saw the face of Satan or Osama bin Laden in it.

perceptual set A habitual way of perceiving, based on expectations.

called a **perceptual set**. Perceptual sets can come in handy; they help us fill in words in sentences, for example, when we haven't really heard every one. But perceptaul sets can also cause misperceptions. In Center Harbor, Maine, local legend has it that veteran newscaster Walter Cronkite was sailing into port one day when he heard a small crowd on shore shouting, "Hello, Walter . . . Hello, Walter." Pleased, he waved and took a bow. Only when he ran aground did he realize what they had really been shouting: "Shallow water . . . shallow water!"

By the way, the previous paragraph has a misspelled word. Did you catch it? If not, probably it was because you expected all the words in this book to be spelled correctly.

Our needs, emotions, expectations, and beliefs are all affected, in turn, by the culture we live in. Different cultures give people practice with different environments. In a classic study done in the 1960s, researchers found that members of some African tribes were much less likely to be fooled by the Müller-Lyer illusion and other geometric illusions than were Westerners. In the West, the researchers observed, people live in a "carpentered" world, full of rectangular structures built with the aid of straightedges and carpenter's squares. Westerners are also used to interpreting two-dimensional photographs and perspective drawings as representations of a three-dimensional world. Therefore, they interpret the kinds of angles used in the Müller-Lyer illusion as right angles extended in space, a habit that would increase susceptibility to the illusion. The rural Africans in the study, living in a less carpentered environment and in round huts, seemed more likely to take the lines in the figures literally, as two-dimensional, which could explain why they were less susceptible to the illusion (Segall, Campbell, & Herskovits, 1966; Segall et al., 1999).

Culture also affects perception by shaping our stereotypes and telling us what is important to notice or ignore. Westerners, for example, tend to focus mostly on the figure when viewing a scene and much less on the ground. East Asians, in contrast, tend to pay attention to the overall context of the scene and the relationship between figure and ground. When Japanese and Americans were shown underwater scenes containing brightly colored fish that were larger and moving faster than other objects in the scene, they reported the same number of details about the fish, but the Japanese reported more details about the background (Masuda & Nisbett, 2001). One of the researchers, Richard Nisbett, commented, "If it ain't moving, it doesn't exist for an American" (quoted in Shea, 2001).

Why should the Japanese pay more attention to context than Americans? One possibility is that a greater concern with the social world directs the attention of the Japanese to contexts of all types. Another possibility is that in Japan, specific objects really do stand out less than in comparable American environments, so living in Japan tends to direct a person's attention to the whole visual field. Indeed, when researchers randomly sampled pictures of hotels, elementary schools, and post offices from small, medium, and large cities in Japan and the United States, they found that the Japanese scenes were more ambiguous and contained more elements than comparable American scenes—just the kind of scenes that encourage attention to context (Miyamoto, Nisbett, & Masuda, 2006).

These photos of a U.S. school (left) and a Japanese school (right) were among a large number of randomly selected photos of schools, hotels, and post offices taken in the two countries. Japanese scenes tend to be more ambiguous and complex than American scenes, which may help explain why the Japanese attend more closely to context than Americans do (Miyamoto, Nisbett, & Masuda, 2006).

QUICK quiz

Direct your perceptual attention now to this quiz.

1. On the visual cliff, 6-month-old babies (a) go right across because they cannot detect depth, (b) cross even though they are afraid, (c) will not cross because they can detect depth, (d) cry or get bored.

2. Newborns and infants (a) have few perceptual abilities, (b) need visual experiences during a critical period for vision to develop normally, (c) see as well as adults.

3. "Have a nice . . ." says Dewey, but then he gets distracted and doesn't finish the thought. Yet Clarence is sure he heard Dewey wish him a nice *day*. Why?

Answers:

1. c 2. b 3. perceptual set due to expectations

WHAT'S *Ahead*

- Can "subliminal perception" tapes help you lose weight or reduce your stress?
- Why are most psychologists skeptical about ESP?

Puzzles of Perception

We come, finally, to two intriguing questions about perception that have captured the public's imagination for years. First, can we ever perceive what is happening in the world when it is below our usual sensory threshold? Second, can we pick up signals from the world or from other people without using our usual sensory channels at all?

Subliminal Perception

As we saw earlier in our discussion of selective attention, even when people are oblivious to speech sounds, they are processing and recognizing those sounds at some level. But these sounds are above people's absolute thresholds. Is it also possible to perceive and respond to messages that are *below* the absolute threshold—too quiet to be consciously heard or too brief or dim to be consciously seen?

Perhaps you have seen ads for products that will supposedly help you learn another language or raise your self-esteem (or, our favorite, learn to love housework) by taking advantage of *subliminal perception*. What are the facts?

Perceiving Without Awareness First, a simple visual stimulus can indeed affect your behavior even when you are unaware that you saw it. For example, people sometimes correctly sense a change in a scene (say, in the color or location of an object) even though the change was shown too quickly to be consciously recognized and identified (Rensink, 2004). And people subliminally exposed to a face will tend to prefer that face over one they did not "see" in this way (Bornstein, Leone, & Galley, 1987). In some studies, researchers have flashed words subliminally in a person's visual field while the person focuses on the middle of a screen. When the words are related to some personality trait, such as honesty, people are more likely later on to judge someone they read about as having that trait. They have been "primed" to evaluate the person in a certain way (Bargh, 1999).

Thus, people often know more than they know they know. In fact, nonconscious processing appears to occur not only in perception but also in memory, thinking, and decision making, as we will see in Chapters 7 and 8. However, even in the laboratory, where researchers have considerable control, the phenomenon can be hard to demonstrate and replicate. The strongest evidence comes from studies using simple stimuli (faces or single words such as *bread*) rather than complex stimuli such as sentences ("Eat whole-wheat bread, not white bread").

Perception Versus Persuasion If subliminal priming can affect judgments and preferences, can it be used to manipulate people's attitudes and behavior? Subliminal persuasion techniques were a hot topic back in the 1950s, when an advertising executive claimed to have

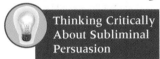
Thinking Critically About Subliminal Persuasion

increased popcorn and Coke sales at a theater by secretly flashing the words EAT POPCORN and DRINK COKE on the movie screen. The claim turned out to be a hoax, devised to save the man's struggling advertising company. Ever since, scientists have been skeptical, and most attempts to demonstrate subliminal persuasion have been disappointing.

That has not deterred people who market subliminal tapes that promise to help you lose weight, stop smoking, relieve stress, read faster, boost your motivation, lower your cholesterol, stop biting your nails, overcome jet lag, or stop taking drugs, all without any effort on your part. If only those claims were true! But in study after study, placebo tapes— tapes that do not contain the messages that participants think they do—are just as "effective" as subliminal tapes (Eich & Hyman, 1992; Merikle & Skanes, 1992; Moore, 1992, 1995). In one typical experiment, people listened to tapes labeled "memory" or "self-esteem," but some heard tapes that were incorrectly labeled. About half showed improvement in the area specified by the label *whether it was correct or not;* the improvement was due to expectations alone (Greenwald et al., 1991).

Three Canadian psychologists have suggested that previous efforts at subliminal persuasion left out an important ingredient: the person's motivation. Instead of trying to influence a person directly by using a subliminal message like "Drink Coke," these researchers used subliminal messages—the words *thirst* and *dry*— to make subjects feel thirsty and prime them to drink. Later, when given a chance to drink, the primed participants did in fact drink more than control subjects did, but only if they had been moderately thirsty to begin with (Strahan, Spencer, & Zanna, 2002).

Does this mean that advertisers can seduce us into buying soft drinks or voting for political candidates by slipping subliminal slogans and images into television and magazine ads? Given the many studies that have found no evidence of subliminal persuasion and the subtlety of the effects that do occur (e.g., you have to be somewhat thirsty already to be primed to want to drink), we think there's little cause for worry about subliminal manipulation. If advertisers want you to buy something, they would probably do better to spend their money on *above*-threshold messages. And if you want to improve yourself or your life, you'll have to do it the old-fashioned way: by working at it consciously.

Extrasensory Perception: Reality or Illusion?

Eyes, ears, mouth, nose, skin—we rely on these organs for our experience of the external world. Some people, however, claim they can send and receive messages about the world without relying on the usual sensory channels, by using *extrasensory perception (ESP)*. Reported ESP experiences involve things like telepathy, the direct communication of messages from one mind to another without the usual sensory signals, and precognition, the perception of an event that has not yet happened.

Most ESP claims challenge everything we currently know to be true about the way the world and the universe operate. A lot of people are ready to accept these claims. Even many college students believe in ESP—in one recent study, 28 percent said they did with another 39 percent "not sure" (Farha & Steward, 2006). And in various polls, about half of all Americans say they believe in it. Is there any scientific evidence for their belief?

"What do you mean you didn't know that we were having a pop quiz today?"

www.CartoonStock.com

Much of the supposed evidence for extrasensory perception comes from anecdotal accounts. But people are not always reliable reporters of their own experiences. They often embellish and exaggerate, or they recall only part of what happened. They also tend to forget incidents that do not fit their beliefs, such as "premonitions" of events that fail to occur. Many ESP experiences could merely be unusual coincidences that are memorable because they are dramatic. What passes for telepathy or precognition could

Thinking Critically About ESP

also be based on what a person knows or deduces through ordinary means. If Joanne's father has had two heart attacks, her premonition that her father will die shortly (followed, in fact, by her father's death) may not be so impressive.

The scientific way to establish a phenomenon is to produce it under controlled conditions. Extrasensory perception has been studied extensively by researchers in the field of **parapsychology**. But ESP studies have often been poorly designed, with inadequate precautions against fraud and improper statistical analysis. After an exhaustive review, the National

Research Council concluded that there was "no scientific justification . . . for the existence of parapsychological phenomena" (Druckman & Swets, 1988).

The issue has not gone away, however. Many people *really, really* want to believe that ESP exists. James Randi, a famous magician who is dedicated to educating the public about psychic deception, has for years offered a million dollars to anyone who can demonstrate ESP or other paranormal powers under close observation. Many have taken up the challenge; no one has succeeded. We think Randi's money is safe.

The history of research on psychic phenomena has been one of initial enthusiasm because of apparently positive results (Bem & Honorton, 1994; Dalton et al., 1996), followed by disappointment when the results cannot be replicated (Milton & Wiseman, 1999, 2001). The thousands of studies done since the 1940s have failed to make a convincing case for ESP. One researcher who tried for 30 years to establish the reality of psychic phenomena finally gave up in defeat. "I found no psychic phenomena," she wrote, "only wishful thinking, self-deception, experimental error, and even an occasional fraud. I became a skeptic" (Blackmore, 2001).

parapsychology The study of purported psychic phenomena such as ESP and mental telepathy.

QUICK quiz

ESP won't help you answer these questions.

1. A study appears to find evidence of "sleep learning"—the ability to perceive and retain material played on an audiotape while a person sleeps. What would you want to know about this research before deciding to tape this chapter and play it by your bedside all night instead of studying it in the usual way?

2. What factors in human perception might explain why so many people interpret unexplained sensations as evidence of ESP, telepathy, or other "psychic" phenomena?

Answers:

1. Was there a control group that listened to, say, a musical selection or white noise? Were the participants really sleeping? How complicated was the material that was allegedly learned—a few key words, whole sentences, a whole lecture by Professor Arbuckle? Were the results large enough to have any practical applications? How did the researchers determine that the participants really were asleep? (When brain-wave measures are used to verify that volunteers are actually sleeping, no "sleep learning" takes place. So if you want to learn the material in this chapter, you'll have to stay awake!) 2. psychological and cultural factors, such as perceptual sets, needs, emotions, wishes, and beliefs

psychology in the news REVISITED

The ancient Greek philosopher Plato once said that "knowledge is nothing but perception." But simple perception is *not* always the best path to knowledge. As we have seen throughout this chapter, we do not passively

register the world "out there"; we mentally construct it. If we are critical thinkers, therefore, we will be aware of how our beliefs and assumptions shape our perceptions.

This means that we should maintain a healthy skepticism when people report seeing spaceships or aliens, as in the story that started this chapter. Some people, as we have noted, are habitual yea-sayers who, because of their expectations, are quick to think they saw something that wasn't there. All of us, even those of us who are not usually gullible, have needs and beliefs that can fool us into seeing things that we want to see. And all of us occasionally read meanings into sensory experiences that are not inherent in the experience itself. Who has not seen nonexistent water on a hot highway or felt a nonexistent insect on the skin after merely thinking about bugs?

Many forces conspire to encourage epidemics of UFO sightings. Some come from the popular media, which generate a lot of money by promoting movies, TV shows, and talk-show accounts about extraterrestrials, and which usually portray skeptics as nerds or narrow-minded debunkers. Other forces are inherent in human psychology, including the fallibility of memory and the power of suggestion after an initial report of a sighting. And some reasons for UFO sightings can be traced to normal distortions of perception: When you are looking up at the sky, where there are few points of reference, it is difficult to judge how far away or how big an object is.

Whenever impartial investigators have looked into UFO reports, they have found that what people really saw were weather balloons, rocket launchings, swamp gas, military aircraft, or (in the vast majority of cases) ordinary celestial bodies, such as planets and meteors. The strange objects in the photo accompanying our news story, which look so much like flying saucers, are really lenticular (lens-shaped) clouds. And the "alien bodies" reported in Roswell were simply test dummies made of rubber, which the Air Force was dropping from high-altitude balloons before subjecting human beings to jumps from the same height. Yet even capable, intelligent people can be fooled. One astronomer who investigates UFO reports says, "I've been with Air Force pilots who thought they were seeing a UFO. But it was actually the moon. I've seen people look at Venus and say they could see portholes on a spaceship" (quoted in Ratcliffe, 2000).

None of this means that the only real world is the mundane one we see in everyday life. Because our sense organs evolved for particular purposes, our sensory windows on the world are partly shuttered. But we can use reason, ingenuity, and science to pry those shutters open. Ordinary perception tells us that the sun circles the earth, but the great astronomer Copernicus was able to figure out nearly five centuries ago that the opposite is true. Ordinary perception will never let us see ultraviolet and infrared rays directly, but we know they are there, and we can measure them. If science can enable us to overturn the everyday evidence of our senses, who knows what surprises science has in store for us?

➤TAKING ➤PSYCHOLOGY ➤WITH ➤YOU

Living with Pain

Temporary pain is an unpleasant but necessary part of life, a warning of disease or injury. Chronic pain is another matter, a serious problem in itself. Back injuries, arthritis, migraine headaches, and serious illnesses can cause unrelieved misery to pain sufferers and their families. Chronic pain can also impair the immune system, putting patients at risk of further complications from their illnesses (Page et al., 1993).

At one time, the only way to combat pain was with drugs or surgery, which often were ineffective. Today, these approaches have improved somewhat, but surgery carries its own risks and drugs often have side effects. Moreover, it has become clear that pain is affected by attitudes, actions, emotions, and circumstances and that treatment must take these influences into account.

Many pain-treatment programs encourage patients to manage their pain themselves instead of relying entirely on health-care professionals. Usually, these programs combine several strategies:

● **Involvement by family and friends.** When a person is in pain, friends and relatives understandably tend to sympathize and to excuse the sufferer from regular responsibilities. The sufferer takes to bed, avoids physical activity, and focuses on the pain. But focusing on pain tends to increase it, and inactivity can lead to shortened muscles, muscle spasms, and fatigue. So sympathy and attention can backfire and may actually prolong the suffering (Flor, Kerns, & Turk, 1987). Many pain experts now encourage family members to reward activity, distraction, and wellness instead of simply offering sympathy. This approach, however, must be used carefully, preferably under the direction of a medical or mental-health professional, because a patient's complaints about pain are an important diagnostic tool for the physician.

● **Self-management.** Patients can learn to identify how, when, and where their pain occurs. This knowledge helps them determine whether the pain is being maintained by external events or is most intense at a certain time of day, and tells them what they might need to do to reduce their pain. Just having a sense of control can have a powerful pain-reducing effect (Cioffi & Holloway, 1993).

● **Relaxation, hypnosis, and acupuncture.** A blue-ribbon panel of experts concluded that relaxation techniques, such as deep breathing, meditating, or focusing on reducing tension in specific muscle groups, can help reduce chronic pain from a variety of medical conditions (NIH Technology Assessment Panel, 1996). Hypnosis can be useful, too, especially when it is combined with behavior modification, physical therapy, and, if the person is anxious or depressed, psychotherapy (Patterson, 2004). Some studies find that acupuncture also helps to reduce some kinds of pain, possibly by stimulating the release of endorphins (Holden, 1997).

● **Cognitive-behavior therapy.** When pain is chronic, people may begin to define themselves in terms of their misery ("I am an ill, suffering person"), which can add to their distress and make the management of the pain more difficult (Pincus & Morley, 2001). Cognitive-behavior therapy teaches people to recognize the connections among thoughts, feelings, and pain; substitute adaptive thoughts for negative ones; and use distraction, relabeling of sensations, and imagery to alleviate suffering (see Chapter 12).

For further information, go to the Internet, where there are many pain-management sites run by reputable institutions such as universities, medical associations, and the federal government. For example, New York's Beth Israel Medical Center runs www.stoppain.org. You can also contact a pain clinic in a teaching hospital or medical school; there are many reputable clinics around the country, some specializing in specific disorders, such as migraines or back injuries. But take care: There are also many untested therapies and quack practitioners who only prey on people's pain.

SUMMARY

- *Sensation* is the detection and direct experience of physical energy as a result of environmental or internal events. *Perception* is the process by which sensory impulses are organized and interpreted.

Our Sensational Senses

- Sensation begins with the *sense receptors*, which convert the energy of a stimulus into electrical impulses that travel along nerves to the brain. Separate sensations can be accounted for by *anatomical codes* (as set forth by the *doctrine of specific nerve energies*) and *functional codes* in the nervous system. In a rare condition called *synesthesia*, sensation in one modality evokes a sensation in another modality, but these experiences are the exception, not the rule.

- Psychologists specializing in *psychophysics* have studied sensory sensitivity by measuring *absolute* and *difference thresholds*. *Signal-detection theory*, however, holds that responses in a detection task consist of both a sensory process and a decision process and will vary with the person's motivation, alertness, and expectations.

- Our senses are designed to respond to change and contrast in the environment. When stimulation is unchanging, *sensory adaptation* occurs. Too little stimulation can cause *sensory deprivation*. Too much stimulation can cause sensory overload. *Selective attention* prevents overload and allows us to focus on what is important, but it also deprives us of sensory information we may need, as in *inattentional blindness*.

Vision

- Vision is affected by the wavelength, intensity, and complexity of light, which produce the psychological dimensions of visual experience—*hue*, *brightness*, and *saturation*. The visual receptors, *rods* and *cones, are* located in the *retina* of the eye. They send signals (via other cells) to the *ganglion cells* and ultimately to the *optic nerve*, which carries visual information to the brain. Rods are responsible for vision in dim light; cones are responsible for color vision. *Dark adaptation* occurs in two stages.

- Specific aspects of the visual world, such as lines at various orientations, are detected by *feature-detector cells* in the visual areas of the brain. Some of these cells respond maximally to complex patterns. A debate is going on about the possible existence of specialized "face modules" in the brain. In general, however, the brain takes in fragmentary information about lines, angles, shapes, motion, brightness, texture, and other features of what we see and comes up with a unified view of the world.

- The *trichromatic* and *opponent-process* theories of color vision apply to different stages of processing. In the first stage, three types of cones in the retina respond selectively to different wavelengths of light. In the second, *opponent-process cells* in the retina and the thalamus respond in opposite fashion to short and long wavelengths of light.

- Perception involves the active construction of a model of the world from moment to moment. The *Gestalt principles* (e.g., *figure and ground*, *proximity*, *closure*, *similarity*, and *continuity*) describe visual strategies used by the brain to perceive forms.

- We localize objects in visual space by using both *binocular* and *monocular cues* to depth. Binocular cues include *convergence* and *retinal disparity*. Monocular cues include *interposition*, *linear perspective*, and other cues. *Perceptual constancies* allow us to perceive objects as stable despite changes in the sensory patterns they produce. *Perceptual illusions* occur when sensory cues are misleading or when we misinterpret cues.

Hearing

- Hearing (*audition*) is affected by the intensity, frequency, and complexity of pressure waves in the air or other transmitting substance, corresponding to the experience of *loudness, pitch*, and *timbre* of the sound. The receptors for hearing are *hair cells* (*cilia*) embedded in the *basilar membrane*, located in the *organ of Corti* in the interior of the *cochlea*. These receptors pass signals along to the *auditory nerve*. The sounds we hear are determined by patterns of hair-cell movement, which produce different neural codes. When we localize sounds, we use as cues subtle differences in how pressure waves reach each of our ears.

Other Senses

- Taste (*gustation*) is a chemical sense. Elevations on the tongue, called *papillae*, contain many *taste buds*, which in turn contain the taste receptors. The basic tastes include salty, sour, bitter, sweet, and probably umami. Responses to a particular taste depend in part on genetic differences among individuals; for example, some people are "supertasters." Taste preferences are also affected by culture and learning and by the texture, temperature, and smell of food.

- Smell (*olfaction*) is also a chemical sense. No basic odors have been identified, and up to a thousand different receptor types exist. But researchers have discovered that distinct odors activate unique combinations of receptor types, and they have identified some of those combinations. Odors also have psychological effects and as we saw in "Close-up on Research," can affect behavior even when people are unaware of their influence.

- The skin senses include touch (pressure), warmth, cold, and pain, and variations such as itch and tickle. Except in the case of pressure, it has been difficult to identify specialized receptors for these senses, but researchers have reported a receptor for one kind of itching and a possible receptor for cold.

- Pain is both a skin sense and an internal sense. According to the *gate-control theory*, the experience of pain depends on whether neural impulses get past a "gate" in the spinal cord and reach the brain. According to a revised version of this theory, a matrix of neurons in the brain can generate pain even in the absence of signals from sensory neurons, which may explain the puzzling phenomenon of *phantom pain*. No one theory, however, completely explains perception of pain, which involves the release of many chemicals all along the pain pathways. Pain comes in many varieties, both physiologically and psychologically, and is affected by genetics, expectations, and culture.

- *Kinesthesis* tells us where our body parts are located and *equilibrium* tells us the orientation of the body as a whole. Together, these two senses provide us with a feeling of physical embodiment.

Perceptual Powers: Origins and Influences

- Many fundamental perceptual skills are inborn or acquired shortly after birth. By using the *visual cliff*, for example, psychologists have learned that babies have depth perception by the age of 6 months and probably even earlier. However, without certain experiences during *critical periods* early in life, cells in the nervous system deteriorate, change, or fail to form appropriate neural pathways, and perception is impaired. This is why efforts to correct congenital blindness or deafness are most successful when they take place early in life.

- Psychological influences on perception include needs, beliefs, emotions, and expectations (which produce *perceptual sets*). These influences are affected by culture, which gives people practice with certain kinds of experiences and influences what they attend to.

Puzzles of Perception

- In the laboratory, simple visual subliminal messages can "prime" certain behaviors, judgments, and motivational states, such as thirst. However, there is no evidence that complex behaviors can be altered by "subliminal perception" tapes or similar subliminal techniques.

- *Extrasensory perception (ESP)* refers to paranormal abilities such as telepathy and precognition. Years of research have failed to produce convincing evidence for ESP.

Psychology in the News, Revisited

- Human perception does not merely capture objective reality but also reflects our needs, biases, and beliefs. Thus our eyes and our ears (and especially our brains) can play tricks on us, as the frequent "sightings" of UFOs illustrate.

KEY TERMS

sensation   185

perception   186

sense receptors   186

anatomical codes   186

doctrine of specific
nerve energies   186

synesthesia   187

functional codes   187

absolute threshold   188

difference threshold   188

signal-detection
theory   189

sensory adaptation   190

sensory deprivation   190

selective attention   190

inattentional
blindness   191

hue   191

brightness   192

saturation   192

retina   192

rods and
cones   192–193

dark adaptation   193

ganglion cells   193

optic nerve   193

feature-detector
cells   195

face module   195

trichromatic
theory   196

opponent-process
theory   196

negative
afterimage   196

figure and ground   197

Gestalt principles   197

binocular cues   199

convergence   199

retinal disparity   199

monocular cues   199

perceptual
constancy   200

perceptual illusion   200

audition   202

loudness   202

pitch   202

frequency (of a sound
wave)   202

timbre   203

organ of Corti   204

cochlea   204

hair cells (cilia)   204

basilar membrane   204

auditory nerve   204

gustation   205

papillae   205

taste buds   205

olfaction   207

gate-control theory of
pain   209

phantom pain   210

kinesthesis   210

equilibrium   211

semicircular canals   211

critical period   212

perceptual set   214

subliminal
perception   215

extrasensory perception
(ESP)   216

parapsychology   217

Sensation is the detection and direct experience of physical energy as a result of environmental or internal events.
Perception is the process by which sensory impulses are organized and interpreted.

The Senses

- Sensation begins with the **sense receptors**, which convert the energy of a stimulus into electrical impulses that travel along the nerves to the brain.
- Anatomical codes (as set forth by the **doctrine of specific nerve energies**) and functional codes in the nervous system account for separate sensations.

Measuring the Senses

- Psychologists specializing in psychophysics have studied sensory sensitivity by measuring **absolute** and **difference thresholds.**
- **Signal-detection theory** holds that responses in a detection task consist of both a sensory process and a decision process and vary with the person's motivation, alertness, and expectations.

Sensory Adaptation

- **Sensory adaptation** occurs when sensation is unchanging.
- **Sensory deprivation** occurs with too little stimulation.

Sensing Without Perceiving

- We use **selective attention** to avoid sensory overload.
- **Inattentional blindness** is a failure to consciously perceive something you are looking at because you are not attending to it.

Hearing

The stimulus for hearing (audition) is a pressure wave or the release of compressed air.

What We Hear

- Intensity corresponds to the experience of **loudness.**
- Frequency corresponds to the experience of **pitch.**
- Complexity corresponds to the experience of **timbre.**

The receptors for hearing are hair cells (cilia) embedded in the basilar membrane of the **organ of Corti** in the interior of the **cochlea.**

Vision

The stimulus for vision is light, which travels in waves.

What We See

- Wavelength of light produces the experience of **hue.**
- Intensity of light produces the experience of **brightness.**
- Complexity of light produces the experience of **saturation.**

Visual Receptors

Visual receptors are located in the **retina** of the eye and send signals to the ganglion cells and ultimately to the optic nerve.
- **Rods** are responsible for vision in dim light
- **Cones** are responsible for color vision.
- **Feature detector cells** in the visual areas of the brain detect specific aspects of the environment, such as line orientation.
- Some researchers believe that certain brain cells comprise a "face module."

Color Vision

- The **trichromatic theory** accounts for the first level of color processing, which occurs in the retina, where three types of cones respond to different wavelengths of light.
- In the second level of color processing, **opponent-process** cells in the retina and thalamus respond in opposite fashion to short and long wavelengths of light.

Gestalt Principles

Gestalt principles such as figure and ground, proximity, closure, similarity, and contnuity describe visual strategies used by the brain to perceive form, distance, and depth.

Depth and Distance Perception

- **Binocular cues** include convergence and retinal disparity.
- **Monocular cues** include, for example, interposition and linear perspective.

Constancies and Illusions

- **Perceptual constancy** is the accurate perception of objects as stable despite changes in the sensory patterns they produce.
- **Perceptual illusions** occur when sensory cues are misleading or we misinterpret them.

(b)

Other Senses

Taste

Taste (gustation) is a chemical sense.

- **Papillae** on the tongue contain **taste buds**, which contain taste receptors.
- The basic tastes are each produced by a different type of chemical: salty, sour, bitter, sweet, and umami.
- Genetic and cultural differences influence responses to a particular taste.

Smell

Smell (olfaction) is also a chemical sense.

- There are up to 1000 different kinds of receptors.
- Distinct odors activate unique combinations of receptors.
- Cultural and individual differences affect people's responses to odors.

Senses of the Skin

Include touch (pressure), warmth, cold, and pain and variations such as itch and tickle.

Pain

Pain is both a skin sense and an internal sense.

Kinesthesis and Equilibrium

Kinesthesis tells us where our body parts are located, and **equilibrium** tells us the orientation of the body as a whole.

Gate control theory holds that the experience of pain depends on whether neural impulses get past a "gate" in the spinal cord and reach the brain.

If "gate" is open, then pain impulses reach the brain

"Gate" closed by incoming impulses from large fibers or from the brain; opened by impulses from smaller fibers

A possible explanation for **phantom pain** is that a matrix of neurons in the brain can generate pain even in the absence of signals from sensory neurons.

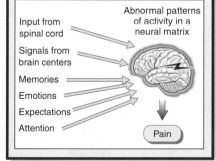

Input from spinal cord

Signals from brain centers

Memories

Emotions

Expectations

Attention

Abnormal patterns of activity in a neural matrix

Pain

Perceptual Powers

Inborn Abilities

- Visual cliff experiments show that even at 6 months, babies have depth perception.
- Without certain experiences during critical periods, perception is impaired.

Psychological Influences on Perception

- Psychological influences on perception include needs, beliefs, emotions, and expectations (which produce **perceptual sets**).
- These influences are affected by culture.

Puzzles of Perception

Subliminal Perception

Simple subliminal messages can "prime" certain behaviors, judgments, and motivational states, but subliminal ads and tapes have no effect.

"ESP"

Years of research have failed to produce convincing evidence for extrasensory perception (ESP).

Man–Machine Chess Match a Draw

NEW YORK, FEBRUARY 8, 2003. A disappointed crowd booed last night after Russian chess master Garry Kasparov agreed to a draw in the final game of a six-match series against Deep Junior, the world champion of chess-playing computers. The series, broadcast live on ESPN2 and the Internet and watched by millions of anxious chess fans around the world, ended in a 3–3 tie.

Kasparov, regarded by many as the greatest chess player of all time, described as "unpleasant" the experience of playing against an opponent that never tires and feels no emotion. "If you make one mistake, you are out of business," he said.

Kasparov has gone up against a computer before. In 1997 he was trounced by a 6-foot-5-inch, 1.4-ton IBM machine named Deep Blue. In that contest, the computer took two games, Kasparov won one, and the other three were a draw. Before the match, Kasparov had boasted that he was "defending human superiority in a purely intellectual field [that] defines human beings." In an interview posted on an IBM Web site, however, he acknowledged that in many ways it was more difficult to play against the computer than against a human opponent. "It never tires," he complained, "never makes tac-tical mistakes from which you can profit. You have to be on full guard every move of the game, which means it is more exhausting. It never gives you a break." Deep Blue, Kasparov admitted, was "stronger than all but a handful of top human players."

Kasparov believed it was important to win that match "to find out whether intuition and experience can outweigh the superior calculation powers of the computer." If he won, he said, he would know that "at least for the time being the human brain still has the edge." After his defeat, he was less than gracious, accusing IBM of secretly providing the com-puter with help from grand masters hidden behind a screen. Chess fans immediately posted dire messages on the Internet. "It's over for mankind," sulked one writer. "This is the moment in which human beings begin to take to the sidelines," wrote another. Deep Blue had no comment, but IBM's stock jumped $5 a share.

Kasparov's latest digital adversary, Deep Junior, boasts four 1.9-GHz Pentium processors and three gigabytes of memory. The computer seems to have earned Kasparov's respect; after the match, he admiringly called Deep Junior's chess program the best in the world.

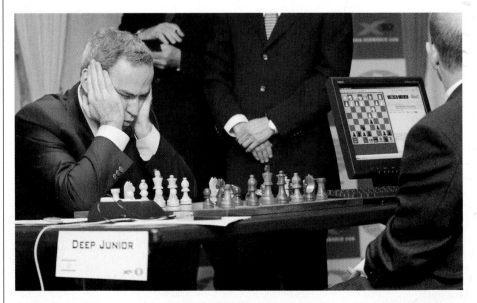

Chess master Garry Kasparov ponders his next move against his mechanical opponent, Deep Junior, in the first of a six-match series. The man at the computer moves pieces on the board when the computer tells him to.

Thinking and Intelligence

At one time, the idea of a machine beating a man at his own game seemed ludicrous, but that is no longer true. Since Kasparov's attempts, other grand masters have tried and failed to beat superfast computers. In 2005, a British grand master was trounced by a machine called Hydra. (One definition of *hydra* is "a persistent or many-sided problem that presents new obstacles as soon as one aspect of the problem is solved.") The computer, with 32 processors, was able to compute 200 million moves per second, and the best the human player could achieve was a draw in one of the seven games played.

Do the achievements of Deep Blue, Deep Junior, and Hydra mean that human beings are not as clever as they think? Are today's superfast, versatile computers more intelligent than we are? Are we really on the threshold of an era when human beings will "take to the sidelines"? To answer these questions, we first need to have a clear understanding of what *human* thinking and intelligence are.

Each day, in the course of ordinary living, we all make plans, draw inferences, analyze relationships, and organize and reorganize our mental world. Descartes' famous declaration "I think, therefore I am" could just as well have been reversed: "I am, therefore I think." Our powers of thought and intelligence inspired our forebears to give our species the immodest name *Homo sapiens*, Latin for wise or rational man. Certainly the human mind, which has managed to come up with poker, penicillin, and pantyhose, is a miraculous thing.

But the human mind has also managed to come up with traffic jams, e-mail spam, and war. To better understand why the same species that figured out how to get to the moon is also capable of breathtaking bumbling here on earth, we will examine in this chapter how people reason, solve problems, and grow in intelligence, as well as some of their mental shortcomings. As you read about the human capacity for thought, ask yourself: Could a machine ever do this?

WHAT'S *Ahead*

- When you think of a bird, why are you more likely to recall a robin than a penguin?

- Does the language you speak affect the way you think?

- How are visual images like images on a computer screen?

- What is happening mentally when you mistakenly take your geography notes to your psychology class?

Thought: Using What We Know

Think for a moment about what thinking does for you. It frees you from the confines of the immediate present: You can think about a trip taken three years ago, a party planned for next Saturday, or the War of 1812. It carries you beyond the boundaries of reality: You can imagine unicorns and utopias, Martians and magic. Because you think, you do not need to grope your way blindly through your problems but can apply knowledge to solve them intelligently and creatively.

To explain such abilities, many cognitive psychologists liken the human mind to an information processor, somewhat analogous to a computer but far more complex. Information-processing approaches capture the fact that the brain does not passively record information but actively alters and organizes it. When we take action, we physically manipulate the environment; when we think, we *mentally* manipulate internal representations of objects, activities, and situations.

The Elements of Cognition

One type of mental representation is the **concept**, a mental category that groups objects, relations, activities, abstractions, or qualities having common properties. The instances of a concept are seen as roughly similar. For example, *golden retriever*, *cocker spaniel*, and *border collie* are instances of the concept *dog*, and *anger*, *joy*, and *sadness* are instances of the concept *emotion*. Concepts simplify and summarize information about the world so that it is manageable, so that we can make decisions quickly and efficiently. You may never have seen a *basenji* or eaten *escargots*, but if you know that the first is an instance of *dog* and the second an instance of *food*, you will know, roughly, how to respond (unless you do not like to eat snails, which is what escargots are).

The qualities associated with a concept do not necessarily apply to every instance: Some apples are not red; some dogs do not bark; some birds do not fly. But all the instances of a concept do share a family resemblance. When we need to decide whether something belongs to a concept, we are likely to compare it to a **prototype**, a representative or most commonplace example of the concept (Rosch, 1973). For instance, which dog is doggier, a golden retriever or a chihuahua? Which fruit is more fruitlike, an apple or a pineapple? Which activity is more representative of sports, football or weight lifting? Most people within a culture can easily tell you which instances of a concept are most representative, or *prototypical*.

The words used to express concepts may influence or shape how we think about them. Many decades ago, Benjamin Lee Whorf, an insurance inspector by profession and a linguist and anthropologist by inclination, proposed that language molds cognition and perception. For example, said Whorf (1956), because English has only one word for snow and Eskimos (the Inuit) have many (for powdered snow, slushy snow, falling snow . . .), the Inuit notice differences in snow that English speakers do not. He also argued that grammar—the way words are formed and arranged to convey tense and other concepts—affects how we think about the world.

Whorf's theory became popular and then fell from favor; English speakers can see all those Inuit kinds of snow, after all, and they have plenty of

concept A mental category that groups objects, relations, activities, abstractions, or qualities having common properties.

prototype An especially representative example of a concept.

Some instances of a concept are more representative or prototypical than others. For example, Hollywood heart throb George Clooney clearly qualifies as a "bachelor," an unmarried man—he is resolutely single! But is the Pope a bachelor? What about Elton John, who has tied the knot with his longtime male partner in a civil union ceremony in England?

adjectives to describe the different varieties. But today Whorf's ideas are once again getting attention. Some researchers are finding that vocabulary and grammar do affect how we perceive the location of objects, think about time, attend to shapes and colors, and remember events (Boroditsky, 2003; Gentner & Goldin-Meadow, 2003). For example, in many languages, speakers must specify whether an object is linguistically masculine or feminine (in Spanish, for example, *la cuenta,* the bill, is feminine but *el cuento,* the story, is masculine). It seems that labeling a concept as masculine or feminine affects the attributes that native speakers ascribe to it. A German speaker will describe a key (masculine in German) as hard, heavy, jagged, metal, serrated, and useful, whereas a Spanish speaker is more likely to describe a key (feminine in Spanish) as golden, intricate, little, lovely, shiny, and tiny. German speakers will describe a bridge (feminine in German) as beautiful, elegant, fragile, peaceful, pretty, and slender, whereas Spanish speakers are more likely to describe a bridge (masculine in Spanish) as big, dangerous, long, strong, sturdy, and towering (Boroditsky, Schmidt, & Phillips, 2003).

Concepts are the building blocks of thought, but they would be of limited use if we merely stacked them up mentally. We must also represent their relationships to one another. One way we ac-complish this may be by storing and using **propositions,** units of meaning that are made up of concepts and that express a unitary idea. A proposition can express nearly any sort of knowledge ("Hortense raises border collies") or belief ("Border collies are smart"). Propositions, in turn, are linked together in complicated networks of knowledge, associations, beliefs, and expectations. These networks, which psychologists call **cognitive schemas**, serve as mental models of aspects of the world. For example, gender schemas represent a person's beliefs and expectations about what it means to be male or female (see Chapter 3). People also have schemas about cultures, occupations, animals, geographical locations, and many other features of the social and natural environment.

Mental images—especially visual images, pictures in the mind's eye—are also important in thinking and in the construction of cognitive schemas. Although no one can directly "see" another person's visual images, psychologists are able to study them indirectly. One method is to measure how long it takes people to rotate an image in their imaginations, scan from one point to another in an image, or read off some detail from an image. The results suggest that visual images are much like images on a computer screen: We can manipulate them, they occur in a mental "space" of

proposition A unit of meaning that is made up of concepts and express-es a single idea.

cognitive schema An integrated mental network of knowledge, beliefs, and expectations concerning a particular topic or aspect of the world.

mental image A mental representation that mir-rors or resembles the thing it represents; men-tal images can occur in many and perhaps all sensory modalities.

a fixed size, and small ones contain less detail than larger ones (Kosslyn, 1980; Shepard & Metzler, 1971). Most people also report auditory images (for instance, a song, slogan, or poem you can hear in your "mind's ear"), and many report images in other sensory modalities as well—touch, taste, smell, or pain. Some even report kinesthetic images, feelings in the muscles and joints.

Here, then, is a visual summary of the elements of cognition:

How Conscious Is Thought?

When we think about thinking, we usually have in mind those mental activities that are carried out in a deliberate way with a conscious goal in mind, such as solving a problem, drawing up plans, or making a decision. However, not all mental processing is conscious.

Subconscious Thinking Some of our cognitive processes lie outside of awareness but can be brought into consciousness with a little effort when necessary. These **subconscious processes** allow us to handle more information and to perform more complex tasks than if we depended entirely on conscious, deliberate thought, and they enable us to perform more than one task simultaneously (Kahneman & Treisman, 1984). Consider all the automatic routines performed "without thinking," though they might once have required careful, conscious attention: knitting, typing, driving a car, decoding the letters in a word in order to read it.

Because of the capacity for automatic processing, people can, with lots of practice, even learn to perform simultaneously such complex tasks as reading and taking dictation, without much loss in accuracy (Hirst, Neisser, & Spelke, 1978). But in ordinary life, "multitasking" is inefficient, even with easy tasks. In fact, far from saving time, toggling between two or more tasks increases the time required to complete them; stress goes up, errors increase, reaction times lengthen, and memory suffers

(Lien, Ruthruff, & Johnston, 2006; Rubinstein, Meyer, & Evans, 2001). Multitasking can even be hazardous to your health. A government study found that dialing a cell phone while driving increases the likelihood of an accident almost three-fold, and other distractions are just as dangerous (Klauer et al., 2006). Participants in the study were caught on camera checking their stocks, fussing with MP3 players, drinking beer, reading e-mails, applying makeup, flossing their teeth, and putting in contact lenses—all while hurtling down the highway at high speeds.

Even when multitasking doesn't put you at risk of crashing your car, it is often a bad idea. When a person does two tasks at once, the amount of brain activity devoted to each task decreases; and while you are switching between tasks, your prefrontal cortex, which prioritizes tasks and enables higher-order thinking, becomes relatively inactive (Jiang, Saxe, & Kanwisher, 2004; Just et al., 2001). So we hope you are not trying to learn these facts while you're also watching TV and messaging your friends!

Nonconscious Thinking Other kinds of thought processes, **nonconscious processes**, remain outside of awareness. You have no doubt had the odd experience of having a solution to a problem pop into mind after you have given up trying to find one. With sudden insight, you see how to solve an equation, assemble a cabinet, or finish a puzzle without quite knowing how you managed to find the solution. Similarly, people

Some well-learned skills do not require much conscious thought and can be performed while doing other things. But multitasking can also get you into trouble. It's not a good idea to talk on your cell phone, eat, and try to drive all at the same time.

subconscious processes Mental processes occurring outside of conscious awareness but accessible to consciousness when necessary.

nonconscious processes Mental processes occurring outside of and not available to conscious awareness.

will often say they rely on intuition—hunches and gut feelings—rather than conscious reasoning to make decisions.

Insight and intuition probably involve two stages of mental processing (Bowers et al., 1990). In the first stage, clues in the problem automatically activate certain memories or knowledge, and you begin to see a pattern or structure in the problem, although you cannot yet say what it is. This nonconscious process guides you toward a hunch or a hypothesis. Then, in the second stage, your thinking becomes conscious, and you become aware of a possible solution. This stage may feel like a sudden revelation ("Aha, I've got it!"), but considerable nonconscious mental work has already occurred.

Sometimes people solve problems or learn new skills without experiencing the second stage at all. For example, some people discover the best strategy for winning a card game without being able to consciously identify what they are doing (Bechara et al., 1997). Psychologists call this phenomenon **implicit learning**: You learn a rule or an adaptive behavior, either with or without a conscious intention to do so, but you don't know how you learned it, and you can't state exactly what it is you have learned (Frensch & Rünger, 2003; Lieberman, 2000). Many of our abilities, from speaking our native language properly to walking up a flight of stairs, are the result of implicit learning.

Mindlessness Even when our thinking is conscious, often we are not thinking very *hard*. We may act, speak, and make decisions out of habit, without stopping to analyze what we are doing or why we are doing it. This sort of *mindlessness*—mental inflexibility, inertia, and obliviousness to the present context—keeps people from recognizing when a change in the situation requires a change in behavior.

In a classic study of mindlessness, a researcher approached people as they were about to use a photocopier and made one of three requests: "Excuse me, may I use the Xerox machine?" "Excuse me, may I use the Xerox machine, because I have to make copies?" or "Excuse me, may I use the Xerox machine, because I'm in a rush?" Normally, people will let someone go before them only if the person has a legitimate reason for doing so, as in the third request. In this study, however, people also complied when the reason sounded like an authentic explanation but was actually meaningless ("because I have to make copies"). They heard the form of the request but they did not hear its content, and they mindlessly stepped aside (Langer, Blank, & Chanowitz, 1978).

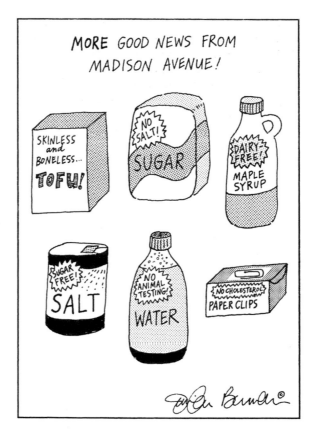

MORE GOOD NEWS FROM MADISON AVENUE!

Advertisers sometimes count on mindlessness in consumers.

Jerome Kagan (1989) has argued that fully conscious awareness is needed only when we must make a deliberate choice, when events happen that can't be handled automatically, and when unexpected moods and feelings arise. "Consciousness," he wrote, "can be likened to the staff of a fire department. Most of the time, it is quietly playing pinochle in the back room; it performs [only] when the alarm sounds." Some researchers go further, arguing that for certain kinds of complex decisions, such as choosing which car or house to buy, "gut feelings" sometimes lead to better choices and more satisfaction than does conscious deliberation (Dijksterhuis et al., 2006). That may be so, but most of us would probably benefit if our mental firefighters paid a little more attention to their jobs. Multitasking, mindlessness, and operating on automatic pilot have their benefits, but they can also lead to errors and mishaps, ranging from the trivial (putting the butter in the dishwasher or locking yourself out of your apartment) to the serious (driving carelessly while daydreaming). Cognitive psychologists have, therefore, devoted a great deal of study to mindful, conscious thought, decision making, and the capacity to reason.

implicit learning
Learning that occurs when you acquire knowledge about something without being aware of how you did so and without being able to state exactly what it is you have learned.

QUICK quiz

Stay fully conscious while taking this quiz.

1. Stuffing your mouth with cotton candy, licking a lollipop, and chewing on a piece of beef jerky are all instances of the _____ *eating*.

2. Which example of the concept *chair* is prototypical: *high chair*, *rocking chair*, or *dining room chair*?

3. In addition to concepts and images, _____, which express a unitary idea, have been suggested as a basic form of mental representation.

4. Peter's mental representation of *Thanksgiving* includes associations (e.g., with turkeys), attitudes ("It's a time to be with relatives"), and expectations ("I'm going to gain weight from all that food"). They are all part of his _____ for the holiday.

5. Zelda discovers that she has mistakenly called her boyfriend's number instead of her mother's. Her error can be attributed to _____.

Answers:

1. concept 2. A plain, straight-backed dining room chair will be prototypical for most people. 3. propositions 4. cognitive schema 5. mindlessness

WHAT'S *Ahead*

- Mentally speaking, why is making a cake, well, a piece of cake?

- Why can't logic solve all of our problems?

- What kind of reasoning do juries need to be good at?

- When people say that all opinions and claims are equally valid, what error are they making?

Reasoning Rationally

reasoning The drawing of conclusions or inferences from observations, facts, or assumptions.

algorithm A problem-solving strategy guaranteed to produce a solution even if the user does not know how it works.

deductive reasoning A form of reasoning in which a conclusion follows necessarily from certain premises; if the premises are true, the conclusion must be true.

inductive reasoning A form of reasoning in which the premises provide support for a conclusion, but it is still possible for the conclusion to be false.

Reasoning is purposeful mental activity that involves operating on information in order to reach conclusions. Unlike impulsive or nonconscious responding, reasoning requires us to draw specific inferences from observations, facts, or assumptions.

Formal Reasoning: Algorithms and Logic

In *formal reasoning problems*—the kind you might find, say, on an intelligence test or a college entrance exam—the information needed for drawing a conclusion or reaching a solution is specified clearly, and there is a single right (or best) answer.

In some formal problems and well-defined tasks, all you have to do is apply an **algorithm**, a set of procedures guaranteed to produce a solution even if you do not know how it works. To solve a problem in long division, you apply a series of operations that you learned in elementary school. To make a cake, you apply an algorithm called a recipe.

For other formal problems, the rules of formal logic are crucial tools to have in your mental toolbox. These tools include (among others) the processes of deductive and inductive reasoning. In **deductive reasoning**, a conclusion *necessarily* follows from a set of observations or propositions (*premises*):

DEDUCTIVE REASONING

For example, if the premises "All human beings are mortal" and "I am a human being" are true, then the conclusion "I am mortal" must also be true.

In contrast, in **inductive reasoning**, a conclusion *probably* follows from certain propositions or premises, but it could conceivably be false:

INDUCTIVE REASONING

For example, if your premises are "I had a delicious meal at Joe's Restaurant on Monday," "I had a delicious meal there again on Tuesday," and "I had another delicious meal there on Wednesday," you might reasonably reach the conclusion that "Joe's Restaurant consistently serves good food." But those meals could have been a fluke: Maybe the regular chef was on vacation and the meals were prepared by a visiting chef.

Informal Reasoning: Heuristics and Dialectical Thinking

Useful as they are, algorithms and logical reasoning cannot solve all of life's problems. In *informal reasoning problems*, there often is no clearly correct solution. Many approaches, viewpoints, or possible solutions may compete, and you may have to decide which one is most reasonable. Further, the information at your disposal may be incomplete, or people may disagree on what the premises should be. Your position on the controversial issue of abortion, for example, will depend on your premises about when meaningful human life begins, what rights an embryo has, and what rights a woman has to control her own body. People on opposing sides of this issue even disagree on how the premises should be phrased, because they have different emotional reactions to terms such as "rights," "meaningful life," and "control over one's body."

Formal and informal reasoning problems usually call for different approaches. Whereas formal problems can often be solved with an algorithm, informal problems often call for a **heuristic**, a rule of thumb that suggests a course of action without guaranteeing an optimal solution. Anyone who has ever played chess or a card game such as hearts is familiar with heuristics ("Get rid of high cards first"). In these games, working out all the possible sequences of moves would be impossible. Heuristics are also useful to an investor trying to predict the stock market ("Buy bonds when interest rates are falling"), a doc-

tor trying to determine the best treatment for a patient ("Use drug X as a first course of action"), and a student trying to decide whether to take a particular course ("Ask friends how they liked the instructor"). All are faced with incomplete information on which to base a decision and may therefore resort to rules of thumb that have proven effective in the past.

In thinking about real-life problems, a person must also be able to use **dialectical reasoning**, the process of comparing and evaluating opposing points of view in order to resolve differences. Philosopher Richard Paul (1984) has described dialectical reasoning as movement "up and back between contradictory lines of reasoning, using each to critically cross-examine the other":

DIALECTAL REASONING

Arguments:

Most reasonable conclusion
based on evidence and logic

Dialectical reasoning is what juries are supposed to do to arrive at a verdict: consider arguments for and against the defendant's guilt, point and counterpoint. It is also what voters are supposed to do when thinking about whether the government should raise taxes or lower them, or about the best way to improve public education.

Reflective Judgment

Many adults clearly have trouble thinking dialectically; they take one position, and that's that. When do people develop the ability to think critically—to

heuristic A rule of thumb that suggests a course of action or guides problem solving but does not guarantee an optimal solution.

dialectical reasoning A process in which opposing facts or ideas are weighed and compared with a view to determining the best solution or to resolving differences.

Practice Your Dialectical Reasoning

Choose a controversial topic, such as whether marijuana should be legalized or the death penalty should be revoked. First list all the arguments you can to support your own position. Then list all the arguments you can on the other side of the issue. You do not have to agree with these arguments; just list them. Do you feel a mental block or emotional discomfort while doing this? Can you imagine how opponents of your position would answer your arguments? Having strong opinions is fine; you should have an informed opinion on matters of public interest. But does that opinion get in the way of even imagining a contrary point of view or of altering your view if the evidence warrants a change?

Talk-radio shows do not exactly encourage reflective judgment!

TALK RADIO JOCKS TACKLE THE BIG ISSUES...

WAR?! WHAT'S UP WITH THAT?
HA HA
STEVE and TINA

TEEN VIOLENCE?! WHO KNEW?
HA HA
TOM and RONA

CANCER. DON'T GET ME STARTED.
HA HA
BRIAN and GINA

DEATH. DON'T GO THERE.
HA HA
KEVIN and MUFFY

humerusjkb@aol.com

question assumptions, evaluate and integrate evidence, consider alternative interpretations, and reach conclusions that can be defended as most reasonable?

To find out, Karen Kitchener and Patricia King interviewed adolescents and adults of all ages and occupations (King & Kitchener, 1994). They began by providing their interviewees with statements that described opposing viewpoints on various topics. Then the interviewer asked: What do you think about these statements? How did you come to hold that point of view? On what do you base your position? Can you ever know for sure that your position is correct? Why do you suppose disagreement exists about this issue? Based on the responses, King and Kitchener identified seven cognitive stages on the road to what they call *reflective judgment* (and we have called critical thinking). At each stage, people make different assumptions about how things are known and use different ways of justifying or defending their beliefs.

In general, people in the two early *prereflective stages* assume that a correct answer always exists and that it can be obtained directly through the senses ("I know what I've seen") or from authorities ("They said so on the news"; "That's what I was brought up to believe"). If authorities do not yet have the truth, prereflective thinkers tend to reach conclusions on the basis of what "feels right" at the moment. They do not distinguish between knowledge and belief or between belief and evidence, and they see no reason to justify a belief (King & Kitchener, 1994). One respondent at this stage, when asked about evolution, said: "Well, some people believe that we evolved from apes and that's the way they want to believe.

But I would never believe that way and nobody could talk me out of the way I believe because I believe the way that it's told in the Bible."

During three *quasi-reflective stages*, people recognize that some things cannot be known with absolute certainty, and they realize that judgments should be supported by reasons, yet they pay attention only to evidence that fits what they already believe. They seem to think that because knowledge is uncertain, any judgment about the evidence is purely subjective. Quasi-reflective thinkers will defend a position by saying that "we all have a right to our own opinion," as if all opinions are created equal. One college student at this stage, when asked whether one opinion on the safety of food additives was right and others were wrong, answered: "No. I think it just depends on how you feel personally because people make their decisions based upon how they feel and what research they've seen. So what one person thinks is right, another person might think is wrong. . . . If I feel that chemicals cause cancer and you feel that food is unsafe without it, your opinion might be right to you and my opinion is right to me."

In the last two stages, a person becomes capable of reflective judgment. He or she understands that although some things can never be known with certainty, some judgments are more valid than others because of their coherence, their fit with the evidence, their usefulness, and so on. People at these *reflective stages* are willing to consider evidence from a variety of sources and to reason dialectically. This interview with a graduate student illustrates reflective thinking:

Interviewer: Can you ever say you know for sure that your point of view on chemical additives is correct?

Student: No, I don't think so [but] I think that we can usually be reasonably certain, given the information we have now, and considering our methodologies. . . . It might be that the research wasn't conducted rigorously enough. In other words, we might have flaws in our data or sample, things like that.

Interviewer: How then would you identify the "better opinion"?

Student: One that takes as many factors as possible into consideration. I mean one that uses the higher percentage of the data that we have, and perhaps that uses the methodology that has been most reliable.

Interviewer: And how do you come to a conclusion about what the evidence suggests?

Student: I think you have to take a look at the different opinions and studies that are offered by different groups. Maybe some studies offered by the chemical industry, some studies by the government, some private studies. . . . You have to try to interpret people's motives and that makes it a more complex soup to try to strain out.

Most people do not show evidence of reflective judgment until their middle or late twenties, if at all. However, when students get support for thinking reflectively and have opportunities to practice it in their courses, their reasoning tends to become more complex, sophisticated, and well grounded (Kitchener et al., 1993). As one writer noted, the gradual development of thinking skills among undergraduates represents an abandonment of "ignorant certainty" in favor of "intelligent confusion" (Kroll, 1992). It may not seem so, but this is a big step forward. You can see why, in this book, we emphasize thinking about and evaluating psychological findings and not just memorizing them.

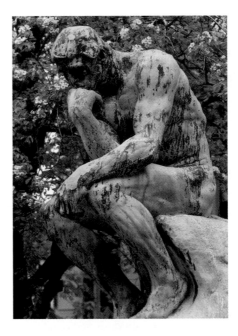

One reason that Auguste Rodin's The Thinker *became world famous and has been much imitated is that it captures so perfectly the universal experience of thinking and reflecting.*

QUICK *quiz*

Reflect on the answers to these questions.

1. Most of the holiday gifts Mervin bought this year cost more than they did last year, so he concludes that inflation is increasing. Is he using inductive, deductive, or dialectical reasoning?

2. Yvonne is arguing with Henrietta about whether real estate is a better investment than stocks. "You can't convince me," says Yvonne. "I just know I'm right." Yvonne needs training in _____ reasoning.

3. Seymour thinks the media have a liberal political bias, and Selena thinks they are too conservative. "Well," says Seymour, "I have my truth and you have yours. It's purely subjective." Which of King and Kitchener's levels of thinking describes Seymour's statement?

4. What kind of evidence might resolve the issue that Seymour and Selena are arguing about?

Answers:

1. inductive   2. dialectical   3. quasi-reflective   4. Researchers might have raters watch a random sample of TV news shows and measure the amount of time devoted to conservative and liberal viewpoints. Or raters could read a random sample of newspaper editorials from all over the country and evaluate the editorials as liberal or conservative in outlook. Perhaps you can think of other strategies. Be careful, though: Ratings can be affected by what people want or expect to perceive.

WHAT'S *Ahead*

- Why do people worry about dying in an airplane crash but ignore dangers that are far more likely?

- How might your physician's choice of words about alternative treatments for your illness affect which one you choose?

- When deciding how to divide up some money, will people always try to maximize their gain?

- When Monday-morning quarterbacks say they knew all along who would win Sunday's big game, what bias might they be showing?

- Why will a terrible hazing make you more loyal to the group that hazed you?

Barriers to Reasoning Rationally

Although most people have the capacity to think logically, reason dialectically, and make judgments reflectively, it is abundantly clear that they don't always do so. One obstacle is the need to be right: If your self-esteem depends on winning every argument, you will find it hard to listen with an open mind to competing views. But human thought processes are also tripped up by many predictable biases and errors. Psychologists have studied dozens of these cognitive pitfalls (Kahneman, 2003). Here we describe just a few.

Exaggerating the Improbable (and Minimizing the Probable)

One common bias is the inclination to exaggerate the probability of rare events—a bias that helps to explain why so many people enter lotteries and why they buy disaster insurance. There are many reasons for this bias. For example, as we discuss in Chapter 9, evolution has equipped us to fear certain things, such as snakes, but the fear has outlasted the actual threat, so we overestimate the danger. The risk of a rattler sinking its fangs into you in Chicago or New York is pretty low! Evolution has also given us brains that are terrific at responding to immediate dangers (say, a threatening animal) or to acts that provoke moral outrage even though they pose no threat to the survival of the species (say, flag burning). But unfortunately, our brains were not designed to become alarmed by serious *future* threats that do not seem to pose much danger right now (such as global warming) (Gilbert, 2006).

When judging probabilities, people are strongly influenced by the **affect heuristic**: the tendency to consult their emotions (affect) instead of judging probabilities objectively (Slovic et al., 2002). Emotions can often help us make decisions by narrowing our options, but emotions can also mislead us by preventing us from accurately assessing risk. One unusual field study looked at how people in France responded to the "mad cow" crisis that occurred a few years ago. (Mad cow disease affects the brain and can be contracted by eating meat from contaminated cows.) Whenever many newspaper articles reported the dangers of "mad cow disease," beef consumption fell during the following month. But when news articles, reporting the same dangers, used the technical names of the disease—Creutzfeldt-Jakob disease or bovine spongiform encephalopathy—beef consumption stayed the same (Sinaceur, Heath, & Cole, 2005). The more popular label caused people to reason emotionally and to overestimate the danger. During the entire period of the supposed crisis, only six people in France were diagnosed with the disease.

Our judgments of risk are also influenced by the **availability heuristic**, the tendency to judge the probability of an event by how easy it is to think of examples or instances of it (Tversky & Kahneman, 1973). The availability heuristic often works hand in hand with the affect heuristic. For example, catastrophes and shocking accidents evoke a strong emotional reaction in us and thus stand out

affect heuristic The tendency to consult one's emotions instead of estimating probabilities objectively.

availability heuristic The tendency to judge the probability of a type of event by how easy it is to think of examples or instances.

Because of the affect and availability heuristics, many of us overestimate the chances of suffering a shark attack. Although shark attacks are extremely rare, they are terrifying and easy to visualize.

in our minds. They are more "available" mentally than are other kinds of negative events. This is why people overestimate the frequency of deaths from tornadoes and underestimate the frequency of deaths from asthma, which occur 20 times as often but do not make headlines (Lichtenstein et al., 1978). It is why a scary film about sharks or news accounts of a shark attack make people fear shark-attack "epidemics," even though such attacks on humans are extremely rare. And it is why, after 9/11, people were afraid to fly in airplanes, even though they took a much greater risk (65 times as great) by driving to their destinations (Sivak & Flannagan, 2003).

Of course, the affect and availability heuristics are not all bad. They can also cause you to overestimate the probability of happy, joyous events—at least, if you're an optimist.

Avoiding Loss

In general, people try to avoid or minimize risks and losses when they make decisions. So when a choice is framed in terms of the risk of losing something, they will respond more cautiously than when the same choice is framed in terms of gain. They will choose a ticket that has a 10 percent chance of winning a raffle rather than one that has a 90 percent chance of losing. Or they will rate a condom as effective when they are told it has a 95 percent success rate in protecting against the AIDS virus, but not when they are told it has a 5 percent failure rate—which is exactly the same thing (Linville, Fischer, & Fischhoff, 1992).

Suppose you had to choose between two health programs to combat a disease expected to kill 600 people. Which would you prefer: a program that would definitely save 200 people or one with a one-third probability of saving all 600 people and a two-thirds probability of saving none? (Problem 1 in Figure 7.1 illustrates this choice.) When asked this question, most people, including physicians, say they prefer the first program. In other words, they reject the riskier though potentially more rewarding solution in favor of a sure gain. However, people will take a risk if they see it as a way to *avoid loss*. Suppose now that you have to choose between a program in which 400 people will definitely die and a program in which there is a one-third probability of nobody dying and a two-thirds probability that all 600 will die. If you think about it, you will see that the alternatives are exactly the same as in the first problem; they are merely worded dif-ferently (see Problem 2 in Figure 7.1). Yet this time, most people choose the second solution. They reject risk when they think of the outcome in terms of lives saved but accept risk when they think of the outcome in terms of lives lost (Tversky & Kahneman, 1981).

Few of us will have to face a decision involving hundreds of lives, but we may have to choose between different medical treatments for ourselves or a relative. Our decision may be affected by whether the doctor frames the choice in terms of chances of surviving or chances of dying.

Unlike this hockey player, most people have a sense of fair play.

The Fairness Bias

Interestingly, in certain circumstances we do not try to avoid loss altogether, because we are subject to a *fairness bias*. Imagine that you are playing a two-person game called the *Ultimatum Game* in which your partner gets $10 and must decide how much to share with you. You can choose to accept your partner's offer, in which case you both get to keep your respective portions, or you can reject the offer, in which case neither of you gets a penny. How low an offer would you accept?

If you think about it, you'll see that it makes sense to accept any amount at all, no matter how paltry, because then at least you will get *something*. But that is not how people respond when playing the Ultimatum Game. If the offer is too low, they are likely to reject it. In industrial societies, offers of 50 percent are typical and offers below 20 or 30 percent are commonly rejected, even when the absolute sums are large. In other societies, the amounts offered and accepted may be higher or lower, but there is always some amount that people consider unfair and refuse to accept (Henrich et al., 2001). People may be competitive and love to win, but they are also powerfully motivated to cooperate and to see fairness prevail.

This finding has intrigued scientists from many disciplines, including psychology, philosophy, economics, anthropology, evolutionary biology, and neuroscience. Using the Ultimatum Game and other laboratory games, they are exploring how a sense of fairness often takes precedence over rational self-interest when people make economic choices. Their work verifies

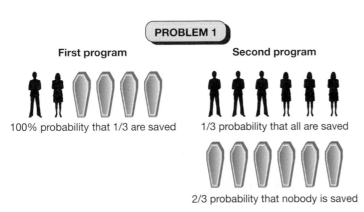

PROBLEM 1

First program

100% probability that 1/3 are saved

Second program

1/3 probability that all are saved

2/3 probability that nobody is saved

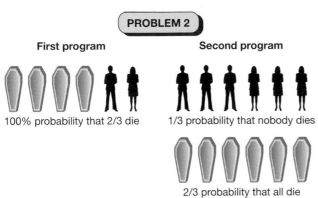

PROBLEM 2

First program

100% probability that 2/3 die

Second program

1/3 probability that nobody dies

2/3 probability that all die

FIGURE 7.1
A Matter of Wording
The decisions we make depend on how the alternatives are framed. When asked to choose between the two programs in Problem 1, which are described in terms of lives saved, most people choose the first program. When asked to choose between the programs in Problem 2, which are described in terms of lives lost, most people choose the second program. Yet the alternatives in the two problems are actually identical.

hindsight bias The tendency to overestimate one's ability to have predicted an event once the outcome is known; the "I knew it all along" phenomenon.

and extends the pioneering work of Nobel Prize winner Herbert Simon (1955), who first showed that economic decisions are not always strictly rational.

Now, if only the desire for fairness didn't lead human beings to inflict suffering so often on those whom they perceive as unfair, and if only their ability to cooperate didn't lead so often to cooperation in waging war.

The Hindsight Bias

Would you have predicted the results of the last election? Would you have predicted the most recent Oscar winner for best picture? When people learn the outcome of an event or the answer to a question, they are often sure that they "knew it all along." Armed with the wisdom of hindsight, they see the outcome that actually occurred as inevitable, and they overestimate their ability to have predicted what happened. Compared with judgments made *before* an event takes place, their judgments about their ability to have predicted the event in advance are inflated (Fischhoff, 1975; Hawkins & Hastie, 1990). This **hindsight bias** shows up all the time in evaluating relationships ("I always knew their marriage wouldn't last"), medical judgments ("I could have told you that mole was cancerous"), and

military opinions ("The generals should have known that the enemy would attempt a surprise attack").

The hindsight bias can be adaptive. When we try to make sense of the past, we focus on explaining just one outcome, the one that occurred, because explaining outcomes that did not take place can be a waste of time. Then, in light of current knowledge, we reconstruct and misremember our previous judgment (Hoffrage, Hertwig, & Gigerenzer, 2000). But as Scott Hawkins and Reid Hastie (1990) wrote, "Hindsight biases represent the dark side of successful learning and judgment." They are the dark side because when we are sure we knew something all along, we are also less willing to find out what we need to know in order to make accurate predictions in the future. In medical conferences, for example, when doctors are told the postmortem findings for a patient who died, they tend to think the case was easier to diagnose than it actually was ("I would have known it was a brain tumor"), and so they learn less from the case than they should (Dawson et al., 1988).

Perhaps you feel that we're not telling you anything new because you have always known about the hindsight bias. But then, you may just have a hindsight bias about the hindsight bias!

GET INVOLVED

Confirming the Confirmation Bias

Suppose someone deals out four cards, each with a letter on one side and a number on the other. You can see only one side of each card:

Your job is to find out whether the following rule is true: "If a card has a vowel on one side, then it has an even number on the other side." Which two cards do you need to turn over to find out?

The vast majority of people say they would turn over the E and the 6, but they are wrong. You do need to turn over the E (a vowel), because if the number on the other side is even, it confirms the rule, and if it's odd, the rule is false. However, the card with the 6 tells you nothing. The rule does not say that a card with an even number must always have a vowel on the other side. So it doesn't matter whether the 6 has a vowel or a consonant on the other side. The card you do need to turn over is the 7, because if it has a vowel on the other side, that fact disconfirms the rule.

People do poorly on this problem because they are biased to look for confirming evidence and because they ignore the possibility of disconfirming evidence. Don't feel bad if you missed it; most judges, lawyers, and people with Ph.D.s do, too.

The Confirmation Bias

When people want to make the most accurate judgment possible, they usually try to consider all of the relevant information. But when they are thinking about issues they already feel strongly about, they often succumb to the **confirmation bias**, paying attention only to evidence that confirms their belief and finding fault with evidence or arguments that point in a different direction (Edwards & Smith, 1996; Kunda, 1990; Nickerson, 1998). You rarely hear someone say, "Oh, thank you for explaining to me why my lifelong philosophy of child rearing (or politics, or investing) is wrong. I'm so grateful for the facts!" The person usually says, "Oh, buzz off, and take your cockamamie ideas with you."

Once you start looking for it, you will see the confirmation bias everywhere. Politicians brag about economic reports that confirm their party's position and dismiss counterevidence as biased or unimportant. Police officers who are convinced of a suspect's guilt take anything the suspect says or does as evidence that confirms it, including the suspect's claims of innocence. The confirmation bias also affects jury members. Instead of considering and weighing possible verdicts against the evidence, many people quickly construct a story about what happened and then consider only the evidence that supports their version of events. These same people are the most confident in their decisions and most likely to vote for an extreme verdict (Kuhn, Weinstock, & Flaton, 1994).

The confirmation bias can affect how you react to what you are learning in school. When students read about scientific findings that dispute one of their own cherished beliefs or that challenge the wisdom of their own actions, they tend to acknowledge but minimize the strengths of the research. In contrast, when a study supports their view, they will acknowledge any flaws (such as a small sample or a reliance on self-reports) but will give these flaws less weight than they otherwise would (Sherman & Kunda, 1989). In thinking critically, people often apply a double standard: They think most critically about results they dislike.

Mental Sets

Another barrier to rational thinking is the development of a **mental set**, a tendency to try to solve new problems by using the same heuristics, strategies, and rules that worked in the past on similar problems. Mental sets make human learning and problem solving efficient; because of them, we do not have to keep reinventing the wheel. But mental sets are not helpful when a problem calls for fresh insights and methods. They cause us to cling rigidly to the same old assumptions, hypotheses, and strategies, blinding us to better or more rapid solutions. (For an illustration of this point, try the Get Involved exercise on this page.)

One general mental set is the tendency to find patterns in events. This tendency is adaptive because it helps us understand and exert some control over what happens in our lives. But it also leads us to see meaningful patterns even when they do not exist. For example, many people with arthritis think that their symptoms follow a pattern

confirmation bias The tendency to look for or pay attention only to information that confirms one's own belief.

mental set A tendency to solve problems using procedures that worked before on similar problems.

GET INVOLVED

Connect The Dots

Copy this figure, and try to connect the dots by using no more than four straight lines, without lifting your pencil or pen. A line must pass through each point. Can you do it?

Most people have difficulty with this problem because they have a mental set to interpret the arrangement of dots as a square. They then assume that they can't extend a line beyond the apparent boundaries of the square. Now that you know this, you might try again if you haven't yet solved the puzzle. Some possible solutions are given on page 261.

cognitive dissonance
A state of tension that occurs when a person simultaneously holds two cognitions that are psychologically inconsistent, or when a person's belief is incongruent with his or her behavior.

dictated by the weather. They suffer more, they say, when the barometric pressure changes or when it's damp or humid out. Yet when researchers followed 18 arthritis patients for 15 months, no association whatsoever emerged between weather conditions and the patients' self-reported pain levels, their ability to function in daily life, or a doctor's evaluation of their joint tenderness (Redelmeier & Tversky, 1996). Of course, because of the confirmation bias, the patients refused to believe the results.

The Need for Cognitive Consistency

Mental sets and the confirmation bias enable us to avoid evidence that contradicts our beliefs. But what happens when disconfirming evidence finally smacks us in the face, and we cannot ignore or discount it any longer? For example, as the twentieth century rolled to an end, predictions of the end of the world escalated. Similar doomsday predictions have been made throughout history and continue to be made today (Kirsch, 2006). When these predictions fail, how come we rarely hear believers say, "Boy, what a fool I was"?

According to the theory of **cognitive dissonance**, people will resolve such conflicts in predictable, though not always obvious, ways (Festinger, 1957). *Dissonance*, the opposite of consistency (*consonance*), is a state of tension that occurs when you simultaneously hold either two cognitions (beliefs, thoughts, attitudes) that are psychologically inconsistent or a belief that is incongruent with your behavior. This tension is uncomfortable, so you will be motivated to reduce it. You may do this by rejecting or modifying one of those inconsistent beliefs, changing your behavior, denying the evidence, or rationalizing:

Many years ago, in a famous field study, Leon Festinger and two associates explored people's reactions to failed prophecies by infiltrating a group of people who thought the world would end on December 21 (Festinger, Riecken, & Schachter, 1956). The group's leader, whom the researchers called Marian Keech, promised that the faithful would be picked up by a flying saucer and whisked to safety at midnight on December 20. Many of her followers quit their jobs and spent all their savings, waiting for the end. What would they do or say, Festinger and his colleagues wondered, to reduce the dissonance between "The world is still muddling along on the 21st" and "I predicted the end of the world and sold off all my worldly possessions"?

The researchers predicted that believers who had made no public commitment to the prophecy, who awaited the end of the world by themselves at home, would simply lose their faith. But those who had acted on their conviction by selling their property and waiting with Keech for the spaceship would be in a state of dissonance. They would have to *increase* their religious belief to avoid the intolerable realization that they had behaved foolishly and others knew it. That is just what happened. At 4:45 A.M., long past the appointed hour of the saucer's arrival, the leader had a new vision. The world had been spared, she said, because of the impressive faith of her little band.

Cognitive-dissonance theory predicts that in more ordinary situations, too, people will resist or rationalize information that conflicts with their existing ideas, just as the people in the arthritis study

COGNITIVE DISSONANCE

Cognitions conflict → Tension (cognitive dissonance)

Behavior conflicts with attitude or belief → Tension (cognitive dissonance)

Tension (cognitive dissonance) → Efforts to reduce dissonance:
Reject belief
Change behavior
Deny the evidence
Rationalize

YESTERDAY IN THIS SPACE I PREDICTED THAT THE WORLD WOULD COME TO AN END. IT DID NOT, HOWEVER. I REGRET ANY INCONVENIENCE THIS MAY HAVE CAUSED.

did. For example, cigarette smokers are often in a state of dissonance, because smoking is dissonant with the fact that smoking causes illness. Smokers might try to reduce the dissonance by trying to quit, by rejecting the evidence that smoking is bad, by persuading themselves that they will quit later on ("after these exams"), by emphasizing the benefits of smoking ("A cigarette helps me relax"), or by deciding that they don't want a long life anyhow ("It will be shorter but sweeter").

You are particularly likely to try to reduce dissonance under three conditions (Aronson, 2004):

1 *When you need to justify a choice or decision that you freely made.* All car dealers know about buyer's remorse: The second that people buy a car, they worry that they made the wrong decision or spent too much—a phenomenon called **postdecision dissonance**. You may try to resolve this dissonance by deciding that the car you chose (or the toaster, or house, or spouse) is really, truly the best in the world. However, if someone else made your decision for you, you will not feel much dissonance if it proves misguided. There is no dissonance between "The Army drafted me; I had no choice about being here" and "I hate basic training."

2 *When you need to justify behavior that conflicts with your view of yourself.* If you consider yourself to be honest, cheating will put you in a state of dissonance. To avoid feeling like a hypocrite, you will try to reduce the dissonance by justifying your behavior ("Everyone else does it"; "I had to do it to get into med school and learn to save lives"). Or if you see yourself as a kind person and you harm someone, you may reduce your dissonance by blaming the person you have victimized (see Chapter 10) or by finding other self-justifying excuses.

3 *When you need to justify the effort you put into a decision or choice.* The harder you work to reach a goal, or the more you suffer for it, the more you will try to convince yourself that you value the goal, even if the goal is not so great after all (Aronson & Mills, 1959). This explains why hazing, whether in social clubs, on athletic teams, or in the military, turns new recruits into loyal members. You might think that people would hate a group that made them suffer. But the cognition "I went through a lot of awful stuff to join this group" is dissonant with the cognition "only to find I hate the group." Therefore, people must decide either that the hazing was not so bad or that they really like the group. This mental reevaluation is called the **justification of effort**, and it

The more effort you put into reaching a goal, the more highly you are likely to value it. Here new cadets at the Virginia Military Institute are forced to crawl through mud until they are covered from head to toe. They will probably become devoted to the military.

is one of the most common methods of reducing dissonance.

Some people are secure enough to own up to their mistakes instead of rationalizing them, or do not have a great need for consistency and so do not experience much cognitive dissonance (Cialdini, Trost, & Newsom, 1995). Moreover, in certain cultures, such as those of East Asia, contradictions and inconsistencies are seen as inevitable in human life, so people are generally less motivated to resolve dissonance than Westerners are (Choi & Nisbett, 2000; Peng & Nisbett, 1999). Still, in many people, a need for cognitive consistency can lead to irrational, self-defeating decisions and actions.

Overcoming Our Cognitive Biases

The fact that our decisions and judgments, and the feelings of regret or pleasure that follow, are not always rational has enormous implications for the legal system, business, medicine, government—in fact, for all areas of life. Sometimes these biases are a good thing. For example, cognitive dissonance reduction helps us preserve our self-confidence, and the fairness bias keeps us from behaving like self-centered louts. From this point of view, such biases are not really so "irrational" after all. Mental biases, however, can also cause us to make poor decisions.

Most people have a "bias blind spot": They acknowledge that *other* people have biases that distort reality, but they think that they themselves are free of bias and see the world as it really is (Pronin, Gilovich, & Ross, 2004). This blind spot is itself a bias! And it is

postdecision dissonance In the theory of cognitive dissonance, tension that occurs when you believe you may have made a bad decision.

justification of effort The tendency of individuals to increase their liking for something that they have worked hard or suffered to attain; a common form of dissonance reduction.

a dangerous one, because it can prevent individuals, nations, ethnic groups, and religious groups from resolving conflicts with others. Each side thinks that its own proposals for ending a conflict are reasonable and fair but the other side's proposals are "biased."

The situation is not entirely hopeless, however. For one thing, people are not equally irrational in all situations. When they are doing things they have some expertise in or are making personal decisions that have serious consequences, cognitive

biases often diminish (Smith & Kida, 1991). Further, once we understand a bias, we may, with some effort, be able to reduce or eliminate it, especially if we make an active, mindful effort to do so and take time to think carefully (Kida, 2006).

Some people, of course, seem to think more rationally than others a great deal of the time; we call them "intelligent." But just what is intelligence, and how can we measure and improve it? We take up these questions next.

QUICK *quiz*

In hindsight, will you say this quiz was easy?

1. In 2001, an unknown person sent anthrax through the United States post office. Many people became afraid to open their mail, although the actual risk for any given individual was extremely small (five people died during the attacks). What heuristics help to explain this reaction?

2. *True or false:* Research on the Ultimatum Game shows that people usually act out of rational self-interest.

3. Stu meets a young woman at the student cafeteria. They hit it off and eventually get married. Says Stu, "I knew that day, when I headed for the cafeteria, that something special was about to happen." What cognitive bias is affecting Stu's thinking, charmingly romantic though it is?

4. In a classic experiment on cognitive dissonance, students did some boring, repetitive tasks and then had to tell another student, who was waiting to participate in the study, that the work was interesting and fun (Festinger & Carlsmith, 1959). Half the students were offered $20 for telling this lie and the others only $1. Based on what you have learned about cognitive dissonance reduction, which students do you think decided later that the tasks had been fun after all? Why?

Answers:

1. the affect and availability heuristics   2. false   3. the hindsight bias   4. The students who got only $1 were more likely to say that the tasks had been fun. They were in a state of dissonance because "The task was as dull as dishwater" is dissonant with "I said I enjoyed it—and for a mere dollar, at that." Those who got $20 could rationalize that the large sum (which really was large in the 1950s) justified the lie.

---

intelligence An inferred characteristic of an individual, usually defined as the ability to profit from experience, acquire knowledge, think abstractly, act purposefully, or adapt to changes in the environment.

factor analysis A statistical method for analyzing the intercorrelations among various measures or test scores; clusters of measures or scores that are highly correlated are assumed to measure the same underlying trait, ability, or aptitude (factor).

g factor A general ability assumed by many theorists to underlie specific mental abilities and talents.

WHAT'S *Ahead*

- How did the original purpose of intelligence testing change when IQ tests came to America?

- Why hasn't it been possible to design intelligence tests that are free of cultural influence?

- Why do some psychologists oppose traditional intelligence testing?

- What kind of intelligence allows you to master the unspoken rules for academic success?

- What is "EQ," and why is it as important as IQ?

Intelligence

Intelligent people disagree on just what intelligence is. Some equate it with the ability to reason abstractly, others with the ability to learn and profit from experience in daily life. Some emphasize the ability to think rationally, others the ability to act

purposefully. These qualities are all probably part of what most people mean by **intelligence**, but theorists weigh them differently.

One of the longest-running debates in psychology is whether an overall quality called "intelligence" even exists. A typical intelligence test asks you to do several things: provide a specific bit of information, notice similarities between objects, solve arithmetic problems, define words, fill in the missing parts of incomplete pictures, arrange pictures in a logical order, arrange blocks to resemble a design, assemble puzzles, use a coding scheme, or judge what behavior would be appropriate in a particular situation. Researchers use a statistical method called **factor analysis** to try to identify which basic abilities underlie performance on the various items. As we saw in Chapter 2, this procedure identifies clusters of correlated items that seem to be measuring some common trait or ability (factor). Most scientists believe that a general ability, or **g factor**, underlies the specific abilities and talents measured by intelligence tests (Gottfredson, 2002; Jensen, 1998; Lubinski,

A psychologist gives a student an intelligence test.

2004; Spearman, 1927; Wechsler, 1955). But others dispute the existence of a g factor on the grounds that a person can excel in some tasks yet do poorly in others (Gould, 1994; Guilford, 1988). Disagreements over how to define intelligence have led some writers to argue, only half jokingly, that intelligence is "whatever intelligence tests measure."

Measuring Intelligence: The Psychometric Approach

The traditional approach to intelligence, the **psychometric** approach, focuses on how well people perform on standardized aptitude tests, which are designed to measure the ability to acquire skills or knowledge. IQ tests, for example, do a pretty good job of predicting how children will do in school.

The Invention of IQ Tests The first widely used intelligence test was devised in 1904, when the French Ministry of Education asked psychologist Alfred Binet (1857–1911) to find a way to identify children who were slow learners so they could be given remedial work. The ministry was reluctant to let teachers identify such children because the teachers might have prejudices about poor children or might assume that shy or disruptive children were mentally impaired. They wanted a more objective approach.

Wrestling with the problem, Binet had a great insight: In the classroom, the responses of "dull" children resembled those of ordinary children of younger ages. Bright children, on the other hand, responded like children of older ages. The thing to measure, then, was a child's **mental age (MA)**, or level of intellectual development relative to other children's. Then instruction could be tailored to the child's capabilities.

The test devised by Binet and his colleague, Théodore Simon, measured memory, vocabulary, and perceptual discrimination. Items ranged from those

that most young children could do easily to those that only older children could handle, as determined by the testing of large numbers of children. A scoring system developed later by others used a formula in which the child's mental age was divided by the child's chronological age to yield an **intelligence quotient**, or **IQ** (a quotient is the result of division). Thus a child of 8 who scored like an average 10-year-old would have a mental age of 10 and an IQ of 125 (10 divided by 8, times 100). All average children, regardless of age, would have an IQ of 100 because mental age and chronological age would be the same.

This method of figuring IQ had serious flaws, however. At one age, scores might cluster tightly around the average, whereas at another age they might be more dispersed. As a result, the score necessary to be in the top 10 or 20 or 30 percent of your age group varied, depending on your age. Also, the IQ formula did not make much sense for adults: A 50-year-old who scores like a 30-year-old does not have low intelligence! Today, therefore, intelligence tests are scored differently. The average is usually set arbitrarily at 100, and tests are constructed so that about two-thirds of all people score between 85 and 115. Individual scores are computed from tables based on established norms. These scores are still informally referred to as IQs, and they still reflect how a person compares with other people, either children of a particular age or adults in general. At all ages, the distribution of scores approximates a normal (bell-shaped) curve, with scores near the average (mean) more common than very high or very low scores (see Figure 7.2).

psychometrics The measurement of mental abilities, traits, and processes.

mental age (MA) A measure of mental development expressed in terms of the average mental ability at a given age.

intelligence quotient (IQ) A measure of intelligence now derived from norms provided for standardized intelligence tests.

FIGURE 7.2
Expected Distribution of IQ Scores
In a large population, IQ scores tend to be distributed on a normal (bell-shaped) curve. On most tests, about 68 percent of all people will score between 85 and 115, about 95 percent will score between 70 and 130, and about 99.7 percent will score between 55 and 145. In any actual sample, however, the distribution will depart somewhat from the theoretical ideal.

In the United States, Stanford psychologist Lewis Terman revised Binet's test and established norms for American children. His version, the *Stanford–Binet Intelligence Scale*, was first published in 1916 and has been updated several times since. The test asks a person to perform a variety of tasks—for example, to fill in missing words in sentences, answer questions requiring general knowledge, predict how a folded paper will look when unfolded, measure a quantity of water using two containers of different sizes, and distinguish between concepts that are similar but not exactly the same (such as, say, vigor and energy). The older the test taker is, the more the test requires in the way of verbal comprehension and fluency, spatial ability, and reasoning.

Two decades later, David Wechsler designed another test expressly for adults, which became the *Wechsler Adult Intelligence Scale (WAIS)*; it was followed by the *Wechsler Intelligence Scale for Children (WISC)*. Although the Wechsler tests produced a general IQ score, they also provided specific scores for different kinds of ability. Verbal items tested a person's vocabulary, arithmetic abilities, immediate memory span, ability to recognize similarities (e.g., "How are books and movies alike?"), and general knowledge and comprehension (e.g., "Who was Thomas Jefferson?" "Why do people who want a divorce have to go to court?"). Performance items tested a range of nonverbal skills, such as the ability to re-create a block design within a specified time limit and to identify a part missing from a picture. The current versions of the Wechsler tests have more subtests and, in addition to an overall IQ score, yield four separate scores: for verbal comprehension, perceptual reasoning, working memory (the ability to hold information in mind so it can be used), and processing speed. (See Figure 7.3 for some sample items.)

Binet had emphasized that his test merely *sampled* intelligence and did not measure everything covered by that term. A test score, he said,

Picture arrangement
(Arrange the panels to make a meaningful story)

Code 1 2 3 4 5

Test 2 1 4 3 5 2 1 3 4 2 1

Object assembly
(Put together a jigsaw puzzle)

Digit symbol
(Using the key at the top, fill in the appropriate symbol beneath each number)

Picture completion
(Supply the missing feature)

Block design
(Copy the design shown, using another set of blocks)

FIGURE 7.3

Performance Tasks on the Wechsler Tests

Nonverbal items such as these are particularly useful for measuring the abilities of those who have poor hearing, are not fluent in the tester's language, have limited education, or resist doing classroom-type problems. A large gap between a person's verbal score and performance on nonverbal tasks such as these sometimes indicates a specific learning problem. (Object assembly, digit symbol, and picture completion adapted from Cronbach, 1990.)

could be useful, along with other information, for predicting school performance, but it should not be confused with intelligence itself. The tests were designed to be given to children individually, so that the test-giver could see whether a child was ill or nervous, had poor vision, or was unmotivated. The purpose was to identify children with learning problems, not to rank all children. But when intelligence testing was brought from France to the United States, its original purpose got lost at sea. In America, IQ tests became widely used not to bring slow learners up to the average, but to categorize people in school and in the armed services according to their presumed "natural ability." The testers overlooked the fact that in America, with its many ethnic groups, people did not all share the same background and experience (Gould, 1996).

An intelligence test is useful only if it is used intelligently. Testing by the U.S. Army during World War I often occurred under noisy, crowded, and confusing conditions, and many items were culturally loaded even though recruits came from diverse cultures. Nevertheless, many people concluded from the results that a high proportion of army recruits were "morons."

Culture and Testing

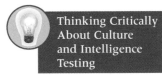

Intelligence tests developed between World War I and the 1960s for use in schools favored city children over rural ones, middle-class children over poor ones, and white children over nonwhite children. One item asked whether the Emperor Concerto was written by Beethoven, Mozart, Bach, Brahms, or Mahler. (The answer is Beethoven.) Critics complained that the tests did not measure the kinds of knowledge and skills that are intelligent in a minority neighborhood or in the hills of Appalachia. They feared that because teachers thought IQ scores revealed the limits of a child's potential, low-scoring children might not get the educational attention or encouragement they needed.

Test-makers responded by trying to construct tests that were unaffected by culture or that incorporated knowledge and skills common to many different cultures. But these efforts were disappointing. One reason was that cultures differ in the problem-solving strategies they emphasize (Serpell, 1994). In the West, white, middle-class children typically learn to classify things by category—to say that an apple and a peach are similar because they are both fruits, and that a saw and a rake are similar because they are both tools. But children who are not trained in middle-class ways of sorting things may classify objects according to their sensory qualities or functions. They may say that an apple and a peach are similar because they both taste good. We think that's a charming and innovative answer, but it is one that testers interpret as less intelligent (Miller-Jones, 1989).

Testing experts also discovered that cultural values and experiences affect many things besides responses to specific test items. These include a person's general attitude toward exams, comfort in the settings required for testing, motivation, rapport with the test-giver, competitiveness, comfort in solving problems independently rather than with others, and familiarity with the conventions for taking tests (Anastasi & Urbina, 1997; López, 1995; Sternberg, 2004).

Moreover, people's performance on IQ and other mental-ability tests depends on their own expectations about how they will do, and those expectations are shaped in part by cultural stereotypes. Stereotypes that portray women or members of particular ethnic, age, or socioeconomic groups as unintelligent can actually depress the performance of people in these groups. You might think that a woman would say, "So sexists think women are dumb at math? I'll show them" or that an African-American would say, "So racists believe that blacks aren't as smart as whites? Just give me that exam." But often that is not what happens.

On the contrary, such individuals commonly feel a burden of doubt about their abilities that Claude Steele (1992, 1997) has labeled **stereotype threat**. The threat occurs when people believe that if they do not do well, they will confirm the stereotypes about their group. Their anxiety may then worsen their performance. Negative thoughts may intrude and disrupt their concentration ("I hate this test," "I'm no good at math") (Cadinu et al., 2005). Or they may cope by "disidentifying" with the test, saying to themselves, in effect, "The outcome of this test has no bearing on how I feel about myself" (Major et al., 1998). As a result, they may not be motivated to do well.

More than 100 studies have shown that stereotype threat can affect the test performance

stereotype threat A burden of doubt a person feels about his or her performance, due to negative stereotypes about his or her group's abilities.

of many African-Americans, Latinos, low-income people, women, and elderly people, all of whom perform better when they are not feeling self-conscious about themselves as members of negatively stereotyped groups (Aronson & Salinas, 1997; Brown & Josephs, 1999; Croizen & Claire, 1998; Inzlicht & Ben-Zeev, 2000; Levy, 1996; Quinn & Spencer, 2001; Steele & Aronson, 1995). Anything that increases the salience of group stereotypes can increase stereotype threat and affect performance, including taking the test in a setting where you are the only member from your group or being asked to state your race before taking the test.

What can be done to reduce stereotype threat? One possibility is simply to tell people about it. When students taking introductory statistics were given a difficult test, with no mention of stereotype threat, women did worse than men. But when students were informed about stereotype threat, the sex difference disappeared (Johns, Schmader, & Martens, 2005). (See how psychology can help people?)

This simple approach is unlikely to eliminate all group differences in test scores, however. And that fact points to a dilemma at the heart of intelligence and mental-ability testing. Intelligence and other mental-ability tests put some groups of people at a disadvantage, yet they also measure skills and knowledge useful in the classroom. How can psychologists and educators recognize and accept cultural differences and, at the same time, promote the mastery of the skills, knowledge, and attitudes that can help people succeed in school and in the larger society?

QUICK quiz

What's your Quiz Quotient (QQ)?

1. What was Binet's great insight?
2. *True or false:* IQ tests designed to avoid cultural bias have failed to eliminate average group differences in IQ scores.
3. Hilda, who is 66, is about to take an IQ test, but she is worried because she knows that older people are often assumed to have diminished mental abilities. Hilda is being affected by _____.

Answers:

1. Mental age does not necessarily correspond to chronological age.   2. true   3. stereotype threat

Dissecting Intelligence: The Cognitive Approach

Critics of standard intelligence tests point out that such tests tell us little about *how* a person goes about answering questions and solving problems. Nor do the tests explain why people with low scores often behave intelligently in real life—making smart consumer decisions, winning at the racetrack, and making wise choices in their relationships instead of repeating the same dumb patterns. Some researchers, therefore, have rejected the psychometric approach to the study and measurement of intelligence and mental abilities in favor of a cognitive approach. Thinking critically, cognitive psychologists have questioned prevailing assumptions about the very meaning of intelligence and the best way to measure it. In contrast to the psychometric approach, which is concerned with how many answers a person gets right on a test, the *cognitive approach* assumes there are many kinds of intelligence and emphasizes the strategies people use when thinking about a problem and arriving at a solution.

Thinking Critically About What It Means to Be Smart

Psychologists who take this approach reject the emphasis on a g factor in research on intelligence. The g factor, in their view, may simply reflect the fact that a variety of different abilities are taught in Western schools and emphasized in Western societies. In countries like Kenya, where children are taught how to succeed in a trade but often not much else, a g factor is less likely to emerge from the children's test scores (Sternberg, 2004).

The Triarchic Theory One well-known cognitive theory is Robert Sternberg's **triarchic theory of intelligence** (1988, 1995) (*triarchic* means "three-part"). Sternberg (2004) defines

triarchic theory of intelligence A theory of intelligence that emphasizes information-processing strategies, the ability to transfer skills to new situations, and the practical application of intelligence.

intelligence as "the skills and knowledge needed for success in life, according to one's own definition of success, within one's sociocultural context." He distinguishes three aspects of intelligence:

1 *Componential intelligence* refers to the information-processing strategies you use when you are thinking intelligently about a problem. These mental "components" include recognizing the problem, selecting a strategy for solving it, mastering and carrying out the strategy, and evaluating the result. This is the type of intelligence generally tapped by IQ tests.

Some of the operations in componential intelligence require not only analytic skills but also **metacognition**, the knowledge or awareness of your own cognitive processes and the ability to monitor and control those processes. Metacognitive skills help you learn. Students who are weak in metacognition fail to notice when a passage in a textbook is difficult, and they do not always realize that they haven't understood what they've been reading. As a result, they spend too little time on difficult material and too much time on material they already know (Nelson & Leonesio, 1988). In contrast, students who are strong in metacognition check their comprehension by restating what they have read, backtracking when necessary, and questioning what they are reading, so they learn better (Bereiter & Bird, 1985).

It works in the other direction, too: The kind of intelligence that enhances academic performance can also help you develop metacognitive skills. Students with poor academic skills typically fail to realize how little they know; they think they're doing fine (Dunning, 2005). The very weaknesses that keep them from doing well on tests or in their courses also keep them from realizing their weaknesses. In one study, students in a psychology course estimated how well they had just done on an exam relative to other students. As you can see in Figure 7.4, those who had performed in the bottom quartile greatly overestimated their own performance (Dunning et al., 2003). In contrast, people with strong academic skills tend to be more realistic. Often they even *underestimate* slightly how their performance compares with the performance of others.

2 *Experiential or creative intelligence* refers to your creativity in transferring skills to new situations. People with experiential intelligence cope well with novelty and learn quickly to make new tasks automatic. Those who are lacking in this area perform well only under a narrow set of circumstances. For example, a student may do well in school, where assignments have specific due dates and feedback is immediate, but be less successful

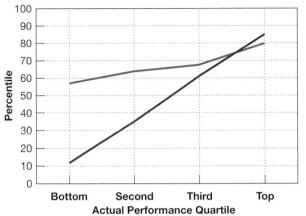

FIGURE 7.4
Ignorance is Bliss
In school and in other settings as well, people who perform poorly often have poor metacognitive skills and, therefore, fail to recognize their own lack of competence. As you can see, the lower students' scores were on an exam, the greater the gap between how they thought they had done and how they actually had done (Dunning et al., 2003).

after graduation if her job requires her to set her own deadlines and her employer doesn't tell her how she is doing.

3 *Contextual or practical intelligence* refers to the practical application of intelligence, which requires you to take into account the different contexts in which you find yourself. If you are strong in contextual intelligence, you know when to adapt to the environment (you are in a dangerous neighborhood, so you become more vigilant). You know when to change environments (you had planned to be a teacher but discover that you dislike working with kids, so you switch to accounting). And you know when to fix the situation (your marriage is rocky, so you and your spouse go for counseling).

Contextual intelligence allows you to acquire **tacit knowledge**—practical, action-oriented strategies for achieving your goals that usually are not formally taught or even verbalized but must instead be inferred by observing others (Sternberg et al., 1995). In studies of college professors, business managers, and salespeople, tacit knowledge and practical intelligence are strong predictors of effectiveness on the job (Sternberg et al., 2000). In college students, tacit knowledge about how to be a good student actually predicts academic success as well as college entrance exams do (Sternberg & Wagner, 1989).

Domains of Intelligence Other psychologists, too, are expanding our understanding of of what it means to be intelligent. They point out that someone who is intelligent in one area, or domain, is not necessarily intelligent in all others. A Nobel Prize winner in medicine may be helpless when it comes to making up a budget; a physicist who is cautious and careful in his own field may uncritically accept pop-psych claims.

metacognition The knowledge or awareness of one's own cognitive processes.

tacit knowledge Strategies for success that are not explicitly taught but that instead must be inferred.

emotional intelligence
The ability to identify your own and other people's emotions accurately, express your emotions clearly, and regulate emotions in yourself and others.

Howard Gardner (1983, 1995) has proposed that the domains of intelligence be expanded to include musical aptitude, kinesthetic intelligence (the bodily grace and physical self-awareness of athletes and dancers), and the capacity for insight into oneself, others, or the natural world. These domains, Gardner argues, are relatively independent and may even have separate neural structures. People with brain damage often lose intelligence in one domain without losing their competence in the others. And some autistic and retarded individuals with *savant syndrome* (*savant* means "learned" in French) have exceptional abilities in one area, such as music, art, or rapid mathematical computation, despite poor functioning in all others.

Two of Gardner's domains, understanding yourself and understanding others, overlap with what some psychologists call **emotional intelligence**, the ability to identify your own and other people's emotions accurately, express your emotions clearly, and manage emotions in yourself and others (Mayer & Salovey, 1997; Salovey & Grewal, 2005). People with high emotional intelligence, popularly known as "EQ," use their emotions to motivate themselves, to spur creative thinking, and to deal empathically with others. People who are lacking in emotional intelligence are often unable to identify their own emotions; they may insist that they're not depressed when a relationship ends, for example, but meanwhile they start drinking too much, become irritable, and stop going out with friends. They may express emotions inappropriately, say by acting violently or impulsively when they are angry or worried. And often they misread nonverbal signals from others; they will give a long-winded account of all their problems even when the listener is obviously bored.

Studies of brain-damaged adults suggest a biological basis for emotional intelligence. Neuroscientist Antonio Damasio (1994) has studied patients with prefrontal-lobe damage that makes them incapable of experiencing strong feelings. Although they score in the normal range on conventional mental tests, these patients persistently make

People with emotional intelligence are skilled at reading nonverbal emotional cues. Which of these boys do you think feels the most confident and relaxed, which one is shyest, and which feels most anxious? What cues are you using to answer?

"dumb," irrational decisions in their lives because they cannot assign values to different options based on their own emotional reactions and cannot read emotional cues from others. As we will see again in Chapter 13, feeling and thinking are not always incompatible, as many people assume; in fact, one requires the other.

Thinking Critically About Intelligence(s)

Not everyone is enthusiastic about the proliferation of new "intelligences." Some argue that emotional intelligence is not a special cognitive ability but a collection of personality traits, such as empathy and extroversion, and that nothing is gained by giving it a trendy name (Davies, Stankov, & Roberts, 1998; Matthews, Zeidner, & Roberts, 2003). Others maintain that abilities such as Gardner's musical and kinesthetic intelligences are better thought of as talents, or else the very concept of intelligence loses all meaning. What is to prevent someone from adding "handicraft intelligence" or "financial intelligence" or "farming intelligence"?

Those who believe that there is a general factor in intelligence can marshal a century of research to

Some theorists would say that the Dixie Chicks have musical intelligence, a surveyor has spatial intelligence, and a compassionate friend has emotional intelligence. Should the definition of intelligence be broadened in this way? Or are these abilities better defined as talents?

support their view (Lubinski, 2004). Tests of g do a better job than measures of personality or specific aptitudes at predicting not only academic achievement but also the cognitive complexity of people's jobs and their occupational success (Kuncel, Hezlett, & Ones, 2004; Schmidt & Hunter, 2004). One longitudinal study followed pairs of brothers who had been reared in the same household but differed in their scores on tests of general intelligence. One brother in each pair had an IQ in the average range (90 to 110) and the other had scored above or below that range. In this sample, in which socioeconomic background was the same for each pair of siblings, IQ strongly predicted which brother finished college, which one earned more money, and which one wound up in a more prestigious occupation (Murray, 1998).

Nonetheless, broadening the notion of intelligence has been extremely useful for several rea-sons. It has forced us to think more critically about what we mean by intelligence and to consider how different kinds of "smarts" help us function in our everyday lives. It has generated research on tests that provide ongoing feedback to the test-taker so that the person can learn from the experience and improve his or her performance (Sternberg, 2004). The cognitive approach has also led to a focus on teaching children strategies for improving their abilities in reading, writing, doing homework, and taking tests. For example, children have been taught to manage their time so they don't procrastinate and to study differently for multiple-choice exams than for essay exams (Sternberg et al., 1995). Most important, new approaches to intelligence encourage us to overcome the mental set of assuming that the only kind of intelligence necessary for a successful life is the kind captured by IQ tests.

QUICK quiz

A good strategy for improving your own test performance is to take the quizzes in this book.

1. What goals do cognitive theories of intelligence have that psychometric theories do not?

2. Logan understands the material in his statistics class, but on tests he spends the entire period on the most difficult problems and never even gets to the problems he can solve easily. According to the triarchic theory of intelligence, which aspect of intelligence does he need to improve?

3. Tracy does not have an unusually high IQ, but at work she was quickly promoted because she knows how to set priorities, communicate with management, and make others feel valued. Tracy has _____ knowledge about how to succeed on the job.

4. What is wrong with defining intelligence as "whatever intelligence tests measure"?

Answers:

1. to understand people's strategies for solving problems and to use this information to improve mental performance   2. componential intelligence (which includes metacognition)   3. tacit   4. This definition implies that a low score must be entirely the scorer's fault rather than the fault of the test. But the test-taker may be intelligent in domains that the test fails to measure, and the test may be measuring traits other than intelligence.

WHAT'S *Ahead*

- To what extent is intelligence heritable?

- What error do many people make when arguing that one group is genetically smarter than another?

- How does the environment nurture or thwart mental ability?

- Why do Asian children perform so much better in school than American students do?

The Origins of Intelligence

"Intelligence," as we have seen, can mean many things. But however we define or measure it, clear-ly some people think and behave more intelligently than others. What accounts for these differences?

Genes and Intelligence

Behavioral geneticists approach this question by doing heritability studies, focusing mainly on the kind of intelligence measured by IQ tests. In Chapter 2, we saw that **heritability** is the proportion of the total variance in a trait within a group that is attributable to genetic variation within the group. This proportion can have a maximum value of 1.0 (which means that the trait is completely heritable). It is usually estimated by doing twin and adoption studies. (You might review pages 55 and 56 if you need to refresh your memory for these procedures.)

heritability A statistical estimate of the proportion of the total variance in some trait that is attributable to genetic differences among individuals within a group.

Genes and Individual Differences

Behavioral-genetic studies show that the kind of intelligence that produces high IQ scores is highly heritable. For children and adolescents, heritability estimates average around .50; that is, about half of the variance in IQ scores is explainable by genetic differences (Chipuer, Rovine, & Plomin, 1990; Devlin, Daniels, & Roeder, 1997; Plomin, 1989). For adults, who are less affected by environmental influences such as schooling, the estimates until middle age are even higher—in the .60 to .80 range (Bouchard, 1995; McClearn et al., 1997; McGue et al., 1993). That is, the genetic contribution becomes relatively larger and the environmental one relatively smaller with age.

In studies of twins, the scores of identical twins are always much more highly correlated than those of fraternal twins, a difference that reflects the influence of genes. In fact, the scores of identical twins reared apart are more highly correlated than those of fraternal twins reared together, as you can see in Figure 7.5. In adoption studies, the scores of adopted children are more highly correlated with those of their birth parents than with those of their biologically unrelated adoptive parents: The higher the birth parents' scores, the higher the child's score is likely to be. As adopted children grow into adolescence, the correlation between their IQ scores and those of their biologically unrelated family members diminishes, and in adulthood the correlation falls to *zero* (Bouchard, 1997b; Scarr, 1993; Scarr & Weinberg, 1994).). (This does not mean that adoption has no positive effects; adopted children score higher on IQ tests than do birth siblings who were not adopted, probably because adoptees grow up in a more enriched environment [van IJzendoorn et al., 2005].)

Researchers are now looking for genes that might influence performance on IQ and other mental tests, and several candidates have been proposed. But progress has been slower than anticipated. Far more genes are likely to be involved than originally thought, and each of these genes is likely to contribute just a tiny piece to the puzzle of genetic variation (Plomin et al., 2003; Posthuma & de Geus, 2006).

The Question of Group Differences

If genes influence individual differences in intelligence, do they also help account for differences *between* groups, as many people assume? This issue has tremendous political and social importance, so we are going to look at it closely.

Most of the focus has been on black–white differences, because African-American children score, on average, some 10 to 12 points lower on IQ tests than do white children. (We are talking about averages; the distributions of scores for black children and white children overlap considerably.) A few psychologists have proposed a genetic explanation of this difference (Jensen, 1969, 1981; Rushton, 1988). As you can imagine, this topic is not merely academic. Racists have used theories of genetic differences between groups to justify their own hatreds, and politicians have used them to argue for cuts in programs that would benefit blacks, other minorities, and poor children. Some researchers themselves have concluded that there is little point in spending money on programs that try to raise the IQs of low-scoring children, of whatever race (Herrnstein & Murray, 1994).

Genetic explanations, however, have a fatal flaw: They use heritability estimates based mainly on white samples to estimate the role of heredity in *group* differences, a procedure that is not valid. This problem sounds pretty technical, but it is not really too difficult to understand, so stay with us.

Thinking Critically About Group Differences in IQ

Consider, first, not people but tomatoes. (Figure 7.6 will help you visualize the following "thought experiment.") Suppose you have a bag of tomato seeds that vary genetically; all things being equal, some will produce tomatoes that are puny and tasteless, and some will produce tomatoes that are plump and delicious. Now you take a bunch of these seeds in your left hand and another bunch from the same bag in your right hand. Though one seed differs genetically from another, there is no average difference between

FIGURE 7.5

Correlations in Siblings' IQ Scores

The IQ scores of identical twins are highly correlated, even when they are reared apart. The data in this graph are based on average correlations across many studies (Bouchard & McGue, 1981).

FIGURE 7.6
The Tomato Plant Experiment
In the hypothetical experiment described in the text, even if the differences among plants within each pot were due entirely to genetics, the average difference between pots could be environmental. The same general principle applies to individual and group differences among human beings.

the seeds in your left hand and those in your right. You plant the left hand's seeds in pot A, with some soil that you have doctored with nitrogen and other nutrients, and you plant the right hand's seeds in pot B, with soil from which you have extracted nutrients. You sing to pot A and put it in the sun; you ignore pot B and leave it in a dark corner.

When the tomato plants grow, they will vary *within* each pot in terms of height, the number of tomatoes produced, and the size of the tomatoes, purely because of genetic differences. But there will also be an average difference between the plants in pot A and those in pot B: The plants in pot A will be healthier and bear more tomatoes. This difference *between* pots is due entirely to the different soils and the care that has been given to the plants—even though the heritability of the *within*-pot differences is 100 percent (Lewontin, 1970, 2001).

The principle is the same for people as it is for tomatoes. Although intellectual differences *within* groups are at least partly genetic, that does not mean that differences *between* groups are genetic. Blacks and whites do not grow up, on average, in the same "pots" (environments). Because of a long legacy of racial hostility and discrimination, black children, as well as Latino and other minority children, often receive far fewer nutrients—literally, in terms of food, and figuratively, in terms of edu-

cation, encouragement by society, and intellectual opportunities. And as we have seen, negative stereotypes about ethnic groups may cause members of these groups to doubt their own abilities, become anxious and self-conscious, and perform more poorly than they otherwise would on tests.

Doing good research on the origins of black–white differences in IQ is extremely difficult in the United States, where racism affects the lives of even affluent, successful African-Americans. However, the few studies that have overcome past methodological problems fail to reveal any genetic differences between blacks and whites in whatever it is that IQ tests measure. One study found that children fathered by black and white American soldiers in Germany after World War II and reared in similar German communities by similar families did not differ significantly in IQ (Eyferth, 1961). Another showed that degree of African ancestry (which can be roughly estimated from skin color, blood analysis, and genealogy) was not related to measured intelligence, as a genetic theory of black–white differences would predict (Scarr et al., 1977). And white and black infants do equally well on a test that measures their preference for novel stimuli, a predictor of later IQ scores (Fagan, 1992).

An intelligent reading of the research on intelligence, therefore, does not direct us to conclude that differences among cultural, ethnic, or national groups are permanent, genetically determined, or signs of any group's innate superiority. On the contrary, the research suggests that we should make sure that all children grow up in the best possible soil, with room for the smartest and the slowest to find a place in the sun.

The Environment and Intelligence

In Chapter 2 we noted that a highly heritable trait can nonetheless be modifiable by the environment and experience. By now you may be wondering what kinds of experiences hinder intellectual development and what kinds of environmental "nutrients" promote it. Here are some of the influences associated with reduced mental ability:

* *Poor prenatal care.* If a pregnant woman is malnourished, contracts infections, takes certain drugs, smokes, is exposed to secondhand smoke, or drinks alcohol regularly, her child is at risk of having learning disabilities and a lower IQ.

* *Malnutrition.* The average IQ gap between severely malnourished and well-nourished children can be as high as 20 points (Stoch & Smythe, 1963; Winick, Meyer, & Harris, 1975).

- *Exposure to toxins.* Lead, especially, can damage the nervous system, even at fairly low levels, producing attention problems, lower IQ scores, and poorer school achievement (Lanphear et al., 2005; Needleman et al., 1996). Many children in the United States are exposed to dangerous levels of lead from dust, contaminated soil, lead paint, and old lead pipes, and the concentration of lead in black children's blood is 50 percent higher than in white children's (Lanphear et al., 2002). Air pollution, which a woman cannot directly control, also appears to be a serious risk factor. A recent longitudinal study of nonsmoking inner-city women found a link between delayed cognitive development in the women's children and the level of pollutants from fossil fuels that the mothers were exposed to during pregnancy (Perera, et al., 2006).

- *Stressful family circumstances.* Factors that predict reduced intellectual competence include, for example, having a father who does not live with the family, a mother with a history of mental illness, parents with limited work skills, and a history of stressful events in early life (Sameroff et al., 1987). On average, each risk factor reduces a child's IQ score by 4 points. Children with seven risk factors score more than *30 points lower* than those with no risk factors.

In contrast, a healthy and stimulating environment can raise mental performance (Guralnick, 1997;

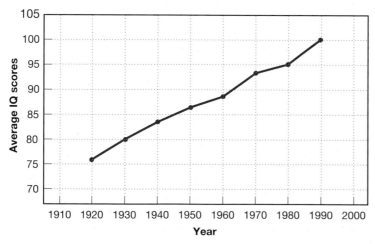

FIGURE 7.7
Climbing IQ Scores
Raw scores on IQ tests have been rising in the developed countries for many decades at a rate much too steep to be accounted for by genetic changes. Because test norms are periodically readjusted to set the average score at 100, most people are unaware of the increase. On this graph, average scores are calibrated according to 1989 norms. As you can see, performance was much lower in 1918 than in 1989. (Adapted from Horgan, 1995.)

Nelson, Westhues, & MacLeod, 2003; Ramey & Ramey, 1998). In one longitudinal study called the Abecedarian Project, inner-city children who got lots of mental enrichment at home and in child care or school, starting in infancy, had much better school achievement than did children in a control group (Campbell & Ramey, 1995). In general, children's mental abilities improve when parents talk to their children about many topics and describe things accurately and fully, encourage them to think things through, read to them, and expect them to do well.

Perhaps the best evidence for the importance of environmental influences on intelligence is the fact that IQ scores in developed countries have been climbing steadily for at least three generations (Flynn, 1987, 1999) (see Figure 7.7). A similar increase was documented in Kenya, a developing country: Rural children ages 6 to 8 scored about 11 points higher in 1998 than their peers did in 1984, the fastest rise in a group's average IQ scores ever reported (Daley et al., 2003). Genes cannot possibly have changed fast enough to account for these findings. Most cognitive psychologists attribute the increases to improvements in education, the growth in jobs requiring abstract thought, and better nutrition and health (Neisser, 1998).

We see, then, that although heredity may provide the range of a child's intellectual potential—a Homer Simpson can never become an Einstein—many other factors affect where in that range the child will fall.

Motivation, Hard Work, and Intellectual Success

Even with a high IQ, emotional intelligence, genetic advantages, talent, and practical know-how, you still might get nowhere at all. Talent, unlike cream, does not inevitably rise to the top; success also depends on drive and determination.

Consider a finding from one of the longest-running psychological studies ever conducted. In 1921, researchers began following more than 1,500 people with childhood IQ scores in the top 1 percent of the distribution. As boys and girls, these people were nicknamed Termites, after Lewis Terman, who originally directed the research. The Termites started out bright, physically healthy, sociable, and well adjusted. As they entered adulthood, most became successful in the traditional ways of the times: men in careers and women as homemakers (Sears & Barbee, 1977; Terman & Oden, 1959). However, some gifted men failed to live up to their early promise, dropping out of school or drifting into

The children of migrant workers (left) often spend long hours in backbreaking field work and may miss out on the educational opportunities and intellectual advantages available to middle-class children (right).

low-level work. When the researchers compared the 100 most successful men with the 100 least successful, they found that motivation made the difference. The successful men were ambitious, were socially active, had many interests, and were encouraged by their parents. The least successful men drifted casually through life. There was no average difference in IQ between the two groups.

CLOSE-UP on Research

Grades, IQ, and Self-Discipline

Once you are motivated to succeed intellectually, you need self-discipline to achieve your goals. Yet there has been remarkably little research on this important trait. This fact prompted Angela Duckworth and Martin Seligman (2005) to **ask an intriguing question**: Which is a better predictor of academic performance among adolescents, IQ or self-discipline? To answer it, they conducted a longitudinal study of ethnically diverse eighth graders attending a magnet school. At the beginning of the semester, they assigned each student a self-discipline score based on a broad range of measures, including self-reports, parents' reports, teachers' reports, and questionnaires. They added a behavioral measure of self-discipline, too: the teenager's ability to delay gratification. The teens had to choose be-

tween taking an envelope containing a dollar or returning it in exchange for getting two dollars a week later. To measure IQ, the researchers used a standard intelligence test. To measure academic performance, they used grades, achievement-test scores, attendance, and selection into a competitive high-school program in the spring semester.

Examining the evidence, the researchers found that self-discipline accounted for more than twice as much of the variance in final grades as IQ did. Compared with their more impulsive classmates, students with strong self-discipline earned higher final grades and achievement-test scores and were more likely to gain admission to the competitive high-school program. As the accompanying graph shows, when the researchers divided the students into five groups (quintiles) based on their IQ scores, final grade point average varied much more steeply as a function of self-discipline than of IQ. That is, overall, correlations between self-discipline and academic performance were much stronger than those between IQ and academic performance. The researchers concluded that "self-discipline has a bigger effect on academic performance than does intellectual talents."

The researchers went on to **consider other interpretations** of the findings, interpretations based on statistical arguments. One was that because the participants attended a school that based admission on their past academic success, and because academic success and self-discipline are highly correlated, the results might not apply to the general population of students, which is more diverse. The researchers

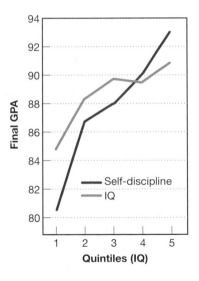

therefore plan to continue their research with more representative samples. They believe, however, that underachievement among American students occurs not because the kids "don't have it in them" but because they don't use it. A failure to exercise self-discipline, the researchers suggest, may be due to American society's emphasis on instant gratification. They therefore argue that "programs that build self-discipline may be the royal road to building academic achievement."

Self-discipline and motivation to work hard at intellectual tasks depend in turn on your attitudes about intelligence and achievement, which are strongly influenced by cultural values. For many years, Harold Stevenson and his colleagues studied such attitudes in Asia and the United States, comparing large samples of grade-school children, parents, and teachers in Minneapolis, Chicago, Sendai (Japan), Taipei (Taiwan), and Beijing (Stevenson & Stigler, 1992). Their results have much to teach us about the cultivation of intellect.

In 1980, the Asian children far outperformed the American children on a broad battery of mathematical tests. On computations and word problems, there was virtually no overlap between schools, with the lowest-scoring Beijing schools doing better than the highest-scoring Chicago schools. (A similar gap occurred in reading scores.) By 1990, the gap between the Asian and the American children had grown even greater. Only 4 percent of the Chinese children and 10 percent of the Japanese children had math scores as low as those of the *average* American child. These differences could not be accounted for by educational resources: The Chinese schools had worse facilities and larger classes than the American ones, and on average, the Chinese parents were poorer and less educated than the American parents. Nor did it have anything to do with intellectual ability in general; the American children were just as knowledgeable and capable as the Asian children on tests of general information.

But this research found that Asians and Americans are worlds apart in their attitudes, expectations, and efforts:

- *Beliefs about intelligence.* American parents, teachers, and children are far more likely than Asians to believe that mathematical ability is innate. Americans tend to think that if you have this ability, you don't have to work hard, and if you don't have it, there's no point in trying.

- *Standards.* American parents have far lower standards for their children's performance; they are satisfied with scores barely above average on a 100-point test. In contrast, Chinese and Japanese parents are happy only with very high scores.

- *Values.* American students do not value education as much as Asian students do, and they are more complacent about mediocre work. When asked what they would wish for if a wizard could give them anything they wanted, more than 60 percent of the Chinese fifth graders named something related to their education. Can you guess what the American children wanted? A majority said money or possessions.

When it comes to intellect, then, it's not just what you've got that counts but what you do with it. Complacency, fatalism, low standards, and a desire for immediate gratification can prevent people from recognizing what they don't know and reduce their efforts to learn.

QUICK quiz

We hope you're not feeling complacent about your quiz performance.

1. On average, behavioral-genetic studies estimate the heritability of intelligence to be (a) about .90, (b) low at all ages, (c) about .50 for children and adolescents.

2. *True or false*: If a trait such as intelligence is highly heritable within a group, then differences between groups must also be due mainly to heredity.

3. The available evidence (does/does not) show that ethnic differences in average IQ scores are due to genetic differences.

4. Name four environmental factors associated with reduced mental ability.

5. According to a recent study of eighth graders, _____ is more strongly correlated with school performance than _____ is.

Answers:

1. c   2. false (can you say why, using the tomato plant analogy?)   3. does not   4. poor prenatal care, malnutrition, exposure to toxins, stressful family circumstances   5. self-discipline, IQ

WHAT'S *Ahead*

- Why do some researchers think that animals can think?
- People love to talk to their pets; can their pets learn to talk back?

Animal Minds

A green heron swipes some bread from a picnicker's table and scatters the crumbs on a nearby stream. When a minnow rises to the bait, the heron strikes, swallowing its prey before you can say "dinner time." A sea otter, floating calmly on its back, bangs a mussel shell against a stone that is resting on its stomach. When the shell cracks apart, the otter devours the tasty morsel inside, tucks the stone under its little arm, and dives for another shell, which it will open in the same way. Incidents such as these have convinced some biologists, psychologists, and ethologists that we are not the only animals with cognitive abilities—that "dumb beasts" are not so dumb after all. But how smart are they?

Animal Intelligence

In the 1920s, Wolfgang Köhler (1925) put chimpanzees in situations in which some tempting bananas were just out of reach and watched to see what the apes would do. Most did nothing, but a few turned out to be quite clever. If the bananas were outside the cage, the animal might pull them in with a stick. If they were hanging overhead, and there were boxes in the cage, the chimpanzee might pile up the boxes and climb on top of them to reach

the fruit. Often the solution came after the animal had been sitting quietly for a while. It appeared as though the chimp had been thinking about the problem and was struck by a sudden insight.

Learning theorists felt that this seemingly impressive behavior could be accounted for perfectly well by standard behavioral principles, without resorting to mental explanations (see Chapter 9). Because of their influence, for years any scientist who claimed that animals could think was likely to get laughed at, or worse. Today, however, the study of animal intelligence is enjoying a resurgence, especially in the interdisciplinary field of **cognitive ethology**. (Ethology is the study of animal behavior, especially in natural environments.) Cognitive ethologists argue that some animals can anticipate future events, make plans and choices, and coordinate their activities with those of their comrades (Griffin, 1992).

When we think about animal cognition, we must be careful, because even complex behavior that appears to be purposeful can be genetically prewired and automatic. The assassin bug of South America catches termites by gluing nest material on its back as camouflage, but it is hard to imagine how the bug's tiny dab of brain tissue could enable it to plan this strategy consciously. Moreover, an animal could be aware of its environment and know some things without knowing that it knows and without being able to think about its own thoughts as human beings do. In short, an animal might have cognition but not metacognition (Budiansky, 1998; Hauser, 2000).

Yet explanations of animal behavior that leave out any sort of consciousness at all and that attribute

How smart is this otter?

cognitive ethology The study of cognitive processes in nonhuman animals.

In an early study of animal intelligence, Sultan, a talented chimpanzee studied by Wolfgang Köhler, was able to figure out how to reach a cluster of bananas by stacking some boxes and climbing on top of them.

Dodger, a 2-year old-dolphin in Shark Bay, Australia, carries a sea sponge on her sensitive beak, apparently as protection against stinging creatures and sharp coral. Recent evidence suggests that dolphin "sponge moms" teach the behavior to their daughters.

animals' actions entirely to instinct do not seem to account for some of the amazing things that animals can do. Like the otter that uses a stone to crack mussel shells, many animals use objects in the natural environment as rudimentary tools, and in some nonhuman primates the behavior is learned. For example, chimpanzee mothers occasionally show their young how to use stone tools to open hard nuts (Boesch, 1991). Orangutans in one particular Sumatran swamp have learned to use stick as tools, held in their mouths, to pry insects from holes in tree trunks and to get seeds out of cracks in a bulb-like fruit, whereas nearby groups of orangutans use only brute force to get to the delicacies (van Schaik, 2006). Even some nonprimates may have the capacity to learn to use tools, although the evidence remains controversial among ethologists. Female bottlenose dolphins off the coast of Australia attach sea sponges to their snouts while hunting for food, which protects them from sharp coral and stinging stonefish, and they seem to acquire this unusual skill from their mothers (Krützen et al., 2005). (Is this yet another case of mothers telling their daughters what to wear?)

In the laboratory, nonhuman primates have accomplished even more surprising things. For example, dozens of studies have found that chimpanzees have a rudimentary sense of number. In one study, chimpanzees compared two pairs of food wells containing chocolate chips. One pair might contain, say, 5 chips and 3 chips, the other 4 chips and 3 chips. Allowed to choose which pair they wanted, the chimps almost always chose the one with the higher combined total, showing some sort of summing ability (Rumbaugh, Savage-Rumbaugh, & Pate, 1988). Chimpanzees can even remember over a period of 20 minutes which of two containers holds more bananas (e.g., 5 versus 8, or 6 versus 10), after watching the bananas being placed one at a time into the containers. In fact, they do as well as young children on this task (Beran & Beran, 2004).

Some researchers (though not all) believe that the great apes—chimpanzees, gorillas, and orangutans—and possibly dolphins and elephants, as well, have an understanding of how their own minds and the minds of others work (de Waal, 2001a; Plotnik de Waal, & Reiss, 2006; Suddendorf & Whiten, 2001). When looking in a mirror, these animals may try to find marks on their bodies that are not directly visible, suggesting self-recognition. In addition, chimpanzees console other chimps who are in distress, use deceptive tactics when competing for food, and point to draw attention to objects; these abilities all imply an ability to grasp what is going on in another individual's mind.

Animals and Language

A primary ingredient of human cognition is *language*, the ability to combine elements that are themselves meaningless into an infinite number of utterances that convey meaning. As we saw in Chapter 3, language allows us to express and comprehend an infinite number of novel utterances, created on the spot. We seem to be the only species that evolved to do this naturally. Other primates use a variety of grunts and screeches to warn each other of danger, to attract attention, and to express emotions, but the sounds are not combined to produce original sentences (at least, as far as we can tell). Bongo may make a certain sound when he finds food, but he cannot say, "The bananas in the next grove are a lot riper than the ones we ate last week and sure beat our usual diet of termites."

Perhaps, however, some animals could acquire language if they got a little help from their human friends. Because the vocal tract of an ape does not permit speech, most researchers have tried innovative approaches that rely on gestures or visual symbols. In one project, chimpanzees learned to use as words various geometric plastic shapes arranged on a magnetic board (Premack & Premack, 1983). In another, they learned to punch symbols on a computer-monitored keyboard (Rumbaugh, 1977). In other projects, chimps and a gorilla named Koko mastered hundreds of signs in American Sign Language (ASL) (Fouts & Rigby, 1977; Gardner & Gardner, 1969; Patterson & Linden, 1981). The animals in these studies learned to follow instructions, answer questions, and make requests. They even seemed to be using their

"It's always 'Sit,' 'Stay,' 'Heel'—never 'Think,' 'Innovate,' 'Be yourself.'"

newfound skills to apologize for being disobedient, scold their trainers, lie when they were naughty, and talk to themselves. Most important, they combined individual signs or symbols into longer utterances that they had never seen before.

Because the apes were lovable and the findings appealing, in early studies it was easy for emotional reasoning to prevail over critical thinking. In their desire to talk to the animals and their affection for their primate friends, some researchers overinterpreted the animals' utterances, reading all sorts of meanings and intentions into a single sign or symbol, and unwittingly giving nonverbal cues that might enable the apes to respond correctly. Further, to some observers, the animals appeared to be stringing signs and symbols together in no particular order instead of using grammatical rules to produce novel utterances. "Me eat banana" seemed to be no different for them than "Banana eat me."

Thinking Critically About Apes and Language

Over the past few decades, however, most researchers have greatly improved their procedures. They have shown that with careful training chimps can indeed acquire the ability to use symbols to refer to objects. Some animals have also used signs spontaneously to converse with each other, suggesting that they are not merely imitating or trying to get a reward (Van Cantfort & Rimpau, 1982). Bonobos (a type of ape) are especially adept at language. One bonobo named Kanzi has learned to understand English words, short sentences, and keyboard symbols without formal training (Savage-Rumbaugh & Lewin, 1994; Savage-Rumbaugh, Shanker, & Taylor, 1998). Kanzi responds correctly to commands such as "Put the key in the refrigerator" and "Go get the ball that is outdoors," even when he has never heard the words combined in that particular way before. He picked up language as children do—by observing others using it and through normal social interaction. He has also learned, with training, to manipulate keyboard symbols to request favorite foods or activities (games, TV, visits to friends) and to announce his intentions.

You do not even have to be a primate to acquire some aspects of language. Dolphins have learned to understand the difference between requests such as "To left Frisbee, right surfboard take" and "To right surfboard, left Frisbee take," communicated in an artificial gestural language (Herman, Kuczaj, & Holder, 1993). And for many years, Irene Pepperberg (2000) has been working with an African gray parrot named Alex, teaching him to count, classify, and compare objects by vocalizing English words. Alex is no birdbrain, even though his brain is the size of a walnut; he shows evidence of both linguistic and

Kanzi, a bonobo with the most advanced linguistic skills yet acquired by a nonhuman primate, answers questions and makes requests by punching symbols on a specially designed computer keyboard. He also understands short English sentences. Kanzi is shown here with researcher Sue Savage-Rumbaugh.

cognitive ability. When he is shown up to six items and is asked how many there are, he responds with spoken (squawked?) English phrases, such as "two cork(s)" or "four key(s)." He can even respond correctly to questions about items specified on two or three dimensions, as in "How many blue key(s)?" or "What matter [material] is orange and three-cornered?" Alex also makes requests ("Want pasta") and answers simple questions about objects ("What color [is this]?" "Which is bigger?"). When he is presented with a blue cork and a blue key and is asked, "What's the same?" he will correctly respond, "Color." He actually scores slightly better with new

Alex is one clever bird. His abilities raise intriguing questions about the intelligence of animals and their capacity for specific aspects of language.

objects than with familiar ones, suggesting that he is not merely "parroting" a set of stock phrases. In recent work, he shows evidence of being able to sum two small sets of objects, such as nuts or jelly beans, for sums up to six (Pepperberg, 2006). In informal interactions, Alex tells Pepperberg, "I love you," "I'm sorry," and "Calm down."

Thinking About the Thinking of Animals

These results on animal language and cognition are impressive, but scientists are still divided over just what they mean. Do the animals have true language? Are they thinking, in human terms? How intelligent are they?

On one side are those who worry about *anthropomorphism*, the tendency to falsely attribute human qualities to nonhuman beings. They tell the story of Clever Hans, a "wonder horse" at the beginning of the twentieth century, who was said to possess mathematical and other abilities (Spitz, 1997). Clever Hans would answer math questions by stamping his hoof the appropriate number of times and respond to other questions by tapping in an established code. But a little careful experimentation by psychologist Oskar Pfungst (1911/1965) revealed that when Hans was prevented from seeing his questioners, or when they did not know the answers themselves, his powers left him. It seems that questioners were staring at the animal's feet and leaning forward expectantly after stating the problem, then lifting their eyes and relaxing as soon as he completed the right number of taps. Clever Hans was indeed clever, but not at math or other human skills. He was merely responding to nonverbal signals that people were inadvertently providing. (Perhaps he had a high EQ.)

This old photo shows Clever Hans in action. His story has taught researchers to beware of anthropomorphism when they interpret findings on animal cognition.

On the other side are those who warn against *anthropodenial*, the tendency to think, mistakenly, that human beings have nothing in common with other animals, who are, after all, our evolutionary cousins (de Waal, 1997, 2001a; Fouts, 1997). The need to see our own species as unique, they say, may keep us from recognizing that other species, too, have cognitive abilities, even if not as intricate as our own. Those who take this position point out that most modern researchers have gone to great lengths to avoid the Clever Hans problem.

The outcome of this debate is bound to have an effect on how we view ourselves and our place among other species. Perhaps, as cognitive ethologist Marc Hauser (2000) has suggested, we can find a way to study and respect animal minds and emotions without assuming sentimentally that they are just like ours.

QUICK quiz

Regrettably, your pet beagle can't help you answer these questions.

1. Which of the following abilities have primates demonstrated, either in the natural environment or the laboratory? (a) the use of objects as simple tools; (b) the summing of quantities; (c) the use of symbols to make requests; (d) an understanding of short English sentences

2. Barnaby thinks that his pet snake Curly is harboring angry thoughts about him because Curly has been standoffish and won't curl around his neck anymore. What error is Barnaby making?

Answers:

1. all of them 2. anthropomorphism

Courtesy of Andrew Toos/CartoonStock.com

We human beings have always thought of ourselves as the smartest species around, and for good reason. We have an astounding ability to adapt to change, solve problems in novel ways, invent endless new gizmos, and use language to create everything from puns to poetry. Yet as this chapter has shown, we are not always as wise in our thinking as we might think, and we may not even be the only animal capable of thought. As if that weren't bad enough, now some people are saying, as in our opening story, that machines are gaining on us in the mental-abilities department—a frequent theme in movies such as the *Matrix* series. Will computers and robots eventually be able to make crucial decisions for us on how to improve public education, manage a baseball team, or schedule the fall TV lineup?

That's hardly likely. Consider the chess-playing accomplishments of Deep Blue, Deep Junior, and Hydra or, more accurately, the accomplishments of the human programmers who wrote the machines' software. Although the computers' feats are impressive, real intelligence is more than the capacity to perform computations with lightning speed. As we have seen, it involves the ability to deal with informal reasoning problems, reason dialectically and reflectively, devise mental shortcuts, read emotions, and acquire tacit knowledge. Intelligence also involves mental efficiency: Human beings are intelligent not because they can consider millions of chess positions a second but because they don't have to! A chess-playing computer's raw calculating power disguises its inefficiency; it wins by rejecting the same moves millions of times (McCarthy, 1997).

From time to time, a commentator will predict that in the near future, computers and robots will be as smart as we are. But most experts disagree. One robot inventor, when asked whether self-reproducing robots could figure out how to become a doomsday machine and threaten the world, said that such a prospect is "as far off as a fax machine is from a Star Trek transporter" (quoted in Chang, 2000). Others point out that robots lack the most important requirement for ruling the universe: a mind of their own. They also lack the feelings and emotional skills that give us emotional intelligence and make our decisions wiser.

Robots and computers, of course, are not the least bit troubled by their lack of cleverness, inasmuch as they lack a mind to be troubled. As computer scientist David Gelernter (1997) wrote after Deep Blue's victory, "How can an object that wants nothing, fears nothing, enjoys nothing, needs nothing, and cares about nothing have a mind?" Because machines are mindless, they also lack a trait that distinguishes human beings not only from computers but also from other species: We try to understand our own misunderstandings. We want to know what we don't know; we are motivated to overcome our mental shortcomings. Our uniquely human capacity for self-examination is probably the best reason to remain optimistic about our cognitive abilities.

Human beings worry that machines will outsmart them, but it's not likely.

➤TAKING ➤PSYCHOLOGY ➤WITH ➤YOU

Becoming More Creative

Take a few moments to answer these items from the Remote Associates Test. Your task is to come up with a fourth word that is associated with each item in a set of three words (Mednick, 1962). For example, an appropriate answer for the set *news–clip–wall* is *paper*. Got the idea? Now try these (the answers are given on page 261):

(1) piggy–green–lash
(2) surprise–political–favor
(3) mark–shelf–telephone
(4) stick–maker–tennis
(5) cream–cottage–cloth

Associating elements in new ways by finding a common connection among them is an important component of creativity. People who are uncreative rely on *convergent thinking*, following a particular set of steps that they think will converge on one correct solution. Once they have solved a problem, they tend to develop a mental set and approach future problems in the same way.

Creative people, in contrast, exercise *divergent thinking*; instead of stubbornly sticking to one tried-and-true path, they explore some side alleys and generate several possible solutions. They come up with new hypotheses, imagine other interpretations, and look for connections that may not be immediately obvious. They can think of many uses for familiar objects, such as, say, unneeded CDs (which can be used as mobiles, Christmas tree decorations, coasters, . . .). As a result, they are able to use familiar concepts in un-expected ways. Creative thinking can be found in the auto mechanic who invents a new tool, the mother who designs and makes her children's clothes, or the office manager who devises a clever way to streamline work flow (Richards, 1991).

A high IQ does not guarantee creativity. Personality characteristics seem more important, especially these three (Helson, Roberts, & Agronick, 1995; MacKinnon, 1968; McCrae, 1987; Schank, 1988):

● **Nonconformity.** Creative individuals are not overly concerned about what others think of them. They are willing to risk ridicule by proposing ideas that may initially appear foolish or off the mark. Geneticist Barbara McClintock's research was ignored or belittled by many for nearly 30 years. But she was sure she could show how genes move around and produce sudden changes in heredity. In 1983, when McClintock won the Nobel Prize, the judges called her work the second greatest genetic discovery of our time, after the discovery of the structure of DNA.

● **Curiosity.** Creative people are open to new experiences; they notice when reality contradicts expectations, and they are curious about the reason. For example, Wilhelm Roentgen, a German physicist, was studying cathode rays when he noticed a strange glow on one of his screens. Other people had seen the glow, but they ignored it because it didn't jibe with their understanding of cathode rays. Roentgen studied the glow, found it to be a new kind of radiation, and thus discovered X-rays (Briggs, 1984).

● **Persistence.** After that imaginary light bulb goes on over your head, you still have to work hard to make the illumination last. Or as Thomas Edison, who invented the real light-bulb, reportedly put it, "Genius is one-tenth inspiration and nine-tenths perspiration." No invention or work of art springs forth full-blown from a person's head. There are many false starts and painful revisions along the way.

In addition to traits that foster creativity, there are *circumstances* that do so. Creativity flourishes when schools and employers encourage intrinsic motivation and not just extrinsic rewards such as gold stars or money (see Chapters 9 and 14). Intrinsic motives include a sense of accomplishment, intellectual fulfillment, the satisfaction of curiosity, and the sheer love of the activity. Creativity also increases when people have control over how to perform a task or solve a problem, are evaluated unobtrusively instead of being constantly observed and judged, and work independently (Amabile, 1983). Organizations encourage creativity when they let people take risks, give them plenty of time to think about problems, and welcome innovation.

In sum, if you hope to become more creative, there are two things you can do. One is to cultivate qualities in you: your skills, intrinsic motivation, and self-discipline. The other is to seek out the kinds of situations that will permit you to express your abilities and experiment with new ideas.

SUMMARY

Thought: Using What We Know

• Thinking is the mental manipulation of information. Our mental representations simplify and summarize information from the environment.

• A *concept* is a mental category that groups objects, relations, activities, abstractions, or qualities that share certain properties. *Prototypical* instances of a concept are more representative than others. The language we use to express concepts may influence how we perceive and think about the world—a notion first proposed years ago by Benjamin Lee Whorf that is now getting renewed attention.

• *Propositions* are made up of concepts and express a unitary idea. They may be linked together to form *cognitive schemas*, which serve as mental models of aspects of the world. *Mental images* also play a role in thinking.

• Not all mental processing is conscious. *Subconscious processes* lie outside of awareness but can be brought into consciousness when necessary. They allow us to perform two or more actions at once when one action is highly automatic. But multitasking is usually inefficient, introduces errors, and can even be dangerous, for example, if done while driving. *Nonconscious processes* remain outside of awareness but nonetheless affect behavior and are involved in what we call "intuition" and "insight" and in *implicit learning*. Conscious processing may be carried out in a *mindless* fashion if we overlook changes in context that call for a change in behavior.

Reasoning Rationally

• *Reasoning* is purposeful mental activity that involves drawing inferences and conclusions from observations or propositions (premises).

• *Formal reasoning problems* can often be solved by applying an *algorithm,* a set of procedures that are guaranteed to produce a solution, or by using logical processes, such as *deductive* and *inductive reasoning*.

• *Informal reasoning problems* often have no clearly correct solution. Disagreement may exist about basic premises, information may be incomplete, and many viewpoints may compete. Such problems often call for the application of *heuristics,* rules of thumb that suggest a course of action without guaranteeing an optimal solution. They may also require *dialectical reasoning* about opposing points of view.

• Studies of *reflective judgment* show that many people have trouble thinking dialectically. People in the *prereflective* stages do not distinguish between knowledge and belief or between belief and evidence. Those in the *quasi-reflective* stages think that because knowledge is sometimes uncertain, any judgment about the evidence is purely subjective. Those who think *reflectively* understand that although some things cannot be known with certainty, some judgments are more valid than others because of their coherence, usefulness, fit with the evidence, and so on. Higher education moves people gradually closer to reflective judgment.

Barriers to Reasoning Rationally

• The ability to reason clearly and rationally is affected by many cognitive biases. People tend to exaggerate the likelihood of improbable events, in part because of the *affect* and *availability heuristics.* They are swayed in their choices by the desire to *avoid loss*. They forego economic gain because of a *fairness bias*. They often overestimate their ability to have made accurate predictions (the *hindsight bias*), attend mostly to evidence that confirms what they want to believe (the *confirmation bias*), and are mentally rigid, forming *mental sets* and seeing patterns where none exists.

• The theory of *cognitive dissonance* holds that people are motivated to reduce the tension that exists when two cognitions conflict—by rejecting or changing a belief, changing their behavior, or rationalizing. People are especially likely to do so when they need to justify a decision (i.e., reduce *postdecision dissonance*), when their actions violate their self-concept, or when they have put hard work into an activity (the *justification of effort*).

Intelligence

• *Intelligence* is hard to define. Some theorists believe that a general ability (a *g factor*) underlies the many specific abilities tapped by intelligence tests, whereas others do not.

• The traditional approach to intelligence, the *psychometric approach,* focuses on how well people perform on standardized aptitude tests. The *intelligence quotient,* or *IQ,* represents how a person has done on an intelligence test, compared to other people. Alfred Binet designed the first widely used intelligence test for the purpose of identifying children who could benefit from remedial work. But in the United States, people assumed that intelligence tests revealed "natural ability," and they used the tests to categorize people in school and in the armed services.

• IQ tests have been criticized for being biased in favor of white, middle-class people. However, efforts to construct tests that are free of cultural influence have been disappointing. Culture affects nearly everything to do with taking a test, from attitudes to problem-solving strategies. Negative stereotypes about a person's ethnicity, gender, or age may cause the person to suffer *stereotype threat,* a burden of doubt about his or her own abilities, which can lead to anxiety or "disidentification" with the test.

• In contrast to the psychometric approach, *cognitive approaches* to intelligence emphasize several kinds of intelligence and the strategies people use to solve problems rather than merely whether they get the right answers. Sternberg's *triarchic theory of intelligence* proposes three aspects of intelligence: *componential* (including *metacognition*), *experiential or creative*, and *contextual or practical*. Contextual intelligence allows you to acquire *tacit knowledge,* practical strategies that are not explicitly taught but are important for success.

• Intelligence in one domain does not necessarily imply intelligence in another. Howard Gardner proposes that there are actually several "intelligences" besides those usually considered, including musical and kinesthetic intelligence, and the capacity to understand the natural world, yourself, or others. The latter two overlap with what some psychologists call *emotional intelligence*.

The Origins of Intelligence

• Behavioral-genetic studies estimate the *heritability* of intelligence (as measured by IQ tests) to be high: about .50 for children and adolescents and .60 to .80 for adults. But these results do not mean that genes determine intelligence, or that group differences in intelligence are genetic. Further, it is not valid to draw conclusions about ethnic differences in intelligence from estimates based on differences within a group. The available evidence fails to support genetic explanations of these differences.

• Environmental factors such as poor prenatal care, malnutrition, exposure to toxins and pollution, and stressful family circumstances are associated with lower performance on mental tests, and a healthy and stimulating environment can improve performance.

• Intellectual achievement also depends on motivation, hard work, and attitudes. As we saw in "Close-up on Research," in teenagers self-discipline predicts grades even better than IQ does. Cross-cultural research shows that beliefs about the origins of mental abilities, parental standards, and attitudes toward education can also help account for differences in academic performance.

Animal Minds

• Some researchers, especially those in the field of *cognitive ethology*, argue that nonhuman animals have greater cognitive abilities than is usually thought. Some animals can use objects as rudimentary tools. Chimpanzees have learned to use numerals to label quantities of items and symbols to refer to objects. Great apes, and possibly other animals, sometimes do things that suggest they may have some understanding of how their own minds and the minds of others work.

• In several projects using visual symbol systems or American Sign Language (ASL), primates have acquired linguistic skills. Some animals (even some nonprimates) seem able to use simple grammatical ordering rules to convey or comprehend meaning. However, scientists are still divided as to how to interpret these findings and the research on animal cognition, with some worrying about *anthropomorphism* and others about *anthropodenial*.

KEY TERMS

concept 226

prototype 226

proposition 227

cognitive schema 227

mental image 227

subconscious
  processes 228

nonconscious
  processes 228

implicit learning 229

mindlessness 229

reasoning 230

formal reasoning
  problems 230

algorithm 230

deductive
  reasoning 230

inductive
  reasoning 230

informal reasoning
  problems 231

heuristic 231

dialectical
  reasoning 231

reflective judgment 232

prereflective
  stages 232

quasi-reflective
  stages 232

reflective stages 232

affect heuristic 234

availability
  heuristic 234

avoidance of loss 235

fairness bias 235

hindsight bias 236

confirmation
  bias 237

mental sets 237

cognitive
  dissonance 238

postdecision
  dissonance 239

justification
  of effort 239

intelligence 240

factor analysis 240

g factor 240

psychometric
  approach to
  intelligence 241

mental age
  (MA) 241

intelligence
  quotient (IQ) 241

Stanford–Binet
  Intelligence
  Scale 242

Answers to the Remote Associates Test on page 258: back, party, book, match, cheese

*Some solutions to the nine-dot problem in the Get Involved exercise on page 237
(from Adams, 1986):*

(a)

(b)

Cut the puzzle apart, tape it together
in a different format, and use
one line.

(c)

(d)

Roll up the puzzle
and draw a spiral
through the dots.

(e)

1 line 0 Folds

Lay the paper on the
surface of the Earth.
Circumnavigate the
globe twice + a few
inches, displacing a little
each time so as to pass
through the next row
on each circuit as you
"Go West, young man."

(f)

~ 2 Lines* 0 Folds

*Statistical

Draw dots as large as
possible. Wad paper into
a ball. Stab with pencil.
Open up and see if you
did it. If not, try again.
"Nobody loses: play
until you win."

(g)

May 30,1974
5 FDR   Navasa
Roosevelt Rds.Na
Ceiba,PR 00635
Dear Prof.James L. Adams,
         My dad and I were
doing Puzzles from "Conceptual
Blockbusting." We were mostly
working on the dot ones,
like ⋮⋮⋮ My dad said a
man found a way to do it
with one line. I tried and
did it. Not with folding,
but I used a fat line. I
does'nt say you can't use
a fat line. Like this➡ ◢
P.S.
acctually you
need a very   Sincerely,
fat writing   Becky Buechel
apparatice.   age:10

(h)

Thought

Elements of Cognition

- **Thinking** is the mental manipulation of information.
- A **concept** is a mental category that groups objects, relations, activities, abstractions, or qualities that share certain properties.
- **Prototypical** instances of a concept are more representative than others.
- The words and grammatical rules used to express concepts may influence how we think about them.
- **Propositions** are made up of concepts and express a unitary idea. They may be linked together to form **cognitive schemas**, which serve as mental models of aspects of the world.
- **Mental images** also play a role in thinking.

How Conscious Is Thought?

- **Subconscious processes** lie outside of awareness but can be brought into consciousness when necessary.
- **Nonconscious processes** remain outside of awareness but are involved in what we call "intuition" and in **implicit learning.**
- **Mindlessness** keeps people from recognizing the need for a change in behavior.

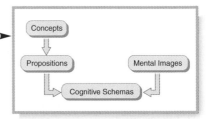

Reasoning Rationally

Reasoning

Reasoning is purposeful mental activity that involves drawing inferences and conclusions from observations or propositions.

Informal Reasoning Problems

Informal reasoning problems often have no clearly correct solution.
- **Heuristics** are rules of thumb that suggest a course of action without guaranteeing an optimal solution.
- **Dialectical** reasoning is a process of comparing and evaluating opposing points of view.

Reflective Judgment

Reflective judgment is the ability to evaluate and integrate evidence, consider alternative interpretations, and reach a defensible conclusion.

Formal Reasoning Problems

Formal reasoning problems can often be solved by:
- Applying an **algorithm**, a set of procedures guaranteed to produce each solution
- Using logical processes
- **Deductive reasoning**

- **Inductive reasoning**

Barriers to Reasoning Rationally

Many cognitive biases are obstacles to rational thinking.
1. Exaggerating the probability of improbable events, in part because of the **affect** and **availability heuristics.**
2. Avoidance of loss
3. The **fairness bias**
4. The **hindsight bias**
5. The **confirmation bias**
6. Formation of **mental sets**
7. Avoidance of **cognitive dissonance**: people are motivated to reduce the tension created when two cognitions or a cognition and a behavior conflict.

Intelligence

Intelligence is an inferred characteristic, usually defined as the ability to profit from experience, acquire knowledge, think abstractly, act purposefully, or adapt to change.

The Origins of Intelligence

Behavioral-genetic studies show the **heritability** of intelligence (as measured by IQ tests) to be high.

The Question of Group Differences

- Genetic explanations of black–white differences in IQ inappropriately use heritability estimates based mainly on white samples.
- Environmental influences on intelligence include:
  — Poor prenatal care
  — Malnutrition
  — Exposure to toxins
  — Stressful family circumstances

Motivation and Intellectual Success

- Intellectual performance is strongly influenced by motivation and self-discipline.
- These in turn are affected by cultural (parental) expectations, attitudes toward education, and beliefs about the origins of mental abilities.

Measuring Intelligence

The **psychometric approach** to intelligence focuses on performance on standardized aptitude tests.
- The **intelligence quotient (IQ)** represents a person's score on a particular test, compared to others' scores.
- Alfred Binet invented IQ tests to objectively identify slow learners for remediation.
- Efforts to create intelligence tests unaffected by culture have been disappointing.
- **Stereotype threat** can affect the test performance of women and minority groups.

Dissecting Intelligence

Cognitive approaches emphasize problem-solving strategies and several kinds of intelligence, rather than a **g factor**.

The **triarchic theory** proposes three aspects of intelligence:
- Componential (includes metacognition)
- Experiential or creative
- Contextual or practical

Other theories propose multiple domains of intelligence. A leading one emphasizes **emotional intelligence**.

Animal Minds

Animal Intelligence

- Some animals can use rudimentary tools.
- Chimpanzees can learn to use numerals and symbols.
- Great apes may have some understanding of their own minds and those of others.

Animals and Language

In several studies, primates and other animals have acquired some aspects of human language.

Wrongly Convicted Man Set Free

THE BRONX, NY, JULY 7, 2006. After spending more than two decades of his life in New York's toughest prisons for a crime he did not commit, Alan Newton, 44, finally became a free man in a Bronx courtroom yesterday, as friends and family clapped and cheered. On hand were two brothers and five sisters, as well as several nieces and nephews who had not yet been born when Newton went to prison.

In 1985, Newton was convicted of brutally raping a 25-year-old woman in an abandoned Bronx building. The victim, who was certain she was identifying the man who had assaulted her, had picked Newton out of a lineup. The use of lineups by police has long been standard operating procedure to help crime victims verify the identity of perpetrators.

Alan Newton was convicted solely on the basis of the victim's testimony that he was the rapist. He was sentenced to up to 40 years in prison. There he remained for over two decades, steadfastly maintaining his innocence. Because he was determined to clear his name, during his long incarceration he refused to improve his chances for parole by changing his plea or by joining a sex offenders rehab group.

In 1994, Newton filed a motion requesting a DNA test, which he was sure would exonerate him, but his request was denied because the evidence was said to be unavailable. Over the years, he kept renewing his requests, but the police insisted three separate times that they could not find the rape kit from the case.

Then, in 2005, the Innocence Project, a nonprofit legal clinic that works for the release of wrongfully convicted inmates, took action on Newton's behalf. At the request of the group's lawyers, the Bronx district attorney's office asked the New York City Police Department to search once again for the kit at an evidence warehouse in Queens. This time the kit turned up, exactly where it had originally been stored and had remained all those years. The results of testing showed conclusively that Newton could not have been the assailant.

After he was freed, Newton said he planned to visit the grave of his mother, who died about 10 years ago. "Mom died of a broken heart," said one of his sisters. Newton also thanked his attorneys and said he felt no bitterness toward the woman whose testimony had led to his confinement at the state's toughest penitentiaries. "My unjust conviction denied both of us justice," he said. "It opens up old wounds and denies her closure. . . . Being angry will not allow you to grow."

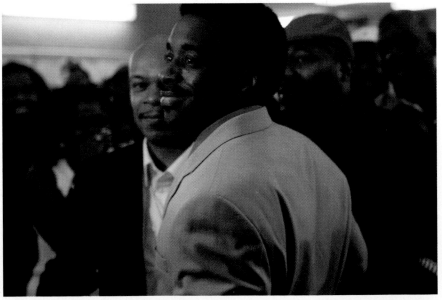

Alan Newton in court after his release from prison. DNA evidence has established that he could not have committed the rape for which he was convicted over 20 years ago.

Ozier Muhammad/The New York Times

Memory

At one time, most prosecutors and juries would have dismissed the testimony of the victim in the Alan Newton case outright. Public opinion tended to blame rape victims for having "provoked" the attack or for failing to fight back strongly enough. As people became more aware of the horrific nature of rape and the unfairness of blaming victims, however, their acceptance of women's testimony increased. Today, some defendants, like Newton, are being sent to prison or even sentenced to death almost solely on the strength of the victim's testimony.

But is an eyewitness's account always reliable? In the absence of corroborating evidence, should a victim's confidence in her memory be sufficient for establishing guilt? Much is at stake in our efforts to answer these questions: getting justice for rape victims and also avoiding the false conviction of men who are innocent.

As you read this chapter, ask yourself: When should we trust our memories, and when should we be cautious about doing so? We all forget a great deal, of course: We watch the evening news and half an hour later cannot recall the main story; we enjoy a meal and quickly forget what we ate. Do we also "remember" things that never happened? Are memory malfunctions the exception to the rule, or are they commonplace? If memory is not always reliable, how can any of us hope to know the story of our own lives? And what are the implications for the legal system, which relies so heavily on the memories of witnesses and crime victims?

WHAT'S *Ahead*

- What's wrong with thinking of memory as a mental movie camera?

- Why do "flashbulb" memories of surprising or shocking events sometimes have less wattage than we think?

- If you have a strong emotional reaction to a remembered event, does that mean your memory is accurate?

Reconstructing the Past

Memory refers to the capacity to retain and retrieve information, and also to the structures that account for this capacity. Human beings are capable of astonishing feats of memory. Most of us can easily remember the tune of our national anthem, how to use an automated teller machine, the most embarrassing experience we ever had, zillions of details about our favorite sports or films, and hundreds of thousands of other bits of information.

Memory confers competence; without it we would be as helpless as newborns, unable to carry out even the most trivial of our daily tasks. Memory also gives us a sense of personal identity; each of us is the sum of our recollections, which is why we feel so threatened when others challenge our memories. Individuals and cultures alike rely on a remembered history for a sense of coherence and meaning; memory gives us our past and guides our future.

The Manufacture of Memory

source misattribution
The inability to distinguish an actual memory of an event from information you learned elsewhere about the event.

In ancient times, philosophers compared memory to a soft wax tablet that would preserve anything that chanced to make an imprint on it. Then, with the advent of the printing press, they began to think of memory as a gigantic library, storing specific events and facts for later retrieval. Today, in the audiovisual age, many people compare memory to a tape recorder or a movie camera, automatically recording every moment of their lives.

Popular and appealing though this belief about memory is, however, it is utterly wrong. Not everything that happens to us or impinges on our senses is tucked away for later use. Memory is selective. If it were not, our minds would be cluttered with mental junk—the temperature at noon on Thursday, the price of turnips two years ago, a phone number needed only once. Moreover, recovering a memory is not at all like replaying a tape of an event; it is more like watching a few unconnected frames and then figuring out what the rest of the scene must have been like.

One of the first scientists to make this point was the British psychologist Sir Frederic Bartlett (1932). Bartlett asked people to read lengthy, unfamiliar stories from other cultures and then tell the stories back to him. As the volunteers tried to recall the stories, they made interesting errors: They often eliminated or changed details that did not make sense to them, and they added other details to make the stories coherent, sometimes even adding a moral. Memory, Bartlett concluded, must therefore be largely a *reconstructive* process. We may reproduce some kinds of simple information by rote, said Bartlett, but when we remember complex information, we typically alter it in ways that help us make sense of the material, based on what we already know or think we know. Since Bartlett's time, hundreds of studies have found this to be true for everything from stories to conversations to personal experiences.

In reconstructing their memories, people often draw on many sources. Suppose someone asks you to describe one of your early birthday parties. You may have some direct recollection of the event, but you may also incorporate information from family stories, photographs, or home videos, and even from accounts of other people's birthdays and reenactments of birthdays on television. You take all these bits and pieces and build one integrated account. Later, you may not be able to separate your original experience from what you added after the fact—a phenomenon called **source misattribution** or sometimes *source confusion* (Johnson, Hashtroudi, & Lindsay, 1993).

A dramatic instance of reconstruction once occurred in the sad case of H. M., whom we described briefly in Chapter 4. Ever since 1953, when much of H. M.'s hippocampus and the adjacent cortex were surgically removed, he has been unable to form lasting

If these children remember this birthday party later in life, their constructions may include information picked up from family photographs, videos, and stories. And they will probably be unable to distinguish their actual memories from information they got elsewhere.

memories for new events, facts, songs, stories, or faces, and so he does not remember much of anything that has happened since his operation (Hilts, 1995; Ogden & Corkin, 1991). To cope with his devastating condition, H. M. has sometimes resorted to reconstructions. On one occasion, after eating a chocolate Valentine's Day heart, H. M. stuck the shiny red wrapping in his shirt pocket. Two hours later, while searching for his handkerchief, he pulled out the paper and looked at it in puzzlement. When a researcher asked why he had the paper in his pocket, he replied, "Well, it could have been wrapped around a big chocolate heart. It must be Valentine's Day!" But a short time later, when she asked him to take out the paper again and say why he had it in his pocket, he replied, "Well, it might have been wrapped around a big chocolate rabbit. It must be Easter!"

H. M. *had* to reconstruct the past; his damaged brain could not recall it in any other way. But those of us with normal memory abilities also reconstruct far more often than we realize.

The Fading Flashbulb

Of course, some unusual, shocking, or tragic events, such as earthquakes or accidents, do hold a special place in memory, especially when we have experienced them personally. Such events seem frozen in time, with all the details intact. Years ago, Roger Brown and James Kulik (1977) labeled these vivid recollections of emotional events *flashbulb memories* because that term captures the surprise, illumination, and seemingly photographic detail that characterize them. They speculated that the capacity for flashbulb memories may have evolved

because such memories had survival value. Remembering the details of a surprising or dangerous experience could have helped our ancestors avoid similar situations.

In some cases, flashbulb memories have lasted for years, even decades. For example, in a Danish study, older people who had lived through the Nazi occupation of their country in World War II often had an accurate memory of verifiable wartime events, such as the time of day that the radio had announced liberation and what the weather had been like at the time (Berntsen & Thomsen, 2005). Despite their intensity, however, even flashbulb memories are not always complete or accurate records of the past. Usually people remember the *gist* of

Thinking Critically About "Flashbulb" Memories

a startling, emotional event they experienced or witnessed, such as a violent shoot-out, the assassination of an admired politician, or the explosion of a space shuttle. But when researchers question them about their memories over time, errors creep into the details, and after a few years, some people even forget the gist (Neisser & Harsch, 1992).

On September 12, 2001, just one day after the attacks on the World Trade Center and the Pentagon, researchers asked 54 college students when they had first heard the news of the attacks, who had told them the news, and what they had been doing at the time. The students were also asked to report details about a mundane event from the days immediately before the attacks, so that

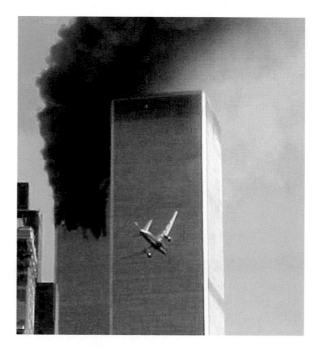

Many people have vivid "flashbulb" memories of the attack on the World Trade Center on September 11, 2001. But even flashbulb memories are not always complete or accurate, and they often change over time. For example, some people are convinced they saw the first attack on television as it was occurring, but that is impossible, as no film crews knew in advance it would happen!

confabulation
Confusion of an event that happened to someone else with one that happened to you, or a belief that you remember something when it never actually happened.

the researchers could compare ordinary memories with flashbulb ones. One group was then retested a week later, a second group 6 weeks later, and a third group 32 weeks later. The students also completed a questionnaire that measured the vividness and emotional intensity of their memories and their confidence in their accuracy. Over time, the vividness of the flashbulb memories and the students' confidence in these memories remained higher than for the everyday memories. Their confidence, however, was misplaced. The details reported by the students became less and less consistent for *both* types of memories; in fact, the flashbulb memories contained just as many inconsistent details as the everyday ones (Talarico & Rubin, 2003).

Even with flashbulb memories, then, facts tend to get mixed with a little fiction. The conclusion is inescapable: Remembering is an active process, one that involves not only dredging up stored information but also putting two and two together to reconstruct the past. And sometimes we put two and two together and get five.

The Conditions of Confabulation

Because memory is reconstructive, it is subject to **confabulation**—confusing an event that happened to someone else with one that happened to you, or coming to believe that you remember something that never really happened. Such confabulations are especially likely under certain circumstances (Garry, Manning, & Loftus, 1996; Hyman & Pentland, 1996; Johnson, 1995):

1 *You have thought, heard, or told others about the imagined event many times.* Suppose that at family gatherings you keep hearing about the time that Uncle Sam scared everyone at a New Year's party by pounding a hammer into the

wall with such force that the wall collapsed. The story is so colorful that you can practically see Uncle Sam in your mind's eye. The more you think about this event, the more likely you are to believe that you were actually there, even if you were sound asleep in another house. This process has been called imagination inflation, because your own active imagination inflates your belief that the event really occurred (Garry & Loftus, 2000). Even merely explaining how a hypothetical childhood experience *could* have happened inflates people's confidence that it really did. Explaining an event makes it seem more familiar and thus real (Sharman, Manning, & Garry, 2005).

2 *The image of the event contains lots of details that make it feel real.* Ordinarily, we can distinguish an imagined event from a real one by the amount of detail we recall; real events tend to produce more details. However, the longer you think about an imagined event, the more details you are likely to add—what Sam was wearing, the fact that he'd had too much to drink, the crumbling plaster, people standing around in party hats—and these details may in turn persuade you that the event really happened and that you have a direct memory of it.

3 *The event is easy to imagine.* If imagining an event takes little effort (as does visualizing a man pounding a wall with a hammer), then we tend to think that our memory is real. In contrast, when we must make an effort to form an image of an experience—for example, of being in a place that we have never seen or doing something that is utterly foreign to us—our cognitive efforts apparently serve as a cue that the event did not really take place, or that we were not there when it did.

As a result of "imagination inflation," you can end up with a memory that feels emotionally, vividly real to you, yet it can be completely false. This means that your feelings about an event, no matter how strong they are, do not guarantee that the event really happened. Consider again our Sam story, which happens to be true. A woman we know believed for years that she had been present in the room as an 11-year-old child when her uncle destroyed the wall. Because the story was so vivid and upsetting to her, she felt angry at him for what she thought was his mean and violent behavior, and she assumed that she must have been angry at the time as well. Then, as an adult, she learned that she was not at the party at all but had merely heard about it repeatedly over

NEVER FORGETS

SOMETIMES FORGETS

ALWAYS FORGETS

the years. Sam had not pounded the wall in anger, but as a joke, to inform the assembled guests that he and his wife were about to remodel their home. Nevertheless, our friend's family has had a hard time convincing her that her "memory" of this event is entirely wrong, and they are not sure she believes them yet.

As the Sam story illustrates, and as laboratory research verifies, false memories can be as stable over time as true ones (Brainerd, Reyna, & Brandse, 1995; Poole, 1995; Roediger & McDermott, 1995). There's just no getting around it: Memory is reconstructive.

In the 1980s, in his best-seller Communion, Whitley Strieber described encounters with nonhuman beings, possibly aliens from outer space. An art director designed this striking cover. Since then, many people have assumed that this is what an extraterrestrial must look like, and some have imported the image into their own confabulated memories of alien abduction.

QUICK quiz

Can you reconstruct what you have read so far in order to answer these questions?

1. Memory is like (a) a wax tablet, (b) a giant file cabinet, (c) a video camera, (d) none of these.

2. *True or false*: Because they are so vivid, flashbulb memories remain perfectly accurate over time.

3. Which of the following confabulated "memories" might people be most inclined to accept as having really happened to them, and why? (a) getting lost in a shopping center at the age of 5, (b) taking a class in astrophysics, (c) visiting a monastery in Tibet as a child, (d) being bullied by another kid in the fourth grade

Answers:

1. d   2. false   3. a and d because they are common events that are easy to imagine in vivid detail. It would be harder to induce someone to believe that he or she had studied astrophysics or visited Tibet, because these are rare events that take an effort to imagine.

WHAT'S *Ahead*

- Can your memories of an event be affected by the way someone questions you about it?

- Can children's testimony about sexual abuse always be trusted?

Memory and the Power of Suggestion

The reconstructive nature of memory helps the mind work efficiently. Instead of cramming our brains with infinite details, we can store the essentials of an experience and then use our knowledge of the world to figure out the specifics when we need them. But precisely because memory is reconstructive, it is also vulnerable to suggestion—to ideas implanted in our minds after the event, which then become associated with it. This fact raises thorny problems in legal cases that involve eyewitness testimony or people's memories of what happened, when, and to whom.

The Eyewitness on Trial

Without the accounts of eyewitnesses, many guilty people would go free. But eyewitness testimony is not always reliable, even when the witness is certain about the accuracy of his or her report. Lineups—a staple of TV shows like *Law and Order*—don't necessarily help, because witnesses may simply identify the person in the line who looks most like the perpetrator of the crime (Wells & Olson, 2003). As a result, some convictions based on eyewitness testimony, like that of Alan Newton, turn out to be tragic mistakes.

Eyewitnesses are especially likely to make mistaken identifications when the suspect's ethnicity differs from their own. When people say of another group, "They all look alike to me," often, unfortunately, they are telling the truth. Because of unfamiliarity with or prejudice toward other ethnic groups, the eyewitness may focus solely on the ethnicity of the person they see committing a crime ("He's black"; "He's white"; "He's an Arab") and ignore the distinctive features that would later make identification more accurate (Levin, 2000; Meissner & Brigham, 2001).

In a program of research spanning more than three decades, Elizabeth Loftus and her colleagues have shown that the memories of eyewitnesses are also influenced by the way in which questions are put to the witness and by suggestive comments made during an interrogation or interview. In one classic study, the researchers showed how even subtle changes in the wording of questions can lead a witness to give different answers. People first viewed short films depicting car collisions. Afterward, the researchers asked some of them, "About how fast were the cars going when they hit each other?"

Other viewers were asked the same question, but with the verb changed to *smashed, collided, bumped,* or *contacted.* Estimates of how fast the cars were going varied, depending on which word was used. *Smashed* produced the highest average speed estimates (40.8 mph), followed by *collided* (39.3 mph), *bumped* (38.1 mph), *hit* (34.0 mph), and *contacted* (31.8 mph) (Loftus & Palmer, 1974).

In a similar study, the researchers asked some participants, "Did you see a broken headlight?" but asked others, "Did you see the broken headlight?" (Loftus & Zanni, 1975). The question with *the* presupposes a broken headlight and merely asks whether the witness saw it, whereas the question with *a* makes no such presupposition. People who received questions with *the* were far more likely to report having seen something that had not really appeared in the film than were those who received questions with *a.* If a tiny word like *the* can lead people to "remember" what they never saw, you can imagine how the leading questions of police detectives and lawyers might influence a witness's recall.

Misleading information from other sources, too, can profoundly alter what witnesses report. Consider what happened when students were shown the face of a young man who had straight hair, then heard a description of the face supposedly written by another witness—a description that wrongly said the man had light, curly hair (see Figure 8.1). When the students reconstructed the face using a kit of facial features, a third of their reconstructions contained the misleading detail, whereas only 5 percent contained it when curly hair was not mentioned (Loftus & Greene, 1980).

Leading questions, suggestive comments, and misleading information affect people's memories not only for events they have witnessed but also for their own experiences. Researchers have successfully used these techniques to induce people to "recall" complicated events from early in life that never actually happened, such as getting lost in a shopping mall, being hospitalized for a high fever, being harassed by a bully, or spilling punch all over the mother of the bride at a wedding (Hyman & Pentland, 1996; Loftus & Pickrell, 1995; Mazzoni et al., 1999). In one such study, when people were shown a phony Disneyland ad featuring Bugs Bunny, about 16 percent later recalled having met a Bugs character at Disneyland (Braun, Ellis, & Loftus, 2002). In later studies, using several versions of the ad, the percentages were even higher. Some people even claimed to remember shaking hands with the character, hugging him, or seeing him in a parade. But these "memories" were impossible, because Bugs Bunny is a Warner Bros. creation and would definitely be rabbit non grata at Disneyland!

Children's Testimony

The power of suggestion can affect anyone, but many people are especially concerned about its impact on children being questioned regarding possible sexual abuse. How can adults find out whether a young child has been sexually molested without influencing or tainting what the child says? The answer is crucial. Throughout the 1980s and 1990s, accusations of child abuse in day-care centers across the United States skyrocketed. After being interviewed by therapists and police investigators, children were claiming that their teachers had molested them in the most terrible ways: hanging them in trees, putting handcuffs on them, raping them, and even forcing them to eat feces. Although in no case had parents actually seen the day-care teachers treating the children badly, although none of the children had complained to their parents, and although none of the parents had noticed any symptoms or problems in their children, most of the accused teachers were sentenced to many years in prison.

Thanks largely to important research by psychological scientists, the hysteria eventually subsided and people were able to assess more clearly what had gone wrong in the interviewing of the children in these cases. Today we know that

FIGURE 8.1
The Influence of Misleading Information
In a study described in the text, students saw the face of a young man with straight hair and then had to reconstruct it from memory. On the left is one student's reconstruction in the absence of misleading information about the man's hair. On the right is another person's reconstruction of the same face after exposure to misleading information that mentioned curly hair (Loftus & Greene, 1980).

although most children *do* recollect accurately much of what they have observed or experienced, many children will say that something happened when it did not. Like adults, they can be influenced by leading questions and suggestions from the person interviewing them (Ceci & Bruck, 1995). Yet many wrongfully convicted teachers remain in prison, and others, though released, must live out their lives as registered sex offenders.

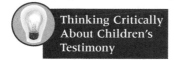
Thinking Critically About Children's Testimony

CLOSE-UP on Research

How Not to Interview Children

Many of the people who interviewed children in the 1980s and 1990s did not **analyze their assumptions and biases**. Some assumed that young children are suggestible and that their testimony is, therefore, almost always unreliable. Others assumed that children never lie about sexual abuse or other distressing experiences. When psychological scientists began to investigate this topic, they realized that both points of view oversimplified. They knew from research that people of any age can be influenced to report things that never happened, and so instead of asking whether children ever lie, they **asked a better question**: "Under what conditions are children apt to be suggestible, to report that something happened to them when in fact it did not?"

In an important field study with real-world relevance, a team of researchers analyzed the actual transcripts of interrogations of children in the first highly publicized sexual abuse case, the McMartin preschool case (which ended in a hung jury). Then they applied the same suggestive techniques in an experiment with preschool children (Garven et al., 1998). A young man visited the children at their school, read them a story, and handed out treats. The man did nothing aggressive, inappropriate, or surprising. A week later the experimenter questioned the children individually about the man's visit. She asked children in one group leading questions ("Did he shove the teacher?" "Did he throw a crayon at a kid who was talking?" "Did he tell

you a secret and tell you not to tell?"). She asked a second group the same questions but also used influence techniques used by interrogators in the McMartin and other day-care cases: for example, telling the children what "other kids" had supposedly said, expressing disappointment if answers were negative, and praising the children for making allegations.

When the researchers **examined the resulting evidence**, they found that in the first group, children said "yes, it happened" to about 17 percent of the false allegations about the man's visit. This finding alone refutes the notion that children never lie, misremember, or make things up. And in the second group, they said "yes" to the false allegations suggested to them a whopping 58 percent of the time. As you can see in the figure below, the 3-year-olds in this group, on average, said "yes" to over 80 percent of the false allegations suggested to them, and the 4- to 6-year-olds said "yes" to over half of the allegations:

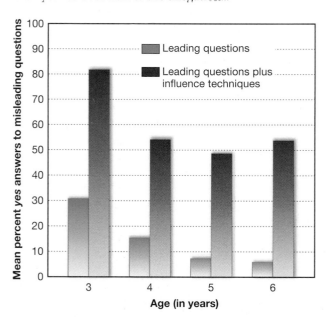

Note that the interviews in this study lasted only 5 to 10 minutes, whereas in actual investigations, interviewers often question children repeatedly over many weeks or months.

This study and many others have clearly established that a child is more likely to give a false report when the interviewer strongly believes the child has been molested and then uses suggestive techniques to get the child to "reveal" molestation (Bruck, 2003). Interviewers who are biased in this way do not think critically. They seek only confirming evidence and ignore discrepant evidence and other explanations for a child's behavior. They reject a child's denial of having been molested and assume the child is "in denial." They use techniques that encourage imagination inflation ("Let's pretend it happened") and that blur reality and fantasy in the child's mind. They praise the child for saying what the interviewer wants to hear—namely, that abuse occurred. They pressure or encourage the child to say that certain terrible things happened, badger the child with repeated questions, tell the child that "everyone else" said it happened, or use bribes and threats (Poole & Lamb, 1998).

Once again, however, we must be careful **not to oversimplify**: Even in the group exposed to the full "package" of influence techniques, some children remained unswayed. Other researchers have asked why that might be, investigating characteristics of the child that might reduce or increase the chances that the child will be vulnerable to leading questions and other influence techniques (Clarke-Stewart, Allhusen, & Malloy, 2004). Children with relatively poor language skills, who are impatient and lack self-control in real-life situations, and who have unsupportive or distant parents are most susceptible. Conversely, children with good verbal comprehension and expression, who have a high degree of self-control, and who enjoy a secure relationship with psychologically healthy parents are best able to resist an interviewer's efforts to influence them.

Finally, researchers have **examined the widely held assumption** that children cannot be induced to make up experiences that are truly traumatic. They have found that this assumption, too, is unsupported. In a study in which schoolchildren were asked for their recollections of an actual sniper incident at their school, many who had been absent from school on that day reported memories of hearing shots, seeing someone lying on the ground, and other details they could not possibly have experienced directly. Apparently, they had been influenced by the accounts of the children who had been there (Pynoos & Nader, 1989). Rumor and hearsay also play a big role in promoting false beliefs and memories in children, just as they do in adults. Young children often think they have experienced an event when in fact they have merely overheard adults or other children talking about it (Principe et al., 2006).

By examining assumptions and avoiding emotional reasoning, researchers have been able to develop better ways of interviewing children that *reduce* the chances of false reporting. For example, if the interviewer says, "Tell me the reason you came to talk to me today," and nothing more, most actual victims will disclose what happened to them (Bruck, 2003). The interviewer must be unbiased and must not assume that the child was molested, must avoid leading or suggestive questions, and must understand that children do not speak the way adults do. Young children often drift from topic to topic, for example, and their words may not be the words adults use (Poole & Lamb, 1998). One little girl thought her "private parts" were her elbows!

In sum, children, like adults, can be accurate in what they report and can also distort, forget, fantasize, and be misled. As research shows, their memory processes are only human.

QUICK quiz

Now see how accurate your own memory processes are.

1. *True or false*: Mistaken identifications are more likely when a suspect's ethnicity differs from that of the eyewitness, even when the witness feels certain about being accurate.

2. Research suggests that the best way to encourage truthful testimony by children is to (a) reassure them that their friends have had the same experience, (b) reward them for telling you that something happened, (c) scold them if you believe they are lying, (d) avoid leading questions.

3. In psychotherapy, hundreds of people have claimed to recall long-buried memories of having taken part in satanic rituals involving animal and human torture and sacrifice. Yet investigators and the FBI have been unable to confirm any of these reports. Based on what you have learned so far, how might you explain such "memories"?

Answers:

1. true   2. d   3. Therapists who uncritically assume that satanic cults are widespread may ask leading questions and otherwise influence their patients. Patients who are susceptible to their therapists' interpretations may then confabulate and "remember" experiences that did not happen, borrowing details from fictionalized accounts or from other troubling experiences in their lives. The result may be source misattribution and the patient's mistaken conviction that the memory is real.

WHAT'S *Ahead*

- In general, which is easier: a multiple-choice question or a short-answer essay question?

- Can you know something without knowing that you know it?

- Why is the computer often used as a metaphor for the mind?

In Pursuit of Memory

Now that we have seen how memory *doesn't* work—namely, like a tape recorder, an infallible filing system, or a journal written in indelible ink—we turn to studies of how it *does* work. The ability to remember is not an absolute talent; it depends on the type of performance being called for. If you have a preference for multiple-choice, essay, or true–false exams, you already know this.

Measuring Memory

Conscious, intentional recollection of an event or an item of information is called **explicit memory**. It is usually measured using one of two methods. The first method tests for **recall**, the ability to retrieve and reproduce information encountered earlier. Essay and fill-in-the-blank exams and memory games such as Trivial Pursuit or Jeopardy require recall. The second method tests for **recognition**, the ability to identify information you have previously observed, read, or heard about. The information is given to you, and all you have to do is say whether it is old or new, or perhaps correct or incorrect, or pick it out of a set of alternatives. The task, in other words, is to compare the information you are given with the information stored in your memory. True–false and multiple-choice tests call for recognition.

Recognition tests can be tricky, especially when false items closely resemble correct ones. Under most circumstances, however, recognition is easier than recall. Recognition for visual images is particularly impressive. If you show people 2,500 slides of faces and places, and later you ask them to identify which ones they saw out of a larger set, they will be able to accurately identify more than 90 percent of the original slides (Haber, 1970).

The superiority of recognition over recall was once demonstrated in a study of people's memories of their high school classmates (Bahrick, Bahrick, & Wittlinger, 1975). The participants, ages 17 to 74, first wrote down the names of as many classmates as they could remember. Recall was poor; even when prompted with yearbook pictures, the youngest people failed to name almost a third of their classmates, and the oldest failed to name most of them. Recognition, however, was far better. When asked to look at a series of cards, each of which contained a set of five photographs, and to say which picture in each set showed a former classmate, recent graduates were right 90 percent of the time—and so were people who had graduated 35 years earlier. The ability to recognize names was nearly as impressive.

Sometimes, information encountered in the past affects our thoughts and actions even though we do not consciously or intentionally remember it—a phenomenon known as **implicit memory** (Graf & Schacter, 1985; Schacter, Chiu, & Ochsner, 1993). To get at this subtle sort of knowledge, researchers must rely on indirect methods instead of the direct ones used to measure explicit memory.

One of the oldest methods of measuring implicit memory, the **relearning method**, or *savings method*, was devised by Hermann Ebbinghaus (1885/1913) in the nineteenth century. The relearning method requires you to relearn information or a task that you have learned earlier. If you master it

explicit memory Conscious, intentional recollection of an event or of an item of information.

recall The ability to retrieve and reproduce from memory previously encountered material.

recognition The ability to identify previously encountered material.

implicit memory Unconscious retention in memory, as evidenced by the effect of a previous experience or previously encountered information on current thoughts or actions.

relearning method A method for measuring retention that compares the time required to relearn material with the time used in the initial learning of the material.

GET INVOLVED

Recalling Rudolph's Friends

You can try this test of recall if you are familiar with the poem "'Twas the Night Before Christmas" or the song "Rudolph the Red-Nosed Reindeer." Rudolph had eight reindeer friends; name as many of them as you can. After you have done your best, turn to the Get Involved exercise on the next page for a recognition test on the same information.

Recognizing Rudolph's Friends

If you took the recall test in the Get Involved exercise on the previous page, now try a recognition test. From the following list, see whether you can identify the correct names of Rudolph the Red-Nosed Reindeer's eight reindeer friends. The answers are at the end of this chapter—but no fair peeking!

Blitzen	Dander	Dancer	Masher
Cupid	Dasher	Prancer	Comet
Kumquat	Donder	Flasher	Pixie
Bouncer	Blintzes	Trixie	Vixen

Which was easier, recall or recognition? Can you speculate on the reason?

---

priming A method for measuring implicit memory in which a person reads or listens to information and is later tested to see whether the information affects performance on another type of task.

more quickly the second time around, you must be remembering something from the first experience.

Today, one of the most common methods in the study of implicit memory, **priming**, asks you to read or listen to some information and then tests you later to see whether the information affects your performance on another type of task. Suppose that you had to read a list of words, some of which began with the letters *def* (such as *define, defend,* or *deform*). Later you might be asked to complete word stems (such as *def-*) with the first word that comes to mind. Even if you could not recognize or recall the original words very well, you would be more likely to complete the word fragments with words from the list than you would be if you had not seen the list. In this procedure, the original words "prime" certain responses on the word-completion task (that is, make them more available), showing that people can retain more knowledge about the past than they realize. They know more than they know that they know (Richardson-Klavehn & Bjork, 1988; Roediger, 1990).

PRIMING

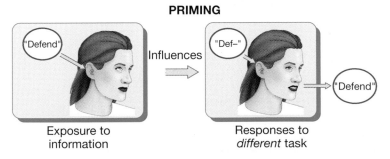

Exposure to information | Influences | Responses to *different* task

Models of Memory

Although people usually refer to memory as a single faculty, as in "I must be losing my memory" or "He has a memory like an elephant's," the term *memory* actually covers a complex collection of abilities and processes. If video or movie cameras are not accurate metaphors for capturing these diverse

components of memory, then what metaphor would be better?

As we saw in Chapter 7, many cognitive psychologists liken the mind to an information processor, along the lines of a computer, though more complex. They have constructed *information-processing models* of cognitive processes, liberally borrowing computer-programming terms such as *input, output, accessing,* and *information retrieval.* When you type something on your computer's keyboard, the machine encodes the information into an electronic language, stores it on a disk, and retrieves it when you need to use it. Similarly, in information-processing models of memory, we *encode* information (convert it to a form that the brain can process and use), *store* the information (retain it over time), and *retrieve* the information (recover it for use). In storage, the information may be represented as concepts, propositions, images, or *cognitive schemas,* mental networks of knowledge, beliefs, and expectations concerning particular topics or aspects of the world. (If you can't retrieve these terms, see Chapter 7.)

In most information-processing models, storage takes place in three interacting memory systems. A *sensory register* retains incoming sensory information for a second or two, until it can be processed further. *Short-term memory (STM)* holds a limited amount of information for a brief period of time, perhaps up to 30 seconds or so, unless a conscious effort is made to keep it there longer. *Long-term memory (LTM)* accounts for longer storage—from a few minutes to decades (Atkinson & Shiffrin, 1968, 1971). Information can pass from the sensory register into short-term memory and in either direction between short-term and long-term memory, as illustrated in Figure 8.2.

This model, which is often informally called the "three-box model," has dominated research on memory since the late 1960s. However, critics of the three-box model note that the human brain does not operate like your average computer. Most computers process instructions and data sequentially, and so the

Retrieved

Sensory register	Short-term memory (STM)	Long-term memory (LTM)
1. Large capacity	1. Limited capacity	1. Unlimited capacity
2. Contains sensory information	2. Brief storage of items (up to 30 seconds if no rehearsal)	2. Storage thought by some to be permanent
3. Very brief retention of images (up to 1/2 second for visual; 2 seconds for auditory)	3. Involved in conscious processing of information	3. Information organized and indexed

Information from environment →

Forgotten   Transferred   Forgotten   Transferred/Retrieved

FIGURE 8.2
Three Memory Systems
In the three-box model of memory, information that does not transfer out of the sensory register or short-term memory is assumed to be forgotten forever. Once in long-term memory, information can be retrieved for use in analyzing incoming sensory information or performing mental operations in short-term memory.

three-box model has emphasized sequential operations. However, the human brain performs many operations simultaneously, in parallel. It recognizes patterns all at once rather than as a sequence of information bits, and it perceives new information, produces speech, and searches memory all at the same time. It can do this because millions of neurons are active at once, and each neuron communicates with thousands of others, which in turn communicate with millions more.

Because of these differences between human beings and machines, some cognitive scientists prefer a **parallel distributed processing (PDP)**, or *connectionist*, model. Instead of representing information as flowing from one system to another, a PDP model represents the contents of memory as connections among a huge number of interacting processing units, distributed in a vast network and all operating in parallel—just like the neurons of the brain (McClelland, 1994; Rumelhart, McClelland, & the PDP Research Group, 1986). As information enters the system, the ability of these units to excite or inhibit each other is constantly adjusted to reflect new knowledge.

Memory researchers are still arguing about which model of memory is most useful. In this chapter, we emphasize the three-box model, but keep in mind that the computer metaphor that inspired it could one day be as outdated as the metaphor of memory as a camera.

QUICK quiz

How well have you encoded and stored what you just learned?

1. Alberta solved a crossword puzzle a few days ago. She no longer recalls the words in the puzzle, but while playing a game of Scrabble, she unconsciously tends to form words that were in the puzzle, showing that she has _____ memories of some of the words.

2. The three basic memory processes are _____, storage, and _____.

3. Do the preceding two questions ask for recall, recognition, or relearning? (And what about *this* question?)

4. One objection to traditional information-processing theories of memory is that, unlike most computers, the brain performs many independent operations _____.

Answers:

1. implicit 2. encoding, retrieval 3. The first two questions both measure recall; the third question measures recognition. 4. simultaneously, or in parallel

WHAT'S *Ahead*

• Why is short-term memory like a leaky bucket?

• When a word is on the tip of your tongue, what errors are you likely to make in recalling it?

• What's the difference between "knowing how" and "knowing that"?

The Three-Box Model of Memory

The information-processing model of three separate memory systems—sensory, short-term, and long-term—remains a leading approach because it offers a convenient way to organize the major

parallel distributed processing (PDP) A model of memory in which knowledge is represented as connections among thousands of interacting processing units, distributed in a vast network and all operating in parallel.

sensory register A memory system that momentarily preserves extremely accurate sensory information before the information fades or moves into short-term memory.

short-term memory (STM) In the three-box model of memory, a limited-capacity memory system involved in the retention of information for brief periods; it is also used to hold information retrieved from long-term memory for temporary use.

working memory Short-term memory plus the mental processes that control retrieval of information from long-term memory and interpret that information appropriately for a given task.

findings on memory, does a good job of accounting for these findings, and is consistent with the biological facts about memory described in Chapter 4. Let us now peer into each of the "boxes."

The Sensory Register: Fleeting Impressions

In the three-box model, all incoming sensory information must make a brief stop in the **sensory register**, the entryway of memory. The sensory register includes a number of separate subsystems, as many as there are senses. Visual images remain in a visual subsystem for a maximum of half a second. Auditory images remain in an auditory subsystem for a slightly longer time, by most estimates up to two seconds or so.

The sensory register acts as a holding bin, retaining information in a highly accurate form until we can select items for attention from the stream of stimuli bombarding our senses. It gives us a brief time to decide whether information is extraneous or important; not everything detected by our senses warrants our attention.

Information that does not quickly go on to short-term memory vanishes forever, like a message written in disappearing ink. That is why people who see an array of 12 letters for just a fraction of a second can report only 4 or 5 of them; by the time they answer, their sensory memories are already fading (Sperling, 1960). The fleeting nature of incoming sensations is actually beneficial; it prevents multiple sensory images—"double exposures"—that might interfere with the accurate perception and encoding of information.

Short-Term Memory: Memory's Scratch Pad

Like the sensory register, **short-term memory (STM)** retains information only temporarily—for up to about 30 seconds by most estimates, although some researchers think that the maximum interval may extend to a few minutes for certain tasks. In short-term memory, the material is no longer an exact sensory image but an encoding of one, such as a word or a phrase. This material either transfers into long-term memory or decays and is lost forever.

Individuals with brain injury, such as H. M., demonstrate the importance of transferring new information from short-term memory into long-term memory. H. M., you will recall, can store information on a short-term basis; he can hold a conversation and he appears to be fine when you first meet him. He also retains implicit memories. However, for the most part, H. M., and other patients like him, cannot retain explicit information about new facts and events for longer than a few minutes. Their terrible memory deficits involve a problem in transferring explicit memories from short-term storage into long-term storage. With a great deal of repetition and drill, they can learn some new visual information, retain it in long-term memory, and recall it normally (McKee & Squire, 1992). But usually information does not get into long-term memory in the first place.

Working Memory Besides retaining new information for brief periods while we are learning it, short-term memory holds information that has been retrieved from long-term memory for temporary use, providing the mental equivalent of a scratch pad while we solve particular problems. Many psychologists now use the term **working memory** to refer to (a) short-term memory plus (b) the mental processes that control the rehearsal and retrieval of information from long-term memory and interpret that information appropriately depending on the task you are doing (Baddeley, 1992). When you do an arithmetic problem, your working memory con-

GET INVOLVED

Your Sensory Register At Work

In a dark room or closet, if you point a flashlight at the wall you'll see a single point of light. But if you swing the flashlight very rapidly in a circle, you will see an unbroken circle of light instead of a series of separate points. The reason: The successive images remain briefly in the sensory register.

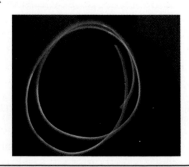

tains the numbers and the instructions for doing the necessary operations, and it also carries out those operations and retains the intermediate results from each step. Working memory may also involve the ability to control attention and avoid distraction in order to maintain information in an accessible or active state and retrieve it easily (Engle, 2002). People who do well on tests of working memory tend to do well in understanding written material, following directions, taking notes, playing bridge, learning new words, and doing many other real-life tasks.

The ability to bring information from long-term memory into short-term memory or to use working memory is not disrupted in patients like H. M. They can not only converse but can also do arithmetic, relate events that predate their injury, and do anything else that requires retrieval of information from long-term into short-term memory. Their problem is with the flow of information in the other direction, from short-term into long-term memory.

People such as H. M. fall at the extreme end on a continuum of forgetfulness, but even those of us with normal memories know from personal experience how frustratingly brief short-term retention can be. We look up a telephone number, are distracted for a moment, and find that the number has vanished from our minds. We meet someone at a gathering and two minutes later find ourselves groping unsuccessfully for the person's name. Is it any wonder that short-term memory has been called a "leaky bucket"?

The Leaky Bucket According to most memory models, if the bucket did not leak it would quickly overflow, because at any given moment, short-term memory can hold only so many items. Years ago, George Miller (1956) estimated its capacity to be "the magical number 7 plus or minus 2." Five-digit zip codes and 7-digit telephone numbers fall conveniently in this range; 16-digit credit card numbers do not. Some researchers have questioned whether Miller's magical number is so magical after all; estimates of STM's capacity have ranged from 2 items to 20, with one more recent estimate putting the "magical number" at around 4 (Cowan, 2001). Everyone agrees, however, that the number of items that short-term memory can handle at any one time is small.

If this is so, then how do we remember the beginning of a spoken sentence until the speaker reaches the end? After all, most sentences are longer than just a few words. According to most information-processing models of memory, we overcome this

If you do not play chess, you probably will not be able to recall the positions of these chess pieces after looking away. But experienced chess players, in the middle of a game, can remember the position of every piece after glancing only briefly at the board. They are able to "chunk" the pieces into a few standard configurations instead of trying to memorize where each piece is located.

problem by grouping small bits of information into larger units, or **chunks.** The real capacity of STM, it turns out, is not a few bits of information but a few chunks. A chunk may be a word, a phrase, a sentence, or even a visual image, and it depends on previous experience. For most Americans, the acronym *FBI* is one chunk, not three, and the date *1492* is one chunk, not four. In contrast, the number *9214* is four chunks and *IBF* is three—unless your address is 9214 or your initials are IBF. To take a more visual example: If you are unfamiliar with football and look at a field full of players, you probably won't be able to remember their positions when you look away. But if you are a fan of the game, you may see a single chunk of information—say, a wishbone formation—and be able to retain it.

Even chunking, however, cannot keep short-term memory from eventually filling up. Information that is needed for longer periods must therefore be transferred to long-term memory. Items that are particularly meaningful or that have an emotional impact may transfer quickly. But items that require more processing will be displaced with new information, and will thus be lost, unless we do something to keep it in STM for a while, as we will discuss shortly.

Long-Term Memory: Final Destination

The third box in the three-box model of memory is **long-term memory (LTM)**. The capacity of long-term memory seems to have no practical limits. The vast amount of information stored there enables us to learn, get around in the environment, and build a sense of identity and a personal history.

Organization in Long-Term Memory

Because long-term memory contains so much information, it must be organized in some way, so that we can find the particular items we

chunk A meaningful unit of information; it may be composed of smaller units.

long-term memory (LTM) In the three-box model of memory, the memory system involved in the long-term storage of information.

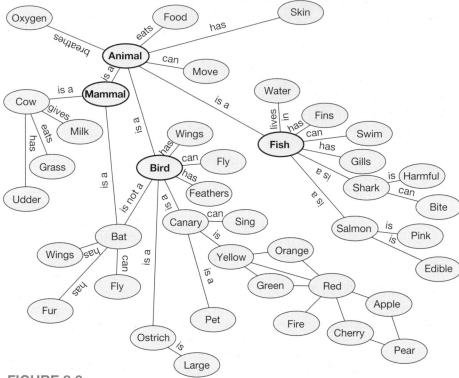

FIGURE 8.3
Part of a Conceptual Grid in Long-Term Memory

Many models of memory represent the contents of long-term semantic memory as an immense network or grid of concepts and the relationships among them. This illustration shows part of a hypothetical grid for animals.

are looking for. One way to organize words (or the concepts they represent) is by the *semantic categories* to which they belong. *Chair*, for example, belongs to the category *furniture*. In a study done many years ago, people had to memorize 60 words that came from four semantic categories: animals, vegetables, names, and professions. The words were presented in random order, but when people were allowed to recall the items in any order they wished, they tended to recall them in clusters corresponding to the four categories (Bousfield, 1953). This finding has been replicated many times.

Evidence on the storage of information by semantic category also comes from cases of people with brain damage. In one such case, a patient called M. D. appeared to have made a complete recovery after suffering several strokes, with one odd exception: He had trouble remembering the names of fruits and vegetables. M. D. could easily name a picture of an abacus or a sphinx but he drew a blank when he saw a picture of an apple or a carrot. He could sort pictures of animals, vehicles, and other objects into their appropriate categories but did poorly with pictures of fruits and vegetables. On the other hand, when M. D. was *given* the names of fruits and vegetables, he immediately pointed to the corresponding pictures (Hart, Berndt, & Caramazza, 1985). Apparently, M. D. still had information stored about fruits and vegetables, but his brain

damage prevented him from using their names to get to the information when he needed it, unless the names were provided by someone else. This evidence suggests that information in memory about a particular concept (such as *orange*) is linked in some way to information about the concept's semantic category (such as *fruit*).

Indeed, many models of long-term memory represent its contents as a vast network of interrelated concepts and propositions (Anderson, 1990; Collins & Loftus, 1975). In these models, a small part of a conceptual network for animals might look something like the one in Figure 8.3. The way people use these networks, however, depends on experience and education. For example, in rural Liberia, the more schooling children have, the more likely they are to use semantic categories in recalling lists of objects (Cole & Scribner, 1974). This makes sense, because in school, children must memorize a lot of information in a short time, and semantic groupings can help. Unschooled children, having less need to memorize lists, do not cluster items and do not remember them as well. But this does not mean that unschooled children have poor memories. When the task is one that is meaningful to them, such as recalling objects that were in a story or a village scene, they remember extremely well (Mistry & Rogoff, 1994).

We organize information in long-term memory not only by semantic groupings but also in terms of the way words sound or look. Have you ever tried to re-

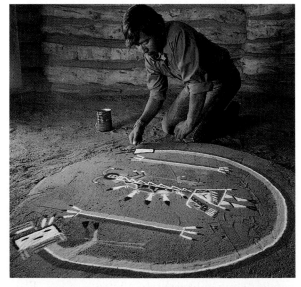

Culture affects the encoding, storage, and retrieval of information in long-term memory. Navajo healers, who use stylized, symbolic sand paintings in their rituals, must commit to memory dozens of intricate visual designs because no exact copies are made and the painting is destroyed after each ceremony.

call some word that was on the "tip of your tongue"? Nearly everyone experiences such *tip-of-the-tongue (TOT) states*, especially when trying to recall the names of acquaintances or famous persons, the names of objects and places, or the titles of movies or books (Burke et al., 1991). TOT states are reported even by users of sign language, who call them tip-of-the-finger states (Thompson, Emmorey, & Gollan, 2005).

When a word is on the tip of the tongue, people tend to come up with words that are similar in meaning to the right one before they finally recall it. But verbal information in long-term memory also seems to be indexed by sound and form, and it is retrievable on that basis. Incorrect guesses often have the correct number of syllables, the correct stress pattern, the correct first letter, or the correct prefix or suffix (Brown & McNeill, 1966). For example, for the target word *sampan* (an Asian boat), a person might say "Siam" or "sarong."

Information in long-term memory may also be organized by its familiarity, relevance, or association with other information. The method used in any given instance probably depends on the nature of the memory; you would no doubt store information about the major cities of Europe differently from information about your first date. To understand the organization of long-term memory, then, we must know what kinds of information can be stored there.

The Contents of Long-Term Memory
Most theories of memory distinguish skills or habits ("knowing how") from abstract or representational knowledge ("knowing that"). **Procedural memories** are memories of knowing how to do something—for example, knowing how to comb your hair, use a pencil, solve a jigsaw puzzle, knit a sweater, or swim. Many researchers consider procedural memories to be implicit, because once skills and habits are learned well they do not require much conscious processing. **Declarative memories**, on the other hand, are memories of knowing that something is true, as in knowing that Ottawa is the capital of Canada; they are usually assumed to be explicit.

Declarative memories, in turn, come in two varieties: semantic memories and episodic memories (Tulving, 1985). **Semantic memories** are internal representations of the world, independent of any particular context. They include facts, rules, and concepts—items of general knowledge. On the basis of your semantic memory of the concept *cat*, you can describe a cat as a small, furry mammal that typically spends its time eating, sleeping, prowling, and staring into space, even though a cat may not be

present when you give this description, and you probably won't know how or when you first learned it. **Episodic memories** are internal representations of personally experienced events. When you remember how your cat once surprised you in the middle of the night by pouncing on your face as you slept, you are retrieving an episodic memory. Figure 8.4 summarizes these kinds of memories.

As we saw in Chapter 4, with sufficient practice, patients such as H. M., who cannot form new declarative memories because of damage to the hippocampus, can acquire new procedural memories; they can learn to solve a puzzle, read mirror-reversed words, or play tennis—even though they do not remember the training sessions in which they learned these skills. Apparently the parts of the brain involved in acquiring procedural memories have remained intact.

From Short-Term to Long-Term Memory: A Puzzle
The three-box model of memory is often invoked to explain an interesting phenomenon called the **serial-position effect**. If you are shown a list of items and are then asked immediately to recall them, your retention of any particular item will depend on its position in the list (Glanzer & Cunitz, 1966). Recall will be best for items at the beginning of the list (the *primacy effect*) and at the end of the list (the *recency effect*). When retention of all the items is plotted, the result will be a U-shaped

procedural memories Memories for the performance of actions or skills ("knowing how").

declarative memories Memories of facts, rules, concepts, and events ("knowing that"); they include semantic and episodic memories.

semantic memories Memories of general knowledge, including facts, rules, concepts, and propositions.

episodic memories Memories of personally experienced events and the contexts in which they occurred.

serial-position effect The tendency for recall of the first and last items on a list to surpass recall of items in the middle of the list.

FIGURE 8.4
Types of Long-Term Memories
This diagram summarizes the distinctions among long-term memories. Can you come up with other examples of each memory type?

FIGURE 8.5
The Serial-Position Effect

When people try to recall a list of similar items immediately after learning it they tend to remember the first and last items best and the ones in the middle worst.

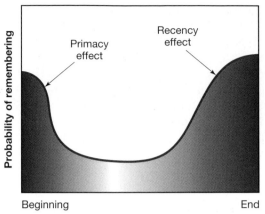

Position of the item in the list

curve, as shown in Figure 8.5. A serial-position effect occurs when you are introduced to a lot of people at a party and find you can recall the names of the first few people you met and the last few, but almost no one in between.

According to the three-box model, the first few items on a list are remembered well because short-term memory was relatively empty when they entered, so these items did not have to compete with others to make it into long-term memory. They were thoroughly processed, so they remain memorable. The last few items are remembered for a different reason: At the time of recall, they are still sitting in short-term memory. The items in the middle of a list, however, are not so well retained because by the time they get into short-term memory, it is already crowded. As a result, many of these items drop out of short-term memory before they can be stored in long-term memory. The problem with this explanation is that the recency effect sometimes occurs even after a considerable delay, when the items at the end of a list can no longer be in short-term memory (Davelaar et al., 2004). The serial-position curve, therefore, remains something of a puzzle.

QUICK quiz

Find out whether the findings just discussed have transferred from your short-term memory to your long-term memory.

1. The _____ holds images for a fraction of a second.

2. For most people, the abbreviation *U.S.A.* consists of _____ informational chunk(s).

3. Suppose you must memorize a long list of words that includes the following: *desk, pig, gold, dog, chair, silver, table, rooster, bed, copper,* and *horse.* If you can recall the words in any order you wish, how are you likely to group them in recall? Why?

4. When you roller-blade, are you relying on procedural, semantic, or episodic memory? How about when you recall the months of the year? Or when you remember falling while roller-blading on an icy January day?

5. If a child is trying to memorize the alphabet, which sequence should present the greatest difficulty: *abcdefg, klmnopq,* or *tuvwxyz?* Why?

Answers:

1. sensory register   2. one   3. *Desk, chair, table,* and *bed* would probably form one cluster; *pig, dog, rooster,* and *horse* a second; and *gold, silver,* and *copper* a third. Concepts tend to be organized in long-term memory in terms of semantic categories, such as *furniture, animals,* and *metals;*   4. procedural; semantic; episodic   5. *klmnopq,* because of the serial-position effect

WHAT'S *Ahead*

- What's wrong with trying to memorize in a rote fashion when you are studying, and what's a better strategy?
- Memory tricks are fun, but are they always useful?

How We Remember

Once we understand how memory works, we can use that understanding to encode and store information so that it "sticks" and will be there when we need it. What are the best strategies to use?

Effective Encoding

Our memories, as we have seen, are not exact replicas of experience. Sensory information is summarized and encoded—for example, as words or images—almost as soon as it is detected. When you hear a lecture you may hang on every word (we hope you do), but you do not memorize those words verbatim. You extract the main points and encode them.

To remember information well, you have to encode it accurately in the first place. With some kinds of information, accurate encoding takes place automatically, without effort. Think about where you usually sit in your psychology class. When were you last there? You can probably provide this information easily, even though you never made a deliberate effort to encode it. But many kinds of information require *effortful encoding*—the plot of a novel, the procedures for assembling a cabinet, the arguments for and against a proposed law. To retain such information, you might have to select the main points, label concepts, or associate the information with personal experiences or with material you already know. Experienced students know that most of the information in a college course requires effortful encoding (otherwise known as studying).

Rehearsal

An important technique for keeping information in short-term memory and increasing the chances of long-term retention is *rehearsal*, the review or practice of material while you are learning it. When people are prevented from rehearsing, the contents of their short-term memories quickly fade (Peterson & Peterson, 1959). You are taking advantage of rehearsal when you look up a telephone number and then repeat it over and over in order to keep it in short-term memory until you no longer need it. And when you can't remember a phone number because you have always used speed dial to call it, you are learning what happens when you *don't* rehearse!

A poignant demonstration of the power of rehearsal once occurred during a session with H. M. (Ogden & Corkin, 1991). The experimenter gave H. M. five digits to repeat and remember, but then

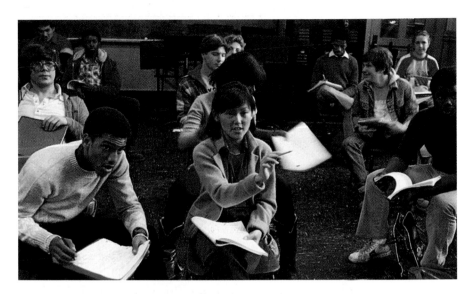

Encoding classroom material for later recall usually requires a deliberate effort. Which of these students do you think will remember best?

she was unexpectedly called away. When she returned after more than an hour, H. M. was able to repeat the five digits correctly. He had been rehearsing them the entire time.

Short-term memory holds many kinds of information, including visual information and abstract meanings. But most people, or at least most hearing people, seem to favor speech for encoding and rehearsing the contents of short-term memory. The speech may be spoken aloud or to oneself. When people make errors on short-term memory tests that use letters or words, they often confuse items that sound the same or similar, such as *d* and *t*, or *bear* and *bare*. These errors suggest that they have been rehearsing verbally.

Elaborative Rehearsal Some strategies for rehearsing are more effective than others. **Maintenance rehearsal** involves merely the rote repetition of the material. This kind of rehearsal is fine for keeping information in STM, but it will not always lead to long-term retention. A better strategy if you want to remember for the long haul is **elaborative rehearsal**, also called *elaboration of encoding* (Cermak & Craik, 1979; Craik & Tulving, 1975). Elaboration involves associating new items of information with material that has already been stored or with other new facts. It can also involve analyzing the physical, sensory, or semantic features of an item.

Suppose that you are studying the hypothalamus, discussed in Chapter 4. Simply memorizing the definition of the hypothalamus in a rote manner is unlikely to help much. But if you can elaborate the concept of the hypothalamus, you are more likely to remember it. For example, knowing

Actors learning a script do not rely on maintenance rehearsal alone. They also use elaborative rehearsal by analyzing the meaning of their lines and by associating their lines with imagined information about the character they are playing.

maintenance rehearsal Rote repetition of material in order to maintain its availability in memory.

elaborative rehearsal Association of new information with already stored knowledge and analysis of the new information to make it memorable.

Unfortunately, the most likely reason for midterm memory loss is not studying enough—or in the right way.

that *hypo* means "under" tells you its location—under the thalamus. Knowing that it is part of the limbic system should clue you that it is probably involved in survival drives and emotion. Many students try to pare down what they're learning to the bare essentials, but in fact, knowing more details about something makes it more memorable; that's what elaboration means.

Deep Processing A related strategy for prolonging retention is **deep processing**, or the processing of meaning (Craik & Lockhart, 1972). If you process only the physical or sensory features of a stimulus, such as how the word *hypothalamus* is spelled and how it sounds, your processing will be shallow even if it is elaborated. If you recognize patterns and assign labels to objects or events ("The *hypo*thalamus is *below* the thalamus"), your processing will be somewhat deeper. If you fully analyze the meaning of what you are trying to remember (for example, by encoding the functions and importance of the hypothalamus), your processing will be deeper yet.

Shallow processing is sometimes useful; when you memorize a poem, for instance, you will want to pay attention to (and elaborately encode) the sounds of the words and the patterns of rhythm in the poem and not just the poem's meaning. Usually, however, deep processing is more effective. That is why, if you try to memorize information that has little or no meaning for you, the information may not stick.

deep processing In the encoding of information, the processing of meaning rather than simply the physical or sensory features of a stimulus.

mnemonics [neh-MON-iks] Strategies and tricks for improving memory, such as the use of a verse or a formula.

Mnemonics

In addition to using elaborative rehearsal and deep processing, people who want to give their powers of memory a boost sometimes use **mnemonics** [neh-MON-iks], formal strategies and tricks for encoding, storing, and retaining information. (Mnemosyne, pronounced neh-MOZ-eh-nee, was the ancient Greek goddess of memory. Can you remember her?) Some mnemonics take the form of easily memorized rhymes (e.g., "Thirty days hath September/April, June, and November . . ."). Others use formulas (e.g., "**E**very **g**ood **b**oy **d**oes **f**ine" for remembering which notes are on the lines of the treble clef in musical notation). Still others use visual images or word associations. The best mnemonics force you to encode material actively and thoroughly. They may also reduce the amount of information by chunking it, which is why, in ads, many companies use words for their phone numbers instead of unmemorable numbers ("Dial GET RICH").

Some stage performers with amazing recall rely on more complicated mnemonics. We are not going to spend time on them here, because for ordinary memory tasks, such tricks are often no more effective than rote rehearsal, and sometimes they are actually worse (Wang, Thomas, & Ouellette, 1992). Most memory researchers do not use such mnemonics themselves (Hébert, 2001). After all, why bother to memorize a grocery list using a fancy mnemonic when you can write down what you need to buy? The fastest route to a good memory is to follow the principles suggested by the findings in this section and by research reviewed in "Taking Psychology with You."

"YOU SIMPLY ASSOCIATE EACH NUMBER WITH A WORD, SUCH AS 'TABLE' AND 3,476,029."

QUICK quiz

Perhaps Mnemosyne will help you answer this question.

Camille is furious with her history professor. "I read the chapter three times, but I still failed the exam," she fumes. "The test must have been unfair." What's wrong with Camille's reasoning, and what are some other possible explanations for her poor performance, based on principles of critical thinking and what you have learned so far about memory?

Answer:

everything instead of being selective.

coding, used maintenance instead of elaborative rehearsal, and used shallow instead of deep processing when she studied. She may also have tried to encode

Camille is reasoning emotionally and is not examining the assumptions underlying her explanations. Perhaps she relied on automatic rather than effortful en-

WHAT'S *Ahead*

- How might new information "erase" old memories?

- What theory explains why you keep dialing an old area code instead of your new one?

- Why is it easier to recall experiences from elementary school if you see pictures of your classmates?

- Why are many researchers skeptical about claims of "repressed" and "recovered" memories?

Why We Forget

Have you ever, in the heat of some deliriously happy moment, said to yourself, "I'll never forget this, never, *never*, NEVER"? Do you find that you can more clearly remember saying those words than the deliriously happy moment itself? Sometimes you encode an event, you rehearse it, you analyze its meaning, you tuck it away in long-term storage—and still you forget it. Is it any wonder that most of us have wished, at one time or another, for a "photographic memory"?

Actually, having a perfect memory is not the blessing that you might suppose. The Russian psychologist Alexander Luria (1968) once told of a

Thinking Critically About Having a Perfect Memory

journalist, S., who could reproduce giant grids of numbers both forward and backward, even after the

passage of many years. S. also remembered the exact circumstances under which he had originally learned the material. To accomplish his astonishing feats, he used mnemonics, especially the formation of visual images. But you should not envy him, for he had a serious problem: He could not forget even when he wanted to. Along with the diamonds of experience, he kept dredging up the pebbles. Images he had formed

in order to remember kept creeping into consciousness, distracting him and interfering with his ability to concentrate. At times he even had trouble holding a conversation because the other person's words would set off a jumble of associations. Eventually, S. took to supporting himself by traveling from place to place, demonstrating his mnemonic abilities for audiences.

Or consider a modern case of a woman called A.J. (Parker, Cahill, & McGaugh, 2006). A.J., who is in her early forties and has average intelligence, possesses an extraordinary memory for her own past. When given any date back to 1980, A.J. is able to say instantly what she was doing, what day of the week it was, and whether anything of great importance happened on that date. A.J. does not have any special talent for memorizing meaningless material such as numbers or letters. Nor does she use mnemonics; rather, she describes her recollections as nonstop and uncontrollable. Like other people who have unusually accurate memories, she finds her abilities to be a mixed blessing. Although she enjoys recalling events from her past, especially happy occasions, she finds it "totally exhausting." "Some call it a gift," she wrote, "but I call it a burden. I run my entire life through my head every day and it drives me crazy!!!"

Paradoxically, then, forgetting is adaptive. We need to forget if we wish to remember efficiently (Bjork, Bjork, & Anderson, 1998). Nonetheless, most of us forget more than we wish to, and we would like to know why. In the early days of psychology, in an effort to measure

WELL, FOR CRYING OUT LOUD! AL TOWBRIDGE! WHAT IS IT, NINE YEARS, SEVEN MONTHS, AND TWELVE DAYS SINCE I LAST RAN INTO YOU? TEN-THIRTY-TWO A.M., A SATURDAY, FELCHER'S HARDWARE STORE. YOU WERE BUYING SEALER FOR YOUR BLACKTOP DRIVEWAY. TELL ME, AL, HOW DID THAT SEALER WORK? DID IT HOLD UP?

MR. TOTAL RECALL

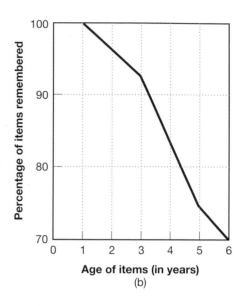

Elapsed time since learning (in days)
(a)

Age of items (in years)
(b)

FIGURE 8.6
Two Kinds of Forgetting Curves
When Hermann Ebbinghaus tested his own memory for nonsense syllables, forgetting was rapid at first and then tapered off (a). In contrast, when Marigold Linton tested her own memory for personal events over a period of several years, her retention was excellent at first, but then it fell off at a gradual but steady rate (b).

pure memory loss independent of personal experience, Hermann Ebbinghaus (1885/1913) memorized long lists of nonsense syllables, such as *bok*, *waf*, or *ged*, and then tested his retention over a period of several weeks. Most of his forgetting occurred soon after the initial learning and then leveled off (see Figure 8.6a). Ebbinghaus's method of studying memory was adopted by generations of psychologists, even though it did not tell them much about the kinds of memories that people care about most.

A century later, Marigold Linton decided to find out how people forget real events rather than nonsense syllables. Like Ebbinghaus, she used herself as a subject, but she charted the curve of forgetting over years rather than days. Every day for 12 years, she recorded on a 4- × 6-inch card two or more things that had happened to her that day. Eventually, she accumulated a catalogue of thousands of discrete events, both trivial ("I have dinner at the Canton Kitchen: delicious lobster dish") and significant ("I land at Orly Airport in Paris"). Once a month, she took a random sampling of all the cards accumulated to that point, noted whether she could remember the events on them, and tried to date the events. Linton (1978) later told how she had expected the kind of rapid forgetting reported by Ebbinghaus. Instead, as you can see in Figure 8.6b, she found that long-term forgetting was slower and proceeded at a much more constant pace, as details gradually dropped out of her memories.

Of course, some memories, especially those that mark important transitions, are more memorable than others. But why did Marigold Linton, like the rest of us, forget so many details? Psychologists have proposed five mechanisms to account for forgetting: decay, replacement of old memories by new ones,

interference, cue-dependent forgetting, and psychological amnesia brought on by repression.

Decay

One commonsense view, the **decay theory**, holds that memory traces fade with time if they are not accessed now and then. We have already seen that decay occurs in the sensory register almost immediately and that it occurs in short-term memory as well unless we keep rehearsing the material. However, the mere passage of time does not account so well for forgetting in long-term memory. People commonly forget things

decay theory The theory that information in memory eventually disappears if it is not accessed; it applies more to short-term than to long-term memory.

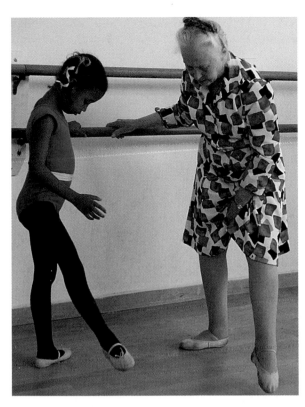

Motor skills, which are stored as procedural memories, can last a lifetime; they never decay.

that happened only yesterday while remembering events from many years ago. Indeed, some memories, both procedural and declarative, can last a lifetime. If you learned to swim as a child, you will still know how to swim at age 30, even if you have not been in a pool or lake for 22 years. Some school lessons also have great staying power. In one study, people did well on a Spanish test 50 years after taking Spanish in high school, even though most had hardly used Span-

ish at all in the intervening years (Bahrick, 1984). Decay alone, although it may play some role, cannot entirely explain lapses in long-term memory.

Replacement

Another theory holds that new information entering memory can wipe out old information, just as rerecording on an audiotape or videotape will obliterate the original material. In a study supporting this view, researchers showed people slides of a traffic accident and used leading questions to get them to think that they had seen a stop sign when they had really seen a yield sign, or vice versa (see Figure 8.7). People in a control group who were not misled in this way were able to identify the sign they had actually seen. Later, all the participants were told the purpose of the study and were asked to guess whether they had been misled. Almost all of those who had been misled continued to insist that they had *really, truly* seen the sign whose existence had been planted in their minds (Loftus, Miller, & Burns, 1978). The researchers interpreted this finding to mean that the subjects had not just been trying to please them and that people's original perceptions had in fact been erased by the misleading information.

Interference

A third theory holds that forgetting occurs because similar items of information interfere with one another in either storage or retrieval; the information may get into memory and stay there, but it becomes confused with other information. Such interference, which occurs in both short- and long-term memory, is especially common when you have to recall isolated facts—names, addresses, personal identification numbers, area codes, and the like.

FIGURE 8.7
The Stop Sign Study
When people who saw a car with a yield sign (left) were later asked if they had seen "the stop sign" (a misleading question), many said they had. Similarly, when those shown a stop sign were asked if they had seen "the yield sign," many said yes. These false memories persisted even after the participants were told about the misleading questions, suggesting that misleading information had erased their original mental representations of the signs (Loftus, Miller, & Burns, 1978).

Suppose you are at a party and you meet someone named Julie. A little later you meet someone named Judy. You go on to talk to other people, and after an hour, you again bump into Julie, but by mistake you call her Judy. The second name has interfered

Retroactive interference

Julie — Learned first
Judy — Learned second

with the first. This type of interference, in which new information interferes with the ability to remember old information, is called **retroactive interference**.

Retroactive interference is illustrated by the story of an absentminded professor of ichthyology (the study of fish) who complained that whenever he learned the name of a new student, he forgot the name of a fish. But whereas with replacement, the new memory erases the old and makes it irretrievable, in retroactive interference, loss of the old memory is sometimes just temporary. With a little concentration, that professor could probably recall his new students and his old fish.

Because new information is constantly entering memory, we are all vulnerable to the effects of retroactive interference, or at least most of us are. H. M. is an exception; his memories of childhood and adolescence are unusually detailed, clear, and unchanging. H. M. can remember actors who were famous when he was a child, the films they were in, and who their costars were. He also knows the names of friends from the second grade. Presumably, these early declarative memories were not subject to interference from memories acquired since the operation because H. M. has not acquired any new memories.

Interference also works in the opposite direction. Old information (such as the Spanish you

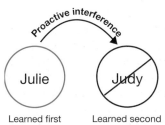

Proactive interference

Julie — Learned first
Judy — Learned second

learned in high school) may interfere with the ability to remember new information (such as the French you are trying to learn now). This type of interference is called **proactive interference**.

Over a period of weeks, months, and years, proactive interference may cause more forgetting than retroactive interference does, because we have stored up so much information that can potentially interfere with anything new.

Cue-Dependent Forgetting

Often, when we need to remember, we rely on *retrieval cues*, items of information that can help us find the

specific information we're looking for. For example, if you are trying to remember the last name of an actor, it might help to know the person's first name or the name of a recent movie the actor starred in.

When we lack retrieval cues, we may feel as if we are lost in the mind's library. In long-term memory, this type of memory failure, called **cue-dependent forgetting**, may be the most common type of all. Willem Wagenaar (1986), who, like Marigold Linton, recorded critical details about events in his life, found that within a year, he had forgotten 20 percent of those details, and after five years, he had forgotten 60 percent. However, when he gathered cues from witnesses about ten events that he thought he had forgotten, he was able to recall something about all ten, which suggests that some of his forgetting was cue dependent.

Cues that were present when you learned a new fact or experienced an event are apt to be especially useful later as retrieval aids. That may explain why remembering is often easier when you are in the same physical environment as you were when an event occurred: Cues in the present context match those from the past. Ordinarily, this overlap helps us remember the past more accurately. But it may also account for the eerie phenomenon of *déjà vu*, the false sense we've all had of having been in exactly the same situation before as we're in now (*déjà vu* means "already seen" in French). Some element in the present situation, familiar from some other context that you cannot identify—even a dream, a novel, or a movie—may make the entire situation seem so familiar that it feels like it happened before (Brown, 2004).

Your mental or physical state may also act as a retrieval cue, evoking a **state-dependent memory**. For example, if you are fearful or relaxed at the time of an event, you may remember that event best when you are once again in the same emotional state (Lang et al., 2001). When victims of violent crimes have trouble recalling details of the experience, it may be in part because they are feeling different emotions than they felt at the time of the crime (Clark, Milberg, & Erber, 1987).

You may also be better able to retrieve a memory when your current mood matches the kind of material you are trying to remember. You are likely to remember happy events better when you are feeling happy than when you are sad (Mayer, McCormick, & Strong, 1995). Similarly, you are likely to remember unhappy events better and remember more of them when you are feeling unhappy, which in turn creates a vicious cycle. The more unhappy memories you recall, the more depressed you feel, and the more depressed you feel, the more unhappy memories you recall . . . so you stay stuck in your depression and make it even worse (Lyubomirsky, Caldwell, & Nolen-

retroactive interference Forgetting that occurs when recently learned material interferes with the ability to remember similar material stored previously.

proactive interference Forgetting that occurs when previously stored material interferes with the ability to remember similar, more recently learned material.

cue-dependent forgetting The inability to retrieve information stored in memory because of insufficient cues for recall.

state-dependent memory The tendency to remember something when the rememberer is in the same physical or mental state as during the original learning or experience.

Charlie Chaplin's film City Lights *provides a classic illustration of state-dependent memory. After Charlie saves a drunken millionaire's life, the two spend the evening carousing. The next day, after sobering up, the millionaire fails to recognize Charlie and gives him the cold shoulder. Then, once again, the millionaire gets drunk—and again greets Charlie as a pal. (This is not an endorsement of drunkenness! Your memory will be best if you are sober during both encoding and recall.)*

Hoeksema, 1998; Wenzel, 2005). You can break out of this trap by deliberately focusing on memories of happy events instead of unpleasant ones.

The Repression Controversy

A final theory of forgetting is concerned with **amnesia**, the loss of memory for important personal information. Amnesia most commonly results from organic conditions such as brain disease or head injury, and is usually temporary. In *psychogenic amnesia*, however, the causes of forgetting are psychological, such as a need to escape feelings of embarrassment, guilt, shame, disappointment, or emotional shock. Psychogenic amnesia begins immediately after the precipitating event, involves massive memory loss including loss of personal identity, and usually ends suddenly, after just a few weeks. Despite its frequent portrayal in films and novels, in real life it is quite rare (McNally, 2003).

Psychologists generally accept the notion of psychogenic amnesia. *Traumatic amnesia*, however, is far more controversial. Traumatic amnesia allegedly involves the burying of specific traumatic events for long periods of time, often for many years. When the memory returns, it is supposedly immune to the usual processes of distortion and confabulation, and is recalled with perfect accuracy. The notion of traumatic amnesia originated with the psychoanalytic theory of Sigmund Freud, who argued that the mind defends itself from unwelcome and upsetting memories through the mechanism of **repression**—the in-

Thinking Critically About Repression and "Traumatic Amnesia"

voluntary pushing of threatening or upsetting information into the unconscious (see Chapter 2).

Most memory researchers reject the notion that a special unconscious mechanism called "repression" is necessary to explain either psychogenic or traumatic amnesia. Richard McNally (2003) reviewed the experimental and clinical evidence carefully and concluded, "The notion that the mind protects itself by repressing or dissociating memories of trauma, rendering them inaccessible to awareness, is a piece of psychiatric folklore devoid of convincing empirical support." The problem for most people who have suffered disturbing experiences is not that they cannot remember, but that they cannot forget: The memories keep intruding. There is no case on record of anyone who has "repressed" the entire memory of being in a concentration camp, being in combat, or being the victim of an earthquake or a terrorist attack, although details of even these horrible experiences are subject to distortion and fading over time, as are all memories.

Further, "repression" is hard to identify or to distinguish from normal forgetting. People who seem to forget disturbing experiences could be intentionally keeping themselves from retrieving their painful memories by distracting themselves whenever a memory is reactivated. Or they may be focusing on positive memories instead. Perhaps, understandably, they are not rehearsing unhappy memories, so the memories fade with time. Perhaps they are simply avoiding the retrieval cues that would evoke the memories. But a reluctance to think about an upsetting experience is not the same as an *inability* to remember it (McNally, 2003).

The debate over traumatic amnesia and repression erupted into the public arena in the 1990s when claims of recovered memories of sexual abuse began to occur. Many women and some men came to believe, during psychotherapy, that they could recall long-buried—"repressed"—memories of having been sexually victimized, usually by a father. For therapists who accepted the notion of repression, such claims were entirely believable (Brown, Scheflin, & Whitfield, 1999; J. Herman, 1992). But most researchers argue that although real abuse certainly occurs, many false memories of victimization have been encouraged by therapists who are unaware of the research we described earlier on the power of suggestion and the dangers of confabulation (Lindsay & Read, 1994; Loftus & Ketcham, 1994; McNally, 2003; Schacter, 2001). By asking leading questions, and by encouraging clients to construct vivid images of abuse, revisit those images frequently, and focus on emotional aspects of the images, such therapists unwittingly set up the very conditions that encourage confabulation and false memories—just as researchers have done purposely in the laboratory.

amnesia The partial or complete loss of memory for important personal information.

repression In psychoanalytic theory, the involuntary pushing of threatening or upsetting information into the unconscious.

In the movie Mysterious Skin, *a young man comes to believe he repressed the memory of being abducted by aliens when he was a child. How can critical thinkers evaluate claims of "repressed" and "recovered" memories?*

Since the 1990s, accusations have steadily declined and many accusers have reconciled with their families, some after realizing that their memories were false (Gardner, 2006; McHugh et al., 2004). The concept of repression, however, refuses to die. In one study, researchers even claimed to have discovered where in the brain repression occurs, by asking people "not to remember" certain words while fMRIs monitored their brain activity (Anderson et al., 2004). Critics, however, quickly pointed out that the study involved the forgetting of mundane words, not the alleged repression of painful memories, and most participants remembered the words they were asked to "repress" anyway (Garry & Loftus, 2004).

Of course, all memory researchers agree that it is possible for someone to forget a single unhappy or deeply unpleasant experience and then recall it years later, just as going back to your elementary school might trigger a memory of the time you were em-barrassed in front of your whole class. How, then, should we respond to an individual's claim to have repressed and later recovered memories of abuse? Given current research on memory, we should be skeptical if the person says that, thanks to therapy, he or she now has memories from the first year or two of life. (As we will see in the next section, this is not possible.) We should be skeptical if a person suddenly recovers a traumatic memory as a result of therapy or after hearing sensational stories in the news. We should be skeptical if, over time, the person's memories become more and more implausible—for instance, the person says that sexual abuse continued day and night for 15 years without ever being remembered and without anyone else in the household noticing anything amiss. And we should hear alarm bells go off if a therapist used suggestive techniques, such as hypnosis, dream analysis, "age regression," guided imagery, and leading questions, to "help" a patient recall the alleged abuse, because these techniques increase confabulation (see Chapter 12). In contrast, a person's recollections are more likely to be trustworthy if there is corroborating evidence from medical records or from the recollections of other family members, and if the person spontaneously recalled the event without pressure from others or the use of suggestive techniques in therapy.

QUICK quiz

If you have not repressed what you just read, try these questions.

1. When reading the novel *Even Cowgirls Get the Blues* years ago, Wilma became a fan of the author, Tom Robbins. Later, she developed a crush on actor/director Tim Robbins, but every time she tried to recall his name she called him "Tom." Why?

2. When a man at his twentieth high school reunion sees his old friends, he recalls incidents he thought were long forgotten. Why?

3. What mechanisms other than repression could account for a person's psychogenic amnesia?

Answers:

1. proactive interference 2. The sight of his friends provides retrieval cues for the incidents. 3. The person could be intentionally avoiding the memory by using distraction or focusing on positive experiences; failure to rehearse the memory may be causing it to fade; or the person may be avoiding retrieval cues that would evoke the memory.

WHAT'S *Ahead*

- Why are the first few years of life a mental blank?
- Why have human beings been called the "storytelling animal"?

Autobiographical Memories

For most of us, our memories about our own experiences are by far the most fascinating. We use them to entertain ("Did I ever tell you about the time . . .?"); we modify them—some people even publish them—in order to create an image of ourselves; we analyze them to learn more about who we are.

Childhood Amnesia: The Missing Years

A curious aspect of autobiographical memory is that most adults cannot recall any events from earlier than the third or fourth year of life. A few people apparently can recall momentous experiences that occurred when they were as young as 2 years old, such as the birth of a sibling, but not earlier ones (Newcombe et al., 2000; Usher & Neisser, 1993). As adults, we cannot remember being fed in infancy by our parents, taking our first steps, or uttering our first halting sentences. We are victims of **childhood amnesia** (sometimes called *infantile amnesia*).

There is something disturbing about childhood amnesia—so disturbing that some people adamantly deny it, claiming to remember events from the

> **Thinking Critically About "Memories" from Infancy**

second or even the first year of life. But like other false memories, these are merely reconstructions based on photographs, family stories, and imagination. The "remembered" event may not even have taken place. Swiss psychologist Jean Piaget (1952b) once reported a memory of nearly being kidnapped at the age of 2. Piaget remembered sitting in his pram, watching his nurse as she bravely defended him from the kidnapper. He remembered the scratches she received on her face. He remembered a police officer with a short cloak and white baton who finally chased the kidnapper away. But when Piaget was 15, his nurse wrote to his parents confessing that she had made up the entire story. Piaget noted, "I therefore must have heard, as a child, the account of this story . . . and projected it into the past in the form of a visual memory, which was a memory of a memory, but false."

Of course, we all retain procedural memories from the toddler stage, when we first learned to use a fork, drink from a cup, and pull a wagon. We also retain semantic memories acquired early in life: the rules of counting, the names of people and things, knowledge about objects in the world, words and meanings. Toddlers who are only 1 to 2 years old often reveal nonverbally that they remember past experiences (for example, by imitating something they saw earlier); and some 4-year-olds can remember experiences that occurred before age $2\frac{1}{2}$ (Bauer & Dow, 1994; McDonough & Mandler, 1994; Tustin & Hayne, 2006). What young children do not do well is encode and retain their early episodic memories—memories of particular events—and carry them into later childhood or adulthood.

Freud thought that childhood amnesia was a special case of repression, but memory researchers today think that repression has nothing to do with it. Biological psychologists believe that childhood amnesia occurs because brain areas involved in the formation or storage of events, and other areas involved in working memory and decision making (such as the prefrontal cortex), are not well devel-

This infant, whose leg is attached by a string to a colorful mobile, will learn within minutes to kick in order to make the mobile move. She may remember the trick a week later—an example of procedural memory. However, when she is older she will not remember the experience itself. Like the rest of us, she will fall victim to childhood amnesia.

oped until a few years after birth (McKee & Squire, 1993; Newcombe et al., 2000). Cognitive psychologists have proposed other explanations, which include the following:

1. *Lack of a sense of self.* In one view, we cannot have an autobiographical memory of ourselves until we have a self to remember. Indeed, autobiographical memories do not begin until the emergence of a self-concept, an event that occurs at somewhat different ages for different children, but not before the age of 2 (Howe, Courage, & Peterson, 1994).

2. *Impoverished encoding.* Preschoolers encode experiences far less elaborately than adults. Young children have not yet mastered the social conventions for reporting events; they do not know what is important and interesting to others. Instead, they tend to rely on adults' questions to provide retrieval cues ("Where did we go for breakfast?" "Who did you go trick-or-treating with?"). This dependency on adults may prevent them from building up a stable core of remembered material that will be available when they are older (Fivush & Hamond, 1991).

childhood (infantile) amnesia The inability to remember events and experiences that occurred during the first two or three years of life.

3 *A focus on the routine.* Preschoolers tend to focus on the routine, familiar aspects of an experience, such as eating lunch or playing with toys, rather than the distinctive aspects that will provide retrieval cues and make an event memorable in the long run (Fivush & Hamond, 1991).

4 *Children's ways of thinking about the world.* The cognitive schemas used by preschoolers are very different from those used by older children and adults. Only after acquiring language and starting school do children learn to think like adults. Their new, adultlike schemas do not contain the information and cues necessary for recalling earlier experiences, so memories of those experiences are lost (Howe & Courage, 1993).

Whatever the explanation for childhood amnesia, our first memories, even when they are not accurate, may provide useful insights into our personalities, current concerns, ambitions, and attitudes toward life. What are *your* first memories—or, at least, what do you think they are?

Memory and Narrative: The Stories of Our Lives

The communications researcher George Gerbner once observed that human beings are unique because they are the only animals that tell stories, and live by the stories they tell. This view of human beings as the "storytelling animal" has had a huge impact in cognitive psychology. The *narratives* we compose to simplify and make sense of our lives have a profound influence on our plans, memories, love affairs, hatreds, ambitions, and dreams.

Thus we say, "I am this way because, as a small child, this happened to me, and then my parents . . . ." We say, "Let me tell you the story of how we fell in love." We say, "When you hear what happened, you'll understand why I felt entitled to take such coldhearted revenge." These stories are not necessarily fiction, as in the child's meaning of "tell me a story." Rather, they are attempts to provide a unifying theme that organizes and gives meaning to the events of our lives. But because these narratives rely heavily on memory, and because memories are reconstructed and are constantly shifting in response to present needs, beliefs, and experiences, our stories are also, to some degree, works of interpretation and imagination. The "spin" you put on a story depends on who the audience is; you are apt to put in, leave out, understate, and embellish different things depending on whether you are relating an event in your life to a therapist, your boss, or a new acquaintance on MySpace.com. Your story is also influenced by your purpose in relating it: for example, to convey facts, entertain, or elicit sympathy. As a result of these influences, distortions are apt to creep in, even when you think you are being accurate. And once those distortions are part of the story, they are likely to become part of your memory of the events themselves (Marsh & B. Tversky, 2004).

Adult memories thus reveal as much about the present as they do about the past. And once we have formulated a story's central theme ("My parents opposed my plans," "My lover was domineering"), that theme may then serve as a cognitive schema that guides what we remember and

---

GET INVOLVED

Analyze a Childhood Memory

Write down as much as you can about an incident from your childhood that stands out in your memory. Now ask a friend or family member who was present at the time to write a description of the same event. Do your accounts differ? If so, why? Did you choose a happy memory or a bleak one, an early one from before age 5 or a later one? What does this exercise tell you about the nature of memory and about your own personality or your present concerns?

what we forget in the future (Mather, Shafir, & Johnson, 2000). The story's theme may also influence our judgments of events and people. If you have a fight with your lover, for example, the central theme in your story about the fight might be negative ("He was a jerk") or neutral ("It was a mutual misunderstanding"). This theme may bias you to blame or forgive your partner long after you have forgotten what the conflict was all about or who said what (McGregor & Holmes, 1999). You can see why you should be careful about the stories you tell!

Think of all the factors you have learned about that can trip you up when you are constructing your life story: confabulation, source misattribution, poor encoding and rehearsal strategies, interference, inadequate retrieval cues, suggestibility, and biases. By now, you should not be surprised that memory can be as fickle as it can be accurate. As cognitive psy-

"And here I am at two years of age. Remember? Mom? Pop? No? Or how about this one. My first day of school. Anyone?"

chologists have shown repeatedly, we are not merely actors in our personal life dramas; we also write the scripts.

psychology in the news REVISITED

The information you have read about in this chapter is having a significant impact on the criminal justice system. In part because of the work of psychological scientists, awareness about the fallibility of memory is growing among police, interrogators, prosecutors, and judges.

The case of Alan Newton, described in our opening news story, is not unusual. When psychological scientists examined 40 cases in which wrongful conviction had been established beyond a doubt, they found that 90 percent of those cases had involved a false identification by one or more eyewitnesses (Wells et al., 1998). Of course, not all eyewitness testimony is erroneous, and such testimony certainly needs to be heard and taken into account. But the potential for errors in identification makes it obvious how important it is to gather evidence carefully, ensure adequate legal representation for defendants, conduct police interviews using proper procedures, reduce pressure on witnesses, and obtain a DNA analysis whenever possible.

Inspired by the Innocence Project, grassroots organizations of lawyers and students in many states have been successfully challenging questionable convictions. Since the early 1990s, these efforts have led to the exoneration of hundreds of innocent people, some of whom had been condemned to death. One man in Illinois, who had been on death row for 16 years, was just hours from execution when a group of Northwestern University journalism students produced evidence that another man had committed the crime. In 2006, a documentary film, "After Innocence," chronicled seven cases of wrongful imprisonment; the men involved are still struggling to get their convictions expunged from their records.

How would you feel if your testimony resulted in the conviction of an innocent person? Would you be able to admit your mistake, or would you, as some have, cling more stubbornly than ever to the accuracy of your memory?

After Ronald Cotton was exonerated of the rape of Jennifer Thompson, the two became friends. Thompson says she has lived with constant anguish because of her mistaken identification.

In one such case, Jennifer Thompson, a rape victim whose testimony had led to the clearance of the actual perpetrator and conviction of the wrong man, later wrote in a *New York Times* editorial (June 18, 2000), "The man I was so sure I had never seen in my life was the man who was inches from my throat, who raped me, who hurt me, who took my spirit away, who robbed me of my soul. And the man I had identified so emphatically on so many occasions was absolutely innocent." Thompson.believes she initially picked out the photo of the innocent man, Ronald Cotton, because, of those presented to her, it most closely resembled the composite sketch she had already provided. Then, when she looked at an actual physical lineup, "I picked out Ronald because, subconsciously, in my mind, he resembled the photo, which resembled the composite, which resembled the attacker. All the images became enmeshed in one image that became Ron, and Ron became my attacker" (quoted in Simon, 2003).

Jennifer Thompson decided to meet Cotton and apologize to him personally. Amazingly, they were both able to put this tragedy behind them, overcome the racial barrier that divided them, and become friends. Nevertheless, she wrote, she still lives "with constant anguish that my profound mistake cost him so dearly. I cannot begin to imagine what would have happened had my mistaken identification occurred in a capital case." Thompson learned from personal experience what you have learned from this chapter: that eyewitnesses can and do make mistakes, that ethnic differences can increase these mistakes, that even memories for shocking or traumatic experiences are vulnerable to distortion and influence by others, and that our confidence in our memories is not a reliable guide to their accuracy.

The most important lesson to be learned from the research in this chapter, the lesson Jennifer Thompson learned to her despair and to her credit, is that human memory has both tremendous strengths and tremendous weaknesses. Because our deepest sense of ourselves relies on our memories, this is a difficult truth to accept. If we can do so, we will be able to respect the great power of memory and at the same time retain humility about our capacity for error, confabulation, and self-deception.

›TAKING ›PSYCHOLOGY ›WITH ›YOU

How to Remember What You Study

Someday in the near future, a "memory pill" may be available to perk up our memories. For the time being, however, those of us who hope to improve our memories must rely on mental strategies. Some simple mnemonics can be useful, but as we have seen, complicated ones are often more bother than they're worth. A better approach is to follow some general guidelines based on the principles in this chapter:

● **Pay attention!** It seems obvious, but often we fail to remember because we never encoded the information in the first place. For example, which of these is the real Lincoln penny?

Most Americans have trouble recognizing the real penny because they have never attended to the details of a penny's design (Nickerson & Adams, 1979). We are not advising you to do so, unless you happen to be a coin collector or a counterfeiting expert. Just keep in mind that when you do have something to remember, such as the material in this book, you will do better if you encode it well. (The real penny, by the way, is the left one in the bottom row.)

● **Encode information in more than one way.** The more elaborate the encoding of information, the more memorable it will be. Use your imagination! For instance, in addition to remembering a telephone number by the sound of the individual digits, you might note the spatial pattern they make as you punch them in on the telephone.

• **Add meaning.** The more meaningful the material, the more likely it is to link up with information already in long-term memory. Meaningfulness also reduces the number of chunks of information you have to learn. Common ways of adding meaning include making up a story about the material, thinking of examples, and forming visual images. (Some people find that the odder the image, the better.) If your license plate happens to be 236MPL, you might think of 236 maples. If you are trying to remember the concept of procedural memory from this chapter, you might make the concept meaningful by thinking of an example from your own life, such as your ability to ride a mountain bike, and then imagine a *P* superimposed on an image of yourself on your bike.

• **Take your time.** Leisurely learning, spread out over several sessions, usually produces better results than harried cramming (although *reviewing* material just before a test can be helpful). In terms of hours spent, "distributed" (spaced) learning sessions are more efficient than "massed" ones; in other words, three separate one-hour study sessions may result in more retention than one session of three hours.

• **Take time out.** If possible, minimize interference by using study breaks for rest or recreation. Sleep is the ultimate way to reduce interference. In a classic study, students who slept for eight hours after learning lists of nonsense syllables retained them better than students who went about their usual business (Jenkins & Dallenbach, 1924). Sleep is not always possible, of course, but periodic mental relaxation usually is.

• **Overlearn.** You can't remember something you never learned well in the first place. Overlearning —studying information even after you think you know it—is one of the best ways to ensure that you'll remember it.

• **Monitor your learning.** Test yourself frequently, rehearse thoroughly, and review periodically to see how you are doing. Don't just evaluate your learning immediately after reading the material, though; because the information is still in short-term memory, you are likely to feel a false sense of confidence about your ability to recall it later. If you delay making a judgment for at least a few minutes, your evaluation will probably be more accurate (Nelson & Dunlosky, 1991).

Whatever strategies you use, you will find that active learning produces more comprehension and better retention than does passive reading or listening. The mind does not gobble up information automatically; you must make the material digestible. Even then, you should not expect to remember everything you read or hear. Nor should you want to. Piling up facts without distinguishing the important from the trivial is just confusing. Popular books and tapes that promise a "perfect," "photographic" memory, or "instant recall" of everything you learn, fly in the face of what psychologists know about how the mind operates. Our advice: Forget them.

SUMMARY

Reconstructing the Past

• Unlike a tape recorder or video camera, human memory is highly selective and is *reconstructive*: People add, delete, and change elements in ways that help them make sense of information and events. They often experience *source misattribution,* the inability to distinguish information stored during an event from information added later. Even vivid *flashbulb memories* tend to become less accurate or complete over time.

• Because memory is reconstructive, it is subject to *confabulation,* the confusion of imagined events with actual ones. Confabulation is especially likely when people have thought, heard, or told others about the imagined event many times and thus experience *imagination inflation,* the image of the event contains many details, or the event is easy to imagine. Confabulated memories can feel emotionally, vividly real yet be false.

Memory and the Power of Suggestion

• The reconstructive nature of memory makes memory vulnerable to suggestion. Eyewitness testimony is especially vulnerable to error when the suspect's ethnicity differs from that of the witness, when leading questions are put to witnesses, or when the witnesses are given misleading information.

• As we saw in "Close-up on Research," findings on memory help clarify the issues in the debate about children's testimony. Like adults, children often remember the essential aspects of an event accurately. However, like adults, they can also be suggestible, especially when responding to biased interviewing by adults—for example, when they are asked questions that blur the line between fantasy and reality or when they are asked leading questions. Children who have strong language skills, have self-control in real-life situations, and have supportive, psychologically healthy parents are best able to resist biased interview techniques.

In Pursuit of Memory

• The ability to remember depends in part on the type of performance called for. In tests of *explicit memory* (conscious recollection), *recognition* is usually better than *recall*. In tests of *implicit memory*, which is measured by indirect methods such as *priming* and the *relearning method*, past experiences may affect current thoughts or actions even when these experiences are not consciously remembered.

• In *information-processing models*, memory involves the *encoding*, *storage*, and *retrieval* of information. In the *three-box model*, there are three interacting systems: the sensory register, short-term memory, and long-term memory. Some cognitive scientists prefer a *parallel distributed processing (PDP)* or *connectionist* model, which represents knowledge as connections among numerous interacting processing units, distributed in a vast network and all operating in parallel. But the three-box model continues to offer a convenient way to organize the major findings on memory.

The Three-Box Model of Memory

• In the three-box model, incoming sensory information makes a brief stop in the *sensory register*, which momentarily retains it in the form of sensory images.

• *Short-term memory (STM)* retains new information for up to 30 seconds by most estimates (unless rehearsal takes place). *Working memory* consists of STM and the mental processes that control the retrieval of information from long-term memory and interpret that information appropriately depending on the task you are doing. Or, alternatively, it may involve the ability to control attention and maintain information in an active, accessible state. The capacity of STM is extremely limited but can be extended if information is organized into larger units by *chunking*.

• *Long-term memory (LTM)* contains an enormous amount of information, which must be organized to make it manageable. Words (or the concepts they represent) are often organized by semantic categories. Many models of LTM represent its contents as a vast network of interrelated concepts. The way people use these networks depends on experience and education. Research on *tip-of-the-tongue (TOT)* states shows that words are also indexed in LTM in terms of sound and form.

• *Procedural memories* ("knowing how") are memories for how to perform specific actions; *declarative memories* ("knowing that") are memories for abstract or representational knowledge. Declarative memories include *semantic memories* (general knowledge) and *episodic memories* (memories for personally experienced events).

• The three-box model is often invoked to explain the *serial-position effect* in memory, but although it can explain the *primacy effect*, it cannot explain why a *recency effect* sometimes occurs after a considerable delay.

How We Remember

• In order to remember material well, we must encode it accurately in the first place. Some kinds of information, such as material in a college course, require *effortful*, as opposed to *automatic*, *encoding*. Rehearsal of information keeps it in short-term memory and increases the chances of long-term retention. *Elaborative rehearsal* is more likely to result in transfer to long-term memory than is *maintenance rehearsal*, and *deep processing* is usually more effective than *shallow processing*.

• *Mnemonics* can also enhance retention by promoting elaborative encoding and making material meaningful, but for ordinary memory tasks, complex memory tricks are often ineffective or even counterproductive.

Why We Forget

• Forgetting can occur for several reasons. Information in sensory and short-term memory appears to *decay* if it does not receive further processing. New information may "erase" and replace old information in long-term memory. *Proactive* and *retroactive interference* may take place. *Cue-dependent forgetting* may occur when *retrieval cues* are inadequate. The most effective retrieval cues are those that were present at the time of the initial experience. A person's mental or physical state may also act as a retrieval cue, evoking a *state-dependent memory*. We tend to remember best those events that are congruent with our current mood.

• *Amnesia*, the forgetting of personal information, usually occurs because of disease or injury to the brain. *Psychogenic amnesia*, which involves a loss of personal identity and has psychological causes, is rare. *Traumatic amnesia*, which allegedly involves the forgetting of specific traumatic events for long periods of time, is highly controversial, as is *repression*, the psychodynamic explanation of traumatic amnesia. Because these concepts lack good empirical support, psychological scientists are skeptical about their validity and about the accuracy of "recovered memories." Critics argue that many therapists, unaware of the power of suggestion and the dangers of confabulation, have encouraged false memories of victimization.

Autobiographical Memories

• Most people cannot recall any events from earlier than the third or fourth year. The reason for such *childhood amnesia* may be partly biological. Cognitive explanations include the lack of a sense of self until the age of 2 or 3, young children's impoverished encoding of their experiences, their focus on routine rather than distinctive aspects of an experience, and their immature cognitive schemas.

• A person's *narrative* "life story" organizes the events of his or her life and gives them meaning. Narratives change as people build up a store of episodic memories, and life stories are, to some degree, works of interpretation and imagination. The stories we tell people are affected by our purpose in telling them and who the audience is. The central themes of our stories can guide recall and influence our judgments of people and events.

Psychology in the News, Revisited

• Across the country, as DNA evidence has exonerated people falsely convicted of rape, murder and other crimes, people are becoming more aware of the limitations of eyewitness testimony and the fallibility of memory.

KEY TERMS

memory 266
reconstructive memory 266
source misattribution 266
flashbulb memories 267
confabulation 268
explicit memory 273
recall 273
recognition 273
implicit memory 273
relearning method 273
priming 274
information-processing models 274
encoding, storage, and retrieval 274

cognitive schemas 274
"three-box model" 274
parallel distributed processing (PDP) model 275
sensory register 276
short-term memory (STM) 276
working memory 276
chunks 277
long-term memory (LTM) 277
semantic categorics 278
tip-of-the-tongue (TOT) state 279
procedural memories 279

declarative memories 279
semantic memories 279
episodic memories 279
serial-position effect 279
primacy and recency effects 279
effortful versus automatic encoding 281
maintenance rehearsal 281
elaborative rehearsal 281
deep versus shallow processing 282
mnemonics 282

decay theory 284
retroactive interference 286
proactive interference 286
retrieval cues 286
cue-dependent forgetting 286
state-dependent memory 286
amnesia (organic) 287
psychogenic amnesia 287
traumatic amnesia 287
repression 287
childhood (infantile) amnesia 289
narratives 290

Memory refers to the capacity to retain and retrieve information, and also to the structures that account for this capacity.

Reconstructing the Past

The Manufacture of Memory

- Human memory is reconstructive: people add, delete, and change elements.
- **Source misattribution** is the inability to distinguish information stored during an event from information added later.
- Flashbulb memories, though emotionally powerful and vivid, are often embellished or change over time.

The Conditions of Confabulation

Confabulation is the confusion of imagined events with real ones, or confusing an event that happened to someone else with one that happened to you. Such confabulations are especially likely under certain circumstances:
- One has thought, heard, or told others about the imagined event many times.
- The image of the event contains lots of details that make it feel real.
- The event is wasy to imagine.

Memory and the Power of Suggestion

The Eyewitness on Trial

Eyewitness testimony is especially vulnerable to error when:
- The suspect's ethnicity differs from the witness's.
- Leading questions are put to the witness.
- Witnesses are given misleading information.

Children's Testimony

Children can be suggestible when:
- Questions blur the lines between reality and fantasy.
- They are asked leading questions.
- They are threatened or urged to give particular answers.
- They are pressured to conform to what other children have said.

In Pursuit of Memory

Measuring Memory

- In tests of **explicit memory**, or conscious recollection, **recognition** is usually better than **recall.**
- In tests of **implicit memory,** which is measured by indirect methods such as **priming** and the **relearning method,** past experiences may affect current thoughts or actions.

Models of Memory

- In information-processing models, memory involves encoding, storage, and retrieval.
- **Parallel distributed processing (PDP):** knowledge is represented as connections among thousands od interacting processing units, all operating in parallel.

The Three-Box Model of Memory

Three Memory Systems

	Sensory register	Short-term memory (STM)	Long-term memory(LTM)
Information from environment	1. Large capacity 2. Contains sensory information 3. Very brief retention of images (up to 1/2 second for visual; 2 seconds for auditory)	1. Limited capacity 2. Brief storage of items (up to 30 seconds if no rehearsal) 3. Involved in conscious processing of information	1. Unlimited capacity 2. Storage thought by some to be permanent 3. Information organized and indexed

Retrieved — Forgotten — Transferred — Forgotten — Transferred/Retrieved

Sensory Register

Incoming information stops in the **sensory register**, which momentarily retains it in the form of sensory images.

Short-Term Memory (STM)

Short-term memory (STM) retains information for up to 30 seconds.
- **Working memory** consists of STM and the mental processes that control the retrieval of information from long-term memory.
- **Chunking** extends the capacity of STM.

How We Remember

- Rehearsal of information keeps it in STM longer and increases the chances of retention.
- **Elaborative rehearsal** is more likely to result in transfer to LTM than is **maintenance rehearsal**.
- **Deep processing** is more effective than shallow processing.
- **Mnemonics** are strategies or tricks for improving memory.

Why We Forget

- **Decay theory** holds that memory eventually disappears if it is not accessed; applies best to sensory and short-term memory.
- Another theory emphasizes the replacement of old information by new information.
- A third theory emphasizes **proactive** and **retroactive interference** in storage or retrieval.
- **Cue-dependent forgetting** may be the most common type of forgetting; it occurs because of inadequate retrieval cues. When one's physical or mental state acts as a retrieval cue, **state-dependent memory** may result.

Autobiographical Memories

Childhood Amnesia

Reasons for **childhood amnesia** may be partly biological and partly due to:
- Lack of sense of self until the age of 2 or 3
- Preschoolers' impoverished encoding of experiences
- Their focus on routine rather than distinctive aspects of experience
- Immature cognitive schemas

Memory and Narrative

- A person's narrative (life story) organizes remembered life events and gives them meaning.
- Adult memories can reveal as much about the present as they do about the past.

The Repression Controversy

- **Amnesia** usually occurs as a result of brain disease or head injury, and is often temporary.
- Psychogenic amnesia has psychological causes and involves a loss of personal identity.
- Traumatic amnesia, which allegedly involves the burying of specific traumatic events for long periods of time, is highly controversial, as is **repression**, the psychodynamic explanation of traumatic amnesia.
- Critics argue that many therapists, unaware of the power of suggestion and the dangers of confabulation, have encouraged false memories of victimization.

Long-Term Memory (LTM)

Information in **long-term memory (LTM)** is organized as a network of interrelated concepts and includes:
- **Procedural memories**
- **Declarative memories**
  — **Semantic**
  — **Episodic**
- The **serial position effect** is the tendency for strongest recall of the first and last items on a list.

psychology in the news

School Orders Mother to Spank Son

CHICAGO, MARCH 6, 2005. Officials at a private school, Schaumberg Christian, have suspended a 6-year-old boy after his mother refused to discipline her son by spanking him.

The first grader, Chandler Scott Fallaw, had been talking in class, chewing gum, bringing toys to school, and failing to do his homework. When his mother, Michelle Fallaw-Gabrielson, arrived to pick him up on Wednesday, an assistant administrator told her to take him to the administrator's office and spank him for the infractions or the boy would be suspended for a day. Fallaw-Gabrielson refused and the next day withdrew him from the school. "I was so shocked that they were putting me in this situation," she said. Although she readily admits that her son is "far from perfect," she says she prefers to use other disciplinary measures, such as time-outs and taking away toys.

The American Civil Liberties Union and other groups concerned about corporal punishment say that the school's requirement, although unusual, seems to be legal. Private schools have wide discretion in disciplinary matters. In nearly half of American states, corporal punishment is also allowed in public schools at the discretion of individual school boards. Although the practice is seldom used, efforts to abolish it often run into strong opposition from some parents and teachers.

Schaumburg Christian's parent-student handbook states that parents may be asked to administer corporal punishment if the school considers it necessary, and parents must sign a "statement of cooperation" with school policies upon enrolling their child. Fallaw-Gabrielson, however, says the policy did not state clearly that the school could issue her an ultimatum and that her son could be suspended if she did not comply. A school administrator, Randy Thaxton, says that situations requiring spanking have been rare at the school. However, inside a desk drawer he keeps a lightweight wooden paddle that can be used for that purpose.

Fallaw-Gabrielson has praise for the school's academic program but feels that school personnel did not deal creatively with her son. Although Chandler is in the first grade, he tests two grade levels higher, so his mother thinks his discipline problems could be due to his feeling restless and bored—something corporal punishment won't change. "I feel like physical [discipline] is not the answer," she says.

Teachers have been disciplining disobedient students ever since schools began and historically, a leading method has been physical punishment. These figurines show a schoolboy forced to hold up heavy bricks with his arms extended and another being hit on his bare buttocks. Spanking students for unruly behavior is still allowed in many U. S. states.

Learning

Is Michelle Fallaw-Gabrielson right, or was the school's demand for corporal punishment justified? Are slapping and spanking sometimes the only recourse for curbing unruly behavior, or are parents who use corporal punishment guilty of child abuse?

The debate over how to discipline children has been with us for a long time. At the core of this debate is a general question: What are the best ways to get people to behave well and to discourage them from behaving badly? It may surprise you to know that this issue is a central one for researchers who study learning. To psychologists, **learning** refers not just to the skills acquired in school but also to *any* relatively permanent change in behavior that occurs because of experience. Experience is the greatest teacher, providing the essential link between the past and the future and enabling a person (or animal) to adapt to changing circumstances. The particular experiences an individual has—both pleasant (like

learning A relatively permanent change in behavior (or behavioral potential) due to experience.

behaviorism An approach to psychology that emphasizes the study of observable behavior and the role of the environment as a determinant of behavior.

conditioning A basic kind of learning that involves associations between environmental stimuli and the organism's responses.

FIGURE 9.1
A Modification of Pavlov's Method

In the apparatus on the right, which was based on Pavlov's techniques, saliva from a dog's cheek flowed down a tube and was measured by the movement of a needle on a revolving drum. In the photo, you can see Ivan Pavlov himself (in the white beard), flanked by his students and a canine subject.

getting a good grade) and unpleasant (like getting paddled or suspended from school)—affect how the person is likely to act in the future.

Research on learning has been heavily influenced by **behaviorism**, the school of psychology that accounts for behavior in terms of observable acts and events, without reference to mental entities, such as "mind" or "will" (see Chapter 1). Behaviorists focus on a basic kind of learning called **conditioning**, which involves associations between environmental stimuli and responses. In fact, behaviorism is sometimes referred to informally as stimulus–reponse ("S–R") psychology.

Behaviorists have shown that two types of conditioning—*classical conditioning* and *operant conditioning*—can explain much of human behavior. But other approaches, including *social-cognitive learning theories*, hold that omitting mental processes from explanations of human learning is like omitting passion from descriptions of sex: You may explain the form, but you miss the essence. To social-cognitive theorists, learning includes not only changes in behavior but also changes in our thoughts, expectations, and knowledge.

As you read about the principles of conditioning and learning in this chapter, ask yourself what they can teach us about the use of punishment to control undesirable behavior. Chandler Fallaw's school believes in the biblical admonition "spare the rod and spoil the child," meaning if that if you do not administer physical punishment (the "rod") when a child misbehaves, you will fail in your duty to raise a well-behaved child. This philosophy is shared by millions of people. But is physical punishment really an effective method of getting students to do their homework or stop chewing gum? What is the best way to modify other people's behavior—and our own?

WHAT'S *Ahead*

- Why would a dog salivate when it sees a light bulb or hears a buzzer?
- How can classical conditioning help explain prejudice?
- If you have learned to fear collies, why might you also be scared of sheepdogs?

Classical Conditioning

At the start of the twentieth century, the great Russian physiologist Ivan Pavlov (1849–1936) was studying salivation in dogs as part of a research program on digestion. His work would shortly win him the Nobel Prize. One of Pavlov's procedures was to make a surgical opening in a dog's cheek and insert a tube that conducted saliva away from the animal's salivary gland so that the saliva could be measured. To stimulate the reflexive flow of saliva, Pavlov placed meat powder or other food in the dog's mouth. This procedure was later refined by others (see Figure 9.1).

Pavlov was a truly dedicated scientific observer. Many years later, as he lay dying, he even dictated his sensations for posterity! And he instilled in his students the same passion for detail. During his salivation studies, one of these students noticed something that most people would have overlooked or dismissed as trivial. After a dog had been brought to the laboratory a number of times, it would start to salivate *before* the food was placed in its mouth. The sight or smell of the food, the dish in which the food was kept, and even the sight of the person who delivered the food each day or the sound of the person's footsteps were enough to start the dog's mouth watering. This new salivary response clearly was not inborn, so it must have been acquired through experience.

At first, Pavlov treated the dog's drooling as merely an annoying secretion. But he quickly realized that his student had stumbled onto an important phenomenon, one that Pavlov came to believe was the basis of all learning in human beings and other animals (Pavlov, 1927). He called that phenomenon a "conditional" reflex—conditional because it depended on environmental conditions. Later, an error in the translation of his writings transformed "conditional" into "conditioned," the word most commonly used today.

Pavlov soon dropped what he had been doing and turned to the study of conditioned reflexes, to which he devoted the last three decades of his life. Why were his dogs salivating to things other than food?

New Reflexes from Old

At first, Pavlov speculated about what his dogs might be thinking and feeling to make them drool before getting their food. Was the doggy equivalent of "Oh boy, this means chow time" going through their minds? Eventually, however, he decided that such speculation was pointless. Instead, he focused on the environment in which the conditioned reflex arose.

The original salivary reflex, according to Pavlov, consisted of an **unconditioned stimulus (US)**, food, and an **unconditioned response (UR)**, salivation. By an unconditioned stimulus, Pavlov meant an event or thing that elicits a response automatically or reflexively. By an unconditioned response, he meant the response that is automatically produced:

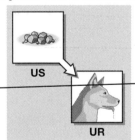

Learning occurs, said Pavlov, when a neutral stimulus (one that does not yet produce a particular response, such as salivation) is regularly paired with an unconditioned stimulus:

The neutral stimulus then becomes a **conditioned stimulus (CS)**, which elicits a learned or conditioned response **(CR)** that is usually similar to the original, unlearned one. In Pavlov's laboratory, the sight of the food dish, which had not previously elicited salivation, became a CS for salivation:

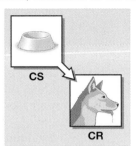

The procedure by which a neutral stimulus becomes a conditioned stimulus eventually became known as **classical conditioning**, also called *Pavlovian* or *respondent conditioning*. Pavlov and his students went on to show that all sorts of things can become conditioned stimuli for salivation if they are paired with food: the ticking of a metronome, the musical tone of a bell or a tuning fork, the vibrating sound of a buzzer, a touch on the leg, a triangle drawn on a large card, even a pinprick or an electric shock. And since Pavlov's day, many automatic, involuntary responses besides salivation have been classically conditioned—for example, heartbeat, stomach secretions, blood pressure, reflexive movements, blinking, and muscle contractions. The optimal interval between the presentation of the neutral stimulus and the presentation of the US depends on the kind of response involved; in the laboratory, the interval is often less than a second.

Principles of Classical Conditioning

Classical conditioning occurs in all species, from worms to *Homo sapiens*. Let's look more closely at some important features of this process: extinction, higher-order conditioning, and stimulus generalization and discrimination.

Extinction   Conditioned responses do not necessarily last forever. If, after conditioning, the conditioned stimulus is repeatedly presented without the unconditioned stimulus, the conditioned response eventually disappears, and **extinction** is said to have occurred (see Figure 9.2). Suppose that you train your dog Milo to salivate to the sound of a bell, but then you ring the bell every five minutes and do *not* follow it with food. Milo will salivate less and less to the bell and will soon stop salivating to the bell altogether; salivation will have been extinguished. However, if you come back the next day

Pavlov = classical.

unconditioned stimulus (US) The classical-conditioning term for a stimulus that elicits a reflexive response in the absence of learning.

unconditioned response (UR) The classical-conditioning term for a reflexive response elicited by a stimulus in the absence of learning.

conditioned stimulus (CS) The classical-conditioning term for an initially neutral stimulus that comes to elicit a conditioned response after being associated with an unconditioned stimulus.

conditioned response (CR) The classical-conditioning term for a response that is elicited by a conditioned stimulus; it occurs after the conditioned stimulus is associated with an unconditioned stimulus.

classical conditioning The process by which a previously neutral stimulus acquires the capacity to elicit a response through association with a stimulus that already elicits a similar or related response.

extinction The weakening and eventual disappearance of a learned response; in classical conditioning, it occurs when the conditioned stimulus is no longer paired with the unconditioned stimulus.

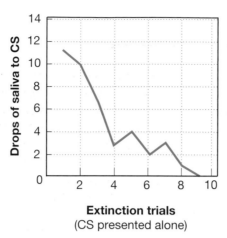

Acquisition trials
(CS paired with US)

Extinction trials
(CS presented alone)

FIGURE 9.2
Acquisition and Extinction of a Salivary Response
A neutral stimulus that is consistently followed by an unconditioned stimulus for salivation will become a conditioned stimulus for salivation (left). But when this conditioned stimulus is then repeatedly presented without the US, the conditioned salivary response will weaken and eventually disappear (right); it has been extinguished.

spontaneous recovery
The reappearance of a learned response after its apparent extinction.

higher-order conditioning In classical conditioning, a procedure in which a neutral stimulus becomes a conditioned stimulus through association with an already established conditioned stimulus.

stimulus generalization
After conditioning, the tendency to respond to a stimulus that resembles one involved in the original conditioning; in classical conditioning, it occurs when a stimulus that resembles the CS elicits the CR.

stimulus discrimination
The tendency to respond differently to two or more similar stimuli; in classical conditioning, it occurs when a stimulus similar to the CS fails to evoke the CR.

and ring the bell, Milo may salivate again for a few trials. The reappearance of the response, called **spontaneous recovery**, explains why completely eliminating a conditioned response usually requires more than one extinction session.

Higher-Order Conditioning

Sometimes a neutral stimulus can become a conditioned stimulus by being paired with an already established CS, a procedure known as **higher-order conditioning**. Say Milo has learned to salivate to the sight of a food dish. Now you flash a bright light before you present the dish. With repeated pairings of the light and the dish, Milo may learn to salivate to the light. The procedure for higher-order conditioning is illustrated in Figure 9.3.

Higher-order conditioning may explain why some words trigger emotional responses in us—why they can inflame us to anger or evoke warm, sentimental feelings. When words are paired with objects or other words that already elicit some emotional response, they, too, may come to elicit that response (Chance, 1999; Staats & Staats, 1957). For example, a child may learn a positive response to the word *birthday* because of its association with gifts and attention. Conversely, the child may learn a negative response to ethnic or national labels, such as *Swede*, *Pole*, or *Jew*, if those words are paired with words that the child has already learned are disagreeable, such as *dumb* or *dirty*. Higher-order conditioning, in other words, may contribute to the formation of prejudices.

Stimulus Generalization and Discrimination

After a stimulus becomes a conditioned stimulus for some response, other, similar stimuli may produce a similar reaction—a phenomenon known as **stimulus generalization**. For example, if you condition your patient pooch Milo to salivate to middle C on the piano, Milo may also salivate to D, which is one tone above C, even though you did not pair D with food. Stimulus generalization is described nicely by an old English proverb: "He who hath been bitten by a snake fears a rope."

The mirror image of stimulus generalization is **stimulus discrimination** in which *different* responses are made to stimuli that resemble the conditioned stimulus in some way. Suppose that you have conditioned Milo to salivate to middle C on the piano by repeatedly pairing the sound with food. Now you play middle C on a guitar, without following it by food (but you continue to follow C on the piano by food). Eventually, Milo will learn to

FIGURE 9.3
Higher-Order Conditioning
In this illustration of higher-order conditioning, the food dish is a previously conditioned stimulus for salivation (left). When the light, a neutral stimulus, is paired with the dish (center), the light also becomes a conditioned stimulus for salivation (right).

GET INVOLVED

Conditioning an Eye-Blink Response

Try out your behavioral skills by conditioning an eye-blink response in a willing friend, using classical-conditioning procedures. You will need a drinking straw and something to make a ringing sound; a spoon tapped on a water glass works well. Tell your friend that you are going to blow in his or her eye through the straw, but do not say why. Immediately before each puff of air, make the ringing sound. Repeat this procedure ten times. Then make the ringing sound while holding the straw up to the person's eye, but *don't* puff. Your friend will probably blink anyway and may continue to do so for one or two more repetitions of the sound before the response extinguishes. Can you identify the US, the UR, the CS, and the CR in this exercise?

---

salivate to a C on the piano and not to salivate to the same note on the guitar; that is, he will discriminate between the two sounds. If you keep at this long enough, you could train Milo to be a pretty discriminating drooler!

What is Actually Learned in Classical Conditioning?

For classical conditioning to be most effective, the stimulus to be conditioned should *precede* the unconditioned stimulus rather than follow it or occur simultaneously with it. This makes sense because in classical conditioning, the conditioned stimulus becomes a signal for the unconditioned stimulus. Classical conditioning is in fact an evolutionary adaptation, one that enables the organism to anticipate and prepare for a biologically important event that is about to happen. In Pavlov's studies, for instance, a bell, buzzer, or other stimulus was a signal that meat was coming, and the dog's salivation was preparation for digesting food.

Today, therefore, many psychologists contend that what an animal or person actually learns in classical conditioning is not merely an association between two paired stimuli that occur close together in time, but rather *information* conveyed by one stimulus about another: for example, "If a tone sounds, food is likely to follow" (Davey, 1992). This view is supported by the research of Robert Rescorla (1988), who showed, in a series of imaginative studies, that the mere pairing of an unconditioned stimulus and a neutral stimulus is not enough to produce learning. To become a conditioned stimulus, the neutral stimulus must reliably signal, or predict, the unconditioned stimulus. If food occurs just as often without a preceding tone as with it, the tone is unlikely to become a condi-

tioned stimulus for salivation, because the tone does not provide any information about the likelihood of getting food.

In everyday life, too, a potential CS may sometimes predict an unconditioned stimulus and sometimes not, so conditioning is less certain than when the CS and US always occur together in the laboratory. A friend of ours, behaviorist Paul Chance, gave us this example: Suppose you work in an office where you are allowed to receive routine calls only from other employees; you may take outside calls only in emergencies. One day, there are three emergencies: Your lover calls to jilt you, the police call to report that your new car was stolen, and your landlord calls to tell you that a broken water pipe has flooded your apartment. If these were the only calls you got, the next time you heard the phone ring (the CS) you might freak out (the CR). But if they occurred randomly among 50 routine business calls, the phone's ringing would probably not upset you (any more than it already has!) because it would not necessarily signal another disaster.

Rescorla (1988) concluded that "Pavlovian conditioning is not a stupid process by which the organism willy-nilly forms associations between any two stimuli that happen to co-occur. Rather, the organism is better seen as an information seeker using logical and perceptual relations among events, along with its own preconceptions, to form a sophisticated representation of its world." Not all learning theorists agree with this conclusion; an orthodox behaviorist would say that it is silly to talk about the preconceptions of a rat. The important point, however, is that concepts such as "information seeking," "preconceptions," and "representations of the world" open the door to a more cognitive view of classical conditioning.

QUICK quiz

Classical-conditioning terms can be hard to learn, so be sure to take this quiz before going on.

A. Name the unconditioned stimulus, unconditioned response, conditioned stimulus, and conditioned response in these two situations:

1. Five-year-old Samantha is watching a storm from her window. A huge bolt of lightning is followed by a tremendous thunderclap, and Samantha jumps at the noise. This happens several more times. There is a brief lull and then another lightning bolt. Samantha jumps in response to the bolt.

2. Gregory's mouth waters whenever he eats anything with lemon in it. One day, while reading an ad that shows a big glass of lemonade, Gregory finds that his mouth has started to water.

B. In the view of many learning theorists, pairing a neutral and an unconditioned stimulus is not enough to produce learning; the neutral stimulus must _____ the unconditioned stimulus.

Answers:

A. 1. US = the thunderclap; UR = jumping elicited by the noise; CS = the sight of the lightning; CR = jumping elicited by the lightning. 2. US = the taste of lemon; UR = salivation elicited by the taste of lemon; CS = the picture of a glass of lemonade; CR = salivation elicited by the picture. B. signal or predict

WHAT'S *Ahead*

- Why do advertisers often include pleasant music and gorgeous scenery in ads for their products?

- How would a classical-conditioning theorist explain your irrational fear of heights or mice?

- If you eat licorice and then happen to get the flu, how might your taste for licorice change?

- How can sitting in a doctor's office make you feel sick?

Classical Conditioning in Real Life

If a dog can learn to salivate to the ringing of a bell, so can you. In fact, you probably have learned to salivate to the sound of a lunch bell, not to mention the phrase *hot fudge sundae*, "mouth-watering" pictures of food in magazines, the sight of a server in a restaurant, and a voice calling out "Dinner's ready!" But the role of classical conditioning goes far beyond the learning of simple reflexive responses; conditioning affects us every day in many ways.

One of the first psychologists to recognize the real-life implications of Pavlovian theory was John B. Watson, who founded American behaviorism and enthusiastically promoted Pavlov's ideas. Watson believed that the whole rich array of human emotion and behavior could be accounted for by conditioning principles. For example, he thought that you learned to love another person when that person was paired with stroking and cuddling. Watson turned out to be wrong about love, which is a lot more complicated than he thought (see Chapter 14). But he was right about the power of classical conditioning to affect our emotions, preferences, and tastes.

Learning to Like

Classical conditioning plays a big role in our emotional responses to objects, events, and places. It can explain why sentimental feelings sweep over us when we see a school mascot, a national flag, or the logo of the Olympic Games: These objects have been associated in the past with positive feelings.

Many Madison Avenue techniques for getting us to like clients' products are also based on the principles first demonstrated by Pavlov, whether advertising executives realize it or not. In one study, college students looked at slides of either a beige pen or a blue pen. During the presentation, half the students heard a song from a recent musical film, and half heard a selection of traditional music from India. (The experimenter made the reasonable assumption that the show tune would be more appealing to the young Americans participating in the study.) Later the students were allowed to choose one of the pens. Almost three-fourths of those who heard the popular music chose a pen that was the same color as the one they had seen in the slides. An equal number of those who heard the Indian music chose a pen that *differed* in color from the one they had seen (Gorn, 1982).

In classical-conditioning terms, the music in this study was an unconditioned stimulus for internal responses associated with pleasure or displeasure, and the pens became conditioned stimuli for similar responses. You can see why television commercials often pair products with music, attractive people, or other appealing sounds and images.

Learning to Fear

Positive emotions are not the only ones that can be classically conditioned; so can dislikes and negative emotions such as fear. A person can learn to fear just about anything if it is paired with something that elicits pain, surprise, or embarrassment. Human beings, however, are biologically primed or "prepared" to learn some kinds of fears more easily than others. It is far easier to establish a conditioned fear of spiders, snakes, and heights than of butterflies, flowers, and toasters (Öhman & Mineka, 2001). The former can be dangerous to your health, so in the process of evolution, human beings acquired a tendency to learn quickly to be wary of them. Some theorists believe that evolution has also instilled in humans a readiness to learn to fear unfamiliar members of ethnic groups other than their own and that this tendency may contribute to the emotional underpinnings of prejudice (Olsson et al., 2005; see Chapter 10).

When fear of an object or situation becomes irrational and interferes with normal activities, it qualifies as a *phobia*. To demonstrate how a phobia might be learned, John Watson and Rosalie Rayner (1920/2000) deliberately established a rat phobia in an 11-month-old boy named Albert. Their goal was to demonstrate how an inborn reaction of fear could transfer to a wide range of stimuli; today we call this stimulus generalization. They also wanted to demonstrate that adult emotional responses, such as specific fears, could originate in early childhood. The procedures and reporting procedures used by Watson and Rayner have been criticized over the years, and for ethical reasons, no psychologist today would attempt to do such a thing to a child. Nevertheless, the study remains a classic, and its main conclusion, that fears can be conditioned, is still well accepted.

"Little Albert" was a placid child who rarely cried. (Watson and Rayner deliberately chose such a child because they thought their demonstration would do him relatively little harm.) When Watson and Rayner gave him a live furry rat to play with, Albert showed no fear; in fact, he was delighted. The same was true when they showed him a variety of other objects, including a rabbit and some cotton wool. However, like most children, Albert was innately afraid of loud noises. When the researchers made a loud noise by striking a steel bar with a hammer, he would jump and fall sideways onto the mattress where he was sitting. The noise made by the hammer was an unconditioned stimulus for the unconditioned response of fear.

Having established that Albert liked rats, Watson and Rayner set about teaching him to fear them. Again they offered him a rat, but this time, as Albert reached for it, one of the researchers struck the steel bar. Startled, Albert fell onto the mattress. A week later, the researchers brought Albert back to the laboratory and repeated this procedure several times. Albert began to whimper and tremble. Finally, the rat was offered alone without the noise. Albert fell over, cried, and crawled away so quickly that he almost reached the edge of the table he was sitting on before an adult caught him; the rat had become a conditioned stimulus for fear (see Figure 9.4). Tests done a few days later showed that Albert's fear had generalized to other hairy or furry

On the TV show Monk, *the lead character has a phobic fear of germs. How did he get to be that way?*

FIGURE 9.4
The Creation of a Fear
In the Little Albert study, noise from a hammer striking a steel bar was an unconditioned stimulus for fear (left). When a white rat, a neutral stimulus, was paired with the noise (center), the rat then became a conditioned stimulus for fear (right).

objects, including white rabbits, cotton wool, a Santa Claus mask, and even John Watson's hair.

Unfortunately, Watson and Rayner lost access to Little Albert, so we do not know how long the child's fears lasted. (We do know, however, that at a final session his fears had already diminished somewhat and had to be "freshened" by repeating the pairing of the conditioned stimuli with the loud noise.) Further, because the study ended early, Watson and Rayner had no opportunity to reverse the conditioning. However, Watson and Mary Cover Jones did reverse another child's conditioned fear—one that was, as Watson put it, "home-grown" rather than psychologist-induced (Jones, 1924). A 3-year-old named Peter was deathly afraid of rabbits. Watson and Jones eliminated this fear with a method called **counterconditioning**, in which a conditioned stimulus is paired with some other stimulus that elicits a response incompatible with the unwanted response. In this case, the rabbit (the CS) was paired with a snack of milk and crackers, and the snack produced pleasant feelings incompatible with the conditioned response of fear. At first, the researchers kept the rabbit some distance from Peter, so that his fear would remain at a low level. Otherwise, Peter might have learned to fear milk and crackers! But gradually, over several days, they brought the rabbit closer and closer. Eventually Peter learned to like rabbits; he was even able to sit with the rabbit in his lap, playing with it with one hand while he ate with the other. A variation of this procedure, called *systematic desensitization*, was later devised for treating phobias in adults (see Chapter 12).

Accounting for Taste

Classical conditioning can also explain how we learn to like and dislike many foods and odors. In the laboratory, researchers have taught animals to dislike foods or odors by pairing them with drugs that cause nausea or other unpleasant symptoms. One researcher trained slugs to associate the smell of carrots, which slugs normally like, with a bitter-tasting chemical that they detest. Soon the slugs were avoiding the smell of carrots. The researcher then demonstrated higher-order conditioning by pairing the smell of carrots with the smell of potato. Sure enough, the slugs began to avoid the smell of potato as well (Sahley, Rudy, & Gelperin, 1981).

Many people have learned to dislike a food after eating it and then falling ill, even when the two events were unrelated. The food, previously a neutral stimulus, becomes a conditioned stimulus for nausea or for other symptoms produced by the

counterconditioning
In classical conditioning, the process of pairing a conditioned stimulus with a stimulus that elicits a response that is incompatible with an unwanted conditioned response.

Whether we say "yuck" or "yum" to a food may depend on a past experience involving classical conditioning.

illness. Psychologist Martin Seligman once told how he himself was conditioned to hate béarnaise sauce. One night, shortly after he and his wife ate a delicious filet mignon with béarnaise sauce, he came down with the flu. Naturally, he felt wretched. His misery had nothing to do with the béarnaise sauce, of course, yet the next time he tried it, he found he disliked the taste (Seligman & Hager, 1972).

Notice that unlike conditioning in the laboratory, Seligman's aversion to the sauce occurred after only one pairing of the sauce with illness and with a considerable delay between the conditioned and unconditioned stimuli. Moreover, Seligman's wife did not become a conditioned stimulus for nausea, and neither did his dinner plate or the server, even though they also had been paired with illness. Why? In earlier work with rats, John Garcia and Robert Koelling (1966) had provided the answer: the existence of a greater biological readiness to associate sickness with taste than with sights or sounds. Later work established the same principle (the "Garcia effect") for many species, including human beings. Like the tendency to acquire certain fears, this biological tendency probably evolved through natural selection because it enhanced survival: Eating bad food is more likely to be followed by illness and death than are particular sights or sounds.

Reacting to Medical Treatments

Because of classical conditioning, medical treatments can create unexpected misery or relief from symptoms for reasons that are entirely unrelated to the treatment itself.

For example, unpleasant reactions to a treatment can generalize to a wide range of other stimuli. This is a particular problem for cancer patients. The nausea and vomiting resulting from chemotherapy often generalize to the place where the therapy takes place, the waiting room, the sound of a nurse's voice, or the smell of rubbing alcohol. The drug treatment is an unconditioned stimulus for nausea and vomiting, and through association, the other previously neutral stimuli become conditioned stimuli for these responses. Even *mental images* of the sights and smells of the clinic may become conditioned stimuli for nausea (Dadds et al., 1997; Redd et al., 1993).

Some cancer patients also acquire a classically conditioned anxiety response to anything associated with their chemotherapy. In one study, patients who drank lemon-lime Kool-Aid before their therapy sessions developed an anxiety response to the drink—an example of higher-order conditioning. They continued to feel anxious even when the drink was offered in their homes rather than at the clinic (Jacobsen et al., 1995).

On the other hand, patients may have *reduced* pain and anxiety when they receive placebos—pills and injections that have no active ingredients or treatments that have no direct physical effect on the problem (see Chapter 1). Placebos can be amazingly powerful, especially when they take the form of a large pill, a pill with a brand name, or an injection (Benedetti & Levi-Montalcini, 2001). Why do they work? Biological psychologists have shown that placebos can actually affect the brain in much the same way as real treatments do (see Chapter 6). Cognitive psychologists emphasize the role of expectations (at least in humans); expectations of getting better may reduce anxiety and thus boost the immune system, or perhaps they encourage

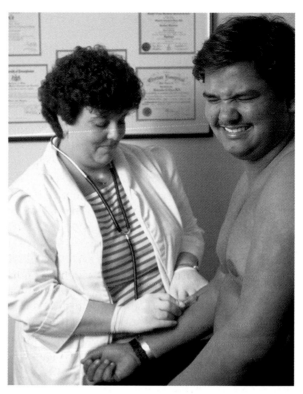

The anxiety that many people feel about having blood drawn can generalize to the nurse, the room, the sight of needles. . . .

us to cope better with our symptoms. Behaviorists, in contrast, argue that the doctor's white coat, the room in the doctor's office or medical clinic, and pills or injections all become conditioned stimuli for relief from symptoms because these stimuli have been associated in the past with *real* drugs (Ader, 2000). The real drugs are the unconditioned stimuli, the relief they bring is the unconditioned response, and the placebos acquire the ability to elicit similar reactions, thereby becoming conditioned responses.

QUICK quiz

We hope you have not acquired a classically conditioned fear of quizzes. See whether you can supply the correct term to describe the outcome in each of these situations.

1. After a child learns to fear spiders, he also responds with fear to ants, beetles, and other crawling bugs.
2. A toddler is afraid of the bath, so her father puts just a little water in the tub and gives the child a lollipop to suck on while she is being washed. Soon the little girl loses her fear of the bath.
3. A factory worker's mouth waters whenever a noontime bell signals the beginning of his lunch break. One day, the bell goes haywire and rings every half hour. By the end of the day, the worker has stopped salivating to the bell.

Answers:

1. stimulus generalization   2. counterconditioning   3. extinction

WHAT'S *Ahead*

• What do praising a child and quitting your nagging have in common?

• How can operant principles account for superstitious rituals?

• What is the best way to discourage a friend from interrupting you while you are studying?

• How do trainers teach guide dogs to perform the amazing services they do for their owners?

Operant Conditioning

▶ **operant conditioning**
The process by which a response becomes more likely to occur or less so, depending on its consequences.

At the end of the nineteenth century, in the first known scientific study of anger, G. Stanley Hall (1899) asked people to describe angry episodes they had experienced or observed. One person told of a 3-year-old girl who broke out in furious, seemingly uncontrollable sobs when she was punished by being kept home from a ride. In the middle of her tantrum, the child suddenly stopped crying and asked her nanny in a perfectly calm voice if her father was in. Told no, she immediately resumed her sobbing.

Children, of course, cry for many valid reasons—pain, discomfort, fear, illness, fatigue—and these cries deserve an adult's sympathy and attention. The child in Hall's study, however, was crying for a different reason. She had learned from prior experience that an outburst of sobbing would bring her attention and possibly the ride she wanted. Her

the neighborhood. Jerry Van Amerongen

STAY OUT

© 1989 Cowles Syndicate, Inc. 10-21

An instantaneous learning experience.

tantrum illustrates one of the most basic laws of learning: *Behavior becomes more likely or less likely depending on its consequences.*

This principle is at the heart of **operant conditioning** (also called *instrumental conditioning*), the second type of conditioning studied by behaviorists. In classical conditioning, it does not matter whether an animal's or person's behavior has consequences; in Pavlov's procedure, for example, the dog got food whether it salivated or not. But in operant conditioning, the organism's response (the little girl's sobbing, for example) *operates* or produces effects on the environment. These effects, in turn, influence whether the response will occur again.

Classical conditioning and operant conditioning also tend to differ in the types of responses they involve. In classical conditioning, the response is typically reflexive, an automatic reaction to something happening in the environment, such as the sight of food or the sound of a bell. Generally, responses in operant conditioning are complex and are not reflexive—for instance, riding a bicycle, writing a letter, climbing a mountain, . . . or throwing a tantrum.

The Birth of Radical Behaviorism

Operant conditioning has been studied since the start of the twentieth century, although it was not called that until later. Edward Thorndike (1898), then a young doctoral candidate, set the stage by observing cats as they tried to escape from a "puzzle box" to reach a scrap of fish that was just outside the box. At first, the cat would scratch, bite, or swat at parts of the cage in an unorganized way. Then, after a few minutes, it would chance on the successful response (loosening a bolt, pulling a string, or hitting a button) and rush out to get the reward. Placed in the box again, the cat now took a little less time to escape, and after several trials, the animal immediately made the correct response. According to Thorndike, the correct response had been "stamped in" by the satisfying result of getting the food. In contrast, annoying or unsatisfying results "stamped out" behavior. Behavior, said Thorndike, is controlled by its consequences.

This general principle was elaborated and extended to more complex forms of behavior by B. F. (Burrhus Frederic) Skinner (1904–1990). Skinner called his approach "radical behaviorism" to distinguish it from the behaviorism of John Watson, who emphasized classical conditioning. Skinner argued that to understand behavior we should focus on the external causes of an action and the action's consequences. He avoided terms that Thorndike used, such as "satisfying" and "annoying," which reflect assumptions about what an organism feels and wants. To explain behavior, he said, we should look outside the individual, not inside.

The Consequences of Behavior

In Skinner's analysis, which has inspired an immense body of research, a response ("operant") can lead to one of three types of consequences.

1 *A neutral consequence neither increases nor decreases the probability that the response will recur.* If a door handle squeaks each time you turn it, but you ignore the sound and it has no effect on your likelihood of opening the door in the future, the squeak is considered a neutral consequence. We will not be concerned further with neutral consequences.

2 **Reinforcement** *strengthens the response or makes it more likely to recur.* When your dog begs for food at the table, and you give her the lamb chop off your plate, her begging is likely to increase:

Response becomes more likely

Reinforcers are roughly equivalent to rewards, and many psychologists use *reward* and *reinforcer* as approximate synonyms. However, strict behaviorists avoid the word *reward* because it implies that something has been earned that results in happiness or satisfaction. To a behaviorist, a stimulus is a reinforcer if it strengthens the preceding behavior, whether or not the organism experiences pleasure or a positive emotion. Conversely, no matter how pleasurable a stimulus is, it is not a reinforcer if it does not increase the likelihood of a response. It's great to get a paycheck, but if you get paid regardless of the effort you put into your work, the money will not reinforce "hard-work behavior."

3 **Punishment** *weakens the response or makes it less likely to recur.* Any aversive (unpleasant) stimulus or event may be a punisher. If your dog begs for food from the table and you sternly say "No," her begging is likely to decrease—as long as you don't then feel guilty and give her the lamb chop anyway:

"No!"   **Response becomes less likely**

[handwritten: Nonshared enviornment]

Parents, employers, and governments resort to reinforcers and punishers all the time—to get kids to behave well, employees to work hard, and constituents to pay taxes—but they do not always use them effectively. For example, they may wait too long to deliver the reinforcer or punisher. In general, the sooner a reinforcer or punisher follows a response, the greater its effect; you are likely to respond more reliably when you do not have to wait ages for a paycheck, a smile, or a grade. When there is a delay, other responses occur in the interval, and the connection between the desired or undesired response and the consequence may not be made.

Primary and Secondary Reinforcers and Punishers

Food, water, light stroking of the skin, and a comfortable air temperature are naturally reinforcing because they satisfy biological needs. They are therefore known as **primary reinforcers**. Similarly, pain and extreme heat or cold are inherently punishing and are therefore known as **primary punishers**. Primary reinforcers and punishers can be very powerful, but they also have some drawbacks, both in real life and in research. For one thing, a primary reinforcer may be ineffective if an animal or person is not in a deprived state; a glass of water is not much of a reward if you just drank three glasses. Also, for obvious ethical reasons, psychologists cannot go around using primary punishers (say, hitting their subjects) or taking away primary reinforcers (say, starving their subjects).

Fortunately, behavior can be controlled just as effectively by **secondary reinforcers** and **secondary punishers**, which are learned. Money, praise, applause, good grades, awards, and gold stars are common secondary reinforcers. Criticism, demerits, catcalls, scolding, fines, and bad grades are common secondary punishers. Most behaviorists believe that secondary reinforcers and punishers

reinforcement The process by which a stimulus or event strengthens or increases the probability of the response that it follows.

punishment The process by which a stimulus or event weakens or reduces the probability of the response that it follows.

primary reinforcer A stimulus that is inherently reinforcing, typically satisfying a physiological need; an example is food.

primary punisher A stimulus that is inherently punishing; an example is electric shock.

secondary reinforcer A stimulus that has acquired reinforcing properties through association with other reinforcers.

secondary punisher A stimulus that has acquired punishing properties through association with other punishers. *[handwritten: fire someone]*

positive reinforcement A reinforcement procedure in which a response is followed by the presentation of, or increase in intensity of, a reinforcing stimulus; as a result, the response becomes stronger or more likely to occur.

negative reinforcement A reinforcement procedure in which a response is followed by the removal, delay, or decrease in intensity of an unpleasant stimulus; as a result, the response becomes stronger or more likely to occur.

acquire their ability to influence behavior by being paired with primary reinforcers and punishers. (If that reminds you of classical conditioning, re-inforce your excellent thinking with a pat on the head! Indeed, secondary reinforcers and punishers are often called *conditioned* reinforcers and punishers.) As a secondary reinforcer, money has considerable power over most people's behavior because it can be exchanged for primary rein-forcers such as food and shelter. It is also associated with other secondary reinforcers, such as praise and respect.

Positive and Negative Reinforcers and Punishers

In our example of the beg-ging dog, something pleasant (getting the lamb chop) followed the dog's begging response, so the response increased. Similarly, if you get a good grade after studying, your efforts to study are likely to continue or increase. This kind of process, in which a pleasant consequence makes a response more likely, is known as **positive reinforcement**. But there is another type of rein-forcement, **negative reinforcement**, which involves the *removal* of something *unpleasant*. For example, if someone nags you all the time to study but stops nagging when you comply, your studying is likely to increase—because you will then avoid the nagging:

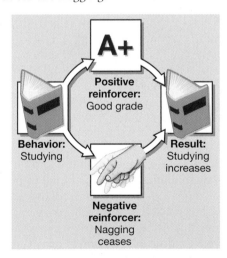

The positive–negative distinction can also be applied to punishment: Something unpleasant may occur following some behavior (positive pun-ishment), or something *pleasant* may be *removed* (negative punishment). For example, if your friends tease you for being an egghead (positive punishment) or if studying makes you lose time with your friends (negative punishment), you may stop studying:

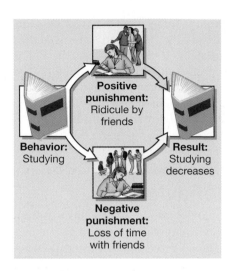

The distinction between positive and negative reinforcement and punishment has been a source of confusion and frustration for generations of stu-dents, turning many strong minds to mush. You will master these terms more quickly if you understand that "positive" and "negative" have nothing to do with "good" or "bad." They refer to procedures—giving something or taking something away.

In the case of reinforcement, think of a positive reinforcer as something that is added or obtained (you might picture a plus sign) and a negative reinforcer as avoidance of, or escape from, something unpleasant (you might picture a minus sign). *In either case, a re-sponse becomes more likely.* Do you recall what happened when Little Albert learned to fear rats through a process of classical conditioning? After he acquired this fear, crawling away was negatively reinforced by escape from the now-fearsome rodent. The negative reinforcement that results from escaping or avoiding something you perceive as unpleasant explains why so many fears are long-lasting. When you avoid a feared object or situation, you also cut off all oppor-tunities for extinguishing your fear.

Understandably, people often confuse negative reinforcement with positive punishment, because both involve an unpleasant stimulus. With punish-ment, though, you are subjected to the unpleasant stimulus, and with negative reinforcement, the un-pleasant stimulus is taken away. To keep these terms straight, remember that punishment, whether pos-itive or negative, *decreases* the likelihood of a response; and reinforcement, whether positive or negative, *increases* it. In real life, punishment and negative re-inforcement often go hand in hand. If you use a choke collar on your dog to teach it to heel, a brief tug on the collar punishes the act of walking ahead of you, but release of the collar negatively reinforces the act of staying by your side.

QUICK quiz

What kind of consequence will follow if you can't answer these questions?

1. A child nags her father for a cookie; he keeps refusing. Finally, unable to stand the nagging any longer, he hands over the cookie. For him, the ending of the child's pleas is a _____. For the child, the cookie is a _____.

2. An able-bodied driver is careful not to park in a handicapped space anymore after paying a large fine for doing so. The loss of money is a _____.

3. Identify which of the following are commonly used as secondary reinforcers: quarters spilling from a slot machine, a winner's blue ribbon, a piece of candy, an A on an exam, frequent-flyer miles.

4. During late afternoon "happy hours," bars and restaurants sell drinks at reduced prices, and appetizers are often free. What undesirable behavior may be rewarded by this practice?

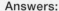

Answers:

1. negative reinforcer;   positive reinforcer   2. punisher—or more precisely, a negative punisher (because something desirable, money, was taken away)   3. All but the candy are secondary reinforcers.   4. One possible answer: The reduced prices, free appetizers, and cheerful atmosphere all reinforce heavy alcohol consumption just before the commuter rush hour, thus possibly contributing to binge drinking and drunk driving.

Principles of Operant Conditioning

Thousands of operant-conditioning studies have been done, many using animals. A favorite experimental tool is the *Skinner box*, a cage equipped with a device that delivers food or water when an animal makes a desired response (see Figure 9.5). In the original version, a machine connected to the cage recorded each response and produced a graph on a piece of paper, showing the cumulative number of responses across time; today computers are used.

Early in his career, Skinner (1938) used the Skinner box for a classic demonstration of operant conditioning. A rat that had previously learned to eat from the food-releasing device was placed in the box. Because no food was present, the animal proceeded to do typical ratlike things, scurrying about the box, sniffing here and there, and randomly touching parts of the floor and walls. Quite by accident, it happened to press a lever mounted on one wall, and immediately a pellet of tasty rat food fell into the food dish. The rat continued its movements and again happened to press the bar, causing another pellet to fall into the dish. With additional repetitions of bar pressing followed by food, the animal began to behave less randomly and to press the bar more consistently. Eventually, Skinner had the rat pressing the bar as fast as it could. Since then, behavioral researchers have used the Skinner box and similar devices to discover many important techniques and applications of operant conditioning.

Light

Bar
Water

Food tray

FIGURE 9.5
The Skinner Box
When a rat in a Skinner box presses a bar, a food pellet or drop of water is automatically released. The photo shows Skinner at work on one of the boxes.

extinction The weakening and eventual disappearance of a learned response; in operant conditioning, it occurs when a response is no longer followed by a reinforcer.

stimulus generalization In operant conditioning, the tendency for a response that has been reinforced (or punished) in the presence of one stimulus to occur (or be suppressed) in the presence of other similar stimuli.

stimulus discrimination In operant conditioning, the tendency of a response to occur in the presence of one stimulus but not in the presence of other, similar stimuli that differ from it on some dimension.

discriminative stimulus A stimulus that signals when a particular response is likely to be followed by a certain type of consequence.

continuous reinforcement A reinforcement schedule in which a particular response is always reinforced.

intermittent (partial) schedule of reinforcement A reinforcement schedule in which a particular response is sometimes but not always reinforced.

Extinction In operant conditioning, as in classical, **extinction** is a procedure that causes a previously learned response to stop. In operant conditioning, extinction takes place when the reinforcer that maintained the response is removed or is no longer available. At first, there may be a spurt of responding, but then the responses gradually taper off and eventually cease. Suppose you put a coin in a vending machine and get nothing back. You may throw in another coin, or perhaps even two, but then you will probably stop trying. The next day, you may put in yet another coin, an example of *spontaneous recovery*. Eventually, however, you will give up on that machine. Your response will have been extinguished.

Stimulus Generalization and Discrimination In operant conditioning, as in classical, **stimulus generalization** may occur. That is, responses may generalize to stimuli that were not present during the original learning situation but that resemble the original stimuli. For example, a pigeon that has been trained to peck at a picture of a circle may also peck at a slightly oval figure. But if you wanted to train the bird to discriminate between the two shapes, you would present both the circle and the oval, giving reinforcers whenever the bird pecked at the circle and withholding reinforcers when it pecked at the oval. Eventually, **stimulus discrimination** would occur.

Sometimes an animal or human being learns to respond to a stimulus only when some other stimulus, called a **discriminative stimulus**, is present. The discriminative stimulus signals whether a response, if made, will pay off. In a Skinner box containing a pigeon, a light may serve as a discriminative stimulus for pecking at a circle. When the light is on, pecking brings a reward; when it is off, pecking is futile. Human behavior is controlled by many discriminative stimuli, both verbal ("Store hours are 9 to 5") and nonverbal (traffic lights, doorbells, the ring of a telephone, other people's facial expressions). We all learn to respond correctly to these stimuli in order to get through the day efficiently and get along with others.

Learning on Schedule When a response is first acquired, learning is usually most rapid if the response is reinforced each time it occurs; this procedure is called **continuous reinforcement**. However, once a response has become reliable, it will be more resistant to extinction if it is rewarded on an **intermittent (partial) schedule of reinforcement**, which involves reinforcing only some responses, not all of them. Skinner (1956) happened

on this fact when he ran short of food pellets for his rats and was forced to deliver reinforcers less often. Not all scientific discoveries are planned!

Intermittent reinforcement helps explain why people often get attached to "lucky" hats, charms, and rituals. A batter pulls his earlobe, gets a home run, and from then on always pulls his earlobe as 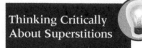 he steps up to the plate. A student takes an exam with a purple pen and gets an A, and from then on will not take an exam without a purple pen. Such rituals persist because sometimes they are followed, purely coincidentally, by a reinforcer—a hit, a good grade—and so they became resistant to extinction.

Skinner (1948) once demonstrated this phenomenon by creating eight "superstitious" pigeons in his laboratory. He rigged the pigeons' cages so that food was delivered every 15 seconds, even if the bird didn't lift a feather. Pigeons are often in motion, so when the food came, each animal was likely to be doing something. That something was then reinforced by delivery of the food. The behavior, of course, was reinforced entirely by chance, but it still became more likely to occur and thus to be reinforced again. Within a short time, six of the pigeons were practicing some sort of consistent ritual—turning in counterclockwise circles, bobbing their heads up and down, or swinging their heads to and fro. None of these activities had the least effect on the delivery of the reinforcer; the birds were behaving "superstitiously," as if they thought their movements were responsible for bringing the food.

Many kinds of intermittent schedules have been studied. Some deliver a reinforcer only after a certain number of responses have occurred; others do so only if a response is made after a certain

Thinking Critically About Superstitions

"Maybe you're right, maybe it won't ward off evil spirits, but maybe it will, and these days who wants to take a chance?"

GET INVOLVED

The Well-Behaved Pet

If you have a pet, you can use operant-conditioning principles to teach your animal something you'd like it to do. Choose something simple. One student we know taught her cat to willingly enter the garage for the night by feeding the animal a special treat there each evening at the same time. Soon the cat was "asking" to get into the garage at bedtime. Another student taught her pastured horse to come to her and submit willingly to the halter by rewarding the animal's occasional approach with a carrot. Soon the horse was approaching regularly and could be put on an intermittent schedule of reinforcement. Be creative, and see whether you can make your pet better behaved or more cooperative in some way.

amount of time has passed since the last reinforcer. The number of responses that must occur or the amount of time that must pass may be fixed (e.g., three responses or five seconds) or may vary around some average. These patterns of reinforcement affect the rate, form, and timing of behavior. The details are beyond the scope of this book, but here is an example. Suppose your sweetheart sends you ten e-mail messages each day, playfully spacing them at unpredictable intervals, although they come on average every hour or so. You will probably check your e-mail regularly at a low but steady rate. But if your sweetheart sends you just one e-mail every day around dinnertime, you will probably start checking around 5:00 P.M., keep doing so until the message arrives (your reward), and then stop looking at all until the next evening.

Now listen up, because here comes one of the most useful things to know about operant conditioning: If you want a response to persist after it has been learned, you should reinforce it *intermittently*, not continuously. If you are giving Harry, your hamster, a treat every time he pushes a ball with his nose, and then you suddenly stop the reinforcement, Harry will soon stop pushing that ball. Because the change in reinforcement is large, from continuous to none at all, Harry will easily discern the change. But if you have been reinforcing Harry's behavior only every so often, the change will not be so dramatic, and your hungry hamster will keep responding for quite a while. Pigeons, rats, and people on intermittent schedules of reinforcement have responded in the laboratory thousands of times without reinforcement before throwing in the towel, especially when the timing of the reinforcer varies. Animals will sometimes work so hard for an unpredictable, infrequent bit of food that the energy they expend is greater than that gained from the reward; theoretically, they could actually work themselves to death!

It follows that if you want to get rid of a response—your own or someone else's—you should be careful *not* to reinforce it intermittently. If you are going to extinguish undesirable behavior by ignoring it—a child's tantrums, a friend's midnight phone calls, a parent's unasked-for advice—you must be absolutely consistent in withholding reinforcement (your attention). Otherwise, the other person will learn that if he or she keeps screaming, calling, or giving advice long enough, it will eventually be rewarded. One of the most common errors people make, from a behavioral point of view, is to reward intermittently the very responses that they would like to eliminate.

Shaping For a response to be reinforced, it must first occur. But suppose you want to train Harry the hamster to pick up a marble, a child to use a fork properly, or a friend to play terrific tennis. Such behaviors, and most others in everyday life, have almost no probability of appearing spontaneously. You could grow old and gray waiting for them to occur so that you could reinforce them. The operant solution to this dilemma is a procedure called **shaping**.

In shaping, you start by reinforcing a tendency in the right direction, and then you gradually require responses that are more and more similar to the final desired response. The responses that you reinforce on the way to the final one are called **successive approximations**. In the case of Harry and the marble, you might deliver a food pellet if the hamster merely turned toward the marble. Once this response was well established, you might then reward Harry for taking a step toward the marble. After that, you could reward him for approaching the marble, then for touching the marble, then for putting both paws on the marble, and finally for holding it. With the achievement of each approximation, the next one would become more likely, making it available for reinforcement.

shaping An operant-conditioning procedure in which successive approximations of a desired response are reinforced.

successive approximations In the procedure of shaping, behaviors that are ordered in terms of increasing similarity or closeness to the desired response.

Behavioral techniques such as shaping have many useful applications. Monkeys have been trained to assist their paralyzed owners by opening doors, helping with feeding, and turning the pages of books. Miniature "guide horses" help blind people navigate city streets. Note the cool protective sneakers!

Using shaping and other techniques, Skinner was able to train pigeons to play Ping-Pong with their beaks and to "bowl" in a miniature alley, complete with a wooden ball and tiny bowling pins. (Skinner had a great sense of humor.) Animal trainers routinely use shaping to teach dogs to act as the "eyes" of the blind and to act as the "limbs" of people with spinal cord injuries; these talented companions learn to turn on light switches, open refrigerator doors, and reach for boxes on shelves.

Biological Limits on Learning

All principles of operant conditioning, like those of classical conditioning, are limited by an animal's genetic dispositions and physical characteristics; if you try to use shaping to teach a fish to dance the samba, you're going to get pretty frustrated (and wear out the fish). Operant-conditioning procedures always work best when they capitalize on inborn tendencies.

Years ago, two psychologists who became animal trainers, Keller and Marian Breland (1961), learned what happens when you ignore biological constraints on learning. They found that their animals were having trouble learning tasks that should have been easy. For example, a pig was supposed to drop large wooden coins in a box. Instead, the pig would drop the coin, push at it with its snout, throw it in the air, and push at it some more. This odd behavior actually delayed delivery of the reinforcer (food, which is *very* reinforcing to a pig), so it was hard to explain in terms of operant principles. The Brelands finally realized that the pig's rooting instinct—using its snout to uncover and dig up edible roots—was keeping it from learning the task. They called such a reversion to instinctive behavior **instinctive drift**.

In human beings, too, operant learning is affected by genetics, biology, and the evolutionary history of our species. As we saw in Chapter 3, human children are biologically disposed to learn language without much effort, and they may be disposed to learn some arithmetic operations, as well (Geary, 1995). Further, as we saw in Chapter 2, temperaments and other inborn dispositions may set limits on how a person responds to reinforcers and punishers. It will be easier to shape belly-dancing behavior if a person is temperamentally disposed to be outgoing and extroverted than if the person is by nature shy.

Skinner: The Man and the Myth

Because of his groundbreaking work on operant conditioning, B. F. Skinner is one of the best known of American psychologists. He is also one of the most misunderstood. For example, many people (even some psychologists) think that Skinner denied the existence of human consciousness and the value of studying it. In reality, Skinner (1972, 1990) maintained that we can study private internal events—what we call perceptions, emotions, and thoughts—by observing our own sensory responses, the verbal reports of others, and the conditions under which such events occur. But he insisted that thoughts and feelings cannot *explain* behavior. These components of consciousness, he said, are themselves simply behaviors that occur because of reinforcement and punishment.

Skinner aroused strong passions in both his supporters and his detractors. Perhaps the issue that most provoked and angered people was his insistence that free will is an illusion. Human beings, he said, just like other animals, are shaped by their environments and their genetic heritage. Skinner

instinctive drift During operant learning, the tendency for an organism to revert to instinctive behavior.

refused to credit personal traits (such as curiosity) or mental events (such as intentions and motives) for anyone's accomplishments, including his own. He regarded himself not as a "self" but as a "repertoire of behaviors" resulting from an environment that encouraged looking, searching, and investigating (Bjork, 1993).

Because Skinner thought that the environment could and should be manipulated to solve people's behavioral problems and improve the world, some critics have portrayed him as cold-blooded. But Skinner, who was a kind and mild-mannered man, felt that it would be unethical not to try to improve human behavior by applying behavioral principles. He practiced what he preached, proposing many ways to advance society and reduce human suffering. At the height of public criticism of Skinner, in 1972, the American Humanist Association recognized his efforts on behalf of humanity by honoring him with its Humanist of the Year Award.

QUICK quiz

Can you apply the principles of operant conditioning? In each of the following situations, choose the best alternative, and give your reason for choosing it.

1. You want your 2-year-old to ask for water with a word instead of a grunt. Should you give him water when he says "wa-wa" or wait until his pronunciation improves?

2. Your roommate keeps interrupting your studying even though you have asked her to stop. Should you ignore her completely or occasionally respond for the sake of good manners?

3. Your father, who rarely calls you, has finally left a voice-mail message. Should you reply quickly or wait a while so he will know how it feels to be ignored?

Answers:

1. You should reinforce "wa-wa," an approximation of *water*, because complex behaviors need to be shaped.   2. From a behavioral view, you should ignore her completely because intermittent reinforcement (attention) could cause her interruptions to persist.   3. If you want to encourage communication, you should reply quickly because immediate reinforcement is more effective than delayed reinforcement.

WHAT'S *Ahead*

- Why do efforts to "crack down" on wrongdoers often go awry?

- What's the best way to discourage a child from throwing tantrums?

- Why does paying children for good grades sometimes backfire?

Operant Conditioning in Real Life

Operant principles can clear up many mysteries about why people behave as they do. They can also explain why people have trouble changing when they want to, in spite of all the well-meaning motivational seminars they attend or resolutions they make. If life at work and at home remains full of the same old reinforcers, punishers, and discriminative stimuli (a grumpy boss, an unresponsive spouse, a refrigerator stocked with fattening goodies), any new responses that have been acquired may fail to generalize.

To help people change unwanted, dangerous, or self-defeating habits, behaviorists have carried operant principles out of the laboratory and into the wider world of the classroom, athletic field, prison, mental hospital, nursing home, rehabilitation ward, child-care center, factory, and office. The use of operant techniques (and classical ones) in such real-world settings is called **behavior modification** (also known as *applied behavioral analysis*).

Behavior modification has had some enormous successes (Kazdin, 2001). Behaviorists have taught parents how to toilet train their children in only a few sessions (Azrin & Foxx, 1974). They have trained disturbed and mentally retarded adults to communicate, mingle socially with others, and earn a living (Lent, 1968; McLeod, 1985). They have taught brain-damaged patients to control inappropriate behavior, focus their attention, and improve their language abilities (McGlynn, 1990). They have developed the most effective programs available for helping autistic children improve their social, language, and academic skills (Green, 1996a, b). And they have helped ordinary folk eliminate unwanted habits, such as smoking and nail biting, or acquire desired ones, such as practicing the piano or studying.

behavior modification The application of conditioning techniques to teach new responses or to reduce or eliminate problematic behavior.

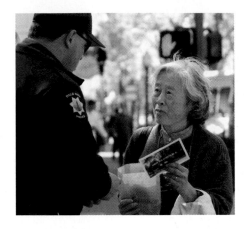

You don't have to be a psychologist to apply behavioral principles. This police officer in Palo Alto, California, is reinforcing law-abiding behavior by giving a gift certificate to a pedestrian.

Yet when nonpsychologists try to apply the principles of conditioning to commonplace problems, their efforts sometimes miss the mark. They may not have a good grasp of the principles you have been learning about in this chapter; for example, they may delay the reinforcer too long or reinforce unwanted behavior intermittently. Further, both punishment and reinforcement have their pitfalls, as we are about to see.

The Pros and Cons of Punishment

In a novel called *Walden Two* (1948/1976), Skinner imagined a utopia in which reinforcers were used so wisely that undesirable behavior was rare. Unfortunately, we do not live in a utopia; bad habits and antisocial acts abound.

Punishment might seem to be an obvious solution. Nearly all Western countries have banned physical punishment of schoolchildren by principals and teachers, but as we saw in our opening story, many American states still permit it for disruptiveness and other misbehavior. The United States is also far more likely than any other developed country to jail its citizens for nonviolent crimes such as drug use and to enact the ultimate punishment—the death penalty—for violent crimes. And, of course, in their relationships people punish one another frequently by yelling, scolding, and sulking. Does all this punishment work?

When Punishment Works Sometimes punishment is unquestionably effective. For example, punishment can deter some young criminals from repeating their offenses. A study of the crimi-

Thinking Critically About Punishment

nal records of all Danish men born between 1944 and 1947 (nearly 29,000 men) examined repeat arrests (recidivism) through age 26 (Brennan & Mednick, 1994). After any given arrest, punishment reduced rates of subsequent arrests for both minor and serious crimes, though recidivism still remained fairly high. Contrary to the researchers' expectations, however, the severity of punishment made no difference: Fines and probation were about as effective as jail time. What mattered most was the *consistency* of the punishment. This is understandable in behavioral terms: When lawbreakers sometimes get away with their crimes, their behavior is

intermittently reinforced and therefore becomes resistant to extinction.

Unfortunately, that is exactly the situation in the United States. Young offenders are punished far less consistently than they are in Denmark, in part because prosecutors, juries, and judges do not want to condemn them to mandatory prison terms. This fact helps to explain why harsh sentencing laws and simplistic efforts to "crack down" on wrongdoers often fail or even backfire. Further, when harsh punishment is imposed, it does not teach young offenders to want to go straight. Indeed, despite its high incarceration rates, the United States has a far higher rate of violent crime than other developed countries do. And within the United States, crime rates are not consistently correlated with rates of incarceration or the imposition of the death penalty (Currie, 1998).

When Punishment Fails What about punishment that occurs every day in families, schools, and workplaces? Laboratory and field studies find that it, too, often fails, for several reasons:

1 *People often administer punishment inappropriately or mindlessly.* They swing in a blind rage, shout things they don't mean, or apply punishment so broadly that it covers all sorts of irrelevant things the target has done.

2 *The recipient of punishment often responds with anxiety, fear, or rage.* Through a process of classical conditioning, these emotional side effects may then generalize to the entire situation in which the punishment occurs—the place, the person delivering the punishment, and the circumstances. These negative emotional reactions can create more problems than the punishment solves. A teenager who has been severely punished may strike back or run away. A spouse who is constantly abused will feel bitter and resentful and is likely to retaliate with small acts of hostility. Being physically punished in childhood is a risk factor for depression, aggression, low self-esteem, and many other problems (Barrish, 1996; Gershoff, 2002; Straus & Kantor, 1994).

3 *The effectiveness of punishment is often temporary, depending heavily on the presence of the punishing person or circumstances.* All of us can probably remember some transgressions of childhood that we never dared commit when our parents were around but that we promptly resumed as soon as they were gone. All we learned was not to get caught.

4 *Most misbehavior is hard to punish immediately.* Punishment, like reward, works best if it quickly follows a response. But outside the laboratory, rapid punishment is often hard to achieve, and during the delay, the behavior may be reinforced many times. For example, if you punish your dog when you get home for getting into the doggie treats and eating them all up, the punishment will not do any good because you are too late: Your pet's misbehavior has already been reinforced by all those delicious treats.

5 *Punishment conveys little information.* If it immediately follows the misbehavior, punishment may tell the recipient what *not* to do, but it does not communicate what the person (or animal) *should* do. Spanking a toddler for messing in her pants will not teach her to use the potty chair, and scolding a student for learning slowly will not teach him to learn more quickly.

6 *An action intended to punish may instead be reinforcing because it brings attention.* Indeed, in some cases, angry attention may be just what the offender is after. If a mother yells at a child who is throwing a tantrum, the very act of yelling may give him what he wants—a reaction

Many harried parents habitually resort to physical punishment without being aware of its many negative consequences for themselves and their children. Based on your reading of this chapter, what alternatives does this father have?

from her. In the schoolroom, teachers who scold children in front of other students, thus putting them in the limelight, often unwittingly reward the very misbehavior they are trying to eliminate.

Because of these drawbacks, most psychologists believe that punishment, especially severe punishment, is a poor way to eliminate unwanted behavior in most situations. When punishment must be used, these guidelines should be kept in mind: (1) It should not involve physical abuse; instead, parents can use time-outs and loss of privileges (negative punishers); (2) it should be accompanied by information about what kind of behavior would be appropriate; and (3) it should be followed, whenever possible, by the reinforcement of desirable behavior.

Fortunately, a good alternative to punishment exists: extinction of the responses you want to discourage. Of course, the simplest form of extinction—ignoring the behavior—is often hard to carry out. It is not easy to ignore a child nagging for a cookie before dinner, a roommate interrupting your concentration, or a dog barking its lungs out. A teacher cannot ignore a child who is hitting a playmate. The dog owner who ignores Fido's backyard barking may soon hear "barking" of another sort from the neighbors. A parent whose child is a video-game addict cannot ignore the behavior because playing video games is rewarding to the child. One solution: Combine extinction of undesirable acts with reinforcement of alternative ones. For example, the parent of a video-game addict might ignore the child's pleas for "just one more game" and at the same time praise the child for doing something else that is incompatible with video-game playing, such as reading or playing basketball.

The Problems with Reward

So far, we have been praising the virtues of reinforcement. But like punishers, rewards do not always work as expected. Let's look at two complications that arise when people try to use them.

Misuse of Rewards   Suppose you are a fourth-grade teacher, and a student has just turned in a paper full of grammatical and punctuation errors. This child has little self-confidence and is easily discouraged. What should you do? Many people think the answer is to give the paper a high mark anyway, in order to bolster the child's self-esteem. Teachers everywhere are handing out

> **Thinking Critically About Rewards**

Gable, Cartoonists & Writers Syndicate/cartoonweb.com

CARTOONISTS & WRITERS SYNDICATE http://CartoonWeb.com

GABLE
THE GLOBE AND MAIL
Toronto
CANADA

lavish praise, happy-face stickers, and high grades in hopes that students' academic performance will improve as they learn to "feel good about themselves," even though study after study has found that high self-esteem does not improve academic performance (Baumeister et al., 2003). One obvious result has been grade inflation at all levels of education. In many colleges and universities, Cs, which once meant average or satisfactory, are nearly extinct.

The problem, from a behavioral point of view, is that to be effective, rewards must be tied to the behavior you are trying to increase. When rewards are dispensed indiscriminately, without being earned, they become meaningless because they no longer reinforce desired behavior; the result is minimal effort and mediocre work. Real self-esteem emerges from effort, persistence, and the gradual acquisition of skills, and is nurtured by a teacher's genuine appreciation of the content of the child's work (Damon, 1995). In the case of the child who turned in a poorly written paper, the teacher could praise its strengths but also give feedback on the paper's weaknesses and show the child how to correct them.

Why Rewards Can Backfire Most of our examples of operant conditioning have involved **extrinsic reinforcers**, which come from an outside source and are not inherently related to the activity being reinforced. Money, praise, gold stars, applause, hugs, and thumbs-up signs are all extrinsic reinforcers. But people (and probably some other animals, too) also work for **intrinsic reinforcers**, such as enjoyment of the task and the satisfaction of accomplishment. As psychologists have applied operant conditioning in real-world settings, they have found that extrinsic reinforcement sometimes becomes too much of a good thing: If you focus on it exclusively, it can kill the pleasure of doing something for its own sake.

extrinsic reinforcers
Reinforcers that are not inherently related to the activity being reinforced, such as money, prizes, and praise.

intrinsic reinforcers
Reinforcers that are inherently related to the activity being reinforced, such as enjoyment of the task and the satisfaction of accomplishment.

GET INVOLVED

What's Reinforcing Your Behavior?

For each activity that you do, indicate whether the reinforcers are extrinsic or intrinsic.

Activity	Mostly extrinsic	Mostly intrinsic	About equally extrinsic and intrinsic
Studying	_____	_____	_____
Housework	_____	_____	_____
Worship	_____	_____	_____
Grooming	_____	_____	_____
Job	_____	_____	_____
Dating	_____	_____	_____
Attending class	_____	_____	_____
Reading unrelated to school	_____	_____	_____
Sports	_____	_____	_____
Cooking	_____	_____	_____

Is there an area of your life in which you'd like intrinsic reinforcement to play a larger role? What can you do to make that happen?

CLOSE-UP on Research

How to Kill Intrinsic Motivation

Consider what happened in a classic study of how praise affects children's intrinsic motivation (Lepper, Greene, & Disbett, 1973). The researchers **asked an interesting question:** Is it possible to reduce children's interest in an activity by making it a means to an end rather than the end itself? When that happens, does play turn into work?

To find out, they first gave nursery-school children the chance to draw with felt-tipped pens during free play and recorded how long each child spontaneously played with the pens. The children clearly enjoyed this activity. Then the researchers told some of the children that if they would draw with felt-tipped pens for a man who had come "to see what kinds of pictures boys and girls like to draw with Magic Markers," afterward they would get a prize—a "Good Player Award" complete with gold seal and red ribbon. After drawing for six minutes, each child got the award as promised. Other children did not expect an award and were not given one. And in a third condition, children were not told there would be an award but got one anyway.

A week later, the researchers again observed the children's free play. Those children who had expected and received an award during the first part of the study spent much less time with the pens than they had before the start of the experiment. In contrast, children who had neither expected nor received an award continued to show as much interest in playing with the pens as they had initially, as you can see in the adjacent figure. Children in the third condition also continued to show a high level of interest in the pens. Similar results have occurred in many other studies when children have been offered a reward for playing with a toy or doing something they already enjoy.

Why should extrinsic rewards undermine the pleasure of doing something for its own sake? Psychologists have **considered alternative interpretations** for this finding. One possibility is that when we are paid for an activity, we interpret it as work. We see our actions as the result of exter-

nal factors instead of our own interests, skills, and efforts. It is as if we say to ourselves, "I'm doing this because I'm being paid for it. Since I'm being paid, it must be something I wouldn't do if I didn't have to." When the reward is withdrawn, we refuse to "work" any longer. This is the explanation that was favored by the researchers in the felt-tipped pen study.

Another possibility is that we tend to regard extrinsic rewards as controlling, so they make us feel pressured and reduce our sense of autonomy and choice ("I guess I have to do what I'm told to do—but *only* what I'm told to do") (Deci et al., 1999).

A third, more behavioral explanation is that extrinsic reinforcement sometimes raises the rate of responding above some optimal, enjoyable level— for example, by causing the children in the felt-tipped pen study to play with the pens longer than they would have on their own. Then the activity really does become work.

We must be careful, however, to **avoid oversimplification**. Extrinsic rewards do not always weaken the impact of intrinsic ones; their effects depend on many factors, including a person's initial motivation, the context in which rewards are achieved, and, when praise is given, the sincerity of the person giving it (Henderlong & Lepper, 2002). If you get praise, money, a high grade, or a trophy for doing a task *well* or for achieving a certain level of performance, rather than for just doing the task, your intrinsic motivation is not likely to decline; in fact, it may increase (Cameron, Banko, & Pierce 2001; Dickinson, 1989). Such rewards are apt to make you feel competent rather than controlled. If rewards are tied to increasingly demanding standards for performance,

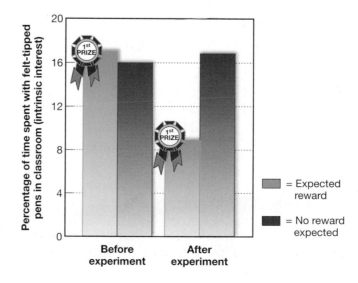

as opposed to an unchanging standard, your intrinsic motivation is especially likely to remain high (Pierce et al., 2003). And if you have always been crazy about reading or playing the banjo, you will probably keep reading or playing even when you do not happen to be getting a grade or applause for doing so. In such cases, you will probably attribute your continued involvement in the activity to your own intrinsic interests and motivation rather than to the reward.

So, what is the take-home message about extrinsic rewards? First, sometimes they are necessary: Few people would trudge off to work every morning if they never got paid; and in the classroom, teachers may need to offer incentives to unmotivated students. Second, extrinsic rewards should be used sparingly, so that intrinsic pleasure in an activity can blossom. As one mother wrote in *Newsweek*, children need to discover for themselves "the joy of music from songs, the power of mathematics from counting and all of human wisdom from reading" (Skreslet, 1987). Finally, educators and employers can avoid the trap of either–or thinking by recognizing that most people do their best when they get tangible rewards for real

"*That is the correct answer, Billy, but I'm afraid you don't win anything for it.*"

achievement *and* when they have interesting, challenging, and varied kinds of work to do.

Effective behavior modification, as you can see, is not only a science but also an art. In "Taking Psychology with You," we offer additional guidelines for mastering that art.

QUICK quiz

Is the art of mastering quizzes intrinsically reinforcing yet?

A. According to behavioral principles, what is happening here?

1. An adolescent whose parents have hit him for minor transgressions since he was small runs away from home.

2. A young woman whose parents paid her to clean her room while she was growing up is a slob when she moves to her own apartment.

3. Two parents scold their young daughter every time they catch her sucking her thumb. The thumb sucking continues anyway.

B. In cities across America, public school systems are now rewarding students for perfect attendance by giving them money, shopping sprees, laptops, video games—even the chance to win a car in a raffle (*The New York Times*, February 5, 2006). What are the pros and cons of such practices?

Answers:

A. 1. The physical punishment was painful, and through a process of classical conditioning, the situation in which it occurred also became unpleasant. Because escape from an unpleasant stimulus is negatively reinforcing, the boy ran away. 2. Extrinsic reinforcers are no longer available, and room-cleaning behavior has been extinguished. Also, extrinsic rewards may have displaced the intrinsic satisfaction of having a tidy room. 3. Punishment has failed, possibly because it rewards thumb sucking with attention or because thumb sucking still brings the child pleasure whenever the parents are not around. B. The rewards may improve attendance (they have in some schools), and students who attend more regularly may wind up more interested in their studies and do better in school. But extrinsic rewards can also decrease intrinsic motivation, and when they are withdrawn (e.g., when the student goes to another school or to college), attendance may plummet ("if there's no reward, why should I attend?"). Further, students may come to expect bigger and bigger rewards, upping the ante. In some schools, especially those that have deemphasized penalties for *poor* attendance, the rewards have backfired and attendance has actually fallen.

WHAT'S *Ahead*

- Can you learn something without any obvious reinforcement?
- Why do two people often learn different lessons from exactly the same experience?
- Does watching violence on TV make people more aggressive?

Learning and the Mind

For half a century, behaviorism was the dominant force in American psychology. Behaviorists liked to compare the mind to an engineer's hypothetical "black box," a device whose workings must be inferred because they cannot be observed directly. To them, the box's contents did not further the understanding of behavior; it was enough to know that pushing a button on the lid would produce a predictable response. But even as early as the 1930s, a few behaviorists could not resist peeking into that black box.

Latent Learning

Behaviorist Edward Tolman (1938) committed virtual heresy at the time by noting that his laboratory rats, when pausing at turning points in a maze, seemed to be *deciding* which way to go. Moreover, the animals sometimes seemed to be learning even without any reinforcement. What, he wondered, was going on in their little rat brains that might account for this puzzle?

In a classic experiment, Tolman and C. H. Honzik (1930) placed three groups of rats in mazes and observed the rats' behavior each day for more than two weeks. The rats in Group 1 always found food at the end of the maze and quickly learned to find it without going down blind alleys. The rats in Group 2 never found food and, as you would expect, followed no particular route. Group 3 was the interesting group. These rats found no food for ten days and seemed to wander aimlessly, but on the eleventh day they received food and then quickly learned to run to the end of the maze. By the next day, they were doing as well as Group 1, which had been rewarded from the beginning (see Figure 9.6).

Group 3 had demonstrated **latent learning**, learning that is not immediately expressed in performance. A great deal of human learning also remains latent until circumstances allow or require it to be expressed. A driver finds her way to Fourth and Kumquat Streets using a new route she has never used before. A little boy observes a parent setting the table or tightening a screw but does not act on this learning for years; then he finds he

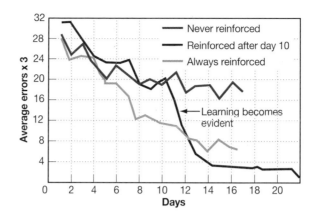

FIGURE 9.6
Latent Learning
In a classic experiment, rats that always found food in a maze made fewer and fewer errors in reaching the food (green curve). In contrast, rats that received no food showed little improvement (blue curve). But rats that got no food for ten days and then were given food on the eleventh day showed rapid improvement from then on (red curve). This suggests that learning involves cognitive changes that can occur in the absence of reinforcement and that may not be acted on until a reinforcer becomes available (Tolman & Honzik, 1930).

knows how to do these things, even though he has never done them before.

Latent learning not only occurs without any obvious reinforcer; it also raises questions about what, exactly, is learned during learning. In the Tolman and Honzik study, the rats that did not get any food until the eleventh day seemed to have acquired a mental representation of the maze. They had been learning the whole time; they simply had no reason to act on that learning until they began to find food. Similarly, the driver taking a new route can do so because she already knows how the city is laid out.

What seems to be acquired in latent learning, therefore, is not a specific response, but knowledge about responses and their consequences. We learn how the world is organized, which paths lead to which places, and which actions can produce which payoffs. This knowledge permits us to be creative and flexible in reaching our goals.

Social-Cognitive Learning Theories

The black box was pried open further in the 1940s, when two social scientists proposed a major modification of radical behaviorism, which they called *social-learning theory* (Dollard & Miller, 1950). Most human learning, they argued, is acquired by observing other people in a social context rather than through standard conditioning procedures. By the 1960s and 1970s, social-learning theory was in full bloom, and a new element had been added: the human capacity for higher-level cognitive processes. Its proponents agreed with behaviorists that human beings, along with the rat and the rabbit, are subject to the laws of operant and classical conditioning. But they added that human beings, unlike the rat and the rabbit, are full of attitudes, beliefs, and expectations that affect the way they acquire information, make decisions, reason, and solve problems.

latent learning A form of learning that is not immediately expressed in an overt response; it occurs without obvious reinforcement.

Today, modern **social-cognitive theories** of learning share an emphasis on the importance of beliefs, perceptions, and observations of others' behavior in determining what we learn and how we behave (Bandura, 1986; Mischel, 1973; Mischel & Schoda, 1995). These mental processes affect what individuals will do at any given moment and also, more generally, the personality traits they develop (see Chapter 2). Social-cognitive theorists note that because people differ in their attitudes, expectations, and perceptions, they can live through the same event yet come away with entirely different lessons from it (Bandura, 2001). All siblings know this. One may regard being grounded by their father as evidence of his all-around meanness, and another may see the same behavior as evidence of his care and concern for his children.

Learning by Observing

Late one night, a friend who lives in a rural area was awakened by a loud clattering and banging. Her whole family raced outside to find the source of the commotion. A raccoon had knocked over a "raccoon-proof" garbage can and seemed to be demonstrating to an assembly of other raccoons how to open it: If you jump up and down on the can's side, the lid will pop off. According to our friend, the observing raccoons learned from this episode how to open stubborn garbage cans, and the observing humans learned how smart raccoons can be. In short, they all benefited from **observational learning**: learning by watching what others do and what happens to them for doing it.

Behaviorists have always acknowledged the importance of observational learning, which they call *vicarious conditioning*, and have tried to explain it in stimulus–response terms. But social-cognitive theorists believe that in human beings, observational learning cannot be fully understood without taking into account the thought processes of the learner (Meltzoff & Gopnik, 1993). They emphasize the knowledge that results when a person sees a *model*—another person—behaving in certain ways and experiencing the consequences (Bandura, 1977).

None of us would last long without observational learning. We would have to learn to avoid oncoming cars by walking into traffic and suffering the consequences or learn to swim by jumping into a deep pool and flailing around. Learning would be not only dangerous but also inefficient. Parents and teachers would be busy 24 hours a day shaping children's behavior. Bosses would have to stand over their employees' desks, rewarding every little link in the complex behavioral chains we call typing, report writing, and accounting.

Many years ago, Albert Bandura and his colleagues showed just how important observational learning is, especially for children who are learning the rules of social behavior (Bandura, Ross, & Ross, 1963). The researchers had nursery-school children watch a short film of two men, Rocky and Johnny, playing with toys. (Apparently the children did not think this behavior was the least bit odd.) In the film, Johnny refuses to share his toys, and Rocky responds by clobbering him. Rocky's aggressive actions are rewarded because he winds up with all the toys. Poor Johnny sits dejectedly in the corner, while Rocky marches off in triumph with a sack full of his loot and a hobbyhorse under his arm.

Like father, like daughter. Parents can be powerful models.

After viewing the film, each child was left alone for 20 minutes in a playroom full of toys, including some of the items shown in the film. Watching through a one-way mirror, the researchers found that the children were much more aggressive in their play than a control group that had not seen the film. Some children imitated Rocky almost exactly. At the end of the session, one little girl even asked the experimenter for a sack!

Of course, children imitate positive activities, too. Matt Groening, the creator of the cartoon show *The Simpsons*, decided it would be funny if the Simpsons' 8-year-old daughter Lisa played the baritone sax. Sure enough, across the country, little girls began imitating her. Cynthia Sikes, a saxophone teacher in New York, told *The New York Times*: "When the show started, I got an influx of girls coming up to me saying, 'I want to play the saxophone because Lisa Simpson plays the saxophone.'"

The Case of Media Violence
These findings on latent learning, the role of perceptions in learning, and observational learning are relevant to an ongoing emotional debate: Does media violence

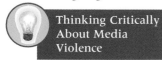
Thinking Critically About Media Violence

make people behave more aggressively? Every time an American child or teenager commits a shocking murder or assault, there is a public outcry over the countless acts of violence that children see on television, in films, and in video games. Politicians and parents blame the media, and the media claim to be blameless. What does the evidence show?

First, since Bandura's early research, hundreds of other experimental studies of children, teenagers, and adults have corroborated his findings, convincing many psychologists that observing aggression does increase aggressiveness (APA Commission on Violence and Youth, 1993; Bushman & Anderson, 2001; Eron, 1995). Meta-analysis shows that the greater the exposure to violence in movies and on television, the stronger the likelihood of a person's behaving aggressively, even after controlling for social class, intelligence, and other factors (Anderson & Bushman, 2001). Moreover, when grade-school children cut back on the time they spend watching TV or playing video games (which are often violent), their aggressiveness declines (Robinson et al., 2001). A review by a group of eminent scientists concluded that "research on violent television and films, video games, and music reveals unequivocal evidence that media violence increases the likelihood of aggressive and violent behavior," both in the short term and long term (Anderson et al., 2003).

But some psychologists and social critics believe that the relationship between media violence and real violence is not strong enough to worry about (Freedman, 2002). Media violence does not cause all viewers, or even most viewers, to become aggressive. Children watch many different programs and movies and have many models to observe besides those they see in the media, including parents and peers. For every teenager who is obsessed with playing *Mortal Kombat* and who entertains violent fantasies of blowing up the world, dozens more think the game is just plain fun and then go off to do their homework. Interestingly, although the number of violent video games increased throughout the 1990s, overall rates of teenage violence actually declined.

Further, cause and effect work in the opposite direction as well: Children and adults who are habitually aggressive like to watch violent shows and are more affected by them than unaggressive people are. After watching violent films, they feel angrier afterward than unaggressive people do and are more likely to behave aggressively toward others (Bushman, 1995).

In the social-cognitive view, both conclusions about the relationship of media violence to violent behavior have merit. Repeated acts of aggression in the media *do* model behavior that some people will imitate, just as media ads influence what many people buy and what many people think the ideal male or female body should look like. Violent media images provide people with "scripts" for behaving aggressively, promote permissive beliefs about aggression as a way to solve problems, and desensitize people to the effects of violence (Anderson et al., 2003). Video games that directly reward violence—for example, by awarding points or moving the player to the next level after a "kill"—increase feelings of hostility, aggressive thinking, and aggressive behavior (Carnagey & Anderson, 2005). But perceptions and interpretations, along with personality dispositions such as aggressiveness and sociability, intervene between what we see, what we learn, and how we respond. One person may learn from seeing people being blown away in a film that violence is cool and masculine; another may conclude that violent images are ugly and stupid, or that they don't mean anything at all—that they are just part of the story.

Does playing violent video games make children more aggressive? The answer is more complicated than "yes" or "no."

What should individuals or society do, if anything, about media violence? Even if only a small percentage of viewers learn to be aggressive from all that violence, the social consequences can be huge, because the total audiences for TV, movies, and video games are immense (Bushman & Anderson, 2001). But censorship, which some people think is the answer, brings its own set of problems: Should we ban *Hamlet*? Cartoons? Batman? Funny Jackie Chan martial-arts films? Fancy special-effects films like *Matrix Reloaded*? All the Star Wars movies except the first one? In the United States, censorship would violate the Constitution, which guarantees freedom of speech. As for voluntary censorship, parents already have the opportunity to install "V-chips" on their TVs to block violent programs, yet only a tiny number of parents actually use them. As you can see, determining a fair and equitable policy regarding media violence will not be easy.

QUICK quiz

In the Harry Potter series, Hermione studies like mad for her wizardry exams. We hope she will serve as a model for you as you take this quiz.

1. A friend asks you to meet her at a new restaurant across town; you have never been there, but you find your way anyway because you have experienced _____ learning.

2. To a social-cognitive theorist, the fact that we can learn without being reinforced for any obvious responses shows that we do not learn specific responses but rather _____.

3. After watching her teenage sister put on some lipstick, a little girl takes a lipstick and applies it to her own lips. She has acquired this behavior through a process of _____.

4. The families of victims shot at a high school by two fellow students claimed in a lawsuit against several video-game manufacturers that the tragedy would not have happened had the killers not had access to violent games. How would you evaluate this claim?

Answers:

1. latent 2. knowledge about responses and their consequences 3. observational learning 4. Although a link has been established between media violence and aggressiveness, it is impossible to prove cause and effect in any given case. Violence has many different causes; for example, some teenagers kill because they have been taunted and rejected by their classmates. Further, a person's response to media violence is influenced by his or her perceptions and attitudes.

psychology in the news REVISITED

How can the behavioral and social-cognitive learning principles covered in this chapter help us think about our opening story, in which Michelle Fallaw-Gabrielson refused to spank her son Chandler after being ordered to do so by his school?

Findings on learning certainly do not rule out all use of punishment, whether by parents or others. As we saw, punishment is sometimes effective; for example, it deters some young criminals from repeating their offenses. And some psychologists argue that the occasional use of moderate punishment in the home, even spanking, has no long-term detrimental outcomes for most middle-class children, so long as it occurs in an otherwise loving context and as a quick action of last resort when a child is misbehaving (Baumrind, Larzelere, & Cowan, 2002).

Yet, as we also saw, punishment often backfires or makes matters worse when it is used as a routine method of discipline, and it can have negative psychological consequences, such as fear, tension, and resentment. When parents insult, humiliate, or ridicule a child, the results are especially devastating. Indeed, from a psychological point of view, the worst thing about spanking is not necessarily the physical pain but rather the humiliation and shame it causes. When severe penalties are imposed for minor infractions, punishment can also make the recipient feel betrayed and angry at the injustice of it. (One of Chandler's offenses, you'll recall, was chewing gum.) Human beings, including children, bring their minds to their experiences, and if they perceive their punishment as being unfair, inequitable, or overly harsh, their bad behavior is unlikely to change.

From a learning perspective, the disciplinary methods used by Chandler's mother—time-outs and taking away toys—are preferable to physical punishment, as long as the parent is consistent (no intermittent reinforcement of bad behavior!), applies the punishment as soon as possible after the behavior occurs, and, most important, remembers to reinforce successive approximations toward desirable behavior. If you have read Chapter 3 of this book, you have also learned about induction as an effective method of discipline—appealing to the child's own resources, abilities, sense of responsibility, and feelings for others.

Finally, a learning theorist would emphasize the role of the environment in causing or maintaining bad behavior, such as a child's rowdiness. For example, one of Chandler's ongoing problems was talking too much in class. There are many possible reasons for his talking, but one likely candidate was suggested by his mother: boredom. Bright or gifted children like Chandler often need a great deal of mental stimulation; their brains are always racing. The quiet, controlled environment of a classroom works fine for many children, but a particularly bright child may be-

come antsy and "too talkative," especially if assignments are below the child's ability level. School personnel may see only a bad child, failing to realize that it's actually the environment that is bad (bad for that particular child, that is). From a learning perspective, instead of trying to change the child by punishing him, adults might try creating or finding a more appropriate environment for him.

For more tips about applying learning principles in your own life, read "Taking Psychology with You." By using the techniques derived from learning theory, we can all learn to fashion healthier environments for ourselves, our families, and our fellow human beings—so long as we exercise those techniques with patience, care, and good judgment.

➤TAKING ➤PSYCHOLOGY ➤WITH ➤YOU

Shape Up!

Operant conditioning can seem deceptively simple—a few rewards here, a bit of shaping there, and you're done. In practice, though, behavior modification can be full of unwanted surprises, even in the hands of experts. Here are a few things to keep in mind if you want to modify someone's behavior:

● **Accentuate the positive.** Most people notice bad behavior more than good and, therefore, miss opportunities to use reinforcers. Parents, for example, often scold a child for bed-wetting but fail to give praise for dry sheets in the morning, or they punish a child for poor grades but fail to reward studying.

● **Reinforce small improvements.** A common error is to withhold reinforcement until behavior is perfect (which may be never). Has your child's grade in math improved from a D to a C? Has your favorite date, who is usually an awful cook, managed to serve up a half-decent omelet? Has your messy roommate left some dirty dishes in the sink but vacuumed the rug? It's probably time for a reinforcer. On the other hand, you do not want to overdo praise or give it insincerely. Gushing about every tiny step in the right direction will cause your praise to lose its value, and soon nothing less than a standing ovation will do.

● **Find the right reinforcers.** You may have to experiment a bit to find which reinforcers a person (or animal) actually wants. Try varying the reinforcers; the same ones used again and again can get boring. Reinforcers,

by the way, do not have to be *things*. You can also use valued activities, such as going out to dinner, to reinforce other behavior.

● **Always examine what you are reinforcing.** It is easy to reinforce undesirable behavior just by responding to it. Suppose someone is always yelling at you at the slightest provocation. If you respond to the yelling at all, whether by crying, apologizing, or yelling back, you are likely to reinforce it. An alternative might be to explain in a calm voice that you will henceforth not respond to complaints unless they are communicated without yelling—and then, if the yelling continues, walk away. When the person does speak civilly, you can reward this behavior with your attention and goodwill.

● **Analyze the reasons for a person's undesirable behavior before responding to it.** A child screaming in a supermarket may be saying, "I'm going out of my head with boredom. Help!" A lover who sulks may be saying, "I'm not sure you really care about me; I'm frightened." Once you understand the purpose of someone's behavior, you may be more effective in dealing with it.

These guidelines apply to your own behavior as well. Assume, for example, that you want to get yourself to study more. Here are some behavioral strategies for increasing the time you spend with your books:

● **Analyze the situation.** Are there circumstances that keep you from studying, such as a friend who is always pressuring

you to go out or a rock band that practices next door? If so, you need to change the discriminative stimuli in your environment during study periods. Try to find a comfortable, cheerful, quiet, well-lit place. Not only will you concentrate better, but you may also have positive emotional responses to the environment, which may generalize to the activity of studying.

● **Set realistic goals.** Goals should be demanding but achievable. If a goal is too vague, as in "I'm going to work harder," you won't know what behavioral changes are necessary to reach it or how to recognize when you have done so (what does "harder" mean?). If your goal is focused, as in "I am going to study two hours every evening instead of one," or "I will read 25 pages instead of 15," you have specified both a course of action and a goal you can achieve (and reward).

● **Keep records.** Chart your progress in some way, perhaps by making a graph. This will keep you honest, and the progress you see on the graph will serve as a secondary reinforcer.

● **Don't punish yourself.** If you did not study enough last week, don't brood about it or berate yourself with self-defeating thoughts, such as "I'll never be a good student" or "I'm a failure." Think about the coming week instead.

Above all, be patient. Shaping behavior is a creative skill that takes time to learn. Like Rome, new habits cannot be built in a day.

SUMMARY

• Research on *learning* has been heavily influenced by *behaviorism*, which accounts for behavior in terms of observable events without reference to mental entities such as "mind" or "will." Behaviorists have focused on two types of *conditioning:* classical and operant.

Classical Conditioning

• *Classical conditioning* was first studied by Russian physiologist Ivan Pavlov. In this type of learning, when a neutral stimulus is paired with an *unconditioned stimulus (US)* that elicits a reflexive *unconditioned response (UR)*, the neutral stimulus comes to elicit a similar or related response. The neutral stimulus then becomes a *conditioned stimulus (CS)*, and the response it elicits is a *conditioned response (CR)*. Nearly any kind of involuntary response can become a CR.

• In *extinction*, the conditioned stimulus is repeatedly presented without the unconditioned stimulus, and the conditioned response eventually disappears—although later it may reappear (*spontaneous recovery*). In *higher-order conditioning*, a neutral stimulus becomes a conditioned stimulus by being paired with an already established conditioned stimulus. In *stimulus generalization*, after a stimulus becomes a conditioned stimulus for some response, other, similar stimuli may produce the same reaction. In *stimulus discrimination*, different responses are made to stimuli that resemble the conditioned stimulus in some way.

• Many theorists believe that what an animal or person learns in classical conditioning is not just an association between the unconditioned and the conditioned stimulus but also information conveyed by one stimulus about another. Indeed, classical conditioning appears to be an evolutionary adaptation that allows an organism to prepare for a biologically important event. Considerable evidence exists that a neutral stimulus does not become a CS unless it reliably signals or predicts the US.

Classical Conditioning in Real Life

• Classical conditioning may account for positive emotional responses to particular objects and events, fears and phobias, the acquisition of likes and dislikes, and reactions to medical treatments and placebos. John Watson showed how fears may be learned and then may be unlearned through a process of *counterconditioning*. Human beings (and many other species) are biologically primed to acquire some adaptive responses easily, such as conditioned taste aversions and certain fears.

Operant Conditioning

• In *operant conditioning*, behavior becomes more likely to occur or less so, depending on its consequences. Responses are generally not reflexive and are more complex than in classical conditioning. Research in this area is closely associated with B. F. Skinner, who called his approach "radical behaviorism."

• In the Skinnerian analysis, *reinforcement* strengthens or increases the probability of a response and *punishment* weakens or decreases the probability of a response. Immediate consequences usually have a greater effect on a response than do delayed consequences.

• Reinforcers are called *primary* when they are naturally reinforcing (e.g., because they satisfy a biological need) and *secondary* when they have acquired their ability to strengthen a response through association with other reinforcers. A similar distinction is made for punishers.

• Reinforcement and punishment may be either positive or negative, depending on whether the consequence involves a stimulus that is presented or one that is removed or avoided. In *positive reinforcement*, something pleasant follows a response; in *negative reinforcement*, something unpleasant is removed following a response. In *positive punishment*, something unpleasant follows the response; in *negative punishment*, something pleasant is removed.

• Using the Skinner box and similar devices, behaviorists have shown that *extinction, stimulus generalization*, and *stimulus discrimination* occur in operant conditioning as well as in classical conditioning. A *discriminative stimulus* signals that a response is likely to be followed by a certain type of consequence.

• The pattern of responding in operant conditioning depends in part on the *schedule of reinforcement*. *Continuous reinforcement* leads to the most rapid learning. However, *intermittent (partial) reinforcement* makes a response more resistant to extinction (and, therefore, helps account for the persistence of superstitious rituals). One of the most common errors people make is to reward intermittently the responses they would like to eliminate.

• *Shaping* is used to train behaviors with a low probability of occurring spontaneously. Reinforcers are given for *successive approximations* to the desired response until the desired response is achieved.

• Biology places limits on what an animal or person can learn through operant conditioning. For example, animals sometimes have trouble learning a task because of *instinctive drift*.

Operant Conditioning in Real Life

• *Behavior modification*, the application of conditioning principles, has been used successfully in many settings, but punishment and reinforcement both have their pitfalls.

• Punishment, when used properly, can discourage undesirable behavior, including criminal behavior. But it is frequently misused and can have unintended consequences. It is often administered inappropriately because of the emotion of the moment; it may produce rage and fear; its effects are often only temporary; it is hard to administer immediately; it conveys little information about the kind of behavior that is desired; and it may provide attention that is rewarding. Extinction of undesirable behavior, combined with reinforcement of desired behavior, is generally preferable to the use of punishment.

• Reinforcers can also be misused. Rewards that are given out indiscriminately, as in efforts to raise children's self-esteem, do not reinforce desirable behavior. And, as we saw in "Close-up on Research," an exclusive reliance on *extrinsic reinforcement* can sometimes undermine the power of *intrinsic reinforcement*. But money and praise do not usually interfere with intrinsic pleasure when a person is rewarded for succeeding or making progress rather than for merely participating in an activity, or when a person is already highly interested in the activity.

Learning and the Mind

• In the 1930s, Edward Tolman studied *latent learning*, in which no obvious reinforcer is present during learning and a response is not expressed until later on when reinforcement does become available. What seems to be acquired in latent learning is not a specific response but rather knowledge about responses and their consequences.

• The 1960s and 1970s saw the increased influence of *social-cognitive theories* of learning, which focus on *observational learning* and the role played by beliefs, interpretations of events, and other cognitions.

• Social-cognitive theorists argue that because people differ in their perceptions and beliefs, they may learn different lessons from the same event or situation. For example, some people become more aggressive after observing violent images, but most people do not. Moreover, cause and effect also work in the opposite direction: Aggressive individuals tend to be drawn to violent images and are more affected by them than other people are.

Psychology in the News, Revisited

• Behavioral and social-cognitive learning theories help us understand when punishment might be constructive and appropriate, and also when it backfires, causing resentment and other undesirable results. The learning perspective also offers good alternatives to physical punishment and helps us appreciate the role of the environment in promoting "bad" behavior. Learning techniques can be enormously helpful for individuals and institutions as long as they are applied wisely and carefully.

KEY TERMS

- **Learning** is any relatively permanent change in behavior resulting from experience.
- **Behaviorism** explains learning as the result of observable acts and events without reference to mental entities, such as "mind" or "will."
- **Conditioning** involves associations between environmental stimuli and responses.

Classical Conditioning

New Reflexes from Old

Classical conditioning is the process by which a previously neutral stimulus acquires the capacity to elicit a response through association with a stimulus that already elicits a similar or related response (first studied by Ivan Pavlov).
- **Unconditioned stimulus (US):** stimulus that elicits a reflexive response in the absence of learning

- **Unconditioned response (UR):** reflexive response elicited by a stimulus in the absence of learning
- **Conditioned stimulus (CS):** initially neutral stimulus that comes to elicit a conditioned response after being associated with an unconditioned stimulus
- **Conditioned response (CR):** response that is elicited by a conditioned stimulus

Principles of Classical Conditioning

- **Extinction:** gradual disappearance of CR after CS is repeatedly presented without US.
- **Higher-order conditioning:** a neutral stimulus becomes a CS after being associated with another CS.

- **Stimulus generalization:** a CR occurs upon presentation of a stimulus similar to the CS.
- **Stimulus discrimination:** stimuli similar to the CS produce different responses.

What is Learned in Classical Conditioning?
- Many psychologists argue that classical conditioning involves information conveyed by one stimulus about another.
- Classical conditioning appears to be an evolutionary adaptation that allows an organism to prepare for a biologically important event.

Classical Conditioning in Real Life

Classical conditioning plays an important role in:
- Positive emotional responses to particular objects and events
- Learned fears and phobias (as demonstrated in the Little Albert study)

- Acquired tastes - likes and dislikes for particular foods and odors
- Unpleasant reactions to stimuli associated with medical treatments and reduced pain or anxiety in response to placebos

The Consequences of Behavior

- A neutral consequence neither increases nor decreases the probability that the response will recur.
- **Reinforcement** strengthens the response or makes it more likely to recur.

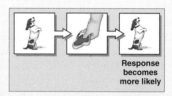

Response becomes more likely

- **Punishment** weakens the response or makes it less likely to recur.

"No!" Response becomes less likely

Primary and Secondary Reinforcers and Punishers

- A **primary reinforcer** strengthens responses because it satisfies a biological need.
- A **secondary reinforcer** strengthens a response because of its association with a primary reinforcer.
- A **primary punisher** is a stimulus that produces discomfort.
- A **secondary punisher** is a stimulus that has acquired punishing properties through association with a primary reinforcer.

Positive and Negative Reinforcers and Punishers

- **Positive reinforcement:** response is followed by the presentation of, or increase in intensity of, a reinforcing stimulus.
- **Negative reinforcement:** response is followed by the removal, delay, or decrease in intensity of an unpleasant stimulus.
- In **positive punishment**, something unpleasant follows the response; in **negative punishment**, something pleasant is removed.

Operant Conditioning

Operant conditioning is the process by which a response becomes more likely or less likely to occur, depending on its consequences; associated with work of B. F. Skinner.

Principles of Operant Conditioning

- **Extinction:** occurs when the behavior is no longer followed by the consequence that reinforced it.
- **Stimulus discrimination:** responses occur in the presence of one stimulus but not to stimuli that resemble the ones originally present but differ from them on some dimension.
- **Stimulus generalization:** responses occur to stimuli that resemble those present during original learning.

- Schedules of reinforcement:
  — **Continuous reinforcement** leads to fastest learning.
  — **Intermittent reinforcement** makes a response resistant to extinction.
- **Shaping:** used to train behaviors through reinforcement of **successive approximations** until the desired behavior occurs.
- **Instinctive drift:** the tendency for an organism to revert to instinctive behavior.

Operant Conditioning in Real Life

Behavior modification: the application of conditioning techniques to teach new responses or eliminate behavior problems.

Pros and Cons of Punishment

- Can effectively discourage undesirable behavior.
- However, often it is used inappropriately; recipients respond with anxiety, fear, or rage; improvement is only temporary; it is too delayed to be effective; it conveys little information about desired behavior; and it involves inadvertent reward by providing attention for undesirable behavior.

Problems with Reward

- It is often misused when rewards are given indiscriminately.
- Exclusive reliance on extrinsic reinforcement can sometimes undermine the power of intrinsic reinforcement, such as enjoyment of the task.

Learning and the Mind

Latent Learning

- Can occur without reinforcers
- Involves aquiring knowledge about responses and their consequences, which permits flexibility in reaching goals

Social-cognitive Learning Theories

- **Social-cognitive** theories focus on **observational learning** and the role played by beliefs, interpretations of events, and other cognitions.

- Social-cognitive theorists argue that because people differ in their perceptions and beliefs, they may learn different lessons from the same situations, as in the case of media violence.

Private England Pleads Guilty in Prisoner Abuse Scandal

FORT HOOD, TX, APRIL 30, 2005. Lawyers for Pfc. Lynndie R. England, the 22-year-old woman who became a vivid symbol of the Abu Ghraib prisoner abuse scandal, announced today that she will plead guilty to reduced charges of conspiracy, dereliction of duty, maltreatment of prisoners, and indecent acts. Private England became an international symbol of cruelty when photos of her participating in abusive, humiliating acts appeared on the Internet. In one photo, she was holding a leash around the neck of a naked Iraqi detainee; in others, she was grinning or giving a thumbs-up over a pile of naked prisoners. The photos set off worldwide outrage against the American military and prompted investigations by Congress and the Pentagon.

England's defense lawyers said they would present evidence that she has a history of mental health problems and learning disabilities. They will also argue that another soldier who was England's boyfriend at the time, Specialist Charles A. Graner, Jr., was the ringleader of the abuses and was a corrupting influence on her.

Six other soldiers have been charged in the abuses committed at Abu Ghraib prison. Four have pleaded guilty in exchange for reduced

England at her trial in the United States.

punishments; a fifth faces a court-martial next month. The sixth, Graner, has already been sentenced to 10 years in prison and dismissed from the military.

The seven soldiers who took part in these incidents defended themselves by saying they were simply following orders. Their families told reporters that the soldiers were kind people who would never voluntarily harm another human being. "Certain people in the Army told her to do what she did. She follows orders," said England's sister. "She's a caring person." Asked if she ever physically abused a detainee, Private England told investigators, "Yes, I stepped on some of them, push them or pull them, but nothing extreme."

This photograph of Pfc. Lynndie England keeping an Iraqi prisoner on a leash at Abu Ghraib prison shocked the world.

Behavior in Social and Cultural Context

Why did the soldiers at Abu Ghraib prison treat the detainees so cruelly? Is Lynndie England a "caring person" who was "simply following orders"? Was she mentally disturbed or cognitively impaired? Was she under the influence of a sadistic boyfriend? Did she and her fellow soldiers behave as they did, not because they were unusually brutal or heartless individuals but because of conditions at the prison where they were ordered to work as guards? Or is the answer to be found in some combination of these explanations?

Researchers in the fields of *social psychology* and *cultural psychology* address these questions, and many other puzzles of human behavior, by examining the influence of the social and cultural environment on the actions of individuals and groups. *Social* psychologists study how social roles, attitudes, relationships, and groups influence people to do things they would not necessarily do on their own—to act bravely, compassionately, aggressively, or even savagely. *Cultural* psychologists study the broader influence of culture and ethnicity on roles and relationships in society. Together these fields explore the reasons for the entire range of good and bad human behavior: the countless examples of kindness, sacrifice, and heroism on the one hand, and of cruelty, selfishness, and war on the other.

In this book, we have included discussions of social and cultural influences on child-rearing practices, moral development, test performance, love and attachment, the communication of emotion, and many other areas of life. In this chapter, we will focus on the basic social and cultural forces that affect behavior and make human beings less independent than they might think. As you read, ask yourself what you think you might have done if you were a solider in charge of detainees at Abu Ghraib. Would you have gone along, either reluctantly or willingly, with how your fellow guards were treating the prisoners? Would you have refused to take part but remained silent? Or would you have "blown the whistle" by reporting your fellow soldiers' abuses to the higher-ups?

WHAT'S *Ahead*

- How do social rules regulate behavior, and what is likely to happen when you violate them?
- Do you have to be mean or disturbed to inflict pain on someone just because an authority tells you to?
- How can ordinary college students be transformed into sadistic prison guards?
- How can people be entrapped into violating their moral principles?

Roles and Rules

"We are all fragile creatures entwined in a cobweb of social constraints," social psychologist Stanley Milgram once said. The constraints he referred to are social **norms**, rules about how we are supposed to act, enforced by threats of punishment if we violate them and promises of reward if we follow them. Norms are the conventions of everyday life that make interactions with other people predictable and orderly; like a cobweb, they are often as invisible as they are strong. Every society has norms for just about everything in human experience: for conducting courtships, for raising children, for making decisions, for behavior in public places. Some norms are enshrined in law, such as "A person may not beat up another person, except in self-defense." Some are unspoken cultural understandings, such as "A man may beat up another man who insults his masculinity." And some are tiny, unspoken regulations that people learn to follow unconsciously, such as "You may not sing at the top of your lungs on a public bus."

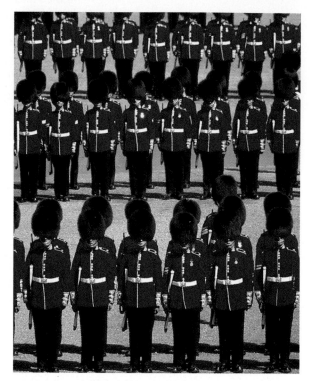

Many roles in modern life require us to give up our individuality. If one of these members of the British Coldstream Guards suddenly broke into a dance, his career would be brief. But when does adherence to a role go too far?

In every society, people also fill a variety of social **roles**, positions that are regulated by norms about how people in those positions should behave. Gender roles define the proper behavior for a man and a woman. Occupational roles determine the correct behavior for a manager and an employee, a professor and a student. Family roles set tasks for parent and child, husband and wife. Certain aspects of every role must be carried out or there will be penalties—emotional, financial, or professional. As a student, for instance, you know just what you have to do to pass your psychology course (or you should by now!). How do you know what a role requirement is? You know when you violate it, intentionally or unintentionally, because you will probably feel awfully uncomfortable, or other people will try to make you feel that way.

Naturally, people bring their own personalities and interests to the roles they play. Just as two actors will play the same part differently although they are reading from the same script, you will have your own "reading" of how to play the role of student, friend, parent, or employer. Nonetheless, the requirements of a social role are strong, so strong that they may even cause you to behave in ways that shatter your fundamental sense of the kind of person you are. We turn now to two classic studies that illuminate the power of social roles in our lives.

- **norms (social)** Rules that regulate social life, including explicit laws and implicit cultural conventions.

- **role** A given social position that is governed by a set of norms for proper behavior.

Dare To Be Different

Either alone or with a friend, try a mild form of "norm violation" (nothing alarming, obscene, dangerous, or offensive). For example, stand backward in line at the grocery store or cafeteria; sit right next to a stranger in the library or at a movie, even when other seats are available; sing or hum loudly for a couple of minutes in a public place; stand "too close" to a friend in conversation. Notice the reactions of onlookers, as well as your own feelings, while you violate this norm. If you do this exercise with someone else, one of you can be the "violator" and the other can write down the responses of others; then switch places. Was it easy to do this exercise? Why or why not?

The Obedience Study

In the early 1960s, Stanley Milgram (1963, 1974) designed a study that would become world-famous. Milgram wanted to know how many people would obey an authority figure when directly ordered to violate their own ethical standards. Participants in the study, however, thought they were part of an experiment on the effects of punishment on learning. Each was assigned, apparently at random, to the role of "teacher." Another person, introduced as a fellow volunteer, was the "learner." Whenever the learner, seated in an adjoining room, made an error in reciting a list of word pairs he was supposed to have memorized, the teacher had to give him an electric shock by depressing a lever on a machine (see Figure 10.1). With each error, the voltage (marked from 0 to 450) was to be increased by another 15 volts. The shock levels on the machine were labeled from SLIGHT SHOCK to DANGER—SEVERE SHOCK and, finally, ominously, XXX. In reality, the learners were confederates of Milgram and did not receive any shocks, but none of the teachers ever realized this during the study. The actor-victims played their parts convincingly: As the study continued, they shouted in pain and pleaded to be released, all according to a pre-arranged script.

Before doing this study, Milgram asked a number of psychiatrists, students, and middle-class adults how many people they thought would "go all the way" to XXX on orders from the researcher. The psychiatrists predicted that most people would refuse to go beyond 150 volts, when the learner first demanded to be freed, and that only one person in a thousand, someone who was disturbed and sadistic, would administer the highest voltage. The nonprofessionals agreed with this prediction, and all of them said that they personally would disobey early in the procedure.

That is not, however, the way the results turned out. Every single person administered some shock to the learner, and about two-thirds of the participants, of all ages and from all walks of life, obeyed to the fullest extent. Many protested to the experimenter, but they backed down when he calmly asserted, "The experiment requires that you continue." They obeyed no matter how much the victim shouted for them to stop and no matter how painful the shocks seemed to be. They obeyed even when they themselves were anguished about the pain they believed they were causing. As Milgram (1974) noted, participants would "sweat, tremble, stutter, bite their lips, groan, and dig their fingernails into their flesh"—but still they obeyed.

FIGURE 10.1
The Milgram Obedience Experiment
On the left is Milgram's original shock machine; in 1963, it looked pretty ominous. On the right, the "learner" is being strapped into his chair by the experimenter and the "teacher."

(left) Archives of the History of American Psychology–The University of Akron
(right) Copyright 1965 by Stanley Milgram. From the film OBEDIENCE, distributed by Penn State Media Sales

In Milgram's study, when the "teacher" had to administer shock directly to the learner, most subjects refused. This one, however, continued to obey.

Over the decades, more than 3,000 people have gone through replications of the Milgram study. Most of them, men and women equally, inflicted what they thought were dangerous amounts of shock to another person. Researchers in other countries have also found high percentages of obedience, ranging to more than 90 percent in Spain and the Netherlands (Meeus & Raaijmakers, 1995; Smith & Bond, 1994).

Milgram and his team subsequently set up several variations of the study to determine the circumstances under which people might disobey the experimenter. They found that virtually nothing the victim did or said changed the likelihood of compliance, even when the victim said he had a heart condition, screamed in agony, or stopped responding entirely, as if he had collapsed. However, people *were* more likely to disobey under the following conditions:

- *When the experimenter left the room,* many people subverted authority by giving low levels of shock but reporting that they had followed orders.

- *When the victim was right there in the room,* and the teacher had to administer the shock directly to the victim's body, many people refused to go on.

- *When two experimenters issued conflicting demands,* with one telling participants to continue the experiment and another saying to stop at once, no one kept inflicting shock.

- *When the person ordering them to continue was an ordinary man,* apparently another volunteer instead of the authoritative experimenter, many participants disobeyed.

- *When the subject worked with peers who refused to go further,* he or she often gained the courage to disobey.

Obedience, Milgram concluded, was more a function of the *situation* than of the particular personalities of the participants. "The key to [their] behavior," Milgram (1974) summarized, "lies not in pent-up anger or aggression but in the nature of their relationship to authority. They have given themselves to the authority; they see themselves as instruments for the execution of his wishes; once so defined, they are unable to break free."

The Milgram study has had its critics. Some consider it unethical because people were kept in the dark about what was really happening until the session was over (of course, telling them in advance would have invalidated the study) and because many

suffered emotional pain (Milgram countered that they would not have felt pain if they had simply disobeyed instructions). Others question the conclusion that personality traits always have less influence on behavior than the demands of the situation; certain traits, such as hostility and rigidity, do increase obedience to authority in real life (Blass, 1993, 2000).

Some psychologists also object to the parallel Milgram drew between the behavior of the study's participants and the brutality of the Nazis and others who have committed acts of barbarism in the name of duty (Darley, 1995). The people in Milgram's study obeyed only when the experimenter was hovering right there, and many of them felt enormous discomfort and conflict. In contrast, most Nazis acted without direct supervision by authorities, without external pressure, and without feelings of anguish.

Nevertheless, this compelling study has had a tremendous influence on public awareness of the dangers of uncritical obedience. As John Darley (1995) observed, "Milgram shows us the beginning of a path by means of which ordinary people, in the grip of social forces, become the origins of atrocities in the real world."

The Prison Study

Another famous demonstration of the power of roles is known as the Stanford Prison Study. Its designers, Philip Zimbardo and Craig Haney, wanted to know what would happen if ordinary college students were randomly assigned to the roles of prisoners and guards (Haney, Banks, & Zimbardo, 1973). And so they set up a serious-looking "prison" in the basement of a Stanford building, complete with individual cells, different uniforms for prisoners and guards (including nightsticks for the guards), and so forth. The students agreed to live there for two weeks.

The results were dramatic. Within a short time, the prisoners became distressed, helpless, and panicky. They developed emotional symptoms and physical ailments. Some became apathetic; others became rebellious. Within an equally short time, the guards began to enjoy their new power. Some tried to be nice, helping the prisoners and doing little favors for them. Some were "tough but fair," holding strictly to "the rules." But about a third became harsh and abusive, even when the prisoners were not resisting in any way. The researchers, who had not expected such a speedy and alarming transformation of healthy students, ended this study after only six days.

Generations of students and the general public have seen emotionally charged clips from the videos

Prisoners and guards quickly learn their respective roles, which often have more influence on their behavior than their personalities do.

made at the time. To the researchers, their study demonstrated the power of roles: The guards' aggression, they said, was entirely a result of wearing a guard's uniform and having the power of the guard's role (Haney, Banks, & Zimbardo, 1973; Haney & Zimbardo, 1998). Recently, however, critics have argued that the prison study is really another example of obedience to authority and of how willingly some people obey instructions—in this case, from Zimbardo himself (Haslam & Reicher, 2003). Consider the briefing that Zimbardo provided to the guards at the beginning of the study:

> You can create in the prisoners feelings of boredom, a sense of fear to some degree, you can create a notion of arbitrariness that their life is totally controlled by us, by the system, you, me, and they'll have no privacy. . . . We're going to take away their individuality in various ways. In general what all this leads to is a sense of powerlessness. That is, in this situation we'll have all the power and they'll have none (The Stanford Prison Study video, quoted in Haslam & Reicher, 2003).

These are pretty powerful suggestions to the guards about how they would be permitted to behave, and they convey Zimbardo's personal encouragement ("*we'll* have all the power"), so it is not surprising that some took Zimbardo at his word and behaved quite brutally. On the other hand, in real prisons, guards do have the kind of power that was given to these students. In any case, the study remains a powerful demonstration of how the *social situation*—whether the role itself or obedience to authority—affects behavior, causing people to behave in ways they might not otherwise choose to do, ways that seem "out of character."

Why People Obey

Of course, obedience to authority or to the norms of a situation is not always harmful or bad. A certain amount of routine compliance with rules is necessary in any group, and obedience to authority has many benefits for individuals and society. A nation could not operate if all its citizens ignored traffic signals, cheated on their taxes, dumped garbage wherever they chose, or assaulted each other. An organization could not function if its members came to work only when they felt like it. But obedience also has a darker aspect. Throughout history, the plea "I was only following orders" has been offered to excuse actions carried out on behalf of orders that were foolish, destructive, or illegal. The writer C. P. Snow once observed that "more hideous crimes have been committed in the name of obedience than in the name of rebellion."

Most people follow orders because of the obvious consequences of disobedience: They can be suspended from school, fired from their jobs, or arrested. They may also obey because of what they hope to gain: being liked, getting certain advantages or promotions from the authority, or learning from the authority's greater knowledge or experience. Primarily, though, people obey because they are deeply convinced of the authority's legitimacy. They obey not in hopes of gaining some tangible benefit, but because they like and respect the authority and value the relationship (Tyler, 1997).

But what about all those obedient people in Milgram's study who felt they were doing wrong and who wished they were free, but who could not untangle themselves from the "cobweb of social constraints?" Why do people obey when it is not in their interests, or when obedience requires them to ignore their own values or even commit a crime? How do they become morally disengaged from the consequences of their actions? Researchers looking at the social context of behavior draw our attention to several factors that cause people to obey when they would rather not (Bandura, 1999; Gourevich, 1998; Kelman & Hamilton, 1989; Staub, 1999):

1 *Allocating responsibility to the authority.* One common way that people justify their behavior is to hand over responsibility to the authority, thereby absolving themselves of accountability for their own actions. In Milgram's study, many who administered the highest levels of shock adopted the attitude "It's his problem; I'm just following orders." In contrast, individuals who refused to give high levels of shock took responsibility for their own actions and refused to

entrapment A gradual process in which individuals escalate their commitment to a course of action to justify their investment of time, money, or effort.

grant the authority legitimacy. "One of the things I think is very cowardly," said a 32-year-old engineer, "is to try to shove the responsibility onto someone else. See, if I now turned around and said, 'It's your fault . . . it's not mine,' I would call that cowardly" (Milgram, 1974).

2 *Routinizing the task.* When people define their actions in terms of routine duties and roles, their behavior starts to feel normal, just a job to be done. Becoming absorbed in busywork distracts them from raising doubts or ethical questions, and it fosters an uncritical, mindless attention to details that obscures the larger picture. In the Milgram study, some people became so fixated on the "learning task" that they shut out any moral concerns about the learner's demands to be let out. Routinization is typically the mechanism by which governments enlist citizens to aid and abet programs of genocide. Nazi bureaucrats kept meticulous records of every victim, and in Cambodia in the 1970s the Khmer Rouge recorded the names and histories of the millions of victims they tortured and killed. "I am not a violent man," said Sous Thy, one of the clerks who recorded these names, to a reporter from *The New York Times*. "I was just making lists."

3 *Wanting to be polite.* Good manners protect people's feelings and make relationships and civilization possible. But once people are caught in what they perceive to be legitimate roles and are obeying a legitimate authority, good manners ensnare them into further obedience. They do not want to rock the boat, appear to doubt the experts, or be rude, because they know they will be disliked for doing so (Collins & Brief, 1995).

Most people learn the language of manners ("please," "thank you," "I'm sorry for missing your birthday"), but they literally lack the words to justify disobedience and rudeness toward an authority they respect. In the Milgram study, many people could not find the words to justify walking out, so they stayed. One woman kept apologizing to the experimenter, trying not to offend him with her worries for the victim: "Do I go right to the end, sir? I hope there's nothing wrong with him there." (She did go right to the end.) A man repeatedly protested and questioned the experimenter, but he too obeyed, even when the victim had apparently collapsed in pain. "He thinks he is killing someone," Milgram (1974) commented, "yet he uses the language of the tea table."

4 *Becoming entrapped.* **Entrapment** is a process in which individuals escalate their commitment to a course of action in order to justify their investment in it (Brockner & Rubin, 1985). The first steps of entrapment pose no difficult choices, but one step leads to another, and before you realize it, you have become committed to a course of action that poses problems. In Milgram's study, once subjects had given a 15-volt shock, they had committed themselves to the experiment. The next level was "only" 30 volts. Because each increment was small, before they knew it most people were administering what they believed were dangerously strong shocks. At that point, it was difficult to explain a sudden decision to quit. Participants who questioned the procedure early were less likely to become entrapped and more likely to eventually disobey (Modigliani & Rochat, 1995).

Individuals and nations alike are vulnerable to the sneaky process of entrapment. You start dating someone you like moderately; before you know it, you have been together so long that you can't break up, although you don't want to become committed, either. Government leaders start a war they think will end quickly. Years later, the nation has lost so many soldiers and so much money that the leaders believe they cannot retreat without losing face.

A chilling study of entrapment was conducted with 25 men who had served in the Greek military police during the authoritarian regime that ended in 1974 (Haritos-Fatouros, 1988). A psychologist interviewed the men, identifying the steps used in training them to use torture in questioning prisoners. First the men were ordered to stand guard outside the interrogation and torture cells. Then they stood guard inside the detention rooms, where they observed the torture of prisoners. Then they helped beat up pris-

Routinization allows people to commit or collaborate in atrocities. More than 16,000 political prisoners were tortured and killed at Tuol Sleng prison by Cambodia's Khmer Rouge, during the genocidal regime of Pol Pot in the 1970s. Authorities kept meticulous records and photos of each victim in order to make their barbarous activities seem mundane and normal. This man, Ing Pech, one of only seven survivors, was spared because he had skills useful to his captors. He now runs a museum at the prison.

Slot machines rely on the principle of entrapment, which is why casinos win millions and most players don't. A person vows to spend only a few dollars but, after losing them, says, "Well, maybe another couple of tries" or "I've spent so much, now I really have to win something to get back what I've lost."

ing torturers. The same procedures have been used to train police interrogators to use torture on political opponents and terrorist suspects all over the world (Huggins, Haritos-Fatouros, & Zimbardo, 2003). In a book appropriately called *Unspeakable Acts, Ordinary People,* John Conroy (2000) documented cases of torture by, among others, Chicago police officers against prisoners, the British army against IRA suspects in Northern Ireland, and Israeli soldiers against Palestinians.

As Milgram would have predicted, even torturers see themselves as otherwise good guys who are just doing their jobs. This is a difficult concept for people who divide the world into "good guys" versus "bad guys" and cannot imagine that good guys might do cruel things. Yet in everyday life, as in the Milgram study, people often set out on a path that is morally ambiguous, only to find that they have traveled a long way toward violating their own principles. From Greece's torturers to the Khmer Rouge's dutiful clerks, from Milgram's well-meaning volunteers to all of us in our everyday lives, people face the difficult task of drawing a line beyond which they will not go. For many, the demands of the role defeat the inner voice of conscience.

oners. Once they had obediently followed these orders and became actively involved, the torturers found their actions easier to carry out.

It is not only "bad" people or "the enemy" who have relied on the principle of entrapment in train-

QUICK quiz

Step into your role of student to answer these questions.

1. About what proportion of the people in Milgram's obedience study administered the highest level of shock? (a) two-thirds, (b) one-half, (c) one-third, (d) one-tenth

2. Which of the following actions by the "learner" reduced the likelihood of being shocked by the "teacher" in Milgram's study? (a) protesting noisily, (b) screaming in pain, (c) complaining of having a heart ailment, (d) nothing he did made a difference

3. A friend of yours, who is moving, asks you to bring over a few boxes. Since you are there anyway, he asks you to fill them with books. Before you know it, you have packed up his entire kitchen, living room, and bedroom. What social-psychological process is at work here?

Answers:

1. a 2. d 3. entrapment

WHAT'S *Ahead*

• What is one of the most common mistakes people make when explaining the behavior of others?

• Why do so many people blame victims of tragedy or crime for having brought their misfortunes on themselves?

• What is the "Big Lie," and why does it work so well?

• What is the difference between ordinary techniques of persuasion and the coercive techniques used by cults?

Social Influences on Beliefs

Social psychologists are interested not only in what people do in social situations but also in what goes on in their heads while they're doing it. Researchers in the area of **social cognition** examine how people's perceptions of themselves and others affect their relationships and how the social environment influences thoughts, beliefs, and values. Some have

social cognition An area in social psychology concerned with social influences on thought, memory, perception, and beliefs.

joined forces with neuroscientists and cognitive psychologists to develop a new specialty called *social-cognitive neuroscience*, which draws upon technologies from neuroscience to study the emotional and social processes underlying beliefs, prejudices, and social behavior (Harris, Todorov, & Fiske, 2005). We will consider two important topics in this area: explanations about behavior and the formation of attitudes.

Attributions

People read detective stories to find out *who* did the dirty deed, but in real life we also want to know *why* people do things. Was it because of a terrible childhood, a mental illness, possession by a demon, or what? According to **attribution theory**, the explanations we make of our behavior and the behavior of others generally fall into two categories. When we make a *situational attribution*, we are identifying the cause of an action as something in the situation or environment: "Joe stole the money because his family is starving." When we make a *dispositional attribution*, we are identifying the cause of an action as something in the person, such as a trait or a motive: "Joe stole the money because he is a born thief."

When people are trying to find reasons for someone else's behavior, they reveal a common bias: They tend to overestimate personality traits and underestimate the influence of the situation (Forgas, 1998; Nisbett & Ross, 1980). In terms of attribution theory, they tend to ignore situational attributions in favor of dispositional ones. This tendency has been called the **fundamental attribution error** (Jones, 1990; Van Boven, Kamada, & Gilovich, 1999). Were the hundreds of people who obeyed Milgram's experimenters sadistic by nature? Were the student guards in the prison study sadistic and the prisoners cowardly? Those who think so are committing the fundamental attribution error. The impulse to explain other people's behavior in terms of their personalities is so strong that we do it even when we know that the other person was *required* to behave in a certain way (Yzerbyt et al., 2001).

People are especially likely to overlook situational attributions when they are in a good mood and not inclined to think about other people's motives critically, or when they are distracted and preoccupied and don't have time to stop and ask themselves, "Why, exactly, *is* Aurelia behaving like such a dimwit today?" (Forgas, 1998). Instead, they leap to the easiest attribution, which is dispositional: It's all because of her dim personality. They are less likely to wonder if Aurelia has recently joined a group of friends who are encouraging dim-witted behavior or if she is under unusual pressure that is making her act "out of character."

Attributions

"Why is Aurelia behaving like a dimwit?"

Situational

"She's under pressure."

Dispositional

"She's self-involved and clueless."

(may lead to)

Fundamental Attribution Error

Ignoring influence of situation on behavior and emphasizing personality traits alone

The fundamental attribution error is especially prevalent in Western nations, where middle-class people tend to believe that individuals are responsible for their own actions. In countries such as India, where everyone is embedded in caste and family networks, and in Japan, China, Korea, and Hong Kong, where people are more group oriented than in the West, people are more likely to be aware of situational constraints on behavior (Choi et al., 2003; Miyamoto & Kitayama, 2002). Thus, if someone is behaving oddly, makes a mistake, or plays badly in a soccer match, a person from India or China is more likely to make a situational attribution of the person's behavior ("He's under pressure") than a dispositional one ("He's incompetent") (Menon et al., 1999).

Westerners do not always prefer dispositional attributions, however. When it comes to explaining their *own* behavior, they often reveal a **self-serving bias**, taking credit for their good actions (a dispositional attribution) but letting the situation account for their failures, embarrassing mistakes, or harmful actions (Mezulis et al., 2004). For instance, most North Americans, when angry, will say, "I am furious for good reason—this situation is intolerable." They are less likely to say, "I am furious because I am an ill-tempered grinch." On the other hand, if they do something admirable, such as donating to charity, they are likely to attribute their motives to a personal disposition ("I'm so generous") instead of the situation ("That guy on the phone pressured me into it").

According to the **just-world hypothesis**, attributions are also affected by the need to believe that the world is fair and that justice prevails and, particularly, that good people are rewarded and bad guys punished. This belief, which is especially prevalent in the United States, helps people make sense out of senseless events and feel safe in the presence of threatening events (Lerner, 1980). When the belief is thrown into doubt, people are motivated to restore it. For example, students who felt most strongly that the world is fair, as measured in their

attribution theory The theory that people are motivated to explain their own and other people's behavior by attributing causes of that behavior to a situation or a disposition.

fundamental attribution error The tendency, in explaining other people's behavior, to overestimate personality factors and underestimate the influence of the situation.

self-serving bias The tendency, in explaining one's own behavior, to take credit for one's good actions and rationalize one's mistakes.

just-world hypothesis The notion that many people need to believe that the world is fair and that justice is served, that bad people are punished and good people rewarded.

replies to a questionnaire before the events of 9/11, later were the most distressed about the attacks and had the strongest desire for revenge (Kaiser, Vick, & Major, 2004).

Unfortunately, one common way of restoring the belief in a just world is to rely on a dispositional attribution called *blaming the victim*. If a friend is fired, a woman is raped, or an innocent bystander is shot by the police, it is reassuring to think that they all must have done something to deserve what happened or to provoke it: The friend wasn't doing his work, the woman was dressed too "provocatively," the bystander shouldn't have been in the way. Blaming the victim is virtually universal when people are ordered to harm others or find themselves entrapped into harming others (Bandura, 1999). In the Milgram study, some "teachers" made comments such as "[The learner] was so stupid and stubborn he deserved to get shocked" (Milgram, 1974).

Of course, sometimes dispositional (personality) attributions *do* explain a person's behavior. The point to remember is that attributions, whether they are accurate or not, have tremendously important consequences. Here's an example that will apply to your own relationships. Happy couples tend to attribute their partners' occasional lapses to something in the

Calvin and Hobbes — by Bill Watterson

situation ("Poor Horace is under a lot of stress") and the partners' positive actions to stable, internal dispositions ("Horace has the sweetest nature"). But unhappy couples do just the reverse. They attribute lapses to their partners' personalities ("Henry is a hopeless mama's boy") and good behavior to the situation ("Yeah, he gave me a present, but only because his mother told him to"). These attributional habits, which can change over time, are strongly related to satisfaction or dissatisfaction with the partner (Karney & Bradbury, 2000). The attributions you make about your partner, your parents, and your friends will make a big difference in how you get along with them—and how long you will put up with their failings.

Children learn the value of self-serving attributions at an early age.

QUICK quiz

To what do you attribute your success in answering these questions?

1. What kind of attribution is being made in each case, situational or dispositional? (a) A man says, "My wife has sure become a grouchy person." (b) The same man says, "I'm grouchy because I've had a bad day at the office." (c) A woman reads about high unemployment in poor communities and says, "Well, if those people weren't so lazy, they would find work."

2. What principles of attribution theory are suggested by the items in the preceding question?

Answers:

1. a. dispositional b. situational c. dispositional   2. Item a illustrates the fundamental attribution error; b, the self-serving bias; and c, blaming the victim, possibly because of the just-world hypothesis.

Attitudes

People hold attitudes about all sorts of things—politics, people, food, children, movies, sports heroes, you name it. An *attitude* is a belief about people, groups, ideas, or activities. Some attitudes are *explicit*: We are aware of them; they shape our conscious decisions and actions; and they can be measured on self-report questionnaires. Others are *implicit*: We are unaware of them; they may influence our behavior in ways we do not recognize; and they are measured

in various indirect ways, as we will see later in discussing the attitudes involved in prejudice (Rudman, 2004; Wilson, Lindsey, & Schooler, 2000).

Shifting Opinions Versus Bedrock Beliefs On most topics, like movies and sports, people easily accept the fact that attitudes range from casual opinions to passionate convictions. If your best friend is neutral about baseball whereas you are an insanely devoted fan, your friendship will probably survive. But when the subject is one

When people hold attitudes that are central to their religious and political philosophies, they often fail to realize that the other side feels just as strongly.

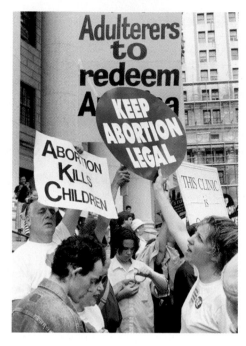

involving beliefs that give meaning and purpose to a person's life—most notably, politics and religion—it's another ball game, so to speak. For example, some people regard the traditions of their religion as sacred sources of guidance, which are to be taken literally and which offer the only possible route to salvation. Others regard the precepts of their religion as general guides that are open to interpretation; they accept some rituals and beliefs but not all of them. Still others find religious beliefs and rituals to be of little personal relevance or actively rebel against them.

Perhaps the one attitude that causes the most controversy and bitterness around the world is the one toward religious diversity: accepting or intolerant. Some people of all religions accept a world of differing religious views and practices; they believe that church and state should be separate. But for many conservatives and fundamentalists (in any religion), religion and politics are inseparable; they believe that one religion should prevail (Jost et al., 2003). You can see, then, why these irreconcilable attitudes cause continuing conflict and are even used to justify war and terrorism.

The Origins of Attitudes Where do attitudes come from, and why do they change or resist change? For decades, social psychologists have assumed that all attitudes are learned, acquired from the groups people belong to, the lessons their parents teach them, the experiences they have, their economic circumstances, and other social and environmental influences. Cer-

tainly, many attitudes are acquired in these ways, and they may change when a person has new experiences or moves into a different social group that has different values and views.

Now, however, it seems that some attitudes are not solely a result of learning. In recent years, social psychologists have been drawing on research from *behavioral genetics*, which has found that some core attitudes stem from personality traits that are highly heritable. That is, the variation among people in these attitudes is due in part to their genetic differences (see Chapter 2). One such trait is "openness to experience." We would expect people who are open to new experiences to hold positive attitudes toward novelty and change in general—say, in religion, art, music, and social and political events in the larger culture. We would expect people who prefer the familiar and conventional to be drawn to conservative politics, religious denominations, and philosophies. And that is what the research is finding.

Religious *affiliation*—whether a person is a Methodist, Muslim, Catholic, Jew, Hindu, and so on—is not heritable; most people choose a religious group because of their parents, ethnicity, culture, and social class. But, as studies of twins reared apart have found, *religiosity*—a person's depth of religious feeling and adherence to a religion's rules—does have a genetic component. In a study of liberal and fundamentalist Protestant Christians, the fundamentalists scored much lower than the liberals on the dimension of openness to experience (Streyffeler & McNally, 1998). When religiosity combines with conservatism and authoritarianism (an unquestioning trust in authority), the result is a deeply ingrained acceptance of tradition and dislike of those who question it (Olson et al., 2001; Saucier, 2000).

Likewise, political *affiliation* is not heritable; it is largely related to your upbringing and to the friends you make in early adulthood, the key years for deciding which party you want to join. Nor do the casual political opinions held by many "swing voters" or people who are politically disengaged have a genetic component. But political conservatism has high heritability: .65 in men and .45 in women (Bouchard, 2004; Bouchard & McGue, 2003). Various political positions on emotionally hot topics that are associated with conservative or liberal views are also partly heritable. A team of researchers discovered this by drawing on two large samples of more than 8,000 sets of twins who had been surveyed about their personality traits, religious beliefs, and political attitudes (Alford, Funk, & Hibbing, 2005). The researchers compared the opinions of fraternal twins (who share, on average, 50 percent of their genes) with those of

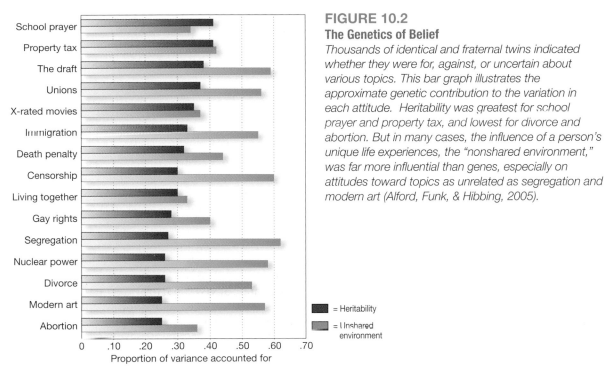

FIGURE 10.2
The Genetics of Belief
Thousands of identical and fraternal twins indicated whether they were for, against, or uncertain about various topics. This bar graph illustrates the approximate genetic contribution to the variation in each attitude. Heritability was greatest for school prayer and property tax, and lowest for divorce and abortion. But in many cases, the influence of a person's unique life experiences, the "nonshared environment," was far more influential than genes, especially on attitudes toward topics as unrelated as segregation and modern art (Alford, Funk, & Hibbing, 2005).

identical twins (who share 100 percent of their genes). They calculated how often the identical twins agreed on each issue, subtracted the rate at which fraternal twins agreed, and ended up with a rough measure of heritability. As you can see in Figure 10.2, the attitudes showing the highest heritability were those toward school prayer and property taxes; attitudes showing the lowest influence of genes included those toward segregation, divorce, and abortion.

These findings are provocative, but it is important not to oversimplify them—say, by incorrectly assuming that everyone's political opinions are hardwired and unaffected by events that happen to them. In fact, the factor that accounted for even *more* of the variation in political attitudes than heritability did was what behavioral geneticists call the *nonshared environment,* an individual's unique life experiences (see Chapter 2). Moreover, given the fact that during most of human evolution there were no schools, military drafts, property taxes, or X-rated movies, what genes might have evolved to shape human beings' later opinions about them? What do you think might be the personality dispositions underlying people's ideological commitments? And what might be the individual life experiences that shape or change them?

Attitudes and behavior can change as a result of new information and experience, but they also change because of a psychological need for consistency. In Chapter 7, we discussed **cognitive dis-** **sonance**, the uncomfortable feeling that occurs when two attitudes, or an attitude and behavior, are in conflict (are dissonant). To resolve this dissonance, one of those attitudes has to change. For example, if a politician or celebrity you admire does something stupid, immoral, or illegal, you can restore consistency by lowering your opinion of the person. Or you can decide that the person's behavior wasn't so stupid or immoral after all . . . and besides, everyone else does it, too.

Friendly Persuasion Core beliefs are obviously going to be resistant to change, especially those that stem from personality traits or from a carefully reasoned philosophy. In contrast, many of our everyday attitudes and beliefs are vulnerable to social influence—efforts by others to get us to believe one thing or another, or to persuade us to change our minds.

All around you, every day, advertisers, politicians, and friends are trying to influence your attitudes. One weapon they use is the drip, drip, drip of a repeated idea. Repeated exposure even to a nonsense syllable such as *zug* is enough to make a person feel more positive toward it (Zajonc, 1968). The attitude-boosting **familiarity effect** of merely seeing the same thing repeatedly is a robust phenomenon. It has been demonstrated across cultures, across species, and across states of consciousness. It works even for stimuli you aren't aware of seeing (Monahan, Murphy, & Zajonc, 2000).

Thinking Critically About the Genetics of Belief

cognitive dissonance A state of tension that occurs when a person simultaneously holds two cognitions that are psychologically inconsistent or when a person's belief is incongruent with his or her behavior.

familiarity effect The tendency of people to feel more positive toward a person, item, product or other stimulus that they have seen often.

The Oreo name on this cereal takes advantage of the familiarity effect. Oreo cookies have been advertised since 1912.

A related phenomenon is the **validity effect**, the tendency of people to believe that something is true simply because it has been repeated many times. Repeat something often enough, even the basest lie, and eventually the public will believe it. Hitler's propaganda minister, Joseph Goebbels, called this technique the "Big Lie."

In a series of experiments, Hal Arkes and his associates demonstrated how the validity effect operates (Arkes, 1993; Arkes, Boehm, & Xu, 1991). In a typical study, people read a list of statements, such as "Mercury has a higher boiling point than copper" or "Over 400 Hollywood films were produced in 1948." They had to rate each statement for its validity, on a scale of 1 (definitely false) to 7 (definitely true). A week or two later, they again rated the validity of some of these statements and also rated others that they had not seen previously. The result: Mere repetition increased the perception that the familiar statements were true. The same effect also occurred for other kinds of statements, including unverifiable opinions (e.g., "At least 75 percent of all politicians are basically dishonest"), opinions that subjects initially felt were true, and even opinions they initially felt were false. "Note that no attempt has been made to persuade," said Arkes (1993). "No supporting arguments are offered. We just have subjects rate the statements. Mere repetition seems to increase rated validity. This is scary."

Another effective technique for influencing people's attitudes is to have arguments presented by someone who is considered admirable, knowledgeable, or beautiful; this is why advertisements are full of sports heroes, experts, and models (Cialdini, 2001; Pratkanis & Aronson, 2001). Persuaders may also try to link their message with a nice, warm, fuzzy feeling. In one early study, students who were given peanuts and Pepsi while listening to a speaker's point of view were more likely to be convinced by it than were students who listened to the same words without the pleasant munchies and soft drinks (Janis, Kaye, & Kirschner, 1965). This finding has been replicated many times, perhaps explaining why so much business is conducted over lunch and so many courtships over dinner!

In sum, here are three good ways to influence attitudes:

```
            Effective Ways to
            Influence Attitudes
        ┌──────────┼──────────┐
  Repetition of   Endorsement   Association
   an idea or     by an admired  of the message
   assertion      or attractive   with a
   (the validity     person      good feeling
    effect)
```

Fear tactics to get people to quit doing risky things usually backfire. But perhaps this campaign to persuade men to quit smoking will be the exception!

On the other hand, one of the most common ways of trying to get people to change their attitudes and behavior, scaring them to death, is actually one of the least effective. Fear tactics are often used to try to persuade people to quit smoking, drive only when sober, use condoms, check for signs of cancer, and, nowadays, prepare for terrorist attacks. But the use of fear can backfire. It often scares people so much that they become defensive or feel hopeless and hence ignore the message ("That will never happen to me, and if it does, there isn't anything I can do about it"). Fear tactics are more effective, however, when the message also provides specific information about how to avoid the danger and when people feel able to take advantage of this information (Cialdini, 2001).

Coercive Persuasion   Every time there is news of a suicide bombing, observers are horrified and deeply puzzled. How could someone strap on a bomb and blow up innocent adults and children at random, sacrificing his or her own life in the process? Why would anyone commit suicide simply because a religious leader instructed them to?

In the 1970s, Jim Jones told members of his "People's Temple" that the time had come to die, and 913 people dutifully lined up to drink Kool-Aid mixed with cyanide, after giving it to their infants and children. In the 1990s, David Koresh, leader of the Branch Davidian cult in Waco, Texas, led his followers to a fiery death in a shoot-out with the FBI. A few years later, Marshall Applewhite, leader of the Heaven's Gate cult in San Diego, persuaded his 38 followers that if they committed suicide, they would travel to heaven in a spaceship in the tail of a comet.

Were all of these people mentally ill? Had they all been "brainwashed"? Brainwashing implies that a person has had a sudden change of mind without being aware of what is happening; it sounds mysterious and strange. In fact, the methods of persuasion involved are neither mysterious nor unusual, but they are indeed *coercive*—that is, designed to suppress an individual's ability to reason, think critically, and make choices in his or her own best interests. Studies of religious, political, and psychological sects and of terrorist cells have identified some of the key processes of coercive persuasion (Bloom, 2005; Moghaddam, 2005; Ofshe & Watters, 1994; Singer, Temerlin, & Langone, 1990; Zimbardo & Leippe, 1991):

Thinking Critically About "Brainwashing"

1 *The person is put under physical or emotional stress.* The individual may not be allowed to eat, sleep, or exercise; may be isolated in a dark room with no stimulation or food; or may be induced into a trancelike state through repetitive chanting or fatigue.

2 *The person's problems are reduced to one simple explanation, which is repeatedly emphasized.* There are as many simplistic explanations as there are groups that offer them. Are you afraid or unhappy? It all stems from the pain of being born. Are you struggling financially? It's your fault for not fervently wanting to be rich. Members may also be taught to simplify their problems by blaming a particular enemy: Jews, the government, nonbelievers. . . .

3 *The leader offers unconditional love, acceptance, and attention.* The new recruit may be given a "love bath" from the group—constant praise and affection. Euphoria and well-being are intense because they typically follow exhaustion and fatigue. In exchange, the leader demands everyone's adoration and obedience.

4 *A new identity based on the group is created.* The recruit is told that he or she is part of the chosen, the elite, or the saved. To foster this new identity, many cults require their members to wear special clothes, eat special diets, or assume a new name.

5 *The person is subjected to entrapment.* At first, the new member agrees only to do small things, but gradually the demands increase: for example, to spend a weekend with the group, then another weekend, then take weekly seminars, then advanced courses, then to contribute money, and so on. No leader ever says to a new recruit at the outset, "If you follow me, you will eventually give up your marriage, home, children, and perhaps your life"; but by the end, that is just what many do.

6 *The person's access to information is severely controlled.* As soon as a person is a committed believer or follower, the group limits the person's choices, denigrates critical thinking, makes fun of doubts, and insists that any private distress is due to lack of belief in the group. Total conformity is demanded. The person may be physically isolated from the outside world and thus from antidotes to the leader's ideas. In many groups, members are required to break all ties with their parents, who are the strongest link to the members' former world and thus the greatest threat to the leader's control.

Some people may be more vulnerable than others to coercive influence, but these techniques are powerful enough to overwhelm even mentally healthy and well-educated individuals. For example, research on contemporary suicide bombers in the Middle East—including Mohamed Atta, one of the 19 hijackers who destroyed the World Trade Center—shows that they had no psychopathology and were often quite educated and affluent (Silke, 2003). Like other revolutionaries, the people who become suicide bombers are idealistic and angry about perceived injustices. But they take extreme measures because they have become entrapped in closed groups led by charismatic leaders. They are separated from their families, are indoctrinated and trained for 18 months

These members of the Aum Shinrikyo ("Supreme Truth") sect in Japan, wearing masks of their leader's face, take the uniformity of cult identity to an extreme. The group's founder instructed his devotees to place nerve gas in a Japanese subway, which killed 10 and sickened thousands of other passengers. One former member said of the sect, "Their strategy is to wear you down and take control of your mind. They promise you heaven, but they make you live in hell."

or more, and eventually become emotionally bonded to the group and the leader (Atran, 2003; Bloom, 2005). Future suicide bombers are also given "love baths"; they are celebrated and honored by their families and communities. In Sri Lanka, where a civil war has been waging for years, pictures of young Tamil suicide bombers are framed with garlands and displayed in training camps, so that other children will come to revere them and learn their names—"the way," one social scientist observed, "young American kids know the names of sports stars. They look up to them, and want to emulate what they have done"

(Bloom, 2005). One expert on suicide bombers observed that the first line of defense against them is for communities to learn "how to minimize the receptivity of *mostly ordinary people* to recruiting organizations" (Atran, 2003; our emphasis).

A key step in increasing people's resistance to coercive persuasion, therefore, is to dispel their illusion of invulnerability to these tactics. Another is to teach people how to articulate and defend their own positions and think critically. These skills prepare people to resist propaganda and make them less vulnerable to manipulation by others (Tormala & Petty, 2002).

QUICK quiz

Now, how can we persuade you to take this quiz without coercing you?

1. Candidate Carson spends $3 million to make sure his name is seen and heard frequently and to repeat unverified charges that his opponent is a thief. What psychological processes is he relying on to win?

2. A friend urges you to join a "life-renewal" group called "The Feeling Life." Your friend has been spending increasing amounts of time with her fellow Feelies, and you have some doubts about them. What questions would you want to have answered before joining up?

Answers:

1. The familiarity effect and the validity effect   2. A few things to consider: Is there an autocratic leader who suppresses all dissent or criticism, while rationalizing this practice as a benefit for members? ("Doubt and disbelief are signs that your feeling side is being repressed.") Have long-standing members given up their friends, families, interests, and ambitions for this group? Does the leader offer simple but unrealistic promises to repair your life and all that troubles you? Are members required to make extreme sacrifices by donating large amounts of time and money?

WHAT'S *Ahead*

• Why do people in groups often go along with the majority even when the majority is dead wrong?

• How can "groupthink" lead to bad, even catastrophic, decisions?

• In an emergency, are you more likely to get help when there are lots of strangers in the area or only a few?

• What enables some people to be nonconformists, take risks to help others, or blow the whistle on wrongdoers?

Individuals in Groups

Even when a group is not at all coercive, something happens to us when we join a bunch of other people. We act differently than we would on our own, regardless of whether the group has convened to solve problems and make decisions, has gathered to have fun, consists of anonymous bystanders or anonymous

members of an Internet chat room, or is just a loose collection of individuals hanging out in a bar. The decisions we make and the actions we take in groups may depend less on our personal desires than on the structure and dynamics of the group itself.

Conformity

One thing people in groups do is conform, taking action or adopting attitudes as a result of real or imagined group pressure.

Suppose that you are required to appear at a psychology laboratory for an experiment on perception. You join seven other students seated in a room. You are shown a 10-inch line and asked which of three other lines is identical to it:

Test line   A   B   C

The correct answer, line A, is obvious, so you are amused when the first person in the group chooses line B. "Bad eyesight," you say to yourself. "He's off by 2 whole inches!" The second person also chooses line B. "What a dope," you think. But by the time the fifth person has chosen line B, you are beginning to doubt yourself. The sixth and seventh students also choose line B, and now you are worried about *your* eyesight. The experimenter looks at you. "Your turn," he says. Do you follow the evidence of your own eyes or the collective judgment of the group?

This was the design for a series of famous studies of conformity conducted by Solomon Asch (1952, 1965). The seven "nearsighted" students were actually Asch's confederates. Asch wanted to know what people would do when a group unanimously contradicted an obvious fact. He found that when people made the line comparisons on their own, they were almost always accurate. But in the group, only 20 percent of the students remained completely independent on every trial, and often they apologized for not agreeing with the others. One-third conformed to the group's incorrect decision more than half the time, and the rest conformed at least some of the time. Whether they conformed or not, the students often felt uncertain of their decision. As one participant later said, "I felt disturbed, puzzled, separated, like an outcast from the rest."

Asch's experiment has been replicated many times and in many countries over the years. In America, conformity has declined since the 1950s, when Asch first did his work, suggesting that conformity reflects social norms, which can change over time (Bond & Smith, 1996). Conformity varies with cultural norms, too. People in individualist cultures, such as the United States, value individual rights and place the "self" above duty to others. They are somewhat less conformist than people in collectivist cultures, who consider social harmony to be more important than individual rights, as in Korea (Kim & Markus, 1999) (see Chapter 2).

Regardless of culture, however, everyone conforms under some circumstances and for similar reasons. Some do so because they identify with group members and want to be like them. Some want to be liked. Some believe the group has knowledge that is superior to their own. And some conform out of pure self-interest, to keep their jobs, win promotions, or win votes. Also, it is not so easy to be a nonconformist! Group members are often uncomfortable with deviants and will try to persuade them to conform. If pleasant persuasion fails, the group may punish, isolate, or reject the nonconformist.

Like obedience, conformity has both positive and negative sides. Society runs more smoothly when people know how to behave in a given situation and when they share the same attitudes and manners. Conformity in dress, preferences, and ideas confers a sense of being "in sync" with friends and colleagues. But conformity can also suppress critical thinking and creativity. In a group, many people will deny their private beliefs, agree with silly notions, and even repudiate their own values.

Groupthink

Close, friendly groups usually work well together. But they face the problem of getting the best ideas and efforts from their members while avoiding an extreme form of conformity called **groupthink**, the tendency to think alike and suppress dissent. According to Irving Janis (1982, 1989), groupthink occurs when a group's need for total agreement

groupthink In close-knit groups, the tendency for all members to think alike for the sake of harmony and to suppress disagreement.

Sometimes people like to conform in order to feel part of the group . . . and sometimes they like to assert their individuality.

diffusion of responsibility In groups, the tendency of members to avoid taking action because they assume that others will.

overwhelms its need to make the wisest decision. The symptoms of groupthink include the following:

- *An illusion of invulnerability.* The group believes it can do no wrong and is 100 percent correct in its decisions.

- *Self-censorship.* Dissenters decide to keep quiet rather than make trouble, offend their friends, or risk being ridiculed.

- *Pressure on dissenters to conform.* The leader teases or humiliates dissenters or otherwise pressures them to go along.

- *An illusion of unanimity.* By discouraging dissent, leaders and group members create an illusion of consensus; they may even explicitly order suspected dissenters to keep quiet.

Throughout history, groupthink has led to disastrous decisions in military and civilian life. In 1961, President John F. Kennedy and his advisers approved a CIA plan to invade Cuba at the Bay of Pigs and try to overthrow the government of Fidel Castro; the invasion was a humiliating defeat. In the mid-1960s, President Lyndon Johnson and his cabinet escalated the war in Vietnam in spite of obvious signs that further bombing and increased troops were not bringing the war to an end. In 1986, NASA officials insulated themselves from the dissenting objections of engineers who warned them that the space shuttle *Challenger* was unsafe; NASA launched it anyway, and it exploded shortly after takeoff. Tragically, when an expert panel warned in 2002 that the space shuttles still had many safety problems, NASA removed five of the panel's nine members and two of its consultants. Early in 2003, the *Columbia* exploded upon reentry, killing its entire crew.

Janis (1982) examined the records of historical military decisions, such as the Bay of Pigs fiasco,

and identified key features of groups that are vulnerable to groupthink: Their members feel that they are part of a tightly connected team; they are isolated from other viewpoints; they feel under pressure from outside forces; and they have a strong, directive leader. Do you notice the similarities between these features and those of coercive groups?

Groupthink can be counteracted by explicitly rewarding the expression of doubt and dissent, protecting and encouraging minority views, generating as many alternative solutions to a problem as group members can think of, and fostering a group identity that encourages members to think of themselves as open-minded problem solvers rather than invulnerable know-it-alls (Turner, Pratkanis, & Samuels, 2003).

The nature of the group is often determined by the leader, of course. For many people in positions of power, from presidents to company executives to movie moguls, the temptation is great to surround themselves with others who agree with what they want to do, and to demote or fire those who disagree on the grounds that they are being "disloyal." Sometimes, though, a great leader rises above this temptation. According to historian Doris Kearns Goodwin (2005), Abraham Lincoln understood the importance of surrounding himself with dissenters. Lincoln invited four of his strongest political competitors to join his cabinet and gave them important posts. As a result of the ensuing debates with his critics, Lincoln was able to avoid the illusion that he had group consensus on every decision, consider alternatives, and eventually enlist the respect and support of his team.

The Anonymous Crowd

Suppose you were in trouble on a city street or in another public place—say, being mugged or having a sudden appendicitis attack. Do you think you would be more likely to get help if (a) one other person was passing by, (b) several other people were in the area, or (c) dozens of people were in the area? Most people would choose the third answer, but that is not how human beings operate. On the contrary, the more people there are around you, the *less* likely it is that one of them will come to your aid. Why?

The answer has to do with a group process called the **diffusion of responsibility**, in which responsibility for an outcome is diffused, or spread, among many people, reducing each individual's personal sense of responsibility. One result is *bystander apathy*: In crowds, when someone is in

People in crowds, feeling anonymous, may do destructive things they would never do on their own. These soccer hooligans are kicking a fan of the opposing team during a night of violence after their team lost.

trouble, individuals often fail to take action or call for help because they assume that someone else will do so (Darley & Latané, 1968). For example, in a case that became famous many years ago, a woman named Kitty Genovese was repeatedly stabbed to death on the street as dozens of her neighbors listened and watched, without ever calling for help. Similar tragedies still happen all too frequently. People are most likely to come to a stranger's aid if they are the only ones around to help, because responsibility cannot be diffused.

In work groups, the diffusion of responsibility sometimes takes the form of *social loafing*: Each member of a team slows down, letting others work harder (Karau & Williams, 1993; Latané, Williams, & Harkins, 1979). Social loafing increases when individual group members are not accountable for the work they do; when people feel that working harder would only duplicate their colleagues' efforts; when workers feel that others are getting a free ride; or when the work itself is uninteresting (Shepperd, 1995). When the challenge of the job is increased or when each member of the group has a different, important job to do, the sense of individual responsibility rises and social loafing declines (Harkins & Szymanski, 1989; Williams & Karau, 1991).

The most extreme instances of the diffusion of responsibility occur in large, anonymous mobs or crowds. The crowds may consist of cheerful sports spectators or angry rioters. Either way, people often

lose all awareness of their individuality and seem to hand themselves over to the mood and actions of the crowd, a state called **deindividuation** (Festinger, Pepitone, & Newcomb, 1952). You are more likely to feel deindividuated in a large city, where no one recognizes you, than in a small town, where it is hard to hide. (You are also more likely to feel deindividuated in large classes, where you might—mistakenly!—think you are invisible to the teacher, than in small ones.) Sometimes organizations actively promote the deindividuation of their members in order to enhance conformity and allegiance to the group. This is an important function of uniforms or masks, which eliminate each member's distinctive identity.

Deindividuation has long been considered a prime reason for mob violence. According to this explanation, because deindividuated people in crowds "forget themselves" and do not feel accountable for their actions, they are more likely to violate social norms and laws than they would be on their own: breaking store windows, looting, getting into fights, or rioting at a sports event. But deindividuation does not always make people more combative. Sometimes it makes them more friendly; think of all the chatty, anonymous people on buses and planes who reveal things to their seatmates they would never tell anyone they knew.

Two classic experiments illustrate the power of the situation to influence what deindividuated people will do. In one, women who wore Ku Klux Klan–like disguises that completely covered their faces and bodies delivered twice as much apparent electric shock to another woman as did women who not only were undisguised but also wore large name tags (Zimbardo, 1970). In a second experiment, women who were wearing nurses' uniforms gave *less* shock than did women in regular dress (Johnson & Downing, 1979). Evidently, the KKK disguises were a signal to behave

Wearing a uniform or disguise increases deindividuation and provides a cue for behavior. The women shown here, wearing Ku Klux Klan–like disguises, behaved more aggressively than individuated women did (Zimbardo, 1970).

aggressively; the nurses' uniforms were a signal to behave nurturantly.

What really seems to be happening when people are in large crowds or anonymous situations, therefore, is not that they become mindless or uninhibited. Rather, they become more likely to conform to the norms of the *specific situation* (Postmes & Spears, 1998). College students who go on wild sprees during spring break may be violating the local laws and norms of Palm Springs or Key West, not because their aggressiveness has been released but because they are conforming to the "let's party!" norms of their fellow students. Crowd norms can also foster helpfulness, as they often do after disasters, when thousands of strangers turn out to help victims by donating food, clothes, and their time.

QUICK quiz

On your own, take responsibility for identifying which phenomenon is illustrated in each of the following situations.

1. The president's closest advisers are afraid to disagree with his views on energy policy.
2. You are at a costume party wearing a silly gorilla suit. When you see a chance to play a practical joke on the host, you do it.
3. Walking down a busy street, you see that fire has broken out in a store window. "Someone must already have called the fire department," you say.

Answers:

1. groupthink   2. deindividuation   3. diffusion of responsibility (causing bystander apathy)

Altruism and Dissent

We have seen how roles, norms, and pressures to obey authority and conform to one's group can cause people to behave in ways they might not otherwise do. Yet throughout history men and women have disobeyed orders they believed to be wrong and have gone against prevailing cultural beliefs; their actions have changed the course of history. In 1956 in Montgomery, Alabama, Rosa Parks refused to give up her seat and move to the back of a bus, as the segregation laws of the time required. She was arrested and convicted of breaking the law. Her calm defiance touched off a boycott in which black citizens refused to ride city buses. It took them over a year, but they won, and the civil rights movement took off.

When people think of heroes, they usually think of men rescuing a child, risking gunfire to bring a fellow soldier to safety, or standing up to a bully. This is the kind of heroism traditionally expected of men, who in general have greater physical strength than women. Indeed, a study of Canadian awards that have been given since 1904 to individuals who risked or lost their lives to save others found that only 9 percent have gone to women. But there are other kinds of heroism that do not require physical strength. During the Holocaust, women in France, Poland, and the Netherlands were as likely as men to risk their lives to save Jews. Women are more likely than men to donate an organ such as a kidney to save another person's life, and women are more likely to volunteer to serve in dangerous postings around the world in the Peace Corps (Becker & Eagly, 2004).

Dissent and *altruism*, the willingness to take selfless or dangerous action on behalf of others, are in part a matter of personal convictions and conscience. However, just as there are situational reasons for obedience and conformity, so there are external influences on a person's decision to state an unpopular opinion, choose conscience over conformity, or help a stranger in trouble. Here are some of the situational factors involved in deciding to behave courageously:

1 *You perceive the need for intervention or help.* It may seem obvious, but before you can take independent action, you must realize that such action is necessary. Sometimes people willfully blind themselves to wrongdoing to justify their own inaction ("I'm just minding my business"; "I have no idea what they're doing over there at that concentration camp"). But blindness to the need for action also occurs when a situation imposes too many demands on people's attention, as it often does for residents of densely populated cities.

2 *The situation increases the likelihood that you will take responsibility.* When you are in a large crowd of observers or in a large organization, it is easy to avoid action because of the diffusion of responsibility. Conversely, when you are in an environment that rewards independent thinking and dissent and discourages social loafing, you may behave accordingly.

3 *Cultural norms encourage you to take action.* Some cultures place a higher value on helping strangers than other cultures do. In Brazil and other Latin American countries, for example, it is important to be *simpático*, a good-natured, kind person who goes out of his or her way to help others. In studies of strangers' helpfulness to one another across 23 U.S. cities and 22 cities in other countries, cultural norms were more important than population density in predicting levels of helpfulness. Pedestrians in busy Copenhagen and Vienna, for example, were kinder to strangers than were passersby in slow-paced Kuala Lumpur or busy New York City (Levine, 2003).

4 *The cost–benefit ratio supports your decision to get involved.* It is easier to be a whistle-blower or to protest a company policy when you know you can find another job, but what if jobs in your field are scarce and you have a family to support? People are less likely to take an independent action if the personal, physical, or financial costs

to them are high. On the other hand, the cost of *not* helping or remaining silent might be guilt, blame from others, loss of honor, or the injury or death of others.

Sadly, the costs of dissent and honesty are often high. Most whistle-blowers, far from being rewarded for their bravery, are punished for it. Three women were named *Time* magazine's Persons of the Year for their courage in exposing wrongdoing in their organizations—Enron, WorldCom, and the FBI—yet all paid a steep professional price for doing so. The two soldiers who first exposed the abuses going on at Abu Ghraib, Samuel J. Provance and James Darby, were shunned by many of their peers and received death threats; one was threatened with a court-martial. Studies of whistle-blowers find that half to two-thirds lose their jobs and have to leave their professions entirely (Alford, 2001).

5 *You have an ally.* In Asch's conformity experiment, the presence of one other person who gave the correct answer was enough to overcome agreement with the majority. In Milgram's experiment, the presence of a peer who disobeyed the experimenter's instruction to shock the learner sharply increased the number of people who also disobeyed. One dissenting member of a group may be viewed as a troublemaker, but two or three are a coalition. An ally reassures a person of the rightness of the protest, and their

When we think of heroes, we tend to think of men like the firefighters who worked so hard to rescue others on 9/11 and the volunteers who saved lives after Hurricane Katrina. But heroism comes in many forms. The three women who exposed wrongdoing in their respective organizations were named Time's Persons of the Year but paid a steep professional price for their courage.

combined efforts may eventually persuade the majority (Wood et al., 1994).

6 *You become entrapped.* Once having taken the initial step of getting involved, most people will increase their commitment. In one study, nearly 9,000 federal employees were asked whether they had observed wrongdoing at work, whether they had told anyone about it, and what happened if they had told. Nearly half of the sample had observed some serious cases of wrongdoing, such as stealing federal funds, accepting bribes, or creating a situation that was dangerous to public safety. Of that half, 72 percent had done nothing at all, but the other 28 percent reported the problem to their immediate supervisors. Once they had taken that step, a majority of the whistle-blowers eventually took the matter to higher authorities (Graham, 1986).

As you can see, certain social and cultural factors make altruism, disobedience, and dissent more likely to occur, just as other factors suppress them.

QUICK quiz

If you weigh the costs and benefits, you'll surely decide to take action and answer this question.

Imagine that you are chief executive officer of a new electric-car company. You want your employees to feel free to offer their suggestions and criticisms to improve productivity and satisfaction. You also want them to inform managers if they find any evidence that the cars are unsafe, even if that means delaying production. What concepts from this chapter could you use in setting company policy?

Answers:

Some possibilities: You could avoid groupthink by encouraging dissenting views and by not requiring unanimity, avoid social loafing and deindividuation by rewarding an employee's innovative suggestions and implementing the best ones, stimulate commitment to the task (building a car that will solve the world's pollution problem), and establish a written policy to protect whistle-blowers. What else can you think of?

WHAT'S *Ahead*

- In what different ways do people balance their ethnic identity and their membership in the larger culture?

- What is an effective antidote to "us–them" thinking?

- How do stereotypes benefit us, and how do they distort reality?

Us Versus Them: Group Identity

Each of us develops a personal identity that is based on our particular traits and unique life history. But we also develop **social identities** based on the groups we belong to, including our national, religious, political, and occupational groups (Brewer & Gardner, 1996; Tajfel & Turner, 1986). Social identities are important because they give us a sense of place and position in the world. Without them, most of us would feel like loose marbles rolling around in an unconnected universe. It feels good to be part of an "us," but does that mean that we must automatically feel superior to "them"?

social identity The part of a person's self-concept that is based on his or her identification with a nation, religious or political group, or other social affiliation.

ethnic identity A person's identification with a religious or ethnic group.

acculturation The process by which members of minority groups come to identify with and feel part of the mainstream culture.

Ethnic Identity

In multicultural societies such as the United States and Canada, different social identities sometimes collide. In particular, people often face the dilemma of balancing an **ethnic identity**, a close identification with a religious or ethnic group, and **acculturation**, identification with the dominant culture (Phinney, 1996; Spencer & Dornbusch, 1990).

There are four ways of balancing ethnic identity and acculturation, depending on whether ethnic identity is strong or weak and whether identification with the larger culture is strong or weak (Berry, 1994; Phinney, 1990). People who are *bicultural* have strong ties both to their ethnicity and to the larger culture: They say, "I am proud of my ethnic heritage, but I identify just as much with my country." They can alternate easily between their culture of origin and the majority culture, slipping into the customs and language of each as circumstances dictate. People who choose *assimilation* have weak feelings of ethnicity but a strong sense of acculturation: Their attitude, for example, might be "I'm an American, period."

Monica Almeida/The New York Times

Ethnic identities are changing these days, as bicultural (and increasingly multiethnic) North Americans blend aspects of mainstream culture with their own traditions. But many people like to celebrate the traditions of their ethnic heritage, as illustrated in these photos of African-American children lighting Kwaanza candles, Ukrainian-American teens wearing national dress, and Japanese-American college students reviving taiko, *traditional Japanese drumming.*

Ethnic separatists have a strong sense of ethnic identity but weak feelings of acculturation: They may say, "My ethnicity comes first; if I join the mainstream, I'm betraying my origins and selling out." And some people feel *marginal*, connected to neither their ethnicity nor the dominant culture: They may not want to identify with any ethnic or national group, or they feel that they don't belong anywhere.

A person's degree of acculturation may change throughout life in response to experiences and societal events. For example, many immigrants arrive in North America with every intention of becoming true Canadians or Americans. If they encounter discrimination or setbacks, however, they may decide that acculturation is harder than they anticipated or that ethnic separatism offers greater solace. In any case, acculturation is rarely a complete accommodation to mainstream culture. Many individuals pick and choose among the values, food, traditions, and customs of the mainstream culture, while also keeping aspects of their heritage that are important to their self-identity (Chun, Organista, & Marin, 2002; Ryder, Alden, & Paulhus, 2000).

On the other hand, it is a sign of our multiethnic times that many people are now refusing to be pigeonholed into any single ethnic category. In the 2000 U.S. census, nearly 7 million people listed themselves as various combinations of identities. New "combo" ethnic identities are emerging out of the traditional, familiar ones such as Latino or Native American: Blaxican (African-American and Mexican), Negripino (African-American and Filipino), Hafu (half Japanese, half something else), or Chino-Latino (Chinese and Hispanic). Some observers believe that America is moving toward a "postethnic" stage, in which young people are becoming less likely to define themselves by their ethnic identity than by their youth identity—a hip-hopper, a *roquero* (rocker), a pop-culture fan, and so forth.

ethnocentrism The belief that one's own ethnic group, nation, or religion is superior to all others.

stereotype A summary impression of a group, in which a person believes that all members of the group share a common trait or traits (positive, negative, or neutral).

Ethnocentrism

Nonetheless, having an ethnic or national identity is still important to most people. Unfortunately, it often leads to **ethnocentrism**, the belief that your own culture or ethnic group is superior to all others. Ethnocentrism is universal, probably because it aids survival by increasing people's attachment to their own group and willingness to work on its behalf. It is even embedded in some languages: The Chinese word for China means "the center of the world" and the Navajo and the Inuit call themselves simply "The People."

Ethnocentrism rests on a fundamental social identity: us. As soon as people have created a category called "us," however, they invariably perceive everybody else as "not-us." This in-group solidarity can be manufactured in a minute in the laboratory, as Henri Tajfel and his colleagues (1971) demonstrated in an experiment with British schoolboys. Tajfel showed the boys slides with varying numbers of dots on them and asked the boys to guess how many dots there were. The boys were arbitrarily told that they were "overestimators" or "underestimators" and were then asked to work on another task. In this phase, they had a chance to give points to other boys identified as overestimators or underestimators. Although each boy worked alone in his cubicle, almost every single one assigned far more points to boys he thought were like him, an overestimator or an underestimator. As the boys emerged from their rooms, they were asked, "Which were you?" The answers received a mix of cheers and boos from the others.

Us–them social identities are strengthened when two groups compete with each other. Years ago, Muzafer Sherif and his colleagues used a natural setting, a Boy Scout camp called Robbers Cave, to demonstrate the effects of competition on hostility and conflict between groups (Sherif, 1958; Sherif et al., 1961). Sherif randomly assigned 11- and 12-year-old boys to two groups, the Eagles and the Rattlers. To build a sense of in-group identity and team spirit, he had each group work together on projects such as making a rope bridge and building a diving board. Sherif then put the Eagles and Rattlers in competition for prizes. During fierce games of football, baseball, and tug-of-war, the boys whipped up a competitive fever that soon spilled off of the playing fields. They began to raid each other's cabins, call each other names, and start fistfights. No one dared to have a friend from the rival group. Before long, the Rattlers and the Eagles were as hostile toward each other as any two gangs fighting for turf or any two nations fighting for dominance. Their hostility continued even when they were just sitting around together watching movies.

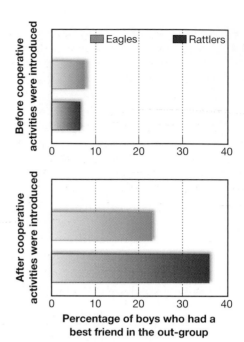

FIGURE 10.3
The Experiment at Robbers Cave
In this study, competitive games fostered hostility between the Rattlers and the Eagles. Few boys had a best friend from the other group (top graph). But after the teams had to cooperate to solve various problems, the percentage who made friends across "enemy lines" shot up (Sherif et al., 1961).

Then Sherif decided to try to undo the hostility he had created and make peace between the Eagles and Rattlers. He and his associates set up a series of predicaments in which both groups needed to work together to reach a desired goal—for example, pooling their resources to get a movie they all wanted to see or pulling a staff truck up a hill on a camping trip. This policy of *interdependence in reaching mutual goals* was highly successful in reducing the boys' "ethnocentrism," competitiveness, and hostility; the boys eventually made friends with their former enemies (see Figure 10.3). Interdependence has a similar effect in adult groups (Gaertner et al., 1990). The reason, it seems, is that cooperation causes people to think of themselves as members of one big group instead of two opposed groups, "us" and "them."

Stereotypes

You can probably think of a million ways that your friends and family members differ: Jeff is stodgy, Ruth is bossy, Farah is outgoing. But if you have never met a person from Turkey or Tibet, you are likely to stereotype Turks and Tibetans. A **stereotype** is a summary impression of a group of people in which all members of the group are viewed as sharing a common trait or traits. Stereotypes may be negative, positive, or neutral. There are stereotypes of people who drive Jeeps or BMWs, of men who wear earrings and of women who wear business suits, of engineering students and art students, of feminists and fraternity men.

Stereotypes aren't necessarily bad. They are, as some psychologists have called them, useful "tools in the mental toolbox"—energy-saving devices that allow us to make efficient decisions (Macrae, Milne, & Bodenhausen, 1994). They help us quickly process new information and retrieve memories. They allow us to organize experience, make sense of differences among individuals and groups, and predict how people will behave. In fact, the brain automatically registers and encodes the basic human categories of gender, race, and age, suggesting that there is a neurological basis for the cognitive efficiency of stereotyping (Ito & Urland, 2003).

However, although stereotypes reflect real differences among people, they also distort that reality in three ways (Judd et al., 1995). First, *they exaggerate differences between groups*, making the stereotyped group seem odd, unfamiliar, or dangerous, not like "us." Second, *they produce selective perception*; people tend to see only the evidence that fits the stereotype and reject any perceptions that do not fit. Third, *they underestimate differences within other groups*. Stereotypes create the false impression that all members of other groups are the same.

Cultural values affect how people evaluate a particular action. Chinese students in Hong Kong, where communalism and respect for elders are valued, think that a student who comes late to class or argues with a parent about grades is being selfish and disrespectful of adults. But Australian students, who value individualism, think that the same behavior is perfectly appropriate (Forgas & Bond, 1985). You can see how the Chinese might form negative stereotypes of "disrespectful" Australians, and how the Australians might form negative stereotypes of the "spineless" Chinese. And it is a small step from negative stereotypes to prejudice.

Which woman is the chemical engineer and which is the assistant? The Western stereotype holds that women are not engineers in the first place, but if they are, they are Western. Actually, the engineer at this refinery is the Kuwaiti woman on the left.

QUICK quiz

Do you have a positive or a negative stereotype of quizzes?

1. Frank, an African-American college student, finds himself caught between two philosophies on his campus. One holds that blacks should move toward full integration into mainstream culture. The other holds that blacks should immerse themselves in the history, values, and contributions of African culture. The first group values _____ whereas the second emphasizes _____.

2. John knows and likes the Mexican minority in his town, but he privately believes that Anglo culture is superior to all others. His belief is evidence of his _____.

3. What strategy does the Robbers Cave study suggest for reducing "us–them" thinking and hostility between groups?

Answers:

1. acculturation, ethnic identity   2. ethnocentrism   3. interdependence in reaching mutual goals

WHAT'S *Ahead*

- Is prejudice more likely to be a *cause* of war or a *result* of it?
- If you believe that women are naturally better than men, are you sexist?
- Is it possible that you have unconscious prejudices? How would you know?
- Why isn't mere contact between cultural groups enough to reduce prejudice between them? What does work?

Group Conflict and Prejudice

A *prejudice* consists of a negative stereotype and a strong, unreasonable dislike or hatred of a group. A central feature of a prejudice is that it remains immune to evidence. In his classic book *The Nature of Prejudice*, Gordon Allport (1954/1979) described the responses characteristic of a prejudiced person when confronted with evidence contradicting his or her beliefs:

Mr. X: The trouble with Jews is that they only take care of their own group.

Mr. Y: But the record of the Community Chest campaign shows that they give more generously, in proportion to their numbers, to the general charities of the community, than do non-Jews.

Mr. X: That shows they are always trying to buy favor and intrude into Christian affairs. They think of nothing but money; that is why there are so many Jewish bankers.

Mr. Y: But a recent study shows that the percentage of Jews in the banking business is negligible, far smaller than the percentage of non-Jews.

Mr. X: That's just it; they don't go in for respectable business; they are only in the movie business or run night clubs.

In times of war, most people fall victim to emotional reasoning about the enemy. They start thinking of "them" as aggressors who are less than human—often as "vermin," dogs, or pigs. After 9/11, anti-American demonstrators in Jakarta portrayed George Bush as a rabid dog, and an American cartoonist lumped all Arab Muslims and nations into a "barrel of vermin."

Notice that Mr. X doesn't even try to respond to Mr. Y's evidence; he just moves along to another reason for his dislike of Jews. That is the slippery nature of prejudice.

The Origins of Prejudice

Prejudice is universal because it has so many sources and functions: psychological, social, cultural, and economic.

1 *Psychological functions.* Prejudice often serves to ward off feelings of doubt and fear. Thus, a straight person who has doubts or anxieties about his own sexuality may develop a hatred of gay people. Prejudice also allows people to use the target group as a scapegoat ("Those people are the source of all my troubles"). And, as research from many nations has confirmed, prejudice is a tonic for low self-esteem: People puff up their own feelings of low self-worth by disliking or hating groups they see as inferior (Islam & Hewstone, 1993; Stephan et al., 1994; Tajfel & Turner, 1986). Prejudice toward a scapegoat may also be a way for people to displace feelings of anger and cope with feelings of powerlessness.

2 *Social and cultural functions.* Not all prejudices have deep-seated psychological roots. Some are acquired through groupthink and other social pressures to conform to the views of friends, relatives, or associates. Some may be passed along mindlessly from one generation to another, as when parents communicate to their children, "We don't associate with people like that." And some unconscious (implicit) prejudices are acquired from advertising, TV shows, and news reports that contain derogatory images and negative stereotypes of certain groups.

Prejudice also serves cultural purposes, bonding people to their own ethnic or national group and its ways; this may be a major evolutionary reason for its universality and persistence (Fishbein, 1996). In this respect, prejudice is the flip side of ethnocentrism; it is not only that *we* are good and kind, but also that *they* are bad or evil. By disliking "them," we feel closer to others who are like "us."

3 *Economic functions.* Prejudice makes official forms of discrimination seem legitimate, by justifying the majority group's dominance, status, or greater wealth (Sidanius, Pratto, & Bobo, 1996). Historically, for example, white men in positions of power have justified their exclusion of women, blacks, and other minorities from the workplace and politics by claiming those minorities were inferior, irrational, and incompetent (Gould, 1996). But any majority group—of any ethnicity, gender, or nationality—that discriminates against a minority will call upon prejudice to legitimize its actions (Islam & Hewstone, 1993).

Although it is widely believed that prejudice is a primary cause of conflict between groups, prejudice is actually more often a *result* of conflict. When any two groups are in direct competition for jobs, or when people are worried about their incomes and the stability of their communities, prejudice between them increases (Doty, Peterson, & Winter, 1991).

Consider the rise and fall of attitudes toward Chinese immigrants in the United States in the nineteenth century, as reported in newspapers of the time (Aronson, 2004). When the Chinese were working in the gold mines and potentially taking jobs from white laborers, whites described them as depraved, vicious, and bloodthirsty. Just a decade later, when the Chinese began working on the transcontinental railroad, doing difficult and dangerous jobs that few white men wanted, prejudice against them declined. Whites described them as

GET INVOLVED

Probing Your Prejudices

Are you prejudiced? No? Is there any group of people you tend to regard in a negative light because of their gender, ethnicity, sexual orientation, nationality, religion, physical appearance, or political views? Write down your deepest thoughts and feelings about this group. Take as long as you want, and do not censor yourself or say what you think you ought to say. Now reread what you have written. Which of the sources of prejudice discussed in the text might be contributing to your views? Do you feel that your attitudes toward the group are legitimate, or are you uncomfortable about having them?

hardworking, industrious, and law-abiding. Then, after the railroad was finished and the Chinese had to compete with Civil War veterans for scarce jobs, white attitudes changed again. Whites now considered the Chinese to be "criminal," "crafty," "conniving," and "stupid." (The white newspapers did not report the attitudes of the Chinese.)

The ultimate competition between groups, of course, is war. When two nations are at war, prejudice against the enemy allows each side to continue feeling righteous about its cause. Drawing on the principles of persuasion and influence described earlier (such as the validity effect), along with propaganda images that demonize and dehumanize the enemy, each side tries to convince its citizens that the enemy is less than human and thus deserves to be killed (Keen, 1986). Fomenting prejudice against the perceived enemy—calling them vermin, rats, mad dogs, heathens, baby killers, or monsters—legitimizes the attackers' motives for war or revenge.

Defining and Measuring Prejudice

Prejudice is like a weasel—hard to grasp and hold on to. One problem is that not all prejudiced people are prejudiced in the same way or to the same extent.

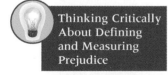
Thinking Critically About Defining and Measuring Prejudice

Suppose that Raymond wishes to be tolerant and open-minded, but he grew up in a small homogeneous community and feels uncomfortable with members of other cultural and religious groups. Should we put Raymond in the same category as Rupert, an outspoken bigot who actively discriminates against others? Do good intentions count? What if Raymond knows nothing about Muslims and mindlessly blurts out a remark that reveals his ignorance? Is that prejudice or thoughtlessness? These questions complicate the measurement of prejudice.

Similar complexities occur in defining "sexism." In research with 15,000 men and women in 19 nations, psychologists found that "hostile sexism," which reflects active dislike of women, is different from "benevolent sexism," in which superficially positive attitudes put women on a pedestal but nonetheless reinforce women's subordination. The latter type of sexism is affectionate but patronizing, conveying the attitude that women are so wonderful, good, kind, and moral that they should stay at home, away from the rough-and-tumble (and power and income) of public life (Glick et al., 2000). In all 19 countries studied, men had significantly higher hostile sexism scores than women did, but in about half the countries, women endorsed benevolent sexism as much as men did.

Because benevolent sexism lacks a tone of hostility to women, it doesn't seem like a prejudice to many people, and many women find it alluring to think they are better than men. But both forms of sexism—whether you think women are too good for equality or not good enough—legitimize gender discrimination and, in some cultures, wife abuse. Studies in Turkey and Brazil found that men who abuse their wives score high not only on hostile sexism but also on benevolent sexism—because if the wife dares to step down from her pedestal, she deserves to be beaten (Glick et al., 2002).

Perhaps you are thinking: "Hey, what about men? There are plenty of prejudices against men, too—that they are sexual predators, emotionally heartless, domineering and arrogant." In fact, when the same group of researchers completed a 16-nation study of attitudes toward men, they found that many people do believe that men are aggressive and predatory, and overall just not as warm and wonderful as women (Glick et al., 2004). This attitude seems hostile to men, the researchers found, but it also reflects and supports gender inequality by characterizing men as being designed for leadership and dominance.

Perhaps the greatest barrier to measuring prejudice today is that most people know they should not have any (Crandall & Eshelman, 2003). If you ask people directly about their prejudices, most will say, in effect, "Me, prejudiced? Not at all!" On surveys in the United States and Canada, the numbers of people who admit to believing that blacks are inferior to whites or women inferior to men have dropped sharply in the last 20 years (Dovidio, 2001; Plant & Devine, 1998).

Pinning Down
Unconscious Prejudices

Some social psychologists, while welcoming the evidence that prejudices have declined, have **asked questions** about how to interpret these surveys. First, do the changing numbers simply reflect a growing awareness that it isn't cool to admit prejudice rather than a real decline in prejudiced feelings? There is considerable **evidence** for that view: In studies of job-hiring practices, most whites do not discriminate against black candidates who have strong qualifications, but they are far more likely to choose *average* white candidates over *average* black ones (Dovidio & Gaertner, 2000). This finding suggests that although old-fashioned discrimination ("We would never hire a black person") may be gone, it lives on in a subtler form ("We would hire Colin Powell and Tiger Woods in a heartbeat, but of course they are exceptional"). Moreover, the same whites who will not admit to disliking African-Americans might agree that "blacks are getting too demanding in their push for equal rights" (Brauer, Wasel, & Niedenthal, 2000).

The next question social psychologists asked was this: Even when people believe they are not prejudiced, or say that they do not want to be, is it possible that they nonetheless are prejudiced at some unconscious level? Years ago, Gordon Allport (1954/1979) observed that "defeated intellectually, prejudice lingers emotionally." That is, people may lose their *explicit*, conscious prejudice toward a group but retain an *implicit*, unconscious prejudice or negative emotional feelings, which they try to suppress in everyday life (Crandall & Eshelman,

2003; Rudman, 2004). So some social psychologists have **redefined their terms** by expanding the definition of prejudice to include an unconscious level of dislike or animosity toward a group. They have **questioned the assumption** that prejudice is primarily conscious. Their own assumption is that implicit attitudes, being automatic and unintentional, are a truer measure of a person's real prejudices (Cunningham, Preacher, & Banaji, 2001). To test their assumption empirically, they have developed several ways of measuring implicit prejudices.

The first method is to pay attention to what people do, not what they say, when they are with a possible object of prejudice, especially when they are angered or stressed (Jones, 1991; Sinclair & Kunda, 1999). In one of the first experiments to do this, white students were asked to administer shock to black or white confederates of the experimenter in what the students believed was a study of biofeedback. In the experimental condition, participants overheard the biofeedback "victim" (who actually received no shock) saying derogatory things about them. In the control condition, participants overheard no such nasty remarks. Then all the participants had another opportunity to shock the victims, and their degree of "aggression" was defined as the amount of shock they administered. As you can see in the figure below, white students actually showed *less* aggression toward blacks than toward whites. But as soon as the white students were angered by overhearing derogatory remarks about themselves, they showed *more* aggression toward blacks than toward whites (Rogers & Prentice-Dunn, 1981).

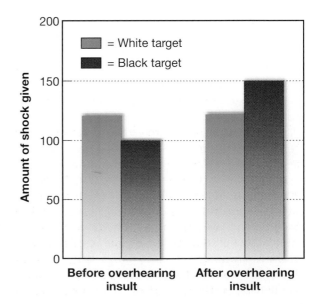

This research has been replicated many times. The same pattern appears in studies of how English-speaking Canadians behave toward French-speaking Canadians (Meindl & Lerner, 1985), straights toward homosexuals, non-Jewish students toward Jews (Fein & Spencer, 1997), and men toward women (Maass et al., 2003). So it seems that many people are willing to control their negative feelings under normal conditions, but as soon as they are angry or frustrated, or get a jolt to their self-esteem, their unconscious prejudice reveals itself.

A second method relies on fMRI and PET scans to determine which parts of the brain are involved in forming stereotypes, holding prejudiced beliefs, and feeling disgust, anger, and other negative feelings about a group (Amodio, Harmon-Jones, & Devine, 2003; Cacioppo et al., 2003; Harris & Fiske, 2006). In one study, when African-Americans and whites saw pictures of each other, activity in the amygdala (the brain structure associated with fear and other negative emotions) was elevated. But it was not elevated when people saw pictures of members of their own group (Hart et al., 2000).

The researchers **did not oversimplify**, for example, by concluding that the negative emotions associated with prejudice are hardwired and thus inevitable. Instead they **asked the next crucial question**: Under what conditions does this brain activation occur in response to pictures of people from other ethnicities? To find out, Mary Wheeler and Susan Fiske (2005) recorded brain activity in the amygdalas of white participants as they looked at photographs of white and black faces. Areas of brain activation depended on what the subjects had been asked to do with the photos. When participants were registering the faces as individuals or as part of a simple visual test rather than as members of the category "blacks," there was no increased activation in the amygdala. The brain may be designed to register differences, it appears, but any negative associations with those differences depend on context and learning.

A third, more controversial method is the *Implicit Association Test* (IAT), which measures the speed of people's positive and negative associations to a target group (Greenwald, McGhee, & Schwartz, 1998). Its proponents have argued that if, for example, white students take longer to respond to black faces associated with positive words (e.g., *triumph, honest*) than to black faces associated with negative words (e.g., *devil, failure*), it must mean that white students have an unconscious prejudice toward blacks. The test has also been used to iden-

tify alleged prejudices toward Asians, women, old people, and other groups (Cunningham, Preacher, & Banaji, 2001; Dovidio, 2001).

We say "alleged" prejudices because other social psychologists have **considered other interpretations** of findings based on the IAT, maintaining that whatever the test measures, it is not a stable prejudice. Two researchers got an IAT effect by matching target faces with nonsense words and neutral words that had no evaluative connotations at all. They concluded that the IAT does not measure emotional evaluations of the target but rather the *salience* of the word associated with it—how much it stands out. (Negative words attract more attention in general.) When the researchers corrected for these factors, the presumed unconscious prejudice faded away (Rothermund & Wentura, 2004).

Moreover, as we saw earlier, people find familiar names, products, and even nonsense syllables to be more pleasant than unfamiliar ones. Some investigators argue that the IAT may simply be measuring, say, white subjects' unfamiliarity with African-Americans and the greater salience of white faces to them, rather than a true prejudice (Kinoshita & Peek-O'Leary, 2005).

As you can see, defining and measuring prejudice are not easy tasks. The research clearly cautions us **not to oversimplify**. To understand prejudice, we must distinguish explicit attitudes from unconscious ones, active hostility from simple discomfort, what people say from what they feel, and what people feel from how they actually behave.

Reducing Conflict and Prejudice

Findings on implicit prejudice suggest that efforts to reduce prejudice by appealing to moral or intellectual arguments are not enough. They must also touch people's deeper insecurities, fears, or negative associations with a group. One study of white students who took a diversity-education course found that the students' prejudices toward African-Americans, both implicit and explicit, had declined by the end of the term, but for different reasons. Their explicit prejudices had been reduced because of a greater understanding of racial issues and a wish to overcome their own biases. But their implicit prejudices were reduced only when they lost their fear of blacks, made black friends in the course, and felt respect and affection for the black professor who taught it (Rudman, 2004).

Just as social psychologists investigate the situations that increase prejudice and animosity toward other groups, they have also examined the conditions that might reduce them. Of course, given the many sources and functions of prejudice, no one method will work in all situations. But social psychologists have identified four external conditions that must be met before conflict and prejudice between groups can be lessened (Dovidio, Gaertner, & Validzic, 1998; Pettigrew, 1998; Slavin & Cooper, 1999; Staub, 1999; Stephan, 1999):

1 *Both sides must have equal legal status, economic opportunities, and power.* This requirement is the spur behind efforts to change laws that permit discrimination. Integration of public facilities in the American South would never have occurred if civil rights advocates had waited for segregation-

ists to have a change of heart. Women would never have gotten the right to vote, attend college, or do "men's work" without persistent challenges to the laws that permitted gender discrimination. But changing the law is not enough if two groups remain in competition for jobs or if one group retains power and dominance over the other.

2 *Authorities and community institutions must provide moral, legal, and economic support for both sides.* Society must establish norms of equality and support them in the actions of its officials— teachers, employers, the judicial system, government officials, and the police. Where segregation is official government policy or an unofficial but established practice, conflict and prejudice not only will continue but also will seem normal and justified.

3 *Both sides must have opportunities to work and socialize together, formally and informally.* According to the *contact hypothesis*, prejudice declines

THE MANY TARGETS OF PREJUDICE

Prejudice has a long and universal history. Why do new prejudices keep emerging, others fade away, and some old ones persist?

Some prejudices rise and fall with events. When France refused to support America's decision to go to war with Iraq in 2003, anti-French anger erupted, as the scrawled sign (immediate right) indicates. Anti-Japanese feelings in the United States ran high in the 1920s (below center), and again in the 1990s, but this prejudice has faded. In contrast, some hatreds, notably homophobia and antisemitism, reflect people's deeper anxieties and are therefore more persistent.

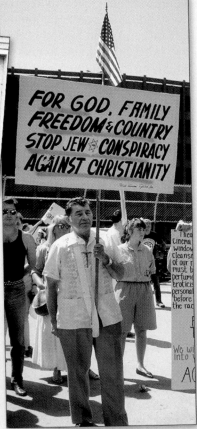

when people have the chance to get used to one another's rules, food, music, customs, and attitudes, thereby discovering their shared interests and shared humanity. Stereotypes are shattered once people realize that "those people" aren't, in fact, "all alike."

The contact hypothesis has been supported by many studies in the laboratory and in the real world: studies of newly integrated housing projects in the American South during the 1950s and 1960s; relationships between German and immigrant Turkish children in German schools; young people's attitudes toward the elderly; healthy people's attitudes toward the mentally ill; nondisabled children's attitudes toward the disabled; and straight people's prejudices toward gay men and lesbians (Fishbein, 1996; Herek & Capitanio, 1996; Tropp & Pettigrew, 2005; Wilner, Walkley, & Cook, 1955).

4 **Both sides must cooperate, working together for a common goal.** Clearly, contact between two groups is not enough; at many multiethnic

Tensions between groups often subside when people work together on a common goal. Here, volunteers from Habitat for Humanity build a new home for low-income people in Los Angeles.

high schools, ethnic groups form cliques and gangs, fighting one another and defending their own ways. To reduce the stereotyping and competition that exist in many schools, Elliot Aronson and his colleagues have developed the "jigsaw" method.

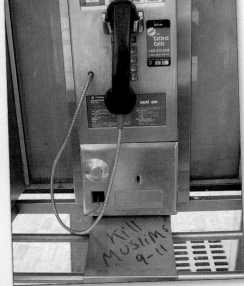

Prejudices toward Native Americans, women, and African-Americans have long been part of American history. Women have been excluded from men's clubs, and segregation of blacks was legal in America until the 1950s. Other prejudices emerge with changing historical events. In the aftermath of 9/11, hostility mounted toward Middle Easterners and Muslims.

Students from different ethnic groups work together on a task that is broken up like a jigsaw puzzle; each person needs to cooperate with the others to put the assignment together. Students in such classes, from elementary school through college, tend to do better, like their classmates better, and become less stereotyped and prejudiced in their thinking than students in traditional classrooms (Aronson, 2000; Aronson & Patnoe, 1997; Slavin & Cooper, 1999). As we saw, cooperation often reduces us–them thinking and prejudice by

creating an encompassing social identity—the Eagles and Rattlers solution.

Each of these four approaches to creating greater harmony between groups is important, but none is sufficient on its own. For example, cooperation in working for a common goal may not work when members of a group have unequal status or believe the teacher or employer is playing favorites. Perhaps one reason that group conflicts and prejudice are so persistent is that all four conditions for reducing them are rarely met at the same time.

QUICK quiz

Try to overcome your prejudice against quizzes by taking this one.

1. What are four important conditions required for reducing prejudice and conflict between groups?

2. Surveys find that large percentages of African-Americans, Asian-Americans, and Latinos hold negative stereotypes of one another and resent other minorities almost as much as they resent whites. What are some reasons that people who have themselves been victims of stereotyping and prejudice would hold the same attitudes toward others?

Answers:

1. Both sides must have equal status and power; have the moral, legal, and economic support of authorities; have opportunities to socialize formally and informally; and cooperate for a common goal. 2. ethnocentrism; low self-esteem; conformity with relatives and friends who share these prejudices; parental lessons and messages conveyed by the media; and economic competition for jobs and resources

After reading this chapter, why do you think the guards at Abu Ghraib abused and humiliated their prisoners? As we have seen, it is not enough to say they were just "bad apples." Philip Zimbardo, who led the prison study, told *The New York Times* (May 6, 2004): "Prisons, where the balance of power is so unequal, tend to be brutal and abusive places . . . At Stanford and in Iraq, it's not that we put bad apples in a good barrel. We put good apples in a bad barrel. The barrel corrupts anything that it touches."

Social psychologists would explain the behavior of Lynndie England and her fellow soldiers by considering the roles they were assigned, which gave them unlimited control over the detainees. They would also emphasize the group norms of the

soldiers' peers. The fact that the guards willingly posed for pictures—in many, they are smiling proudly—indicates that they were showing off for their friends and that they believed their behavior was normal and appropriate. In all likelihood, they were able to justify their behavior by blaming the victims, saying that the detainees, who had not been found guilty of any crime, deserved whatever harsh treatment they got.

As for the soldiers' defense that they were "only following orders," this did not appear to be the case. There *should* have been orders from higher-ups, or at least clear rules for the treatment of detainees. But Pentagon investigations concluded that no one authorized or encouraged the soldiers' treatment of prisoners, such as forcing detainees to masturbate or pile naked on top of one another to form a pyramid. The investigations also revealed that the detention center was chaotic and

These paintings done during wartime poignantly illustrate one child's effort to portray the horror of war and another's dream of peace. Can we learn to design a world in which conflicts and group differences, though inevitable, need not lead to violence?

poorly run, and rules on treatment of detainees were so vague and changed so frequently that even higher-ranking soldiers did not know the difference between abuse and acceptable interrogation techniques. In the midst of this chaos, the soldiers made up their own rules and group norms, and once those norms were in place, most guards went along with their peers.

The good news in this bleak picture is that the barrel does not actually "corrupt anything that it touches." Not every soldier at Abu Ghraib humiliated and tortured the detainees. Some refused to participate. Some informed their commanding officers. Some eventually blew the whistle publicly. These individuals did not mindlessly pass along responsibility for their actions to their senior officers.

Throughout this chapter, we have seen that "human nature" contains the potential for unspeakable acts of cruelty and inspiring acts of goodness. Most people believe that some cultures and individuals are inherently good or evil; if we can just get rid of those few evil ones, everything will be fine. But from the standpoint of social and cultural psychology, all human beings, like all cultures, contain the potential for both.

Thinking Critically About "Evil" Cultures

In this respect, virtually no country has bloodless hands. The Nazis, of course, systematically exterminated millions of Jews, Gypsies, homosexuals, disabled people, and anyone else not of the "pure" Aryan "race." But Americans and Canadians slaughtered native peoples in North America, Turks slaughtered Armenians, the Khmer Rouge slaughtered millions of fellow Cambodians, the Spanish conquistadors slaughtered native peoples in Mexico and South America, Idi Amin waged a reign of terror against his own people in Uganda, the Japanese slaughtered Koreans and Chinese, Iraqis slaughtered Kurds, despotic political regimes in Argentina and Chile killed thousands of dissidents and rebels, the Hutu in Rwanda murdered thousands of Tutsi, and in the former Yugoslavia, Bosnian Serbs massacred thousands of Bosnian Muslims in the name of "ethnic cleansing."

It is easy to conclude that such outbreaks of violence are a result of inner aggressive drives, the sheer evilness of the perpetrators, or age-old tribal hatreds. But in the social-psychological view, they result from the all-too-normal processes we have discussed in this chapter, including ethnocentrism, obedience to authority, conformity, groupthink, deindividuation, stereotyping, and prejudice. These processes are especially likely to be activated when a government feels weakened and vulnerable. By generating an outside enemy, rulers create "us–them" thinking to impose order and cohesion among their citizens and to create a scapegoat for the country's economic problems (Smith, 1998; Staub, 1996). Yet when circumstances within a nation change, societies can also change from being warlike to being peaceful. Sweden was once one of the most warlike nations on earth, but today it is among the most pacifistic and egalitarian.

The philosopher Hannah Arendt covered the trial of Adolf Eichmann, a Nazi officer who supervised the deportation and death of millions of Jews. Arendt (1963) used the phrase *the banality of evil* to describe how it was possible for Eichmann and other ordinary people in Nazi Germany to commit the atrocities they did. (*Banal* means "commonplace" or "unoriginal.") The compelling evidence for the banality of evil is, perhaps, the hardest lesson in psychology. The research discussed in this chapter suggests that aggression, ethnocentrism, and prejudice will always be with us, as long as differences exist among groups. But it can also help us formulate realistic yet nonviolent ways of living in a diverse world. By identifying the conditions that create the banality of evil, perhaps we can create others that foster the "banality of virtue"—everyday acts of kindness, selflessness, and generosity.

➤TAKING ➤PSYCHOLOGY ➤WITH ➤YOU

Travels Across the Cultural Divide

A French salesman worked for a company that was bought by Americans. When the new American manager ordered him to step up his sales within the next three months, the employee quit in a huff, taking his customers with him. Why? In France, it takes years to develop customers; in family-owned businesses, relationships with customers may span generations. The American wanted instant results, as Americans often do, but the French salesman knew this was impossible and quit. The American view was "He wasn't up to the job; he's lazy and disloyal, so he stole my customers." The French view was "There is no point in explaining anything to a person who is so stupid as to think you can acquire loyal customers in three months" (Hall & Hall, 1987).

Both men were committing the fundamental attribution error: assuming that the other person's behavior was due to personality rather than the situation, in this case a situation governed by cultural rules. Many corporations now realize that such rules are not trivial and that success in a global economy depends on understanding them. You, too, can benefit from the psychological research on cultures, whether you plan to do business abroad, intend to visit as a tourist, or just want to get along better in your own society.

● **Be sure you understand the other culture's rules, manners, and customs.** If you find yourself getting angry over something a person from another culture is doing, try to find out whether your expectations and perceptions of that person's behavior are appropriate. For example, Koreans typically do not shake hands when greeting strangers, whereas most North Americans and Europeans do. People who shake hands as a gesture of friendship and courtesy are likely to feel insulted if another person refuses to do the same, unless they understand this cultural difference.

Or suppose that you are shopping in the Middle East or Latin America, where bargaining on a price is the usual practice. If you are not used to bargaining, the experience is likely to be exasperating because you will not know whether you got taken or got a great deal. On the other hand, if you are from a bargaining culture, you will feel just as exasperated if a seller offers you a flat price. "Where's the fun in this?" you'll say. "The whole human transaction of shopping is gone!"

Whichever kind of culture you come from, you may need a "translator" to help you navigate the unfamiliar system. In Los Angeles, a physician we know could not persuade his Iranian patients that office fees are fixed, not negotiable. They kept offering him half, then 60 percent . . . and each time he said "no" they thought he was just taking a hard negotiating position. It took a bicultural relative of the patients to explain the odd American custom of fixed prices for services.

● **When in Rome, do as the Romans do—as much as possible.** Most of the things you really need to know about a culture are not to be found in guidebooks. To learn the unspoken rules of a culture, look, listen, and observe. What is the pace of life like? Do people regard brash individuality and loud speech as admirable or embarrassing? When customers enter a shop, do they greet and chat with the shopkeeper or ignore the person as they browse?

Remember, though, that even when you know the rules, you may find it difficult to carry them out. In the Middle East, two men will look directly at one another as they talk, but such direct gazes would be deeply uncomfortable to most Japanese and a sign of insult or confrontation to some African-Americans (Keating, 1994). Knowing this fact about gaze rules can help people accept the reality of different customs, but most of us will still feel uncomfortable trying to change our own ways.

● **Avoid stereotyping.** Try not to let your awareness of general cultural differences cause you to overlook individual variations within cultures. During a dreary Boston winter, Roger Brown (1986) went to the Bahamas for a vacation. To his surprise, he found the people he met unfriendly, rude, and sullen. As a social psychologist, he came up with a situational attribution for their behavior: He decided that the reason was that Bahamians had to deal with spoiled, demanding foreigners. He tried out this hypothesis on a cab driver. The cab driver looked at Brown in amazement, smiled cheerfully, and told him that Bahamians don't mind tourists—just *unsmiling* tourists.

And then Brown realized what had been going on. "Not tourists generally, but this tourist, myself, was the cause," he wrote. "Confronted with my unrelaxed wintry Boston face, they had assumed I had no interest in them and had responded noncommittally, inexpressively. I had created the Bahamian national character. Everywhere I took my face it sprang into being. So I began smiling a lot, and the Bahamians changed their national character. In fact, they lost any national character and differentiated into individuals."

Wise travelers can use their knowledge of cultural differences while avoiding the trap of stereotyping. Sociocultural research teaches us to appreciate the many cultural rules that govern people's behavior, values, and attitudes. Yet we should not forget Roger Brown's lesson that every human being is an individual: one who not only reflects his or her culture but also shares the common concerns of all humanity.

SUMMARY

- Social and cultural psychologists emphasize environmental influences on behavior. *Social psychologists* study how social roles, attitudes, relationships, and groups influence individuals; *cultural psychologists* study the influence of culture on human behavior.

Roles and Rules

- Two classic studies illustrate the power of *norms* and *roles* to affect individual actions. In Milgram's obedience study, most people in the role of "teacher" inflicted what they thought was extreme shock on another person because of the authority of the experimenter. In Zimbardo's prison study, college students quickly fell into the role of "prisoner" or "guard."

- Obedience to authority contributes to the smooth running of society, but obedience can also lead to actions that are deadly, foolish, or illegal. People obey orders because they can be punished if they do not, out of respect for the authority, and to gain advantages. Even when they would rather not obey, they may do so because they hand over responsibility for their actions to the authority, because their role is routinized into duties that are performed mindlessly, because they are embarrassed to violate the rules of good manners and lack the words to protest, or because they have been *entrapped*.

Social Influences on Beliefs

- Researchers in the area of *social cognition* study how people's relationships and social environment affect their beliefs and perceptions. *Social-cognitive neuroscientists* draw upon technologies from neuroscience to study the emotional and social processes underlying beliefs, prejudices, and social behavior. According to *attribution theory*, people are motivated to search for causes to which they can attribute their own and other people's behavior. Their attributions may be *situational* or *dispositional*. The *fundamental attribution error* occurs when people overestimate personality traits as a cause of behavior and underestimate the influence of the situation. A *self-serving bias* allows people to excuse their mistakes by blaming the situation yet taking credit for their good deeds. According to the *just-world hypothesis*, most people need to believe that the world is fair and that people get what they deserve. To preserve this belief, they may blame victims of abuse or injustice for provoking or deserving it.

- People hold many *attitudes* about people, things, and ideas. Attitudes may be *explicit* (conscious) or *implicit* (unconscious). Many attitudes are acquired through learning and social influence, but some are associated with personality traits that have a genetic component and are deeply ingrained. Religious and political affiliations are not heritable, but religiosity and certain political attitudes do have relatively high heritability. Attitudes are also profoundly affected by the *nonshared environment,* an individual's unique life experiences. Attitudes and behavior may change as an effort to reduce *cognitive dissonance.*

- One powerful way to influence attitudes is through the *familiarity effect* and the *validity effect*: Simply exposing people repeatedly to a name or product makes them like it more, and repeating a statement over and over again makes it seem more believable. Other techniques of attitude change include associating a product or message with someone who is famous, attractive, or expert, and linking the product with good feelings. Fear tactics tend to backfire.

- Tactics of *coercive persuasion* include putting a person under extreme stress; defining problems simplistically; offering the appearance of unconditional love and acceptance in exchange for unquestioning loyalty; creating a new identity for the person; using entrapment; and controlling access to outside information. Even ordinary people without any psychopathology can be vulnerable to these techniques.

Individuals in Groups

- In groups, individuals often behave differently than they would on their own. Conformity has many benefits; it permits the smooth running of society and allows people to feel in harmony with others like them. As the famous Asch experiment showed, most people will conform to the judgments of others even when the others are plain wrong. People in collectivist cultures value conformity and the sense of group harmony it creates more than do people in individualist cultures. But everyone conforms under some conditions.

• Most people conform to social pressure because they identify with a group, trust the group's judgment or knowledge, hope for personal gain, or wish to be liked. But they also may conform mindlessly and self-destructively, violating their own preferences and values because "everyone else is doing it."

• Groups that are strongly cohesive, are isolated from other views, are under outside pressure, and have strong leaders are vulnerable to *groupthink*, the tendency of group members to think alike, censor themselves, actively suppress disagreement, and feel that their decisions are invulnerable. Groupthink often produces faulty decisions because group members fail to seek disconfirming evidence for their ideas. However, groups can be structured to counteract groupthink.

• *Diffusion of responsibility* in a group can lead to inaction on the part of individuals, such as *bystander apathy* or, in work groups, *social loafing*. The diffusion of responsibility is likely to occur under conditions that promote *deindividuation*, the loss of awareness of one's individuality. Deindividuation increases when people feel anonymous, as in a large group or crowd, or when they are wearing masks or uniforms. In some situations, crowd norms lead deindividuated people to behave aggressively, but in others, crowd norms foster helpfulness.

• The willingness to speak up for an unpopular opinion, blow the whistle on illegal practices, or help a stranger in trouble and perform other acts of *altruism* is partly a matter of personal belief and conscience. But several situational factors are also important: The person perceives that help is needed; cultural norms support taking action; the situation increases the likelihood that the person will take responsibility; the costs of not doing anything are greater than the costs of getting involved; the person has an ally; and the person becomes entrapped in a commitment to help or dissent.

Us Versus Them: Group Identity

• People develop *social identities* based on their group affiliations, including nationality, ethnicity, gender, and other social memberships. Social identities provide a feeling of place and connection in the world.

• In culturally diverse societies, many people face the problem of balancing their *ethnic identity* with *acculturation* into the larger society. Depending on whether ethnic identity and acculturation are strong or weak, a person may become *bicultural*, choose *assimilation*, become an *ethnic separatist*, or feel *marginal*.

• *Ethnocentrism*, the belief that one's own ethnic group or nation is superior to all others, promotes "us–them" thinking. One effective strategy for reducing us–them thinking and hostility between groups is cooperation, when both sides must work together to reach a common goal.

• *Stereotypes* help people rapidly process new information, organize experience, and predict how others will behave. But they distort reality by exaggerating differences between groups, underestimating the differences within groups, and producing selective perception.

Group Conflict and Prejudice

• A *prejudice* is an unreasonable negative feeling toward a category of people. Prejudice has psychological, social-cultural, and economic functions. Psychologically, it wards off feelings of anxiety and doubt, provides a simple explanation of complex problems, and bolsters self-esteem when a person feels threatened. But other causes of prejudice are social: People acquire prejudices through conformity and groupthink, parental lessons, and media images. Prejudice has the cultural purpose of bonding people to their social groups and nations. Prejudice also serves to justify a majority group's economic interests and dominance and even to legitimize war. During times of economic insecurity and competition for jobs, prejudice rises significantly.

• Prejudice is a challenge to define and measure. For example, "hostile sexism" is different from "benevolent sexism," though both legitimize gender discrimination. As discussed in "Close-up on Research," psychologists disagree on whether racism and other prejudices are declining or have merely taken new forms. Because many people are unwilling to admit their prejudices openly, some researchers are trying to measure prejudice indirectly: by seeing whether people are more likely to behave aggressively toward a target when they are stressed or insulted; by observing changes in the brain; or by assessing unconscious positive or negative associations with a group, as with the *Implicit Association Test* (IAT). However, the IAT has many critics who claim it is not capturing true prejudice.

• Four external conditions are required for reducing prejudice and conflict between groups: Both sides must have equal legal status, economic standing, and power; both sides must have the legal, economic, and moral support of authorities and cultural institutions; both sides must have opportunities to work and socialize together (the *contact hypothesis*); and both sides must work together for a common goal.

Psychology in the News, Revisited

• Although many people believe that only bad or evil people do bad deeds, the principles of social and cultural psychology show that under certain conditions, good people are often induced to do bad things too. All individuals are affected by the rules of their peer groups and the norms of their cultures. And everyone is influenced to one degree or another by the social processes of obedience and conformity, persuasion, bystander apathy, groupthink, deindividuation, ethnocentrism, stereotyping, and prejudice.

KEY TERMS

social psychology   331

cultural
  psychology   331

norms (social)   332

role   332

entrapment   336

social cognition   337

social-cognitive
  neuroscience   338

attribution theory   338

situational
  attributions   338

dispositional
  attributions   338

fundamental attribution
  error   338

self-serving bias   338

just-world
  hypothesis   338

blaming the victim   339

attitude   339

explicit and implicit
  attitudes   339

nonshared
  environment   341

cognitive
  dissonance   341

familiarity effect   341

validity effect   342

coercive
  persuasion   342

groupthink   345

diffusion of
  responsibility   346

bystander apathy   346

social loafing   347

deindividuation   347

altruism   348

social identity   350

ethnic identity   350

acculturation   350

bicultural, assimilated,
  ethnic separatist,
  and marginal
  identities   350–351

ethnocentrism   352

stereotype   352

prejudice   353

Implicit Association
  Test   357

contact hypothesis   358

- Social psychologists study how social roles, attitudes, relationships, and groups influence individuals.
- Cultural psychologists study the influence of culture on human behavior.

Roles and Rules

Two Classic Studies

- In Milgram's obedience study, most people inflicted what they thought was extreme shock on another person because of the experimenter's authority.
- In Zimbardo's prison study, students quickly took on the role of "prisoner" or "guard."

- **Norms**: rules that regulate social life, including explicit laws and implicit cultural conventions
- **Roles**: social positions that are regulated by norms about how people in those positions should behave

Why People Obey

Several factors cause people to obey, including:
1. Allocating responsibility to the authority
2. Routinizing the task
3. Wanting to be polite
4. Becoming **entrapped**: increasing their commitment to a course of action in order to justify their investment in it

Social Influences on Beliefs

- **Social cognition**: how people's perceptions of themselves and others affect their relationships and how the social environment influences thoughts, beliefs, and values.
- Social-cognitive neuroscience draws upon technologies from neuroscience to study the emotional and social processes underlying beliefs, prejudices, and social behavior.

Attributions

Attribution theory holds that people explain their own and other people's behavior by attributing its causes to a situation or disposition.
- The **fundamental attribution** error is the tendency to ignore situational factors in favor of dispositional ones.
- Because of the **self-serving bias,** people blame the situation for their bad behavior but take credit for their good deeds.
- According to the **just-world hypothesis,** people have a need to believe the world is fair.

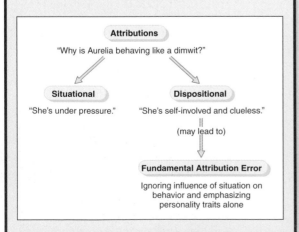

Attitudes

Attitudes may be:
- Implicit (unconscious) or explicit (conscious)
- Resistant to change
- Subject to social influence

- Highly heritable (e.g., religiosity and certain political attitudes)
- Influenced by the "unshared environment"
- Altered because of the need to reduce cognitive dissonance

Friendly Persuasion

Efforts to get people to change their attitudes often rely on:
- The **familiarity effect**
- The **validity effect**

Coercive Persuasion

Coercive efforts to change attitudes include:
1. Putting a person under physical or emotional stress
2. Defining problems simplistically
3. Offering unconditional love in exchange for unquestioning loyalty
4. Creating a new identity for the person
5. Using entrapment
6. Controlling access to outside information

Individuals in Groups

Conformity

The Asch experiment shows that most people will conform to others' judgments, even when others are obviously wrong.

Groupthink

Groupthink, an extreme form of conformity, leads to faulty decisions because group members are vulnerable to:
1. An illusion of invulnerability
2. Self-censorship
3. Pressure on dissenters to conform
4. An illusion of unanimity

The Anonymous Crowd

When people are part of large, anonymous groups, two processes may occur:
1. **Diffusion of responsibility**, the spreading out of responsibility among many people. It can lead to:
   — Bystander apathy
   — Social loafing
2. **Deindividuation**, the loss of awareness of one's own individuality:
   — Increases as group gets larger
   — Increases when group members wear masks or uniforms
   — May increase helpfulness as well as destructiveness depending on social norms

Altruism and Dissent

Altruism and dissent are partly a matter of personal convictions and conscience, but situational factors also make them more likely, including:
• Perceiving that help is needed
• Being in a situation that rewards independent thinking and discourages social loafing
• Deciding that the costs of not acting are greater than those of taking action
• Having an ally
• Becoming entrapped in a commitment to help or dissent

Us Versus Them: Group Identity

Social identities are based on a person's identification with a nation, religion, political group, or other important affiliations.

Ethnic Identity

• People often face the dilemma of balancing an **ethnic identity**, a close identification with a religious or ethnic group, and **acculturation**, identification with the dominant culture.
• Four ways a person may balance ethnic identity and acculturation:
   1. Become bicultural
   2. Choose assimilation
   3. Become an ethnic separatist
   4. Feel marginal

Ethnocentrism

Ethnocentrism, the belief that one's own ethnic group or nation is superior to all others, can create "us-them" thinking and hostile competition.

Stereotypes

Stereotypes can be efficient cognitive summaries of other groups, but they distort reality by:
1. Exaggerating differences between groups
2. Producing selective perception
3. Underestimating the differences *within* other groups

Group Conflict and Prejudice

A **prejudice** consists of a negative stereotype and a persistent, unreasonable negative feeling toward a category of people.

Origins of Prejudice

1. Psychological: prejudice wards off feelings of anxiety and doubt, simplifies complex problems, boosts self-esteem.
2. Social: prejudice bonds people to their social group and nation.
3. Economic: prejudice justifies a majority group's economic interests and legitimizes war.

Defining and Measuring Prejudice

• Prejudice is a challenge to define and measure; for example, "hostile sexism" is different from "benevolent sexism," though both legitimize gender discrimination.
• Psychologists disagree on whether racism and other prejudices are declining or have merely taken new forms.
• Some researchers are trying to measure prejudice indirectly:
— By seeing whether people are more likely to behave aggressively toward a target when they are stressed or insulted
— By observing changes in the brain
— By assessing unconscious positive or negative associations with a group, as with the Implicit Association Test (IAT); however, the IAT has critics who claim it is not capturing true prejudice

Reducing Conflict and Prejudice

1. Both sides must have equal legal status, economic standing, and power.
2. Both sides must have the legal and moral support of authorities and cultural institutions.
3. Both sides must have opportunities to work and socialize together (the contact hypothesis).
4. Both sides must work toward a common goal.

psychology in the news

Internet Addiction Growing

For Some "Internet Vampires," Lure of the Internet Is Stronger Than That of Sleep, Classes, or Meals

MANCHESTER, NH, SEPTEMBER 2, 2005. Matthew Small had a 4.0 average at Saint Anselm College—until he entered Azeroth, the virtual World of Warcraft. For seven months, he immersed himself in this world, in which his character, a warrior-healer, accomplished glorious feats. A sophomore, Mr. Small spent a minimum of six hours a day collecting armor, swords, and other cyber-gear for his character, gloating to his friends about his "accomplishments" in the game. His friends were not impressed. "They told me the game was completely stupid," he says, and that he was wasting his time, but he ignored their warnings.

Matthew Small's college work suffered. His papers, he admits, were awful. His close friends drifted away, and his grades slipped. Then, one day, in what addicts call "a moment of clarity," he realized that he had logged more than 1,000 hours playing the game and finally decided it was time to turn in his armor.

According to surveys of students across the country, "Internet dependence" and addiction are growing problems. In the 2004 National College Health Assessment, a survey of 47,000 students, 13 percent said that their time on the Internet and playing computer games had affected their grades for the worse. "We had an honors student who was spending 12 to 15 hours a day on the Internet, and essentially flunked out of school," said one psychologist at the University of Maryland. Barbara McMullen, director of e-commerce initiatives at Marist College in Poughkeepsie, New York, calls these students "Internet vampires," because they sleep all day and then stay up all night online, sending countless e-mails to their friends or playing games.

The problem is also being reported in many countries outside of North America. In China, for example, some experts put the number of Internet addicts at 2.5 million, and this year China recently opened the first official treatment clinic in Beijing. Some of its patients have reportedly had trouble distinguishing between reality and virtual worlds.

So widespread is the problem that the Internet itself now has more than 3,000 "Internet addiction" message boards and support groups. One student wrote that his time online was "seriously hurting both my schoolwork and my social life, and therefore it must stop. But I'm not sure what to do to keep myself off the net. My self-discipline isn't what it should be."

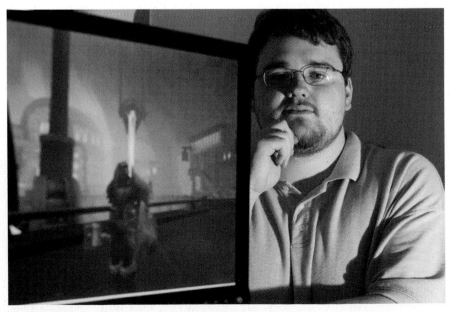

Matthew Small with the former object of his addiction.

Psychological Disorders

Do students such as

Matthew Small really have an addiction, a mental disorder comparable to alcohol or drug addiction? Or do they simply have a plain old problem that has always been familiar to students everywhere—the problem of not being able to organize their time, of wanting to procrastinate and have fun rather than study? How broadly should we define the term *addiction*? Should it include not only compulsive Internet use but also habitual shopping, eating too much chocolate, and watching TV for hours on end?

You don't have to be a psychologist to recognize the most extreme forms of abnormal behavior. When people think of "mental illness," they usually think of people with delusions, people who behave in bizarre ways, or people who commit random murders and other heartless crimes. But most psychological problems, like those of students who spend too much time on the Internet for their own good, are far less dramatic and far more common. Some people go through episodes of complete inability to function, yet get along fine between those episodes. Many people function adequately, yet suffer constant anxiety or melancholy. In this chapter, you will learn about the range of psychological

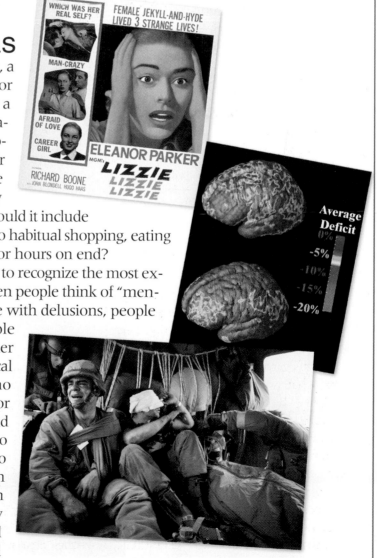

What is normal? In many places, it is normal for women and men to create scars on their bodies for decoration or symbolic meaning. In Papua New Guinea, all young men to go through an initiation rite in which small, deep cuts are made on their backs to create permanent scars that signify a crocodile's scales (left). In contrast, in most places it is abnormal to mutilate oneself for the sole purpose of inflicting injury and pain, as the patient on the right has done. But what about the decorative scars on the arm of the 23-year-old American woman (middle), who had them made by a "body artist"? She also has scars on her leg and her stomach. Is her behavior "normal" or "abnormal"?

disorders, from the mildly troubling to the severely incapacitating. But you will also learn why diagnosing mental problems is not the same as diagnosing medical problems such as diabetes or appendicitis.

One of the most common worries that people have is "Am I normal?" It is normal to fear being abnormal—especially when you are reading about psychological problems! But it is also normal to have problems. As you read, ask yourself how you would pinpoint precisely when "normal" problems shade into "abnormal" ones on the spectrum of human behavior.

WHAT'S *Ahead*

- What are three approaches to defining mental disorder?
- Why is the standard guide to the diagnosis of mental disorders controversial?
- Why were slaves who tried to escape once considered to be mentally ill?
- How reliable are "projective" tests like the popular Rorschach Inkblot Test?

Defining and Diagnosing Disorder

Many people confuse abnormal behavior—behavior that deviates from the norm—with mental disorder, but the two are not the same. A person may behave in ways that are statistically rare (collecting ceramic pigs, being a genius at math, committing murder) without having a mental disorder. Conversely, some mental disorders, such as depression and anxiety, are extremely common.

People also confuse mental disorder and insanity. In the law, the definition of *insanity* rests primarily on whether a person is aware of the consequences of his or her actions and can control his or her behavior. But *insanity* is a legal term only; a person may have a mental disorder and yet be considered sane by the court.

If frequency of the problem is not a guide, and insanity reflects only one extreme kind of mental illness, how then should we define a "mental disorder"?

Dilemmas of Definition

One problem is that the definition of a disorder depends on whether we are taking society's point of view, the view of people who are affected by the troubled individual, or the perspective of troubled individuals themselves.

1 *Mental disorder as a violation of cultural standards.* One approach to defining mental disorder emphasizes the roles and rules of the culture. Every society sets up standards for its members to follow, and those who break the most important rules are usually considered deviant or disturbed. However, many of these rules are specific to a particular time or group. For example, it is not uncommon for bereaved people to have momentary visions of a deceased relative or to "hear" the person's voice. But in most of North America, these hallucinations are considered abnormal, and people who have them often fear they might be "crazy." In contrast, the Chinese, the Hopi, and members of many other cultures regard such visions as perfectly normal.

2 *Mental disorder as emotional distress.* A second approach identifies mental disorder in terms of a person's own suffering—as from depression, anxiety, incapacitating fears, or problems with drugs. In this definition, a behavior that is unendurable or upsetting for one person, such as lack of interest in sex, may be acceptable and normal for another. But it does not cover the behavior of people who are clearly disturbed and dangerous to others yet are not troubled about their actions.

3 *Mental disorder as behavior that is self-destructive or harmful to others.* A third approach emphasizes the negative consequences of a person's behavior. Some behavior is harmful to the individual sufferer—such as the behavior of a woman who is so afraid of crowds that she cannot leave her house, a man who drinks so much that he cannot keep a job, and a student who is so anxious that he cannot take exams. In other cases, the individual may report feeling fine and deny that anything is wrong, yet behave in ways that are disruptive, dangerous, or out of touch with reality—as when a child sets fires, a compulsive gambler loses the family savings, or a woman hears voices telling her to stalk a celebrity.

In this chapter, we define **mental disorder** broadly, as any behavior or emotional state that causes a person great suffering, is self-destructive, seriously impairs the person's ability to work or get along with others, or endangers others or the community. By this definition, nearly half of all Americans will have some mental-health problem in the course of their lives, or one of their loved ones will (Kessler et al., 2005).

Dilemmas of Diagnosis

Even armed with a general definition of mental disorder, psychologists have found that classifying mental disorders into distinct categories is not an easy task. In this section we will examine why this is so.

Classifying Disorders: The DSM

The standard reference manual used to diagnose all mental disorders is the *Diagnostic and Statistical Manual of Mental Disorders* (DSM), published by the American Psychiatric Association (1994, 2000). The DSM's primary aim is *descriptive:* to provide clear diagnostic categories so that clinicians and researchers can agree on which disorders they are talking about and can then study and treat these disorders. For a list of the DSM's major categories, see Table 11.1.

The DSM lists the symptoms of each disorder and, wherever possible, gives information about the typical age of onset, predisposing factors, course of the disorder, prevalence of the disorder, sex ratio of those affected, and cultural issues that might affect diagnosis. When clinicians make a diagnosis, the DSM encourages them to take into account many factors, such as the client's personality traits, medical conditions, stresses at work and at home, and the duration and severity of the problem.

The DSM has had an extraordinary impact worldwide. Virtually all textbooks in psychiatry and psychology base their discussions of mental disorders on the DSM. Attorneys and judges often refer to the manual's list of mental disorders, even though the DSM warns that its categories "may not be wholly relevant to legal judgments." With each new edition of the manual, the number of mental disorders has grown (see Figure 11.1). The first edition, in 1952, was only 86 pages long and contained about 100 diagnoses. The DSM-IV, published in 1994 and revised slightly in 2000, is 900 pages long and contains nearly 400 diagnoses.

What is the reason for this explosion of "mental disorders"? Supporters of the new categories answer that it is important to distinguish disorders precisely in order to treat them properly. Critics point to an economic reason: Insurance companies require clinicians to assign their clients an appropriate DSM code number for the diagnosed disorder, which puts pressure on compilers of the manual to add more diagnoses so that physicians and psychologists will be compensated.

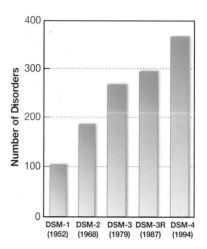

FIGURE 11.1
The Rising Number of DSM Disorders
Mental disorders in the DSM have increased nearly fourfold since the first edition (Houts, 2002).

Problems with the DSM Because of the DSM's powerful influence, critics maintain that it is important to be aware of its limitations and some inherent problems in the very effort to classify and label mental disorders:

> **Thinking Critically About Diagnosing Disorders**

1 *The danger of overdiagnosis.* "If you give a small boy a hammer," wrote Abraham Kaplan (1967), "it will turn out that everything he runs into needs pounding." Likewise, say critics, if you give mental-health professionals a diagnostic label, it will turn out that everyone they run into has the symptoms of the new disorder. Consider "attention deficit/hyperactivity disorder" (ADHD), a label given to children (and

mental disorder Any behavior or emotional state that causes a person great suffering, is self–destructive, seriously impairs the person's ability to work or get along with others, or endangers others or the community.

TABLE 11.1
Major Diagnostic Categories in the DSM-IV

Disorders usually first diagnosed in infancy, childhood, or adolescence include mental retardation, attention deficit disorders (such as hyperactivity or an inability to concentrate), and developmental problems.

Delirium, dementia, amnesia, and other cognitive disorders are those resulting from brain damage, degenerative diseases such as syphilis or Alzheimer's, toxic substances, or drugs.

Substance-related disorders are problems associated with excessive use of or withdrawal from alcohol, amphetamines, caffeine, cocaine, hallucinogens, nicotine, opiates, or other drugs.

Schizophrenia and other psychotic disorders are disorders characterized by delusions, hallucinations, and severe disturbances in thinking and emotion.

Mood disorders include major depression, bipolar disorder (manic depression), and dysthymia (chronic depressed mood).

Anxiety disorders include generalized anxiety disorder, phobias, panic attacks with or without agoraphobia, posttraumatic stress disorder, and obsessive thoughts or compulsive rituals.

Eating disorders include anorexia nervosa (self-starvation because of an irrational fear of being or becoming fat) and bulimia nervosa (episodes of binge eating and vomiting).

Dissociative disorders include dissociative amnesia (in which important events cannot be remembered after a traumatic event) and dissociative identity disorder, characterized by the presence of two or more distinct identities or personalities.

Sexual and gender identity disorders include problems of sexual (gender) identity, such as transsexualism (wanting to be the other sex), problems of sexual performance (such as premature ejaculation or lack of orgasm), and paraphilias (needing unusual or bizarre imagery or acts for sexual arousal).

Impulse control disorders involve an inability to resist an impulse to perform some act that is harmful to the individual or to others, such as pathological gambling, stealing (kleptomania), setting fires (pyromania), or having violent rages.

Personality disorders are inflexible and maladaptive patterns that cause distress to the individual or impair the ability to function; they include paranoid, narcissistic, and antisocial personality disorders.

Additional conditions that may be a focus of clinical attention include "problems in living" such as bereavement, academic difficulties, spiritual problems, and acculturation problems.

---

adults) who are impulsive, restless, and easily frustrated and who have trouble concentrating. Since ADHD was added to the DSM, it has become the fastest-growing disorder in America, where it is diagnosed at least ten times as often as it is in Europe. Critics, therefore, fear that parents, teachers, and mental-health professionals are overusing this diagnosis, especially with boys, who make up 80 to 90 percent of all ADHD cases. The critics argue that normal boyish behavior—being rambunctious, refusing to nap, being playful, not listening to teachers in school—is often being turned into an illness (Panksepp, 1998). A longitudinal study of more than a hundred 4- to 6-year-olds found that the number of children who met the criteria for ADHD declined over time. Some remained highly impul-

sive and unable to concentrate, but others, it seems, simply matured (Lahey et al., 2005).

2 *The power of diagnostic labels.* Being given a diagnosis reassures people who are seeking an explanation for their emotional symptoms or problems ("Whew! So *that's* what I've got!"). But once a person has been given a diagnosis, other people begin to see that person primarily in terms of the label; it sticks like lint. For example, when a rebellious, disobedient teenager is diagnosed as having oppositional defiant disorder, people tend to see him as a person with a permanent, official disorder; something is wrong with his personality. They therefore overlook other possible explanations of his actions: Maybe he is defiant because he has been mistreated or because his parents never listen to him. And once he is labeled, observers tend to ignore changes in his behavior and the times when he is not being defiant.

3 *The confusion of serious mental disorders with normal problems.* The DSM is not called "The Diagnostic and Statistical Manual of Mental Disorders and a Whole Bunch of Everyday Problems." Yet each edition adds more everyday problems, including "disorder of written expression" (having trouble writing clearly), "mathematics disorder" (not doing well in math), "religious or spiritual problem," and "caffeine-induced sleep disorder" (which at least is easy to cure; just switch to decaf). Some critics fear that by lumping together such ordinary difficulties with true mental illnesses, such as schizophrenia, the DSM implies that everyday problems are comparable to disorders—and equally likely to require treatment (Houts, 2002).

4 *The illusion of objectivity and universality.* Finally, some psychologists argue that the whole enterprise of the DSM is a vain attempt to impose a veneer of science on an inherently subjective process (Houts, 2002; Kutchins & Kirk, 1997; Tiefer, 2004). Many decisions about what to include as a disorder, say these critics, are based not on empirical evidence but on group consensus. The problem is that group consensus often reflects prevailing attitudes and prejudices rather than objective evidence.

It is easy to identify prejudices in *past* notions of mental problems. In the early years of the nineteenth century, a physician named Samuel Cartwright argued that many slaves were suffering from *drapetomania*, an urge to escape from slavery (Kutchins & Kirk, 1997; Landrine, 1988). (He made up the word from *drapetes*, the Latin word for "runaway slave," and *mania*, meaning "mad" or "crazy.") Thus, doctors could assure slave owners that a mental illness, not the intolerable condition of slavery, made slaves seek freedom. Today, of course, "drapetomania" seems foolish and cruel.

Over the years, psychiatrists have quite properly rejected many other "disorders" that reflected cultural prejudices and lacked empirical validation, such as lack of vaginal orgasm, childhood masturbation disorder, and homosexuality (Wakefield, 1992). But critics argue that many disorders in the DSM are just as affected by contemporary prejudices and values. Today you don't have a disorder if you want to have sex "too often" (once called, in women, "nymphomania"), but you do if you do not want to have sex often "enough" (hypoactive sexual desire disorder)

Harriet Tubman (on the left) poses with some of those she helped to escape from slavery on the "underground railroad." Slaveholders welcomed the idea that Tubman and others who insisted on their freedom had a mental disorder called "drapetomania."

(Groneman, 2000; Tiefer, 2004). Emotional problems allegedly associated with menstruation remain in the DSM, but behavioral problems associated with testosterone have never even been considered for inclusion. In short, critics maintain, many diagnoses still depend on a cultural consensus about what constitutes normal behavior, as well as what constitutes a mental disorder.

Advantages of the DSM Defenders of the DSM agree that the boundaries between "normal problems" and "mental disorder" are fuzzy and often difficult to determine (Kessler et al., 2005). They also recognize that many psychological symptoms fall along a continuum, ranging from mild to severe. However, they point out that new studies are improving empirical support for many of the DSM's categories (Beutler & Malik, 2002; Widiger & Clark, 2000). Defenders argue, further, that when the manual is used correctly and diagnoses are made with valid objective tests, the DSM improves the reliability of diagnosis (Wittchen et al., 1995). The DSM's categories help clinicians distinguish among disorders that might share certain symptoms (such as anxiety, irritability, or delusions) in order to select the most appropriate treatment.

Moreover, the DSM-IV included, for the first time, a list of *culture-bound syndromes*, disorders that are specific to particular cultural contexts. All students will surely sympathize with the West African disorder of "brain fag," mental exhaustion due to excessive studying! Other culture-bound syndromes include *amok* in Malaysia, brooding followed by a violent outburst; *shin-byung* in Korea, a syndrome of anxiety and bodily complaints accompanied by feelings of being possessed by ancestral spirits; *taijin-kyofu-sho* in Japan, an intense fear that one is offending or embarrassing others; and *ataque de nervios* throughout Latin America, an episode of uncontrollable shouting, crying, trembling, and verbal or physical aggression. The DSM acknowledges that these syndromes rarely overlap with DSM diagnostic categories yet can cause great mental suffering in the cultures where they occur. At the same time, DSM defenders argue, some disorders are universal, although they may take different forms. All over the world, from the Inuit of Alaska to the Yoruba of Nigeria, some individuals have delusions, are severely depressed, suffer panic attacks, or cannot control their behavior (Butcher, Lim, & Nezami, 1998; Kleinman, 1988).

Dilemmas of Measurement

Clinical psychologists and psychiatrists usually make a diagnosis by interviewing a patient and observing the person's behavior when he or she arrives at the office, hospital, or clinic. But many also use psychological tests to help them decide on a diagnosis. Such tests are also commonly used in schools (e.g., to determine whether a child has a learning disorder or emotional problem) and in court settings (e.g., to try to determine which parent should have custody in a divorce case).

Projective Tests **Projective tests** consist of ambiguous pictures, sentences, or stories that the test taker interprets or completes. A child or adult may be asked to draw a person, a house, or some other object, or to finish a sentence (such as "My father . . . " or "Women are . . . "). The psychodynamic assumption behind all projective tests is that the person's unconscious thoughts and feelings will be "projected" onto the test and revealed in the person's responses. (See Chapter 2 for a discussion of psychodynamic theories and their emphasis on unconscious motives and conflicts.)

projective tests
Psychological tests used to infer a person's motives, conflicts, and unconscious dynamics on the basis of the person's interpretations of ambiguous stimuli.

Rorschach Inkblot Test
A projective personality test that requires respondents to interpret abstract, symmetrical inkblots.

Thinking Critically About Projective Tests

Projective tests can help clinicians establish rapport with their clients and can encourage clients to open up about anxieties and conflicts they might be ashamed to discuss. But the evidence is overwhelming that these tests lack reliability and validity, which makes them inappropriate for their most common uses, assessing personality traits or diagnosing mental disorders (Dawes, 1994; Wood et al., 2003). They lack reliability because different clinicians often interpret the same person's scores differently, perhaps projecting their own beliefs and assumptions when they decide what a specific response means. The tests have low validity because they fail to measure what they are supposed to measure. One reason is that responses to a projective test are significantly affected by sleepiness, hunger, medication, worry, verbal ability, the clinician's instructions, the clinician's own personality (friendly and warm, or cool and remote), and other events occurring that day.

One of the most popular projectives is the **Rorschach Inkblot Test**, which was devised by Swiss psychiatrist Hermann Rorschach in 1921. It consists of ten cards with symmetrical abstract patterns, originally formed by spilling ink on paper and folding the paper in half. The test taker reports what he or she sees in the inkblots, and the clinician interprets the answers according to the symbolic meanings emphasized by psychodynamic theories. One kind of response, for instance, might be interpreted as evidence of a person's dependency.

Although the Rorschach is widely used among clinicians, efforts to confirm its reliability and validity have repeatedly failed (Wood et al., 2003). The Rorschach does not reliably diagnose depression,

What do you see in this Rorschach inkblot?

posttraumatic stress reactions, personality disorders, serious mental disorders, or evidence of sexual abuse. Claims of the Rorschach's success often come from workshops where clinicians are taught how to use the test, which is hardly an impartial way of assessing it (Wood et al., 2003).

Many psychotherapists use projective tests with young children to help them express feelings they cannot reveal verbally. But during the 1980s, some therapists began using projective methods for another purpose: to determine whether a child had been sexually abused. They claimed they could identify a child who had been abused by observing how the child played with "anatomically detailed" dolls (dolls with realistic genitals), and that is how many of them testified in hundreds of court cases (Ceci & Bruck, 1995).

Unfortunately, these therapists had not tested their beliefs by using a fundamental scientific procedure: comparison with a control group (see Chapter 1). They had not asked, "How do *nonabused* children play with these dolls?" When psychological scientists conducted controlled research to answer this question, they found that large percentages of nonabused children are also fascinated with the doll's genitals. They will poke at them, grab them, pound sticks into a female doll's vagina, and do other things that alarm adults. The crucial conclusion was that you cannot reliably diagnose sexual abuse on the basis of children's doll play (Bruck et al., 1995; Hunsley, Lee, & Wood, 2003; Koocher et al., 1995; Wood et al., 2003). You can see how someone who did not understand the problems with projective tests might end up making inferences about a child's behavior that were dangerously wrong.

Another situation in which projective tests are also used widely yet often inappropriately is in child-custody assessments. Understandably, when faced with divorcing partners who are bitterly quarreling, calling each other names, and accusing each other of being a terrible parent, the courts long for an objective way to determine which one is better suited to have custody. But when a panel of researchers impartially examined the leading psychological assessment measures, most of which are projective tests, they found that "these measures assess ill-defined constructs, and they do so poorly, leaving no scientific justification for their use in child custody evaluations" (Emery, Otto, & O'Donohue, 2005).

Objective Tests Many clinicians also use **objective tests (inventories)**. As we discussed in Chapter 2, these are standardized questionnaires that ask about the test taker's behavior and feelings. Some inventories, such as the Beck Depression Inventory, the Spielberger State-Trait Anger Inventory, and the Taylor Manifest Anxiety Scale, assess specific emotional problems. The most widely used objective test for assessing disorders, the **Minnesota Multiphasic Personality Inventory (MMPI)**, is organized into ten categories, or *scales*, covering such problems as depression, paranoia, schizophrenia, and introversion.

Inventories are generally more reliable and more valid than either projective methods or subjective clinical judgments (Dawes, 1994; Meyer et al., 2001). But inventories also have some problems. In spite of recent revisions of the MMPI, one continuing problem is that it often fails to take into account differences among cultural, regional, and socioeconomic groups. For example, Mexican, Puerto Rican, and Argentine respondents score differently from non-Hispanic Americans, on average, on the test's Masculinity–Femininity Scale—a reflection not of emotional problems but of traditional Latino attitudes toward sex roles (Cabiya et al., 2000). Also, the MMPI has a significant rate of false positives; that is, it sometimes labels a person's responses as evidence of mental disorder when no abnormality actually exists (Guthrie & Mobley, 1994). And, finally, objective tests such as the MMPI are often inappropriately used in business, industry, legal settings, and schools by persons who are not well trained in testing (or in psychology).

We turn now to a closer examination of some of the disorders described in the DSM. Of course, we cannot cover all of them in one chapter, so we have singled out several that illustrate the range of psychological problems that afflict humanity, from the common to the very rare.

For years, many therapists used anatomically detailed dolls as a projective test to determine whether a child had been sexually abused, but this practice has not been supported by empirical evidence.

objective tests (inventories) Standardized objective questionnaires requiring written responses; they typically include scales on which people are asked to rate themselves.

Minnesota Multiphasic Personality Inventory (MMPI) A widely used objective personality test.

QUICK quiz

Your mental health will be enhanced if you can answer these questions.

1. Ruthie is afraid to leave her apartment unless she is with a close friend or relative, yet she says she feels fine and angrily resists her friends' advice that she get help. What definition of mental disorder does Ruthie's behavior meet?

2. The primary purpose of the DSM is to (a) provide descriptive criteria for diagnosing mental disorders, (b) help psychologists assess normal as well as abnormal behavior, (c) describe the causes of common disorders, (d) keep the number of diagnostic categories of mental disorders to a minimum.

3. List four criticisms of the DSM.

4. What is the advantage of inventories, compared with clinical judgments and projective tests, in diagnosing mental disorders?

Answers:

1. behavior that is self-destructive   2. a   3. It can foster overdiagnosis; it overlooks the power of diagnostic labels on the perceptions of clinicians and the behavior of clients; it confuses serious mental disorders with everyday problems in living; and it falsely implies that its diagnoses apply universally and are always based on objective evidence. 4. Inventories have better reliability and validity.

WHAT'S *Ahead*

- What is the difference between ordinary anxiety and an anxiety disorder?

- Why is the most disabling of all phobias known as the "fear of fear"?

- When is checking the stove before leaving home a sign of caution, and when does it signal a disorder?

Anxiety Disorders

Anyone who is waiting for important news, or living in a situation that is unpredictable and uncontrollable, quite sensibly feels anxiety, a general state of apprehension or psychological tension. And anyone who is in a dangerous and unfamiliar situation, such as making a first parachute jump or facing an annoyed hippopotamus, quite sensibly feels flat-out fear. In the short run, these emotions are adaptive because they energize us to cope with danger. They ensure that we don't make that first jump without knowing how to operate the parachute and that we get away from that hippo as fast as we can.

But sometimes fear and anxiety become detached from any actual danger, or these feelings continue even when danger and uncertainty are past. The result may be chronic anxiety, marked by long-lasting feelings of apprehension and doom; *panic attacks*, short-lived but intense feelings of spontaneous anxiety; *phobias*, excessive fears of specific things or situations; or *obsessive-compulsive disorder*, in which repeated thoughts and rituals are used to ward off anxious feelings.

generalized anxiety disorder A continuous state of anxiety marked by feelings of worry and dread, apprehension, difficulties in concentration, and signs of motor tension.

Anxiety and Panic

The chief characteristic of **generalized anxiety disorder** is continuous, uncontrollable anxiety—a feeling of foreboding and dread—that occurs on a majority of days during a six-month period and that is not brought on by physical causes such as disease, drugs, or drinking too much coffee. Symptoms include restlessness or feeling keyed up, difficulty concentrating, jitteriness, irritability, disturbed sleep, and unwanted, intrusive worries.

Some people suffer from generalized anxiety disorder without having lived through any specific anxiety-producing event. They may have a physiological tendency to experience anxiety symptoms—sweaty palms, a racing heart, shortness of breath—when they are in unfamiliar, challenging, or uncontrollable situations. Other chronically anxious people may have a history, starting in childhood, of being unable to control or predict their environments (Barlow, 2000; Mineka & Zinbarg, 2006). Whatever the origins of their anxiety, people with generalized anxiety disorder have mental habits that foster their worries and keep their anxiety bubbling along; they perceive everything as an opportunity for disaster (Riskind et al., 2000).

Posttraumatic Stress Disorder Stress symptoms, including insomnia, agitation, and jumpiness, are entirely normal in the immediate aftermath of any crisis or trauma, such as war, rape, torture, natural disasters, sudden bereavement, or terrorist attacks. But if the symptoms persist for one month or longer and begin to impair a person's functioning, the sufferer may

This grief-stricken soldier has just learned that the body bag on the flight with him contains the remains of a close friend who was killed in action. Understandably, soldiers like him suffer posttraumatic stress symptoms. But why do most people eventually recover, whereas others have PTSD for many years?

have **posttraumatic stress disorder (PTSD)**. Typical symptoms of PTSD include reliving the trauma in recurrent, intrusive thoughts; a sense of detachment from others and a loss of interest in familiar activities; and increased physiological arousal, reflected in insomnia, irritability, and impaired concentration.

Most people who live through a traumatic experience eventually recover. One major national survey of Americans found that about 60 percent had experienced a traumatic event, but only 8 percent of the men and 20 percent of the women developed PTSD (Kessler et al., 1995). Some experts predicted an epidemic of PTSD after 9/11, but it never materialized (Bonanno et al., 2006). Why, then, if most people recover from a trauma, do some have PTSD symptoms for years? One answer may involve a genetic predisposition. Behavioral-genetic studies of twins in the general population as well as among combat veterans have found that PTSD symptoms have a significantly heritable component (Stein et al., 2002).

Another answer is that people who develop long-lasting PTSD have often had a prior family history of psychological problems and other traumatic experiences, with poor emotional adjustment to them (Ozer et al., 2003). One reason for this poor adjustment is that they are more likely to have self-defeating, anxiety-producing ways of thinking in general—for example, they tend to "catastrophize"

about every little thing that goes wrong, to believe they are inadequate, and to feel that no one can be trusted (Bryant & Guthrie, 2005). Many seem to lack the psychological and neurological resources to deal with their difficult experiences. They are more likely than more resilient people to have the personality trait of neuroticism (negative emotionality, described in Chapter 2) and to have lower-than-average intelligence, which may impair their ability to cope cognitively with trauma (McNally, 2003).

Interestingly, in PTSD sufferers, the hippocampus is apt to be smaller than average (McNally, 2003). The hippocampus is crucially involved in autobiographical memory. An abnormally small one may figure in the difficulty of some trauma survivors to react to their memories as events from their past, which may be why they keep reliving them in the present.

Originally, researchers thought that severe trauma caused neuron damage or loss of cells in the hippocampus, producing PTSD symptoms—impaired memory, recurrent fears, and so forth. But this hypothesis has been refuted. One team used MRIs to measure hippocampal size in identical twins, only one of whom in each pair had been in combat in Vietnam. If trauma affects the hippocampus, then the size of the hippocampus should have been different in the veterans who developed PTSD and their identical twins. But this was not what the researchers found. Two things were necessary for a vet to develop chronic PTSD: serving in combat *and* having a smaller hippocampus than normal (Gilbertson et al., 2002). Twins who had the smaller hippocampus but no military service did not develop PTSD, and neither did the twins who *did* experience combat but who had normal-sized hippocampi.

Many cases of PTSD, therefore, seem to be a result of impaired neurological and cognitive functioning that existed *before* the trauma took place, triggered by the eventual traumatic experience (McNally, 2003).

Panic Disorder   Another kind of anxiety disorder is **panic disorder**, in which a person has recurring attacks of intense fear or panic, often with feelings of impending doom or death. These panic attacks may last from a few minutes to (more rarely) several hours. Symptoms include trembling and shaking, dizziness, chest pain or discomfort, rapid heart rate, feelings of unreality, hot and cold flashes, sweating, and, as a result of all these physical reactions, a fear of dying, going crazy, or losing control. Many sufferers fear they are having a heart attack.

posttraumatic stress disorder (PTSD) An anxiety disorder in which a person who has experienced a traumatic or life-threatening event has symptoms such as psychic numbing, reliving of the trauma, and increased physiological arousal.

panic disorder An anxiety disorder in which a person experiences recurring panic attacks, periods of intense fear, and feelings of impending doom or death, accompanied by physiological symptoms such as rapid heart rate and dizziness.

Although panic attacks seem to occur out of nowhere, they in fact usually occur in the aftermath of stress, prolonged emotion, specific worries, or frightening experiences (McNally, 1998). For example, a friend of ours was on a plane that was a target of a bomb threat while airborne at 33,000 feet. He coped beautifully at the time, but two weeks later, seemingly out of nowhere, he had a panic attack.

Such delayed attacks after life-threatening scares are common. The essential difference between people who develop panic disorder and those who do not lies in *how they interpret their bodily reactions* (Barlow, 2000). Healthy people who have occasional panic attacks see them correctly as a result of a passing crisis or period of stress, comparable to another person's migraines. But people who develop panic disorder regard the attack as a sign of illness or impending death, and they begin to live their lives in restrictive ways, trying to avoid future attacks. It is this self-imposed restriction that makes this disorder so difficult for its sufferers (and their families).

People who have panic disorder are found throughout the world, but culture influences the particular symptoms they experience (Barlow, Chorpita, & Turovsky, 1996). Feelings of choking or being smothered, numbness, and fear of dying are most common in Latin America and southern Europe; fear of public places is most common in northern Europe and America; and a fear of going crazy is more common in the Americas than in Europe. In Greenland, some fishermen suffer from "kayak-angst"—a sudden attack of dizziness and fear that occurs while they are fishing in small, one-person kayaks (Amering & Katschnig, 1990).

Fears and Phobias

Are you afraid of bugs, snakes, or dogs? Are you vaguely uncomfortable with them or so afraid that you can't stand to be around one? A **phobia** is an exaggerated fear of a specific situation, activity, or thing. Some common phobias—such as fear of snakes, insects, heights (acrophobia), or enclosed spaces (claustrophobia)—may have evolved to be easily acquired in human beings because these fears reflected real dangers for the species (Öhman & Mineka, 2003). Other phobias, such as a fear of cats or the color purple (porphyrophobia), may be acquired through classical conditioning, as we saw in Chapter 9, or through observational learning—watching a frightening event that is happening to someone else (Mineka & Zinbarg, 2006). Still other phobias, such as fear of dirt and germs (mysophobia) or of the number 13 (triskaidekaphobia), may reflect personality differences or cultural traditions. Whatever its source,

THE FAR SIDE®   BY GARY LARSON

© 1985 FarWorks, Inc. All Rights Reserved/Dist. by Creators Syndicate

The Far Side® by Gary Larson © 1985 FarWorks, Inc. All Rights Reserved. The Far Side® and the Larson® signature are registered trademarks of FarWorks, Inc. Used with permission.

Luposlipaphobia: The fear of being pursued by timber wolves around a kitchen table while wearing socks on a newly waxed floor.

a phobia is truly frightening and often incapacitating for its sufferer. It is not just a tendency to say "ugh" at tarantulas or skip the snake display at the zoo.

People who have a *social phobia* become extremely anxious in situations in which they will be observed by others—eating in a restaurant, speaking in front of a group or crowd, having to perform for others. They worry that they will do or say something that will be excruciatingly humiliating or embarrassing. Again, these phobias are more severe forms of the occasional shyness and social anxiety that everyone experiences. For people with a social phobia, the mere thought of being in a new situation with unfamiliar people is scary enough to cause sweating, trembling, nausea, and an overwhelming feeling of inadequacy. So they don't go, increasing their isolation and imagined fears.

By far the most disabling fear disorder is **agoraphobia**. In ancient Greece, the *agora* was the social, political, business, and religious center of town, the public meeting place away from home. The fundamental fear in agoraphobia is of being trapped in a crowded public place, where escape might be difficult or where help might be unavailable if the person has a panic attack. Individuals with agoraphobia report many specific fears—of being in a crowded movie theater, driving in traffic or tunnels, or going to parties—but the underlying

phobia An exaggerated, unrealistic fear of a specific situation, activity, or object.

agoraphobia A set of phobias, often set off by a panic attack, involving the basic fear of being away from a safe place or person.

What Scares You?

Everyone fears something. Stop for a moment to think about what you fear most. Heights? Snakes? Speaking in public? Ask yourself these questions: (1) How long have you feared this thing or situation? (2) How would you respond if you could not avoid this thing or situation? (3) How much would you be willing to rearrange your life to avoid this feared thing or situation? After considering these questions, would you regard your fear as a full-blown phobia? What are your criteria for deciding?

---

fear is of being away from a safe place, usually home, or a safe person, usually a parent or spouse.

Agoraphobia typically begins with a panic attack that seems to have no cause (McNally, 1998). The attack is so unexpected and scary that the agoraphobic-to-be begins to avoid situations that he or she thinks may provoke another one. A woman we know had a panic attack while driving on a freeway. This was a perfectly normal posttraumatic response to the suicide of her husband a few weeks earlier. But thereafter she avoided freeways—as if the freeway, and not the suicide, had caused the attack. Because so many of the actions associated with agoraphobia arise as a mistaken effort to avoid a panic attack, psychologists regard agoraphobia as a "fear of fear" rather than simply a fear of places.

Obsessions and Compulsions

Obsessive-compulsive disorder (OCD) is characterized by recurrent, persistent, unwished-for thoughts or images (*obsessions*) or by repetitive, ritualized, stereotyped behaviors that the person feels must be carried out to avoid disaster (*compulsions*). Of course, many people have trivial compulsions and practice superstitious rituals. Baseball players are famous for them—one won't change his socks and another will eat chicken every day of the week while they are on a hitting streak. Obsessions and compulsions become a disorder when they become uncontrollable and interfere with a person's life.

People who have obsessive thoughts often find them frightening or repugnant—thoughts of killing a child, of becoming contaminated by a handshake, or of having unknowingly hurt someone in a traffic accident. Obsessive thoughts take many forms, but they are alike in reflecting impaired ways of reasoning and processing information.

People who suffer from compulsions likewise feel they have no control over them. The most common compulsions are hand washing, counting, touching, and checking. A woman *must* check the furnace, lights,

locks, oven, and fireplace three times before she can sleep; or a man *must* wash his hands and face precisely eight times before he leaves the house. Most sufferers do not enjoy such rituals and realize that the behavior is senseless. But if they try to forgo the ritual, they feel mounting anxiety that is relieved only by giving in to it. For one young man with OCD, stairs became a treadmill he could not get off. "At first I'd walk up and down the stairs only three or four times," he recalled. "Later I had to run up and down 63 times in 45 minutes. If I failed, I had to start all over again from the beginning" (quoted in King, 1989).

In many people with OCD, the prefrontal cortex is depleted of serotonin, which creates a kind of cognitive rigidity—an inability to let go of certain thoughts (Clarke et al., 2004). In addition, several parts of the brain are hyperactive (Schwartz et al., 1996). Normally, once danger is past or a person realizes that there is no cause for fear, the brain's alarm signal turns off. In people with OCD, however, false alarms keep clanging and the emotional networks

obsessive-compulsive disorder (OCD) An anxiety disorder in which a person feels trapped in persistent thoughts (*obsessions*) and repetitive, ritualized behaviors (*compulsions*) designed to reduce anxiety.

In the apartment of a woman with OCD, nearly every inch is covered with stuff—junk mail, wrapping paper, broken electric toothbrushes, empty tissue boxes, and clothes. The woman becomes extremely anxious at even the thought of throwing anything out. She keeps only one spot uncluttered: the half of the bed she sleeps on.

keep sending out mistaken "fear!" messages. The sufferer feels in a constant state of danger and tries repeatedly to reduce the resulting anxiety.

New biological research suggests that OCD is not a single, unified disorder (Taylor, McKay, & Abramowitz, 2005). One "subtype" of OCD afflicts pathological hoarders who fill their homes with newspapers, bags of old clothing, used tissue boxes— all kinds of junk. They cannot let go because they are tormented by fears of throwing out something they will need later. A PET-scan study that compared obsessive hoarders with other people with obsessive symptoms found that hoarders had less activity in parts of the brain involved in decision making, problem solving, spatial orientation, and memory (Saxena et al., 2004). Perhaps these deficits explain why hoarders keep things (their inability to decide what to throw away creates a constant struggle) and why they often keep their papers and junk in the living room, kitchen, or even on the bed. They have trouble remembering where things are and thus feel the need to have them in sight.

QUICK quiz

We hope you don't feel anxious about matching each term on the left with its description on the right.

1. social phobia
2. generalized anxiety disorder
3. posttraumatic stress disorder
4. agoraphobia
5. compulsion
6. obsession

a. need to perform a ritual
b. fear of fear; fear of being trapped with no way of escape
c. continuing sense of doom and worry
d. repeated, unwanted thoughts
e. fear of meeting new people
f. anxiety following a severe shock

Answers:

1.e 2.c 3.f 4.b 5.a 6.d

WHAT'S *Ahead*

• How can you tell whether you have major depression or just the blues?

• What are the "poles" in bipolar disorder?

• How do some people think themselves into depression?

Mood Disorders

In the DSM, *mood disorders* include disturbances in mood ranging from extreme depression to extreme mania. Of course, most people feel sad from time to time, and also joyful. And most people, at some time in their lives, will know the wild grief that accompanies tragedy and bereavement. These normal feelings, however, are a far cry from the clinical disorders described by the DSM.

Depression

Anxiety, painful though it is, is at least a sign that a person is engaged in the future: It reflects the belief that something bad will happen. But depressed people feel burned out about the future: They are sure that nothing good will ever happen. Some people go through life with constant but low-grade unhappiness; they can do what they need to but nearly always report their mood as sad or "down in the dumps." Others suffer from **major depression**, a serious mood disorder that involves emotional, behavioral, cognitive, and physical changes severe enough to disrupt a person's ordinary functioning. The writer William Styron, who fought and recovered from major depression, used the beginning of Dante's classic poem *The Divine Comedy* to convey his suffering:

> *In the middle of the journey of our life*
> *I found myself in a dark wood.*
> *For I had lost the right path.*

"For those who have dwelt in depression's dark wood," wrote Styron in *Darkness Visible*, "and known its inexplicable agony, the return from the abyss is not unlike the ascent of the poet, trudging upward and upward out of hell's black depths and at last emerging into what he saw as 'the shining world.'"

People with major depression feel despairing and hopeless. They may think often of death or sui-

major depression A mood disorder involving disturbances in emotion (excessive sadness), behavior (loss of interest in one's usual activities), cognition (thoughts of hopelessness), and body function (fatigue and loss of appetite).

cide. They lose interest or pleasure in their usual activities. They feel unable to get up and do things; it takes an enormous effort even to get dressed. Their thinking patterns feed their bleak moods. They exaggerate minor failings, ignore or discount positive events, and interpret any little thing that goes wrong as evidence that nothing will ever go right. Emotionally healthy people who are sad or grieving do not see themselves as completely worthless and unlovable. But depressed people interpret losses as signs of personal failure and conclude that they will never be happy again.

Depression is accompanied by physical changes as well. The depressed person may overeat or stop eating, have difficulty falling asleep or sleeping through the night, have trouble concentrating, and feel tired all the time. Some sufferers have other physical reactions, such as headaches or inexplicable pain.

Major depression occurs at least twice as often among women as among men, all over the world. However, because women are more likely to talk

Even people who are rich, successful, and adored by millions can suffer from major depression. The suicide of Nirvana's lead singer, Kurt Cobain, shocked and saddened his many fans.

about their feelings than men and more likely to seek help, depression in males may be underdiagnosed. Men who are depressed often try to mask the feeling by withdrawing, drinking heavily or abusing other drugs, or behaving violently (Canetto, 1992; Kessler et al., 1995). As one depression researcher put it, "Women think and men drink."

Bipolar Disorder

At the opposite pole from depression is *mania*, an abnormally high state of exhilaration. You might think it's impossible to feel too good, but mania is not the normal joy of being in love or winning the Pulitzer Prize. Instead of feeling fatigued and listless, the manic person is excessively "wired." Instead of feeling hopeless and powerless, the person feels powerful and is full of plans—but these plans are usually based on delusional ideas, as in thinking that he or she has solved the world's problems. People in a state of mania often get into terrible trouble, going on extravagant spending sprees, making impulsive and bad decisions, or having risky sexual adventures.

When people experience at least one episode of mania alternating with episodes of depression, they are said to have **bipolar disorder** (formerly called *manic-depressive disorder*). This is a rarer problem than depression and distinctly different. Although more women than men suffer from depression, bipolar disorder occurs equally in both sexes. The great humorist Mark Twain had bipolar disorder, which he described as "periodical and sudden changes of mood . . . from deep melancholy to half-insane tempests and cyclones." Other writers, artists, musicians, and scientists have suffered from this disorder, (Jamison, 1992). During the highs, many of these artists create their best work, but the price of the lows is disastrous relationships, bankruptcy, and sometimes suicide.

Theories of Depression

Psychologists have investigated four contributing factors to major depression: genetic factors, life experiences, problems with close attachments, and cognitive habits. Few researchers think that any one of these factors alone produces chronic depression. Most researchers now emphasize a **vulnerability-stress model** of mental disorder, in which a person's vulnerabilities (in genetic predispositions, personality traits, or habits of thinking) *interact* with stressful events (such as sexual victimization, violence, or loss of a close relationship) to produce any given case (Hankin & Abramson,

bipolar disorder A mood disorder in which episodes of both depression and mania (excessive euphoria) occur.

vulnerability-stress models Approaches that emphasize how individual vulnerabilities (e.g., in genes or personality traits) interact with external stresses or circumstances to produce mental disorders.

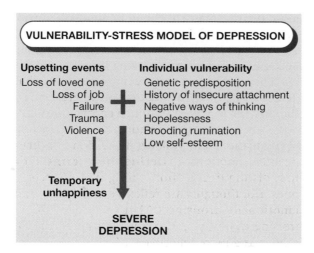

2001). Let's consider the evidence for each contributing factor in depression:

1 *Genetic factors.* Studies of adopted children and twins support the notion that major depression is a moderately heritable disorder (Bierut et al., 1999; Kendler et al., 1993). Psychologists are hunting for the genes that might be involved, although it is unlikely that a single gene directly or inevitably "causes" severe depression. As in the case of posttraumatic stress disorder, a genetic predisposition must interact with stressful events to create the disorder.

Psychologists have recently identified one gene (called 5-HTT) that comes in two forms: a long form that apparently helps protect people from depression, and a short form that makes them more vulnerable to it (Caspi et al., 2003). In a study of 847 New Zealanders who were followed from birth to age 26, the researchers found that 43 percent of those who possessed two copies of the short form of this gene (one from each parent) became severely depressed in the aftermath of major stress (such as the loss of a job, disabling injuries, a death in the family, or abuse suffered in childhood). Yet only 17 percent of those with two copies of the long form of this gene became depressed, *even when they suffered the same stresses.* And people who inherited one long form of the gene from one parent and a short form from the other fell in between in their susceptibility to depression (33 percent).

Genes may exert their effects on depression by affecting levels of serotonin and other neurotransmitters in the brain. Genes may also affect production of the stress hormone cortisol, which, at high levels, can damage cells in the hippocampus and amygdala (Sapolsky, 2000; Sheline, 2000). In de-

pressed patients, the system that regulates reactions to stress is in overdrive; it doesn't shut down when it should, and it keeps overproducing cortisol (Plotsky, Owens, & Nemeroff, 1998).

Nonetheless, genes cannot account for all cases of depression; even among the New Zealanders with the greatest genetic vulnerability, more than half did not become depressed. Nor do genes seem to account for the sex difference in depression rates. In the New Zealand study, women were no more likely than men to have the short form of the 5-HTT gene.

2 *Life experiences and circumstances.* One powerful experience that often generates depression is violence. Inner-city adolescents of both sexes who are exposed to high rates of violence report higher levels of depression and more attempts to commit suicide than those who are not subjected to constant violence in their lives or communities (Mazza & Reynolds, 1999). Women who suffer from domestic violence are also more likely to become depressed and anxious (Ehrensaft, Moffitt, & Caspi, 2006). In addition, the conditions of people's lives—the roles they occupy, their status, their satisfactions with work and family—can affect their likelihood of becoming depressed. Men are more likely than women to be both married and working full time, a combination of roles that is strongly associated with mental health and lower rates of depression (Brown, 1993), and women are more likely to live in poverty, endure discrimination, and be sexually abused, all of which increase the likelihood of depression (Belle & Doucet, 2003; Weiss, Longhurst, & Mazure, 1999).

3 *Losses of important relationships.* A third line of investigation emphasizes the loss of important relationships in setting off depression in vulnerable individuals. Many depressed people have a history of separations and losses, both past and present; insecure attachments; and rejection by parents or peers (Nolan, Flynn, & Garber, 2003; Weissman, Markowitz, & Klerman, 2000).

4 *Cognitive habits.* Finally, depression involves specific, negative ways of thinking about one's situation (Beck, 2005). Typically, depressed people believe that their situation is *permanent* ("Nothing good will ever happen to me") and *uncontrollable* ("I'm depressed because I'm ugly and horrible and I can't do anything about it"). Expecting nothing to get better, they do nothing to improve their lives and therefore remain unhappy. They feel hopeless and pessimistic, believing that they are powerless to change the future (Abramson, Metalsky, & Alloy, 1989; Seligman, 1991).

One of the strongest bad cognitive habits associated with depression is *rumination*—brooding about everything that is wrong in your life, sitting alone thinking about how unmotivated you feel, and persuading yourself that no one loves you or ever will. People with ruminating cognitive styles that foster hopelessness are at greater risk of developing full-blown major depression than are people who are able to distract themselves, look outward, and seek solutions (Chorpita & Barlow, 1998). Beginning in adolescence, women are more likely than men to develop a ruminating, introspective style, rehearsing the reasons for their unhappiness. This tendency contributes both to longer-lasting depressions in women and to the sex difference in reported rates (Nolen-Hoeksema, 2002, 2004).

CLOSE-UP on Research

Rumination Versus Reflection

The findings about rumination are pretty interesting, because just about all of us know what it feels like to think that everything is hopeless, to brood over hurt feelings, to rehearse real and imagined insults ("who does he think he is, anyway?"), and to wallow in our anxieties ("I'm never going to do well in this course—I can't possibly keep up"). When we think of examples like these, we can see why rumination might keep us stuck in an anxious, angry, or gloomy frame of mind.

Three psychological scientists—Ethan Kross, Ozlem Ayduk, and Walter Mischel (2005)—decided to **ask questions** about this common mental habit, such as "How does rumination differ from thinking about a problem constructively?" and "How can we face our normal, negative emotions without becoming overwhelmed by them?" They **examined the widespread assumption** that often it is necessary to confront anxiety, anger, and depression in order to learn to

regulate and manage them. When, they wondered, is it a good idea to think about what's wrong in your life, and when do such thoughts become self-defeating?

The researchers did an experiment that demonstrated why we should **not oversimplify** the answer to this question. Perhaps, they hypothesized, it's not rumination alone, but a *kind* of rumination, that prolongs depression and other negative emotions. To **define their terms**, they first distinguished "hot" thoughts from "cool" ones. Hot thoughts are reflexive, automatic, and emotionally arousing ("That rat! How dare he treat me that way!"). Cool thoughts are distanced, calmer, and more reflective ("It's very odd for him to be acting in that rat-like way. I wonder what's going on with him"). They next distinguished "self-immersed" thinking from taking a "self-distancing" perspective. When you are self-immersed, you can't think beyond your own immediate feelings or what is happening to *you*. When you distance yourself, you can see yourself as another person might, more dispassionately, because your ego isn't as involved.

The investigators asked 155 students to think about an experience in which they felt overwhelming anger and hostility. Half of the students were instructed to recall this experience in a self-immersed way ("relive the situation as if it were happening to you all over again") and the other half in a self-distancing way ("take a few steps back . . . watch the conflict unfold as if it were happening all over again to the distant you"). Each group was split in half again, with some asked to focus on *what* they were feeling and the others to focus on *why* they were feeling it. As you can see in the figure, the students who both distanced themselves from the experience *and* tried to explain the reasons for it (the "whys") felt less angry and upset overall than did any of the other groups.

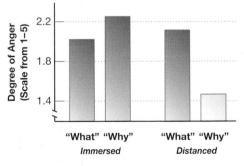

The researchers did not examine the particular kind of rumination that is involved in depression, and so we will have to **tolerate uncertainty** until the results are replicated to see if they will apply to that emotion, too. If they do, we may learn that one reason that rumination prolongs depression is that it tends to be hot and self-focused. Learning to take a cooler perspective, on our feelings and on our own behavior, can help us break out of negative emotions instead of feeding them and keeping them alive. This strategy is, in fact, the basis of cognitive therapy, which we will discuss in the next chapter.

The factors we have described—genetic, situational, and cognitive—combine in different ways to produce any given case of depression. That is why the same precipitating event can affect two people entirely differently: why one is able to roll with the punches of life and another is knocked flat.

QUICK quiz

Don't let another quiz make you vulnerable to depression!

1. Biological researchers find that depressed people have unusually high levels of the stress hormone _____.

2. Depressed people tend to believe that the reasons for their unhappiness are (a) controllable, (b) temporary, (c) out of their hands, (d) caused by the situation.

3. A news headline announces that a gene has been identified as the cause of depression. Does this mean that everyone with the gene will become depressed? How should critical thinkers interpret this research?

Answers:

1. cortisol 2. c 3. No, it means that people with the gene are *more likely* to become depressed if they also undergo severely stressful experiences. Critical thinkers would also want to make sure the research is replicated, and they would realize that not all kinds of depression might be influenced by genetics.

WHAT'S *Ahead*

- When does being self-centered become a disorder?
- What do a charming but heartless tycoon and a remorseless killer have in common?
- Why are some people seemingly incapable of feeling guilt and shame?

Personality Disorders

Personality disorders involve unchanging, maladaptive traits that cause great distress or an inability to get along with others. The DSM-IV describes such a disorder as "an enduring pattern of inner experience and behavior that deviates markedly from the expectations of the individual's culture [and] is pervasive and inflexible." Personality disorders are not caused by medical conditions, stress, or situations that temporarily induce a person to behave in ways that are out of character.

Problem Personalities

Personality disorders come in many varieties. One, **paranoid personality disorder**, involves pervasive, unfounded suspiciousness and mistrust of other people, irrational jealousy, secretiveness, and doubt about the loyalty of others. People with paranoid personalities have delusions of being persecuted by everyone from their closest relatives to government agencies, and their beliefs are immune to disconfirming evidence.

Narcissistic personality disorder involves an exaggerated sense of self-importance and self-absorption. The word *narcissism* gets its name from the Greek myth of Narcissus, a beautiful young man who fell in love with his own image. Narcissistic individuals are preoccupied with fantasies of their own importance, power, and brilliance. They demand constant attention and admiration and feel

Narcissus fell in love with his own image, and now he has a personality disorder named after him—just what a narcissist would expect!

personality disorders Rigid personality patterns that cause personal distress or an inability to get along with others.

paranoid personality disorder A disorder characterized by unreasonable, excessive suspiciousness and mistrust, and irrational feelings of being persecuted by others.

narcissistic personality disorder A disorder characterized by an exaggerated sense of self-importance and self-absorption.

entitled to special favors, without, however, being willing to reciprocate.

Given this description, do you know a narcissist or two? Of course you do—and that is the problem. It is hard to know where value judgments end (say, about someone's selfishness) and a clear disorder begins (Maddux & Mundell, 1997). Cultures differ too in how they draw the line. American society often encourages people to pursue dreams of unlimited success, physical beauty, and ideal love, but such dreams might be considered signs of serious disturbance in a more group-oriented society.

Criminals and Psychopaths

Throughout history, people have been fascinated and horrified by the "bad seeds" among them—people who, even as children, are ready to break the rules and seem unable to be socialized. Societies have also recognized and feared the few members in their midst who lack all human connection to anyone else, people who can cheat, con, and kill without flinching.

In 1976, Hervey Cleckley popularized and standardized the term *psychopath* to describe a person who lacks all conscience. A key characteristic of **psychopathy**, said Cleckley, is an inability to feel normal emotions. Psychopaths are incapable not only of remorse but also of fear of punishment and of shame, guilt, and empathy for the misery they cause others. Because they lack emotional connections to others, they often behave cruelly and irresponsibly—usually more for the thrill than for personal gain.

If caught in a lie or a crime, psychopaths may seem sincerely sorry and promise to make amends, but it is all an act. They can be utterly charming, but they use their charm to manipulate and deceive others (Cleckley, 1976; Hare, Hart, & Harpur, 1991). Some psychopaths are violent and sadistic, able to kill a pet, a child, or a random adult without a twinge of regret, but others direct their energies into con games or career advancement, abusing other people emotionally or economically rather than physically (Robins, Tipp, & Przybeck, 1991). A leading researcher in this field, Robert Hare, calls corporate psychopaths "snakes in suits."

In the 1990s, the clinicians who were revising the DSM decided to replace the term *psychopathy* with **antisocial personality disorder (APD)**, which applies to people who show "a pervasive pattern of disregard for, and violation of, the rights of others." People with APD repeatedly break the law; they are impulsive and seek quick thrills; they show reckless disregard for their own safety or that of others; they often get into physical fights or assault others; and they are irresponsible, failing to hold jobs or meet obligations (Widiger et al., 1996). Crucially for the diagnosis, they have had a history of these behavioral problems since childhood; they aren't just teenage delinquents who have been hanging out with a bad peer group. In people with APD, as one researcher found, rule breaking and irresponsibility start in early childhood and then take different forms at different ages: "biting and hitting at age 4, shoplifting and truancy at age 10, selling drugs and stealing cars at age 16, robbery and rape at age 22, and fraud and child abuse at age 30" (Moffitt, 1993).

The DSM made the change in labeling to emphasize the *behavioral* signs of antisocial personality disorder. But to many clinicians, the defining essence of psychopaths is their heartlessness and conniving charm. People who commit violent crimes may be antisocial, reckless, and irresponsible, these clinicians point out, yet differ greatly in their motivations for behaving this way. People with APD also vary widely in their capacity for empathy, remorse, guilt, anxiety, or loyalty (Hare, Hart, & Harpur, 1991). Thus, not all people with APD are psychopaths. Conversely, as we just noted, not all psychopaths are antisocial and aggressive in the typical ways that people with APD are. However, sometimes the two disorders converge, as in the case of sadistic or "cold-blooded" killers.

Causes of APD Something certainly seems to be amiss in the emotional wiring of psychopaths and people with APD—the wiring that allows all primates to feel connected to others of their kind. When that wiring goes awry, even some chimpanzees behave in ways that are comparable to the actions of human psychopaths! They, too, deceive and manipulate others to get their way and are unmoved by the suffering of others of their kind (Lilienfeld et al., 1999).

Researchers have identified a number of factors involved in these disorders:

1 *Abnormalities in the central nervous system.* The inability of psychopaths and most people with APD to feel emotional arousal—empathy, guilt, fear of punishment, and anxiety under stress—suggests some aberration in the central nervous system (Hare, 1965, 1996; Lykken, 1995; Raine et al., 2000). Indeed, psychopaths do not respond physiologically to the threat of punishment the way other people do; this may be why they can behave fearlessly in situations that would scare others to death. Normally, when a person is anticipating danger, pain, or punishment, the electrical conductance of the skin changes, a classically conditioned response that indicates anxiety or fear. But

antisocial personality disorder (APD) A disorder characterized by antisocial behavior such as lying, stealing, manipulating others, and sometimes violence; and a lack of guilt, shame, and empathy.

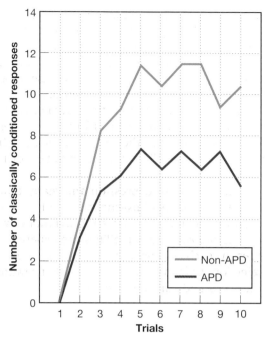

FIGURE 11.2
Emotions and Antisocial Personality Disorder
In several experiments, people with antisocial personality disorder (APD) were less likely than others to develop classically conditioned responses to anticipated danger, pain, or shock—responses that indicate normal anxiety (Hare, 1965). This deficit may be related to the ability of people with APD to act without remorse or regard for the consequences.

psychopaths are slow to develop such responses, which suggests that they are unable to feel the anxiety necessary for learning that their actions will have unpleasant consequences (see Figure 11.2). Their lack of empathy for others who are suffering also seems to have a physiological basis. When psy-

chopaths are shown pictures of people crying and in distress, their skin conductance barely shifts, in contrast to that of nonpsychopaths, which shoots up (Blair et al., 1997).

This emotional flatness may help distinguish psychopaths from other aggressive people with antisocial personality disorder (Lorber, 2004). For example, antisocial, violent adolescents who have normal levels of physiological arousal in response to danger and threat, and whose responses can be classically conditioned, do not usually get involved in a life of crime as adults, suggesting that they outgrow the disorder with maturity (Raine & Liu, 1998). But those who are likely to become career criminals have the same unusually low levels of physiological arousal that psychopaths do.

2 Impaired frontal-lobe functioning. One trait shared by psychopaths and people with APD is impulsivity, an inability to control responses to frustration and provocation (Luengo et al., 1994; Raine, 1996). Such an inability, which often leads to breaking rules and laws, may have a biological basis. Many psychopaths have abnormalities in the prefrontal cortex, which, as we saw in Chapter 4, is responsible for planning and impulse control. They don't do as well as healthy individuals on neuropsychological tests of frontal-lobe functioning, and they have less gray matter in the frontal lobes than other people do (Dinn & Harris, 2000). One PET-scan study found that predatory murderers had less brain activity in the frontal lobe than did men who murdered in the heat of passion or controls who had not murdered anybody (Raine et al., 1998).

One reason for these frontal-lobe abnormalities may be brain damage resulting from physical

Some people with APD are psychopathic. Gary L. Ridgway (left), the deadliest convicted serial killer in U.S. history, strangled 48 women, placing their bodies in clusters around the country. He did this because, he said coolly, he wanted to keep track of them. "I killed so many women, I have a hard time keeping them straight," he told the court. But other people with APD use charm and elaborate scams to deceive and defraud. Babyfaced Christopher Rocancourt (right, wearing tie), shown with actor Mickey Rourke, conned celebrities and others into giving him money and doing him favors (some illegal) by adopting countless false identities, such as movie producer, cat burglar, diamond smuggler, or financier. After he was finally arrested on charges of passport counterfeiting, he persuaded authorities to free him on bond—and promptly jumped bail.

neglect, accidents, battering, or injury. Men convicted of violent crimes are more likely than nonviolent criminals and noncriminals to have been severely battered as children (Lewis, 1992; Milner & McCanne, 1991; Raine et al., 2001). And an indepth analysis of two young adults whose prefrontal cortex was damaged in infancy—one was run over by a car when she was 15 months old, and the other had a brain tumor removed—showed that both grew up to be compulsive liars, thieves, and heartless rule breakers. They could not hold jobs or plan for the future, could not distinguish right from wrong, and lacked empathy (Anderson et al., 1999).

3 *Genetic influences.* More than 100 studies have investigated the role of genetic influences, and meta-analyses find that genes account for 40 to 50 percent of the variation in antisocial

behavior (Moffitt, 2005). In a longitudinal study of boys who had been physically abused in childhood, those who had a deficiency in a crucial gene later had far more arrests for violent crimes than did abused boys who had a normal gene (Caspi et al., 2002). Although only 12 percent of the abused boys had this genetic deficiency, they accounted for nearly half of all later convictions for violent crimes. However, boys who had the deficient gene but who were not maltreated did not grow up to be violent.

In short, as with depression and many other disorders, the causes of psychopathy and APD reflect an interaction between an individual's own genetic or biological vulnerabilities and experiences or stressors such as physical abuse, parental neglect or rejection, or living in a subculture that rewards ruthlessness and hard-heartedness.

QUICK quiz

There is (as yet) no diagnosis of Test-Avoidance Personality Disorder, so take this quiz.

A. Can you diagnose each of the following disorders?
1. Ann can barely get out of bed in the morning. She feels that life is hopeless and despairs of ever feeling good about herself.
2. Connie constantly feels a sense of impending doom; for days her heart has been beating rapidly, and she can't relax.
3. Damon is totally absorbed in his own feelings and wishes.
4. Edna believes that everyone is out to get her and no one can be trusted.

B. What is the central difference in the diagnosis of psychopathy and antisocial personality disorder?

C. Suppose you read about an unusually brutal assault committed by a gang member during a robbery. Should you assume that he has an antisocial personality disorder? Why or why not?

Answers:

A. 1. major depression 2. generalized anxiety disorder 3. narcissistic personality disorder 4. paranoid personality disorder B. 1. Psychopathy is characterized by lack of remorse, guilt, shame, and empathy, whereas antisocial personality disorder is characterized by a lifelong history of reckless rule breaking, aggression, and irresponsibility. C. 1. Committing a violent act does not necessarily mean a person has antisocial personality disorder. This gang member may have acted violently as a way of conforming to the norms of his fellow gang members or because he felt afraid of getting caught during the robbery.

WHAT'S *Ahead*
- In what ways might genes contribute to alcoholism?
- Why is alcoholism more common in Ireland than in Italy?
- Why don't policies of abstinence from alcohol reduce problem drinking?
- If you take morphine to control chronic pain, does that mean you will become addicted to it?

Drug Abuse and Addiction

Most people who use drugs (legal, illegal, or prescription) use them in moderation; but some people depend too much on them, and others abuse drugs even at the cost of their own health. The DSM-IV defines *substance abuse* as "a maladaptive pattern of substance use leading to clinically significant impairment or distress." Symptoms of such impairment include failure to hold a job, care for children, or complete schoolwork; use of the drug in hazardous situations (e.g., while driving a car or operating machinery); and frequent conflicts with others about use of the drug or as a result of using the drug.

In Chapter 5, we described the major psychoactive drugs and their effects. In this section, focusing on the example of alcoholism, we will consider the two dominant approaches to understanding addiction and drug abuse—the biological model and the learning model—and then see how they might be reconciled.

Biology and Addiction

The *biological model* holds that addiction, whether to alcohol or any other drug, is due primarily to a person's biochemistry, metabolism, and genetic predisposition. Most of the genetic evidence comes from twin and family studies of alcoholism. These studies show that although genes are involved, it is too simple to say, as some people do, that "genes cause alcoholism." Evidence of an inherited vulnerability to alcohol is stronger for men than for women, but even this link depends on the *kind* of alcoholism (Cloninger, 1990; Goodwin et al., 1994;

McGue, 1999; Schuckit & Smith, 1996). There is a heritable component in the kind of alcoholism that begins in adolescence and is linked to impulsivity, antisocial behavior, and criminality (Bohman et al., 1987; McGue, 1999). But for male alcoholics who begin drinking heavily in adulthood, genetic factors are only weakly involved, if at all.

For a while researchers thought they had found an "alcoholism gene" that affected brain receptors for dopamine, a neurotransmitter involved in the sensation of pleasure. This hypothesis has not been well supported (Plomin & McGuffin, 2003). Actually, the strongest evidence to date is that genes are involved not with alcoholism but with protection *against* alcoholism. There is a genetic factor that causes low activity of an enzyme that is important in the metabolism of alcohol. People who lack this enzyme respond to alcohol with unpleasant symptoms, such as flushing and nausea. This genetic protection is common among Asians but rare among Europeans, which may be one reason that rates of alcoholism are much lower in Asian than in Caucasian populations (Heath et al., 2003). On the other hand, Native Americans often have the same genetic protection that Asians do, yet they have much higher rates of alcoholism.

Within populations, genes might contribute to traits or temperaments (such as impulsivity) that predispose a person to become alcoholic. Genes may also affect how much a person needs to drink before feeling high. In an ongoing longitudinal study of 450 young men (half of whom had alcoholic fathers and half of whom did not), the men who at age 20 had to drink more than others to feel any reaction were at increased risk of becoming alcoholic within the decade. This was true regardless of their initial drinking habits or family history (Schuckit, 1998; Schuckit & Smith, 1996). Some people may inherit not only a general susceptibility to substance abuse but also a vulnerability to specific drugs—heroin, alcohol, cocaine, or nicotine (Tsuang et al., 2001). As with so many other disorders, however, tracking down the genes involved has been difficult.

The usual way of looking at the relationship between biological factors and addiction is to assume that the former cause the latter. However, there is strong evidence that the relationship also works the other way: *Addictions can result from the abuse of drugs* (Crombag & Robinson, 2004). Drugs change the brain. Heavy drinking alters brain function, reduces the level of painkilling endorphins, produces nerve damage, shrinks the cerebral cortex, and damages the liver. As you can see in Figure 11.3, heavy use of alcohol, cocaine, heroin, metham-

By poking fun at the things people do to make themselves feel better, this cartoon reminds us that many "addictions" are not biochemical.

FIGURE 11.3
The Addicted Brain
PET-scan studies show that the brains of cocaine addicts have fewer receptors for dopamine, a neurotransmitter involved in pleasurable sensations. (The more yellow and red in the brain image, the more receptors there are.) The brains of people addicted to methamphetamine, alcohol, and even food show a similar pattern (Volkow et al., 2001).

phetamine, or other drugs also reduces the number of receptors for dopamine (Volkow et al., 2001). These changes can then create addiction, a craving for more of the drug. Thus, drug abuse, which begins as a voluntary action, can turn into drug addiction, a compulsive behavior that the addict finds almost impossible to control.

Learning, Culture, and Addiction

The *learning model* examines the role of the environment, learning, and culture in encouraging or discouraging drug abuse and addiction. Four major findings underscore the importance of understanding these factors:

1 *Addiction patterns vary according to cultural practices and the social environment.* Alcoholism is much more likely to occur in societies that forbid children to drink but condone drunkenness in adults (as in Ireland) than in societies that teach children how to drink responsibly and moderately but condemn adult drunkenness (as in Italy, Greece, and France). In cultures with low rates of alcoholism (except for those committed to a religious rule that forbids use of all psychoactive drugs), adults demonstrate correct drinking habits to their children, gradually introducing them to alcohol in safe family settings. Alcohol is not used as a rite of passage into adulthood, nor is it associated with masculinity and power (Peele &

Brodsky, 1991; Vaillant, 1983). Abstainers are not sneered at, and drunkenness is not considered charming, comical, or manly; it is considered stupid or obnoxious.

Within a particular country, addiction rates can rise or fall rapidly in response to cultural changes. In colonial America, the average person actually drank two to three times the amount of liquor consumed today, yet alcoholism was not a serious problem. Drinking was a universally accepted social activity; families drank and ate together. Alcohol was believed to produce pleasant feelings and relaxation, and Puritan ministers endorsed its use (Critchlow, 1986). Then, between 1790 and 1830, when the American frontier was expanding, drinking came to symbolize masculine independence and toughness. The saloon became the place for drinking away from home. As people stopped drinking in moderation, with their families, alcoholism rates shot up—as the learning model would predict.

Substance abuse and addiction problems also increase when people move from their culture of origin into another that has different drinking rules (Westermeyer, 1995). For example, in most Latino cultures, such as those of Mexico and Puerto Rico, drinking and drunkenness are considered male activities. Thus, Latina women tend to drink rarely, if at all, and they have few drinking problems—until they move into an Anglo environment, where their rates of alcoholism rise (Canino, 1994). Likewise, the cultural norm of moderate drinking among college women has been changing; college women are

Alcoholism rates vary with cultural practices. They are lowest in cultures in which people drink moderately with meals and children learn the rules of social drinking from their families, as at this Jewish family's Passover seder.

much more likely to drink in binges than they formerly were. Binge drinking itself depends on a student's social environment. In a survey a few years ago, 75 percent of students who were living in fraternities or sororities reported binge drinking, compared with 51 percent in regular dormitories and 25 percent who were living at home *(Los Angeles Times,* March 25, 2002).

2 *Policies of total abstinence tend to increase rates of addiction rather than reduce them.* In the United States, the temperance movement of the early twentieth century held that drinking inevitably leads to drunkenness and drunkenness to crime. The solution it won for the Prohibition years (1920 to 1933) was national abstinence. But this victory backfired: Again in accordance with the learning model, Prohibition reduced rates of drinking overall, but it *increased* rates of alcoholism among those who did drink. Because people were denied the opportunity to learn to drink moderately, they drank excessively when given the chance (McCord, 1989). And, of course, when a substance is forbidden, it becomes more attractive to some people.

3 *Not all addicts have withdrawal symptoms when they stop taking a drug.* When heavy users of a drug stop taking it, they often suffer such unpleasant symptoms as nausea, abdominal cramps, depression, and sleep problems, depending on the drug. But these symptoms are far from universal. During the Vietnam War, nearly 30 percent of American soldiers were taking heroin in doses far stronger than those available on the streets of U.S. cities. These men believed themselves to be addicted, and experts predicted a drug-withdrawal disaster among the returning veterans. It never materialized; over 90 percent of the men simply gave up the drug, without significant withdrawal pain, when they came home to new circumstances (Robins, Davis, & Goodwin, 1974). Similarly, the majority of people who are addicted to cigarettes, tranquilizers, or painkillers are able to stop taking these drugs without outside help and without severe withdrawal symptoms (Prochaska, Norcross, & DiClemente, 1994). Many people find this information startling, even unbelievable. That is because people who can quit without help aren't entering programs to help them quit, so they are invisible to the general public and to the medical and therapeutic world. But they have been identified in random-sample community surveys.

4 *Addiction does not depend on properties of the drug alone but also on the reasons for taking it.* For decades, doctors were afraid to treat people with chronic pain by giving them narcotics, fearing they would become addicts. As a result of this belief, millions of people were condemned to live with chronic suffering from back injury, arthritis, nerve disorders, and other conditions. Then researchers found that the vast majority of pain sufferers—who use morphine and other opiates not to escape from the world, as addicts do, but to function in the world—do not become addicted (Portenoy, 1994). This was such good news that many researchers then went to the opposite extreme, optimistically believing that no one would become addicted to slow-release narcotic painkillers such as OxyContin. But again they underestimated the importance of the motives for taking the drugs. People who are searching for escape and euphoria will find a way to abuse *any* mood-altering drug, or, as many teenagers are now doing, to create drug "cocktails" to give them a high. That is why the abuse of narcotic painkillers and even the stimulants in common flu medication has become a significant social problem.

In the case of alcohol, most people drink simply to be sociable, to conform to the group they are with, or to relax when they are stressed, and these people are unlikely to become addicted. The problem occurs when people drink in order to disguise or suppress their anxiety or depression, or when they drink alone to drown their sorrows and forget

The Rastafarian church in Jamaica regards marijuana as a "wisdom weed" and even young children smoke it as part of their religious tradition. Under such circumstances, its use does not lead to addiction or the use of harder drugs.

Test Your Motives for Drinking

If you drink, why do you do so? Check all of the motives that apply to you:

_____ to relax

_____ to be sociable

_____ to escape from worries

_____ to cope with depression

_____ to enhance a good meal

_____ to get drunk and lose control

_____ to conform to peers

_____ to rebel against authority

_____ to express anger or other uncomfortable feelings

_____ to relieve boredom

_____ other (specify)

Do your reasons promote abuse or responsible use? How do you respond physically to alcohol? What have you learned about drinking from your family, your friends, and cultural messages? What do your answers tell you about your own vulnerability to addiction?

---

their worries (Cooper et al., 1995; Mohr et al., 2001). College students who feel alienated and uninvolved with their studies are more likely than their happier peers to go binge drinking, with the conscious intention of getting drunk (Flacks & Thomas, 1998). In many cases, then, the decision to start abusing drugs depends more on your motives, and on the norms of your friends, than on the chemical properties of the drug itself.

Debating Solutions to Addiction

The biological and learning models both contribute to our understanding of drug use and addiction.

Thinking Critically About Theories of Addiction

Yet among many researchers and public-health professionals, these views are quite polarized. What we have here is a case of either–or thinking on a national scale: Either complete abstinence is the solution, or it is the problem.

Those who advocate the disease model say that all alcoholics and problem drinkers must abstain completely; once an addict has even a single drink, he or she will not be able to stop. Those who champion the learning model argue that some problem drinkers can learn to drink moderately if they learn safe-drinking skills, acquire other ways of coping with stress, and avoid friends and situations that pressure them to drink excessively (Denning, Little, & Glickman, 2004; Marlatt et al., 1998; Sobell & Sobell, 1993).

How can we assess these two positions critically? Because alcoholism and problem drinking occur for many reasons, neither model offers the only solution. Many alcoholics cannot learn to drink moderately, especially if they have been drinking heavily for many years—by which time, as we saw earlier, physiological changes in their brains and bodies may have turned them from drug abusers into drug addicts. On the other hand, total-abstinence groups like Alcoholics Anonymous (AA) are ineffective for many people. According to its own surveys and those done independently, one-third to one-half of all people who join AA drop out. Many of these dropouts benefit from programs such as Harm Reduction, Rational Recovery, Moderation Management, and DrinkWise, which teach people how to drink moderately and keep their drinking under control (Denning, Little, & Glickman, 2004; Fletcher, 2001; Marlatt, 1996; Peele & Brodsky, 1991; Rosenberg, 1993).

So instead of asking, "Can addicts and problem drinkers learn to drink moderately?" we should ask, "What are the factors that make it more likely that someone can learn to control problem drinking?" Problem drinkers who are most likely to become moderate drinkers have a history of less severe dependence on the drug. They lead more stable lives and have jobs and families. In contrast, those who are at greater risk of drug abuse or alcoholism have these risk factors: (1) They have a physiological vulnerability to a drug or have been using a drug long enough for it to damage or change their brain; (2) they believe that they have no control over the drug; (3) they live in a culture or a peer group that promotes and rewards binge drinking and discourages moderate drug use; (4) they have come to rely on the drug as a way of avoiding problems, suppressing anger or fear, or coping with stress.

QUICK quiz

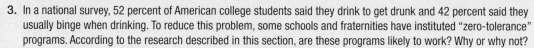

If you are addicted to passing exams, answer these questions.

1. What is the most reasonable conclusion about the role of genes in alcoholism? (a) Without a key gene, a person cannot become alcoholic; (b) the presence of a key gene will almost always cause a person to become alcoholic; (c) genes may increase a person's vulnerability to some kinds of alcoholism.

2. Which cultural practice is associated with *low* rates of alcoholism? (a) gradual introduction to drinking in family settings, (b) infrequent binge drinking, (c) drinking as a rite of passage into adulthood, (d) policies of prohibition

3. In a national survey, 52 percent of American college students said they drink to get drunk and 42 percent said they usually binge when drinking. To reduce this problem, some schools and fraternities have instituted "zero-tolerance" programs. According to the research described in this section, are these programs likely to work? Why or why not?

Answers:

1. c 2. a 3. Zero-tolerance and other abstinence programs are not likely to be successful because they do not address the *reasons* that students binge, do not affect the student culture that fosters binge drinking, and do not teach students how to drink moderately.

WHAT'S *Ahead*

- Why are many clinicians and researchers skeptical about multiple personality disorder?

- Why did the number of "multiple personality" cases jump from a handful to many thousands in only a decade?

Dissociative Identity Disorder

In this section we will examine one of the most controversial diagnoses ever to arise in psychiatry and psychology: **dissociative identity disorder,** formerly and still popularly called *multiple personality disorder* (MPD). This disorder describes the apparent emergence, within one person, of two or more distinct identities, each with its own name, memories, preferences, and personality traits.

The MPD Controversy Cases of multiple personality portrayed on TV, in popular books, and in films such as *The Three Faces of Eve* and *Sybil* have captivated the public for years. In 2005, Robert Oxnam wrote a book claiming that his alcoholism, bulimia, and rages were a result of having 11 competing "personalities," some old, some young, some male, some female. Among mental-health professionals, however, two competing views of MPD exist. On one side are those who think that MPD is common but often unrecognized or misdiagnosed. They believe the disorder originates in childhood as a means of coping with unspeakable horrors, such as torture (Gleaves, 1996). In this view, the trauma produces a mental "splitting" (*dissociation*): One personality emerges to handle everyday experiences, another personality (called an "alter") to cope with the bad ones. MPD patients are frequently described as having lived for years with several alters of which they were unaware, until hypnosis revealed them in therapy.

On the other side are those who believe that most cases of MPD are unwittingly generated by clinicians themselves, during their interactions with vulnerable clients who have other psychological problems (Lilienfeld & Lohr, 2003). They point out that before 1980, only a handful of MPD cases had ever been diagnosed anywhere in the world; yet by the mid-1990s, *tens of thousands* of cases had been reported. MPD became a lucrative business, benefiting hospitals that opened MPD clinics, therapists who had a new disorder to treat, and psychiatrists and patients who wrote best-selling books. Skeptics think the sudden increase in cases was a sign that the disorder was being wildly overdiagnosed by its proponents. Clinicians who deeply believed in the prevalence of MPD may even have been creating the disorder in their clients through suggestive techniques, like hypnosis, and through the power of suggestion, sometimes bordering on coercion (Merskey, 1995; Rieber, 2006; Spanos, 1996).

You can see this pressure at work in the comments of psychiatrist Richard Kluft (1987), who wrote that efforts to determine the presence of MPD—that is, to get the person to reveal a "dissociated" personality—may require "between 2 1/2 and 4 hours of continuous interviewing. Interviewees must be prevented from taking breaks to regain composure . . . In one recent case of singular difficulty, the first sign of dissociation was noted in the 6th hour, and a definitive spontaneous switching of

dissociative identity disorder A controversial disorder marked by the apparent appearance within one person of two or more distinct personalities, each with its own name and traits; commonly known as *multiple personality disorder* (MPD).

personalities occurred in the 8th hour." Mercy! After eight hours of "continuous interviewing" without a single break, how many of us wouldn't do what the interviewer wanted?

Clinicians who conducted such interrogations argued that they were merely *permitting* other personalities to reveal themselves. However, in numerous malpractice cases across the country, courts have ruled, on the basis of the testimony of scientific experts in psychiatry and psychology, that it is more likely that these clinicians were actively creating personalities through suggestion and sometimes outright intimidation (Loftus, 1996). The MPD clinics in hospitals closed, psychiatrists became more wary, and the number of cases dropped sharply almost overnight.

The Sociocognitive Explanation

No one disputes that some troubled, highly imaginative individuals can produce many different "personalities" when asked. But the *sociocognitive explanation* of MPD holds that this phenomenon is simply an extreme form of the ability we all have to present different aspects of our personalities to others (Spanos, 1996). In this view, the diagnosis of MPD provides a culturally acceptable way for some troubled people to make sense of their problems (Hacking, 1995; Showalter, 1997). It allows them to account for sexual or criminal behavior that they now regret or find intolerably embarrassing; they can claim their "other personality did it." In turn, therapists who are looking for MPD reward such patients with attention and praise for revealing more and more personalities (Piper & Merskey, 2004).

Thinking Critically About "Multiple Personality Disorder"

The story of the rise and fall of MPD offers an important lesson in critical thinking, because unskeptical media coverage of sensational MPD cases played a major role in fostering the rise of MPD diagnoses. When Canadian psychiatrist Harold Merskey (1992) reviewed the published cases of MPD, he was unable to find a single one in which a patient developed MPD without being influenced by the therapist's suggestions or reports about the disorder in books and the media. Even the famous case of "Sybil," a huge hit as a book, film, and television special, was a hoax. Sybil never had a traumatic childhood of sexual abuse, she did not have multiple personality disorder, and her "symptoms" were largely generated by her psychiatrist (Borch-Jacobson, 1997; Rieber, 2006).

Of course, there have been legitimate examples of this rare disorder. But even the authors of *The Three Faces of Eve* became alarmed by the media hype and proliferation of questionable cases. Thirty years later, they reported that of the hundreds of possible MPD cases that had been referred to them in the intervening years, they thought only one was a genuine multiple personality (Thigpen & Cleckley, 1984). Each case, therefore, must be examined on its own merits. But the story of MPD teaches us to think critically about disorders that become trendy—to consider other explanations, to examine assumptions and biases, and to demand good evidence.

Popular books and films about multiple personality spawned countless imitators like Lizzie—and thousands of reported cases. Most of this increase was a result of unwitting therapist influence and sensational stories in the media.

QUICK quiz

Any one of your personalities may answer this question.

In August 2003, Donna Walker was arrested for trying to convince an Indiana couple that she was their long-missing daughter. She claimed that her "bad girl" personality (Allison) was responsible for this deception and also for her long history of perpetrating hoaxes on police, friends, and the media. Her "good girl" personality (Donna), she said, was a victim of childhood sexual abuse who spent years working as an FBI informant. The FBI verified that Walker had worked for them, although some of her reports were fabricated. One agent said that Walker has as many as seven personalities who come and go. As a critical thinker, what questions would you want to ask about Walker and her multiple-personality defense?

Answer:

Some possible questions to ask: Is there corroborating evidence for Walker's claims that she was sexually molested as a child? (She said she was abused from ages 4 to 13 by a family member and then by the minister of her church and that she was sent to a psychiatric hospital at 13.) How much of the rest of her life story can be independently corroborated? Did Walker only claim to have "other personalities" when she was in a jam with the law or was there evidence of MPD throughout her life? Could she have another mental disorder, such as schizophrenia or antisocial personality disorder?

WHAT'S *Ahead*

- What's the difference between schizophrenia and a "split personality"?
- Is schizophrenia partly heritable?
- Could schizophrenia begin in the womb?

Schizophrenia

To be schizophrenic is best summed up in a repeating dream that I have had since childhood. In this dream I am lying on a beautiful sunlit beach but my body is in pieces. . . . I realize that the tide is coming in and that I am unable to gather the parts of my dismembered body together to run away. . . . This to me is what schizophrenia feels like; being fragmented in one's personality and constantly afraid that the tide of illness will completely cover me (Quoted in Rollin, 1980).

In 1911, Swiss psychiatrist Eugen Bleuler coined the term **schizophrenia** to describe cases in which the personality loses its unity. Contrary to popular belief, people with schizophrenia do not have a "split" or "multiple" personality. As this haunting quotation illustrates, schizophrenia is a fragmented condition in which words are split from meaning, actions from motives, perceptions from reality. It is an example of a **psychosis**, a mental condition that involves distorted perceptions of reality and an inability to function in most aspects of life.

Symptoms of Schizophrenia

Schizophrenia is the cancer of mental illness: elusive, complex, and varying in form. The disorder typically involves the following symptoms:

1 **Bizarre delusions,** such as the belief that dogs are extraterrestrials disguised as pets. Some people with schizophrenia have delusions of identity, believing that they are Moses, Jesus, or another famous person. Some have paranoid delusions, taking innocent events—a stranger's cough, a helicopter overhead—as evidence that everyone is plotting against them. They often report that their thoughts have been inserted into their heads by someone controlling them or are being broadcast on television. And some people have delusional obsessions. A woman named Margaret Mary Ray believed with all her heart that late-night talk-show host David Letterman was in love with her. She stalked him day and night for a decade, writing him letters and repeatedly breaking into his house. (Eventually, she committed suicide.)

2 **Hallucinations,** false sensory experiences that feel intensely real. By far the most common hallucination among people with schizophrenia is hearing voices; it is virtually a hallmark of the disease. Some sufferers of schizophrenia are so tormented by these voices that they commit suicide to escape them. One man described how he heard as many as 50 voices cursing him, urging him to steal other people's brain cells, or ordering him to kill himself. Once he picked up a ringing telephone and heard them screaming, "You're guilty!" over and over. They yelled "as loud as humans with megaphones," he told a reporter. "It was utter despair. I felt scared. They were always around" (Goode, 2003).

3 **Disorganized, incoherent speech,** consisting of an illogical jumble of ideas and symbols, linked by meaningless rhyming words or by remote associations called *word salads*. A patient of Bleuler's wrote, "Olive oil is an Arabian liquor-sauce which the Afghans, Moors and Moslems use in ostrich farming. The Indian plantain tree is the whiskey of the Parsees and Arabs. Barley, rice and sugar cane called artichoke, grow remarkably well in India. The Brahmins live as castes in Baluchistan. The Circassians occupy Manchuria and China. China is the Eldorado of the Pawnees" (Bleuler, 1911/1950).

4 **Grossly disorganized and inappropriate behavior,** which may range from childlike silliness to unpredictable and violent agitation. The person may wear three overcoats and gloves on a hot day, start collecting garbage, or hoard scraps of food.

5 **Impaired cognitive abilities.** People with schizophrenia do much worse than healthy people in almost every cognitive domain, especially verbal learning and recall of words and stories, perception, working memory, selective attention, and problem solving (Barch, 2003; Uhlhaas & Silverstein, 2005). Their speech is often impoverished; they make only brief, empty replies in conversation, because of diminished thought rather than an unwillingness to speak. Many of these cognitive impairments emerge in vulnerable children long before an actual schizophrenic breakdown occurs, and they last after the patient's psychotic symptoms subside as a result of medication (Heinrichs, 2005).

schizophrenia A psychotic disorder marked by delusions, hallucinations, disorganized and incoherent speech, inappropriate behavior, and cognitive

psychosis An extreme mental disturbance involving distorted perceptions and irrational behavior; it may have psychological or organic causes.

Other symptoms may appear months before hallucinations or delusions do, and they often persist even when more dramatic symptoms are in remission. For example, many people with schizophrenia lose the motivation to take care of themselves and interact with others; they may stop working or bathing and become isolated and withdrawn. They seem emotionally "flat"; their facial expressions are unresponsive and they make poor eye contact. Some completely withdraw into a private world, sitting for hours without moving, a condition called *catatonic stupor*. (Catatonic states can also produce frenzied, purposeless behavior that goes on for hours.)

Although signs of schizophrenia may emerge early, the first full-blown psychotic episode typically occurs in late adolescence or early adulthood. In some individuals, the breakdown occurs suddenly; in others, it is more gradual, a slow change in personality. The more breakdowns and relapses the individual has had, the poorer the chances for complete recovery. Yet many people suffering from this illness learn to control the symptoms, often with the help of antipsychotic medication and community programs (see Chapter 12), and are able to work and have good family relationships (Harding, Zubin, & Strauss, 1992).

The mystery of this disease is that some people with schizophrenia are almost completely impaired in all spheres; others do well in certain areas. Still others have normal moments of lucidity in otherwise withdrawn lives. One adolescent crouched in a rigid catatonic posture in front of a television for the month of October; later, he was able to report on all the highlights of the World Series he had seen. A middle-aged man, hospitalized for 20 years, believing he was a prophet of God and that monsters were coming out of the walls, was able to interrupt his ranting to play a good game of chess (Wender & Klein, 1981).

Origins of Schizophrenia

Any disorder that has so many variations and symptoms will pose many problems for those trying to find its origins. Early psychodynamic and learning theories, which held that schizophrenia results from being raised by an erratic, cold, rejecting mother or from living in an unpredictable environment, have not been supported. Most researchers now believe that schizophrenia is caused by genetic problems that produce subtle abnormalities in the brain. However, genes must interact with certain stressors in the environment during prenatal development,

When people with schizophrenia are asked to draw pictures, their drawings are often distorted, lack color, include words, and reveal flat emotion. One patient was asked to copy a picture of flowers from a magazine (top right). The initial result is shown on the left. The drawing in the center shows improvement, and the drawing on the right shows how much the patient progressed after several months of treatment.

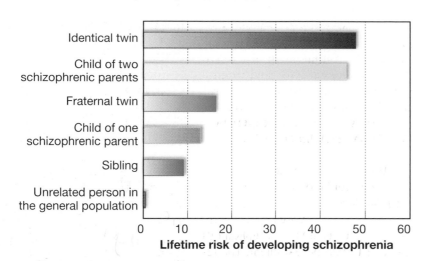

FIGURE 11.4
Genetic Vulnerability to Schizophrenia
This graph, based on combined data from 40 European twin and adoption studies, shows that the closer the genetic relationship to a person with schizophrenia, the higher the risk of developing the disorder. (Based on Gottesman, 1991.)

birth, or adolescence. Here is some evidence on the contributing factors:

1 **Genetic predispositions.** A person has a much greater risk of developing schizophrenia if an identical twin develops the disorder, even if the twins are reared apart (Gottesman, 1991; Heinrichs, 2005). Children with one schizophrenic parent have a lifetime risk of 12 percent, and children with two schizophrenic parents have a lifetime risk of 35–46 percent, compared to a risk in the general population of only 1–2 percent (Goldstein, 1987). (See Figure 11.4.) In a Finnish study of identical twins, fully 83 percent of the variation

in the risk of becoming schizophrenic was due to combined genetic factors and only 17 percent to unique environmental factors (Cannon et al., 1998). Researchers all over the world are trying to track down genes that might be involved in specific symptoms, such as hallucinations, sensitivity to sounds, and cognitive impairments. One team has identified a gene whose chromosomal aberrations are involved in schizophrenia and bipolar disorder, which share severe disturbances of emotion and cognition (Millar et al., 2005).

2 **Structural brain abnormalities.** Most individuals with schizophrenia have abnormalities in the brain, including a decrease in the volume of the temporal lobe or hippocampus, reduced numbers of neurons in the prefrontal cortex, or enlargement of the *ventricles*, spaces in the brain that are filled with cerebrospinal fluid (see Figure 11.5) (Akbarian et al., 1996; Heinrichs, 2005; Zorrilla et al., 1997). Schizophrenics are also more likely than healthy individuals to have abnormalities in the thalamus, the traffic-control center that filters sensations and focuses attention (Andreasen et al., 1994; Gur et al., 1998). Schizophrenics also may have abnormalities in the auditory cortex and Broca's and Wernicke's areas, all involved in speech perception and processing. Such abnormalities might explain the nightmare of voice hallucinations.

3 **Neurotransmitter abnormalities.** Abnormalities in several neurotransmitters, including serotonin, glutamate, and dopamine, have been associated with schizophrenia (Sawa & Snyder, 2002). However, similar neurotransmitter abnormalities are also found in many other mental disorders, such as depression and alcoholism, making it

FIGURE 11.5
Schizophrenia and the Brain
MRI scans show that a person with schizophrenia (left) is more likely than a healthy person (right) to have enlarged ventricles, or spaces, in the brain (see arrows) (Andreasen et al., 1994).

difficult to know whether these abnormalities play a specific role in schizophrenia.

4 ***Prenatal problems or birth complications.*** Damage to the fetal brain significantly increases the likelihood of schizophrenia later in life. Such damage may occur if the mother suffers from malnutrition; schizophrenia rates rise during times of famine, as happened in China and elsewhere (St. Clair et al., 2005). Damage may also occur if the mother gets the flu virus during the first four months of prenatal development, which triples the risk of schizophrenia (Brown et al., 2004; Mednick, Huttunen, & Machón, 1994). And it may occur if there are complications during birth that injure the baby's brain or deprive it of oxygen (Cannon et al., 2000). However, prenatal stress—on the mother or the fetus—is a risk factor for the development of other psychological disorders later in life, too, not only schizophrenia (Huizink, Mulder, & Buitelaar, 2004).

5 ***Adolescent abnormalities in brain development.*** The last factor contributing to schizophrenia occurs in adolescence, when the brain undergoes a natural pruning away of synapses in the brain. Normally, this pruning helps make the brain more efficient in handling the new challenges of adulthood. But it appears that in schizophrenic brains, too many synapses are pruned away, which may explain why

the first schizophrenic episode typically occurs in adolescence or early adulthood (Thompson et al., 2001). The reason for the excessive pruning is not yet known, but it may involve genetic dispositions, fetal brain damage, or stressful life experiences (McGlashan & Hoffman, 2000).

Thus, the developmental pathway of schizophrenia looks like something of a relay. It starts with a genetic predisposition, which must combine with prenatal risk factors or birth complications that affect brain development. The resulting vulnerability then awaits events in adolescence—synaptic pruning within the brain or external stressors—that serve as a trigger for the disease (Conklin & Iacono, 2002). This model explains why one identical twin may develop schizophrenia but not the other: Both may have the genetic susceptibility, but only one was exposed to other risk factors in the womb, birth complications, or stressful life events. These factors may combine in different ways as well, explaining why some schizophrenics recover and others do not. The riddle of schizophrenia is likely to be several riddles, waiting to be solved.

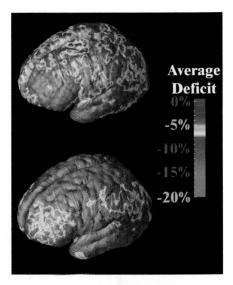

These dramatic images highlight areas of gray-matter loss in adolescents with schizophrenia over five years. The areas of greatest tissue loss (regions that control memory, hearing, motor functions, and attention) are shown in red and magenta. A healthy brain (top) would look almost entirely blue.

QUICK quiz

The following quiz is not a hallucination.

1. What are the five major kinds of symptoms in schizophrenia?
2. *True or false:* The vast majority of people with schizophrenia do not have a schizophrenic parent.
3. What are the three likely stages in the "relay race" that produces schizophrenia?

Answers:

1. delusions, hallucinations, disorganized speech, inappropriate behavior, and impaired cognitive abilities   2. true   3. Genetic predispositions; prenatal risk factors or birth complications; events during adolescence, such as excessive pruning of synapses in the brain or external stressors

psychology in the news REVISITED

We have come to the end of a long walk along the spectrum of psychological problems—from those that are normal conditions of life, such as occa-

sional anxiety or "caffeine-induced sleep disorder," to mental disorders that are severely disabling, such as schizophrenia. Where on this spectrum would you place Internet dependence, the complaint of the students in our opening story?

Some psychologists think that Internet addiction is a true disorder, comparable to drug addiction or to any other compulsive behavior. After all, it meets some of the criteria for a mental disorder: It can be maladaptive, disrupting the lives of those who spend thousands of hours in cyberspace instead of the real world; it often causes them emotional distress; and it often upsets and worries their friends and family. Like drug addicts and people with obsessive-compulsive disorder, some individuals claim they have no control over their behavior, in this case the time they spend on the Internet.

Other psychologists, however, think that students who spend too much time online are no different from previous generations who also found plenty of ways to distract themselves and avoid the common problems facing students everywhere—insecurity, worry about grades, a disappointing social life. This is not a "mental disorder," they say; it's a normal problem, called Learning to Pass Courses and Figure Out Life.

One of the great debates generated by all diagnoses of mental disorder concerns the question of

Thinking Critically About Mental Disorders and Responsibility

personal responsibility. In law and in everyday life, many people reach for a psychological reason to exonerate themselves of responsibility for their actions. Romance writer Janet Dailey, accused of plagiarizing whole passages from another writer's work, said she was suffering from "a psychological problem that I never even suspected I had." Elizabeth Roach embezzled nearly $250,000 from her employer to finance shopping binges and then claimed she was a "shopaholic" who went on sprees to "self-medicate" her depression. Do you find these excuses convincing, or do you think they are efforts to avoid responsibility for illegal or irresponsible actions?

Now consider a more serious example, the tragic story of Andrea Yates, a Texas woman who killed her five young children in a state of extreme despair. She had suffered from clinical depression and psychotic episodes for years and in her blackest depressions became mute and catatonic. She tried to kill herself twice. Her father, two brothers, and a sister had suffered varying degrees of mental illness, including depression. Yates was overwhelmed by the burden of raising and home-schooling all of her children with no help from her husband, who reportedly permitted her two hours a week of personal time. Although she suffered a postpartum psychotic episode

Andrea Yates was convicted of the murder of her children and sent to a mental institution. Do you agree that this was the appropriate punishment? Why or why not?

after the birth of their fourth child and a clinical psychologist warned her against having another baby, her husband refused to consider birth control, although not for religious reasons. "We want as many as nature will allow," he said (Yardley, 2001). In 2002, Yates was convicted of murder and sentenced to life in prison after a jury rejected her claim that she was so psychotic that she thought she was saving the souls of her children by killing them. That conviction was overturned on appeal. In 2006, another jury found her not guilty by reason of insanity and she was sent to a mental institution.

Does Andrea Yates deserve our condemnation for her horrible acts of murder or our pity? Was her punishment appropriate? Unquestionably, many people do suffer from mental disorders that make it difficult or even impossible for them to control their behavior. How can we distinguish impairments that legitimately reduce a person's responsibility for his or her actions from unjustified excuses?

We noted at the beginning of this chapter that "insanity" refers only to the defendant's ability to know right from wrong at the time the crime was committed. It is invoked in only a tiny percentage of all criminal cases. But in some jurisdictions, a defendant may claim to have diminished responsibility for a crime. This claim does not free the defendant, but it may result in reducing the charges from premeditated first-degree murder to manslaughter. A diminished-capacity defense holds that the defendant lacked the mental capacity to form a calculated and malicious plan but instead was impaired by mental illness or the great provocation of the situation. In some jurisdictions, diminished capacity and other mitigating factors are considered only at the sentencing phase, once the defendant has been found guilty.

When thinking about the relationship of mental disorder to personal responsibility, we face a dilemma. The law recognizes, rightly, that people who are mentally incompetent, delusional, or disturbed should not be judged by the same standards as mentally healthy individuals. At the same time, society has an obligation to protect its citizens from harm and to reject easy excuses for violations of the law. To balance these two positions, we need to find ways to ensure that people who commit crimes or behave reprehensibly face the consequences of their behavior. We also must ensure that people who are suffering from psychological problems have the compassionate support of society in their search for help. After all, psychological problems of one kind or another are challenges that all of us will face at some time in our lives.

➤TAKING ➤PSYCHOLOGY ➤WITH ➤YOU

When a Friend Is Suicidal

Suicide can be frightening to those who find themselves fantasizing about it, and it is devastating to the family and friends of those who go through with it. In the United States, it is the ninth leading cause of death, far surpassing homicide. The suicide rate is highest among white men over the age of 65, but suicide rates have nearly tripled in the past 40 years among adolescents and young adults, especially among college students and African-American teenagers. Every year about 1,300 college students commit suicide, and nearly 32,000 more make an unsuccessful attempt (Farrell, 2005).

Women are more likely than men to attempt suicide, primarily as a cry for help, whereas men are four times more likely than women to succeed. Moreover, men's efforts to commit suicide are not always obvious: Some men provoke confrontations with the police, hoping to be shot; some intentionally kill themselves in car accidents; and men are more likely than women to destroy themselves with drugs.

Because of the many widespread myths about suicide, it is important to become informed and know what to do in a crisis:

● **Take all suicide threats seriously.** Some people assume they can't do anything when a friend talks about committing suicide. "He'll just do it at another place, another time," they think. In fact, most suicides occur during an acute crisis. Once the person gets through the crisis, the desire to die fades. Others believe that if a friend is *talking* about committing suicide, he or she won't really *do* it. This belief also is false. Few people commit suicide without signaling their intentions. Most are ambivalent: "I want to kill myself, but I don't want to be dead—at least not forever." Most suicidal people want relief from the terrible pain of feeling that nobody cares and that life is not worth living. Getting these thoughts and fears out in the open is an important first step.

● **Know the danger signs.** A person is at risk of trying to commit suicide if he or she has tried to do it before; has become withdrawn and listless; has a history of depression; reveals specific plans for carrying out the suicide or gives away cherished possessions; expresses no concern about religious prohibitions or the impact on family members; and has access to a lethal method, such as a gun.

● **Get involved: Ask questions and get help.** If you believe a friend is suicidal, do not be afraid to ask, "Are you thinking of suicide?" This question does not "put the idea" in anyone's mind. If your friend is contemplating the action, he or she will probably be relieved to talk about it, which in turn will reduce feelings of isolation and despair. Don't try to talk your friend out of it by debating whether suicide is right or wrong, and don't put on phony cheerfulness. If your friend's words scare you, say so. By allowing your friend to unburden his or her grief, you help the person get through the immediate crisis.

● **Do not leave your friend alone.** If necessary, get the person to a clinic or a hospital emergency room, or call a local suicide hot line. Don't worry about doing the wrong thing. In an emergency, the worst thing you can do is nothing at all.

● **If you are the one who is contemplating suicide, remember that you are not alone and that help is a phone call or an e-mail away.** You can call the national hot-line number, 1-800-SUICIDE, or your school's counseling services. For more information, the Centers for Disease Control and Prevention have a Web site that provides facts about suicide (www.cdc.gov/safeusa/suicide.htm). Many students fear to get help because they think no one will understand, or they fear they will be made fun of by their friends, or they believe they cannot be helped. Wrong, wrong, wrong.

In her revealing book *Night Falls Fast: Understanding Suicide*, Kay Jamison (1999), a psychologist who suffers from bipolar disorder, explored this difficult subject from the standpoint both of a mental-health professional and of a person who has "been there." In describing the aftermath of her own suicide attempt, she wrote: "I do know . . . that I should have been dead but was not—and that I was fortunate enough to be given another chance at life, which many others were not."

SUMMARY

Defining and Diagnosing Disorder

• When defining *mental disorder*, mental-health professionals emphasize the violation of cultural standards, emotional suffering, and whether the behavior is harmful to others or society.

• *The Diagnostic and Statistical Manual of Mental Disorders* (DSM) is designed to provide objective criteria and categories for diagnosing mental disorder. Critics argue that the diagnosis of mental disorders is inherently a subjective process that can never be entirely objective. They believe the DSM fosters overdiagnosis, overlooks the influence of diagnostic labels on clients and therapists, confuses serious mental disorders with everyday problems in living, and creates an illusion of objectivity and universality.

• Supporters of the DSM believe that when the DSM criteria are used correctly and when empirically validated objective tests are used, reliability in diagnosis improves. The DSM now lists many *culture-bound syndromes* in addition to disorders, such as depression and schizophrenia, in addition to disorders found all over the world.

• In diagnosing psychological disorders, clinicians often use *projective tests* such as the Rorschach Inkblot Test or, with children, the use of anatomically detailed dolls. These methods have low reliability and validity, creating problems when they are used in the legal arena, as in custody disputes, or in diagnosing disorders. In general, *objective tests (inventories)*, such as the *MMPI*, are more reliable and valid than projective ones.

Anxiety Disorders

• *Generalized anxiety disorder* involves continuous, chronic anxiety, with signs of nervousness, worry, and irritability. When anxiety results from exposure to uncontrollable or unpredictable danger, it can lead to *posttraumatic stress disorder*, which involves mentally reliving the trauma, emotional detachment, and increased physiological arousal.

• Most people who live through a trauma eventually recover, but some develop PTSD. The reasons include having a history of psychological problems and other traumatic experiences, lacking social support and psychological resources, having lower-than-average intelligence, having a relatively smaller hippocampus than normal, and having a genetic vulnerability.

• *Panic disorder* involves sudden, intense attacks of profound fear. Panic attacks are common in the aftermath of stress or frightening experiences; those who go on to develop a disorder tend to interpret the attacks as a sign of impending disaster.

• *Phobias* are unrealistic fears of specific situations, activities, or things. Common *social phobias* include fears of speaking in public, using public rest rooms, or being observed by others. *Agoraphobia*, the fear of being away from a safe place or person, is the most disabling phobia—a "fear of fear." It often begins with a panic attack, which the person tries to avoid in the future by staying close to "safe" places or people.

• *Obsessive-compulsive disorder (OCD)* involves recurrent, unwished-for thoughts or images (obsessions) and repetitive, ritualized behaviors (compulsions) that a person feels unable to control. Parts of the brain involved in fear and responses to threat are also more active than normal in people with OCD; the "alarm mechanism," once activated, does not turn off when danger is past. One kind of OCD creates pathological hoarding and may involve deficits in other parts of the brain.

Mood Disorders

• Symptoms of *major depression* include distorted thinking patterns, low self-esteem, physical ailments such as fatigue and loss of appetite, and prolonged grief and despair. Women are twice as likely as men to suffer from major depression, but depression in men may be underdiagnosed. In *bipolar disorder*, a person experiences episodes of both depression and *mania* (excessive euphoria). It is equally common in both sexes.

• *Vulnerability-stress models* of depression look at interactions between individual vulnerabilities and stressful experiences. Some people have a genetic predisposition to become depressed when they undergo severe stress, and others may be genetically protected. Genes may affect levels of serotonin and the stress hormone cortisol. For some vulnerable individuals, repeated losses of important people can set off episodes of major depression. Life experiences that increase the risk of depression include violence, problems with work and family life, poverty, discrimination, and sexual abuse. Cognitive habits also play an important role: believing that the origin of one's unhappiness is permanent and uncontrollable, feeling hopeless and pessimistic, and brooding or ruminating about one's problems.

• "Close-up on Research" examines the differences between unproductive rumination and the kind of thoughts that can lead to solving problems.

Personality Disorders

• *Personality disorders* are characterized by rigid, self-destructive traits that cause distress or an inability to get along with others. They include, among others, *paranoid*, *narcissistic*, and *antisocial personality disorders*.

• The term *psychopath* describes people who lack conscience and emotional connection to others; they don't feel remorse, shame, guilt, or anxiety over wrongdoing, and they can charm and con others with ease. *Antisocial personality disorder* (APD) applies to people with a lifelong pattern of aggressive, reckless, impulsive, and criminal behavior. Not all psychopaths have APD, and not all people with APD are psychopaths, but in some individuals the two disorders converge. Researchers have identified abnormalities in the central nervous system and prefrontal cortex that are associated with lack of emotional responsiveness and with impulsivity. APD has a genetic component, but biological vulnerabilities must interact with stressful or violent environments to produce the disorder.

Drug Abuse and Addiction

• The effects of drugs depend on whether they are used moderately or are abused. Signs of *substance abuse* include impaired ability to work or get along with others, use of the drug in hazardous situations, recurrent arrests for drug use, and conflicts with others caused by drug use.

• According to the *biological model* of addiction, some people have a biological vulnerability to alcoholism and other addictions, due to genetic factors that affect their metabolism, biochemistry, or personality traits. But heavy drug abuse also changes the brain in ways that make addiction more likely.

• Advocates of the *learning model* of addiction point out that addiction patterns vary according to culture, learning, and accepted practice; that many people can stop taking drugs without experiencing withdrawal symptoms; that drug abuse depends on the reasons for taking a drug; and that abuse increases when people are not taught moderate use.

• Although the biological and learning models are polarized on many issues, the evidence suggests that addiction and abuse result from an interaction between biological and psychological vulnerability and a person's culture, learning history, motives for taking a drug, and situation.

Dissociative Identity Disorder

• In *dissociative identity disorder* (commonly called *multiple personality disorder*, or MPD), two or more distinct personalities and identities appear to split off (*dissociate*) within one person. Considerable controversy surrounds the validity and nature of MPD. Some clinicians think it is common, often goes undiagnosed, and originates in childhood trauma. Others offer a *sociocognitive* explanation. They argue that most cases result from pressure and suggestion by clinicians who believe in the disorder, interacting with vulnerable patients who find MPD a plausible explanation for their problems. Media coverage of sensational alleged cases of MPD contributed greatly to the rise in the number of cases after 1980.

Schizophrenia

• *Schizophrenia* is a psychotic disorder involving delusions, hallucinations, disorganized speech (*word salads*), inappropriate behavior, and severe cognitive impairments. Other symptoms, such as loss of motivation and emotional flatness, may appear before a psychotic episode and persist even when the more dramatic symptoms are in remission. Some people with schizophrenia fall into a *catatonic stupor*. Cases of schizophrenia vary in their specific symptoms, severity, duration, and prognosis.

• Schizophrenia appears to involve genetic predispositions that lead to structural brain abnormalities, such as enlarged ventricles and neurotransmitter abnormalities. However, in the "relay" that produces the disorder, genetic predispositions must interact with certain stressors in the environment during prenatal development (such as the mother's malnutrition or a prenatal viral infection), birth complications, and excessive pruning of synapses during adolescence.

Psychology in the News, Revisited

• When people claim to have a mental disorder, psychologists and others struggle to decide whether the claim is an excuse for illegal or destructive actions, or whether these individuals truly have a disorder that reduces their ability to control their behavior.

KEY TERMS

insanity 370

mental disorder 371

Diagnostic and Statistical Manual of Mental Disorders (DSM) 371

projective tests 374

Rorschach Inkblot Test 374

objective tests (inventories) 375

Minnesota Multiphasic Personality Inventory (MMPI) 375

generalized anxiety disorder 376

posttraumatic stress disorder (PTSD) 377

panic disorder (panic attack) 377

phobia 378

social phobia 378

agoraphobia 378

obsessive-compulsive disorder (OCD) 379

mood disorder 380

major depression 380

mania 381

bipolar disorder 381

vulnerability-stress model of depression 381

personality disorders 384

paranoid personality disorder 384

narcissistic personality disorder 384

psychopathy 385

antisocial personality disorder (APD) 385

substance abuse 387

biological model of addiction 388

learning model of addiction 389

dissociative identity disorder (multiple

personality disorder, MPD) 392

dissociation 392

sociocognitive explanation of MPD 393

schizophrenia 394

psychosis 394

"word salad" 394

catatonic stupor 395

Defining and Diagnosing Disorder

When defining **mental disorder**, mental-health professionals emphasize the violation of cultural standards, emotional suffering caused by the behavior, and whether the behavior is harmful to others or society.

Dilemmas of Diagnosis

The Diagnostic and Statistical Manual of Mental Disorders (DSM) is designed to provide objective criteria and categories for diagnosing mental disorders.

Problems with the DSM include:
- Dangers of overdiagnosis
- Overlooking the influence of diagnostic labels themselves
- Confusing serious mental disorders with everyday problems
- Creating the illusion of objectivity and universality

Advantages of the DSM include:
- Reliability in diagnosis improves
- Identifies many universal disorders

Measuring Disorders

Projective tests, such as the **Rorschach Inkblot Test,** have low reliability and validity.

Objective tests (inventories), such as the **Minnesota Multiphasic Personality Inventory (MMPI),** have high reliability and validity.

Mood Disorders

1. **Major depression** involves prolonged grief, hopelessness, and loss of energy, appetite, and interest in activities.
2. **Bipolar disorder** involves episodes of both depression and mania (excessive euphoria).

Theories of Depression

Vulnerability-stress models of depression look at interactions between individual vulnerabilities and stressful experiences.

VULNERABILITY-STRESS MODEL OF DEPRESSION

Upsetting events	Individual vulnerability
Loss of loved one	Genetic predisposition
Loss of job	History of insecure attachment
Failure	Negative ways of thinking
Trauma	Hopelessness
Violence	Brooding rumination
	Low self-esteem

Temporary unhappiness

SEVERE DEPRESSION

Four contributing factors:
1. Genetic factors that may protect against depression or create a predisposition toward it
2. Life experiences and circumstances, including violence, sexual abuse, discrimination, and poverty
3. Losses of important relationships
4. Cognitive habits, such as believing that unhappiness is permanent and uncontrollable, ruminating about problems, and feeling hopeless

Anxiety Disorders

- **Generalized anxiety disorder** involves continuous chronic anxiety.
- **Posttraumatic stress disorder** involves reliving the trauma in recurrent, intrusive thoughts; a sense of detachment; and increased physiological arousal.
- **Panic disorder** involves sudden, intense attacks of profound fear.
- **Phobias** are unrealistic fears of specific situations, activities, or things, or, in the case of **agoraphobia**, being away from a safe place.
- **Obsessive-compulsive disorder (OCD)** involves recurrent, unwished-for thoughts or images (obsessions) and repetitive, ritualized behaviors (compulsions).

Personality Disorders

Personality disorders are characterized by rigid, self-destructive traits that cause distress or an inability to get along with others.

Antisocial Personality Disorder

- **Psychopaths** and people with **antisocial personality disorder** are unable to feel normal remorse and empathy, lack conscience, and behave in antisocial ways.
- The two disorders are not exactly the same, but certain factors are involved in both:
— Abnormalities in the CNS
— Impaired frontal-lobe functioning
— Genetic influences

Dissociative Identity Disorder

Dissociative identity disorder, formerly called multiple personality disorder (MPD), involves two or more identities that appear to split off within one person.
- Some clinicians believe MPD is common and originates in childhood trauma; others believe that most cases result from suggestion by clinicians themselves.
- Media coverage has contributed to the rise in MPD diagnoses.
- The sociocognitive explanation of MPD holds that it is simply an extreme form of the ability we all have to present different aspects of our personalities to others.

Drug Abuse and Addiction

Substance Abuse

Signs of substance abuse:
- Impaired ability to work or get along with others
- Use of the drug in hazardous situations
- Conflicts with others caused by drug use

Models of Addiction

The **biological model** holds that some people are genetically predisposed to addiction, or develop addictions as a result of the biological changes in the brain caused by heavy drug abuse.

The **learning model** holds that most kinds of addiction stem from conditions that encourage or discourage drug abuse. Evidence:
1. Addiction patterns vary according to culture.
2. Many people stop taking drugs without withdrawal symptoms.
3. Drug abuse depends on the reasons for taking the drug.
4. Abuse increases when people are not taught moderate use.

Schizophenia

Schizophenia is a fragmented condition in which words are split from meaning, actions are split from motives, and perceptions are split from reality.

Symptoms of schizophrenia:
- Bizarre delusions
- Hallucinations, sometimes visual but usually auditory
- Disorganized, incoherent speech ("word salads")
- Disorganized and inappropriate behavior
- Impaired cognitive abilities
- Loss of motivation and affect

Causes of Schizophenia

1. Genetic predispositions
2. Structural brain abnormalities
3. Neurotransmitter abnormalities
4. Prenatal problems or birth complications
5. Adolescent abnormalities in brain development

Schizophrenia and the Brain

psychology in the news

Colorado Girl Dies After Controversial Therapy

DENVER, CO, MAY 23, 2000. Police have charged four people with causing the death of 10-year-old Candace Newmaker during a session of "rebirthing" therapy at a Denver counseling center. The procedure, aimed at helping adopted children form attachments to their adoptive parents by "reliving" birth, was captured on closed-circuit television as the girl's mother watched in a nearby room.

The child was completely wrapped in a blanket that supposedly simulated the womb, and was surrounded by large pillows. Clinic counselors Connell Watkins and Julie

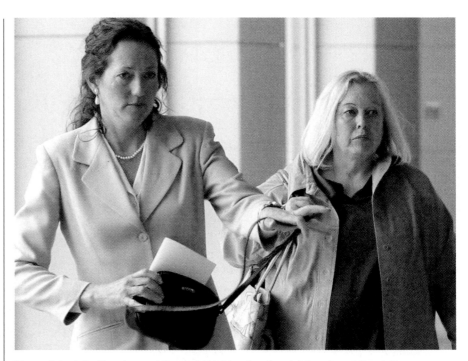

Therapists Julie Ponder and Connell Watkins (on the right) arrive at the Jefferson County District Court for a hearing on charges of "reckless child abuse" in the death of Candace Newmaker.

Candace Newmaker, age 10.

Ponder, along with two assistants, then pressed in on the pillows to simulate contractions and told the girl to push her way out of the blanket over her head. Candace repeatedly said that she could not breathe and felt she was going to die. But instead of unwrapping her, the therapists said, "You've got to push hard if you want to be born—or do you want to stay in there and die?"

Rebirthing therapy is one of various kinds of "attachment therapies" that are supposed to help rebellious children or those with emotional disorders bond to their parents. Most of these therapies involve physically restraining the child in some way.

The girl, who was adopted four years ago and had been treated for attention deficit disorder and depression, lost consciousness and was rushed to a local hospital, where she died the next day. Watkins, an unlicensed social worker who operated the counseling center, and her three employees were charged with reckless child abuse resulting in death.

Approaches to Treatment and Therapy

Were the techniques used by the Colorado therapists in this story standard practice in psychotherapy? How is a layperson like Jeane Newmaker, who wanted to help her troubled adopted child, supposed to tell the difference between good therapy and bad? When does psychotherapy help people with their problems and when does it do emotional damage—or cause even greater harm? These questions are especially pressing today, when new kinds of therapies keep emerging, all claiming successful cures.

Most people get through the normal problems of life with the healing help of time and friends. Some people, however, develop one or more of the disorders described in the previous chapter, such as depression, panic attacks, obsessive-compulsive disorder, phobias, posttraumatic stress disorder, or schizophrenia. What kind of therapy might help them? People have plenty of ordinary difficulties too, from marital conflict to coping with the loss of a loved one. What kind of therapy might help them?

In this chapter, we will evaluate two major approaches to treatment. *Biological treatments* include drugs or direct intervention in brain function; they are primarily prescribed by psychiatrists or other physicians in a hospital or on an outpatient basis. *Psychotherapy* covers an array of psychological approaches, including psychodynamic therapies, cognitive and behavioral therapies, family therapy, and humanist therapies.

Each of these approaches can successfully handle some problems but not others. Each can help some people but not others. And in some cases, the misuse of medication or of therapeutic techniques can be harmful. At the end of this chapter we will tell you what happened to the four people who caused the death of Candace Newmaker and what the status is of "attachment therapy." As you read, see whether you can come up with some things you would want to know when evaluating any form of therapy, including unorthodox ones such as rebirthing.

WHAT'S *Ahead*

- What kinds of drugs are used to treat psychological disorders?

- Are antidepressants always the best treatment for depression?

- Can mental disorders be cured by brain surgery?

- Why is "shock therapy" hailed by some clinicians but condemned by others?

Biological Treatments for Mental Disorders

For hundreds of years, people have tried to find the origins of mental illness, attributing the causes at various times to evil spirits, pressure in the skull, disease, or bad environments. The contemporary mental-health world continues to alternate between viewing mental disorders as diseases that can be treated medically and as emotional problems that must be treated psychologically (Luhrmann, 2000). Today, biological explanations and treatments are in the ascendance. This is partly because of evidence that some disorders have a genetic component or involve a biochemical or neurological abnormality (see Chapter 11) and partly because economic and social forces are fostering biomedical solutions (Angell, 2004; Healy, 2002).

The Question of Drugs

The most commonly used biological treatment is medication. Because drugs are so widely prescribed these days, both for severe disorders such as schizophrenia and for more common problems such as anxiety and depression, consumers need to understand what these drugs are, how they can best be used, and their limitations.

Drugs Commonly Prescribed for Mental Disorders The main classes of drugs used in the treatment of mental disorders are these:

1 **Antipsychotic drugs**, also called *neuroleptics*—older ones such as Thorazine and Haldol and newer, second-generation ones such as Clozaril and Risperdal—are used primarily in the treatment of schizophrenia and other psychoses, though increasingly they are being used for nonpsychotic disorders such as severe depression, impulse control problems, and bipolar disorder. Many antipsychotic drugs are designed to block or reduce the sensitivity of brain receptors that respond to dopamine. Some also increase levels of serotonin, a neurotransmitter that inhibits dopamine activity. Antipsychotic drugs can reduce agitation, delusions, and hallucinations, and they can shorten schizophrenic episodes. However, they offer little relief from other symptoms, such as jumbled thoughts, difficulty concentrating, apathy, emotional flatness, or inability to interact with others (see Chapter 11).

Although the newer drugs have been promoted as being safer and more effective, a large federally funded study found that the older medications often alleviate schizophrenia symptoms about as well as the newer, far more expensive ones do (Lieberman et al., 2005). The new antipsychotics are as likely as the older ones to cause troubling negative side effects, especially muscle rigidity, hand tremors, and other involuntary muscle movements that can develop into a neurological disorder. Some of the newer drugs also have other risks, including weight gain that can lead to severe diabetes, which can cause medical complications and death (Masand, 2000). In 2003, the makers of Risperdal cautioned physicians to stop prescribing the drug to

antipsychotic drugs
Drugs used primarily in the treatment of schizophrenia and other psychotic disorders.

These photos show the effects of antipsychotic drugs on the symptoms of a young man with schizophrenia. In the top photo, he was unmedicated; in the photo below, he had taken medication. However, these drugs do not help all people with psychotic disorders.

elderly patients with dementia because it can cause strokes and is ineffective for this population. Although antipsychotic medication allows many people to be released from hospitals, these individuals cannot always care for themselves, and they often fail to keep taking their medication because of the unpleasant and sometimes dangerous side effects.

2 **Antidepressant drugs** are used primarily in the treatment of depression, anxiety, phobias, and obsessive-compulsive disorder. *Monoamine oxidase inhibitors (MAOIs)*, such as Nardil, elevate the levels of norepinephrine and serotonin in the brain by blocking or inhibiting an enzyme that deactivates these neurotransmitters. *Tricyclic antidepressants*, such as Elavil, boost norepinephrine and serotonin levels by preventing the normal reabsorption, or

"reuptake," of these substances by the cells that have released them. *Selective serotonin reuptake inhibitors (SSRIs)*, such as Prozac, work on the same principle as the tricyclics but specifically target serotonin. Cymbalta and Remeron target both serotonin and norepinephrine.

Antidepressants are nonaddictive, but they can produce some unpleasant physical reactions, including dry mouth, headaches, constipation, nausea, restlessness, gastrointestinal problems, weight gain, and, in as many as one-third of all patients, decreased sexual desire and blocked or delayed orgasm (Hollon, Thase, & Markowitz, 2002). MAOIs interact with foods containing a chemical found in cheese and beer, so dietary restrictions may be required.

Some investigators are studying herbs like St. John's wort. A meta-analysis of clinical studies found that St. John's wort was more effective than a placebo for milder forms of depression (Kim, Streltzer, & Goebert, 1999), but the efficacy of this herb remains in dispute. Also, the herb is now known to affect metabolism and to interact with about half of all prescription medications, including birth-control pills, blood thinners, and some AIDS drugs (Markowitz et al., 2003). Anyone taking St. John's wort along with a prescription drug should inform his or her physician.

3 **Tranquilizers**, such as Valium and Xanax, increase the activity of the neurotransmitter gamma-aminobutyric acid (GABA). Although they were developed to treat people with mild anxiety, they are often overprescribed by general

"Before Prozac, she loathed company."

antidepressant drugs Drugs used primarily in the treatment of mood disorders, especially depression and anxiety.

tranquilizers Drugs commonly but often inappropriately prescribed for patients who complain of unhappiness, anxiety, or worry.

lithium carbonate A drug frequently given to people suffering from bipolar disorder.

placebo effect The apparent success of a medication or treatment that is due to the patient's expectations or hopes rather than to the drug or treatment itself.

physicians for patients who complain of more serious mood disorders. Tranquilizers may help people with panic disorder and individuals who are having an acute anxiety attack (Ballenger et al., 1988), but they are not considered the treatment of choice over a long period of time. Symptoms almost always return if the medication is stopped, and a significant percentage of people who take tranquilizers overuse them and develop problems with withdrawal and tolerance (i.e., they need larger and larger doses).

4 A special category of drug, a salt called **lithium carbonate**, often helps people who suffer from bipolar disorder (depression alternating with euphoria) (Keck & McElroy, 1998). It may produce its effects by moderating levels of norepinephrine or by protecting brain cells from being overstimulated by another neurotransmitter, glutamate (Nonaka, Hough, & Chuang, 1998). Lithium must be given in exactly the right dose, and bloodstream levels of the drug must be carefully monitored, because too little will not help and too much is toxic—sometimes even fatal. Unfortunately, in some people, lithium produces short-term side effects (tremors) and long-term problems (kidney damage). Newer drugs for people with bipolar disorder include Tegretol, Depakote, and some of the newer antipsychotics (Bowden et al., 2000; McElroy & Keck, 2000).

For a review of these drugs and their uses, see Table 12.1.

Some Cautions About Drug Treatments Without question, drugs have rescued some people from emotional despair, suicide, obsessive-compulsive disorder, and panic attacks. They have enabled severely depressed or mentally disturbed people to function and respond to psychotherapy. Yet many psychiatrists and drug companies are trumpeting the benefits of medication without informing the public of its limitations, so a few words of caution are in order.

Thinking Critically About Drug Treatments

1 *The placebo effect.* New drugs, like new psychotherapies, often promise quick and effective cures, as was the case with the arrival of Clozaril, Xanax, and Prozac. But the **placebo effect** ensures that many people will respond positively to a new drug just because of the enthusiasm surrounding it and their own expectations that the drug will make them feel better. After a while, when placebo effects decline, many drugs turn out to be neither as effective as promised nor as widely applicable. This has happened repeatedly with each new generation of tranquilizers and each new "miracle" antipsychotic drug and antidepressant, including Clozaril and Prozac (Healy, 2004; Moncrieff, 2001).

In fact, some investigators maintain that much of the effectiveness of antidepressants is due to a placebo effect (Khan et al., 2003; Kirsch &

TABLE 12.1
Drugs Used in the Treatment of Psychological Disorders

	Antipsychotics (Neuroleptics)	Antidepressants	Tranquilizers	Lithium Carbonate
Example	Thorazine	Prozac (SSRI)	Valium	
	Haldol	Nardil (MAOI)	Xanax	
	Clozaril	Elavil (tricyclic)		
	Risperdal	Paxil (SSRI)		
		Wellbutrin (other)		
		Cymbalta (other)		
Primarily used for	Schizophrenia	Depression	Mood disorders	Bipolar disorder
	Other psychoses	Anxiety disorders	Panic disorder	
	Impulsive anger	Panic disorder		
	Bipolar disorder	Obsessive-compulsive disorder		

Sapirstein, 1998). Even researchers who quarrel with that strong conclusion acknowledge that the drugs are less effective than commonly believed. Overall, only about half of all depressed patients respond positively to any given antidepressant medication, and of those, only about 40 percent are actually responding to the specific biological effects of the drugs (Hollon, Thase, & Markowitz, 2002). New research in neuroscience is illuminating the reason that placebos work for some people: The psychological expectation of improvement actually produces some of the same brain changes that medication does (Benedetti et al., 2005).

2 *High dropout and relapse rates.* A person may have short-term success with antipsychotic or antidepressant drugs. However, in part because of these drugs' unpleasant side effects, one-half to two-thirds of people eventually stop taking them. When they do, they are quite likely to relapse, especially if they have not learned how to cope with their problems (Hollon, Thase, & Maskowitz, 2002).

3 *Dosage problems.* The challenge with drugs is to find the *therapeutic window*, the amount that is enough but not too much. This problem is compounded by the fact that the same dose of a drug may be metabolized differently in men and women, old people and young people, and different ethnic groups. When psychiatrist Keh-Ming Lin moved from Taiwan to the United States, he was amazed to learn that the dosage of antipsychotic drugs given to American patients with schizophrenia was often ten times higher than the dose for Chinese patients. In subsequent studies, Lin and his colleagues confirmed that Asian patients require significantly lower doses of the medication for optimal treatment (Lin, Poland, & Chien, 1990). Similarly, African-Americans suffering from depression or bipolar disorder seem to need lower dosages of tricyclic antidepressants and lithium than other ethnic groups do (Strickland et al., 1991, 1995). Groups may differ in the dosages they can tolerate because of variations in metabolic rates, amount of body fat, the number or type of drug receptors in the brain, or cultural practices such as smoking cigarettes and eating certain foods.

4 *Unknown long-term risks.* As we saw, antipsychotic drugs can have dangerous and even fatal consequences if taken for many years. Antidepressants, in contrast, are assumed to be quite safe, but the effects of taking them indefi-

nitely are still unknown. One problem is that many of the studies that get no results or that demonstrate a drug's hazards go unpublished (Krimsky, 2003). In 2003, British drug authorities reported that nine unpublished studies of Paxil found that it tripled the risk of suicidal thoughts and suicide attempts in young people who were taking the drug, compared to those given a placebo (Harris, 2003). Paxil and other SSRIs can cause a severe form of restlessness and agitation in the first few weeks they are taken, and this reaction might push vulnerable young people to a precipice. Today, the U.S. Food and Drug Administration (FDA) has required warning labels on SSRIs and has cautioned against prescribing them to anyone under 18.

The general public and even many physicians do not realize that new drugs are often tested on only a few hundred people for only a few weeks or months, even when the drug is one that patients might take for years. (The cost of bringing most new drugs to market is very high, and manufacturers feel they cannot afford to wait years to determine whether there might be long-term hazards.) Many physicians and laypersons, feeling reassured if a drug is effective in the short run, overlook the possibility of long-term dangers, as well as the potential risks of drug interactions. Yet psychiatrists, understandably frustrated by the failure of existing antipsychotics and antidepressants to help all of their clients, are increasingly prescribing "cocktails" of medications—this one for anxiety,

"I think the dosage needs adjusting. I'm not nearly as happy as the people in the ads."

plus this one for depression, plus another to manage the side effects. They report anecdotal success in some cases, but as yet there has been virtually no research on the benefits and risks of these combination approaches over time.

Medications have saved lives and improved the lives of thousands of people suffering from severe mental illness, as well as those suffering from milder forms of depression, anxiety, and other emotional problems. Yet the cautions we have listed are the reason that it is important to think critically about this issue. The popularity of drugs has been fueled by pressure from managed-care organizations, which prefer to pay for one patient visit for a prescription rather than ten visits for psychotherapy, and by drug company advertising. In 1997 the Food and Drug Administration (FDA) permitted pharmaceutical companies to advertise directly to consumers, a practice still forbidden in Canada and Europe; sales of new drugs skyrocketed.

Yet most consumers do not realize that once a drug is approved by the FDA, doctors are permitted to prescribe it for different conditions and for populations other than those on which it was originally tested. That is why antidepressants are now being marketed for "social phobias"; why Prozac, when its patent expired, was renamed Sarafem and marketed to women for "Premenstrual Dysphoric Disorder"; why Ritalin, widely given to school-aged children, is now being prescribed for 2- and 3-year-olds; and why antipsychotics such as Risperdal are being used for nonpsychotic disorders such as impulsive aggression. Most worrisome for the future of impartial research is that most researchers who are studying the effectiveness of medication have strong financial ties to the pharmaceutical industry in the form of consulting fees, funding for studies, stock investments, and patents (Angell, 2004; Healy, 2002; Krimsky, 2003).

The overprescription of drugs for mood disorders in North America also occurs because of a common but mistaken assumption: that if a disorder appears to have biological origins or involve biochemical abnormalities, then biological treatments must be most appropriate. But, in fact, changing your behavior and thoughts—through psychotherapy or other new experiences—can also change the way your brain functions. This point was dramatically illustrated in two PET-scan studies of people with obsessive-compulsive disorder. Among those who were taking Prozac, the metabolism of glucose in the brain improved, suggesting that the drug was having a beneficial effect. But exactly the *same* brain changes occurred in people who were getting cognitive-behavior

psychosurgery Any surgical procedure that destroys selected areas of the brain believed to be involved in emotional disorders or violent, impulsive behavior.

FIGURE 12.1
Psychotherapy and the Brain
These PET scans show the brain of a person with obsessive-compulsive disorder before and after behavior therapy. Before therapy, the glucose metabolic rates in the right caudate nucleus (rCd) were elevated. After therapy, this area calmed down, becoming less active, just as it did with medication (Schwartz et al., 1996).

therapy and no medication (see Figure 12.1) (Baxter et al., 1992; Schwartz et al., 1996). And unlike antidepressants, cognitive-behavior therapy also restores depressed people's brain-wave patterns during sleep to normal (Thase et al., 1998).

In sum, consumers must critically weigh the benefits and limitations of medication for psychological problems. If ever a question required us not to oversimplify, this one is it. Drugs for mental disorders are neither totally miraculous, as some of their promoters say, nor totally worthless, as some of their critics maintain. Their effectiveness depends on why the individual is taking them, how severe the problem is, and whether the person learns how to function better and cope with the problem.

Direct Brain Intervention

For most of human history, a person suffering from mental illness often got a rather extreme form of "help." A well-meaning tribal healer or, later, a doctor would try to release the "psychic pressures" believed to be causing the symptoms by drilling holes in the victim's skull. (It didn't work.) However, the basic impulse—to try to cure mental illness by intervening directly in the brain—has continued.

One effort is through **psychosurgery**, surgery designed to destroy selected areas of the brain thought to be responsible for emotional disorders or disturbed behavior. The most famous form of modern psychosurgery was invented in 1935, when a Portuguese neurologist, Antonio Egas Moniz, drilled two holes into the skull of a mental patient and used a specially designed instrument to cut or crush nerve fibers running from the prefrontal lobes to other areas. This operation, called a *prefrontal lobotomy*, was supposed to reduce the patient's emotional symptoms without impairing intellectual ability. The procedure—which, incredibly, was never assessed or validated scientifically—was performed on tens of thousands of people. Tragically, lobotomies left many patients apathetic, withdrawn, and unable to care for themselves (Valenstein, 1986). Yet Moniz won a Nobel prize for his work.

Today, psychosurgery is rare, but some neurosurgeons have not given up on the effort to cure mental illness by operating on the brain. Some are burning holes in the frontal lobes of the brain as a last resort for people with intractable cases of obsessive-compulsive disorder and severe depression, people who have not responded to drugs or psychotherapy (Cosgrove & Rauch, 2003). Unfortunately, reports of success are largely anecdotal and no controlled studies have been conducted on any of the new forms of psychosurgery (Lopes et al., 2004).

Instead of operating on the brain, therefore, other psychiatrists and neurologists prefer to stimulate it electrically. The oldest method is **electroconvulsive therapy (ECT)**, or "shock therapy," which is used for the treatment of severe depression, although no one knows how or why it works. An electrode is placed on one side of the head (rarely on both), and a brief current is turned on. The current triggers a seizure that typically lasts one minute, causing the body to convulse. Today, unlike in the past, patients are given muscle relaxants and anesthesia, so they sleep through the procedure and their convulsions are minimized. ECT has helped some people who are suicidal and who have not responded to medication

or any other treatments. However, the mood-improving effect of ECT is usually short-lived, and the depression almost always returns within a few weeks or months (Hollon, Thase, & Markowitz, 2002). And ECT is *ineffective* with other disorders, such as schizophrenia or alcoholism, though it is occasionally misused for these conditions.

ECT's supporters cite research showing that when ECT is used properly, it is safe and causes no long-term cognitive impairment, significant memory loss, or detectable brain damage (Abrams, 1997; Fink, 1999). Critics counter that ECT is often used improperly and that it can in fact damage the brain. While this debate continues, researchers are looking for milder ways to electrically stimulate the brains of severely depressed individuals. One method, *transcranial magnetic stimulation (TMS)*, involves the use of a pulsing magnetic coil held to a person's skull over the left prefrontal cortex. This area of the brain is less active in people with depression, and repeated TMS seems to give it a boost. The patient stays awake, and the procedure does not cause memory loss or other side effects (Wasserman & Lisanby, 2001). In one well-controlled study of depressed patients who had not improved on medication, those who were given TMS treatments every day for four weeks were more likely to improve than those given a sham treatment with no stimulation (Fitzgerald et al., 2003). Nonetheless, as yet, no one knows why magnetic stimulation might ease a patient's emotional suffering.

George Ruhe/The New York Times

Top, a man receives ECT; below, a researcher demonstrates transcranial magnetic stimulation (TMS), a newer method for treating depression.

QUICK quiz

No amount of electric shock will stimulate test-taking ability.

A. Match these treatments with the problems for which they are typically used.

   1. antipsychotic drugs
   2. antidepressant drugs
   3. lithium carbonate
   4. electroconvulsive therapy

   a. suicidal depression
   b. bipolar disorder
   c. schizophrenia
   d. depression and anxiety
   e. obsessive-compulsive disorder

B. Give four reasons to be cautious about claims that drugs for psychological disorders are miracle cures.

C. Jezebel has had occasional episodes of depression that seem to be getting worse. Her physician prescribes an antidepressant. Before taking it, what questions should Jezebel ask herself and the doctor?

Answers:

A. 1. c 2. d, e 3. b 4. a B. Placebo effects are common; dropout and relapse rates are high; appropriate dosages can be difficult to determine and can vary by sex, age, and ethnicity; and some drugs have unknown or long-term risks. C. Has the physician prescribed the drug without taking her full medical and psychological history? Has the physician considered all possible reasons for her depression? Would psychotherapy be appropriate, either with or without medication? Does the medication have any unpleasant side effects or long-term risks? Will the doctor continue to monitor her reactions to the drug on a regular basis?

electroconvulsive therapy (ECT) A procedure used in cases of prolonged and severe major depression, in which a brief brain seizure is induced.

WHAT'S *Ahead*

- Why are psychodynamic therapies called "depth" therapies?
- How can therapies based on learning principles help you change your bad habits?
- How do cognitive therapists help people get rid of self-defeating thoughts?
- Why do humanist therapists focus on the "here and now" instead of the "why and how"?
- Why do family therapists prefer to treat families rather than individuals?

Kinds of Psychotherapy

All good psychotherapists want to help clients think about their lives in new ways and find solutions to the problems that plague them. In this section we will consider the major schools of psychotherapy. To illustrate the philosophy and methods of each one, we will focus on a fictional fellow named Murray. Murray is a smart guy whose problem is all too familiar to many students: He procrastinates. He just can't seem to settle down and write his term papers. He keeps getting incompletes, and before long the incompletes turn to F's. Why does Murray procrastinate, manufacturing his own misery? What kind of therapy might help him?

Psychodynamic Therapy

Sigmund Freud was the father of the "talking cure," as one of his patients called it. In his method of **psychoanalysis**, patients talk not about their immediate problems but about their dreams and memories of childhood. Freud believed that intensive analysis of these dreams and memories would give patients insight into the unconscious reasons for their symptoms and unhappiness. With insight and emotional release, the person's symptoms would disappear.

In orthodox psychoanalysis, which is rarely practiced today, the client meets with the therapist as often as several times a week for a period of years. The client lies on a sofa, with the analyst sitting out of view, and says whatever comes to mind without censoring, a technique called **free association**. (The popular image of therapy in cartoons and movies still often includes a person lying on a couch.) The analyst listens to the client's free associations and dreams but rarely comments. There is no rush to solve the problem that brought the client into therapy. In fact, a person may come in complaining of a symptom, such as anxiety or headaches, and the therapist may not get around to that symptom for months or even years. The analyst views the symptom as only the tip of the mental iceberg.

Freud's psychoanalytic method has evolved into many different forms of **psychodynamic therapy**, which share the goal of exploring the unconscious dynamics of personality, such as defenses and conflicts (see Chapter 2). Proponents of these therapies often refer to them as "depth" therapies because the goal is to delve into the deep, unconscious processes believed to be the source of the patient's problems rather than to concentrate on "superficial" symptoms and conscious beliefs.

A major element of all psychodynamic therapies, from Freudian to present forms, is **transference**, the client's transfer (displacement) of emotional elements of his or her inner life—usually feelings about the client's parents—outward onto the analyst. Have you ever found yourself responding to a new acquaintance with unusually quick affection or dislike, and later realized it was because the person reminded you of a relative whom you loved or loathed? That experience is similar to transference. In therapy, a woman who has failed to resolve her Oedipal love for her father might believe she has fallen in love with the analyst. A man who is unconsciously angry at his mother for rejecting him might become furious with his analyst for going on vacation. Through analysis of transference in the therapy setting, psychodynamic therapists believe, clients can see their emotional conflicts in action and can work through and resolve them.

Today, most psychodynamic therapists reject the orthodox psychoanalytic approach, while retaining

"HAVE A COUPLE OF DREAMS, AND CALL ME IN THE MORNING."

psychoanalysis A method of "depth" psychotherapy developed by Sigmund Freud, emphasizing the exploration of unconscious motives and conflicts.

free association In psychodynamic therapies, the process of saying freely whatever comes to mind in connection with dreams, memories, fantasies, or conflicts.

psychodynamic therapies Psychotherapies that share the goal of exploring the unconscious dynamics of personality, although they differ from Freudian analysis in various ways.

transference In psychodynamic therapies, a critical process in which the client transfers unconscious emotions or reactions, such as emotional feelings about his or her parents, onto the therapist.

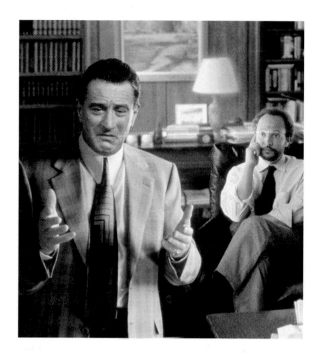

Many popular TV shows and movies, such as The Sopranos *and* Analyze This *(with Robert DeNiro as a mobster patient and Billy Crystal as his psychoanalyst), feature psychodynamic therapists. This is one reason that many people mistakenly think that all therapies are psychodynamic.*

the key goals of examining transference, probing for unconscious motives and patterns that stem from childhood experiences, and breaking through the client's unconscious defenses (Schafer, 1992; Westen, 1998). They sit facing the client, they participate more actively, and they are more goal directed than traditional analysts. Many practice time-limited therapy, consisting of 15, 20, or 25 sessions. Without delving into the client's entire history, the therapist listens to the client's problems and formulates the main issue (Groves, 1996). The rest of the therapy focuses on the person's self-defeating habits and recurring problems. For example, our friend Murray might gain the insight that he procrastinates as a way of expressing anger toward his parents. He might realize that he is angry because they insist that he study for a career he dislikes. Ideally, Murray will come to this insight by himself. If the analyst suggests it, Murray might feel too defensive to accept it.

Behavior and Cognitive Therapy

Unlike psychodynamic therapists, psychologists who practice behavior therapy or cognitive therapy would not worry much about Murray's past, his parents, or his unconscious anxieties. Psychologists who practice behavior therapy would get right to the problem: What are the reinforcers in Murray's environment that are maintaining his behavior? "Mur," they would say, "forget about insight. You have lousy study habits." Psychologists who practice cognitive therapy would focus on helping Murray understand how his beliefs about studying, writing papers, and success are woefully unrealistic. Often these two approaches are combined.

Behavioral Techniques

Behavior therapy is based on *applied behavioral analysis*, the application of techniques derived from the behavioral principles of classical and operant conditioning that we discussed in Chapter 9. (You may want to review those principles before going on.) Here are some of these methods (Kazdin, 2001):

1 *Exposure.* The most widely used behavioral approach for treating fears and panic is **graduated exposure**. When people are afraid of some situation, object, or upsetting memory, they usually do everything they can to avoid confronting or thinking of it. Naturally, this only makes the fear worse. Exposure treatments, either in the client's imagination or in actual situations, are aimed at reversing this tendency. In graduated exposure, the client controls the degree of confrontation with the source of the fear. For example, someone who is trying to avoid thinking of a traumatic event might be asked to imagine the event over and over, until it no longer evokes the same degree of panic. A more dramatic form of exposure is **flooding**, in which the therapist takes the client directly into the feared situation and remains there until the client's panic and anxiety decline. Thus a person suffering from agoraphobia might be taken into a department store or a

behavior therapy A form of therapy that applies principles of classical and operant conditioning to help people change self-defeating or problematic behaviors.

graduated exposure In behavior therapy, a method in which a person suffering from an anxiety disorder, such as a phobia or panic attacks, is gradually confronted with the feared object or situation until the anxiety subsides.

flooding In behavior therapy, a form of exposure treatment in which the client is taken directly into the feared situation until his or her panic subsides.

In this "virtual reality" version of graduated exposure, people with spider phobias are gradually exposed to computerized but extremely lifelike images of spiders in a realistic, three-dimensional environment.

Cure Your Fears

See whether systematic desensitization will help you conquer your greatest fear. Write down a list of situations that evoke your fear, starting with one that produces little anxiety (e.g., looking down from a second-floor window) and ending with the most frightening one (e.g., looking straight down from a fiftieth-floor window). Then find a quiet room where you will have no distractions, sit in a comfortable chair, and relax all the muscles of your body. Breathe slowly and deeply. Imagine the first, easiest scene, remaining as relaxed as possible. Do this until you can confront the image without becoming anxious. When that happens, go on to the next scene in your hierarchy. Do not try this all at once; space out your sessions over time. Does it work?

---

subway, an action that would normally be terrifying to contemplate. Notice how different this approach is from the psychodynamic one, in which the goal is to uncover the presumably unconscious reason that the agoraphobic feels afraid of going out.

2 **Systematic desensitization.** Systematic desensitization is an older behavioral method, a step-by-step process of breaking down a client's conditioned associations with a feared object or experience (Wolpe, 1958). It is based on the classical-conditioning procedure of *counterconditioning*, in which a stimulus (such as a dog) for an unwanted response (such as fear) is paired with some other stimulus or situation that elicits a response incompatible with the undesirable one (see Chapter 9). In this case, the incompatible response is usually relaxation. The client learns to relax deeply while imagining or looking at a sequence of feared stimuli, arranged in a hierarchy from the least frightening to the most frightening. The hierarchy itself is provided by the client. The sequence for a person who is terrified of spiders might be to read the classic children's story *Charlotte's Web*, then look at pictures of small, cute spiders, then look at pictures of tarantulas, then move on to observing a real spider, and so on. At each step the person must become relaxed and comfortable before going on. Eventually, the fear responses are extinguished.

3 **Behavioral self-monitoring.** Before people can change their behavior, they have to identify the reinforcers that are supporting their unwanted habits: attention from others, temporary relief from tension or unhappiness, or tangible rewards such as money or a good meal. One way to do this is for the client to keep a record of the behavior that he or she wishes to change. A man who wants to curb his overeating may not be aware of how much he eats throughout the day to relieve tension; a behavioral record might show that he eats more junk food than he realized in the late afternoon. A mother might complain that her child "always" has temper tantrums; a behavioral record will show when, where, and with whom they occur. Once the unwanted behavior is identified, along with the reinforcers that have been maintaining it, a treatment program can be designed to change it. For instance, the man might find other ways to reduce stress and make sure that he is nowhere near junk food in the late afternoon. The mother can learn to respond to her child's tantrum not with her attention (or a cookie to buy silence) but with a time-out: banishing the child to a corner where no positive reinforcers are available.

4 **Skills training.** It is not enough to tell someone "Don't be shy" if the person does not know how to make small talk with others, or "Don't yell!" if the person does not know how to express feelings calmly. Therefore, some behavior therapists use operant-conditioning techniques, modeling, and role-playing to teach the skills a client might lack. For example, a shy person might learn how to converse in social settings by focusing on other people rather than on his or her own insecurity. Skills-training programs have been designed for all kinds of behavioral problems, such as teaching parents how to discipline their children, impulsive adults how to manage anger, and people with schizophrenia how to get along in the world.

A behaviorist would treat Murray's procrastination in several ways. Murray might not know how he actually spends his time when he is avoiding his studies. Afraid that he hasn't time to do everything,

---

systematic desensitization In behavior therapy, a step-by-step process of desensitizing a client to a feared object or experience; it is based on the classical-conditioning procedure of counterconditioning.

behavioral self-monitoring In behavior therapy, a method of keeping careful data on the frequency and consequences of the behavior to be changed.

skills training In behavior therapy, an effort to teach the client skills that he or she may lack, as well as new constructive behaviors to replace self-defeating ones.

he does nothing. Monitoring his own behavior with a diary would let Murray know exactly how he spends his time, and how much time he should realistically allot to a project. Instead of having a vague, impossibly huge goal, such as "I'm going to reorganize my life," Murray would establish specific small goals, such as reading the two books necessary for an English paper and writing one page of an assignment. If Murray does not know how to write clearly, however, even writing one page might feel overwhelming; he might also need some skills training, such as a basic composition class. Most important, the therapist would change the reinforcers that are maintaining Murray's "procrastination behavior"—perhaps the immediate gratification of partying with friends—and replace them with reinforcers for getting the work done.

Cognitive Techniques

Of course, people's thoughts and motivations can influence their behavior. **Cognitive therapy** helps clients identify the beliefs and expectations that might be unnecessarily prolonging their anger, fear, depression, conflicts, and other problems (Persons, Davidson, & Tompkins, 2001). Clients examine the evidence for their beliefs—say, that everyone is mean and selfish, that ambition is hopeless, or that love is doomed. They learn to consider other explanations of the behavior of people who annoy them: Perhaps their father's strict discipline was intended not to control but to protect them. By requiring people to identify their assumptions and biases, examine the evidence, and consider other interpretations, cognitive therapy, as you can see, teaches critical thinking!

One of the best-known contemporary schools of cognitive therapy is Albert Ellis's **rational emotive behavior therapy** (Ellis, 1993; Ellis & Blau, 1998). In this approach, which reflects Ellis's own no-nonsense, get-on-with-it attitude, the therapist uses rational arguments to directly challenge a client's unrealistic beliefs or expectations. Ellis has pointed out that people who are emotionally upset often *overgeneralize*: They decide that one annoying act by someone means that person is totally bad in every way, or that a normal mistake they made is evidence that they are rotten to the core. Many people also *catastrophize*, transforming a small problem into a disaster: "I failed this test, and now I'll flunk out of school, and no one will ever like me, and even my cat will hate me, and I'll never get a job." The therapist challenges these thoughts directly, showing the client why they are irrational and misguided.

Another leading form of cognitive therapy, devised by Aaron Beck (1976, 2005), avoids direct challenges to the client's beliefs. Beck pioneered in the application of cognitive therapy for depression. As we saw in Chapter 11, depression often arises from specific pessimistic thoughts—for example, that the sources of your misery are permanent and that nothing good will ever happen to you again. For Beck, these beliefs are not "irrational"; rather, they are unproductive or based on misinformation. A therapist using Beck's approach would encourage you to test your beliefs against the evidence. If you say, "But I *know* no one likes me," the therapist might say, "Oh, yes? How do you know? Do you really not have a single friend? Has anyone in the past year been nice to you?"

Cognitive therapists encourage clients to emphasize the positive (the early sunny signs of spring) rather than always focusing on the negative (the lingering icy clutch of winter). Poet Michael Casey described the first daffodil that bravely rises through the snow as "a gleam of laughter in a sullen face."

GET INVOLVED

Mind Over Mood

See whether cognitive-therapy techniques can help you control your moods. Think of a time recently when you felt a particularly strong emotion, such as depression, anger, or anxiety. On a piece of paper, record (1) the situation—who was there, what happened, and when; (2) the intensity of your feeling at the time, from weak to strong; and (3) the thoughts that were going through your mind (e.g., "She never cares about what I want to do"; "I hate being angry"; "He's going to leave me").

Now examine your thoughts. What is the worst thing that can happen if those thoughts are true? Are your thoughts accurate or are you "mind-reading" the other person's intentions and motives? Is there another way to think about this situation or the other person's behavior? If you practice this exercise repeatedly, you may learn how your thoughts affect your moods—and find out that you have more control over your feelings than you realized (from Greenberger & Padesky, 1995).

cognitive therapy A form of therapy designed to identify and change irrational, unproductive ways of thinking and, hence, to reduce negative emotions and their behavioral consequences.

rational emotive behavior therapy A form of cognitive therapy devised by Albert Ellis, designed to challenge the client's unrealistic or irrational thoughts.

A cognitive therapist might treat Murray's procrastination by having Murray write down his thoughts about work, read the thoughts as if someone else had said them, and then write a rational response to each one. This technique would encourage Murray to examine the validity of his assumptions and beliefs. Many procrastinators are perfectionists; if they cannot do something perfectly, they will not do it at all. Unable to accept their limitations, they set impossible standards and catastrophize:

Negative Thought	Rational Response
If I don't get an A+ on this paper, my life will be ruined.	My life will be a lot worse if I keep getting incompletes. It's better to get a B or even a C than to do nothing at all.
My professor is going to think I'm an idiot when he reads this. I'll feel humiliated by his criticism.	He hasn't accused me of being an idiot yet. If he makes some criticisms, I can learn from them and do better next time.

Strict behaviorists consider thoughts to be "behaviors" that are modifiable by learning principles; they do not regard thoughts as causes of behavior. But most psychologists believe that thoughts and behavior influence each other, which is why *cognitive-behavior therapy* is more common than either form alone.

Humanist and Existential Therapy

Humanist therapy, like its parent philosophy humanism, starts from the assumption that people seek self-actualization and self-fulfillment. The humanist therapist generally does not dig into past conflicts but aims instead to help clients feel better about themselves and free themselves from self-imposed limits. Humanist therapists want to know how clients subjectively perceive their own situations, so they can help them develop the will and confidence to bring about change. That is why they explore what is going on "here and now," not the issues of "why and how."

In **client-centered (nondirective) therapy**, developed by Carl Rogers, the therapist's role is to listen to the client's needs in an accepting, nonjudgmental way and offer what Rogers called *unconditional positive regard* (see Chapter 2). Whatever the client's specific complaint is, the goal is to build the client's self-esteem and self-acceptance and help the client find a more productive way of seeing his or her problems. Thus a Rogerian might assume that Murray's procrastination masks his low self-regard, and that Murray is out of touch with his real feelings and wish-

es. Perhaps he is not passing his courses because he is trying to please his parents by majoring in prelaw, when he would secretly rather become an artist.

Rogers (1951, 1961) believed that effective therapists must be warm and genuine in expressing their feelings and must respect their clients' feelings, too. For Rogers, *empathy*, the therapist's ability to understand and accept what the client says, is the crucial ingredient of successful therapy. The therapist shows a basic level of empathy by listening carefully and being able to restate accurately the client's remarks: "You tell me that you feel frustrated, Murray, because no matter how hard you try, you don't succeed." But the therapist shows advanced empathy by understanding the *meaning* of the client's remarks: "Working that hard without results must really make you unhappy and maybe make you feel a bit sorry for yourself." The client, according to Rogers, will eventually internalize the therapist's support and become more self-accepting.

Existential therapy helps clients explore the meaning of existence and face with courage the great questions of life, such as death, freedom, alienation from oneself and others, loneliness, and meaninglessness. Existential therapists, like humanist therapists, believe that our lives are not inevitably determined by our pasts or our circumstances—that we have the power to choose our own destinies. As Irvin Yalom (1989) explained, "The crucial first step in therapy is the patient's assumption of responsibility for his or her life predicament. As long as one believes that one's problems are caused by some force or agency outside oneself, there is no leverage in therapy."

Client-centered therapy emphasizes the importance of the therapist's warmth and empathy.

humanist therapy A form of psychotherapy based on the philosophy of humanism, which emphasizes people's free will to change, not past conflicts.

client-centered (nondirective) therapy A humanist approach to therapy devised by Carl Rogers, which emphasizes the therapist's empathy with the client and the use of unconditional positive regard.

existential therapy A form of therapy designed to help clients explore the meaning of existence and face the great questions of life, such as death, freedom, alienation, and loneliness.

Yalom argues that the goal of therapy is to help clients cope with the inescapable realities of life and death and the struggle for meaning. However grim our experiences may be, he believes, "they contain the seeds of wisdom and redemption." Perhaps the most remarkable example of a man able to find seeds of wisdom in a barren landscape was Victor Frankl (1905–1997), who developed a form of existential therapy after surviving a Nazi concentration camp. In that pit of horror, Frankl (1955) observed, some people maintained their sanity because they were able to find meaning in the experience, shattering though it was.

Some observers believe that, ultimately, all therapies are existential. In different ways, therapy helps people determine what is important to them, what values guide them, and what changes they will have the courage to make. An existential therapist might help Murray think about the significance of his procrastination, what his ultimate goals in life are, and how he might find the strength to carry out his ambitions.

Family and Couples Therapy

Murray's situation is getting worse. His father has begun to call him Tomorrow Man, which upsets his mother, and his younger brother, the math major, has been calculating how much tuition money Murray's incompletes are costing. His older sister Isabel, the biochemist who never had an incomplete in her life, now proposes that all of them go to a family therapist. "Murray's not the only one in this family with complaints," she says.

Family therapists would maintain that Murray's problem developed in the context of his family, that it is sustained by the dynamics of his family, and that any change he makes will affect all members of his family (McDaniel, Lusterman, & Philpot, 2001). One of the most famous early family therapists, Salvador Minuchin (1984), compared the family to a kaleidoscope, a changing pattern of mosaics in which the pattern is larger than any one piece. In this view, efforts to isolate and treat one member of the family without the others are doomed. Only if all family members reveal their differing perceptions of each other can mistakes and misperceptions be identified. A teenager, for instance, may see his mother as crabby and nagging when actually she is tired and worried. A parent may see a child as rebellious when in fact the child is lonely and desperate for attention.

Family members are usually unaware of how they influence one another. By observing the entire family, the family therapist hopes to discover tensions and imbalances in power and communication. For example, in some families a child may

have a chronic illness or a psychological disorder, such as anorexia, that affects the workings of the whole family. One parent may become overinvolved with the sick child while the other parent retreats, and each may start blaming the other. The child, in turn, may cling to the illness or disorder as a way of expressing anger, keeping the parents together, getting the parents' attention, or asserting control (Kerr & Bowen, 1998; Luepnitz, 1988).

Even when it is not possible to treat the whole family, some therapists will treat individuals in a **family-systems perspective**, which recognizes that people's behavior in a family is as interconnected as that of two dancers (Bowen, 1978; Carter & McGoldrick, 1988; Lerner, 1989). Clients learn that if they change in any way, even for the better, their families may protest noisily or may send subtle messages that read, "Change back!" Why? Because when one family member changes, each of the others must change too. As the saying goes, it takes two to tango, and if one dancer stops, so must the other. But most people do not like change. They are comfortable with old patterns and habits, even those that cause them trouble. They want to keep dancing the same old dance, even if their feet hurt.

When a couple is arguing frequently about issues that never seem to get resolved, they may benefit from *couples therapy*, which is designed to help couples understand and resolve the inevitable conflicts that occur in all relationships (Christensen & Jacobson, 2000). Couples therapists generally insist on seeing both partners, so that they will hear both sides of the story. They cut through the blaming and attacking ("She never listens to me!" "He never does anything!") and focus on helping the couple get over hurt and blame and make specific

family-systems perspective An approach to doing therapy with individuals or families by emphasizing how each family member forms part of a larger interacting system.

Some family therapists use photographs to help people identify themes and problems in their family histories. Does this picture convey a happy and cohesive family to you or a divided one? Shortly after it was taken, the couple divorced; the father took custody of the children . . . and the mother kept the dog (Entin, 1992).

behavioral changes to reduce anger and conflict. Recently, many couples therapists have been moving away from the "fix all the differences" approach and are instead helping couples learn to accept and live with qualities, in both partners, that aren't going to change much (Hayes, 2004). For example, a wife can stop trying to turn her calm, steady husband into a spontaneous adventurer ("After all, that's what I originally loved about him—he's as steady as a rock") and a husband can stop trying to make his shy wife more assertive ("I have always loved her serenity").

Family and couples therapists may use psychodynamic, behavioral, cognitive, or humanist approaches in their work; they share only a focus on the family or the couple. In Murray's case, a family therapist would observe how Murray's procrastination fits his family dynamics. Perhaps it allows Murray to get his father's attention and his mother's sympathy. Perhaps it keeps Murray from facing his greatest fear: that if he does finish his work, it will not measure up to his father's high standards. The therapist will not only help Murray change his work habits but also help his family deal with a changed Murray.

Psychotherapy in Practice

The kinds of psychotherapy that we have discussed are all quite different in theory, and so are their techniques (see Table 12.2). Yet in practice, many

TABLE 12.2
The Major Schools of Therapy Compared

	Primary Goal	Methods
Psychodynamic		
Psychoanalytic	Insight into unconscious motives and feelings	Probing unconscious motives through dream analysis, free association, transference
Modern Psychodynamic	Same	Analyst more active and directive; therapy briefer
Cognitive-Behavior		
Behavioral	Modification of self-defeating behaviors	Systematic desensitization, exposure (flooding), behavioral records, skills training
Cognitive	Modification of irrational or unvalidated beliefs	Challenging unwarranted beliefs, catastrophizing, and mind reading, or prompting client to test beliefs against evidence
Humanist and Existential		
Humanist	Insight; self-acceptance and self-fulfillment; new, optimistic perceptions of self and world	Providing a nonjudgmental setting in which to discuss life issues; use of empathy and unconditional positive regard by therapist
Existential	Finding meaning in life and accepting inevitable losses	Varies with therapist; philosophical discussions about meaning of life, client's goals, finding courage
Family and Couples		
Family	Modification of family patterns	May use any of the preceding methods to change family patterns that perpetuate problems and conflicts
Couples	Resolution of conflicts, breaking out of destructive habits, accepting differences	May use any of the preceding methods to help the couple communicate better, resolve conflicts, or accept what cannot be changed

psychotherapists take an *integrative approach*, drawing on methods and ideas from various schools and avoiding strong allegiances to any one theory. This flexibility enables them to treat clients with whatever methods work best.

All successful therapies, regardless of approach, share a key element: They are able to motivate the client into wanting to change, and they replace a client's pessimistic or unrealistic story—the story each of us develops over time to explain our lives and problems—with one that is more hopeful or attainable (Freedman & Combs, 1996; Howard, 1991; Schafer, 1992). Some therapists explicitly focus on helping clients change their life narratives

and their own role in them. For example, David Epston worked with an immigrant woman named Marisa, who had been abused and rejected all her life. "To tell a story about your life turns it into a history," he told her, "one that can be left behind, and makes it easier for you to create a future of your own design" (quoted in O'Hanlon, 1994). Marisa came to see that she could tell a new story about her experiences. Instead of seeing the tragedies that had befallen her as evidence that she was a worthless victim, as she always had, she now saw the same events as evidence of her strength and endurance. "My life has a future now," she told him. "It will never be the same again."

QUICK quiz

Don't be a procrastinator like our friend Murray; take this quiz now.

Match each method or concept with the therapy associated with it.

1. transference
2. systematic desensitization
3. facing the fear of death
4. reappraisal of thoughts
5. unconditional positive regard
6. exposure to feared situation
7. avoidance of "catastrophizing"
8. analysis of generational patterns

a. cognitive therapy
b. psychodynamic therapy
c. humanist therapy
d. behavior therapy
e. family therapy
f. existential therapy

Answers:

1.b 2.d 3.f 4.a 5.c 6.d 7.a 8.e

WHAT'S *Ahead*

- What is the "therapeutic alliance" and why does it matter?
- What sorts of people make the best therapists and the best clients?
- What is the "scientist–practitioner gap" and why has it been widening?
- Which form of psychotherapy is most likely to help if you are anxious or depressed?
- Under what conditions can psychotherapy be harmful?

Evaluating Psychotherapy

Poor Murray! He is getting a little baffled by all these therapies. He wants to make a choice soon—no sense in procrastinating about that, too! Is there

any scientific evidence, he wonders, that might help him decide which therapy will be best for him?

The Therapeutic Alliance

Psychotherapy is, first and foremost, a relationship. As in all relationships, its success depends on the qualities that each person brings to the encounter. Successful therapy often also depends on the bond the therapist and client establish between them, called the **therapeutic alliance**. When both parties respect and understand one another and agree on the goals of treatment, the client is more likely to improve, regardless of the specific techniques the therapist uses (Klein et al., 2003).

Qualities of the Participants Clients who are most likely to do well in therapy are, not surprisingly, motivated to improve and solve their problems (Orlinsky & Howard, 1994). They tend

therapeutic alliance
The bond of confidence and mutual understanding established between therapist and client, which allows them to work together to solve the client's problems.

to have support from their families and a personal style of dealing actively with problems instead of avoiding them. Personality traits also influence whether a person will be able to change in therapy. As we saw in Chapter 2, some people are characteristically negative and bitter; others are more agreeable and positive, even in the midst of emotional crises. Hostile, negative individuals are more resistant to therapy and less likely to benefit from it; so are people with long-standing personality problems or psychotic disorders (Kopta et al., 1994). The personality of the therapist affects the outcome of therapy, too, particularly the qualities that Carl Rogers praised: empathy, warmth, and genuineness. The most successful therapists make their clients feel respected, accepted, and understood (Miller, 2000).

Culture and the Therapeutic Connection

Many therapists and clients establish successful therapeutic alliances in spite of coming from different backgrounds. But sometimes cultural differences cause misunderstandings that result from ignorance or prejudice (Comas-Díaz & Greene, 1994). A lifetime of experience with racism and a general cultural distrust may keep some African-Americans from revealing feelings that they believe a white therapist would not understand or accept (Whaley, 2001). Misunderstandings and prejudice may be one reason that Asian-American, Latino, and African-American clients are more likely to stay in therapy when their therapists' ethnicity matches their own. But a cultural match is also important because it often makes it more likely that clients and therapists will share perceptions of what the client's problem is, agree on the best way of coping, and have the same expectations about what therapy can accomplish (Zone et al., 2005).

In establishing a bond with clients, therapists must distinguish normal cultural patterns from individual psychological problems. An Irish-American family therapist, Monica McGoldrick (1996), described some problems that are typical of Irish-American families. These problems arise from Irish history and religious beliefs, and they are deeply ingrained. "In general, the therapist cannot expect the family to turn into a physically affectionate, emotionally intimate group, or to enjoy being in therapy very much," she observed. "The notion of Original Sin—that you are guilty before you are born—leaves them with a heavy sense of burden. Someone not sensitized to these issues may see this as pathological. It is not. But it is also not likely to change and the therapist should help the family tolerate this inner guilt rather than try to get rid of it."

More and more psychotherapists are becoming "sensitized to the issues" caused by cultural differences (Arredondo et al., 2005). For example, many Latino and Asian clients are likely to react to a formal interview with a therapist with relative passivity and deference, leading some therapists to misdiagnose this cultural norm as a problem with shyness. In Latin American cultures, *susto*, or "loss of the soul," is a

Some psychotherapists fit their approach to the client's cultural background. For example, most Puerto Rican children know the tales of Juan Bobo (left), a foolish child ("bobo") who is always getting into trouble. The therapists on the right have adapted these stories for Puerto Rican children who are coping with new problems and temptations in America. The children and their mothers watch a videotape of the folktale, discuss it together, and later role-play its major themes, such as controlling aggression and distinguishing right from wrong. This method has been more successful than traditional therapies in reducing the children's anxieties and improving their attention spans and imaginations (Costantino & Malgady, 1996).

common response to extreme grief or fright; the person believes that his or her soul has departed along with that of the deceased relative. A psychotherapist unfamiliar with this culturally determined response might conclude that the sufferer was delusional or psychotic. Latino clients are also more likely than Anglos to value harmony in their relationships, which often translates into an unwillingness to express negative emotions or confront family members or friends directly, so therapists need to help such clients find ways to communicate better within that cultural context (Arredondo & Perez, 2003).

Being aware of cultural differences, however, does not mean that the therapist should stereotype clients. Some Asians, after all, do have problems with excessive shyness, some Latinos do have emotional disorders, and some Irish do not carry burdens of guilt! It does mean that therapists must ensure that their clients find them to be trustworthy and effective, and it means that clients must be aware of their own prejudices, too.

The Scientist–Practitioner Gap

Now suppose that Murray has found a nice psychotherapist who seems pretty smart and friendly. Is a good alliance enough? How important is the *kind* of therapy that an individual practices? Have some methods of psychotherapy been scientifically shown to be more effective than others, are some totally useless, and are some potentially harmful?

These questions have generated a huge debate among clinical practitioners and psychological scientists. Many psychotherapists believe that trying to evaluate psychotherapy using standard empirical methods is an exercise in futility: Numbers and graphs, they say, cannot possibly capture the complex exchange that takes place between a therapist and a client. What "works" in psychotherapy is usually not a good technique but a good *relationship*. Psychotherapy, they maintain, is an art that you acquire from clinical experience; it is not a science. You can't measure its effectiveness the way you can measure, say, the effectiveness of a new drug, because so many diverse ingredients go into a good psychotherapeutic experience (Wampold, 2001). Other clinicians fear that efforts to measure the effectiveness of psychotherapy oversimplify the process because, among other reasons, many patients have an assortment of emotional problems and need therapy for a longer time than research can reasonably allow (Westen, Novotny, & Thompson-Brenner, 2004).

Thinking Critically About Research and Psychotherapy

For their part, psychological scientists agree that therapy is often a complex process, but, they argue, that is no reason it cannot be scientifically investigated, just like any other complex psychological process such as the development of language or personality (Crits-Christoph, Wilson, & Hollon, 2005). Moreover, they are concerned that when therapists fail to keep up with empirical findings in the field, their clients may suffer. It is crucial, scientists say, for therapists to be aware of research findings on the most beneficial methods for particular problems, on ineffective or potentially harmful techniques, and on topics relevant to their practice, such as memory, hypnosis, and child development (Lilienfeld, Lynn, & Lohr, 2003).

Over the years, the breach between scientists and therapists has widened, creating what is commonly called the *scientist–practitioner gap*. One reason for the growing split has been the rise of professional schools that are not connected to academic psychology departments and that train students solely to do therapy. Graduates of these schools sometimes know little about research methods or even about research assessing different therapy techniques (Peterson, 2003).

The scientist–practitioner gap has also widened because of the proliferation of new therapies trying to gain a foothold in a crowded market. Some of these therapies are packaged and promoted without any scientific support at all (Beyerstein, 1999). One such therapy, Neurolinguistic Programming (NLP), claims to match people's learning styles with their "brain types" and thereby enhance their communication skills. The U.S. National Research Council concluded that there is no credible evidence for NLP's claims or methods (Druckman & Swets, 1988).

Other therapies repackage established techniques, using a new name and terminology. For example, Eye Movement Desensitization and Reprocessing (EMDR) is built on the tried-and-true behavioral techniques of desensitization and exposure for treating anxiety

randomized controlled trials Research designed to determine the effectiveness of a new medication or form of therapy, in which people with a given problem or disorder are randomly assigned to one or more treatment groups or to a control group.

(Lohr, Tolin, & Lilienfeld, 1998). EMDR's founder, Francine Shapiro (1995), added eye-movement exercises: Clients move their eyes from side to side, following the therapist's moving finger, while concentrating on the memory to be desensitized. Shapiro's (1994) explanation for why such eye movements work is that "the system may become unbalanced due to a trauma or through stress engendered during a developmental window, but once appropriately catalyzed and maintained in a dynamic state by EMDR, it transmutes information to a state of therapeutically appropriate resolution." (If you do not understand that, don't worry; we don't either.)

Thousands of therapists have been trained to do EMDR, and they have claimed success in treating everything from posttraumatic stress disorder and panic attacks to eating disorders and sexual dysfunction. EMDR has even won endorsements from some prominent psychologists. Yet there is no evidence from controlled studies that it is any better than standard exposure treatments (Goldstein et al., 2000; Lohr et al., 1999; Taylor et al., 2003). One clinical researcher who reviewed the evidence concluded that the eye movements that are supposedly essential to this technique do not constitute "anything more than pseudoscientific window dressing" (Lilienfeld, 1996).

Problems in Assessing Therapy

Because of the proliferation of therapies, including many that are questionable at best, and because of economic pressures on insurers and rising health costs, clinical psychologists are increasingly being called on to provide empirical assessments of therapy. But you can't just ask people if the therapy helped them, because no matter what kind of therapy is involved, clients

are motivated to tell you it worked. "Dr. Blitznik is a genius!" they will exclaim. "I would *never* have taken that job (or moved to Cincinnati, or found my true love) if it hadn't been for Dr. Blitznik!" Every kind of therapy ever devised produces enthusiastic testimonials from people who feel it saved their lives.

The problem with testimonials is that none of us can be our own control group. How do people know they wouldn't have taken the job, moved to Cincinnati, or found true love anyway—maybe even sooner, if Dr. Blitznik had not kept them in treatment? Second, Dr. Blitznik's success could be due to the placebo effect: The client's anticipation of success and the buzz about Dr. B.'s fabulous new method might be the active ingredients rather than Dr. B.'s therapy itself. And third, notice that you never hear testimonials from the people who dropped out, who weren't helped, or who actually got worse. So researchers cannot be satisfied with testimonials, no matter how glowing. They know that thanks to the *justification of effort* effect (see Chapter 7), people who have put time, money, and effort into something will tell you it was worth it. No one wants to say, "Yeah, I saw Dr. Blitznik for five years, and boy, was it ever a waste of time."

To guard against these problems, some clinical researchers conduct **randomized controlled trials**, in which people with a given problem or disorder are randomly assigned to one or more treatment groups or to a control group.

CLOSE-UP on Research

Each school of therapy approaches problems differently! Empirical research helps determine which method is best suited for which problem.

Does Crisis Debriefing Help?

Sometimes the results of randomized controlled trials have been surprising, even shocking. For example, in the aftermath of natural and human-made disasters, such as earthquakes or terrorist attacks, disaster therapists often arrive on the scene to treat survivors for symptoms of trauma, hoping to prevent survivors from later developing posttraumatic stress disorder (PTSD). In one of the most popular interventions, called Critical Incident Stress Debriefing (CISD), survivors gather in a group for "debriefing," which generally lasts from one to three hours. Participants are expected to disclose their thoughts and emotions about the traumatic experience, and the group leader warns members about possible trauma symptoms that might develop.

Several independent investigators have **analyzed the assumptions** that underlie CISD: that a traumatic experience almost invariably causes long-lasting posttraumatic stress disorder (as we saw in Chapter 11, it does not); that venting negative emotions is cathartic and helps you get rid of them (as we will see in Chapter 13, it often does just the opposite); and that early intervention—getting to survivors in the immediate aftermath of a disaster—is necessary to head off the development of serious PTSD. All of these assumptions seem to be perfectly reasonable, but when psychological scientists **avoided emotional reasoning** ("It feels reasonable, so it must be true") and **examined the evidence** for them, they were in for a surprise.

Richard Gist, a community psychologist who works with firefighters and has witnessed many tragedies and disasters in that capacity, investigated the efficacy of debriefing following a plane crash in Sioux City, Iowa, in which 112 of 296 passengers died. Rescue teams faced with the grisly job of recovering bodies were randomly assigned to either CISD or no treatment and were followed up two years later (Gist, Lubin, & Redburn, 1998). The researchers found no evidence that debriefed firefighters were doing any better than those who had not had the intervention; in fact, there was a slight but statistically significant trend toward the *worsening* of anxiety symptoms in those who had been in CISD. The rescuers who were doing the best had relied on informal souces of support and help—friends and co-workers who had shared the experience.

Researchers have **considered other explanations** for these findings. Perhaps the results were unique to the kind of disaster or to the kind of survivors, in this case professional firefighters who are used to dealing with traumatic events. But many other studies have replicated and extended these findings with a wide assortment of human tragedies and with all sorts of people, including victims of burns, accidents, miscarriages, violent crimes, and combat (van Emmerik et al., 2002; McNally, Bryant, & Ehlers, 2003).

For example, in a randomized controlled trial, people who were victims of serious car accidents were followed for three years; some had received the CISD intervention and some had not. As you can see in the above figure, almost everyone had re-

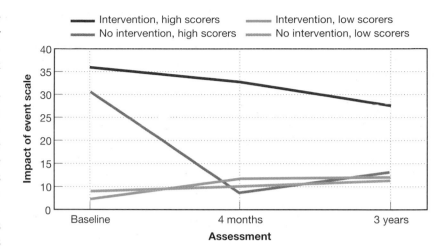

covered in only four months and remained fine after three years. The researchers, however, **did not oversimplify** their results. They divided the survivors into two groups: those who had had a highly emotional reaction to the accident at the outset and those who had not. For the latter group (green and gold lines), the intervention made no difference. But look at what happened to the people who really were traumatized by the accident (purple and red lines, the "high stress" scorers): If they did *not* get CISD, they were fine in four months, too, like everyone else. But for those who *did* get the intervention, CISD actually blocked their improvement, and they had higher stress symptoms than all the others in the study even after three years. The researchers concluded that "psychological debriefing is ineffective and has adverse long-term effects. It is not an appropriate treatment for trauma victims" (Mayou et al., 2000). In 2005, the World Health Organization, which deals with survivors of trauma around the world, agreed with this assessment (van Ommeren, Saxena, & Saraceno, 2005).

You can see, then, why the scientific assessment of psychotherapeutic claims and methods is so important.

What Works?   We turn now to the evidence showing the benefits of psychotherapy and which therapies work best. There have been a number of important efforts to review the overall effectiveness of different therapeutic approaches for different disorders (e.g., Chambless et al., 1998; Chambless & Ollendick, 2001; Hollon, Thase, & Markowitz, 2002). For many problems and most emotional disorders, cognitive and behavior therapies (CBT) have emerged as the methods of choice. These therapies are particularly effective for the following problems:

- *Depression.* Cognitive therapy's greatest success has been in the treatment of mood disorders, especially depression (Beck, 2005). It is often as effective as antidepressants, and people in cognitive therapy are less likely than those on drugs to relapse when the treatment is over. The reason may be that the lessons learned in cognitive therapy last a long time after treatment (Antonuccio et al., 1999; Hollon, Thase, & Markowitz, 2002; McNally, 1994; Seligman et al., 1999). In one randomized controlled study, 120 adults who had attempted suicide and been sent to an emergency room were assigned to one of two conditions. Some were given 10 sessions of cognitive therapy; the rest were simply given referrals for help and later called to see how they were doing. Those who received cognitive therapy were only about half as likely to attempt suicide again in the next 18 months and scored significantly lower on tests of depression and hopelessness (Brown et al., 2005).

- *Anxiety disorders.* Exposure techniques are more effective than any other treatment for posttraumatic stress disorder, agoraphobia, and specific phobias, such as fear of dogs or of public speaking. And cognitive-behavior therapy is often more effective than medication for panic disorder, generalized anxiety disorder, and obsessive-compulsive disorder (Dalgleish, 2004; Mitte, 2005).

- *Anger and impulsive violence.* Cognitive therapy is often successful in reducing chronic anger, abusiveness, and hostility, and it also teaches people how to express anger more calmly and constructively (Deffenbacher et al., 2003; Kassinove, 1995).

- *Health problems.* Cognitive and behavior therapies are highly successful in helping people cope with pain, chronic fatigue syndrome, headaches, and irritable bowel syndrome; quit smoking or overcome other addictions; recover from eating disorders such as bulimia and binge eating; improve their sleeping patterns; and manage other health problems (Butler et al., 1991; Crits-Christoph, Wilson, & Hollon, 2005; Skinner et al., 1990; Stepanski & Perlis, 2000; Wilson & Fairburn, 1993).

- *Childhood and adolescent behavior problems.* Behavior therapy is the most effective treatment for behavior problems that range from bedwetting to impulsive anger, and even for problems that have biological origins (Green, 1996a; Weisz et al., 1995).

IN THE BLEACHERS By Steve Moore

Batters overcoming *bonkinogginophobia*, a fear of the ball.

- *Relapse prevention.* Cognitive-behavioral approaches have also been highly effective in reducing the rate of relapse in high-risk situations for people with problems such as substance abuse, depression, sexual offending, and even schizophrenia (Witkiewitz & Marlatt, 2004).

However, no single type of therapy can help everyone. Recall that depression has different origins and comes in different degrees of intensity, so the same intervention—whether a medication or a form of psychotherapy—will not benefit all sufferers (Parker, Parker, & Kerrie, 2003). Cognitive-behavior therapy is designed for specific identifiable problems, but some people may not be motivated to do the "homework" that this therapy requires. Others may seek therapy for less clearly defined difficulties, wishing to introspect about their feelings and lives, find solace and courage, or explore moral issues. And some people are too deeply troubled by personality disorders or psychoses to respond well to any kind of psychotherapy.

Some problems, and some clients, are immune to any single kind of therapy but may respond to combined methods. For example, people who have severe, recurrent depressions often do better on a combination of antidepressants and psychotherapy than with either method alone (Hollon, Thase,

& Markowitz, 2002; Keller et al., 2000). A leading treatment for sex offenders combines cognitive therapy, behavioral techniques, sex education, group therapy, and social-skills training (Abel et al., 1988; Kaplan, Morales, & Becker, 1993). Young adults with schizophrenia are greatly helped by family intervention therapies that teach parents behavioral skills for dealing with their troubled children and that educate the family about how to cope with the illness constructively (Chambless et al., 1998; Goldstein & Miklowitz, 1995). Nine studies found that over a two-year period, only 30 percent of the schizophrenic patients in such family intervention treatments relapsed compared to 65 percent of those whose families were not involved.

An important invervention called *multisystemic therapy* (MST) has been highly successful in reducing teenage violence, criminal activity, drug abuse, and school problems in troubled inner-city communities. Its practitioners combine family systems techniques with behavioral methods, but apply them in the context of forming "neighborhood parnerships" with local leaders, residents, parents, and teachers to help prevent or reduce teenagers' problems (Henggeler et al., 1998; Swenson et al., 2005). The premise of multisystemic therapy is that because aggressiveness and drug abuse are often reinforced or caused by the adolescent's family, classroom, peers, and local culture, you can't successfully treat the adolescent without also treating his or her environment. Indeed, MST has been shown to be more effective than other methods on their own (Schaeffer & Borduin, 2005).

In sum, as you can see in Figure 12.2, the factors contributing to successful therapy are the qualities of the participants, the strength of the therapeutic alliance, and the specific methods of the therapy.

When Therapy Harms

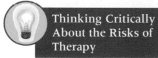
Thinking Critically About the Risks of Therapy

Every treatment and intervention, including aspirin, carries risks, and so does psychotherapy. But the risks to clients increase when any of the following occurs:

1 *The use of empirically unsupported, potentially dangerous techniques.* In Chapter 8 we saw that memory does not work like a videocamera or tape recorder; memories are not "buried" in the brain, awaiting magic methods to root them out. Yet many therapists claim that they can help clients accurately retrieve painful old memories through the use of unreliable methods such as hypnosis, sodium amytal (a barbiturate mislead-

FIGURE 12.2
The Ingredients of Successful Therapy

ingly called "truth serum"), guided imagery, and dream analysis. These techniques all enhance the client's suggestibility (Mazzoni, Loftus, & Kirsch, 2001). For example, when a therapist tells clients that their dreams are memories of something that really happened, many clients begin to confuse their dreams with reality (Mazzoni et al., 1999).

Many research psychologists are greatly concerned that a significant minority of registered, licensed psychotherapists—between one-fourth and one-third of them—have used one or more of these inappropriate techniques specifically to help clients "retrieve" memories of sexual abuse, as you can see in Figure 12.3 (Poole et al., 1995). Research in the United States and Canada finds that the percentages have not declined appreciably in recent years (Katz, 2001; Nunez, Poole, & Memon, 2002; Polusny & Follette, 1996).

2 *Inappropriate or coercive influence, which can create new problems for the client.* In a healthy therapeutic alliance, therapists and clients come to agree on an explanation for the client's problems. Of course, the therapist will influence this explanation, according to his or her training and philosophy. Some therapists, however, cross the line. They so zealously believe in the prevalence of certain disorders that they actually induce the client to produce the symptoms they are looking for (McHugh, 1993; McNally, 2003; Merskey, 1995; Watters & Ofshe, 1999). Therapist influence, and sometimes downright coercion, is a likely reason for the huge numbers of people who were diagnosed with multiple personality disorder in the 1980s and 1990s (see Chapter 11) and for an epidemic of recovered memories of sexual abuse during that period (see Chapter 8).

3 *Prejudice or cultural ignorance on the part of the therapist.* Some therapists may be prejudiced against some clients because of the client's

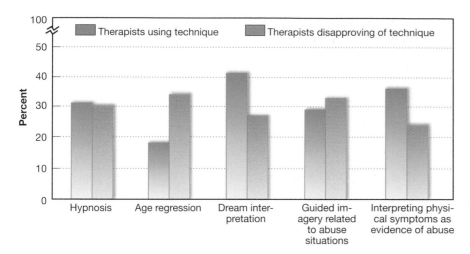

FIGURE 12.3
Psychotherapists' Attitudes Toward Suggestive Techniques
Although suggestive techniques can produce false memories, between one-fourth and one-third of licensed clinical psychologists use these methods regularly "to help clients recall memories of sexual abuse." About the same percentages disapprove of using such techniques. (The rest neither use the methods nor disapprove of them.) The percentages are from two combined random samples of American clinical psychologists with Ph.D.s (Poole et al., 1995). The numbers have not changed appreciably in recent years.

gender, culture, religion, or sexual orientation. A therapist may try to induce a client to conform to the therapist's standards and values, even if they are not appropriate for the client or in the client's best interest. For example, for many years gay men and lesbians who entered therapy were told that homosexuality was a mental illness that could be cured. Some of the so-called treatments were harsh, such as electric shock for "inappropriate" arousal. Although these methods were discredited many years ago (Davison, 1976), other kinds of "reparative" therapies that supposedly turn gay men and lesbians into heterosexuals still surface from time to time. They are often promoted in campaigns by conservative Christians who believe that homosexuality is a sin, with testimonials from alleged converts. But there is no reliable empirical evidence from scientifically designed studies supporting these claims, and both the American Psychological Association and the American Psychiatric Association have gone on record opposing reparative therapies on ethical and scientific grounds.

4 *Sexual intimacies or other unethical behavior on the part of the therapist.* The APA's ethical guidelines prohibit therapists from having any sexual intimacies with their clients or violating other professional boundaries. Occasionally, some therapists behave like cult leaders, persuading their clients that their mental health depends on staying in therapy and severing their connections to their "toxic" families (Singer, 1995; Watters & Ofshe, 1999). Such "psychotherapy cults" are created by

In many movies, therapists behave unethically, crossing professional boundaries with their clients. In Prince of Tides, *Barbra Streisand played a psychiatrist who becomes sexually involved with her client's brother, who then becomes her client too. Such films simply that this behavior is common and harmless, but it is prohibited by the APA's ethical guidelines.*

the therapist's use of techniques that foster the client's dependency and isolation, prevent the client from terminating therapy, and reduce the client's ability to think critically (see Chapter 10).

To avoid these risks and benefit from what good, effective psychotherapy has to offer, people looking for a therapy that can help them must become educated consumers.

QUICK quiz

Find out if you are an educated consumer of psychotherapy by taking this quiz.

1. Which of the following is the most important predictor of successful therapy? (a) how long it lasts, (b) the insight it provides the client, (c) the bond between therapist and client, (d) whether the therapist and client are matched according to gender

2. In general, which type of psychotherapy is most effective for anxiety and depression?

3. What are four possible sources of harm in psychotherapy?

4. Ferdie is spending too much time playing softball and not enough time studying, so he signs up for "sportaholic therapy" (ST). The therapist tells him the cure is to quit softball cold turkey and tap his temples three times whenever he feels the urge to play. After a few months, Ferdie announces that ST isn't helping and he's going to quit. The therapist gives him testimonials of other clients who swear by ST, adding that Ferdie's doubts are actually a sign that the therapy is working. What are some problems with this argument? (Bonus: What kind of therapy might help Ferdie manage his time better?)

Answers:

1. c 2. cognitive-behavior 3. unethical behavior, prejudice or biased treatment, inappropriate or coercive influence, and the use of empirically unsupported techniques 4. The therapist has violated the principle of falsifiability (see Chapter 1). If Ferdie is helped by the treatment, that shows it works; if he is not helped, that still shows it works and Ferdie is simply "in denial" about its benefits. Also, Ferdie is not hearing testimonials from people who have dropped out of ST and were not helped by it. (Bonus: A good behavioral time-management program might help, so Ferdie can play softball and get other things done, too.)

Now that we have reviewed the major kinds of psychotherapy, along with their successes and risks, let's return to the issues raised by the case against the "rebirthing" therapists in Colorado. Connell Watkins and Julie Ponder, the two social workers who ran the counseling center where Candace Newmaker died in "treatment," were sentenced to 16 years in prison for reckless child abuse resulting in death. Their two assistants, Brita St. Clair and Jack McDaniels, were sentenced to 10 years' probation.

Rebirthing is just one technique used in attachment therapies (AT), which include "holding therapy" and "therapeutic parenting." Attachment therapy methods, which are aimed at getting children to "bond" with their parents, include withholding food, isolating the children for extended periods, humiliating them, restraining them by wrapping them in sheets or blankets, and pressing great weights upon them. At least eight children have died from one form or another of AT. The American Psychiatric Association officially opposes attachment therapies, noting that "there is *no* scientific evidence to support the effectiveness of such interventions." The American Professional Society on the Abuse of Children has also taken a strong stand condemning attachment therapies and the unvalidated assumptions on which they are based.

How can you, as a potential consumer of psychological services, distinguish between techniques that are beneficial and techniques that can harm? As a critical thinker, what questions should you ask about the therapist and the therapist's approach?

The first step is to make sure you are dealing with a reputable individual with appropriate credentials and training. As we saw in Chapter 1, to become a licensed psychologist, a person must have an advanced degree and a period of supervised training. However, the title *psychotherapist* is unregulated; anyone can set up any kind of program and call it "therapy." In the United States and Canada, people can get credentialed as "experts" in various techniques and therapies simply by attending a weekend seminar or a training program lasting a week or two.

In Colorado, for example, it is legal to practice psychotherapy without a license, although therapists must register with the state. Watkins and Ponder were both unlicensed, and their registrations had lapsed. They had been trained in rebirthing by a California promoter of the method in a two-week training course. One of the members of the Colorado Mental Health Grievance Board noted with dismay that her *hairdresser's* training took 1,500 hours, whereas anyone could take a quickie course and become "certified" in a method that could take a child's life.

Second, it is important to ask whether a therapist practices one of the empirically supported methods described in this chapter, and whether the basic assumptions of the therapist are likewise validated by empirical research. There is nothing especially new about rebirthing therapy, which has been around since the 1970s, when its founder claimed he had reexperienced his own birth while taking a bath. (Many psychological problems, he somehow decided, can be traced to a traumatic experience in the womb or during birth.) Many of rebirthing's practitioners even have advanced degrees and licenses.

But the basic assumptions of this method and other forms of AT—that children can recover from trauma, insecure attachment, or other psychological problems by reliving their births or by being forcibly restrained or harshly punished in other ways—are utterly unsupported by the vast research on infancy, learning, attachment, memory, or posttraumatic stress disorder. For that matter, why should the experience of being born be traumatic? Isn't it pretty nice to be let out of cramped quarters and see daylight and beaming parental faces?

Besides choosing a therapist carefully, consumers need to be realistic about what they expect of psychotherapy. In the hands of an empathic and knowledgeable practitioner, psychotherapy can help you make decisions and clarify your values and goals. It can teach you new skills and new ways of thinking. It can help you get along better with your family and break out of destructive family patterns. It can get you through bad times when no one seems to care or to understand what you are feeling. It can teach you how to manage depression, anxiety, and anger.

However, despite its many benefits, psychotherapy cannot transform you into someone you're not. It cannot turn an introvert into an extrovert. It cannot cure an emotional disorder overnight. It cannot provide a life without problems. And it is not intended to substitute for experience—for work that is satisfying, relationships that are sustaining, activities that are enjoyable. As Socrates knew, the unexamined life is not worth living. But as we would add, the unlived life is not worth examining.

►TAKING ►PSYCHOLOGY ►WITH ►YOU

How to Evaluate Self-Help Groups and Books

Not all psychological problems require the aid of a professional. Nowadays, thousands of programs and books are designed to help people help themselves. In the United States, more than 2,000 self-help books are published every year, and an estimated 7 to 15 million adults belong to self-help groups. Do these books and groups help?

Self-help groups are available (online and in person) for alcoholics, relatives of alcoholics, people suffering from depression, anorexia, or schizophrenia, women with breast cancer, parents of murdered children, diabetics, rape victims, stepparents, relatives of Alzheimer's patients, and people with just about any other concern you can think of (Davison, Pennebaker, & Dickerson, 2000). Members say that the primary benefits are the awareness that they are not alone, encouragement when they are feeling down, and help in feeling better about themselves.

Self-help groups offer understanding, empathy, and solutions to shared problems. Such groups can be reassuring and supportive in ways that family, friends, and psychotherapists may not be. For example, people with disabilities face unique challenges that involve coping not only with physical problems but also with the condescension, hostility, and prejudice of many nondisabled people (Linton, 1998). Other disabled people, who share these challenges, can offer the right kind of empathy and useful advice.

Self-help groups do not provide psychotherapy, and they are not designed to help people with serious psychological difficulties. They are not regulated by law or by professional standards, and they vary widely in their philosophies and methods. Some are accepting and tolerant, offering support and spiritual guidance. Others are confrontational and coercive, and members who disagree with the premises of the group may be made to feel deviant, crazy, or "in denial." If you choose to become part of a support group, be sure it falls in the first category.

As for self-help books, there is one for every problem, from how to toilet train your children to how to find happiness in seven steps. When self-help books propose a specific, well-supported program for the reader to follow, they can actually be as effective as treatment administered by a therapist—*if* the reader follows through with the program (Rosen, Glasgow, & Moore, 2003). Unfortunately, most books do not do this. After serving as chair of the APA's Task Force on Self-Help Therapies, Gerald Rosen (1981) concluded, "Psychologists have published untested materials, advanced exaggerated claims, and accepted the use of misleading titles that encourage unrealistic expectations regarding outcome." That was written more than 20 years ago, and the situation is worse today. The information in this chapter suggests some guidelines for evaluating a self-help book:

● **The book's advice should be based on sound scientific theory and should propose a program that has been empirically supported.** It should not be based on the author's pseudoscientific theories, armchair observations, or political views. This criterion rules out, among other kinds of books, most of the love manuals in which the author's own lovelorn stories or tales of woe with the other sex become the basis of an entire philosophy of love, marriage, and happiness. Personal accounts by people who have survived difficulties can be helpful and inspirational,

of course, but an author's own experience is not grounds for generalizing to everyone.

● **The book should not promise the impossible.** This lets out books that promise you perfect sex, total love, or high self-esteem in 30 days. It also lets out books or tapes that promote techniques whose effectiveness has been disconfirmed by research, such as dream analysis or "subliminal" messages.

● **The advice should be organized in a systematic program.** It should be given

step by step, not as a vague pep talk to "take charge of your life" or "find love in your heart," and the reader should be told how to evaluate his or her progress.

Some books do meet these criteria. One is *Changing for Good* (Prochaska, Norcross, & DiClemente, 1994), which describes the ingredients of effective change that apply to people in and out of therapy. But as long as people yearn for a magic bullet to cure their problems, quick-fix solutions will find a ready audience.

Formal and informal support groups provide a setting for sharing concerns and exchanging constructive advice, as these men with AIDS are doing.

SUMMARY

Biological Treatments For Mental Disorders

• Over the centuries, people trying to understand and treat psychological disorders have alternated between biological and psychological explanations. Today, biological treatments are in the ascendance because of research findings on the genetic and biological causes of some disorders and because of economic and social factors.

• The medications most commonly prescribed for mental disorders include *antipsychotic drugs*, used in treating schizophrenia and other psychotic disorders; *antidepressants*, used in treating depression,

anxiety disorders, and obsessive-compulsive disorder; *tranquilizers*, often prescribed for emotional problems; and *lithium carbonate*, a salt used to treat bipolar disorder.

• Drawbacks of drug treatment include the *placebo effect*; high dropout and relapse rates among people who take medications without also learning how to cope with their problems; the difficulty of finding the correct dose (the *therapeutic window*) for each individual, compounded by the fact that a person's ethnicity, sex, and age can influence a drug's effectiveness; and the long-term risks of medication, known and unknown, and of possible drug interactions when several are combined. Medication can be helpful and can even save lives, but in an age when commercial interests are heavily invested in promoting drugs for psychological problems, the public is largely unaware of drugs' limitations. Medication should not be prescribed uncritically and routinely, especially when nondrug therapies can work as well as drugs for many mood and behavioral problems.

• When drugs or psychotherapy have failed to help seriously disturbed people, some psychiatrists have intervened directly in the brain. *Psychosurgery*, which destroys selected areas of the brain thought to be responsible for a mental disorder, is rarely done today. *Electroconvulsive therapy (ECT)*, in which a brief current is sent through the brain, has been used successfully to treat suicidal depression. However, controversy exists about its effects on the brain and the appropriateness of its use. A newer method, *transcranial magnetic stimulation*, is being studied as a way of treating severe depression.

Kinds of Psychotherapy

• *Psychodynamic ("depth") therapies* include Freudian *psychoanalysis*, which is traditionally lengthy, and its modern variations, which are briefer and in which the therapist plays a more active role. These therapies explore unconscious dynamics by using *free association* and focusing on the process of *transference*.

• *Behavior therapists* draw on classical and operant principles of learning, called *applied behavioral analysis*. Behavior therapists use such methods as *graduated exposure*, and sometimes immediate exposure, called *flooding; systematic desensitization*, based on *counterconditioning; behavioral self-monitoring;* and *skills training*.

• *Cognitive therapists* aim to change the irrational thoughts involved in negative emotions and self-defeating actions. Albert Ellis's *rational emotive behavior therapy (REBT)* and Aaron Beck's form of cognitive therapy are two leading approaches.

• *Humanist therapy* attempts to help people feel better about themselves by focusing on here-and-now issues and on the human capacity for self-fulfillment and self-actualization. Carl Rogers's *client-centered (nondirective) therapy* emphasizes the importance of the therapist's empathy and ability to provide *unconditional positive regard*. *Existential therapy* helps people cope with philosophical dilemmas, such as the meaning of life and the fear of death.

• *Family therapists* share the view that individual problems develop in the context of the whole family network. They tend to share a *family-systems perspective*, understanding that any one person's behavior in the family affects everyone else. In *couples therapy*, the therapist sees both partners in a relationship to help them resolve ongoing quarrels and disputes or learn to accept and live with both partners' traits.

• In practice, many therapists are *integrative*, drawing on different methods and ideas. Whatever their approach, successful therapies share the goal of helping people form more adaptive "life stories."

Evaluating Psychotherapy

• Successful therapy requires a *therapeutic alliance* between the therapist and the client, so that they understand each other and can work together. The clients who benefit most from psychotherapy are motivated to solve their problems; hostile, negative individuals are more resistant to treatment. For their part, good therapists are empathic and constructive. They must also be sensitive to cultural differences and be able to distinguish normal cultural patterns from mental disorders.

• A *scientist–practitioner gap* has developed because of the different assumptions held by researchers and many clinicians regarding the value of empirical research for doing psychotherapy and for assessing its effectiveness. The gap has led to a proliferation of scientifically unsupported psychotherapies.

• In assessing the effectiveness of psychotherapy, researchers must control for the placebo effect and the *justification of effort* effect. They rely on *randomized controlled trials* to determine which therapies are empirically supported. For example, as the "Close-up on Research" discusses, randomized controlled trials have shown that post-crisis debriefing programs are usually ineffective at best and can even slow recovery for some survivors.

• Some psychotherapies are better than others for specific problems. Behavior therapy and cognitive-behavior therapy are the most effective for depression, anxiety disorders, anger problems, certain health problems (such as pain, insomnia, and eating disorders), childhood and adolescent behavior problems, and relapse prevention. People with some problems, including severe depression and schizophrenia, may respond best to combined therapeutic approaches. *Multisystemic therapy*, which combines family systems and behavioral methods in a community context, is beneficial in reducing adolescent violence, drug abuse, and school problems.

• In some cases, therapy is harmful. The therapist may use empirically unsupported and potentially harmful techniques, such as unreliable methods of "recovering" memories of abuse; inadvertently create disorders through undue influence or suggestion; be prejudiced against a client; or behave unethically.

Psychology in the News, Revisited

• Because of the growing number of unlicensed psychotherapists and the rise of new therapies with methods and assumptions that have little or no empirical validation, consumers need to choose a therapist carefully, select the kind of therapy best suited for their problem, and be realistic about what they expect of psychotherapy.

KEY TERMS

antipsychotic drugs (neuroleptics)   406

antidepressant drugs   407

monoamine oxidase inhibitors (MAOIs)   407

tricyclic antidepressants   407

selective serotonin reuptake inhibitors (SSRIs)   407

tranquilizers   407

lithium carbonate   408

placebo effect   408

therapeutic window   409

psychosurgery   410

prefrontal lobotomy   410

electroconvulsive therapy (ECT)   411

transcranial magnetic stimulation (TMS)   411

psychoanalysis   412

free association   412

psychodynamic ("depth") therapies   412

transference   412

behavior therapy   413

applied behavior analysis   413

graduated exposure   413

flooding   413

systematic desensitization   414

counterconditioning   414

behavioral self-monitoring   414

skills training   414

cognitive therapy   415

rational emotive behavior therapy   415

cognitive-behavior therapy   416

humanist therapy   416

client-centered (nondirective) therapy   416

unconditional positive regard   416

existential therapy   416

family therapy   417

family-systems perspective   417

couples therapy   417

integrative approach to psychotherapy   419

therapeutic alliance   419

scientist–practitioner gap   421

randomized controlled trials   422

multisystemic therapy   425

Biological Treatments of Mental Disorders

Drugs

Drugs commonly prescribed for mental disorders include:
- **Antipsychotics**: used in treating schizophrenia and other psychotic disorders
- **Antidepressants**: used in treating depression, anxiety disorders, and obsessive-compulsive disorder
- **Tranquilizers**: often prescribed for emotional problems
- **Lithium carbonate**: a salt used to treat bipolar disorder

Cautions About Drug Treatments

Drawbacks of drug treatment include:
- The placebo effect
- High dropout and relapse rates among people who take medications without also learning how to cope with their problems
- The difficulty of finding the correct dose (the therapeutic window)
- The long-term risks of many medications are unknown

Direct Brain Intervention

- **Psychosurgery** destroys selected areas of the brain thought to be responsible for a mental disorder but is rarely used today.
- **Electroconvulsive therapy (ECT)**, in which a brief current is sent through the brain, has been used successfully to treat suicidal depression, but its use is controversial.
- **Transcranial magnetic stimulation**, in which a pulsing magnetic coil is held over the left prefrontal cortex, is being used with depression but its effectiveness is still uncertain.

Kinds of Psychotherapy

Psychodynamic Therapy

Psychodynamic ("depth") therapies, including Freudian **psychoanalysis** and its modern variations, explore the unconscious, through:
- **Free association**
- The process of **transference**

Humanist and Existential Therapy

Humanist therapy focuses on the capacity for self-fulfillment and self-actualization.
- Carl Rogers's **client-centered therapy** emphasizes the therapist's role in providing unconditional positive regard for the client.

Existential therapy helps people cope with philosophical issues such as the meaning of life.

Behavior and Cognitive Therapy

Behavior therapy applies principles of classical and operant conditioning to help change problematic behaviors. Uses such methods as:
- **Graduated exposure** and **flooding**
- **Systematic desensitization**
- **Behavioral self-monitoring**
- **Skills training**

Cognitive therapy, such as Ellis's **rational emotive behavior therapy,** is designed to identify and change irrational, unproductive ways of thinking, and reduce negative emotions and their behavioral consequences.

Family and Couples Therapies

- Family therapies tend to share a **family-systems perspective,** understanding that one person's behavior affects the whole family.
- Couples therapy is designed to help couples understand and resolve the inevitable conflicts that occur in all relationships.

Evaluating Psychotherapy

The Scientist-Practitioner Gap

A scientist-practitioner gap has developed, leading to a proliferation of scientifically unsupported therapies, such as Critical Incident Stress Debriefing.

Evaluations of psychotherapy must control for:
• The placebo effect
• Justification of effort
Scientific assessments of therapy rely on **randomized controlled trials.**

Therapeutic Alliance

• Qualities of the participants
• Mutual understanding of cultural issues

When Therapy Harms

Psychotherapy can be risky for clients if the therapist:
1. Uses empirically unsupported and potentially harmful techniques
2. Inadvertently creates disorders through suggestion
3. Is prejudiced against a client
4. Is unethical

What Works?

Cognitive-behavior therapy (CBT) is most effective for:
• Depression
• Anxiety disorders
• Anger problems
• Health problems
• Child and adolescent behavior problems
• Preventing relapse

Combined methods may help particular individuals or difficult problems:
• Multisystemic therapy for troubled, violent adolescents
• Antidepressants and CBT for severe depression
• Family therapy and behavior therapy for schizophrenia

Qualities of client (e.g., motivated to change) + Qualities of therapist (e.g., warmth, empathy)

Therapeutic alliance + Effective method for given problem → Successful Outcome

TABLE 12.2
The Major Schools of Therapy Compared

	Primary Goal	Methods
Psychodynamic		
Psychoanalytic	Insight into unconscious motives and feelings	Probing unconscious motives through dream analysis, free association, transference
Modern Psychodynamic	Same	Analyst more active and directive; therapy briefer
Cognitive-Behavior		
Behavioral	Modification of self-defeating behaviors	Systematic desensitization, exposure (flooding), behavioral records, skills training
Cognitive	Modification of irrational or unvalidated beliefs	Challenging unwarranted beliefs, catastrophizing, and mind reading, or prompting client to test beliefs against evidence
Humanist and Existential		
Humanist	Insight; self-acceptance and self-fulfillment; new, optimistic perceptions of self and world	Providing a nonjudgmental setting in which to discuss life issues; use of empathy and unconditional positive regard by therapist
Existential	Finding meaning in life and accepting inevitable losses	Varies with therapist; philosophical discussions about meaning of life, client's goals, finding courage
Family and Couples		
Family	Modification of family patterns	May use any of the preceding methods to change family patterns that perpetuate problems and conflicts
Couples	Resolution of conflicts, breaking out of destructive habits, accepting differences	May use any of the preceding methods to help the couple communicate better, resolve conflicts, or accept what cannot be changed

Woman Who Ran Over Spouse Sentenced to 20 Years

HOUSTON, TX, FEBRUARY 15, 2003. Clara Harris, a 45-year-old dentist and mother of twin boys, was sentenced today to 20 years in prison and a $10,000 fine for the first-degree murder of her husband, David Harris. Dr. Harris stood quietly without emotion as the decision was read.

The jury of nine women and three men ruled that the defendant, a former beauty queen, had acted with "sudden passion" when she killed her husband by running him over repeatedly with her Mercedes-Benz in the parking lot of the hotel where they had been married 11 years before. Witnesses testified that David Harris's body was thrown about 25 feet by the impact of the car, as the defendant's stepdaughter, Lindsey Harris, 17, watched in horror. "He was really scared," she said. "He was trying to get away and he couldn't."

Clara Harris testified that she had become frightened, angry, and humiliated when she learned that her husband was having an affair. When her husband told her she was "too big" but his mistress had a "perfect body," Dr. Harris said she joined a fitness club, went to the hairdresser every day, and made plans to have liposuction and breast-enlargement surgery. Later, suspecting that her husband had not broken off his affair, she hired a private detective to follow him. The detective alerted her to the fact that her husband and his mistress were at the hotel, and she confronted them. At that point in her account of events, Dr. Harris's testimony became erratic and she claimed she had a "blackout." Running him over "happened in a fraction of a second," she said. "I didn't have time to think."

Because the jury found that Clara Harris had killed in a "sudden passion" rather than with cold deliberation, she will be eligible for parole in 10 years. Otherwise, her conviction for first-degree murder could have sent her to prison for up to 99 years.

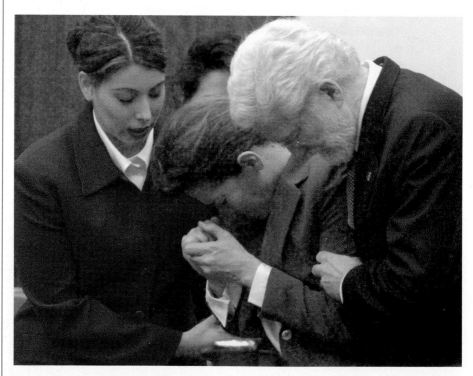

Clara Harris, supported by her attorneys, collapses after a jury sentenced today her to 20 years in prison for the murder of her husband.

Emotion, Stress, and Health

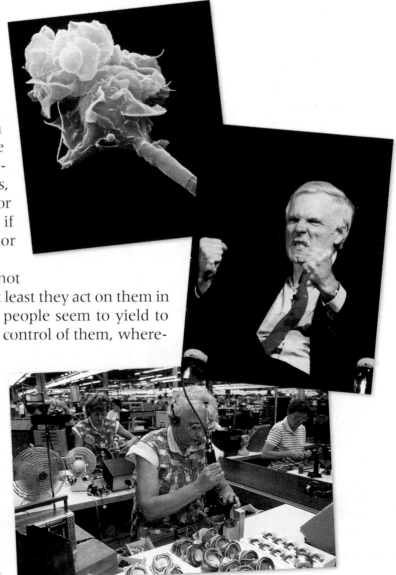

Almost everyone can understand Clara Harris's feelings. Most of us will, at some time, taste the bitterness of rejection and learn firsthand how excruciating the pangs of embarrassment and humiliation can be. In those moments, we want to sink into the ground or indulge ourselves in the furious, if fleeting, impulse for retaliation or revenge.

Fortunately, most people do not act on their furious impulses, or at least they act on them in nonviolent ways. Why do some people seem to yield to their emotions, apparently losing control of them, whereas others are able to keep rage and other unpleasant feelings from turning into violent or self-destructive actions?

In this chapter we will explore this question and others, as we examine the physiology and psychology of emotions and stress. Prolonged negative emotions such as anger can certainly be stressful, and stress can certainly produce negative emotions. But both of these processes are shaped by how we interpret the events that happen to us, by the demands of the situation we are in, and by the rules of our culture. As you read, see whether you can think of some explanations for Clara Harris's behavior other than "she couldn't help it." And see whether you can come up with some ideas for reducing unpleasant emotions and stressful experiences in your own life.

WHAT'S *Ahead*

- Which facial expressions of emotion do most people recognize the world over?

- Which little structure in the brain sees to it that you cross the street *fast* when a truck is headed toward you?

- Which two hormones can make you too excited to eat?

- In a competition, who is likely to be happier, the third-place winner or the second-place winner?

- Why can't an infant feel shame or guilt?

The Nature of Emotion

People often curse their emotions, wishing to be freed from anger, jealousy, shame, guilt, and grief. Yet imagine a life without emotions. You would be unmoved by the magic of music. You would never care about losing someone you love, not only because you would not know sadness but also because you would not know love. You would never laugh because nothing would strike you as funny. And you would be a social klutz because you would not be able to know what other people were feeling.

Because emotions can get us into trouble, for centuries emotion was regarded as the opposite of thinking, and an inferior opposite at that. The heart (emotion) was said to be part of our "irrational" mammalian heritage, in contrast to our "rational" human capacity for thought and logic. Today, psychologists avoid such either–or thinking.

Thinking Critically About "Irrational" Emotions

As we have seen in other chapters, normal thought processes involve many "irrational" biases, such as the confirmation bias, the hindsight bias, the self-serving bias, and biases in the construction of memories. Conversely, emotions are not always irrational, even when they are uncomfortable. Emotions bind people together, motivate them to achieve their goals, and help them make decisions and plans (Damasio, 1994). When you are faced with a decision between two appealing and justifiable career alternatives,

emotion A state of arousal involving facial and bodily changes, brain activation, cognitive appraisals, subjective feelings, and tendencies toward action.

primary emotions Emotions that are considered to be universal and biologically based.

secondary emotions Emotions that are specific to certain cultures.

for example, your sense of which one "feels right" emotionally may help you make the better choice. Disgust, which is pretty disgusting, probably evolved as a mechanism that protects infants and adults from eating tainted or poisonous food. Even embarrassment, so painful to the individual, serves important functions: It appeases others when you feel you have made a fool of yourself, broken a moral rule, or violated a social norm (Keltner & Anderson, 2000).

In defining **emotion**, psychologists focus on three major components: *physiological* changes in the face, brain, and body; *cognitive* processes such as interpretations of events; and *cultural* influences that shape the experience and expression of emotion. If we compare human emotions to a tree, the biological capacity for emotion is the trunk and root system; thoughts and explanations create the many branches; and culture is the gardener that shapes the tree and prunes it, cutting off some limbs and cultivating others. Let's begin with the trunk.

Emotion and the Body

Research on the physiological aspects of emotion suggests that people everywhere are born with certain basic or **primary emotions**, which typically include fear, anger, sadness, joy, surprise, disgust, and contempt. These emotions have distinctive physiological patterns and corresponding facial expressions, and the situations that evoke them are the same all over the world: Everywhere, sadness follows perception of loss, fear follows perception of threat and bodily harm, anger follows perception of insult or injustice, and so forth (Scherer, 1997). In contrast, **secondary emotions** include all the variations and blends of emotion that vary from one culture to another and develop gradually with increasing cognitive maturity.

Neuroscientists and other researchers are studying the biological aspects of emotions: facial expressions, brain regions and circuits, and the autonomic nervous system.

The Face of Emotion

The most obvious place to look for emotion is on the face, where emotions are often visibly expressed. In 1872, Charles Darwin argued that human facial expressions—the smile, the frown, the grimace, the glare—are as innate as the wing flutter of a frightened bird, the purr of a contented cat, and the snarl of a threatened wolf. Such expressions evolved, he said, because they allowed our forebears to tell at a glance the difference between a friendly stranger and a hostile one.

Modern psychologists have supported Darwin's idea by showing that certain emotional displays are recognized the world over (see Figure 13.1). Paul Ekman and his colleagues have gathered abundant

Jessica Tracy, University of British Columbia. Tracy, J.L., & Robins, R.W. (2004). Show your pride: Evidence for a discrete emotion expression. Psychological Science, 15, 194–197.

FIGURE 13.1
Some Universal Expressions
Can you tell what feelings are being conveyed here? Most people around the world can readily identify expressions of surprise, disgust, happiness, sadness, anger, fear, and contempt—no matter what the age, culture, sex, or historical era of the person conveying the emotion. Some researchers think that pride might also be a universal emotion. Can you find the face of pride in this group?

evidence for the universality of seven basic facial expressions of emotion—expressions that correspond to the list of emotions usually identified as primary: anger, happiness, fear, surprise, disgust, sadness, and contempt (Ekman, 2003; Ekman et al., 1987). In every culture they have studied—in Brazil, Chile, Estonia, Germany, Greece, Hong Kong, Italy, Japan, New Guinea, Scotland, Sumatra, Turkey, and the United States—a large majority of people recognize the emotional expressions portrayed by those in other cultures. Even most members of isolated tribes who have never watched a movie or read *People* magazine, such as the Foré of New Guinea or the Minangkabau of West Sumatra, can recognize the emotions expressed in pictures of people who are entirely foreign to them, and we can recognize theirs. Lately, some researchers have argued that

pride is also a basic human emotion. Children as young as 4 years old, and people from an isolated culture in Africa, can reliably identify facial and bodily expressions of pride (Tracy & Robins, 2004; Tracy, Robins, & Lagattuta, 2005).

Ekman and his associates developed a special coding system to analyze and identify each of the nearly 80 muscles of the face, as well as the combinations of muscles associated with various emotions (Ekman, 2003). When people try to hide their feelings and put on an emotion, they generally use different groups of muscles than they do for authentic ones. For example, when people try to pretend that they feel sad, only 15 percent manage to get the eyebrows, eyelids, and forehead wrinkle exactly right, mimicking the way true grief is expressed spontaneously. Authentic smiles last only 2

GREAT MOMS IN HISTORY.

IT WON'T KILL YOU TO SMILE A LITTLE, MONA!

Great moms have always understood the importance of facial feedback.

seconds; false smiles may last 10 seconds or more (Ekman, Friesen, & O'Sullivan, 1988).

The Functions of Facial Expressions

Interestingly, facial expressions not only can reflect our internal feelings; they also may *influence* them. In the process of **facial feedback**, the facial muscles send messages to the brain about the basic emotion being expressed: A smile tells us that we're happy, a frown that we're angry or perplexed (Izard, 1990). When people are told to smile and look pleased or happy, their positive feelings increase; when they are told to look angry, displeased, or disgusted, positive feelings decrease (Kleinke, Peterson, & Rutledge, 1998).

Facial feedback affects emotional states even when people are not specifically asked to imitate an emotion, but just to alter their facial muscles. For example, when people are told to contract the facial muscles involved in smiling (though not actually instructed to smile) and are then shown cartoons, they find the cartoons funnier than if they are contracting their muscles in a way that is incompatible with smiling (Strack, Martin, & Stepper, 1988). And when they are asked to contort their facial muscles into patterns associated with anger, that is often the emotion they feel. As one young man put it, "When my jaw was clenched and my brows down, I tried not to be angry but it just fit the position" (Laird, 1974). If you put on an "angry" face, your heart rate will rise faster than if you put on a "happy" face (Levenson, Ekman, & Friesen, 1990). The next time you are feeling sad or afraid, try purposely smiling, even if no one is around. Keep smiling. Does facial feedback work for you?

As Darwin suggested, facial expressions also probably evolved to help us communicate our emotional states to others and provoke a response from them—"Come help me!" "Get away!" (Fridlund, 1994). This signaling function begins in infancy. A baby's expressions of misery, angry frustration, or disgust are apparent to most parents, who respond by soothing an uncomfortable baby, feeding a grumpy one, or removing unappealing food from a disgusted one (Izard, 1994b; Stenberg & Campos, 1990). And an infant's smile of joy usually melts the heart of the weariest parent, provoking a happy cuddle. Obviously a baby's facial expressions have survival

value! Babies seem primed to respond to adults' expressions, too. Tiny newborns will suck longer on a pacifier if it produces a happy face than if it produces a face with a neutral or negative expression (Walker-Andrews, 1997). (If you become a parent, remember this.)

Starting at the end of their first year, babies begin to alter their own behavior in reaction to their parents' facial expressions of emotion, and this ability, too, has survival value. Do you recall the visual-cliff studies described in Chapter 6? These studies were originally designed to test for depth perception, which emerges early in infancy. But in one experiment, 1-year-old babies were put on a more ambiguous visual cliff that did not drop off sharply and thus did not automatically evoke fear, as the original cliff did. In this case, the babies' behavior depended on their mothers' expressions: 74 percent crossed the cliff when their mothers put on a happy, reassuring expression, but not a single infant crossed when the mother showed an expression of fear (Sorce et al., 1985). If you have ever watched a toddler take a tumble and then look at his or her parent before deciding whether to cry or to forget it, you will understand the influence of parental facial expressions. And you can see why they have had such survival value for babies: An infant needs to be able to read the parent's facial signals of alarm or safety because young children do not yet have the experience necessary for judging danger.

Finally, facial expressions of emotion can generate emotions in others, which is why moods can literally be contagious. When people see pictures of facial expressions of emotion or other nonverbal emotional signals, their own facial and other bodily muscles subtly mimic the ones they are observing. This unconscious process often activates a similar emotional state in themselves (Dimberg, Thunberg, & Elmehed, 2000). Have you ever been in a cheerful mood, had lunch with a depressed friend, and come away feeling vaguely depressed yourself? Have you ever stopped to have a chat with a friend who was nervous about an upcoming exam and ended up feeling edgy yourself? That's *mood contagion* at work. In daily life, if you are intentionally trying to create rapport with another person, you are, without realizing it, likely to start mimicking that person's facial expressions and other nonverbal cues. If someone mimics *your* expressions and body language, you are more likely to be helpful toward that person (Lakin & Chartrand, 2003; van Baaren et al., 2004). When two people are talking, the greater their synchrony, the higher the rapport and emotional harmony they will feel toward one another (see Figure 13.2).

facial feedback The process by which the facial muscles send messages to the brain about the basic emotion being expressed.

FIGURE 13.2
The Contagion of Emotion
These volunteers, videotaped in a study of conversational synchrony, are obviously in sync with one another, even though they have just met. The degree to which two people's gestures and expressions are synchronized affects the rapport they feel with one another. Such synchrony can also create a contagion of moods (Bernieri et al., 1991, 1996).

Facial expressions, then, are important clues to a person's emotions, but they are only part of the emotional picture. People can feel sad, anxious, or angry without letting it show. And, of course, people often use facial expressions to lie about their feelings as well as to express them. In Shakespeare's play *Henry VI*, the villain who will become the evil King Richard III says,

Why, I can smile, and murder while I smile;
And cry content to that which grieves my heart;
And wet my cheeks with artificial tears,
And frame my face to all occasions.

Emotion and the Brain Another line of research seeks to identify parts of the brain that are involved in specific emotions or that are responsible for different aspects of emotional experience: recognizing another person's emotion, feeling an emotion, expressing an emotion, and acting on an emotion. For example, people who have a stroke that affects two areas involved in disgust are often unable to feel disgusted! One young man with stroke damage in these regions could recognize all of the basic facial expressions except for disgust, and he had little or no emotional response to images and ideas that would be disgusting to most people, such as feces-shaped chocolate (Calder et al., 2000). Are you making a disgusted expression as you read that? He couldn't.

Most emotions motivate a response of some sort: to embrace or approach the person who instills joy in you, attack a person who makes you angry, withdraw

from a scene that disgusts you, or flee from a person or situation that frightens you. The prefrontal regions of the brain are involved in these impulses to approach or withdraw. Regions of the *right* prefrontal region are specialized for withdrawal or escape (as in disgust and fear) (Harmon-Jones & Sigelman, 2001). Regions of the *left* prefrontal cortex are specialized for the motivation to approach others (as with happiness, a positive emotion, and anger, a negative one) (Pizzagalli et al., 2005). People who have greater-than-average activation of this left area, compared with the right, have more positive feelings, a quicker ability to recover from negative emotions, and a greater ability to suppress negative emotions (Urry et al., 2004). People with damage to this area often lose the capacity for joy.

The *amygdala*, a small structure in the brain's limbic system, plays a key role in emotion, especially anger and fear. The amygdala is responsible for evaluating sensory information, quickly determining its emotional importance, and making the initial decision to approach or withdraw from a person or situation (Adolphs, 2001; LeDoux, 1996). The amygdala quickly assesses danger or threat, which is a good thing, because otherwise you could be standing in the street asking, "Is it wise to cross now, while that very large truck is coming toward me?" The amygdala's initial response may then be overridden by a more accurate appraisal from the cortex. This is why you

2. The cerebral cortex generates a more complete picture; it can override signals sent by the amygdala ("It's only Mike in a down coat").

1. The amygdala scrutinizes information for its emotional importance ("It's a bear! Be afraid! Run!").

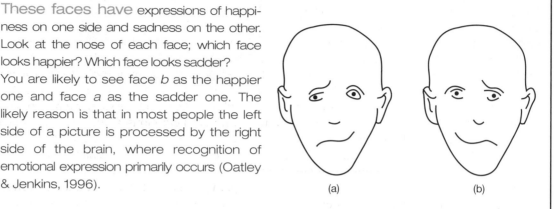

Turn On Your Right Hemisphere

These faces have expressions of happiness on one side and sadness on the other. Look at the nose of each face; which face looks happier? Which face looks sadder?

You are likely to see face *b* as the happier one and face *a* as the sadder one. The likely reason is that in most people the left side of a picture is processed by the right side of the brain, where recognition of emotional expression primarily occurs (Oatley & Jenkins, 1996).

(a) (b)

mirror neurons Brain cells that fire when a person or animal observes others carrying out an action; they are involved in empathy, imitation, and reading emotions.

jump with fear when you suddenly feel a hand on your back in a dark alley, and why your fear evaporates when the cortex registers that the hand belongs to a friend whose lousy idea of humor is to scare you in a dark alley.

If either the amygdala or critical areas of the cortex are damaged, abnormalities in the ability to process fear result. People with damage in the amygdala often have difficulty recognizing fear in others (Adolphs, 2001). One such woman could accurately *display* fear and other emotions herself, but she could not *perceive* or recognize expressions of fear in others (Anderson & Phelps, 2000). In contrast, people with damage to areas of the cortex often lose the capacity to put aside their fear when the emotion is no longer necessary. The result can be constant, irrational feelings of impending doom and anxiety and obsessive thoughts of danger.

Recently, neuroscientists have discovered the existence of **mirror neurons**, specific cells in the brain that are activated when an animal or a person ob-

serves others doing a specific task. Research with fMRI and other brain-imaging technologies has suggested that human mirror neurons, which are found in several key areas of the brain, are far more complex and evolved than those of monkeys. Mirror neurons specialize in helping us identify with what others are feeling, imitate their actions, and read their emotions (Arbib, 2005; Buxbaum, Kyle, & Menon, 2005; Molnar-Szakacs et al., 2005). For example, when you see another person in pain, one reason you feel a jolt of empathy is that mirror neurons involved in pain are firing. When you watch a spider crawl up someone's leg, one reason you have a creepy sensation is that your mirror neurons are firing—the same ones that would fire if the spider were crawling up your own leg. Incredibly, human mirror neurons do not simply recognize another person's action; they actually provide a neural basis for helping us code the intentions of that person's action (Iacoboni et al., 2005). Mirror neurons thus appear to be the underlying mechanism for human empathy, nonverbal rapport, and the contagion of moods we mentioned earlier.

The Energy of Emotion When the amygdala and prefrontal cortex signal "Danger! Get outta here!" you need to be able to move fast. The next stage of the emotional relay is the release of hormones, which produces the energy of emotion. When you are under stress or experience an intense emotion, the sympathetic division of the autonomic nervous system spurs the adrenal glands to send out two hormones, *epinephrine* and *norepinephrine* (see Chapter 4). These chemical messengers produce a state of arousal and alertness. The pupils dilate, widening to allow in more light; the heart beats faster; breathing speeds up; and blood sugar rises, providing the body with more energy to act. Digestion slows down, so that blood flow can be diverted from the

Mirror neurons are clearly at work in this conversation.

stomach and intestines to the muscles and surface of the skin. (This is why, when you are excited, scared, furious, or wildly in love, you may not want to eat.) The ultimate purpose of all these physiological changes is to prepare the body to respond quickly to danger or threat, excitement or challenge.

The adrenal glands produce epinephrine and norepinephrine in response to many challenges in the environment. These hormones will surge if you are laughing at a comedian, playing a video game, worrying about an exam, cheering at a sports event, reacting to an insult, or driving on a hot day in terrible traffic. Epinephrine in particular provides the energy of an emotion, that familiar tingle of excitement. At high levels, it can create the sensation of being "seized" or "flooded" by an emotion that is out of your control. In a sense, you *are* out of control, because people cannot consciously alter their heart rate, blood pressure, and digestive tract. However, you can learn to control your *actions* when you are under the sway of an emotion, even one that feels as intense as anger. And no emotion, no matter how urgent or compelling, lasts forever. As arousal subsides, anger may pale into annoyance, ecstasy into contentment, fear into suspicion, past emotional whirlwinds into calm breezes.

Although epinephrine and norepinephrine are released during many emotional states, emotions also differ from one another physiologically: Fear, disgust, anger, sadness, surprise, and happiness are associated with different patterns of brain activity and autonomic nervous system activity, as measured by heart rate, electrical conductivity of the skin, and finger temperature (Damasio et al., 2000; Levenson, 1992). These distinctive patterns may explain why people all over the world use similar terms to describe basic (primary) emotions, saying they feel "hot and bothered" when they are angry, feel "cold and clammy" when they are afraid, and have a "lump in the throat" when they are sad. These metaphors capture what is going on in their bodies (Oatley & Duncan, 1994).

In sum, the physiology of emotion involves characteristic facial expressions; activity in specific parts of the brain, notably the amygdala, specialized regions of the prefrontal cortex, and mirror neurons; and sympathetic nervous system activity that prepares the body for action. But these physical changes cannot explain why, of two students about to take an exam, one feels psyched up and the other feels overwhelmed by anxiety. And hormones alone won't tell you whether you are thrilled or frightened, sick or just in love.

QUICK *quiz*

We hope that a little surge of hormonal energy will help you answer these questions.

1. A 3-year-old sees her dad dressed as a gorilla and runs away in fear. What brain structure is probably involved in her emotional reaction?

2. Ana Maria is watching an old Laurel and Hardy film, which makes her chuckle and makes her want to see more funny movies. Which side of her prefrontal cortex is likely to be most active?

3. Casey is watching *Horrible Hatchet Homicides in the Haunted House.* What cells in his brain are making him wince when the hero is being attacked?

4. Casey is watching *Horrible Hatchet Homicides in the Haunted House II.* What hormones are causing his heart to pound and his palms to sweat when the murderer is stalking an unsuspecting victim?

Answers:

1. the amygdala   2. the left   3. mirror neurons   4. epinephrine and norepinephrine

Emotion and the Mind

Two friends of ours returned from a mountain-climbing trip to Nepal. One said, "I was ecstatic! The crystal-clear skies, the millions of stars, the friendly people, the majestic mountains, the harmony of the universe!" The other said, "I was miserable! The bedbugs and fleas, the lack of toilets, the yak-butter tea, the awful food, the unforgiving mountains!"

Same trip, two different reactions to it. Why? In the first century A.D., the Stoic philosophers suggested an answer: People do not become angry or sad or ecstatic because of actual events, but because of their explanations of those events. Modern psychologists have verified the Stoics' ideas experimentally and are identifying the cognitive processes involved in emotions.

Many years ago, Stanley Schachter and Jerome Singer (1962) argued that the experience of emotion

GET INVOLVED

Examining Your Emotions After An Exam

After your next psychology test, write down the reasons you think you got the grade you did. Do you attribute the grade to your own efforts or perhaps a lack of effort? If you did not do as well as you hoped, do you blame yourself or do you blame your teacher for being too hard or "unfair"? If you did do well, do you take credit for your good grade, or do you think your success was just a lucky fluke? How are these explanations related to your feelings about your grade?

depends both on physiological arousal and on how you interpret and explain that arousal. Your body may be churning away in high gear, but unless you can explain and label those changes, you will not feel a true emotion. This idea spurred other investigators to study how emotions are created or influenced by beliefs, perceptions of the situation, expectations, and *attributions*—the explanations that people make of their own and other people's behavior (see Chapter 10). Human beings, after all, are the only species that can say, "The more I thought about it, the madder I got." In fact, we often do think ourselves into an emotional state—in this case, anger—and by implication, we can think ourselves out of it.

Surprisingly, third-place winners tend to be happier about their performance than those who come in second. Certainly, Olympic fencing bronze medalist Jean-Michel Henry of France (left) looks happier than silver medalist Pavel Kolobkov of the Unified Team (right). (Eric Strecki, center, won the gold for France.)

Psychologists have studied the role of cognitions in all kinds of emotions, from joy to sadness. For example, imagine that you get an A on your psychology midterm; how will you feel? Or perhaps you get a D on that midterm; how will you feel then? Most people assume that success brings happiness and failure brings unhappiness, but the emotions you feel will depend more on how you explain your grade than on what you actually get. Do you attribute your grade to your own efforts (or lack of them) or to the teacher, fate, or luck? In a series of experiments, students who believed they did well because of their own efforts tended to feel proud, competent, and satisfied. Those who believed they did well because of a lucky fluke or chance tended to feel gratitude, surprise, or guilt ("I don't deserve this"). Those who believed their failures were their own fault tended to feel regretful, guilty, or resigned. And those who blamed others tended to feel angry (Weiner, 1986).

Here is a more surprising example of how thoughts affect emotions. Of two Olympic finalists, one who wins a second-place silver medal and one who wins a third-place bronze medal, who will feel happier? Won't it be the silver medalist? Nope. In a study of athletes' reactions to placing second and third in the 1992 Olympics and the 1994 Empire State Games, the bronze medalists were happier than the silver medalists (Medvec, Madey, & Gilovich, 1995). Apparently, the athletes were comparing their performance to what might have been. The second-place winners, comparing themselves to the gold medalists, were unhappy that they didn't get the gold. But the third-place winners, comparing themselves to those who did worse than they, were happy that they earned a medal at all!

Cognitions and physiology are inextricably linked in the experience of emotion. Thoughts affect emotions, and emotional states influence thoughts (Gray, 2004). For example, blaming others for your woes can make you feel angry, but once you are angry you may be more inclined to think the worst of other people's motives. The complicated mix of emotions that people feel when they have "disappointing wins" (outcomes that were not as good as they had expected) or "relieving losses" (bad outcomes that could have been worse) shows how powerfully thoughts affect emotional responses. It is why we can even feel two emotions, such as pleasure and regret, simultaneously (Larsen et al., 2004).

Some emotions require only minimal, simple cognitions or are primitive feelings that occur beneath awareness (Winkielman & Berridge, 2004). A conditioned sentimental response to a patriotic symbol or a warm, fuzzy feeling toward a familiar souvenir involves simple, nonconscious reactions (Izard, 1994a; Murphy, Monahan, & Zajonc, 1995). An infant's primitive emotions do not have much mental sophistication: "Hey, I'm mad because no one is feeding me!" As a child's cerebral cortex matures, however, cognitions become more complex, and so do emotions: "Hey, I'm mad because this situation is entirely unfair!" Some emotions depend completely on the maturation of higher cognitive capacities. Shame and guilt, for example, do not occur until a child is 2 or 3 years old. These *self*-conscious emotions require the emergence of a sense of self and the ability to perceive that you have behaved badly or let another person down (Baumeister, Stillwell, & Heatherton, 1994; Tangney et al., 1996).

Today, almost all theories of emotion hold that attributions, beliefs, and the meanings people give to events are essential to the creation of most cmo-

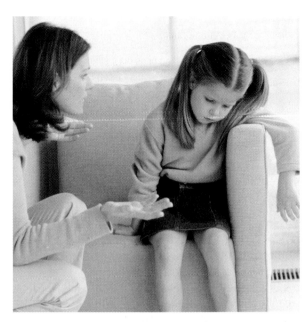

Children need to have a sense of self before they can feel the moral emotions of shame, guilt, or remorse.

tions. But where do these attributions, beliefs, and meanings come from? When people decide that it is shameful for a man to dance on a table with a lampshade on his head, or for a woman to walk down a street with her arms and legs uncovered, where do their ideas about shame originate? If you are a person who loudly curses others when you are angry, where did you learn that cursing is acceptable? To answer these questions, we turn to the third major aspect of emotional experience: the role of culture.

QUICK quiz

How are your thoughts affecting your feelings about this quiz?

1. Dara and Dinah get B's on their psychology midterm, but Dara is ecstatic and proud, and Dinah is furious. What expectations and attributions are probably affecting their emotional reactions?

2. At a party, you see a stranger flirting with your date. You are flooded with jealousy. What cognitions might be causing this emotion? *Be specific.* What alternative thoughts might reduce your jealous feelings?

Answers:

1. Dara was probably expecting a lower grade and is attributing her B to her own efforts; Dinah was probably expecting a higher grade and is attributing her B to the instructor's unfairness, bad luck, or other external reasons.   2. Possible thoughts causing jealousy are "My date finds other people more attractive," "That person is trying to steal my date," or "My date's behavior is humiliating me." But you could be thinking, "It's a compliment to me that other people find my date attractive" or "It pleases me that my date is getting such deserved attention."

WHAT'S *Ahead*

- Why does one person find bugs disgusting, whereas another considers them a culinary treat?

- Do Germans, Japanese, and Americans always mean the same thing when they smile at others?

- Why do people show sadness at funerals even when they are not feeling sad?

- Are women really more "emotional" than men?

Emotion and Culture

A young wife leaves her house one morning to draw water from the local well as her husband watches from the porch. On her way back from the well, a male stranger stops her and asks for some water. She gives him a cupful and then invites him home to dinner. He accepts. The husband, wife, and guest have a pleasant meal together. The husband, in a gesture of hospitality, invites the guest to spend the night—with his wife. The guest accepts. In the morning, the husband leaves early to bring home breakfast. When he returns, he finds his wife again in bed with the visitor.

At what point in this story will the husband feel angry? The answer depends on his culture (Hupka, 1981, 1991). A North American husband would feel rather angry at a wife who had an extramarital affair, and a wife would feel rather angry at being offered to a guest as if she were a lamb chop. But these reactions are not universal. A Pawnee husband of the nineteenth century would be enraged at any man who dared ask his wife for water. An Ammassalik Inuit husband finds it perfectly honorable to offer his wife to a stranger, but

In some cultures, such as the Inuit, anger is not tolerated because it threatens the community's need for closeness and cooperation. Inuit mothers like this one often will ignore an angry baby, thus teaching the child that angry complaints are unwelcome.

only once; he would be angry to find his wife and the guest having a second encounter. And a century ago, a Toda husband in India would not be angry at all because the Todas allowed both husband and wife to take lovers. Both spouses might feel angry, though, if one of them had a *sneaky* affair, without announcing it publicly.

People in most cultures feel angry in response to insult and the violation of social rules. But as this story shows, they often disagree about what an insult is or what the correct rule should be. In this section, we will explore how culture influences the emotions we feel and the ways in which we express them.

How Culture Shapes Emotions

Are some emotions specific to particular cultures and not found elsewhere? What does it mean, for example, that some languages have words for subtle emotional states that other languages lack? The Germans have *schadenfreude*, a feeling of joy at another's misfortune. The Japanese speak of *hagaii*, helpless anguish tinged with frustration. And Tahitians have *mehameha*, a trembling sensation that Tahitians feel when ordinary categories of perception are suspended—at twilight, in the brush, watching fires glow without heat. In the West, an event that cannot be identified is usually greeted with fear. Yet *mehameha* does not describe what Westerners call fear or terror (Levy, 1984).

Do these interesting linguistic differences mean that Germans are more likely than others actually to feel *schadenfreude*, the Japanese to feel *hagaii*, and the Tahitians to feel *mehameha*? Or are they just more willing to give these subtle emotions a single name? Certainly many non-German Westerners feel something like *schadenfreude* at the downfall or humiliation of their political opponents who once defeated them, ex-lovers who once jilted them, or, as one study confirmed, the ultimate defeat of a rival who has beaten them in a sporting event (Leach et al., 2003).

Many psychologists would say that all human beings are capable of feeling the primary, hardwired emotions, the ones that have distinctive physiological hallmarks in the brain, face, and nervous system. But individuals might indeed differ in their abilities to experience secondary emotions, including variations such as *schadenfreude, hagaii*, or *mehameha*.

The difference between primary emotions and more complex cultural variations is reflected in language all over the world. In Chapter 7, we noted that a *prototype* is a typical representative of a class of things. People everywhere consider the primary emotions to be prototypical examples of the concept *emotion*: For example, most people will say that *anger* and *sadness* are more representative of an emotion than *irritability* and *nostalgia* are. Prototypical emotions are reflected in the emotion words that young children learn first: *happy, sad, mad,* and *scared*. As children develop, they begin to draw emotional distinctions that are less prototypical and more specific to their language and culture, such as *ecstatic, depressed, hostile,* or *anxious* (Hupka, Lenton, & Hutchison, 1999; Russell & Fehr, 1994; Shaver, Wu, & Schwartz, 1992). In this way, they come to experience the nuances of emotional feeling that their cultures emphasize.

Some psychologists, however, don't think much of the primary–secondary distinction because, for them, there is *no* aspect of any emotion that is not influenced by culture or context, and there is no "pure" emotion with clear-cut boundaries that separate it

> **Thinking Critically About "Basic" Emotions**

from other emotions (Barrett, 2006; Elfenbein & Ambady, 2003). Anger may be universal, but the way it is experienced and expressed will vary from culture to culture—whether it feels good or bad, useful or destructive. Culture even affects which emotions are defined as basic or primary. Anger is regarded as a primary emotion by individualistic Western psychologists; but in collectivist cultures, described in Chapter 2, shame and loss of face are more central emotions (Kitayama & Markus, 1994). And on the tiny Micronesian atoll of Ifaluk, everyone would say that *fago* is the most fundamental emotion. *Fago*, translated as "compassion/love/sadness," reflects the sad feeling one has when a loved one is absent or in need, and the pleasurable sense of compassion in being able to care and help (Lutz, 1988).

What, then, would theories of primary emotions look like from a non-Western perspective? They might start with shame and *fago*, which are just blips on the radar screen of Western emotion research. And they might also include empathy, envy, regret, greed, and love, which are felt by human beings everywhere yet are omitted from most lists of "universals" because they don't seem to have corresponding facial expressions (Zajonc, 2003).

Everyone agrees, however, that cultures determine much of what people feel emotional *about*. As we saw, disgust is universal, but the content of what produces disgust changes as an infant matures, and it varies across cultures. People in some cultures learn to become disgusted by bugs (which other people find beautiful or tasty), unfamiliar sexual practices, dirt, death, "contamination" by a handshake with a stranger, or particular foods (e.g., meat if they are vegetarian, or pork if they are Muslims or Orthodox Jews). Most people feel disgust when their culture's moral rules are broken (Rozin, Lowery, & Ebert, 1994).

Communicating Emotions

Suppose that someone who was dear to you died. Would you cry, and if so, would you do it alone or in public? Would you wail and tear your clothes, or try to keep your feelings to yourself? Your answer will depend in part on your culture's **display rules** for emotion (Ekman et al., 1987; Gross, 1998). In some cultures, grief is expressed by weeping; in others, by tearless resignation; and in still others by dance, drink, and song. Once you feel an emotion, how you express it is rarely a matter of "I say what I feel." You may be obliged to disguise what you feel. You may wish you could feel what you say.

Even the smile, which seems a straightforward signal of friendliness, has many meanings and uses that are not universal. Americans smile more frequently than Germans, not because Americans are inherently friendlier but because they differ in their notions of when a smile is appropriate. After a German–American business meeting, Americans often complain that the Germans were cold and aloof, and the Germans often complain that the Americans were excessively cheerful, hiding their real feelings under the mask of a smile (Hall & Hall, 1990). The Japanese smile even more than Americans, to disguise

display rules Social and cultural rules that regulate when, how, and where a person may express (or suppress) emotions.

Around the world, the cultural rules for expressing emotions (or suppressing them) differ. The display rule for a formal Japanese wedding portrait is "no direct expressions of emotion"—but not every member of this family has learned that rule yet.

emotion work
Expression of an emotion, often because of a role requirement, that a person does not really feel.

embarrassment, anger, or other negative emotions whose public display is considered rude and incorrect.

Display rules also govern *body language*, nonverbal signals of body movement, posture, gesture, and gaze (Birdwhistell, 1970). Most aspects of body language are specific to particular languages and cultures, which makes even the simplest gesture subject to misunderstanding and offense. The sign of the University of Texas football team, the Longhorns, is to extend the index finger and the pinkie. Be careful where you make this gesture! In Italy and other parts of Europe, it means you're saying a man's wife has been unfaithful to him—a serious insult.

When people are talking to each other, mismatched body language will make their conversation feel out of sync; they may feel as confused and emotionally upset as if they had had a verbal misunderstanding. When people feel uncomfortable with someone from another culture, the reason may simply be that they are not "speaking" the same body language.

Display rules tell us not only what to do when we *are* feeling an emotion but also how and when to show an emotion we do *not* feel. Most people are expected to demonstrate sadness at funerals, happiness at weddings, and affection toward relatives. What if we don't actually feel sad, happy, or affectionate? Acting out an emotion we do not really feel because we believe it is socially appropriate is called **emotion work**. It is part of our efforts to regulate our emotions when we are with others (Gross, 1998). Sometimes emotion work is a job requirement: Flight attendants, waiters, and customer-service representatives must put on a happy face to convey cheerfulness, even if they are privately angry about a rude or drunken customer. And bill collectors must put on a stern face to convey threat, even if they feel sorry for the person they are collecting money from (Hochschild, 1983).

Gender and Emotion

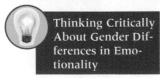

Thinking Critically About Gender Differences in Emotionality

"Women are too emotional," men often complain. "Men are too uptight," women often reply. This is one of the oldest gender stereotypes. But what does "too emotional" mean? We need to define our terms and examine our assumptions.

Although women are more likely than men to suffer from the mood disorder of severe depression (see Chapter 11), there is little evidence that one sex feels any of the everyday emotions more often than the other, whether the emotion is anger, worry, embarrassment, anxiety, love, or grief (Archer, 2004;

Deffenbacher et al., 2003; Fischer et al., 1993; Harris, 2003; Kring & Gordon, 1998; Shields, 2005). The major difference between the sexes has less to do with whether they *feel* emotions than with how and when their emotions are *expressed*.

In North America, women, on the average, smile more than men do, gaze at their listeners more, have more emotionally expressive faces, use more expressive hand and body movements, and touch others more (DePaulo, 1992; Kring & Gordon, 1998). Women also smile more than men to pacify others, convey deference to someone of higher status, or smooth over conflicts (Hess, Adams, & Kleck, 2005; Shields, 2005). In fact, women who don't smile when others expect them to do so are often disliked, even if they are actually smiling as often as men would.

Women also talk about their emotions more than men do. They are far more likely to cry and to acknowledge emotions that reveal vulnerability and weakness, such as "hurt feelings," fear, sadness, loneliness, shame, and guilt (Grossman & Wood, 1993; Timmers, Fischer, & Manstead, 1998). In contrast, most North American men express only one emotion more freely than women: anger toward strangers, especially other men. Otherwise, men are expected to control and mask negative feelings. When they are worried or afraid, they are more likely than women to use vague terms, saying that they feel moody, frustrated, or "on edge" (Fehr et al., 1999; Smith & Reise, 1998).

However, the influence of a particular situation often overrides gender rules (LaFrance, Hecht, & Paluck, 2003). You won't find many gender differences in emotional expressiveness at a football game or the World Series—everyone gets to cheer and boo! Another important situational constraint on emotional expression is the status of the participants (Snodgrass, 1992). A man is as likely as a woman to control his temper when the target of anger is someone with higher status or power; few people, no matter how angry, will readily sound off at a professor, police officer, or employer. And the sexes do similar emotion work

"It's truly remarkable, Louis, thirty-seven years next Tuesday and never a cross word between us."

Both sexes feel emotionally attached to friends, but often they express their affections differently. From childhood on, girls tend to prefer "face-to-face" friendships based on shared feelings; boys tend to prefer "side-by-side" friendships based on shared activities.

when the situation or job requires it. A male flight attendant has to smile as much with passengers as a female one does, and a female FBI agent has to be as emotionally strong and controlled as a male agent does.

Moreover, North American gender differences are by no means universal. Italian, French, Spanish, and Middle Eastern men can have entire conversations using highly expressive hand gestures and facial expressions, and you won't find sex differences in nonverbal expressiveness in their cultures. In contrast, in Asian cultures, both sexes are taught to control emotional expression (Matsumoto, 1996; Mesquita & Frijda, 1992). Cultures also determine which emotions men and women express most freely. Israeli and Italian men are more likely than

women to mask feelings of sadness, but British, Spanish, Swiss, and German men are more likely than their female counterparts to *express* this emotion (Wallbott, Ricci-Bitti, & Bänninger-Huber, 1986).

In sum, the answer to "Which sex is more emotional?" is: sometimes men, sometimes women, and sometimes neither, depending on the circumstances and their culture.

The emotion "tree," as we have seen, can take many shapes, depending on physiology, cognitive processes, and cultural rules. Next we will see how these three factors can help us understand those difficult situations in which stress and negative emotions threaten to overwhelm us and even to make us ill.

QUICK quiz

Please do not display anger if you miss a question.

1. In Western theories of emotion, anger would be called a _____ emotion, whereas *fago* would be called a _____ emotion.

2. Maureen is working in a fast-food restaurant and is becoming irritated with a customer who isn't ordering fast enough. She is supposed to be pleasant to all customers, but instead she snaps, "Hey, whaddaya want to order, slowpoke?" To keep her job and her temper, Maureen needs practice in _____.

3. In a class discussion, a student says something that embarrasses a student from another culture. The second student smiles to disguise his discomfort; the first student, thinking he is not being taken seriously, gets angry. This misunderstanding reflects the students' different _____ for the expression of embarrassment and anger.

4. *True or false:* Throughout the world, women are more emotionally expressive than men.

Answers:

1. primary, secondary   2. emotion work   3. display rules   4. false

The Nature of Stress

general adaptation syndrome According to Hans Selye, a series of physiological reactions to sress occuring in three phases: alarm, resistance, and exhaustion.

No life is entirely free of stress. We are all vulnerable to *stressors*—conflicts that annoy us, pressures that fatigue us, and tragedies and losses that temporarily shatter our lives. The question that most fascinates everyone is whether these events are linked to illness, and whether, by controlling our emotional reactions to events, we can improve our health and well-being.

Stress and the Body

The modern era of stress research began in 1956, when the Canadian physician Hans Selye (1907–1982) published *The Stress of Life*. Environmental stressors such as heat, cold, pain, toxins, and danger, Selye wrote, disrupt the body's equilibrium. The body then mobilizes its resources to fight off these stressors and restore normal functioning. Selye described the body's response to external stressors of all kinds as a **general adaptation syndrome**, physiological reactions that occur in three phases:

1 *The alarm phase*, in which the body mobilizes the sympathetic nervous system to meet the immediate threat. The threat could be anything from taking a test you haven't studied for to running from a rabid dog. As we saw earlier, the release of adrenal hormones, epinephrine and norepinephrine, occurs with any intense emotion and produces a boost in energy, tense muscles, reduced sensitivity to pain, the shutting down of digestion (so that blood will flow more efficiently to the brain, muscles, and skin), and a rise in blood pressure. Decades before Selye, psychologist Walter Cannon (1929) described these changes as the "fight or flight" response, a phrase still in use.

Stress hormones elevated

Blood flow increases

Heart rate speeds up

Digestion slows

Muscles tense

2 *The resistance phase*, in which your body attempts to resist or cope with a stressor that cannot be avoided. During this phase, the physiological responses of the alarm phase continue, but these very responses make the body more vulnerable to other stressors. For example, when your body has mobilized to fight off the flu, you may find you are more easily annoyed by minor frustrations. In most cases, the body will eventually adapt to the stressor and return to normal.

3 *The exhaustion phase*, in which persistent stress depletes the body of energy, thereby increasing vulnerability to physical problems and illness. The same reactions that allow the body to respond effectively in the alarm and resistance phases are unhealthy as long-range responses. Tense muscles can cause headache and neck pain. Increased blood pressure can become chronic hypertension. If normal digestive processes are interrupted or shut down for too long, digestive disorders may result.

Selye did not believe that people should aim for a stress-free life. Some stress, he said, is positive and productive, even if it also requires the body

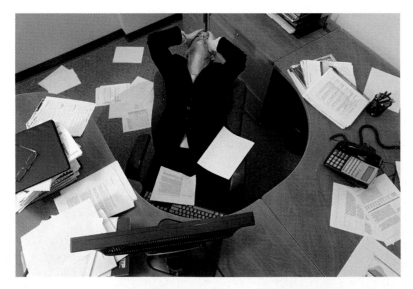

Do you feel overwhelmed by assignments you think you'll never finish, or do you feel challenged by having them? The answer affects how stressed you are.

Alas, the same stress hormones that help in the short run can have unwanted long-term consequences.

to produce short-term energy: competing in an athletic event, falling in love, working hard on a project you enjoy. And some negative stress is simply unavoidable; it's called life!

Current Approaches Many of Selye's ideas proved to be particularly insightful, such as his observation that the same biological changes that are adaptive in the short run, because they permit the body to respond quickly to danger, can become hazardous in the long run (McEwen, 1998). Modern researchers are learning exactly how this happens.

When you are under stress, your brain's hypothalamus sends messages to the endocrine glands along two major pathways. One, as Selye observed, activates the sympathetic division of the autonomic nervous system for fight or flight. In the second, the hypothalamus releases chemical messengers that spur the adrenal cortex to secrete *cortisol* and other hormones that elevate blood sugar and protect the body's tissues from inflammation in case of injury. The result is increased energy, which is crucial for short-term responses to stress (Kemeny, 2003). But if cortisol and other stress hormones stay high too long, they can contribute to hypertension and other physical disorders, possibly depression and other emotional disorders, and even a craving for rich "comfort" foods that are stored as fat in case of emergency. Interestingly, not all stressors produce a rise in cortisol. Cortisol is most likely to be triggered by *psychological* stressors: when people's self-preservation is threatened, when they have no control over the task at hand, or when they feel that they are being judged negatively by others (Dickerson & Kemeny, 2004).

Selye thought that all stressors affect the body in roughly the same ways, but we now know that different stressors may evoke somewhat different responses. Also, people's responses to the same stressor vary widely, depending on their learning history, gender, preexisting medical conditions, and genetic pre-

dispositions for high blood pressure, obesity, diabetes, or other problems (McEwen, 2000; Røysamb et al., 2003; Taylor et al., 2000b). This is why some people respond to the same stressor with much greater increases in blood pressure, heart rate, and hormone levels than other individuals do, and their physical changes take longer to subside back to normal. These hyperresponsive individuals may be the ones most at risk for eventual illness.

Of the many bodily systems affected by stress, one of the most intensively studied has been the immune system, which enables the body to fight disease and infection. The white blood cells of the immune system are designed to recognize foreign substances (*antigens*), such as flu viruses, bacteria, and tumor cells, and then destroy or deactivate them. When an antigen invades the body, the immune system deploys different kinds of white blood cells as

The immune system consists of fighter cells that look more fantastical than any alien creature Hollywood could design. This one is about to engulf and destroy a cigarette-shaped parasite that causes a tropical disease.

weapons, depending on the nature of the enemy. Prolonged stress can suppress some or many of these white blood cells. In one study of medical students who had the herpes virus, herpes outbreaks were more likely to occur when the students were feeling lonely or were under pressure from exams. Loneliness and tension apparently suppressed the immune system's capabilities, permitting the existing herpes virus to erupt (Kiecolt-Glaser et al., 1985a).

Stressors Affecting the Body
Some kinds of stressors are especially likely to affect the immune system, thereby increasing the risk of illness or poor health:

1 *Work-related problems.* Because work is central in most people's lives, the effects of unemployment or of a chronically stressful work environment can be especially severe. Work-related stress can even increase your vulnerability to the common cold. In one study, heroic volunteers were given either ordinary nose drops or nose drops containing a cold virus, and then quarantined for five days. The people most likely to come down with a cold's miserable symptoms were those who had been underemployed or unemployed for at least a month (see Figure 13.3). The longer the work problems had lasted, the greater the likelihood of illness (Cohen et al., 1998).

2 *Noise.* Children who live or go to school near noisy airports have higher blood pressure and higher levels of stress hormones, are more distractible, and have more learning and attention difficulties than do children in quieter environments (Cohen et al., 1980; Evans, Bullinger, & Hygge, 1998). In adults, constant loud noise contributes to cardiovascular problems, irritability, fatigue, and aggressiveness (Staples, 1996).

3 *Bereavement and loss.* In the two years following bereavement, widowed people, especially men, are more susceptible to illness and their mortality rate is higher than would otherwise be expected (Stroebe, Stroebe, & Schut, 2001).

4 *Poverty, powerlessness, and low status.* People at the lower rungs of the socioeconomic ladder have worse health and higher mortality rates for almost every disease and medical condition than do those at the top (Adler & Snibbe, 2003). In America, one obvious reason is that poor people cannot afford medical care. They are also more likely to eat high-calorie, fast-food diets that increase the risk of obesity and diabetes. Another reason for the poorer health of low-income people is that they often live with continuous environmental stressors: higher crime rates, discrimination, fewer community services, run-down housing, and greater exposure to hazards such as chemical contamination, as well as emotional stressors of constant anger, fear, and anxiety (Gallo & Matthews, 2003). These conditions affect urban blacks disproportionately and may help account for their relatively high incidence of hypertension, which can lead to kidney disease, strokes, and heart attacks (Clark et al., 1999).

FIGURE 13.3
Stress and the Common Cold
Chronic stress lasting a month or more boosts the risk of catching a cold. The risk is increased among people undergoing problems with their friends or loved ones; it is highest among people who are out of work (Cohen et al., 1998).

Before you try to persuade your instructors that the stress of chronic studying is bad for your health, however, consider this mystery: None of the chronic stressors we just discussed leads in a direct, simple way to illness or affects everyone in the same way. Although some people's health is affected by noise, bereavement, losing a job, poverty, or discrimination, *most* individuals living with these stressors do not get sick; indeed, the great majority are resilient (Bonanno, 2004; Taylor, Repetti, & Seeman, 1997). Some people exposed to a flu virus are sick all winter; others don't even get the sniffles. Why?

The answer, as we will see next, depends in large part on how people think about their experiences and what they do when they feel stressed or under pressure.

Stress and the Mind

Some people manufacture their own misery. Send them to a beach for a week to escape the pressures of civilization, and they take along a suitcase full of worries and irritations. Others stay serene in the midst of chaos and conflict; they seem to carry along their own inner tranquilizer. These two kinds of people are distinguished by how they explain events and by the degree of control they feel they have over what happens to them.

Optimism and Pessimism
When something bad happens to you, what is your first reaction? Do you tell yourself that you will somehow come through it okay, or do you gloomily mutter, "More proof that if something can go wrong for me, it will"?

In a fundamental way, optimism—the general expectation that things will go well in spite of occasional setbacks—makes life possible. If people are in a jam but believe things will get better eventually, they will keep striving to make that prediction come true. Even despondent fans of the Chicago Cubs, who have not won the World Series in living memory, maintain a lunatic optimism that "there's always next year." If the Boston Red Sox could do it in 2004, their first World Series win since 1918, surely there is hope!

Optimism is also a lot better for your health and well-being than pessimism is (Carver & Scheier, 1999; Peterson, 2000). This does not mean that an optimistic outlook will always prolong the life of a person who already has a serious illness: A team of Australian researchers who followed 179 patients with lung cancer over a period of eight years found that optimism made no difference at all in who lived, or in how long they lived (Schofield et al., 2004). But optimism does seem to produce good health and even prolong life in people without life-threatening illnesses, whereas the "catastrophizing" style of pessimists is associated with untimely death (Maruta et al., 2000; Peterson et al., 1998).

Optimists do not deny their problems or avoid facing bad news; rather, they regard the problems and bad news as difficulties they can overcome. They may have better health than pessimists, therefore, partly because they take better care of themselves. They are more likely than pessimists to be active problem solvers, get support from friends, and seek information that can help them (Brissette, Scheier, & Carver, 2002). They do not give up at the first sign of a setback or escape into wishful thinking. They keep their sense of humor, plan for the future, and reinterpret the situation in a positive light (Aspinwall & Brunhart, 1996; Chang, 1998). Pessimists, in contrast, often do self-destructive things: They drink too much, smoke, fail to wear seat belts, drive too fast, and refuse to take medication for illness. This may be why pessimists, especially males, are more likely than optimists to die in accidents or as a result of violence (Peterson et al., 1998).

Pessimists, naturally, accuse optimists of being unrealistic, and often that is true! Yet health and well-being often depend on having some "positive illusions" about yourself, your abilities, and your circumstances (Taylor et al., 2000a). Positive illusions have both psychological benefits and physiological ones. Optimism is directly associated with

CartoonStock Ltd. CSL

locus of control A general expectation about whether the results of your actions are under your own control (internal locus) or beyond your control (external locus).

better immune function, such as a rise in the natural killer cells that fight infection (Räikkönen et al., 1999; Segerstrom et al., 1998). And people who see themselves in "self-enhancing" ways—thinking, for example, that they are smarter and healthier than average—also show immunological benefits. They have lower physiological activation in the face of chronic difficulties, thereby reducing the wear and tear on their body's regulatory systems (Taylor et al., 2003).

Can pessimists be cured of their gloomy outlook? Optimists, naturally, think so. One way is by teaching pessimists to follow the oldest advice in the world: to count their blessings instead of their burdens. Even among people with serious illnesses, such as a neuromuscular disease, a focus on the positive aspects of life increases well-being and reduces the number of physical symptoms they report (Emmons & McCullough, 2003).

The Sense of Control
Optimism is related to another important cognitive ingredient in health: having an internal locus of control. **Locus of control** refers to your general expectation about whether you can control the things that happen to you (Rotter, 1990). People who have an *internal locus of control* ("internals") tend to believe that they are responsible for what happens to them. Those who have an *external locus of control* ("externals") tend to believe that their lives are controlled by luck, fate, or other people. Having an internal locus of control is associated with good health, academic achievement, political activism, and emotional well-being (Lang & Heckhausen, 2001; Strickland, 1989).

Most people can tolerate all kinds of stressors if they feel able to predict or control them. The crowd you choose to join for a football game is not as stressful as the crowd you cannot escape on a busy street; the music you choose to play at ear-splitting volume is not as stressful as the rotten music you are forced to listen to when you are put on hold on the phone. People who have the greatest control over their work pace and activities, such as executives and managers, have fewer illnesses and stress symptoms than do employees who have little control, who feel trapped doing repetitive tasks, and who have a low chance of promotion (Karasek & Theorell, 1990). The greatest threat to health and well-being occurs when people feel caught in a situation they cannot escape, one that goes on without a foreseeable end. Conversely, feelings of control can reduce or even eliminate the link between stressors and illness that we described earlier. People who have an internal locus of control are better able than externals to resist infection by cold viruses and even the health-impairing effects of poverty and discrimination (Cohen, Tyrrell, & Smith, 1993; Krieger & Sidney, 1996; Lachman & Weaver, 1998).

Feeling in control affects the immune system, which may be why it helps to speed up recovery from surgery and some diseases (E. Skinner, 1996). As with optimism, feeling in control also makes people more likely to take action to improve their health when necessary. In a group of patients recovering from heart attacks, for example, those who believed the heart attack occurred because they smoked, didn't exercise, or had a stressful job were more likely to change their bad habits and recover quickly. In contrast, those who thought their

 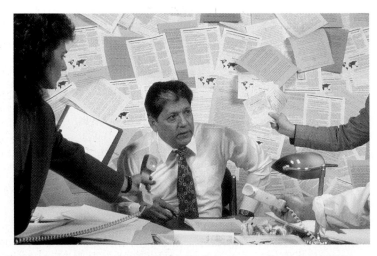

Who has more stress—corporate managers in highly competitive jobs or assembly-line workers in routine and predictable jobs? Research finds that people who are bossed suffer more from job stress than their bosses do, especially if the employees cannot control many aspects of their work (Karasek & Theorell, 1990).

illness was due to bad luck or fate—factors outside their control—were less likely to generate plans for recovery and more likely to resume their old unhealthy habits (Affleck et al., 1987; Ewart, 1995).

The Limits of Control Overall, then, a sense of control is a good thing. But the question must be asked: control over what? It is surely not beneficial for people to believe they can control absolutely every aspect of their lives; some things, such as death, taxes, or being a random victim of a crime, are out of anyone's control. Health and well-being are not enhanced by self-blame ("Whatever goes wrong with my health is my fault") or the belief that all disease can be prevented by doing the right thing ("If I take vitamins and hold the right positive attitude, I'll never get sick").

> **Thinking Critically About the Benefits of Control**

Eastern and Western cultures tend to hold different attitudes toward the ability and desirability of controlling one's own life. In general, Western cultures celebrate **primary control**, in which people try to influence events by trying to exert direct control over them: If you are in a bad situation, you are supposed to change it, fix it, or fight it. The Eastern approach emphasizes **secondary control**, in which people try to accommodate to a bad situation by changing their own aspirations or desires: If you have a problem, you are supposed to live with it or act in spite of it (Rothbaum, Weisz, & Snyder, 1982).

People who are ill or under stress can reap the benefits of both Western and Eastern forms of control by avoiding either–or thinking: for example, by taking responsibility for future actions while not blaming themselves unduly for past ones. Among college freshmen who are doing poorly in their classes, future success depends on maintaining enough primary control to keep working hard and learning to study better, *and* on the ability to come to terms with the fact that success is not going to drop into their laps without effort (Hall et al., 2006). Among women who are recovering from sexual assault or coping with cancer, adjustment is related to a woman's belief that she is not to blame for being raped or for getting sick but that she *is* in charge of taking care of herself from now on (Frazier, 2003; Taylor, Lichtman, & Wood, 1984). "I felt that I had lost control of my body somehow," said one cancer survivor, "and the way for me to get back some control was to find out as much as I could." This way of thinking allows a person to avoid guilt and self-blame while retaining a sense of self-efficacy, the belief that you are basically in charge of your own life and can take steps to get better.

Many problems require us to decide what we can change and to accept what we cannot; perhaps the secret of healthy control lies in knowing the difference.

primary control An effort to modify reality by changing other people, the situation, or events; a "fighting back" philosophy.

secondary control An effort to accept reality by changing your own attitudes, goals, or emotions; a "learn to live with it" philosophy.

QUICK quiz

We hope these questions are not sources of stress for you.

1. Steve is unexpectedly called on in class to discuss a question. He hasn't the faintest idea of the answer, and he feels his heart start to pound and his palms to sweat. According to Selye, Steve is in the _____ phase of his stress response.

2. Maria has worked as a file clerk for 17 years in a job that is closely supervised and boring. Her boss must make many rapid-fire decisions every day and is always complaining of the pressures of responsibility. Which of them probably has the more stressful job? (a) Maria, (b) the boss, (c) both equally, (d) neither job is stressful (*Bonus:* Why?)

3. Anika usually takes credit for doing well on her work assignments and blames her failures on lack of effort. Benecia attributes her successes to luck and blames her failures on the fact that she is an indecisive Gemini. Anika has an _____ locus of control whereas Benecia has an _____ locus.

4. Adapting to the reality that you are getting older is an example of (primary/secondary) control; joining a protest to make a local company clean up its hazardous wastes is an example of (primary/secondary) control.

5. On television, a self-described health expert explains that "no one gets sick if they don't want to be sick," because we can all control our bodies. As a critical thinker, how should you assess this claim?

Answers:

1. alarm   2. a, because Maria has less control than her boss does over every aspect of her work.   3. internal; external   4. secondary; primary   5. Skeptically. First, you would want to define your terms: What does "control" mean, and what kind of control is the supposed expert referring to? People can control some things, such as how much they exercise and whether they smoke, and they can control some aspects of treatment once they become ill, but they cannot control everything that happens to them. Second, you would examine the assumption that control is always a good thing; the belief that we have total control over our lives could lead to depression and unwarranted self-blame when illness strikes.

WHAT'S *Ahead*

- Why are people who are chronically angry and mistrustful their own worst enemy?

- Which disease is depression most clearly linked to?

- Can revealing your unresolved emotions help your health?

Stress and Emotion

Perhaps you have heard people say things like "She was so depressed, it's no wonder she got cancer" or "He's always so angry, he's going to give himself a heart attack one day." Are negative emotions, especially anger and depression, hazardous to your health?

Once a person already has a virus or medical condition or is living in a chronically stressful situation, negative emotions can indeed increase the risk of illness and affect the course of recovery. Feeling anxious, helpless, and depressed, for example, can delay the healing of wounds after surgery, whereas feeling hopeful can significantly speed healing (Kiecolt-Glaser et al., 1998). People who become depressed after a heart attack are significantly more likely to die from cardiac causes in the succeeding year, even controlling for severity of the disease and other risk factors (Frasure-Smith et al., 1999). But can negative emotions, all on their own, make you sick?

Hostility and Depression

One of the first modern efforts to link emotions and illness occurred in the 1970s, with research on the "Type A" personality, a set of qualities thought to be associated with heart disease—ambitiousness, impatience, anger, working hard, and having high standards for oneself. Later work ruled out all of these factors except one: The toxic ingredient in the Type A personality turned out to be hostility.

By "hostility" we do not mean the irritability or anger that everyone feels on occasion, but *cynical* or *antagonistic hostility*, which characterizes people who are mistrustful of others and always ready to provoke mean, furious arguments (Marshall et al., 1994; T. Miller et al., 1996). In a study of male physicians who had been interviewed as medical students 25 years earlier, those who were chronically angry and resentful were five times as likely as nonhostile men to get heart disease, even when other risk factors such as smoking and a poor diet were taken into account (Ewart & Kolod-

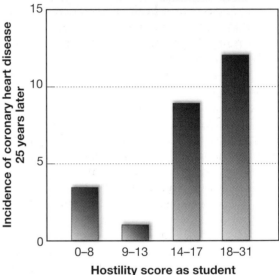

FIGURE 13.4
Hostility and Heart Disease
Anger is more hazardous to health than a heavy workload. Men who had the highest hostility scores as young medical students were the most likely to have coronary heart disease 25 years later (Williams, Barefoot, & Shekelle, 1985).

ner, 1994; Williams, Barefoot, & Shekelle, 1985) (see Figure 13.4). These findings have been replicated in other large-scale studies, with African-Americans and whites, and with women as well as men (Williams et al., 2000). Proneness to anger is a significant risk factor, all on its own, for impairments of the immune system, elevated blood pressure, and heart disease.

Clinical depression, too, is linked to at least a doubled risk of heart attack and cardiovascular disease, according to several large-scale longitudinal studies that found that chronic, severe depression precedes the development of heart disease by many years (Frasure-Smith & Lespérance, 2005; Schulz et al., 2000). A recent theory suggests that because depression, anxiety, and anger-hostility often occur together, like bunches of grapes, the real culprit in heart disease may be a general disposition toward negative emotions (Suls & Bunde, 2005). However, no connection has been found to date between depression and cancer or AIDS (Wulsin, Vaillant, & Wells, 1999).

Positive Emotions: Do They Help?

Just as negative emotions can be unhealthful, positive emotions seem to be healthful (Fredrickson et al., 2003). Consider the findings from a study of 180 Catholic nuns. Researchers examined autobiographies composed by the nuns when the women were about 22 years old, to see whether the quality of their writing predicted the onset of Alzheimer's disease later in life. (It did.) When other researchers scored the writings for their emotional content, they found a strong association between the frequency of positive emotions described—such as happiness, interest, love, hope, gratitude, contentment, amusement, relief—and longevity six decades later (Danner, Snowdon, & Friesen, 2001). The nuns whose life stories contained the most words describing positive emotions lived, on average, nine years longer than nuns who reported the fewest positive feelings. These differences in longevity could not have been due to, say, the stress of poverty, raising children, or particular experiences. The women all had the same experiences and standard of living, at least after they entered the convent.

Psychologists are trying to find out just what it is about feeling happy, cheerful, and hopeful that could protect a person from getting sick. Of course, perhaps the cheerfulness of the long-lived nuns simply reflected an easygoing temperament or other genetic influences that promote long life. But positive emotions could also be physically beneficial because they soften or counteract the high arousal caused by negative emotions or chronic stressors. They may dispose people to think more creatively about their opportunities and choices and to take action to achieve their goals. People who express positive feelings are more likely to attract friends and supporters, too, than are people who are always bitter and brooding, and, as we will see, social support contributes to good health (Pressman & Cohen, 2005).

Hostility is hazardous, but humor is healthful!

If you don't feel bouncy and happy all the time, don't worry; everyone feels grumpy, irritable, and unhappy on occasion. But according to one study in which college students kept a daily diary of their positive and negative emotions for 28 days, the students who were really flourishing, who had the greatest emotional well-being, had a ratio of positive to negative emotions of at least 3 to 1 (Fredrickson & Losada, 2005). You might want to keep track of your own positive-to-negative emotion ratio for the next month to see where yours falls. Are positive emotions more typical of your emotional life than negative ones, or is it the other way around?

Emotional Inhibition and Expression

If positive emotions are beneficial and negative emotions are risky, you might assume that the safest thing to do when you feel angry, depressed, or worried is to try to suppress the feeling. But anyone who has tried to banish an unwelcome thought, a bitter memory, or pangs of longing for an ex-lover knows how hard it can be to do this. When you are trying to avoid a thought, you are in fact processing the thought more frequently, rehearsing it. That is why, when you are obsessed with someone you were once romantically involved with, trying not to think of the person actually prolongs your emotional responsiveness to him or her (Wegner & Gold, 1995).

Moreover, the continued inhibition of thoughts and emotions requires physical effort that can be

True Confessions

To see whether the research on the benefits of confession will be helpful to you, take a moment to jot down your deepest thoughts and feelings about being in college, your past, a secret, your future . . . anything you have never told anyone. Do this again tomorrow and then again for a few days in a row. Note your feelings after writing, too. Are you upset, troubled, sad, or relieved? Does your account change over time? Research suggests that if you do this exercise now, you may have fewer colds, headaches, and trips to the doctor over the next few months (Pennebaker, Colder, & Sharp, 1990).

stressful to the body. People who are able to express matters of great emotional importance to them show elevated levels of disease-fighting white blood cells, whereas people who suppress such feelings tend to have decreased levels (Petrie, Booth, & Pennebaker, 1998).

Given the findings on the harmful effects of feeling negative emotions and also of suppressing them, what is a person supposed to do with them? Occasional feelings of anger, anxiety, and sadness are, of course, inevitable. It is only when people hold on to them too long, rehearsing them and brooding about them, that they can create problems.

Everyone has secrets and private moments of sad reflection. But when you feel sad or fearful for too long, keeping your feelings to yourself may increase your stress.

The Benefits of Confession
One way to get rid of negative emotions comes from research on the benefits of confession: divulging private thoughts and feelings that make you ashamed, worried, or sad (Pennebaker, 2002). Such feelings can be created by holding on to painful secrets, but they can also be produced by normal but stressful transitions, such as starting college.

In one study, freshmen who wrote about their "deepest thoughts and feelings" about being in college reported greater short-term homesickness and anxiety, compared to students who wrote about trivial topics. But by the end of the school year they had had fewer bouts of flu and fewer visits to the infirmary than the control group did (Pennebaker, Colder, & Sharp, 1990). This finding has been replicated in other studies, including among college students in Romania (Opre et al., 2005). The method is even more powerful when people write about traumatic experiences. Another group of college students was asked to write about either a personal, traumatic experience or a neutral topic for 20 minutes a day for four days. Those who were asked to reveal their feelings about a traumatic event all had something to talk about. Many told stories of sexual coercion, physical beatings, humiliation, or parental abandonment. Yet most had never discussed these experiences with anyone. The researchers collected data on the students' physical symptoms, white blood cell counts, emotions, and visits to the health center. On every measure, the students who wrote about traumatic experiences were better off than those who did not (Pennebaker, Kiecolt-Glaser, & Glaser, 1988).

Of course, confession can make you feel worse if you reveal your secrets to a confidant who is judgmental, is unable to help, or betrays your confidence. Moreover, confession's benefits occur only when the revelation produces insight and understanding, thereby ending the stressful repetition of obsessive thoughts and unresolved feelings (Kennedy-Moore & Watson, 2001; Lepore, Ragan, & Jones, 2000). One young woman, who had been molested at the age of 9 by a boy a year older, at first wrote about her feelings of embarrassment and guilt. By the third day, she was writing about how angry she felt at the boy. By the last day, she had begun to see the whole event differently; he was a child too, after all. When the study was over, she said, "Before, when I thought about it, I'd lie to myself. . . . Now, I don't feel like I even have to think about it because I got it off my chest. I finally admitted that it happened."

The Benefits of Letting Grievances Go
Another important way of letting go of negative emotions is to give up the thoughts that produce grudges and replace them with a different perspective. In recent years, there has been a surge of research on anger's antidote: forgiveness. When people rehearse their grievances and hold grudges, their blood pressure, heart rate, and skin conductance rise. Forgiving thoughts (as in the preceding example—"he was a child too") reduce these signs of physiological arousal and restore feelings of control (Witvliet, Ludwig, & Vander Laan, 2001).

(See Figure 13.5.) Forgiveness, like confession when it works, helps people see events in a new light. It promotes empathy, the ability to see the situation from another person's perspective. It strengthens and repairs relationships (Karremans et al., 2003).

Forgiveness does *not* mean that the offended person denies, ignores, or excuses the offense, which might be serious. It does mean that the victim is able, finally, to come to terms with the injustice and let go of obsessive feelings of hurt, rage, and vengefulness. As the Chinese proverb says, "He who pursues revenge should dig two graves."

In sum, health psychology suggests a middle path between "keeping your cool" and "getting hot and bothered": learning to identify, express, and deal with negative emotions, without ruminating on them and letting them erode your relationships or your own well-being.

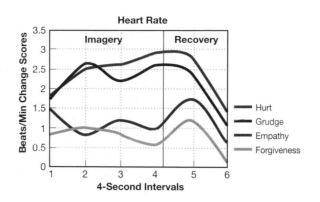

FIGURE 13.5
Heartfelt Forgiveness
Participants in this study were asked to think of someone who they felt had offended or hurt them. Then they were asked to imagine unforgiving reactions (rehearsing the hurt and harboring a grudge) and forgiving reactions (feeling empathy, forgiving). People's heart rates increased much more sharply, and took longer to return to normal, when their thoughts were unforgiving.

QUICK quiz

You'll reduce your stress if you can answer these questions.

1. Which aspect of Type A behavior is most hazardous to the heart? (a) working hard, (b) being in a hurry, (c) cynical hostility, (d) high physical reactivity to work, (e) general grumpiness

2. Amber has many worries about being in college, but she is afraid to tell anyone. What might be the healthiest solution for her? (a) trying not to think about her problems, (b) writing down her feelings in a diary, (c) talking frequently to strangers who won't judge her, (d) expressing her fears whenever she feels them

Answers:

1.c 2.b

WHAT'S *Ahead*

- When you're feeling overwhelmed, what are some ways to calm yourself?

- Why is it important to move beyond the emotions caused by a problem and deal with the problem itself?

- How can you learn to rethink your problems?

- When do friends reduce your stress and when do they just make matters worse?

Emotions, Stress, and Health: How to Cope

We have noted that most people who are under stress, even those living in difficult situations, do not become ill. In addition to feeling optimistic and in control, and not wallowing around in negative emotions, how do they manage to cope? The word coping implies that people are behaving in ways

that barely help them keep their heads above water ("How are you doing?" "Oh, I'm coping"). But some people cope in ways that do more than help them *survive* adversity. They *thrive*, by learning from their experiences and coming out stronger because of them (Joseph & Linley, 2005; see Figure 13.6).

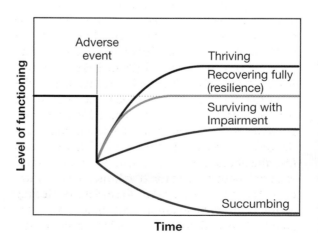

FIGURE 13.6
Succumbing, Surviving, or Thriving
People may respond to adversity by giving up, surviving with some impairment, recovering fully, or thriving—learning from the experience and coming out stronger because of it (Carver, 1998).

These people know all about surviving and thriving.

FIGURE 13.7
Fitness and Health
Among people under low stress, aerobically fit individuals had about the same number of health problems as those who were less fit. But among people under high stress, fit individuals had fewer health problems (Roth & Holmes, 1985).

Cooling Off

The most immediate way to cope with the physiological tension of stress and negative emotions is to calm down: to take time out and reduce the body's physical arousal through meditation or relaxation. For example, *progressive relaxation* training—learning to alternately tense and relax the muscles, from toes to head, and to meditate by clearing your mind—lowers blood pressure, stress hormones, and feelings of anger or anxiety,

and improves immune function (Scheufele, 2000). So does the ancient Buddhist practice of "mindfulness meditation," which teaches, among other things, an ability to focus attention on a single object or idea and to cultivate emotional tranquility (Davidson et al., 2003).

Another effective buffer between stressors and illness is exercise. People who are physically fit have fewer health problems than people who are less fit even when they are under the same pressures. They also show lower physiological arousal to stressors (see Figure 13.7). The more that people exercise, the less anxious, depressed, and irritable they are, and the fewer colds and other illnesses they have (Hendrix et al., 1991; Vita et al., 1998).

Perhaps you can think of other ways to calm down when you're hot and bothered. Many people, from infants to the old, respond beneficially to the soothing touch of massage (Moyer, Rounds, & Hannum, 2004). Other methods include listening to soothing music, writing in a journal, and baking bread. Such activities give the body a chance to recover from the alarm phase of its stress response and from the intensity of negative emotions. But some problems call for more than cooling off. If your house has burned down or you need a serious operation, jogging and meditating will not be enough. Sometimes other coping strategies are necessary.

Solving the Problem

Years ago, at the age of 23, a friend of ours named Simi Linton was struck by tragedy. Linton, her new husband, and her best friend were in a horrific car accident. When she awoke in a hospital room, with only a vague memory of a crash and an ambulance, she learned that her husband and friend had been killed and that she herself had permanent spinal injury and would never walk again.

How in the world does anyone recover from such a devastating event? Some people advise survivors of disaster or tragedy to "get it out of your system" or to "get in touch with your feelings." But survivors know they feel miserable. What should they *do*? This question gets to the heart of the difference between *emotion-focused* and *problem-focused coping* (Lazarus, 2000; Lazarus & Folkman, 1984). Emotion-focused coping concentrates on the emotions the problem has caused, whether anger, anxiety, or grief. For a period of time after any tragedy or disaster, it is normal to give in to these emotions and feel overwhelmed by them. In this stage, people often need to

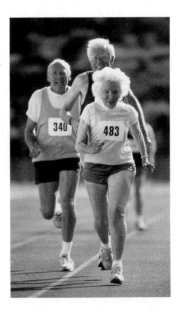

Health problems chart (Low / High Life stress) with High aerobic fitness and Low aerobic fitness.

talk obsessively about the event in order to come to terms with it, make sense of it, and decide what to do about it (Lepore, Ragan, & Jones, 2000).

Eventually, though, most people become ready to concentrate on solving the problem itself. The specific steps in problem-focused coping depend on the nature of the problem: whether it is a pressing but one-time decision; a continuing difficulty, such as living with a disability; or an anticipated event, such as having an operation. Once the problem is identified, the coper can learn as much as possible about it from professionals, friends, books, and others in the same predicament (Clarke & Evans, 1998). Becoming informed increases the feeling of control and can speed recovery (Doering et al., 2000).

As for Simi Linton, she learned more about her medical condition; she learned how to do just about everything in her wheelchair (including dancing!); and she went back to school. She got a Ph.D. in psychology, remarried, and became a highly respected teacher, counselor, writer, and activist committed to improving conditions and opportunities for people with disabilities (Linton, 2006).

Rethinking the Problem

Some problems cannot be solved; these are the unavoidable facts of life, such as an inability to have children, losing your job, or developing a chronic illness. Even when you cannot fix a problem, however, you can change the way you think about it. Here are three effective cognitive coping methods.

1 *Reappraising the situation.* Although you may not be able to get rid of a stressor, you can choose to think about it differently, a process called *reappraisal*. Reappraisal can turn anger into sympathy, worry into determination, and feelings of loss into feelings of opportunity. Maybe that job you lost was pretty dismal but you were too afraid to quit and look for another; now you can. Reappraisal improves well-being and reduces negative emotions, whereas just trying to suppress your negative emotions actually makes them worse (Gross & John, 2003).

2 *Learning from the experience.* Most victims of traumatic events and life-threatening illnesses report that the experience made them stronger, more resilient, even better human beings (McFarland & Alvaro, 2000). The ability to find meaning and benefits even in the worst adver-

The ultimate example of rethinking your problems.

sity seems crucial to psychological recovery. It even slows the course of serious diseases. In a longitudinal study of men with HIV who had been recently bereaved, those who "tried not to think about it" showed sharper declines in immune function and were more likely to die during the follow-up period than were men who found meaning and purpose in the loss. The latter said they had acquired greater appreciation of the loved one, a perception of life as being fragile and precious, or other benefits. "I would say that his death lit up my faith," said one man (Taylor et al., 2000a).

3 *Making social comparisons.* In a difficult situation, successful copers often compare themselves to others who are (they feel) less fortunate. Even if they have fatal diseases, they find someone who is worse off (Taylor & Lobel, 1989; Wood, Michela, & Giordano, 2000). One AIDS sufferer said in an interview, "I made a list of all the other diseases I would rather not have than AIDS. Lou Gehrig's disease, being in a wheelchair; rheumatoid arthritis, when you are in knots and in terrible pain." Another said: "I really have an advantage in a sense over other people. . . . I have the opportunity to look at my life, to make changes, and to deeply appreciate the time that I have" (Reed, 1990).

Drawing on Social Support

A final way to deal with negative emotions and stress is to reach out to others. Your health depends not only on what is going on in your body and mind but also on what is going on in your relationships: what you take from them, and what you give to them.

Friends can be our greatest source of warmth, support, and fun . . .

When Friends Help You Cope . . .

Think of all the ways in which family members, friends, neighbors, and co-workers can help you. They can offer concern and affection. They can help you evaluate problems and plan a course of action. They can offer resources and services such as lending you money or a car, or taking notes in class for you when you are sick. Most of all, they are sources of attachment and connection, which everyone needs throughout life.

Friends are nice to have, and they even improve your health. Remember the study we described earlier, showing that stress increases your risk of getting a cold? Well, having a lot of friends and social contacts reduces that risk. In a group of nearly 300 volunteers exposed to a flu virus, those with the most friends were the least likely to get sick (Cohen et al., 1997). Social support is especially important for people who have stressful jobs that require high cardiovascular responsiveness day after day, such as firefighters. Having social support helps the heart rate and stress hormones return to normal more quickly after a stressful episode (Roy, Steptoe, & Kirschbaum, 1998).

People who live in a network of close connections even live longer than those who do not. In studies that followed thousands of adults for ten years, people who had many friends, connections, or memberships in church and other groups lived longer, on average, than those who had few. The importance of having social networks was unrelated to physical health at the time the studies began, to socioeconomic status, and to risk factors like smoking (Berkman & Syme, 1979; House, Landis, & Umberson, 1988).

CLOSE-UP on Research

Hugs and Health

One of the greatest benefits of social support is the physical affection and comfort it provides. Those close to us do not just touch us emotionally; they also touch us physically. One research team discovered the power of touch when they **asked a question** that has long intrigued psychologists: Why do happily married couples enjoy better health, on average, than their single friends? One answer—that husbands and wives monitor one another's health, for example by limiting how much the other smokes or drinks—is partially true, but not enough to account for married people's better health in relation to singles.

The researchers—James Coan, Hillary Schaefer, and Richard Davidson (2006)—recruited 16 couples who filled out an in-depth questionnaire on their coping styles, degree of emotional intimacy, mutual interests, and happiness in their marriage. The wives then lay in an MRI machine, periodically receiving a mild electric shock on the ankle. The husbands were told to reach into the imaging machine at a particular time and hold their wives' hands. (For comparison, a stranger to the women also provided a comforting touch.) Naturally, the women felt pretty apprehensive about the MRI and the shocks, and their brain images showed activation in the hypothalamus and other regions involved with pain, physical arousal, and negative emotions.

When the researchers **examined the evidence**, they found that the moment the women felt a husband's reassuring hand, their brain activation subsided in all the regions that had been revved up to cope with threat and fear. The investigators **considered other explanations**: Perhaps it was touch alone that was important, regardless of who was providing it. But holding hands with a stranger, while comforting, did not produce as great a decrease in brain activation as did a husband's touch. Moreover, as you can see in the figure below, the women who showed the least activation were those in "super-couples," whose scores on the questionnaire showed an unusual degree of closeness and intimacy. For these women, the hypothalamus and other areas of the brain associated with the anticipation of pain were particularly soothed. Because physical pain is influenced so much by anticipation and fear, a supportive touch from a close partner literally blunted the sensation of pain.

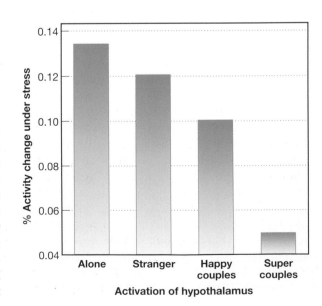

Of course, **we don't want to oversimplify**. The meaning of a touch—why it is offered and how it is interpreted by the person receiving it—is probably critical. But if the touch is an affectionate and welcome one, it can actually elevate some "therapeutic" hormones. Evidence for this idea comes from another study, in which 59 women ages 20 to 49, all in close relationships with a stable partner, reported how often they and their partners were physically affectionate in their everyday lives, for example by holding hands and hugging (Light, Grewen, & Amico, 2005). The researchers measured the women's heart rates, blood pressure, and levels of *oxytocin*, the hormone that induces relaxation and is associated with mothering and attachment. The women were then asked to sit and talk with their partners for a few minutes about a warm shared memory, watch a short romantic video, and give one another a hug. Finally the women were separated from their partners and were asked to write and deliver a speech about a recent experience that was stressful or made them angry.

The women who had the highest oxytocin levels had lower blood pressure and heart rates throughout the experiment, including during the stressful phase, and the women who reported getting the most hugs from their partners had the highest oxytocin levels, also at all phases of the study. The researchers concluded that oxytocin might be a key link between hugging and lower blood pressure. And because high blood pressure is associated with heart disease, well, do the math . . . and do the hugging.

. . . And Coping with Friends

Of course, sometimes other people *aren't* helpful. Sometimes they themselves are the source of unhappiness, stress, and anger.

In close relationships, the same person who is a source of support can also become a source of stress, especially if the two parties are arguing all the time. Being in an unhappy, bitter, uncommunicative marriage can significantly impair health. It makes the partners depressed and angry, affects their health habits, and also directly influences their cardiovascular, endocrine, and immune systems (Kiecolt-Glaser & Newton, 2001). Married couples who argue in a hostile fashion—criticizing, interrupting, or insulting the other person, and becoming angry and defensive—show significant elevations of stress hormones and poorer immune function afterward. In fact, any wounds or blisters

. . . and also sources of exasperation, anger, and misery.

a hostile couple has actually heal more slowly than they do in couples who do not argue in a hostile way (Kiecolt-Glaser et al., 2005). Couples who argue in a positive fashion—trying to find common ground, compromising, listening to each other's concerns, and using humor to defuse tension—do not show these impairments (Kiecolt-Glaser et al., 1993). As one student of ours observed, "This study gives new meaning to the accusation 'You make me sick!'" It also suggests that learning to argue fairly and constructively has physical as well as psychological benefits.

In addition to being sources of conflict, friends and relatives may be unsupportive in times of trouble simply out of ignorance or awkwardness. They may abandon you or say something stupid and hurtful. Sometimes they actively block your efforts to change bad health habits—say, to cut down on binge drinking or smoking—by making fun of you or pressuring you to conform to what "everyone" does. And sometimes, because they have never been in the same situation and do not know what to do to help, they offer the wrong kind of support. For example, they may try to cheer you up, saying, "Everything will be fine," rather than let you talk about your fears or find solutions. That is why support groups of people experiencing the same illness (such as breast cancer or AIDS), problem (such as a parent's alcoholism), or disfiguring disease are often more helpful than friends who haven't "been there" (Davison, Pennebaker, & Dickerson, 2000).

Finally, we should not forget the benefits of giving support, rather than always being on the receiving end. Julius Segal (1986), a psychologist who worked with Holocaust survivors, hostages, refugees, and other survivors of catastrophe, wrote that a key element in their recovery was compassion for others, "healing through helping." People who frequently help their friends and family with practical and emotional support also live longer than self-oriented nonhelpers (Brown et al., 2003). Why? The ability to look outside yourself is related to all of the successful coping mechanisms we have discussed. It encourages you to solve problems instead of blaming others or just venting your emotions, helps you reappraise the situation by seeing it from another person's perspective, fosters forgiveness, and allows you to gain perspective on your own problems. "Healing through helping" thus helps you live with situations that are facts of life.

QUICK quiz

Can you cope with these questions?

1. You accidentally broke your glasses. Which response is an example of cognitive reappraisal? (a) "I am such a stupid, clumsy idiot!" (b) "I never do anything right." (c) "What a shame, but I've been wanting new frames anyway." (d) "I'll forget about it in aerobics class."

2. Finding out what your legal and financial resources are when you have been victimized by a crime is an example of (a) problem-focused coping, (b) emotion-focused coping, (c) distraction, (d) reappraisal.

3. "This class drives me crazy, but I'm better off than my friends who aren't in college" is an example of (a) distraction, (b) social comparison, (c) denial, (d) empathy.

4. What hormone is elevated when happy couples hug one another?

5. Your roommate has turned your room into a garbage dump, filled with rotten leftover food and unwashed clothes. Assuming that you don't like living with rotting food and dirty clothes, what coping strategies described in this section might help you?

Answers:

1. c   2. a   3. b   4. oxytocin   5. You might solve the problem by finding a compromise (e.g., cleaning the room together). You could reappraise the seriousness of the problem ("I only have to live with this person until the end of the term") or compare your roommate to others who are worse ("at least mine is generous and friendly"). And you might mobilize some social support, perhaps by offering your friends a pizza dinner if they help you clean up.

psychology in the news REVISITED

Let us return now to the case of Clara Harris, who was so angry at her unfaithful husband that she murdered him by running him over with her car. The law acknowledges the difference between illegal actions committed in "the heat of anger" and those committed with "cool" premeditation. Harris could have been sentenced to prison for up to 99 years, but "sudden passion" reduced her sentence to 20 years, and she will be eligible for parole in 10. Sudden passion made an 89-year difference in her punishment!

This chapter described the connections among emotion, cognition, and stress. When we are feeling extreme emotions or when major stressors require the body to cope with threat, fear, or danger, the body whirls into action to give us the energy to respond. Just about everyone, for example, has had the unpleasant experience of a racing heart, sweaty palms, and other emotional symptoms upon seeing a former lover with a new partner, let alone a current partner. When Harris found her husband in the hotel lobby with his lover, we can all imagine how emotionally upset she was.

But, as we also saw, biology does not give us the whole picture. It is equally important to understand the role of perceptions, beliefs, and expectations in generating emotions and stress. It may seem obvious that Harris blamed her husband for having an affair, and that her rage resulted from her perception of be-

trayal. But what if she had been able to interpret his behavior another way, for example as evidence of his selfishness and unworthiness? Perhaps then she might have reacted to his affair with other emotions, such as relief to be through with the guy. What if she had focused not on the reasons for her anger but on the reasons for her sadness—say, at how painful it is to lose a close partner? Perhaps then her dominant feelings would have been sorrow and regret.

This chapter also examined the importance of having a sense of control over events, noting the helplessness and panic that can ensue when people lose their feelings of control. Westerners, particularly, tend to have a philosophy of fighting back against unwelcome events rather than of accepting disappointments and losses. When Harris, a former beauty queen, discovered her husband's affair, she tried to recover control of her marriage and win her husband back by having her hair done every day and making plans to have cosmetic surgery. When these efforts failed, she did not know what else to do.

Finally, we saw that there are better ways of coping than by murdering the person causing your anger and stress! These include rethinking the problem, learning from it, comparing oneself to others less fortunate, helping others, and finding a good, strong support group. Clara Harris might not have been able to control her pounding heart and emotional distress when she saw her husband with another woman. But if she had known better ways of managing her distress, she could have controlled her behavior. She could have walked away. (In "Taking Psychology with You," we offer further suggestions for handling anger.)

Keep in mind, though, that successful coping does not mean eliminating all sources of stress or all difficult emotions. It does not mean constant happiness or a life without pain and frustration. The healthy person faces problems, deals with them, and gets beyond them, but the problems are necessary if the person is to ac-quire coping skills that endure. To wish for a life with-out stress, or a life without emotion, would be like wishing for a life without friends. The result might be calm, but it would be joyless. Daily hassles, chronic problems, and occasional tragedies are inescapable. How we handle them is the test of our humanity.

►TAKING ►PSYCHOLOGY ►WITH ►YOU

The Dilemma of Anger: "Let It Out" or "Bottle It Up"?

What do you do when you feel angry? Do you tend to brood and sulk, collecting your right-eous complaints like acorns for the winter, or do you erupt, hurling your wrath upon anyone or anything at hand? Do you discuss your feel-ings when you have calmed down? Does "let-ting anger out" get rid of it for you, or does it only make it more intense? The answers are crucial for how you get along with your fami-ly, neighbors, employers, and strangers.

Chronic feelings of anger and an inabili-ty to control anger can be as emotionally devastating and unhealthy as chronic prob-lems with depression or anxiety. In contrast to much pop-psych advice, research shows that expressing anger does not always get it "out of your system"; often people feel worse after an angry confrontation, both physically and mentally. When people brood and ruminate about their anger, talk to oth-ers incessantly about how angry they are, or ventilate their feelings in hostile acts, their blood pressure shoots up, they often feel angrier, and they behave even *more* aggressively later than if they had just let their feelings of anger subside (Bushman et al., 2005; Tavris, 1989). Conversely, when people learn to control their tempers and express anger constructively, they usually feel better, not worse; calmer, not angrier.

When people are feeling angry, they have a choice of doing any number of things. First, they can try to rethink the situation to reduce its emotional impact; this approach nips anger in the bud and is often more effective than trying to suppress the feeling completely or just venting it (Gross, 2001). Once people are feeling angry, they have several options about how to behave: They can write letters, play the piano, jog, try to solve the problem that is causing their anger, abuse their friends or fam-ily, hit a punching bag, or yell. If a particular ac-tion soothes their feelings or gets the desired response from others, they are likely to ac-quire a habit. Soon that habit feels "natural," as if it could never be changed. Some habits

are better than others, though. Baking bread is fine, whereas many people justify their vio-lent tempers by saying, "I couldn't help my-self." But they can. If you have acquired an abusive or aggressive habit, the research in this chapter offers practical suggestions for learning constructive ways of managing anger:

● **Don't sound off in the heat of anger; let bodily arousal cool down.** Whether your arousal comes from background stress-es such as heat, crowds, or loud noise or from conflict with another person, take time to relax. Time allows you to decide whether you are really angry or just tired and tense. Other cooling-off strategies include taking a time-out in the middle of an argument, meditating or relaxing, and calming yourself with a distracting activity.

● **Don't take it personally.** If you feel that you have been insulted, check your percep-tion for its accuracy. Could there be another reason for the behavior you find offensive? Peo-ple who are quick to feel anger tend to interpret other people's actions as intentional offenses. People who are slow to anger tend to give oth-ers the benefit of the doubt, and they are not as focused on their own injured pride. Empa-thy ("Poor guy, he's feeling rotten") is usually incompatible with anger, so practice seeing the situation from the other person's perspective.

● **Beware of road rage—yours and the other person's.** Driving increases every-one's level of physiological arousal, but not everyone becomes a hotheaded driver. Some drivers make themselves angry by having vengeful and retaliatory thoughts about other drivers (who have the nerve to change lanes or who dare to drive at the speed limit). Hotheaded drivers take more risks while driving (rapidly switching lanes), behave more aggressively (swearing at other drivers), and have more accidents (Deffen-bacher et al., 2003).

● **If you decide that expressing anger is appropriate, be sure you use the right**

verbal and nonverbal language to make yourself understood. Because cultures (and families) have different display rules, be sure the recipient of your anger under-stands what you are feeling and what com-plaint you are trying to convey. If your way of expressing anger is to sulk, expecting everyone else to read your mind, you are not communicating clearly.

● **Think carefully about how to express anger so that you will get the results you want.** What do you want your anger to ac-complish? Do you just want to make the other person feel bad, or do you want the other person to understand your concerns and make amends? Shouting "You moron! How *could* you be so stupid!" might accom-plish the former goal, but it's not likely to get the person to apologize, let alone to change his or her behavior. If your goal is to improve a bad situation or achieve justice, then learn-ing how to express anger so the other per-son will listen is essential.

Of course, if you just want to blow off steam, go right ahead—but you risk be-coming a hothead.

Would anyone in the group like to respond to the way Frank is dealing with his anger?

SUMMARY

The Nature of Emotion

• Thoughts and emotions are not "opposites" each influences the other. Both processes can be rational or irrational, and both are necessary for making plans and wise decisions. The experience of *emotion* involves physiological changes in the face, brain, and autonomic nervous system; cognitive processes; and cultural norms and regulations. *Primary emotions* are thought to be universal, whereas *secondary emotions* are specific to cultures.

• Some basic facial expressions—anger, fear, sadness, happiness, disgust, surprise, contempt, and possibly pride—are widely recognized across cultures. They probably evolved to foster communication with others, enhance survival, and signal our intentions to others. As studies of *facial feedback* show, they also help us to identify our own emotional states. Facial expressions can also generate emotions in others through unconscious mimicry, which is why people can "catch" each other's moods. The ability to synchronize moods through facial expressions and other nonverbal cues is important for establishing rapport and interacting smoothly. However, because people can and do disguise their emotions, their expressions do not always communicate accurately.

• Many aspects of emotion are associated with specific parts of the brain. The *amygdala* is responsible for initially evaluating the emotional importance of incoming sensory information and is especially involved in fear. The *cerebral cortex* provides the cognitive ability to override this initial appraisal. Emotions generally involve the motivation to approach or withdraw; regions of the *left* prefrontal cortex appear to be specialized for the motivation to approach others (as with happiness and anger), whereas regions of the *right* prefrontal region are specialized for withdrawal or escape (as with disgust and fear). *Mirror neurons* throughout the brain are activated when people observe others. These neurons are involved in empathy, imitation, synchrony, and understanding another person's intentions.

• During the experience of any emotion, *epinephrine* and *norepinephrine* produce a state of physiological arousal to prepare the body for an output of energy. But different emotions are also associated with different patterns of autonomic nervous system activity.

• Cognitive approaches to emotion emphasize the perceptions and *attributions* that are involved in different emotions. Some emotions involve simple, nonconscious reactions, such as a conditioned response to an emotional symbol. Others, such as shame and guilt, require complex cognitive capacities.

Emotion and Culture

• Most psychologists believe that all human beings share the ability to experience primary emotions, whereas secondary emotions may be culture specific—a view supported by research on emotion *prototypes*. But others believe that culture affects every aspect of emotional experience, including which emotions are considered basic and what people feel emotional about.

• Culture strongly influences the *display rules* that regulate how and whether people express their emotions. The ability to synchronize moods through *body language* is important for rapport and smooth interactions. *Emotion work* is the effort a person makes to display an emotion he or she does not feel but feels obliged to convey.

• Women and men are equally likely to feel all emotions, from love to anger, although gender rules shape differences in emotional expression. On average, in North America, women are more verbally and nonverbally expressive than men except for anger at strangers. But the situation can override gender rules; both sexes are less expressive to a person of higher status than they, both sexes will do the emotion work their job requires, and some situations foster expressiveness in everybody. Gender differences also vary across cultures.

The Nature of Stress

• Hans Selye argued that environmental stressors such as heat, pain, and danger produce a *general adaptation syndrome*, in which the body responds in three stages: *alarm, resistance*, and *exhaustion*. If a stressor persists, it may overwhelm the body's ability to cope, and fatigue or illness may result. Studies of the immune system have confirmed that stress can suppress the activity of disease-fighting white blood cells and make illness more likely.

• Modern research has supported and added to Selye's work. When a person is under stress, the hypothalamus sends messages to the endocrine glands along two major pathways. One activates the sympathetic division of the autonomic nervous system. In the other, the hypothalamus releases chemical messengers that spur production of *cortisol* and other hormones that increase energy. Excess levels of cortisol can become harmful in the long run. Responses to stress differ across individuals, depending on the type of stressor and the individual's own genetic predispositions.

• Several chronic stressors increase the risk of illness: constant, uncontrollable noise; bereavement and loss; unemployment and work-related problems; and poverty and powerlessness. However, most people who experience these stressors do not become ill. Health psychologists study the psychological, social, and biological factors that explain why only some people get sick.

• Two important psychological factors that affect health are having an *optimistic explanatory style* (in contrast to a *pessimistic* one) and having an *internal locus of control*. Optimism and control improve immune function and also increase a person's ability to tolerate pain, live with ongoing problems, and recover from illness. Health and well-being may depend on the right combination of *primary control*, trying to change the stressful situation, and *secondary control*, learning to accept and accommodate to the stressful situation. Cultures differ in the kind of control they emphasize and value.

Stress and Emotion

• Researchers have sought links between emotions and illness. Chronic anger, especially in the form of *cynical* or *antagonistic* hostility, is a strong risk factor in heart disease. Chronic depression also seems to be related to heart disease, but its link to other illnesses remains unclear.

• People who are emotionally inhibited are at greater risk of illness than people who acknowledge and cope with negative emotions. The effort to suppress worries, secrets, and memories of upsetting experiences can paradoxically lead to obsessively ruminating on these thoughts and become stressful to the body.

• Two ways of letting go of negative emotions include revealing them on paper or to others, if this produces new insight and understanding, and forgiving or letting go of grudges.

Emotions, Stress, and Health: How to Cope

• One way to cope with stress and negative emotions is to reduce their physical effects, for example through relaxation and exercise. Another is to focus on solving the problem (*problem-focused coping*) rather than on venting the emotions caused by the problem (*emotion-focused coping*). A third is to rethink the problem, which involves *reappraisal*, learning from the experience, and comparing oneself to others.

• *Social support* is essential in maintaining physical health and emotional well-being; it even prolongs life and speeds recovery from illness. As the "Close-up on Research" discussion shows, a touch or a hug from a supportive partner calms the alarm circuits of the brain and raises levels of *oxytocin*, which may result in reduced heart rate and blood pressure. However, friends and family can also be sources of stress. In close relationships, couples who fight in a hostile and negative way show impaired immune function. *Giving* support to others—"healing through helping"—is also associated with health and hastens recovery from traumatic experiences.

Psychology in the News, Revisited

• We may not always be able to control the physiological arousal produced by stress or intense emotions, but we generally are able to decide how to behave when we are upset. Coping with stress does not mean trying to live without pain or problems. It means learning how to live with them.

KEY TERMS

The Nature of Emotion

Emotion involves physiological changes in the face, brain, and autonomic nervous system; cognitive interpretations of events; and tendencies toward action, all influenced by cultural norms.

Emotion and the Body

- **Primary emotions** are biologically based and thought to be universal.
- **Secondary emotions** include all the variations and blends of emotion that vary from one culture to another.

Some facial expressions are recognized across cultures and thus seem to reflect a key set of primary emotions: anger, fear, sadness, happiness, disgust, surprise, contempt, and possibly pride.

Functions of facial expressions include:
- Communicating emotion
- Identifying our own emotions through **facial feedback**
- Generating moods in others through mood contagion
- Allowing us to lie about our true feelings

Brain areas associated with emotion:
- The amygdala evaluates incoming emotion, especially anger and fear.

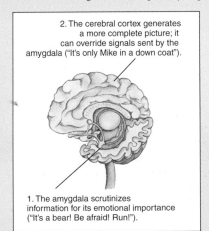

2. The cerebral cortex generates a more complete picture; it can override signals sent by the amygdala ("It's only Mike in a down coat").

1. The amygdala scrutinizes information for its emotional importance ("It's a bear! Be afraid! Run!").

- The left prefrontal cortex specializes in approach motivation and positive emotions; the right prefrontal cortex specializes in escape and negative emotions.
- **Mirror neurons** are brain cells that are activated when an animal or person observes others doing a specific task; they are involved in empathy, imitation, and reading emotions.

During experience of any emotion, two hormones produce a state of arousal: epinephrine and norepinephrine.

Emotion and the Mind

People's perceptions, beliefs, and interpretations of events generate different emotions.
- Some emotions are cognitively primitive.
- As the cortex matures, cognitions become more complex, permitting the emergence of more complex and self-conscious emotions such as shame and guilt.

Emotion and Culture

- Most psychologists believe that all human beings share the ability to experience primary emotions.
- Some psychologists believe that culture affects every aspect of emotional experience.

Communicating Emotions

- **Display rules** regulate how and whether people show emotion.
- Body language communicates emotions nonverbally.
- **Emotion work** is the effort to display an emotion a person does not feel because it is socially appropriate or required.

Gender and Emotion

- The sexes do not differ in how often they feel the range of everyday emotions.
- North American women are more verbally and nonverbally expressive than men.
- Men are more likely to express anger at strangers.

Situations can override gender rules:
- Both sexes are less expressive to a person of higher status.
- Both sexes do "emotion work" associated with their jobs.
- Some situations foster emotion in everybody.
- Gender differences vary across cultures.

The Nature of Stress

Stress and the Body

Hans Selye argued that environmental stressors produce a **general adaptation syndrome**, physiological reactions that occur in three phases:
1. Alarm
2. Resistance
3. Exhaustion

Stress hormones elevated

- Blood flow increases
- Heart rate speeds up
- Digestion slows
- Muscles tense

Physical Changes

When a person is under stress, the hypothalamus sends messages to the endocrine glands along two major pathways in order to:
1. Activate the sympathetic nervous system for "fight or flight"
2. Release chemical messengers that spur production of **cortisol** and other hormones to release energy

Chronic stressors that affect the immune system and increase the risk of illness include:
- Unemployment and work-related problems
- Constant, uncontrollable noise
- Bereavement
- Poverty, powerlessness, and low status

Psychological Factors

Two psychological factors that can increase a person's ability to tolerate pain, live with ongoing problems, and recover from illness:
- Being **optimistic**
- Having an **internal locus of control**

Health and well-being may depend on a combination of:
- **Primary control,** trying to change the stressful situation
- **Secondary control,** learning to accept and to accommodate to the stressful situation

Stress and Emotion

Emotional factors that increase the risk of heart disease and other illness:
- Cynical or antagonistic hostility
- Chronic depression
- Prolonged inhibition of negative emotions

Letting Go of Negative Emotions

Two ways of letting go of negative emotions:
1. Confession: revealing private thoughts and feelings
2. Forgiveness: coming to terms with the injustice

Heartfelt Forgivness

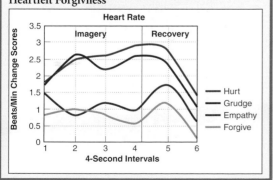

Emotions, Stress, and Health: How to Cope

1. Reducing the physical effects of negative emotion through relaxation and exercise
2. Relying on problem-focused coping rather than emotion-focused coping
3. Rethinking the problem:
   - Reappraising the situation
   - Learning from the experience
   - Comparing yourself to others
4. Drawing on social support or giving it to others can speed recovery from illness and prolong life, although the wrong kind of social support can be detrimental.

psychology in the news

Modern Casanova Admits Courting 50 Women

FORT BRAGG, NC, JUNE 11, 2003. Col. Kassem Saleh didn't do anything illegal, but he is in hot water anyway. Col. Saleh, a 29-year veteran of the United States Army, apparently courted and proposed to more than 50 women whom he met through Internet dating services. They are not happy. In fact, they are demanding that the Army punish him. The women, ages 33 to 50, said he was "beautifully romantic" in his e-mails. Some had received engagement rings and others were planning weddings, though none had actually met him. "We are not a group of stupid, naive women," said one. "We are bright, intellectual, professional women. I can't tell you how much he wooed us with his words. He made us feel like goddesses, fairy princesses, Cinderellas. We had all found our Superman."

Fugitive Rapist Captured

PUNTA DE MITAS, MEXICO, JUNE 22, 2003. Andrew Luster, 39, the wealthy great-grandson of cosmetics magnate Max Factor, was captured today in a small fishing village on the coast of Mexico. Luster had fled during his trial on charges of raping three women after drugging them with the date-rape drug Liquid X (GHB), a powerful sedative that can induce coma, and then videotaping himself having sex with the women after they passed out. He was convicted in absentia and sentenced to 124 years in prison. Luster, who eluded capture for five months, was finally nabbed by a bounty hunter.

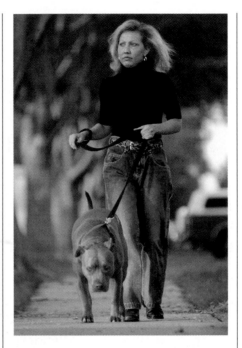

Jennifer Rosenthal needed a liver transplant after she took usnic acid to "stay in shape."

Dying to Be Thin

LONG BEACH, CA, MARCH 4, 2003. A young woman is recovering after nearly killing herself by taking an unproven weight-loss drug. Jennifer Rosenthal, 28, decided to try usnic acid to "stay in shape," although she was not overweight, because the label on the bottle said the chemical would make her body burn calories at an accelerated rate. Rosenthal took the pills for 17 days. A month later she suffered complete liver failure and went into a coma. If she had not received an emergency liver transplant, she would have died. Usnic acid has now been implicated in liver disease or death in numerous cases. One weight-loss product containing a form of usnic acid has been taken off the market, but its manufacturer continues to sell other pills that allegedly build muscle and burn fat.

Armstrong Wins Seven in a Row

PARIS, FRANCE, JULY 24, 2005. Lance Armstrong has won the grueling, 2,125-mile-long Tour de France for the seventh time today, the first man ever to have done so in the history of this arduous biking race over the mountains of France. Armstrong's victories and motivation to keep racing have astonished and delighted the world because of his 1996 recovery from testicular cancer, which had spread to his abdomen, lungs, and brain. Armstrong had decided at the time to retire from the sport, but eventually he came back to win this most difficult of bicycle races, not just once but repeatedly.

The Major Motives of Life: Love, Sex, Food, and Work

What explains the allure of romantic love stories, the kind Colonel Saleh was so good at spinning? Why would attractive, wealthy men like Andrew Luster resort to sexual coercion and rape? Why do so many people struggle to lose weight, even subjecting themselves to the risks of drugs and surgery, and why do so many dieters fail? What motivates people like Lance Armstrong to pursue their dreams in spite of illness and setbacks that would cause many others to give up?

The word *motivation*, like the word *emotion*, comes from the Latin root meaning "to move," and the psychology of motivation is indeed the study of what moves us, why we do what we do. To psychologists, **motivation** refers to an inferred process within a person or animal, which causes that organism to move toward a goal or away from an unpleasant situation. The goal may be to get married or avoid marriage. The goal may be to eat or avoid eating. The goal may be to satisfy a biological need, as in eating a

motivation An inferred process within a person or animal that causes movement either toward a goal or away from an unpleasant situation.

intrinsic motivation The desire to do something for its own sake and for the internal pleasure it provides.

extrinsic motivation The desire to do something for the sake of external rewards, such as money or fame.

sandwich to reduce hunger, or to fulfill a psychological ambition, such as being the first person to row across the Atlantic in a dinghy. But whereas the things that motivate, say, a rabbit are pretty basic (keep eating, keep running from danger, keep multiplying), human motivation is more complex, because people are conscious creatures who think and plan ahead, set goals for themselves, and plot strategies to reach those goals.

In this chapter, we will examine four central areas of human motivation: love, sex, food, and achievement. We will see how happiness and well-being are affected by the kinds of goals we set for ourselves, and by whether we are spurred to reach those goals because of **intrinsic motivation**, enjoyment of an activity for its own sake, or **extrinsic motivation**, pursuit of a goal for external rewards.

As you read, see whether this information helps you understand the enduring appeal of romantic love, the reasons for Andrew Luster's cruel rapes, the desperate risks some people take to lose weight, and the determination of Lance Armstrong to conquer both his illness and the mountains of France.

WHAT'S *Ahead*

- When someone says "I love you," can you be sure what the person means?
- Do men and women differ in the ability to love?
- How are your beliefs about love affected by your income?

The Social Animal: Motives to Love

Do you have a favorite love story? Is it one where the couple falls madly in love at first sight and, after a couple of silly misunderstandings, lives happily ever after without a single quarrel or miserable moment? Or is it more a story of lifelong mutual respect and companionship? What *is* love, anyway—the crazy, passionate, heart-palpitating feeling of falling for another person, or the steady, stable feeling of deep and abiding attachment and trust?

The Biology of Love

Psychologists who study love (a tough job, but someone has to do it) distinguish *passionate* (*"romantic"*) love, characterized by a whirlwind of intense emotions and sexual passion, from *companionate love,* characterized by affection and trust (Hatfield & Rapson, 1996). Passionate love is the stuff of crushes, infatuations, "love at first sight," and the early stage of love affairs. It may burn out completely or evolve into companionate love.

In this era of PET scans and biotechnical advances, it was inevitable that researchers would seek to explain passionate love by rummaging around in the brain. Neuroscientists hope to find answers to the great mysteries of attraction: why people often are hopelessly smitten with someone who is "unsuitable," why the heart seems to overrule the head in matters of love ("He/she is perfectly nice, but I just didn't feel any *chemistry*"), and why many people feel obsessed with a new beloved and can barely sleep or eat when they are parted.

Many biologically oriented researchers believe that the neurological origins of passionate love begin in infancy, in the baby's attachment to the mother. In this view, maternal and romantic love, the deepest of human attachments, share a common evolutionary purpose—preserving the species—and so they share common neural mechanisms, the ones that make attachment and pair-bonding feel good. And, in fact, certain key neurotransmitters and hormones that are involved in pleasure and reward are activated in the mother–baby pair-bond and later in the pair-bond of adult lovers and even of passionate friends (Bartels & Zeki, 2004;

Adult romantic love, with its exchange of loving gazes and depth of passionate attachment, may have its origins in the biology of the baby–mother bond.

Diamond, 2004). The hormone *oxytocin* plays a crucial role in the attachment–caregiving system, influencing feelings and expressions of love, caring, and trust not only between mothers and babies but also between friends and between lovers (Taylor et al., 2000b). In one study, couples given oxytocin through a nasal spray increased their nonverbal expressions of love for one another (Gonzaga et al., 2006). We can just imagine what the pharmaceutical industry will try to do with this information!

Studies of animals also find that the characteristic feelings and actions that occur during attachment are mediated by "reward" circuits in the brain and involve the release of *endorphins,* the brain's natural opiates. When baby mice and other animals are separated from their mothers, they cry out in distress, and the mother's touch (or lick) releases endorphins that soothe the infant. But when puppies, guinea pigs, and chicks are injected with low doses of either morphine or endorphins, the animals show much less distress than usual when separated from their mothers; the chemicals seem to be a biological replacement for mom (Panksepp et al., 1980). And when mice are genetically engineered to lack certain opioid receptors, they become less attached to their mothers and do not show signs of distress when separated from them. This is the same kind of social aloofness that autistic children display (Moles, Kieffer, & D'Amato, 2004).

These findings suggest that endorphin-stimulated euphoria may be a child's initial motive for seeking affection and cuddling—that, in effect, a child attached to a parent is a child addicted to love. The addictive quality of adult passionate love, and the physical and emotional distress that lovers feel when they are apart, may involve the same biochemistry (Diamond, 2004).

Clearly, then, the bonds of attachment are biologically based. Yet, as always, it is important to avoid biological reductionism and the conclusion that "love is all in our hormones" or "love occurs in this corner of the brain but not that one." Human love affairs involve many other factors that affect whom we choose, how we get along, and whether we stay with a partner over the years.

The Psychology of Love

Many romantics believe there is only one true love awaiting them. Considering that there are $6\frac{1}{2}$ billion people on the planet, the odds of finding said person are a bit daunting! What if you're in Omaha or Winnipeg and your True Love is in Dubrovnik or Kankakee? You could wander for years and never cross paths.

Internet services capitalize on the fact that like attracts like. "What type turns you on?" The type that is similar to you!

Fortunately, evolution has made it possible to form deep and lasting attachments without traveling the world. In fact, the first major predictor of whom we love is plain *proximity*: The people who are nearest to you are most likely to be dearest to you, too. We choose our friends and lovers from the set of people who live close by, or who study or work near us. Of course, today's love-seekers can find remote kindred spirits on the Internet, but proximity remains a highly desirable attribute; dating sites can filter out anyone who is geographically undesirable. And *similarity*—in looks, attitudes, beliefs, values, personality, and interests—is the second key predictor of whom we love (Berscheid & Reis, 1998). Although some romantics believe that "opposites attract," the fact is that we tend to choose friends and loved ones who are most like us. Many students use Facebook to find romantic prospects who share their love of poker, the TV show *Smallville*, the hip-hop band Jurassic 5, or any other passion.

The Attachment Theory of Love

Once you find someone to love, *how* do you love? According to Phillip Shaver and Cindy Hazan (1993), adults, just like babies, can be *secure, anxious,* or *avoidant* in their attachments (see Chapter 3). Securely attached lovers are, well, secure: They are rarely jealous or worried about being abandoned. They are more compassionate and helpful than insecurely attached people and are quicker to understand and forgive their partners if the partner does something thoughtless or annoying (Mikulincer et al., 2005; Shaver & Mikulincer, 2006). Anxious lovers are always agitated about their relationships; they want to be close but worry that their partners will leave them. Other

An avoidant lover in action.

"My preference is for someone who's afraid of closeness, like me."

people often describe them as clingy, which may be why they are more likely than secure lovers to suffer from unrequited love (Aron, Aron, & Allen, 1998). Avoidant people distrust and avoid intimate attachments.

Where do these differences come from? According to the *attachment theory of love*, people's attachment styles as adults derive in large part from how their parents cared for them (Fraley & Shaver, 2000; Mikulincer & Goodman, 2006). As children, they form internal "working models" of relationships: Can I trust others? Am I worthy of being loved? Will my parents leave me? If a child's parents were cold and rejecting and provided little or no emotional and physical comfort, the child learns to expect other relationships to be the same. If children form secure attachments to trusted parents, they become more trusting of others, expecting to form other secure attachments with friends and lovers in adulthood (Feeney & Cassidy, 2003).

The distribution of the three basic styles of attachment among adults is in fact very similar to that found for infants: about 64 percent are secure, 25 percent are avoidant, and 11 percent are anxious. Further, the kinds of relationships that people have as adults are strongly related to their reports of how their parents treated them (Mickelson, Kessler, & Shaver, 1997). Securely attached adults report having had warm, close relationships with their parents. Although they recognize their parents' flaws, they describe their parents as having been more loving and kind than insecurely attached people do. Anxious people feel more ambivalence toward their parents, especially their mothers, and also describe their parents ambivalently, as having been both harsh and kind. And people with an avoidant attachment style describe their parents in almost entirely negative terms. These individuals are most likely to report having had cold, rejecting parents, extended periods of separation from their mothers, or childhood environments that prevented them from forging close ties with others (Hazan & Shaver, 1994; Klohnen & Bera, 1998).

Keep in mind, though, that a person's own temperament could also account for the consistency of attachment styles from childhood to adulthood, as well as for the "working models" of relationships that are formed during childhood. Certainly some parents are cold, punitive, and rejecting. But a child who is temperamentally fearful or whose "reward circuits" do not function normally may reject even a kind parent's efforts to console and cuddle, and that child may, therefore, come to believe that all relationships are untrustworthy.

The Ingredients of Love   When people are asked to define the key ingredients of love, most agree that love is a mix of passion, intimacy, and commitment (Aron & Westbay, 1996; Lemieux & Hale, 2000; Sternberg, 1997). However, in most relationships, over the years, romantic passion subsides and intimacy increases. Intimacy is based on deep knowledge of the other person, which accumulates gradually, but passion is based on emotion, which is generated by novelty and change. That is why passion is usually highest at the beginning of a relationship, when two people begin to disclose things about themselves to each other, and lowest when knowledge of the other person's beliefs and

JUMP START reprinted by permission of United Feature Syndicate, Inc.

GET INVOLVED

What Is Your Love Attachment Style?

Which of the following three statements, adapted from Hazan and Shaver (1994), best describes how you typically feel in your romantic relationships?

Secure style: I find it relatively easy to get close to others and am comfortable depending on them and having them depend on me. I don't often worry about being abandoned or about someone getting too close.

Avoidant style: I am somewhat uncomfortable being close; I find it difficult to trust others completely and difficult to allow myself to depend on them. I am nervous when anyone gets close, and often love partners want me to be more intimate than I feel comfortable being.

Anxious style: I find that others are reluctant to get as close as I would like. I often worry that my partner doesn't really love me or won't stay with me. I want to merge completely with another person, and this desire sometimes scares people away.

If you are currently in a dating relationship—and have the nerve!—ask your partner how he or she would reply. Are you well matched?

---

habits is at its maximum, when it seems that there is nothing left to learn about the beloved. Biological factors such as the brain's opiate system may contribute to early passion, as we noted, but most psychologists believe that the factors that contribute to a long and intimate love relationship have more to do with the couple's attitudes, values, temperaments, power balance, and personalities than with hormones.

The critical-thinking guideline "define your terms" may never be more important than in matters of love. The way we define love deeply affects our satisfaction with relationships and even whether our relationships last. After all, if you believe that the only real love is romantic love, that

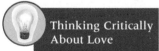
Thinking Critically About Love

love is defined by sexual passion and hot emotion, then you may decide you are out of love when the initial phase of attraction fades, as it eventually must, and you will be repeatedly disappointed. Robert Solomon (1994) argued that "We conceive of [love] falsely . . . We expect an explosion at the beginning powerful enough to fuel love through all of its ups and downs instead of viewing love as a process over which we have control, a process that tends to increase with time rather than wane."

Gender, Culture, and Love

Which sex is more romantic? Which sex truly understands true love? Which sex falls in love but won't commit? Pop-psych books are full of answers, along with advice for dealing with all those love-challenged

heartbreakers who love you and leave you (fools that they are). But all stereotypes oversimplify. Neither sex loves more than the other in terms of love at first sight, passionate love, or companionate love over the long haul (Dion & Dion, 1993; Fehr, 1993; Hatfield & Rapson, 1996). Men and women are equally likely to suffer the heart-crushing torments of unrequited love. They are equally likely to be securely or insecurely attached (Feeney & Cassidy, 2003). Both sexes suffer mightily when a love relationship ends, assuming they did not want it to.

However, women and men do differ, on average, in how they *express* love. Males in many cultures learn early that revelations of emotion can be construed as evidence of vulnerability and weakness, which are considered unmasculine. Thus, men in such cultures often develop ways of revealing love that differ from the ways women do. In contemporary Western society, many women express feelings of love in words, whereas many men express these feelings in actions—doing things for the partner, supporting the family financially, or just sharing the same activity, such as watching TV or a football game together (Baumeister & Bratslavsky, 1999; Cancian, 1987; Swain, 1989). Similarly, many women tend to define intimacy as shared revelations of feelings, but many men define intimacy as just hanging out together.

These gender differences in ways of expressing the universal motives of love and intimacy do not just pop up out of nowhere; they reflect social, economic, and cultural forces. For example, for many years, Western men were more romantic than women in their choice of partner, and women in turn were far more pragmatic than men. One reason was

Marriage for financial security is still the only option for many women from impoverished nations—like this bride, whose husband chose her from a mail-order catalogue.

that a woman did not just marry a man; she married a standard of living. Therefore, she could not afford to marry someone unsuitable or waste her time in a relationship that was not going anywhere, even if she loved the guy. She married, in short, for extrinsic reasons rather than intrinsic ones. In contrast, a man could afford to be sentimental in his choice of partner. In the 1960s, two-thirds of a sample of college men said they would not marry someone they did not love, but only one-fourth of the women ruled out the possibility (Kephart, 1967).

As women entered the workforce and as two incomes became necessary in most families, however, the gender difference in romantic love faded, and

so did economic motivations to marry, all over the world. Nowadays, in every developed nation, only tiny numbers of women and men would consider marrying someone they did not love, even if the person had all the right qualities. Pragmatic reasons for marriage, with romantic love being a remote luxury, persist only in countries where the extended family still controls female sexuality and the financial terms of marriage (Hatfield & Rapson, 1996). Yet even in these countries, such as India and Pakistan, the tight rules governing marriage choices are loosening. So are the rules forbidding divorce, even in extremely traditional nations such as Japan and South Korea.

As you can see, our motivations to love may start with biology and the workings of the brain, but they are shaped and directed by our early experiences with parents, the culture we live in, and something as utterly unromantic as economic dependency or self-sufficiency.

QUICK quiz

Are you passionately committed to quizzes yet?

1. How are adult passionate love and infant–mother love biologically similar?

2. Tiffany is wildly in love with Timothy, and he with her, but she can't stop worrying about him and doubting his love. She wants to be with him constantly, but when she feels jealous she pushes him away and finds it hard to forgive him. According to the attachment theory of love, which style of attachment does Tiffany have?

3. *True or false:* Until recently, most men in Western societies were more likely than women to marry for love.

Answers:

1. Both involve the release of neurotransmitters, the hormone oxytocin, and endorphins that make attachment literally feel good by activating the pleasure-reward circuits in the brain.   2. anxious   3. true

WHAT'S *Ahead*

- Is one kind of orgasm better or healthier for women than another?

- What part of the anatomy do psychologists think is the "sexiest sex organ"?

- How do the sexual rules for heterosexual couples foster misunderstandings?

- Can psychological theories about smothering mothers or absent fathers explain why some men are gay?

The Erotic Animal: Motives for Sex

Most people believe that sex is a biological drive, merely a matter of doing what comes naturally. It is certainly true that in most other species, sexual behavior is genetically programmed. Without

instruction, a male stickleback fish knows exactly what to do with a female stickleback, and a whooping crane knows when to whoop. But as sex researcher Leonore Tiefer (2004) has observed, for human beings "sex is not a natural act." For one thing, the activities that one culture considers natural—say, mouth-to-mouth kissing or oral sex—are often considered unnatural in another culture or historical time. For another, people have to learn from experience and culture what they are supposed to do with their sexual desires and how they are expected to behave. Human sexuality is a blend of biological, psychological, and cultural factors.

The Biology of Desire

Biological researchers have contributed to our understanding of sexual motivation by sweeping away the cobwebs of superstition and ignorance about how the body works.

Desire and sensuality are lifelong pleasures.

Hormones and Sexual Response

One biological factor that seems to promote sexual desire in both sexes is the hormone testosterone. Its role has been documented in studies of men who have been given synthetic hormones that suppress the production of testosterone, of men and women who have abnormally low testosterone levels, and of women who have kept diaries of their sexual activity while also having their hormone levels periodically measured (Bradford & Pawlak, 1993; Dabbs, 2000; Sherwin, 1998b).

This evidence has led pharmaceutical companies and some physicians to promote testosterone treatments for women and men who complain of low sexual desire. But there are significant problems with this apparent solution. One is that there is no consensus on how much sexual activity is "not enough" or on the difference between normally low and abnormally deficient levels of testosterone. Measures of testosterone taken at different intervals do not correlate strongly because the hormone fluctuates. The symptoms of androgen deficiency (low libido, fatigue, lack of well-being) are also those of depression and marital problems. And, in a significant number of cases, the side effects range from unpleasant to harmful (International Consensus Conference, 2002). Moreover, hormones and behavior travel a two-way street: Testosterone does contribute to sexual arousal, but sexual activity also produces higher levels of testosterone (Sapolsky, 1997).

Arousal and Orgasm

Physiological research has dispelled a lot of nonsense written about female sexuality, such as the once-common notions that "good" women don't have orgasms or that mature women should have the "right kind" of orgasm (Ehrenreich, 1978).

The first modern attack on these beliefs came from Alfred Kinsey and his associates (1948, 1953),

in their pioneering books on male and female sexuality. Kinsey's team surveyed thousands of Americans about their sexual attitudes and behavior, and they also reviewed the existing research on sexual physiology. In *Sexual Behavior in the Human Female*, they observed that "males would be better prepared to understand females, and females to understand males, if they realized that they are alike in their basic anatomy and physiology." For example, the penis and the clitoris develop from the same embryonic tissues; they differ in size, of course, but not in sensitivity.

The idea that men and women are sexually similar in any way was extremely shocking in 1953. At that time many people believed that women were not as sexually motivated as men and that women cared more about affection than sexual satisfaction—notions soundly refuted by Kinsey's interviews. Kinsey did believe, however, that women overall have a "lesser sexual capacity" than men, reflected in women's lower frequency of masturbation and orgasm. Although he acknowledged that many women are taught to avoid, dislike, or feel ambivalent about sex, he tended to attribute this gender difference to biology.

The next wave of sex research began in the 1960s with the laboratory research of physician William Masters and his associate Virginia Johnson (1966). In studies of physiological changes during sexual arousal and orgasm, Masters and Johnson confirmed that male and female orgasms are indeed remarkably similar and that all orgasms are physiologically the same, regardless of the source of stimulation. But Masters and Johnson disagreed with Kinsey's assertion that women have a lesser

The "Kinsey Report" on women, officially titled Sexual Behavior in the Human Female, *was not exactly greeted with praise and acceptance—or with clear thinking.*

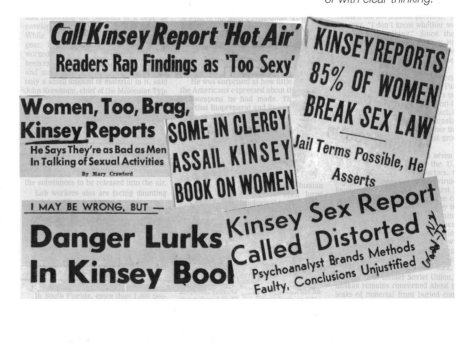

sexual capacity than men. On the contrary, they argued, women's capacity for sexual response "infinitely surpasses that of men" because a woman, unlike most men, is able to have repeated orgasms until exhaustion or a ringing telephone makes her stop.

However, just as Kinsey might have underestimated women's sexual capacity, Masters and Johnson might have overestimated it. Their research was limited by the selection of a sample consisting only of men and women who were easily orgasmic, and they did not investigate how people's physiological responses might vary according to their age, experience, and culture (Tiefer, 2004). Thus, in their eagerness to show that the physiology of arousal and orgasm was the same in both sexes, Masters and Johnson tended to overlook individual differences (Irvine, 1990). Since Masters and Johnson's studies, sex researchers have learned much more about individual variation in sexual physiology and responsiveness (Ellison, 2000; Tiefer, 2004).

Sex and the "Sex Drive"

The question of whether men and women are alike or different in some underlying, biologically based sex drive continues to provoke lively debate. Although women on average are certainly as capable as men of sexual pleasure, men have higher rates of almost every kind of sexual behavior, including masturbation, erotic fantasies, and orgasm (Oliver & Hyde, 1993; Peplau, 2003). These sex differences occur even when men are forbidden by cultural or religious rules to engage in sex at all; for example, Catholic priests have more of these sexual experiences than Catholic nuns do (Baumeister, Catanese, & Vohs, 2001).

Biological psychologists argue that these differences occur universally because the hormones and brain circuits involved in sexual behavior differ for men and women. They maintain that for men, the wiring for sex overlaps with that for dominance and aggression, which is why sex and aggression are more likely to be linked in men than women. For women, the circuits and hormones governing sexuality and nurturance seem to overlap, which is why sex and love are more likely to be linked in women than in men (Diamond, 2004).

Other psychologists, however, maintain that most gender differences in sexual behavior reflect women's and men's different roles and experiences in life and have little or nothing to do with biologically based drives or brain circuits (Eagly & Wood, 1999). They maintain that as long as large numbers of women learn to fear, dislike, or avoid sex, whether through cultural and familial messages or through coercive or unpleasant sexual experiences, it is impossible to know what women's sexual drive might really be like (Kaschak & Tiefer, 2002). A middle view is that men's sexual behavior is more biologically influenced than is women's, whereas women's sexual desires and responsiveness are more affected by circumstances, the specific relationship, and cultural norms (Baumeister, 2000; Peplau et al., 2000).

Evolution and Sex

Evolutionary psychologists believe that sex differences in sex drive and in courtship and mating practices evolved in response to species' survival needs (Buss, 1994). In this view, it was evolutionarily adaptive for males to compete with other males for access to young and fertile females and to try to win and then inseminate as many females as possible. The more females a male mates with, the more genes he can pass along. The human record in this regard was achieved by a man who fathered 899 children (Daly & Wilson, 1983). (What else he did with his time is not known.)

In contrast, according to evolutionary psychologists, females need to shop for the best genetic deal, because they can conceive and bear only a limited number of offspring. Having such a large biological investment in each pregnancy, they can't afford to make mistakes. Besides, mating with a lot of different males would produce no more offspring than staying with just one. So, in the evolutionary view, females try to attach themselves to dominant

"It's a guy thing."

This Kenyan man has 40 wives and 349 children (all of whom, apparently, come to visit). Although he is unusual, in societies around the world it is more common for men to have many wives than for women to have many husbands. Evolutionary psychologists think the reason is that men have evolved to sow as many wild oats as they can, whereas women have evolved to be happy with just a few grains.

males, who have resources and status and are likely to have superior genes.

In human beings and other species, according to proponents of this view, the result of these two opposite sexual strategies is that males generally want sex more often than females do; males are often fickle and promiscuous, whereas females are usually devoted and faithful; males are drawn to sexual novelty, whereas females want stability and security; males will sometimes resort to sexual coercion and rape; males are relatively undiscriminating in their choice of partners, whereas females are cautious and choosy; and males are competitive and concerned about dominance, whereas females are less so.

In human beings, some of these sex differences do appear to be universal or at least very common. In one massive international project, scientists studied many thousands of people in cultures all across the globe (Buss, 1994; Schmitt, 2003). Around the world, men are more interested in the youth and beauty of their sexual partners, presumably because youth is associated with fertility. They are more sexually jealous and possessive, presumably because males can never be 100 percent sure that their children are really theirs genetically. They are quicker to have sex with partners they don't know well and more inclined toward promiscuity, presumably so that their sperm will be distributed as widely as possible. Women, in contrast, tend to emphasize the financial resources or prospects of a potential mate, his status, and his willingness to commit to a relationship (Bailey et al., 1994; Buss, 1996, 2000; Buunk et al., 1996; Mealey, 2000; Sprecher, Sullivan, & Hatfield, 1994).

Evolution, Culture, and Sex One problem with evolutionary theories of sex differences is that many of those differences are stereotypes. For example, the actual behavior of human beings and other animals often contradicts the image of the sexually promiscuous male and the coy and choosy female (Barash & Lipton, 2001; Birkhead, 2001; Fausto-Sterling, 1997; Hrdy, 1994; Roughgarden, 2004). In species after species—birds, fish, and mammals, including human beings—females are sexually ardent and often have many male partners. The female's sexual behavior does not seem to depend only on the goal of being fertilized by the male: Females have sex when they are not ovulating and even when they are already pregnant. And in many species, from penguins to primates, males do not just mate and run, as the photos on the next page illustrate. They stick around, feeding the infants, carrying them, and protecting them against predators (Hrdy, 1988; Snowdon, 1997).

A second problem with evolutionary explanations is that human sexual behavior is remarkably varied and changeable. Cultures range from those in which women have many children to those in which they have very few; from those in which men are intimately involved in child rearing to those in which they do nothing at all; from those in which women may have many lovers to those in which women may be killed if they have sex outside of marriage (Hatfield & Rapson, 1996). In many places, the chastity of a potential mate is much more important to men than to women, but elsewhere it is important to both sexes—or to neither (see Figure 14.1).

Thinking Critically About Evolutionary Theories of Sex

FIGURE 14.1
Attitudes Toward Chastity
In many places, men care more about a partner's chastity than women do, as evolutionary psychologists would predict. But culture has a powerful effect on these attitudes, as this graph shows. Notice that in China, both partners prefer a partner who has not yet had intercourse, whereas in Sweden, chastity is a nonissue (from Buss, 1995).

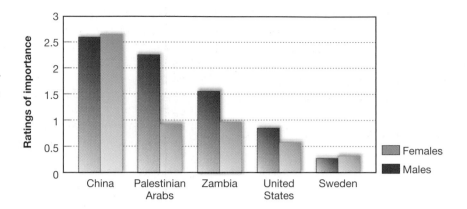

People's attitudes and sexual practices can change rapidly within a culture, too. For example, a meta-analysis of 530 studies, involving nearly 270,000 individuals, showed that in America, young people's sexual attitudes and behavior changed dramatically between 1943 and 1999, with the largest changes occurring among girls and young women (Wells & Twenge, 2005). Approval of premarital sex leapt from 12 percent to 73 percent among young women and from 40 percent to 79 percent among young men; feelings of sexual guilt decreased sharply for both sexes; and, for women, average age at first intercourse dropped from 19 to 15.

Likewise, although in the evolutionary view women supposedly value commitment to a relationship more than men do and are more dedicated to parenting, that is not what recent studies of American adults find. Researchers at the Centers for Disease Control and Prevention (CDC) interviewed more than 12,000 men and women ages 15 to 44 about sex, living together, marriage, divorce, and parenting (Martinez et al., 2006). Fully two-thirds of the men, compared to only 51 percent of the women, agreed with the statement "It is better to get married than go through life single." Most women *and* men agreed that "It is more important for a man to spend a lot of time with his family than be successful at his career." Among fathers in their first marriage, 90 percent were living with their kids and spent considerable time feeding and bathing them, helping with homework, and taking them to activities. And 94 percent of both sexes agreed that "The rewards of being a parent are worth it despite the cost and work it takes."

A final problem with evolutionary theories of sexuality is that the ideal partners that people say they would like on a questionnaire may not have anything to do with their actual choices. Plenty of women don't date or marry rich men, nor do all men date or marry stereotypically beautiful women. Many happily find partners who are plain, financially challenged, or merely average Joes and Janes. As we saw in discussing love, most people choose partners based on their proximity and similarity. Actually, this makes good evolutionary sense, because our prehistoric ancestors, unlike undergraduates filling out questionnaires about their ideal mate, did not have 5,000 fellow students to choose from. They lived in small bands, so if they were lucky they might get to choose between Urp and Ork, and that was about it. They could not hold out for some knockout or rich guy down the road (Hazan & Diamond, 2000).

This evidence, say the critics, argues against a universal, genetically determined sexual strategy. What evolution *has* bestowed on us, they say, is an amazingly flexible brain. Biology influences sexual behavior but it is only one influence among many, as we shall see next.

The Psychology of Desire

Psychologists are fond of observing that the sexiest sex organ is the brain, where perceptions begin. People's values, fantasies, and beliefs profoundly affect their sexual desire and behavior. That is why a touch on the knee by an exciting new date feels terrifically sexy, but the same touch by a creepy stranger on a bus feels disgusting. It is why a worried thought can kill sexual arousal in a second, and why a fantasy can be more erotic than reality.

The Many Motives for Sex To most people, the primary motives for sex are pretty obvious: to enjoy the pleasure of it, to express love and intimacy, or to make babies. But there are other motives too, not all of them so positive. Studies of several hundred college students and more than 1,500 older adults identified six factors

Ah, father love! Evolutionary approaches to sex assume that males across species have only a minimal investment in caring for offspring. But there are many exceptions. Male snow monkeys and lions are doting dads.

underlying the many reasons that people give for having sex (Cooper, Shapiro, & Powers, 1998):

- *Enhancement*—the emotional satisfaction or physical pleasure of sex.
- *Intimacy*—emotional closeness with the partner.
- *Coping*—dealing with negative emotions and disappointments.
- *Self-affirmation*—reassurance that one is attractive or desirable.
- *Partner approval*—the desire to please or appease one's partner, perhaps to avoid the partner's anger or rejection.
- *Peer approval*—the wish to impress one's friends, be part of the group, and conform to what everyone else seems to be doing.

In this research, men and women did not differ in their motives for intimacy, but men were much more likely to have had sex for all the other motives, especially peer approval. The older that people were, the more likely they were to have sex for intimacy and for self-enhancement (pleasure) and the less likely they were to have sex for peer or partner approval. White adolescents were more often motivated by a desire for intimacy than black adolescents were, and black teenagers were more often motivated by coping and peer pressure.

Perhaps you can think of other motives for sex, too: spiritual transcendence, money, duty, power over the partner, submission to the partner, rebellion . . .

People's motives for having sex affect many aspects of their sexual behavior, including whether they engage in sex in the first place, whether they enjoy it, whether they have unprotected or otherwise risky sex, and whether they have few or many partners (Browning et al., 2000). Extrinsic motives, such as having sex for purposes of coping and gaining approval, are most strongly associated with risky sexual behavior, including having many partners and not using birth control (Cooper, Shapiro, & Powers, 1998; Hamby & Koss, 2003; Impett, Peplau, & Gable, 2005).

Unfortunately, significant numbers of women and men are having sex for extrinsic rather than intrinsic motives. In one study, college students in dating relationships kept a daily diary of their sexual experiences. Fifty percent of the women and 26 percent of the men reported consenting to unwanted sexual activity during that time (O'Sullivan & Allgeier, 1998). Men typically do so because of peer pressure, inexperience, a desire for popularity, or a fear of seeming homosexual or unmasculine. Women typically do so because they do not want to lose the relationship; because they feel obligated, once the partner has spent time and money on them; because the partner makes them feel guilty; or because they want to satisfy the partner and avoid conflict (Impett, Gable, & Peplau, 2005).

People's motives for consenting to unwanted sex depend in part on their own feelings of security in the relationship. In a study of 125 college women,

The many motivations for sex range from sex for profit to sex for fun.

one-half to two-thirds of Asian-American, white, and Latina women had consented to unwanted sex, and all of the African-American women said they had. Do you remember the attachment theory of love discussed earlier? Anxiously attached women were the most willing to consent to unwanted sex, especially if they feared their partners were less committed than they were. They reported that they often had sex out of feelings of obligation and to prevent the partner from leaving. Securely attached women also occasionally had unwanted sex, but their reasons were different: to gain sexual experience, to satisfy their curiosity, or to actively please their partners and further the intimacy between them (Impett, Gable, & Peplau, 2005).

Sexual Coercion and Rape

One of the most persistent differences in the sexual experiences of women and men has to do with their perceptions of, and experiences with, sexual coercion. In a nationally representative survey of more than 3,000 Americans ages 18 to 59, nearly one-fourth of the women said that a man, usually a husband or boyfriend, had forced them to do something sexually that they did not want to do (Laumann et al., 1994). But only about 3 percent of the men said they had ever forced a woman into a sexual act. Obviously, what many women regard as coercion is not always seen as coercive by men. On the other hand, about half of all women who report a sexual assault that meets the legal definition of rape do not label it as such (McMullin & White, 2006). College women tend to define rape as being forced into intercourse by an acquaintance or stranger or having been molested as a child. They are least likely to call their experience rape if they were sexually assaulted by a boyfriend, were drunk or otherwise drugged, or were forced to have oral or digital sex (Kahn, 2004).

Although the public image of the rapist tends to be one of a menacing stranger, in most cases the rapist is known to the victim. They may have dated once or a few times; they may even be married (Koss, 1993; Russell, 1990). What causes some men to rape? There appear to be several different motivations:

- *Peer approval.* College men who have physically coerced their dates into having sex have often been pressured by male friends to prove their masculinity by scoring (Kanin, 1985).

- *Anger, revenge, or a desire to dominate or humiliate the victim.* This motive is apparent among soldiers who rape captive women during war and then often kill them (Olujic, 1998). Similarly, reports of the systematic rapes of female cadets at the U.S. Air Force Academy suggest that the rapists' motives were to humiliate the women and get women to leave the Academy. Aggressive motives also occur in the rape of men by other men, usually by anal penetration (King & Woollett, 1997). This form of rape typically occurs in youth gangs, where the intention is to humiliate rival gang members, and in prison, where again the motive is to conquer and degrade the victim.

- *Having the personality traits of narcissism, insecurity, defensiveness, or hostility toward women.* Sexually aggressive males often are narcissistic, are unable to empathize with women, and feel entitled to have sexual relations with whatever woman they choose. They misperceive women's behavior in social situations, equate feelings of power with sexuality, and accuse women of provoking them (Bushman et al., 2003; Drieschner & Lange, 1999; Malamuth et al., 1995; Zurbriggen, 2000).

- *Contempt for the victim and a sadistic pleasure in inflicting pain.* A minority of rapists are men who are primarily motivated to injure or murder their victims.

You can see that the answer to the question "Why do people have sex?" is not at all obvious. It is not a simple matter of "doing what's natural." In addition to the intrinsic motives of intimacy, pleasure, procreation, and love, extrinsic motives include intimidation, dominance, insecurity, appeasing the partner, approval from peers, and the wish to prove oneself a real man or a desirable woman.

The Culture of Desire

Think about kissing. Westerners like to think about kissing, and to do it, too. But if you think kissing is natural, try to remember your first serious kiss and all you had to learn about noses, breathing, and the position of teeth and tongue. The sexual kiss is so complicated that some cultures have never even

This ad, which is directed at men, emphasizes the importance of respect and communication in sexual relationships. Do you think it is effective? Why or why not?

SAN FRANCISCO COMMISSION ON THE STATUS OF WOMEN

The sexiest thing you can say to a woman is, "Is this okay with you?"

RESPECT IS WHAT'S SEXY

Kissing is a learned skill—one that some people start practicing earlier than others.

gotten around to it. They think that kissing another person's mouth—the very place that food enters!—is disgusting (Tiefer, 2004). Others have elevated the sexual kiss to high art; why do you suppose one version is called French kissing?

As the kiss illustrates, having the physical equipment to perform a sexual act is not all there is to sexual motivation. People have to learn, from cultural norms, peers, and parental lessons, what is supposed to turn them on (or off), which parts of the body and what activities are erotic (or repulsive), and even how to have pleasurable sexual relations (Laumann & Gagnon, 1995). To men in cultures where women are required to cover up completely in public, the sight of a woman's ankle can be arousing; to Western men today, an ankle doesn't do it. In some cultures, oral sex is regarded as a bizarre sexual deviation; in others, it is not only considered normal but also supremely desirable. In some cultures, sex is seen as something joyful and beautiful, an art to be cultivated as one might cultivate the skill of gourmet cooking. In oth-

ers, it is considered ugly and dirty, something to be gotten through as quickly as possible.

Sexual Scripts   How do cultures transmit their rules and attitudes about sex to their members? During childhood and adolescence, people learn their culture's *gender roles,* collections of rules that determine the proper attitudes and behavior for men and women, sexual and otherwise. Just as an actor in the role of Hamlet needs a script to learn his part, a person following a gender role needs a **sexual script** that instructs men and women on how to behave in sexual situations (Gagnon & Simon, 1973; Laumann & Gagnon, 1995). If you are a teenage girl, are you supposed to be sexually adventurous and assertive or sexually modest and passive? How about if you are a teenage boy? What if you are an older woman or an older man? The answers differ from culture to culture, as members act in accordance with the sexual scripts for their gender, age, religion, social status, and peer group.

In many parts of the world, boys acquire their attitudes about sex in a competitive atmosphere where the goal is to impress other males, and they talk and joke about masturbation and other sexual experiences with their friends. While boys are learning to value physical sex, girls are learning to value relationships and to make themselves attractive. Many learn that their role is to be sexually desirable (which is good), but not to indulge in their own sexual pleasures (which would be bad)—unless they are following the sexual scripts of the characters in *Grey's Anatomy* or *Sex and the City!* Gay men and lesbians follow sexual scripts, too. But theirs tend to be more flexible than heterosexual scripts in establishing rules for the relationship because most partners are not following a traditional gender role (Kurdek, 2005; Peplau & Spalding, 2000).

sexual scripts   Sets of implicit rules that specify proper sexual behavior for a person in a given situation, varying with the person's gender, age, religion, social status, and peer group.

These teenagers are following the sexual scripts for their gender—the boys, by ogling and making sexual remarks about girls in order to impress their peers, and the girls, by preening and wearing makeup to look good for boys.

Is the Double Standard Still Alive?

Think of all the words you know to describe a sexually active woman and then think of words for a sexually active man. Is one list longer than the other? Are the two lists equally negative or positive in their connotations? Ask a few people who are at least 20 years older than you how they would answer. Does your list agree with theirs? What does this exercise tell you about the survival of the double standard and your culture's sexual scripts?

When gender roles change because of social and economic shifts in society, so do sexual scripts. Whenever women have needed marriage to ensure their social and financial security, they have generally regarded sex as a bargaining chip, an asset to be rationed rather than an activity to be enjoyed for its own sake (Hatfield & Rapson, 1996). A woman with no economic resources of her own cannot afford a sexual relationship if that means risking an unwanted pregnancy, the security of marriage, her reputation in society, her physical safety, or, in some cultures, her very life. When women become self-supporting and able to control their own fertility, however, they are more likely to want sex for pleasure rather than as a means to another goal.

Nicole Bengiveno/The New York Times

Evidence of same-sex sexual activity has been found in more than 450 nonhuman species. These young male penguins, Squawk and Milou, entwine their necks, kiss, call to each other, and have sex—and they firmly reject females. Another male pair in the same zoo, Silo and Roy, seemed so desperate to incubate an egg together that they put a rock in their nest and sat on it. Their human keeper was so touched that he gave them a fertile egg to hatch. Silo and Roy sat on it for the necessary 34 days until their chick, Tango, was born, and then they raised Tango beautifully.

The Riddle of Sexual Orientation

Why do most people become heterosexual, some homosexual, and others bisexual? Many psychological explanations for homosexuality have been proposed over the years, but none of them has been supported. Homosexuality is not a result of having a smothering mother, an absent father, or emotional problems. It is not caused by same-sex sexual play in childhood or adolescence, which is actually quite common (Lamb, 2002). It is not caused by seduction by an older adult (Rind, Tromovich, & Bauserman, 1998). It is not caused by parental practices or role models. Most gay men recall that they rejected the typical boy role and boys' toys and games from a very early age in spite of enormous pressures from their parents and peers to conform to the traditional male role (Bailey & Zucker, 1995). Conversely, the overwhelming majority of children of gay parents do not become gay, as a learning model would predict, although they are more likely than the children of straight parents to be open-minded about homosexuality and gender roles (Bailey et al., 1995; Patterson, 1992, 1995).

Many researchers, therefore, have been turning to biological explanations of sexual orientation. One line of supporting evidence is that homosexual behavior—including courtship displays, sexual activity, and rearing of young by two males or two females—has been documented in some 450 species, including bottlenose dolphins, penguins, and primates (Bagemihl, 1999). Sexual orientation also seems to be moderately heritable, particularly in men (Bailey, Dunn, & Martin, 2000; Rahman & Wilson, 2003). But the large majority of gay men and lesbians do not have a close gay relative, and their siblings, including twins, are overwhelmingly likely to be heterosexual (Peplau et al., 2000).

In the early 1990s, a few studies of gay men reported associations between sexual orientation and specific areas of the brain (Allen & Gorski, 1992; LeVay, 1991). These studies got lots of press, but they

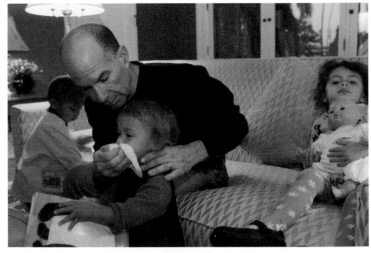

Gay and lesbian couples have all the joys and problems of straight couples. On the left, Phyllis Lyon and Del Martin, who have been together for more than 50 years, embrace after their marriage at City Hall in San Francisco. On the right, Tom Howard is shown with the three children he is raising with his partner. Howard left his job as a professor in order to be a stay-at-home dad.

have not been replicated (Byne, 1995). Researchers have also examined the role of prenatal exposure to androgens (Bailey & Pillard, 1995; Gladue, 1994). Female babies accidentally exposed in the womb to masculinizing hormones are more likely than other girls to become bisexual or lesbian and to prefer typical boys' toys and activities (Collaer & Hines, 1995; Meyer-Bahlburg et al., 1995). However, most androgenized girls do not become lesbians, and most lesbians were not exposed to atypical prenatal hormones (Peplau et al., 2000).

One new line of research is investigating the possibility that other prenatal events might predispose a child toward a same-sex orientation. For example, more than a dozen studies have found that the probability of a man's becoming gay rises significantly according to the number of older brothers he has—gay or not—when these brothers are born of the same mother. (Remember, though, that the percentage of males who become homosexual is very small.) A recent study of 944 homosexual and heterosexual men suggests that this "brother effect" has nothing to do with family environment but rather with conditions within the womb before birth (Bogaert, 2006). In this study, the only factor that predicted sexual orientation was having older biological brothers; growing up with older stepbrothers or adoptive brothers (or sisters) had no influence at all. The increased chance of homosexuality occurred even when men had older brothers born to the same mother but raised in a different home. No one yet has any idea, however, what prenatal influence might account for these results.

The basic problem with trying to find a single origin of sexual orientation is that sexual identity and behavior take different forms, and they don't correlate strongly (Savin-Williams, 2006). Some people are heterosexual in behavior but have homosexual fantasies and even define themselves as gay or lesbian. Some men, such as prisoners, are homosexual in behavior because they lack opportunities for heterosexual sex, but they do not define themselves as gay and prefer women as sexual partners. In some cultures, teenage boys go through a homosexual phase that they do not define as homosexual and that does not affect their future relations with women (Herdt, 1984). Some gay men are feminine in interests and manner, but many are not; some lesbians are "butch" (i.e., masculine) in interests and manner, but many other lesbians are not (Singh et al., 1999).

Moreover, although some lesbians have an exclusively same-sex orientation their whole lives, many have more fluid sexual orientations: They have sex with the person they fall in love with, male or female (Peplau et al., 2000). Some women are lesbian for a particular time in their lives, as reflected in the joking term LUG—lesbian until graduation (Diamond, 2003). In Lesotho, in South Africa, women have intimate relations with other women, including passionate kissing and oral sex, but they do not define these acts as sexual, as they do when a man is the partner (Kendall, 1999).

Biological factors cannot account for the diversity of such customs or for the diversity of experience among gay men and lesbians. At present, therefore, we must tolerate uncertainty about the origins of sexual orientation. Perhaps the origins will turn out to differ, on average, for males and females and also differ among individuals, whatever their primary orientation.

Now, how are you reacting to these findings? Your responses are probably affected by your feelings

Thinking Critically About Findings on Homosexuality

about homosexuality. Many gay men and lesbians welcome biological research on the grounds that it supports what they have been saying all along: Sexual orientation is not a matter of choice but a fact of nature. Others fear that people who are prejudiced against homosexuals will use this research to argue that gay people have a biological defect that should be eradicated. But people who are hostile to homosexuals can use any theory, biological or psychological, to justify their wish to eliminate homosexuality. They have often used learning theories to argue, mistakenly, that "if it's learned, it can be unlearned," and thus to subject gay men, and even "unboyish" boys as young as 3 years old, to harsh and punitive forms of behavior modification (Burke, 1996).

Political storms about sex research are no less heated today than they were in Kinsey's time. Some conservative and evangelical Christians, including the Traditional Values Coalition, are trying to block research on sexual behavior they say the Bible disapproves of, such as masturbation, homosexuality, and any form of sexual behavior outside marriage. Other conservative Christians, however, call upon modern research to make the case that homosexuality is not a preference but a natural disposition. In their book *What God Has Joined Together: A Christian Case for Gay Marriage*, David Myers and Letha Scanzoni (2005) argue that the Bible's seven brief comments opposing same-sex behavior are really condemnations of the exploitation of children, promiscuity, idolatry, and acting against one's nature, and that these verses pale in importance beside the Bible's thousands of verses about love, compassion, and empathy.

As you see, research on sexuality can be used for many purposes and political goals, depending on the values and attitudes of the culture in which such findings emerge and people's own religious passions or personal beliefs. But as long as people are morally opposed to homosexuality, preconceptions and prejudice are likely to cloud their reactions to anything that psychologists learn about it.

QUICK quiz

Were you motivated to learn about sexual motivation?

1. Biological research finds that (a) male and female sexual responses are physiologically very different, (b) all women can have multiple orgasms, (c) testosterone promotes sexual desire in both sexes.

2. Research on the motives of rapists finds that rape is usually a result of (a) thwarted sexual desire, (b) hostility or a need for peer approval, (c) crossed signals, (d) female provocation.

3. Under what conditions are women most likely to use sex as a "bargaining chip"? (a) when they are employed and thus have their own money to bargain with, (b) when they don't know how to play poker, (c) when they are using birth control, (d) when they are financially dependent

4. *True or false:* Exclusively psychological theories of the origins of homosexuality have never been supported.

Answers:

1.c 2.b 3.d 4.true

WHAT'S *Ahead*

- Is being overweight usually a result of psychological problems?

- What theory explains why it's so hard for heavy people to lose weight, and just as hard for thin people to gain it?

- Why are people all over the world getting fatter?

- Why are so many competent professional women determined to be very thin?

The Hungry Animal: Motives to Eat

Many people spend a lot of time and energy thinking about their bodies and wanting to fix them. They long to be thin, or thinner, struggling unsuccessfully their whole lives to shed pounds. Others think that fat is just fine. How much do genes, psychology, and environment affect our motivation to eat or not to eat?

The Genetics of Weight

At one time, most psychologists thought that being overweight was a sign of emotional disturbance. If you were fat, it was because you hated your mother, feared intimacy, or were trying to fill an emotional hole in your psyche by loading up on rich desserts. The evidence for psychological theories of overweight, however, came mainly from self-reports and from flawed studies that lacked control groups or objective measures of how much people were actually eating. When researchers did controlled experiments, they learned that fat people, on average, are no more and no less emotionally disturbed than average-weight people (Stunkard, 1980).

Even more surprising, studies showed that heaviness is not always caused by overeating. Many heavy people do eat large quantities of food, but so do some thin people. In one study, in which volunteers gorged themselves for months, it was as hard for slender people to gain weight as it is for most heavy people to lose weight. The minute the study was over, the slender people lost weight as fast as dieters gained it back (Sims, 1974).

The leading explanation for such findings has been that a biological mechanism keeps your body weight at a genetically influenced **set point**, the weight you stay at when you are not trying to gain or lose (Lissner et al., 1991). The set point can vary about 10 percent in either direction. For example, a woman with a set point of 150 pounds might weigh anywhere from 135 to 165. But if her weight dips below 135 or goes above 165, her body will produce either an insatiable urge to eat or a loss of appetite to bring its fat levels back into line.

Set-point research has focused on how the body regulates appetite, eating, and weight gain and loss.

Everyone has a genetically programmed *basal metabolism rate*, the rate at which the body burns calories for energy, and a fixed number of fat cells, which store fat for energy and thus can change in size. A complex interaction of metabolism, fat cells, and hormones keeps people at the weight their bodies are designed to be, much as a thermostat keeps a house at a preset temperature. When a heavy person diets, the body's metabolism slows down to conserve energy and fat reserves. When a thin person overeats, metabolism speeds up, burning energy. In one study, in which 16 slender volunteers ate 1,000 extra calories every day for 8 weeks, their metabolisms sped up to burn the excess calories. They were like hummingbirds, in constant movement: fidgeting, pacing, changing their positions frequently while seated, and so on (Levine, Eberhardt, & Jensen, 1999).

Set-point theory predicts that the heritability of weight and body fat should be high, and indeed it is: In twin and adoption studies, heritability estimates fall between .40 and .70 (Comuzzie & Allison, 1998). Pairs of adult identical twins who grow up in different families are just as similar in body weight and shape as twins raised together. When identical twins gain weight, they usually gain it in the same place: Some pairs store extra pounds

set point The genetically influenced weight range for an individual, maintained by biological mechanisms that regulate food intake, fat reserves, and metabolism.

Body weight and shape are strongly affected by genetic factors. The Pimas of the American Southwest gain weight easily but lose it slowly, whereas the Bororo nomads of Nigeria can eat a lot of food yet remain slender.

around their waists, others on their hips and thighs (C. Bouchard et al., 1990).

Genes are also involved in some causes of overweight. In a study of 171 Pima Indians in Arizona, two-thirds of the women and half of the men became heavier over time, and the slower their metabolisms, the greater the weight gain. After adding anywhere from 20 to 45 pounds, however, the Pimas stopped gaining weight. Their metabolism rates rose, and their weights stabilized at the new, higher level (Ravussin et al., 1988). Many Pimas apparently have a set point for plumpness.

When there is a mutation in the genes that regulate normal eating and weight control, the result may be obesity. For example, one gene, called *obese*, or *ob* for short, causes fat cells to secrete a protein, which researchers have named *leptin* (from the Greek *leptos*, "slender"). Leptin travels through the blood to the brain's hypothalamus, which is involved in the regulation of appetite. When leptin levels are normal, people eat just enough to maintain their weight. When a mutation of the *ob* gene causes leptin levels to be too low, however, the hypothalamus thinks the body lacks fat reserves and signals the individual to overeat (Zhang et al., 1994). Injecting leptin into leptin-deficient mice reduces the animals' appetites, speeds up their metabolisms, and makes them more active; as a result, the animals shed weight (Friedman, 2003).

Studies of mice suggest that leptin plays its most crucial role early in life by altering the brain chemistry that influences how much an animal or person later eats. More specifically, leptin helps regulate body weight by strengthening neural circuits in the hypothalamus that reduce appetite and by weakening circuits that stimulate it (Elmquist & Flier, 2004). During a critical period in infancy, leptin influences the formation of those neural connections, and the set point is, well, set (Bouret, Draper, & Simerly, 2004). Some researchers speculate that because of this early neural plasticity, overfeeding infants while the hypothalamus is developing may later produce childhood obesity.

The story of leptin is, however, a good cautionary tale for consumers. When the effects of leptin were discovered in mice and the presence of leptin was discovered in humans, one pharmaceutical company thought it had a surefire obesity drug at hand: Take leptin, lose weight! It seemed to be too good to be true, and, alas, it was. The role of leptin in human obesity is more complicated than it is in mice. For most obese people, leptin does not play a major role, and taking more of it does not produce much weight loss (Comuzzie & Allison, 1998).

Researchers have identified a number of other genes that are linked to obesity (Farooqi & O'Rahilly, 2004; Friedman, 2003; Herbert et al., 2006). For example, they have discovered a gene that modulates production of a protein that apparently converts excess calories into heat rather than fat. Possession of this gene may be the reason that slim people stay slim even when they overeat (Arsenijevic et al., 2000).

But be cautious about the enthusiasm that always accompanies such findings. Critical thinkers should be wary of oversimplified claims that a gene or a hormone "determines" anything or that its discovery is "a major breakthrough." Dozens of genes and body chemicals are involved in appetite, metabolism rates, and weight regulation. Moreover, these elements often conflict. You have receptors in your nose and mouth that keep urging you to eat more ("The food is right there! It's good! Eat!"), receptors in your gut telling you to quit ("You've had enough already!"), and leptins and other chemicals telling you that you have stored enough fat or not enough. One hormone makes you hungry and eager to eat more, and another turns off your appetite after a meal, making you eat less. The complexity of the mechanisms governing appetite and weight explains why appetite-suppressing drugs inevitably fail in the long run: They target only one of the many factors that conspire to keep you the weight you are.

Thinking Critically About Weight-Loss "Breakthroughs"

Culture, Psychology, and Weight

If genes are so strongly implicated in weight and body shape, and if most people have normal set points, why are so many people, all over the world, getting fatter? More than half of all American adults, and at least 25 percent of all children and teenagers, are now overweight or obese. The increase has been greatest among the very fat: The number of Americans who are at least 100 pounds overweight has quadrupled since the 1980s. Increases in obesity rates have occurred in both sexes, all social classes, and all age groups, and in many other countries (Taubes, 1998). The United Nations, so used to dealing with problems of starvation, has announced that "Obesity is the dominant unmet

Both of these mice have a mutation in the ob *gene, which usually makes mice chubby, like the one on the left. But when leptin is injected daily, the mice eat less and burn more calories, becoming slim, like his friendly pal.*

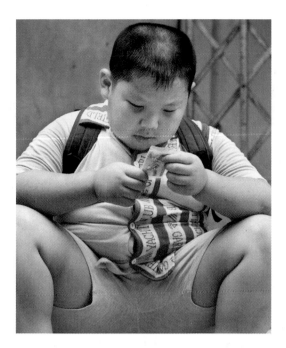

Obesity is a global problem. Children around the world are eating more fast food, while exercising less.

global health issue," especially in the United States, Canada, Great Britain, Japan, and Australia, and even in coastal China and Southeast Asia.

The Environment and Obesity

The leading environmental culprits causing the worldwide weight-gain epidemic are (1) the increased abundance of low-cost, varied, high-calorie foods; (2) the habit of eating high-calorie food on the run rather than in leisurely meals; (3) the rise in energy-saving devices, such as remote controls; (4) the speed and convenience of driving rather than walking or biking; (5) the growing sizes of typical servings of food and drink, and (6) the preference for watching television and videos rather than doing anything active (Critser, 2002; Robinson, 1999). The reason for the rising numbers of overweight people is simple: Calorie consumption is up and exercise is down.

Most human beings are predisposed to gain weight when rich food is abundant because, in the past, starvation was all too often a real possibility. Therefore, a tendency to store calories in the form of fat provided a definite survival advantage. Unfortunately, evolution did not design a comparable mechanism to prevent people who do not have hummingbird metabolisms from gaining excess weight when food is easily available, tasty, rich, varied, and cheap. That, of course, is precisely the situation today, surrounded as we are by $^3/_4$ = pound burgers, fries, chips, tacos, candy bars, and pizzas. Moreover, in American culture, food and drink portions have become supersized, double or triple the size they were only one generation ago. Even babies and toddlers up to 2 years of age are being fed as much as 30 percent more calories than they need (Fox et al., 2004). When people from other cultures move to the United States, they often put on pounds because of the change in dietary habits (Sundquist & Winkleby, 2000).

Another major influence on weight is exercise, which boosts the body's metabolic rate, even in people who are genetically susceptible to obesity (Esparza et al., 2000). When obese women are put on severely restricted diets, their metabolic rates drop sharply, as set-point theory would predict. But when they combine the diet with moderate physical activity—daily walking—they lose weight and their metabolic rates rise almost to previous levels (Wadden et al., 1990).

Cultural Attitudes

Eating habits and activity levels, in turn, are shaped by a culture's customs and standards of what the ideal body should look like: fat, thin, muscular, soft. In many places around the world, especially in those where famine and crop failures are common, fat is taken as a sign of health, affluence in men, and sexual desirability in women (Stearns, 1997). Among the Calabari of Nigeria, brides are put in special fattening huts where they do nothing but eat, so as to become plump enough to please their husbands. And at the Hangandi festival in Niger, the fattest woman wins the beauty contest.

Cultural influences on obesity can also be observed among white farm families. Farmers originally ate large amounts of food for *intrinsic* reasons: When you do hard, labor-intensive work, you need a lot of calories. But today many farm families eat for *extrinsic* motives: to be sociable and conform to family tradition. In the Farm Belt states of the American Midwest, people are expected to eat huge, hearty meals and plenty of sweet desserts. If you don't join in, an anthropologist from Iowa told *The New York Times,* you are being antisocial, insulting your hosts and rejecting your kin (Angier, 2000).

Ironically, while people of all ethnicities and social classes have been getting fatter, the cultural ideal for women in the United States, Canada, and Europe has been getting thinner. The ideal of the voluptuously curvy woman, big-breasted and big-hipped, was popular before World War I and after World War II. But in the flapper era of the 1920s and again starting in the 1960s, big breasts and hips became

During the 1950s, actresses like Jayne Mansfield embodied the postwar ideal: curvy, buxom, and "womanly." In the 1980s and 1990s, many women struggled to be skinny and boyish; today, they want to be thin but also have prominent breasts, like Naomi Watts. Men, too, have been caught up in body-image changes. The 1960s' ideal was the soft and scrawny hippie; today's ideal man is tough and muscular.

bulimia An eating disorder characterized by episodes of bingeing and purging.

anorexia (nervosa) An eating disorder characterized by fear of being fat, a distorted body image, radically reduced consumption of food, and emaciation.

unfashionable. Today the American female ideal is an odd combination: big breasts but no hips. The cultural ideal for American men has changed, too. Until relatively recently, most heavily muscled men were laborers and farmers, so being physically strong and muscular was a sign of being working class. In the past decade, pressures have increased for middle-class men to be buff and strong (Bordo, 2000).

Why did these changes occur? One explanation is that white men and women are more likely than African-Americans or Latinos to associate overweight with softness, laziness, and weakness (Crandall & Martinez, 1996). And they associate the curvy, big-breasted female body with femininity, nurturance, and motherhood. So big breasts are fashionable in eras that celebrate women's role as mothers, such as after World War II, when women were encouraged to give up their wartime jobs and have many children (Stearns, 1997). However, among many whites, femininity is also associated, alas, with incompetence. Thus, whenever women have entered traditionally male spheres of education and work, as they did in the 1920s and again since the 1970s, professionally ambitious women have tried to look boyishly thin and muscular in order to avoid appearing soft, feminine, and dumb (Silverstein & Perlick, 1995; Silverstein, Peterson, & Perdue, 1986). Today's big-breasted but otherwise skinny female ideal may reflect cultural ambivalence about whether women's proper role is domestic or professional. As for men, having a strong, muscular body is now a sign of affluence rather than poverty. It means a man has the money and time to join a gym and work out.

Weight and Health: Biology Versus Culture

What happens when your genetic disposition clashes with your culture's notions of the ideal body? The battle between biology and culture can cause physical and emotional problems, because being extremely overweight or starving to be underweight can both be harmful.

Cultures that regard overweight as a sign of health and sexiness are obviously more accepting of people who are heavy. But obesity can cause serious health problems. When combined with a lack of aerobic fitness, it is a leading risk factor in diabetes, high blood pressure, heart disease, stroke, cancer, infertility, sleep apnea, and many other disorders. About 67 percent of all black women are overweight, compared to 47 percent of white women, and 1 in 10 middle-aged black women is more than 100 pounds overweight—explaining in part why black women are four times as likely as white women to die young of heart disease (Angier, 2000).

Efforts to match a cultural standard of excessive thinness can also pose serious risks to health. Evolution has programmed women for a reserve of fat necessary for the onset of menstruation, healthy childbearing, nursing, and, after menopause, the production and storage of estrogen. In cultures that think women should be very thin, many women become obsessed with weight and are continually dieting, forever fighting their bodies' need for a certain degree of roundness. In addition, a significant minority develop serious eating disorders that reflect an irrational terror of being fat. In **bulimia**, the person binges (eats vast quantities of rich food) and then purges by inducing vomiting or using laxatives. In **anorexia**, the person eats hardly anything and therefore becomes dangerously thin; anorexics have severely distorted body images, thinking they are fat even when they are emaciated. Although many people with these disorders recover, others damage their health permanently or, in the case of anorexia, die of heart or kidney failure or complications of osteoporosis. Their weakened bones simply collapse.

Eating disorders and body-image distortions among boys and men are increasing, too, though they take different forms (Bordo, 2000). Just as anorexic women see their gaunt bodies as being too fat, some men have the delusion that their muscular bodies are too puny. So they abuse steroids and exercise or pump iron compulsively (Pope, Phillips, & Olivardia, 2000). Men who live in cultures in which this body image is not promoted or considered de-

sirable, such as Chinese men in Taiwan and pastoral nomads of northern Kenya, have fewer body-image disorders than American men do and virtually no interest in muscle-building drugs (Campbell, Pope, & Filiault, 2005; Yang, Gray, & Pope, 2005).

Genes may play a role in the development of eating disorders. However, genetic dispositions clearly interact with cultural pressures and with a person's psychological conflicts. Ballerinas, models, actresses, and jockeys are under enormous professional pressure to be superthin. Some of the psychological factors that contribute to eating disorders include depression and anxiety, low self-esteem, perfectionism, a distorted body image, drug use, and perceived pressure from peers to lose weight (Presnell, Bearman, & Stice, 2004; Ricciardelli & McCabe, 2004).

In sum, genetic predispositions for a certain body weight and metabolism interact with psychological needs, cultural norms, and individual habits to shape, in this case quite literally, who we are.

Anorexics cannot see the difference between being fashionably thin and being dangerously skeletal. This anorexic woman died.

QUICK quiz

Is all this information about eating making you hungry for knowledge?

1. *True or false:* Most fat people are heavy because their emotional problems cause them to overeat.
2. What theory seems to explain why thin people rarely become fat and fat people have so much trouble losing weight?
3. Which hormone helps regulate appetite by telling the hypothalamus that the body has stored enough fat?
4. Rising rates of obesity can best be explained by (a) genetic changes over the past few decades, (b) a lack of willpower, (c) an abundance of high-calorie food and sedentary lifestyles, (d) the increase in eating disorders.
5. Bill, who is thin, reads in the newspaper that genes set the range of body weight and shape. "Oh, good," he exclaims, "now I can eat all the junk food I want; I was born to be skinny." What's wrong with Bill's conclusion?

Answers:

1. false 2. set-point theory 3. leptin 4. c 5. Bill is right to recognize that there may be limits to how heavy he can become. But he is oversimplifying and jumping to conclusions. Many people who have a set point for leanness will gain considerable weight on fatty foods and excess calories, especially if they don't exercise. Also, junk food is unhealthy for reasons that have nothing to do with becoming overweight.

WHAT'S *Ahead*

- Why is doing your best an ineffective goal to set for yourself?
- When you are learning a new skill, which should you concentrate on: mastering it or performing it well in front of others?
- Which aspects of a job are more important than money in increasing your work satisfaction and involvement?
- How is the *desire* to achieve affected by the *opportunity* to achieve?

The Competent Animal: Motives to Achieve

Almost every adult works. But work does not only mean paid employment. Students work at studying. Homemakers work, often more hours than salaried employees, at running a household. Artists, poets, and actors work, even if they are paid erratically (or not at all). Most people are motivated to work in

"Finish it? Why would I want to finish it?"

order to meet the basic needs for food and shelter. Yet survival does not explain why some people want to do their work well and others just want to get it done. And it does not explain why some people work merely to make a living and put their passions for achievement into unpaid activities—learning to become an accomplished trail rider or traveling to Madagascar to catch sight of a rare bird for their bird-watching list.

Psychologists, particularly those in the field of *industrial/organizational psychology*, have measured the psychological qualities that spur achievement and success and also the environmental conditions that influence productivity and satisfaction. Their findings apply not only to understanding why people thrive or wilt at their jobs, but also to understanding people's aspirations and achievements in general.

The Effects of Motivation on Work

In the early 1950s, David McClelland and his associates (1953) speculated that some people have a **need for achievement** that motivates them as much as hunger motivates people to eat. To measure the strength of this motive, McClelland used a variation of the **Thematic Apperception Test (TAT)**, which requires the test-taker to make up a story about a set of ambiguous pictures, such as a young man sitting at a desk. (The TAT is one of many *projective tests*, which are based on the assumption that a person will project unconscious motives and feelings onto an ambiguous stimulus; see Chapter 11.) The strength of the achievement motive, said McClelland (1961), is captured in the fantasies the test-taker reveals. "In fantasy any-

THE MANY MOTIVES OF ACCOMPLISHMENT

◄ **IMMORTALITY**
WILLIAM FAULKNER
(1897–1962)
Novelist

"Really the writer doesn't want success . . . He wants to leave a scratch on that wall [of oblivion]—Kilroy was here—that somebody a hundred or a thousand years later will see."

◄ **JUSTICE**
MARTIN LUTHER KING, JR.
(1929–1968)
Civil rights activist

"I have a dream . . . that my four little children will one day live in a nation where they will not be judged by the color of their skin but the content of their character."

KNOWLEDGE ►
HELLEN KELLER
(1880–1968)
Blind/deaf author and lecturer

"Knowledge is happiness, because to have knowledge broad, deep knowledge—is to know true ends from false, and lofty things from low."

AUTONOMY ►
GEORGIA O'KEEFFE
(1887–1986)
Artist

"[I] found myself saying to myself—I can't live where I want to, go where I want to, do what I want to . . . I decided I was a very stupid fool not to at least paint as I wanted to."

thing is at least symbolically possible," he explained. "A person may rise to great heights, sink to great depths, kill his grandmother, or take off for the South Sea Islands on a pogo stick."

The TAT is one of the few projective tests that have modest empirical support for the measurement of achievement motivation. But it does not have strong test–retest reliability, meaning that people's responses are easily influenced by what is going on at that moment in their lives rather than by some inner drive to succeed. Some people might tell stories of achieving against all odds not because they are determined to do so, but because they are idly daydreaming about dazzling the competition. Also, it isn't clear that the TAT tells researchers anything they would not learn by just *asking* people about their ambitions (Lilienfeld, Wood, & Garb, 2000). But the method launched many investigations into the question of why some people seem to have a drive to excel, no matter what, and others just drift along.

The Importance of Goals Today the predominant approach to understanding achievement motivation emphasizes goals rather than inner drives: What you accomplish depends on the goals you set for yourself and the reasons you pursue them. Not just any old goals will promote achievement, though. A goal is most likely to improve your motivation and performance when three conditions are met (Higgins, 1998; Locke & Latham, 2002):

- *The goal is specific.* Defining a goal vaguely, such as "doing your best," is as ineffective as having no goals at all. You need to be specific about what you are going to do and when you are going to do it: "I will write four pages of this paper today."

- *The goal is challenging but achievable.* You are apt to work harder for tough but realistic goals, which make you feel gratified when you reach them, than for either easy goals that pose no challenge or impossible goals that can never be attained.

need for achievement A learned motive to meet personal standards of success and excellence in a chosen area.

Thematic Apperception Test (TAT) A projective test that asks respondents to interpret drawings showing scenes of people; scored for unconscious traits and motives, such as the need for achievement, power, or affiliation.

DUTY ▶
ELANOR ROOSELVELT
(1884–1962)
Humanitarian, lecturer, stateswoman
"As for accomplishments, I just did what I had to do as things came along."

GREED ▶
IVAN BOESKY
(b. 1937)
Financier, convicted of insider trading violations
"Greed is all right . . . I think greed is healthy. You can be greedy and still feel good about yourself."

◀ POWER
HENRY KISSINGER
(b. 1923)
Former Secretary of State
"Power is the ultimate aphrodisiac."

◀ EXCELLENCE
FLORENCE GRIFFITH JOYNER
(1959-1998)
Olympic gold medalist
"When you've been second best for so long, you can either accept it, or try to become the best. I made the decision to try and be the best."

approach goals Goals framed in terms of desired outcomes or experiences, such as learning to scuba dive.

avoidance goals Goals framed in terms of avoiding unpleasant experiences, such as trying not to look foolish in public.

performance goals Goals framed in terms of performing well in front of others, being judged favorably, and avoiding criticism.

mastery (learning) goals Goals framed in terms of increasing one's competence and skills.

• *The goal is framed in terms of getting what you want rather than avoiding what you do not want.* **Approach goals** are positive experiences that you seek directly, such as learning to scuba dive or trying to get a better grade. **Avoidance goals** involve the effort to avoid unpleasant experiences, such as trying not to make a fool of yourself at parties or trying to avoid being dependent.

People who frame their goals in specific, achievable approach terms (e.g., "I'm going to lose weight by jogging three times a week") feel better about themselves, feel more competent, are more optimistic, and are less depressed than people who frame the same goals in avoidance terms (e.g., "I'm going to lose weight by staying away from rich foods") (Coats, Janoff-Bulman, & Alpert, 1996; Updegraff, Gable, & Taylor, 2004). Framing goals in terms of approach or avoidance can even affect the quality of close relationships. For example, people who have sex for *approach* motives—to enjoy their own physical pleasure, to promote a partner's happiness, or to seek enhanced intimacy—tend to have happier and less conflicted relationships than those who have sex to *avoid* a partner's loss of interest or quarrels with the partner (Impett, Peplau, & Gable, 2005).

Can you guess why approach goals produce better results than avoidance goals? Approach goals allow you to focus on what you can actively do to accomplish them and on the intrinsic pleasure of the activity. Avoidance goals make you focus on what you have to give up (Elliot & Sheldon, 1998).

CLOSE-UP on Research

Motivating Children (and Ourselves) to Learn

Defining your goals is only the first step on the road to success; next you need to know what to do when you hit a pothole. Some people give up when a goal becomes difficult or they are faced with a setback, whereas others become even more determined to succeed. Carol Dweck and her colleagues **asked this question**: If talent, ambition, and IQ alone do not predict who will push on and who will give up, what does? The familiar answer is that you have it or you don't, but the researchers **considered other explanations**. The crucial factor, they proposed, is the

type of goal the person is working to achieve: Does the person want to show off in front of others or learn the task for the satisfaction of it?

First, the researchers **defined their terms** by distinguishing performance goals from mastery goals. People who are motivated by **performance goals** are concerned primarily with being judged favorably and avoiding criticism. Those who are motivated by **mastery (learning) goals** are concerned with increasing their competence and skills and finding intrinsic pleasure in what they are learning (Dweck & Sorich, 1999; Grant & Dweck, 2003). Dweck hypothesized that when people who are motivated by performance goals do poorly, they will often decide the fault is theirs and stop trying to improve. Because their goal is to demonstrate their abilities, they set themselves up for grief when they temporarily fail, as all of us must if we are to learn anything new. In contrast, people who are motivated to master new skills will generally regard failure as a source of useful information that will help them improve. Failure and criticism are less likely to discourage them because they know that learning takes time.

But why do some children choose performance goals and others choose mastery goals? To find out, and to pinpoint the different consequences of having one goal or the other, Claudia Mueller and Dweck (1998) conducted a series of experiments with young children. Having **examined the previous evidence**, they suspected that a leading influence on children's goals was whether parents and teachers praised them for their "natural" intelligence or for their diligent efforts.

In one study, 128 Anglo, African-American, and Hispanic fifth graders were asked to work independently on sets of puzzle problems. After four minutes, the experimenter came in, told the children to stop, and scored their results. She then gave them one of two types of feedback that constituted the experimental manipulation. She told all of them that

Why do some kids get immersed in a task and keep at it, while others get bored and give up?

they had done well, but she praised some of them for their ability ("You must be smart at these problems!") and others for their effort ("You must have worked hard at these problems!"). (Children in the control condition received no additional feedback.) The children then got another four minutes to work on a more difficult set of problems, but this time the experimenter told them they had done a lot worse. Finally, the children described which goals they preferred to work for: performance (e.g., doing "problems that aren't too hard, so I don't get many wrong") or mastery (e.g., doing "problems that I'll learn a lot from, even if I won't look so smart"). They also rated their desire to persist on the problems and their enjoyment in doing them and explained why they thought they had failed. At the end of the experiment, the researcher informed the children that the second set of problems was for older seventh graders, so that the children would not go home feeling defeated or unhappy with their scores.

The researchers found that children praised for being smart rather than for working hard tended to lose the pleasure of learning and focused instead on how well they were doing. After these children failed the second set of problems, they tended to give up on subsequent ones, enjoyed them less, and actually performed less well than children who had been praised for their efforts. As you can see in the figure below, nearly 70 percent of fifth graders who were praised for their intelligence later chose performance goals rather than learning goals, compared to fewer than 10 percent of children who were praised for their efforts. The graph also reveals another unwelcome side effect of being praised for intelligence rather than effort: The children were much more likely to lie to other kids about how well they had done. After all, showing off was what mattered to them.

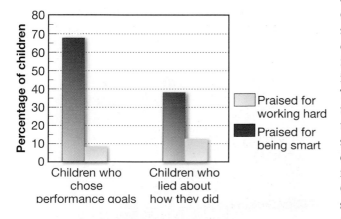

Mueller and Dweck **analyzed an assumption** that is widely held in American society: that intelligence and ability are fixed traits that you can't do

anything about. This assumption often makes it difficult for people to **avoid emotional reasoning:** They decide that if they fail, they are stupid and they might as well give up. But Dweck and her colleagues showed that when children realize that all effort is subject to improvement, they realize that they can always try again. That is the key to mastery. As one learning-oriented child said to the experimenters, "Mistakes are our friends" (Dweck & Sorich, 1999).

Mastery goals are powerful intrinsic motivators at all levels of education and throughout life. Students who are in college primarily to master new areas of knowledge choose more challenging projects, persist in the face of difficulty, use deeper and more elaborate study strategies, are less likely than other students to cheat, and *enjoy* learning more than do students who are there only to get a degree and a meal ticket (Grant & Dweck, 2003; Elliot & McGregor, 2001). Researchers who study work motivation, however, are careful to **avoid oversimplification**. After all, people who are motivated by performance goals, as Olympic athletes and world-class musicians certainly are, often do improve their performance. Ambitious individuals who are determined to become the best in their field are able to successfully blend performance and mastery goals (Barron & Harackiewicz, 2001).

Expectations and Self-Efficacy

How hard you work for something also depends on your expectations. If you are fairly certain of success, you will work harder to reach your goal than if you are fairly certain of failure.

A classic experiment showed how quickly experience affects these expectations. Young women were asked to solve 15 anagram puzzles. Before working on each one, they had to estimate their chances of solving it. Half of the women started off with very easy anagrams, but half began with insoluble ones. Sure enough, those who started with the easy ones increased their estimates of success on later ones. Those who began with the impossible ones decided they would all be impossible. These expectations, in turn, affected the young women's ability to actually solve the last 10 anagrams, which were the same for everyone. The higher the expectation of success, the more anagrams the women solved (Feather, 1966). Once acquired, therefore, expectations can create a **self-fulfilling prophecy** (Merton, 1948): Your expectations make you behave in ways that make the expectation come true. You expect to succeed, so you work hard—and succeed. Or you expect to fail, so you don't do much work—and do poorly.

self-fulfilling prophecy An expectation that is fulfilled because of the tendency of the person holding it to act in ways that bring it about.

self-efficacy A person's belief that he or she is capable of producing desired results, such as mastering new skills and reaching goals.

But where do expectations come from? One source is your level of confidence in your abilities. Do you feel able to handle challenges? No one is born with the feeling of **self-efficacy**. You acquire it through experience in mastering new skills, overcoming obstacles, and learning from occasional failures. Self-efficacy also comes from having successful role models who teach you that your ambitions are possible and from having people around to give you constructive feedback and encouragement (Bandura, 1997, 2001, 2006).

People who have a strong sense of self-efficacy are quick to cope with problems rather than stewing and brooding about them. Studies in North America, Europe, and Russia find that self-efficacy has a positive effect on just about every aspect of people's lives: how well they do on a task, how persistently they pursue their goals, the kind of career choices they make, their ability to solve complex problems, their motivation to work for political and social goals, their health habits, and even their chances of recovery from heart attack (Bandura et al., 2001; Ewart, 1995; Maddux, 1995; Stajkovic & Luthans, 1998).

The Effects of Work on Motivation

Imagine that you live in a town that has one famous company, Boopsie's Biscuits & Buns. Everyone in the town is grateful for the 3B company and goes to work there with high hopes. Soon, however, an odd thing starts happening to many employees. They complain of fatigue and irritability. They are taking lots of sick leave. Productivity declines. What's going on at Boopsie's Biscuits & Buns? Is everybody suffering from sheer laziness?

Most people would answer that something is wrong with those employees. But what if something is wrong with Boopsie's? Some people undoubtedly do lack motivation, but accomplishment does not de-

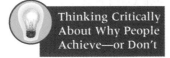
Thinking Critically About Why People Achieve—or Don't

pend on internal motives alone. Psychologists also want to know how the work we do, as well as the conditions under which we do it, nurture or crush our motivation to succeed.

Working Conditions Several aspects of the work environment are likely to increase work motivation and satisfaction and reduce the chances of emotional burnout (Bond et al., 2004; Maslach et al., 2001; Rhoades & Eisenberger, 2002):

- The work feels meaningful and important to employees.
- Employees have control over many aspects of their work, such as setting their own hours and making decisions.

- Tasks are varied rather than repetitive.
- The company maintains clear and consistent rules.
- Employees have supportive relationships with their superiors and co-workers.
- Employees receive useful feedback about their work, so they know what they have accomplished and what they need to do to improve.
- The company offers opportunities for its employees to learn and advance.

Companies that foster these conditions tend to have more productive and satisfied employees. Workers tend to become more creative in their thinking and feel better about themselves and their work than they do if they feel stuck in routine, boring jobs that give them no flexibility or control over their daily tasks (Karasek & Theorell, 1990; Locke & Latham, 1990). Conversely, when people are put in situations that frustrate their desire and ability to succeed, they become dissatisfied and stressed out, and their desire to succeed declines (Jenkins, 1994).

Did you notice anything missing from that list of beneficial working conditions? Where is money, supposedly the great motivator? Actually, work motivation is related not to the amount of money you get but to how and when you get it. The strongest motivator is *incentive pay*, bonuses that are given upon completion of a goal rather than as an automatic raise (Locke et al., 1981). Incentive pay increases people's feelings of competence and accomplishment ("I got this raise because I deserved it"). This doesn't mean that people should accept low pay so they will like their jobs better or that they should never demand cost-of-living raises!

Opportunities to Achieve Another important working condition that affects achievement is having the opportunity to achieve. When

Like employees, students can have poor working conditions that affect their motivation. They may have to study in crowded quarters or may have small siblings who interrupt and distract them.

someone does not do well at work, others are apt to say it is the individual's own fault because he or she lacks the internal drive to make it. But what the person may really lack is a fair chance to make it, and this is especially true for those who have been subjected to systematic discrimination. At one time, for example, women were said to be less successful than men in the workplace because women had an internalized "fear of success." Yet this apparent internal motive vanished as opportunities for women improved and sex discrimination was made illegal.

One external factor that affects many people's motivation to work in a particular field is the proportion of men and women in it (Kanter, 1977/1993). When occupations are segregated by gender, many people form gender stereotypes about the requirements of such careers: Female jobs require kindness and nurturance; male jobs require strength and smarts. These stereotypes, in turn, stifle many people's aspirations to enter a nontraditional career and also create prejudices in employers (Agars, 2004; Cejka & Eagly, 1999). When law, veterinary medicine, and bartending were almost entirely male professions, and nursing, teaching, and child care almost entirely female, few women aspired to enter the "male" professions and few men to enter the "female" ones. As job segregation began breaking down, however, people's career motivations changed. Today, it isn't at all unusual to see a female lawyer, vet, or bartender or a male nurse or even nanny. And although

women are still a minority in engineering, math, and science, their numbers are rising: In 1970–1971, women earned 0.6 percent of the doctorates in engineering, 7.6 percent of those in mathematics, and 16.3 percent of those in biological sciences. By 2001–2002, the percentages had jumped to 17.3 percent, 29 percent, and 44.3 percent respectively (Cox & Alm, 2005). As these numbers have increased, the view that women are not suited to engineering, math, and science has been fading, though slowly.

As you can see, work motivation and satisfaction depend on the right fit between qualities of the individual and conditions of the work. The following illustration summarizes the factors within individuals and in their environments that promote or inhibit intrinsic motivation:

QUICK quiz

Work on your understanding of work motivation.

1. Horatio wants to earn a black belt in karate. Which way(s) of thinking about this goal are most likely to help him reach it? (a) "I should do the best I can," (b) "I should be sure not to lose many matches," (c) "I will set specific goals that are tough but attainable," (d) "I will set specific goals that I know I can reach easily," (e) "I will strive to achieve key milestones on the way to my goal."

2. Ramón and Ramona are learning to ski. Every time she falls, Ramona says, "This is the most humiliating experience I've ever had! Everyone is watching me behave like a clumsy dolt!" When Ramón falls, he says, "&*!!@$@! I'll show these dratted skis who's boss!" Why is Ramona more likely than Ramón to give up? (a) She is a clumsy dolt; (b) she is less competent at skiing; (c) she is focused on learning; (d) she is focused on performance.

3. Which of these factors significantly increase work motivation? (a) specific goals, (b) regular pay, (c) feedback, (d) general goals, (e) being told what to do, (f) being able to make decisions, (g) the chance of promotion, (h) having routine, predictable work

4. An employer is annoyed by the behavior of an employee and is thinking of firing her. Her work is competent, but she rarely arrives on time, doesn't seem as motivated as others to do well, and has begun to take an unusual number of sick days. The boss has decided she is lazy and unmotivated to succeed. What guidelines of critical thinking is the boss overlooking, and what should the boss consider before firing her?

Answers:

1. c, e   2. d   3. a, c, f, g   4. The boss is jumping to the conclusion that the woman has low work motivation. This may be true, but because her work is competent, the boss should *consider other explanations* and *examine the evidence*. Perhaps the work conditions are unsatisfactory; there may be few opportunities for promotion; she may get no feedback; perhaps the company does not provide child care, so she arrives late because she has child-care obligations. What other possible explanations come to mind?

WHAT'S *Ahead*

- Does more money produce more happiness?

- What kind of conflict do you have when you want to study for a big exam but you also want to go out partying?

- Do you have to satisfy basic needs for security and belonging before you can become "self-actualized"?

Motives, Values, and Well-Being

In all the domains of human motivation that we have examined, a key conclusion emerges: People who are motivated by the intrinsic satisfaction of an activity are happier and more satisfied than those motivated solely by extrinsic rewards (Deci & Ryan, 1985; Kasser & Ryan, 2001). We saw, too, how intrinsic motivation will rise or fall depending on the goals we choose and the reasons we pursue them. Goals, in turn, are determined by our values about what is important in life: freedom, religion, equality, wealth, fame, wisdom, serenity, salvation, sexual passion, the desire to improve the world, or anything else. Psychological research cannot tell us which values to choose, but it does help illuminate the consequences of our choices.

For example, although American culture puts a high value on accumulating wealth, the pursuit of material things for their own sake has a dark side. According to studies conducted in both America (an affluent nation) and Russia (a struggling nation), people who are primarily motivated to get rich have poorer psychological adjustment and lower well-being than do people whose primary values are self-acceptance, affiliation with others, or wanting to make the world a better place (Kasser & Ryan, 1996; Ryan et al., 1999). This is especially true when the reasons for striving for money are, again, extrinsic (e.g., you do it to impress others) rather than intrinsic (e.g., you do it so you can afford to do the volunteer work you love) (Carver & Baird, 1998; Srivastava, Locke, & Bartol, 2001). Research finds repeatedly that having positive, intrinsically enjoyable *experiences* makes most people happier than having *things:* Doing is more satisfying than buying (Van Boven & Gilovich, 2003). Although people imagine that greater wealth will bring greater happiness, once they are at a level that provides basic comfort and security, more isn't better. They adjust quickly to the greater wealth and then think they need even more of it to be happier (Gilbert, 2006).

Thinking Critically About Money and Happiness

THE FAR SIDE® BY GARY LARSON

© 1985 FarWorks, Inc. All Rights Reserved/Dist. by Creators Syndicate

DAMNED if you do

DAMNED if you don't

"C'mon, c'mon—it's either one or the other."

The Far Side® by Gary Larson © 1985 FarWorks, Inc. All Rights Reserved. The Far Side® and the Larson® signature are registered trademarks of FarWorks, Inc. Used with permission.

A classic avoidance–avoidance conflict.

Whichever values and goals you choose, if they are in conflict, the discrepancy can produce emotional stress and unhappiness. Two motives conflict when the satisfaction of one leads to the inability to act on the other—when, that is, you want to have your cake and eat it, too. Researchers have identified three kinds of motivational conflicts (Lewin, 1948):

1 *Approach–approach conflicts* occur when you are equally attracted to two or more possible activities or goals. For example, you would like to be a veterinarian *and* a rock singer; you would like to go out Tuesday night with friends *and* study like mad for an exam Wednesday.

2 *Avoidance–avoidance conflicts* require you to choose between the lesser of two evils because you dislike both alternatives. Novice parachute jumpers, for example, must choose between the fear of jumping and the fear of losing face if they don't jump.

3 *Approach–avoidance conflicts* occur when a single activity or goal has both a positive and a negative aspect. In culturally diverse nations, differing cultural values produce many approach–avoidance conflicts, as our students have revealed. A Chicano student said he wants to become a lawyer, but his parents, valuing family closeness, worry that if he goes to graduate school, he will become independent and feel superior to his working-class family. An African-American student from a poor neighborhood, in college on scholarship, is torn between wanting to leave his background behind him forever and returning to help his home community. And a white student wants to be a marine biologist, but her friends tell her that only nerdy guys and dweebs go into science.

Conflicts like these are inevitable, part of the price and pleasure of living. But if conflicts remain unresolved, they can take an emotional toll. In students, high levels of conflict and ambivalence about goals and values are associated with anxiety, depression, headaches and other symptoms, and more visits to the health center (Emmons & King, 1988). In contrast, students who strive for goals that are consistent with the qualities they value are healthier and have a greater sense of meaning and purpose in life than do those who are pursuing goals discrepant with their core values (McGregor & Little, 1998; Sheldon & Houser-Marko, 2001).

Are some psychological goals more important to our well-being than others? The humanist psychologist Abraham Maslow (1970) thought so. Maslow envisioned people's motives as forming a pyramid, a *hierarchy of needs*. At the bottom level of the pyramid were basic survival needs for food, sleep, and water; at the next level were security needs, for shelter and safety; at the third level were social needs, for belonging and affection; at the fourth level were esteem needs, for self-respect and the respect of others; and at the top were needs for self-actualization and self-transcendence. Maslow argued that your needs must be met at each level before you can even think of the matters posed by the level above it. You can't worry about achievement if you are hungry, cold, and poor. You can't become self-actualized if you haven't satisfied your needs for self-esteem and love. Human beings behave badly, he argued, only when their lower needs are frustrated.

This theory, which seemed logical and was so optimistic about human progress, became immensely popular. Motivational speakers still often refer to it, using colorful pictures of Maslow's pyramid. But the theory, which was based mostly on Maslow's observations and intuitions, has had little empirical support (Sheldon et al., 2001; Smither, 1998). On the contrary, people may have *simultaneous* needs for comfort and safety *and* for attachments, self-esteem, and competence. And individuals who have met their lower needs do not inevitably seek higher ones, nor is it the case that people behave badly only when their lower needs are frustrated. Higher needs may even supersede lower ones. History is full of examples of people who would rather die of torture or starvation than sacrifice their convictions, or who would rather explore, risk, or create than be safe and secure at home.

A different way of thinking about universal psychological needs has been developed by researchers who studied large samples of students in the United States and South Korea (Sheldon et al., 2001). Although students are not actually typical of all human beings on the planet, the findings are provocative and support many of the points of this chapter. The top four psychological needs turned out to be *autonomy* (feeling that you are making choices based on your "true interests and values"), *competence* (feeling able to master challenges), *relatedness* (feeling close to others who are important to you), and *self-esteem* (having self-respect). Other needs were of lesser importance, including pleasure, self-actualization (which was at the top of Maslow's list), popularity, and, at the bottom, once again . . . money and luxury.

In sum, psychological well-being depends on finding activities and choosing goals that are intrinsically satisfying, on being able to resolve conflicts between competing goals, and on feeling that we have the freedom to choose which goals we want to pursue.

QUICK quiz

Do you wish to approach or avoid this quiz?

1. A Pakistani student says she desperately wants an education and a career as a pharmacist, but she also does not want to be disobedient to her parents, who have arranged a marriage for her back home. Which kind of conflict does she have?
2. Maslow's popular hierarchy of needs has several flaws. What are they?
3. Letitia just got her law degree. She wanted to work in environmental law, but a corporate firm specializing in real-estate contracts has offered her a job and an enormous salary that seem too good to refuse. Why should she think carefully and critically in making a decision?

Answers:

1. approach–avoidance   2. It was not based on extensive empirical research; it has not been well supported by research; the needs he proposed can be simultaneous rather than hierarchical; "higher" needs often supersede "lower" ones.   3. Taking a job primarily for its extrinsic benefits might suppress her intrinsic satisfaction in the work. Also, people motivated solely to acquire money often have poorer psychological adjustment and lower well-being than others. And although money provides material benefits, psychological needs are also important, such as autonomy, competence, self-esteem, and connection to others.

psychology in the news
REVISITED

Understanding the biological, psychological, and cultural influences on motivation can help us understand the stories that opened this chapter and other stories that make the news every day.

Colonel Saleh, who wooed and won more than 50 women with romantic e-mails, took advantage of the modern ideal of romantic, passionate love, the kind that involves emotional turmoil, sexual longing, and idealization of the loved one. As pragmatic reasons for marriage have faded, especially among women, this ideal has become increasingly popular throughout the world. The women who succumbed to Saleh's persuasive words had jobs and considered themselves to be "bright, intellectual, professional women." Yet even they fell for a man who made them feel "like goddesses, fairy princesses, Cinderellas." (Because Saleh continued writing to so many women, they must have made *him* feel like a god, a prince, a hero!)

Yet, as we saw, passionate romance is only one element of love. It characterizes the early stage of love affairs, when the lovers still don't know much about each other, and it often creates unrealistic expectations that can lead to disappointment. If a relationship is to last, the lovers must also pass the tests of intimacy and commitment. What would have happened to these women had they married their suitor? (Not that he was actually available, inasmuch as he was already married.) Would they have been as happy clearing the table with him and diapering the baby as they were in the fantasy dreams of an Internet correspondence?

Our second news item, about the rape conviction of Andrew Luster, illustrates some of the unpleasant motivations that some people bring to their sexual encounters. As we saw, the motives for sex among men who rape have less to do with physical pleasure than with hostility toward women, peer pressure to prove their masculinity, narcissism, and a cultural script that endorses or tolerates promiscuous, impersonal sex for men. The fact that Luster had to drug his victims into a stupor to have sex with them also suggests, perhaps, a deep fear of women who are sexually assertive.

The news item about the risks of diet drugs reveals the problems that arise when people seek quick cures for their weight problems. Jennifer Rosenthal's near death from usnic acid came right on the heels of the death of Steve Bechler, a 23-year-old pitcher for the Baltimore Orioles, who collapsed and died during a spring-training workout. His death was linked to ephedra, another substance widely promoted for weight loss, one that has caused strokes, seizures, heart disorders, and psychotic breakdowns. Unfortunately, Jennifer Rosenthal never thought to ask whether usnic acid had been tested on humans or studied for its effectiveness, risks, and side effects. She did not ask whether it had been approved by the FDA. "I didn't think about that kind of stuff," she told a reporter from *The New York Times.* "Not very smart."

Rosenthal's story is an object lesson in why consumers should call upon their critical-thinking skills to assess claims of "miracle pills." As we saw in this chapter, the mechanisms that govern weight gain and loss, appetite, eating, and hunger are enormously complex and interrelated, involving genetics, hormones, exercise, portion sizes, social pressures, and culture. No wonder so many people yearn for a simple solution, one that does not require them to change their eating or exercise habits.

Finally, the story of Lance Armstrong shows the importance of having self-efficacy, setting challenging but achievable goals, and persisting in the pursuit of your dreams despite inevitable failures. After winning his war with cancer, Armstrong was ready to give up bicycle racing, but his coaches wouldn't let him. They took him on a week-long training retreat in the mountains, where they all rode hard for hours a day, just for the pleasure of riding. There, Armstrong realized how much he loved racing. Today he thrives on the inspiration he offers to other cancer survivors. He calls this role "the obligation of the cured."

Abraham Maslow may have been wrong about a universal hierarchy of motives, but perhaps each of us develops our own hierarchy as we grow from childhood to old age. For some people, the needs for love, security, or safety will dominate. For others, the need for achievement or power will rule. Some of us will wrestle with conflicting motives; for others, one consuming ambition will hold sway over all others. The motives and goals that inspire us, and the choices we make in their pursuit, are what give our lives passion, color, and meaning. Choose wisely.

➤TAKING ➤PSYCHOLOGY ➤WITH ➤YOU

Get Motivated!

At the end of the first chapter of this book, we discussed not only what psychology can do for you but also what it cannot. As we hope this final chapter has shown, psychology can teach us a great deal about the many motives of human life: the meanings of love, the mysteries of sex, the dilemmas we create for ourselves about eating and weight, and the conditions that enhance or suppress the pursuit of achievement. Psychology cannot tell us which motives, goals, and values to choose in the first place: love, wealth, security, passion, freedom, fame, the desire to improve the world, or anything else. However, it can tell us how to achieve the goals that are important to us and how to ensure that those goals are intrinsically satisfying.

Think for a moment about your own values and goals, for now and for the future. Would you like to improve your love life? Enjoy school more? Lose weight? Become a better tennis player? If the theories and findings in this chapter—indeed, in this book—are to be of long-lasting personal value to you, they must jump off the printed page and into your daily life. And so, in this final "Taking Psychology with You," let's apply the lessons of motivational research to your own life.

● **Seek activities that are intrinsically pleasurable, even if they don't pay off.** If you really, really want to study Swahili or Swedish even though these languages are not in your prelaw requirements, try to find a way to do it. If you are not enjoying your major or your job, consider finding a career that would be more intrinsically pleasurable, or at least make sure you have other projects and activities that you do enjoy for their own sake. The overriding conclusion of this chapter is that people feel happier and are healthier when they feel intrinsically motivated in their work and family lives rather than motivated only by external rewards or obligations.

● **Focus on learning goals rather than on performance goals.** In general, you will be better able to cope with setbacks if your goal is to learn rather than to show how good you are. Regard failure as a chance to learn rather than as a sign of incompetence. The more you are able to focus on improvement, the better your performance will be—in any activity, from cooking to studying to learning to play an instrument to making friends.

● **Assess your working conditions.** Remember that everyone has working conditions, whether you are a student, a self-employed writer, or a homemaker. If your motivation and well-being are starting to wilt, check out your environment. Are you getting support from others? Do you have opportunities to develop ideas and vary your routine, or are you expected to toe the line and do the same thing day after day? Are there barriers that might limit your advancement in your chosen field?

● **Take steps to resolve motivational conflicts.** Are you torn between competing goals? For instance, are you unhappily stuck between the goal of achieving independence and a desire to be cared for by your parents? The reconciliation of conflicts like these is important for your well-being (Emmons & King, 1988).

Most of all, think critically about the goals you have chosen for yourself: Are they what you want to do or what someone else wants you to do? Do they reflect your values? In a commencement address some years ago, Mario Cuomo, the former governor of New York, had these words of wisdom for the graduating students: "When you've parked the second car in the garage, and installed the hot tub, and skied in Colorado, and wind-surfed in the Caribbean, when you've had your first love affair and your second and your third, the question will remain: Where does the dream end for me?"

SUMMARY

• *Motivation* refers to an inferred process within a person or animal that causes that organism to move toward a goal—to satisfy a biological need or achieve a psychological ambition—or away from an unpleasant situation. Motivation may be *intrinsic*, for the inherent pleasure of an activity, or *extrinsic*, for external rewards.

The Social Animal: Motives to Love

• All human beings have a *need for affiliation*—for connection, attachment, and love. Two strong predictors of whom people will love are *proximity* and *similarity*. But love itself takes various forms and has different meanings. Traditionally, *passionate* ("romantic") *love* has been distinguished from *companionate love*. For most people, love consists of passion, intimacy, and commitment. *Attachment the-ory* views adults' love relationships, like those of infants, as being secure, avoidant, or anxious.

• Men and women are equally likely to feel love and need attachment, but they differ, on average, in how they express feelings of love and how they define intimacy. In Western societies, women often express love in words, whereas men express it in actions. But as women have entered the workforce in large numbers and pragmatic reasons for marriage have faded, the two sexes have become more alike in endorsing romantic love as a requirement for marriage.

The Erotic Animal: Motives for Sex

• Biological research finds that testosterone influences sexual desire in both sexes, although hormones do not "cause" sexual behavior in a simple, direct way. The Kinsey surveys of male and female sexuality and the laboratory research of Masters and Johnson showed that physiologically, there is no right kind of orgasm for women to have, and that both sexes are capable of sexual arousal and response.

• Some researchers believe that men have a higher frequency of many sexual behaviors, on average, because they have a stronger sex drive than women do. Others believe that gender differences in sexual motivation and behavior are a result of differences in roles, cultural norms, and opportunity. A compromise view is that male sexuality is more biologically influenced than is women's, whereas female sexuality is more governed by circumstances, relationships, and cultural norms.

• Evolutionary psychologists argue that men and women have evolved different sexual strategies and behavior in response to survival problems faced in the distant past. In this view, it has been adaptive for males to be promiscuous, to be attracted to young partners, and to want sexual novelty, and for females to be monogamous, to be choosy about partners, and to prefer security to novelty. Critics counter that human sexual behavior is too varied and flexible to fit a single evolutionary explanation; that the evolutionary portrait of sex differences is a stereotype, and most men and women are more alike than different; and that our ancestors probably did not have a wide range of partners to choose from. What may have evolved is mate selection based on *proximity* and *similarity*.

• Psychological, social, and cultural approaches to sexual motivation emphasize the ways that values, beliefs, and fantasies affect sexual desire and response. Men and women have sex to satisfy many different psychological motives, including pleasure, intimacy, coping, self-affirmation, the partner's approval, or peer approval. Extrinsic motives for sex, such as peer approval, are associated with riskier sexual behavior than intrinsic motives are. Both sexes may agree to intercourse for nonsexual motives: Men sometimes feel obligated to make a move to prove their masculinity, and women sometimes feel obliged to give in to preserve the relationship. People's motives for consenting to unwanted sex vary, depending on their own feelings of security and commitment in the relationship.

• A major gender difference in sexual experience has to do with rape and perceptions of sexual coercion: What many women regard as coercion is not always seen as such by men. Men who rape do so for diverse reasons, including peer pressure; anger, revenge, or a desire to humiliate the victim; narcissism and hostility toward women; and sometimes sadism.

• Cultures differ widely in determining what parts of the body people learn are erotic, which sexual acts are considered erotic or repulsive, and whether sex itself is good or bad. Cultures transmit these ideas through *gender roles* and *sexual scripts*, which specify appropriate sexual behavior given a person's gender, age, and sexual orientation. As in the case of love, gender differences (and growing similarities) in sexuality are strongly affected by cultural and economic factors.

• The origins of sexual orientation are still unknown. Traditional psychological explanations have not been supported. Genetic, hormonal, and prenatal factors may be involved. Biology, culture, learning, and circumstance probably interact in complex ways to produce a given person's orientation. Research on this issue is sensitive because people often confuse scientific questions about the origins of homosexuality with their own emotional and religious feelings about the topic.

The Hungry Animal: Motives to Eat

• Overweight and obesity are not simply a result of failed willpower, emotional disturbance, or overeating. Hunger, weight, and eating are regulated by a set of bodily mechanisms, such as *basal metabolism rate* and number of fat cells, that keep people close to their genetically influenced *set point*. Genes influence body shape, extent of weight gain, and percentage of fat in the body. Genes also account for certain types of obesity; the *ob* gene regulates *leptin*, which enables the hypothalamus to regulate appetite and metabolism.

• Set-point theory alone cannot explain why rates of overweight and obesity are rising all over the world, among all social classes, ethnicities, and ages. The reasons reflect the interaction of an evolved genetic disposition to gain weight when rich food is plentiful and an environment that provides cheap, varied, high-calorie food and rewards sedentary lifestyles. Eating habits and activity levels are also affected by cultural standards of what the ideal body should look like—heavy or thin, soft or muscular.

• When genetic predispositions clash with culture, health problems and eating disorders can result. In cultures that foster overeating and regard overweight as a sign of attractiveness and health, obesity is acceptable, but obesity has many health risks. In cultures that foster unrealistically thin bodies, eating disorders increase, especially *bulimia* and *anorexia*. These disorders are far more common in women than in men, but as pressures on men to have muscular bodies have increased, body-image problems in men are increasing too.

The Competent Animal: Motives to Achieve

• The study of the *need for achievement* began with research using the *Thematic Apperception Test (TAT)*. People who are motivated by a high need for achievement set high but realistic standards for success and excellence. The TAT has empirical problems, but it launched the study of the factors that motivate achievement.

• People achieve more when they have specific, focused goals; when they set high but achievable goals for themselves; and when they have *approach goals* (seeking a positive outcome) rather than *avoidance goals* (avoiding an unpleasant outcome).

• As discussed in "Close-up on Research," the motivation to achieve depends not only on ability, but also on whether people set *mastery (learning) goals*, in which the focus is on learning the task well, or *performance goals*, in which the focus is on performing well for others. Mastery goals lead to persistence in the face of failures and setbacks; performance goals often lead to giving up. People's expectations can create *self-fulfilling prophecies* of success or failure. These expectations stem in part from one's level of *self-efficacy*.

• Work motivation also depends on circumstances of the job itself. Working conditions that promote motivation and satisfaction are those that provide workers with a sense of meaningfulness, control, variation in tasks, clear rules, supportive relationships, feedback, and opportunities for advancement and learning. *Incentive pay* is more effective than predictable raises in elevating work motivation. One factor in the motivation to enter a career is its gender ratio. A person's motivation to achieve also depends on the person's having the opportunity to be promoted.

Motives, Values, and Well-Being

• Satisfaction and well-being increase when people enjoy the intrinsic satisfaction of an activity and when their goals and values are in harmony. In an *approach–approach conflict*, a person is equally attracted to two goals. In an *avoidance–avoidance conflict*, a person is equally repelled by two goals. An *approach–avoidance* conflict is the most difficult to resolve, because the person is both attracted to and repelled by the same goal. Prolonged conflict can lead to physical symptoms and reduced well-being.

• Abraham Maslow believed that human motives could be ranked along a *hierarchy of needs*, from basic biological needs for survival to higher psychological needs for self-actualization. This popular theory has not been well supported empirically. Another approach suggests that people have four major psychological needs: for autonomy, competence, relatedness, and self-esteem.

KEY TERMS

motivation   469

intrinsic
  motivation   470

extrinsic
  motivation   470

passionate and
  companionate
  love   470

oxytocin   471

proximity and
  similarity   471

attachment theory
  of love   472

gender roles   481

sexual scripts   481

set point   485

basal metabolism
  rate   485

leptin   486

bulimia   488

anorexia   489

industrial/organizational
  psychology   490

need for
  achievement   490

Thematic Apperception
  Test (TAT)   490

approach goals versus
  avoidance goals   492

performance goals   492

mastery (learning)
  goals   492

self-fulfilling
  prophecy   493

self-efficacy   494

incentive pay   494

approach and avoidance
  conflicts   496

Maslow's hierarchy
  of needs   497

Motivation refers to an inferred process within a person or animal that causes that organism to move toward a goal or away from an unpleasant situation.
• **Intrinsic motivation** is for the inherent pleasure of an activity.
• **Extrinsic motivation** is for external reward, such as money or fame.

The Social Animal: Motives to Love

The Biology of Love

Biological origins of passionate love may begin in infancy, when mother-infant bond releases neuro-transmitters and hormones involved in pleasure and reward:
• oxytocin
• endorphins

The Psychology of Love

Predictors of whom people will love:
1. Proximity: The people nearest are most likely dearest
2. Similarity: Like attracts like

Attachment Theory of Love

Attachment theory views adults' love relationships, like those of infants, as:
• Secure
• Avoidant
• Anxious-ambivalent

Gender, Culture, and Love

• In Western societies, the sexes do not differ in their feelings of love but in how they express those feelings:
— Women often express love in words.
— Men often express love in actions.
• Gender differences in love reflect economic and social forces, such as whether a person can afford to marry for love.

The Erotic Animal: Motives for Sex

The Biology of Desire

• Testosterone influences sexual desire in both sexes but does not "cause" sexual behavior.
• The Kinsey surveys of male and female sexuality and the lab research of Masters and Johnson showed that:
— There is no "right" kind of orgasm for women to have.
— Both sexes are capable of sexual arousal and response.
Sex and the "sex drive":
• On average, men have a higher frequency of many sexual behaviors than women do.
• Some researchers believe the reason for this difference is that men have a stronger sex drive.
• Others believe the difference is a result of differences in roles and cultural norms.

The Riddle of Sexual Orientation

• Homosexuality is not a result of psychological factors or of having gay parents.
• Same-sex behavior has been documented in more than 450 species.
• There is some evidence for prenatal and genetic contributions to homosexuality, but to date biological explanations cannot account for the sexual orientation of most gay men and lesbians.

Evolution and Sex

Evolutionary psychologists argue that men and women have evolved different sexual strategies and behavior in response to survival problems faced in the distant past.

In this view, it has been adaptive for males to:
• Be promiscuous
• Be attracted to young partners
• Want sexual novelty

Females have evolved to:
• Be monogamous
• Be choosy about partners
• Prefer security to novelty

Critics counter that:
• The assumption that males are promiscuous and females are choosy is a stereotype; in many species, males care for their young and females have multiple partners.
• Human sexual behavior is too varied to favor a single evolutionary explanation.
• Human sexual behavior changes with cultural changes.
• What people say is their ideal partner on a survey is not necessarily whom they choose.

The Culture of Desire

Cultures differ in determining:
• Which body parts are considered erotic
• Which sexual acts are considered erotic
• Whether sex itself is good or bad

Cultures transmit sexual norms through:
• Gender roles
• **Sexual scripts**

The Psychology of Desire

Psychological approaches to sexual motivation emphasize the influences of values, beliefs, expectations, and fantasies. The many motives for having sex include:
• Pleasure
• Intimacy
• Coping
• Self-affirmation
• The partner's approval
• Peer approval

Extrinsic motives for sex (e.g., for peer approval or fear of losing the relationship) are associated with risky sexual behavior and consenting to unwanted sex.

Sexual Coercion and Rape

Women and men differ in their views of rape and sexual coercion. Motives for rape include:
• peer pressure
• anger, revenge, or desire to humiliate
• hostility toward women
• sadism

The Hungry Animal: Motives to Eat

The Genetics of Weight

Hunger, weight, and eating are governed by a genetically influenced **set point**, which regulates food intake, fat reserves, and basal metabolism rate. Genes also influence:
- Body shape
- Extent of weight gain
- Percentage and distribution of body fat
- Certain types of obesity
— The obese (ob) gene causes fat cells to secrete **leptin**, which helps the hypothalamus to regulate appetite.
— Other genes and chemicals are involved in appetite, metabolism, and weight gain.

Culture, Psychology, and Weight

Environment and Obesity

The primary environmental causes of the worldwide epidemic of overweight and obesity are:
- The prevalence of inexpensive, high-calorie fast food
- The habit of eating on the run
- The use of energy-saving devices
- The use of cars rather than walking or biking
- Increased portion sizes
- Preference for sedentary activities over exercise

Cultural Attitudes

- Eating habits are influenced by cultural standards of the ideal body—e.g., fat, thin, soft, muscular.
- These standards vary across cultures and may change within a culture, e.g., as gender roles change.
- When people believe that their bodies do not match the cultural ideal, eating disorders such as **bulimia** and **anorexia** may increase.
- Eating disorders are more common in women than in men, although body-image disorders among men are increasing.

The Competent Animal: Motives to Achieve

The Effects of Motivation on Work

The **need for achievement** was first studied using the **Thematic Apperception Test** (TAT).

Expectations and Self-Efficacy

- Expectations of success or failure can create a **self-fulfilling prophecy**.
- Expectations of success stem in part from feelings of **self-efficacy**.

The Importance of Goals

People achieve more and feel better about themselves when goals are:
- Specific rather than vaguely defined
- Challenging but achieveable
- Framed as **approach goals** rather than as **avoidance goals**

Most people develop higher intrinsic pleasure in learning when they are motivated by:
- **Mastery (performance) goals**, learning the task well, rather than by
- **Performance goals**, showing off for others.
- Top performers, however, such as world-class athletes and musicians, are motivated by both kinds of goals.

The Effects of Work on Motivation

Working conditions increase employees' satisfaction and motivation, especially when employees:
- Feel their work is meaningful
- Have control over many aspects of their work
- Have varied tasks
- Know the company has clear and consistent rules
- Have supportive relationships
- Get useful feedback
- Have opportunities to learn and advance

Motives, Values, and Well-Being

Motivational Conflicts

- Approach-approach conflict: A person is equally attracted to two goals.
- Avoidance-avoidance conflict: A person is equally repelled by two goals.
- Approach-avoidance conflict: A person is both attracted to, and repelled by, the same goal.

Psychological Needs

- Abraham Maslow believed that human motives could be ranked in a hierarchy of needs, but this theory has had little empirical support.
- Another approach suggests that four major psychological needs are important cross-culturally:
— Autonomy
— Competence
— Relatedness
— Self-esteem

appendix
statistical methods

Nineteenth-century English statesman Benjamin Disraeli reportedly once named three forms of dishonesty: "lies, damned lies, and statistics." It is certainly true that people can lie with the help of statistics. It happens all the time: Advertisers, politicians, and others with some claim to make either use numbers inappropriately or ignore certain critical ones. (When hearing that "four out of five doctors surveyed" recommended some product, have you ever wondered just how many doctors were surveyed and whether they were representative of all doctors?) People also use numbers to convey a false impression of certainty and objectivity when the true state of affairs is uncertainty or ignorance. But it is people, not statistics, that lie. When statistics are used correctly, they neither confuse nor mislead. On the contrary, they expose unwarranted conclusions, promote clarity and precision, and protect us from our own biases and blind spots.

If statistics are useful anywhere, it is in the study of human behavior. If human beings were all alike, and psychologists could specify all the influences on behavior, there would be no need for statistics. But any time we measure human behavior, we are going to wind up with different observations or scores for different individuals. Statistics can help us spot trends amid the diversity.

This appendix will introduce you to some basic statistical calculations used in psychology. Reading the appendix will not make you into a statistician, but it will acquaint you with some ways of organizing and assessing research data. If you suffer from a "number phobia," relax: You do not need to know much math to understand this material. However, you should have read Chapter 1, which discussed the rationale for using statistics and described various research methods. You may want to review the basic terms and concepts covered in that chapter. Be sure that you can define *hypothesis, sample, correlation, independent variable, dependent variable, random assignment, experimental group, control group, descriptive statistics, inferential statistics* and *test of statistical significance*. (Correlation coefficients, which are described in some detail in Chapter 1, will not be covered here.)

To read the tables in this appendix, you will also need to know the following symbols:

N = the total number of observations or scores in a set

X = an observation or score

Σ = the Greek capital letter sigma, read as "the sum of"

$\sqrt{}$ = the square root of

(*Note:* Boldfaced terms in this appendix are defined in the glossary at the end of the book.)

Organizing Data

Before we can discuss statistics, we need some numbers. Imagine that you are a psychologist and that you are interested in that most pleasing of human qualities, a sense of humor. You suspect that a well-developed funny bone can protect people from the negative emotional effects of stress. You already know that in the months following a stressful event, people who score high on sense-of-humor tests tend to feel less tense and moody than more sobersided individuals do. You realize, though, that this correlational evidence does not prove cause and effect. Perhaps people with a healthy sense of humor have other traits, such as flexibility or creativity, that act as the true stress buffers. To find out whether humor itself really softens the impact of stress, you do an experiment.

First, you randomly assign subjects to two groups, an experimental group and a control group. To keep our calculations simple, let's assume there are only 15 people per group. Each person individually views a silent film that most North Americans find fairly stressful, one showing Australian aboriginal boys undergoing a puberty rite involving genital mutilation. Subjects in the experimental group are instructed to make up a humorous monologue while watching the film. Those in the control group are told to make up a straightforward narrative. After the film, each person answers a mood questionnaire that measures current feelings of tension, depression, aggressiveness, and anxiety. A person's overall score on the questionnaire can range from 1 (no mood disturbance) to 7 (strong mood

Table A.1
Some Hypothetical Raw Data

These scores are for the hypothetical humor-and-stress study described in the text.

Experimental group
4,5,4,4,3,6,5,2,4,3,5,4,4,3,4

Control group
6,4,7,6,6,4,6,7,7,5,5,5,7,6,6

disturbance). This procedure provides you with 15 "mood disturbance" scores for each group. Have people who tried to be humorous reported less disturbance than those who did not?

Constructing a Frequency Distribution

Your first step might be to organize and condense the "raw data" (the obtained scores) by constructing a **frequency distribution** for each group. A frequency distribution shows how often each possible score actually occurred. To construct one, you first order all the possible scores from highest to lowest. (Our mood disturbance scores will be ordered from 7 to 1.) Then you tally how often each score was actually obtained. Table A.1 gives some hypothetical raw data for the two groups, and Table A.2 shows the two frequency distributions based on these data. From these distributions you can see that the two groups differed. In the experimental group, the extreme scores of 7 and 1 did not occur at all, and the most common score was the middle one, 4. In the control group, a score of 7 occurred four times, the most common score was 6, and no one obtained a score lower than 4.

Because our mood scores have only seven possible values, our frequency distributions are quite manageable. Suppose, though, that your questionnaire had yielded scores that could range from 1 to 50. A frequency distribution with 50 entries would be cumbersome and might not reveal trends in the data clearly. A solution would be to construct a *grouped frequency distribution* by grouping adjacent scores into equal-sized *classes* or *intervals*. Each interval could cover, say, five scores (1–5, 6–10, 11–15, and so forth). Then you could tally the frequencies within each *interval*. This procedure would reduce the number of entries in each distribution from 50 to only 10, making the overall results much easier to grasp. However, information would be lost. For example, there would be no way of knowing how many people had a score of 43 versus 44.

Table A.2
Two Frequency Distributions

The scores are from Table A.1.

Experimental Group			Control Group		
Mood Disturbance Score	Tally	Frequency	Mood Disturbance Score	Tally	Frequency
7		0	7	////	4
6	/	1	6	ʰʰ /	6
5	///	3	5	///	3
4	ʰʰ //	7	4	//	2
3	///	3	3		0
2	/	1	2		0
1		0	1		0
	$N = 15$			$N = 15$	

Graphing the Data

As everyone knows, a picture is worth a thousand words. The most common statistical picture is a **graph**, a drawing that depicts numerical relationships. Graphs appear at several points in this book, and are routinely used by psychologists to convey their findings to others. From graphs, we can get a general impression of what the data are like, note the relative frequencies of different scores, and see which score was most frequent.

In a graph constructed from a frequency distribution, the possible score values are shown along a horizontal line (the *x-axis* of the graph) and frequencies along a vertical line (the *y-axis*), or vice versa. To construct a **histogram**, or **bar graph**, from our mood scores, we draw rectangles (bars) above each score, indicating the number of times it occurred by the rectangle's height (Figure A.1).

A slightly different kind of "picture" is provided by a **frequency polygon**, or **line graph**. In a frequency polygon,

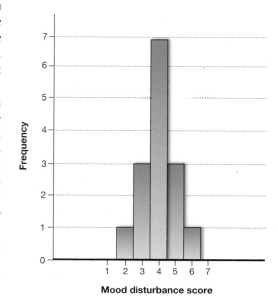

FIGURE A.1
A Histogram
This graph depicts the distribution of mood disturbance scores shown on the left side of Table A.2.

FIGURE A.2
A Frequency Polygon
This graph depicts the same data as Figure A.1.

the frequency of each score is indicated by a dot placed directly over the score on the horizontal axis, at the appropriate height on the vertical axis. The dots for the various scores are then joined together by straight lines, as in Figure A.2. When necessary an "extra" score, with a frequency of zero, can be added at each end of the horizontal axis, so that the polygon will rest on this axis instead of floating above it.

A word of caution about graphs: They may either exaggerate or mask differences in the data, depending on which units are used on the vertical axis. The two graphs in Figure A.3, although they

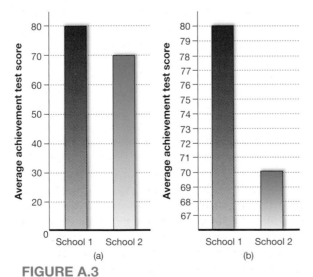

FIGURE A.3
Same Data, Different Impressions
These two graphs depict the same data, but have different units on the vertical axis.

look quite different, actually depict the same data. Always read the units on the axes of a graph; otherwise, the shape of a histogram or frequency polygon may be misleading.

Describing Data

Having organized your data, you are now ready to summarize and describe them. As you will recall from Chapter 1, procedures for doing so are known as **descriptive statistics**. In the following discussion, the word *score* will stand for any numerical observation.

Measuring Central Tendency

Your first step in describing your data might be to compute a **measure of central tendency** for each group. Measures of central tendency characterize an entire set of data in terms of a single representative number.

The Mean The most popular measure of central tendency is the arithmetic mean, usually called simply the **mean**. It is often expressed by the symbol *M*. Most people are thinking of the mean when they say "average." We run across means all the time: in grade point averages, temperature averages, and batting averages. The mean is valuable to the psychologist because it takes all the data into account and it can be used in further statistical analyses. To compute the mean, you simply add up a set of scores and divide the total by the number of scores in the set. Recall that in mathematical notation, Σ means "the sum of," X stands for the individual scores, and N represents the total number of scores in a set. Thus the formula for calculating the mean is:

$$M = \frac{\Sigma X}{N}$$

Table A.3 shows how to compute the mean for our experimental group. Test your ability to perform this calculation by computing the mean for the control group yourself. (You can find the answer, along with other control group statistics, on page A-7.) Later, we will describe how a psychologist would compare the two means statistically to see if there is a significant difference between them.

The Median Despite its usefulness, sometimes the mean can be misleading, as we noted in Chapter 1. Suppose you piled some children on a seesaw in such a way that it was perfectly balanced, and then a 200-pound adult came and sat on one end. The center of gravity would quickly shift toward the adult. In the same way, one extremely high score can dramatically raise the mean (and one extremely low score can dramatically lower it). In real life, this can be a serious problem. For example, in the calculation of a town's mean income, one millionaire would offset hundreds of poor people. The mean income would be a misleading indication of the town's actual wealth.

When extreme scores occur, a more representative measure of central tendency is the **median**, or midpoint in a set of scores or observations ordered from highest to lowest. In any set of scores, the same *number* of scores falls above the median as below it. The median is not affected by extreme scores. If you were calculating the median income of that same town, the one millionaire would offset only one poor person.

When the number of scores in the set is odd, calculating the median is a simple matter of counting in from the ends to the middle. However, if the number of scores is even, there will be two middle scores. The simplest solution is to find the mean of those two scores and use that number as the median. (When the data are from a grouped frequency distribution, a more complicated procedure is required, one beyond the scope of this appendix.) In our experimental group, the median score is 4 (see Table A.3 again). What is it for the control group?

The Mode A third measure of central tendency is the **mode**, the score that occurs most often. In our experimental group, the modal score is 4. In our control group, it is 6. In some distributions, all scores occur with equal frequency, and there is no mode. In others, two or more scores "tie" for the distinction of being most frequent. Modes are used less often than other measures of central tendency. They do not tell us anything about the other scores in the distribution; they often are not very "central"; and they tend to fluctuate from one random sample of a population to another more than either the median or the mean.

Measuring Variability

A measure of central tendency may or may not be highly representative of other scores in a distribution. To understand our results, we also need a **measure of variability** that will tell us whether our scores are clustered closely around the mean or widely scattered.

The Range The simplest measure of variability is the **range**, which is found by subtracting the

Table A.3
Calculating a Mean and a Median

The scores are from the left side of Table A.1.

Mean (*M*)

$$M = \frac{4 + 5 + 4 + 4 + 3 + 6 + 5 + 2 + 4 + 3 + 5 + 4 + 4 + 3 + 4}{15}$$

$$= \frac{60}{15}$$

$$= 4$$

Median

Scores, in order: 2, 3, 3, 3, 4, 4, 4, $\boxed{4}$, 4, 4, 4, 5, 5, 5, 6

↑

Median

lowest score from the highest one. For our hypothetical set of mood disturbance scores, the range in the experimental group is 4 and in the control group it is 3. Unfortunately, though, simplicity is not always a virtue. The range gives us some information about variability but ignores all scores other than the highest and lowest ones.

The Standard Deviation A more sophisticated measure of variability is the **standard deviation (SD)**. This statistic takes every score in the distribution into account. Loosely speaking, it gives us an idea of how much, on the average, scores in a distribution differ from the mean. If the scores were all the same, the standard deviation would be zero. The higher the standard deviation, the more variability there is among scores.

To compute the standard deviation, we must find out how much each individual score deviates from the mean. To do so we simply subtract the mean from each score. This gives us a set of *deviation scores*. Deviation scores for numbers above the mean will be positive, those for numbers below the mean will be negative, and the positive scores will exactly balance the negative ones. In other words, the sum of the deviation scores will be zero. That is a problem, since the next step in our calculation is to add. The solution is to *square* all the deviation scores (that is, to multiply each score by itself). This step gets rid of negative values. Then we can compute the average of the squared deviation scores by adding them up and dividing the sum by the number of scores (*N*). Finally, we take the square root of the result, which takes us from squared units of measurement back to the same units that were used originally (in this case, mood disturbance levels).

The calculations just described are expressed by the following formula:

$$SD = \sqrt{\frac{\Sigma(X - M)^2}{N}}$$

Table A.4 shows the calculations for computing the standard deviation for our experimental group. Try your hand at computing the standard deviation for the control group.

Remember, a large standard deviation signifies that scores are widely scattered, and that therefore the mean is not terribly typical of the entire population. A small standard deviation tells us that most scores are clustered near the mean, and that therefore the mean is representative. Suppose two classes took a psychology exam, and both classes had the same mean score, 75 out of a possible 100. From the means alone, you might conclude that the classes were similar in performance. But if Class A had a standard deviation of 3 and Class B had a standard deviation of 9, you would know that there was much more variability in performance in Class B. This information could be useful to an instructor in planning lectures and making assignments.

Transforming Scores

Sometimes researchers do not wish to work directly with raw scores. They may prefer numbers that are more manageable, such as when the raw scores are tiny fractions. Or they may want to work with scores that reveal where a person stands relative to others. In such cases, raw scores can be transformed to other kinds of scores.

Percentile Scores One common transformation converts each raw score to a **percentile score** (also called a *centile rank*). A percentile score gives the percentage of people who scored at or below a given raw score. Suppose you learn that you have scored 37 on a psychology exam. In the absence of any other information, you may not know whether to celebrate or cry. But if you are told that 37 is equivalent to a percentile score of 90, you know that you can be pretty proud of yourself; you have scored as well as, or higher than, 90 percent of those who have taken the test. On the other hand, if you are told that 37 is equivalent to a percentile score of 50, you have scored only at the median—only as well as, or higher than, half of the other students. The highest possible percentile rank is 99, or more precisely, 99.99, because you can never do better than 100 percent of a group when you are a member of the group. (Can you say what the lowest possible percentile score is? The answer is on page A-7.) Standardized tests such as those described in previous chapters often come with tables that allow for the easy conversion of any raw score to the appropriate percentile score, based on data from a larger number of people who have already taken the test.

Percentile scores are easy to understand and easy to calculate. However, they also have a drawback: They merely rank people and do not tell us how far apart people are in terms of raw scores. Suppose you scored in the 50th percentile on an exam, June scored in the 45th, Tricia scored in the 20th, and Sean scored in the 15th. The difference between you and June may seem identical to that between Tricia and Sean (five percentiles). But in terms of raw scores you and June are probably more alike than Tricia and Sean, because exam scores usually cluster closely together around the midpoint of the distribution and are farther apart at

Table A.4
Calculating a Standard Deviation

Scores (X)	Deviation scores (X − M)	Squared deviation scores (X − M)²
6	2	4
5	1	1
5	1	1
5	1	1
4	0	0
4	0	0
4	0	0
4	0	0
4	0	0
4	0	0
4	0	0
3	-1	1
3	-1	1
3	-1	1
2	-2	4
	0	14

$$SD = \sqrt{\frac{\Sigma(X - M)^2}{N}} = \sqrt{\frac{14}{15}} = \sqrt{.93} = .97$$

Note: When data from a sample are used to estimate the standard deviation of the population from which the sample was drawn, division is by $N - 1$ instead of N, for reasons that will not concern us here.

the extremes. Because percentile scores do not preserve the spatial relationships in the original distribution of scores, they are inappropriate for computing many kinds of statistics. For example, they cannot be used to calculate means.

Z-scores Another common transformation of raw scores is to **z-scores**, or **standard scores**. A z-score tells you how far a given raw score is above or below the mean, using the standard deviation as the unit of measurement. To compute a z score, you subtract the mean of the distribution from the raw score and divide by the standard deviation:

$$z = \frac{X - M}{SD}$$

Unlike percentile scores, z-scores preserve the relative spacing of the original raw scores. The mean itself always corresponds to a z-score of zero, since it cannot deviate from itself. All scores above the mean have positive z-scores and all scores below the mean have negative ones. When the raw scores form a certain pattern called a *normal distribution* (to be described shortly), a z-score tells you how high or low the corresponding raw score was, relative to the other scores. If your exam score of 37 is equivalent to a z-score of +1.0, you have scored 1 standard deviation above the mean. Assuming a roughly normal distribution, that's pretty good, because in a normal distribution only about 16 percent of all scores fall at or above 1 standard deviation above the mean. But if your 37 is equivalent to a z-score of −1.0, you have scored 1 standard deviation below the mean—a poor score.

Z-scores are sometimes used to compare people's performance on different tests or measures. Say that Elsa earns a score of 64 on her first psychology test and Manuel, who is taking psychology from a different instructor, earns a 62 on his first test. In Elsa's class, the mean score is 50 and the standard deviation is 7, so Elsa's z-score is (64 − 50)/7 = 2.0. In Manuel's class, the mean is also 50, but the standard deviation is 6. Therefore, his z-score is also 2.0 [(62 − 50)/6]. Compared to their respective classmates, Elsa and Manuel did equally well. But be careful: This does not imply that they are equally able students. Perhaps Elsa's instructor has a reputation for giving easy tests and Manuel's for giving hard ones, so Manuel's instructor has attracted a more industrious group of students. In that case, Manuel faces stiffer competition than Elsa does, and even though he and Elsa have the same z-score, Manuel's performance may be more impressive.

You can see that comparing z-scores from different people or different tests must be done with caution. Standardized tests, such as IQ tests and various personality tests, use z-scores derived from a large sample of people assumed to be representative of the general population taking the tests. When two tests are standardized for similar populations, it is safe to compare z-scores on them. But z-scores derived from special samples, such as students in different psychology classes, may not be comparable.

Curves

In addition to knowing how spread out our scores are, we need to know the pattern of their distribution. At this point we come to a rather curious phenomenon. When researchers make a very large number of observations, many of the physical and psychological variables they study have a distribution that approximates a pattern called a **normal distribution**. (We say "approximates" because a perfect normal distribution is a theoretical construct and is not actually found in nature.) Plotted in a frequency polygon, a normal distribution has a symmetrical, bell-shaped form known as a **normal curve** (see Figure A.4).

A normal curve has several interesting and convenient properties. The right side is the exact mirror image of the left. The mean, median, and mode all have the same value and are at the exact center of the curve, at the top of the "bell." Most observations or scores cluster around the center of the curve, with

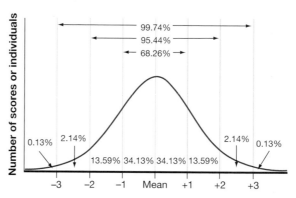

FIGURE A.4
A Normal Curve
When standard deviations (or z-scores) are used along the horizontal axis of a normal curve, certain fixed percentages of scores fall between the mean and any given point. As you can see, most scores fall in the middle range (between +1 and −1 standard deviations from the mean).

far fewer out at the ends, or "tails" of the curve. Most important, as Figure A.4 shows, when standard deviations (or z-scores) are used on the horizontal axis of the curve, the percentage of scores falling between the mean and any given point on the horizontal axis is always the same. For example, 68.26 percent of the scores will fall between plus and minus 1 standard deviation from the mean; 95.44 percent of the scores will fall between plus and minus 2 standard deviations from the mean; and 99.74 percent of the scores will fall between plus and minus 3 standard deviations from the mean. These percentages hold for any normal curve, no matter what the size of the standard deviation. Tables are available showing the percentages of scores in a normal distribution that lie between the mean and various points (as expressed by z-scores).

The normal curve makes life easier for psychologists when they want to compare individuals on some trait or performance. For example, since IQ scores from a population form a roughly normal curve, the mean and standard deviation of a test are all the information you need in order to know how many people score above or below a particular score. On a test with a mean of 100 and a standard deviation of 15, about 68.26 percent of the population scores between 85 and 115—1 standard deviation below and 1 standard deviation above the mean (see Chapter 7).

Not all types of observations, however, are distributed normally. Some curves are lopsided, or *skewed,* with scores clustering at one end or the other of the horizontal axis (see Figure A.5). When the "tail" of the curve is longer on the right than on the left, the curve is said to be positively, or right, skewed.

When the opposite is true, the curve is said to be negatively, or left, skewed. In experiments, reaction times typically form a right-skewed distribution. For example, if people must press a button whenever they hear some signal, most will react quite quickly; but a few will take an unusually long time, causing the right "tail" of the curve to be stretched out.

Knowing the shape of a distribution can be extremely valuable. Paleontologist Stephen Jay Gould (1985) once told how such information helped him cope with the news that he had a rare and serious form of cancer. Being a researcher, he immediately headed for the library to learn all he could about his disease. The first thing he found was that it was incurable, with a median mortality of only eight months after discovery. Most people might have assumed that a "median mortality of eight months" means "I will probably be dead in eight months." But Gould realized that although half of all patients died within eight months, the other half survived longer than that. Since his disease had been diagnosed in its early stages, he was getting top-notch medical treatment, and he had a strong will to live, Gould figured he could reasonably expect to be in the half of the distribution that survived beyond eight months. Even more cheering, the distribution of deaths from the disease was right-skewed: The cases to the left of the median of eight months could only extend to zero months, but those to the right could stretch out for years. Gould saw no reason why he should not expect to be in the tip of that right-hand tail.

For Stephen Jay Gould, statistics, properly interpreted, were "profoundly nurturant and life-giving." They offered him hope and inspired him to fight his disease. The initial diagnosis was made in July of 1982. Gould remained professionally active for 20 more years. When he died in 2002, it was from an unrelated type of cancer.

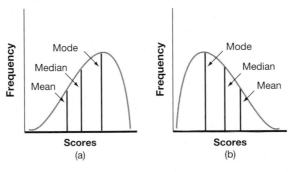

FIGURE A.5
Skewed Curves
Curve (a) is skewed negatively, to the left. Curve (b) is skewed positively, to the right. The direction of a curve's skewness is determined by the position of the long tail, not by the position of the bulge. In a skewed curve, the mean, median, and mode fall at different points.

Answers to questions in this chapter:

Control group statistics:

$$\text{Mean} = \frac{\Sigma X}{N} = \frac{87}{15} = 5.8$$

Median = 6

$$\text{Standard Deviation} = \sqrt{\frac{\Sigma(X - M)^2}{N}} = \sqrt{\frac{14.4}{15}}$$

$$= \sqrt{.96} = .98$$

Lowest possible percentile score: 1 (or, more precisely, .01)

Drawing Inferences

Once data are organized and summarized, the next step is to ask whether they differ from what might have been expected purely by chance (see Chapter 1). A researcher needs to know whether it is safe to infer that the results from a particular sample of people are valid for the entire population from which the sample was drawn. **Inferential statistics** provide this information. They are used in both experimental and correlational studies.

The Null Versus the Alternative Hypothesis

In an experiment, the scientist must assess the possibility that his or her experimental manipulations will have no effect on the subjects' behavior. The statement expressing this possibility is called the **null hypothesis**. In our stress-and-humor study, the null hypothesis states that making up a funny commentary will not relieve stress any more than making up a straightforward narrative will. In other words, it predicts that the difference between the means of the two groups will not deviate significantly from zero. Any obtained difference will be due solely to chance fluctuations. In contrast, the **alternative hypothesis** (also called the *experimental* or *research hypothesis*) states that on the average the experimental group will have lower mood disturbance scores than the control group.

The null hypothesis and the alternative hypothesis cannot both be true. Our goal is to reject the null hypothesis. If our results turn out to be consistent with the null hypothesis, we will not be able to do so. If the data are inconsistent with the null hypothesis, we will be able to reject it with some degree of confidence. Unless we study the entire population, though, we will never be able to say that the alternative hypothesis has been proven. No matter how impressive our results are, there will always be some degree of uncertainty about the inferences we draw from them. Since we cannot prove the alternative hypothesis, we must be satisfied with showing that the null hypothesis is unreasonable.

Students are often surprised to learn that in traditional hypothesis testing it is the null hypothesis, not the alternative hypothesis, that is tested. After all, it is the alternative hypothesis that is actually of interest. But this procedure does make sense. The null hypothesis can be stated precisely and tested directly. In the case of our fictitious study, the null hypothesis predicts that the difference between the two means will be zero.

The alternative hypothesis does not permit a precise prediction because we don't know how much the two means might differ (if, in fact, they do differ). Therefore, it cannot be tested directly.

Testing Hypotheses

Many computations are available for testing the null hypothesis. The choice depends on the design of the study, the size of the sample, and other factors. We will not cover any specific tests here. Our purpose is simply to introduce you to the kind of reasoning that underlies hypothesis testing. With that in mind, let us return once again to our data. For each of our two groups we have calculated a mean and a standard deviation. Now we want to compare the two sets of data to see if they differ enough for us to reject the null hypothesis. We wish to be reasonably certain that our observed differences did not occur entirely by chance.

What does it mean to be "reasonably certain"? How different from zero must our result be to be taken seriously? Imagine, for a moment, that we had infinite resources and could somehow repeat our experiment, each time using a new pair of groups, until we had "run" the entire population through the study. It can be shown mathematically that if only chance were operating, our various experimental results would form a normal distribution. This theoretical distribution is called "the sampling distribution of the difference between means," but since that is quite a mouthful, we will simply call it the *sampling distribution* for short. If the null hypothesis were true, the mean of the sampling distribution would be zero. That is, on the average, we would find no difference between the two groups. Often, though, because of chance influences or *random error*, we would get a result that deviated to one degree or another from zero. On rare occasions, the result would deviate a great deal from zero.

We cannot test the entire population, though. All we have are data from a single sample. We would like to know whether the difference between means that we actually obtained would be close to the mean of the theoretical sampling distribution (if we could test the entire population) or far away from it, out in one of the "tails" of the curve. Was our result highly likely to occur on the basis of chance alone or highly unlikely?

Before we can answer that question, we must have some precise way to measure distance from the mean of the sampling distribution. We must know exactly how far from the mean our obtained result must be to be considered "far away." If only we knew the standard deviation of the sampling distribution, we could use it as our unit of measurement. We don't know it, but fortunately, we can use the standard deviation of our *sample* to estimate it. (We will not go into the reasons that this is so.)

Now we are in business. We can look at the mean difference between our two groups and figure out how far it is (in terms of standard deviations) from the mean of the sampling distribution. As mentioned earlier, one of the convenient things about a normal distribution is that a certain fixed percentage of all observations falls between the mean of the distribution and any given point above or below the mean. These percentages are available from tables. Therefore, if we know the "distance" of our obtained result from the mean of the theoretical sampling distribution, we automatically know how likely our result is to have occurred strictly by chance.

To give a specific example, if it turns out that our obtained result is 2 standard deviations above the mean of the theoretical sampling distribution, we know that the probability of its having occurred by chance is less than 2.3 percent. If our result is 3 standard deviations above the mean of the sampling distribution, the probability of its having occurred by chance is less than .13 percent—less than 1 in 800. In either case, we might well suspect that our result did not occur entirely by chance after all. We would call the result **statistically significant**. (Psychologists usually consider any highly unlikely result to be of interest, no matter which direction it takes. In other words, the result may be in either tail of the sampling distribution.)

To summarize: Statistical significance means that if only chance were operating, our result would be highly improbable, so we are fairly safe in concluding that more than chance was operating—namely, the influence of our independent variable. We can reject the null hypothesis, and open the champagne. As we noted in Chapter 1, psychologists usually accept a finding as statistically significant if the likelihood of its occurring by chance is 5 percent or less (see Figure A.6). This cutoff point gives the researcher a reasonable chance of confirming reliable results as well as reasonable protection against accepting unreliable ones.

Some cautions are in order, though. As noted in Chapter 1, conventional tests of statistical significance have drawn serious criticisms in recent years. Statistically significant results are not always psychologically interesting or important. Further, statistical significance is related to the size of the sample. A large sample increases the likelihood of reliable results. But there is a trade-off: The larger the sample,

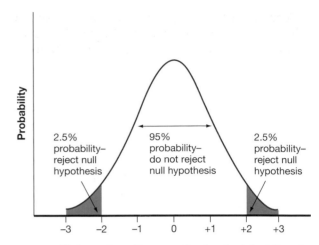

FIGURE A.6
Statistical Significance
This curve represents the theoretical sampling distribution discussed in the text. The curve is what we would expect by chance if we did our hypothetical stress-and-humor study many times, testing the entire population. If we used the conventional significance level of .05, we would regard our obtained result as significant only if the probability of getting a result that far from zero by chance (in either direction) totaled 5 percent or less. As shown, the result must fall far out in one of the tails of the sampling distribution. Otherwise, we cannot reject the null hypothesis.

the more probable it is that a small result having no practical importance will reach statistical significance. On the other hand, with the sample sizes typically used in psychological research, there is a good chance of falsely concluding that an experimental effect has not occurred when one actually has (Hunter, 1997). For these reasons, it is always useful to know how much of the total variability in scores was accounted for by the independent variable (the **effect size**). (The computations are not discussed here.) If only 3 percent of the variance was accounted for, then 97 percent was due either to chance factors or to systematic influences of which the researcher was unaware. Because human behavior is affected by so many factors, the amount of variability accounted for by a single psychological variable is often modest. But sometimes the effect size is considerable even when the results don't quite reach significance.

Oh, by the way, findings on humor turn out to be pretty complicated. They depend on how you define "sense of humor," how you do the study, and what aspects of humor you are investigating. Researchers are learning that a sense of humor probably doesn't help people live longer, avoid the flu, or recover from injury faster. On the other hand, during times of stress, humor is more emotionally beneficial than fuming or moping around (as long as it's not of the hostile or sarcastic variety). So, when gravity gets you down, try a little levity.

SUMMARY

• When used correctly, statistics expose unwarranted conclusions, promote precision, and help researchers spot trends amid diversity.

• Often, the first step in data analysis is to organize and condense data in a *frequency distribution*, a tally showing how often each possible score (or interval of scores) occurred. Such information can also be depicted in a *histogram* (bar graph) or a *frequency polygon* (line graph).

• Descriptive statistics summarize and describe the data. *Central tendency* is measured by the *mean, median,* or, less frequently, the *mode*. Since a measure of central tendency may or may not be highly representative of other scores in a distribution, it is also important to analyze variability. A large *standard deviation* means that scores are widely scattered about the mean; a small one means that most scores are clustered near the mean.

• Raw scores can be transformed into other kinds of scores. *Percentile scores* indicate the percentage of people who scored at or below a given raw score. *Z-scores (standard scores)* indicate how far a given raw score is above or below the mean of the distribution.

• Many variables have a distribution approximating a *normal distribution,* depicted as a *normal curve*. The normal curve has a convenient property: When standard deviations are used as the units on the horizontal axis, the percentage of scores falling between any two points on the horizontal axis is always the same. Not all types of observations are distributed normally, however. Some distributions are *skewed* to the left or right.

• Inferential statistics can be used to test the *null hypothesis* and to tell a researcher whether a result differed significantly from what might have been expected purely by chance. Basically, hypothesis testing involves estimating where the obtained result would have fallen in a theoretical *sampling distribution* based on studies of the entire population in question. If the result would have been far out in one of the tails of the distribution, it is considered statistically significant. A statistically significant result may or may not be psychologically interesting or important, so many researchers also compute the *effect size*.

KEY TERMS

frequency distribution   A-2

graph   A-2

histogram/bar graph   A-2

frequency polygon/line graph   A-2

descriptive statistics   A-3

measure of central tendency   A-3

mean   A-3

median   A-4

mode   A-4

measure of variability   A-4

range   A-4

standard deviation   A-4

deviation score   A-4

percentile score (centile rank)   A-5

z-score (standard score)   A-6

normal distribution   A-6

normal curve   A-6

right- and left-skewed distributions   A-7

inferential statistics   A-8

null hypothesis   A-8

alternative hypothesis   A-8

sampling distribution   A-8

statistically significant   A-9

effect size   A-9

glossary

absolute threshold   The smallest quantity of physical energy that can be reliably detected by an observer.

acculturation   The process by which members of minority groups come to identify with and feel part of the mainstream culture.

action potential   A brief change in electrical voltage that occurs when a neuron is stimulated; it serves to produce an electrical impulse.

activation-synthesis theory   The theory that dreaming results from the cortical synthesis and interpretation of neural signals triggered by activity in the lower part of the brain.

adrenal hormones   Hormones that are produced by the adrenal glands and that are involved in emotion and stress.

affect heuristic   The tendency to consult one's emotions instead of estimating probabilities objectively.

agoraphobia   A set of phobias, often set off by a panic attack, involving the basic fear of being away from a safe place or person.

algorithm   A problem-solving strategy guaranteed to produce a solution even if the user does not know how it works.

alternative hypothesis   An assertion that the independent variable in a study will have a certain predictable effect on the dependent variable; also called an experimental or research hypothesis.

amnesia   The partial or complete loss of memory for important personal information.

amygdala [uh-MIG-dul-uh]   A brain structure involved in the arousal and regulation of emotion and the initial emotional response to sensory information.

anorexia (nervosa)   An eating disorder characterized by fear of being fat, a distorted body image, radically reduced consumption of food, and emaciation.

antidepressant drugs   Drugs used primarily in the treatment of mood disorders, especially depression and anxiety.

antipsychotic drugs   Drugs used primarily in the treatment of schizophrenia and other psychotic disorders.

antisocial personality disorder (APD)   A disorder characterized by antisocial behavior such as lying, stealing, manipulating others, and sometimes violence; and a lack of guilt, shame, and empathy.

applied psychology   The study of psychological issues that have direct practical significance; also, the application of psychological findings.

approach goals   Goals framed in terms of desired outcomes or experiences, such as learning to scuba dive.

archetypes [AR-ki-types]   Universal, symbolic images that appear in myths, art, stories, and dreams; to Jungians, they reflect the collective unconscious.

arithmetic mean   An average that is calculated by adding up a set of quantities and dividing the sum by the total number of quantities in the set.

attribution theory   The theory that people are motivated to explain their own and other people's behavior by attributing causes of that behavior to a situation or a disposition.

autonomic nervous system   The subdivision of the peripheral nervous system that regulates the internal organs and glands.

availability heuristic   The tendency to judge the probability of a type of event by how easy it is to think of examples or instances.

avoidance goals   Goals framed in terms of avoiding unpleasant experiences, such as trying not to look foolish in public.

axon   A neuron's extending fiber that conducts impulses away from the cell body and transmits them to other neurons or to muscle or gland cells.

basic psychology   The study of psychological issues in order to seek knowledge for its own sake rather than for its practical application.

behavior modification   The application of conditioning techniques to teach new responses or to reduce or eliminate problematic behavior.

behavior therapy   A form of therapy that applies principles of classical and operant conditioning to help people change self-defeating or problematic behaviors.

behavioral genetics   An interdisciplinary field of study concerned with the genetic bases of individual differences in behavior and personality.

behavioral self-monitoring   In behavior therapy, a method of keeping careful data on the frequency and consequences of the behavior to be changed.

behaviorism   An approach to psychology that emphasizes the study of observable behavior and the role of the environment as a determinant of behavior.

binocular cues   Visual cues to depth or distance requiring two eyes.

biological perspective   A psychological approach that emphasizes bodily events and changes associated with actions, feelings, and thoughts.

biological rhythm   A periodic, more or less regular fluctuation in a biological system; it may or may not have psychological implications.

bipolar disorder   A mood disorder in which episodes of both depression and mania (excessive euphoria) occur.

brain stem   The part of the brain at the top of the spinal cord, consisting of the medulla and the pons.

brightness   Lightness or luminance; the dimension of visual experience related to the amount (intensity) of light emitted from or reflected by an object.

bulimia   An eating disorder characterized by episodes of bingeing and purging.

case study   A detailed description of a particular individual being studied or treated.

cell body   The part of the neuron that keeps it alive and determines whether it will fire.

central nervous system (CNS)   The portion of the nervous system consisting of the brain and spinal cord.

cerebellum   A brain structure that regulates movement and balance and that is involved in some cognitive tasks.

cerebral cortex   A collection of several thin layers of cells covering the cerebrum; it is largely responsible for higher mental functions. *Cortex* is Latin for "bark" or "rind."

cerebral hemispheres The two halves of the cerebrum.

cerebrum [suh-REE-brum] The largest brain structure, consisting of the upper part of the brain; it is in charge of most sensory, motor, and cognitive processes. From the Latin for "brain."

childhood (infantile) amnesia The inability to remember events and experiences that occurred during the first two or three years of life.

chunk A meaningful unit of information; it may be composed of smaller units.

circadian [sur-CAY-dee-un] rhythm A biological rhythm with a period (from peak to peak or trough to trough) of about 24 hours; from the Latin *circa*, "about," and *dies*, "a day."

classical conditioning The process by which a previously neutral stimulus acquires the capacity to elicit a response through association with a stimulus that already elicits a similar or related response.

client-centered (nondirective) therapy A humanist approach to therapy devised by Carl Rogers, which emphasizes the therapist's empathy with the client and the use of unconditional positive regard.

cochlea [KOCK-lee-uh] A snail-shaped, fluid-filled organ in the inner ear, containing the organ of Corti, where the receptors for hearing are located.

coefficient of correlation A measure of correlation that ranges in value from −1.00 to +1.00.

cognitive dissonance A state of tension that occurs when a person simultaneously holds two cognitions that are psychologically inconsistent or when a person's belief is incongruent with his or her behavior.

cognitive ethology The study of cognitive processes in nonhuman animals.

cognitive perspective A psychological approach that emphasizes mental processes in perception, memory, language, problem solving, and other areas of behavior.

cognitive schema An integrated mental network of knowledge, beliefs, and expectations concerning a particular topic or aspect of the world.

cognitive therapy A form of therapy designed to identify and change irrational, unproductive ways of thinking and, hence, to reduce negative emotions and their behavioral consequences.

collective unconscious In Jungian theory, the universal memories and experiences of humankind, represented in the symbols, stories, and images (archetypes) that occur across all cultures.

collectivist cultures Cultures in which the self is regarded as embedded in relationships, and harmony with one's group is prized above individual goals and wishes.

concept A mental category that groups objects, relations, activities, abstractions, or qualities having common properties.

conditioned response (CR) The classical-conditioning term for a response that is elicited by a conditioned stimulus; it occurs after the conditioned stimulus is associated with an unconditioned stimulus.

conditioned stimulus (CS) The classical-conditioning term for an initially neutral stimulus that comes to elicit a conditioned response after being associated with an unconditioned stimulus.

conditioning A basic kind of learning that involves associations between environmental stimuli and the organism's responses.

cones Visual receptors involved in color vision.

confabulation Confusion of an event that happened to someone else with one that happened to you, or a belief that you remember something when it never actually happened.

confirmation bias The tendency to look for or pay attention only to information that confirms one's own belief.

conservation The understanding that the physical properties of objects—such as the number of items in a cluster or the amount of liquid in a glass—can remain the same even when their form or appearance changes.

contact comfort In primates, the innate pleasure derived from close physical contact; it is the basis of an infant's first attachment.

continuous reinforcement A reinforcement schedule in which a particular response is always reinforced.

control condition In an experiment, a comparison condition in which subjects are not exposed to the same treatment as are those in the experimental condition.

convergence The turning inward of the eyes, which occurs when they focus on a nearby object.

corpus callosum [CORE-pus ca-LOW-suhm] The bundle of nerve fibers connecting the two cerebral hemispheres.

correlation A measure of how strongly two variables are related to each other.

correlational study A descriptive study that looks for a consistent relationship between two phenomena.

counterconditioning In classical conditioning, the process of pairing a conditioned stimulus with a stimulus that elicits a response that is incompatible with an unwanted conditioned response.

critical thinking The ability and willingness to assess claims and make objective judgments on the basis of well-supported reasons and evidence rather than emotion or anecdote.

cross-sectional study A study in which individuals of different ages are compared at a given time.

crystallized intelligence Cognitive skills and specific knowledge of information acquired over a lifetime; it is heavily dependent on education and tends to remain stable over the lifetime.

cue-dependent forgetting The inability to retrieve information stored in memory because of insufficient cues for recall.

culture A program of shared rules that govern the behavior of members of a community or society and a set of values, beliefs, and attitudes shared by most members of that community.

dark adaptation A process by which visual receptors become maximally sensitive to dim light.

decay theory The theory that information in memory eventually disappears if it is not accessed; it applies more to short-term than to long-term memory.

declarative memories Memories of facts, rules, concepts, and events ("knowing that"); they include semantic and episodic memories.

deductive reasoning A form of reasoning in which a conclusion follows necessarily from certain premises; if the premises are true, the conclusion must be true.

deep processing In the encoding of information, the processing of meaning rather than simply the physical or sensory features of a stimulus.

defense mechanisms Methods used by the ego to prevent unconscious anxiety or threatening thoughts from entering consciousness.

deindividuation   In groups or crowds, the loss of awareness of one's own individuality.

dendrites   A neuron's branches that receive information from other neurons and transmit it toward the cell body.

dependent variable   A variable that an experimenter predicts will be affected by manipulations of the independent variable.

depressants   Drugs that slow down activity in the central nervous system.

descriptive methods   Methods that yield descriptions of behavior but not necessarily causal explanations.

descriptive statistics   Statistics that organize and summarize research data.

dialectical reasoning   A process in which opposing facts or ideas are weighed and compared with a view to determining the best solution or to resolving differences.

difference threshold   The smallest difference in stimulation that can be reliably detected by an observer when two stimuli are compared; also called *just noticeable difference* (*jnd*).

diffusion of responsibility   In groups, the tendency of members to avoid taking action because they assume that others will.

discriminative stimulus   A stimulus that signals when a particular response is likely to be followed by a certain type of consequence.

display rules   Social and cultural rules that regulate when, how, and where a person may express (or suppress) emotions.

dissociation   A split in consciousness in which one part of the mind operates independently of others.

dissociative identity disorder   A controversial disorder marked by the apparent appearance within one person of two or more distinct personalities, each with its own name and traits; commonly known as *multiple personality disorder* (*MPD*).

doctrine of specific nerve energies   The principle that different sensory modalities exist because signals received by the sense organs stimulate different nerve pathways leading to different areas of the brain.

double-blind study   An experiment in which neither the participants nor the individuals running the study know which participants are in the control group and which are in the experimental group until after the results are tallied.

effect size   In an experiment, the amount of variance in the data accounted for by the independent variable.

ego   In psychoanalysis, the part of personality that represents reason, good sense, and rational self-control.

egocentric thinking   Seeing the world from only your own point of view; the inability to take another person's perspective.

elaborative rehearsal   Association of new information with already stored knowledge and analysis of the new information to make it memorable.

electroconvulsive therapy (ECT)   A procedure used in cases of prolonged and severe major depression, in which a brief brain seizure is induced.

electroencephalogram (EEG)   A recording of neural activity detected by electrodes.

emotion   A state of arousal involving facial and bodily changes, brain activation, cognitive appraisals, subjective feelings, and tendencies toward action.

emotion work   Expression of an emotion, often because of a role requirement, that a person does not really feel.

emotional intelligence   The ability to identify your own and other people's emotions accurately, express your emotions clearly, and regulate emotions in yourself and others.

empirical   Relying on or derived from observation, experimentation, or measurement.

endocrine glands   Internal organs that produce hormones and release them into the bloodstream.

endogenous   Generated from within rather than by external cues.

endorphins [en-DOR-fins]   Chemical substances in the nervous system that are similar in structure and action to opiates; they are involved in pain reduction, pleasure, and memory and are known technically as *endogenous opioid peptides*.

entrapment   A gradual process in which individuals escalate their commitment to a course of action to justify their investment of time, money, or effort.

episodic memories   Memories of personally experienced events and the contexts in which they occurred.

equilibrium   The sense of balance.

ethnic identity   A person's identification with a religious or ethnic group.

ethnocentrism   The belief that one's own ethnic group, nation, or religion is superior to all others.

evolutionary psychology   A field of psychology emphasizing evolutionary mechanisms that may help explain human commonalities in cognition, development, emotion, social practices, and other areas of behavior.

existential therapy   A form of therapy designed to help clients explore the meaning of existence and face the great questions of life, such as death, freedom, alienation, and loneliness.

existentialism   A philosophical approach that emphasizes the inevitable dilemmas and challenges of human existence.

experiment   A controlled test of a hypothesis in which the researcher manipulates one variable to discover its effect on another.

experimenter effects   Unintended changes in subjects' behavior due to cues inadvertently given by the experimenter.

explicit memory   Conscious, intentional recollection of an event or of an item of information.

extinction   The weakening and eventual disappearance of a learned response. In classical conditioning, it occurs when the conditioned stimulus is no longer paired with the unconditioned stimulus; in operant conditioning, it occurs when a response is no longer followed by a reinforcer.

extrinsic motivation   The desire to do something for the sake of external rewards, such as money or fame.

extrinsic reinforcers   Reinforcers that are not inherently related to the activity being reinforced, such as money, prizes, and praise.

facial feedback   The process by which the facial muscles send messages to the brain about the basic emotion being expressed.

factor analysis   A statistical method for analyzing the intercorrelations among various measures or test scores; clusters of measures or scores that are highly correlated are assumed to measure the same underlying trait, ability, or aptitude (factor).

familiarity effect   The tendency of people to feel more positive toward a person, item, product or other stimulus that they have seen often.

family-systems perspective   An approach to doing therapy with individuals or families by emphasizing how each family member forms part of a larger interacting system.

feature-detector cells   Cells in the visual cortex that are sensitive to specific features of the environment.

field research   Descriptive or experimental research conducted in a natural setting outside the laboratory.

flooding   In behavior therapy, a form of exposure treatment in which the client is taken directly into the feared situation until his or her panic subsides.

fluid intelligence   The capacity for deductive reasoning and the ability to use new information to solve problems; it is relatively independent of education and tends to decline in old age.

free association   In psychodynamic therapies, the process of saying freely whatever comes to mind in connection with dreams, memories, fantasies, or conflicts.

frequency distribution   A summary of how frequently each score in a set occurred.

frequency polygon (line graph)   A graph showing a set of points obtained by plotting score values against score frequencies; adjacent points are joined by straight lines.

frontal lobes   Lobes at the front of the brain's cerebral cortex; they contain areas involved in short-term memory, higher-order thinking, initiative, social judgment, and (in the left lobe, typically) speech production.

functionalism   An early psychological approach that emphasized the function or purpose of behavior and consciousness.

fundamental attribution error   The tendency, in explaining other people's behavior, to overestimate personality factors and underestimate the influence of the situation.

g factor   A general ability assumed by many theorists to underlie specific mental abilities and talents.

ganglion cells   Neurons in the retina of the eye, which gather information from receptor cells (by way of intermediate bipolar cells); their axons make up the optic nerve.

gate-control theory   The theory that the experience of pain depends in part on whether pain impulses get past a neurological "gate" in the spinal cord and thus reach the brain.

gender identity   The fundamental sense of being male or female; it is independent of whether the person conforms to the social and cultural rules of gender.

gender schema   A cognitive schema (mental network) of knowledge, beliefs, metaphors, and expectations about what it means to be male or female.

gender typing   The process by which children learn the abilities, interests, personality traits, and behaviors associated with being masculine or feminine in their culture.

general adaptation syndrome   According to Hans Selye, a series of physiological reactions to stressors occurring in three phases: alarm, resistance, and exhaustion.

generalized anxiety disorder   A continuous state of anxiety marked by feelings of worry and dread, apprehension, difficulties in concentration, and signs of motor tension.

genes   The functional units of heredity; they are composed of DNA and specify the structure of proteins.

Gestalt principles   Principles that describe the brain's organization of sensory information into meaningful units and patterns.

glia [GLY-uh or GLEE-uh]   Cells that support, nurture, and insulate neurons, remove debris when neurons die, and modify neuronal functioning.

graduated exposure   In behavior therapy, a method in which a person suffering from an anxiety disorder, such as a phobia or panic attacks, is gradually confronted with the feared object or situation until the anxiety subsides.

graph   A drawing that depicts numerical relationships.

groupthink   In close-knit groups, the tendency for all members to think alike for the sake of harmony and to suppress disagreement.

heritability   A statistical estimate of the proportion of the total variance in some trait that is attributable to genetic differences among individuals within a group.

heuristic   A rule of thumb that suggests a course of action or guides problem solving but does not guarantee an optimal solution.

higher-order conditioning   In classical conditioning, a procedure in which a neutral stimulus becomes a conditioned stimulus through association with an already established conditioned stimulus.

hindsight bias   The tendency to overestimate one's ability to have predicted an event once the outcome is known; the "I knew it all along" phenomenon.

hippocampus   A brain structure involved in the storage of new information in memory.

histogram (bar graph)   A graph in which the heights (or lengths) of bars are proportional to the frequencies of individual scores or classes of scores in a distribution.

hormones   Chemical substances, secreted by organs called glands, that affect the functioning of other organs.

hue   The dimension of visual experience specified by color names and related to the wavelength of light.

humanist psychology   A psychological approach that emphasizes free will, personal growth, resilience, and the achievement of human potential.

humanist therapy   A form of psychotherapy based on the philosophy of humanism, which emphasizes people's free will to change, not past conflicts.

hypnosis   A procedure in which the practitioner suggests changes in the sensations, perceptions, thoughts, feelings, or behavior of the subject.

hypothalamus   A brain structure involved in emotions and drives vital to survival; it regulates the autonomic nervous system.

hypothesis   A statement that attempts to predict or to account for a set of phenomena; scientific hypotheses specify relationships among events or variables and are empirically tested.

id   In psychoanalysis, the part of personality containing inherited psychic energy, particularly sexual and aggressive instincts.

implicit learning   Learning that occurs when you acquire knowledge about something without being aware of how you did so and without being able to state exactly what it is you have learned.

implicit memory   Unconscious retention in memory, as evidenced by the effect of a previous experience or previously encountered information on current thoughts or actions.

inattentional blindness   Failure to consciously perceive something you are looking at because you are not attending to it.

independent variable   A variable that an experimenter manipulates.

individualist cultures   Cultures in which the self is regarded as autonomous, and individual goals and wishes are prized above duty and relations with others.

induction   A method of child rearing in which the parent appeals to the child's own resources, abilities, sense of responsibility, and feelings for others in correcting misbehavior.

inductive reasoning   A form of reasoning in which the premises provide support for a conclusion, but it is still possible for the conclusion to be false.

inferential statistics   Statistical procedures that allow researchers to draw inferences about how statistically meaningful a study's results are.

informed consent   The doctrine that human research subjects must participate voluntarily and must know enough about a study to make an intelligent decision about whether to participate.

instinctive drift   During operant learning, the tendency for an organism to revert to instinctive behavior.

intelligence   An inferred characteristic of an individual, usually defined as the ability to profit from experience, acquire knowledge, think abstractly, act purposefully, or adapt to changes in the environment.

intelligence quotient (IQ)   A measure of intelligence now derived from norms provided for standardized intelligence tests.

intermittent (partial) schedule of reinforcement   A reinforcement schedule in which a particular response is sometimes but not always reinforced.

internal desynchronization   A state in which biological rhythms are not in phase (synchronized) with one another.

intersex conditions (intersexuality)   Conditions, occurring in about one of every 2,000 births, in which chromosomal or hormonal anomalies cause a child to be born with ambiguous genitals, or genitals that conflict with the infant's chromosomes.

intrinsic motivation   The desire to do something for its own sake and for the internal pleasure it provides.

intrinsic reinforcers   Reinforcers that are inherently related to the activity being reinforced, such as enjoyment of the task and the satisfaction of accomplishment.

justification of effort   The tendency of individuals to increase their liking for something that they have worked hard or suffered to attain; a common form of dissonance reduction.

just-world hypothesis   The notion that many people need to believe that the world is fair and that justice is served, that bad people are punished and good people rewarded.

kinesthesis [KIN-es-THEE-sis]   The sense of body position and movement of body parts; also called *kinesthesia*.

language acquisition device   According to many psycholinguists, an innate mental module that allows young children to develop language if they are exposed to an adequate sampling of conversation.

latent learning   A form of learning that is not immediately expressed in an overt response; it occurs without obvious reinforcement.

lateralization   Speciali zation of the two cerebral hemispheres for particular operations.

learning   A relatively permanent change in behavior (or behavioral potential) due to experience.

learning perspective   A psychological approach that emphasizes how the environment and experience affect a person's or animal's actions; it includes behaviorism and social-cognitive learning theories.

libido (li-BEE-do)   In psychoanalysis, the psychic energy that fuels the life or sexual instincts of the id.

limbic system   A group of brain areas involved in emotional reactions and motivated behavior.

lithium carbonate   A drug frequently given to people suffering from bipolar disorder.

localization of function   Specialization of particular brain areas for particular functions.

locus of control   A general expectation about whether the results of your actions are under your own control (internal locus) or beyond your control (external locus).

longitudinal study   A study in which individuals are followed and periodically reassessed over a period of time.

long-term memory (LTM)   In the three-box model of memory, the memory system involved in the long-term storage of information.

loudness   The dimension of auditory experience related to the intensity of a pressure wave.

lucid dream   A dream in which the dreamer is aware of dreaming.

maintenance rehearsal   Rote repetition of material in order to maintain its availability in memory.

major depression   A mood disorder involving disturbances in emotion (excessive sadness), behavior (loss of interest in one's usual activities), cognition (thoughts of hopelessness), and body function (fatigue and loss of appetite).

mastery (learning) goals   Goals framed in terms of increasing one's competence and skills.

mean   See arithmetic mean.

measure of central tendency   A number intended to characterize an entire set of data.

measure of variability   A number that indicates how dispersed scores are around the mean of the distribution.

median   A measure of central tendency; the value at the midpoint of a distribution of scores when the scores are ordered from highest to lowest.

medulla [muh-DUL-uh]   A structure in the brain stem responsible for certain automatic functions, such as breathing and heart rate.

melatonin   A hormone, secreted by the pineal gland, that is involved in the regulation of daily biological (circadian) rhythms.

menarche [men-ARR-kee]   The onset of menstruation.

menopause   The cessation of menstruation and of the production of ova; it is usually a gradual process lasting up to several years.

mental age (MA)   A measure of mental development expressed in terms of the average mental ability at a given age.

mental disorder   Any behavior or emotional state that causes a person great suffering, is self-destructive, seriously impairs the person's ability to work or get along with others, or endangers others or the community.

mental image   A mental representation that mirrors or resembles the thing it represents; mental images can occur in many and perhaps all sensory modalities.

mental set   A tendency to solve problems using procedures that worked before on similar problems.

meta-analysis   A procedure for combining and analyzing data from many studies; it determines how much of the variance in scores across all studies can be explained by a particular variable.

metacognition   The knowledge or awareness of one's own cognitive processes.

Minnesota Multiphasic Personality Inventory (MMPI)   A widely used objective personality test.

mirror neurons   Brain cells that fire when a person or animal observes others carrying out an action; they are involved in empathy, imitation, and reading emotions.

mnemonics [neh-MON-iks] Strategies and tricks for improving memory, such as the use of a verse or a formula.

mode A measure of central tendency; the most frequently occurring score in a distribution.

monocular cues Visual cues to depth or distance that can be used by one eye alone.

motivation An inferred process within a person or animal that causes movement either toward a goal or away from an unpleasant situation.

MRI (magnetic resonance imaging) A method for studying body and brain tissue, using magnetic fields and special radio receivers.

myelin sheath A fatty insulation that may surround the axon of a neuron.

narcissistic personality disorder A disorder characterized by an exaggerated sense of self-importance and self-absorption.

narcolepsy A sleep disorder involving sudden and unpredictable daytime attacks of sleepiness or actual sleep.

need for achievement A learned motive to meet personal standards of success and excellence in a chosen area.

negative correlation An association between increases in one variable and decreases in another.

negative reinforcement A reinforcement procedure in which a response is followed by the removal, delay, or decrease in intensity of an unpleasant stimulus; as a result, the response becomes stronger or more likely to occur.

nerve A bundle of nerve fibers (axons and sometimes dendrites) in the peripheral nervous system.

neuron A cell that conducts electrochemical signals; the basic unit of the nervous system; also called a *nerve cell*.

neurotransmitter A chemical substance that is released by a transmitting neuron at the synapse and that alters the activity of a receiving neuron.

nonconscious processes Mental processes occurring outside of and not available to conscious awareness.

nonshared environment Unique aspects of a person's environment and experience that are not shared with family members.

normal curve A symmetrical, bell-shaped frequency polygon representing a normal distribution.

normal distribution A theoretical frequency distribution having certain special characteristics. For example, the distribution is symmetrical; the mean, mode, and median all have the same value; and the farther a score is from the mean, the less the likelihood of obtaining it.

norms In test construction, established standards of performance.

norms (social) Rules that regulate social life, including explicit laws and implicit cultural conventions.

null hypothesis An assertion that the independent variable in a study will have no effect on the dependent variable.

object permanence The understanding, which develops throughout the first year, that an object continues to exist even when you cannot see it or touch it.

objective tests (inventories) Standardized objective questionnaires requiring written responses; they typically include scales on which people are asked to rate themselves.

object-relations school A psychodynamic approach that emphasizes the importance of the infant's first two years of life and the baby's formative relationships, especially with the mother.

observational learning A process in which an individual learns new responses by observing the behavior of another (a model) rather than through direct experience; sometimes called *vicarious conditioning*.

observational study A study in which the researcher carefully and systematically observes and records behavior without interfering with the behavior; it may involve either naturalistic or laboratory observation.

obsessive-compulsive disorder (OCD) An anxiety disorder in which a person feels trapped in persistent thoughts (*obsessions*) and repetitive, ritualized behaviors (*compulsions*) designed to reduce anxiety.

occipital [ahk-SIP-uh-tuhl] lobes Lobes at the lower back part of the brain's cerebral cortex; they contain areas that receive visual information.

Oedipus complex In psychoanalysis, a conflict occurring in the phallic (Oedipal) stage, in which a child desires the parent of the other sex and views the same-sex parent as a rival.

operant conditioning The process by which a response becomes more likely to occur or less so, depending on its consequences.

operational definition A precise definition of a term in a hypothesis, which specifies the operations for observing and measuring the process or phenomenon being defined.

opiates Drugs, derived from the opium poppy, that relieve pain and commonly produce euphoria.

opponent-process theory A theory of color perception that assumes that the visual system treats pairs of colors as opposing or antagonistic.

organ of Corti [CORE-tee] A structure in the cochlea containing hair cells that serve as the receptors for hearing.

oxytocin A hormone, secreted by the pituitary gland, that stimulates uterine contractions during childbirth, facilitates the ejection of milk during nursing, and seems to promote, in both sexes, attachment and trust in relationships.

panic disorder An anxiety disorder in which a person experiences recurring panic attacks, periods of intense fear, and feelings of impending doom or death, accompanied by physiological symptoms such as rapid heart rate and dizziness.

papillae [pa-PILL-ee] Knoblike elevations on the tongue, containing the taste buds. (Singular: *papilla*.)

parallel distributed processing (PDP) A model of memory in which knowledge is represented as connections among thousands of interacting processing units, distributed in a vast network and all operating in parallel.

paranoid personality disorder A disorder characterized by unreasonable, excessive suspiciousness and mistrust, and irrational feelings of being persecuted by others.

parapsychology The study of purported psychic phenomena such as ESP and mental telepathy.

parasympathetic nervous system The subdivision of the autonomic nervous system that operates during relaxed states and that conserves energy.

parietal [puh-RYE-uh-tuhl] lobes Lobes at the top of the brain's cerebral cortex; they contain areas that receive information on pressure, pain, touch, and temperature.

percentile score   A score that indicates the percentage of people who scored at or below a given raw score; also called *centile rank*.

perception   The process by which the brain organizes and interprets sensory information.

perceptual constancy   The accurate perception of objects as stable or unchanged despite changes in the sensory patterns they produce.

perceptual set   A habitual way of perceiving, based on expectations.

performance goals   Goals framed in terms of performing well in front of others, being judged favorably, and avoiding criticism.

peripheral nervous system (PNS)   All portions of the nervous system outside the brain and spinal cord; it includes sensory and motor nerves.

personality   A distinctive and relatively stable pattern of behavior, thoughts, motives, and emotions that characterizes an individual.

personality disorders   Rigid personality patterns that cause personal distress or an inability to get along with others.

PET scan (positron-emission tomography)   A method for analyzing biochemical activity in the brain, using injections of a glucoselike substance containing a radioactive element.

phantom pain   The experience of pain in a missing limb or other body part.

phobia   An exaggerated, unrealistic fear of a specific situation, activity, or object.

phrenology   The now discredited theory that different brain areas account for specific character and personality traits, which can be "read" from bumps on the skull.

pitch   The dimension of auditory experience related to the frequency of a pressure wave; it is related to the height or depth of a tone.

pituitary gland   A small endocrine gland at the base of the brain that releases many hormones and regulates other endocrine glands.

placebo   An inactive substance or fake treatment used as a control in an experiment.

placebo effect   The apparent success of a medication or treatment that is due to the patient's expectations or hopes rather than to the drug or treatment itself.

plasticity   The brain's ability to change and adapt in response to experience, for example, by reorganizing or growing new neural connections.

pons   A structure in the brain stem involved in, among other things, sleeping, waking, and dreaming.

positive correlation   An association between increases in one variable and increases in another or between decreases in one and in the other.

positive reinforcement   A reinforcement procedure in which a response is followed by the presentation of, or increase in intensity of, a reinforcing stimulus; as a result, the response becomes stronger or more likely to occur.

postdecision dissonance   In the theory of cognitive dissonance, tension that occurs when you believe you may have made a bad decision.

posttraumatic stress disorder (PTSD)   An anxiety disorder in which a person who has experienced a traumatic or life-threatening event has symptoms such as psychic numbing, reliving of the trauma, and increased physiological arousal.

power assertion   A method of child rearing in which the parent uses punishment and authority to correct the child's misbehavior.

primary control   An effort to modify reality by changing other people, the situation, or events; a "fighting back" philosophy.

primary emotions   Emotions that are considered to be universal and biologically based.

primary punisher   A stimulus that is inherently punishing; an example is electric shock.

primary reinforcer   A stimulus that is inherently reinforcing, typically satisfying a physiological need; an example is food.

priming   A method for measuring implicit memory in which a person reads or listens to information and is later tested to see whether the information affects performance on another type of task.

principle of falsifiability   The principle that a scientific theory must make predictions that are specific enough to expose the theory to the possibility of disconfirmation.

proactive interference   Forgetting that occurs when previously stored material interferes with the ability to remember similar, more recently learned material.

procedural memories   Memories for the performance of actions or skills ("knowing how").

projective tests   Psychological tests used to infer a person's motives, conflicts, and unconscious dynamics on the basis of the person's interpretations of ambiguous stimuli.

proposition   A unit of meaning that is made up of concepts and expresses a single idea.

prototype   An especially representative example of a concept.

psychedelic drugs   Consciousness-altering drugs that produce hallucinations, change thought processes, or disrupt the normal perception of time and space.

psychoactive drug   A drug capable of influencing perception, mood, cognition, or behavior.

psychoanalysis   A theory of personality and a method of psychotherapy developed by Sigmund Freud; it emphasizes unconscious motives and conflicts.

psychodynamic perspective   A psychological approach that emphasizes unconscious dynamics within the individual, such as inner forces, conflicts, or the movement of instinctual energy.

psychodynamic theories   Theories that explain behavior and personality in terms of unconscious dynamics within the individual.

psychodynamic therapies   Psychotherapies that share the goal of exploring the unconscious dynamics of personality, although they differ from Freudian analysis in various ways.

psychological tests   Procedures used to measure and evaluate personality traits, emotional states, aptitudes, interests, abilities, and values.

psychology   The discipline concerned with behavior and mental processes and how they are affected by an organism's physical state, mental state, and external environment; often represented by ψ, the Greek letter psi (usually pronounced "sy").

psychometrics   The measurement of mental abilities, traits, and processes.

psychosis   An extreme mental disturbance involving distorted perceptions and irrational behavior; it may have psychological or organic causes.

psychosurgery Any surgical procedure that destroys selected areas of the brain believed to be involved in emotional disorders or violent, impulsive behavior.

puberty The age at which a person becomes capable of sexual reproduction.

punishment The process by which a stimulus or event weakens or reduces the probability of the response that it follows.

random assignment A procedure for assigning people to experimental and control groups in which each individual has the same probability as any other of being assigned to a given group.

randomized controlled trials Research designed to determine the effectiveness of a new medication or form of therapy, in which people with a given problem or disorder are randomly assigned to one or more treatment groups or to a control group.

range A measure of the spread of scores, calculated by subtracting the lowest score from the highest score.

rapid eye movement (REM) sleep Sleep periods characterized by eye movement, loss of muscle tone, and dreaming.

rational emotive behavior therapy A form of cognitive therapy devised by Albert Ellis, designed to challenge the client's unrealistic or irrational thoughts.

reasoning The drawing of conclusions or inferences from observations, facts, or assumptions.

recall The ability to retrieve and reproduce from memory previously encountered material.

reciprocal determinism In social-cognitive theories, the two-way interaction between aspects of the environment and aspects of the individual in the shaping of personality traits.

recognition The ability to identify previously encountered material.

reinforcement The process by which a stimulus or event strengthens or increases the probability of the response that it follows.

relearning method A method for measuring retention that compares the time required to relearn material with the time used in the initial learning of the material.

reliability In test construction, the consistency of test scores from one time and place to another.

representative sample A group of individuals, selected from a population for study, which matches that population on important characteristics such as age and sex.

repression In psychoanalytic theory, the involuntary pushing of threatening or upsetting information into the unconscious.

reticular activating system (RAS) A dense network of neurons in the core of the brain stem; it arouses the cortex and screens incoming information.

retina Neural tissue lining the back of the eyeball's interior, which contains the receptors for vision.

retinal disparity The slight difference in lateral separation between two objects as seen by the left eye and the right eye.

retroactive interference Forgetting that occurs when recently learned material interferes with the ability to remember similar material stored previously.

rods Visual receptors that respond to dim light.

role A given social position that is governed by a set of norms for proper behavior.

Rorschach Inkblot Test A projective personality test that requires respondents to interpret abstract, symmetrical inkblots.

saturation Vividness or purity of color; the dimension of visual experience related to the complexity of light waves.

schizophrenia A psychotic disorder marked by delusions, hallucinations, disorganized and incoherent speech, inappropriate behavior, and cognitive impairments.

seasonal affective disorder (SAD) A controversial disorder in which a person experiences depression during the winter and an improvement of mood in the spring.

secondary control An effort to accept reality by changing your own attitudes, goals, or emotions; a "learn to live with it" philosophy.

secondary emotions Emotions that are specific to certain cultures.

secondary punisher A stimulus that has acquired punishing properties through association with other punishers.

secondary reinforcer A stimulus that has acquired reinforcing properties through association with other reinforcers.

selective attention The focusing of attention on selected aspects of the environment and the blocking out of others.

self-efficacy A person's belief that he or she is capable of producing desired results, such as mastering new skills and reaching goals.

self-fulfilling prophecy An expectation that is fulfilled because of the tendency of the person holding it to act in ways that bring it about.

self-serving bias The tendency, in explaining one's own behavior, to take credit for one's good actions and rationalize one's mistakes.

semantic memories Memories of general knowledge, including facts, rules, concepts, and propositions.

semicircular canals Sense organs in the inner ear, which contribute to equilibrium by responding to rotation of the head.

sensation The detection of physical energy emitted or reflected by physical objects.

sense receptors Specialized cells that convert physical energy in the environment or the body to electrical energy that can be transmitted as nerve impulses to the brain.

sensory adaptation The reduction or disappearance of sensory responsiveness that occurs when stimulation is unchanging or repetitious.

sensory deprivation The absence of normal levels of sensory stimulation.

sensory register A memory system that momentarily preserves extremely accurate sensory information before the information fades or moves into short-term memory.

separation anxiety The distress that most children develop, at about 6 to 8 months of age, when their primary caregivers temporarily leave them with others.

serial-position effect The tendency for recall of the first and last items on a list to surpass recall of items in the middle of the list.

set point The genetically influenced weight range for an individual, maintained by biological mechanisms that regulate food intake, fat reserves, and metabolism.

sex hormones Hormones that regulate the development and functioning of reproductive organs and that stimulate the development of male and female sexual characteristics; they include androgens, estrogens, and progesterone.

sexual scripts Sets of implicit rules that specify proper sexual behavior for a person in a given situation, varying with the person's gender, age, religion, social status, and peer group.

shaping An operant-conditioning procedure in which successive approximations of a desired response are reinforced.

short-term memory (STM) In the three-box model of memory, a limited-capacity memory system involved in the retention of information for brief periods; it is also used to hold information retrieved from long-term memory for temporary use.

signal-detection theory A psychophysical theory that divides the detection of a sensory signal into a sensory process and a decision process.

significance tests Statistical tests that assess how likely it is that a study's results occurred merely by chance.

single-blind study An experiment in which subjects do not know whether they are in an experimental or a control group.

skills training In behavior therapy, an effort to teach the client skills that he or she may lack, as well as new constructive behaviors to replace self-defeating ones.

sleep apnea A disorder in which breathing briefly stops during sleep, causing the person to choke and gasp.

social cognition An area in social psychology concerned with social influences on thought, memory, perception, and beliefs.

social identity The part of a person's self-concept that is based on his or her identification with a nation, religious or political group, or other social affiliation.

social-cognitive learning theory A major contemporary learning view of personality, which holds that personality traits result from a person's learning history and his or her expectations, beliefs, perceptions of events, and other cognitions.

social-cognitive theories Theories that emphasize how behavior is learned and maintained through observation and imitation of others, positive consequences, and cognitive processes such as plans, expectations, and beliefs.

socialization The process by which children learn the behaviors, attitudes, and expectations required of them by their society or culture.

sociocultural perspective A psychological approach that emphasizes social and cultural influences on behavior.

somatic nervous system The subdivision of the peripheral nervous system that connects to sensory receptors and to skeletal muscles; sometimes called the *skeletal nervous system.*

source misattribution The inability to distinguish an actual memory of an event from information you learned elsewhere about the event.

spinal cord A collection of neurons and supportive tissue running from the base of the brain down the center of the back, protected by a column of bones (the spinal column).

spinal reflexes Automatic behaviors produced by the spinal cord without brain involvement.

spontaneous recovery The reappearance of a learned response after its apparent extinction.

standard deviation A commonly used measure of variability that indicates the average difference between scores in a distribution and their mean; more precisely, the square root of the average squared deviation from the mean.

standardize In test construction, to develop uniform procedures for giving and scoring a test.

state-dependent memory The tendency to remember something when the rememberer is in the same physical or mental state as during the original learning or experience.

statistically significant A term used to refer to a result that is extremely unlikely to have occurred by chance.

stem cells Immature cells that renew themselves and have the potential to develop into mature cells; given encouraging environments, stem cells from early embryos can develop into any cell type.

stereotype A summary impression of a group, in which a person believes that all members of the group share a common trait or traits (positive, negative, or neutral).

stereotype threat A burden of doubt a person feels about his or her performance, due to negative stereotypes about his or her group's abilities.

stimulants Drugs that speed up activity in the central nervous system.

stimulus discrimination The tendency to respond differently to two or more similar stimuli. In classical conditioning, it occurs when a stimulus that resembles the conditioned stimulus fails to evoke the conditioned response. In operant conditioning, it occurs when an organism learns to make a response in the presence of one stimulus but not in the presence of other, similar stimuli that differ from it on some dimension.

stimulus generalization After conditioning, the tendency to respond to a stimulus that resembles one involved in the original conditioning. In classical conditioning, it occurs when a stimulus that resembles the conditioned stimulus elicits the conditioned response. In operant conditioning, it occurs when a response that has been reinforced (or punished) in the presence of one stimulus occurs (or is suppressed) in the presence of other, similar stimuli.

subconscious processes Mental processes occurring outside of conscious awareness but accessible to consciousness when necessary.

successive approximations In the procedure of shaping, behaviors that are ordered in terms of increasing similarity or closeness to the desired response.

superego In psychoanalysis, the part of personality that represents conscience, morality, and social standards.

suprachiasmatic [soo-pruh-kie-az-MAT-ick] nucleus (SCN) An area of the brain containing a biological clock that governs circadian rhythms.

surveys Questionnaires and interviews that ask people directly about their experiences, attitudes, or opinions.

sympathetic nervous system The subdivision of the autonomic nervous system that mobilizes bodily resources and increases the output of energy during emotion and stress.

synapse The site where transmission of a nerve impulse from one nerve cell to another occurs; it includes the axon terminal, the synaptic cleft, and receptor sites in the membrane of the receiving cell.

synesthesia A rare condition in which stimulation of one sense also evokes a sensation in another.

systematic desensitization In behavior therapy, a step-by-step process of desensitizing a client to a feared object or experience; it is based on the classical-conditioning procedure of counterconditioning.

tacit knowledge Strategies for success that are not explicitly taught but that instead must be inferred.

taste buds Nests of taste-receptor cells.

telegraphic speech A child's first word combinations, which omit (as a telegram did) unnecessary words.

temperaments Physiological dispositions to respond to the environment in certain ways; they are present in infancy and are assumed to be innate.

temporal lobes Lobes at the sides of the brain's cerebral cortex; they contain areas involved in hearing, memory, perception, emotion, and (in the left lobe, typically) language comprehension.

thalamus A brain structure that relays sensory messages to the cerebral cortex.

Thematic Apperception Test (TAT) A projective test that asks respondents to interpret drawings showing scenes of people; scored for unconscious traits and motives, such as the need for achievement, power, or affiliation.

theory An organized system of assumptions and principles that purports to explain a specified set of phenomena and their interrelationships.

theory of mind The human ability to think about the way one's own mind and the minds of others work, and how cognitions and feelings affect behavior.

therapeutic alliance The bond of confidence and mutual understanding established between therapist and client, which allows them to work together to solve the client's problems.

timbre The distinguishing quality of a sound; the dimension of auditory experience related to the complexity of the pressure wave.

tolerance Increased resistance to a drug's effects accompanying continued use.

trait A characteristic of an individual, describing a habitual way of behaving, thinking, or feeling.

tranquilizers Drugs commonly but often inappropriately prescribed for patients who complain of unhappiness, anxiety, or worry.

transcranial magnetic stimulation (TMS) A method of stimulating brain cells, using a powerful magnetic field produced by a wire coil placed on a person's head; it can be used by researchers to temporarily inactivate neural circuits and is also being used therapeutically.

transference In psychodynamic therapies, a critical process in which the client transfers unconscious emotions or reactions, such as emotional feelings about his or her parents, onto the therapist.

triarchic theory of intelligence A theory of intelligence that emphasizes information-processing strategies, the ability to transfer skills to new situations, and the practical application of intelligence.

trichromatic theory A theory of color perception that proposes three mechanisms in the visual system, each sensitive to a certain range of wavelengths; their interaction is assumed to produce all the different experiences of hue.

unconditional positive regard To Carl Rogers, love or support given to another person with no conditions attached.

unconditioned response (UR) The classical-conditioning term for a reflexive response elicited by a stimulus in the absence of learning.

unconditioned stimulus (US) The classical-conditioning term for a stimulus that elicits a reflexive response in the absence of learning.

validity The ability of a test to measure what it was designed to measure.

validity effect The tendency of people to believe that a statement is true or valid simply because it has been repeated many times.

variables Characteristics of behavior or experience that can be measured or described by a numeric scale; variables are manipulated and assessed in scientific studies.

volunteer bias A shortcoming of findings derived from a sample of volunteers instead of a representative sample; the volunteers may differ from those who did not volunteer.

vulnerability-stress models Approaches that emphasize how individual vulnerabilities (e.g., in genes or personality traits) interact with external stresses or circumstances to produce mental disorders.

withdrawal Physical and psychological symptoms that occur when someone addicted to a drug stops taking it.

working memory Short-term memory plus the mental processes that control retrieval of information from long-term memory and interpret that information appropriately for a given task.

z-score (standard score) A number that indicates how far a given raw score is above or below the mean, using the standard deviation of the distribution as the unit of measurement.

references

Abel, Gene G.; Mittelman, Mary; Becker, Judith V.; et al. (1988). Predicting child molesters' response to treatment. *Annals of the New York Academy of Sciences, 528,* 223–234.

Abrahamson, Amy C.; Baker, Laura A.; & Caspi, Avshalom (2002). Rebellious teens? Genetic and environmental influences on the social attitudes of adolescents. *Journal of Personality and Social Psychology, 83,* 1392–1408.

Abrams, David B., & Wilson, G. Terence (1983). Alcohol, sexual arousal, and self-control. *Journal of Personality and Social Psychology, 45,* 188–198.

Abrams, R. (1997). *Electroconvulsive therapy* (3rd ed.). Oxford, England: Oxford University Press.

Abramson, Lyn Y.; Metalsky, Gerald I.; & Alloy, Lauren B. (1989). Hopelessness depression: A theory-based subtype of depression. *Psychological Review, 96,* 358–372.

Adams, James L. (1986). *Conceptual blockbusting: A guide to better ideas* (3rd ed.). Boston: Addison-Wesley.

Ader, Robert (2000). True or false: The placebo effect as seen in drug studies is definitive proof that the mind can bring about clinically relevant changes in the body: The placebo effect: If it's all in your head, does that mean you only think you feel better? *Advances in Mind-Body Medicine, 16,* 7–11.

Adler, Nancy E., & Snibbe, Alana C. (2003). The role of psychosocial processes in explaining the gradient between socioeconomic status and health. *Current Directions in Psychological Science, 12,* 119–123.

Adolphs, Ralph (2001). Emotion, social cognition, and the human brain. Invited address presented at the annual meeting of the American Psychological Society, Toronto.

Affleck, Glenn; Tennen, Howard; Croog, Sydney; & Levine, Sol (1987). Causal attribution, perceived control, and recovery from a heart attack. *Journal of Social and Clinical Psychology, 5,* 339–355.

Agars, Mark D. (2004). Reconsidering the impact of gender stereotypes on the advancement of women in organizations. *Psychology of Women Quarterly, 28,* 103–111.

Ainsworth, Mary D. S. (1973). The development of infant–mother attachment. In B. M. Caldwell & H. N. Ricciuti (Eds.), *Review of child development research* (Vol. 3). Chicago: University of Chicago Press.

Ainsworth, Mary D. S. (1979). Infant–mother attachment. *American Psychologist, 34,* 932–937.

Akbarian, Schahram; Kim, J. J.; Potkin, Steven G.; et al. (1996). Maldistribution of interstitial neurons in prefrontal white matter of the brains of schizophrenic patients. *Archives of General Psychiatry, 53,* 425–436.

Alford, C. Fred (2001). *Whistleblowers: Broken lives and organizations.* Ithaca, NY: Cornell University Press.

Alford, John R.; Funk, Carolyn L.; & Hibbing, John R. (2005). Are political orientations genetically transmitted? *American Political Science Review, 99,* 153–167.

Allen, Laura S., & Gorski, Robert A. (1992). Sexual orientation and the size of the anterior commissure in the human brain. *Proceedings of the National Academy of Sciences, 89,* 7199–7202.

Allport, Gordon W. (1937). *Personality: A psychological interpretation.* New York: Holt, Rinehart and Winston.

Allport, Gordon W. (1954/1979). *The nature of prejudice.* Reading, MA: Addison-Wesley.

Allport, Gordon W. (1961). *Pattern and growth in personality.* New York: Holt, Rinehart and Winston.

Amabile, Teresa M. (1983). *The social psychology of creativity.* New York: Springer-Verlag.

Amedi, Amir; Merabet, Lotfi; Bermpohl, Felix; & Pascual-Leone, Alvaro (2005). The occipital cortex in the blind: Lessons about plasticity and vision. *Current Directions in Psychological Science, 14,* 306–311.

American Psychiatric Association (1994). *The diagnostic and statistical manual of mental disorders* (4th ed.). Washington, DC: American Psychiatric Association.

American Psychiatric Association (2000). *The diagnostic and statistical manual of mental disorders, IV-TR.* Washington, DC: American Psychiatric Association.

Amering, Michaela, & Katschnig, Heinz (1990). Panic attacks and panic disorder in cross-cultural perspective. *Psychiatric Annals, 20,* 511–516.

Amodio, David M.; Harmon-Jones, Eddie; & Devine, Patricia G. (2003). Individual differences in the activation and control of affective race bias as assessed by startle eyeblink response and self-report. *Journal of Personality and Social Psychology, 84,* 738–753.

Anastasi, Anne, & Urbina, Susan (1997). *Psychological testing* (7th ed.). Upper Saddle River, NJ: Prentice Hall.

Anderson, Adam K., & Phelps, Elizabeth A. (2000). Expression without recognition: Contributions of the human amygdala to emotional communication. *Psychological Science, 11,* 106–111.

Anderson, Amanda (2005). *The way we argue now: A study in the cultures of theory.* Princeton, NJ: Princeton University Press.

Anderson, Cameron; Keltner, Dacher; & John, Oliver P. (2003). Emotional convergence between people over time. *Journal of Personality and Social Psychology, 84,* 1054–1068.

Anderson, Craig A., & Bushman, Brad J. (2001). Effects of violent video games on aggressive behavior, aggressive cognition, aggressive affect, physiological arousal, and prosocial behavior: A meta-analytic review of the scientific literature. *Psychological Science, 12,* 353–359.

Anderson, John R. (1990). *The adaptive nature of thought.* Hillsdale, NJ: Erlbaum.

Anderson, Michael C.; Ochsner, Keven N.; Kuhl, Brice; et al. (2004). Neural systems underlying the suppression of unwanted memories. *Science, 303,* 232–235.

Anderson, S. W.; Bechara, A.; Damasio, H.; Tranel, D.; & Damasio, A. R. (1999). Impairment of social and moral behavior related to early damage in human prefrontal cortex. *Nature Neuroscience, 2,* 1032–1037.

Andreasen, Nancy C.; Arndt, Stephan; Swayze, Victor, II; et al. (1994). Thalamic abnormalities in schizophrenia visualized through magnetic resonance image averaging. *Science, 266,* 294–298.

Angell, Marcia (2004). *The truth about the drug companies: How they deceive us and what to do about it.* New York: Random House.

Angier, Natalie (2000, November 7). Who is fat? It depends on culture. *The New York Times,* Science Times, D1–2.

Antonova, Irina; Arancio, Ottavio; Trillat, Anne-Cecile; et al. (2001). Rapid increase in clusters of presynaptic proteins at onset of long-lasting potentiation. *Science, 294,* 1547–1550.

Antonuccio, David O.; Danton, William G.; & DeNelsky, Garland Y.; et al. (1999). Raising questions about antidepressants. *Psychotherapy and Psychosomatics, 68,* 3–14.

Antrobus, John (1991). Dreaming: Cognitive processes during cortical activation and high afferent thresholds. *Psychological Review, 98,* 96–121.

Antrobus, John (2000). How does the dreaming brain explain the dreaming mind? *Behavioral and Brain Sciences, 23,* 904–907.

APA Commission on Violence and Youth (1993). *Violence and youth: Psychology's response.* Washington, DC: American Psychological Association.

Arbib, Michael A. (2005). From monkey-like action recognition to human language: An evolutionary framework for neurolinguistics. *Behavioral and Brain Sciences, 28,* 105–167

Archer, John (2004). Sex differences in aggression in real-world settings: A meta-analytic review. *Review of General Psychology, 8,* 291–322

Arendt, Hannah (1963). *Eichmann in Jerusalem: A report on the banality of evil.* New York: Viking.

Arkes, Hal R. (1993). Some practical judgment and decision-making research. In N. J. Castellan, Jr., et al. (Eds.), *Individual and group decision making: Current issues.* Hillsdale, NJ: Erlbaum.

Arkes, Hal R.; Boehm, Lawrence E.; & Xu, Gang (1991). The determinants of judged validity. *Journal of Experimental Social Psychology, 27,* 576–605.

Arnett, Jeffrey J. (2000). Emerging adulthood: A theory of development from the late teens through the twenties. *American Psychologist, 55,* 469–480.

Aron, Arthur; Aron, Elaine N.; & Allen, Joselyn (1998). Motivations for unreciprocated love. *Personality and Social Psychology Bulletin, 24,* 787–796.

Aron, Arthur, & Westbay, Lori (1996). Dimensions of the prototype of love. *Journal of Personality and Social Psychology, 70,* 535–551.

Aronson, Elliot (2000). *Nobody left to hate.* New York: Freeman.

Aronson, Elliot (2004). *The social animal* (9th ed.). New York: Worth.

Aronson, Elliot, & Mills, Judson (1959). The effect of severity of initiation on liking for a group. *Journal of Abnormal and Social Psychology, 59,* 177–181.

Aronson, Elliot, & Patnoe, Shelley (1997). *Cooperation in the classroom: The jigsaw method.* New York: Longman.

Aronson, Joshua, & Salinas, Moises F. (1997). Stereotype threat, attribution ambiguity, and Latino underperformance. Unpublished manuscript, University of Texas, Austin.

Arredondo, Patricia, & Perez, Patricia (2003). Counseling paradigms and Latina/o Americans. In F. Harper & J. McFadden (Eds.), *Culture and counseling: New approaches.* Boston: Allyn & Bacon.

Arredondo, Patricia; Rosen, Daniel C.; Rice, Tiffany; Perez, Patricia; & Tovar-Gamero, Zoila G. (2005). Multicultural counseling: A 10-year content analysis of the *Journal of Counseling & Development. Journal of Counseling and Development, 83,* 155–161.

Arroyo, Carmen G., & Zigler, Edward (1995). Racial identity, academic achievement, and the psychological well-being of economically disadvantaged adolescents. *Journal of Personality and Social Psychology, 69,* 903–914.

Arsenijevic, D.; Onuma, H.; Pecqueur, C.; et al. (2000, December 26). Disruption of the uncoupling protein-2 gene in mice reveals a role in immunity and reactive oxygen species production. *Nature Genetics, 4,* 387–388.

Asch, Solomon E. (1952). *Social psychology.* Englewood Cliffs, NJ: Prentice-Hall.

Asch, Solomon E. (1965). Effects of group pressure upon the modification and distortion of judgments. In H. Proshansky & B. Seidenberg (Eds.), *Basic studies in social psychology.* New York: Holt, Rinehart and Winston.

Aserinsky, Eugene, & Kleitman, Nathaniel (1955). Two types of ocular motility occurring in sleep. *Journal of Applied Physiology, 8,* 1–10.

Aspinwall, Lisa G., & Brunhart, Susanne M. (1996). Distinguishing optimism from denial: Optimistic beliefs predict attention to health threats. *Personality and Social Psychology Bulletin, 22,* 993–1003.

Atkinson, Richard C., & Shiffrin, Richard M. (1968). Human memory: A proposed system and its control processes. In K. W. Spence & J. T. Spence (Eds.), *The psychology of learning and motivation: Vol. 2. Advances in research and theory.* New York: Academic Press.

Atkinson, Richard C., & Shiffrin, Richard M. (1971, August). The control of short-term memory. *Scientific American, 225*(2), 82–90.

Atran, Scott (2003, March 7). Geneis of suicide terrorism. *Science, 299,* 1534–1539.

AuBuchon, Peter G., & Calhoun, Karen S. (1985). Menstrual cycle symptomatology: The role of social expectancy and experimental demand characteristics. *Psychosomatic Medicine, 47,* 35–45.

Axel, Richard (1995, October). The molecular logic of smell. *Scientific American,* 154–159.

Azrin, Nathan H., & Foxx, Richard M. (1974). *Toilet training in less than a day.* New York: Simon & Schuster.

Baddeley, Alan D. (1992). Working memory. *Science, 255,* 556–559.

Bagemihl, Bruce (1999). *Biological exuberance: Animal homosexuality and natural diversity.* New York: St. Martin's Press.

Bahrick, Harry P. (1984). Semantic memory content in permastore: Fifty years of memory for Spanish learned in school. *Journal of Experimental Psychology: General, 113,* 1–29.

Bahrick, Harry P.; Bahrick, Phyllis O.; & Wittlinger, Roy P. (1975). Fifty years of memory for names and faces: A cross-sectional approach. *Journal of Experimental Psychology: General, 104,* 54–75.

Bailey, J. Michael; Bobrow, David; Wolfe, Marilyn; & Mikach, Sarah (1995). Sexual orientation of adult sons of gay fathers. *Developmental Psychology, 31,* 124–129.

Bailey, J. Michael; Dunne, Michael P.; & Martin, Nicholas G. (2000). Genetic and environmental influences on sexual orientation and its correlates in an Australian twin sample. *Journal of Personality and Social Psychology, 78,* 524–536.

Bailey, J. Michael; Gaulin, Steven; Agyei, Yvonne; & Gladue, Brian A. (1994). Effects of gender and sexual orientation on evolutionarily relevant aspects of human mating psychology. *Journal of Personality and Social Psychology, 66,* 1081–1093.

Bailey, J. Michael, & Pillard, Richard C. (1995). Genetics of human sexual orientation. *Annual Review of Sex Research, 6,* 126–150.

Bailey, J. Michael, & Zucker, Kenneth J. (1995). Childhood sex-typed behavior and sexual orientation: A conceptual analysis and quantitative review. *Developmental Psychology, 31,* 43–55.

Baillargeon, Renée (1994). How do infants learn about the physical world? *Current Directions in Psychological Science, 5,* 133–140.

Baillargeon, Renée (1999). Young infants' expectations about hidden objects: A reply to three challenges. *Developmental Science, 2,* 115–163.

Baker, Mark C. (2001). *The atoms of language: The mind's hidden rules of grammar.* New York: Basic Books.

Bakermans-Kranenburg, Marian J.; van IJzendoorn, Marinus H.; & Juffer, Femmie (2003). Less is more: Meta-analyses of sensitivity and attachment interventions in early childhood. *Psychological Bulletin, 129,* 195–215.

Ball, K.; Berch, D. B.; Helmers, K. F.; et al. (2002, November 13). Effects of cognitive training interventions with older adults: A randomized controlled trial. *Journal of the American Medical Association, 288*, 2271–2281.

Ballenger, James C.; Burrows, Graham D.; DuPont, Robert L.; et al. (1988). Alprazolam in panic disorder and agoraphobia: Results from a multicenter trial. *Archives of General Psychiatry, 45*, 413–421.

Bandura, Albert (1977). *Social learning theory*. Englewood Cliffs, NJ: Prentice-Hall.

Bandura, Albert (1986). *Social foundations of thought and action: A social cognitive theory*. Englewood Cliffs, NJ: Prentice-Hall.

Bandura, Albert (1997). *Self-efficacy: The exercise of control*. New York: Freeman.

Bandura, Albert (1999). Moral disengagement in the perpetration of inhumanities. *Personality and Social Psychology Review, 3*, 193–209.

Bandura, Albert (2001). Social cognitive theory: An agentic perspective. *Annual Review of Psychology, 52*, 1–26. Palo Alto, CA: Annual Reviews.

Bandura, Albert (2006). Toward a psychology of human agency. *Perspectives on Psychological Science, 1*, 164–180.

Bandura, Albert; Caprara, Gian Vittorio; Barbaranelli, Claudio; Pastorelli, Concetta; & Regalia, Camillo (2001). Sociocognitive self-regulatory mechanisms governing transgressive behavior. *Journal of Personality and Social Psychology, 80*, 125–135.

Bandura, Albert; Ross, Dorothea; & Ross, Sheila A. (1963). Vicarious reinforcement and imitative learning. *Journal of Abnormal and Social Psychology, 67*, 601–607.

Banks, Martin S. (with Philip Salapatek) (1984). Infant visual perception. In P. Mussen (Series Ed.), M. M. Haith & J. J. Campos (Vol. Eds.), *Handbook of child psychology: Vol. II. Infancy and developmental psychobiology* (4th ed.). New York: Wiley.

Barash, David P., & Lipton, Judith Eve (2001). *The myth of monogamy: Fidelity and infidelity in animals and people*. New York: W. H. Freeman.

Barbuto, J. E. (1997). A critique of the Myers-Briggs Type Indicator and its operationalization of Carl Jung's psychological types. *Psychological Reports, 80*, 611–625.

Barch, Deanna M. (2003). Cognition in schizophrenia: Does working memory work? *Current Directions in Psychological Science, 12*, 146–150.

Bargh, John A. (1999, January 29). The most powerful manipulative messages are hiding in plain sight. *The Chronicle of Higher Education*, B6.

Barinaga, Marcia (1992). Challenging the "no new neurons" dogma. *Science, 255*, 1646.

Barlow, David H. (2000). Unraveling the mysteries of anxiety and its disorders from the perspective of emotion theory. *American Psychologist, 55*, 1247–1263.

Barlow, David H.; Chorpita, Bruce F.; & Turovsky, Julia (1996). Fear, panic, anxiety, and disorders of emotion. In D. A. Hope et al. (Eds.), *Nebraska Symposium on Motivation, 1995: Perspectives on anxiety, panic, and fear*. Lincoln, NE: University of Nebraska Press.

Barrett, Deirdre (2001). *The committee of sleep*. New York: Crown/Random House.

Barrett, Lisa F. (2006). Are emotions natural kinds? *Perspectives on Psychological Science, 1*, 28–58.

Barrish, Barbara M. (1996). The relationship of remembered parental physical punishment to adolescent self-concept. *Dissertation Abstracts International, Section B, 57*, 2171.

Barron, Kenneth S., & Harackiewicz, Judith M. (2001). Achievement goals and optimal motivation: Testing multiple goal models. *Journal of Personality and Social Psychology, 80*, 706–722.

Barsky, S. H.; Roth, M. D.; Kleerup, E. C.; Simmons, M.; & Tashkin, D. P. (1998). Histopathologic and molecular alterations in bronchial epithelium in habitual smokers of marijuana, cocaine, and/or tobacco. *Journal of the National Cancer Institute, 90*, 1198–1205.

Bartels, Andreas, & Zeki, Semir (2004). The neural correlates of material and romantic love. *NeuroImage, 21*, 1155–1166.

Bartlett, Frederic C. (1932). *Remembering*. Cambridge, England: Cambridge University Press.

Bartoshuk, Linda M. (1998). Born to burn: Genetic variation in taste. Paper presented at the annual meeting of the American Psychological Association, San Francisco.

Bartoshuk, Linda M.; Duffy, V. B.; Lucchina, L. A.; et al. (1998). PROP (6-n-propylthiouracil) supertasters and the saltiness of NaCl. *Annals of the New York Academy of Sciences, 855*, 793–796.

Bassetti, C.; Vella, S.; Donati, F.; et al. (2000). SPECT during sleepwalking. *Lancet, 356*, 484–485.

Basson, Rosemary; McInnis, Rosemary; Smith, Mike D.; Hodgson, Gemma; & Koppiker, Nandan (2002). Efficacy and safety of sidenafil citrate in women with sexual dysfunction associated with female sexual arousal disorder. *Journal of Women's Health and Gender-Based Medicine, 11*, 367–377.

Bauer, Patricia J., & Dow, Gina Annunziato (1994). Episodic memory in 16- and 20-month-old children: Specifics are generalized but not forgotten. *Developmental Psychology, 30*, 403–417.

Baumeister, Roy F. (2000). Gender differences in erotic plasticity: The female sex drive as socially flexible and responsive. *Psychological Bulletin, 126*, 347–374.

Baumeister, Roy F., & Bratslavsky, Ellen (1999). Passion, intimacy, and time: Passionate love as a function of change in intimacy. *Personality and Social Psychology Review, 3*, 49–67.

Baumeister, Roy F.; Campbell, Jennifer D.; Krueger, Joachim I.; & Vohs, Kathleen D. (2003). Does high self-esteem cause better performance, interpersonal success, happiness, or healthier lifestyles? *Psychological Science in the Public Interest, 4*(1)[whole issue].

Baumeister, Roy F.; Catanese, Kathleen R.; & Vohs, Kathleen D. (2001). Is there a gender difference in strength of sex drive? Theoretical views, conceptual distinctions, and a review of relevant evidence. *Personality and Social Psychology Review, 5*, 242–273.

Baumeister, Roy F.; Dale, Karen; & Sommer, Kristin L. (1998). Freudian defense mechanisms and empirical findings in modern social psychology: Reaction formation, projection, displacement, undoing, isolation, sublimation, and denial. *Journal of Personality, 66*, 1081–1124.

Baumeister, Roy F.; Stillwell, Arlene M.; & Heatherton, Todd F. (1994). Guilt: An interpersonal approach. *Psychological Bulletin, 115*, 243–267.

Baumrind, Diana (1989). Rearing competent children. In W. Damon (Ed.), *Child development today and tomorrow*. San Francisco: Jossey-Bass.

Baumrind, Diana (1991). Parenting styles and adolescent development. In R. Lerner, A. C. Petersen, & J. Brooks-Gunn (Eds.), *The encyclopedia of adolescence*. New York: Garland.

Baumrind, Diana; Larzelere, Robert E.; & Cowan, Philip (2002). Ordinary physical punishment—Is it harmful? Commentary on Gershoff's Review. *Psychological Bulletin, 128*, in press.

Baxter, Lewis R.; Schwartz, Jeffrey M.; Bergman, Kenneth S.; et al. (1992). Caudate glucose metabolic rate changes with both drug and behavior therapy for obsessive-compulsive disorder. *Archives of General Psychiatry, 49*, 681–689.

Bechara, Antoine; Dermas, Hanna; Tranel, Daniel; & Damasio, Antonio R. (1997). Deciding advantageously before knowing the advantageous strategy. *Science, 275*, 1293–1294.

Beck, Aaron T. (1976). *Cognitive therapy and the emotional disorders.* New York: International Universities Press.

Beck, Aaron T. (2005). The current state of cognitive therapy: A 40-year retrospective. *Archives of General Psychiatry, 62,* 953–959.

Becker, Selwyn W., & Eagly, Alice H. (2004). The heroism of women and men. *American Psychologist, 59,* 163–178.

Beer, Jeremy M.; Arnold, Richard D.; & Loehlin, John C. (1998). Genetic and environmental influences on MMPI factor scales: Joint model fitting to twin and adoption data. *Journal of Personality and Social Psychology, 74,* 818–827.

Belle, Deborah, & Doucet, Joanne (2003). Poverty, inequality, and discrimination as sources of depression among U.S. women. *Psychology of Women Quarterly, 27,* 101–113.

Belsky, Jay; Hsieh, Kuang-Hua; & Crnic, Keith (1996). Infant positive and negative emotionality: One dimension or two? *Developmental Psychology, 32,* 289–298.

Bem, Daryl J., & Honorton, Charles (1994). Does psi exist? Replicable evidence for an anomalous process of information transfer. *Psychological Bulletin, 115,* 4–18.

Bem, Sandra L. (1993). *The lenses of gender.* New Haven, CT: Yale University Press.

Benedetti, Fabrizio, & Levi-Montalcini, Rita (2001). Opioid and non-opioid mechanisms of placebo analgesia. Paper presented at the annual meeting of the American Psychological Society, Toronto.

Benedetti, Fabrizio; Mayberg, Helen S.; Wager, Tor D. ; et al. (2005, November 9). Neurobiological mechanisms of the placebo effect. *The Journal of Neuroscience, 45,* 10390–10402.

Benjamin, Ludy T., Jr. (1998). Why Gorgeous George, and not Wilhelm Wundt, was the founder of psychology: A history of popular psychology in America. Invited address presented at the National Institute on the Teaching of Psychology, St. Petersburg Beach.

Benjamin, Ludy T., Jr. (2003). Why can't psychology get a stamp? *Journal of Applied Psychoanalytic Studies, 5,* 443–454.

Beran, Michael J., & Beran, Mary M. (2004). Chimpanzees remember the results of one-by-one addition of food items to sets over extended time periods. *Psychological Science, 15,* 94–99.

Bereiter, Carl, & Bird, Marlene (1985). Use of thinking aloud in identification and teaching of reading comprehension strategies. *Cognition and Instruction, 2,* 131–156.

Berenbaum, Sheri A., & Bailey, J. Michael (2003). Effects on gender identity of prenatal androgens and genital appearance: Evidence from girls with congenital adrenal hyperplasia. *Journal of Clinical Endocrinology and Metabolism, 88,* 1102–1106.

Berger, F.; Gage, F. H.; & Vijayaraghavan, S. (1998). Nicotinic receptor-induced apoptotic cell death of hippocampal progenitor cells. *Journal of Neuroscience, 18,* 6871–6881.

Berkman, Lisa F., & Syme, S. Leonard (1979). Social networks, host resistance, and mortality: A nine-year follow-up study of Alameda County residents. *American Journal of Epidemiology, 109,* 186–204.

Berkowitz, Marvin W., & Grych, John H. (2000). Early character development and education. *Early Education & Development, 11,* 55–72.

Bernieri, Frank J.; Davis, Janet M.; Rosenthal, Robert; & Knee, C. Raymond (1991). *Interactional synchrony and the social affordance of rapport: A validation study.* Unpublished manuscript, Oregon State University, Corvallis.

Bernieri, Frank J.; Gillis, John S.; Davis, Janet M.; & Grahe, Jon E. (1996). Dyad rapport and the accuracy of its judgment across situations: A lens model analysis. *Journal of Personality and Social Psychology, 71,* 110–129.

Berntsen, Dorthe, & Thomsen, Dorthe K. (2005). Personal memories for remote historical events: Accuracy and clarity of flashbulb memories related to World War II. *Journal of Experimental Psychology: General, 134,* 242–257.

Berry, John W. (1994). Acculturative stress. In W. J. Lonner & R. S. Malpass (Eds.), *Psychology and culture.* Needham Heights, MA: Allyn & Bacon.

Berscheid, Ellen, & Reis, Harry T. (1998). Attraction and close relationships. In D. T. Gilbert, S. T. Fiske, & G. Lindzey (Eds.), *The handbook of social psychology, Vol. 2* (4th ed.). New York: McGraw-Hill.

Beutler, Larry E. (2000). David and Goliath: When empirical and clinical standards of practice meet. *American Psychologist, 55,* 997–1007.

Beutler, Larry E., & Malik, Mary L. (Eds.) (2002). *Rethinking the DSM: A psychological perspective.* Washington, DC: American Psychological Association.

Beyerstein, Barry L. (1996). Graphology. In G. Stein (Ed.), *The encyclopedia of the paranormal.* Amherst, NY: Prometheus Books.

Beyerstein, Barry L. (1999). Fringe psychotherapies: The public at risk. In W. Sampson (Ed.), *A Guide to Alternative Medicine.* London: Gordon and Breech.

Bierut, Laura Jean; Heath, Andrew C.; Bucholz, Kathleen K.; et al. (1999). Major depressive disorder in a community-based twin sample: Are there different genetic contributions for men and women? *Archives of General Psychiatry, 56,* 557–563.

Birdwhistell, Ray L. (1970). *Kinesics and context: Essays on body motion communication.* Philadelphia: University of Pennsylvania Press.

Birkhead, Tim (2001). *Promiscuity: An evolutionary history of sperm competition.* Cambridge, MA: Harvard University Press.

Bischof, Matthias, & Bassetti, Claudio L. (2004). Total dream loss: A distinct neuropsychological dysfunction after bilateral PCA stroke. *Annals of Neurology,* published online Sept. 10, 2004. (DOI: 10.1002/ana.20246.)

Bjork, Daniel W. (1993). *B. F. Skinner: A life.* New York: Basic Books.

Bjork, Elizabeth L.; Bjork, Robert A.; & Anderson, M. C. (1998). Varieties of goal-directed forgetting. In J. M. Golding & C. M. MacLeod (Eds.), *Intentional forgetting.* Mahwah, NJ: Erlbaum.

Bjork, Robert A. (October, 2000). Human factors 101: How about just trying things out? *APS Observer, 13,* 3, 30.

Bjorkland, D. F. (2000). *Children's thinking: Developmental function and individual differences.* Belmont, CA: Wadsworth.

Blackmore, Susan (2001, March/April). Giving up the ghosts: End of a personal quest. *Skeptical Inquirer, 25.*

Blagrove, Mark (1996). Problems with the cognitive psychological modeling of dreaming. *Journal of Mind and Behavior, 17,* 99–134.

Blair, R. D. J.; Jones, L.; Clark, F.; & Smith, M. (1997). The psychopathic individual: A lack of responsiveness to distress cues? *Psychophysiology, 45,* 192–198.

Blakemore, Colin, & Cooper, Grahame F. (1970). Development of the brain depends on the visual environment. *Nature, 228,* 477–478.

Blass, Thomas (1993). What we know about obedience: Distillations from 30 years of research on the Milgram paradigm. Paper presented at the annual meeting of the American Psychological Association, Toronto.

Blass, Thomas (Ed.) (2000). *Obedience to authority: Current perspectives on the Milgram paradigm.* Mahwah, NJ: Erlbaum.

Blazer, Dan G.; Kessler, Ronald C.; & Swartz, Marvin S. (1998). Epidemiology of recurrent major and minor depression with a seasonal pattern: The National Comorbidity Survey. *British Journal of Psychiatry, 172,* 164–167.

Bleuler, Eugen (1911/1950). *Dementia praecox or the group of schizophrenias.* New York: International Universities Press.

Bliss, T. V., & Collingridge, G. L. (1993). A synaptic model of memory: Long-term potentiation in the hippocampus. *Nature, 361*(6407), 31–39.

Bloom, Mia (2005). *Dying to kill: The allure of suicide terror.* New York: Columbia University Press.

Blum, Deborah (2002). *Love at Goon Park: Harry Harlow and the science of affection.* Cambridge, MA: Perseus Books.

Boesch, Cristophe (1991). Teaching among wild chimpanzees. *Animal Behavior, 41,* 530–532.

Bogaert, Anthony F. (2006, June 28). Biological versus nonbiological older brothers and men's sexual orientation. *Proceedings of the National Academy of Sciences,* published online June 28, 2006, 10.1073/pnas.0511152103.

Bohannon, John N., & Stanowicz, Laura (1988). The issue of negative evidence: Adult responses to children's language errors. *Developmental Psychology, 24,* 684–689.

Bohannon, John N., & Symons, Victoria (1988). Conversational conditions of children's imitation. Paper presented at the biennial Conference on Human Development, Charleston, South Carolina.

Bohman, Michael; Cloninger, R.; Sigvardsson, S.; & von Knorring, Anne-Liis (1987). The genetics of alcoholisms and related disorders. *Journal of Psychiatric Research, 21,* 447–452.

Bonanno, George A. (2004). Loss, trauma, and human resilience. *American Psychologist, 59,* 20–28.

Bonanno, George A.; Galea, Sandro; Bucciarelli, Angela; & Vlahov, David (2006). Psychological resilience after disaster. *Psychological Science, 17,* 181–186.

Bond, Meg A.; Punnett, Laura; Pyle, Jean L.; et al. (2004). Gendered work conditions, health, and work outcomes. *Journal of Occupational Health Psychology, 91,* 28–45.

Bond, Rod, & Smith, Peter B. (1996). Culture and conformity: A meta-analysis of studies using Asch's (1952b, 1956) line judgment task. *Psychological Bulletin, 119,* 111–137.

Bonnet, Michael H. (1990). The perception of sleep onset in insomniacs and normal sleepers. In R. R. Bootzin, J. F. Kihlstrom, & D. L. Schacter (Eds.), *Sleep and cognition.* Washington, DC: American Psychological Association.

Booth, Frank W., & Neufer, P. Darrell (2005). Exercise controls gene expression. *American Scientist, 93,* 28–35.

Borch-Jacobsen, Mikkel (1997, April 24). Sybil—The making of a disease: An interview with Dr. Herbert Spiegel. *The New York Review of Books,* 60–64.

Bordo, Susan (2000). *The male body.* New York: Farrar, Straus and Giroux.

Bornstein, Robert F.; Leone, Dean R.; & Galley, Donna J. (1987). The generalizability of subliminal mere exposure effects: Influence of stimuli perceived without awareness on social behavior. *Journal of Personality and Social Psychology, 53,* 1070–1079.

Boroditsky, Lera (2003). Linguistic relativity. In L. Nadel (Ed.), *Encyclopedia of cognitive science.* London: Nature Publishing Group.

Boroditsky, Lera; Schmidt, Lauren; & Phillips, Webb (2003). Sex, syntax, and semantics. In D. Gentner & S. Goldin-Meadow (Eds.), *Language in mind: Advances in the study of language and thought.* Cambridge: MIT Press.

Bosworth, Hayden B., & Schaie, K. Warner (1999). Survival effects in cognitive function, cognitive style, and sociodemographic variables in the Seattle Longitudinal Study. *Experimental Aging Research, 25,* 121–139.

Bouchard, Claude; Tremblay, A.; Despres, J. P.; et al. (1990, May 24). The response to long-term overfeeding in identical twins. *New England Journal of Medicine, 322,* 1477–1482.

Bouchard, Thomas J., Jr. (1995). Nature's twice-told tale: Identical twins reared apart—what they tell us about human individuality. Paper presented at the annual meeting of the Western Psychological Association, Los Angeles.

Bouchard, Thomas J., Jr. (1997a). The genetics of personality. In K. Blum & E. P. Noble (Eds.), *Handbook of psychiatric genetics.* Boca Raton, FL: CRC Press.

Bouchard, Thomas J., Jr. (1997b). IQ similarity in twins reared apart: Findings and responses to critics. In R. J. Sternberg & E. Grigorenko (Eds.), *Intelligence: Heredity and environment.* New York: Cambridge University Press.

Bouchard, Thomas J., Jr. (2004). Genetic influence on human psychological traits: A survey. *Current Directions in Psychological Science, 13,* 148–151.

Bouchard, Thomas J., Jr., & McGue, Matthew (1981). Familial studies of intelligence: A review. *Science, 212,* 1055–1058.

Bouchard, Thomas J., Jr., & McGue, Matthew (2003). Genetic and environmental influences on human psychological differences. *Journal of Neurobiology, 54,* 4–45.

Bouret, Sebastien G.; Draper, Shin J.; & Simerly, Richard B. (2004). Trophic action of leptin on hypothalamic neurons that regulate feeding. *Science, 304,* 108–110.

Bousfield, W. A. (1953). The occurrence of clustering in the recall of randomly arranged associates. *Journal of General Psychology, 49,* 229–240.

Bowden, Charles L.; Calabrese, Joseph R.; McElroy, Susan L.; et al. (2000). A randomized, placebo-controlled 12-month trial or divalproex and lithium in treatment of outpatients with bipolar I disorder. *Archives of General Psychiatry, 57,* 481–489.

Bowen, Murray (1978). *Family therapy in clinical practice.* New York: Jason Aronson.

Bower, Bruce (1998, February 21). All fired up: Perception may dance to the beat of collective neuronal rhythms. *Science News, 153,* 120–121.

Bowers, Kenneth S.; Regehr, Glenn; Balthazard, Claude; & Parker, Kevin (1990). Intuition in the context of discovery. *Cognitive Psychology, 22,* 72–110.

Bowlby, John (1982). *Attachment and loss. Vol. 1.* Attachment (Rev. ed.). New York: Basic Books.

Bradford, John M., & Pawlak, Anne (1993). Effects of cyproterone acetate on sexual arousal patterns of pedophiles. *Archives of Sexual Behavior, 22,* 629–641.

Brainerd, C. J.; Reyna, V. F.; & Brandse, E. (1995). Are children's false memories more persistent than their true memories? *Psychological Science, 6,* 359–364.

Brauer, Markus; Wasel, Wolfgang; & Niedenthal, Paula (2000). Implicit and explicit components of prejudice. *Review of General Psychology, 4,* 79–101.

Braun, Kathryn A.; Ellis, Rhiannon; & Loftus, Elizabeth F. (2002). Make my memory: How advertising can change our memories of the past. *Psychology & Marketing, 19,* 1–23.

Braungert, J. M.; Plomin, Robert; DeFries, J. C.; & Fulker, D. W. (1992). Genetic influence on tester-rated infant temperament as assessed by Bayley's Infant Behavior Record: Nonadoptive and adoptive siblings and twins. *Developmental Psychology, 28,* 40–47.

Brazelton, Timony R.; Rossi, Fabio M.; Keshet, Gilmor I.; & Blau, Helen M. (2000). From marrow to brain: expression of neuronal phenotypes in adult mice. *Science, 290,* 1775–1779.

Breland, Keller, & Breland, Marian (1961). The misbehavior of organisms. *American Psychologist, 16,* 681–684.

Brennan, Patricia A., & Mednick, Sarnoff A. (1994). Learning theory approach to the deterrence of criminal recidivism. *Journal of Abnormal Psychology, 103,* 430–440.

Brewer, Marilynn B., & Gardner, Wendi (1996). Who is this "we"? Levels of collective identity and self representations. *Journal of Personality and Social Psychology, 71,* 83–93.

Briggs, John (1984, December). The genius mind. *Science Digest, 92*(12), 74–77, 102–103.

Brissette, Ian; Scheier, Michael F.; & Carver, Charles S. (2002). The role of optimism in social network development, coping, and psychological adjustment during a life transition. *Journal of Personality and Social Psychology, 82,* 102–111.

Brockner, Joel, & Rubin, Jeffrey Z. (1985). *Entrapment in escalating conflicts: A social psychological analysis.* New York: Springer-Verlag.

Broks, Paul (2004). *Into the silent land: Travels in neuropsychology* New York: Grove Press.

Brooks-Gunn, J. (1986). Differentiating premenstrual symptoms and syndromes. *Psychosomatic Medicine, 48,* 385–387.

Brown, Alan S. (2004). *The déjà vu experience: Essays in cognitive psychology.* New York: Psychology Press.

Brown, Alan S.; Begg, M. D.; Gravenstein, S.; et al. (2004). Serologic evidence of prenatal influenza in the etiology of schizophrenia. *Archives of General Psychiatry, 61,* 774–780.

Brown Center on Education Policy (2003). *Do students have too much homework?* Washington, DC: Brookings Institution.

Brown, D., Scheflin, A. W., & Whitfield, C. L. (1999). Recovered memories: The current weight of the evidence in science and in the courts. *Journal of Psychiatry and Law, 27,* 5–156.

Brown, George W. (1993). Life events and affective disorder: Replications and limitations. *Psychosomatic Medicine, 55,* 248–259.

Brown, Gregory K.; Ten Have, Thomas; Henriques, Gregg R.; et al. (2005, August 3). Cognitive therapy for the prevention of suicide attempts. *Journal of the American Medical Association, 294,* 563–570.

Brown, Roger (1986). *Social psychology* (2nd ed.). New York: Free Press.

Brown, Roger; Cazden, Courtney; & Bellugi, Ursula (1969). The child's grammar from I to III. In J. P. Hill (Ed.), *Minnesota Symposium on Child Psychology* (Vol. 2). Minneapolis: University of Minnesota Press.

Brown, Roger, & Kulik, James (1977). Flashbulb memories. *Cognition, 5,* 73–99.

Brown, Roger, & McNeill, David (1966). The "tip of the tongue" phenomenon. *Journal of Verbal Learning and Verbal Behavior, 5,* 325–337.

Brown, Ryan P., & Josephs, Robert A. (1999). A burden of proof: Stereotype relevance and gender differences in math performance. *Journal of Personality and Social Psychology, 76,* 246–257.

Brown, Stephanie L.; Nesse, Randolph M.; Vinokur, Amiram D.; & Smith, Dylan M. (2003). Providing social support may be more beneficial than receiving it: Results from a prospective study of mortality. *Psychological Science, 14,* 320–327.

Browning, James R.; Hatfield, Elaine; Kessler, Debra; & Levine, Tim (2000). Sexual motives, gender, and sexual behavior. *Archives of Sexual Behavior, 29,* 135–153.

Bruck, Maggie (2003). Effects of suggestion on the reliability and credibility of children's reports. Invited address at the annual meeting of the American Psychological Society, Atlanta.

Bruck, Maggie; Ceci, Stephen J.; Francoeur, E.; & Renick, A. (1995). Anatomically detailed dolls do not facilitate preschoolers' reports of a pediatric examination involving genital touching. *Journal of Experimental Psychology: Applied, 1,* 95–109.

Bryant, Richard A., & Guthrie, Rachel M. (2005). Maladaptive appraisals as a risk factor for posttraumatic stress. *Psychological Science, 16,* 749–752.

Buchert, R.; Thomasius, R.; Nebeling, B.; et al. (2003). Long-term effects of "ecstasy" use on serotonin transporters of the brain investigated by PET. *Journal of Nuclear Medicine, 44,* 375–384.

Buck, Linda, & Axel, Richard (1991). A novel multigene family may encode odorant receptors: A molecular basis for odor recognition. *Cell, 65,* 175–187.

Budiansky, Stephen (1998). *If a lion could talk: Animal intelligence and the evolution of consciousness.* New York: Free Press.

Bukowski, William M. (2001). Friendship and the worlds of childhood. In D. W. Nangle & C. A. Erdley (Eds.), The role of friendship in psychological adjustment. *New directions for child and adolescent development, No. 91.* San Francisco, CA: Jossey-Bass.

Burke, Deborah M.; MacKay, Donald G.; Worthley, Joanna S.; & Wade, Elizabeth (1991). On the tip of the tongue: What causes word finding failures in young and older adults? *Journal of Memory and Language, 30,* 237–246.

Burke, Deborah M., & Shafto, Meredith A. (2004). Aging and language production. *Current Directions in Psychological Science, 13,* 21–24.

Burke, Phyllis (1996). *Gender shock.* New York: Basic Books.

Burnham, Denis; Kitamura, Christine; & Vollmer-Conna, Uté (2002, May 24). What's new, pussycat? On talking to babies and animals. *Science, 296,* 1435.

Bushman, Brad J. (1995). Moderating role of trait aggressiveness in the effects of violent media on aggression. *Journal of Personality and Social Psychology, 69,* 950–960.

Bushman, Brad J., & Anderson, Craig A. (2001). Media violence and the American public: Scientific facts versus media misinformation. *American Psychologist, 56,* 477–489.

Bushman, Brad J.; Bonacci, Angelica M.; Pedersen, William C.; et al. (2005). Chewing on it can chew you up: Effects of rumination on triggered displaced aggression. *Journal of Personality and Social Psychology, 88,* 969–983.

Bushman, Brad; Bonacci, Angelica M.; van Dijk, Mirjam; & Baumeister, Roy F. (2003). Narcissism, sexual refusal, and aggression: Testing a narcissistic reactance model of sexual coercion. *Journal of Personality and Social Psychology, 84,* 1027–1040.

Buss, David M. (1994). *The evolution of desire: Strategies of human mating.* New York: Basic Books.

Buss, David M. (1995). Evolutionary psychology: A new paradigm for psychological science. *Psychological Inquiry, 6,* 1–30.

Buss, David M. (1996). Sexual conflict: Can evolutionary and feminist perspectives converge? In D. M. Buss & N. Malamuth (Eds.), *Sex, power, conflict: Evolutionary and feminist perspectives.* New York: Oxford University Press.

Bussey, Kay, & Bandura, Albert (1992). Self-regulatory mechanisms governing gender development. *Child Development, 63,* 1236–1250.

Bussey, Kay, & Bandura, Albert (1999). Social-cognitive theory of gender development and differentiation. *Psychological Review, 106,* 676–713.

Butcher, James N.; Lim, Jeeyoung; & Nezami, Elahe (1998). Objective study of abnormal personality in cross-cultural settings: The MMPI-2. *Journal of Cross-Cultural Psychology, 29,* 189–211.

Butler, S.; Chalder, T.; Ron, M.; et al. (1991). Cognitive behaviour therapy in chronic fatigue syndrome. *Journal of Neurology, Neurosurgery & Psychiatry, 54,* 153–158.

Button, T. M. M.; Thapar, A.; & McGuffin, P. (2005). Relationship between antisocial behaviour, attention-deficit hyperactivity disorder and maternal prenatal smoking. *British Journal of Psychiatry. 187*, 155–160.

Buunk, Bram; Angleitner, Alois; Oubaid, Viktor; & Buss, David M. (1996). Sex differences in jealousy in evolutionary and cultural perspective: Tests from the Netherlands, Germany, and the United States. *Psychological Science, 7*, 359–363.

Buxbaum, Laurel J.; Kyle, Kathleen M.; & Menon, Rukmini (2005). On beyond mirror neurons: Internal representations subserving imitation and recognition of skilled object-related actions in humans. *Cognitive Brain Research, 25*, 226–239.

Byne, William (1995). Science and belief: Psychobiological research on sexual orientation. *Journal of Homosexuality, 28*, 303–344.

Cabiya, Jose J.; Lucio, Emilia; Chavira, Denise A.; et al. (2000). MMPI-2 scores of Puerto Rican, Mexican, and U.S. Latino college students: A research note. *Psychological Reports, 87*, 266–268.

Cacioppo, J. T.; Berntson, G. G.; Lorig, Tyler S.; et al. (2003). Just because you're imaging the brain doesn't mean you can stop using your head: A primer and set of first principles. *Journal of Personality and Social Psychology, 85*, 650–661.

Cadinu, Mara; Maass, Anne; Rosabianca, Alessandra; & Kiesner, Jeff (2005). Why do women underperform under stereotype threat? Evidence for the role of negative thinking. *Psychological Science, 16*, 472–578.

Cahill, Larry (2005, May). His brain, her brain. *Scientific American, 292*, 40–47.

Cahill, Larry; Prins, Bruce; Weber, Michael; & McGaugh, James L. (1994). ß-adrenergic activation and memory for emotional events. *Nature, 371*, 702–704.

Calder, A. J.; Keane, J.; Manes, F.; Antoun, N.; & Young, A. W. (2000). Impaired recognition and experience of disgust following brain injury. *Nature Neuroscience, 3*, 1077–1078.

Cameron, Judy; Banko, Katherine M.; & Pierce, W. David (2001). Pervasive negative effects of rewards on intrinsic motivation: The myth continues. *Behavior Analyst, 24*, 1–44.

Campbell, Benjamin C.; Pope, Harrison G.; & Filiault, Shaun (2005). Body image among Ariaal men from Northern Kenya. *Journal of Cross-Cultural Psychology, 36*, 371–379.

Campbell, Frances A., & Ramey, Craig T. (1995). Cognitive and school outcomes for high risk students at middle adolescence: Positive effects of early intervention. *American Educational Research Journal, 32*, 743–772.

Campbell, Jennifer; Trapnell, Paul D.; Heine, Steven J.; et al. (1996). Self-concept clarity: Measurement, personality correlates, and cultural boundaries. *Journal of Personality and Social Psychology, 70*, 141–156.

Campbell, Joseph (1949/1968). *The hero with 1,000 faces* (2nd ed.). Princeton, NJ: Princeton University Press.

Cancian, Francesca M. (1987). *Love in America: Gender and self-development*. Cambridge, England: Cambridge University Press.

Canetto, Silvia S. (1992). Suicide attempts and substance abuse: Similarities and differences. *Journal of Psychology, 125*, 605–620.

Canino, Glorisa (1994). Alcohol use and misuse among Hispanic women: Selected factors, processes, and studies. *International Journal of the Addictions, 29*, 1083–1100.

Cannon, Tyrone D.; Huttunen, Matti O.; Loennqvist, Jouko; et al. (2000). The inheritance of neuropsychological dysfunction in twins discordant for schizophrenia. *American Journal of Human Genetics, 67*, 369–382.

Cannon, Tyrone D.; Kaprio, Jaakko; Loennqvist, Jouko; Huttunen, Matti O.; & Koskenvuo, Markku (1998). The genetic epidemiology of schizophrenia in a Finnish twin cohort: A population-based modeling study. *Archives of General Psychiatry, 55*, 67–74.

Cannon, Walter B. (1929). *Bodily changes in pain, hunger, fear and rage* (2nd ed.). New York: Appleton.

Capaldi, Deborah M.; Pears, Katherine C.; Patterson, Gerald R.; & Owen, Lee D. (2003). Continuity of parenting practices across generations in an at-risk sample: A prospective comparison of direct and mediated associations. *Journal of Abnormal Child Psychology, 31*, 127–142.

Carnagey, Nicholas L., & Anderson, Craig A. (2005). The effects of reward and punishment in violent video games on aggressive affect, cognition, and behavior. *Psychological Science, 16*, 882–889.

Carskadon, Mary A.; Mitler, Merrill M.; & Dement, William C. (1974). A comparison of insomniacs and normals: Total sleep time and sleep latency. *Sleep Research, 3*, 130 [Abstract].

Carter, Betty, & McGoldrick, Monica (Eds.) (1988). *The changing family life cycle: A framework for family therapy* (2nd ed.). New York: Gardner Press.

Cartwright, Rosalind (1977). *Night life: Explorations in dreaming*. Englewood Cliffs, NJ: Prentice-Hall.

Cartwright, Rosalind D. (1996). Dreams and adaptations to divorce. In D. Barrett (Ed.), *Trauma and dreams*. Cambridge: Harvard University Press.

Cartwright, Rosalind D.; Young, Michael A.; Mercer, Patricia; & Bears, Michael (1998). Role of REM sleep and dream variables in the prediction of remission from depression. *Psychiatry Research, 80*, 249–255.

Carver, Charles S. (1998). Resilience and thriving: Issues, models, and linkages. *Journal of Social Issues, 54*, 245–266.

Carver, Charles S., & Baird, Eryn (1998). The American dream revisited: Is it *what* you want or *why* you want it that matters? *Psychological Science, 9*, 289–292.

Carver, Charles S., & Scheier, Michael F. (1999). Optimism. In C. R. Snyder (Ed.), *Coping: The psychology of what works*. New York: Oxford University Press.

Caspi, Avshalom (2000). The child is father of the man: Personality continuities from childhood to adulthood. *Journal of Personality and Social Psychology, 78*, 158–172.

Caspi, Avshalom; McClay, Joseph; Moffitt, Terrie E.; et al. (2002, August 2). Role of genotype in the cycle of violence in maltreated children. *Science, 297*, 851–857.

Caspi, Avshalom, & Moffitt, Terrie E. (1991). Individual differences are accentuated during periods of social change: The sample case of girls at puberty. *Journal of Personality and Social Psychology, 61*, 157–168.

Caspi, Avshalom; Sugden, Karen; Moffitt, Terrie E.; et al. (2003). Influence of life stress on depression: Moderation by a polymorphism in the 5-HTT gene. *Science, 301*, 386–389.

Cattell, Raymond B. (1965). *The scientific analysis of personality*. Baltimore, MD: Penguin.

Cattell, Raymond B. (1973). *Personality and mood by questionnaire*. San Francisco: Jossey-Bass.

Ceci, Stephen J., & Bruck, Maggie (1995). *Jeopardy in the courtroom: A scientific analysis of children's testimony*. Washington, DC: American Psychological Association.

Cejka, Mary Ann, & Eagly, Alice H. (1999). Gender-stereotypic images of occupations correspond to the sex segregation of employment. *Personality and Social Psychology Bulletin, 25*, 413–423.

Cermak, Laird S., & Craik, Fergus I. M. (Eds.) (1979). *Levels of processing in human memory*. Hillsdale, NJ: Erlbaum.

Cervone, Daniel, & Shoda, Yuichi (1999). Beyond traits in the study of personality coherence. *Current Directions in Psychological Science, 8*, 27–32.

Chambless, Dianne L., & Ollendick, T. H. (2001). Empirically supported psychological interventions: Controversies and evidence. *Annual Review of Psychology, 52,* 685–716.

Chambless, Dianne L.; & the Task Force on Psychological Interventions (1998). Update on empirically validated therapies II. *The Clinical Psychologist, 51,* 3–16.

Chance, Paul (1999). *Learning and behavior* (4th ed.). Pacific Grove: Brooks/Cole.

Chandra, R. K. (2001). Effect of vitamin and trace-element supplementation on cognitive function in elderly subjects. *Nutrition, 17,* 709–712.

Chang, Edward C. (1998). Dispositional optimism and primary and secondary appraisal of a stressor. *Journal of Personality and Social Psychology, 74,* 1109–1120.

Chang, Kenneth (2000, September 12). Can robots rule the world? Not yet. *New York Times, Science section,* B1.

Charles, S. T., & Carstensen, Laura L. (2004). A life-span view of emotional functioning in adulthood and old age. In P. Costa (Ed.), *Recent advances in psychology and aging* (Vol. 15). Amsterdam: Elsevier.

Charles, Susan T.; Reynolds, Chandra A.; & Gatz, Margaret (2001). Age-related differences and change in positive and negative affect over 23 years. *Journal of Personality and Social Psychology, 80,* 136–151.

Chaudhari, Nirupa ; Landin, A. M.; & Roper, S. D. (2000). A metabotropic glutamate receptor variant functions as a taste receptor. *Nature Neuroscience, 3,* 113–119.

Chaves, J. F. (1989). Hypnotic control of clinical pain. In N. P. Spanos & J. F. Chaves (Eds.), *Hypnosis: The cognitive-behavioral perspective.* Buffalo, NY: Prometheus Books.

Chehab, Farid F.; Mounzih, K.; Lu, R.; & Lim, M. E. (1997, January 3). Early onset of reproductive function in normal female mice treated with leptin. *Science, 275,* 88–90.

Chipuer, Heather M.; Rovine, Michael J.; & Plomin, Robert (1990). LISREL modeling: Genetic and environmental influences on IQ revisited. *Intelligence, 14,* 11–29.

Choi, Incheol; Dalal, Reeshad; Kim-Prieto, Chu; & Park, Hyekyung (2003).Culture and judgment of causal relevance. *Journal of Personality and Social Psychology, 84,* 46–59.

Choi, Incheol, & Nisbett, Richard (2000). Cultural psychology of surprise: Holistic theories and recognition of contradiction. *Journal of Personality and Social Psychology, 79,* 890–905.

Chomsky, Noam (1957). *Syntactic structures.* The Hague, Netherlands: Mouton.

Chomsky, Noam (1980). Initial states and steady states. In M. Piatelli-Palmerini (Ed.), *Language and learning: The debate between Jean Piaget and Noam Chomsky.* Cambridge, MA: Harvard University Press.

Chorpita, Bruce F., & Barlow, David H. (1998). The development of anxiety: The role of control in the early environment. *Psychological Bulletin, 124,* 3–21.

Chrisler, Joan C. (2000). PMS as a culture-bound syndrome. In J. C. Chrisler, C. Golden, & P. D. Rozee (Eds.), *Lectures on the psychology of women* (2nd ed.). New York: McGraw-Hill.

Christakis, Dimitri A.; Zimmerman, Frederick J.; DiGiuseppe, David L.; & McCarty, Carolyn A. (2004). Early television exposure and subsequent attentional problems in children. *Pediatrics, 113,* 708–713.

Christensen, Andrew, & Jacobson, Neil S. (2000). *Reconcilable differences.* New York: Guilford.

Christensen, Larry, & Burrows, Ross (1990). Dietary treatment of depression. *Behavior Therapy, 21,* 183–194.

Chun, Kevin M.; Organista, Pamela B.; & Marin, Gerardo (Eds.) (2002). *Acculturation: Advances in theory, measurement, and applied research.* Washington, DC: American Psychological Association.

Chung, Young; Klimanskaya, Irina; Becker, Sandy; et al. (2005). Embryonic and extraembryonic stem cell lines derived from single mouse blastomeres. *Nature, 439,* 216–219.

Church, A. Timothy, & Lonner, Walter J. (1998). The cross-cultural perspective in the study of personality: Rationale and current research. *Journal of Cross-Cultural Psychology, 29,* 32–62.

Cialdini, Robert B. (2001). *Influence: Science and practice* (4th ed.). Boston: Allyn & Bacon.

Cialdini, Robert B.; Trost, Melanie R.; & Newsom, Jason T. (1995). Preference for consistency: The development of a valid measure and the discovery of surprising behavioral implications. *Journal of Personality and Social Psychology, 69,* 318–328.

Cinque, Guglielmo (1999). *Adverbs and functional heads: A cross-linguistic approach.* New York: Oxford University Press.

Cioffi, Delia, & Holloway, James (1993). Delayed costs of suppressed pain. *Journal of Personality and Social Psychology, 64,* 274–282.

Cioffi, Frank (1998). *Freud and the question of pseudoscience.* Chicago, IL: Open Court.

Clancy, Susan A. (2005). *Abducted: How people come to believe they were kidnapped by aliens.* Cambridge, MA: Harvard University Press.

Clark, Margaret S.; Milberg, Sandra; & Erber, Ralph (1987). Arousal state dependent memory: Evidence and some implications for understanding social judgments and social behavior. In K. Fiedler & J. P. Forgas (Eds.), *Affect, cognition and social behavior.* Toronto, Canada: Hogrefe.

Clark, Rodney; Anderson, Norman B.; Clark, Vernessa R.; & Williams, David R. (1999). Racism as a stressor for African Americans: A biopsychosocial model. *American Psychologist, 54,* 805–816.

Clarke, H. F.; Dalley, J. W.; Crofts, H. S.; et al. (2004, May 7). Cognitive inflexibility after prefrontal serotonin depletion. *Science, 304,* 878–880.

Clarke, Peter, & Evans, Susan H. (1998). *Surviving modern medicine.* Rutgers, NJ: Rutgers University Press.

Clarke-Stewart, Allison; Malloy, Lindsay C.; & Allhusen, Virginia D. (2004). Verbal ability, self-control, and close relationships with parents protect children against misleading suggestions. *Applied Cognitive Psychology, 18,* 1037–1058.

Cleckley, Hervey (1976). *The mask of sanity* (5th ed.). St. Louis, MO: Mosby.

Cloninger, C. Robert (1990). *The genetics and biology of alcoholism.* Cold Springs Harbor, ME: Cold Springs Harbor Press.

Coan, James A.; Schaefer, Hillary; & Davidson, Richard J. (2006). Lending a hand: Social regulation of the neural response to threat. *Psychological Science, 17.*

Coats, Erik J.; Janoff-Bulman, Ronnie; & Alpert, Nancy (1996). Approach versus avoidance goals: Differences in self-evaluation and well-being. *Personality and Social Psychology Bulletin, 22,* 1057–1067.

Cohen, David B. (1999). *Stranger in the nest: Do parents really shape their child's personality, intelligence, or character?* New York: Wiley.

Cohen, Dov (1998). Culture, social organization, and patterns of violence. *Journal of Personality and Social Psychology, 75,* 408–419.

Cohen, Dov; Nisbett, Richard E.; Bowdle, Brian F.; & Schwarz, Norbert (1996). Insult, aggression, and the Southern culture of honor: An "experimental ethnography." *Journal of Personality and Social Psychology, 70,* 945–960.

Cohen, Sheldon; Doyle, W. J.; Skoner, D. P.; et al. (1997). Social ties and susceptibility to the common cold. *Journal of the American Medical Association, 277,* 1940–1944.

Cohen, Sheldon; Evans, Gary W.; Krantz, David S.; & Stokols, Daniel (1980). Physiological, motivational, and cognitive effects of aircraft noise on children. *American Psychologist, 35,* 231–243.

Cohen, Sheldon; Frank, Ellen; Doyle, William J.; et al. (1998). Types of stressors that increase susceptibility to the common cold in healthy adults. *Health Psychology, 17,* 214–223.

Cohen, Sheldon; Tyrrell, David A.; & Smith, Andrew P. (1993). Negative life events, perceived stress, negative affect, and susceptibility to the common cold. *Journal of Personality and Social Psychology, 64,* 131–140.

Colcombe, Stanley, & Kramer, Arthur F. (2003). Fitness effects on the cognitive function of older adults: A meta-analytic study. *Psychological Science, 14,* 125–130.

Cole, Michael, & Scribner, Sylvia (1974). *Culture and thought.* New York: Wiley.

Collaer, Marcia L., & Hines, Melissa (1995). Human behavioral sex differences: A role for gonadal hormones during early development? *Psychological Bulletin, 118,* 55–107.

Collins, Allan M., & Loftus, Elizabeth F. (1975). A spreading-activation theory of semantic processing. *Psychological Review, 82,* 407–428.

Collins, Barry E., & Brief, Diana E. (1995). Using person-perception vignette methodologies to uncover the symbolic meanings of teacher behaviors in the Milgram paradigm. *Journal of Social Issues, 51,* 89–106.

Collins, W. Andrew; Maccoby, Eleanor E.; Steinberg, Laurence; Hetherington, E. Mavis; & Bornstein, Marc H. (2000). Contemporary research on parenting: The case of nature and nurture. *American Psychologist, 55,* 218–232.

Comas-Díaz, Lillian, & Greene, Beverly (1994). *Women of color: Integrating ethnic and gender identities in psychotherapy.* New York: Guilford.

Comuzzie, Anthony G., & Allison, David B. (1998). The search for human obesity genes. *Science, 280,* 1374–1377.

Conklin, Heather M., & Iacono, William G. (2002). Schizophrenia: A neurodevelopmental perspective. *Current Directions in Psychological Science, 11,* 33–37.

Conroy, John (2000). *Unspeakable acts, ordinary people: The dynamics of torture.* New York: Knopf.

Cooper, M. Lynne; Frone, Michael R.; Russell, Marcia; & Mudar, Pamela (1995). Drinking to regulate positive and negative emotions: A motivational model of alcohol use. *Journal of Personality and Social Psychology, 69,* 990–1005.

Cooper, M. Lynne; Shapiro, Cheryl M.; & Powers, Anne M. (1998). Motivations for sex and risky sexual behavior among adolescents and young adults: A functional perspective. *Journal of Personality and Social Psychology, 75,* 1528–1558.

Corkin, Suzanne (1984). Lasting consequences of bilateral medial temporal lobectomy: Clinical course and experimental findings in H. M. *Seminars in Neurology, 4,* 249–259.

Corkin, Suzanne; Amaral, David G.; Gonzalez, R. Gilberto; et al. (1997). H. M.'s medial temporal lobe lesion: Findings from magnetic resonance imaging. *Journal of Neuroscience, 17,* 3964–3979.

Cosgrove, G. R., & Rauch, S. L. (2003). Stereotactic cingulotomy. *Neurosurg Clin North America, 14,* 225–235.

Costa, Paul T., Jr.; McCrae, Robert R.; Martin, Thomas A.; et al. (1999). Personality development from adolescence through adulthood: Further cross-cultural comparisons of age differences. In V. J. Molfese & D. Molfese (Eds.), *Temperament and personality development across the life span.* Hillsdale, NJ: Erlbaum.

Costantino, Giuseppe, & Malgady, Robert G. (1996). Culturally sensitive treatment: Cuento and hero/heroine modeling therapies for Hispanic children and adolescents. In E. D. Hibbs & P. S. Jensen (Eds.), *Psychosocial treatments for child and adolescent disorders: Empirically based strategies for clinical practice.* Washington, DC: American Psychological Association.

Cota-Robles, S.; Neiss, M.; & Rowe, D. C. (2002). The role of puberty in violent and nonviolent delinquency among Anglo American, Mexican American, and African American boys. *Journal of Adolescent Research, 17,* 364–376.

Council, J. R.; Kirsch, Irving; & Grant, D. L. (1996). Imagination, expectancy and hypnotic responding. In R. G. Kunzendorf, N. K. Spanos, & B. J. Wallace (Eds.), *Hypnosis and imagination.* Amityville, NY: Baywood.

Courage, Mary L., & Howe, Mark L. (2002). From infant to child: The dynamics of cognitive change in the second year of life. *Psychological Bulletin, 128,* 250–277.

Cowan, Nelson (2001). The magical number 4 in short-term memory: A reconsideration of mental storage capacity. *Behavioral and Brain Sciences, 24,* 87–185.

Cowen, Emory L.; Wyman, Peter A.; Work, William C.; & Parker, Gayle R. (1990). The Rochester Child Resilience Project (RCRP): Overview and summary of first year findings. *Development and Psychopathology, 2,* 193–212.

Cox, W. Michael, and Alm, Richard (2005, February 28). Scientists are made, not born. *The New York Times* op-ed page (online).

Craik, Fergus I. M. & Lockhart, Robert (1972). Levels of processing: A framework for memory research. *Journal of Verbal Learning and Verbal Behavior, 11,* 671–684.

Craik, Fergus I. M., & Tulving, Endel (1975). Depth of processing and the retention of words in episodic memory. *Journal of Experimental Psychology: General, 104,* 268–294.

Crair, Michael C.; Gillespie, Deda C.; & Stryker, Michael P. (1998). The role of visual experience in the development of columns in cat visual cortex. *Science, 279,* 566–570.

Cramer, Phebe (2000). Defense mechanisms in psychology today: Further processes for adaptation. *American Psychologist, 55,* 637–646.

Crandall, Christian S., & Eshelman, Amy (2003). A justification-suppression model of the expression and experience of prejudice. *Psychological Bulletin, 129,* 414–446.

Crandall, Christian S., & Martinez, Rebecca (1996). Culture, ideology, and antifat attitudes. *Personality and Social Psychology Bulletin, 22,* 1165–1176.

Crews, Frederick (Ed.) (1998). *Unauthorized Freud: Doubters confront a legend.* New York: Viking.

Critchlow, Barbara (1986). The powers of John Barleycorn: Beliefs about the effects of alcohol on social behavior. *American Psychologist, 41,* 751–764.

Crits-Christoph, Paul; Wilson, G. Terence; & Hollon, Steven D. (2005). Empirically supported psychotherapies: Comment on Westen, Novotny, and Thompson-Brenner (2004). *Psychological Bulletin, 131,* 412–417.

Critser, Greg (2002). *Supersize.* New York: Houghton-Mifflin.

Croizen, Jean-Claude, & Claire, Theresa (1998). Extending the concept of stereotype threat to social class: The intellectual underperformance of students from low socioeconomic backgrounds. *Personality and Social Psychology Bulletin, 24,* 588–594.

Crombag, Hans S., & Robinson, Terry E. (2004). Drugs, environment, brain, and behavior. *Current Directions in Psychological Science, 13,* 107–111.

Cronbach, Lee (1990). *Essentials of psychological testing* (5th ed.). New York: Harper & Row.

Cummings, Brian J.; Uchida, Nobuko; Tamaki, Stanley J.; et al. (2005). Human neural stem cells differentiate and promote locomotor recovery in spinal cord–injured mice. *Proceedings of the National Academy of Science, 102,* 14069–14074.

Cunningham, William A.; Preacher, Kristopher J.; & Banaji, Mahzarin R. (2001). Implicit attitude measures: Consistency, stability, and convergent validity. *Psychological Science, 12,* 163–170.

Currie, Elliot (1998). *Crime and punishment in America.* New York: Henry Holt.

Curtiss, Susan (1977). *Genie: A psycholinguistic study of a modern-day "wild child."* New York: Academic Press.

Curtiss, Susan (1982). Developmental dissociations of language and cognition. In L. Obler & D. Fein (Eds.), *Exceptional language and linguistics.* New York: Academic Press.

Cytowic, Richard E. (2002). *Synethesia: A union of the senses* (2nd ed.). Cambridge, MA: MIT Press.

Czeisler, Charles A.; Duffy, Jeanne F.; Shanahan, Theresa L.; et al. (1999). Stability, precision, and near-24-hour period of the human circadian pacemaker. *Science, 284,* 2177–2181.

Dabbs, James M., Jr. (2000). *Heroes, rogues, and lovers: Testosterone and behavior.* New York: McGraw-Hill.

Dadds, Mark R.; Bovbjerg, Dana H.; Redd, William H.; & Cutmore, Tim R. H. (1997). Imagery in human classical conditioning. *Psychological Bulletin, 122,* 89–103.

Daley, Tamara C.; Whaley, Shannon E.; Sigman, Marian D.; et al. (2003). IQ on the rise: The Flynn Effect in rural Kenyan children. *Psychological Science, 14,* 215–219.

Dalgleish, Tim (2004). Cognitive approaches to posttraumatic stress disorder: The evolution of multirepresentational theorizing. *Psychological Bulletin, 130,* 228–260.

Dalton, K. S.; Morris, D. L.; Delanoy, D. I.; et al. (1996). Security measures in an automated ganzfeld system. *Journal of Parapsychology, 60,* 129–147.

Daly, Martin, & Wilson, Margo (1983). *Sex, evolution, and behavior* (2nd ed.). Belmont, CA: Wadsworth.

Damak, Sami; Rong, Minqing; Yasumatsu, Keiko; et al. (2003). Detection of sweet and umami taste in the absence of taste receptor T1r3. *Science, 301,* 850–853.

Damasio, Antonio R. (1994). *Descartes' error: Emotion, reason, and the human brain.* New York: Grosset/Putnam.

Damasio, Antonio R. (2003). *Looking for Spinoza: Joy, sorrow, and the feeling brain.* San Diego: Harcourt.

Damasio, A. R.; Grabowski, T. J.; Bechara, A.; et al. (2000). Subcortical and cortical brain activity during the feeling of self-generated emotions. *Nature Neuroscience, 3,* 1049–1056.

Damasio, Hanna; Grabowski, Thomas J.; Frank, Randall; et al. (1994). The return of Phineas Gage: Clues about the brain from the skull of a famous patient. *Science, 264,* 1102–1105.

Damasio, Hanna; Grabowski, Thomas J.; Tranel, Daniel; et al. (1996). A neural basis for lexical retrieval. *Nature, 380,* 499–505.

Damon, William (1995). *Greater expectations.* New York: Free Press.

Danner, Deborah D.; Snowdon, David A.; & Friesen, Wallace V. (2001). Positive emotions in early life and longevity: Findings from the nun study. *Journal of Personality and Social Psychology, 80,* 804–813.

Darley, John M. (1995). Constructive and destructive obedience: A taxonomy of principal agent relationships. In A. G. Miller, B. E. Collins, & D. E. Brief (Eds.), Perspectives on obedience to authority: The legacy of the Milgram experiments. *Journal of Social Issues, 51*(3), 125–154.

Darley, John M., & Latane, Bibb (1968). Bystander intervention in emergencies: Diffusion of responsibility. *Journal of Personality and Social Psychology, 8,* 377–383.

Dasen, Pierre R. (1994). Culture and cognitive development from a Piagetian perspective. In W. J. Lonner & R. S. Malpass (Eds.), *Psychology and culture.* Needham Heights, MA: Allyn & Bacon.

Daum, Irene, & Schugens, Markus M. (1996). On the cerebellum and classical conditioning. *Psychological Science, 5,* 58–61.

Davelaar, Eddy J.; Goshen-Gottstein, Yonatan; Ashkenazi, Amir; et al. (2004). The demise of short-term memory revisited: Empirical and computational investigations of recency effects. *Psychological Review, 112,* 3–42.

Davey, Graham C. (1992). Classical conditioning and the acquisition of human fears and phobias: A review and synthesis of the literature. *Advances in Behaviour Research and Therapy, 14,* 29–66.

Davidson, Richard J.; Abercrombie, H.; Nitschke, J. B.; & Putnam, K. (1999). Regional brain function, emotion, and disorders of emotion. *Current Opinion in Neurobiology, 9,* 228–234.

Davidson, Richard J.; Kabat-Zinn, J.; Schumacher, J.; et al. (2003). Alterations in brain and immune function produced by mindfulness meditation. *Psychosomatic Medicine, 65,* 564–570.

Davies, Michael J.; Baer, David J.; Judd, Joseph T; et al. (2002). Effects of moderate alcohol intake on fasting insulin and glucose concentrations and insulin sensitivity in postmenopausal women: A randomized controlled trial. *Journal of the American Medical Association, 287,* 2559–2562.

Davies, Michaela; Stankov, Lazar; & Roberts, Richard D. (1998). Emotional intelligence: In search of an elusive construct. *Journal of Personality and Social Psychology, 75,* 989–1015.

Davis, B. E.; Moon, R. Y.; Sachs, H. C.; & Ottolini, M. C. (1998). Effects of sleep position on infant motor development. *Pediatrics, 102,* 1135–1140.

Davis, Karen D.; Kiss, Z. H.; Luo, L.; et al. (1998). Phantom sensations generated by thalamic microstimulation. *Nature, 391,* 385–387.

Davison, Gerald C. (1976). Homosexuality: The ethical challenge. *Journal of Consulting and Clinical Psychology, 44,* 157–162.

Davison, Kathryn P.; Pennebaker, James W.; & Dickerson, Sally S. (2000). Who talks? The social psychology of illness support groups. *American Psychologist, 55,* 205–217.

Dawes, Robyn M. (1994). *House of cards: Psychology and psychotherapy built on myth.* New York: Free Press.

Dawson, Neal V.; Arkes, Hal R.; Siciliano, C.; et al. (1988). Hindsight bias: An impediment to accurate probability estimation in clinicopathologic conferences. *Medical Decision Making, 8*(4), 259–264.

Dean, Geoffrey (1992). The bottom line: Effect size. In B. Beyerstein & D. Beyerstein (Eds.), *The write stuff: Evaluations of graphology-The study of handwriting analysis.* Buffalo, NY: Prometheus Books.

Deci, Edward L.; Koestner, Richard; & Ryan, Richard M. (1999). A meta-analytic review of experiments examining the effects of extrinsic rewards on intrinsic motivation. *Psychological Bulletin, 125,* 627–668.

Deci, Edward L., & Ryan, Richard M. (1985). *Intrinsic motivation and self-determination of human behavior.* New York: Plenum.

Deffenbacher, Jerry L.; Deffenbacher, David M.; Lynch, Rebekah S.; & Richards, Tracy L. (2003). Anger, aggression and risky behavior: A comparison of high and low anger drivers. *Behaviour Research and Therapy, 41,* 701–718.

Dement, William (1978). *Some must watch while some must sleep.* New York: Norton.

Dement, William (1992). *The sleepwatchers.* Stanford, CA: Stanford Alumni Association.

Dennett, Daniel C. (1991). *Consciousness explained.* Boston: Little, Brown.

Denning, Patt; Little, Jeannie; & Glickman, Adina (2004). *Over the influence: The harm reduction guide for managing drugs and alcohol.* New York: Guilford.

Denny, Dallas (Ed.) (1998). *Current concepts in transgender identity.* New York: Garland Press.

DePaulo, Bella M. (1992). Nonverbal behavior and self-presentation. *Psychological Bulletin, 111,* 203–243.

de Rivera, Joseph (1989). Comparing experiences across cultures: Shame and guilt in America and Japan. *Hiroshima Forum for Psychology, 14,* 13–20.

De Robertis, Michael M., & Delaney, Paul A. (2000). A second survey of the attitudes of university students to astrology and astronomy. *Journal of the Royal Astronomical Society of Canada, 94,* 112–122.

DeValois, Russell L., & DeValois, Karen K. (1975). Neural coding of color. In E. C. Carterette & M. P. Friedman (Eds.), *Handbook of perception* (Vol. 5). New York: Academic Press.

Devlin, B.; Daniels, Michael; & Roeder, Kathryn (1997). The heritability of IQ. *Nature, 388,* 468–471.

de Waal, Frans (1997, July). Are we in anthropodenial? *Discover,* 50–53.

de Waal, Frans (2001a). *The ape and the sushi master: Cultural reflections by a primatologist.* New York: Basic Books.

De Wolff, Marianne, & van Ijzendoorn, Marinus H. (1997). Sensitivity and attachment: A meta-analysis on parental antecedents of infant attachment. *Child Development, 68,* 571–591.

Diamond, Lisa M. (2003). Was it a phase? Young women's relinquishment of lesbian/bisexual identities over a 5-year period. *Journal of Personality and Social Psychology, 84,* 352–364.

Diamond, Lisa M. (2004). Emerging perspectives on distinctions between romantic love and sexual desire. *Current Directions in Psychological Science, 13,* 116–119.

Diamond, Marian C. (1993, Winter–Spring). An optimistic view of the aging brain. *Generations, 17,* 31–33.

Dickerson, Sally S., & Kemeny, Margaret E. (2004). Acute stressors and cortisol responses: A theoretical integration and synthesis of laboratory research. *Psychological Bulletin, 130,* 355–391.

Dickinson, Alyce M. (1989). The detrimental effects of extrinsic reinforcement on "intrinsic motivation." *The Behavior Analyst, 12,* 1–15.

Dien, Dora S. (1999). Chinese authority-directed orientation and Japanese peer-group orientation: Questioning the notion of collectivism. *Review of General Psychology, 3,* 372–385.

Digman, John M., & Shmelyov, Alexander G. (1996). The structure of temperament and personality in Russian children. *Journal of Personality and Social Psychology, 71,* 341–351.

Dijksterhuis, Ap; Bos, Maarten W.; Nordgren, Loran F.; & van Baaren, Rick B. (2006). On making the right choice: The deliberation-without-attention effect. *Science, 311,* 1005–1007.

Dimberg, Ulf; Thunberg, Monika; & Elmehed, Kurt (2000). Unconscious facial reactions to emotional facial expressions. *Psychological Science, 11,* 86–89.

Dinges, David F.; Whitehouse, Wayne G.; Orne, Emily C.; Powell, John W.; Orne, Martin T.; & Erdelyi, Matthew H. (1992). Evaluating hypnotic memory enhancement (hypermnesia and reminiscence) using multitrial forced recall. *Journal of Experimental Psychology: Learning, Memory, and Cognition, 18,* 1139–1147.

Dinn, W. M., & Harris, C. L. (2000). Neurocognitive function in antisocial personality disorder. *Psychiatry Research, 97,* 173–190.

Dion, Kenneth L., & Dion, Karen K. (1993). Gender and ethnocultural comparisons in styles of love. *Psychology of Women Quarterly, 17,* 463–474.

Doering, Stephan; Katzlberger, Florian; Rumpold, Gerhard; et al. (2000). Videotape preparation of patients before hip replacement surgery reduces stress. *Psychosomatic Medicine, 62,* 365–373.

Dollard, John, & Miller, Neal E. (1950). *Personality and psychotherapy: An analysis in terms of learning, thinking, and culture.* New York: McGraw-Hill.

Dolnick, Edward (1990, July). What dreams are (really) made of. *The Atlantic Monthly, 226,* 41–45, 48–53, 56–58, 60–61.

Domhoff, G. William (1996). *Finding meaning in dreams: A quantitative approach.* New York: Plenum.

Domhoff, G. William (2003). *The scientific study of dreams: Neural networks, cognitive development, and content analysis.* Washington, DC: American Psychological Association.

Doty, Richard M.; Peterson, Bill E.; & Winter, David G. (1991). Threat and authoritarianism in the United States, 1978–1987. *Journal of Personality and Social Psychology, 61,* 629–640.

Dovidio, John F. (2001). On the nature of contemporary prejudice: The third wave. *Journal of Social Issues, 57,* 829–849.

Dovidio, John F., & Gaertner, Samuel L. (2000). Aversive racism and selection decisions: 1989 and 1999. *Psychological Science, 11,* 315–319.

Dovidio, John F.; Gaertner, Samuel L.; & Validzic, Ana (1998). Intergroup bias: Status, differentiation, and a common in-group identity. *Journal of Personality and Social Psychology, 75,* 109–120.

Drevets, W. C. (2000). Neuroimaging studies of mood disorders. *Biological Psychiatry, 48,* 813–829.

Drieschner, K., & Lange, A. (1999). A review of cognitive factors in the etiology of rape: Theories, empirical studies, and implications. *Clinical Psychology Review, 19,* 57–77.

Druckman, Daniel, & Swets, John A. (Eds.) (1988). *Enhancing human performance: Issues, theories, and techniques.* Washington, DC: National Academy Press.

Duckworth, Angela L., & Seligman, Martin E. P. (2005). Self-discipline outdoes IQ in predicting academic performance of adolescents. *Psychological Science, 16,* 939–944.

Dumit, Joseph (2004). *Picturing personhood: Brain scans and biomedical identity.* Princeton, NJ: Princeton University Press.

Dunbar, R. I. M. (2004). Gossip in evolutionary perspective. *Review of General Psychology, 8,* 100–110.

Duncan, Paula D.; Ritter, Philip L.; Dornbusch, Sanford M.; et al. (1985). The effects of pubertal timing on body image, school behavior, and deviance. *Journal of Youth and Adolescence, 14,* 227–235.

Dunning, David (2005). *Self-insight: Roadblocks and detours on the path to knowing thyself.* New York: Psychology Press.

Dunning, David; Heath, Chip; & Suls, Jerry M. (2004). Flawed self-assessment: Implications for health, education, and the workplace. *Psychological Science in the Public Interest, 5,* 69–106.

Dunning, David; Johnson, Kerri; Ehrlinger, Joyce; & Kruger, Justin (2003). Why people fail to recognize their own incompetence. *Current Directions in Psychological Science, 12,* 83–87.

Durga, Jane; van Boxtel, M. P.; Schouten, E. G.; et al. (2006). Folate and the methylenetetrahydrofolate reductase 667 → T mutation correlate with cognitive performance. *Neurobiology of Aging, 27,* 334–343.

Dweck, Carol S. (2006). *Mindset: The new psychology of success.* New York: Random House.

Dweck, Carol S., & Sorich, Lisa A. (1999). Mastery-oriented thinking. In C. R. Snyder (Ed.), *Coping: The psychology of what works*. New York: Oxford University Press.

Eagly, Alice H., & Wood, Wendy (1999). The origins of sex differences in human behavior: Evolved dispositions versus social roles. *American Psychologist, 54*, 408–423.

Earl-Novell, Sarah L., & Jessup, Donna C. (2005). The relationship between perceptions of premenstrual syndrome and degree performance. *Assessment & Evaluation in Higher Education, 30*, 343–352.

Ebbinghaus, Hermann M. (1885/1913). *Memory: A contribution to experimental psychology* (H. A. Ruger & C. E. Bussenius, Trans.). New York: Teachers College Press, Columbia University.

Edwards, Kari, & Smith, Edward E. (1996). A disconfirmation bias in the evaluation of arguments. *Journal of Personality and Social Psychology, 71*, 5–24.

Efran, Jay S.; Greene, Mitchell A.; & Gordon, Don E. (1998, March/April). Lessons of the new genetics: Finding the right fit for our clients. *Family Therapy Networker, 22*, 26–41.

Ehrenreich, Barbara (1978). *For her own good: 150 years of the experts' advice to women*. New York: Doubleday.

Ehrenreich, Barbara (2001, June 4). What are they probing for? [Essay.] *Time*, 86.

Ehrensaft, Miriam K.; Moffitt, Terrie E.; & Caspi, Avshalom (2006). Is domestic violence followed by an increased risk of psychiatric disorders among women but not among men? A longitudinal cohort study. *American Journal of Psychiatry, 163*, 885–892.

Eich, E., & Hyman, R. (1992). Subliminal self-help. In D. Druckman & R. A. Bjork (Eds.), *In the mind's eye: Enhancing human performance*. Washington, DC: National Academy Press.

Eisenberg, Nancy; Guthrie, Ivanna K.; Cumberland, Amanda; et al. (2002). Prosocial development in early adulthood: A longitudinal study. *Journal of Personality and Social Psychology, 82*, 993–1006.

Ekman, Paul (2003). *Emotions revealed*. New York: Times Books.

Ekman, Paul; Friesen, Wallace V.; & O'Sullivan, Maureen (1988). Smiles when lying. *Journal of Personality and Social Psychology, 54*, 414–420.

Ekman, Paul; Friesen, Wallace V.; O'Sullivan, Maureen; et al. (1987). Universals and cultural differences in the judgments of facial expression of emotion. *Journal of Personality and Social Psychology, 53*, 712–717.

Ekman, Paul, & Heider, Karl G. (1988). The universality of a contempt expression: A replication. *Motivation and Emotion, 12*, 303–308.

Elfenbein, Hillary A., & Ambady, Nalini (2002). On the universality and cultural specificity of emotion recognition: A meta-analysis. *Psychological Bulletin, 128*, 203–235.

Elliot, Andrew J., & McGregor, Holly A. (2001). A 2 X 2 achievement goal framework. *Journal of Personality and Social Psychology, 80*, 501–519.

Elliot, Andrew J., & Sheldon, Kennon M. (1998). Avoidance personal goals and the personality-illness relationship. *Journal of Personality and Social Psychology, 75*, 1282–1299.

Ellis, Albert (1993). Changing rational-emotive therapy (RET) to rational emotive behavior therapy (REBT). *Behavior Therapist, 16*, 257–258.

Ellis, Albert, & Blau, S. (1998). Rational emotive behavior therapy. *Directions in Clinical and Counseling Psychology, 8*, 41–56.

Ellison, Carol R. (2000). *Women's sexualities*. Oakland, CA: New Harbinger.

Elmquist, Joel K., & Flier, Jeffrey S. (2004, April 2). The fat-brain axis enters a new dimension. *Science, 304*, 63–64.

Else-Quest, Nicole M.; Hyde, Janet S.; Goldsmith, H. Hill; & Can Hulle, Carol A. (2006). Gender differences in temperament: A meta-analysis. *Psychological Bulletin, 132*, 33–72.

Emery, Robert E., & Laumann-Billings, Lisa (1998). An overview of the nature, causes, and consequences of abusive family relationships. *American Psychologist, 53*, 121–135.

Emery, Robert E.; Otto, Randy K.; & O'Donohue, William T. (2005). A critical assessment of child custody evaluations: Limited science and a flawed system. *Psychological Science in the Public Interest, 6*, 1–29.

Emmons, Robert A., & King, Laura A. (1988). Conflict among personal strivings: Immediate and long-term implications for psychological and physical well-being. *Journal of Personality and Social Psychology, 54*, 1040–1048.

Emmons, Robert A., & McCullough, Michael E. (2003). Counting blessings versus burdens: An experimental investigation of gratitude and subjective well-being in daily life. *Journal of Personality and Social Psychology, 84*, 377–389.

Englander-Golden, Paula; Whitmore, Mary R.; & Dienstbier, Richard A. (1978). Menstrual cycle as focus of study and self-reports of moods and behavior. *Motivation and Emotion, 2*, 75–86.

Engle, Randall W. (2002). Working memory capacity as executive attention. *Current Directions in Psychological Science, 11*, 19–23.

Entin, Alan D. (1992). Family photographs: Visual icons and emotional history. Paper presented at the annual meeting of the American Psychological Association, Washington, DC.

Ericksen, Julia A., & Steffen, Sally A. (1999). *Kiss and tell: Surveying sex in the twentieth century*. Cambridge, MA: Harvard University Press.

Erikson, Erik H. (1950/1963). *Childhood and society* (2nd ed.). New York: Norton.

Erikson, Erik H. (1982). *The life cycle completed*. New York: Norton.

Eriksson, P. S.; Perfilieva, E; Bjork-Eriksson, T.; et al. (1998). Neurogenesis in the adult human hippocampus. *Nature Medicine, 4*, 1313–1317.

Eron, Leonard D. (1995). *Media violence: How it affects kids and what can be done about it*. Invited address presented at the annual meeting of the American Psychological Association, New York.

Ervin-Tripp, Susan (1964). Imitation and structural change in children's language. In E. H. Lenneberg (Ed.), *New directions in the study of language*. Cambridge, MA: MIT Press.

Escera, Carles; Cilveti, Robert; & Grau, Carles (1992). Ultradian rhythms in cognitive operations: Evidence from the P300 component of the event-related potentials. *Medical Science Research, 20*, 137–138.

Esparza, J.; Fox, C.; Harper, I. T.; et al. (2000, January 24). Daily energy expenditure in Mexican and USA Pima Indians: Low physical activity as a possible cause of obesity. *International Journal of Obesity and Related Metabolic Disorders, 1*, 55–59.

Evans, Christopher (1984). *Landscapes of the night* (edited and completed by Peter Evans). New York: Viking.

Evans, Gary W.; Bullinger, Monika; & Hygge, Staffan (1998). Chronic noise exposure and physiological response: A prospective study of children living under environmental stress. *Psychological Science, 9*, 75–77.

Ewart, Craig K. (1995). Self-efficacy and recovery from heart attack. In J. E. Maddux (Ed.), *Self-efficacy, adaptation, and adjustment: Theory, research, and application*. New York: Plenum.

Ewart, Craig K., & Kolodner, Kenneth B. (1994). Negative affect, gender, and expressive style predict elevated ambulatory blood pressure in adolescents. *Journal of Personality and Social Psychology, 66*, 596–605.

Eyer, Diane E. (1992). *Mother-infant bonding: A scientific fiction*. New Haven, CT: Yale University Press.

Eyferth, Klaus (1961). [The performance of different groups of the children of occupation forces on the Hamburg-Wechsler Intelligence Test for Children.] *Archiv für die Gesamte Psychologie, 113,* 222–241.

Fagan, Joseph F., III (1992). Intelligence: A theoretical viewpoint. *Current Directions in Psychological Science, 1,* 82–86.

Fagot, Beverly I. (1993, June). Gender role development in early childhood: Environmental input, internal construction. Invited address presented at the annual meeting of the International Academy of Sex Research, Monterey, CA.

Fagot, Beverly I.; Hagan, R.; Leinbach, Mary D.; & Kronsberg, S. (1985). Differential reactions to assertive and communicative acts of toddler boys and girls. *Child Development, 56,* 1499–1505.

Fagot, Beverly I., & Leinbach, Mary D. (1993). Gender-role development in young children: From discrimination to labeling. *Developmental Review, 13,* 205–224.

Falk, Ruma, & Greenbaum, Charles W. (1995). Significance tests die hard: The amazing persistence of a probabilistic misconception. *Theory & Psychology, 5*(1), 75–98.

Fallon, James H.; Keator, David B.; Mbogori, James; et al. (2004). Hostility differentiates the brain metabolic effects of nicotine. *Cognitive Brain Research, 18,* 142–148.

Fallone, Gahan; Acebo, Christine; Seifer, Ronald; & Carskadon, Mary A. (2005). Experimental restriction of sleep opportunity in children: Effects on teacher ratings. *Sleep, 28,* 1280–1286.

Farha, Bryan, & Steward, Gary Jr. (2006, January/February). Paranormal beliefs: An analysis of college students. *Skeptical Inquirer,* 37–40.

Farooqi, I. Sadaf, & O'Rahilly, Stephen (2004). Monogenic human obesity syndromes. *Recent Progress in Hormone Research, 59,* 409–424.

Farrell, Elizabeth F. (2005, December 16). Need therapy? Check your in box. *Chronicle of Higher Education,* A35.

Fausto-Sterling, Anne (1997). Beyond difference: A biologist's perspective. *Journal of Social Issues, 53,* 233–258.

FDA Drug Bulletin (1990, April). Two new psychiatric drugs. *20*(1), 9.

Feather, N. T. (1966). Effects of prior success and failure on expectations of success and subsequent performance. *Journal of Personality and Social Psychology, 3,* 287–298.

Feeney, Brooke C., & Cassidy, Jude (2003). Reconstructive memory related to adolescent-parent conflict interactions. *Journal of Personality and Social Psychology, 85,* 945–955.

Fehr, Beverley (1993). How do I love thee . . . Let me consult my prototype. In S. Duck (Ed.), *Individuals in relationships* (Vol. 1). Newbury Park, CA: Sage.

Fehr, Beverley; Baldwin, Mark; Collins, Lois; et al. (1999). Anger in close relationships: An interpersonal script analysis. *Personality and Social Psychology Bulletin, 25,* 299–312.

Fein, Steven, & Spencer, Steven J. (1997). Prejudice as self-image maintenance: Affirming the self through derogating others. *Journal of Personality and Social Psychology, 73,* 31–44.

Fellows, J. L.; Trosclair, A.; Adams, E. K.; & Rivera, C. C. (2002). Annual smoking attributable mortality, years of potential life lost and economic costs: United States 1995–1999. *Morbidity and Mortality Weekly Report, 51,* 300–303.

Fernald, Anne, & Mazzie, Claudia (1991). Prosody and focus in speech to infants and adults. *Developmental Psychology, 27,* 209–221.

Fernandez, Ephrem, & Turk, Dennis C. (1992). Sensory and affective components of pain: Separation and synthesis. *Psychological Bulletin, 112,* 205–217.

Festinger, Leon (1957). *A theory of cognitive dissonance.* Evanston, IL: Row, Peterson.

Festinger, Leon, & Carlsmith, J. Merrill (1959). Cognitive consequences of forced compliance. *Journal of Abnormal and Social Psychology, 58,* 203–210.

Festinger, Leon; Pepitone, Albert; & Newcomb, Theodore (1952). Some consequences of deindividuation in a group. *Journal of Abnormal and Social Psychology, 47,* 382–389.

Festinger, Leon; Riecken, Henry W.; & Schachter, Stanley (1956). *When prophecy fails.* Minneapolis: University of Minnesota Press.

Fields, Howard (1991). Depression and pain: A neurobiological model. *Neuropsychiatry, Neuropsychology, and Behavioral Neurology, 4,* 83–92.

Fields, R. Douglas (2004, April). The other half of the brain. *Scientific American,* 54–61.

Fiez, J. A. (1996). Cerebellar contributions to cognition. *Neuron, 16,* 13–15.

Fine, Ione; Wade, A. R.; Brewer, A. A.; et al. (2003). Long-term deprivation affects visual perception and cortex. *Nature Neuroscience, 6,* 915–916.

Fink, Max (1999). *Electroshock: Restoring the mind.* New York: Oxford University Press.

Fischer, Pamela C.; Smith, Randy J.; Leonard, Elizabeth; et al. (1993). Sex differences on affective dimensions: Continuing examination. *Journal of Counseling and Development, 71,* 440–443.

Fischhoff, Baruch (1975). Hindsight is not equal to foresight: The effect of outcome knowledge on judgment under uncertainty. *Journal of Experimental Psychology: Human Perception and Performance, 1,* 288–299.

Fishbein, Harold D. (1996). *Peer prejudice and discimination.* Boulder, CO: Westview Press.

Fisher, S., & Greenberg, R. (1996). *Freud scientifically appraised.* New York: John Wiley.

Fitzgerald, P. B.; Brown, T. L.; Marston, N. A.; et al. (2003). Transcranial magnetic stimulation in the treatment of depression: a double-blind, placebo-controlled trial. *Archives of General Psychiatry, 60,* 1002–1008.

Fivush, Robyn, & Hamond, Nina R. (1991). Autobiographical memory across the school years: Toward reconceptualizing childhood amnesia. In R. Flacks & S. L. Thomas (1998, November 27). Among affluent students, a culture of disengagement. *Chronicle of Higher Education,* p. A48.

Flacks, Richard, & Thomas, Scott L. (1998, November 27). Among affluent students, a culture of disengagement. *Chronicle of Higher Education,* p. A48.

Flavell, John H. (1999). Cognitive development: Children's knowledge about the mind. *Annual Review of Psychology, 50,* 21–45.

Fleeson, William (2004). Moving personality beyond the person-situation debate. *Current Directions in Psychological Science, 13,* 83–87.

Fletcher, Anne M. (2001). *Sober for good.* New York: Houghton-Mifflin.

Flor, Herta; Kerns, Robert D.; & Turk, Dennis C. (1987). The role of spouse reinforcement, perceived pain, and activity levels of chronic pain patients. *Journal of Psychosomatic Research, 31,* 251–259.

Flynn, James R. (1987). Massive IQ gains in 14 nations: What IQ tests really measure. *Psychological Bulletin, 95,* 29–51.

Flynn, James R. (1999). Searching for justice: the discovery of IQ gains over time. *American Psychologist, 54,* 5–20.

Forgas, Joseph P. (1998). On being happy and mistaken: Mood effects on the fundamental attribution error. *Journal of Personality and Social Psychology, 75,* 318–331.

Forgas, Joseph P., & Bond, Michael H. (1985). Cultural influences on the perception of interaction episodes. *Personality and Social Psychology Bulletin, 11,* 75–88.

Foulkes, D. (1962). Dream reports from different states of sleep. *Journal of Abnormal and Social Psychology, 65,* 14–25.

Foulkes, David (1999). *Children's dreaming and the development of consciousness.* Cambridge, MA: Harvard University Press.

Fouts, Roger S. (with Stephen T. Mills) (1997). *Next of kin: What chimpanzees have taught me about who we are.* New York: Morrow.

Fouts, Roger S., & Rigby, Randall L. (1977). Man–chimpanzee communication. In T. A. Seboek (Ed.), *How animals communicate.* Bloomington: University of Indiana Press.

Fox, Mary Kay; Pac, Susan; Devaney, Barbara; & Jankowski, Linda (2004). Feeding infants and toddlers study: What foods are infants and toddlers eating? *Journal of the American Dietetic Association, 104,* 22–30.

Fox, Nathan A.; Henderson, Heather A.; Marshall, Peter J.; et al. (2005a). Behavioral inhibition: Linking biology and behavior within a developmental framework. *Annual Review of Psychology, 56,* 235–262.

Fox, Nathan A.; Nichols, Kate E.; Henderson, Heather A.; et al. (2005b). Evidence for a gene–environment interaction in predicting behavioral inhibition in middle childhood. *Psychological Science, 16,* 921–926.

Fraley, R. Chris, & Shaver, Phillip (2000). Adult romantic attachment: Theoretical developments, emerging controversies, and unanswered questions. *Review of General Psychology, 4,* 132–154.

Frankl, Victor E. (1955). *The doctor and the soul: An introduction to logotherapy.* New York: Knopf.

Frasure-Smith, Nancy, & Lespérance, Francois (2005). Depression and coronary heart disease: Complex synergism of mind, body, and environment. *Current Directions in Psychological Science, 14,* 39–43.

Frasure-Smith, Nancy; Lesperance, F., Juneau, M.; Talajic, M.; & Bourassa, M. G. (1999). Gender, depression, and one-year prognosis after myocardial infarction. *Psychosomatic Medicine, 61,* 26–37.

Frazier, Patricia A. (2003). Perceived control and distress following sexual assault: A longitudinal test of a new model. *Journal of Personality and Social Psychology, 84,* 1257–1269.

Fredrickson, Barbara L., & Losada, Marcial F. (2005). Positive affect and the complex dynamics of human flourishing. *American Psychologist, 60,* 678–686.

Fredrickson, Barbara L.; Tugade, Michele M.; Waugh, Christian E.; & Larkin, Gregory R. (2003). What good are positive emotions in crises? *Journal of Personality and Social Psychology, 84,* 365–376.

Freedman, Hill, & Combs, Gene (1996). *Narrative therapy.* New York: Norton.

Freedman, Jonathan (2002). *Media violence and its effect on aggression.* Toronto, Ontario, Canada: University of Toronto Press.

Frensch, Peter A.; & Rünger, Dennis (2003). Implicit learning. *Current Directions in Psychological Science, 12,* 13–18.

Freud, Anna (1967). *Ego and the mechanisms of defense* (The writings of Anna Freud, Vol. 2) (rev. ed.). New York: International Universities Press.

Freud, Sigmund (1900/1953). The interpretation of dreams. In J. Strachey (Ed.), *The standard edition of the complete psychological works of Sigmund Freud* (Vols. 4 and 5). London: Hogarth Press.

Freud, Sigmund (1905). Three essays on the theory of sexuality. In J. Strachey (Ed.), *Standard edition* (Vol. 7).

Freud, Sigmund (1920/1960). *A general introduction to psychoanalysis* (Joan Riviere, Trans.). New York: Washington Square Press.

Freud, Sigmund (1923/1962). *The ego and the id* (Joan Riviere, Trans.). New York: Norton.

Freud, Sigmund (1924a). The dissolution of the Oedipus complex. In J. Strachey (Ed.), *Standard edition* (Vol. 19).

Freud, Sigmund (1924b). Some psychical consequences of the anatomical distinction between the sexes. In J. Strachey (Ed.), *Standard edition* (Vol. 19).

Freud, Sigmund (1961). *Letters of Sigmund Freud, 1873–1939.* Edited by Ernst L. Freud. London: Hogarth Press.

Fridlund, Alan J. (1994). *Human facial expression: An evolutionary view.* San Diego: Academic Press.

Friedman, Jeffrey M. (2003). A war on obesity, not the obese. *Science, 299,* 856–858.

Friedrich, William; Fisher, Jennifer; Broughton, Daniel; et al. (1998). Normative sexual behavior in children: A contemporary sample. *Pediatrics, 101,* 1–8. See also http://www.pediatrics.org/cgi/content/full/101/4/e9.

Frome, Pamela M., & Eccles, Jacquelynne S. (1998). Parents' influence on children's achievement-related perceptions. *Journal of Personality and Social Psychology, 74,* 435–452.

Frye, Richard E.; Schwartz, B. S.; & Doty, Richard L. (1990). Dose-related effects of cigarette smoking on olfactory function. *Journal of the American Medical Association, 263,* 1233–1236.

Fuchs, C. S.; Stampfer, M. J.; Colditz, G. A.; et al. (1995, May 11). Alcohol consumption and mortality among women. *New England Journal of Medicine, 332,* 1245–1250.

Gable, Shelly L., & Haidt, Jonathan (2005). What (and why) is positive psychology? *Review of General Psychology, 9,* 103–110.

Gaertner, Samuel L.; Mann, Jeffrey A.; Dovidio, John F.; et al. (1990). How does cooperation reduce intergroup bias? *Journal of Personality and Social Psychology, 59,* 692–704.

Gage, Fred H.; Kempermann, G.; Palmer, T. D.; et al. (1998). Multipotent progenitor cells in the adult dentate gyrus. *Journal of Neurobiology, 36,* 249–266.

Gagnon, John, & Simon, William (1973). *Sexual conduct: The social sources of human sexuality.* Chicago: Aldine.

Galanter, Eugene (1962). Contemporary psychophysics. In R. Brown, E. Galanter, H. Hess, & G. Mandler (Eds.), *New directions in psychology.* New York: Holt, Rinehart and Winston.

Gallant, Jack L.; Braun, Jochen; & Van Essen, David C. (1993). Selectivity for polar, hyperbolic, and Cartesian gratings in macaque visual cortex. *Science, 259,* 100–103.

Gallant, Sheryle J.; Hamilton, Jean A.; Popiel, Debra A.; et al. (1991). Daily moods and symptoms: Effects of awareness of study focus, gender, menstrual-cycle phase, and day of the week. *Health Psychology, 10,* 180–189.

Gallo, Linda C., & Matthews, Karen A. (2003). Understanding the association between socioeconomic status and physical health: Do negative emotions play a role? *Psychological Bulletin, 129,* 10–51.

Gao, Jia-Hong; Parsons, Lawrence M.; Bower, James M.; et al. (1996). Cerebellum implicated in sensory acquisition and discrimination rather than motor control. *Science, 272,* 545–547.

Garbarino, James, & Bedard, Claire (2001). *Parents under siege.* New York: The Free Press.

Garcia, John, & Koelling, Robert A. (1966). Relation of cue to consequence in avoidance learning. *Psychonomic Science, 4,* 23–124.

Gardner, Howard (1983). *Frames of mind: The theory of multiple intelligences.* New York: Basic Books.

Gardner, Howard (1995). Perennial antinomies and perpetual redrawings: Is there progress in the study of mind? In R. L. Solso & D. W. Massar (Eds.), *The science of the mind: 2001 and beyond.* New York: Oxford University Press.

Gardner, Martin (2006, January/February). The memory wars: Part I. *Skeptical Inquirer, 30,* 28–31.

Gardner, R. Allen, & Gardner, Beatrice T. (1969). Teaching sign language to a chimpanzee. *Science, 165*, 664–672.

Garmezy, Norman (1991). Resilience and vulnerability to adverse developmental outcomes associated with poverty. *American Behavioral Scientist, 34*, 416–430.

Garry, Maryanne, & Loftus, Elizabeth F. (2000). Imagination inflation is not a statistical artifact. Paper presented at the annual meeting of the American Psychological & Law Society, New Orleans.

Garry, Maryanne, & Loftus, Elizabeth F. (May/June, 2004). I am Freud's brain. *Skeptical Inquirer,* 16–18.

Garry, Maryanne; Manning, Charles G.; & Loftus, Elizabeth F. (1996). Imagination inflation: Imagining a childhood event inflates confidence that it occurred. *Psychonomic Bulletin & Review, 3*, 208–214.

Garven, Sena; Wood, James M.; Malpass, Roy S.; & Shaw, John S., III (1998). More than suggestion: The effect of interviewing techniques from the McMartin Preschool case. *Journal of Applied Psychology, 83*, 347–359.

Gauthier, Irene; Skudlarksi, P.; Gore, J. C.; & Anderson, A. W. (2000). Expertise for cars and birds recruits brain areas involved in face recognition. *Nature Neuroscience, 3*, 191–197.

Gauthier, Yvon (2003, May–June). Infant mental health as we enter the third millennium: Can we prevent aggression? *Infant Mental Health Journal, 243*, 296–308.

Gawande, Atul (1998, September 21). The pain perplex. *The New Yorker, 86*, 88, 90, 92–94.

Gazzaniga, Michael S. (1967). The split brain in man. *Scientific American, 217*(2), 24–29.

Gazzaniga, Michael S. (1983). Right hemisphere language following brain bisection: A 20-year perspective. *American Psychologist, 38*, 525–537.

Gazzaniga, Michael S. (1985). *The social brain: Discovering the networks of the mind.* New York: Basic Books.

Gazzaniga, Michael S. (1988). *Mind matters.* Boston: Houghton Mifflin.

Gazzaniga, Michael S. (1998). *The mind's past.* Berkeley, CA: University of California Press.

Geary, David C. (1995). Reflections of evolution and culture in children's cognition: Implications for mathematical development and instruction. *American Psychologist, 50*, 24–37.

Gelernter, David (1997, May 19). How hard is chess? *Time,* 72–73.

Gentner, Dedre, & Goldin-Meadow, Susan (Eds.) (2003). *Language in mind: Advances in the study of language and thought.* Cambridge: MIT Press.

Gershoff, Elizabeth T. (2002). Parental corporal punishment and associated child behaviors and experiences: A meta-analytic and theoretical review. *Psychological Bulletin, 128*, 539–579.

Gibson, Eleanor, & Walk, Richard (1960). The "visual cliff." *Scientific American, 202*, 80–92.

Gilbert, Daniel (2006). *Stumbling on happiness.* New York: Knopf.

Gilbert, Daniel (2006, July 2). If only gay sex caused global warming. *Los Angeles Times,* Comment section, pp. M1, M6.

Gilbertson, Mark W.; Shenton, Martha E.; Ciszewski, Aleksandra; et al. (2002). Hippocampal volume predicts pathologic vulnerability to psychological trauma. *Nature Neuroscience, 5*, 1242–1247.

Gilmore, David D. (1990). *Manhood in the making: Cultural concepts of masculinity.* New Haven, CT: Yale University Press.

Gist, Richard, & Lubin, Bernard (Eds.) (1999). *Response to disaster: Psychosocial, community, and ecological approaches.* Philadelphia, PA: Brunner/Mazel (Taylor & Francis).

Gladue, Brian A. (1994). The biopsychology of sexual orientation. *Current Directions in Psychological Science, 3*, 150–154.

Gladwell, Malcolm (2004, September 20). Personality plus. *The New Yorker,* 42–48.

Glanzer, Murray, & Cunitz, Anita R. (1966). Two storage mechanisms in free recall. *Journal of Verbal Learning and Verbal Behavior, 5*, 351–360.

Gleaves, David H. (1996). The sociocognitive model of dissociative identity disorder: A reexamination of the evidence. *Psychological Bulletin, 120*, 42–59.

Glick, Peter; Fiske, Susan T.; Mladinic, Antonio; et al. (2000). Beyond prejudice as simple antipathy: Hostile and benevolent sexism across cultures. *Journal of Personality and Social Psychology, 79*, 763–775.

Glick, Peter; Lameiras, Maria; Fiske, Susan T.; et al. (2004). Bad but bold: Ambivalent attitudes toward men predict gender inequality in 16 nations. *Journal of Personality and Social Psychology, 86*, 713–728.

Glick, Peter; Sakalli-Ugurlu, Nuray; Ferreira, Maria Cristina; & de Souza, Marcos Aguiar (2002). Ambivalent sexism and attitudes toward wife abuse in Turkey and Brazil. *Psychology of Women Quarterly, 26*, 292–297.

Golden, Robert M.; Gaynes, Bradley N.; Ekstrom, R. David; et al. (2005). The efficacy of light therapy in the treatment of mood disorders: A review and meta-analysis of the evidence. *American Journal of Psychiatry, 162*, 656–662.

Goldin-Meadow, Susan (2003). *The resilience of language.* New York: Psychology Press.

Goldman-Rakic, Patricia S. (1996). Opening the mind through neurobiology. Invited address at the annual meeting of the American Psychological Association, Toronto, Canada.

Goldstein, Alan J.; de Beurs, Edwin; Chambless, Dianne L.; & Wilson, Kimberly A. (2000). EMDR for panic disorder with agoraphobia: Comparison with waiting list and credible attention-placebo control conditions. *Journal of Consulting and Clinical Psychology, 68*, 947–956.

Goldstein, Eda G. (2002). *Object relations theory and self psychology in social work practice.* New York: Free Press.

Goldstein, Jill M.; Seidman, Larry J.; Horton, Nicholas J.; et al. (2001). Normal sexual dimorphism of the adult human brain assessed by in vivo magnetic resonance imaging. *Cerebral Cortex, 11*, 490–497.

Goldstein, Michael J. (1987). Psychosocial issues. *Schizophrenia Bulletin, 13*(1), 157–171.

Goldstein, Michael, & Miklowitz, David (1995). The effectiveness of psychoeducational family therapy in the treatment of schizophrenic disorders. *Journal of Marital and Family Therapy, 21*, 361–376.

Golinkoff, Roberta M., & Hirsh-Pasek, Kathy (2006). Baby wordsmith: From associationist to social sophisticate. *Current Directions in Psychological Science, 15*, 30–33.

Golombok, Susan, & Fivush, Robyn (1994). *Gender development.* New York: Cambridge University Press.

Golub, Sharon (1992). *Periods: From menarche to menopause.* Newbury Park, CA: Sage.

Gonzaga, Gian C.; Turner, Rebecca A.; Keltner, Dacher; et al. (2006). Romantic love and sexual desire in close relationships. *Emotion, 6*, 163–179.

Goode, Erica (2003, May 6). Experts see mind's voices in new light. *The New York Times,* Science Times, pp. D1, D4.

Goodwin, Donald W.; Knop, Joachim; Jensen, Per; et al. (1994). Thirty-year follow-up of men at high risk for alcoholism. In T. F. Babor & V. M. Hesselbrock (Eds.), *Types of alcoholics: Evidence from clinical, experimental, and genetic research.* New York: New York Academy of Sciences.

Goodwin, Doris Kearns (2005). *Team of rivals: The political genius of Abraham Lincoln.* New York: Simon & Schuster.

Goodwyn, Susan, & Acredolo, Linda (1998). Encouraging symbolic gestures: A new perspective on the relationship between gesture and speech. In J. Iverson & S. Goldin-Meadow (Eds.), *The nature and functions of gesture in children's communication*. San Francisco: Jossey-Bass.

Gordon, Peter (2004). Numerical cognition without words: Evidence from Amazonia. *Science,* published online August 19, 2004; 10.1126/science.1094492.

Gorn, Gerald J. (1982). The effects of music in advertising on choice behavior: A classical conditioning approach. *Journal of Marketing, 46,* 94–101.

Gosling, Samuel D. (2001). From mice to men: What can we learn about personality from animal research? *Psychological Bulletin, 127,* 45–86.

Gosling, Samuel D., & John, Oliver P. (1999). Personality dimensions in nonhuman animals: A cross-species review. *Current Directions in Psychological Science, 8,* 69–75.

Gosling, Samuel D.; Kwan, Virginia S. Y.; & John, Oliver P. (2003). A dog's got personality: A cross-species comparative approach to personality judgments in dogs and humans. *Journal of Personality and Social Psychology, 85,* 1161–1169.

Gosling, Samual D.; Vazire, Simine; Srivatava, Sanjay; & John, Oliver P. (2004). Should we trust web-based studies? A comparative analysis of six preconceptions about Internet questionnaires. *American Psychologist, 59,* 93–104.

Gottesman, Irving I. (1991). *Schizophrenia genesis: The origins of madness.* New York: Freeman.

Gottfredson, Linda S. (2002). g: Highly general and highly practical. In R. J. Sternberg & E. I. Grigorenko (Eds.), *The general intelligence factor: How general is it?* Mahway, NJ: Erlbaum.

Gougoux, Frederic; Zatorre, Robert J.; Lassonde, Maryse; et al. (2005). A functional neuroimaging study of sound localization: Visual cortex activity predicts performance in early-blind individuals. *PloS Biology, 3,* 324–333.

Gould, Elizabeth; Beylin, A; Tanapat, Patima; et al. (1999). Learning enhances adult neurogenesis in the hippocampal formation. *Nature Neuroscience, 2,* 260–265.

Gould, Elizabeth; Reeves, Alison J.; Graziano, Michael S. A.; & Gross, Charles G. (1999). Neurogenesis in the neocortex of adult primates. *Science, 286,* 548–552.

Gould, Elizabeth; Tanapat, Patima; McEwen, Bruce S.; et al. (1998). Proliferation of granule cell precursors in the dentate gyrus of adult monkeys is diminished by stress. *Proceedings of the National Academy of Science, 95,* 3168–3171.

Gould, Stephen Jay (1994, November 28). Curveball. [Review of *The Bell Curve,* by Richard J. Herrnstein and Charles Murray.] *New Yorker,* 139–149.

Gould, Stephen Jay (1996). *The mismeasure of man* (Rev. ed.). New York: Norton.

Gourevich, Philip (1998). *We wish to inform you that tomorrow we will be killed with our families: Stories from Rwanda.* New York: Farrar, Straus & Giroux.

Graf, Peter, & Schacter, Daniel A. (1985). Implicit and explicit memory for new associations in normal and amnesic subjects. *Journal of Experimental Psychology: Learning, Memory, and Cognition, 11,* 501–518.

Graham, Jill W. (1986). Principled organizational dissent: A theoretical essay. *Research in Organizational Behavior, 8,* 1–52.

Grant, Heidi, & Dweck, Carol S. (2003). Clarifying achievement goals and their impact. *Journal of Personality and Social Psychology, 85,* 541–553.

Grant, Igor; Gonzalez, Raul; Carey, Catherine L.; et al. (2003). Nonacute (residual) neurocognitive effects of cannabis use: a meta-analytic study. *Journal of the International Neuropsychological Society, 9,* 679–689.

Gray, Jeremy R. (2004). Integration of emotion and cognitive control. *Current Directions in Psychological Science, 13,* 46–49.

Green, Gina (1996a). Behavioral treatment of autistic persons: A review of research from 1980 to the present. *Research in Developmental Disabilities, 17,* 433–465.

Green, Gina (1996b). Early behavioral intervention for autism: What does research tell us? In C. Maurice, G. Green, & S. C. Luce (Eds.), *Behavioral Intervention for Young Children with Autism.* Austin, TX: PRO-ED.

Greenberger, Dennis, & Padesky, Christine A. (1995). *Mind over mood: A cognitive therapy treatment manual for clients.* New York: Guilford.

Greenough, William T., & Anderson, Brenda J. (1991). Cerebellar synaptic plasticity: Relation to learning vs. neural activity. *Annals of the New York Academy of Sciences, 627,* 231–247.

Greenough, William T., & Black, James E. (1992). Induction of brain structure by experience: Substrates for cognitive development. In M. Gunnar & C. A. Nelson (Eds.), *Behavioral developmental neuroscience: Vol. 24. Minnesota Symposia on Child Psychology.* Hillsdale, NJ: Erlbaum.

Greenwald, Anthony G.; McGhee, Debbie E.; & Schwartz, Jordan L. K. (1998). Measuring individual differences in implicit cognition: The Implicit Association Test. *Journal of Personality and Social Psychology, 74,* 1464–1480.

Greenwald, Anthony G.; Spangenberg, Eric R.; Pratkanis, Anthony R.; & Eskenazi, Jay (1991). Double-blind tests of subliminal self-help audiotapes. *Psychological Science, 2,* 119–122.

Gregory, Richard L. (1963). Distortion of visual space as inappropriate constancy scaling. *Nature, 199,* 678–679.

Griffin, Donald R. (1992). *Animal minds.* Chicago: University of Chicago Press.

Grinspoon, Lester, & Bakalar, James B. (1993). *Marihuana, the forbidden medicine.* New Haven, CT: Yale University Press.

Groneman, Carol (2000). *Nymphomania: A history.* New York: Norton.

Gross, James J. (1998). The emerging field of emotion regulation: An integrative review. *Review of General Psychology, 2,* 271–299.

Gross, James J. (2001). Emotion regulation in adulthood: Timing is everything. *Current Directions in Psychological Science, 10,* 214–219.

Gross, James J., & John, Oliver, P. (2003). Individual differences in two emotion regulation processes: Implications for affect, relationships, and well-being. *Journal of Personality and Social Psychology, 85,* 348–362.

Grossman, Michele, & Wood, Wendy (1993). Sex differences in intensity of emotional experience: A social role interpretation. *Journal of Personality and Social Psychology, 65,* 1010–1022.

Groves, James E. (Ed.) (1996). *Essential papers on short-term dynamic therapy.* New York: New York University Press.

Guan, Kaomei; Nayernia, Karim; Maier, Lars S.; et al. (2006). Pluripotency of spermatogonial stem cells from adult mice testes. *Nature, 440,* 1199–1203. [Letter.]

Guilford, J. P. (1988). Some changes in the structure-of-intellect model. *Educational and Psychological Measurement, 48,* 1–4.

Gur, R. C.; Gunning-Dixon, Faith; Bilker, Wareen B.; & Gur, Raquel E. (2002). Sex differences in temporo-limbic and frontal brain volumes of healthy adults. *Cerebral Cortex, 12,* 998–1003.

Gur, R. E.; Maany, V.; Mozley, P. D.; et al. (1998). Subcortical MRI volumes in neuroleptic-naive and treated patients with schizophrenia. *American Journal of Psychiatry, 155,* 1711–1717.

Guralnick, M. J. (Ed.) (1997). *The effectiveness of early intervention.* Baltimore: Brookes.

Guthrie, Paul C., & Mobley, Brenda D. (1994). A comparison of the differential diagnostic efficiency of three personality disorder inventories. *Journal of Clinical Psychology, 50*, 656–665.

Guzman-Marin, Ruben; Suntsova, Natalia; Methippara, Melvi; et al. (2005). Sleep deprivation suppresses neurogenesis in the adult hippocampus of rats. *European Journal of Neuroscience, 22*, 2111–2116.

Haber, Ralph N. (1970, May). How we remember what we see. *Scientific American, 222*, 104–112.

Hacking, Ian (1995). *Rewriting the soul: Multiple personality and the sciences of memory.* Princeton: Princeton University Press.

Haimov, I., & Lavie, P. (1996). Melatonin—A soporific hormone. *Current Directions in Psychological Science, 5*, 106–111.

Hall, Calvin (1953a). A cognitive theory of dreams. *Journal of General Psychology, 49*, 273–282.

Hall, Calvin (1953b). *The meaning of dreams.* New York: McGraw-Hill.

Hall, Edward T. (1959). *The silent language.* Garden City, NY: Doubleday.

Hall, Edward T. (1976). *Beyond culture.* New York: Anchor.

Hall, Edward T. (1983). *The dance of life: The other dimension of time.* Garden City, NY: Anchor Press/Doubleday.

Hall, Edward T., & Hall, Mildred R. (1987). *Hidden differences: Doing business with the Japanese.* Garden City, NY: Anchor Press/Doubleday.

Hall, Edward T., & Hall, Mildred R. (1990). *Understanding cultural differences.* Yarmouth, ME: Intercultural Press.

Hall, Nathan C.; Perry, Raymond P.; Ruthig, Joelle C.; et al. (2006). Primary and secondary control in achievement settings: A longitudinal field study of academic motivation, emotions, and performance. *Journal of Applied Social Psychology, 36*, 1430–1470.

Halliday, G. (1993). Examination dreams. *Perceptual and Motor Skills, 77*, 489–490.

Halpern, Diane (2002). *Thought and knowledge: An introduction to critical thinking* (4th ed.). Hillsdale, NJ: Erlbaum.

Hamby, Sherry L., & Koss, Mary P. (2003). Shades of gray: A qualitative study of terms used in the measurement of sexual victimization. *Psychology of Women Quarterly, 27*, 243–255.

Hancox, Robert J.; Milne, Barry J.; & Poulton, Richie (2005). Association of television viewing during childhood with poor educational achievement. *Archives of Pediatric and Adolescent Medicine, 259*, 614–618.

Haney, Craig; Banks, Curtis; & Zimbardo, Philip (1973). Interpersonal dynamics in a simulated prison. *International Journal of Criminology and Penology, 1*, 69–97.

Haney, Craig, & Zimbardo, Philip (1998). The past and future of U.S. prison policy: Twenty-five years after the Stanford Prison Experiment. *American Psychologist, 53*, 709–727.

Hankin, Benjamin L., & Abramson, Lyn Y. (2001). Development of gender differences in depression: An elaborated cognitive vulnerability-transactional stress theory. *Psychological Bulletin, 127*, 773–796.

Hardie, Elizabeth A. (1997). PMS in the workplace: Dispelling the myth of cyclic function. Journal of *Occupational and Organizational Psychology, 70*, 97–102.

Harding, Courtenay M.; Zubin, Joseph; & Strauss, John S. (1992). Chronicity in schizophrenia: Revisited. *British Journal of Psychiatry, 161*(Suppl. 18), 27–37.

Hare, Robert D. (1965). Temporal gradient of fear arousal in psychopaths. *Journal of Abnormal Psychology, 70*, 442–445.

Hare, Robert D. (1993). *Without conscience: The disturbing world of the psychopaths among us.* New York: Pocket Books.

Hare, Robert D. (1996). Psychopathy: A clinical construct whose time has come. *Criminal Justice and Behavior, 23*, 24–54.

Hare, Robert D.; Hart, Stephen D.; & Harpur, Timothy J. (1991). Psychopathy and the DSM-IV criteria for antisocial personality disorder. *Journal of Abnormal Psychology, 100*, 391–398.

Haritos-Fatouros, Mika (1988). The official torturer: A learning model for obedience to the authority of violence. *Journal of Applied Social Psychology, 18*, 1107–1120.

Harkins, Stephen G., & Szymanski, Kate (1989). Social loafing and group evaluation. *Journal of Personality and Social Psychology, 56*, 934–941.

Harlow, Harry F. (1958). The nature of love. *American Psychologist, 13*, 673–685.

Harlow, Harry F., & Harlow, Margaret K. (1966). Learning to love. *American Scientist, 54*, 244–272.

Harmon-Jones, Eddie, & Sigelman, Jonathan (2001). State anger and prefrontal brain activity: Evidence that insult-related relative left-prefrontal activation is associated with experienced anger and aggression. *Journal of Personality and Social Psychology, 80*, 797–803.

Harris, Gardiner (2003, August 7). Debate resumes on the safety of depression's wonder drugs. *The New York Times*, pp. A1, C4.

Harrls, Judith R. (1998) *The nurture assumption.* New York: The Free Press.

Harris, Judith R. (2006). *No two alike: Human nature and human individuality.* New York: Norton.

Harris, Lasana T., & Fiske, Susan T. (2006). Dehumanizing the lowest of the low: Neuro-imaging responses to extreme outgroups. *Psychological Science*, in press.

Harris, Lasana T.; Todorov, Alexander; & Fiske, Susan T. (2005). Attributions on the brain: Neuro-imaging dispositional inferences, beyond theory of mind. *NeuroImage, 28*, 763–769.

Hart, A. J.; Whalen, P. J.; Shin, L. M.; et al. (2000). Differential response in the human amygdala to racial outgroup vs. ingroup face stimuli. *NeuroReport, 11*, 2351–2355.

Hart, John, Jr.; Berndt, Rita S.; & Caramazza, Alfonso (1985, August 1). Category-specific naming deficit following cerebral infarction. *Nature, 316*, 339–340.

Hartup, William (1999). Peer experience and its developmental significance. In M. Bennett (Ed.), *Developmental Psychology: Achievements and prospects.* Philadelphia: Psychology Press.

Haslam, S. Alexander, & Reicher, Stephen (2003, Spring). Beyond Stanford: Questioning a role-based explanation of tyranny. *Society for Experimental Social Psychology Dialogue, 18*, 22–25.

Hatfield, Elaine, & Rapson, Richard L. (1996). *Love and sex. Cross cultural perspectives.* Boston: Allyn & Bacon.

Hauser, Marc (2000). *Wild minds: What animals really think.* New York: Holt.

Haut, Jennifer S.; Beckwith, Bill E.; Petros, Thomas V.; & Russell, Sue (1989). Gender differences in retrieval from long-term memory following acute intoxication with ethanol. *Physiology and Behavior, 45*, 1161–1165.

Hawkins, Scott A., & Hastie, Reid (1990). Hindsight: Biased judgments of past events after the outcomes are known. *Psychological Bulletin, 107*, 311–327.

Hayes, Steven C. (2004). Acceptance and commitment therapy and the new behavior therapies: Mindfulness, acceptance, and relationship. In S. C. Hayes, V. M. Follette, & M. M. Linehan (2004), *Mindfulness and acceptance: Expanding the cognitive-behavioral tradition.* New York: Guilford.

Hayman, Ronald (2001). *A life of Jung.* New York: W. W. Norton.

Hazan, Cindy, & Diamond, Lisa M. (2000). The place of attachment in human mating. *Review of General Psychology, 4,* 186–204.

Hazan, Cindy, & Shaver, Phillip R. (1994). Attachment as an organizational framework for research on close relationships. *Psychological Inquiry, 5,* 1–22.

Healy, David (2002). *The creation of psychopharmacology.* Cambridge, MA: Harvard University Press.

Healy, David (2004). *Let them eat Prozac.* New York: New York University Press.

Heath, A. C.; Madden, P. A. F.; Bucholz, K. K.; et al. (2003). Genetic and genotype x environment interaction effects on risk of dependence on alcohol, tobacco, and other drugs: new research. In R Plomin et al. (Eds.), *Behavioral genetics in the postgenomic era.* Washington, DC: APA Books.

Hébert, Richard (2001, September). Code overload: Doing a number on memory. *APS Observer, 14,* 1, 7–11.

Heinrichs, R. Walter (2005). The primacy of cognition in schizophrenia. *American Psychologist, 60,* 229–242.

Helson, Ravenna; Roberts, Brent; & Agronick, Gail (1995). Enduringness and change in creative personality and the prediction of occupational creativity. *Journal of Personality and Social Psychology, 6,* 1173–1183.

Henderlong, Jennifer, & Lepper, Mark R. (2002). The effects of praise on children's intrinsic motivation: A review and synthesis. *Psychological Bulletin, 128,* 774–795.

Hendrix, William H.; Steel, Robert P.; Leap, Terry L.; & Summers, Timothy P. (1991). Development of a stress-related health promotion model: Antecedents and organizational effectiveness outcomes. *Journal of Social Behavior and Personality 6, 141–162.*

Henggeler, Scott W.; Schoenwald, Sonya K.; Borduin, Charles M.; et al. (1998). *Multisystemic treatment of antisocial behavior in children and adolescents.* New York: Guilford Press.

Henrich, Joseph; Boyd, Robert; Bowles, Samuel; et al. (2001). In search of Homo Economicus: Behavioral experiments in 15 small scale societies. *American Economics Review, 91,* 73–78.

Herbert, Alan; Gerry, Norman P.; McQueen, Matthew B.; et al. (2006, April 14). A common genetic variant is associated with adult and childhood obesity. *Science, 312,* 279–283.

Herdt, Gilbert (1984). *Ritualized homosexuality in Melanesia.* Berkeley: University of California Press.

Herek, Gregory M., & Capitanio, J. P. (1996). "Some of my best friends": Intergroup contact, concealable stigma, and heterosexuals' attitudes toward gay men and lesbians. *Personality and Social Psychology Bulletin, 22,* 412–424.

Herman, John H. (1992). Transmutative and reproductive properties of dreams: Evidence for cortical modulation of brainstem generators. In J. Antrobus & M. Bertini (Eds.), *The neuropsychology of dreaming.* Hillsdale, NJ: Erlbaum.

Herman, Judith (1992). *Trauma and recovery.* New York: Basic Books.

Herman, Louis M.; Kuczaj, Stan A.; & Holder, Mark D. (1993). Responses to anomalous gestural sequences by a language-trained dolphin: Evidence for processing of semantic relations and syntactic information. *Journal of Experimental Psychology: General, 122,* 184–194.

Heron, Woodburn (1957). The pathology of boredom. *Scientific American, 196*(1), 52–56.

Herrnstein, Richard J., & Murray, Charles (1994). *The bell curve: Intelligence and class structure in American life.* New York: Free Press.

Herz, Rachel S., & Cupchik, Gerald C. (1995). The emotional distinctiveness of odor-evoked memories. *Chemical Senses, 20,* 517–528.

Hess, Thomas M. (2005). Memory and aging in context. *Psychological Bulletin, 131,* 383–406.

Hess, Ursula; Adams, Reginald B., Jr.; & Kleck, Robert (2005). Who may frown and who should smile? Dominance, affiliation, and the display of happiness and anger. *Cognition & Emotion, 19,* 515–536.

Higgins, E. Tory (1998). Promotion and prevention: Regulatory focus as a motivational principle. *Advances in Experimental Social Psychology, 30,* 1–46.

Hilgard, Ernest R. (1977). *Divided consciousness: Multiple controls in human thought and action.* New York: Wiley-Interscience.

Hilgard, Ernest R. (1986). *Divided consciousness: Multiple controls in human thought and action* (2nd ed.). New York: Wiley.

Hilts, Philip J. (1995). *Memory's ghost: The strange tale of Mr. M. and the nature of memory.* New York: Simon & Schuster.

Hirsch, Helmut V. B., & Spinelli, D. N. (1970). Visual experience modifies distribution of horizontally and vertically oriented receptive fields in cats. *Science, 168,* 869–871.

Hirst, William; Neisser, Ulric; & Spelke, Elizabeth (1978, January). Divided attention. *Human Nature, 1,* 54–61.

Hobson, J. Allan (1988). *The dreaming brain.* New York: Basic Books.

Hobson, J. Allan (1990). Activation, input source, and modulation: A neurocognitive model of the state of the brain mind. In R. R. Bootzin, J. F. Kihlstrom, & D. L. Schacter (Eds.), *Sleep and cognition.* Washington, DC: American Psychological Association.

Hobson, J. Allan (2002). *Dreaming: An introduction to the science of sleep.* New York: Oxford University Press.

Hobson, J. Allan; Pace-Schott, Edward F.; & Stickgold, Robert (2000). Dreaming and the brain: Toward a cognitive neuroscience of consicous states. *Behavioral and Brain Sciences, 23,* 793–842, 904–1018, 1083–1121.

Hochschild, Arlie (1983). *The managed heart.* Berkeley: University of California Press.

Hodges, Ernest V. E., & Perry, David G. (1999). Personal and interpersonal antecedents and consequences of victimization by peers. *Journal of Personality and Social Psychology, 76,* 677–685.

Hoffman, Martin L. (1994). Discipline and internalization. *Developmental Psychology, 30,* 26–28.

Hoffrage, Ulrich; Hertwig, Ralph; & Gigerenzer, Gerd (2000). Hindsight bias: A by-product of knowledge updating? *Journal of Experimental Psychology: Learning, Memory, & Cognition, 26,* 566–581.

Hofstede, Geert, & Bond, Michael H. (1988). The Confucius connection: From cultural roots to economic growth. *Organizational Dynamics,* 5–21.

Holden, Constance (1997). Thumbs up for acupuncture. [News report.] *Science, 278,* 1231.

Holden, George W., & Miller, Pamela C. (1999). Enduring and different: A meta-analysis of the similarity in parents' child rearing. *Psychological Bulletin, 125,* 223–254.

Holland, Rob W.; Hendriks, Merel; & Aarts, Henk (2005). Smells like clean spirit: Nonconscious effects of scent on cognition and behavior. *Psychological Science, 16,* 689–693.

Hollon, Steven D.; Thase, Michael E.; & Markowitz, John C. (2002). Treatment and prevention of depression. *Psychological Science in the Public Interest, 3,* 39–77.

Hooker, Evelyn (1957). The adjustment of the male overt homosexual. *Journal of Projective Techniques, 21,* 18–31.

Horgan, John (1995, November). Get smart, take a test: A long-term rise in IQ scores baffles intelligence experts. *Scientific American, 273,* 12,14.

Horney, Karen (1926/1973). The flight from womanhood. *The International Journal of Psycho-Analysis, 7,* 324–339. Reprinted in J. B. Miller (Ed.), *Psychoanalysis and women.* New York: Brunner/Mazel, 1973.

Hotz, Robert Lee (2000, November 29). Women use more of brain when listening, study says. *Los Angeles Times,* A1, A18–19.

House, James S.; Landis, Karl R.; & Umberson, Debra (1988, July 19). Social relationships and health. *Science, 241,* 540–545.

Houts, Arthur C. (2002). Discovery, invention, and the expansion of the modern *Diagnostic and Statistical Manuals of Mental Disorders.* In L. E. Beutler & M. L. Malik (Eds.), *Rethinking the DSM: A psychological perspective.* Washington, DC: American Psychological Association.

Howard, George S. (1991). Culture tales: A narrative approach to thinking, cross-cultural psychology, and psychotherapy. *American Psychologist, 46,* 187–197.

Howe, Mark L., & Courage, Mary L. (1993). On resolving the enigma of infantile amnesia. *Psychological Bulletin, 113,* 305–326.

Howe, Mark L.; Courage, Mary L.; & Peterson, Carole (1994). How can I remember when "I" wasn't there? Long-term retention of traumatic experiences and emergence of the cognitive self. *Consciousness and Cognition, 3,* 327–355.

Howe, Neil, & Strauss, William (2003). *Millennials go to college.* American Association of Collegiate Registrars and Admissions Officers, and Life-Course Associates, available at http://www.aacrao.org.

Hrdy, Sarah B. (1988). Empathy, polyandry, and the myth of the coy female. In R. Bleier (Ed.), *Feminist approaches to science.* New York: Pergamon.

Hrdy, Sarah B. (1994). What do women want? In T. A. Bass (Ed.), *Reinventing the future: Conversations with the world's leading scientists.* Reading, MA: Addison-Wesley.

Hrdy, Sarah B. (1999). *Mother nature.* New York: Pantheon.

Huang, L.; Shanker, Y. G.; Dubauskaite, J.; et al. (1999). Ggamma13 colocalizes with gustducin in taste receptor cells and mediates IP3 responses to bitter denatonium. *Nature Neuroscience, 2,* 1055–1062.

Hubel, David H., & Wiesel, Torsten N. (1962). Receptive fields, binocular interaction and functional architecture in the cat's visual cortex. *Journal of Physiology* (London), *160,* 106–154.

Hubel, David H., & Wiesel, Torsten N. (1968). Receptive fields and functional architecture of monkey striate cortex. *Journal of Physiology* (London), *195,* 215–243.

Huggins, Martha K.; Haritos-Fatouros, Mika; & Zimbardo, Philip G. (2003). *Violence workers: Police torturers and murderers reconstruct Brazilian atrocities.* Berkeley, CA: University of California Press.

Huizink, Anja C.; Mulder, Edu J. H.; & Buitelaar, Jan K. (2004). Prenatal stress and risk for psychopathology: Specific effects or induction of general susceptibility? *Psychological Bulletin, 130,* 115–142.

Hulbert, Ann (2003). *Raising America: Experts, parents and a century of advice about children.* New York: Knopf.

Hultsch, David F.; Hertzog, Christopher; Small, Brent J.; & Dixon, Roger A. (1999). Use it or lose it: Engaged lifestyle as a buffer of cognitive decline in aging? *Psychology and Aging, 14,* 245–263.

Hunsley, John; Lee, Catherine M.; & Wood, James (2003). Controversial and questionable assessment techniques. In S. O. Lilienfeld, S. J. Lynn, & J. M. Lohn (Eds.), *Science and pseudoscience in clinical psychology.* New York: Guilford.

Hunter, John E. (1997). Needed: A ban on the significance test. *Psychological Science, 8,* 3–7.

Hupka, Ralph B. (1981). Cultural determinants of jealousy. *Alternative Lifestyles, 4,* 310–356.

Hupka, Ralph B. (1991). The motive for the arousal of romantic jealousy. In P. Salovey (Ed.), *The psychology of jealousy and envy.* New York: Guilford Press.

Hupka, Ralph B.; Lenton, Alison P.; & Hutchison, Keith A. (1999). Universal development of emotion categories in natural language. *Journal of Personality and Social Psychology, 77,* 247–278.

Hur, Yoon-Mi; Bouchard, Thomas J., Jr.; & Lykken, David T. (1998). Genetic and environmental influence on morningness-eveningness. *Personality and Individual Differences, 25,* 917–925.

Hyde, Janet S. (2000). A gendered brain? [Review of *Sex and cognition,* by Doreen Kimura.] *Journal of Sex Research, 37,* 191.

Hyde, Janet S. (2005). The gender similarities hypothesis. *American Psychologist, 60,* 581–592.

Hyman, Ira E., Jr., & Pentland, Joel (1996). The role of mental imagery in the creation of false childhood memories. *Journal of Memory and Language, 35,* 101–117.

Iacoboni, Marco; Molnar-Szakacs, Istvan; Gallese, Vittorio; et al. (2005). Grasping the intentions of others with one's own mirror neuron system. *Public Library of Science: Biology 3*(3): e79. DOI: *10.1371/journal.pbio.003079.*

Ikonomidou, Chrysanthy; Bittigau, Petra; Ishimaru, Masahiko J.; et al. (2000, February 11). Ethanol-induced apoptotic neurodegeneration and fetal alcohol syndrome. *Science, 287,* 1056–1060.

Impett, Emily A.; Gable, Shelly; & Peplau, Letitia A. (2005). Giving up and giving in: The costs and benefits of daily sacrifice in intimate relationships. *Journal of Personality and Social Psychology, 89,* 327–344.

Impett, Emily A.; Peplau, Letitia A.; & Gable, Shelly (2005). Approach and avoidance sexual motives: Implications for personal and interpersonal well-being. *Personal Relationships, 12,* 465–482.

Ingram, J. L.; Stodgell, C. J.; Hyman S. L.; et al. (2000). Discovery of allelic variants of HOXA2 and HOXB1: Genetic susceptibility to autism spectrum disorders. *Teratology, 62,* 393–405.

International Consensus Conference (2002, June). *Female Androgen Deficiency Syndrome: Definition, Diagnosis, and Classification: International Consensus* Conference, Princeton, NJ. http://www.medscape.com/viewprogram/302.

Inzlicht, Michael, & Ben-Zeev, Talia (2000). A threatening intellectual environment: Why females are susceptible to experiencing problem-solving deficits in the presence of males. *Psychological Science, 11,* 365–371.

Irvine, Janice M. (1990). *Disorders of desire: Sex and gender in modern American sexology.* Philadelphia: Temple University Press.

Islam, Mir Rabiul, & Hewstone, Miles (1993). Intergroup attributions and affective consequences in majority and minority groups. *Journal of Personality and Social Psychology, 64,* 936–950.

Ito, Tiffany A., & Urland, Geoffrey R. (2003). Race and gender on the brain: Electrocortical measures of attention to the race and gender of multiply categorizable individuals. *Journal of Personality and Social Psychology, 85,* 616–626.

Izard, Carroll E. (1990). Facial expressions and the regulation of emotions. *Journal of Personality and Social Psychology, 58,* 487–498.

Izard, Carroll E. (1994a). Four systems for emotion activation: Cognitive and noncognitive processes. *Psychological Review, 100,* 68–90.

Izard, Carroll E. (1994b). Innate and universal facial expressions: Evidence from developmental and cross-cultural research. *Psychological Bulletin, 115,* 288–299.

Izumikawa, Masahiko; Minoda, Ryosei; Kawamoto, Karen A.; et al. (2005). Auditory hair cell replacement and hearing improvement by *Atoh1* gene therapy in deaf mammals. *Nature Medicine, 11,* 271–276.

Jacobs, Gregg D.; Pace-Schott, Edward F.; Stickgold, Robert; & Otto, Michael W. (2004). Cognitive behavior therapy and pharmacotherapy for chronic insomnia: A randomized controlled trial and direct comparison. *Archives of Internal Medicine, 164,* 1888–1896.

Jacobsen, Paul B; Bovbjerg, Dana H.; Schwartz, Marc D.; et al. (1995). Conditioned emotional distress in women receiving chemotherapy for breast cancer. *Journal of Consulting & Clinical Psychology, 63,* 108–114.

Jaffe, Eric (2005). How random is that? Students are convenient research subjects but they're not a simple sample. *APS Observer, 18,* 19–30.

James, William (1890/1950). *Principles of psychology* (Vol. 1). New York: Dover.

James, William (1902/1936). *The varieties of religious experience.* New York: Modern Library.

Jamison, Kay (1992). *Touched with fire: Manic depressive illness and the artistic temperament.* New York: Free Press.

Jamison, Kay (1999). *Night falls fast: Understanding suicide.* New York: Knopf.

Jancke, Lutz; Schlaug, Gottfried; & Steinmetz, Helmuth (1997). Hand skill asymmetry in professional musicians. *Brain and Cognition, 34,* 424–432.

Jang, Kerry L.; McCrae, Robert R.; Angleitner, Alois; et al. (1998). Heritability of facet-level traits in a cross-cultural twin sample: Support for a hierarchical model of personality. *Journal of Personality and Social Psychology, 74,* 1556–1565.

Janis, Irving L. (1982). *Groupthink: Psychological studies of policy decisions and fiascoes* (2nd ed.). Boston: Houghton Mifflin.

Janis, Irving L. (1989). *Crucial decisions: Leadership in policymaking and crisis management.* New York: Free Press.

Janis, Irving L.; Kaye, Donald; & Kirschner, Paul (1965). Facilitating effects of "eating while reading" on responsiveness to persuasive communications. *Journal of Personality and Social Psychology, 1,* 181–186.

Jenkins, John G., & Dallenbach, Karl M. (1924). Obliviscence during sleep and waking. *American Journal of Psychology, 35,* 605–612.

Jenkins, Sharon Rae (1994). Need for power and women's careers over 14 years: Structural power, job satisfaction, and motive change. *Journal of Personality and Social Psychology, 66,* 155–165.

Jensen, Arthur R. (1969). How much can we boost IQ and scholastic achievement? *Harvard Educational Review, 39,* 1–123.

Jensen, Arthur R. (1981). *Straight talk about mental tests.* New York: Free Press.

Jensen, Arthur R. (1998). *The g factor: The science of mental ability.* Westport, CT: Praeger/Greenwood.

Jiang, Yuhong; Saxe, Rebecca; & Kanwisher, Nancy (2004). Functional magnetic resonance imaging provides new constraints on theories of the psychological refractory period. *Psychological Science, 15,* 390–396.

Johns, Michael; Schmader, Toni; & Martens, Andy (2005). Knowing is half the battle: Teaching stereotype threat as a means of improving women's math performance. *Psychological Science, 16,* 175–179.

Johnson, Marcia K. (1995). The relation between memory and reality. Paper presented at the annual meeting of the American Psychological Association, New York.

Johnson, Marcia K.; Hashtroudi, Shahin; & Lindsay, D. Stephen (1993). Source monitoring. *Psychological Bulletin, 114,* 3–28.

Johnson, Robert, & Downing, Leslie (1979). Deindividuation and valence of cues: Effects of prosocial and antisocial behavior. *Journal of Personality and Social Psychology, 37,* 1532–1538.

Jones, Amanda C., & Gosling, Samuel D. (2005). Temperament and personality in dogs (Canis familiaris): A review and evaluation of past research. *Applied Animal Behaviour Science, 95,* 1–53.

Jones, Edward E. (1990). *Interpersonal perception.* New York: Macmillan.

Jones, James M. (1991). Psychological models of race: What have they been and what should they be? In J. D. Goodchilds (Ed.), *Psychological perspectives on human diversity in America.* Washington, DC: American Psychological Association.

Jones, Mary Cover (1924). A laboratory study of fear: The case of Peter. *Pedagogical Seminary, 31,* 308–315.

Joseph, Stephen, & Linley, P. Alex (2005). Positive adjustment to threatening events: An organismic valuing theory of growth through adversity. *Review of General Psychology, 9,* 262–280.

Jost, John T.; Glaser, Jack; Kruglanski, Arie W.; & Sulloway, Frank J. (2003). Political conservatism as motivated social cognition. *Psychological Bulletin, 129,* 339–375.

Judd, Charles M.; Park, Bernadette; Ryan, Carey S.; et al. (1995). Stereotypes and ethnocentrism: Diverging interethnic perceptions of African American and white American youth. *Journal of Personality and Social Psychology, 69,* 460–481.

Jung, Carl (1967). *Collected works.* Princeton, NJ: Princeton University Press.

Jusczyk, Peter W. (2002). How infants adapt speech-processing capacities to native-language structure. *Current Directions in Psychological Science, 11,* 15–18.

Jusczyk, Peter W.; Houston, D.; & Newsome, M. (1999). The beginnings of word segmentation in English-learning infants. *Cognitive Psychology, 39,* 159–207.

Just, Marcel A.; Carpenter, Patricia A.; Keller, T. A.; et al. (2001). Interdependence of nonoverlapping cortical systems in dual cognitive tasks. *NeuroImage, 14,* 417–426.

Kagan, Jerome (1984). *The nature of the child.* New York: Basic Books.

Kagan, Jerome (1997). Temperament and the reactions to unfamiliarity. *Child Development, 68,* 139–143.

Kahn, Arnold S. (2004). 2003 Carolyn Sherif Award Address: What college women do and do not experience as rape. *Psychology of Women Quarterly, 28,* 9–15.

Kahneman, Daniel (2003). A perspective on judgment and choice: Mapping bounded rationality. *American Psychologist, 58,* 697–720.

Kahneman, Daniel, & Treisman, Anne (1984). Changing views of attention and automaticity. In R. Parasuraman, D. R. Davies, & J. Beatty (Eds.), *Varieties of attention.* New York: Academic Press.

Kaiser, Cheryl R.; Vick, S. Brooke; & Major, Brenda (2004). A prospective investigation of the relationship between just-world beliefs and the desire for revenge after September 11, 2001. *Psychological Science, 15,* 503–506.

Kanin, Eugene J. (1985). Date rapists: Differential sexual socialization and relative deprivation. *Archives of Sexual Behavior, 14,* 219–231.

Kanter, Rosabeth M. (1977/1993). *Men and women of the corporation.* New York: Basic Books.

Kanwisher, Nancy (2000). Domain specificity in face perception. *Nature Neuroscience, 3,* 759.

Kaplan, Abraham (1967). A philosophical discussion of normality. *Archives of General Psychiatry, 17,* 325–330.

Kaplan, Meg S.; Morales, Miguel; & Becker, Judith V. (1993). The impact of verbal satiation of adolescent sex offenders: A preliminary report. *Journal of Child Sexual Abuse, 2,* 81–88.

Karasek, Robert, & Theorell, Tores (1990). *Healthy work: Stress, productivity, and the reconstruction of working life.* New York: Basic Books.

Karau, Steven J., & Williams, Kipling D. (1993). Social loafing: A meta-analytic review and theoretical integration. *Journal of Personality and Social Psychology, 65,* 681–706.

Karney, Benjamin, & Bradbury, Thomas N. (2000). Attributions in marriage: State or trait? A growth curve analysis. *Journal of Personality and Social Psychology, 78,* 295–309.

Karni, Avi; Tanne, David; Rubenstein, Barton S.; Askenasy, Jean J. M.; & Sagi, Dov (1994). Dependence on REM sleep of overnight improvement of a perceptual skill. *Science, 265,* 679–682.

Karraker, Katherine H.; Vogel, Dena A.; & Lake, Margaret A. (1995). Parents' gender-stereotyped perceptions of newborns: The eye of the beholder revisited. *Sex Roles, 33,* 687–701.

Karremans, Johan C.; Van Lange, Paul A. M.; Ouwerkerk, Jaap W.; & Kluwer, Esther S. (2003). When forgiving enhances psychological well-being: The role of interpersonal commitment. *Journal of Personality and Social Psychology, 84,* 1011–1026.

Kaschak, Ellyn, & Tiefer, Leonore (Eds.) (2002). *A new view of women's sexual problems.* Binghamton, NY: Haworth Press.

Kashima, Yoshihisa; Yamaguchi, Susumu; Kim, Uichol; et al. (1995). Culture, gender, and self: A perspective from individualism–collectivism research. *Journal of Personality and Social Psychology, 69,* 925–937.

Kasser, Tim, & Ryan, Richard M. (1996). Further examining the American dream: Correlates of financial success as a central life aspiration. *Personality and Social Psychology Bulletin, 22,* 280–287.

Kasser, Tim, & Ryan, Richard M. (2001). Be careful what you wish for: Optimal functioning and the relative attainment of intrinsic and extrinsic goals. In P. Schmuck & K. M. Sheldon (Eds.), *Life goals and well-being.* Lengerich, Germany: Pabst Science Publishers.

Kassinove, Howard (Ed.) (1995). *Anger disorders: Definition, diagnosis, treatment.* Washington, DC: Taylor & Francis.

Katigbak, Marcia S.; Church, A. Timothy; Guanzon-Lapeña, Ma. Angeles; et al. (2002). Are indigenous personality dimensions culture specific? Philippine inventories and the Five-Factor model. *Journal of Personality and Social Psychology, 82,* 89–101.

Katz, Zender (2001). Canadian psychologists' education, trauma history, and the recovery of memories of childhood sexual abuse. (Doctoral Dissertation, Simon Fraser University, 2001.) *Dissertations Abstracts International, 61,* 3848.

Kaufman, Joan, & Zigler, Edward (1987). Do abused children become abusive parents? *American Journal of Orthopsychiatry, 57,* 186–192.

Kazdin, Alan E. (2001). *Behavior modification in applied settings* (6th ed.). Belmont, CA: Wadsworth.

Keating, Caroline F. (1994). World without words: Messages from face and body. In W. J. Lonner & R. Malpass (Eds.), *Psychology and culture.* Needham Heights, MA: Allyn & Bacon.

Keck, Paul E., Jr., & McElroy, Susan L. (1998). Pharmacological treatment of bipolar disorders. In P. E. Nathan & J. M. Gorman (Eds.), *A guide to treatments that work.* New York: Oxford University Press.

Keen, Sam (1986). *Faces of the enemy: Reflections of the hostile imagination.* San Francisco: Harper & Row.

Keller, Heidi; Abels, Monika; Lamm, Bettina; et al. (2005). Ecocultural effects on early infant care: A study in Cameroon, India, and Germany. *Ethos, 33,* 512–541.

Keller, Martin B.; McCullough, James P.; Klein, Daniel N.; et al. (2000, May 18). A comparison of nefazodone, the cognitive behavioral-analysis system of psychotherapy, and their combination for the treatment of chronic depression. *New England Journal of Medicine, 342,* 1462–1470.

Kelman, Herbert C., & Hamilton, V. Lee (1989). *Crimes of obedience: Toward a social psychology of authority and responsibility.* New Haven, CT: Yale University Press.

Keltner, Dacher, & Anderson, Cameron (2000). Saving face for Darwin: The functions and uses of embarrassment. *Current Directions in Psychological Science, 9,* 187–192.

Kemeny, Margaret E. (2003). The psychobiology of stress. *Current Directions in Psychological Science, 12,* 124–129.

Kempermann, G.; Brandon, E. P., & Gage, F. H. (1998). Environmental stimulation of 120/SvJ mice causes increased cell proliferation and neurogenesis in the adult dentate gyrus. *Current Biology, 8,* 939–942.

Kendall [no first name] (1999). Women in Lesotho and the (Western) construction of homophobia. In E. Blackwood & S. E. Wieringa (Eds.), *Female desires: Same-sex relations and transgender practices across cultures.* New York: Columbia University Press.

Kendler, Kenneth S.; Pedersen, Nancy; Johnson, Lars; Neale, Michael C.; & Mathie, A. (1993). A Swedish pilot twin study of affective illness, including hospital and population-ascertained subsamples. *Archives of General Psychiatry, 50,* 699–706.

Kennedy, Donald, & Norman, Colin (2005). Introduction to special issue: What don't we know? *Science, 309,* 75.

Kennedy-Moore, Eileen, & Watson, Jeanne C. (2001). How and when does emotional expression help? *Review of General Psychology, 5,* 187–212.

Kephart, William M. (1967). Some correlates of romantic love. *Journal of Marriage and the Family, 29,* 470–474.

Kerr, Michael E., & Bowen, Murray (1988). *Family evaluation: An approach based on Bowen theory.* New York: Norton.

Kessler, Ronald C.; Chiu, W. T.; Demler, O.; Merikangas, K. R.; & Walters, E. E. (2005). Prevalence, severity, and comorbidity of 12-month DSM-IV disorders in the National Comorbidity Survey Replication. *Archives of General Psychiatry, 62,* 590–592.

Kessler, Ronald C.; Sonnega, A.; Bromet, E.; et al. (1995). Posttraumatic stress disorder in the National Comorbidity Survey. *Archives of General Psychiatry, 52,* 1048–1060.

Khan, A.; Detke, M.; Khan, S. R.; & Mallinckrodt, C. (2003). Placebo response and antidepressant clinical trial outcome. *Journal of Nervous and Mental Diseases, 191,* 211–218.

Kida, Thomas (2006). *Don't believe everything you think: The 6 basic mistakes we make in thinking.* Amherst, NY: Prometheus Books.

Kiecolt-Glaser, Janice K.; Garner, Warren; Speicher, Carl; et al. (1985). Psychosocial modifiers of immunocompetence in medical students. *Psychosomatic Medicine, 46,* 7–14.

Kiecolt-Glaser, Janice K.; Loving, T. J.; Stowell, J. R.; et al. (2005). Hostile marital interactions, proinflammatory cytokine production, and wound healing. *Archives of General Psychiatry, 62,* 1377–1384.

Kiecolt-Glaser, Janice K.; Malarkey, William B.; Chee, MaryAnn; et al. (1993). Negative behavior during marital conflict is associated with immunological down-regulation. *Psychosomatic Medicine, 55,* 395–409.

Kiecolt-Glaser, Janice K., & Newton, Tamara L. (2001). Marriage and health: His and hers. *Psychological Bulletin, 127,* 472–503.

Kiecolt-Glaser, Janice K.; Page, Gayle G.; Marucha, Phillip T.; et al. (1998). Psychological influences on surgical recovery: Perspectives from psychoneuroimmunology. *American Psychologist, 53,* 1209–1218.

Kihlstrom, John F. (1994). Hypnosis, delayed recall, and the principles of memory. *International Journal of Clinical and Experimental Hypnosis, 40,* 337–345.

Kihlstrom, John F. (1995). From a subject's point of view: The experiment as conversation and collaboration between investigator and subject. Invited address presented at the annual meeting of the American Psychological Society, New York.

Killeen, Peter R. (2005). An alternative to null-hypothesis significance. *Psychological Science, 16,* 345–353.

Kim, Hannah L.; Streltzer, Jon; & Goebert, Deborah (1999). St. John's wort for depression: A meta-analysis of well-defined clinical trials. *Journal of Nervous and Mental Diseases, 187,* 532–538.

Kim, Heejung, & Markus, Hazel Rose (1999). Deviance or uniqueness, harmony or conformity? A cultural analysis. *Journal of Personality and Social Psychology, 77,* 785–800.

King, M., & Woollett, E. (1997). Sexually assaulted males: 115 men consulting a counseling service. *Archives of Sexual Behavior, 26,* 579–588.

King, Pamela (1989, October). The chemistry of doubt. *Psychology Today, 58,* 60.

King, Patricia M., & Kitchener, Karen S. (1994). *Developing reflective judgment: Understanding and promoting intellectual growth and critical thinking in adolescents and adults.* San Francisco: Jossey Bass.

Kinoshita, Sachiko, & Peek-O'Leary, Marie (2005). Does the compatibility effect in the race Implicit Association Test reflect familiarity or affect? *Psychonomic Bulletin & Review, 12,* 442–452.

Kinsey, Alfred C.; Pomeroy, Wardell B.; & Martin, Clyde E. (1948). *Sexual behavior in the human male.* Philadelphia: Saunders.

Kinsey, Alfred C.; Pomeroy, Wardell B.; Martin, Clyde E.; & Gebhard, Paul H. (1953). *Sexual behavior in the human female.* Philadelphia: Saunders.

Kirsch, Irving (1997). Response expectancy theory and application: A decennial review. *Applied and Preventive Psychology, 6,* 69–70.

Kirsch, Irving, & Lynn, Steven J. (1995). The altered state of hypnosis: Changes in the theoretical landscape. *American Psychologist, 50,* 846–858.

Kirsch, Irving, & Lynn, Steven J. (1998). Dissociation theories of hypnosis. *Psychological Bulletin, 123,* 100–113.

Kirsch, Irving; Montgomery, G.; & Sapirstein, G. (1995). Hypnosis as an adjunct to cognitive behavioral psychotherapy: A meta-analysis. *Journal of Consulting and Clinical Psychology, 63,* 214–220.

Kirsch, Irving; Silva, Christopher E.; Carone, James E.; Johnston, J. Dennis; & Simon, B. (1989). The surreptitious observation design: An experimental paradigm for distinguishing artifact from essence in hypnosis. *Journal of Abnormal Psychology, 98,* 132–136.

Kirsch, Jonathan (2006). *A history of the end of the world.* San Francisco: HarperSanFrancisco.

Kish, Stephen J. (2003) What is the evidence that Ecstasy (MDMA) can cause Parkinson's disease? *Movement Disorders 18,* 1219–1223.

Kitayama, Shinobu, & Markus, Hazel R. (1994). Introduction to cultural psychology and emotion research. In S. Kitayama & H. R. Markus (Eds.), *Emotion and culture: Empirical studies of mutual influence.* Washington, DC: American Psychological Association.

Kitchener, Karen S.; Lynch, Cindy L.; Fischer, Kurt W.; & Wood, Phillip K. (1993). Developmental range of reflective judgment: The effect of contextual support and practice on developmental stage. *Developmental Psychology, 29,* 893–906.

Klauer, Sheila G.; Dingus, Thomas A.; Neale, Vicki L., et al. (2006). *The impact of driver inattention on near- crash/crash risk: An analysis using the 100-car naturalistic driving study data*[pdf]. Performed by Virginia Tech Transportation Institute, Blacksburg, VA, sponsored by National Highway Traffic Safety Administration, Washington, DC, DOT HS 810 594.

Kleim, J. A.; Swain, R. A.; Armstrong, K. A.; et al. (1998). Selective synaptic plasticity within the cerebellar cortex following complex motor skill learning. *Neurobiology of Learning and Memory, 69,* 274–289.

Klein, Daniel N.; Schwartz, Joseph E.; Santiago, Neil J.; et al. (2003). Therapeutic alliance in depression treatment: Controlling for prior change and patient characteristics. *Journal of Consulting & Clinical Psychology, 71,* 997–1006.

Klein, Raymond, & Armitage, Roseanne (1979). Rhythms in human performance: 1 1/2-hour oscillations in cognitive style. *Science, 204,* 1326–1328.

Klein, Stanley B.; Cosmides, Leda; Costabile, Kristi A.; & Mei, Lisa (2002). Is there something special about the self? A neuropsychological case study. *Journal of Research in Personality, 36,* 490–506.

Kleinke, Chris L.; Peterson, Thomas R.; & Rutledge, Thomas R. (1998). Effects of self-generated facial expressions on mood. *Journal of Personality and Social Psychology, 74,* 272–279.

Kleinman, Arthur (1988). *Rethinking psychiatry: From cultural category to personal experience.* New York: Free Press.

Klima, Edward S., & Bellugi, Ursula (1966). Syntactic regularities in the speech of children. In J. Lyons & R. J. Wales (Eds.), *Psycholinguistics papers.* Edinburgh, Scotland: Edinburgh University Press.

Klimoski, R. (1992). Graphology and personnel selection. In B. Beyerstein & D. Beyerstein (Eds.), *The write stuff: Evaluations of graphology—The study of handwriting analysis.* Buffalo, NY: Prometheus Books.

Kling, Kristen C.; Hyde, Janet S.; Showers, Carolin J.; & Buswell, Brenda N. (1999). Gender differences in self-esteem: A meta-analysis. *Psychological Bulletin, 125,* 470–500.

Klohnen, Eva C., & Bera, Stephan (1998). Behavioral and experiential patterns of avoidantly and securely attached women across adulthood: A 31-year longitudinal perspective. *Journal of Personality and Social Psychology, 74,* 211–223.

Kluft, Richard P. (1987). The simulation and dissimulation of multiple personality disorder. *American Journal of Clinical Hypnosis, 30,* 104–118.

Kochanska, Grazyna; Forman, David R.; Aksan, Nazan; & Dunbar, Stephen B. (2005). Pathways to conscience: Early mother-child mutually responsive orientation and children's moral emotion, conduct, and cognition. *Journal of Child Psychology and Psychiatry, 46,* 19–34.

Kochanska, Grazyna, & Knaack, Amy (2003). Effortful control as a personality characteristic of young children: Antecedents, correlates, and consequences. *Journal of Personality, 71,* 1087–1112.

Kohlberg, Lawrence (1964). Development of moral character and moral ideology. In M. Hoffman & L. W. Hoffman (Eds.), *Review of child development research.* New York: Russell Sage Foundation.

Köhler, Wolfgang (1925). *The mentality of apes.* New York: Harcourt, Brace.

Köhler, Wolfgang (1929). *Gestalt psychology.* New York: Horace Liveright.

Kolb, Bryan; Gibb, Robbin; & Robinson, Terry E. (2003). Brain plasticity and behavior. *Current Directions in Psychological Science, 12,* 1–5.

Koocher, Gerald P.; Goodman, Gail S.; White, C. Sue; et al. (1995). Psychological science and the use of anatomically detailed dolls in child sexual-abuse assessments. *Psychological Bulletin, 118,* 199–222.

Kopta, Stephen M.; Howard, Kenneth I.; Lowry, Jenny L.; & Beutler, Larry E. (1994). Patterns of symptomatic recovery in psychotherapy. *Journal of Consulting and Clinical Psychology, 62,* 1009–1016.

Koss, Mary P. (1993). Rape: Scope, impact, interventions, and public policy responses. *American Psychologist, 48,* 1062–1069.

Kosslyn, Stephen M. (1980). *Image and mind.* Cambridge, MA: Harvard University Press.

Kosslyn, Stephen M.; Pascual-Leone, A.; Felician, O.; et al. (1999). The role of area 17 in visual imagery: convergent evidence from PET and rTMS. *Science, 284,* 167–170.

Koyama, Tetsua; McHaffie, John G.; Laurienti, Paul J.; & Coghill, Robert C. (2005). The subjective experience of pain: Where expectations become reality. *Proceedings of the National Academy of Sciences, 102,* 12950–12955.

Kraft, Ulrich (2005, October). Mending the spinal cord. *Scientific American Mind,* pp. 68–73.

Krieger, Nancy, & Sidney, S. (1996). Racial discrimination and blood pressure: The CARDIA study of young black and white adults. *American Journal of Public Health, 86,* 1370–1378.

Krimsky, Sheldon (2003). *Science in the private interest.* Lanham, MD: Rowman & Littlefield.

Kring, Ann M., & Gordon, Albert H. (1998). Sex differences in emotion: Expression, experience, and physiology. *Journal of Personality and Social Psychology, 74,* 686–703.

Kripke, Daniel F. (1974). Ultradian rhythms in sleep and wakefulness. In E. D. Weitzman (Ed.), *Advances in sleep research* (Vol. 1). Flushing, NY: Spectrum.

Kroll, Barry M. (1992). *Teaching hearts and minds: College students reflect on the Vietnam War in literature.* Carbondale: Southern Illinois University Press.

Kross, Ethan; Ayduk, Ozlem; & Mischel, Walter (2005). When asking "why" does not hurt: Distinguishing rumination from reflective processing of negative emotions. *Psychological Science, 16,* 709–715.

Krueger, Robert F. (2000). Phenotypic, genetic, and nonshared environmental parallels in the structure of personality: A view from the Multidimensional Personality Questionnaire. *Journal of Personality and Social Psychology, 79,* 1057–1067.

Krueger, Robert F.; Hicks, Brian M.; & McGue, Matt (2001). Altruism and antisocial behavior: Independent tendencies, unique personality correlates, distinct etiologies. *Psychological Science, 12,* 397–402.

Krupa, David J.; Thompson, Judith K.; & Thompson, Richard F. (1993). Localization of a memory trace in the mammalian brain. *Science, 260,* 989–991.

Krützen, Michael; Mann, Janet; Heithaus, Michael R.; et al. (2005). Cultural transmission of tool use in bottlenose dolphins. *Proceedings of the National Academy of Sciences, 102,* 8939–8943; published online before print as 10.1073/pnas.0500232102.

Kuhl, Patricia K.; Williams, Karen A.; Lacerda, Francisco; et al. (1992, January 31). Linguistic experience alters phonetic perception in infants by 6 months of age. *Science, 255,* 606–608.

Kuhn, Deanna; Weinstock, Michael; & Flaton, Robin (1994). How well do jurors reason? Competence dimensions of individual variation in a juror reasoning task. *Psychological Science, 5,* 289–296.

Kuncel, Nathan R.; Hezlett, Sarah A.; & Ones, Deniz S. (2004). Academic performance, career potential, creativity, and job performance: Can one construct predict them all? *Journal of Personality and Social Psychology, 86,* 148–161.

Kunda, Ziva (1990). The case for motivated reasoning. *Psychological Bulletin, 108,* 480–498.

Kurdek, Lawrence A. (2005). What do we know about gay and lesbian couples? *Current Directions in Psychological Science, 14,* 251–254.

Kutchins, Herb, & Kirk, Stuart A. (1997). *Making us crazy: DSM. The psychiatric bible and the creation of mental disorders.* New York: Free Press.

LaBerge, Stephen, & Levitan, Lynne (1995). Validity established of DreamLight cues for eliciting lucid dreaming. *Dreaming: Journal of the Association for the Study of Dreams, 5,* 159–168.

Lachman, Margie E., & Weaver, Suzanne L. (1998). The sense of control as a moderator of social class differences in health and well-being. *Journal of Personality and Social Psychology, 74,* 763–773.

Lachman, Sheldon J. (1996). Processes in perception: Psychological transformations of highly structured stimulus material. *Perceptual and Motor Skills, 83,* 411–418.

LaFrance, Marianne; Hecht, Marvin A.; & Paluck, Elizabeth L. (2003). The contingent smile: A meta-analysis of sex differences in smiling. *Psychological Bulletin, 129,* 305–334.

Lahey, B. B.; Pelham, W. E.; Loney, J.; et al. (2005). Instability of the DSM-IV subtypes of ADHD from preschool through elementary school. *Archives of General Psychiatry, 62,* 896–902.

Lai, Hui-Ling, & Good, Marion (2005). Music improves sleep quality in older adults. *Journal of Advanced Nursing, 49,* 234–244.

Laird, James D. (1974). Self-attribution of emotion: The effects of expressive behavior on the quality of emotional experience. *Journal of Personality and Social Psychology, 29,* 475–486.

Lakin, Jessica L., & Chartrand, Tanya L. (2003). Using nonconscious behavioral mimicry to create affiliation and rapport. *Psychological Science, 14,* 334–339.

Lakoff, Robin T., & Coyne, James C. (1993). *Father knows best: The use and abuse of power in Freud's case of "Dora."* New York: Teachers College Press.

Lamb, Sharon (2002). *The secret lives of girls.* New York: The Free Press.

Landrine, Hope (1988). Revising the framework of abnormal psychology. In P. Bronstein & K. Quina (Eds.), *Teaching a psychology of people.* Washington, DC: American Psychological Association.

Lang, Ariel J.; Craske, Michelle G.; Brown, Matt; & Ghaneian, Atousa (2001). Fear-related state dependent memory. *Cognition & Emotion, 15,* 695–703.

Lang, Frieder R., & Heckhausen, Jutta (2001). Perceived control over development and subjective well-being: Differential benefits across adulthood. *Journal of Personality and Social Psychology, 81,* 509–523.

Langer, Ellen J. (1983). *The psychology of control.* Beverly Hills, CA: Sage.

Langer, Ellen J.; Blank, Arthur; & Chanowitz, Benzion (1978). The mindlessness of ostensibly thoughtful action: The role of placebic information in interpersonal interaction. *Journal of Personality and Social Psychology, 36,* 635–642.

Lanphear, B. P.; Hornung, R.; Ho, M.; et al. (2002). Environmental lead exposure during early childhood. *Journal of Pediatrics, 140,* 40–47.

Lanphear, B. P.; Hornung, R.; Khoury, J.; et al. (2005). Low-level environmental lead exposure and children's intellectual function: An international pooled analysis. *Environmental Health Perspectives, 113,* 894–899.

Larsen, Jeff T.; McGraw, A. Peter; Mellers, Barbara A.; & Cacioppo, John T. (2004). The agony of victory and the thrill of defeat. *Psychological Science, 15,* 325–330.

Latané, Bibb; Williams, Kipling; & Harkins, Stephen (1979). Many hands make light the work: The causes and consequences of social loafing. *Journal of Personality and Social Psychology, 37,* 822–832.

Laumann, Edward O., & Gagnon John H. (1995). A sociological perspective on sexual action. In R. G. Parker & J. H. Gagnon (Eds.), *Conceiving sexuality: Approaches to sex research in a postmodern world.* New York: Routledge.

Laumann, Edward O.; Gagnon, John H.; Michael, Robert T.; & Michaels, Stuart (1994). *The social organization of sexuality.* Chicago: University of Chicago Press.

Laurence, J. R., & Perry, C. (1988). *Hypnosis, will, and memory: A psycholegal history.* New York: Guilford Press.

Lavie, Peretz (1976). Ultradian rhythms in the perception of two apparent motions. *Chronobiologia, 3,* 21–218.

Lazarus, Richard S. (2000). Toward better research on stress and coping. *American Psychologist, 55,* 665–673.

Lazarus, Richard S., & Folkman, Susan (1984). *Stress, appraisal, and coping.* New York: Springer.

Leach, Colin W.; Spears, Russell; Branscombe, Nyla R.; & Doosje, Bertjan (2003). Malicious pleasure: Schadenfreude at the suffering of another group. *Journal of Personality and Social Psychology, 84,* 932–943.

LeDoux, Joseph E. (1996). *The emotional brain.* New York: Simon & Schuster.

Leinbach, Mary D.; Hort, Barbara E.; & Fagot, Beverly I. (1997). Bears are for boys: Metaphorical associations in young children's gender stereotypes. *Cognitive Development, 12,* 107–130.

Lemieux, Robert, & Hale, Jerold L. (2000). Intimacy, passion, and commitment among married individuals: Further testing of the Triangular Theory of Love. *Psychological Reports, 87,* 941–948.

Lent, James R. (1968, June). Mimosa cottage: Experiment in hope. *Psychology Today,* 51–58.

Lepore, Stephen J.; Ragan, Jennifer D.; & Jones, Scott (2000). Talking facilitates cognitive-emotional processes of adaptation to an acute stressor. *Journal of Personality and Social Psychology, 78,* 499–508.

Lepowsky, Maria (1994). *Fruit of the motherland: Gender in an egalitarian society.* New York: Columbia University Press.

Lepper, Mark R.; Greene, David; & Nisbett, Richard E. (1973). Undermining children's intrinsic interest with extrinsic rewards. *Journal of Personality and Social Psychology, 28,* 129–137.

Leproult, Rachel; Van Reeth, Olivier; Byrne, Maria M.; et al. (1997). Sleepiness, performance, and neuroendocrine function during sleep deprivation: Effects of exposure to bright light or exercise. *Journal of Biological Rhythms, 12,* 245–258.

Lerner, Harriet G. (1989). *The dance of intimacy.* New York: Harper & Row.

Lerner, Melvin J. (1980). *The belief in a just world: A fundamental delusion.* New York: Plenum.

Lester, Barry M.; LaGasse, Linda L.; & Seifer, Ronald (1998, October 23). Cocaine exposure and children: The meaning of subtle effects. *Science, 282,* 633–634.

LeVay, Simon (1991). A difference in hypothalamic structure between heterosexual and homosexual men. *Science, 253,* 1034–1037.

Levenson, Robert W. (1992). Autonomic nervous system differences among emotions. *Psychological Science, 3,* 23–27.

Levenson, Robert W.; Ekman, Paul; & Friesen, Wallace V. (1990). Voluntary facial action generates emotion-specific autonomic nervous system activity. *Psychophysiology, 27,* 363–384.

Levin, Daniel T. (2000). Race as a visual feature: Using visual search and perceptual discrimination tasks to understand face categories and the cross-race recognition deficit. *Journal of Experimental Psychology. General, 129,* 559–574.

Levine, James A.; Eberhardt, Norman L.; & Jensen, Michael D. (1999, January 8). Role of nonexercise activity thermogenesis in resistance to fat gain in humans. *Science, 283,* 212–214.

Levine, Robert V. (2003, May-June). The kindness of strangers. *American Scientist, 91,* 227–233.

Levy, Becca. (1996). Improving memory in old age through implicit self-stereotyping. *Journal of Personality and Social Psychology, 71,* 1092–1107.

Levy, David A. (1997). *Tools of critical thinking: Metathoughts for psychology.* Boston: Allyn & Bacon.

Levy, Jerre; Trevarthen, Colwyn; & Sperry, Roger W. (1972). Perception of bilateral chimeric figures following hemispheric deconnection. *Brain, 95,* 61–78.

Levy, Robert I. (1984). The emotions in comparative perspective. In K. R. Scherer & P. Ekman (Eds.), *Approaches to emotion.* Hillsdale, NJ: Erlbaum.

Lewin, Kurt (1948). *Resolving social conflicts.* New York: Harper.

Lewis, Dorothy O. (1992). From abuse to violence: Psychophysiological consequences of maltreatment. *Journal of the American Academy of Child and Adolescent Psychiatry, 31,* 383–391.

Lewontin, Richard C. (1970). Race and intelligence. *Bulletin of the Atomic Scientists, 26*(3), 2–8.

Lewontin, Richard C. (2001, March 5). Genomania: A disorder of modern biology and medicine. Invited address at the University of California, Los Angeles.

Lewy, Alfred J.; Ahmed, Saeeduddin; Jackson, Jeanne L.; & Sack, Robert L. (1992). Melatonin shifts human circadian rhythms according to a phase response curve. *Chronobiology International, 9,* 380–392.

Li, Shu-Chen; Lindenberger, Ulman; Hommel, Bernhard; et al. (2004). Transformations in the couplings among intellectual abilities and constituent cognitive processes across the life span. *Psychological Science, 15,* 155–163.

Lichtenstein, Sarah; Slovic, Paul; Fischhoff, Baruch; et al. (1978). Judged frequency of lethal events. *Journal of Experimental Psychology: Human Learning and Memory, 4,* 551–578.

Lickona, Thomas (1983). *Raising good children.* New York: Bantam.

Lieberman, J. A.; Stroup, T. S.; McEvoy, J. P.; et al. (2005, September 22). Effectiveness of antipsychotic drugs in patients with chronic schizophrenia. *New England Journal of Medicine, 353,* 1209–1223.

Lieberman, Matthew (2000). Intuition: A social cognitive neuroscience approach. *Psychological Bulletin, 126,* 109–137.

Lien, Mei-Ching; Ruthruff, Eric; & Johnston, James C. (2006). Attentional limitations in doing two tasks at once: The search for exceptions. *Current Directions in Psychological Science, 16,* 89–93.

Liepert, J.; Bauder, H.; Miltner, W. H.; et al. (2000). Treatment-induced cortical reorganization after stroke in humans. *Stroke, 31,* 1210–1216.

Light, Kathleen C.; Grewen, Karen M.; & Amico, Janet A. (2005). More frequent partner hugs and higher oxytocin levels are linked to lower blood pressure and heart rate in premenopausal women. *Biological Psychology, 69,* 5–21.

Lilienfeld, Scott O. (1996, January/February). EMDR treatment: Less than meets the eye? *Skeptical Inquirer,* 25–31.

Lilienfeld, Scott O.; Gershon, Jonathan; Duke, Marshall; Marino, Lori; & De Waal, Frans B. M. (1999). A preliminary investigation of the construct of psychopathic personality (psychopathy) in chimpanzees (Pan troglodytes). *Journal of Comparative Psychology, 113,* 365–375.

Lilienfeld, Scott O., & Lohr, Jeffrey (2003). Dissociative identity disorder: Multiple personalities, multiple controversies. In S.O. Lilienfeld, S. J. Lynn, & J. M. Lohr (Eds.), *Science and pseudoscience in clinical psychology.* New York: Guilford.

Lilienfeld, Scott O.; Lynn, Steven Jay; & Lohr, Jeffrey M. (Eds.) (2003). *Science and pseudoscience in clinical psychology.* New York: Guilford.

Lilienfeld, Scott O.; Wood, James M.; & Garb, Howard N. (2000). The scientific status of projective techniques. *Psychological Science in the Public Interest, 1,* 27–66.

Lillard, Angeline S. (1998). Ethnopsychologies: Cultural variations in theories of mind. *Psychological Bulletin, 123,* 3–32.

Lin, Keh-Ming; Poland, Russell E.; & Chien, C. P. (1990). Ethnicity and psychopharmacology: Recent findings and future research directions. In E. Sorel (Ed.), *Family, culture, and psychobiology.* New York: Legas.

Lin, L.; Hungs, M.; & Mignot, E. (2001). Narcolepsy and the HLA region. *Journal of Neuroimmunology, 117,* 9–20.

Lindsay, D. Stephen, & Read, J. D. (1994). Psychotherapy and memories of childhood sexual abuse: A cognitive perspective. *Applied Cognitive Psychology, 8,* 281–338.

Linton, Marigold (1978). Real-world memory after six years: An in vivo study of very long-term memory. In M. M. Gruneberg, P. E. Morris, & R. N. Sykes (Eds.), *Practical aspects of memory.* London: Academic Press.

Linton, Simi (1998). *Claiming disability: Knowledge and identity.* New York: New York University Press.

Linton, Simi (2006). *My body politic.* Ann Arbor, MI: University of Michigan Press.

Linville, P. W.; Fischer, G. W.; & Fischhoff, B. (1992). AIDS risk perceptions and decision biases. In J. B. Pryor & G. D. Reeder (Eds.), *The social psychology of HIV infection.* Hillsdale, NJ: Erlbaum.

Lipps, Jere H. (2004, January/February). Judging authority. *Skeptical Inquirer,* 35–37.

Lissner, L.; Odell, P. M.; D'Agostino, R. B.; et al. (1991, June 27). Variability of body weight and health outcomes in the Framingham population. *New England Journal of Medicine, 324,* 1839–1844.

Locke, Edwin A., & Latham, Gary P. (1990). Work motivation and satisfaction: Light at the end of the tunnel. *Psychological Science, 1,* 240–246.

Locke, Edwin A., & Latham, Gary P. (2002). Building a practically useful theory of goal setting and task motivation. *American Psychologist, 57,* 705–717.

Locke, Edwin A.; Shaw, Karyll; Saari, Lise; & Latham, Gary (1981). Goal-setting and task performance: 1969–1980. *Psychological Bulletin, 90,* 125–152.

Loehlin, John C. (1992). *Genes and environment in personality development.* Newbury Park CA: Sage.

Loehlin, John C.; Horn, J. M.; & Willerman, L. (1996). Heredity, environment, and IQ in the Texas adoption study. In R. J. Sternberg & E. Grigorenko (Eds.), *Intelligence: Heredity and environment.* New York: Cambridge University Press.

Loftus, Elizabeth F. (1996). Memory distortion and false memory creation. *Bulletin of the American Academy of Psychiatry and the Law, 24,* 281–295.

Loftus, Elizabeth F., & Greene, Edith (1980). Warning: Even memory for faces may be contagious. *Law and Human Behavior, 4,* 323–334.

Loftus, Elizabeth F., & Ketcham, Katherine (1994). *The myth of repressed memory.* New York: St. Martin's Press.

Loftus, Elizabeth F.; Miller, David G.; & Burns, Helen J. (1978). Semantic integration of verbal information into a visual memory. *Journal of Experimental Psychology: Human Learning and Memory, 4,* 19–31.

Loftus, Elizabeth F., & Palmer, John C. (1974). Reconstruction of automobile destruction: An example of the interaction between language and memory. *Journal of Verbal Learning and Verbal Behavior, 13,* 585–589.

Loftus, Elizabeth F., & Pickrell, Jacqueline E. (1995). The formation of false memories. *Psychiatric Annals, 25,* 720–725.

Loftus, Elizabeth F., & Zanni, Guido (1975). Eyewitness testimony: The influence of the wording of a question. *Bulletin of the Psychonomic Society, 5,* 86–88.

Lohr, Jeffrey M.; Montgomery, Robert W.; Lilienfeld, Scott O.; & Tolin, David F. (1999). Pseudoscience and the commercial promotion of trauma treatments. In R. Gist & B. Lubin (Eds.), *Response to disaster: Psychosocial, community, and ecological approaches.* Philadelphia, PA: Brunner/Mazel (Taylor & Francis).

Lohr, Jeffrey M.; Tolin, D. F.; & Lilienfeld, Scott O. (1998). Efficacy of eye movement desensitization and reprocessing: Implications for behavior therapy. *Behavior Therapy, 29,* 123–156.

Lonner, Walter J. (1995). Culture and human diversity. In E. Trickett, R. Watts, & D. Birman (Eds.), *Human diversity: Perspectives on people in context.* San Francisco: Jossey-Bass.

Lopes, A. C.; de Mathis, M. E.; Canteras, M. M.; et al. (2004). Update on neurosurgical treatment for obsessive compulsive disorder [original article in Portuguese]. *Rev bras Psiquiatr, 26,* 62–66.

Lopez, N. L.; Bonenberger, J. L.; & Schneider, H. G. (2001). Parental disciplinary history, current levels of empathy, and moral reasoning in young adults. *North American Journal of Psychology, 3,* 193–204.

López, Steven R. (1995). Testing ethnic minority children. In B. B. Wolman (Ed.), *The encyclopedia of psychology, psychiatry, and psychoanalysis.* New York: Holt.

Lorber, Michael F. (2004). Psychophysiology of aggression, psychopathy, and conduct problems: A meta-analysis. *Psychological Bulletin, 130,* 531–552.

Lubinski, David (2004). Introduction to the special section on cognitive abilities: 100 years after Spearman's (1904) "'General intelligence,' objectively determined and measured." *Journal of Personality and Social Psychology, 86,* 96–111.

Lucchina, L. A.; Curtis, O. F.; Putnam, P.; et al. (1998). Psychophysical measurement of 6-n-propylthiouracil (PROP) taste perception. *Annals of the New York Academy of Sciences, 855,* 816–819.

Luders, Eileen; Narr, Katherine L.; Thompson, Paul M.; et al. (2004). Gender differences in cortical complexity. *Nature Neuroscience, 7,* 799–800.

Luengo, M. A.; Carrillo-de-la-Peña, M. T.; Otero, J. M.; & Romero, E. (1994). A short-term longitudinal study of impulsivity and antisocial behavior. *Journal of Personality and Social Psychology, 66,* 542–548.

Luepnitz, Deborah A. (1988). *The family interpreted: Feminist theory in clinical practice.* New York: Basic Books.

Lugaresi, Elio; Medori, R.; Montagna, P.; et al. (1986, October 16). Fatal familial insomnia and dysautonomia with selective degeneration of thalamic nuclei. *New England Journal of Medicine, 315,* 997–1003.

Luhrmann, T. M. (2000). *Of two minds: the growing disorder in American psychiatry.* New York: Knopf.

Luna, Beatriz; Garver, Krista E.; Urban, Trinity A.; et al. (2004). Maturation of cognitive processes from late childhood to adulthood. *Child Development, 75,* 1357–1372.

Luria, Alexander R. (1968). *The mind of a mnemonist* (L. Soltaroff, Trans.). New York: Basic Books.

Luria, Alexander R. (1980). *Higher cortical functions in man* (2nd rev. ed.). New York: Basic Books.

Lutz, Catherine (1988). *Unnatural emotions.* Chicago: University of Chicago Press.

Lykken, David T. (1995). *The antisocial personalities.* Hillsdale, NJ: Erlbaum.

Lykken, David T., & Tellegen, Auke (1996). Happiness is a stochastic phenomenon. *Psychological Science, 7,* 186–189.

Lynn, Steven Jay; Rhue, Judith W.; & Weekes, John R. (1990). Hypnotic involuntariness: A social cognitive analysis. *Psychological Review, 97,* 69–184.

Lytton, Hugh, & Romney, David M. (1991). Parents' differential socialization of boys and girls: A meta-analysis. *Psychological Bulletin, 109,* 267–296.

Lyubomirsky, Sonja; Caldwell, Nicole D.; & Nolen-Hoeksema, Susan (1998). Effects of ruminative and distracting responses to depressed mood on retrieval of autobiographical memories. *Journal of Personality and Social Psychology, 75,* 166–177.

Maas, James B. (1998). *Power sleep.* New York: Villard.

Maass, Anne; Cadinu, Mara; Guarnieri, Gaia; & Grasselli, Annalisa (2003). Sexual harassment under social identity threat: The computer harassment paradigm. *Journal of Personality and Social Psychology, 85*, 853–870.

MacArthur Foundation Research Network on Successful Midlife Development (1999). Report of latest findings (Orville G. Brim, director; 2145 14th Avenue, Vero Beach, FL 32960).

Maccoby, Eleanor E. (1998). *The two sexes: Growing up apart, coming together.* Cambridge, MA: Belknap Press/Harvard University Press.

Maccoby, Eleanor E. (2002). Gender and group process: A developmental perspective. *Current Directions in Psychological Science, 11*, 54–58.

Mack, Arien (2003). Inattentional blindness: Looking without seeing. *Current Directions in Psychological Science, 12*, 180–184.

MacKinnon, Donald W. (1968). Selecting students with creative potential. In P. Heist (Ed.), *The creative college student: An unmet challenge.* San Francisco: Jossey-Bass.

MacLean, Paul (1993). Cerebral evolution of emotion. In M. Lewis & J. M. Haviland (Eds.), *Handbook of emotions.* New York: Guilford Press.

Macleod John; Oakes Rachel; Copello, Alex; et al. (2004). Psychological and social sequelae of cannabis and other illicit drug use by young people: a systematic review of longitudinal, general population studies. *The Lancet, 363*, 1568–1569.

Macmillan, Malcolm (2000). *An odd kind of fame: Stories of Phineas Gage.* Cambridge: MIT Press.

Macrae, C. Neil; Kelley, William M.; & Heatherton, Todd F. (2004). A self less ordinary: The medial prefrontal cortex and you. In M. S. Gazzaniga (Ed.), *Cognitive Neurosciences III.* Cambridge, MA: MIT Press.

Macrae, C. Neil; Milne, Alan B.; & Bodenhausen, Galen V. (1994). Stereotypes as energy-saving devices: A peek inside the cognitive toolbox. *Journal of Personality and Social Psychology, 66*, 37–47.

Maddux, James E. (Ed.) (1995). *Self-efficacy, adaptation, and adjustment: Theory, research, and application.* New York: Plenum.

Maddux, James E., & Mundell, Clare E. (1997). Disorders of personality. In V. Derlega, B. Winstead, & W. Jones (Eds.), *Personality: Contemporary theory and research* (2nd ed.). Chicago: Nelson-Hall.

Maguire, Eleanor A.; Gadian, David G.; Johnsrude, Ingrid S.; et al. (2000). Navigation-related structural change in the hippocampi of taxi drivers. *Proceedings of the National Academy of Sciences, 97*, 4398–4403.

Major, Brenda; Spencer, Steven; Schmader, Toni; et al. (1998). Coping with negative stereotypes about intellectual performance: The role of psychological disengagement. *Personality and Social Psychology Bulletin, 24*, 34–50.

Maki, Pauline M.; & Resnick, Susan M. (2000). Longitudinal effects of estrogen replacement therapy on PET cerebral blood flow and cognition. *Neurobiology of Aging, 21*, 373–383.

Malamuth, Neil M.; Linz, Daniel; Heavey, Christopher L.; et al. (1995). Using the confluence model of sexual aggression to predict men's conflict with women: A 10-year follow-up study. *Journal of Personality and Social Psychology, 69*, 353–369.

Malaspina, Dolores (2001). Paternal factors and schizophrenia risk: De novo mutations and imprinting. *Schizophrenia Bulletin, 27*, 379–393.

Mansfield, Elizabeth D., & McAdams, Dan P. (1996). Generativity and themes of agency and community in adult autobiography. *Personality and Social Psychology Bulletin, 22*, 721–731.

Maquet, Pierre; Laereys, S.; Peigneux, P.; et al. (2000). Experience-dependent changes in cerebral activation during human REM sleep. *Nature Neuroscience, 8*, 831–836.

Marcus, Gary F. (1999). *The algebraic mind.* Cambridge, MA: MIT Press.

Marcus, Gary F.; Pinker, Steven; Ullman, Michael; et al. (1992). Over-regularization in language acquisition. *Monographs of the Society for Research in Child Development, 57* (Serial No. 228), 1–182.

Marcus, Gary F.; Vijayan, S.; Rao, S. Bandi; & Vishton, P. M. (1999). Rule learning by seven-month-old infants. *Science, 283*, 77–80.

Marcus-Newhall, Amy; Pedersen, William C.; Carlson, Mike; & Miller, Norman (2000). Displaced aggression is alive and well: A meta-analytic review. *Journal of Personality and Social Psychology, 78*, 670–689.

Margolin, Gayla, & Gordis, Elana B. (2004). Children's exposure to violence in the family and community. *Current Directions in Psychological Science, 13*, 152–155.

Markowitz, J. S.; Donovan, J. L.; DeVane, C. L.; et al. (2003, September 17). Effect of St John's wort on drug metabolism by induction of cytochrome P450 3A4 enzyme. *Journal of the American Medical Association, 290*, 1519–1520.

Markus, Hazel R., & Kitayama, Shinobu (1991). Culture and the self: Implications for cognition, emotion, and motivation. *Psychological Review, 98*, 224–253.

Markus, Rob; Panhuysen, Geert; Tuiten, Adriaan; & Koppeschaar, Hans (2000). Effects of food on cortisol and mood in vulnerable subjects under controllable and uncontrollable stress. *Physiology and Behavior, 70*, 333–342.

Marlatt, G. Alan (1996). Models of relapse and relapse prevention: A commentary. *Experimental and Clinical Psychopharmacology, 4*, 55–60.

Marlatt, G. Alan; Baer, John S.; Kivlahan, Daniel R.; et al. (1998) Screening and brief intervention for high-risk college student drinkers. *Journal of Consulting and Clinical Psychology, 66*, 604–615.

Marlatt, G. Alan, & Rohsenow, Damaris J. (1980). Cognitive processes in alcohol use: Expectancy and the balanced placebo design. In N. K. Mello (Ed.), *Advances in substance abuse* (Vol. 1). Greenwich, CT: JAI Press.

Marsh, Elizabeth J., & Tversky, Barbara (2004). Spinning the stories of our lives. *Applied Cognitive Psychology, 18*, 491–503.

Marshall, Grant N.; Wortman, Camille B.; Vickers, Ross R., Jr.; et al. (1994). The five-factor model of personality as a framework for personality health research. *Journal of Personality and Social Psychology, 67*, 278–286.

Martin, Carol Lynn, & Ruble, Diane (2004). Children's search for gender cues. *Current Directions in Psychological Science, 13*, 67–70.

Martin, Carol Lynn; Ruble, Diane N.; & Szkrybalo, Joel (2002). Cognitive theories of early gender development. *Psychological Bulletin, 128*, 903–933.

Martinez, Gladys M.; Chandra, Anjani; Abma, Joyce C.; et al. (2006). Fertility, Contraception, and Fatherhood: Data on Men and Women From Cycle 6 of the 2002 National Survey of Family Growth. DHHS Publication No. (PHS) 2006–1978. Washington, DC: Centers for Disease Control.

Martino, Gail, & Marks, Lawrence E. (2001). Synesthesia: Strong and weak. *Current Directions in Psychological Science, 10*, 61–69.

Maruta, T.; Colligan R. C.; Malinchoc, M.; & Offord, K. P. (2000). Optimists vs. pessimists: Survival rate among medical patients over a 30-year period. *Mayo Clinic Proceedings, 75*, 140–143.

Masand, P. S. (2000). Side effects of antipsychotics in the elderly. *Journal of Clinical Psychiatry, 61*(suppl. 8), 43–49.

Maslach, Christina; Schaufeli, Wilmar B.; & Leiter, Michael P. (2001). Job burnout. *Annual Review of Psychology, 52*, 397–422.

Maslow, Abraham H. (1970). *Motivation and personality* (2nd ed.). New York: Harper & Row.

Maslow, Abraham H. (1971). *The farther reaches of human nature.* New York: Viking.

Masten, Ann S. (2001). Ordinary magic: Resilience processes in development. *American Psychologist, 56,* 227–238.

Masters, William H., & Johnson, Virginia E. (1966). *Human sexual response.* Boston: Little, Brown.

Masuda, Takahiko, & Nisbett, Richard E. (2001). Attending holistically versus analytically: Comparing the context sensitivity of Japanese and Americans. *Journal of Personality and Social Psychology, 81,* 922–934.

Mather, Jennifer A., & Anderson, Roland C. (1993). Personalities of octopuses (Octopus rubescens). *Journal of Comparative Psychology, 197,* 336–340.

Mather, Mara; Shafir, Eldar; & Johnson, Marcia K. (2000). Misremembrance of options past: Source monitoring and choice. *Psychological Science, 11,* 132–138.

Matsumoto, David (1996). *Culture and psychology.* Pacific Grove, CA: Brooks-Cole.

Matthews, Gerald; Zeidner, Moshe; & Roberts, Richard D. (2003). *Emotional intelligence: Science and myth.* Cambridge, MA: MIT Press/ Bradford Books.

Maurer, Daphne; Lewis, Terri L.; Brent, Henry P.; & Levin, Alex V. (1999). Rapid improvement in the acuity of infants after visual input. *Science, 286,* 108–110.

Max, M.; Shanker, Y. G.; Huang, L.; et al. (2001). Tas1r3, encoding a new candidate taste receptor, is allelic to the sweet responsiveness locus Sac. *Nature Genetics, 28,* 58–63.

Maxfield, Michael, & Widom, Cathy S. (1996). The cycle of violence. Revisited 6 years later. *Archives of Pediatric and Adolescent Medicine, 150,* 390–395.

Mayberry, Rachel I., & Nicoladis, Elena (2000). Gesture reflects language development: Evidence from bilingual children. *Current Directions in Psychological Science, 9,* 192–196.

Mayer, John D.; McCormick, Laura J.; & Strong, Sara E. (1995). Mood-congruent memory and natural mood: New evidence. *Personality and Social Psychology Bulletin, 21,* 736–746.

Mayer, John D., & Salovey, Peter (1997). What is emotional intelligence? In P. Salovey & D. Sluyter (Eds.), *Emotional development and emotional intelligence: Implications for educators.* New York: Basic Books.

Mayou, R. A.; Ehlers, A.; & Hobbs, M. (2000). Psychological debriefing for road traffic accident victims. *British Journal of Psychiatry, 176,* 589–593.

Mazza, James J., & Reynolds, William M. (1999). Exposure to violence in young inner-city adolescents: Relationships with suicidal ideation, depression, and PTSD symptomatology. *Journal of Abnormal Child Psychology, 27,* 203–213.

Mazzoni, Giuliana A.; Loftus, Elizabeth F.; & Kirsch, Irving (2001). Changing beliefs about implausible autobiographical events: A little plausibility goes a long way. *Journal of Experimental Psychology: Applied, 7,* 51–59.

Mazzoni, Giuliana A.; Loftus, Elizabeth F.; Seitz, Aaron; & Lynn, Steven J. (1999). Changing beliefs and memories through dream interpretation. *Applied Cognitive Psychology, 13,* 125–144.

McCarthy, John (1997). AI as sport [Review of Kasparov versus Deep Blue: Computer chess comes of age, by Monty Newborn]. *Science, 276,* 1518–1519.

McClearn, Gerald E.; Johanson, Boo; Berg, Stig; et al. (1997). Substantial genetic influence on cognitive abilities in twins 80 or more years old. *Science, 176,* 1560–1563.

McClelland, David C. (1961). *The achieving society.* New York: Free Press.

McClelland, David C.; Atkinson, John W.; Clark, Russell A.; & Lowell, Edgar L. (1953). *The achievement motive.* New York: Appleton-Century-Crofts.

McClelland, James L. (1994). The organization of memory: A parallel distributed processing perspective. *Revue Neurologique, 150,* 570–579.

McCord, Joan (1989). Another time, another drug. Paper presented at conference on Vulnerability to the Transition from Drug Use to Abuse and Dependence, Rockville, MD.

McCrae, Robert R.; Costa, Paul T., Jr.; Ostendorf, Fritz; et al. (2000). Nature over nurture: Temperament, personality, and life span development. *Journal of Personality and Social Psychology, 78,* 173–186.

McCrae, Robert R.; Terracciano, Antonio; Costa, Paul T. Jr.; & Ozer, Daniel J. (2006). Person-factors in the California adult Q-set: Closing the door on personality trait types? *European Journal of Personality, 20,* 29–44.

McCrae, Robert R.; Terracciano, Antonio; & members of the Personality Profiles of Cultures Project (2005). Universal features of personality traits from the observer's perspective: Data from 50 cultures. *Journal of Personality and Social Psychology, 88,* 547–561.

McDaniel, Susan H.; Lusterman, Don-David; & Philpot, Carol L. (Eds.) (2001). *Casebook for integrating family therapy: An ecosystemic approach.* Washington, DC: American Psychological Association.

McDonough, Laraine, & Mandler, Jean M. (1994). Very long-term recall in infancy. *Memory, 2,* 339–352.

McElroy, Susan I., & Keck, Paul E., Jr. (2000). Pharmacologic agents for the treatment of acute bipolar mania. *Biological Psychiatry, 48,* 539–557.

McEwen, Bruce S. (1998). Protective and damaging effects of stress mediators. *New England Journal of Medicine, 338,* 171–179.

McEwen, Bruce S. (2000). Allostasis and allostatic load: Implications for neuropsychopharmacology. *Neuropsychopharmacology 22,* 108–124.

McFarland, Cathy, & Alvaro, Celeste (2000). The impact of motivation on temporal comparisons: Coping with traumatic events by perceiving personal growth. *Journal of Personality and Social Psychology, 79,* 327–343.

McFarlane, Jessica; Martin, Carol L.; & Williams, Tannis M. (1988). Mood fluctuations: Women versus men and menstrual versus other cycles. *Psychology of Women Quarterly, 12,* 201–223.

McFarlane, Jessica M., & Williams, Tannis M. (1994). Placing premenstrual syndrome in perspective. *Psychology of Women Quarterly, 18,* 339–373.

McGaugh, James L. (1990). Significance and remembrance: The role of neuromodulatory systems. *Psychological Science, 1,* 15–25.

McGlashan, Thomas H., & Hoffman, Ralph E. (2000). Schizophrenia as a disorder of developmentally reduced synaptic connectivity. *Archives of General Psychiatry, 57,* 637–648.

McGlynn, Susan M. (1990). Behavioral approaches to neuropsychological rehabilitation. *Psychological Bulletin, 108,* 420–441.

McGoldrick, Monica (1996). Irish families. In M. McGoldrick, J. Giordano, & J. K. Pearce (Eds.), *Ethnicity and family therapy* (2nd ed.). New York: Guilford.

McGregor, Ian, & Holmes, John G. (1999). How storytelling shapes memory and impressions of relationship events over time. *Journal of Personality and Social Psychology, 76,* 403–419.

McGregor, Ian, & Little, Brian R. (1998). Personal projects, happiness, and meaning: On doing well and being yourself. *Journal of Personality and Social Psychology, 74,* 494–512.

McGue, Matt (1999). The behavioral genetics of alcoholism. *Current Directions in Psychological Science, 8,* 109–115.

McGue, Matt; Bouchard, Thomas J., Jr.; Iacono, William G.; & Lykken, David T. (1993). Behavioral genetics of cognitive ability: A life-span perspective. In R. Plomin & G. E. McClearn (Eds.), *Nature, nurture, and psychology.* Washington, DC: American Psychological Association.

McGue, Matt, & Lykken, David T. (1992). Genetic influence on risk of divorce. *Psychological Science, 3,* 368–373.

McHugh, Paul R. (1993, December). Psychotherapy awry. *American Scholar,* 17–30.

McHugh, Paul R.; Lief, Harold I.; Freyd, Pamela P.; & Fetkewicz, Janet M. (2004). From refusal to reconciliation: Family relationships after an accusation based on recovered memories. *Journal of Nervous and Mental Disease, 192,* 525–531.

McKee, Richard D., & Squire, Larry R. (1992). Equivalent forgetting rates in long-term memory for diencephalic and medial temporal lobe amnesia. *Journal of Neuroscience, 12,* 3765–3772.

McKee, Richard D., & Squire, Larry R. (1993). On the development of declarative memory. *Journal of Experimental Psychology: Learning, Memory, and Cognition, 19,* 397–404.

McKemy, D. D.; Neuhausser, W. M.; & Julius, D. (2002). Identification of a cold receptor reveals a general role for TRP channels in thermosensation. *Nature, 416,* 52–58.

McKinlay, John B.; McKinlay, Sonja M.; & Brambilla, Donald (1987). The relative contributions of endocrine changes and social circumstances to depression in mid-aged women. *Journal of Health and Social Behavior, 28,* 345–363.

McLeod, Beverly (1985, March). Real work for real pay. *Psychology Today,* 42–44, 46, 48–50.

McMullin, Darcy, & White, Jacqueline W. (2006). Long-term effects of labeling a rape experience. *Psychology of Women Quarterly, 30,* 96–105.

McNally, Richard J. (1994). *Panic disorder: A critical analysis.* New York: Guilford.

McNally, Richard J. (1998). Panic attacks. In *Encyclopedia of mental health* (Vol. 3). New York: Academic Press.

McNally, Richard J. (2003). *Remembering trauma.* Cambridge, MA: Harvard University Press.

McNally, Richard J.; Bryant, Richard A.; & Ehlers, Anke (2003). Does early psychological intervention promote recovery from posttraumatic stress? *Psychological Science in the Public Interest, 4,* 45–79.

McNeill, David (1966). Developmental psycholinguistics. In F. L. Smith & G. A. Miller (Eds.), *The genesis of language: A psycholinguistic approach.* Cambridge, MA: MIT Press.

Mealey, Linda (2000). *Sex differences: Developmental and evolutionary strategies.* San Diego: Academic Press.

Medawar, Peter B. (1982). *Pluto's republic.* Oxford, England: Oxford University Press.

Mednick, Sara C.; Nakayama, Ken; Cantero, Jose L.; et al. (2002). The restorative effect of naps on perceptual deterioration. *Nature Neuroscience, 5,* 677–681.

Mednick, Sarnoff A. (1962). The associative basis of the creative process. *Psychological Review, 69,* 220–232.

Mednick, Sarnoff A.; Huttunen, Matti O.; & Machón, Ricardo (1994). Prenatal influenza infections and adult schizophrenia. *Schizophrenia Bulletin, 20,* 263–267.

Medvec, Victoria H.; Madey, Scott F.; & Gilovich, Thomas (1995). When less is more: Counterfactual thinking and satisfaction among Olympic medalists. *Journal of Personality and Social Psychology, 69,* 603–610.

Meeus, Wim H. J., & Raaijmakers, Quinten A. W. (1995). Obedience in modern society: The Utrecht studies. In A. G. Miller, B. E. Collins, & D. E. Brief (Eds.), *Perspectives on obedience to authority: The legacy of the Milgram experiments. Journal of Social Issues, 51*(3), 155–175.

Meindl, James R., & Lerner, Melvin J. (1985). Exacerbation of extreme responses to an out-group. *Journal of Personality and Social Psychology, 47,* 71–84.

Meissner, Christian A. & Brigham, John C. (2001). Thirty years of investigating the own-race bias in memory for faces: A meta-analytic review. *Psychology, Public Policy, & Law, 7,* 3–35.

Meltzoff, Andrew N., & Gopnik, Alison (1993). The role of imitation in understanding persons and developing a theory of mind. In S. Baron-Cohen, H. Tager-Flusberg, & D. Cohen (Eds.), *Understanding other minds.* New York: Oxford University Press.

Melzack, Ronald (1992, April). Phantom limbs. *Scientific American, 266,* 120–126. [Reprinted in the special issue *Mysteries of the Mind,* 1997.]

Melzack, Ronald (1993). Pain: Past, present and future. *Canadian Journal of Experimental Psychology, 47,* 615–629.

Melzack, Ronald, & Wall, Patrick D. (1965). Pain mechanisms: A new theory. *Science, 13,* 971–979.

Mennella, Julie A.; Jagnow, C. P.; & Beauchamp, Gary K. (2001). Prenatal and postnatal flavor learning by human infants. *Pediatrics, 107,* E88.

Menon, Tanya; Morris, Michael W.; Chiu, Chi-yue; & Hone, Ying-yi (1999). Culture and the construal of agency: Attribution to individual versus group dispositions. *Journal of Personality and Social Psychology, 76,* 701–717.

Mercer, Jean (2006). *Understanding attachment.* Westport, CT: Praeger.

Merikle, Philip M., & Skanes, Heather E. (1992). Subliminal self-help audiotapes: A search for placebo effects. *Journal of Applied Psychology, 77,* 772–776.

Merskey, Harold (1992). The manufacture of personalities: The production of MPD. *British Journal of Psychiatry, 160,* 327–340.

Merskey, Harold (1995). The manufacture of personalities: The production of multiple personality disorder. In L. M. Cohen, J. N. Berzoff, & M. R. Elin (Eds.), *Dissociative identity disorder: Theoretical and treatment controversies.* Northvale, NJ: Aronson.

Merton, Robert K. (1948). The self-fulfilling prophecy. *Antioch Review, 8,* 193–210.

Mesquita, Batja, & Frijda, Nico H. (1992). Cultural variations in emotions: A review. *Psychological Bulletin, 112,* 179–204.

Meyer, Gregory J.; Finn, Stephen E.; Eyde, Lorraine D.; et al. (2001). Psychological testing and psychological assessment. *American Psychologist, 56,* 128–165.

Meyer-Bahlburg, Heino F. L.; Ehrhardt, Anke A.; Rosen, Laura R.; et al. (1995). Prenatal estrogens and the development of homosexual orientation. *Developmental Psychology, 31,* 12–21.

Mezulis, Amy H.; Abramson, Lyn Y.; Hyde, Janet S.; & Hankin, Benjamin L. (2004). Is there a positivity bias in attributions? *Psychological Bulletin, 130,* 711–747.

Mickelson, Kristin D.; Kessler, Ronald C.; & Shaver, Phillip R. (1997). Adult attachment in a nationally representative sample. *Journal of Personality and Social Psychology, 73,* 1092–1106.

Mieda, Michihiro; Willie, Jon T.; Hara, Junko; et al. (2004). Orexin peptides prevent cataplexy and improve wakefulness in an orexin neuron-ablated model of narcolepsy in mice. *Proceedings of the National Academy of Science, 101,* 4649–4654.

Mikulincer, Mario, & Goodman, Gail (Eds.) (2006). *Dynamics of romantic love: Attachment, caregiving, and sex.* New York: Guilford.

Mikulincer, Mario; Shaver, Phillip R.; Gillath, Omri; & Nitzberg, R. E. (2005). Attachment, caregiving, and altruism: Boosting attachment security increases compassion and helping. *Journal of Personality and Social Psychology, 89,* 817–839.

Mikulincer, Mario; Shaver, Phillip R.; & Horesh, Nita (2006). Attachment bases of emotion regulation and posttraumatic adjustment. In D. K. Snyder, J. A. Simpson, & J. N. Hughes (Eds.), *Emotion regulation in couples and families: Pathways to dysfunction and health*. Washington, DC: American Psychological Association.

Milgram, Stanley (1963). Behavioral study of obedience. *Journal of Abnormal and Social Psychology, 67,* 371–378.

Milgram, Stanley (1974). *Obedience to authority: An experimental view*. New York: Harper & Row.

Millar, J. Kirsty; Pickard, Benjamin S.; Mackie, Shaun; et al. (2005, November 18). DISC1 and PDE4B are interacting genetic factors in schizophrenia that regulate cAMP signaling. *Science, 310,* 1187–1191.

Miller, Bruce L.; Seeley, William W.; Mychack, Paula; et al. (2001). Neuroanatomy of the self: Evidence from patients with frontotemporal dementia. *Neurology, 57,* 817–821.

Miller, George A. (1956). The magical number seven, plus or minus two: Some limits on our capacity for processing information. *Psychological Review, 63,* 81–97.

Miller, Gregory E., & Cohen, Sheldon (2001). Psychological interventions and the immune system: A meta-analytic review and critique. *Health Psychology, 20,* 47–63.

Miller, Inglis J., & Reedy, Frank E. (1990). Variations in human taste bud density and taste intensity perception. *Physiology and Behavior, 47,* 1213–1219.

Miller, Neal E. (1978). Biofeedback and visceral learning. *Annual Review of Psychology, 29,* 421–452.

Miller, Todd Q.; Smith, Timothy W.; Turner, Charles W.; et al. (1996). A meta-analytic review of research on hostility and physical health. *Psychological Bulletin, 119,* 322–348.

Miller, William R. (2000). Rediscovering fire: Small interventions, large effects. *Psychology of Addictive Behaviors, 14,* 6–18.

Miller-Jones, Dalton (1989). Culture and testing. *American Psychologist, 44,* 360–366.

Milner, Brenda (1970). Memory and the temporal regions of the brain. In K. H. Pribram & D. E. Broadbent (Eds.), *Biology of memory*. New York: Academic Press.

Milner, J. S., & McCanne, T. R. (1991). Neuropsychological correlates of physical child abuse. In J. S. Milner (Ed.), *Neuropsychology of aggression*. Norwell, MA: Kluwer Academic.

Milton, Julie, & Wiseman, Richard (1999). Does psi exist? Lack of replication of an anomalous process of information transfer. *Psychological Bulletin, 125,* 387–391.

Milton, Julie, & Wiseman, Richard (2001). Does psi exist? Reply to Storm and Ertel (2001). *Psychological Bulletin, 127,* 434–438.

Mineka, Susan, & Zinbarg, Richard (2006). A contemporary learning theory perspective on the etiology of anxiety disorders. *American Psychologist, 61,* 10–26.

Minuchin, Salvador (1984). *Family kaleidoscope*. Cambridge, MA: Harvard University Press.

Mischel, Walter (1973). Toward a cognitive social learning reconceptualization of personality. *Psychological Review, 80,* 252–253.

Mischel, Walter, & Shoda, Yuichi (1995). A cognitive affective system theory of personality: Reconceptualizing situations, dispositions, dynamics, and invariance in personality structures. *Psychological Review, 102,* 246–268.

Mistry, Jayanthi, & Rogoff, Barbara (1994). Remembering in cultural context. In W. J. Lonner & R. Malpass (Eds.), *Psychology and culture*. Needham Heights, MA: Allyn & Bacon.

Mitte, Kristin (2005). Meta-analysis of cognitive-behavioral treatments for generalized anxiety disorder: A comparison with pharmacotherapy. *Psychological Bulletin, 131,* 785–795.

Miyamoto, Yuri, & Kitayama, Shinobu (2002). Cultural variation in correspondence bias: The critical role of attitude diagnosticity of socially constrained behavior. *Journal of Personality and Social Psychology, 83,* 1239–1248.

Miyamoto, Yuri; Nisbett, Richard E.; & Masuda, Takahiko (2006). Culture and the physical environment: Holistic versus analytic perceptual affordances. *Psychological Science, 17,* 113–119.

Modigliani, Andre, & Rochat, François (1995). The role of interaction sequences and the timing of resistance in shaping obedience and defiance to authority. In A. G. Miller, B. E. Collins, & D. E. Brief (Eds.), Perspectives on obedience to authority: The legacy of the Milgram experiments. *Journal of Social Issues, 51*(3), 107–125.

Moen, Phyllis, & Wethington, Elaine (1999). Midlife development in a life course context. In S. L. Willis & J. E. Reid (Eds.), Life in the middle: *Psychological and social development in middle age*. San Diego, CA: Academic Press.

Moffitt, Terrie E. (1993). Adolescence-limited and life-course-persistent antisocial behavior: A developmental taxonomy. *Psychological Review, 100,* 674–701.

Moffitt, Terrie E. (2005). The new look of behavioral genetics in developmental psychopathology: Gene–environment interplay in antisocial behaviors. *Psychological Bulletin, 131,* 533–554.

Moghaddam, Fathali M. (2005). The staircase to terrorism: A psychological exploration. *American Psychologist, 60,* 161–169.

Mohr, Cynthia; Armeli, Stephen; Tennen, Howard; et al. (2001). Daily interpersonal experiences, context, and alcohol consumption: Crying in your beer and toasting good times. *Journal of Personality and Social Psychology, 80,* 489–500.

Moles, Anna; Kieffer, Brigitte; & D'Amato, Francesca (2004). Deficit in attachment behavior in mice lacking the μ-opioid receptor gene. *Science, 304,* 1983–1986.

Molnar-Szakacs, Istvan; Iacoboni, Marco; Koski, Lisa; & Mazziotta, John C. (2005). Functional segregation within pars opercularis of the inferior frontal gyrus: evidence from fMRI studies of imitation and action observation. *Cerebral Cortex, 15,* 986–994.

Molteni, Raffaella; Barnard, R. J.; Ying, Zhe; et al. (2002). A high-fat, refined sugar diet reduces hippocampal brain-derived neurotrophic factor, neuronal plasticity, and learning. *Neuroscience 112,* 803–814.

Monahan, Jennifer L.; Murphy, Sheila T.; & Zajonc, R. B. (2000). Subliminal mere exposure: Specific, general, and diffuse effects. *Psychological Science, 11,* 462–466.

Moncrieff, Joanna (2001). Are antidepressants overrated? A review of methodological problems in antidepressant trials. *Journal of Nervous and Mental Disease, 189,* 288–295.

Montmayeur, J. P.; Liberies, S. D.; Matsunami, H.; & Buck, L. B. (2001). A candidate taste receptor gene near a sweet taste locus. *Nature Neuroscience, 4,* 492–498.

Moore, Robert Y. (1997). Circadian rhythms: Basic neurobiology and clinical applications. Annual Review of Medicine, 48, 253–266.

Moore, Timothy E. (1992, Spring). Subliminal perception: Facts and fallacies. *Skeptical Inquirer, 16,* 273–281.

Moore, Timothy E. (1995). Subliminal self-help auditory tapes: An empirical test of perceptual consequences. *Canadian Journal of Behavioural Science, 27,* 9–20.

Moore, Timothy E., & Pepler, Debra J. (2006). Wounding words: Maternal verbal aggression and children's adjustment. *Journal of Family Violence, 21,* 89–93.

Morin, Charles M. (2004). Cognitive-behavioral approaches to the treatment of insomnia. *Journal of Clinical Psychiatry, 65*[suppl. 16], 33–40.

Morris, Martha C.; Evans, Denis A.; Bienias, Julia L. et al. (2004). Dietary niacin and the risk of Alzheimer's disease and cognitive decline. *Journal of Neurology, Neurosurgery, and Psychiatry, 75,* 1039–1093.

Moscovitch, Morris; Winocur, Gordon; & Behrmann, Marlene (1997). What is special about face recognition? Nineteen experiments on a person with visual object agnosia and dyslexia but normal face recognition. *Journal of Cognitive Neuroscience, 9,* 555–604.

Moyer, Christopher A.; Rounds, James; & Hannum, James W. (2004). A meta-analysis of massage therapy research. *Psychological Bulletin, 130,* 3–18.

Mozell, Maxwell M.; Smith, Bruce P.; Smith, Paul E.; Sullivan, Richard L.; & Swender, Philip (1969). Nasal chemoreception in flavor identification. *Archives of Otolaryngology, 90,* 367–373.

Mroczek, D. K., & Spiro, A., III (2005). Changes in life satisfaction during adulthood: Findings from the Veterans Affairs normative aging study. *Journal of Personality and Social Psychology, 88,* 189–202.

Mueller, Claudia M., & Dweck, Carol S. (1998). Praise for intelligence can undermine children's motivation and performance. *Journal of Personality and Social Psychology, 75,* 33–52.

Mukamal, Kenneth J.; Conigrove, Katherine M; Mittleman, Murray A.; et al. (2003). Roles of drinking pattern and type of alcohol consumed in coronary heart disease in men. *New England Journal of Medicine, 348,* 109–118.

Müller, Ralph-Axel; Courchesne, Eric; & Allen, Greg (1998). The cerebellum: So much more. [Letter.] *Science, 282,* 879–880.

Murphy, Sheila T.; Monahan, Jennifer L.; & Zajonc, R. B. (1995). Additivity of nonconscious affect: Combined effects of priming and exposure. *Journal of Personality and Social Psychology, 69,* 589–602.

Murray, Charles (1998). *Income, inequality, and IQ.* Washington, DC: American Enterprise Institute.

Myers, David G., & Scanzoni, Letha D. (2005). *What God has joined together: The Christian case for gay marriage.* San Francisco: HarperSanFrancisco.

Myers, Ronald E., & Sperry, R. W. (1953). Interocular transfer of a visual form discrimination habit in cats after section of the optic chiasm and corpus callosum. *Anatomical Record, 115,* 351–352.

Nash, Michael R. (1987). What, if anything, is regressed about hypnotic age regression? A review of the empirical literature. *Psychological Bulletin, 102,* 42–52.

Nash, Michael R., & Barnier, Amanda J. (2007). *The Oxford handbook of hypnosis.* Oxford, UK: Oxford University Press.

Nash, Michael R., & Nadon, Robert (1997). Hypnosis. In D. L. Faigman, D. Kaye, M. J. Saks, & J. Sanders (Eds.), *Modern scientific evidence: The law and science of expert testimony.* St. Paul, MN: West.

National Science Board (2000). *Science & engineering indicators 2000.* Chapter 8: Science and technology: Attitudes and public understanding. Arlington, VA: National Science Foundation. [A reprint of the relevant section of this chapter can be found in the January/February 2001 issue of *Skeptical Inquirer,* 12–15.]

Needleman, Herbert L.; Riess, Julie A.; Tobin, Michael J.; et al. (1996). Bone lead levels and delinquent behavior. *Journal of the American Medical Association, 275,* 363–369.

Neher, Andrew (1996). Jung's theory of archetypes: A critique. *Journal of Humanistic Psychology, 36,* 61–91.

Neisser, Ulric (Ed.) (1998). *The rising curve: Long-term gains in IQ and related measures.* Washington, DC: American Psychological Association.

Neisser, Ulric, & Harsch, Nicole (1992). Phantom flashbulbs: False recollections of hearing the news about *Challenger.* In E. Winograd & U. Neisser (Eds.), *Affect and accuracy in recall: Studies of "flashbulb memories."* New York: Cambridge University Press.

Nelson, C. A.; Thomas, K.; & de Haan, M. (2006). Neural bases of cognitive development. In D. Kuhn & R. S. Siegler (Eds.), *Handbook of child psychology: Vol. 2. Cognition, perception, and language* (6th ed.). Hoboken, NJ: Wiley.

Nelson, Geoffrey; Westhues, Anne; & MacLeod, Jennifer (2003). A meta-analysis of longitudinal research on preschool prevention programs for children. *Prevention & Treatment, 6,* article 31. [Posted online, December 18, 2003.]

Nelson, Thomas O., & Dunlosky, John (1991). When people's judgments of learning (JOLs) are extremely accurate at predicting subsequent recall: The "delayed JOL effect." *Psychological Science, 2,* 267–270.

Nelson, Thomas O., & Leonesio, R. Jacob (1988). Allocation of self-paced study time and the "labor in vain effect." *Journal of Experimental Psychology: Learning, Memory, and Cognition, 14,* 676–686.

Ness, Jose; Aronow, Wilbert S.; & Beck, Gwen (2006). Menopausal symptoms after cessation of hormone replacement therapy. *Maturitas, 53,* 356–361.

Neugarten, Bernice (1979). Time, age, and the life cycle. *American Journal of Psychiatry, 136,* 887–894.

Newcombe, Nora S.; Drummey, Anna B.; Fox, Nathan A.; et al. (2000). Remembering early childhood: How much, how, and why (or why not). *Current Directions in Psychological Science, 9,* 55–58.

Newland, M. Christopher, & Rasmussen, Erin B. (2003). Behavior in adulthood and during aging is affected by contaminant exposure in utero. *Current Directions in Psychological Science, 12,* 212–217.

NICHD Early Child Care Research Network (2002). Child-care structure-process-outcome: Direct and indirect effects of child-care quality on young children's development. *Psychological Science, 13,* 199–206.

NICHD Early Child Care Research Network (2006). Infant–mother attachment classification: Risk and protection in relation to changing maternal caregiving quality. *Developmental Psychology, 42,* 38–58.

Nickerson, Raymond A., & Adams, Marilyn Jager (1979). Long-term memory for a common object. *Cognitive Psychology, 11,* 287–307.

NIH Technology Assessment Panel on Integration of Behavioral and Relaxation Approaches into the Treatment of Chronic Pain and Insomnia (1996). *Journal of the American Medical Association, 276,* 313–318.

Nisbett, Richard E. (1993). Violence and U.S. regional culture. *American Psychologist, 48,* 441–449.

Nisbett, Richard E., & Ross, Lee (1980). *Human inference: Strategies and shortcomings of social judgment.* Englewood Cliffs, NJ: Prentice-Hall.

Nolan, Susan A.; Flynn, Cynthia; & Garber, Judy (2003). Prospective relations between rejection and depression in young adolescents. *Journal of Personality and Social Psychology, 85,* 745–755.

Nolen-Hoeksema, Susan (2002). Gender differences in depression. In I. H. Gotlib & C. Hammen (Eds.), *Handbook of depression.* New York: Guilford.

Nolen-Hoeksema, Susan (2004). Lost in thought: Rumination and depression. Paper presented at the National Institute on the Teaching of Psychology, St. Petersburg, Florida.

Nonaka, S.; Hough, C. J.; & Chuang, De-Maw (1998, March 3). Chronic lithium treatment robustly protects neurons in the central nervous system against excitotoxicity by inhibiting N-methyl-D-aspartate receptor-mediated calcium influx. *Proceedings of the National Academy of Sciences, 95,* 2642–2647.

Norcross, John C.; Kohout, Jessica L.; & Wicherski, Marlene (2005). Graduate study in psychology: 1971 to 2004. *American Psychologist, 60,* 959–975.

Norman, Donald A. (1988). *The psychology of everyday things.* New York: Basic Books.

Nunez, Narina; Poole, Debra A.; & Memon, Amina (2002). Psychology's two cultures revisited: Implications for the integration of science with practice. *Scientific Review of Mental Health Practice, 1.*

Nunn, J. A.; Gregory, L. J.; Brammer, M.; et al. (2002). Functional magnetic resonance imaging of synesthesia: Activation of V4/V8 by spoken words. *Nature Neuroscience, 5,* 371–375.

Ó Scalaidhe, Séamas P.; Wilson, Fraser A. W.; & Goldman-Rakic, Patricia S. (1997). A real segregation of face-processing neurons in prefrontal cortex. *Science, 278,* 1135–1138.

Oatley, Keith, & Jenkins, Jennifer M. (1996). *Understanding emotions.* Cambridge, MA: Blackwell.

Ofshe, Richard J., & Watters, Ethan (1994). *Making monsters: False memory, psychotherapy, and sexual hysteria.* New York: Scribners.

Ogbu, John U. (2003). *Black American students in an affluent suburb: A study of academic disengagement.* Mahwah, NJ: Erlbaum.

Ogden, Jenni A., & Corkin, Suzanne (1991). Memories of H. M. In W. C. Abraham, M. C. Corballis, & K. G. White (Eds.), *Memory mechanisms: A tribute to G. V. Goddard.* Hillsdale, NJ: Erlbaum.

O'Hanlon, Bill (1994, November/December). The third wave. *Family Therapy Networker,* 18–29.

Öhman, Arne, & Mineka, Susan (2001). Fears, phobias, and preparedness: Toward an evolved module of fear and fear learning. *Psychological Review, 108,* 483–522.

Öhman, Arne, & Mineka, Susan (2003). The malicious serpent: Snakes as a prototypical stimulus for an evolved module of fear. *Current Directions in Psychological Science, 12,* 5–9.

Oliver, Mary Beth, & Hyde, Janet S. (1993). Gender differences in sexuality: A meta-analysis. *Psychological Bulletin, 114,* 29–51.

Olson, James M.; Vernon, Philip A.; Harris, Julie Aitken; & Jang, Kerry L. (2001). The heritability of attitudes: A study of twins. *Journal of Personality and Social Psychology, 80,* 845–850.

Olsson, Andreas; Ebert, Jeffrey; Banaji, Mahzarin; & Phelps, Elizabeth A. (2005). The role of social groups in the persistence of learned fear. *Science, 309,* 785–787.

Olujic, M. B. (1998). Embodiment of terror: Gendered violence in peacetime and wartime in Croatia and Bosnia-Herzegovina. *Medical Anthropology Quarterly, 12,* 31–50.

Opre, Adrian; Coman, Alin; Kallay, Eva; et al. (2005). Reducing distress in college students by expressive writing. A pilot study on a Romanian sample. *Cognitie Creier Comportament, 9,* 53–64. Romanian Association for Cognitive Science, Romania, www.cognitrom.ro.

O'Rahilly, Ronan, & Müller, Fabiola (2001). *Human embryology and teratology.* New York: Wiley.

Orlinsky, David E., & Howard, Kenneth I. (1994). Unity and diversity among psychotherapies: A comparative perspective. In B. Bongar & L. E. Beutler (Eds.), *Foundations of psychotherapy: Theory, research, and practice.* New York: Oxford University Press.

O'Sullivan, L. F., & Allgeier, Elizabeth R. (1998). Feigning sexual desire: Consenting to unwanted sexual activity in heterosexual dating relationships. *Journal of Sex Research, 35,* 234–243.

Ozer, Emily J.; Best, Suzanne R.; Lipsey, Tami L.; & Weiss, Daniel S. (2003). Predictors of posttraumatic stress disorder and symptoms in adults: A meta-analysis. *Psychological Bulletin, 129,* 52–73.

Page, Gayle G.; Ben-Eliyahu, Shamgar; Yirmiya, Raz; & Liebeskind, John C. (1993). Morphine attenuates surgery-induced enhancement of metastatic colonization in rats. *Pain, 54,* 21–28.

Pagel, James F. (2003). Non-dreamers. *Sleep Medicine, 4,* 235–241.

Panksepp, Jaak (1998). Attention deficit hyperactivity disorders, psychostimulants, and intolerance of childhood playfulness: A tragedy in the making? *Current Directions in Psychological Science, 7,* 91–98.

Panksepp, Jaak; Herman, B. H.; Vilberg, T.; et al. (1980). Endogenous opioids and social behavior. *Neuroscience and Biobehavioral Reviews, 4,* 473–487.

Park, Robert L. (2000). *Voodoo science: The road from foolishness to fraud.* New York: Oxford University Press.

Parker, Elizabeth S.; Birnbaum, Isabel M.; & Noble, Ernest P. (1976). Alcohol and memory: Storage and state dependency. *Journal of Verbal Learning and Verbal Behavior, 15,* 691–702.

Parker, Elizabeth S.; Cahill, Larry; & McGaugh, James L. (2006). A case of unusual autobiographical remembering. *Neurocase, 12,* 35–49.

Parker, Gordon; Parker, Kay; & Eyers, Kerrie (2003). Cognitive behavior therapy for depression: Choose horses for courses. *American Journal of Psychiatry, 160,* 825–834.

Parlee, Mary B. (1982). Changes in moods and activation levels during the menstrual cycle in experimentally naive subjects. *Psychology of Women Quarterly, 7,* 119–131.

Parlee, Mary B. (1994). The social construction of premenstrual syndrome: A case study of scientific discourse as cultural contestation. In M. G. Winkler & L. B. Cole (Eds.), *The good body: Asceticism in contemporary culture.* New Haven, CT: Yale University Press.

Pascual-Leone, Alvaro; Amedi, Amir; Fregni, Felipe; & Merabet, Lofte B. (2005). The plastic human brain cortex. *Annual Review of Neuroscience, 28,* 377–401.

Patterson, Charlotte J. (1992). Children of lesbian and gay parents. *Child Development, 63,* 1025–1042.

Patterson, Charlotte J. (1995). Sexual orientation and human development: An overview. *Developmental Psychology, 31,* 3–11.

Patterson, David R. (2004). Treating pain with hypnosis. *Current Directions in Psychological Science, 13,* 252–255.

Patterson, David R., & Jensen, Mark P. (2003). Hypnosis and clinical pain. *Psychological Bulletin, 129,* 495–521.

Patterson, Francine, & Linden, Eugene (1981). *The education of Koko.* New York: Holt, Rinehart and Winston.

Paul, Annie M. (2004). *The cult of personality.* New York: The Free Press.

Paul, Richard W. (1984, September). Critical thinking: Fundamental to education for a free society. *Educational Leadership,* 4–14.

Paunonen, Sampo V. (2003). Big Five factors or personality and replicated predictions of behavior. *Journal of Personality & Social Psychology, 84,* 411–422.

Paunonen, Sampo V., & Ashton, Michael C. (2001). Big Five factors and facets and the prediction of behavior. *Journal of Personality and Social Psychology, 81,* 524–539.

Pavlov, Ivan P. (1927). *Conditioned reflexes* (G. V. Anrep, Trans.). London: Oxford University Press.

Pearlin, Leonard (1982). Discontinuities in the study of aging. In T. K. Hareven & K. J. Adams (Eds.), *Aging and life course transitions: An interdisciplinary perspective*. New York: Guilford.

Peele, Stanton, & Brodsky, Archie, with Mary Arnold (1991). *The truth about addiction and recovery*. New York: Simon & Schuster.

Peier, A. M.; Moqrich, A.; Hergarden, A. C.; et al. (2002). A TRP channel that senses cold stimuli and menthol. *Cell, 108*, 705–715.

Peng, Kaiping, & Nisbett, Richard E. (1999). Culture, dialectics, and reasoning about contradiction. *American Psychologist, 54*, 741–754.

Pennebaker, James W. (2002). Writing, social processes, and psychotherapy: From past to future. In S. J. Lepore and J. M. Smyth (Eds.), *The writing cure: How expressive writing promotes health and emotional well-being*. Washington, DC: American Psychological Association.

Pennebaker, James W.; Colder, Michelle; & Sharp, Lisa K. (1990). Accelerating the coping process. *Journal of Personality and Social Psychology, 58*, 528–527.

Pennebaker, James W.; Kiecolt-Glaser, Janice; & Glaser, Ronald (1988). Disclosure of traumas and immune function: Health implications for psychotherapy. *Journal of Consulting and Clinical Psychology, 56*, 239–245.

Peplau, Letita Anne (2003). Human sexuality: How do men and women differ? *Current Directions in Psychological Science, 12*, 37–40.

Peplau, Letitia Anne, & Spalding, Leah R. (2000). The close relationships of lesbians, gay men and bisexuals. In C. Hendrick & S. Hendrick (Eds.), *Close relationships: A sourcebook*. Thousand Oaks, CA: Sage.

Peplau, Letitia Anne; Spalding, Leah R.; Conley, Terri D.; & Veniegas, Rosemary C. (2000). The development of sexual orientation in women. *Annual Review of Sex Research, 10*, 70–99.

Pepperberg, Irene (2000). *The Alex studies: Cognitive and communicative abilities of grey parrots*. Cambridge, MA: Harvard University Press.

Pepperberg, Irene M. (2006). Grey parrot (Psittacus erithacus) numerical abilities: Addition and further experiments on a zero-like concept. *Journal of Comparative Psychology, 120*, 1–11.

Perera, Frederica P.; Rauh, Virginia; Whyatt, Robin M.; et al. (2006). Effect of prenatal exposure to airborne polycyclic aromatic hydrocarbons on neurodevelopment in the first three years of life among inner-city children. *Environmental Health Perspectives*, published online April 24, doi:10.1289/ehp.9084.

Persons, Jacqueline; Davidson, Joan; & Tompkins, Michael A. (2001). *Essential components of cognitive-behavior therapy for depression*. Washington, DC: American Psychological Association.

Pert, Candace B., & Snyder, Solomon H. (1973). Opiate receptor: Demonstration in nervous tissue. *Science, 179*, 1011–1014.

Peterson, Christopher (2000). The future of optimism. *American Psychologist, 55*, 44–55.

Peterson, Christopher; Seligman, Martin E. P.; Yurko, Karen H.; et al. (1998). Catastrophizing and untimely death. *Psychological Science, 9*, 127–130.

Peterson, Donald R. (2003). Unintended consequences: Ventures and misadventures in the education of professional psychologists. *American Psychologist, 58*, 791–800.

Peterson, Lloyd R., & Peterson, Margaret J. (1959). Short-term retention of individual verbal items. *Journal of Experimental Psychology, 58*, 193–198.

Peterson, Robert A. (2001). On the use of college students in social science research: Insights from a second-order meta-analysis. *Journal of Consumer Research, 28*, 450–461.

Petrie, Keith J.; Booth, Roger J.; & Pennebaker, James W. (1998). The immunological effects of thought suppression. *Journal of Personality and Social Psychology, 75*, 1264–1272.

Pettigrew, Thomas F. (1998). Intergroup contact theory. *Annual Review of Psychology, 49*, 65–85. Palo Alto, CA: Annual Reviews.

Pfungst, Oskar (1911/1965). *Clever Hans (The horse of Mr. von Osten): A contribution to experimental animal and human psychology*. New York: Holt, Rinehart and Winston.

Phillips, Micheal D.; Lowe, M. J.; Lurito, J. T.; et al. (2001). Temporal lobe activation demonstrates sex-based differences during passive listening. *Radiology, 220*, 202–207.

Phinney, Jean S. (1990). Ethnic identity in adolescents and adults: Review of research. *Psychological Bulletin, 108*, 499–514.

Phinney, Jean S. (1996). When we talk about American ethnic groups, what do we mean? *American Psychologist, 51*, 918–927.

Piaget, Jean (1929/1960). *The child's conception of the world*. Paterson, NJ: Littlefield, Adams.

Piaget, Jean (1952). Play, dreams, and imitation in childhood. New York: W. W. Norton.

Piaget, Jean (1984). Piaget's theory. In P. Mussen (Series Ed.) & W. Kessen (Vol. Ed.), *Handbook of child psychology: Vol. 1. History, theory, and methods* (4th ed.). New York: Wiley.

Pierce, W. David; Cameron, Judy; Banko, Katherine M.; & So, Sylvia (2003). Positive effects of rewards and performance standards on intrinsic motivation. *Psychological Record, 53*, 561–579.

Pincus, Tamar, & Morley, Stephen (2001). Cognitive-processing bias in chronic pain: A review and integration. *Psychological Bulletin, 127*, 599–617.

Pinker, Steven (1994). *The language instinct: How the mind creates language*. New York: Morrow.

Pinker, Steven (1999). *Words and rules: The ingredients of language*. New York: Basic Books.

Piper, August, & Merskey, Harold (2004). The persistence of folly: A critical examination of dissociative identity disorder. Part I: The excesses of an improbable concept. *Canadian Journal of Psychiatry, 49*, 592–600. [Note: Part II (The defence and decline of multiple personality or dissociative identity disorder) appeared in the following issue of the *Canadian Journal of Psychiatry, 49*, 678–683.]

Pittenger, David J. (1993). The utility of the Myers-Briggs Type Indicator. *Review of Educational Research, 63*, 467–488.

Pizzagalli, Diego A.; Sherwood, Rebecca A.; Henriques, Jeffrey B.; & Davidson, Richard J. (2005). Frontal brain asymmetry and reward responsiveness: A source-localization study. *Psychological Science, 16*, 805–813.

Plant, E. Ashby, & Devine, Patricia G. (1998). Internal and external motivation to respond without prejudice. *Journal of Personality and Social Psychology, 75*, 811–832.

Plomin, Robert (1989). Environment and genes: Determinants of behavior. *American Psychologist, 44*, 105–111.

Plomin, Robert; Asbury, Kathryn; & Dunn, Judith F. (2001). Why are children in the same family so different? Nonshared environment a decade later. *Canadian Journal of Psychiatry, 46*, 225–233.

Plomin, Robert; Corley, Robin; DeFries, J. C.; & Fulker, D. W. (1990). Individual differences in television viewing in early childhood: Nature as well as nurture. *Psychological Science, 1*, 371–377.

Plomin, Robert, & DeFries, John C. (1985). *Origins of individual differences in infancy: The Colorado Adoption Project*. New York: Academic Press.

Plomin, Robert; DeFries, John C.; Craig, Ian W.; & McGuffin, Peter (2003). *Behavioral genetics in the postgenomic era*. Washington, DC: American Psychological Association.

Plomin, Robert; DeFries, John C.; McClearn, Gerald E.; & McGuffin, Peter (2001). *Behavioral genetics* (4th ed.). New York: Worth.

Plomin, Robert, & McGuffin, Peter (2003). Psychopathology in the postgenomic era. *Annual Review of Psychology, 54,* 205–228.

Plotnik, Joshua M.; de Waal, Frans B. M.; & Reiss, Diana (2006). Self-recognition in an Asian elephant. *Proceedings of the National Academy of Science,* published online October 30, 10.1073/pnas.0608062103.

Plotsky, Paul M.; Owens, Michael J.; & Nemeroff, Charles B. (1998). Psychoneuroendocrinology of depression: Hypothalamic-pituitary-adrenal axis. *Psychoneuroendocrinology, 21,* 293–307.

Polusny, Melissa A., & Follette, Victoria M. (1996). Remembering childhood sexual abuse: A national survey of psychologists' clinical practices, beliefs, and personal experiences. *Professional Psychology: Research and Practice, 27,* 41–52.

Poole, Debra A. (1995). Strolling fuzzy-trace theory through eyewitness testimony (or vice versa). *Learning and Individual Differences, 7,* 87–93.

Poole, Debra A., & Lamb, Michael E. (1998). *Investigative interviews of children.* Washington, DC: American Psychological Association.

Poole, Debra A.; Lindsay, D. Stephen; Memon, Amina; & Bull, Ray (1995). Psychotherapy and the recovery of memories of childhood sexual abuse: U.S. and British practitioners' opinions, practices, and experiences. *Journal of Consulting and Clinical Psychology, 63,* 426–437.

Pope, Harrison G., Jr.; Phillips, Katharine A.; & Olivardia, Roberto (2000). *The Adonis complex: The secret crisis of male body obsession.* New York: Free Press.

Portenoy, Russell K. (1994). Opioid therapy for chronic nonmalignant pain: Current status. In H. L. Fields & J. C. Liebeskind (Eds.), *Progress in pain research and management. Pharmacological approaches to the treatment of chronic pain: Vol. 1.* Seattle: International Association for the Study of Pain.

Posthuma, Danielle, & de Geus, Eco J. C. (2006). Progress in the molecular-genetic study of intelligence. *Current Directions in Psychological Science, 15,* 151–155.

Postmes, Tom, & Spears, Russell (1998). Deindividuation and antinormative behavior: A meta-analysis. *Psychological Bulletin, 123,* 238–259.

Potter, W. James (1987). Does television viewing hinder academic achievement among adolescents? *Human Communication Research, 14,* 27–46.

Poulin-Dubois, Diane; Serbin, Lisa A.; Kenyon, Brenda; & Derbyshire, Alison (1994). Infants' intermodal knowledge about gender. *Developmental Psychology, 30,* 436–442.

Powell, Russell A., & Boer, Douglas P. (1995). Did Freud misinterpret reported memories of sexual abuse as fantasies? *Psychological Reports, 77,* 563–570.

Pratkanis, Anthony, & Aronson, Elliot (2001). *The age of propaganda.* (Rev. ed.). New York: W. H. Freeman.

Premack, David, & Premack, Ann James (1983). *The mind of an ape.* New York: Norton.

Presnell, Katherine; Bearman, Sarah Kate; & Stice, Eric (2004). Risk factors for body dissatisfaction in adolescent boys and girls: A prospective study. *International Journal of Eating Disorders, 36,* 389–401.

Pressman, Sarah D., & Cohen, Sheldon (2005). Does positive affect influence health? *Psychological Bulletin, 131,* 925–971.

Preston, Jesse, & Epley, Nicholas (2005). Explanations versus applications: The explanatory power of valuable beliefs. *Psychological Science, 16,* 826–832.

Principe, Gabrielle; Kanaya, Tamoe; Ceci, Stephen J.; & Singh, Mona (2006). Believing is seeing: How rumors can engender false memories in preschoolers. *American Psychologist, 17,* 243–248.

Prochaska, James O.; Norcross, John C.; & DiClemente, Carlo C. (1994). *Changing for good.* New York: Morrow.

Pronin, Emily; Gilovich, Thomas; & Ross, Lee (2004). Objectivity in the eye of the beholder: Divergent perceptions of bias in self versus others. *Psychological Review, 111,* 781–799.

Ptito, Maurice; Moesgaard, Solvej M.; Gjedde, Albert; & Kupers, Ron (2005). Cross-modal plasticity revealed by electrotactile stimulation of the tongue in the congenitally blind. *Brain, 128,* 606–614.

Punamaeki, Raija-Leena, & Joustie, Marja (1998). The role of culture, violence, and personal factors affecting dream content. *Journal of Cross-Cultural Psychology, 29,* 320–342.

Pynoos, R. S., & Nader, K. (1989). Children's memory and proximity to violence. *Journal of the American Academy of Child and Adolescent Psychiatry, 28,* 236–241.

Quinn, Diane M., & Spencer, Steven J. (2001). The interference of stereotype threat with women's generation of mathematical problem-solving strategies. *Journal of Social Issues, 57,* 55–71.

Quinn, Paul (2002). Category representation in young infants. *Current Directions in Psychological Science, 11,* 66–70.

Quinn, Paul, & Bhatt, Ramesh (2005). Learning perceptual organization in infancy. *Psychological Science, 16,* 511–515.

Radetsky, Peter (1991, April). The brainiest cells alive. *Discover, 12,* 82–85, 88, 90.

Radford, Benjamin (2005, June). Psychic predictions (and rationalizations) fail again. *Skeptical Briefs, 15,* 529.

Raffaelli, Marcela; Crockett, Lisa J.; & Shen, Yuh-ling (2005). Developmental stability and change in self-regulation from childhood to adolescence. *The Journal of Genetic Psychology, 166,* 54–75.

Rahman, Qazi, & Wilson, Glenn D. (2003). Born gay? The psychobiology of human sexual orientation. *Personality and Individual Differences, 34,* 1337–1382.

Räikkönen, Katri; Matthews, Karen A.; Flory, Janine D.; et al. (1999). Effects of optimism, pessimism, and trait anxiety on ambulatory blood pressure and mood during everyday life. *Journal of Personality and Social Psychology, 76,* 104–113.

Raine, Adrian (1996). Autonomic nervous system factors underlying disinhibited, antisocial, and violent behavior. Biosocial perspectives and treatment implications. *Annals of the New York Academy of Sciences, 794,* 46–59.

Raine, Adrian; Lencz, Todd; Bihrle, Susan; LaCasse, Lori; & Colletti, Patrick (2000). Reduced prefrontal gray matter volume and reduced autonomic activity in antisocial personality disorder. *Archives of General Psychiatry, 57,* 119–127.

Raine, Adrian, & Liu, Jiang-Hong (1998). Biological predispositions to violence and their implications for biosocial treatment and prevention. *Psychology, Crime & Law, 4,* 107–125.

Raine, Adrian; Meloy, J. R.; Bihrle, S.; et al. (1998). Reduced prefrontal and increased subcortical brain functioning assessed using positron emission tomography in predatory and affective murderers. *Behavioral Science and Law, 16,* 319–332.

Raine, Adrian; Park, Sohee; Lencz, Todd; et al. (2001). Reduced right hemisphere activation in severely abused violent offenders during a working memory task: An fMRI study. *Aggressive Behavior, 27,* 111–129.

Ramey, Craig T., & Ramey, Sharon Landesman (1998). Early intervention and early experience. *American Psychologist, 53,* 109–120.

Rapkin, Andrea J.; Chang, Li C.; & Reading, Anthony E. (1988). Comparison of retrospective and prospective assessment of premenstrual symptoms. *Psychological Reports, 62,* 55–60.

Ratcliffe, Heather (2000, January 28). Midwest UFO sightings get once-over from scientists. *Detroit News,* Religion Section [online version].

Rathbun, Constance; DiVirgilio, Letitia; & Waldfogel, Samuel (1958). A restitutive process in children following radical separation from family and culture. *American Journal of Orthopsychiatry, 28,* 408–415.

Rauschecker, Josef P. (1999). Making brain circuits listen. *Science, 285,* 1686–1687.

Ravussin, Eric; Lillioja, Stephen; Knowler, William; et al. (1988). Reduced rate of energy expenditure as a risk factor for body-weight gain. *New England Journal of Medicine, 318,* 467–472.

Redd, W. H.; Dadds, M. R.; Futterman, A. D.; Taylor, K.; & Bovbjerg, D. (1993). Nausea induced by mental images of chemotherapy. *Cancer, 72,* 629–636.

Redelmeier, Donald A., & Tversky, Amos (1996). On the belief that arthritis pain is related to the weather. *Proceedings of the National Academy of Sciences, 93,* 2895–2896.

Reed, Geoffrey M. (1990). Stress, coping, and psychological adaptation in a sample of gay and bisexual men with AIDS. Unpublished doctoral dissertation, University of California, Los Angeles.

Reedy, F. E.; Bartoshuk, L. M.; Miller, I. J.; Duffy, V. B.; Lucchina, L.; & Yanagisawa, K. (1993). Relationships among papillae, taste pores, and 6-n-propylthiouracil (PROP) suprathreshold taste sensitivity. *Chemical Senses, 18,* 618–619.

Reichenberg, Abraham; Gross, Raz; Weiser, Mark; Bresnahan, Michealine; et al. (2006). Advancing paternal age and autism. *Archives of General Psychiatry, 63,* 1026–1032.

Reid, R. L. (1991). Premenstrual syndrome. *New England Journal of Medicine, 324,* 1208–1210.

Reiner, William G., & Gearhart, John P. (2004, January 22). Discordant sexual identity in some genetic males with cloacal exstrophy assigned to female sex at birth. *New England Journal of Medicine, 350,* 333–341.

Rensink, Ronald (2004). Visual sensing without seeing. *Psychological Science, 15,* 27–32.

Repetti, Rena L.; Taylor, Shelley E.; & Seeman, Teresa E. (2002). Risky families: Family social environments and the mental and physical health of offspring. *Psychological Bulletin, 128,* 330–366.

Rescorla, Robert A. (1988). Pavlovian conditioning: It's not what you think it is. *American Psychologist, 43,* 151–160.

Restak, Richard (1983, October). Is free will a fraud? *Science Digest, 91*(10), 52–55.

Restak, Richard M. (1994). *The modular brain.* New York: Macmillan.

Revell, Victoria L., & Eastman, Charmane I. (2005). How to fool Mother Nature into letting you fly around or stay up all night. *Journal of Biological Rhythms, 20,* 353–365.

Reynolds, Brent A., & Weiss, Samuel (1992). Generation of neurons and astrocytes from isolated cells of the adult mammalian central nervous system. *Science, 255,* 1707–1710.

Reynolds, Kristi; Lewis, L. Brian; Nolen, John David L.; et al. (2003). Alcohol consumption and risk of stroke: A meta-analysis. *Journal of the American Medical Association, 289,* 579–588.

Rhoades, Linda, & Eisenberger, Robert (2002). Perceived organizational support: A review of the literature. *Journal of Applied Psychology, 87,* 698–714.

Ricciardelli, Lina A., & McCabe, Marita P. (2004). A biopsychosocial model of disordered eating and the pursuit of muscularity in adolescent boys. *Psychological Bulletin, 130,* 179–205.

Rice, Mabel L. (1990). Preschoolers' QUIL: Quick incidental learning of words. In G. Conti-Ramsden & C. E. Snow (Eds.), *Children's language* (Vol. 7). Hillsdale, NJ: Erlbaum.

Richards, Ruth L. (1991). Everyday creativity and the arts. Paper presented at the annual meeting of the American Psychological Association, San Francisco.

Richardson, John T. E. (Ed.) (1992). *Cognition and the menstrual cycle.* New York: Springer-Verlag.

Richardson-Klavehn, Alan, & Bjork, Robert A. (1988). Measures of memory. *Annual Review of Psychology, 39,* 475–543.

Ridley-Johnson, Robyn; Cooper, Harris; & Chance, June (1983). The relation of children's television viewing to school achievement and I.Q. *Journal of Educational Research, 76,* 294–297.

Rieber, Robert W. (2006). *The bifurcation of the self.* New York: Springer.

Rind, Bruce; Tromovitch, Philip; & Bauserman, Robert (1998). A meta-analytic examination of assumed properties of child sexual abuse using college samples. *Psychological Bulletin, 124,* 22–53.

Riskind, John H.; Williams, Nathan L.; Gessner, Theodore L.; et al. (2000). The looming maladaptive style: Anxiety, danger, and schematic processing. *Journal of Personality and Social Psychology, 79,* 837–852.

Roan, Shari (2002, April 29). Late-late motherhood. *The Los Angeles Times,* pp. S1, S6.

Roberts, Brent W.; Caspi, Avshalom; & Moffitt, Terrie F. (2001). The kids are alright: Growth and stability in personality development from adolescence to adulthood. *Journal of Personality and Social Psychology, 81,* 670–683.

Roberts, Brent W.; Walton, Kate E.; & Viechtbauer, Wolfgang (2006). Patterns of mean-level change in personality traits across the life course: A meta-analysis of longitudinal studies. *Psychological Bulletin, 132,* 1–25.

Robins, Lee N.; Davis, Darlene H.; & Goodwin, Donald W. (1974). Drug use by U.S. Army enlisted men in Vietnam: A follow-up on their return home. *American Journal of Epidemiology, 99,* 235–249.

Robins, Lee N.; Tipp, Jayson; & Przybeck, Thomas R. (1991). Antisocial personality. In L. N. Robins & D. A. Regier (Eds.), *Psychiatric disorders in America.* New York: Free Press.

Robinson, Thomas N. (1999, October 27). Reducing children's television viewing to prevent obesity: A randomized controlled trial. *Journal of the American Medical Association, 282,* 1561–1567.

Robinson, Thomas; Wilde, M. L.; Navracruz, L. C.; et al. (2001). Effects of reducing children's television and video game use on aggressive behavior: a randomized controlled trial. *Archives of Pediatric and Adolescent Medicine, 155,* 13–14.

Rocha, Beatriz A.; Scearce-Levie, Kimberly; Lucas, Jose J.; et al. (1998). Increased vulnerability to cocaine in mice lacking the serotonin-1B receptor. *Nature, 393,* 175–178.

Roediger, Henry L. (1990). Implicit memory: Retention without remembering. *American Psychologist, 45,* 1043–1056.

Roediger, Henry L., & McDermott, Kathleen B. (1995). Creating false memories: Remembering words not presented in lists. *Journal of Experimental Psychology; Learning, Memory, & Cognition, 21,* 803–814.

Rogers, Carl (1951). *Client-centered therapy: Its current practice, implications, and theory.* Boston: Houghton Mifflin.

Rogers, Carl (1961). *On becoming a person.* Boston: Houghton Mifflin.

Rogers, Ronald W., & Prentice-Dunn, Steven (1981). Deindividuation and anger-mediated interracial aggression: Unmasking regressive racism. *Journal of Personality and Social Psychology, 41,* 63–73.

Rogoff, Barbara (2003). *The cultural nature of human development.* New York: Oxford University Press.

Rollin, Henry (Ed.) (1980). *Coping with schizophrenia.* London: Burnett.

Rosch, Eleanor H. (1973). Natural categories. *Cognitive Psychology, 4,* 328–350.

Rosen, Gerald M. (1981). Guidelines for the review of do-it-yourself treatment books. *Contemporary Psychology, 26,* 189–191.

Rosen, Gerald M.; Glasgow, Russell E.; & Moore, Timothy E. (2003). Self-help therapy: The science and business of giving psychology away. In S. O. Lilienfeld, S. J. Lynn, & J. M. Lohr (Eds.), *Science and pseudoscience in clinical psychology.* New York: Guilford.

Rosenberg, Harold (1993). Prediction of controlled drinking by alcoholics and problem drinkers. *Psychological Bulletin, 113,* 129–139.

Rosenthal, Norman E. (1998). *Winter blues: Seasonal affective disorder: What it is and how to overcome it.* New York: Guilford Press.

Rosenthal, Robert (1994). Interpersonal expectancy effects: A 30-year perspective. *Current Directions in Psychological Science, 3,* 176–179.

Rosenzweig, Mark R. (1984). Experience, memory, and the brain. *American Psychologist, 39,* 365–376.

Roser, Matt E., & Gazzaniga, Michael S. (2004). Automatic brains: Interpretive minds. *Current Directions in Psychological Science, 13,* 56–59.

Roth, David L.; & Holmes, David S. (1985). Influence of physical fitness in determining the impact of stressful life events on physical and psychologic health. *Psychosomatic Medicine, 47,* 164–173.

Rothbart, Mary K.; Ahadi, Stephan A.; & Evans, David E. (2000). Temperament and personality: Origins and outcomes. *Journal of Personality and Social Psychology, 78,* 122–135.

Rothbaum, Fred; Weisz, John; Pott, Martha; et al. (2000). Attachment and culture: Security in the United States and Japan. *American Psychologist, 55,* 1093–1104.

Rothbaum, Fred M.; Weisz, John R.; & Snyder, Samuel S. (1982). Changing the world and changing the self: A two-process model of perceived control. *Journal of Personality and Social Psychology, 42,* 5–37.

Rothermund, Klaus, & Wentura, Dirk (2004). Underlying processes in the Implicit Association Test: Dissociating salience from associations. *Journal of Experimental Psychology: General, 133,* 139–165.

Rotter, Julian B. (1990). Internal versus external control of reinforcement: A case history of a variable. *American Psychologist, 45,* 489–493.

Roughgarden, Joan (2004). *Evolution's rainbow: Diversity, gender, and sexuality in nature and people.* Berkeley: University of California Press.

Roy, Mark P.; Steptoe, Andrew; & Kirschbaum, Clemens (1998). Life events and social support as moderators of individual differences in cardiovascular and cortisol reactivity. *Journal of Personality and Social Psychology, 75,* 1273–1281.

Røysamb, Espen; Tambs, Kristian; Reichborn-Kjennerud, Ted; et al. (2003). Happiness and health: Environmental and genetic contributions to the relationship between subjective well-being, perceived health, and somatic illness. *Journal of Personality and Social Psychology, 85,* 1136–1146.

Rozin, Paul; Lowery, Laura; & Ebert, Rhonda (1994). Varieties of disgust faces and the structure of disgust. *Journal of Personality and Social Psychology, 66,* 870–881.

Rubinstein, Joshua S.; Meyer, David E.; & Evans, Jeffrey E. (2001). Executive control of cognitive processes in task switching. *Journal of Experimental Psychology: Human Perception and Performance, 27,* 763–797.

Rudman, Laurie A. (2004). Sources of implicit attitudes. *Current Directions in Psychological Science,* in press.

Ruggiero, Vincent R. (1988). *Teaching thinking across the curriculum.* New York: Harper & Row.

Rumbaugh, Duane M. (1977). *Language learning by a chimpanzee: The Lana project.* New York: Academic Press.

Rumbaugh, Duane M.; Savage-Rumbaugh, E. Sue; & Pate, James L. (1988). Addendum to "Summation in the chimpanzee (*Pan troglodytes*)." *Journal of Experimental Psychology: Animal Behavior Processes, 14,* 118–120.

Rumelhart, David E.; McClelland, James L.; & the PDP Research Group (1986). *Parallel distributed processing: Explorations in the microstructure of cognition* (Vols. 1 and 2). Cambridge, MA: MIT Press.

Rushton, J. Philippe (1988). Race differences in behavior: A review and evolutionary analysis. *Personality and Individual Differences, 9,* 1009–1024.

Russell, Diana E. H. (1990). *Rape in marriage* (Rev. ed.). Bloomington: Indiana University Press.

Russell, James A., & Fehr, Beverley (1994). Fuzzy concepts in a fuzzy hierarchy: Varieties of anger. *Journal of Personality and Social Psychology, 67,* 186–205.

Rutter, Michael; O'Connor, Thomas G.; & the English and Romanian Adoptees (ERA) Study Team (2004). Are there biological programming effects for psychological development? Findings from a study of Romanian adoptees. *Developmental Psychology, 40,* 81–94.

Rutter, Michael; Pickles, Andrew; Murray, Robin; & Eaves, Lindon (2001). Testing hypotheses on specific environmental causal effects on behavior. *Psychological Bulletin, 127,* 291–324.

Ryan, Richard M.; Chirkov, Valery I.; Little, Todd D.; et al. (1999). The American dream in Russia: Extrinsic aspirations and well-being in two cultures. *Personality and Social Psychology Bulletin, 25,* 1509–1524.

Ryder, Andrew G.; Alden, Lynn E.; & Paulhus, Delroy L. (2000). Is acculturation unidimensional or bidimensional? A head-to-head comparison in the prediction of personality, self-identity, and adjustment. *Journal of Personality and Social Psychology, 79,* 49–65.

Rymer, Russ (1993). *Genie: An abused child's flight from silence.* New York: HarperCollins.

Sack, Robert L., & Lewy, Alfred J. (1997). Melatonin as a chronobiotic: Treatment of circadian desynchrony in night workers and the blind. *Journal of Biological Rhythms, 12,* 595–603.

Sacks, Oliver (1985). *The man who mistook his wife for a hat and other clinical tales.* New York: Simon & Schuster.

Saffran, J. R.; Aslin, R. N.; & Newport, E. L. (1996). Statistical learning by 8-month-old infants. *Science, 274,* 1926–1928.

Sagan, Eli (1988). *Freud, women, and morality: The psychology of good and evil.* New York: Basic Books.

Sage, Cyrille; Huang, Mingqian; Karimi, Kambiz; et al. (2005). Proliferation of functional hair cells in vivo in the absence of the retinoblastoma protein. *Science, 307,* 114–118.

Sahley, Christie L.; Rudy, Jerry W.; & Gelperin, Alan (1981). An analysis of associative learning in a terrestrial mollusk: 1. Higher-order conditioning, blocking, and a transient US preexposure effect. *Journal of Comparative Physiology, 144,* 1–8.

Salovey, Peter, & Grewal, Daisy (2005). The science of emotional intelligence. *Current Directions in Psychological Science, 14,* 281–285.

Salthouse, Timothy A. (2006). Mental exercise and mental aging: Evaluating the validity of the "use it or lose it" hypothesis. *Perspectives on Psychological Science, 1,* 68–87.

Sameroff, Arnold J.; Seifer, Ronald; Barocas, Ralph; et al. (1987). Intelligence quotient scores of 4-year-old children: Social-environmental risk factors. *Pediatrics, 79,* 343–350.

Sampson, Paul D.; Streissguth, Ann P.; Bookstein, Fred L.; & Barr, Helen M. (2000). On categorizations in analyses of alcohol teratogenesis. *Environmental Health Perspectives, 108,* 421–428.

Sapolsky, Robert M. (1997). *The trouble with testosterone.* New York: Touchstone.

Sapolsky, Robert M. (2000). The possibility of neurotoxicity in the hippocampus in major depression: A primer on neuron death. *Biological Psychiatry, 48,* 755–765.

Sarbin, Theodore R. (1991). Hypnosis: A fifty year perspective. *Contemporary Hypnosis, 8,* 1–15.

Saucier, Deborah M., & Kimura, Doreen (1998). Intrapersonal motor but not extrapersonal targeting skill is enhanced during the midluteal phase of the menstrual cycle. *Developmental Neuropsychology, 14,* 385–398.

Saucier, Gerard (2000). Isms and the structure of social attitudes. *Journal of Personality and Social Psychology, 78,* 366–385.

Savage-Rumbaugh, Sue, & Lewin, Roger (1994). *Kanzi: The ape at the brink of the human mind.* New York: Wiley.

Savage-Rumbaugh, Sue; Shanker, Stuart; & Taylor, Talbot (1998). *Apes, language and the human mind.* New York: Oxford University Press.

Savin-Williams, Ritch C. (2006). Who's gay? Does it matter? *Current Directions in Psychological Science, 15,* 40–44.

Sawa, Akira, & Snyder, Solomon H. (2002, April 26). Schizophrenia: Diverse approaches to a complex disease. *Science, 296,* 692–694.

Saxena, S.; Brody, A. L.; Maidment, K. M.; et al. (2004). Cerebral glucose metabolism in obsessive-compulsive hoarding. *American Journal of Psychiatry, 161,* 1038–1048.

Scarr, Sandra (1993). Biological and cultural diversity: The legacy of Darwin for development. *Child Development, 64,* 1333–1353.

Scarr, Sandra; Pakstis, Andrew J.; Katz, Soloman H.; & Barker, William B. (1977). Absence of a relationship between degree of white ancestry and intellectual skill in a black population. *Human Genetics, 39,* 69–86.

Scarr, Sandra, & Weinberg, Robert A. (1994). Educational and occupational achievement of brothers and sisters in adoptive and biologically related families. *Behavioral Genetics, 24,* 301–325.

Schachter, Stanley, & Singer, Jerome E. (1962). Cognitive, social, and physiological determinants of emotional state. *Psychological Review, 69,* 379–399.

Schacter, Daniel L. (2001). *The seven sins of memory: How the mind forgets and remembers.* Boston: Houghton Mifflin.

Schacter, Daniel L.; Chiu, C. Y. Peter; & Ochsner, Kevin N. (1993). Implicit memory: A selective review. *Annual Review of Neuroscience, 16,* 159–182.

Schaeffer, Cindy M., & Borduin, Charles M. (2005). Long-term follow-up to a randomized clinical trial of multisystemic therapy with serious and violent juvenile offenders. *Journal of Consulting and Clinical Psychology, 73,* 445–453.

Schafer, Roy (1992). *Retelling a life: Narration and dialogue in psychoanalysis.* New York: Basic Books.

Schaie, K. Warner (1993). The Seattle longitudinal studies of adult intelligence. *Current Directions in Psychological Science, 2,* 171–175.

Schaie, K. Warner, & Willis, Sherry L. (2002). *Adult development and aging* (5th ed.). Upper Saddle River, NJ: Prentice Hall.

Schaie, K. Warner, & Zuo, Yan-Ling (2001). Family environments and cognitive functioning. In R. J. Sternberg & E. Grigorenko (Eds.), *Cognitive development in context.* Hillsdale, NJ: Erlbaum.

Schank, Roger, with Peter Childers (1988). *The creative attitude.* New York: Macmillan.

Scherer, Klaus R. (1997). The role of culture in emotion-antecedent appraisal. *Journal of Personality and Social Psychology, 73,* 902–922.

Scheufele, Peter M. (2000). Effects of progressive relaxation and classical music on measurements of attention, relaxation, and stress responses. *Journal of Behavioral Medicine, 23,* 207–228.

Schiff, Nicholas D.; Rodriguez-Moreno, Diana; Kamal, Ayeesha; et al. (2005). fMRI reveals large-scale network activation in minimally conscious patients. *Neurology, 64,* 514–523.

Schlossberg, Nancy K., & Robinson, Susan P. (1996). *Going to plan B.* New York: Simon & Schuster/Fireside.

Schlosser, Eric (2003). *Reefer madness: Sex, drugs, and cheap labor in the American black market.* Boston: Houghton-Mifflin.

Schmelz, M.; Schmidt, R.; Bickel, A.; et al. (1997). Specific C-receptors for itch in human skin. *Journal of Neuroscience, 17,* 8003–8008.

Schmidt, Frank L., & Hunter, John (2004). General mental ability in the world of work: Occupational attainment and job performance. *Journal of Personality and Social Psychology, 86,* 162–173.

Schmitt, David P. (2003). Universal sex differences in the desire for sexual variety: Tests from 52 nations, 6 continents, and 13 islands. *Journal of Personality and Social Psychology, 85,* 85–104.

Schnell, Lisa, & Schwab, Martin E. (1990, January 18). Axonal regeneration in the rat spinal cord produced by an antibody against myelin-associated neurite growth inhibitors. *Nature, 343,* 269–272.

Schofield, P.; Ball, D.; Smith, J. G.; et al. (2004). Optimism and survival in lung carcinoma patients. *Cancer, 100,* 1276–1282.

Schuckit, Marc A. (1998). Relationship among genetic, environmental, and psychological variables in predicting alcoholism. Invited address presented at the annual meeting of the American Psychological Association, San Francisco.

Schuckit, Marc A., & Smith, T. L. (1996). An 8-year follow-up of 450 sons of alcoholic and control subjects. *Archives of General Psychiatry, 53,* 202–210.

Schulz, Richard; Beach, S. R.; Ives, D. G.; et al. (2000). Association between depression and mortality in older adults: The Cardiovascular Health Study. *Archives of Internal Medicine, 160,* 1761–1768.

Schwartz, Jeffrey; Stoessel, Paula W.; Baxter, Lewis R.; et al. (1996). Systematic changes in cerebral glucose metabolic rate after successful behavior modification treatment of obsessive–compulsive disorder. *Archives of General Psychiatry, 53,* 109–113.

Sears, Pauline, & Barbee, Ann H. (1977). Career and life satisfactions among Terman's gifted women. In J. C. Stanley, W. C. George, & C. H. Solano (Eds.), *The gifted and the creative: A fifty-year perspective.* Baltimore, MD: Johns Hopkins University Press.

Segal, Julius (1986). *Winning life's toughest battles.* New York: McGraw-Hill.

Segall, Marshall H.; Campbell, Donald T.; & Herskovits, Melville J. (1966). *The influence of culture on visual perception.* Indianapolis, IN: Bobbs-Merrill.

Segall, Marshall H.; Dasen, Pierre R.; Berry, John W.; & Poortinga, Ype H. (1999). *Human behavior in global perspective: An introduction to cross-cultural psychology* (2nd ed.). Boston: Allyn & Bacon.

Segerstrom, Suzanne C.; Taylor, Shelley E.; Kemeny, Margaret E.; & Fahey, John L. (1998). Optimism is associated with mood, coping, and immune change in response to stress. *Journal of Personality and Social Psychology, 74,* 1646–1655.

Seidenberg, Mark S.; MacDonald, Maryellen C.; & Saffran, Jenny R. (2002). Does grammar start where statistics stop? *Science, 298,* 553–554.

Seifer, Ronald; Schiller, Masha; Sameroff, Arnold; et al. (1996). Attachment, maternal sensitivity, and infant temperament during the first year of life. *Developmental Psychology, 32,* 12–25.

Sekuler, Robert, & Blake, Randolph (1994). *Perception* (3rd ed.). New York: Knopf.

Seligman, Martin E. P. (1991). *Learned optimism.* New York: Knopf.

Seligman, Martin E. P., & Csikszentmihaly, Mihaly (2000). Positive psychology: An introduction. *American Psychologist, 55,* 5–14.

Seligman, Martin E. P., & Hager, Joanne L. (1972, August). Biological boundaries of learning: The sauce-béarnaise syndrome. *Psychology Today,* 59–61, 84–87.

Seligman, Martin E. P.; Schulman, Peter; DeRubeis, Robert J.; & Hollon, Steven D. (1999). The prevention of depression and anxiety. *Prevention & Treatment, 2,* electronic posting December 21, 1999 on the Website of the American Psychological Association.

Selye, Hans (1956). *The stress of life.* New York: McGraw-Hill.

Senghas, Ann, & Coppola, Marie (2001). Children creating language: How Nicaraguan Sign Language acquired a spatial grammar. *Psychological Science, 12,* 323–328.

Serbin, Lisa A.; Powlishta, Kimberly K.; & Gulko, Judith (1993). The development of sex typing in middle childhood. *Monographs of the Society for Research in Child Development, 58(2), Serial No. 232,* v-74.

Serpell, Robert (1994). The cultural construction of intelligence. In W. J. Lonner & R. S. Malpass (Eds.), *Psychology and culture.* Needham Heights, MA: Allyn & Bacon.

Shapiro, Francine (1994). EMDR: In the eye of a paradigm shift. *Behavior Therapist, 17,* 153–156.

Shapiro, Francine (1995). *Eye movement desensitization and reprocessing: Basic principles, protocols, and procedures.* New York: Guilford.

Sharman, Stephanie J.; Manning, Charles G.; & Garry, Maryanne (2005). Explain this: Explaining childhood events inflates confidence for those events. *Applied Cognitive Psychology, 19,* 16–74.

Shatz, Marilyn, & Gelman, Rochel (1973). The development of communication skills: Modifications in the speech of young children as a function of the listener. *Monographs of the Society for Research in Child Development, 38.*

Shaver, Phillip R., & Hazan, Cindy (1993). Adult romantic attachment: Theory and evidence. In D. Perlman & W. H. Jones (Eds.), *Advances in personal relationships* (Vol. 4). London: Kingsley.

Shaver, Phillip R., & Mikulincer, Mario (2006). Attachment and forgiveness in romantic relationships. Paper presented at the annual meeting of the Society for Personality and Social Psychology, Palm Springs, CA.

Shaver, Phillip R.; Wu, Shelley; & Schwartz, Judith C. (1992). Cross-cultural similarities and differences in emotion and its representation: A prototype approach. In M. S. Clark (Ed.), *Review of Personality and Social Psychology* (Vol. 13). Newbury Park, CA: Sage.

Shaywitz, Bennett A.; Shaywitz, Sally E.; Pugh, Kenneth R.; et al. (1995). Sex differences in the functional organization of the brain for language. *Nature, 373,* 607–609.

Shea, Christopher (2001, September). White man can't contextualize. *Lingua Franca,* 44–47, 49–51.

Sheldon, Kennon M.; Elliot, Andrew J.; Kim, Youngmee; & Kasser, Tim (2001). What is satisfying about satisfying events? Testing 10 candidate psychological needs. *Journal of Personality and Social Psychology, 80,* 325–339.

Sheldon, Kennon M., & Houser-Marko, Linda (2001). Self-concordance, goal attainment, and the pursuit of happiness: Can there be an upward spiral? *Journal of Personality and Social Psychology, 80,* 152–165.

Sheline, Yvette I. (2000). 3D MRI studies of neuroanatomic changes in unipolar major depression: The role of stress and medical comorbidity. *Biological Psychiatry, 48,* 791–800.

Shepard, Roger N., & Metzler, Jacqueline (1971). Mental rotation of three-dimensional objects. *Science, 171,* 701–703.

Shepperd, James A. (1995). Remedying motivation and productivity loss in collective settings. *Current Directions in Psychological Science, 4,* 131–140.

Sherif, Muzafer (1958). Superordinate goals in the reduction of intergroup conflicts. *American Journal of Sociology, 63,* 349–356.

Sherif, Muzafer; Harvey, O. J.; White, B. J.; Hood, William; & Sherif, Carolyn (1961). *Intergroup conflict and cooperation: The Robbers Cave experiment.* Norman: University of Oklahoma Institute of Intergroup Relations.

Sherman, Bonnie R., & Kunda, Ziva (1989). Motivated evaluation of scientific evidence. Paper presented at the annual meeting of the American Psychological Society, Arlington, VA.

Shermer, Michael (1997). *Why people believe weird things: Pseudoscience, superstition, and other confusions of our time.* New York: Freeman.

Sherwin, Barbara B. (1998a). Estrogen and cognitive functioning in women. *Proceedings of the Society for Experimental Biological Medicine, 217,* 17–22.

Sherwin, Barbara B. (1998b). Use of combined estrogen-androgen preparations in the postmenopause: Evidence from clinical studies. *International Journal of Fertility & Women's Medicine, 43,* 98–103.

Shields, Stephanie A. (2005). The politics of emotion in everyday life: "Appropriate" emotion and claims on identity. *Review of General Psychology, 9,* 3–15.

Showalter, Elaine (1997). *Hystories: Hysterical epidemics and modern culture.* New York: Columbia University Press.

Sidanius, Jim; Pratto, Felicia; & Bobo, Lawrence (1996). Racism, conservatism, affirmative action, and intellectual sophistication: A matter of principled conservatism or group dominance? *Journal of Personality and Social Psychology, 70,* 476–490.

Siegel, Ronald K. (1989). *Intoxication: Life in pursuit of artificial paradise.* New York: Dutton.

Siegler, Robert S. (2006). Microgenetic analyses of learning. In D. Kuhn & R. S. Siegler (Eds.), *Handbook of child psychology: Vol. 2. Cognition, perception, and language* (6th ed.). New York: Wiley.

Silke, Andrew (Ed.) (2003). *Terrorists, victims, and society: Psychological perspectives on terrorism and its consequences.* New York: Wiley.

Silverstein, Brett, & Perlick, Deborah (1995). *The cost of competence: Why inequality causes depression, eating disorders, and illness in women.* New York: Oxford University Press.

Silverstein, Brett; Peterson, Barbara; & Perdue, Lauren (1986). Some correlates of the thin standard of bodily attractiveness in women. *International Journal of Eating Disorders, 5,* 145–155.

Simon, Herbert A. (1955). A behavioral model of rational choice. *Quarterly Journal of Economics, 69,* 99–118.

Simon, Taryn (2003, January 26). Freedom row. *The New York Times Magazine,* pp. 32, 37.

Simons, Daniel J., & Chabris, Christopher F. (1999). Gorillas in our midst: Sustained inattentional blindness for dynamic events. *Perception, 28,* 1059–1974.

Sims, Ethan A. (1974). Studies in human hyperphagia. In G. Bray & J. Bethune (Eds.), *Treatment and management of obesity.* New York: Harper & Row.

Sinaceur, Marwan; Heath, Chip; & Cole, Steve (2005). Emotional and deliberative reactions to a public crisis: Mad Cow disease in France. *Psychological Science, 16,* 247–254.

Sinclair, Lisa, & Kunda, Ziva (1999). Reactions to a Black professional: Motivated inhibition and activation of conflicting stereotypes. *Journal of Personality and Social Psychology, 77,* 885–904.

Singer, Margaret T. (with Janja Lalich) (1995). *Cults in our midst.* San Francisco: Jossey-Bass.

Singer, Margaret T.; Temerlin, Maurice K.; & Langone, Michael D. (1990). Psycotherapy cults. *Cultic Studies Journal, 7,* 101–125.

Singh, Devendra; Vidaurri, Melody; Zambarano, Robert J.; & Dabbs, James M., Jr. (1999). Lesbian erotic role identification: Behavioral, morphological, and hormonal correlates. *Journal of Personality and Social Psychology, 76,* 1035–1049.

Sivak, Michael, & Flannagan, Michael J. (2003). Flying and driving after the September 11 attacks. *American Scientist, 91,* 6–8.

Skinner, B. F. (1938). *The behavior of organisms: An experimental analysis.* New York: Appleton-Century-Crofts.

Skinner, B. F. (1948/1976). *Walden Two.* New York: Macmillan.

Skinner, B. F. (1956). A case history in the scientific method. *American Psychologist, 11,* 221–233.

Skinner, B. F. (1972). The operational analysis of psychological terms. In B. F. Skinner, *Cumulative record* (3rd ed.). New York: Appleton-Century-Crofts.

Skinner, B. F. (1990). Can psychology be a science of mind? *American Psychologist, 45,* 1206–1210.

Skinner, Ellen A. (1996). A guide to constructs of control. *Journal of Personality and Social Psychology, 71,* 549–570.

Skinner, J. B.; Erskine, A.; Pearce, S. A.; et al. (1990). The evaluation of a cognitive behavioural treatment programme in outpatients with chronic pain. *Journal of Psychosomatic Research, 34,* 13–19.

Skreslet, Paula (1987, November 30). The prizes of first grade. *Newsweek, 8.*

Slade, Pauline (1984). Premenstrual emotional changes in normal women: Fact or fiction? *Journal of Psychosomatic Research, 28,* 1–7.

Slavin, Robert E., & Cooper, Robert (1999). Improving intergroup relations: Lessons learned from cooperative learning programs. *Journal of Social Issues, 55,* 647–663.

Slovic, Paul; Finucane, Melissa L.; Peters, Ellen.; & MacGregor, Donald G. (2002). The affect heuristic. In T. Gilovich, D. Griffin, & D. Kahneman (Eds.), *Heuristics and biases: The psychology of intuitive judgment.* New York: Cambridge University Press.

Smith, David N. (1998). The psychocultural roots of genocide: Legitimacy and crisis in Rwanda. *American Psychologist, 53,* 743–753.

Smith, James F., & Kida, Thomas (1991). Heuristics and biases: Expertise and task realism in auditing. *Psychological Bulletin, 109,* 472–489.

Smith, Larissa L., & Reise, Steven P. (1998). Gender differences on negative affectivity: An IRT study of differential item functioning on the Multidimensional Personality Questionnaire Stress Reaction Scale. *Journal of Personality and Social Psychology, 75,* 1350–1362.

Smith, Peter B., & Bond, Michael H. (1994). *Social psychology across cultures: Analysis and perspectives.* Boston: Allyn & Bacon.

Smither, Robert D. (1998). *The psychology of work and human performance* (3rd ed.). New York: Longman.

Snodgrass, Sara E. (1992). Further effects of role versus gender on interpersonal sensitivity. *Journal of Personality and Social Psychology, 62,* 154–158.

Snowdon, Charles T. (1997). The "nature" of sex differences: Myths of male and female. In P.A. Gowaty (Ed.), *Feminism and evolutionary biology.* New York: Chapman and Hall.

Snyder, C. R., & Shenkel, Randee J. (1975, March). The P. T. Barnum effect. *Psychology Today,* 52–54.

Sobell, Mark B., & Sobell, Linda C. (1993). *Problem drinkers: Guided self-change treatment.* New York: Guilford.

Solomon, Paul R. (1979). Science and television commercials: Adding relevance to the research methodology course. *Teaching of Psychology, 6,* 26–30.

Solomon, Robert C. (1994). *About love.* Lanham, MD: Littlefield Adams.

Somer, Oya, & Goldberg, Lewis R. (1999). The structure of Turkish trait-descriptive adjectives. *Journal of Personality and Social Psychology, 76,* 431–450.

Sommer, Robert (1969). *Personal space: The behavioral basis of design.* Englewood Cliffs, NJ: Prentice-Hall.

Sorce, James F.; Emde, Robert N.; Campos, Joseph; & Klinnert, Mary D. (1985). Maternal emotional signaling: Its effect on the visual cliff behavior of 1-year-olds. *Developmental Psychology, 21,* 195–200.

Spanos, Nicholas P. (1991). A sociocognitive approach to hypnosis. In S. J. Lynn & J. W. Rhue (Eds.), *Theories of hypnosis: Current models and perspectives.* New York: Guilford Press.

Spanos, Nicholas P. (1996). *Multiple identities and false memories: A sociocognitive perspective.* Washington, DC: American Psychological Association.

Spanos, Nicholas P.; Burgess, Cheryl A.; Roncon, Vera; et al. (1993). Surreptitiously observed hypnotic responding in simulators and in skill-trained and untrained high hypnotizables. *Journal of Personality and Social Psychology, 65,* 391–398.

Spanos, Nicholas P.; Menary, Evelyn; Gabora, Natalie J.; et al. (1991). Secondary identity enactments during hypnotic past-life regression: A sociocognitive perspective. *Journal of Personality and Social Psychology, 61,* 308–320.

Spanos, Nicholas P.; Stenstrom, Robert J.; & Johnson, Joseph C. (1988). Hypnosis, placebo, and suggestion in the treatment of warts. *Psychosomatic Medicine, 50,* 245–260.

Spear, Linda P. (2000). Neurobiological changes in adolescence. *Current Directions in Psychological Science, 9,* 111–114.

Spearman, Charles (1927). *The abilities of man.* London: Macmillan.

Spelke, Elizabeth S. (2000). Core knowledge. *American Psychologist, 55,* 1233–1243.

Spencer, M. B., & Dornbusch, Sanford M. (1990). Ethnicity. In S. S. Feldman & G. R. Elliott (Eds.), *At the threshold: The developing adolescent.* Cambridge, MA: Harvard University Press.

Sperling, George (1960). The information available in brief visual presentations. *Psychological Monographs, 74*(498).

Sperry, Roger W. (1964). The great cerebral commissure. *Scientific American, 210*(1), 42–52.

Sperry, Roger W. (1982). Some effects of disconnecting the cerebral hemispheres. *Science, 217,* 1223–1226.

Spilich, George J.; June, Lorraine; & Renner, Judith (1992). Cigarette smoking and cognitive performance. *British Journal of Addiction, 87,* 113–126.

Spitz, Herman H. (1997). *Nonconscious movements: From mystical messages to facilitated communication*. Mahwah, NJ: Erlbaum.

Sprecher, Susan; Sullivan, Quintin; & Hatfield, Elaine (1994). Mate selection preferences: Gender differences examined in a national sample. *Journal of Personality and Social Psychology, 66,* 1074–1080.

Spring, Bonnie; Chiodo, June; & Bowen, Deborah J. (1987). Carbohydrates, tryptophan, and behavior: A methodological review. *Psychological Bulletin, 102,* 234–256.

Springer, Sally P., & Deutsch, Georg (1998). Left brain, right brain: *Perspectives from cognitive neuroscience*. New York: Freeman.

Squier, Leslie H., & Domhoff, G. William (1998). The presentation of dreaming and dreams in introductory psychology textbooks: A critical examination with suggestions for textbook authors and course instructors. *Dreaming, 8,* 149–168.

Squire, Larry R. (1987). *Memory and the brain*. New York: Oxford University Press.

Squire, Larry R., & Zola-Morgan, Stuart (1991). The medial temporal lobe memory system. *Science, 253,* 1380–1386.

Srivastava, Abhishek; Locke, Edwin A.; & Bartol, Kathryn M. (2001). Money and subjective well-being: It's not the money, it's the motives. *Journal of Personality and Social Psychology, 80,* 959–971.

Staats, Carolyn K., & Staats, Arthur W. (1957). Meaning established by classical conditioning. *Journal of Experimental Psychology, 54,* 74–80.

Stajkovic, Alexander D., & Luthans, Fred (1998). Self-efficacy and work-related performance: A meta-analysis. *Psychological Bulletin, 124,* 240–261.

Stanovich, Keith (1996). *How to think straight about psychology* (4th ed.). New York: HarperCollins.

Stanwood, Gregg D., & Levitt, Pat (2001). *The effects of cocaine on the developing nervous system*. In C. A. Nelson & M. Luciana (Eds.), *Handbook of developmental cognitive neuroscience*. Cambridge, MA: The MIT Press.

Staples, Susan L. (1996). Human response to environmental noise: Psychological research and public policy. *American Psychologist, 51,* 143–150.

Stattin, Haken, & Magnusson, David (1990). *Pubertal maturation in female development*. Hillsdale, NJ: Erlbaum.

Staub, Ervin (1996). Cultural-social roots of violence. *American Psychologist, 51,* 117–132.

Staub, Ervin (1999). The roots of evil: Social conditions, culture, personality, and basic human needs. *Personality and Social Psychology Review, 3,* 179–192.

St. Clair, D.; Xu, M.; Wang, P.; et al. (2005, August 3). Rates of adult schizophrenia following prenatal exposure to the Chinese famine of 1959–1961. *Journal of the American Medical Association, 294,* 557–562.

Stearns, Peter N. (1997). *Fat history: Bodies and beauty in the modern West*. New York: New York University Press.

Steele, Claude M. (1992, April). Race and the schooling of Black Americans. *Atlantic Monthly,* 68–78.

Steele, Claude M. (1997). A threat in the air: How stereotypes shape intellectual identity and performance. *American Psychologist, 52,* 613–629.

Steele, Claude M., & Aronson, Joshua (1995). Stereotype threat and the intellectual test performance of African-Americans. *Journal of Personality and Social Psychology, 69,* 797–811.

Stein, M. B.; Jang, K. L.; Taylor, S.; Vernon, P. A.; & Livesley, W. J. (2002). Genetic and environmental influences on trauma exposure and posttraumatic stress disorder symptoms: A general population twin study. *American Journal of Psychiatry, 159,* 1675–1681.

Steinberg, Laurence D.; Dornbusch, Sanford M.; & Brown, B. Bradford (1992). Ethnic differences in adolescent achievement: An ecological perspective. *American Psychologist, 47,* 723–729.

Stenberg, Craig R., & Campos, Joseph (1990). The development of anger expressions in infancy. In N. Stein, B. Leventhal, & T. Trabasso (Eds.), *Psychological and biological approaches to emotion*. Hillsdale, NJ: Erlbaum.

Stepanski, Edward, & Perlis, Michael (2000). Behavioral sleep medicine: An emerging subspecialty in health psychology. *Journal of Psychosomatic Research, 49,* 343–347.

Stephan, Walter G. (1999). *Reducing prejudice and stereotyping in schools*. New York: Teachers College Press.

Stephan, Walter G.; Ageyev, Vladimir; Coates-Shrider, Lisa; et al. (1994). On the relationship between stereotypes and prejudice: An international study. *Personality and Social Psychology Bulletin, 20,* 277–284.

Stern, Daniel (1985). *The interpersonal world of the infant.,* New York: Basic Books.

Stern, Marilyn, & Karraker, Katherine H. (1989). Sex stereotyping of infants: A review of gender labeling studies. *Sex Roles, 20,* 501–522.

Sternberg, Robert J. (1988). *The triarchic mind: A new theory of human intelligence*. New York: Viking.

Sternberg, Robert J. (1995). *In search of the human mind*. Orlando, FL: Harcourt Brace.

Sternberg, Robert J. (1997). Construct validation of a triangular love scale. *European Journal of Social Psychology, 27,* 313–335.

Sternberg, Robert J. (2004). Culture and intelligence. *American Psychologist, 59,* 325–338.

Sternberg, Robert J.; Forsythe, George B.; Hedlund, Jennifer; et al. (2000). *Practical intelligence in everyday life*. New York: Cambridge University Press.

Sternberg, Robert J., & Wagner, Richard K. (1989). Individual differences in practical knowledge and its acquisition. In P. Ackerman, R. J. Sternberg, & R. Glaser (Eds.), *Individual differences*. New York: Freeman.

Sternberg, Robert J.; Wagner, Richard K.; Williams, Wendy M.; & Horvath, Joseph A. (1995). Testing common sense. *American Psychologist, 50,* 912–927.

Stevenson, Harold W., & Stigler, James W. (1992). *The learning gap*. New York: Summit.

Stickgold, Robert (2005). Sleep-dependent memory consolidation. *Nature, 437,* 1272–1278.

Stoch, M. B., & Smythe, P. M. (1963). Does undernutrition during infancy inhibit brain growth and subsequent intellectual development? *Archives of Diseases in Childhood, 38,* 546–552.

Strack, Fritz; Martin, Leonard L.; & Stepper, Sabine (1988). Inhibiting and facilitating conditions of the human smile: A nonobtrusive test of the facial-feedback hypothesis. *Journal of Social and Personality Psychology, 54,* 768–777.

Strahan, Erin J.; Spencer, Steven J.; & Zanna, Mark P. (2002). Subliminal priming and persuasion: Striking while the iron is hot. *Journal of Experimental Social Psychology, 38,* 556–568.

Straus, Murray A., & Kantor, Glenda Kaufman (1994). Corporal punishment of adolescents by parents: A risk factor in the epidemiology of depression, suicide, alcohol abuse, child abuse, and wife beating. *Adolescence, 29,* 543–561.

Streissguth, Ann P. (2001). Recent advances in fetal alcohol syndrome and alcohol use in pregnancy. In D. P. Agarwal & H. K. Seitz (Eds.), *Alcohol in health and disease*. New York: Marcel Dekker.

Streyffeler, Lisa L., & McNally, Richard J. (1998). Fundamentalists and liberals: personality characteristics of Protestant Christians. *Personality and Individual Differences, 24,* 579–580.

Strickland, Bonnie R. (1989). Internal–external control expectancies: From contingency to creativity. *American Psychologist, 44,* 1–12.

Strickland, Tony L.; Lin, Keh-Ming; Fu, Paul; et al. (1995). Comparison of lithium ratio between African-American and Caucasian bipolar patients. *Biological Psychiatry, 37,* 325–330.

Strickland, Tony L.; Ranganath, Vijay; Lin, Keh-Ming; et al. (1991). Psychopharmacological considerations in the treatment of black American populations. *Psychopharmacology Bulletin, 27,* 441–448.

Stroebe, Margaret; Strobe, Wolfgang; & Schut, Henk (2001). Gender differences in adjustment to bereavement: An empirical and theoretical review. *Review of General Psychology, 5,* 62–83.

Stroebe, Wolfgang; Stroebe, Margaret; Abakoumkin, Georgios; & Schut, Henk (1996). The role of loneliness and social support in adjustment to loss: A test of attachment versus stress theory. *Journal of Personality and Social Psychology, 70,* 1241–1249.

Stunkard, Albert J. (Ed.) (1980). *Obesity.* Philadelphia: Saunders.

Suddendorf, Thomas, & Whiten, Andrew (2001). Mental evolution and development: Evidence for secondary representation in children, great apes, and other animals. *Psychological Bulletin, 127,* 629–650.

Suedfeld, Peter (1975). The benefits of boredom: Sensory deprivation reconsidered. *American Scientist, 63*(1), 60–69.

Sullivan, Michael J. L.; Tripp, Dean A.; & Santor, Darcy (1998). Gender differences in pain and pain behaviour: The role of catastrophizing. Paper presented at the annual meeting of the American Psychological Association, San Francisco.

Sulloway, Frank J. (1992). *Freud, biologist of the mind: Beyond the psychoanalytic legend* (Rev. ed.). Cambridge, MA: Harvard University Press.

Suls, Jerry, & Bunde, James (2005). Anger, anxiety, and depression as risk factors for cardiovascular disease: The problems and implications of overlapping affective dispositions. *Psychological Bulletin, 131,* 260–300.

Sundquist, J., & Winkleby, M. (2000, June). Country of birth, acculturation status and abdominal obesity in a national sample of Mexican-American women and men. *International Journal of Epidemiology, 29,* 470–477.

Swain, Scott (1989). Covert intimacy: Closeness in men's friendships. In B. J. Risman & P. Schwartz (Eds.), *Gender in intimate relationships.* Belmont, CA: Wadsworth.

Swenson, Cynthia C.; Henggeler, Scott W.; Taylor, Ida S.; & Addison, Oliver W. (2005). *Multisystemic therapy and neighborhood partnerships: Reducing adolescent violence and substance abuse.* New York: Guilford Press.

Tajfel, Henri; Billig, M. G.; Bundy, R. P.; & Flament, C. (1971). Social categorization and intergroup behavior. *European Journal of Social Psychology, 1,* 149–178.

Tajfel, Henri, & Turner, John C. (1986). The social identity theory of intergroup behavior. In S. Worchel & W. G. Austin (Eds.), *Psychology of intergroup relations.* Chicago: Nelson-Hall.

Talarico, Jennifer M., & Rubin, David C. (2003). Confidence, not consistency, characterizes flashbulb memories. *Psychological Science, 14,* 455–461.

Tangney, June P.; Wagner, Patricia E.; Hill-Barlow, Deborah; et al. (1996). Relation of shame and guilt to constructive versus destructive responses to anger across the lifespan. *Journal of Personality and Social Psychology, 70,* 797–809.

Taubes, Gary (1998). As obesity rates rise, experts struggle to explain why. *Science, 280,* 1367–1368.

Tavris, Carol (1989). *Anger: The misunderstood emotion* (Rev. ed.). New York: Simon & Schuster/Touchstone.

Taylor, Annette Kujawski, & Kowalski, Patricia (2004). Naïve psychological science: The prevalence, strength, and sources of misconceptions. *Psychological Record, 54,* 15–25.

Taylor, Shelley E.; Kemeny, Margaret E.; Reed, Geoffrey M.; Bower, Julienne E.; & Gruenewald, Tara L. (2000a). Psychological resources, positive illusions, and health. *American Psychologist, 55,* 99–109.

Taylor, Shelley E.; Klein, Laura C.; Lewis, Brian P.; et al. (2000b). Biobehavioral responses to stress in females: Tend-and-befriend, not fight-or-flight. *Psychological Review, 107,* 411–429.

Taylor, Shelley E.; Lichtman, Rosemary R.; & Wood, Joanne V. (1984). Attributions, beliefs about control, and adjustment to breast cancer. *Journal of Personality and Social Psychology, 46,* 489–502.

Taylor, Shelley E., & Lobel, Marci (1989). Social comparison activity under threat: Downward evaluation and upward contacts. *Psychological Review, 96,* 569–575.

Taylor, Shelley E.; Repetti, Rena; & Seeman, Teresa (1997). Health psychology: What is an unhealthy environment and how does it get under the skin? *Annual Review of Psychology* (Vol. 48). Palo Alto, CA: Annual Reviews.

Taylor, Steven; McKay, Dean; & Abramowitz, Jonathan S. (2005). Is obsessive-compulsive disorder a disturbance of security motivation? *Psychological Review, 112,* 650–657.

Taylor, Steven; Thordarson, Dana S.; Maxfield, Louise; et al. (2003). Comparative efficacy, speed, and adverse effects of three PTSD treatments: Exposure therapy, EMDR, and relaxation training. *Journal of Consulting and Clinical Psychology, 71,* 330–338.

Terman, Lewis M., & Oden, Melita H. (1959). *Genetic studies of genius: Vol. 5. The gifted group at mid-life.* Stanford, CA: Stanford University Press.

Terracciano, Antonio, & McCrae, Robert R. (2006, February). "National character does not reflect mean personality traits levels in 49 cultures": Reply. *Science, 311,* 777–779.

Thase, Michael E.; Fasiczka, Amy L.; Berman, Susan R.; et al. (1998). Electroencephalographic sleep profiles before and after cognitive behavior therapy of depression. *Archives of General Psychiatry, 55,* 138–144.

Thigpen, Corbett H., & Cleckley, Hervey M. (1984). On the incidence of multiple personality disorder: A brief communication. *International Journal of Clinical and Experimental Hypnosis, 32,* 63–66.

Thompson, Clara (1943/1973). Penis envy in women. *Psychiatry, 6,* 123–125. Reprinted in J. B. Miller (Ed.), *Psychoanalysis and women.* New York: Brunner/Mazel, 1973.

Thompson, Paul M.; Vidal, Christine N.; Giedd, Jay N.; et al. (2001). Mapping adolescent brain change reveals dynamic wave of accelerated gray matter loss in very early-onset schizophrenia. *Proceedings of the National Academy of Sciences of the USA, 98,* 11650–11655.

Thompson, Robin; Emmorey, Karen; & Gollan, Tamar H. (2005). "Tip of the fingers" experiences by deaf signers. *Psychological Science, 16,* 856–860.

Thorndike, Edward L. (1898). Animal intelligence: An experimental study of the associative processes in animals. *Psychological Review Monograph Supplement, 2* (Whole No. 8).

Thorndike, Edward L. (1903). *Educational psychology.* New York: Columbia University Teachers College.

Tiefer, Leonore (2004). *Sex is not a natural act, and other essays* (Rev. ed.). Boulder, CO: Westview.

Timmers, Monique; Fischer, Agneta H.; & Manstead, Antony S. R. (1998). Gender differences in motives for regulating emotions. *Personality and Social Psychology Bulletin, 24,* 974–985.

Tolman, Edward C. (1938). The determiners of behavior at a choice point. *Psychological Review, 45,* 1–35.

Tolman, Edward C., & Honzik, Chase H. (1930). Introduction and removal of reward and maze performance in rats. *University of California Publications in Psychology, 4,* 257–275.

Toma, J. G.; Akhavan, M.; Frenandes, K. J.; et al. (2001). Isolation of multipotent adult stem cells from the dermis of mammalian skin. *Nature Cell Biology, 3,* 778–784.

Tomasello, Michael (2000). Culture and cognitive development. *Current Directions in Psychological Science, 9,* 37–40.

Tomlinson, Mark; Cooper, Peter; & Murray, Lynne (2005). The mother–infant relationship and infant attachment in a South African peri-urban settlement. *Child Development, 76,* 1044–1054.

Tormala, Zakary L., & Petty, Richard E. (2002). What doesn't kill me makes me stronger: The effects of resisting persuasion on attitude certainty. *Journal of Personality and Social Psychology, 83,* 1298–1313.

Tracy, Jessica L., & Robins, Richard W. (2004). Show your pride: Evidence for a discrete emotion expression. *Psychological Science, 15,* 194–197.

Tracy, Jessica L., Robins, Richard W.; & Lagattuta, Kristin H. (2005). Can children recognize pride? *Emotion, 5,* 251–257.

Travis, John (2000). Snap, crackle, and feel good? Magnetic fields that map the brain may also treat its disorders. *Science News.*

Triandis, Harry C. (1996). The psychological measurement of cultural syndromes. *American Psychologist, 51,* 407–415.

Tronick, Edward Z.; Morelli, Gilda A.; & Ivey, Paula K. (1992). The Efe forager infant and toddler's pattern of social relationships: Multiple and simultaneous. *Developmental Psychology, 28,* 568–577.

Tropp, Linda R., & Pettigrew, Thomas F. (2005). Relationships between intergroup contact and prejudice among minority and majority status groups. *Psychological Science, 16,* 951–957.

Tsuang, Ming T.; Bar, Jessica L.; Harley, Rebecca M.; Lyons, Michael J. (2001). The Harvard Twin Study of Substance Abuse: What we have learned. *Harvard Review of Psychiatry, 9,* 267–279.

Tulving, Endel (1985). How many memory systems are there? *American Psychologist, 40,* 385–398.

Turati, Chiara (2004). Why faces are not special to newborns: An alternative account of the face preference. *Current Directions in Psychological Science, 13,* 5–8.

Turkheimer, Eric (2000). Three laws of behavior genetics and what they mean. *Current Directions in Psychological Science, 9,* 160–164.

Turner, C. F.; Ku, L.; Rogers, S. M.; et al. (1998). Adolescent sexual behavior, drug use, and violence: Increased reporting with computer survey technology. *Science, 280,* 867–873.

Turner, Marlene E.; Pratkanis, Anthony R.; & Samuels, Tara (2003). Identity metamorphosis and groupthink prevention: Examining Intel's departure from the DRAM industry. In A. Haslam, D. van Knippenberg, M. Platow, & N. Ellemers (Eds.), *Social identity at work: Developing theory for organizational practice.* Philadelphia, PA: Psychology Press.

Tustin, Karen, & Hayne, Harlene (2005). A new method to measure childhood amnesia in children, adolescents, and adults. Poster presented at the annual meeting of the International Society for the Study of Behavioural Development, Melbourne, Australia.

Tversky, Amos, & Kahneman, Daniel (1973). Availability: A heuristic for judging frequency and probability. *Cognitive Psychology, 5,* 207–232.

Tversky, Amos, & Kahneman, Daniel (1981). The framing of decisions and the psychology of choice. *Science, 211,* 453–458.

Tyler, Tom R. (1997). The psychology of legitimacy: A relational perspective on voluntary deference to authorities. *Personality and Social Psychology Review, 1,* 323–345.

Uhlhaas, Peter J., & Silverstein, Steven M. (2005). Perceptual organization in schizophrenia spectrum disorders: Empirical research and theoretical implications. *Psychological Bulletin, 131,* 618–632.

Ullian, E. M.; Chrisopherson, K. S.; & Barres, B. A. (2004). Role for glia in synaptogenesis. *Glia, 47,* 209–216.

Updegraff, John A.; Gable, Shelly L.; & Taylor, Shelley E. (2004). What makes experiences satisfying? The interaction of approach-avoidance motivations and emotions in well-being. *Journal of Personality and Social Psychology, 86,* 496–504.

Urry, Heather L.; Nitschke, Jack B.; Dolski, Isa; et al. (2004). Making a life worth living: Neural correlates of well-being. *Psychological Science, 15,* 367–372.

Usher, JoNell A., & Neisser, Ulric (1993). Childhood amnesia and the beginnings of memory for four early life events. *Journal of Experimental Psychology: General, 122,* 155–165.

Vaillant, George E. (1983). *The natural history of alcoholism: Causes, patterns, and paths to recovery.* Cambridge, MA: Harvard University Press.

Vaillant, George E. (Ed.) (1992). *Ego mechanisms of defense.* Washington, DC: American Psychiatric Press.

Valenstein, Elliot (1986). *Great and desperate cures: The rise and decline of psychosurgery and other radical treatments for mental illness.* New York: Basic Books.

Van Baaren, Rick B.; Holland, Rob W.; Kawakami, Kerry; & van Knippenberg, Ad (2004). Mimicry and prosocial behavior. *Psychological Science, 15,* 71–74.

Van Boven, Leaf, & Gilovich, Thomas (2003). To do or to have? That is the question. *Journal of Personality and Social Psychology, 85,* 1193–1202.

Van Boven, Leaf; Kamada, Akiko; & Gilovich, Thomas (1999). The perceiver as perceived: Everyday intuitions about the correspondence bias. *Journal of Personality and Social Psychology, 77,* 1188–1199.

Van Cantfort, Thomas E., & Rimpau, James B. (1982). Sign language studies with children and chimpanzees. *Sign Language Studies, 34,* 15–72.

Van de Castle, R. (1994). *Our dreaming mind.* New York: Ballantine Books.

Vandello, Joseph A., & Cohen, Dov (1999). Patterns of individualism and collectivism across the United States. *Journal of Personality and Social Psychology, 77,* 279–292.

Vandello, Joseph A., & Cohen, Dov (2003). Male honor and female fidelity: Implicit cultural scripts that perpetuate domestic violence. *Journal of Personality & Social Psychology, 84,* 997–1010.

Van Emmerik, Arnold A.; Kamphuis, Jan H.; Hulsbosch, Alexander M.; & Emmelkamp, Paul M. G. (2002, September 7). Single session debriefing after psychological trauma: A meta-analysis. *The Lancet, 360,* 766–771.

van Ijzendoorn, Marinus H.; Juffer, Femmie; & Klein Poelhuis, Caroline W. (2005). Adoption and cognitive development: A meta-analytic comparison of adopted and nonadopted children's IQ and school performance. *Psychological Bulletin, 131,* 301–316.

van Ommeren, Mark; Saxena, Shekhar; & Saraceno, Benedetto (2005, January). Mental and social health during and after acute emergencies: emerging consensus?. *Bulletin of the World Health Organization, 83,* 71–76.

van Praag, H.; Kempermann, G.; & Gage, F. H. (1999). Running increases cell proliferation and neurogenesis in the adult mouse dentate gyrus. *Nature Neuroscience, 2,* 266–270.

van Schaik, Carel (2006 April). Why are some animals so smart? *Scientific American,* 64–71.

van Tilburg, Miranda A. L.; Becht, Marleen C.; & Vingerhoets, Ad J. J. M. (2003). Self-reported crying during the menstrual cycle: Sign of discomfort and emotional turmoil or erroneous beliefs? *Journal of Psychosomatic Obstetrics & Gynecology, 24,* 247–255.

Vecera, Shaun P.; Vogel, Edward, K.; & Woodman, Geoffrey F. (2002). Lower region: A new cue for figure-ground assignment. *Journal of Experimental Psychology: General, 131,* 194–205.

Vila, J., & Beech, H. R. (1980). Premenstrual symptomatology: An interaction hypothesis. *British Journal of Social and Clinical Psychology, 19,* 73–80.

Vita, A. J.; Terry, R. B.; Hubert, H. B.; & Fries, J. F. (1998). Aging, health risks, and cumulative disability. *New England Journal of Medicine, 338,* 1035–1041.

Volkow, Nora D.; Chang, Linda; Wang, Gene-Jack; et al. (2001). Association of dopamine transporter reduction with psychomotor impairment in methamphetamine abusers. *American Journal of Psychiatry, 158,* 377–382.

Voyer, Daniel; Voyer, Susan; & Bryden, M. P. (1995). Magnitude of sex differences in spatial abilities: A meta-analysis and consideration of critical variables. *Psychological Bulletin, 117,* 250–270.

Vroon, Piet (1997). *Smell: The secret seducer.* [Trans. by Paul Vincent.] New York: Farrar, Straus & Giroux.

Wadden, Thomas A.; Foster, G. D.; Letizia, K. A.; & Mullen, J. L. (1990, August 8). Long-term effects of dieting on resting metabolic rate in obese outpatients. *Journal of the American Medical Association, 264,* 707–711.

Wagenaar, Willem A. (1986). My memory: A study of autobiographical memory over six years. *Cognitive Psychology, 18,* 225–252.

Wagner, Ullrich; Gais, Steffen; Haider, Hilde; et al. (2004). Sleep inspires insight. *Nature, 427,* 304–305.

Wakefield, Jerome C. (1992). Disorder as harmful dysfunction: A conceptual critique of DSM-III-R's definition of mental disorder. *Psychological Review, 99,* 232–247.

Walker, Anne (1994). Mood and well-being in consecutive menstrual cycles: Methodological and theoretical implications. *Psychology of Women Quarterly, 18,* 271–290.

Walker, Elaine F. (2002). Adolescent neurodevelopment and psychopathology. *Current Directions in Psychological Science, 11,* 24–28.

Walker-Andrews, Arlene S. (1997). Infants' perception of expressive behaviors: Differentiation of multimodal information. *Psychological Bulletin, 121,* 437–456.

Wallbott, Harald G.; Ricci-Bitti, Pio; & Bänninger-Huber, Eva (1986). Non-verbal reactions to emotional experiences. In K. R. Scherer, H. G. Wallbott, & A. B. Summerfield (Eds.), *Experiencing emotion: A cross-cultural study.* Cambridge, England: Cambridge University Press.

Waller, Niels G.; Kojetin, Brian A.; Bouchard, Thomas J., Jr.; et al. (1990). Genetic and environmental influences on religious interests, attitudes, and values: A study of twins reared apart and together. *Psychological Science, 1,* 138–142.

Wampold, Bruce (2001). *The great psychotherapy debate: Models, methods, and findings.* Mahwah, NJ: Erlbaum.

Wang, Alvin Y.; Thomas, Margaret H.; & Ouellette, Judith A. (1992). The keyword mnemonic and retention of second-language vocabulary words. *Journal of Educational Psychology, 84,* 520–528.

Warren, Gayle H., & Raynes, Anthony E. (1972). Mood changes during three conditions of alcohol intake. *Quarterly Journal of Studies on Alcohol, 33,* 979–989.

Wasserman, Eric W., & Lisanby, Sarah H. (2001). Therapeutic application of repetitive transcranial magnetic stimulation: A review. *Clinical Neurophysiology, 112,* 1367–1377.

Watson, David; Hubbard, Brock; & Wiese, David (2000). Self-other agreement in personality and affectivity: The role of acquaintanceship, trait visibility, and assumed similarity. *Journal of Personality and Social Psychology, 78,* 546–558.

Watson, John B. (1925). *Behaviorism.* New York: Norton.

Watson, John B., & Rayner, Rosalie (1920). Conditioned emotional reactions. *Journal of Experimental Psychology, 3,* 1–14. (Reprinted in *American Psychologist, 55,* March 2000, 313–317.)

Watters, Ethan, & Ofshe, Richard (1999). *Therapy's delusions.* New York: Scribner.

Webster, Richard (1995). *Why Freud was wrong.* New York: Basic Books.

Wechsler, David (1955). *Manual for the Wechsler Adult Intelligence Scale.* New York: Psychological Corporation.

Wegner, Daniel M., & Gold, Daniel B. (1995). Fanning old flames: Emotional and cognitive effects of suppressing thoughts of a past relationship. *Journal of Personality and Social Psychology, 68,* 782–792.

Wehr, Thomas A.; Duncan, Wallace C.; Sher, Leo; et al. (2001). A circadian signal of change of season in patients with seasonal affective disorder. *Archives of General Psychiatry, 58,* 1108–1114.

Weil, Andrew T. (1972/1986). *The natural mind: A new way of looking at drugs and the higher consciousness.* Boston: Houghton Mifflin.

Weiner, Bernard (1986). *An attributional theory of motivation and emotion.* New York: Springer-Verlag.

Weiss, Erica; Longhurst, James G.; & Mazure, Carolyn M. (1999). Childhood sexual abuse as a risk factor for depression in women: Psychological and neurological correlates. *American Journal of Psychiatry, 156,* 816–828.

Weissman, Myrna M.; Markowitz, John C.; & Klerman, Gerald L. (2000). *Comprehensive guide to interpersonal psychotherapy.* New York: Basic Books.

Weisz, John R.; Weiss, Bahr; Han, Susan S.; et al. (1995). Effects of psychotherapy with children and adolescents revisited: A meta-analysis of treatment outcome studies. *Psychological Bulletin, 117,* 450–468.

Wellman, H. M.; Cross, D.; & Watson, J. (2001). Meta-analysis of theory-of-mind development: The truth about false belief. *Child Development, 72,* 655–684.

Wells, Brooke E., & Twenge, Jean (2005). Changes in young people's sexual behavior and attitudes, 1943–1999: A cross-temporal meta-analysis. *Review of General Psychology, 9,* 249–261.

Wells, Gary L., & Olson, Elisabeth A. (2003). Eyewitness testimony. *Annual Review of Psychology, 54,* 277–295.

Wells, Gary L.; Small, Mark; Penrod, Steven; et al. (1998). Eyewitness identification procedures: Recommendations for lineups and photospreads. *Law and Human Behavior, 22,* 602–647.

Wender, Paul H., & Klein, Donald F. (1981). *Mind, mood, and medicine: A guide to the new biopsychiatry.* New York: Farrar, Straus and Giroux.

Wenzel, Amy (2005). Autobiographical memory tasks in clinical research. In A. Wenzel & D. C. Rubin, *Cognitive methods and their application to clinical research*. Washington, DC: American Psychological Association.

Werner, Emmy E. (1989). High-risk children in young adulthood: A longitudinal study from birth to 32 years. *American Journal of Orthopsychiatry, 59*, 72–81.

Wertheimer, Michael (1958). Principles of perceptual organization. In D. C. Beardslee & M. Wertheimer (Eds.), *Readings in perception*. Princeton, NJ: Van Nostrand. [Original work published 1923.]

West, Melissa O., & Prinz, Ronald J. (1987). Parental alcoholism and childhood psychopathology. *Psychological Bulletin, 102*, 204–218.

Westen, Drew (1998). The scientific legacy of Sigmund Freud: Toward a psychodynamically informed psychological science. *Psychological Bulletin, 124*, 333–371.

Westen, Drew; Novotny, Catherine M.; & Thompson-Brenner, Heather (2004). The empirical status of empirically supported psychotherapies: Assumptions, findings, and reporting in controlled clinical trials. *Psychological Bulletin, 130*, 631–663.

Westen, Drew, & Shedler, Jonathan (1999). Revising and assessing axis II, Part II: Toward an empirically based and clinically useful classification of personality disorders. *American Journal of Psychiatry, 156*, 273–285.

Westermeyer, Joseph (1995). Cultural aspects of substance abuse and alcoholism: Assessment and management. *Psychiatric Clinics of North America, 18*, 589–605.

Wethington, Elaine (2000). Expecting stress: Americans and the "midlife crisis." *Motivation & Emotion, 24*, 85–103.

Whaley, Arthur L. (2001). Cultural mistrust: An important psychological construct for diagnosis and treatment of African Americans. *Professional Psychology: Research & Practice, 32*, 555–562.

Wheeler, David L. (1998, September 11). Neuroscientists take stock of brain-imaging studies. *Chronicle of Higher Education*, pp. A20–A21.

Wheeler, Mary E., & Fiske, Susan T. (2005). Controlling racial prejudice: Social-cognitive goals affect amygdala and stereotype activation. *Psychological Science, 16*, 56–63.

Whorf, Benjamin L. (1956). *Language, thought and reality*. Cambridge, MA: MIT Press. [Original work published 1940.)

Wickelgren, Ingrid (1997). Estrogen stakes claim to cognition. *Science, 276*, 675–678.

Widiger, Thomas; Cadoret, Remi; Hare, Robert; et al. (1996). DSM-IV antisocial personality disorder field trial. *Journal of Abnormal Psychology, 105*, 3–16.

Widiger, Thomas, & Clark, Lee Anna (2000). Toward DSM-V and the classification of psychopathology. *Psychological Bulletin, 126*, 946–963.

Williams, Janice E.; Paton, Catherine C.; Siegler, Ilene C.; et al. (2000). Anger proneness predicts coronary heart disease risk. *Circulation, 101*, 2034–2039.

Williams, Kipling D., & Karau, Steven J. (1991). Social loafing and social compensation: The effects of expectations of co-worker performance. *Journal of Personality and Social Psychology, 61*, 570–581.

Williams, Redford B., Jr.; Barefoot, John C.; & Shekelle, Richard B. (1985). The health consequences of hostility. In M. A. Chesney & R. H. Rosenman (Eds.), *Anger and hostility in cardiovascular and behavioral disorders*. New York: Hemisphere.

Wilner, Daniel; Walkley, Rosabelle; & Cook, Stuart (1955). *Human relations in interracial housing*. Minneapolis: University of Minnesota Press.

Wilson, G. Terence, & Fairburn, Christopher G. (1993). Cognitive treatments for eating disorders. *Journal of Consulting and Clinical Psychology, 61*, 261–269.

Wilson, Timothy D.; Lindsey, S.; & Schooler, T. Y. (2000). A model of dual attitudes. *Psychological Review, 107*, 101–126.

Winick, Myron; Meyer, Knarig Katchadurian; & Harris, Ruth C. (1975). Malnutrition and environmental enrichment by early adoption. *Science, 190*, 1173–1175.

Winkielman, Piotr, & Berridge, Kent C. (2004). Unconscious emotion. *Current Directions in Psychological Science, 13*, 120–126.

Winnicott, D. W. (1957/1990). *Home is where we start from*. New York: Norton.

Wirz-Justice, Anna; Benedetti, Francesco; Berger, Mathias; et al. (2005). Chronotherapeutics (light and wake therapy) in affective disorders. *Psychological Medicine, 35*, 939–944.

Wispé, Lauren G., & Drambarean, Nicholas C. (1953). Physiological need, word frequency, and visual duration thresholds. *Journal of Experimental Psychology, 46*, 25–31.

Witelson, Sandra F.; Glazer, I. I.; & Kigar, D. L. (1994). Sex differences in numerical density of neurons in human auditory association cortex. *Society for Neuroscience Abstracts, 30* (Abstr. No. 582.12).

Witkiewitz, Katie, & Marlatt, G. Alan (2004). Relapse prevention for alcohol and drug problems: That was Zen, this is Tao. *American Psychologist, 59*, 224–235.

Wittchen, Hans-Ulrich; Kessler, Ronald C.; Zhao, Shanyang; & Abelson, Jamie (1995). Reliability and clinical validity of UM-CIDI DSM-III-R generalized anxiety disorder. *Journal of Psychiatric Research, 29*, 95–110.

Witvliet, Charlotte vanOyen; Ludwig, Thomas E.; & Vander Laan, Kelly L. (2001). Granting forgiveness or harboring grudges: Implications for emotion, physiology, and health. *Psychological Science, 12*, 117–123.

Wolfson, Amy R., and Carskadon, Mary A. (1998). Sleep schedules and daytime functioning in adolescents. *Child Development, 69*, 875–887.

Wolpe, Joseph (1958). *Psychotherapy by reciprocal inhibition*. Palo Alto, CA: Stanford University Press.

Wood, James M.; Nezworski, M. Teresa; Lilienfeld, Scott O.; & Garb, Howard N. (2003). *What's wrong with the Rorschach?* San Francisco: Jossey-Bass.

Wood, Joanne V.; Michela, John L.; & Giordano, Caterina (2000). Downward comparison in everyday life: Reconciling self-enhancement models with the mood-cognition priming model. *Journal of Personality and Social Psychology, 79*, 563–579.

Wood, Wendy; Lundgren, Sharon; Ouellette, Judith A.; et al. (1994). Minority influence: A meta-analytic review of social influence processes. *Psychological Bulletin, 115*, 323–345.

Woody, Erik Z., & Bowers, Kenneth S. (1994). A frontal assault on dissociated control. In S. J. Lynn & J. W. Rhue (Eds.), *Dissociation: Clinical, theoretical and research perspectives*. New York: Guilford.

Wu, Aiguo; Ying, Zhe; & Gómez-Pinilla, Fernando (2004). Dietary omega-3 fatty acids normalize BDNF levels, reduce oxidative damage, and counteract learning disability after traumatic brain injury in rats. *Journal of Neurotrauma, 21*, 1457–1467.

Wulsin, L. R.; Vaillant, G. E.; & Wells, V. E. (1999). A systematic review of the mortality of depression. *Psychosomatic Medicine, 61*, 6–17.

Wyrobek, A. J.; Eskenazi, B.; Young, S.; et al. (2006, June 9). Advancing age has differential effects on DNA damage, chromatin integrity, gene mutations, and aneuploidies in sperm. *Proceedings of the National Academy of Sciences, 103*, 9601–9606.

Yalom, Irvin D. (1989). *Love's executioner and other tales of psychotherapy*. New York: Basic Books.

Yang, Chi-Fu Jeffrey; Gray, Peter; & Pope, Harrison G. Jr. (2005). Male body image in Taiwan versus the West: Yanggang Zhiqi meets the Adonis Complex. *American Journal of Psychiatry, 162,* 263–269.

Yapko, Michael (1994). *Suggestions of abuse: True and false memories of childhood sexual trauma.* New York: Simon & Schuster.

Yardley, Jim (2001, September 8). Despair plagued mother held in children's deaths. *The New York Times,* p. A16.

Young, Malcolm P., & Yamane, Shigeru (1992). Sparse population coding of faces in the inferotemporal cortex. *Science, 256,* 1327–1331.

Yzerbyt, Vincent Y.; Corneille, Olivier; Dumont, Muriel; & Hahn, Kirstin (2001). The dispositional inference strikes back: Situational focus and dispositional suppression in causal attribution. *Journal of Personality and Social Psychology, 81,* 365–376.

Zajonc, R. B. (1968). Attitudinal effects of mere exposure. *Journal of Personality and Social Psychology, 9, Monograph Supplement 2,* 1–27.

Zajonc, R. B. (2003). The power of words. Invited address presented to the American Psychological Society, Atlanta.

Zhang, Yiying; Hoon, M. A.; Chandrashekar, J.; et al. (2003). Coding of sweet, bitter, and umami tastes: different receptor cells sharing similar signaling pathways. *Cell, 112,* 293–301.

Zhang, Yiying; Proenca, Ricardo; Maffei, Margherita; et al. (1994). Positional cloning of the mouse obese gene and its human homologue. *Nature, 372*(6505), 425–432.

Zhu, L. X.; Sharma, S.; Stolina, M.; et al. (2000). Delta-9-tetrahydrocannabinol inhibits antitumor immunity by a CB2 receptor-mediated, cytokine-dependent pathway. *Journal of Immunology, 165,* 373–380.

Zimbardo, Philip G. (1970). The human choice: Individuation, reason, and order versus deindividuation, impulse, and chaos. In W. J. Arnold & D. Levine (Eds.), *Nebraska Symposium on Motivation, 1969.* Lincoln, NE: University of Nebraska Press.

Zimbardo, Philip G., & Leippe, Michael R. (1991). *The psychology of attitude change and social influence.* New York: McGraw-Hill.

Zimmer, Lynn, & Morgan, John P. (1997). *Marijuana myths, marijuana fact: A review of the scientific evidence.* New York: Lindesmith Center.

Zone, Nolon; Sue, Stanley; Chang, Janer; et al. (2005). Beyond ethnic match: Effects of client–therapist cognitive match in problem perception, coping orientation, and therapy goals on treatment outcomes. *Journal of Community Psychology, 33,* 569–585.

Zorrilla, L. T.; Cannon, T. D.; Kronenberg, S.; et al. (1997, December 15). Structural brain abnormalities in schizophrenia: A family study. *Biological Psychiatry, 42,* 1080–1086.

Zou, Zhihua, & Buck, Linda (2006). Combinatorial effects of odorant mixes in olfactory cortex. *Science, 311,* 1477–1481.

Zubieta, Jon-Kar; Heitzeg, M. M.; Smith, Y. R.; et al. (2003). COMT val158met genotype affects mu-opioid neurotransmitter responses to a pain stressor. *Science, 299,* 1240–1243.

Zucker, Kenneth J. (1999). Intersexuality and gender identity differentiation. *Annual Review of Sex Research, 10,* 1–69.

Zurbriggen, Eileen L. (2000). Social motives and cognitive power-sex associations: Predictors of aggressive sexual behavior. *Journal of Personality and Social Psychology, 78,* 559–581.

credits

Photos and Cartoons

Chapter 1 *Page 2 (left):* Jim Winstead, Jr.; *p. 2 (center):* James Nielsen/ZUMA Press; *p. 3 (top):* Kashi Photography; *p. 3 (center):* Jupiter Images-Comstock Images; *p. 3 (bottom):* Folio, Inc.; *p. 5:* © Punch/Rothco; *p. 7:* Courtesy of the Library of Congress; *p. 8:* Jupiter Images-Comstock Images; *p. 12 (top):* George Ruhe Photography; *p. 12 (center):* Michael Newman/PhotoEdit Inc.; *p. 12 (bottom):* Kashi Photography; *p. 15:* © The New Yorker Collection 1989 Lee Lorenz from cartoonbank.com. All Rights Reserved; *p. 16:* Andre Kole; *p. 17 (top):* Jose L. Pelaez/Corbis/Stock Market; *p. 17 (bottom):* Unicorn Stock Photos; *p. 18:* AP Wide World Photos; *p. 20:* Figure from Genie: A Psycholinguistic Study of a Modern Day "Wild Child" by Susan Curtiss, © 1977, Elsevier Science (USA), reproduced by permission of the publisher; *p. 21:* Redux Pictures; *p. 22:* © The New Yorker Collection 1998 Roz Chast from cartoonbank.com All Rights Reserved; *p. 23:* © The New Yorker Collection 1970 Henry Martin from cartoonbank.com. All Rights Reserved; *p. 30:* Grant V. Faint/Getty Images Inc.-Image Bank; *p. 32:* © 1990 Creators Syndicate Inc. By permission of Mell Lazarus and Creators Syndicate, Inc.; *p. 34 (top left):* Folio, Inc.; *p. 34 (bottom left):* David Young-Wolff/PhotoEdit Inc.; *p. 34 (center):* William Thompson/Index Stock Imagery, Inc.; *p. 34 (right):* Robert Stolarik/Gamma Press USA, Inc.; *p. 35:* St. Petersburg Times; *p. 37 (top):* Jose L. Pelaez/Corbis/Stock Market; *p. 37 (bottom):* Unicorn Stock Photos.

Chapter 2 *Page 40 (bottom):* Getty Images, Inc.; *p. 40 (top left):* Reuters NewMedia Inc./Corbis/Bettmann; *p. 40 (top right):* Getty Images, Inc.; *p. 41 (top):* ZUMA Press; *p. 41 (center):* Fujifotos/The Image Works; *p. 41 (bottom):* Catherine Karnow/Woodfin Camp & Associates; *p. 43 (left):* Courtesy of A.W. Freud et al./Collection of the Library of Congress; *p. 43 (right):* ScienceCartoonsPlus.com; *p. 44:* © The New Yorker Collection 1985 Joseph Mirachi from cartoonbank.com. All Rights Reserved; *p. 45:* Ericka McConnell/Getty Images, Inc.-Taxi; *p. 47 (left):* Photofest; *p. 47 (right):* Donna Day/Getty Images Inc.-Stone Allstock; *p. 48:* Corbis/Sygma; *p. 50:* The Far Side® by Gary Larson © 1990 FarWorks, Inc. All Rights Reserved. Used with Permission; *p. 51:* Catherine Karnow/Woodfin Camp & Associates; *p. 53:* ScienceCartoonsPlus.com; *p. 54:* Henry Horenstein/CORBIS- NY; *p. 55 (left):* Ellen Senisi/Ellen Senisi; *p. 55 (right):* Dr. Stephen J. Suomi; *p. 56:* Peter Byron/PhotoEdit Inc.; *p. 57:* © Tee and Charles Addams Foundation; *p. 58 (left):* Marcel Thomas/Cashew1digitalfotos.com; *p. 58 (right):* ZUMA Press; *p. 60:* Richard Hutchings/PhotoEdit Inc.; *p. 62 (top):* Timothy Eagan/Woodfin Camp & Associates; *p. 62 (bottom):* Fujifotos/The Image Works; *p. 63:* Robert Azzi/Woodfin Camp & Associates; *p. 64 (top left):* Peter Finger/CORBIS/CORBIS-NY; *p. 64 (top right):* Alan Keohane © Dorling Kindersley; *p. 66:* AP Wide World Photos; *p. 67:* ScienceCartoonsPlus.com; *p. 73 (left):* Peter Byron/PhotoEdit Inc.; *p. 73 (right):* Robert Azzi/Woodfin Camp & Associates.

Chapter 3 *Page 74:* Vadim Ghirda/AP Wide World Photos; *p. 75 (top):* Nancy Richmond/The Image Works; *p. 75 (center):* Charles Gupton/Charles Gupton Photography; *p. 75 (bottom):* Richard Hutchings/Photo Researchers, Inc.; *p. 76:* Theo Westenberger Photography; *p. 77:* © Baby Blues Partnership. Reprinted with special permission of King Features Syndicate; *p. 78:* Laura Dwight/Corbis/Bettmann; *p. 79 (left):* Martin Rogers/Woodfin Camp & Associates; *p. 79 (right):* Martin Rogers/Woodfin Camp & Associates; *p. 80:* © The New Yorker Collection 1985 Lee Lorenz from cartoonbank.com. All Rights Reserved; *p. 82:* Erika Stone; *p. 83:* © "Baby Blues Partnership. Reprinted with special permission of King Features Syndicate."; *p. 84:* Ann Senghas/Ann Senghas; *p. 85:* Michael Newman/PhotoEdit Inc.; *p. 86 (left and right):* Laura Dwight/Laura Dwight Photography; *p. 89:* Mandal Ranjit/Photo Researchers, Inc.; *p. 90 (top left):* Nancy Richmond/The Image Works; *p. 90 (bottom right):* Tony Freeman/PhotoEdit Inc.; *p. 91:* PhotoEdit Inc.; *p. 94 (left):* The Granger Collection, New York; *p. 94 (center):* National Museum of Natural History, © 2004 Smithsonian Institution; *p. 94 (right):* George Ruhe/The New York Times; *p. 95:* Laura Dwight Photography; *p. 96 (left):* Getty Images, Inc-Liaison; *p. 96 (right):* Brenda Black and Louis Toby/Black/Toby Photography; *p. 97:* CATHY © Cathy Guisewite. Reprinted with permission of UNIVERSAL PRESS SYNDICATE. All rights reserved; *p. 99:* Richard Hutchings/Photo Researchers, Inc.; *p. 100:* © The New Yorker Collection 2001 Barbara Smaller from cartoonbank.com. All Rights Reserved; *p. 102:* Tom McCarthy/Index Stock Imagery, Inc.; *p. 103:* DOONESBURY © G. B. Trudeau. Reprinted with permission of UNIVERSAL PRESS SYNDICATE. All rights reserved; *p. 105 (top left):* Charles Gupton/Charles Gupton Photography; *p. 105 (top right):* Abigail Heyman; *p. 107:* © Bogdan Cristel/CORBIS All Rights Reserved; *p. 112 (left):* Erika Stone; *p. 112 (right):* Martin Rogers/Woodfin Camp & Associates.

Chapter 4 *Page 114 (bottom):* © CORBIS All Rights Reserved; *p. 114 (top):* AP Wide World Photos; *p. 115 (top):* Ron Sachs/Corbis/Sygma; *p. 115 (center):* Keith Brofsky/Getty Images, Inc.-Photodisc; *p. 115 (bottom):* Dennis Kunkel/Phototake NYC; *p. 116:* Dan McCoy/Rainbow; *p. 120:* Biophoto Associates/Photo Researchers, Inc.; *p. 121:* Marc Lieberman/Salk Institute; *p. 122:* Dennis Kunkel/Phototake NYC; *p. 125:* Ron Sachs/Corbis/Sygma; *p. 126:* ScienceCartoonsPlus.com; *p. 128 (left):* Keith Brofsky/Getty Images, Inc.-Photodisc; *p. 128 (right):* Photo Lennart Nilsson/Albert Bonniers Forlag AB; *p. 129 (top left):* Hank Morgan/Science Source/Photo Researchers, Inc.; *p. 129 (top right):* Michael E. Phelps/Mazziotta UCLA School of Medicine; *p. 129 (bottom):* Howard Sochurek, Inc.; *p. 135 (left):* The Warren Anatomical Museum, Francis A. Countway Library of Medicine, Harvard Medical School; *p. 135 (right):* from: Damasio H, Grabowski T, Frank R, Galaburda AM, Damasio AR: "The Return of Phineas Gage: Clues about the brain from a famous patient." "Science," 264: 1102–1105, 1994. Department of Neurology and Image Analysis Facility, University of Iowa; *p. 138:* CartoonStock Ltd. CSL; *p. 140:* ScienceCartoonsPlus.com; *p. 141:* Radiological Society of North America, Radiology 2001; 220: 202–207, Figure 3; *p. 142:* Jennifer Berman/Jennifer K. Berman; *p. 143:* Dr. Ronald Cranford/TERRIPAC; *p. 148:* Howard Sochurek, Inc.

Chapter 5 *Page 150:* Kevin Wolf/AP Wide World Photos; *p. 151 (top):* Tibor Hirsch/Photo Researchers, Inc.; *p. 151 (center):* J. Hobson/Photo Researchers, Inc.; *p. 151 (bottom):* R. Hutchings/PhotoEdit Inc.; *p. 153 (left and right):* Tom Ives/Corbis/Sygma; *p. 154 (top):* ScienceCartoonsPlus.com; *p. 154 (bottom):* Jeff Greenberg/PhotoEdit Inc.; *p. 155:* Bryan and Cherry Alexander; *p. 156:* Amy Etra/PhotoEdit Inc.; *p. 158:* © The New Yorker Collection 1999 William Haefeli from cartoonbank.com. All Rights Reserved; *p. 160 (left and right):* Chandoha Photography; *p. 161 (top):* Jessica T. Offir; *p. 161 (center):* R. Hutchings/PhotoEdit Inc.; *p. 161 (bottom):* Earl Roberge/Photo Researchers, Inc.; *p. 162:* © The New Yorker Collection (1990) (Koren) from cartoonbank.com. All Rights Reserved; *p. 164:* © The New Yorker Collection 1973 Dana Fradon from cartoonbank.com. All Rights Reserved; *p. 165 (left to right):* J. Hobson/Photo Researchers, Inc.; *p. 168:* Bookstaver/AP Wide World Photos; *p. 169:* ScienceCartoonsPlus.com;

of Neuro Imaging"; *p. 369 (bottom):* David Turnley/Corbis/Bettmann; *p. 370 (left):* © Bojan Brecelj/CORBIS All Rights Reserved; *p. 370 (center):* Al Campanie/The Image Works; *p. 370 (right):* Elena Dorfman/Redux Pictures; *p. 373:* Sophia Smith Collection, Smith College; *p. 374:* Yoav Levy/Phototake NYC; *p. 375:* Corbis/Bettmann; *p. 377:* David Turnley/Corbis/Bettmann; *p. 378:* The Far Side® by Gary Larson © 1985 FarWorks, Inc. All Rights Reserved. Used with Permission; *p. 379:* © 2000, The Washington Post, reprinted with permission; *p. 381:* Mick Hutson/Retna Ltd.; *p. 384:* Corbis/Bettmann; *p. 386 (left):* AP Wide World Photos; *p. 386 (right):* Don Camp/Don Camp Photography; *p. 388:* Universal Press Syndicate; *p. 389 (top left):* Brookhaven National Laboratory; *p. 389 (bottom right):* Leland Bobbe/Getty Images Inc.-Stone Allstock; *p. 390:* © Daniel Laine/CORBIS All Rights Reserved; *p. 393:* Photofest/Jagarts; *p. 395 (left to right):* Al Vercoutere; *p. 396 (bottom, left and right):* © Howard Sochurek. All Rights Reserved; *p. 397:* "Courtesy, Dr. Arthur W. Toga, Laboratory of Neuro Imaging"; *p. 398:* AP Wide World Photos; *p. 403 (left and right):* © Howard Sochurek. All Rights Reserved.

Chapter 12 *Page 404 (bottom left):* AP Wide World Photos; *p. 404 (top right):* AP Wide World Photos; *p. 405 (top):* George Ruhe/The New York Times; *p. 405 (center):* Photofest; *p. 405 (bottom):* University of Washington HIT Lab/Mary Levin; *p. 407 (left, top and bottom):* Alvin H. Perlmutter Inc.; *p. 407 (bottom right):* © The New Yorker Collection 1993 Lee Lorenz from cartoonbank.com. All Rights Reserved; *p. 409:* © The New Yorker Collection 2001 Barbara Smaller from cartoonbank.com. All Rights Reserved; *p. 410:* Top two images: Sanjaya Saxena, MD and J.M. Schwartz, M.D.-UCLA Neuropsychiatric Institute (unpublished data, 1996). Bottom two images: Copyright © 1996, American Medical Association, from Schwartz, J.M. et. al, "Archives of General Psychiatry", February 1996, Volume 53, p.s 109–113.; *p. 411 (top):* W McIntyre/Photo Researchers, Inc.; *p. 411 (bottom):* George Ruhe/The New York Times; *p. 412:* ScienceCartoonsPlus.com; *p. 413 (top left):* Photofest; *p. 413 (bottom right):* University of Washington HIT Lab/Mary Levin; *p. 415:* Getty Images/Retrofile; *p. 416:* Michael Newman/PhotoEdit Inc.; *p. 417:* Courtesy of Alan Entin, Ph. D., family psychologist; *p. 420 (left):* Giuseppe Costantino, Ph.D., Director; *p. 420 (right):* Government of Puerto Rico Economic Development Administration; *p. 421:* ScienceCartoonsPlus.com; *p. 422:* Sydney Harris; *p. 424:* IN THE BLEACHERS © Steve Moore. Reprinted with permission of UNIVERSAL PRESS SYNDICATE. All rights reserved; *p. 426:* Everett Collection; *p. 429:* Michael Schumann/Corbis/SABA Press Photos, Inc.; *p. 432:* George Ruhe/ The New York Times.

Chapter 13 *Page 434:* AP Wide World Photos; *p. 435 (top):* Juergen Berger, Max-Planck Institute/Science Photo Library/Photo Researchers, Inc., *p. 435 (center):* Fred Prouser/Corbis/Reuters America LLC; *p. 435 (bottom):* Michael Greenlar/The Image Works; *p. 437 (top, left to right):* Michael Newman/PhotoEdit Inc.; Erika Stone; Laura Dwight Photography; Eric Gay/AP Wide World Photos; *p. 437 (bottom, left to right):* Fred Prouser/Corbis/Reuters America LLC; Jessica Tracy, University of British Columbia, Tracy, J.L., & Robins, R.W. (2004). Show your pride: Evidence for a discrete emotion expression. Psychological Science, 15, 194–197; Michael Philip Manheim/ImageState/International Stock Photography Ltd.; Itar-Tass/Sovfoto; *p. 438:* Heidi S. Mario; *p. 439 (top, left and right):* Frank J. Bernieri, PhD; *p. 440 (bottom left):* Michael Nichols/National Geographic Society; *p. 442:* PCN Photography; *p. 443:* Darama/Corbis/Bettmann; *p. 444:* Bryan and Cherry Alexander; *p. 445:* Magnum Photos, Inc.; *p. 446:* © Charles Barsotti from cartoonbank.com. All Rights Reserved; *p. 447 (left):* Janice Rubin; *p. 447 (right):* Robb Kendrick/Aurora & Quanta Productions Inc; *p. 448:* Getty Images, Inc.; *p. 449 (top):* CATHY '2000 Cathy Guisewite. Reprinted with permission of UNIVERSAL PRESS SYNDICATE. All rights reserved; *p. 449 (bottom right):* Juergen Berger, Max-Planck Institute/Science Photo Library/Photo Researchers, Inc.; *p. 450*

(right): Dion Ogust/The Image Works; *p. 451:* CartoonStock Ltd. CSL; *p. 452 (left):* Michael Greenlar/The Image Works; *p. 452 (right):* Stephen Agricola Photography/The Image Works; *p. 454 (top):* Bill Varie/Corbis/Bettmann; *p. 455:* Barry Lewis/Barry Lewis; *p. 456:* Barbara Singer/Getty Images-Photonica Amana America, Inc.; *p. 458 (top left):* Los Angeles Times Photo By Gina Ferazzi; *p. 458 (bottom left):* Ken Fisher/Getty Images Inc.-Stone Allstock; *p. 459:* Mary Hancock; *p. 460:* Chris Haston/Picture Desk, Inc./Kobal Collection; *p. 461:* NBC Universal, Inc.; *p. 463:* © Dan Piraro. Reprinted with special permission of King Features Syndicate.

Chapter 14 *Page 468 (top left):* Ann Johansson/Ann Johansson; *p. 468 (bottom right):* © Stefano Rellandini/CORBIS All Rights Reserved; *p. 469 (top):* Corbis/Bettmann; *p. 469 (center):* Guang Niu/Corbis/Reuters America LLC; *p. 469 (bottom):* Nicole Bengiveno/The New York Times; *p. 470 (left and right):* Picture Press Bild- und Textagentur GmbH, Munich, Germany; *p. 471:* David Young-Wolff/PhotoEdit Inc.; *p. 472 (top left):* © The New Yorker Collection, 1989 Robert Weber from cartoonbank.com. All Rights Reserved; *p. 472 (bottom):* JUMP START reprinted by permission of United Feature Syndicate, Inc.; *p. 474:* Magnum Photos, Inc.; *p. 475 (top left):* Bruce Ayres/Getty Images Inc.-Stone Allstock; *p. 475 (bottom right):* Reprinted by permission of The Kinsey Institute for Research in Sex, Gender, and Reproduction, Inc.; *p. 476:* © The New Yorker Collection 1995 Donald Reilly from cartoonbank.com. All Rights Reserved; *p. 477:* Magnum Photos, Inc.; *p. 478 (top):* Getty Images, Inc.; *p. 478 (bottom):* C&M Denis Huot/Peter Arnold, Inc.; *p. 479 (left):* Getty Images, Inc-Liaison; *p. 479 (right):* Carol Ford/Getty Images Inc.-Stone Allstock; *p. 480:* Rachel Epstein/PhotoEdit Inc.; *p. 481 (top left):* Unicorn Stock Photos; *p. 481 (bottom left):* Jupiter Images-FoodPix-Creatas-Brand X-Banana Stock-PictureQuest; *p. 481 (bottom right):* Cassy Cohen/PhotoEdit Inc.; *p. 482:* Nicole Bengiveno/The New York Times; *p. 483 (left):* CORBIS-NY; *p. 483 (right):* Stephanie Diani/The New York Times; *p. 485 (left):* Dennis Stock/Magnum Photos, Inc.; *p. 485 (right):* Victor Englebert/Photo Researchers, Inc.; *p. 486:* Remi Banali/Gamma Press USA, Inc.; *p. 487:* Guang Niu/Corbis/Reuters America LLC; *p. 488 (left to right):* CinemaPhoto/Corbis/Bettmann; CORBIS-NY; Frank Siteman/Stock Boston; Phil McCarten/PhotoEdit Inc.; *p. 489:* William Thompson/Index Stock Imagery, Inc.; *p. 490 (top left):* © The New Yorker Collection 1985 W.B. Park from cartoonbank.com. All Rights Reserved; *p. 490 (bottom, left to right):* Courtesy of the Library of Congress; Corbis/Bettmann; Flip Schulke/Black Star; Corbis/Bettmann; *p. 491 (bottom, left to right):* Corbis/Sygma; Marvin Koner/Black Star; Corbis/Sygma; Carol Halebian/Getty Images, Inc-Liaison; *p. 492:* Daniel Bosler/Getty Images Inc.-Stone Allstock; *p. 494:* Spencer Grant/Index Stock Imagery, Inc.; *p. 496:* The Far Side® by Gary Larson © 1985 FarWorks, Inc. All Rights Reserved. Used with Permission.

Figures and Tables

Chapter 1 *Page 25:* Figure 1.2 (a) & (b): Adaptation of fig. 1.2 from UNDERSTANDING STATISTICS: An Informal Introduction for the Behavioral Sciences 1st ed. by Wright. Copyright © 1976. Reprinted by permission of Wadsworth, a division of Thomson Learning: "http://www.thomsonrights.com" Fax 800 730-2215; Figure 1.2 (c): From INTRODUCTION TO THE PRACTICE OF STATISTICS by David S. Moore and George P. McCabe. Copyright © 1989, 1993, 1999 by W. H. Freeman and Company. Reprinted with permission of W. H. Freeman and Company; *p. 29:* Figure 1.4: Basson et al., 2002.

Chapter 2 *page 51:* Get Involved: Rate Your Traits: From Appendix A, p. 525 in "A Very Brief Measure of the Big Five Personality Domains" by S. D. Gosling, P. J. Rentfrow, & W. B. Swann, Jr., *Journal of Research in Personality, 37.* Copyright © 2003. Reprinted by permission of Elsevier; *p. 52:* Figure 2.1: From Costa, P. T., Jr, McCrae, R. R., & Martin, T. A. et al. (1999). Personality development from adolescence through adulthood: Further cross-cultural comparisons of age differences. In V. J. Molfese & D. Molfese (eds.), *Temperament and Personality Development across the Life Span*. Hillsdale, NJ: Erlbaum; *p. 64:* From "Insult, Aggression, and the Southern Culture of Honor" by Cohen, et al., *Journal of Personality and Social Psychology, 70.* Copyright © 1996 by the American Psychological Association. Reprinted in accordance with APA guidelines.

Chapter 3 *Page 88:* Figure 3.3: From "How Do Infants Learn About the Physical World?" by Rene Baillargeon, *Current Directions in Psychology, 5.* Copyright © 1994 by Blackwell Publishing Ltd. Reprinted by permission; *p. 100:* Figure 3.4: Figure 2 from "Gender Differences in Self-Esteem" by K. C. Kling, J. S. Hyde, C. J. Showers & B. N. Buswell, *Psychological Bulletin, 125,* (1999). Copyright © 1999 by the American Psychological Association. Reprinted by permission; *p. 103:* Figure 3.5: From "Conceptions of the Transition to Adulthood From Adolescence Through Mid-Life" by Jeffrey Arnett, *Journal of Adult Development, 8,* (2), April 2001. Copyright © 2001 by Kluwer Academic/Plenum Publishers. By permission of Springer Science and Business Media.

Chapter 4 *Page 123:* From fig. 5, p. 329 in "A Functional Neuroimaging Study of Sound Localization: Visual Cortex Activity Predicts Performance In Early-Blind Individuals" by F. Gougoux, R. J. Zatorre, M. Lassonde, et al., *PloS Biology,* Volume 3, Issue 2 (2005). Published by the Public Library of Science.

Chapter 5 *Page 157:* McFarlane, Martin & Williams, 1988.

Chapter 6 *Page 208:* Figure 1, p. 690 from "Smells Like Clean Spirit: Nonconscious Effects of Scent on Cognition and Behavior" by R. W. Holland, M. Hendriks, & H. Aarts, *Psychological Science, 16,* (9). Copyright © 2005. Reprinted by permission of Blackwell Publishing; *p. 206:* Figure 6.10: From "Taste Test" by Mozell, et al., *Archives of Otolarynology, 90,* (1969). Copyright © 1969 by American Medical Association. Reprinted by permission.

Chapter 7 *Page 237:* From CONCEPTUAL BLOCKBUSTING by James Adams. Copyright © 1986 by James Adams. Reprinted by permission of DeCapo Press, a member of Perseus Books Group; *p. 242:* Figure 7.3: From p. 208 in ESSENTIALS OF PSYCHOLOGICAL TESTING 4th edition by Lee J. Cronbach. Copyright © 1984 by HarperCollins Publishers. Reprinted by permission; *p. 254:* Figure 7.4: Dunning, et al., 2003; *p. 248:* Figure 7.5: Bouchard & McGue, 1981; *p. 250:* Figure 7.7: Adapted from p. 14 in "Get Smart: Take a Test: A Long-Term Rise in IQ Scores Baffles Intelligence Experts" by J Horgan, *Scientific American,* November 1995. Copyright © 1995. Reprinted by permission of Dimitry Schildlovsky; *p. 251:* Graph, p. 943 from "Self-Discipline Outdoes IQ in Predicting Academic Performance of Adolescents" by A. L. Duckworth & M. E. P. Seligman, (2005), *Psychological Science, 16.* Copyright © 2005. Reprinted by permission of Blackwell Publishing; *p. 261:* From CONCEPTUAL BLOCKBUSTING by James Adams. Copyright © 1986 by James Adams. Reprinted by permission of DeCapo Press, a member of Perseus Books Group.

Chapter 8 *Page 271:* Garven et al., 1998.

Chapter 9 *Page 302:* Figure 9.2: From "Acquisition and Extinction of a Salivary Response" by Ivan P. Pavlov in CONDITIONED RESPONSES translated by G. V. Anrep. Copyright 1927. Reprinted by permission of Oxford University Press, UK; *p. 311:* Figure 9.5: From p. 96 in "Teaching Machines" by B. F. Skinner, *Scientific American,* November 1961. Copyright © 1961. Reprinted by permission; *p. 319:* From "Turning Play into Work" by David Green and Mark R. Lepper, *Psychology Today,* September 1974. Copyright © 1974 by Sussex Publishers, Inc. Reprinted by permission of *Psychology Today* Magazine; *p. 321:* Figure 9.6: From "Introduction and Removal of Reward and Maze Performance in Rate" by E. C. Tolman and C. H. Honzik, *Psychology, 4* (1930). Reprinted by permission.

Chapter 10 *Page 341:* Figure 10.2: Abridged Table 1, p. 159 from "Are Political Orientations Genetically Transmitted?" by Alford, Funk & Hibbing, *American Political Science Review, 99,* (2), May 2005. Copyright © 2005. Reprinted by permission of Cambridge University Press and the author; *p. 352:* Figure 10.3: From "The Robbers Cave Experiment" by Muzafer Sherif. Copyright © 1988 University Press of New England. Reprinted by permission; *p. 356:* From "Deindividuation and Anger-Mediated Interracial Agression: Unmasking Regressive Racism" by R. W. Rogers & S. Prentice-Dunn, *Journal of Personality and Social Psychology, 41* (1981. Copyright © 1981 by the American Psychological Association. Reprinted in accordance with APA guidelines.

Chapter 11 *Page 371:* Figure 11.1: Houts, 2002; *p. 383:* Adapted figure, p. 712, from "When Asking ëWhy' Does Not Hurt: Distinguishing Rumination from Reflective Processing of Negative Emotions" by E. Kross, O. Ayduk, & W. Mischel, *Psychological Science, 16,* (2005). (Blackwell Publishers, UK); *p. 386:* Figure 11.2: Hare, 1985; *p. 396:* Figure 11.4: Based on Gottesman, 1991; *p. 396:* Figure 11.5: Andreasen et al., 1994.

Chapter 13 *Page 450:* Figure 13.3: From "Stress and the Common Cold" by Cohen et al. in *The New York Times,* May 12, 1998. Copyright © 1998 by The New York Times Co. Reprinted with permission; *p. 454:* Figure 13.4: Williams, Barefoot, & Shekelle, 1985; *p. 457:* Figure 13.5: From p. 165, "Granting Forgiveness" by Witvliet, Ludwig & Vander Laan, *Psychological Science, 12* (2001). Copyright © 2001 by Blackwell Publishing. Reprinted by permission of the publisher; *p. 457:* Figure 13.6: From p. 127 in "Resilience and Thriving in Response to Challenge: An Opportunity for a Paradigm Shift in Women's Health" by V. E. O'Leary & J. R. Ickovics in *Women's Health: Research on Gender, Behavior and Policy, 1* (1994). Copyright © 1994. Reprinted by permission of Lawrence Erlbaum Associates; *p. 458:* Figure 13.7: From "Fitness and Health" in ABNORMAL PSYCHOLOGY by David Holmes. Copyright © 1991 by Addison Wesley Longman Publishers. Reprinted by permission of Addison Wesley Longman Publishers.

Chapter 14 *Page 478:* Figure 14.1: From "Evolutionary Psychology: A New Paradigm for Psychological Science" by D. M. Buss, *Psychological Inquiry, 6,* (1995). Copyright © 1995 by Lawrence Erlbaum Associates, Inc. Reprinted by permission; *p. 493:* From "Praise for Intelligence can Undermine Children's Motivation and Performance" by C. M. Muller and C. S. Dweck, *Journal of Personality and Social Psychology, 75,* (1998). Copyright © 1998 by the American Psychological Association. Reprinted in accordance with APA guidelines.

name index

subject index